THE FLORA OF THE PRESIDENCY OF BOMBAY

THE FLORA OF THE PRESIDENCY OF BOMBAY

THEODORE COOKE

GYAN

Published by

GYAN

Gyan Publishing House
5, Ansari Road
Daryaganj, New Delhi-110002
Phone: 011-47034999, 9811692060
E-mail: books@gyanbooks.com

Distribution Network
gyanbooks.com
India, USA, Canada, UK, Australia

ISBN: 978-93-7169-638-8 (PB)

First Published, 1934

2nd Impression 2026

Printed at: Gyan Press, Delhi.

THE FLORA OF THE PRESIDENCY OF BOMBAY

Author: THEODORE COOKE

FLORA

OF

BOMBAY.

Dates of Publication of the Several Parts of this Volume.

PART	I.	pp. 1–192	was published	*July* 1901.
„	II.	pp. 193–408	„	*April* 1902.
„	III.	pp. 409 to end	„	*May* 1903.

THE

FLORA OF THE PRESIDENCY OF BOMBAY.

BY

THEODORE COOKE, C.I.E.

M.A., M.A.I., LL.D., F.L.S., F.G.S., M.INST.C.E.I.

FORMERLY PRINCIPAL OF THE COLLEGE OF SCIENCE AT POONA AND DIRECTOR OF THE BOTANICAL SURVEY OF WESTERN INDIA.

VOL. I.

RANUNCULACEÆ TO RUBIACEÆ.

PUBLISHED UNDER THE AUTHORITY OF THE SECRETARY OF STATE FOR INDIA IN COUNCIL.

LONDON:
TAYLOR AND FRANCIS,
RED LION COURT, FLEET STREET.
1903.

PREFACE.

THE necessity for "local" or "regional" Floras to supplement Sir Joseph Hooker's great work, 'The Flora of British India,' which deals with several thousand species of plants drawn from a very wide area and grown under diverse climatic conditions, has been fully recognized by the highest botanical authorities. The inauguration of the Botanical Survey of India and the subdivision of the great Indian continent into regions, each forming a branch of the Survey, under the general supervision of Major Prain, I.M.S., Director of the Royal Botanic Gardens, Calcutta, has secured the collection of sufficient material to warrant the preparation of regional Floras for certain portions of the entire area. On the extension of the Survey to the Western Presidency, I was appointed by the Government of Bombay Honorary Director of the Botanical Survey of Western India, with Mr. G. M. Woodrow as Assistant; and I was further allowed the services of a paid Herbarium-keeper, a few native plant-collectors, and a small annual grant to provide for travelling-allowances and other incidental expenses. A Herbarium * was established at the College of Science at Poona, of which I was at that time Principal, and a real advance was soon made in our knowledge of the botany of the Bombay Presidency. Since my retirement, after 30 years' actual residence in India, I have been selected by the Government of Bombay to carry out this, the first of a series of regional Floras projected by the Director of the Survey.

The Presidency of Bombay, including Sind and Baroda (which latter State, containing 4400 square miles, though removed in 1875 from the

* The Herbarium at the College of Science which had grown largely and had developed into a highly efficient institution, was wholly destroyed by fire in May 1902; but as I fortunately possessed a good collection of my own, amassed during many years' travel in the Presidency, I was able to present that Herbarium with another collection of Bombay plants.—T. C.

administrative control of the Government of Bombay, is, for botanical purposes, included within the limits of the Presidency), extends from 13° 53′ to 28° 47′ N. lat. and from 66° 43′ to 76° 30′ E. long., and contains about 196,000 square miles, an area more than 1½ times that of Great Britain and Ireland.

To the north of the Tapti river, which passes the town of Surat, stretches the flat alluvial and fertile plain of Gujarat, much of it without a hill to break the monotony of the landscape for miles. Sind, still further to the north-west, separated from Baluchistan by the Kirthar mountains which sometimes rise to a height of 7000 feet, is much of it a plain of desert sand with occasional ridges of low sand-hills.

South of the Tapti river the country gradually becomes interspersed with hills, and further south the Western Gháts (Sahyádris) run parallel to the sea-coast for about 500 miles, with a general elevation of nearly 2000 feet, though occasionally hills rise to a height of 4000 feet or more above the sea-level.

The low-lying plain between the foot of the Western Gháts and the sea, interspersed with hills and with a heavy rainfall and a humid and enervating climate, is known as the Konkan, while the Deccan is the extensive elevated plateau behind the Gháts, interspersed with numerous hills which are either isolated or in short ranges, with a generally light rainfall and a dry climate.

The rock of which the Gháts are composed is trap, which, from its peculiarity of breaking away along vertical planes, gives rise to precipitous scarps and hills of strange fantastic form, whose summits are sometimes inaccessible. From the top of Mahableshwar, the chief sanatorium of Bombay, a hill of considerable extent standing at an elevation of 4500 feet above the sea, magnificent views of some of the hill-ranges may be obtained. From a well-known locality on that hill named Elphinstone Point, one can look down into the valley below, a sheer drop of about 3000 feet, while extending for miles rise tier on tier of precipitous hills on many of which the foot of a European has never stepped. The trap-hills are very often bare of vegetation on their summits, except where, as at Mahableshwar and Matheran (another sanatorium rising to about 2500 feet above the sea), a capping of laterite covers the trap, in which case the vegetation is varied and abundant.

The highest hill in the Bombay Presidency (except the Kirthar mountains) is a peak in the Deccan rising to 5427 feet above the sea.

The rainfall varies in the Bombay Presidency from 3 or 4 inches, or even less in the almost rainless districts of Sind, to upwards of 300 inches on the Western Ghâts. The average annual rainfall of some of the most important stations is as follows (neglecting decimals):—

	in.		in.
Jacobabad (Sind)	4	Bombay	80
Karachi	7	Karwar	116
Poona	28	Lanoli	165
Baroda	39	Matheran	242
Belgaum	49	Mahableshwar	263

Under such diverse conditions of elevation and rainfall the climate is naturally variable, being excessively humid in some regions and intensely arid in others, while, as a matter of course, the character of the vegetation varies with the climatic conditions. For example, in the exceptionally arid climate of Sind plants occur which do not appear elsewhere in India, and a very large proportion of the Sind vegetation consists of plants which are indigenous in Africa.

The earliest essay at a Flora of Bombay was that of Mr. John Graham, Deputy Postmaster General, who published in 1839 a Catalogue of the plants grown in Bombay and its vicinity. Graham died at the early age of 34, before the work was entirely completed, and its final 50 pages were carried through the press by Mr. Nimmo. Although a mere list, as its title implies, for no descriptions of the plants enumerated are given which is much to be regretted, still the work is excellent as far as it goes, and gives, what is most valuable in a work of the kind, the localities from which the several plants were obtained. Considering the means of communication that existed at the time, for there were no railways, and travelling was difficult and tedious, one cannot help being struck with admiration at the number of plants brought together in this Catalogue, all of which were, as Mr. Graham states, personally examined either by himself or by Mr. Nimmo, and most of which were correctly named.

The next work was the 'Bombay Flora' (published in 1861) by two well-known botanists, Dalzell and Gibson. The descriptions are somewhat meagre and no distinguishing characters are given of Orders and Genera, an omission which has made the work less useful to the student of Indian botany than it might otherwise have been.

Since the date of Dalzell and Gibson's 'Bombay Flora,' thanks chiefly to the work done by the Botanical Survey, the number of species of plants known to occur in Bombay has greatly increased. As an instance, I may mention that, under the Natural Orders Leguminosæ and Rubiaceæ the present volume contains respectively 284 and 80 species of indigenous or naturalized plants, while the same Orders in Dalzell and Gibson's 'Flora' contain 179 and 56.

I have, as far as possible, given the vernacular names of plants, but it may be as well to caution students of Indian Botany against blindly accepting the name given to a plant by a native coolie. Natives who spend most of their lives in the jungle and who are really *woodmen*, are generally correct in their nomenclature; but the ordinary coolie is often utterly ignorant, yet, rather than confess his ignorance, will sometimes invent a name to satisfy the "sahib." The names, too, often vary in different districts, and it is not uncommon to find the same vernacular name applied to entirely distinct plants. Still the native names, if honestly given and not manufactured for the occasion, may often prove valuable, as I have frequently found to be the case.

Prior to the establishment of the Survey, botanical work was the duty of no official. All the botanical work was carried on, as a labour of love, by gentlemen engaged in various branches of the public service, who devoted to their beloved science all the time that could be spared from their legitimate avocations. The work done in the Konkan and Sind by Dr. J. Ellerton Stocks of the Indian Medical Service, that done in the Konkan by Mr. Law of the Civil Service, and in Belgaum and Kanara by Dr. Ritchie, are matters of botanical history, and to these pioneers, as well as to Messrs. Nimmo, John Graham, Dalzell and Gibson, all of whom worked under no inconsiderable difficulties, botanical science owes a deep and lasting debt of gratitude. I must not omit to mention the excellent work done by Mr. G. M. Woodrow, who after many years of arduous labour in the botanic field, at first as my assistant and subsequently as Director of the Botanical Survey of Western India, has recently returned to Europe, nor of Mr. George Gammie who has succeeded Mr. Woodrow. Mr. Talbot, of the Indian Forest Service, whose labours in N. Kanara, where he has discovered several new species of plants, are well known, is still at work in India, and we may expect further valuable results from his untiring energy.

It can hardly be expected that the present 'Flora' will be an absolutely exhaustive one, although I have every reason to believe that the plants which still remain undiscovered are few. When we consider that a very large area (more than $1\frac{1}{2}$ times that of the British Isles) has to be examined, that the facilities for travelling leave much to be desired, that the staff to carry out the exploration is a very limited one, that some of the jungles are rife with malaria at certain seasons, and that certain of the Ghát districts are difficult of access and some of them yet unexplored, it will be admitted that the task botanists still have to face is a formidable one.

My sincere thanks are due to the Director and Staff of the Royal Botanical Gardens at Kew, who have given me every possible assistance during the progress of this work, as well as to Sir George King, F.R.S., and Mr. C. B. Clarke, F.R.S., both of whom have been constant workers side by side with me in the Kew Herbarium, and have given me much aid and friendly counsel. Lastly, I would express my thanks to the Government of Bombay for the confidence they have reposed in me by selecting me for the pleasing duty of preparing the Flora of the Presidency, a confidence which I trust will not be misplaced.

THEODORE COOKE.

KEW, 27th April, 1903.

NOTE

During the 40 years that have elapsed since the publication of the 'Flora of Bombay' (1861) by Dalzell and Gibson, our knowledge of the botany of the Presidency has largely increased, especially during the last 10 years, as a consequence of the inauguration of the Botanical Survey of India under Sir G. King. The present volume appears as the first of a series of regional Floras of India which has been organized by the present Director of that Survey; and as this, the first Part of the work (comprising 192 pages), contains descriptions of more than 130 species which find no place in the corresponding portion of Dalzell's 'Flora,' the necessity for the undertaking is sufficiently evident.

A difficulty which occurs in the preparation of a local Flora such as the present, embracing as it does a very wide area, is the want, in many cases, of information as to the precise localities in which specimens have been collected. The older botanists Stocks, Dalzell, Law, &c., who collected in the Presidency, rarely furnished more definite localities than Konkan, Deccan, Sind and the like; and there are now in the Kew Herbarium hundreds of specimens supplied by Dr. Stocks, one of the most indefatigable of Bombay collectors, which afford no further information on their labels than "Konkan, Stocks." As the Konkan is a wide area, including Kanara geographically, and comprising within its limits low-lying coast as well as elevated hilly districts, it is obvious that more precise information as to locality would be very desirable. I have given all the information in my power in this direction, and it is to be hoped that future collectors will endeavour to further supply the need. It would also be a great advantage if the color of the flowers and the habit of the plants were entered on the labels, a kind of information which can rarely be obtained from dried specimens. The Director of the Botanical Survey of India, Major D. Prain, I.M.S., 'Memoirs and Memoranda' (1894), pp. 392-406, has given excellent instructions, especially designed for Indian collectors, as to the best mode of preparing specimens for the Herbarium, a copy of which may be obtained through the College of Science at Poona.

I have adhered to the main divisions of the Presidency that Dalzell and Gibson seem to have worked to, viz. Konkan, Deccan, Gujarat, Southern Mahratta Country and Sind, as being the most convenient to follow. The S. M. Country, which includes the Collectorates of Belgaum and Dharwar, is not a geographical division of the Presidency, but the term is well understood and is more intelligible to most of its inhabitants than the term "Karnatak." Kanara, which should be strictly included within the Konkan, possesses so many plants of interest occurring solely within its area, that I have thought it well to keep it separate. In Dalzell's time the botany of the Southern Ghâts was little known, and it is to the untiring zeal of Mr. Talbot that our present knowledge of the botany of N. Kanara is mainly due.

In citing the names of collectors and authorities as to the distribution of plants, I have appended a ! in all cases where the actual specimens referred to have been seen and verified by me.

I have given throughout references to Dr. Watt's valuable 'Dictionary of the Economic Products of India.'

I take this opportunity of expressing my sincere thanks to the Director of the Royal Gardens and the Staff of the Herbarium at Kew, for their unvarying kindness, as well as for the valuable advice and assistance they have always been ready to afford.

T. C.

Kew, July 1901.

FLORA OF BOMBAY.

ORDER I. RANUNCULACEÆ.

Annual or perennial herbs, more rarely shrubs. Leaves radical or alternate (opposite in *Clematis* and *Naravelia*), entire or divided; stipules 0, or adnate to the petioles, rarely free. Flowers regular (irregular in *Delphinium*), 1–2-sexual, rarely bracteate. Sepals 3–many, (usually 5), often petaloid, imbricate (valvate in *Clematis*). Petals imbricate, isomerous with the sepals or many, hypogynous, free, sometimes minute or deformed or 0. Stamens indefinite, hypogynous; anthers usually adnate and dehiscing laterally. Carpels many, rarely solitary, free or rarely subconnate, 1-celled; ovules 1 or more on the ventral suture, anatropous, erect with a ventral raphe, or pendulous with a dorsal raphe; style simple. Fruit of numerous, dry, 1-seeded, indehiscent achenes, or many-seeded follicles, rarely baccate. Seeds small; albumen copious; embryo minute.—DISTRIB. Abundant in temperate and cold regions; genera 30; species about 500.

Climbing shrubs; leaves opposite.
- Flowers apetalous; terminal leaflet not transformed into a tendril .... 1. CLEMATIS.
- Flowers with petals and sepals; terminal leaflet usually transformed into a tendril .... 2. NARAVELIA.

Herbs; leaves alternate.
- Flowers regular.
  - Sepals petaloid .... 3. THALICTRUM.
  - Sepals herbaceous .... 4. RANUNCULUS.
- Flowers irregular; posterior sepal spurred .... 5. DELPHINIUM.

1. CLEMATIS, Linn.

Woody undershrubs, usually climbing. Leaves opposite, usually compound, exstipulate; petioles often twining but not changed into tendrils. Inflorescence axillary or terminal; flowers solitary or panicled. Sepals usually 4 (rarely 5–8), petaloid, imbricate or valvate. Petals 0. Stamens many. Carpels many; ovule 1, pendulous. Fruit a head of sessile or stalked achenes; style persistent, naked or bearded.—DISTRIB. All temperate regions; less common in the tropics; species 180.

Filaments glabrous.
- Flowers exceeding 1 in. in diam.
  - Leaves large; flowers purple .... 1. *C. smilacifolia.*
  - Leaves small; flowers white .... 2. *C. triloba.*
- Flowers less than 1 in. in diam.
  - Connective of anthers not produced .... 3. *C. Gouriana.*
  - Connective of anthers much produced .... 4. *C. hedysarifolia.*

Filaments hairy; flowers yellow .... 5. *C. Wightiana.*

1. **Clematis smilacifolia,** *Wall. in Asiat. Res.* v. 13 (1820) p. 402. A woody climber, glabrous except the inflorescence; stems sulcate. Lower leaves 3–8 by 1–6 in., ovate, acute or acuminate, entire or shortly serrate, base rounded or cordate, 5–9- (frequently 7-) nerved from the base; petioles reaching 6 in. long, twining. Upper leaves sometimes once ternate; blades smaller, narrower, cuneate at the base. Flowers large, exceeding 1 in. in diam., in long, axillary panicles; pedicels reaching 3 in. long, glabrous. Sepals 4–5, oblong, ¾–1 in. long, spreading from the base, at length reflexed, clothed outside with velvety brown tomentum, purple inside. Filaments linear, glabrous, the outer longer than the inner with shorter anthers; connective produced. Achenes ovoid, compressed, pubescent with thickened margins and long feathery tails. Fl. B. I. v. 1, p. 3; Dalz. & Gibs. p. 1; Kuntze, Monogr. Clem. in Verh. Bot. ver. Brandenb. 26 (1885) p. 120; Trim. Fl. Ceyl. v. 1, p. 1; Talb. Trees, Bomb. p. 1; Woodr. in Journ. Bomb. Nat. v. 11 (1897) p. 119.—Flowers: Oct.

Not very common in the Bombay Presidency. KONKAN: *Stocks*!, *Law*!; in evergreen forests, not common, *Talbot*. DECCAN: Phunda Ghát, *Dalzell & Gibson*. KANARA: *Stocks*!; near Nilkund (N. Kanara), *Gibson*!; N. Kanara, *Talbot*.—DISTRIB. Java, Borneo, Philippines.

2. **Clematis triloba,** *Heyne, in Roth. Nov. Sp.* (1821) p. 251. An extensive climber, but often found trailing amongst grass; whole plant except the older stems sericeo-villous or tomentose; stems sulcate. Leaves simple or once ternate, entire or shallowly 1–7-lobed, the lobes usually mucronate; blades 1–2 in. long, from ovate, acute, to orbicular, base rounded, cuneate or cordate; petioles slender, twining, ¾–3 in. long; petiolules ¼–¾ in. long. Flowers white, more than 1½ in. across, in axillary, corymbose panicles; bracts foliaceous, ovate, acute. Sepals 4–6, stellately spreading, pubescent outside, glabrous inside, oblong or obovate, terminated by a tomentose mucro. Stamens ¼–⅜ in. long; filaments ligulate, glabrous; connective not produced. Achenes ovoid, compressed, silky-villous, with long feathery tails. Fl. B. I. v. 1, p. 3; Dalz. & Gibs. p. 1; Kuntze, Monogr. Clem. in Verh. Bot. ver. Brandenb. 26 (1885) p. 150; Talb. Trees, Bomb. p. 1; Woodr. in Journ. Bomb. Nat. v. 11 (1897) p. 119; Watt, Dict. Econ. Prod. v. 2, p. 370.—Flowers: Sept.–Nov. VERN. *Mor-vel*; *Rânjai*.

Very common throughout the Deccan. KONKAN: *Law*! DECCAN: *Gibson*!; Kartriz Ghát near Poona, *Law*!; Garada, 12 miles S. of Poona, *Gokhale*!; Tulligaum, near Poona, *Cooke*!; Dongergaon, near Ahmednagar, *Cooke*!; hills near Poona, *Woodrow*!; Mawal district of Poona Collectorate, *Dalzell & Gibson*.

3. **Clematis Gouriana,** *Roxb. Hort. Beng.* (1814) p. 43. Climbing to a great height, usually glabrous, except the young parts; stems grooved, brown. Leaves pinnate, bipinnate or tripinnate; leaflets 1–5 by ½–1½ in., ovate or oblong, acuminate, entire or coarsely toothed, rounded or cordate at the base, strongly nerved and reticulately veined, upper surface shining; petioles long, slender. Flowers small, scarcely reaching ½ in. in diam., in much-branched, decompound panicles, yellowish or greenish-white; peduncles and pedicels more or less pubescent. Sepals 4, obovate or oblong, puberulous on both surfaces. Filaments narrow-linear, glabrous; connective not produced. Achenes ovoid, hairy, with long feathery tails. Fl. B. I. v. 1, p. 4; Grah. Cat. p. 1;

Dalz. & Gibs. p. 1; Trim. Fl. Ceyl. v. 1, p. 2; Talb. Trees, Bomb. p. 1; Woodr. in Journ. Bomb. Nat. v. 11 (1897) p. 119; Watt, Dict. Econ. Prod. v. 2, p. 369. *C. vitalba*, var. *Gauriana*, Kuntze, Monogr. Clem. in Verh. Bot. ver. Brandenb. 26 (1885) p. 100.—Flowers: Oct.-Nov. VERN. *Mor-vel.*

In thickets on the Ghâts, common. KONKAN: *Law*!; Matheran, *Cooke*!; Amboli Ghât, *Cooke*! DECCAN: Nasik, *Woodrow*; Koina valley, below Mahableshwar, *Cooke*! S. M. COUNTRY: Belgaum, *Ritchie*!—DISTRIB. Java, Philippines.

4. **Clematis hedysarifolia,** *DC. Syst.* v. 1 (1818) p. 148. A woody climber; branches furrowed, the younger parts puberulous, the older glabrous. Leaves pinnate; leaflets 3-5, coriaceous, $1\frac{1}{2}$-$4\frac{1}{2}$ by $\frac{3}{4}$-$2\frac{1}{2}$ in., ovate-lanceolate, acuminate, cordate or rounded at the base, entire or irregularly toothed, glabrous, shining, very closely reticulately veined, the reticulations prominent on the upper surface; petioles up to 3 in. long, twining. Flowers about $\frac{3}{4}$ in. in diam., in many-flowered, decompound panicles; pedicels pubescent; bracts foliaceous. Sepals 4, ovate or oblong, densely pubescent outside, at length deflexed. Filaments ligulate, $\frac{1}{16}$ in. broad, glabrous; connective much produced. Achenes ovoid, compressed, hairy, with thickened, tubercular margins and long, feathery tails. Fl. B. I. v. 1, p. 4; Kuntze, Monogr. Clem. in Verh. Bot. ver. Brandenb. 26 (1885) p. 151; Talb. Trees, Bomb. p. 1; Woodr. in Journ. Bomb. Nat. v. 11 (1897) p. 120.—Flowers: Oct.-Nov. VERN. *Bendrichi-vel.*

KONKAN: *Law*! DECCAN: Koina valley below Mahableshwar, *Cooke*!; Singhad, 12 miles from Poona, *Woodrow*! GUJARAT: Dang jungles, *Woodrow*. S. M. COUNTRY: Londa, *Cooke*!; Belgaum, *Ritchie*! KANARA: N. Kanara, *Woodrow*!, *Talbot*!

5. **Clematis Wightiana,** *Wall. Cat.* (1828) 4674. A woody climber; branches clothed with appressed hairs. Leaves pinnate; leaflets 3-5, silky-villous on both surfaces, 1-$2\frac{1}{2}$ by $\frac{3}{4}$-$\frac{1}{2}$ in., orbicular or broadly ovate, cordate, irregularly toothed or lobed; nerves and veins prominent beneath; petioles up to 4 in. long, more or less clothed with silky hairs. Flowers $1\frac{3}{4}$-$2\frac{1}{4}$ in. in diam., in panicles longer than the leaves; bracts foliaceous, lobed or toothed, silky-villous. Sepals 4, pale golden yellow, $\frac{7}{8}$ by $\frac{3}{8}$ in., ovate, clothed with silky hairs outside, glabrous inside. Stamens shorter than the sepals; filaments hairy for a short distance below the middle, the upper portion and the base being glabrous: connective not produced. Achenes ovoid, compressed, densely silky and with long feathery tails. Fl. B. I. v. 1, p. 5; Grah. Cat. p. 1; Dalz. & Gibs. p. 1; Talb. Trees, Bomb. p. 2; Woodr. in Journ. Bomb. Nat. v. 11 (1897) p. 120. *C. orientalis*, var. *Wightiana*, Kuntze, Monogr. Clem. in Verh. Bot. ver. Brandenb. 26 (1885) p. 125.—Flowers: Jan.

A very handsome species confined to the highest Ghâts of the Presidency; very common at Mahableshwar. DECCAN: Mahableshwar, *Cooke*!, *Dr. Lush*!

2. NARAVELIA, DC.

Stem woody, scandent. Leaves opposite, bifoliolate from the terminal leaflet being transformed into a tendril. Flowers panicled. Sepals 4-5. Petals many, linear or clavate, distinct from the stamens. Carpels many; ovule pendulous. Achenes with a short, thick, hollow stalk and long, bearded styles.—DISTRIB. S. Asia and the Indian Archipelago; species 3.

Differs from *Clematis* by the presence of petals and tendrils.

1. **Naravelia zeylanica,** *DC. Syst.* v. 1 (1818) p. 167. A climbing shrub. Leaves 2-foliolate, the third or terminal leaflet having been transformed into a long slender tendril which terminates in three pointed, hooked branches; leaflets broadly ovate, acuminate, often unequal at the base, entire or rarely coarsely toothed, pubescent beneath; petioles $1\frac{1}{2}$–$2\frac{1}{2}$ in. long. Flowers small, $\frac{1}{2}$–$\frac{3}{4}$ in. in diam. Sepals 4–5, ovate-oblong, densely pubescent externally, caducous. Petals 6–12, linear-spathulate, usually a little longer than the sepals. Filaments ligulate, glabrous; connective produced. Achenes shortly stalked, hairy, with long feathery tails. Fl. B. I. v. 1, p. 7; Grah. Cat. p. 1; Dalz. & Gibs. p. 1; Trim. Fl. Ceyl. v. 1, p. 2; Talb. Trees, Bomb. p. 2; Woodr. in Journ. Bomb. Nat. v. 11 (1897) p. 120; Watt, Dict. Econ. Prod. v. 5, p. 317.—Flowers: Oct.–Dec.

KANARA: *Law*! ; moist forests, *Talbot*; Divimana, on the Kumpta and Sirsi Road (N. Kanara), *Woodrow*! S. M. COUNTRY: Dharwar districts, *Law*! *Dalzell & Gibson* (Bo. Fl. l. c.) give as the habitat of this plant "Southern Ghâts only." The specimens I have seen were obtained from Kanara and the Dharwar districts.—DISTRIB. Ceylon, Java.

3. THALICTRUM, Linn.

Erect herbs with a perennial root. Leaves compound; petioles sheathing, often auricled or stipulate. Flowers usually small, panicled or racemed, often polygamous. Sepals 4–5, petaloid, imbricate in bud. Petals 0. Stamens many. Carpels usually many; ovule 1, pendulous. Fruit a small head of sessile or stalked achenes; style persistent or deciduous, ecaudate.—DISTRIB. Temperate regions of the N. hemisphere; a few in tropical India and the Cape; species 50.

1. **Thalictrum Dalzellii,** *Hook. Ic. Pl.* v. 9 (1852) t. 868. A rigid plant, about 1 ft. high; stem and branches slender, grooved, light-colored, glabrous. Leaves 3-foliolate (except the uppermost which are usually 1-foliolate); leaflets 1–2 in. in diam., glabrous, pale beneath, suborbicular or reniform, with a deep acute sinus (uppermost subsessile), margins crenately and irregularly lobed and toothed; nerves and veins prominent on both surfaces; petioles of lower leaves $1\frac{1}{2}$–2 in. long, deeply grooved, glabrous; petiolules $\frac{1}{2}$–1 in. long; stipules $\frac{3}{8}$ in. long, oblong, membranous, strongly nerved. Flowers $\frac{1}{4}$ in. in diam., in small leafy panicles crowded at the ends of the branches. Sepals 4, nerved, oblong, obtuse, as long as the stamens. Filaments filiform; anthers muticous. Achenes less than $\frac{1}{8}$ in. long, many in each head, shortly stalked, narrow-oblong, deeply furrowed, glabrous, with a hooked tip. Fl. B. I. v. 1, p. 13; Dalz. & Gibs. p. 2; Woodr. in Journ. Bomb. Nat. v. 11 (1897) p. 120.—Flowers: Aug.

A rare plant found in a few mountainous districts. KONKAN: Ghâts, *Stocks*!, *Dalzell*!; Ghâts near Vingorla, *Dalzell*. DECCAN: Purandhar, *Cooke*!, *Woodrow*!; Harishchandar, *Dalzell & Gibson*.

4. RANUNCULUS, Linn.

Annual or perennial, often acrid herbs. Leaves entire or divided. Flowers white, yellow or red, terminal, solitary or panicled, rarely axillary and sessile. Sepals 3–5, caducous. Petals as many or more numerous, with a basal, nectariferous pit or scale. Stamens usually numerous, shorter than the sepals or petals. Carpels many; ovule 1, ascending; style short. Achenes capitate or spicate, apiculate or beaked. —DISTRIB. All temperate regions; species about 160.

1. **Ranunculus sceleratus,** *Linn. Sp. Pl.* (1753) p. 551. Annual, erect, 1–2 ft. high; stems and branches hollow, deeply furrowed, glabrous. Radical leaves ¾–1½ in. in diam., reniform, 3-partite almost to the base; segments obovate, cuneate, again variously lobed or notched. Upper cauline leaves 3-partite, the segments narrow-oblong, entire or toothed, glabrous. Petioles sheathing, those of the radical leaves variable in length, from 1–6 in. long, those of the cauline leaves becoming shorter upwards, glabrous. Flowers ¼–½ in. in diam. Sepals oblong, about equalling the petals, pubescent, caducous. Petals 4–5, elliptic-oblong, white. Anthers yellow. Head of achenes cylindric, ¼–⅜ in. long; achenes small, numerous, apiculate. Fl. B. I. v. 1, p. 19; K. Prantl, in Engl. & Prantl, Pflanzenf. v. 3, part 2, p. 64, fig. 48, C, D; Woodr. in Journ. Bomb. Nat. v. 11 (1897) p. 120; Watt, Dict. Econ. Prod. v. 6, part 1, p. 392.—Flowers: Feb.–Mar.

SIND: Banks of the Indus, common, *Stocks*!; Sukkur, banks of the Indus, *Woodrow*! —DISTRIB. Europe, N. Asia, China, N. Africa, temperate America.

5. DELPHINIUM, Linn.

Annual or perennial herbs. Leaves alternate, palmately lobed or divided. Flowers large, racemed or panicled, blue, purple, rosy or white, very rarely yellow. Sepals 5, subconnate at base, the upper produced into a spur. Petals 2 or 4, small, the two upper produced into a spur-like appendage within the spur of the calyx, the two lateral spurless or wanting. Filaments sometimes dilated at the base. Follicles 1–7, sessile, free, many-ovuled. Seeds numerous, subfleshy.—DISTRIB. Temperate zone of the N. hemisphere; species about 40.

1. **Delphinium dasycaulon,** *Fres. Mus. Senckenb.* v. 2 (1837) p. 272. Herbaceous, erect, 1½–3 ft. high; stem hollow, terete, hairy. Radical leaves large, reaching 6 in. across, reniform, 5–7-lobed; lobes trapezoidal, again variously divided, usually mucronate. Cauline leaves more deeply divided into narrower segments, with a few hairs on the upper surface and on the nerves beneath. Petioles sheathing, those of the radical leaves very long, reaching 1 ft. in length, more or less hairy, those of the cauline leaves shorter. Flowers bright blue, in lax racemes; bracts subulate, 1 at the base, and 2 alternate ones about the middle of each pedicel; pedicels about equalling the flowers. Sepals ¾ in. long, pubescent outside, marked with a white, hairy spot near the top; spur conical, about ⅜ in. long, slightly recurved, hairy outside. Petals: the upper cartilaginous, the lower 2-lobed, hairy. Filaments much dilated at the base. Follicles 3, straight. Fl. B. I. v. 1, p. 25; Dalz. & Gibs. p. 2; Woodr. in Journ. Bomb. Nat. v. 11 (1897) p. 120.—Flowers: Aug.–Sept.

A rare plant. DECCAN: Junnar, *Stocks*!, *Woodrow*!, *Dalzell & Gibson*; Kadkala 20 miles W. of Poona, *Cooke*!—DISTRIB. Abyssinia.

ORDER II. DILLENIACEÆ.

Trees or shrubs. Leaves alternate, with sheathing petioles, exstipulate, or rarely with lateral, deciduous stipules. Flowers yellow or white. Sepals 5, imbricate, persistent. Petals 5 or fewer, deciduous. Stamens numerous, hypogynous, many-seriate; anthers innate, dehiscing by lateral slits or terminal pores. Carpels 1 or more, free or cohering in the axis; ovules amphitropous, solitary or few and ascending, or many and attached to the ventral suture; styles distinct. Fruit follicular, or indehiscent and sub-baccate. Seeds 1, or many, arillate (except *Dillenia*); testa crustaceous; raphe short; albumen fleshy; embryo minute, next the hilum.—DISTRIB. Tropics of both hemispheres and Australia; genera 16; species about 200.

1. DILLENIA, Linn.

Trees. Leaves large, with parallel nerves. Flowers handsome, lateral, solitary or fascicled. Sepals 5, spreading. Petals 5, usually large, Stamens nearly free; anthers linear, the inner erect or recurved, introrse, the outer recurved, extrorse. Carpels 5-20, cohering in the axis, many-ovuled, indehiscent, when ripe united into a globose fruit enveloped in the sepals. Seeds not, or sometimes, immersed in pulp, exarillate.—DISTRIB. Tropical Asia, Australia; species 15.

Flowers large, often 6 in. in diam. .... 1. *D. indica*.
Flowers small, scarcely 1 in. in diam. .... 2. *D. pentagyna*.

1. **Dillenia indica,** *Linn. Sp. Pl.* (1753) p. 535. A middle-sized tree; trunk straight but not high; branches spreading, forming a round, shady head. Leaves fascicled at the ends of the branches, oblong-lanceolate, acuminate, 8–12 by about 4 in., sharply serrate, the nerves close, running into the serratures, not forking at the margins, upper surface and the nerves beneath more or less pubescent; petioles 1–2 in. long, channelled, sheathing. Flowers often exceeding 6 in. in diam., white, fragrant, appearing with the leaves, usually solitary towards the end of each branchlet; pedicels about 3 in. long, clavate, round, smooth. Sepals orbicular, concave, thick and fleshy. Petals oblong. Stamens many, the inner larger, and arching over the shorter outer ones. Fruit large, 3–4 in. in diam., hard outside, fleshy within. Seeds many, imbedded in glutinous pulp, compressed, with hairy margins. Fl. B. I. v. 1, p. 36; E. Gilg. in Engl. & Prantl, Pflanzenf. v. 3, part 6, p. 124, fig. 65; Talb. Trees, Bomb. p. 2; Woodr. in Journ. Bomb. Nat. v. 11 (1897) p. 120; Watt, Dict. Econ. Prod. v. 3, p. 113. *D. speciosa*, Thunb. in Trans. Linn. Soc. v. 1 (1791) p. 200; Grah. Cat. p. 2; Dalz. & Gibs. p. 2.—Flowers: June. VERN. *Mota-karmal.*

KONKAN: Banda, Alibag, *Dalzell & Gibson*; S. Konkan, *Graham*; Sawantwari, *Talbot*, *Woodrow*. S. M. COUNTRY: Belgaum, *Talbot*.

The thick sepals have an agreeable acid flavor and are eaten by the natives. When added to syrup they are used as a cough mixture (Dalzell & Gibson).

2. **Dillenia pentagyna,** *Roxb. Cor. Pl.* v. 1 (1795) p. 21, t. 20. A middle-sized tree with erect trunk; branches straggling, numerous, ascending, with drooping ends. Leaves at the extremities of the branches, very large, reaching 2 ft. and upwards in length, by 1 ft. in

breadth (the leaves of young trees larger than those of older, often attaining a length of 4 ft. or more), smooth and shining when old, downy when young, the nerves of very young leaves densely clothed with white hairs, nerves many, often forking towards the margins, margins with sharp villous teeth at the extremities of the main nerves and of each of the furcations; petioles about 2 in. long, channelled, sheathing. Flowers scarcely 1 in. in diam., fragrant, appearing before the leaves, in fascicles from tuberosities on the naked, woody, 2- or 3-years' old branchlets; pedicels 1½ in. long, erect, terete, glabrous. Sepals ovate, obtuse, ½ in. long. Petals oblong-lanceolate, yellow. Filaments numerous, the outer erect, the inner spreading, twice as long as the outer. Ovaries 5; styles short; stigmas spreading. Fruit edible, pendulous, size of a small nutmeg, the fleshy sepals entirely enclosing 5 small, soft capsules. Seeds reniform, 1 (rarely 2) ripening in each capsule. Fl. B. I. v. 1, p. 38; Grah. Cat. p. 2; Dalz. & Gibs. p. 2; Bedd. Flor. Sylv. t. 104; Talb. Trees, Bomb. p. 2; Woodr. in Journ. Bomb. Nat. v. 11 (1897) p. 120; Watt, Dict. Econ. Prod. v. 3, p. 114.—Flowers: Mar.-Apr. VERN. *Karmal.*

Common along the Western face of the Ghâts. KONKAN: Matheran, *Cooke*!; Sakarpathár, *Woodrow*. GUJARAT: Dang jungles, *Woodrow*. S. M. COUNTRY: banks of Gatparba river, *Graham*; S. M. Country and Ghâts up to Lat. 19°, *Dalzell & Gibson*. KANARA: Ghâts and Kalanaddi, *Ritchie*!

The large leaves are used to form a substratum for roof thatch and sold in bundles for the purpose.

ORDER III. MAGNOLIACEÆ.

Trees or shrubs, often aromatic. Leaves alternate, undivided, entire or toothed, stipulate or not. Flowers axillary and terminal, usually showy. Sepals and petals hypogynous, very deciduous, imbricate, arranged in whorls of 3. Stamens indefinite, hypogynous; anther-cells adnate, bursting longitudinally. Carpels many, free or partly cohering, in one or more whorls on an elongate axis; ovules 2 or more; styles usually short. Seeds few, sometimes pendulous from a long funicle; testa single and crustaceous, or double and the outer fleshy; albumen granular, or fleshy and oily; embryo minute; cotyledons spreading.—DISTRIB. Tropical Eastern Asia, N. America; genera 9; species 70.

1. MICHELIA, Linn.

Trees. Leaf-buds enveloped in convolute deciduous stipules which are connate in pairs. Sepals and petals similar, concolorous, 9 or more, 3- or more-seriate, imbricate. Stamens numerous, many-seriate; anthers linear, adnate, introrse. Gynophore stipitate. Carpels many, persistent, 2-valved, arranged in a lax or elongate spike, dehiscing dorsally; ovules 2, or more. Seeds pendulous by a long funicle.—DISTRIB. Temperate and subtropical mountains of India, also in Sumatra, Java and China; species about 12.

1. **Michelia Champaca,** *Linn. Sp. Pl.* (1753) p. 536. A tall, handsome, evergreen tree with a straight trunk; branches ascending, spreading, forming a close head. Leaves 7–10 by 2–3½ in., lanceolate, acute or acuminate, entire, glabrous above (except when young), glabrous

or more or less pubescent beneath; petioles $\frac{3}{4}$–1 in. long. Flowers about 2–$2\frac{1}{2}$ in. in diam., very fragrant, axillary, solitary, each enclosed in bud by a greyish-yellow pubescent, spathaceous, coriaceous, deciduous bract. Sepals and petals 15 or more, deep yellow or orange; the outer oblong, acute; the inner linear; pedicels $\frac{1}{4}$ in. long, stout, wrinkled, marked with an annular scar round the middle. Capsules $\frac{3}{4}$ in., dark brown, opening on the back by two valves; valves woody, orbicular, covered with white warty excrescences. Seeds 1–12, brown, polished, variously angled, rounded on the back. Fl. B. I. v. 1, p. 42; Talb. Trees, Bomb. p. 2; Woodr. in Journ. Bomb. Nat. v. 11 (1897) p. 120; Watt, Dict. Econ. Prod. v. 5, p. 241. *M. Rheedii*, Wight, Ill. v. 1, p. 14; Grah. Cat. p. 2.—Flowers: Apr.–Sept. VERN. *Sonchápha*; *Pivala-Chápha*.

Not wild in the Bombay Presidency. The tree is commonly planted near temples; the fragrant flowers are used in religious ceremonies and also by women for ornamenting their hair.—DISTRIB. Java.

ORDER IV. ANONACEÆ.

Trees or shrubs, often climbing, frequently aromatic. Leaves alternate, quite entire, exstipulate. Flowers hermaphrodite, rarely unisexual. Sepals 3 (rarely 2), distinct or united into a 3-lobed or 3-dentate calyx, usually valvate. Petals usually thick and fleshy, generally 6, biseriate, hypogynous, valvate or slightly imbricate, the inner sometimes absent. Stamens usually many, in many series, on a thick torus; filaments short or 0; anthers adnate, 2-celled, cells extrorse or sublateral, dehiscing by a longitudinal slit; connective usually produced into an oblong, dilated or truncate head. Ovaries 1 or more, apocarpous, very rarely (*Anona*) syncarpous, with distinct or agglutinated stigmas; ovules 1 or more; styles short or almost 0. Fruit of one or more sessile or stalked, 1- or many-seeded, usually indehiscent carpels. Seeds arillate or naked; albumen copious, ruminate; embryo minute; cotyledons divaricating.—DISTRIB. Chiefly in the tropics of the Old World; genera 40; species 400.

Anther-cells concealed by the overlapping connective.
  Petals 2-seriate, one or both series imbricate in bud...... 1. UVARIA.
  Petals valvate.
    Petals subequal.
      Petals conniving at the concave base .... 2. ARTABOTRYS.
      Petals flat, spreading from the base.
        Ovules 2 or more, 1-seriate on the ventral suture .... 3. UNONA.
        Ovules 1–2, basal or sub-basal .... 4. POLYALTHIA.
    Inner petals $\frac{1}{3}$ shorter than the outer, clawed ...... 5. GONIOTHALAMUS.
    Inner petals minute, or 0 .... 6. ANONA.
Anther-cells not concealed by the overlapping connective.
  Petals valvate, the inner longest.
    Ovules 1–2; inner petals not saccate .... 7. MILIUSA.
    Ovules 6 or more; inner petals saccate at the base. 8. SACCOPETALUM.
  Petals valvate, the inner shortest .... 9. OROPHEA.
  Petals imbricate, subequal .... 10. BOCAGEA.

1. UVARIA, Linn.

Scandent or sarmentose shrubs, stellately pubescent or tomentose. Inflorescence terminal or leaf-opposed, rarely axillary; flowers hermaphrodite. Sepals 3, often connate at the base, broad, valvate. Petals 6, orbicular, ovate or oblong, imbricate in 2 series, sometimes connate at the base. Stamens indefinite; connective produced beyond the cells, subfoliaceous or truncate. Torus depressed, pubescent or tomentose. Ovaries indefinite, linear-oblong; ovules many, 2-seriate; style short, thick. Ripe carpels numerous, dry or berried, few- or many-seeded.—DISTRIB. Tropical Asia and Africa with a few Australian species; species about 110.

Capsules blunt at each end; peduncles slender; seeds in a single row .... 1. *U. Narum.*
Capsules tapering to each end; peduncles thick; seeds in a double row .... 2. *U. Hookeri.*

1. **Uvaria Narum,** *Blume, Fl. Java, Anon.* (1828) p. 5. A large climber. Leaves 2–6 by 1–1½ in., oblong-lanceolate, acute or acuminate, glabrous on both surfaces, reticulately veined; petioles short, less than ¼ in. long. Flowers reddish, 1 in. in diam., solitary, terminal; pedicels 1–1½ in. long. Sepals orbicular-ovate, connate at the base, reflexed, minutely stellately tomentose. Petals usually 6, sometimes 7–8, ovate or oblong, connate at the base. Connective of anthers produced at the apex, broad, truncate. Carpels ⅝–¾ in. long, and about ⅓ in. in diam., numerous, scarlet, glabrous, slightly torulose, on slender stalks ⅝–¾ in. long. Seeds chestnut-brown, suborbicular, in a single row, usually 4–5, those at the ends of the carpels plano-convex, the intermediate ones compressed, nearly flat. Fl. B. I. v. 1, p. 50; Grah. Cat. p. 3; Dalz. & Gibs. p. 3; Trim. Fl. Ceyl. p. 19; King, in Ann. Roy. Bot. Gard. Calcutta, v. 4, part 1 (1893) p. 27, and part 2, t. 21; Talb. Trees, Bomb. p. 3; Woodr. in Journ. Bomb. Nat. v. 11 (1897) p. 120; Watt, Dict. Econ. Prod. v. 6, part 4, p. 217. *Uvaria lurida*, Dalz. & Gibs. p. 3 (*not* of Fl. B. I.).—Flowers: Nov.

KONKAN: *Dalzell* !, *Law* !, *Stocks* ! S. M. COUNTRY: Párwa Ghât, *Woodrow*. KANARA: *Talbot*.

2. **Uvaria Hookeri,** *King, in Ann. Roy. Bot. Gard. Calcutta*, v. 4, part 1 (1893) p. 28. A climbing shrub; all parts except the inflorescence glabrous. Leaves as in *U. Narum*, but larger (6–9 in. long). Flowers as in *U. Narum*, but larger (1–1½ in. in diam.). Carpels ovoid, tapering to the end, their peduncles thick, 1½–2 in. long. Seeds in two rows. Otherwise as in *U. Narum*. *U. Narum*, Wall. Cat. 6473 (in part); Wight, Ill. v. 1, p. 19, t. 6; Hook. f. & Thoms. Fl. Ind. p. 102 (in part); Dalz. & Gibs. p. 3. Var. 2, *macrophylla*, Hook. f. Fl. B. I. v. 1, p. 50.

In the Fl. Ind. of Hook. f. & Thoms. p. 102, the authors remarked that it was not improbable that more than one species had been confounded under *U. Narum*. Sir George King has separated *U. Narum* into 2 species, founding the new species *U. Hookeri*, which differs from his *U. Narum* in having biseriate seeds, carpels tapering at one end, larger leaves and flowers, and longer and thicker stalks to the carpels.

Forests of the Western Ghâts, *King*, l. c.

2. ARTABOTRYS, R. Br.

Shrubs, usually sarmentose or scandent. Flowers solitary or fascicled, often fragrant, usually on woody, hooked, recurved branches (*peduncles*).

Sepals 3, valvate, cohering at the base. Petals 6, biseriate, valvate, concave at the base, constricted around the organs, again spreading. Stamens indefinite, oblong or cuneate; connective truncate or produced; anther-cells dorsal. Torus flat or convex. Ovaries many or few; ovules 2, erect, collateral; style oblong or columnar. Ripe carpels berried.—DISTRIB. Tropical Africa, China, Malaya; species about 30.

1. **Artabotrys odoratissimus,** *R. Br. in Bot. Reg.* (1820) t. 423. A shrub, often scandent. Leaves up to 7 by 1½–2 in., oblong-lanceolate, shortly acuminate, glabrous, shining, acute at the base; petioles ¼–⅜ in. long. Flowers yellow, solitary or in pairs, 1¼–1½ in. long; pedicels ¾ in. long. Sepals ¼ in. long, connate below, ovate, acute, tips reflexed. Petals lanceolate above the saccate base, clothed with appressed silky hairs. Ripe carpels 6–10, obovoid, glabrous, ¾–1½ in. long, by ⅞ in. in diam., yellow. Seeds oblong, a little flattened, deeply grooved on one side, more than ½ in. long. Fl. B. I. v. 1, p. 54; Grah. Cat. p. 4; Dalz. & Gibs. Suppl. p. 2 (*odoratissima*); King, in Ann. Roy. Bot. Gard. Calcutta, v. 4, part 1 (1893) p. 44, and part 2, t. 55; Trim. Fl. Ceyl. v. 1, p. 21; Talb. Trees, Bomb. p. 3; Woodr. in Journ. Bomb. Nat. v. 11 (1897) p. 120; Watt, Dict. Econ. Prod. v. 1, p. 322. VERN. *Hirva-chápha*; *Kála-chápha*.

Not indigenous to the Bombay Presidency, but cultivated largely for its fragrant flowers. Sir G. King (l. c.) says that it is wild in the southern parts of India and Ceylon.—DISTRIB. Java, S. China.

2. **Artabotrys zeylanicus,** *Hook. f. & Thoms. Fl. Ind.* v. 1 (1855) p. 128. A strong climber. Leaves 4–6 by 1½–2½ in., oblong-lanceolate, oblanceolate or elliptic, acute or shortly acuminate, entire, glabrous on both surfaces; petioles ¼ in. long. Flowers solitary or fascicled; peduncles leaf-opposed, thickened, hooked, flattened, with 1 or more pedicels ½ in. long starting from the bend of the hook and 1 more from its extremity; bracts at base of pedicel small, acute, rusty-pubescent. Sepals 3, about ¼ in. long, broadly ovate, acute, cohering below, rusty-tomentose outside. Petals 1–1½ by ¼ in., densely tomentose on both surfaces, oblong-lanceolate. Anthers sessile. Fruit of 7–10 carpels, ovoid, mucronate, sessile, somewhat rugose, ½–1 in. long, by ⅜–¾ in. in diam. Seeds ¾ in. long, oblong-ovoid, brown. Fl. B. I. v. 1, p. 54; King, in Ann. Roy. Bot. Gard. Calcutta, v. 4, part 1 (1893) p. 43, and part 2, t. 53; Trim. Fl. Ceyl. v. 1, p. 22; Woodr. in Journ. Bomb. Nat. v. 11 (1897) p. 120.—Flowers: Nov.–Feb.

Rare, except in Kanara. KANARA: *Stocks*!, *Dalzell*!; evergreen forests of N. Kanara, towards the south; abundant in the forests near the Gairsoppa Falls, *Talbot*; Divimana (N. Kanara), *Woodrow*!—DISTRIB. Ceylon.

3. UNONA, Linn.

Trees or scandent shrubs. Flowers usually solitary, axillary or extra-axillary, rather large. Sepals 3, valvate. Petals 6, valvate in æstivation, 2-seriate, the 3 inner rarely absent. Stamens many, cuneate, the apex of the produced connective subglobose or truncate. Torus flat or slightly concave. Ovaries many; ovules 2 or more, 1-seriate (rarely sub-2-seriate); style ovoid or oblong, recurved, grooved. Ripe carpels usually stalked, elongate and constricted between the seeds or baccate.

Seeds few or many.—DISTRIB. Tropical Asia and Africa; species about 50.

1. **Unona pannosa,** *Dalz. in Hook. Kew Journ. Bot.* v. 3 (1851) p. 207. A tree; young parts puberulous. Leaves lanceolate, rarely elliptic, acuminate, 2½–4½ by 1–1¾ in., glabrous above, more or less pubescent beneath, sometimes pellucido-punctate, base acute or rounded; petioles short, less than ¼ in. long. Flowers axillary or terminal, solitary, straw-colored; pedicels ¼–¾ in. long. Sepals ¼–⅜ in. long, ovate, acute, pubescent. Petals in 2 series; outer 1–1½ in. long, oblong, acute or subobtuse, covered on both surfaces with fuscous, velvety tomentum, clawed, the claw rugose outside, glabrous within; inner petals narrower and shorter than the outer. Ovaries 10–12, strigose; ovules 2–6. Carpels 5–7, ovoid or obovoid, ¾ in. long, rounded or pointed, pubescent or tomentose, rarely slightly torulose. Fl. B. I. v. 1, p. 58; King, in Ann. Roy. Bot. Gard. Calcutta, v. 4, part 1 (1893) p. 55, and part 2, t. 72; Talb. Trees, Bomb. p. 4; Watt, Dict. Econ. Prod. v. 6, part 4, p. 211. *Unona farinosa*, Dalz. & Gibs. p. 3; Woodr. in Journ. Bomb. Nat. v. 11 (1897) p. 120. Flowers: Mar.–Oct.

KONKAN: Hathkambe near Ratnagiri, *Woodrow.* S. M. COUNTRY: Párwa Ghát, *Dalzell & Gibson.*

2. **Unona discolor,** *Vahl, Symb.* v. 2 (1791) p. 63, t. 36. A shrub, sometimes climbing. Leaves 3–7 by 1–2 in., oblong-lanceolate, acute or acuminate, glabrous and shining above, glaucous, smooth or scarcely pubescent beneath, base rounded; petioles ¼ in. long. Flowers 2–2½ in. long, extra-axillary, solitary, fragrant; pedicels 1–2 in. long, slender, pubescent, thickening in fruit, with a minute, linear bract below the middle. Sepals ⅛–⅝ in. long, lanceolate, spreading, subglabrous. Ovaries oblong, hairy; stigma laterally grooved. Ripe carpels numerous, ¾–1½ in. long, on stalks ¼ in. long, constricted between the seeds; joints 2–5, marked with a ring of pubescence at the constrictions. Fl. B. I. v. 1, p. 59; Grah. Cat. p. 3; Dalz. & Gibs. p. 3; King, in Ann. Roy. Bot. Gard. Calcutta, v. 4, part 1 (1893) p. 56, and part 2, t. 74; Talb. Trees, Bomb. p. 4; Woodr. in Journ. Bomb. Nat. v. 11 (1897) p. 120. *Unona Dunalii*, Hook. f. & Thoms. Fl. Ind. p. 131; Dalz. & Gibs. p. 3.—Flowers: Aug.

KONKAN: Sivapur in the Wari country, *Dalzell & Gibson, Woodrow.* KANARA: in evergreen forests, *Talbot.*—DISTRIB. Malaya.

3. **Unona Lawii,** *Hook. f. & Thoms. Fl. Ind.* (1855) p. 132. A climbing shrub with slender leafy branches; young parts silky-pubescent. Leaves 2–4 by 1–1½ in., oblong-lanceolate, acute or acuminate, glabrous above, glaucous and more or less pubescent beneath, base rounded; petioles scarcely exceeding ⅛ in. long. Flowers extra-axillary, solitary; pedicels slender, ¾–1¼ in. long, inserted opposite to and a little below the insertion of the leaf, with a minute, ovate, acute bract below the middle. Sepals ¼–⅜ in. long, ovate-lanceolate, acute, tomentose without. Petals: the exterior up to 2½ in. long, rarely reaching ¼ in. in breadth

(usually about $\frac{1}{8}$ in.); the interior shorter, narrow-linear, silky-pubescent on both surfaces, with a slightly enlarged, villous claw which is tubercular within. Ovaries 2–3-ovuled. Carpels many, on a stalk about $\frac{1}{4}$ in. long, mucronate; joints 1–3, oblong-ovoid. Fl. B. I. v. 1, p. 59; Dalz. & Gibs. p. 3; King, in Ann. Roy. Bot. Gard. Calcutta, v. 4, part 1 (1893) p. 57, and part 2, t. 77, A; Talb. Trees, Bomb. p. 4; Woodr. in Journ. Bomb. Nat. v. 11 (1897) p. 120.—Flowers: Apr.–Aug.

KONKAN: *Stocks*!, *Law*!, *Dalzell*!; Wari, *Ritchie*! KANARA: N. Kanara, *Talbot*.

4. **POLYALTHIA,** Blume.

Trees or shrubs. Flowers solitary or fascicled, axillary or leaf-opposed. Sepals 3, valvate or slightly imbricate. Petals 6, valvate, 2-seriate, flat, subequal, ovate or narrow. Stamens many, cuneate; connective truncately dilated beyond the cells. Ovaries indefinite; ovules 1–2, basal and erect or sub-basal and ascending; style usually oblong. Ripe carpels berried, globose or oblong, stalked, 1-seeded.—DISTRIB. Tropical Asia, Africa and Australia; species about 50.

Flowers in fascicles or cymes, axillary or from branches below the leaves; petals linear.
  Leaves narrow-lanceolate, the margins undulate; flowers not fragrant .... 1. *P. longifolia.*
  Leaves elliptic, the margins not undulate; flowers fragrant. 2. *P. fragrans.*
Flowers solitary or 1–3 together, axillary; petals ovate .... 3. *P. cerasoides.*

1. **Polyalthia longifolia,** *Benth. & Hook. f. ex Fl. B. I.* v. 1 (1875) p. 62. A tall handsome tree; young branches slender, glabrous. Leaves membranous, 3–9 by $\frac{3}{4}$–$1\frac{1}{2}$ in., narrowly lanceolate, tapering to a fine point, shining, both surfaces glabrous, margins undulate; petioles about $\frac{1}{4}$ in. long. Flowers 1–$1\frac{1}{2}$ in. across, yellowish-green, in fascicles or shortly peduncled umbels; pedicels slender, 1–$1\frac{1}{2}$ in. long, with a small, pubescent, deciduous bract about or above the middle. Sepals $\frac{1}{8}$ in. long, triangular, pubescent, the tips reflexed. Petals subequal, linear, spreading, tapering to a point. Ripe carpels $\frac{3}{4}$ in. long, numerous, stalked, ovoid, obtuse at both ends, glabrous; stalk $\frac{1}{2}$ in. long, stout, glabrous. Seeds smooth, shining. Fl. B. I. v. 1, p. 62; King, in Ann. Roy. Bot. Gard. Calcutta, v. 4, part 1 (1823) p. 72, and part 2, t. 99; Trim. Fl. Ceyl. v. 1, p. 24; Woodr. in Journ. Bomb. Nat. v. 11 (1897) p. 120; Watt, Dict. Econ. Prod. v. 6, part 1, p. 313. *Guatteria longifolia*, Wall. Cat. 6442; Grah. Cat. p. 4; Dalz. & Gibs. Suppl. p. 2. Flowers: Apr.–June. VERN. *Asok*; *Rát*; *Asupála* (Gujarati).

Not indigenous. Planted as an avenue tree in many stations in the Presidency. May be seen at the Sangam, Poona.—DISTRIB. Ceylon.

2. **Polyalthia fragrans,** *Benth. & Hook. f. ex Fl. B. I.* v. 1 (1875) p. 63. A tree; young parts fuscous-tomentose. Leaves 5–8 by $1\frac{1}{2}$–$3\frac{1}{4}$ in., membranous, elliptic, acute, obtuse or acuminate, upper surface glabrous, shining, lower subglabrous; nerves many pairs, prominent on the underside; petioles $\frac{1}{3}$–$\frac{1}{2}$ in. long. Flowers in short-peduncled, tomentose cymes from tubercles on the branches; pedicels very short in bud, lengthening in flower, up to 1 in. long, with a suborbicular bract about the middle; peduncles and pedicels becoming thickened and

woody in fruit. Sepals small, orbicular. Petals subequal, narrow-linear, 1–1½ in. long, by ¼ in. broad, puberulous. Carpels numerous (10–20), oblique, 1–1½ in. long, ovoid, blunt; pericarp very brittle. Seeds orbicular-ovoid; endosperm transversely fibrous. Fl. B. I. v. 1, p. 63; King, in Ann. Roy. Bot. Gard. Calcutta, v. 4, part 1 (1893) p. 72, and part 2, t. 100, A; Talb. Trees, Bomb. p. 4; Woodr. in Journ. Bomb. Nat. v. 11 (1897) p. 120. *Guatteria fragrans*, Dalz. in Hook. Kew Journ. Bot. v. 3 (1851) p. 206; Dalz. & Gibs. p. 4.

KONKAN: *Law!*, *Stocks!*; Sivapur (Wari Country), *Woodrow*. KANARA: *Stocks!*; on the Southern Ghâts of N. Kanara, common in evergreen forests, *Talbot*.

3. **Polyalthia cerasoides,** *Hook. f. & Benth. ex Fl. B. I.* v. 1 (1875) p. 63. A shrub or small tree with light grey bark; young branches minutely rufous-tomentose, the older glabrous. Leaves membranous, 3–6 by 1–1½ in., oblong-lanceolate, acute or acuminate, glabrous above, pubescent (afterwards glabrous) beneath, base rounded or subacute; petioles less than ¼ inch long, tomentose. Flowers axillary, 1–3 together from short woody tubercles, greenish; pedicels tomentose, ¾–1 in. long, becoming woody in fruit with 1 or 2 large, ovate, pubescent bracts below the middle. Sepals ¼ in. long, ovate, acute, with appressed hairs on the outside, glabrous inside, reflexed. Petals fleshy, incurved, ⅜ in. long by ⅛ in. broad, oblong-ovate, obtuse or subacute, puberulous. Carpels many (usually more than 20), ⅜ in. long, ovoid, apiculate, stalked; stalks ¾–1 in. long. Fl. B. I. v. 1, p. 63; Bedd. Fl. Sylv. t. 1; King, in Ann. Roy. Bot. Gard. Calcutta, v. 4, part 1 (1893) p. 65, and part 2, t. 86, B; Talb. Trees, Bomb. p. 4; Woodr. in Journ. Bomb. Nat. v. 11 (1897) p. 120; Watt, Dict. Econ. Prod. v. 6, part 1, p. 313. *Guatteria cerasoides*, W. & A. Prod. p. 10; Grah. Cat. p. 4; Dalz. & Gibs. p. 3.—Flowers: Mar. VERN. *Hum*; *Vabbina*.

KONKAN: Thal Ghât, Jowar forests, *Graham, Dalzell & Gibson, Woodrow*.

5. GONIOTHALAMUS, Blume.

Shrubs or small trees. Leaves shining above with oblique, parallel, distant, not prominent nerves, forming intra-marginal loops. Flowers solitary or fascicled, axillary or extra-axillary. Sepals 3, usually large, valvate. Petals 6, valvate, in 2 series, thickly coriaceous, the outer flat, ovate or elongate, the inner united into a conical cap over the stamens and ovary, narrowed at the base into a short claw. Stamens many; the produced connective ovate or capitate. Ovaries many; ovules 2, superposed; style oblong or elongate. Ripe carpels 1-seeded.—DISTRIB. Tropical Asia and the Indian Archipelago; species about 40.

1. **Goniothalamus Cardiopetalus,** *Hook. f. & Thoms. Fl. Ind.* (1855) p. 107. A shrub or small tree. Leaves membranous, 5–8 by 2–2½ in., oblong-lanceolate or oblanceolate, suddenly and shortly acuminate; both surfaces glabrous, margins minutely waved, base cuneate; petioles ⅙ in. long. Flowers usually supra-axillary, solitary, or 2–3 in a vertical line above the petiole, sericeo-villous when young, afterwards glabrescent; pedicels ¼–½ in. long, 2–3-bracteate at base; bracts minute. Sepals small, ¼ in. long, orbicular, with appressed, fulvous hairs on the outside. Petals velvety; the outer ½–¾ in. long, concave, cucullate, oblong-ovate, acute; the inner ⅓ shorter and united into a mitreform

column. Style elongate; stigma 2-lobed; ovule solitary. Ripe carpels ¾ in. long, oblong, apiculate, sessile. Fl. B. I. v. 1, p. 75; King, in Ann. Roy. Bot. Gard. Calcutta, v. 4, part 1 (1893) p. 93, and part 3, t. 129; Talb. Trees, Bomb. p. 5; Woodr. in Journ. Bomb. Nat. v. 11 (1897) p. 120; Watt, Dict. Econ. Prod. v. 3, p. 533.—Flowers: Mar.

KANARA: N. Kanara, *Gibson!*, *Stocks!*; Divimana Ghát, *Cooke!*; Nilkund (N. Kanara), *Talbot!*; N. Kanara, in evergreen forests; common on the Ankola Ghát, *Talbot*; N. Kanara, *Woodrow*.

6. ANONA, Linn.

Trees or shrubs. Peduncles 1-flowered; flowers terminal or leaf-opposed. Sepals 3, small, valvate. Petals usually 6, valvate, in 2 series, the exterior fleshy, concave at base, the inner subsimilar or smaller, rarely wanting. Stamens many, the produced connective ovoid at top. Ovaries many, often connate; ovule 1, erect; style oblong. Ripe carpels confluent in a multilocular, ovoid or globose, many-seeded fruit.—DISTRIB. Chiefly tropical American; a few species inhabiting tropical Africa and Asia; species about 400.

Fruit tubercled .... 1. *A. squamosa.*
Fruit smooth, slightly areolate.. 2. *A. reticulata.*

1. **Anona squamosa,** *Linn. Sp. Pl.* (1753) p. 537. A tree about 20 ft. high. Leaves 1½–3 by ¾–1½ in., oblong-lanceolate or elliptic, obtuse or subacute, pellucido-punctate, glabrous above, glaucous and pubescent beneath when young; lateral nerves 8–11 pairs; petioles ½ in. long. Flowers solitary, leaf-opposed, or 2–4, on short, extra-axillary branchlets; pedicels ½–¾ in. long, bracteate below the middle. Sepals minute, triangular, pubescent. Petals pubescent on both surfaces; the exterior about 1 by ¼ in.; the interior minute or sometimes wanting. Fruit globose, 2–4 in. in diam., usually with a glaucous bloom on the surface when young, yellowish-green when ripe, easily broken into large pieces; areoles well-marked, granulate or tuberculate, 5–6-gonous; pulp denser than in *Anona reticulata* and sweeter. Seeds brownish-black, smooth. Fl. B. I. v. 1, p. 78; Grah. Cat. p. 3; Blume, Fl. Java, Anon. p. 107, t. 53, B; Mart. in Fl. Bras. v. 13 (1841) p. 14, t. 5, fig. 1; Dalz. & Gibs. Suppl. p. 2; K. Prantl, in Engl. & Prantl, Pflanzenf. v. 3, part 2, p. 37, fig. 31, B, C; Talb. Trees, Bomb. p. 5; Woodr. in Journ. Bomb. Nat. v. 11 (1897) p. 120; Watt, Dict. Econ. Prod. v. 1, p. 259. —Flowers: May–July. VERN. *Sitaphal.*

The *Custard Apple* of Anglo-Indians; the *Sweet Sop* of the W. Indies. Cultivated and becoming naturalized throughout India, where the fruit is highly valued. The bruised leaves are used for destroying worms bred in sores (*Dalz. & Gibs.* l. c.).

2. **Anona reticulata,** *Linn. Sp. Pl.* (1753) p. 537. A small tree; young branches tomentose, the older glabrous. Leaves membranous, 4–7 by 1–1¾ in., oblong-lanceolate, acute or obtuse, cuneate or rounded at the base, minutely pellucido-punctate, the upper surface glabrous, the lower with a few scattered hairs; nerves 15–18 pairs; petioles ¼–¾ in. long. Flowers 2–4, on lateral pedicels; pedicels about ½ in. long, elongating and becoming thick and woody in fruit. Sepals small, $\frac{3}{16}$ in. long, broadly ovate, acute, tomentose. Petals: the exterior 1¼ in. long by ¼ in. broad, tomentose on both surfaces; the interior minute,

shorter than the sepals. Fruit 4–6 in. in diam., subglobose or somewhat heart-shaped, roughish outside, yellow or yellowish-red when ripe; areoles pentagonal, lightly marked. Seeds smooth, blackish. Differs from *Anona squamosa* in the larger fruit, the areoles of which are not so distinctly marked as in that species, in the larger and more pointed leaves, and in the greater number of nerves. Fl. B. I. v. 1, p. 78; Grah. Cat. p. 3; Dalz. & Gibs. Suppl. p. 2; Talb. Trees, Bomb. p. 5; Woodr. in Journ. Bomb. Nat. v. 11 (1897) p. 120; Watt, Dict. Econ. Prod. v. 1, p. 258.—Flowers: June. VERN. *Rámphal.*

The *Bullock's heart* or *Custard Apple* of the West Indies. Cultivated, but not so extensively as the preceding species. The fruit is largely eaten by the natives, more rarely by Europeans.—DISTRIB. Tropical America.

Anona muricata, Linn., the *Sour Sop* of the West Indies, has been occasionally cultivated in Bombay, but not to any extent.

7. MILIUSA, Leschen.

Middle-sized or low trees. Flowers 1–2-sexual, solitary or fascicled, axillary or extra-axillary. Sepals 3, minute, valvate. Petals 6, valvate, in 2 series, the exterior minute, sepaloid, the interior much larger and thinly coriaceous, often cohering. Stamens many; anthers sub-didymous, cells contiguous, ovoid, extrorse; connective hardly apiculate. Ovaries many; ovules 1–2, rarely 3–4; style oblong or very short. Ripe carpels globose or oblong, 1-many-seeded.—DISTRIB. Species 8, all Indian.

1. **Miliusa indica,** *Leschen. in A. DC. Mém. Fam. Anonacées* (1832) p. 37. A much-branched, variable shrub; young parts fusco-pubescent. Leaves thinly coriaceous, 1¼–3 by ¾–1½ in., oblong-elliptic or oblong-lanceolate, obtuse or acute, glabrous above, glabrous or pubescent beneath, base usually rounded, a little oblique, sometimes subcordate; petioles short, less than ⅛ in. long, pubescent. Flowers axillary, solitary; pedicels slender, ¼–½ in. long, bracteate at the base. Sepals small, ovate, pubescent outside, reflexed. Petals purple; the exterior sepaloid, broadly ovate, about twice as long as the sepals, pubescent; the interior ovate, acuminate, thrice as long as the exterior petals. Stamens numerous, intermixed with stiff hairs; connective slightly produced, rounded. Ovaries densely pilose, oblong, 1–2-ovuled. Ripe carpels numerous, ovoid or obovoid, subsessile, silky-pubescent. Fl. B. I. v. 1, p. 86; K. Prantl, in Engl. & Prantl, Pflanzenf. v. 3, part 2, p. 29, fig. 23, A, B; Trim. Fl. Ceyl. v. 1, p. 34; King, in Ann. Roy. Bot. Gard. Calcutta, v. 4, part 1 (1893) p. 157, and part 3, t. 205, A; Talb. Trees, Bomb. p. 5; Woodr. in Journ. Bomb. Nat. v. 11 (1897) p. 120.—Flowers throughout the year.

Common in N. Kanara in the Ghát forests. KANARA: Nilkund (N. Kanara), *Woodrow*; Poteli (N. Kanara), *Talbot*!

8. SACCOPETALUM, Bennett.

Trees. Leaves deciduous. Flowers axillary, solitary or fascicled. Sepals 3, small, valvate. Petals 6, valvate, in 2 series, the outer small sepaloid, the inner much larger, erect or conniving and saccate at the base. Stamens many; the produced connective conspicuously apiculate. Ovaries many, 6 or more. Ripe carpels subglobose.

Reduced to *Miliusa* by Baillon (*Hist. des Plantes*, 244), from which it differs chiefly by its saccate petals.—DISTRIB. Species 5, of which 2 are Indian, 1 an inhabitant of Java, 1 of the Philippines, and 1 Australian.

1. **Saccopetalum tomentosum,** *Hook. f. & Thoms. Fl. Ind.* (1855) p. 152. A large tree; young branches tomentose, afterwards glabrous. Leaves membranous, 4–7 by 2½–3 in., ovate-oblong, acute, rounded or subacute at the base, glabrous or glabrescent above (except the pubescent midrib), pubescent or tomentose at length glabrous beneath, the midrib sometimes tubercular; petioles ⅛ in. long. Flowers 1 in. in diam.; peduncles leaf-opposed or subterminal, 0–½ in. long, 1–many-flowered; pedicels very slender, 1¾–2½ in. long, bracteate at the base. Sepals minute. Petals: the exterior small, longer than the sepals, linear, acute; the interior about ½ in. long, ovate-oblong, obtuse, saccate at the base, both surfaces pubescent. Stamens numerous, in several rows, shortly apiculate. Ovaries broadly ovate, hirsute at the base; ovules 4–6, in two rows; stigma sessile. Ripe carpels 5–15, about 1 in. long, stalked, subglobose, tapering slightly towards the base, succulent, purple when ripe; stalks ½–1 in. long. Fl. B. I. v. 1, p. 88; Dalz. & Gibs. p. 4; King, in Ann. Roy. Bot. Gard. Calcutta, v. 4, part 1 (1893) p. 159, and part 3, t. 207; Talb. Trees, Bomb. p. 5; Woodr. in Journ. Bomb. Nat. v. 11 (1897) p. 121; Watt, Dict. Econ. Prod. v. 6, part 2, p. 381.—Flowers: Apr.

Western Ghâts. KANARA: Kurli, *Ritchie*!; Talkat Ghât, *Dalzell*! S. M. COUNTRY: Padshapur (Belgaum districts), *Ritchie*!

9. OROPHEA, Blume.

Trees or shrubs. Leaves small. Flowers axillary, solitary, fascicled or cymose. Sepals 3. Petals 6, valvate, in 2 series; the exterior oval; the interior clawed and cohering by their margins into a cap. Stamens 6–12, ovoid, fleshy; anther-cells dorsal; connective sometimes prolonged into a conical, apical point, not truncate. Staminodes 0 or 3–6. Ovaries 3–15; ovules 4; style short or 0. Ripe carpels 1- or more-seeded, globular or oblong.—DISTRIB. Tropical Asia and the Indian Archipelago; species about 25.

1. **Orophea zeylanica,** *Hook. f. & Thoms. Fl. Ind.* (1855) p. 111. A much branched shrub or small tree; young parts fusco-pubescent. Leaves thinly coriaceous, glabrous, 2–4 by 1–1¾ in., oblong-elliptic, shortly and obtusely acuminate, base narrowed or rounded, suboblique; petioles $\frac{1}{10}$ in. long. Flowers green, less than ½ in. in diam.; peduncles extra-axillary, ½–1 in. long, 1–3-flowered; pedicels very slender, variable in length (frequently about 1 in. long), with a bract at the base of each pedicel and sometimes another above its middle. Sepals orbicular, tomentose. Petals: the exterior ¼ in. long, similar to the sepals but larger, broadly-ovate, acute; the interior ⅓ in. long, trapezoidal, glabrous, with pubescent margins. Stamens 6, in a row, their apices pointed. Ovaries 12–15, glabrous, obovoid, 2-ovuled; stigma oblong, subsessile. Carpels ⅓–½ in. in diam., smooth, glabrous, shortly stalked, 1–2-seeded; stalks $\frac{1}{10}$ in. long. Fl. B. I. v. 1, p. 90; King, in Ann. Roy. Bot. Gard. Calcutta, v. 4, part 1 (1893) p. 104, and part 3, t. 146, B; Trim. Fl.

Ceyl. v. 1, p. 35; Talb. Trees, Bomb. p. 6; Woodr. in Journ. Bomb. Nat. v. 11 (1897) p. 121.—Flowers: Feb.

KANARA: on the Ghâts, *Stocks*!, *Dalzell*!; N. Kanara, *Talbot*; Bodeli, in fruit, in April, *Woodrow*.—DISTRIB. Ceylon.

10. BOCAGEA, St. Hilaire.

Trees or shrubs. Leaves often pellucido-punctate. Flowers small, terminal, axillary or fascicled, on woody tubercles, 1–2-sexual. Sepals ovate or orbicular, scarcely connate at the base. Petals 6, imbricate, in 2 series, subequal, orbicular or concave. Stamens 6–18, thick; connective produced. Ovaries 3-6, attenuated into a short style; ovules 1 or 2–8 on the ventral suture; stigma capitate or obtuse. Ripe carpels stalked, globose.—DISTRIB. Tropical Asia and S. America; species 12.

1. **Bocagea Dalzelli,** *Hook. f. Fl. B. I.* v. 1 (1875) p. 92. A small, handsome, laurel-like tree; branches slender. Leaves coriaceous, 4–8 by $1\frac{1}{2}$–$2\frac{1}{2}$ in., oblong-lanceolate, acute or acuminate, upper surface shining, glabrous, lower dull, paler, base narrowed or rounded; petioles $\frac{1}{4}$–$\frac{3}{8}$ in. long, transversely rugose. Flowers small, white, solitary or in fascicles of 2–10, on small woody tubercles on the branches below the leaves; pedicels $\frac{1}{2}$ in. long, with numerous scaly bracts at the base. Sepals orbicular, connate at the base, glabrous, ciliate. Petals: the exterior $\frac{1}{4}$ in. long, orbicular, concave; the interior a little shorter, ciliate. Stamens 12–18, the outer row sometimes imperfect; connective broad, projecting above the dorsal anthers. Ovaries 3–5, oblong, hairy; style short, lateral, glabrous; stigma small. Ripe carpels 1 in. in diam., smooth, globose, sessile. Fl. B. I. v. 1, p. 92; Talb. Trees, Bomb. p. 6; Woodr. in Journ. Bomb. Nat. v. 11 (1897) p. 121. *Guatteria laurifolia*, Grah. Cat. p. 4. *Sageræa laurina*, Dalz. & Gibs. p. 2; King, in Ann. Roy. Bot. Gard. Calcutta, v. 4, part 1 (1893) p. 7, and part 2, t. 35, B.—Flowers: Nov. VERN. *Sageri*; *Andi*.

The Konkan and Kanara on the hills. KONKAN: *Stocks*!, *Dalzell*!; ravines at the western side of the Ghâts and hills at Nagotna, *Graham*; Matheran, *Cooke*!, *Woodrow*! KANARA: N. Kanara, in evergreen forests, *Talbot*.

ORDER V. MENISPERMACEÆ.

Scandent or twining shrubs. Leaves alternate, usually palminerved, entire or lobed, exstipulate. Flowers diœcious, small or minute, fascicled, panicled or racemose, rarely solitary. Sepals usually 6 (rarely 1–4 or 9–12), imbricate in 2–4 series, the outer often minute. MALE FLOWERS: Stamens hypogynous, equal in number and opposite to the petals; filaments free or connate; anthers various, usually adnate, extrose or lateral. FEMALE FLOWERS: Staminodes 6 or 0. Ovaries 3 (rarely 1 or 6–12); ovules solitary, usually amphitropous; styles usually recurved, simple or lobed. Ripe carpels drupaceous; style-scar subterminal or, by excentric growth, sub-basal. Seeds usually hooked or reniform, often curved round an intrusion of the endocarp (*condyle*, Miers); albumen even, or ruminate, or 0; cotyledons flat or semiterete, foliaceous or fleshy, appressed or spreading.—DISTRIB. Chiefly in the tropics of both hemispheres; genera 32; species about 100.

Ovaries 3 or more.
  Seed oblong or globose.
    Style-scar subterminal; filaments free .... 1. TINOSPORA.
    Style-scar sub-basal; filaments connate .... 2. ANAMIRTA.
  Seed horseshoe-shaped.
    Petals 6, minute, cuneate .... 3. TILIACORA.
    Petals 6, auricled .... 4. COCCULUS.
Ovary solitary.
  Sepals free.
    Petals of male and female 3–5, free .... 5. STEPHANIA.
    Petals of male 4, connate, of female 1 .... 6. CISSAMPELOS.
  Sepals connate .... 7. CYCLEA.

1. TINOSPORA, Miers.

Climbing shrubs. Leaves cordate or truncate at the base. Flowers in axillary or terminal elongate racemes or panicles. Sepals 6, in 2 series, the inner larger, membranous. Petals 6, smaller than the sepals. MALE FLOWERS: Stamens 6; filaments free, thickened at the apex; anther-cells dehiscing longitudinally by an oblique, almost marginal slit. FEMALE FLOWERS: Staminodes 6, clavate. Ovaries 3; stigmas forked. Drupes 1–3, ovoid; style-scar subterminal; endocarp rugose, dorsally keeled, ventrally concave. Seed meniscoid, grooved ventrally or curved round the intruded sub-2-lobed endocarp; albumen ruminate on the ventral side only; embryo slightly curved; cotyledons foliaceous, ovate, divaricate.—DISTRIB. Tropical Asia, Africa, and Australia; species about 8.

Leaves large, 4–6 in. in diam., tomentose or woolly beneath...... 1. *T. malabarica.*
Leaves smaller, 2–3½ in. in diam., glabrous..................... 2. *T. cordifolia.*

1. **Tinospora malabarica,** *Miers, in Ann. & Mag. Nat. Hist.* ser. 2, v. 7 (1851) p. 38, & *Contrib.* v. 3 (1864) p. 32. A large climber; young parts clothed with whitish hairs; stems ½ in. in diam.; smooth and shining, with light-colored, papery bark more or less warty. Leaves membranous, 4–6 by 3½–5 in., 7-nerved, broadly ovate, cordate, acuminate, pubescent above, whitish-tomentose beneath; petioles reaching 5 in. long, thickened and twisted at the base. Flowers green, in racemes 3–6 in. long; pedicels slender, clustered. Sepals 6, the outer small, ovate-oblong, obtuse, the inner larger, oblong or suborbicular, concave. Petals in the male flowers obovate, cuneate, rounded at the apex, not embracing the stamens. Drupes 1–3 (usually 2), ovoid, smooth, red, on thick stalks; endocarp marked externally with many sharp-pointed tubercles. Fl. B. I. v. 1, p. 96; Dalz. & Gibs. p. 5, Trim. Fl. Ceyl. v. 1, p. 38; Talb. Trees, Bomb. p. 6; Woodr. in Journ. Bomb. Nat. v. 11 (1897) p. 121. *Cocculus malabaricus*, DC. Syst. v. 1, p. 518; Grah. Cat. p. 4.

The Konkan and Kanara, not common. KONKAN: *Dalzell & Gibson*; in fruit in January, *Woodrow*; S. Konkan, *Nimmo* (ex *Graham*). KANARA: moist forests of N. Kanara, *Talbot.*

2. **Tinospora cordifolia,** *Miers, in Ann. & Mag. Nat. Hist.* ser. 2, v. 7 (1851) p. 38, & *Contrib.* v. 3 (1864) p. 31. An extensive glabrous climber; bark corky, grooved. Leaves membranous, 7-nerved, 2–3½ in. long, roundish or subdeltoid, cordate with a broad sinus, reticulately veined, glabrous on both surfaces, subglaucous beneath; petioles up to

3 in. long. Racemes often much longer than the leaves, axillary, terminal or from the old wood. Flowers yellow, the males fascicled, the females usually solitary; pedicels slender; bracts lanceolate-subulate, the lower sometimes foliaceous. MALE FLOWERS: Sepals: the 3 outer very small, ovate-oblong acute; the 3 inner larger, membranous, suborbicular, concave. Petals: each loosely embracing a stamen, claw cuneate, lamina triquetrous or subtrilobed, reflexed at the apex. FEMALE FLOWERS: Petals cuneate-oblong, with entire (*not* reflexed) margins. Drupes 1–3, dorsally convex, ventrally nearly flat, red, size of a large pea; style-scar subterminal. Fl. B. I. v. 1, p. 97; Dalz. & Gibs. p. 5; Talb. Trees, Bomb. p. 6; Woodr. in Journ. Bomb. Nat. v. 11 (1897) p. 121; Watt, Dict. Econ. Prod. v. 6, part 4, p. 63. *Cocculus cordifolius*, DC. Syst. v. 1, p. 518; Grah. Cat. p. 4.—Flowers: Apr. VERN. *Gul-vel.*

Very common in thickets throughout the Presidency; frequently planted. KONKAN: *Dalzell & Gibson, Graham.* DECCAN: *Woodrow*!; Poona, *Woodrow*! S. M. COUNTRY: Belgaum, *Ritchie*!; Badami, *Cooke*!

2. ANAMIRTA, Colebr.

A climbing shrub. Flowers panicled. Sepals 6, with 2 appressed bracts. Petals 0. MALE FLOWERS: Anthers sessile on a stout column, 2-celled, bursting transversely. FEMALE FLOWERS: Staminodes 9, clavate, 1-seriate. Ovaries 3, on a short gynophore; stigma subcapitate, reflexed. Drupes on a 3-fid gynophore, obliquely ovoid, dorsally gibbous; style-scar sub-basal; endocarp woody. Seed globose, embracing the subglobose, hollow, intruded endocarp; albumen dense, of horny granules; embryo curved; cotyledons narrow-oblong, thin, spreading.

1. **Anamirta paniculata,** *Colebr.* (1819) *in Trans. Linn. Soc.* v. 13 (1821) p. 66. A shrub, climbing to a considerable height; bark ash-colored, vertically furrowed; young parts glabrous. Leaves subcoriaceous, 4–8 by 3–5 in., broadly ovate, cordate or truncate (rarely attenuated) at the base, acute or acuminate (rarely obtuse), 5- (rarely 3-) nerved, glabrous above, pale beneath, with a tuft of hairs in the axils of the nerves except the basal ones; petioles terete, striate, glabrous, thickened at base and apex. Flowers $\frac{1}{4}$ in. in diam., in branched glabrous panicles, 10–14 in. long, on the old branches; branches of the panicle 1–2 in. long, many-flowered; buds globular; pedicels short, $\frac{1}{4}$–$\frac{1}{3}$ in. long, divaricate. Sepals subequal, deciduous, ovate-oblong, concave, quite glabrous. Anthers, in the male flowers, forming a globose head on the short stout column of adherent filaments. Ovaries 3, on a very short smooth gynophore, surrounded at base by a ring of minute, fleshy, bifid staminodes; stigmas reflexed. Ripe carpels 1–3 (usually 2), $\frac{1}{2}$ in. in diam. on the thickened branches of the enlarged gynophore, smooth, black. Miers, Contrib. v. 3, p. 51; Trim. Fl. Ceyl. v. 1, p. 40. *Anamirta Cocculus*, W. & A. Prodr. p. 446; Fl. B. I. v. 1, p. 98; Dalz. & Gibs. p. 4; Talb. Trees, Bomb. p. 7; Woodr. in Journ. Bomb. Nat. v. 11 (1897) p. 121; Watt, Dict. Econ. Prod. v. 1, p. 235. *Cocculus suberosus*, DC. Syst. v. 1, p. 519; Grah. Cat. p. 4. VERN. *Kákaphal*; *Kákamari*; *Vátoli.*

KONKAN: common, *Dalzell & Gibson*; in fruit, January, *Woodrow.* KANARA: *Talbot.*

3. **TILIACORA,** Colebr.

A climbing shrub. Leaves ovate. Flowers in elongate panicles. Sepals 6, in 2 series, the outer small, the inner much larger, scarcely imbricate. Petals 6, minute, cuneate. MALE FLOWERS: Stamens 6, free; anthers 2-celled, introrse. FEMALE FLOWERS: Ovaries 3–12; styles short, subulate. Drupes obovoid, stalked, laterally compressed; style-scar sub-basal; endocarp thin, obscurely ribbed, grooved on both sides. Seed hooked; albumen oily, ruminate; embryo nearly as long as the seed; cotyledons fleshy, appressed.—DISTRIB. East Indies; species 1.

1. **Tiliacora racemosa,** *Colebr. in Trans. Linn. Soc.* v. 13 (1821) p. 67. A woody climber; branches cinereous, striate; young shoots glabrous. Leaves 3–6 by 1½–4 in., 3–5-nerved, ovate, acuminate, cordate, truncate, or rounded at the base, glabrous on both surfaces, shining above, very prominently reticulately veined beneath, margins undulate; petioles ½–¾ in long. Flowers yellow, ¼ in. across, in elongate, lax, axillary, racemose panicles up to 12 in. long; branches 1 in. long, puberulous, at length glabrous, male 3–7-flowered at the apex, female 1-flowered; bracts subulate, hairy. Sepals alike in both sexes; the 3 outer ovate, acute, ciliolate, much shorter than the inner; the inner oblong, obtuse. Petals in both sexes obovate or suborbicular, slightly emarginate, much shorter than the stamens. Drupes 1–10, reddish, ¼ in. long, ovate, compressed, shortly stalked. Fl. B. I. v. 1, p. 99; Trim. Fl. Ceyl. v. 1, p. 42; Talb. Trees, Bomb. p. 7; Watt, Dict. Econ. Prod. v. 6, part 4, p. 56. *Tiliacora acuminata*, Miers, in Ann. & Mag. Nat. Hist. ser. 2, v. 7, p. 39; Hook. f. & Thoms. Fl. Ind. p. 187. *Cocculus acuminatus*, DC. Prodr. v. 1, p. 99; Grab. Cat. p. 5.—Flowers: Jan.–Feb.

KONKAN: *Nimmo*, fide *Graham*, l. c., and fide *Hook. f.* and *Thoms.* l. c.

4. **COCCULUS,** DC.

Climbing or sarmentose shrubs. Flowers in axillary, usually short panicles. Sepals 6, in 2 series, the inner larger. *Petals* 6, shorter than the sepals, usually auricled. MALE FLOWERS: Stamens embraced by the petals; anthers subglobose, cells bursting transversely. FEMALE FLOWERS: Staminodes 6 or 0. Ovaries 3; styles usually cylindric. Drupes laterally compressed; endocarp horseshoe-shaped, dorsally keeled and tuberculate, sides excavate. Seeds horseshoe-shaped; albumen scanty; cotyledons linear, flat, appressed.—DISTRIB. All warm climates.

Leaves suborbicular, glabrous; panicles large .... 1. *C. macrocarpus.*
Leaves deltoid or hastate, villous; panicles short .... 2. *C. villosus.*
Leaves oblong or trapezoidal, at length glabrous; male flowers fascicled, female solitary .... 3. *C. Laeba.*

1. **Cocculus macrocarpus,** *Wight & Arn. Prodr.* (1834) p. 12. A shrub, climbing to a great height; trunk sometimes reaching nearly 1 ft. in diam. with wrinkled bark; young branches dark brown, striate. Leaves variable in shape, usually broader than long, 2–4 by 2½–4½ in., 5-nerved, reticulately veined, rotund or reniform (rarely broadly ovate, acute), truncate or cordate at the base, mucronate, glabrous above,

glaucous beneath, margins somewhat undulate; petioles 2–5 in. long, slender, yellowish, more or less inserted within the margin of the blade. Inflorescence in large, much-branched, glabrous, pendulous panicles 1½–2 ft. long; peduncles usually many, in divergent fascicles from the old wood; flowers yellow, faintly fragrant, in fascicles or umbels along the rhachis; pedicels slender. Sepals thinly membranous, marked (as are the petals and the ovaries) with purple lines and spots; the inner sepals obovate-oblong, rather larger than the outer. Petals broadly cuneate, 3-lobed; the middle lobe emarginate, rarely acute; the lateral lobes embracing the stamens. Anthers subglobose. Ovaries oblong, incurved. Ripe carpels 1–2, nearly sessile, ⅞–1 in. long, obovate-oblong, compressed, tapering to a short neck, glaucous; style-scar conspicuous, basal; endocarp transversely ridged. Seed doubled into a hook. Fl. B. I. v. 1, p. 101; Grah. Cat. p. 5; Dalz. & Gibs. p. 5; Trim. Fl. Ceyl. v. 1, p. 43; Talb. Trees, Bomb. p. 7; Woodr. in Journ. Bomb. Nat. v. 11 (1897) p. 121.—Flowers: Feb.–Mar. VERN. *Rámrik*; *Waten-vel.*

In the Konkan and N. Kanara; abundant at Matheran. KONKAN: *Dalzell & Gibson*, *Law*!, *Gibson*!; Matheran, *Cooke*!, *Woodrow*! KANARA: N. Kanara, on banks of rivers and in moist forests, locally abundant, *Talbot*. S. M. COUNTRY: Belgaum, *Ritchie*!—DISTRIB. China.

2. **Cocculus villosus,** *DC. Syst.* v. 1 (1818) p. 525. A straggling, scandent shrub; young parts densely and softly villous; branches striate. Leaves 1½–2½ by ½–1½ in., 3–5-nerved, ovate-oblong, subdeltoid or subhastate, obtuse, subacute or retuse, apiculate, subcordate or truncate at the base, softly villous on both surfaces, at length nearly glabrous; petioles ⅛ in. long, densely villous. MALE FLOWERS in small axillary cymose panicles; pedicels slender; bracts minute, subulate, hairy. Sepals oblong-ovate, hairy outside, the 3 inner the larger. Petals thinly membranous, obovate, emarginate, embracing the stamens, smaller than the petals of the female flowers. FEMALE FLOWERS in axillary clusters, 2–3 together, rarely racemose. Petals thick and fleshy, divided at the apex into two triangular lobes with swollen bases, claw hairy. Ovaries 3, smooth; stigmas terete, thick, reflexed. Drupe size of a small pea, keeled, transversely rugose. Fl. B. I. v. 1, p. 101; Dalz. & Gibs. p. 5; Talb. Trees, Bomb. p. 7; Woodr. in Journ. Bomb. Nat. v. 11 (1897) p. 121; Watt, Dict. Econ. Prod. v. 2, p. 397.—Flowers: Dec. VERN. *Vásan-vel*; *Páravel.*

Common in hedges throughout the Presidency. KONKAN: *Law*! DECCAN: Poona, *Woodrow*! GUJARAT: Porbandar, *Cooke*!

3. **Cocculus Leaeba,** *DC. Syst.* (1818) p. 529. A scandent shrub; branches cinereous, striate, glabrous; branchlets long, slender, puberulous, at length glabrate. Leaves very variable, ¾–1½ by ⅜–¾ in., 3–5-nerved, oblong, or trapezoidal with rounded angles, subhastate, or sometimes linear-oblong, usually obtuse, mucronate, glabrous (except when young), base cuneate or rounded; petioles ⅛–¼ in. long, hairy. Flowers axillary, small, inserted in a hairy tubercle, the males clustered in dense axillary fascicles, the females solitary (rarely twin). Petals of the male flowers deeply and acutely emarginate, with 2 lateral lobes embracing the stamens. Ovaries 3. Drupe obovoid, keeled, compressed; style-scar basal. Fl. B. I. v. 1, p. 102; Talb. Trees, Bomb. p. 7; Woodr. in Journ. Bomb. Nat. v. 11 (1897) p. 121; Watt, Dict. Econ. Prod.

v. 2, p. 397. *Cocculus glaber*, W. & A. Prodr. p. 13.—Flowers: Nov.–Dec.

In Sind and Gujarat. SIND: near Karachi, *Cooke*!, *Woodrow*! GUJARAT: Dwarka, *Woodrow*!; Porbandar, *Cooke*!—DISTRIB. Afghanistan, Arabia, Africa.

5. STEPHANIA, Loureiro.

Climbing shrubs. Leaves usually peltate. Flowers umbellate. MALE FLOWERS: Sepals 6–10, free, 2-seriate. Petals 3–5, shorter than the sepals, obovate, fleshy. Anthers 6, connate into a ring encircling the top of the staminal column, bursting transversely. FEMALE FLOWERS: Sepals 3–5. Petals as in the male. Staminodes 0. Ovary 1; style 3-6-partite. Drupe glabrous; endocarp compressed, horseshoe-shaped, dorsally tubercled, sides hollow and perforate. Seed almost annular; cotyledons long, slender, ½-terete, appressed.—DISTRIB. Tropics of the Old World and Australia; species 4.

1. **Stephania hernandifolia,** *Walp. Rep.* v. 1 (1842) p. 96. A slender twining shrub; branchlets striate; young shoots glabrous. Leaves peltate, thinly coriaceous, 3–5 by 2½–4 in., ovate or subdeltoid, acute, acuminate, or subobtuse, mucronate, rounded or truncate at the base, glabrous on both surfaces or slightly puberulous on the nerves, glaucescent beneath; petioles 1¼–3 in. long, inserted more than ½ in. within the basal margin, slender, striate, glabrous. Flowers minute, nearly sessile, in small umbels at the ends of long-stalked axillary umbels; bracts subulate. Peduncles about 1 in. long, very slender, glabrous; rays 8–12. Sepals: in the male 6, the outer smaller than the inner, obovate, subobtuse; in the female usually 3–4, ovate, acute. Petals 3–4, obovate-cuneate in both sexes, about half the length of the sepals. Drupes solitary, subsessile, ⅓ in. long, obovoid, compressed, glabrous; endocarp deeply and sharply transversely ridged. Seed curved almost into a ring. Fl. B. I. v. 1, p. 103; Dalz. & Gibs. p. 6; Trim. Fl. Ceyl. v. 1, p. 45; Talb. Trees, Bomb. p. 8; Woodr. in Journ. Bomb. Nat. v. 11 (1897) p. 121; Watt, Dict. Econ. Prod. v. 6, part 3, p. 359.—Flowers: July–Aug.

KONKAN: *Law*!, *Dalzell & Gibson*, *Talbot*. DECCAN: hills near Junnar, *Woodrow*!; Khandala, *Woodrow*!; Lanoli, *Cooke*! KANARA: N. Kanara, *Talbot*.—DISTRIB. Malaya, tropical Africa and Australia.

6. CISSAMPELOS, Linn.

Suberect or climbing shrubs. Leaves often peltate. MALE FLOWERS cymose. Sepals 4. Petals 4, connate into a subentire, short cup. Anthers 2–4, sessile, connate, encircling the top of the peltate staminal column, bursting transversely. FEMALE FLOWERS racemose, crowded in the axils of roundish, leafy bracts. Sepals and petals 1 of each, 2-nerved, adnate to the bracts. Staminodes 0. Ovary 1; style short, 3-fid or 3-toothed. Drupe subglobose; style-scar sub-basal; endocarp compressed, dorsally tubercled, the sides excavated. Seed horseshoe-shaped; embryo linear; cotyledons appressed.—DISTRIB. America, tropical Asia, tropical and S. Africa; species about 18.

1. **Cissampelos Pereira,** *Linn. Sp. Pl.* (1753) p. 1031. A climbing shrub; branches striate, pubescent or subglabrous. Leaves peltate,

$1\frac{1}{2}$–4 in. in diam., orbicular or reniform, often slightly broader than long, cordate or truncate at the base, mucronate, pubescent on both surfaces when young, at length glabrous, underside pale or subglaucous, margins ciliate; petiole $1\frac{1}{2}$–4 in. long, pubescent, inserted $\frac{1}{8}$–$\frac{1}{4}$ in. within the basal margin. Flowers minute, yellowish. MALE FLOWERS pedicelled in nearly axillary cymes; peduncles filiform, $\frac{3}{4}$ in. long, pubescent; bracts small, subulate. Sepals 4, hairy outside, obovate-oblong, concave. Petals combined into a cyathiform corolla, hairy without, glabrous within, half the length of the sepals. Filaments longer than the corolla. FEMALE FLOWERS in elongate, solitary or twin, axillary racemes; pedicels very short, pubescent or villous; bracts foliaceous, more or less stalked or nearly sessile, orbicular or reniform, mucronate, usually softly villous (sometimes glabrous), ciliate, persistent. Sepal 1, ovate-oblong, villous on the outside. Petal 1, subrotund, about half the length of the sepal. Drupe subglobose, compressed, hairy, red; endocarp transversely ridged. Fl. B. I. v. 1, p. 103; Dalz. & Gibs. p. 5; K. Prantl, in Engl. & Prantl, Pflanzenf. v. 3, part 2, pp. 84, 85, fig. 62, A–F; Trim. Fl. Ceyl. v. 1, p. 46; Talb. Trees, Bomb. p. 8; Woodr. in Journ. Bomb. Nat. v. 11 (1897) p. 121; Watt, Dict. Econ. Prod. v. 2, p. 327. *Cissampelos convolvulacea*, Willd. Sp. Pl. v. 4, p. 863; Grah. Cat. p. 5. Flowers: July–Sept. VERN. *Paháḍmul*; *Paháḍvel*.

KONKAN: *Law*!, *Dalzell & Gibson*, *Talbot*. DECCAN: hills near Junnar, *Woodrow*!; Lanoli, *Cooke*!; Khandala, *Woodrow*! KANARA: N. Kanara, *Talbot*.

7. CYCLEA, Arnott.

Shrubs, usually climbing. Leaves peltate or broadly cordate. Flowers in axillary panicles. MALE FLOWERS: Sepals 4–8, connate into a campanulate or inflated globose calyx. Petals as many as the sepals, more or less connate. Anthers 4–6, connate, crowning the staminal column, bursting transversely. FEMALE FLOWERS: Sepal 1, oblong. Petal 1, orbicular. Ovary 1; style short, 3–5-lobed, lobes radiating. Drupe subglobose; style-scar sub-basal; endocarp horseshoe-shaped, dorsally tubercled, sides not excavated, convex. Seed horseshoe-shaped; albumen scanty; cotyledons slender, $\frac{1}{2}$-terete, appressed.—DISTRIB. Tropical Asia; species 3.

Calyx globose; teeth 4–8, short .... 1. *C. Burmanni.*
Calyx campanulate, divided nearly to the base; lobes 4–5 .... 2. *C. peltata.*

1. **Cyclea Burmanni,** *Miers, in Ann. & Mag. Nat. Hist.* ser. 2, v. 7 (1851) p. 41, & *Contrib.* v. 3 (1871) p. 239, t. 121. A climbing shrub; branches slender, terete, striate, hairy when young, glabrous when older. Leaves thinly coriaceous, peltate, 2–5 by $1\frac{1}{4}$–$3\frac{1}{2}$ in., elongate-deltoid, often panduriformly sinuate below the middle, sinuate-truncate or scarcely cordate at the base with rounded angles, shining, glabrous or with a few scattered hairs above, pubescent and reticulately veined beneath, margins slightly repand, nerves hairy; petioles 1–$1\frac{1}{2}$ in. long, hairy, inserted $\frac{1}{2}$–$\frac{3}{4}$ in. within the basal margin. MALE FLOWERS in axillary panicles much longer than the leaf, laxly branched, puberulous; branches remote, elongate, filiform; pedicels slender. Calyx subglobose, shortly 4–8- (often 6-) toothed, hairy without, puberulous or glabrous within. Corolla cyathiform, glabrous, fleshy, margin subentire, involute. FEMALE FLOWERS in axillary racemes about as long as the petiole, pubescent.

Sepal 1, suborbicular, pilose outside. Petal 1, orbicular, glabrous and fleshy, a little smaller than the sepal, to which it is adnate at the base. Drupe white when ripe; endocarp muriculate in lines on the back. Fl. B. I. v. 1, p. 104; Dalz. & Gibs. p. 6; Trim. Fl. Ceyl. v. 1, p. 47; Talb. Trees, Bomb. p. 8; Woodr. in Journ. Bomb. Nat. v. 11 (1897) p. 121. *Clypea Burmanni*, W. & A. Prodr. p. 14 (in part); Grah. Cat. p. 5.—Flowers: Jan. VERN. *Pākar.*

Hilly parts of the Konkan and Ghâts, *Dalzell & Gibson.* KONKAN: *Stocks*!, *Dalzell*!, *Gibson*!; Western Ghâts, *Woodrow.* S. M. COUNTRY: Belgaum, *Ritchie*, 976!

2. **Cyclea peltata,** *Hook. f. & Thoms. Fl. Ind.* (1855) p. 201. Similar in general appearance and habit to the preceding species. Leaves 3–6 by 2–4½ in., deltoid or ovate, acute, truncate or slightly sinuate at the base with rounded angles, mucronate, more or less hairy on the nerves and veins, margins often ciliate. Flowers minute, smaller than in the preceding. MALE PANICLES axillary, slender, much-branched; branches remote, divaricate, the lower the longer, gradually becoming shorter upwards, the uppermost very short or obsolete; flowers subsessile, interruptedly spicate or collected into heads. Calyx campanulate, divided nearly to the base into 4 (rarely 5) segments, pilose without. Corolla 4-(rarely 5-) fid. FEMALE PANICLES racemose, much shorter than the male. Sepal oblong, glabrous. Petal orbicular, much shorter than the sepal. Ovary pilose. Drupe pilose. Fl. B. I. v. 1, p. 104; Dalz. & Gibs. p. 6; Miers, Contrib. v. 3, p. 236; Trim. Fl. Ceyl. v. 1, p. 47; Talb. Trees, Bomb. p. 8; Woodr. in Journ. Bomb. Nat. v. 11 (1897) p. 121.

Distinguished from *C. Burmanni* by the more ovate leaves and by the calyx, which is campanulate (almost funnel-shaped) instead of globose, and which is divided almost to the base, instead of being shortly toothed. The corolla too is more deeply divided than in the preceding species.

The plant is by no means common in the Bombay Presidency. It may be found occasionally on some of the Konkan hills, but not nearly so frequently as *Cyclea Burmanni.*

ORDER VI. NYMPHÆACEÆ.

Aquatic, perennial herbs, with a submerged rhizome. Leaves usually floating, rarely emersed, usually peltate, involute in vernation, the submerged leaves never divided; petioles long. Flowers usually floating or sometimes emersed, handsome; scapes 1-flowered, naked; floral whorls all free, hypogynous or adnate to a fleshy disk which surrounds or envelops the carpels. Sepals 3–5. Petals 3–5 or many. Stamens 6–many; anthers erect. Carpels 3 or more in one whorl, free or connate or irregularly sunk in pits of the disk; stigmas as many, peltate or decurrent. Ovules few or many, scattered over the walls of the cells, anatropous or orthotropous. Fruit emersed or maturing beneath the water, formed of the connate carpels, or of separate and indehiscent carpels, or of the enlarged, turbinate, flat-topped disk with the nut-like carpels sunk in its crown. Seeds naked or immersed in a fleshy or pulpous aril; albumen floury or 0; embryo enclosed in the enlarged amniotic sac.—DISTRIB. Throughout the world; genera 8; species about 35.

Carpels confluent with the disk into one ovary; ovules many; seeds albuminous .... 1. NYMPHÆA.
Carpels irregularly scattered, sunk in pits of the turbinate disk; ovules 1-2; seeds exalbuminous .... 2. NELUMBIUM.

1. NYMPHÆA, Linn.

Large aquatic herbs; rootstock creeping. Flowers large, floating, on long, radical scapes, expanded. Sepals 4, inserted at the base of the torus. Petals 12–28, in many series, the inner gradually transformed into stamens, all adnate to the base of the disk. Filaments petaloid, 40–60 in many series. Anthers narrow-linear; slits introrse. Ovaries many, immersed in a fleshy torus and combined with it, forming a many-celled ovary, crowned by the connate, radiating, furrowed stigmas; ovules numerous, anatropous. Fruit a soft spongy berry, ripening under water, bursting irregularly. Seeds minute, nesting in pulp, enclosed in a sac-like, fleshy aril, albuminous.—DISTRIB. Throughout the greater part of the world; species about 25.

Anthers without appendages; stigmatic rays with clavate appendages. 1. *N. Lotus.*
Anthers with appendages; stigmatic rays without appendages .... 2. *N. stellata.*

1. **Nymphæa Lotus,** *Linn. Sp. Pl.* (1753) p. 511. Rootstock tuberous, short, erect, roundish. Leaves peltate, 6–10 in. in diam., orbicular or reniform (the younger subsagittate), deeply cordate at the base the sinus 2½–3 in. deep, sharply and irregularly sinuate-dentate, with very sharp hard teeth, glabrous and often nigro-punctate above, velvety-pubescent and prominently veined beneath; petioles very long, cylindric, submerged, glabrous or puberulous, inserted ½–¾ in. within the basal margin. Flowers solitary, 3–8 in. across, red, pale rose, or white, open in the mornings only; peduncles very long, usually pubescent. Sepals oblong, obtuse, 5–10-ribbed. Petals about 12, oblong, obtuse, about thrice as long as broad. Stamens about 40; anthers without appendages; filaments much dilated at the base; pollen smooth. Stigmatic rays 10–20, with clavate appendages. Fruit 1¼ in. in diam., fleshy, globose, green, ripening beneath the water. Seeds ovoid, rough; aril white, transparent. Fl. B. I. v. 1, p. 114; Dalz. & Gibs. p. 6; R. Caspary, in Engl. & Prantl, Pflanzenf. v. 3, part 2, p. 8, fig. 9, A, B; Trim. Fl. Ceyl. v. 1, p. 40; Woodr. in Journ. Bomb. Nat. v. 11 (1897) p. 121; Watt, Dict. Econ. Prod. v. 5, p. 436. *Nymphæa rubra*, Roxb. ex Salisb. Parad. Lond. 1, sub t. 14; Grah. Cat. p. 5.—Flowers all the year. VERN. *Kamal.*

Common throughout India in the warmer parts; cultivated in the Bombay Presidency.—DISTRIB. Africa, Hungary, Java, Philippines.

VAR. 1. *pubescens*, Hook. f. & Thoms. Fl. Ind. (1855) p. 241. Leaves more densely pubescent beneath. Flowers smaller, 3–4 in. in diam. Sepals oblong, acute. *Nymphæa pubescens*, Willd. Sp. Pl. v. 2, p. 1154; Grah. Cat. p. 6.

Equally common with the former. Both are cultivated in the Bombay Presidency. The roots and seeds are eaten in times of scarcity.

2. **Nymphæa stellata,** *Willd. Sp. Pl.* v. 2 (1797) p. 1153. Rootstock ovoid, short, acute. Leaves peltate, 5–8 in. in diam., orbicular or elliptic (the younger sagittate), obtusely sinuate-dentate or entire, with a narrow sinus 2–3 in. deep, glabrous on both surfaces, often blotched

with purple beneath; petioles long, slender, submerged. Flowers solitary, 3–6 in. in diam., usually pale violet, less commonly light blue or purple, sometimes faintly fragrant, open all the day; peduncles long. Sepals many-veined, not ribbed, oblong-lanceolate, acute or subobtuse, streaked with purple lines. Petals linear-oblong or lanceolate. Filaments 10–50, dilated at the base; anthers with a lingual appendage; pollen smooth. Stigmatic rays 10–30, without appendages. Fruit globular. Seeds longitudinally striate. Fl. B. I. v. 1, p. 114; Grah. Cat. p. 5; Dalz. & Gibs. p. 6; Trim. Fl. Ceyl. v. 1, p. 50; Woodr. in Journ. Bomb. Nat. v. 11 (1897) p. 121; Watt, Dict. Econ. Prod. v. 5, p. 438.—Flowers all the year. VERN. *Uplia-Kamal.*

Common throughout the warmer parts of India; cultivated in the Bombay Presidency, but not so extensively as the preceding species. The roots and seeds are eaten in times of scarcity.—DISTRIB. Africa.

2. NELUMBIUM, Juss.

Aquatic herbs; juice milky; rhizome horizontal. Leaves peltate, much raised out of the water. Scapes 1-flowered. Flowers handsome, rosy, white or yellow. Sepals 4–5, inserted on the top of the scape, caducous. Petals and stamens numerous, hypogynous, many-seriate, caducous. Anthers appendaged. Ovaries many, 1-celled, sunk in the flat top of an obconic fleshy torus; ovules 1–2, pendulous; style very short, exserted; stigmas terminal, subdilated. Carpels ovoid, loose in the cavities of the large spongy torus; pericarp bony, smooth. Seed filling the carpel; testa spongy; albumen 0; cotyledons thick, fleshy, enclosing the large folded plumule.—DISTRIB. Species 2, one West Indian, the other Asiatic and Australian.

1. **Nelumbium speciosum,** *Willd. Sp. Pl.* v. 2, p. 1258. A large aquatic herb with slender, elongate, branched, creeping stems sending out roots at the nodes. Leaves membranous, 1–2 ft. or more in diam., orbicular, concave or cupped, erect, exactly peltate, entire, radiately nerved, glaucous, glabrous; petioles very long, rough with small distant prickles, otherwise smooth. Flowers solitary, 4–10 in. in diam., white or rosy; peduncles coming off from the nodes of the stem, sheathing at the base. Sepals small. Petals 2–5 in. long, elliptic, obtuse, finely veined, concave, at first erect, afterwards spreading. Anthers with a clavate appendage. Torus ¾ in. high, spongy; the top flat, 1 in. broad, becoming enlarged in fruit to a breadth of 2–4 in. Ripe carpels ½ in. long, ovoid, glabrous. Fl. B. I. v. 1, p. 116; Grah. Cat. p. 5; Dalz. & Gibs. p. 7; Trim. Fl. Ceyl. v. 1, p. 51; Woodr. in Journ. Bomb. Nat. v. 11 (1867) p. 121; Watt, Dict. Econ. Prod. v. 5, p. 343.—Flowers: July. VERN. *Kamal*; *Kankadi.*—DISTRIB. Persia, Malaya, China, Japan, tropical Australia.

In tanks throughout the warmer parts of India, a doubtful native; cultivated in the Bombay Presidency. The tender roots and rhizomes are eaten in times of scarcity and with the seeds and petals are used medicinally by the natives.

ORDER VII. PAPAVERACEÆ.

Annual or perennial herbs; juice milky or colored. Leaves radical or alternate, exstipulate. Flowers often large, nodding in bud, regular, hermaphrodite; perianth and stamens very caducous. Sepals 2–3, hypogynous, concave. Petals 4, large, crumpled, 2-seriate. Stamens very many; filaments slender; anthers erect, slits lateral. Ovary 1-celled or 2–4-celled by the produced placentas; ovules many-seriate, parietal, anatropous; style short or 0; stigmas radiating, connate and opposite the placentas or free and alternating with them. Carpels dehiscing by pores or valves. Seeds many, small; albumen oily and fleshy; embryo minute, 2-lobed or 2-fid.—DISTRIB. N. temperate zone; species about 65.

1. ARGEMONE, Linn.

Branching, glaucescent herbs with yellow juice. Leaves inciso-pinnatifid, usually spinoso-dentate or rigidly setose. Flowers handsome, terminal, white or yellow; buds usually erect. Sepals 2–3. Petals 4–6. Stamens indefinite. Ovary 1-celled; ovules many, on 4–7 parietal, filiform placentas; style scarcely any; stigma 4–7-lobed. Capsule oblong, short, dehiscing at top by short valves alternating with the stigmas and placentas. Seeds many, scrobiculate, not crested.—DISTRIB. American plants, of which one, *Argemone mexicana*, has been naturalized in India.

1. **Argemone mexicana,** *Linn. Sp. Pl.* (1753) p. 508. A prickly herb 2–4 ft. high, divaricately branched. Leaves sessile, ½-amplexicaul, variegated with white, 3–6 by 1–2½ in., sinuato-pinnatifid; the segments inciso-dentate, spiny on the margins, the midrib and the veins beneath, lower surface very pale; prickles very sharp, yellow. Flowers 1–3 in. across; peduncles prickly. Sepals 2–3, concave, nearly valvate in æstivation, prickly outside, horned at the apex, very caducous. Petals 1–1¼ in. long, twice as many (4–6) as the sepals, imbricate in 2 series, more or less crumpled in æstivation, obovate, cuneiform, yellow with darker parallel veins, deciduous; bracts foliaceous. Ovary covered with soft spines; stigma red. Capsules ¾–1½ in. long, oblong or elliptic, prickly, rarely unarmed. Seeds blackish-brown, deeply reticulato-scrobiculate. Fl. B. I. v. 1, p. 117; Grah. Cat. p. 6; Dalz. & Gibs. Suppl. p. 3; Bot. Mag. (1794) v. 7, t. 243; Asa Gray & Sprague, Gen. Pl. U. States, v. 1, p. 111, t. 47; Woodr. in Journ. Bomb. Nat. v. 11 (1897) p. 121; Watt, Dict. Econ. Prod. v. 1, p. 306.—Flowers all the year. VERN. *Pivala-dhotara*.—DISTRIB. Tropical America, but naturalized in most warm countries.

The plant has been widely established, and is to be met with along roadsides and as a weed in cultivated fields throughout India. The yellow juice is used medicinally by the natives and oil is expressed from the seeds.

ORDER VIII. FUMARIACEÆ.

Annual or perennial herbs with watery juice. Leaves alternate, usually divided; segments not jointed. Flowers small, racemed, hermaphrodite. Sepals 2, scale-like, deciduous. Petals 4, in dissimilar pairs; the 2 outer larger, one or both gibbous or spurred; the two inner smaller, erect, tips often cohering. Stamens 6, in two bundles opposite the outer petals; anther of central stamen in each bundle 2-celled, of lateral stamens 1-celled. Ovary 1-celled; ovules 2 or more, amphitropous, parietal; stigma obtuse or lobed. Fruit a 2-valved, many-seeded capsule or an indehiscent, 1-seeded nut. Seeds albuminous; raphe sometimes appendaged; embryo minute.—DISTRIB. Widely diffused throughout the temperate and warm regions of the N. hemisphere and extratropical Africa; genera 7; species 130.

1. FUMARIA, Linn.

Herbs, usually annual, often diffuse or scandent. Leaves multisect; segments usually narrow. Flowers small, white, rosy, or purplish, in terminal or leaf-opposed racemes. Sepals 2, small. Petals 4, erect or connivent; the 2 outer dissimilar, the lower flat or concave, the upper gibbous or spurred at the base; the 2 inner clawed, keeled, tips free or coherent. Stamens 6, diadelphous, with a basal spur enclosed in the spur of the petal. Ovary 1-celled; style filiform; stigma entire or shortly 2-lobed. Fruit 1-seeded, indehiscent, subglobose.—DISTRIB. Europe, Central Asia and extratropical Africa; species 8.

1. **Fumaria parviflora,** *Lam. Encyc.* v. 2 (1786) p. 567, var. *Vaillantii*, *Loisel* (sp.) *in Desv. Journ. Bot.* v. 2 (1809) p. 358. Diffuse, 6 in.–2 ft. high; stem and branches glabrous or faintly puberulous. Leaves multifid, glaucous; segments flat, narrow-linear, acute, mucronate. Racemes lax, 1–2½ in. long; flowers ¼–⅓ in. long, white or pale rose with purple tips; fruiting pedicels ⅛ in. long; bracts membranous, lanceolate, shorter than or equalling the fruiting pedicels. Sepals minute, caducous. Capsule globose, not pointed, slightly verrucose, polished. Fl. B. I. v. 1, p. 128; Grah. Cat. p. 6; Dalz. & Gibs. p. 7; DC. Prodr. v. 1, p. 130; W. & A. Prodr. p. 18; Syme, Eng. Bot. v. 1, ed. 3, p. 113, t. 77; Woodr. in Journ. Bomb. Nat. v. 11 (1897) p. 121; Watt, Dict. Econ. Prod. v. 3, p. 454.—Flowers: Jan. VERN. *Pitpápda.*

A weed found usually in cultivated fields in the Deccan and Sind. DECCAN: *Dalzell & Gibson*, *Woodrow*; Sirur, *Graham*; Khandesh, *Woodrow*!, *Dalzell & Gibson*. SIND: *Stocks*, 687!; *Cooke*!

ORDER IX. CRUCIFERÆ.

Annual or perennial herbs, rarely shrubs, with watery, often acrid juice. Leaves radical or alternate, exstipulate. Flowers usually racemose. Sepals 4, free, the 2 lateral often large and saccate at the base, imbricate. Petals 4 (rarely 0), placed crosswise, imbricate. Stamens 6, 2-seriate, hypogynous; the 2 outer opposite the lateral sepals; the 4 inner larger, in pairs, opposite the other sepals; filaments subulate. Disk with usually 4 glands opposite the sepals. Ovary 2-celled, by a septum joining the placentas, or 1-celled or with superimposed cellules; ovules many (rarely 1–2), 1–2-seriate, on 2 parietal placentas; style short or 0; stigma simple, or with 2 lobes opposite the placentas. Fruit a long or short, 2-celled and 2-valved pod, the valves deciduous and leaving the seeds on the persistent placentas (*replum*), or indehiscent, or of superposed 1-seeded joints. Seeds small; albumen 0; cotyledons large, plano-convex or longitudinally concave or folded, foliaceous in germination; radicle turned up on the back of one cotyledon (*incumbent*) or facing their edges (*accumbent*).—DISTRIB. All temperate and cold regions, chiefly of the Old World; genera 172; species about 1200.

Pods long, dehiscing throughout their whole length, terete, 4-angled or dorsally compressed (parallel to the septum).
Lateral sepals not saccate at the base.
Pods spreading or ascending; cotyledons accumbent.
Pods tumid, not compressed; seeds 2-seriate .... 1. NASTURTIUM.
Pods narrow-linear, compressed; seeds 1-seriate .... 2. CARDAMINE.
Pods closely appressed to the axis .... 4. ERUCA.
Lateral sepals saccate at the base.
A twiggy undershrub; leaves small, linear-oblong; cotyledons accumbent .... 3. FARSETIA.
Branched herb, woody at the base; leaves large, elliptic oblong; cotyledons incumbent...... 5. MORICANDIA.
Pods short, dehiscing throughout their whole length, compressed at right angles to the narrow septum.
Valves not winged.
Pods many-seeded .... 6. CAPSELLA.
Pods 2-seeded .... 7. SENEBIERA.
Valves with broad wings .... 8. THLASPI.
Pods long or short, transversely jointed; joints indehiscent or the lower 2-valved.
A leafy undershrub; pods 2-jointed, lower joint seedless, 2-valved .... 9. PHYSORHYNCHUS.

1. NASTURTIUM, R. Br.

Terrestrial or aquatic, branched herbs, glabrous or clothed with simple hairs. Leaves entire, lobed or pinnatifid. Flowers small, yellow, rarely white, sometimes bracteate. Sepals short, spreading, equal. Petals short, narrowed at the base, scarcely clawed or 0. Stamens, 2, 4 or 6; filaments without wings or teeth. Pods not compressed, subterete; valves faintly 1-nerved; septum hyaline; style short or long and slender; stigma simple or 2-lobed. Seeds small, turgid, usually 2-seriate; cotyledons accumbent.—DISTRIB. Throughout the world; species 20–25.

Aquatic herb .... 1. *N. officinale.*
Terrestrial herb .... 2. *N. indicum.*

1. **Nasturtium officinale,** *R. Br. in Ait. Hort. Kew.* ed. 2, v. 4, p. 110. An aquatic herb; stem 2–4 ft. long, procumbent and rooting, fistular, often floating. Leaves green or olive-brown, pinnate; leaflets sessile, 3–5 pairs and a terminal one, ovate-oblong or sinuately-lobed, obtuse. Flowers small, $\frac{1}{8}$–$\frac{1}{4}$ in. in diam., in short racemes. Petals exceeding the sepals. Pods $\frac{1}{2}$–1 in. long, shortly cylindric, stalked, spreading or curved upwards; fruiting pedicels about equalling the pods. Seeds minute, muriculate, not winged, red. Fl. B. I. v. 1, p. 133; Grah. Cat. p. 7; Dalz. & Gibs. Suppl. p. 4; Syme, Engl. Bot. v. 1, p. 176, t. 125; Watt, Dict. Econ. Prod. v. 5, p. 342.

The Water-cress, introduced into India. It now grows wild in many watercourses and is cultivated in many places in the vicinity of Indian stations, the leaves being collected and sold in the markets chiefly for the use of Europeans.—DISTRIB. Afghanistan, temperate Europe and Asia.

2. **Nasturtium indicum,** *DC. Syst.* v. 2 (1821) p. 199. Erect, 6–18 in. high, glabrous or hairy; stem branched from the base, terete, slender. Leaves ovate-lanceolate, runcinate-dentate; lower leaves 3 by 1 in., usually petioled, inciso-pinnatifid or lobed at the base, the lobes acute on both sides irregularly dentate from the middle to the apex; upper leaves subsessile, dentate above the base, subentire at the apex. Racemes terminal, many-flowered, much elongate; flowers small, yellow; pedicels $\frac{1}{8}$–$\frac{1}{4}$ in. long, ebracteate. Pods $\frac{1}{2}$–$\frac{3}{4}$ in. long, straight or slightly curved, subterete, spreading or ascending. Seeds numerous, minute, ellipsoid, 2-seriate, red, not winged. Fl. B. I. v. 1, p. 134; Woodr. in Journ. Bomb. Nat. v. 11 (1897) p. 121. *Nasturtium madagascariense,* W. & A. Prodr. p. 19.

Tolerably common throughout the Presidency in damp places. KONKAN: *Stocks*!, *Law*! S. M. COUNTRY: Belgaum, *Ritchie*, 21!—DISTRIB. China, Malaya.

2. CARDAMINE, Linn.

Annual or perennial, often glabrous herbs. Leaves entire, lobed or pinnate. Flowers white or purplish (rarely yellow), ebracteate, arranged in corymbs or short racemes which afterwards elongate. Sepals equal at the base. Petals clawed. Pods narrow-linear, compressed, tapering at both ends; valves opening elastically; septum membranous; stigma simple or 2-lobed. Seeds compressed, 1-seriate, not winged; cotyledons accumbent.—DISTRIB. Temperate and cold regions of the globe; species about 60.

1. **Cardamine subumbellata,** *Hook. f. & T. Anders. Fl. B. I.* v. 1 (1875) p. 138. A small much-branched herb, 6–10 in. high; stem and branches angled, often tinged with purple. Leaves (including petioles) 2–2$\frac{3}{4}$ in. long, pinnate; leaflets 5–7, about $\frac{1}{2}$–$\frac{1}{3}$ in. in diam. (the terminal leaflet larger), ovate or suborbicular, irregularly crenate or lobed, usually shortly and obliquely cuneate at the base, sparingly hairy; radical leaves absent or few, when present not forming a rosette and with smaller leaflets than the stem-leaves; petiolules of the lateral leaflets $\frac{1}{8}$–$\frac{1}{4}$ in. long, those of the terminal leaflets $\frac{1}{4}$–$\frac{1}{2}$ in. long. Flowers small, few, pale-yellow, at first corymbose, afterwards racemose; pedicels short, slender. Stamens 6. Pods $\frac{3}{4}$–1 in. long by $\frac{1}{16}$–$\frac{1}{12}$ in. broad, linear-lanceolate, much flattened. Seeds 4–8, broad-oblong, distant. Trim. Fl. Ceyl. v. 1, p. 53; Woodr. in Journ. Bomb. Nat. v. 11 (1897) p. 122. *Cardamine hirsuta*, var. *subumbellata*, Dalz. in Hook. Kew Journ. Bot. v. 4 (1852) p. 294; Dalz. & Gibs. p. 7. *Cardamine hirsuta*, var. *sylvatica*, (Link) Woodr. in Journ. Bomb. Nat. v. 11 (1897) p. 122.—Flowers: July–Sept.

On high hills throughout the Southern districts of the Presidency; abundant at Mahableshwar. KONKAN: *Law*! DECCAN: Khandala, *Woodrow*; Mahableshwar, *Cooke*!; Karli, *Jacquemont*, 761! S. M. COUNTRY: hills near Belgaum, *Dalzell*!—DISTRIB. Temperate and subtropical regions.

3. FARSETIA, Desv.

Herbs or branched undershrubs, often twiggy, hoary or tomentose. Leaves small, quite entire, alternate. Flowers spicate or racemed, white, pink or yellow, sometimes minute. Sepals usually erect, the lateral ones saccate at the base. Petals clawed. Pods sessile, oblong or linear, much compressed; valves flat or convex, with or without a midrib; septum membranous, veined. Seeds 1-2-seriate, suborbicular, with a broad membranous wing; cotyledons accumbent.—DISTRIB. S. Europe, N. Africa, Asia Minor, Persia, Arabia; species about 20.

Flowers large; seeds 2-seriate .... 1. *F. Jacquemontii.*
Flowers small; seeds 1-seriate .... 2. *F. Hamiltonii.*

1. **Farsetia Jacquemontii,** *Hook. f. & Thoms. in Journ. Linn. Soc.* v. 5 (1861) p. 148. An erect, rigid shrub, clothed with appressed hairs attached by tho middle; branches terete, slender. Leaves $\frac{1}{4}$–$1\frac{1}{2}$ by $\frac{1}{16}$–$\frac{1}{10}$ in., linear-lanceolate; petioles very short. Flowers large, pink, in long slender, lax racemes; buds ellipsoid; pedicels short. Calyx cylindric; Sepals $\frac{1}{8}$–$\frac{1}{4}$ in. long, linear-oblong, acute, hairy. Petals $\frac{3}{16}$–$\frac{3}{8}$ in. long. Pods stalked, $1\frac{1}{4}$–2 in. long by $\frac{1}{8}$–$\frac{1}{6}$ in. broad, flat, faintly 1-nerved or nerveless; stalks $\frac{1}{8}$–$\frac{1}{6}$ in. long. Seeds 2-seriate, flattened, furnished with a broad membranous wing, brown. Fl. B. I. v. 1, p. 140; Woodr. in Journ. Bomb. Nat. v. 11 (1897) p. 122; Watt, Dict. Econ. Prod. v. 3, p. 320.

SIND: *Dalzell*!, *Woodrow*!; Sehwan, *Cooke*!—DISTRIB. N. India, Afghanistan and Beluchistan.

2. **Farsetia Hamiltonii,** *Royle, Ill. Bot. Himal.* (1839) p. 71. Twiggy; branches numerous, long, slender, covered with dense appressed hairs attached by the middle. Leaves linear, very narrow, $\frac{1}{4}$–$\frac{1}{2}$ by $\frac{1}{32}$ in. Flowers small, pink, in long spicate racemes. Sepals $\frac{1}{10}$–$\frac{1}{8}$ in. long, oblong, obtuse, hairy, the margins scarious. Petals obovate, a little longer than the sepals. Pods $\frac{1}{2}$–$\frac{3}{4}$ in. long by $\frac{1}{8}$–$\frac{1}{6}$ in. broad, flattened; style slender. Seeds brown, 1-seriate, with broad, membranous margins. Fl. B. I. v. 1, p. 140; Woodr. in Journ. Bomb. Nat. v. 11 (1897) p. 122; Watt, Dict. Econ. Prod. v. 3, p. 320.

SIND: *Woodrow*.—DISTRIB. Afghanistan, Arabia, Algeria.

4. ERUCA, Tourn.

Annual or biennial herbs, erect, branching. Leaves lyrato-pinnatifid. Flowers white, yellow or violet, veined; pedicels slender. Sepals erect, equal at the base. Stamens free, not toothed. Pods ovoid-oblong, turgid, terete, with an ensiform seedless beak; valves concave, 3-nerved; septum membranous; stigma simple. Seeds numerous, 2-seriate; cotyledons conduplicate.—DISTRIB. Europe, Western Asia; species 3.

1. **Eruca sativa,** *Mill. Gard. Dict.* ed. 8 (1768) n. 1. Erect, branched, 2–3 ft. high; stems and branches glabrous or with a few scattered hairs. Leaves petioled, lyrato-pinnatifid, sinuate-dentate, rarely entire. Flowers white or yellow. Sepals $\frac{3}{8}$ in. long, oblong, acute, often tipped with hairs. Petals $\frac{5}{8}$ in. long, obovate, veined; pedicels $\frac{1}{8}$ in. long. Pod turgid, 1 in. long, closely appressed to the axis; beak flattened, 3-nerved, glabrous. Seeds 2-seriate, subglobose. Fl. B. I. v. 1, p. 158; Woodr. in Journ. Bomb. Nat. v. 11 (1897) p. 122; Watt, Dict. Econ. Prod. v. 3, p. 266. VERN. *Safed-sarsu.*

A weed of cultivation, found in cultivated places throughout the Presidency. The plant is extensively cultivated as a cold season crop in the North Western Provinces and in the Punjab, oil being expressed from the seeds.—DISTRIB. Shores of the Mediterranean, Western Asia.

5. MORICANDIA, DC.

Branched herbs, often woody at the base, glaucous, glabrous. Leaves entire, amplexicaul or pinnatisect. Flowers large, violet, purple or rosy. Sepals erect, the lateral saccate at the base. Petals clawed. Pods linear, elongate, with or without a flattened, 1-seeded beak; valves flat or bluntly keeled; stigmatic lobes united into a short cone. Seeds numerous, 1–2-seriate, compressed, sometimes winged; cotyledons incumbent, conduplicate.—DISTRIB. The Mediterranean region, Arabia, W. Asia; species about 5.

1. **Moricandia tortuosa,** *H. f. & Thoms. in Journ. Linn. Soc.* v. 5 (1861) p. 172. Whole plant glaucous and glabrous. Leaves thick, mucronate; the lower petioled, 2–5 by 1–2 in., elliptic-obovate, acute or acuminate, cuneate at base, attenuated into the petiole, the margins sinuato-crenate; the upper stem-leaves sessile, lanceolate. Flowers large, erect, in long few-flowered racemes; buds ellipsoid, acuminate; pedicels ⅛ in. long. Sepals up to ⅓ in. long, linear-oblong, acute. Petals obovate, pale rose-colored, about twice as long as the sepals. Pods linear, elongate, subterete, striate; beak subcylindric, ⅛ in. long; style short, conical. Seeds oblong-ellipsoid, with an ear-shaped wing at the base and microscopically margined on the sides, chestnut-brown. Fl. B. I. v. 1, p. 158; Woodr. in Journ. Bomb. Nat. v. 11 (1897) p. 122.

SIND: *Woodrow.*

6. CAPSELLA, Medik.

Annual, branched, often weak herbs, glabrous or hairy. Radical leaves rosulate, entire, lobed or pinnatifid. Flowers racemed, small, white; pedicels slender. Sepals spreading, equal at the base. Petals short. Stamens free, not toothed. Pods obcordate, cuneate, laterally compressed; valves boat-shaped, keeled; septum membranous; style short. Seeds numerous, 2-seriate, ellipsoid; cotyledons incumbent.—DISTRIB. Temperate regions of both hemispheres; species 6.

1. **Capsella Bursa-pastoris,** *Medik. Pflanzen.* (1792) p. 85. An erect herb, 6–24 in. high, glabrous or hairy; branches terete. Leaves: the radical rosulate, 2–4 (including the petioles if present) by ½–1 in., oblong, acute or oblanceolate, toothed or inciso-pinnatifid, the lobes acute on both sides, sometimes entire; stem-leaves distant, 1–2½ in. long, oblong-lanceolate, amplexicaul, hastate or sagittate at the base with acute parallel or diverging auricles. Flowers at first corymbose, afterwards elongating into a raceme 8–9 in. long. Sepals oblong, obtuse. Petals oblanceolate, white, about half as long again as the sepals. Pods glabrous, ⅜ in. long, by ⅛–¼ in. broad at top; pedicels slender, smooth, terete, ebracteate. Seeds numerous, ellipsoid, reddish-brown. Fl. B. I. v. 1, p. 159; Moench, Method. Pl. (1794) p. 271; Syme, Eng. Bot. v. 1, p. 211, t. 152; Trim. Fl. Ceyl. v. 1, p. 54; Woodr. in Journ. Bomb. Nat. v. 11 (1897) p. 122; Watt, Dict. Econ. Prod. v. 2, p. 134.—Flowers: Jan.

Mahableshwar, ex *Woodrow*, l. c.—DISTRIB. A weed of cultivation; Europe, Persia, Asia.

7. SENEBIERA, Poir.

Annual or biennial, branched herbs. Leaves alternate, entire or pinnatisect. Flowers in short, leaf-opposed racemes, minute, white (rarely purple), sometimes apetalous. Sepals short, spreading, equal at the base. Stamens free, not toothed, small, sometimes 0. Pod short, didymous, laterally compressed, indehiscent; valves subglobose, rugose or crested; style short or 0. Seeds 1 in each cell; cotyledons incumbent, gradually narrowed into the incumbent radicle.—DISTRIB. Temperate and warm regions of both hemispheres; species 6.

1. **Senebiera pinnatifida,** *DC. Mém. Soc. Hist. Par.* (1799) p. 144, t. 9. An annual herb, 6–18 in. high, diffuse or procumbent, much-branched from the base; branches glabrescent or with scattered, white hairs. Leaves somewhat fleshy, glabrous or sparsely pubescent: radical leaves 2–4 in. long, pinnate, the pinnæ 6–10 pairs, inciso-dentate; cauline leaves $\frac{3}{4}$–1 in. long, pinnatisect or pinnatifid, the segments 3–7, inciso-dentate, $\frac{1}{4}$ by $\frac{1}{8}$ in., the ultimate segments oblanceolate, entire, shortly mucronate. Flowers $\frac{1}{20}$ in. across, in leaf-opposed corymbs, at first sessile, afterwards racemose. Sepals ovate, obtuse. Petals often absent, when present white, as long as the sepals, linear or spathulate. Stamens usually 2 bearing anthers, with 4 filaments (?) not bearing anthers 1 at each side of a perfect stamen; filaments subulate; anthers globose, didymous. Fruiting racemes 1–2 in. long; pods $\frac{1}{16}$ in. long by $\frac{1}{10}$ in. broad, didymous, compressed, notched about equally at the base and apex, reticulato-rugose; fruiting pedicels very slender, $\frac{1}{8}$–$\frac{3}{16}$ in. long, often slightly hairy. Seeds yellowish-brown, reniform, minutely punctulate.—Flowers: Feb. Not in Fl. B. I.; Sprague & Gray, Gen. Pl. U. States, v. 1, t. 72. *Senebiera didyma,* Woodr. in Journ. Bomb. Nat. v. 11 (1897) p. 122.

SIND: Ruk Junction on the Railway Line in Upper Sind, *Cooke!, Woodrow.*—DISTRIB. Temperate S. America.

8. THLASPI, Linn.

Annual or perennial herbs, usually glabrous. Radical leaves rosulate; cauline oblong hastate, auricled. Flowers racemose, ebracteate, white or rosy. Sepals erect, equal at the base. Petals obovate. Pod short, orbicular, obovate or obcordate, laterally compressed, emarginate; valves keeled or winged; septum narrow, membranous; style short or long; stigma emarginate. Seeds 2 (rarely more), in each cell, not winged; radicle accumbent.—DISTRIB. Europe, Asia, N. America; species 30.

1. **Thlaspi arvense,** *Linn. Sp. Pl.* (1753) p. 646. A glabrous herb, 6–18 in. high, often corymbosely branched; stems striate. Leaves: the lower up to 4 in. long, oblong-obovate, obtuse, sinuate-dentate or entire, much attenuated at the base; the upper amplexicaul, with acute diverging auricles, oblong, acute or obtuse, toothed or rarely entire. Flowers $\frac{1}{5}$ in. across, in dense, corymbose racemes, afterwards elongating. Sepals oblong, obtuse. Petals spathulate, half as long again as the sepals, truncate or slightly emarginate at the apex. Fruiting raceme long; pedicels $\frac{3}{8}$–$\frac{3}{4}$ in. long, spreading. Pods flat, $\frac{3}{4}$–$\frac{7}{8}$ in. in diam. including the wing, or $\frac{1}{2}$–$\frac{5}{8}$ by $\frac{3}{8}$ excluding it, suborbicular, obcordate, with a deep sinus at the apex; wing gradually increasing in width from

the base upwards, the lobes contiguous or sometimes slightly overlapping at the apex; style very short. Seeds 4-6 in each cell, irregularly ovoid, with raised, concentric ridges, black. Fl. B. I. v. 1, p. 162; Syme, Eng. Bot. v. 1, p. 202, t. 144; Woodr. in Journ. Bomb. Nat. v. 11 (1897) p. 122.—Flowers: Mar.

SIND: Kirthar mountains, *Woodrow*.—DISTRIB. Europe, N. Africa, W. Asia; a weed of cultivation.

9. PHYSORHYNCHUS, Hook.

A branched, leafy undershrub. Leaves fleshy; the lower petioled; the upper contracted at the base, auricled. Flowers rather large, in elongate, ebracteate racemes; pedicels very short. Sepals erect, equal at the base. Stamens free, not toothed. Pod short, indehiscent, jointed, the lower joint longitudinally 2-celled with small spurious valves, the upper joint much larger, ovoid, beaked, 2-celled, cells 2-4-seeded; septum thin; style conical; stigma subcapitate. Seeds pendulous from the side of the cell; cotyledons conduplicate.—DISTRIB. Afghanistan, Beluchistan; species 1.

1. **Physorhynchus brahuicus,** *Hook. Icon. Pl.* (1852) tt. 821, 822. Perennial, erect, about 2 ft. high, glaucous, glabrous; stem woody at the base. Leaves thick, entire or sinuate-dentate; lower 2-5 by 1-3 in., obovate, rounded or acute at the base, attenuated into the petiole; upper smaller, sessile, oblong-lanceolate, semi-amplexicaul, auricled. Racemes elongate, much divaricate in fruit; flowers white; pedicels ¼ in. long, erect, thickened at top. Sepals ovate-oblong, ⅜ in. long. Petals obovate, twice as long as the sepals. Pods ½-¾ in. long; valves of the lower joint deciduous. Seeds subtriangular, globose, punctate. Fl. B. I. v. 1, p. 165; Ait. Pb. & Sind Pl. p. 8; Woodr. in Journ. Bomb. Nat. v. 11 (1897) p. 122.—Flowers: Aug.

SIND: *Stocks*!; Brahuic hills, *Stocks*!; Thano-Bula-Khan, *Woodrow*.—DISTRIB. Afghanistan, Beluchistan, S. Persia.
Stocks says the leaves are eaten like cabbage and are an excellent vegetable.

CULTIVATED ECONOMIC PLANTS.

A number of plants of the Order (*Cruciferæ*) are cultivated throughout the Presidency, either as vegetables, or for the oil obtainable from the seeds. Of these the most important are the several species and varieties of the genus *Brassica*.

BRASSICA NIGRA, Koch. Black mustard. *Vern.* Rai; Mohári. Fl. B. I. v. 1, p. 156; Watt, Dict. Econ. Prod. v. 1, p. 530. Cultivated in fields.

BRASSICA CAMPESTRIS, Linn., of which the following subspecies are more or less cultivated: Subsp. 1, CAMPESTRIS proper. The Swedish turnip. Rarely cultivated in the Bombay Presidency. Subsp. 2, NAPUS. The rape or coleseed. *Vern.* Sarsan; Pivli-rai. Cultivated in fields. Subsp. 3, RAPA. The common turnip. *Vern.* Shalgam. Grown in gardens as a vegetable, chiefly for the use of Europeans. The knol-kohl or kohl-rabi largely takes the place of the turnip as a culinary vegetable, being a plant better adapted for cultivation in a hot climate.

BRASSICA OLERACEA, Linn.; Watt, Dict. Econ. Prod. v. 1, p. 533, of which the following varieties are more or less grown for food, especially in districts where water is procurable for irrigation: *acephala*, Scotch kail, borecole; *bullata*, the Savoy cabbage; *gemmifera*, Brussels sprouts; *capitata*, red and white cabbage, the former rarely grown; *caulorapa*, the knol-kohl or kohl-rabi; *botrytis*, the cauliflower, largely cultivated.

BRASSICA JUNCEA, Hook. f. & Thoms. *Vern.* Mohári. Fl. B. I. v. 1, p. 157; Watt, Dict. Econ. Prod. v. 1, p. 528. Cultivated as a cold season crop.

A full account of the varieties of the genus grown in India will be found in Watt, Dict. Econ. Prod. v. 1, pp. 520-534.

The following are also extensively grown :—

RAPHANUS SATIVUS, Linn. The radish. *Vern.* Mula. Fl. B. I. v. 1, p. 166; Watt, Dict. Econ. Prod. v. 6, part 1, p. 393. Cultivated throughout the Presidency. The common Indian radish is larger and coarser than the English plant, and is eaten both raw and cooked.

RAPHANUS SATIVUS, var. *caudatus*, Linn., the rat-tail radish, or Java radish, is widely grown, especially in Gujarat. *Vern.* Mougri. The long whip-like purple pods often attain a length of 2 feet or more, and are eaten raw or cooked. The seeds, according to the younger Linnæus, were introduced into India from Java.

LEPIDIUM SATIVUM, Linn. The cress. *Vern.* Aliv. Fl. B. I. v. 1, p. 159; Watt, Dict. Econ. Prod. v. 4, p. 627. Widely cultivated, not only for Europeans, but also as a potherb for native use. The seeds are imported into Bombay in considerable quantities from Persia.

ORDER X. CAPPARIDACEÆ.

Herbs, shrubs, or trees, erect or climbing. Leaves alternate (rarely opposite); stipules 2 or 0, sometimes spinescent. Flowers usually 2-sexual, axillary, fascicled or solitary, or terminal and corymbose or racemose, regular or irregular, often handsome. Sepals 4-8, free or connate, 1-2-seriate, valvate or imbricate, rarely open in bud. Petals 4 (rarely 0, very rarely 5 or 8), sessile or clawed, imbricate or open, very rarely valvate in bud, hypogynous or seated on the disk. Stamens inserted at the base or apex of the torus, few or very many, equal or unequal, all fertile or some without anthers; anthers oblong, basifixed. Disk 0, or tumid, or lining the calyx-tube. Ovary sessile, or with a long or short stalk (*gynophore*), 1-celled; ovules numerous, on 2-4 parietal placentas; style short or 0; stigma usually orbicular. Fruit capsular or baccate, or dry and indehiscent, very rarely drupaceous. Seeds reniform or angled; albumen 0 or thin; embryo incurved.—DISTRIB. Chiefly tropical; genera 23; species about 300.

Herbs; fruit capsular.
  Stamens sessile on the disk .... 1. CLEOME.
  Stamens inserted on a gynophore .... 2. GYNANDROPSIS.
An undershrub, 6-20 in. high; fruit with a membranous wing, indehiscent, 1-seeded .... 3. DIPTERYGIUM.

Trees or shrubs; fruit berried or capsular.
Sepals combined at the base into a tube .... 4. Mærua.
Sepals distinct, inserted on the edge of the disk .... 5. Cratæva.
Sepals biseriate.
Stamens 4–6, inserted half way up the gynophore...... 6. Cadaba.
Stamens 8–∞, inserted at the base of the gynophore... 7. Capparis.

1. CLEOME, Linn.

Herbs. Leaves simple or 3–9-foliolate, entire or serrulate. Flowers solitary or racemose, white, yellow, pink or purple. Sepals 4, spreading. Petals 4, subequal, sometimes subunilateral. Stamens 4–8, inserted on the torus. Ovary sessile or with a very short gynophore; ovules many, on 2 parietal placentas; style short or 0. Capsule usually elongate, sometimes inflated, sessile or stalked, 1-celled, 2-valved; valves membranous, separating from the persistent placentas. Seeds reniform.—Distrib. In tropical or warm regions throughout the world; species about 90.

Leaves simple.
Stamens 6 or less.
Leaves oblong-lanceolate, penninerved; bracts petiolate. 1. *C. monophylla.*
Leaves ovate, cordate, penninerved; bracts small, sessile .... 2. *C. papillosa.*
Leaves suborbicular, palmately 5-nerved; bracts leafy... 3. *C. quinquenervia.*
Leaves fleshy, ovate or obovate, 3-nerved; bracts small. 4. *C. Stocksiana.*
Stamens 10–12.
Leaves oblong-lanceolate; bracts leafy .... 5. *C. simplicifolia.*
Leaves compound.
Stamens 6; leaflets not exceeding ½ in.; capsule sessile.
Herb with an odor of musk or rue; stem without prickles .... 6. *C. brachycarpa.*
Herb with distant prickles on the stem and leaves ...... 7. *C. aspera.*
Stamens 6; leaflets 1 in.; capsule stalked..................... 8. *C. Burmanni.*
Stamens 10 or more.
Capsule glandular-pubescent; flowers yellow .... 9. *C. viscosa.*
Capsule smooth; flowers rosy .... 10. *C. Chelidonii.*

1. **Cleome monophylla,** *Linn. Sp. Pl.* (1753) p. 672. Erect, branched, 1–2 ft. high, more or less hairy or pubescent; stems striate. Leaves simple, 1–3 by ¾–⅞ in., passing gradually into bracts above, oblong-lanceolate, base truncate, rounded or cordate; petioles slender, 1–1½ in. long. Flowers pink (not yellow as erroneously described by Linnæus), solitary in the axils of stalked, leafy bracts, in a long erect raceme; pedicels slender; bracts ovate or subdeltoid, cordate, strongly pubescent. Stamens 6. Sepals linear, acute, ciliate with gland-tipped hairs. Petals oblong, rounded at top, clawed. Capsules 2½–3½ by $\frac{1}{12}$–⅛ in., subcylindric, pointed, striate, clothed with short stout hairs. Gynophore very short or 0. Seeds transversely rugose. Fl. B. I. v. 1, p. 168; Grah. Cat. p. 7; Dalz. & Gibs. p. 8; Trim. Fl. Ceyl. v. 1, p. 55; Woodr. in Journ. Bomb. Nat. v. 11 (1897) p. 122.—Flowers: Nov.

A common weed. Deccan: Gokak, *Woodrow.* Gujarat: *Woodrow.* S. M. Country: Belgaum, *Ritchie,* 24! Badami, *Cooke*!, *Woodrow*!—Distrib. Tropical Africa.

2. **Cleome papillosa,** *Steud. Nomen.* ed. 2 (1840) v. 1, p. 382. A much-branched plant, rough with glandular hairs; branches slender. Leaves ¼–1 in. in diam., elliptic-ovate to orbicular, entire, rounded or cordate at the base, scabrid and papillose; petioles of the lower leaves

½–1 in. long, those of the upper leaves very short. Flowers small, pink, in long slender bracteate racemes; pedicels filiform; bracts small (the uppermost flowers of raceme ebracteate). Sepals lanceolate, glandular. Petals clawed. Stamens 6. Capsules glabrous or slightly papillose, striate, very slender, ¾–1½ in. long by $\frac{1}{33}$ in. in diam. Gynophore almost 0. Seeds minute, brown-black, glabrous, granulate. Fl. B. I. v. 1, p. 168; Woodr. in Journ. Bomb. Nat. v. 11 (1897) p. 122.—Flowers: Aug.

SIND: *Dalzell*, 34!, *Stocks*!, *Vicary*!; Rocks in Sind, *Stocks*!; Thano-Bula-Khan Road, 34 miles from Karachi, *Woodrow*.—DISTRIB. Abyssinia, Nubia, Kordofan, Arabia.

3. **Cleome quinquenervia,** *DC. Prodr.* v. 1 (1824) p. 239. Glaucous, 6–12 in. high, the whole plant clothed with glandular hairs; branches many from a woody base, rigid, terete. Leaves ½–1 in. in diam., ovate or suborbicular, subcordate, palmately 5-nerved from the base, margins ciliate with gland-tipped hairs; petioles glandular-hairy, those of the lower leaves 1–1½ in. long, those of the upper leaves shorter. Flowers pale pink, in the axils of leafy bracts on short racemes; bracts ovate, acute, subsessile; pedicels slender, ¼–⅜ in. long. Sepals linear, acute, half as long as the petals, ciliate with gland-tipped hairs. Petals ovate, acute, with a crested appendage across the inside a little above the base, glabrous except the tips. Stamens 4. Capsules 1–1¼ by ⅛–⅙ in., narrow-oblong, acute at both ends, straight or slightly curved, rough with short, thick, gland-tipped hairs. Gynophore 0. Seeds minute, numerous, smooth, chestnut-brown. Fl. B. I. v. 1, p. 168; T. Anders., Fl. Aden., in Journ. Linn. Soc. v. 5, Suppl. 1, p. 3; Griff. Itin. notes, 322, n. 1261; Woodr. in Journ. Bomb. Nat. v. 11 (1897) p. 122. *Cleome pentanervia*, Ait. Cat. Pb. & Sind Pl. p. 9.—Flowers: Oct.

SIND: Laki (Karachi district), *Woodrow*!; hills in Sind, *Vicary*!—DISTRIB. Persia, Afghanistan, Arabia.

4. **Cleome Stocksiana,** *Boiss. Diag.* ser. 2 (1853) fasc. 1, p. 47. Perennial, branched from the base, the lower branches striate, subglabrous, the upper glandular. Leaves fleshy, ½–1¼ by ¼–¾ in., glandular-pubescent or subglabrous, palmately 3-nerved; petioles ¼–1 in. long, glandular or smooth. Flowers small, in the axils of leafy bracts on an elongate raceme; pedicels glandular, ¼–⅜ in. long; bracts elliptic or obovate, shortly stalked, glandular. Sepals elliptic-oblong. Petals obovate-spathulate, veined with dark purple veins, clawed. Capsules broadly linear, 1½ by ⅙ in., gland-dotted, reticulately veined, shining inside, pendulous. Gynophore very short. Seeds in 2 series, at first hairy, the hairs soon falling off, globose, chestnut-brown. Fl. B. I. v. 1, p. 169; Boiss. Fl. Orient. v. 1, p. 414; Griff. Itin. notes, 225, n. 183; Ait. Cat. Pb. & Sind Pl. p. 9; Woodr. in Journ. Bomb. Nat. v. 11 (1897) p. 122.—Flowers: Oct.

SIND: Boogta Hills, *Vicary*!; Laki (Karachi district), *Woodrow*!—DISTRIB. Beluchistan.

5. **Cleome simplicifolia,** *Hook. f. & Thoms.* in *Fl. B. I.* v. 1, p. 169. Annual, 6–18 in. high; whole plant clothed with short, rigid, spinulose hairs from glandular bases; branches many from the base, ascending, furrowed. Leaves ½–1½ by ½–¾ in., obovate or oblong-elliptic, strigose

on both surfaces; petioles of the lower leaves $\frac{1}{2}$–$\frac{3}{4}$ in. long, those of the upper gradually becoming shorter. Flowers violet, solitary in the axils of leafy bracts on elongate racemes; pedicels filiform, $\frac{1}{2}$ in. long, hairy at top; bracts narrow-oblong, subsessile. Stamens 12; filaments enlarged at the apex. Sepals small, $\frac{1}{12}$ in. long, ovate, acute, pilose. Petals $\frac{1}{8}$ in. long, oblong, acute, veined with dark purple veins, glabrous. Capsules $\frac{3}{4}$–1 by $\frac{1}{8}$ in., long-beaked, glabrous, striate, slightly compressed, torulose. Gynophore 0. Seeds large, yellowish-brown, smooth. Woodr. in Journ. Bomb. Nat. v. 11 (1897) p. 122. *Polanisia simplicifolia*, Camb. in Jacq. Voy. Bot. p. 20, t. 20; Dalz. & Gibs. p. 8.—Flowers: July–Aug.

A common weed in the Deccan. KONKAN: *Stocks*!; Bombay, *Law*! DECCAN: Poona Collectorate, *Dalzell & Gibson*; near Poona, *Dalzell*!; Poona, *Jacquemont*, 813!, 814!, *Woodrow*. S. M. COUNTRY: Belgaum, *Ritchie*, 1018!

6. **Cleome brachycarpa,** *Vahl*, (ined.) *ex DC. Prodr.* v. 1 (1824) p. 240. A perennial herb, 6–18 in. high, with an odor of rue; stems many from a woody base, the older subglabrous, the younger glandular or viscid-pubescent. Leaves 3–5-foliolate; petioles $\frac{1}{8}$–$\frac{1}{4}$ in. long; leaflets $\frac{1}{4}$–$\frac{3}{8}$ by $\frac{1}{10}$–$\frac{1}{4}$ in., obovate-oblong, viscidly puberulous; petiolules very short. Flowers yellow, in the axils of leafy bracts, in lax racemes; pedicels $\frac{3}{8}$–$\frac{1}{2}$ in. long, filiform; bracts 3-foliolate or simple, subsessile. Sepals $\frac{1}{10}$ in. long, ovate-lanceolate, much shorter than the petals, glandular-pubescent outside. Petals $\frac{1}{4}$–$\frac{3}{8}$ in. long, ovate-oblong, subacute, glabrous, furnished inside with a small scale-like appendage above the short claw. Stamens 6. Capsules $\frac{3}{8}$–$\frac{1}{2}$ by $\frac{1}{10}$–$\frac{1}{8}$ in., oblong, inflated, glandular; style about $\frac{1}{4}$ in. long, filiform. Gynophore 0. Seeds minute, smooth. Fl. B. I. v. 1, p. 169; T. Anders., Fl. Aden., in Journ. Linn. Soc. v. 5, Suppl. 1 (1860) p. 4; Woodr. in Journ. Bomb. Nat. v. 11 (1897) p. 122. *Cleome Vahliana*, Fresen. in Mus. Senckenb. v. 2, p. 110; Ait. Cat. Pb. & Sind Pl. p. 9. *Cleome Ruta*, Cambess. in Jacq. Voy. Bot. p. 19, t. 19; Ait. Cat. Pb. & Sind Pl. p. 9.—Flowers: Nov.–May. VERN. *Kásturi*.

Very abundant throughout Sind. SIND: *Dalzell*, 32!; hills in Sind, *Stocks*, 456!; Boogta Hills, *Vicary*!; Karachi, *Woodrow*!; Sukkur, *Cooke*!—DISTRIB. N. Africa, Arabia.

7. **Cleome aspera,** *Kœn.* (ined.) *ex DC. Prodr.* v. 1 (1824) p. 241. Annual, 6–18 in. high, much-branched from the base; branches ascending, grooved, glabrous, armed with small distant prickles from triangular bases. Leaves trifoliolate; petioles $\frac{1}{8}$–$\frac{3}{4}$ in. long; leaflets $\frac{1}{4}$–1 in. long (the terminal much the largest), oblong-lanceolate or oblanceolate, glandular and prickly; petiolules very short or 0. Flowers small, pink, solitary in the axils of floral leaves (bracts); pedicels filiform, $\frac{1}{4}$–$\frac{1}{2}$ in. long; bracts subsessile, simple or trifoliolate. Sepals oblong-lanceolate, $\frac{1}{32}$ in. long. Petals $\frac{3}{16}$ in. long, obovate-oblong. Capsules 1–1$\frac{1}{4}$ by $\frac{1}{10}$–$\frac{1}{8}$ in., striate, subterete, scarcely torulose, tapering at both ends but quite sessile, glabrous. Gynophore 0. Seeds yellowish-brown, almost orange, transversely and sharply ridged, subglobose. Fl. B. I. v. 1, p. 169; Trim. Fl. Ceyl. v. 1, p. 56; Woodr. in Journ. Bomb. Nat. v. 11 (1897) p. 123. —Flowers: Aug.

Southern Districts, rare. S. M. COUNTRY: Dharwar, *Woodrow*; Badami, *Cooke*!, *Woodrow*

8. **Cleome Burmanni,** *Wight & Arn. Prodr.* (1834) p. 22. Annual, 6–18 in. high; stem (but not the leaves) rough with minute scattered prickles. Leaves 3-foliolate; leaflets ovate-oblong or obovate, those of the lower leaves shorter than the petioles, those of the upper much longer, glabrous. Capsules 1½–2 by $\frac{1}{16}$ in., subterete, striate, attenuated at the base, stalked, glabrous. Gynophore ⅛ in. long. Seeds as in the preceding species. Fl. B. I. v. 1, p. 170; Grah. Cat. p. 7; Trim. Fl. Ceyl. v. 1, p. 56; Woodr. in Journ. Bomb. Nat. v. 11 (1897) p. 123.

Very similar to *Cleome aspera*, from which it differs chiefly by the presence of a distinct gynophore. Trimen (Fl. Ceyl. v. 1, p. 56) considers it doubtfully distinct from that plant.

SIND: Hyderabad, *W. Strachan* (fide *Woodrow*, l. c.).

9. **Cleome viscosa,** *Linn. Sp. Pl.* (1753) p. 672. Annual, erect, 1–3 ft. high; stems grooved, densely clothed with glandular and simple hairs. Leaves 3–5-foliolate; petioles of the lower leaves 1–2 in. long, gradually becoming shorter upwards; the floral leaves (bracts) often subsessile. Leaflets elliptic-oblong or obovate, acute or obtuse, the terminal the largest and reaching 1¾ by 1 in. (when 5-foliolate the basal pair much reduced); petiolules short, hairy. Flowers yellow, axillary, growing out into a lax raceme; pedicels slender, terete, hairy. Sepals $\frac{3}{16}$ in. long, oblong-lanceolate, glandular-pubescent outside. Petals oblong-obovate, about ½ in. long, veined. Stamens exceeding 20. Capsules 2–2½ by ¼ in., erect, hairy, obliquely striate, compressed, tapering towards both ends, terminated by a style ⅛ in. long. Seeds brown-black when ripe, finely transversely striate, subglobose. Fl. B. I. v. 1, p. 170; Trim. Fl. Ceyl. v. 1, p. 57; Woodr. in Journ. Bomb. Nat. v. 11 (1897) p. 123; Watt, Dict. Econ. Prod. v. 2, p. 371. *Polanisia icosandra*, W. & A. Prodr. p. 22; Grah. Cat. p. 8; Dalz. & Gibs. p. 8.—Flowers: Sept.–June. VERN. *Pivli-tilwân.*

A common weed, widely distributed throughout the Presidency; very common in the Deccan and about Poona. KONKAN: near the lighthouse at Vingorla, *Nairne*. DECCAN: widely, *Woodrow*; Poona, *Cooke*!

10. **Cleome Chelidonii,** *Linn. f. Suppl.* (1781) p. 300. Annual, erect, much-branched, 1–3 ft. high; stem and branches striate, glabrous except for a few scattered hairs from glandular bases. Leaves 3–9-(commonly 7-) foliolate, (the number of leaflets diminishing upwards), passing into simple, linear bracts above; leaflets up to 2½ in. long, oblong-obovate, or the upper narrow-linear, appressedly pubescent; petioles reaching 4 in. long, glabrous except for a few glandular hairs. Flowers rosy, in terminal and axillary racemes, becoming corymbose; pedicels 1–1½ in. long. Sepals small, ovate, acute. Petals ⅜–½ in. long, obovate, mucronate. Stamens indefinite. Capsules 2–4 in. long, slender, cylindric, tapering at both ends, finely striate. Gynophore 0. Seeds yellowish-brown, echinate. Fl. B. I. v. 1, p. 170; Woodr. in Journ. Bomb. Nat. v. 11 (1897) p. 123. *Polanisia Chelidonii*, DC. Prodr. v. 1, p. 242; W. & A. Prodr. p. 22; Grah. Cat. p. 7; Dalz. & Gibs. p. 8.—Flowers: July–Feb.

In moist places throughout the Presidency. KONKAN: *Stocks*! DECCAN: Bojapore on the road to Poona, *Dalzell & Gibson*; Khadkala, *Woodrow*; between Poona and Karli, *Jacquemont*, 812!; Lanoli, *Cooke*!; near Poona, *Woodrow*! GUJARAT: Dang jungles, *Woodrow*. S. M. COUNTRY: Belgaum, *Ritchie*, 23!—DISTRIB. Java.

2. GYNANDROPSIS, DC.

Annual herbs, usually glandular-pubescent. Leaves 3–7-foliolate. Flowers racemose. Sepals 4, spreading, deciduous. Petals 4, with long slender claws, imbricate or open in bud. Stamens 6; filaments adnate to a slender gynophore, spreading above, subequal. Ovary stalked; ovules many. Capsule usually stalked, compressed or subterete, usually elongate. Seeds reniform or orbicular; testa rugose; cotyledons incurved, accumbent.—DISTRIB. Tropical regions of both hemispheres; species 10.

1. **Gynandropsis pentaphylla**, *DC. Prodr.* v. 1 (1824) p. 238. Annual, erect, branched, 2–4 ft. high; stems and branches striate, more or less clothed with white spreading hairs. Leaves 3–5-foliolate; petioles 2–3 in. long, sometimes armed with small distant prickles; leaflets subsessile, $\frac{3}{4}$–$1\frac{1}{2}$ by $\frac{1}{2}$–1 in., elliptic-obovate, obtuse, acute or acuminate, cuneate at the base, pubescent on both sides, margins crenate-dentate or subentire. Flowers at first corymbose, elongating into a dense bracteate raceme; pedicels $\frac{1}{2}$–$\frac{3}{4}$ in. long, viscid-pubescent; bracts subsessile, trifoliolate, with small obovate leaflets. Sepals lanceolate, glandular-pubescent, green with white veins. Petals pale pink, $\frac{5}{8}$ in. long, broadly obovate or suborbicular with a long narrow claw. Gynophore $\frac{3}{4}$–1 in. long. Stamens purple, inserted about $\frac{1}{2}$ way up the gynophore. Ovary linear-oblong, glandular, seated on the top of the gynophore; style almost 0. Capsules 2–$3\frac{1}{2}$ by $\frac{3}{16}$ in., viscid-pubescent, tapering at both ends, obliquely striate. Seeds muricate, dark brown. Fl. B. I. v. 1, p. 171; Grah. Cat. p. 7; Dalz. & Gibs. p. 7; Eichler in Mart. Fl. Bras. v. 13, part 1 (1865) p. 261, t. 58, fig. 3; Watt, Dict. Econ. Prod. v. 4, p. 190.—Flowers: June. VERN. *Pándri-tilwán.*

A common weed in waste places. DECCAN: *Woodrow*!; Ahmednagar, *Cooke*!; Poona, in cultivated fields, *Jacquemont*, 810! GUJARAT: *Woodrow*. S. M. COUNTRY: Belgaum, *Ritchie*, 1158!

Gynandropsis speciosa, DC., with large rose-colored flowers is often grown as an ornamental plant in gardens.

3. DIPTERYGIUM, Decaisne.

A twiggy, divaricately-branched undershrub. Leaves small, petioled, scattered, ovate-oblong, acute, quite entire. Flowers small, bracteate. Sepals small, equal at the base. Stamens 6, equal. Ovary 1-celled; ovules 1–2 in each cell, often 4-winged, the wings afterwards disappearing; style elongate; stigma capitate. Fruit indehiscent, small, pendulous, ellipsoid, compressed, surrounded by a membranous wing, 1-seeded. Seeds erect, curved; cotyledons concave; embryo incumbent.—DISTRIB. Arabia, Nubia; species 1.

1. **Dipterygium glaucum,** *Decaisne, in Ann. Sc. Nat.* ser. 2, v. 4 (1835) p. 67. A shrub 6–20 in. high; branches slender, terete, grooved. Leaves $\frac{1}{4}$–$\frac{1}{2}$ by $\frac{1}{12}$–$\frac{1}{10}$ in., few, and as well as the stems rough with viscid glands; petioles short. Flowers in long, bracteate racemes; pedicels short, filiform. Sepals small, ovate, acute. Petals white, ovate, obtuse, shortly clawed. Fruit transversely wrinkled. Fl. B. I. v. 1, p. 164 (under N.O. *Cruciferæ*); F. Pax, in Engl. & Prantl, Pflanz. v. 3,

part 2, p. 225, fig. 135; Woodr. in Journ. Bomb. Nat. v. 11 (1897) p. 122.—Flowers: Sept.

SIND: near Jacobabad, *Cooke*!, *Woodrow*!—DISTRIB. Arabia, N.E. Africa.

4. **MÆRUA**, Forsk.

Climbing unarmed shrubs, often glaucous. Leaves simple, quite entire. Flowers corymbose. Sepals 4, united at the base into a persistent infundibuliform tube forming a 4-lobed calyx; lobes valvate. Petals 4, smaller than the calyx-lobes, inserted on the edge of the cup-shaped disk. Disk infundibuliform, lining the calyx-tube, elongated in the middle into a columnar obconic receptacle or torus, equalling or slightly exceeding the calyx-tube. Stamens many, inserted on the torus; filaments free or connate at the base. Ovary seated on a long gynophore, 1–2-celled; placentas 2–4, parietal or cohering in the middle; ovules many; stigma subsessile. Berry fleshy, elongate, moniliform, 1- or more-seeded. Seeds large; cotyledons fleshy, convolute.—DISTRIB. Tropical Africa, Arabia; species about 20.

1. **Mærua ovalifolia,** *Cambess. in Jacquemont, Voy. Bot.* (1844) p. 23, t. 24. A climbing shrub with divaricate branches; bark smooth, pale. Leaves 1–2 by $\frac{3}{8}$–1 in., elliptic-oblong, obtuse or retuse, mucronate, glaucous, glabrous; petioles stout, $\frac{1}{8}$–$\frac{1}{4}$ in. long. Flowers in corymbs, greenish-white, terminal or on lateral shoots; pedicels $\frac{1}{2}$–$\frac{3}{4}$ in. long, glabrous; bract 1 at the base of each pedicel, small, ovate, acuminate, rigid, yellow. Calyx-lobes ovate, acute, $\frac{1}{2}$ in. long, hooded at the apex, with a short horn behind the hood and with a line of dense white pubescence on the margin. Calyx-tube $\frac{1}{8}$ in. long, lined with an infundibuliform disk as long as the tube with truncate margins, the columnar torus slightly exceeding the calyx-tube. Petals ovate-lanceolate, acute, with slightly undulate margins, half as long as the calyx-lobes and alternate with them or nearly so, inserted on the margin of the cup-shaped disk. Stamens many, inserted on the torus. Gynophore $\frac{3}{4}$ in. long. Ovary cylindric, truncate; style 0; stigma large. Fruit pale brown, constricted between the seeds, forming an elongate twisted and knotted berry, each lobe or knot 1-seeded. Seeds brown, globose, echinate. *Mærua arenaria*, Hook. f. & Thoms. in Fl. B. I. v. 1, p. 171; Trim. Fl. Ceyl. v. 1, p. 58; Talb. Trees, Bomb. p. 9; Woodr. in Journ. Bomb. Nat. v. 11 (1897) p. 123. *Niebuhria oblongifolia*, Royle, Ill. Him. Bot. p. 73; Grah. Cat. p. 8; Dalz. & Gibs. p. 8. *Capparis heteroclita*, Roxb. Fl. Ind. v. 2, p. 570.—Flowers: Nov.–Mar.

KONKAN: N. & S. Konkan, *Law*! DECCAN: Yeoat, near Poona, *Cooke*!, *Woodrow*!; between Wai and the Kamatki Ghát, *Graham*; hedges in the Deccan, *Dalzell & Gibson*. GUJARAT: Deesa, *Law* (fide *Graham*); hedges in Gujarat, *Dalzell & Gibson*. S. M. COUNTRY: Dharwar, *Talbot*.

5. **CRATÆVA**, Linn.

Trees. Leaves 3-foliolate. Flowers in axillary and terminal corymbs, handsome, usually polygamous. Sepals inserted on the edge of the disk, deciduous, imbricate. Petals 4, with long claws, open in bud. Disk hemispheric, lobed, lining the bottom of the calyx. Stamens 8–20, nserted on the margin of the disk; filaments filiform, elongate. Ovary ovoid, on a long gynophore, 1-2-celled; placentas 2; ovules many, in many series; stigma sessile, discoid. Berry rather large, globose or ovoid. Seeds few or many, reniform, imbedded in pulp.—DISTRIB. Tropical regions of the world; species 6.

1. **Cratæva religiosa,** *Forst. f. Prodr.* (1786) p. 35. A small tree with a much-branched head. Leaves deciduous, 3-foliolate; petioles 1½–3 in. long; leaflets 2–6 by 1½–2½ in., ovate, lanceolate or obovate, acute or acuminate, attenuated at the base, entire, glabrous on both surfaces, pale beneath and reticulately veined, the lateral leaflets oblique at the base; petiolules ¼–⅜ in. long. Flowers many, in dense terminal corymbs, greenish-white; pedicels 1–1¾ in. long, stout, glabrous. Sepals petaloid, small, distant, ovate, acute. Petals (including the claw) nearly 1 by ⅝ in.; claw up to ¼ in. long, very narrow. Stamens longer than the petals, spreading. Gynophore nearly 2 in. long, terete, smooth. Ovary ellipsoid; stigma flat. Fruit a globose or ovoid, woody, smooth or scurfy berry, on the thickened gynophore. Seeds imbedded in pulp, nearly smooth, brown. Fl. B. I. v. 1, p. 172; Pax, in Engl. & Prantl, Pflanzenf. v. 3, part 2 (1891) pp. 227, 228, fig. 137; Talb. Trees, Bomb. p. 9; Woodr. in Journ. Bomb. Nat. v. 11 (1897) p. 123; Watt, Dict. Econ. Prod. v. 2, p. 583.—DISTRIB. Tropical Africa.

VAR. 1. *Nurvala*, Hook. f. & Thoms. Fl. B. I. v. 1, p. 172. Leaflets ovate-lanceolate, taper-pointed. Berry ovoid. *Cratæva Nurvala*, Buch.-Ham. in Trans. Linn. Soc. v. 15 (1827) p. 121; Dalz. & Gibs. p. 8. *Cratæva Roxburghii*, Grah. Cat. p. 8.—Flowers: Mar. VERN. *Vâya-varna.*

KONKAN: *Stocks*!, *Law*!; Byculla (Bombay), *Graham*; Karanja Hill, *Dalzell & Gibson*; Wari Country, *Dalzell & Gibson*. KANARA: Chandwar, *Ritchie*, 29!; Hulical, *Woodrow*!

The tree is often planted near temples and tombs.

VAR. 2. *Roxburghii*, Hook. f. & Thoms. Fl. B. I. v. 1, p. 172. Leaflets ovate or obovate, abruptly acuminate. Berry globose. *Cratæva Roxburghii*, Br. in Denh. & Clapp. Travels, App. (1826) p. 224; Dalz. & Gibs. p. 8; Trim. Fl. Ceyl. v. 1, p. 59.

KONKAN: *Law*!; Wari jungles, *Dalzell & Gibson*. GUJARAT: banks of the Narbada near Chandod, *Dalzell & Gibson*.

6. CADABA, Forsk.

Unarmed shrubs. Leaves simple or trifoliolate. Flowers axillary, solitary, racemose or corymbose. Sepals 4, unequal or 2-seriate, the 2 outer valvate. Petals 2–4, rarely 0, clawed. Disk prolonged into a trumpet-shaped or spathulate process with a tubular claw. Stamens 4–6; filaments filiform, exserted, spreading. Ovary 1-celled, on the top of a long gynophore; ovules many, on 2–4 parietal placentas; stigma sessile. Fruit fleshy, long, cylindric, berried, or dehiscing tardily by 2 valves which leave the pulpy placentas. Seeds subglobose; testa cartilaginous; cotyledons convolute.—DISTRIB. Tropical and subtropical E. and W. Africa, Arabia; species 12.

Shrubs; limb of petals spathulate.
  Stamens 4 .... 1. *C. indica.*
  Stamens 5 .... 2. *C. farinosa.*
A tree; limb of petals suborbicular .... 3. *C. heterotricha.*

1. **Cadaba indica,** *Lam. Encyc.* v. 1 (1783) p. 544. A straggling, much-branched shrub; stems terete, the older smooth, purplish, the younger pubescent, yellowish-brown. Leaves simple, entire, $\frac{3}{4}$–$1\frac{1}{2}$ by $\frac{3}{8}$–$\frac{1}{2}$ in., elliptic-oblong, obtuse (rarely retuse), mucronate, reticulately veined, glabrous, base rounded; petioles $\frac{1}{10}$–$\frac{1}{8}$ in. long. Flowers dirty white, in few-flowered, terminal, 1-sided racemes, the upper flowers corymbose; pedicels $\frac{3}{8}$–$\frac{3}{4}$ in. long, pubescent; bract 1 at the base of each pedicel, subulate. Sepals subequal, ovate-oblong, acute, exceeding $\frac{1}{2}$ in. long, pubescent outside. Petals spathulate, about equalling the sepals; claw long, very narrow. Disk prolonged into a funnel-shaped process $\frac{3}{8}$ in. long, expanded and toothed at the apex, mouth oblique. Stamens 4, inserted about $\frac{1}{2}$ way up the gynophore, much exserted. Gynophore $\frac{3}{4}$–$\frac{7}{8}$ in. long. Ovary oblong; style 0. Fruit dehiscent, 1–2 in. by $\frac{1}{8}$ in., cylindric, irregularly torulose, pubescent or smooth. Seeds numerous, striate, surrounded by an orange-red aril. Fl. B. I. v. 1, p. 172; Grah. Cat. p. 8; Dalz. & Gibs. p. 9; Trim. Fl. Ceyl. v. 1, p. 60; Talb. Trees, Bomb. p. 9; Woodr. in Journ. Bomb. Nat. v. 11 (1897) p. 123.—Flowers: Nov.–Mar.

KONKAN: *Law*!; Cross island (Bombay harbour), *Stocks*! DECCAN: *Dalzell & Gibson*; Bijapur, *Cooke*!, *Woodrow*! GUJARAT: *Dalzell & Gibson*; Junaghad, *Cooke*!; Porbandar, *Cooke*!; Surat, *Woodrow*. S. M. COUNTRY: Belgaum, *Ritchie*, 980!; Dharwar, *Cooke*!

2. **Cadaba farinosa,** *Forsk. Fl. Ægypt.-Arab.* (1775) p. 68. A much-branched, hoary, wiry shrub. Leaves $\frac{1}{4}$–$\frac{1}{2}$ in. long, ovate or oblong, obtuse or retuse, glaucous, or whitish and mealy at first, at length glabrate; petioles $\frac{1}{10}$ in. long. Flowers as in *Cadaba indica*, the limb of the petals narrower. Stamens 5; filaments inserted about $\frac{1}{2}$ way up the gynophore. Fruit subterete or slightly torulose, 1–2 in. long, on a gynophore $\frac{1}{2}$–1 in. long. Seeds reniform-rotundate, compressed. Fl. B. I. v. 1, p. 173; Ait. Cat. Pb. & Sind Pl. p. 10; Talb. Trees, Bomb. p. 9; Watt, Dict. Econ. Prod. v. 2, p. 3.

A rare plant, found in Sind. SIND: *Stocks*!, *Dalzell*!

3. **Cadaba heterotricha,** *Stocks, in Hook. Icon. Pl.* v. 9 (1852) t. 839. A small tree, 12–20 ft. high, glaucous and pulverulent; branches hoary. Leaves petioled, orbicular, emarginate, pubescent with stellate or glandular hairs, often cuneate at the base. Petals 4, orbicular, clawed. Disk elongated into a process about $\frac{2}{3}$ as long as the gynophore, bilabiate, lower lip truncate, the upper elongate, reflexed, 2–3-crenate at the apex. Filaments 5, glabrous, free. Ovary and gynophore glandular-pubescent. Fruit unknown.

Stocks says (l. c.).—"The hairs on this plant are of 3 kinds. The herbaceous parts have an ashy, glaucous look from minute, sessile, stellate hairs covering the whole epidermis. Mixed with these stellate hairs are pedicelled ones, forked at the summit. These give a farinaceous look to the young shoots. Together with these, there are always present glandular, capitate hairs, few and inconspicuous." Fl. B. I. v. 1, p. 173; Talb. Trees, Bomb. p. 9.

A very rare plant. SIND: *Stocks*!; on rocks near Cape Monze, *Stocks* ex Fl. B. I. (l. c.).

7. CAPPARIS, Linn.

Trees or shrubs, often scandent, unarmed or with stipular thorns. Leaves simple, rarely 0. Inflorescence various; flowers white or colored, often showy, usually bracteate. Sepals 4, free or connate at the very base, in 2 series, imbricate, or the 2 exterior subvalvate. Petals 4, imbricate. Torus short. Stamens usually many, inserted on the torus at the base of a long gynophore. Ovary stalked, 1-4-celled; ovules many, on 2-6 parietal placentas; stigma sessile. Berry stalked, globose or cylindric, often elongate, rarely dehiscent. Seeds many, imbedded in pulp; testa crustaceous or coriaceous; embryo convolute.—DISTRIB. In both tropics and in the warm regions of Europe and Asia; species 120.

Flowers axillary, solitary or in fascicles of 2-3.
- Prostrate shrub; leaves orbicular; thorns usually hooked. ... 1. *C. spinosa.*
- Erect shrub; leaves ovate-lanceolate; thorns straight...... 2. *C. zeylanica.*
- Erect shrub; leaves elliptic-lanceolate; thorns minute or 0 ... 3. *C. Heyneana.*
- Shrub or small tree; leaves narrow-oblong; thorns straight. 4. *C. divaricata.*

Flowers corymbose (sometimes racemose in *C. grandis*).
- Leafless except on the young shoots, on which the leaves are linear ... 5. *C. aphylla.*
- Leaves oblong with a callous tip, glabrous; flowers 4-5 in. in diam. ... 6. *C. Moonii.*
- Leaves oblong or obovate, glabrous; flowers 1½ in. in diam. 7. *C. Roxburghii.*
- Leaves elliptic-obovate, olive-green-pubescent when young; flowers 1 in. in diam. ... 8. *C. grandis.*

Flowers in shortly peduncled umbels.
- An erect shrub; flowers small, few... 9. *C. pedunculosa.*
- A woody climber ... 10. *C. sepiaria.*

Flowers supra-axillary in a vertical line on the branches.
- A large climber; young parts fuscous-tomentose ... 11. *C. horrida.*
- A slender climbing shrub; young parts glabrous ... 12. *C. tenera.*

1. **Capparis spinosa,** *Linn. Sp. Pl.* (1753) p. 503. A diffuse, prostrate shrub; branches terete, glabrous or pubescent. Leaves variable, ½-1¼ in. in diam., glaucescent, orbicular or from broadly ovate to obovate, retuse or sometimes acute, mucronate, entire, rounded or cuneate at the base, glabrous or more or less pubescent; petioles about ⅛ in. long; stipules of 2 hooked (rarely straight), orange-colored thorns. Flowers handsome, axillary, solitary; pedicels 1-2 in. long, thickened in fruit. Sepals subequal. Petals white, 1-1¼ in. long, exceeding the sepals. Filaments purple, longer than the petals. Gynophore 2-3 in. long. Fruit 1-2 in. long, obovoid, ribbed, red when ripe. Seeds globose, smooth, brown. Fl. B. I. v. 1, p. 173; PAX, in Engl. & Prantl, Pflanzenf. v. 3, part 2, p. 226, fig. 136, A, B, C, D; Talb. Trees, Bomb. p. 10; Woodr. in Journ. Bomb. Nat. v. 11 (1897) p. 123; Watt, Dict. Econ. Prod. v. 2, p. 133. *Capparis Murrayana*, Grah. Cat. p. 9; Dalz. & Gibs. p. 9.—Flowers: Jan.-Mar. The *Caper* plant; the pickled flower-buds constitute the capers of commerce. VERN. *Kabar*; *Kalvári.*

In dry beds of streams in many places throughout the Presidency. KONKAN: *Law*!; Raighar, *Dalzell*! DECCAN: Mahableshwar, *Cooke*!, *Dalzell & Gibson*, *Woodrow*; Harishchandar, *Gibson* (fide *Graham*, l. c.). SIND: *Stocks*!; Kirthar mountains, *Woodrow*; Ruk Junction on the Railway Line, Upper Sind, *Cooke*!—DISTRIB. Europe (the Mediterranean region), Asia, N. Africa, Australia.

VAR. *galeata*, Hook. f. & Thoms. in Fl. B. I. v. 1, p. 173. Leaves fleshy, ovate-orbicular, tipped with a more or less curved mucro; lower sepal very saccate. *Capparis galeata*, Fresen. in Mus. Senckenb. v. 2, p. 111; Oliver, Fl. Trop. Afr. v. 1, p. 95.

A maritime plant, growing on the Sind coasts. SIND: *Dalzell*!; rocks by the sea and saltwater creeks, Karachi, *Stocks*!—DISTRIB. Arabia and E. Africa near the sea.

2. **Capparis zeylanica,** *Linn. Sp. Pl.* ed. 2 (1762) p. 720. A rigid, much-branched shrub; young shoots glabrous. Leaves coriaceous, 1½–2½ by ¾–1½ in., elliptic or broadly lanceolate, acute or obtuse, entire, glabrous on both surfaces, prominently reticulately veined, pale beneath, base subacute or rounded; petioles ⅛ in. long; stipular thorns short, straight. Flowers 1¾–2 in. in diam., axillary, solitary or 2–3 together on a short shoot; pedicels slender, 1–1½ in. long. Sepals nearly equal, concave. Petals ⅞ in. long, white, oblong, obtuse, undulate, the lower pair spreading, the upper approximate and with a colored spot at the base. Gynophore ½–¾ in. long. Ovary oblong, pubescent. Fruit irregularly ovoid, 2–2½ by 1–1¼ in., pointed or blunt, bright scarlet. Seeds numerous, imbedded in a white fetid pulp. Fl. B. I. v. 1, p. 174; Trim. Fl. Ceyl. v. 1, p. 61; Talb. Trees, Bomb. p. 10; Woodr. in Journ. Bomb. Nat. v. 11 (1897) p. 123; Watt, Dict. Econ. Prod. v. 2, p. 134. *Capparis brevispina*, DC. Prodr. v. 1, p. 246; Grah. Cat. p. 8; Dalz. & Gibs. p. 9.—Flowers: Feb.–Apr. VERN. *Wagdti*; *Govindphal.*

KONKAN: near Vingorla, *Dalzell & Gibson*. DECCAN: W. Deccan, *Dalzell & Gibson*; Alandi (near Poona), *Woodrow*. KANARA: N. Kanara, *Talbot*. S. M. COUNTRY: Dharwar, *Woodrow*, *Talbot*.

3. **Capparis Heyneana,** *Wall. Cat.* (1828) 6985. An erect shrub, unarmed or with minute, straight, stipular thorns. Leaves 3–5 by 1–2 in., elliptic-lanceolate, acute or acuminate, narrowed at the base, reticulately veined, the younger clothed with ferruginous, stellate tomentum, the older glabrous, shining above; petioles ¼ in. long. Flowers very large, 4–5 in. in diam., white or pale blue, arranged in corymbose, 2–6-flowered racemes, terminal or at the ends of short axillary branches; pedicels 1–1½ in. long and together with the subulate bracts ferrugino-tomentose. Sepals obtuse, tomentose within. Petals flat, obovate, spreading, the 2 lower much approximated and with a yellow, pubescent, basal spot. Filaments as long as the petals. Gynophore 1–1½ in. long. Ovary oblong, tomentose. Fruit not seen. Fl. B. I. v. 1, p. 174; Grah. Cat. p. 9; Talb. Trees, Bomb. p. 10; Woodr. in Journ. Bomb. Nat. v. 11 (1897) p. 123; Watt, Dict. Econ. Prod. v. 2, p. 131. *Capparis formosa*, Dalz. in Hook. Kew Journ. v. 2 (1850) p. 40; Dalz. & Gibs. p. 9.—Flowers: Apr.–May. VERN. *Chayruka.*

KONKAN: *Dalzell*!, *Law*! Ghâts of the S. Konkan, *Talbot*. KANARA: *Ritchie*, 1614!; in evergreen forests, N. Kanara, *Talbot*; Divimana (N. Kanara), *Woodrow*.

4. **Capparis divaricata,** *Lam. Encyc.* v. 1 (1783) p. 606. A much-branched shrub or small tree. Leaves 1¼–2½ by ⅜–¾ in., 5–7-nerved from the base, narrow-oblong, obtuse or retuse, rarely acute, mucronate, rounded at the base, the young leaves tomentose, the older glabrous; petioles ⅛–³⁄₁₆ in. long; stipular thorns stout, straight or slightly curved. Flowers 2¼ in. in diam., axillary, solitary, greenish; buds beaked, tomentose; pedicels ½–¾ in. long, stout, tomentose. Sepals ovate, acute, araneoso-tomentose on both surfaces. Petals oblong, acute or rounded at the top, araneoso-tomentose on both surfaces. Gynophore ¾ in. long.

Ovary glabrous, ribbed. Fruit 2 in. in diam., subglobose, scarlet, warted, 5–6-ribbed, obtusely beaked, seated on the elongate and greatly thickened gynophore. Fl. B. I. v. 1, p. 174; Trim. Fl. Ceyl. v. 1, p. 61; Talb. Trees, Bomb. p. 10; Woodr. in Journ. Bomb. Nat. v. 11 (1897) p. 123. *Capparis stylosa*, DC. Prodr. v. 1, p. 246; Grah. Cat. p. 8; Dalz. & Gibs. p. 10.—Flowers: Feb.–Apr.

DECCAN: common all over the Deccan, *Dalzell & Gibson*, *Talbot*; Rajewadi, *Woodrow*; Alandi, *Woodrow*. S. M. COUNTRY: Badami, *Woodrow*!, *Cooke*!

5. **Capparis aphylla,** *Roth, Nov. Pl. Sp.* (1821) p. 238. A straggling, glabrous shrub; branches terete, smooth, green. Leaves on the young shoots only (the older branches leafless), small, less than ½ in. long, linear-oblong, acute, spinous-pointed; petioles very short or 0; stipular thorns long, sharp, straight, orange-yellow. Flowers in many-flowered corymbs, from the old branches, or from short lateral shoots; pedicels slender, about ½ in. long. Sepals: the outer pubescent, ciliate, subvalvate, the lower sepal very saccate, acuminate, the upper much smaller, ovate-oblong, concave; inner sepals elliptic, acute, with floccose margins. Petals red, narrow-oblong, ⅜ by ⅛ in. Gynophore ½ in. long. Fruit globular, size of a small cherry, glabrous, beaked. Fl. B. I. v. 1, p. 174; Grah. Cat. p. 9; Dalz. & Gibs. p. 9; Talb. Trees, Bomb. p. 10; Woodr. in Journ. Bomb. Nat. v. 11 (1897) p. 123; Watt, Dict. Econ. Prod. v. 2, p. 130. *Sodada decidua*, Forsk. Fl. Ægypt. (1775) p. 81. *Capparis decidua*, Pax, in Engl. & Prantl, Pflanzenf. v. 3, part 2, pp. 230, 231, fig. 139 (*not* of Edgew.).—Flowers: Nov.–Mar. VERN. *Nepti*.

Throughout the driest parts of the Presidency; very common in Sind. DECCAN: *Dalzell & Gibson*; widely, *Woodrow*; Yeoat, near Poona, *Woodrow*!; island in the Poona river, *Cooke*! GUJARAT: *Dalzell & Gibson*. SIND: *Cooke*!—DISTRIB. Arabia, N. tropical Africa, Egypt.

6. **Capparis Moonii,** *Wight, Ill.* v. 1 (1840) p. 35. A large climbing shrub; stems reaching 6 in. in diam.; young branches purple, glabrous, shining. Leaves 3–4 by 1¼–2 in., elliptic-oblong, obtuse or acute, with a short callous tip, glabrous on both surfaces, shining above, paler beneath; petioles ½–¾ in. long; stipular thorns short, stout, hooked. Flowers white, 4–5 in. in diam., in terminal corymbs; pedicels 1½–2½ in. long, stout, flattened, glabrous. Sepals: the outer 1 in. in diam., orbicular, deeply cupped, much imbricate; the inner broadly oblong, finely tomentose outside. Petals spreading, pubescent on the upper surface. Stamens very numerous, 2–2½ in. long. Gynophore 2–3 in. long. Ovary ovoid, glabrous. Fruit 2–4 in. in diam., subglobose, pointed, seated on the much thickened woody stalk. Seeds numerous, ¾ in. in diam. Fl. B. I. v. 1, p. 175; Trim. Fl. Ceyl. v. 1, p. 62; Talb. Trees, Bomb. p. 10; Woodr. in Journ. Bomb. Nat. v. 11 (1897) p. 123. —Flowers: Dec.–Jan. VERN. *Wagáti*.

KONKAN: *Stocks*!, *Law*!; W. Gháts widely, *Woodrow*. DECCAN: Khandala, *Stocks*!, *Cooke*!, *Woodrow*. S. M. COUNTRY: Ramghát, *Ritchie*, 26! KANARA: evergreen forests along the N. Kanara Gháts, *Talbot*.

7. **Capparis Roxburghii,** *DC. Prodr.* v. 1 (1824) p. 247. A large woody climber; young branches fuscous- or hoary-pubescent. Leaves 1½–2½ by 1–1½ in., oblong or obovate, acute or shortly acuminate narrowed or cuneate at the base, glabrous, shining, pale beneath;

petioles ¼-½ in. long; stipular thorns stout, hooked. Flowers white, 1-1½ in. in diam., in corymbs at the extremities of the branches or on short axillary branches; buds tomentose; pedicels 1-1¾ in. long, pubescent or tomentose. Sepals as in the preceding species, but much smaller, the outer less than ½ in. in diam. Petals broadly obovate-cuneate. Gynophore 2 in. long. Ovary subglobose, pointed, glabrous. Fruit 1½-2 in. in diam., dark purple (*Roxb.* l. c.), globose, umbonate. Seeds numerous. Fl. B. I. v. 1, p. 175; Grah. Cat. p. 9; Dalz. & Gibs. p. 9 (?); Trim. Fl. Ceyl. v. 1, p. 62; Talb. Trees, Bomb. p. 10; Woodr. in Journ. Bomb. Nat. v. 11 (1897) p. 123. *Capparis corymbosa*, Roxb. Fl. Ind. v. 2, p. 569.—Flowers: Aug. VERN. *Wagáti.*

Very like the preceding, from which it differs chiefly in size and pubescence. In the description by Dalzell & Gibson (Bombay Flora, p. 9), it seems doubtful whether the plant described as *C. Roxburghii* may not be *C. Moonii.*

KANARA: *Stocks!*; Kumpta and Ankola Ghát, in evergreen forests, *Talbot.*

8. **Capparis grandis,** *Linn. f. Suppl.* (1781) p. 263. A small tree; young shoots covered with olive-green tomentum. Leaves 1-2½ by 1-1½ in., elliptic-obovate, obtuse (rarely retuse), sometimes mucronate, the younger clothed with olive green velvety pubescence, the older subglabrous, except the midrib; petioles ¼-½ in. long; stipular thorns usually absent, when present hooked. Flowers about 1 in. in diam., in terminal, many-flowered, densely pubescent corymbs, or sometimes in racemes the lower pedicels of which are furnished with stalked, leafy, the upper with small, deciduous bracts; pedicels ¾-1 in. long. Sepals: the outer ¼-$\frac{5}{16}$ in. long, covered with olive-colored pubescence outside, boat-shaped, valvate; the inner broadly elliptic, ciliate. Petals oblong-obovate, the inner surface pubescent. Gynophore usually ¾-1 in. long, sometimes only ⅛ in. Ovary ovoid, very acute, glabrous. Fruit the size of a nutmeg, subglobose, purple, smooth, 2-6-seeded. Fl. B. I. v. 1, p. 176; Grah. Cat. p. 9; Dalz. & Gibs. p. 10; Trim. Fl. Ceyl. v. 1, p. 63; Woodr. in Journ. Bomb. Nat. v. 11 (1897) p. 123; Watt, Dict. Econ. Prod. v. 2, p. 131.—Flowers: Apr.-May. VERN. *Pachunda.*

DECCAN: *Gibson!*; in the forts of Sholapore and Miraj, *Dalzell & Gibson*; Buleshwar Hill, Yeoat, 30 miles E. of Poona, *Woodrow!*; islet in the Mutha-Mula River, Poona, *Kanitkar!*; near Poona, *Cooke!* KANARA: *Law!* S. M. COUNTRY: in the forests of the Dharwar district, *Talbot*; Belgaum, *Ritchie*, 919!

9. **Capparis pedunculosa,** *Wall. Cat.* (1828) 6999. An erect shrub with wiry branches; young parts pubescent. Leaves bifarious, very close together, ⅜-1 in. in diam., broad-elliptic or orbicular, obtuse or acute, usually mucronate, glabrous, base rounded or subcordate; petioles very short; stipular spines hooked. Flowers white, in simple terminal and axillary short-peduncled umbels; pedicels ¾-1 in. long, filiform. Sepals less than ¼ in. long, reflexed, glabrous. Petals as long as the sepals. Gynophore 1 in. long, filiform. Fruit subglobose, size of a pea, smooth. Fl. B. I. v. 1, p. 176 (amending citation of no. in Wall. Cat.); Dalz. & Gibs. p. 9; Trim. Fl. Ceyl. v. 1, p. 63; Talb. Trees, Bomb. p. 11; Woodr. in Journ. Bomb. Nat. v. 11 (1897) p. 123.

I have seen no specimens from Bombay. Dalzell & Gibson (l. c.) give Mahábleshwar as a locality in which *Capparis pedunculosa* proper occurs. I consider this an error. I have *personally* examined numerous specimens of the Mahableshwar plant *in situ*, and all of them belonged to the var. *longispina*, which is very abundant on the hill.

VAR. *longispina*, Hook. f. & Thoms. (sp.) in Fl. B. I. v. 1, p. 176. Stipular spines straight, acicular, divaricate, sometimes reaching $\frac{1}{2}$ in. long. Leaves dark green, the upper surface shining, the lower more or less pubescent.—Flowers: Mar. VERN. *Kolisna.*

KONKAN: dense woods of the Ghâts, *Stocks*!, *Law*!; Matheran, *Cooke*! DECCAN: *Gibson*!; Mahableshwar, *Cooke*!, *Woodrow*! KANARA: along the N. Kanara Ghâts, *Talbot.*

10. **Capparis sepiaria,** *Linn. Syst.* ed. 10 (1759) p. 1071. A much-branched, woody climber; young shoots more or less pubescent. Leaves $\frac{3}{4}$–$1\frac{1}{2}$ by $\frac{1}{2}$–$\frac{7}{8}$ in., oblong-elliptic or obovate, obtuse, emarginate, rarely acute, the younger more or less pubescent, the older glabrous; petioles $\frac{1}{10}$–$\frac{1}{8}$ in. long, pubescent; stipular spines hooked. Flowers white, $\frac{1}{4}$–$\frac{3}{8}$ in. in diam., in dense, short-peduncled or sessile umbels; pedicels $\frac{1}{2}$–$\frac{3}{4}$ in. long, filiform. Gynophore $\frac{1}{4}$–$\frac{3}{8}$ in. long, filiform. Ovary ovoid, pointed, glabrous or very minutely pubescent. Fruit $\frac{1}{4}$–$\frac{3}{8}$ in. in diam., globose, smooth, black when ripe. Fl. B. I. v. 1, p. 177; Grah. Cat. p. 9; Dalz. & Gibs. p. 10; Trim. Fl. Ceyl. v. 1, p. 64; Talb. Trees, Bomb. p. 11; Woodr. in Journ. Bomb. Nat. v. 11 (1897) p. 123; Watt, Dict. Econ. Prod. v. 2, p. 132.—Flowers: Feb.–May. VERN. *Kanthar.*

Common in dry parts of the Presidency. DECCAN: widely, *Woodrow*; Nasik, *Cooke*! KANARA: Haliyal, *Ritchie*, 1617!

11. **Capparis horrida,** *Linn. f. Suppl.* (1781) p. 264. A climbing shrub; branches terete; young parts clothed with rufous tomentum. Leaves 1–3 by $\frac{3}{4}$-2 in., elliptic-oblong, obtuse, acute or retuse, with a long, stout mucro, narrowed at the base, reticulately veined, glabrous and shining above; petioles $\frac{1}{4}$ in. long; stipular spines hooked. Flowers supra-axillary, solitary or 2–3, one above the other in a vertical line, the upper the longest. Sepals $\frac{3}{8}$ in. long, densely rufous-pubescent outside, very concave. Petals twice as long as the sepals, densely villous. Gynophore $1\frac{1}{4}$ in. long. Ovary ellipsoid, apiculate. Fruit subglobose, $1\frac{1}{4}$ in. in diam., on a greatly thickened stalk, obtusely 4-angled, red-brown. Seeds many. Fl. B. I. v. 1, p. 178; Grah. Cat. p. 9; Dalz. & Gibs. p. 10; Trim. Fl. Ceyl. v. 1, p. 64; Talb. Trees, Bomb. p. 11; Woodr. in Journ. Bomb. Nat. v. 11 (1897) p. 123; Watt, Dict. Econ. Prod. v. 2, p. 131.—Flowers: Nov.–Apr. VERN. *Tarati.*

Throughout the Presidency and Sind, tolerably common. KONKAN: *Stocks*! DECCAN: *Woodrow*; Poona, *Cooke*! S. M. COUNTRY: Belgaum, *Ritchie*, 25! SIND: *Woodrow.*

12. **Capparis tenera,** *Dalz. in Hook. Kew Journ. Bot.* v. 2 (1850) p. 41. A climbing shrub; branches slender, terete, glabrous. Leaves membranous, 1–$2\frac{1}{2}$ by $\frac{3}{4}$-$1\frac{1}{4}$ in., ovate-oblong or lanceolate, acuminate, glabrous; petioles $\frac{1}{8}$ in. long; stipular spines hooked. Flowers white, $\frac{1}{2}$ in. in diam., supra-axillary, usually solitary or sometimes 2 (rarely 3) together in a vertical line, one above the other; pedicels filiform, $\frac{3}{4}$–$1\frac{1}{4}$ in. long. Sepals linear-lanceolate, deflexed. Petals oblong, acute, longer than the sepals, pubescent. Gynophore $\frac{3}{4}$ in. long, filiform. Ovary ovoid, long-pointed, glabrous. Fruit pisiform, $\frac{3}{8}$ in. in diam., usually 4-seeded. Fl. B. I. v. 1, p. 179; Dalz. & Gibs. p. 9; Trim. Fl. Ceyl.

v. 1, p. 65; Talb. Trees, Bomb. p. 11; Woodr. in Journ. Bomb. Nat. v. 11 (1897) p. 123.—Flowers: Mar.-May.

On the Ghâts, rare, *Dalzell & Gibson*. KONKAN: *Stocks*! KANARA: *Law*!; Kála naddi, *Ritchie*, 1613!; Kumpta-Sirsi Road, *Woodrow*; S. Ghâts of N. Kanara, *Talbot*.

ORDER XI. RESEDACEÆ.

Herbs, rarely shrubs. Leaves alternate, entire or pinnatisect; stipules 0, or glandular. Flowers small, racemose or spicate, bracteate. Calyx persistent, 4–7-partite, irregular; lobes imbricate in bud. Petals 2–7, hypogynous, entire or lobed, equal, or the upper larger, open in bud. Disk conspicuous, hypogynous (0 in *Oligomeris*). Stamens usually many, seated on the disk, free or connate, equal or unequal. Ovary 1-celled, of 2–6 connate carpels, often lobed at the top and open between the lobes which bear the sessile stigmas; ovules on 2–6 parietal placentas, amphitropous or campylotropous. Fruit capsular (a berry in *Ochradenus*), open at the top. Seeds many, reniform; albumen 0; embryo curved or folded; cotyledons incumbent.—DISTRIB. S. Europe, N. and S. Africa, N. Asia; genera 6; species about 30.

Fruit capsular.
Petals 4–7 .... 1. RESEDA.
Petals 2 .... 2. OLIGOMERIS.
Fruit a berry; petals 0.. 3. OCHRADENUS.

1. RESEDA, Linn.

Erect or decumbent herbs. Leaves entire, lobed or pinnatisect; stipules glandular. Flowers small, racemose, bracteate. Calyx 4–7-partite. Petals 4–7, unequal, multifid, the upper with a membranous appendage above the claw. Disk subsessile, broad, dilated on the upper side. Stamens 10–40, inserted within the disk. Ovary sessile or stalked, 3-lobed at the apex; placentas 3–6; ovules many. Capsule indehiscent, open at top. Seeds numerous.—DISTRIB. N. Africa, W. Asia; species 26.

Leaves narrow-linear, the upper 3–5-divided .... 1. *R. pruinosa.*
Leaves obovate, the upper undivided .... 2. *R. Aucheri.*

1. **Reseda pruinosa,** *Delile, Flor. Ægypt. Illustr.* (1812) p. 63. An erect perennial, 1–1½ ft. high; branches terete, glabrous, more or less papillose. Leaves papillose; the lower linear-lanceolate; the upper deeply 3–5-divided, the segments narrow-linear. Flowers minute, subsessile, in a dense, terminal, spiciform raceme 6–9 in. long; pedicels very short when in flower, elongating to $\frac{1}{10}$–$\frac{1}{8}$ in. in fruit; bracts linear-subulate, deciduous. Sepals 6–7, oblong-lanceolate, with hyaline and papillose margins. Petals white. Capsules $\frac{1}{3}$ in. long, oblong-obovoid, slightly contracted at the mouth, erect, appressed to the axis. Seeds yellowish-white, smooth, subglobose. Fl. B. I. v. 1, p. 181; Woodr. in Journ. Bomb. Nat. v. 11 (1897) p. 123; Watt, Dict. Econ. Prod. v. 6, part 1, p. 436.—Flowers: Mar.

SIND: *Stocks*, 587!; Boogta hills, *Vicary*!; Bullo Khan, *Woodrow*.

2. **Reseda Aucheri,** *Boiss. Diag.* ser. 1 (1842) fasc. 1, p. 5. An erect, branched perennial, 1–2 ft. high, glabrous or slightly papillose. Leaves 1–2 in. long, entire, oblong-obovate or lanceolate, acute or obtuse, tapering into a long petiole, glabrous, glaucous. Flowers yellowish-white, in dense spiciform racemes; pedicels scarcely $\frac{1}{12}$ in. long. Sepals 6–7, half as long as the petals, linear, acute, with hyaline margins. Petals $\frac{1}{8}$–$\frac{1}{6}$ in. long, the upper 9–11-partite for $\frac{1}{3}$ of their length, the entire portion oblong-obovate. Capsules as in the preceding. Fl. B. I. v. 1, p. 181; Boiss. Fl. Orient. v. 1, p. 434; Watt, Dict. Econ. Prod. v. 6, part 1, p. 436.

SIND: rare, *Dalzell*!, *Stocks*!

R. odorata, Linn. (*Mignionette*), is often cultivated, especially in the gardens of Europeans.

2. OLIGOMERIS, Camb.

Herbs. Leaves linear, entire, scattered or fascicled. Flowers small, in terminal spikes. Calyx 4-partite. Petals 2, distinct or connate at the base. Disk 0. Stamens 3–8, hypogynous; filaments free or monadelphous. Ovary sessile, 4-angled, 4-cuspidate; placentas 4, many-ovuled. Capsules angled, open at top. Seeds many.—DISTRIB. Species 4, of which 3 are S. African and the fourth distributed through N. Africa, Syria and Persia to India.

1. **Oligomeris glaucescens,** *Camb. in Jacquemont, Voy. Bot.* (1844) p. 24, t. 25. An annual erect glaucous herb; stems many, erect, sulcate, glabrescent. Leaves sessile, 1–2 by $\frac{1}{8}$ in., narrow-linear, acute, glabrous. Flowers greenish-white, in terminal spikes, the upper portion of the spikes dense, the lower lax; bract lanceolate, longer than the calyx. Calyx glabrous; lobes unequal, lanceolate, acute. Petals equalling the calyx, connate more than $\frac{1}{2}$-way up. Stamens 3, a little shorter than the petals; filaments connate at the base. Ovary sessile, depressed-globose, 4-cuspidate, 4-furrowed lengthwise; stigmas obtuse. Capsules very small, membranous. Seeds minute, shining, $\frac{1}{40}$ in. in diam. Fl. B. I. v. 1, p. 181; Woodr. in Journ. Bomb. Nat. v. 11 (1897) p. 123.

SIND: *Stocks*, 585! and 591!; Kirthar Mountains, *Woodrow*.—DISTRIB. Beluchistan, and westward to Spain and the Canaries.

3. OCHRADENUS, Delile.

Branched glabrous herbs; branches slender, twiggy. Leaves small, linear, on the younger branches only, solitary or fascicled. Flowers small, spicate or racemose, often polygamous. Calyx 5-fid. Corolla 0. Disk unilateral. Stamens 10–20, inserted within the disk. Ovary sessile, ovoid, closed at the top, 3-cuspidate; placentas 3; ovules many. Fruit a many-seeded berry.—DISTRIB. Species 2, one Spanish, the other the following, distributed to Syria and Egypt.

1. **Ochradenus baccatus,** *Delile, Flor. d'Egypte,* (1812) p. 236, t. 31. Shrubby, 6–12 ft. high; branches terete, striate, glabrous. Leaves $\frac{1}{2}$–$1\frac{1}{2}$ by $\frac{1}{12}$ in., entire, scattered near the base of the branches, olive-green, fleshy, narrow-linear, spathulate, with a callous tip, glabrous. Flowers yellowish, minute, shortly pedicelled, laxly arranged in rigid racemes, 1–2-sexual. Calyx 5–6-lobed. Petals 0. Stamens 10–12. Berry small, $\frac{1}{8}$ in. in diam., shortly stalked, obovoid, attenuated at the base, the apex

rounded and obtusely 3-denticulate. Seeds few, pale brown. Fl. B. I. v. 1, p. 182; Woodr. in Journ. Bomb. Nat. v. 11 (1897) p. 123.

SIND: Hyderabad; Karachi, *Woodrow*.—DISTRIB. Westwards to Syria and Egypt.

ORDER XII. VIOLACEÆ.

Herbs or shrubs. Leaves alternate, entire or pinnatisect; stipules foliaceous or small, commonly deciduous in the shrubby species. Flowers regular or irregular. Sepals 5, usually persistent, equal or unequal, imbricate in bud. Petals 5, hypogynous, equal or unequal, imbricate or contorted in bud. Stamens 5; filaments short, broad; anthers free or connate; connective broad, produced beyond the cells. Ovary sessile, 1-celled; ovules many, on 3 parietal placentas, anatropous; stigma capitate, truncate or cupular, entire or lobed. Fruit a 3-valved capsule, rarely baccate. Seeds small; albumen fleshy; embryo straight; cotyledons flat.—DISTRIB. Throughout almost the whole world, the herbaceous chiefly in the temperate, the shrubby species more frequent in tropical regions; genera 21; species 240.

Sepals produced at the base .... 1. VIOLA.
Sepals not produced at the base.. 2. IONIDIUM.

1. VIOLA, Linn.

Herbs, rarely shrubs. Leaves alternate; stipules persistent, often foliaceous. Flowers on 1- (rarely 2-) flowered axillary peduncles, often dimorphic, some large-petalled which ripen few seeds, others small-petalled or apetalous and prolific. Sepals subequal, produced below their insertion at the base. Petals usually spreading, the inner (lower by the torsion of the pedicels) often the larger, spurred or saccate at the base. Anthers connate; the connectives of the two lower often spurred at the base. Style clavate, or variously dilated, sometimes straight with a terminal stigma, or more or less curved with a stigma facing the lower petal. Capsule elastically 3-valved. Seeds ovoid or globose.—DISTRIB. Chiefly in the temperate regions of the N. hemisphere and S. America; species about 100.

1. **Viola Stocksii**, *Boiss. Fl. Orient.* v. 1 (1867) p. 453. A low much-branched herb, 3–6 in. high, with woody base; branches glabrous. Leaves (including the petioles) $\frac{1}{2}$–1 by $\frac{1}{4}$–$\frac{1}{2}$ in., oblong-obovate, or elliptic-lanceolate, acute, apiculate, decurrent into the petiole, glabrous, entire or obscurely crenulate (rarely dentate); stipules fimbriate. Flowers small, $\frac{1}{4}$ in. in diam., white with a violet blotch on the uppermost petal; pedicels $\frac{3}{4}$–$1\frac{1}{2}$ in. long, slender, glabrous; bracts $\frac{3}{16}$ in. long, subulate, attached near the top of the pedicels. Sepals $\frac{3}{16}$ in. long, lanceolate, tapering to a fine point, glabrous, spur very short, rounded. Style clavate, compressed; stigma of 2 oblong, parallel disks. Capsules $\frac{1}{6}$–$\frac{1}{4}$ in. long, smooth, cylindric, pointed at both ends. Seeds ovoid, pointed, white, polished. *Viola cinerea*, Hook. f. & Thoms. in Fl. B. I. v. 1, p. 185 (*not* of Boiss.); Woodr. in Journ. Bomb. Nat. v. 11 (1897) p. 124; Watt, Dict. Econ. Prod. v. 6, part 4, p. 244.—Flowers: July–Aug.

GUJARAT: (Rajkot (Kathiawar), *C. Macnaghten*!; Thorala (Kathiawar), *C. Macnaghten*! SIND: *Dalzell*, 73!, *Cooke*!, *Woodrow*!; Margalli, *Vicary*!; Moosa-Khail, *Vicary*, 11!—DISTRIB. Beluchistan, Afghanistan.

2. IONIDIUM, Ventenat.

Herbs or undershrubs. Leaves alternate, rarely opposite. Flowers axillary, orange or purple. Sepals 5, subequal, not produced at the base. Petals 5, the lower larger, clawed, saccate or spurred at the base. Anthers connate or free, 2 or 4 of them gibbous or spurred at the back. Style clavate, incurved; stigma oblique. Capsule elastically 3-valved. Seeds globose; testa crustaceous.—Distrib. Chiefly tropical American, a few in Africa, Asia and Australia; species 40.

1. **Ionidium heterophyllum,** *Ventenat, Jard. de la Malm.* (1803) fol. 27 *verso.* A small suffrutescent perennial herb, 6–12 in. high, with many diffuse or ascending branches, glabrous or more or less pubescent. Leaves linear or lanceolate, $1\frac{1}{2}$–2 by $\frac{1}{8}$–$\frac{1}{3}$ in., subsessile, entire, or with serrated margins; stipules gland-tipped, subulate. Flowers red, axillary, solitary; pedicels shorter than the leaves, $\frac{1}{4}$–$\frac{1}{2}$ in. long, erect, slender; bracts small, above the middle of the pedicel. Sepals $\frac{1}{10}$ in. long, lanceolate, very acute, keeled. Petals unequal, the 2 upper ones oblong, slightly longer than the sepals, the 2 lateral longer, falcate, the lowest much larger than the others, having an orbicular or obovate limb with a long claw which is curved behind into a short spur. Capsules about $\frac{1}{4}$ in. in diam., subglobose. Seeds ovoid, acute, longitudinally striate, yellowish-white, about $\frac{1}{18}$ in. long. *Ionidium suffruticosum,* Ging, in DC. Prodr. v. 1, p. 311; Fl. B. I. v. 1, p. 185; Grah. Cat. p. 11; Woodr. in Journ. Bomb. Nat. v. 11 (1897) p. 124; Watt, Dict. Econ. Prod. v. 4, p. 475. *Ionidium enneaspermum* and *I. hexaspermum,* Dalz. & Gibs. p. 12.—Flowers: Oct.-Dec. Vern. *Ratanparas.*

Konkan: *Stocks*! Gujarat: Broach, *Woodrow.* S. M. Country: Belgaum, *Ritchie,* 675!; Badami, *Woodrow*!; Dharwar, *Cooke*!

Order XIII. BIXACEÆ.

Trees or shrubs. Leaves alternate; stipules minute or 0. Flowers regular, 1–2-sexual. Sepals 4–5, rarely 2–6, imbricate (rarely completely connate), deciduous. Petals 4–5 or 0, imbricate or contorted in bud, deciduous. Stamens hypogynous or scarcely subperigynous, indefinite, rarely definite; anthers 2-celled, bursting by slits or pores. Disk thickened, often glandular. Ovary 1- (rarely many-) celled; ovules 2-many on each placenta, amphitropous or anatropous; style and stigmas free or united. Fruit fleshy or dry, indehiscent or valvular, the valves bearing the seeds in the middle. Seeds arillate or testa pulpy; albumen fleshy, rarely thin; embryo axile; cotyledons foliaceous, often cordate. —Distrib. Throughout the tropics of both hemispheres; genera 30; species 160.

Flowers bisexual.
- Leaves palmately divided; flowers 4–5 in. in diam....... 1. Cochlospermum.
- Leaves simple; flowers 2 in. in diam.......... 2. Bixa.
- Flowers small.......... 3. Scolopia.

Flowers diœcious.
- Petals 0 .... 4. Flacourtia.
- Petals 5, with a scale opposite to each .... 5. Hydnocarpus.

1. **COCHLOSPERMUM,** Kunth.

Trees or shrubs, with yellow or red juice. Leaves palmately or digitately divided. Flowers hermaphrodite, large, yellow, handsome. Sepals 5, imbricate, deciduous. Petals 5, large, contorted in bud. Stamens many, inserted on an eglandular disk; anthers oblong or linear, sometimes apiculate beyond the cells. Ovary globose; ovules many, on 3–5 parietal placentas; style simple; stigma minutely denticulate. Capsule 3–5-valved, incompletely 3–5-celled. Seeds cochleate; testa hard, woolly; embryo curved; cotyledons ovate.—DISTRIB. Tropical regions of the world; species 11.

1. **Cochlospermum Gossypium,** *DC. Prodr.* v. 1 (1824) p. 527. A small tree, 8–18 ft. high, with a branching head; bark smooth, ash-colored. Leaves scattered about the ends of the branchlets, 3–7 in. in diam., palmately 3–5-lobed, glabrous above, white-tomentose beneath; lobes entire, acute; petioles 4–7 in. long, pubescent when young. Flowers 4–5 in. in diam., in terminal subcorymbose panicles, bright yellow, appearing before the leaves; pedicels stout, 2–5 in. long, grooved and twisted, pubescent. Sepals unequal, oblong, concave, silky outside. Petals obovate, deeply emarginate. Capsules 2–3 in. long, obovoid, striate outside. Seeds ¼ in. long, cochleate, covered with an abundance of white silky wool. Fl. B. I. v. 1, p. 190; Grah. Cat. p. 22; Talb. Trees, Bomb. p. 12; Woodr. in Journ. Bomb. Nat. v. 11 (1897) p. 124; Watt, Dict. Econ. Prod. v. 2, p. 412. *Bombax gossypinum*, Linn. Syst. ed. 12, v. 2, p. 457; Roxb. Fl. Ind. v. 3, p. 169. *Bombax Gossypium*, Cav. Diss. p. 297.—Flowers: Feb.–Apr. VERN. *Ganeri.*

Found on a few of the Konkan and Deccan hills; often planted near temples. KONKAN: *Stocks*!; in gardens, Bombay, *Graham*. DECCAN: Chattersinghi hill, Poona Collectorate, *Woodrow*!; Kartriz Ghát, *Cooke*!; hill near Poona, *Woodrow*!; Khandesh hills, *Talbot*. S. M. COUNTRY: Belgaum, *Ritchie*, 998! GUJARAT; Sátpura jungles, *Dr. Gibson ex Graham*.

2. **BIXA,** Linn.

Small trees with yellow or red juice. Leaves large, quite entire, penninerved. Flowers hermaphrodite, terminal, panicled, handsome; pedicels 5-glandular beneath the calyx. Sepals 5, imbricate, deciduous. Petals 5, large, contorto-imbricate. Stamens many, inserted on a thick torus; anthers oblong, dehiscing at the apex by 2 short slits confluent into a pore. Ovary 1-celled; ovules many, on 2 parietal placentas; style slender, curved; stigma very shortly 2-lobed. Capsule densely echinate-setose, loculicidally 2-valved; valves thick, placentiferous in the middle. Seeds obovoid or trigonous; funicle dilated at the apex; testa subfleshy; embryo large; cotyledons flat.—DISTRIB. Species not more than about 2. The following species is cultivated throughout the tropics for the coloring matter afforded by the testa of the seeds.

1. **Bixa Orellana,** *Linn. Sp. Pl.* (1753) p. 512. A small evergreen tree. Leaves 4–8 by 2½–5 in., ovate, acute or acuminate, truncate or subcordate at the base, glabrous on both surfaces; petioles 2–3 in. long. Flowers 2 in. in diam., in terminal panicles; pedicels pubescent. Sepals: the two smaller concave; the three larger oblong or suborbicular. Petals white or pink, obovate. Capsules ovoid or subglobose, clothed with long

soft prickles. Seeds trigonous, rounded and grooved on the back, covered with a red pulp. Fl. B. I. v. 1, p. 190; Grah. Cat. p. 10; Dalz. & Gibs. Suppl. p. 5; Eichler, in Mart. Fl. Bras. v. 13, part 1, p. 433, t. 87; Warburg, in Engl. & Prantl, Pflanzenf. v. 3, part 6, pp. 310–311, fig. 142; Talb. Trees, Bomb. p. 12; Woodr. in Journ. Bomb. Nat. v. 11 (1897) p. 124; Watt, Dict. Econ. Prod. v. 1, p. 454. —Flowers: Aug.–Sept. VERN. *Kisri*; *Shendri*.

Originally a native of America the plant is largely cultivated throughout India.—The pulp which surrounds the seeds, known in commerce as "*Arnatto*," is used in dyeing silk and is largely employed for giving cloths a temporary dye during certain of the native festivals. The pulp is also used in India by the native milkmen for coloring butter and is imported in considerable quantities from the W. Indies into Europe, where it is used for coloring cheese, chocolate, butter and other edibles. See Watt, Dict. Econ. Prod. l. c.

3. **SCOLOPIA,** Schreb.

Trees with axillary spines, rarely unarmed. Leaves alternate, penninerved, entire or toothed, sometimes 2-glandular at the apex of the petiole. Flowers hermaphrodite, small, axillary, racemose. Sepals 4–6, slightly imbricate or subvalvate. Petals as many as, and subsimilar to, the sepals. Stamens many, inserted on a glandular or eglandular disk; anthers ovoid; connective produced. Ovary 1-celled; ovules few, on 3–4 parietal placentas; style filiform; stigma entire or 3–4-lobed. Berry pulpy within, 2–4-seeded. Seeds with long funicles; testa hard; cotyledons foliaceous, slender.—DISTRIB. S. and E. Africa, tropical Asia and N. Australia; species 15.

1. **Scolopia crenata,** *Clos. in Ann. Sc. Nat.* ser. 4, v. 8 (1857) p. 250. A small tree; branches with straight, simple spines when young, afterwards unarmed. Leaves 2–6 by 1–2½ in., ovate, acute or acuminate, narrowed at the base, glabrous, margins usually with minute, distant glandular teeth; petioles ¼–½ in. long. Flowers small, pale pink, numerous, in axillary panicles shorter than the leaves; pedicels ¼–½ in. long; bracts deciduous. Sepals 5–6, broad-oblong, obtuse, somewhat fleshy. Petals smaller than the sepals, obovate. Stamens numerous; connective of anthers produced, glabrous; filaments filiform. Style stout, grooved, ¼ in. long. Berry ½–⅝ in. in diam., ovoid or globose, pointed. Fl. B. I. v. 1, p. 191; Talb. Trees, Bomb. p. 12; Woodr. in Journ. Bomb. Nat. v. 11 (1897) p. 124; Watt, Dict. Econ. Prod. v. 6, part 2, p. 491. *Scolopia acuminata*, Clos. l. c. p. 251; Trim. Fl. Ceyl. v. 1, p. 70. *Phoberos crenatus*, W. & A. Prodr. p. 29; Dalz. & Gibs. p. 11.—Flowers: Mar.

Southern Ghâts, not common. KONKAN: *Law* !, *Stocks* !; on the Ghâts to the S. of Ramghât, *Dalzell & Gibson*; W. Ghâts, *Woodrow*. KANARA: Ghâts and forests near Nilkund (N. Kanara), *Talbot*.—DISTRIB. China, Philippines.

4. **FLACOURTIA,** Commers.

Trees or shrubs, often spinous. Leaves shortly petioled, toothed or crenate. Flowers small, diœcious. Sepals 4–5, small, imbricate. Petals 0. Stamens many, sometimes surrounded by glands; anthers versatile, short. Ovary on a glandular disk, 2–5-celled; styles 2 or more, distinct or connate at the base; stigmas notched or 2-lobed.

Fruit indehiscent; endocarp hard, with as many cells as seeds. Seeds obovoid; testa thinly coriaceous; cotyledons orbicular.—DISTRIB. The warmer parts of Africa, Asia and the adjacent islands; species 12.

Thorns not bearing flowers and fruit.
  Drupe size of a cherry, scarlet when ripe .... 1. *F. montana.*
  Drupe size of a plum, purple when ripe........................ 2. *F. Cataphracta.*
  Drupe size of a pea.
    Stigmas 5–11 .... 3. *F. Ramontchi.*
    Stigmas 3–4 .... 4. *F. latifolia.*
Thorns bearing flowers and fruit........................ 5. *F. sepiaria.*

1. **Flacourtia montana,** *Grah. Cat. Bomb. Pl.* (1839) p. 10. A very thorny tree. Leaves 4–7 by 1½–3 in., 3–5-nerved from the base, ovate, acute or acuminate, crenate, glabrous and shining above, glabrate beneath except the midrib, base acute or rounded; petioles ⅓ in. long. Flowers diœcious, in fascicled densely pubescent racemes. Fruit globose, obtusely ribbed, size of a cherry, of an agreeable acid flavor, scarlet when ripe, edible. Fl. B. I. v. 1, p. 192; Dalz. & Gibs. p. 10; Talb. Trees, Bomb. p. 12; Woodr. in Journ. Bomb. Nat. v. 11 (1897) p. 124; Watt, Dict. Econ. Prod. v. 3, p. 398.—Flowers: Nov.–Dec. Fruit ripe in March. VERN. *Attak.*

On the Ghâts rare, *Graham.* KONKAN: *Law!*, *Stocks!*; Bombay, *Dalzell!*; W. Ghâts, *Woodrow.* KANARA: N. Kanara, in evergreen forests, *Talbot*; Ankola, *Woodrow*; Kanara, *Law!*; Kála naddi, *Ritchie*, 1619!

Graham describes the fruit as of the size of a crab-apple, but it is not larger than a cherry. Dalzell & Gibson (*l. c.*) notice that it is in perfection in March.

2. **Flacourtia Cataphracta,** *Roxb. in Willd. Sp. Pl.* v. 4 (1805) p. 830. A small tree; branches white-dotted, glabrous, the young ones armed; spines compound. Leaves membranous, 2–4 by 1–1¾ in., oblong or oblong-lanceolate, long-acuminate, (the lower leaves on the branches often obtuse), quite glabrous, crenate-serrate; petioles ¼–½ in. long. Flowers very small, $\frac{1}{10}$–⅛ in. in diam., diœcious, in irregular glabrous racemes. Ovary flask-shaped, neck contracted; stigmas 4–6, capitate. Fruit the size of a small plum, very acid. Fl. B. I. v. 1, p. 193; Talb. Trees, Bomb. p. 13; Watt, Dict. Econ. Prod. v. 3, p. 398.

This species is included on the authority of *Dalzell & Gibson* (Bomb. Fl. p. 10), by whom it is stated to have been found in the Wari country on the banks of rivers.—It does not appear to have been found by any other collector and Wight & Arnott do not mention it.

3. **Flacourtia Ramontchi,** *L'Hérit. Stirp.* (1784) p. 59, tt. 30, 30, β. A small tree, armed. Leaves glabrous, 1½–3 by 1–1½ in., elliptic, acute or acuminate, attenuated at the base, coarsely crenate or serrate; petioles ⅛–¼ in. long, puberulous. Flowers in short-branched glabrous or puberulous racemes. Sepals ovate, ciliate. Stigmas 5–11, free or connate. Fruit size of a pea. Fl. B. I. v. 1, p. 193; Grah. Cat. p. 10; Watt, Dict. Econ. Prod. v. 3, p. 399.

VAR. 1. *sapida.* A small tree, often with large compound branched spines on the trunk; young shoots pubescent. Leaves 1½–3½ by 1–1½ in., broadly elliptic or obovate, usually acuminate, crenate or serrate, glabrous or pubescent on the veins beneath, base acute; petioles ¼–⅓ in. long. Flowers in small, axillary, racemose clusters; pedicels jointed above the middle. Sepals ciliate, very small, ovate or orbicular. Disk with crenate margin. Stigmas 5–6, nearly sessile. Fruit globular, ½ in. in diam., dark purple. Fl. B. I. v. 1, p. 193; Trim. Fl. Ceyl. v. 1, p. 73. *Flacourtia sapida* (sp.), Roxb. Cor. Pl. v. 1, p. 49, t. 69; Grah. Cat. p. 10. *Flacourtia Ramontchi*, Dalz. & Gibs. p. 10. VERN. *Panavla.*

Hills of the Konkan and Deccan. KONKAN: *Law*!, *Stocks*! S. M. COUNTRY: Belgaum, *Ritchie*, 982!; Chorla Ghát, *Dalzell & Gibson.*

VAR. 2. *occidentalis.* Branchlets and young parts more or less tomentose. Leaves 1½–3 by 1–2 in., oblong-elliptic, obovate or lanceolate, rounded or acute at the apex, narrowed at the base, crenate or serrate, more or less tomentose. Spines slender, straight. Sepals ovate, ciliate.

Rare in the Bombay Presidency. KONKAN: *Gibson*!, *Stocks*!

4. **Flacourtia latifolia,** *T. Cooke.* A small tree armed with long, straight, sharp, naked spines which are often compound on the older stems, sometimes unarmed. Leaves coriaceous, 3–5 by 2–3 in., broadly elliptic, acute or acuminate (rarely obtuse), crenate-serrate, glabrous, narrowed at the base, reticulately veined, the veins prominent on the lower surface; petioles ¼–½ in. long, more or less puberulous, those of the young leaves red. Flowers from the branches, in short pubescent racemes, yellowish-white; pedicels jointed near the middle. Sepals obovate or orbicular, ciliate. Stigmas 3–4 (usually 3), sessile. Fruit size of a pea, dark purple. *F. Ramontchi*, var. *latifolia*, Fl. B. I. v. 1, p. 193. *F. inermis* (?), Grah. Cat. p. 10 (*not* of Roxb.).—Flowers: Mar. VERN. *Támbat.*

Common at Mahableshwar, apparently confined to a limited range of the higher Ghâts. DECCAN: Mahableshwar, *Cooke*! S. M. COUNTRY: Chuta hill near Belgaum, *Ritchie*, 189!

I have made this a distinct species instead of a variety of *F. Ramontchi.* The presence of 3 (rarely 4) stigmas and the larger leaves seem to justify the separation. The tree, which is abundant at Mahableshwar, has always been a puzzle. Nairne remarks (Fl. Plts. W. I. p. 20)—"What the *támbat* at Mahableshwar is it is beyond me to decide."

5. **Flacourtia sepiaria,** *Roxb. Cor. Pl.* v. 1 (1795) p. 48, t. 68. A much-branched, thorny shrub; spines usually bearing flowers and fruit. Leaves on the young shoots alternate, on the older fascicled, ½–1½ by ½ in., elliptic, obovate or obcordate, cuneate or narrowed at the base, more or less crenate-serrate, glabrous, stiff; petioles ⅛–¼ in. long. Flowers diœcious, axillary, very small, greenish, solitary or in racemose clusters shorter than the leaves. Male sepals ovate, obtuse; female orbicular. Stigmas 3–4, on very short styles. Fruit globular, ⅓ in. in diam., smooth. Fl. B. I. v. 1, p. 194; Grah. Cat. p. 10; Dalz. & Gibs. p. 11; Trim. Fl. Ceyl. v. 1, p. 73; Talb. Trees, Bomb. p. 13; Woodr. in Journ. Bomb. Nat. v. 11 (1897) p. 124; Watt, Dict. Econ. Prod. v. 3, p. 399.—Flowers: Mar. VERN. *Támbat.*

Common in the hilly parts of the Konkan and Deccan. KONKAN: hilly parts, *Graham*; Western Ghâts, widely, *Woodrow.* DECCAN: towards the Ghâts, *Dalzell & Gibson*, *Talbot.* S. M. COUNTRY: Dharwar, *Cooke*!

5. HYDNOCARPUS, Gærtner.

Trees. Leaves alternate, serrate or entire; stipules deciduous. Flowers axillary, solitary or in few-flowered racemes or fascicles, diœcious.

Sepals 5, much imbricate in bud. Petals 5, with a scale at the base of each. MALE FLOWERS: Stamens 5–8; anthers oblong or reniform; connective broad. Ovary 0, or rudimentary. FEMALE FLOWERS: Stamens as in the male, but without pollen or reduced to staminodes. Ovary 1-celled; ovules many, on 3–6 parietal placentas; stigmas 3–6, sessile or subsessile, spreading, dilated, lobed. Berry large, subglobose; pericarp woody. Seeds numerous; testa crustaceous; albumen oily; cotyledons foliaceous, broadly ovate, flat.—DISTRIB. Tropical Asia; species about 6.

1. **Hydnocarpus Wightiana,** *Blume, Rumphia*, v. 4 (1848) p. 22. A tree, reaching 40–50 ft. in height. Leaves 5–9 by 1½–3 in., ovate, oblong or lanceolate, acuminate, entire or serrate, glabrous, base rounded or acute; petioles ¼–⅝ in. long; stipules lanceolate, deciduous. Flowers ⅜–½ in. in diam., solitary or in small racemes. Sepals 5, the outer ovate, the 3 inner much larger, very concave. Petals 5, broadly oblong or orbicular, rounded at the top, fringed with soft white hairs; scales about ½ the size of the petals, ovate, densely hairy. MALE FLOWERS: Stamens 5, opposite the petals; filaments subulate, hairy at the base, about equalling the petals. FEMALE FLOWERS: Stamens 5, as in the male; anthers without pollen. Ovary globose, hairy; stigmas flat on the top of the ovary, each cuneate and 2-lobed. Berry globose or obovoid, size of a small apple, tomentose. Seeds obtusely angular, numerous, yellowish. Fl. B. I. v. 1, p. 196; Dalz. & Gibs. p. 11; Talb. Trees, Bomb. p. 13; Woodr. in Journ. Bomb. Nat. v. 11 (1897) p. 124; Watt, Dict. Econ. Prod. v. 4, p. 308. *Hydnocarpus inebrians*, Wall. Cat. 6670; Wight, Ill. v. 1, t. 16; Grah. Cat. p. 10.—Flowers: Jan.–Apr. VERN. *Kadu-Kavath.*

The Konkans and Kanara, chiefly on hill ranges near the coast. KONKAN: *Stocks*!, *Law*!; near Goa, *Stocks*!, *Dalzell*!; Vingorla, *Ritchie*, 31!; S. Konkan, *Talbot*, *Dalzell & Gibson*; W. Ghâts, widely, *Woodrow*. KANARA: N. Kanara, *Ritchie*, 31!; evergreen forests, *Talbot*.

ORDER XIV. PITTOSPORACEÆ.

Shrubs or small trees. Leaves alternate or subverticillate, usually quite entire, exstipulate. Flowers usually hermaphrodite and regular, terminal or axillary. Sepals 5, imbricate, free or rarely connate at the base. Petals 5, hypogynous, imbricate, longer than the sepals. Stamens 5, hypogynous, free, alternating with the petals; anthers versatile. Torus small. Ovary 1-celled with 2–5 parietal placentas, or 2–5-celled by the projection of the placentas; ovules many, parietal or axile, anatropous; style simple; stigma terminal, entire or lobed. Fruit capsular or indehiscent. Seeds usually numerous; testa thin, smooth or rarely rugose; albumen hard; embryo minute; radicle next the hilum; cotyledons short or indistinct.—DISTRIB. Genera 9; species about 90, chiefly Australian.

1. PITTOSPORUM, Banks.

Erect shrubs or small trees, usually evergreen, glabrous or rarely tomentose. Leaves entire or sinuato-dentate, subverticillate at the apices of the branches in some species. Sepals free or connate at the base. Petals connivent at the base or beyond the middle into a tube or coherent, rarely spreading from the base. Filaments subulate; anthers erect, 2-celled, bursting by slits. Ovary sessile or shortly stalked, incompletely 2–3-celled; style short. Capsule 1-celled, woody, 2- rarely 3-valved; valves placentiferous in the middle. Seeds smooth, usually imbedded in a viscous pulp.—DISTRIB. Subtropical Asia and Australia; species about 50.

Leaves and branches glabrous; capsule size of a pea, glabrous... 1. *P. floribundum.*
Young branches and inflorescence pubescent or tomentose; capsule size of a small cherry, tomentose .... 2. *P. dasycaulon.*

1. **Pittosporum floribundum,** *Wight & Arn. Prodr.* (1834) p. 154. A small tree; bark light-colored, dotted with lighter specks. Leaves thinly coriaceous, 3–6 by $1\frac{1}{4}$–$2\frac{1}{4}$ in., lanceolate or oblong-lanceolate, acute or acuminate, glabrous and shining above, paler beneath, undulate; petioles $\frac{1}{2}$–$\frac{3}{4}$ in. long. Flowers numerous, in much-branched, terminal, compound corymbs; pedicels glabrous or pubescent. Sepals $\frac{1}{10}$ in. long, ovate, acute or obtuse, pubescent outside. Petals yellow, $\frac{1}{4}$–$\frac{5}{16}$ in. long, narrow-oblong. Ovary very hairy in the lower part; ovules about 12; style simple, glabrous; stigma 2-lobed. Capsules pisiform, $\frac{1}{4}$ in. in diam., 2-valved, about 6-seeded. Seeds obtusely angular, smooth, black. Fl. B. I. v. 1, p. 199; Grah. Cat. p. 38; Dalz. & Gibs. p. 44; Talb. Trees, Bomb. p. 13; Woodr. in Journ. Bomb. Nat. v. 11 (1897) p. 124; Watt, Dict. Econ. Prod. v. 6, part 1, p. 283.—Flowers: Apr.–Sept. VERN. *Yekadi.*

Tolerably common along the range of the Ghâts. KONKAN: in the Ghât forests, *Talbot, Law*! DECCAN: Rotunda Ghât, Mahableshwar, *Woodrow*; Khandala, pretty common, *Graham*; Khandala valley, *Cooke*! KANARA: N. Kanara, in the Ghât forests, *Talbot.*

2. **Pittosporum dasycaulon,** *Miquel, Anal. Bot. Ind.* pars 3 (1852) p. 5. A shrub or small tree; young branches clothed with yellowish tomentum. Leaves 2–5 by 1–2 in., lanceolate, acute or acuminate, glabrous or the midrib beneath downy; petioles $\frac{1}{4}$–$\frac{3}{8}$ in. long, those of the young leaves tomentose. Flowers in dense terminal corymbs, clothed with yellowish tomentum. Sepals $\frac{1}{10}$ in. long, ovate, very acute, densely pubescent outside, ciliate. Petals yellow, $\frac{3}{8}$–$\frac{1}{2}$ in. long, narrow-oblong. Capsules larger than in the preceding species, $\frac{3}{8}$–$\frac{1}{2}$ in. in diam., compressed, densely tomentose before dehiscence, 2-valved, about 6-seeded. Fl. B. I. v. 1, p. 199; Talb. Trees, Bomb. p. 13; Woodr. in Journ. Bomb. Nat. v. 11 (1897) p. 124.—Flowers: Nov.–Jan. VERN. *Gápsundi.*

Rare; sparingly distributed throughout the Western Ghâts. KONKAN: *Stocks*!, *Dalzell*! S. M. COUNTRY: Belgaum, *Ritchie*, 131!; Ramghât, *Ritchie*!; near Hubli, ex *Miquel*, l. c. (*Metz.* 775)! KANARA: Yacombi (N. Kanara), *Woodrow*!; evergreen forests, *Talbot.*

ORDER XV. POLYGALACEÆ.

Herbs or erect or scandent shrubs, rarely small trees. Leaves alternate (rarely whorled), simple or occasionally reduced to scales or 0, exstipulate. Flowers irregular, hermaphrodite, 3-bracteate. Sepals 5, free, much imbricate in bud, the 2 inner larger, sometimes very large, often petaloid (wing sepals). Petals 5 or 3, hypogynous, distinct, unequal, the inferior usually keel-shaped. Stamens 8 (in *Salomonia* 4–5), hypogynous; filaments united into a sheath, rarely distinct; anthers opening by terminal pores, rarely by slits. Torus small, rarely expanded into an annular disk. Ovary free, 1–3-celled; ovules 1 or more in each cell, anatropous; style usually curved. Fruit generally a 2-celled, 2-seeded, loculicidal capsule, or indehiscent, or of 3 indehiscent carpels. Seed pendulous, often strophiolate, usually albuminous, often pilose.—DISTRIB. Genera 15; species 400–500, throughout the warm regions of the world, except New Zealand.

1. POLYGALA, Linn.

Herbs, rarely shrubs. Leaves alternate, rarely opposite or verticillate. Flowers spicate or racemose. Sepals unequal, the 2 inner larger (wings) usually petaloid. Petals 3, united at the base with the staminal sheath, the lower one keeled and generally crested. Stamens 8; filaments united for their lower half into a split sheath; anthers opening by pores. Ovary 2-celled; ovule 1 in each cell, pendulous. Capsule 2-celled, loculicidal, 2-seeded. Seeds pilose or glabrous, almost always strophiolate and albuminous.—DISTRIB. Throughout the warm regions of the globe, except New Zealand and Tasmania; species more than 200.

Seeds with a strophiole.
  Wings obtuse.
    Leaves lanceolate; wings petaloid, glabrous; capsule margined.......... 1. *P. persicariæfolia.*
    Leaves narrow-linear; wings with a green midrib; capsule not margined .... 2. *P. erioptera.*
  Wings acute or acuminate.
    Racemes long; capsule not or scarcely ciliate .... 3. *P. elongata.*
    Racemes short, almost capitate; capsule densely ciliate. 4. *P. chinensis.*
Seeds without a strophiole .... 5. *P. irregularis.*

1. **Polygala persicariæfolia,** *DC. Prodr.* v. 1 (1824) p. 326. Stem erect, 6–18 in. high, simple or branching, slender, grooved, pubescent. Leaves subsessile, 1–2 by $\frac{1}{4}$–$\frac{5}{8}$ in., oblong-lanceolate, mucronate, glabrous on both surfaces or with a few scattered hairs, paler beneath, margins ciliolate. Flowers rose-colored, in terminal and extra-axillary racemes; corolla much shorter than the wings; crest a broad membranous appendage with a multifid limb; pedicels $\frac{1}{10}$–$\frac{1}{8}$ in. long, filiform, curved downwards; bracts small, linear-lanceolate, acute. Outer sepals $\frac{1}{8}$ in. long, ovate-oblong, slightly deflexed. Wings membranous, broadly ovate or suborbicular, with 3–5 conspicuous looping nerves, glabrous. Capsules elliptic-oblong, emarginate, shorter than the wings, margins thickened, ciliate. Seeds oblong, clothed with dense subappressed hairs; strophiole smooth, hemispheric, not appendiculate at the base. Fl. B. I. v. 1, p. 202; Dalz. & Gibs. p. 13; Woodr. in Journ. Bomb. Nat. v. 11 (1897) p. 124; Chodat, Monogr. Polygal. part 2, p. 331, t. 27, figs. 22–23.—Flowers: Aug.–Sept.

On the highest Ghâts east of Bombay, *Dalzell & Gibson*. KONKAN: Ghâts, *Stocks*! DECCAN: Mahableshwar, *Cooke*!; Panchgani, *Cooke*!; Bowdhan hill near Poona, *Woodrow*! KANARA: *Law*! S. M. COUNTRY: Belgaum, *Ritchie*, 34!—DISTRIB. Tropical Africa and Australia.

2. **Polygala erioptera,** *DC. Prodr.* v. 1 (1824) p. 326. Annual, 6–15 in. high, usually branched from the base or nearly so; branches ascending, numerous, terete, pubescent or glabrescent. Leaves ½–1½ by $\frac{1}{12}$–¼ in., very variable in form, from oblong-obovate to very narrow linear, narrowed at the base, apex rounded or subacute, sometimes mucronate, clothed on both surfaces with minute simple hairs; petioles about $\frac{1}{32}$ in. long. Flowers yellow, in axillary or extra-axillary, very short few-flowered racemes; crest dorsal, of many bifid or linear filaments arranged in 2 bundles; pedicels slender, hairy, ⅛ in. long; bracts minute, ovate, hairy. Outer sepals $\frac{1}{16}$ in. long, ovate, pubescent. Wings ⅛–$\frac{3}{16}$ in. long, obliquely ovate-oblong, pubescent, a little longer than the capsule, with a strong, green midrib and membranous, ciliate margins. Capsules oblong-elliptic, not margined, pubescent, ciliate, shorter and narrower than the wings, obliquely emarginate. Seeds oblong, densely pilose; strophiole galeate, horny, smooth and shining or sometimes with a few hairs, obscurely 3-lobed. Fl. B. I. v. 1, p. 203; Chodat, Monogr. Polygal. part 2, p. 342, t. 28, figs. 1–4; Woodr. in Journ. Bomb. Nat. v. 11 (1897) p. 124. *Polygala Vahliana*, DC. Prodr. v. 1, p. 326; Dalz. & Gibs. p. 13.—Flowers: Aug.

Pretty common in Gujarat and Sind. KONKAN: *Stocks*! DECCAN: dry fields near Poona, *Woodrow*! GUJARAT: Broach, *Woodrow*; Ankleswar (near Broach), *Woodrow*!, *Cooke*! SIND: Karachi, *Dalzell*!; Jemadar ka Landa (near Karachi), *Stocks*, 471!—DISTRIB. Arabia, tropical Asia and Africa.

The leaves of the Sind specimens are usually very narrow.

3. **Polygala elongata,** *Klein, ex Willd. Sp. Pl.* v. 3 (1800) p. 879. Annual, 6–18 in. high, erect or ascending; branches slender, terete, glabrous or pubescent. Leaves ¾–1½ by ⅛–⅙ in., subsessile, linear-oblong, obtuse, mucronate. Flowers yellow, in lax supra-axillary racemes 3–9 in. long; crest of a single tubular appendage multifid only at the apex; pedicels $\frac{1}{16}$ in. long; bracts small, membranous, ovate, acute, ciliate, persistent. Outer sepals $\frac{1}{12}$ in. long, lanceolate, acute, with membranous, ciliolate margins. Wings ⅕ in. long, very oblique, ovate or subfalcate, acute or mucronulate, a little longer than the capsule, glabrous or slightly pubescent, not ciliate. Capsules emarginate, very unequal-sided, oblong, glabrescent, narrowly margined. Seeds pyriform, clothed with short, appressed, silky hairs; strophiole 3-lobed, very shortly appendaged, smooth. Fl. B. I. v. 1, p. 203; Chodat, Monogr. Polygal. part 2, p. 387, t. 29, figs. 47–48; Woodr. in Journ. Bomb. Nat. v. 11 (1897) p. 124. *Polygala campestris*, Dalz. in Hook. Kew Journ. Bot. v. 2 (1850) p. 40; Dalz. & Gibs. p. 13.—Flowers: Aug.–Nov.

KONKAN: *Dalzell*!; Malwan, ex *Dalzell* in Hook. Journ. l. c.; Sawantwari, *Cooke*!, *Woodrow*! KANARA: Tinai (N. Kanara), *Talbot*!; Kanara, *Thomson*! S. M. COUNTRY: Badami, *Woodrow*; Belgaum, *Ritchie*!

4. **Polygala chinensis,** *Linn. Sp. Pl.* (1753) p. 704. Annual, 4–10 in. high, erect, branched from the base, glabrous or pubescent. Leaves very variable, ½–1½ in. long, obovate, suborbicular or linear-oblong, rather thick, coriaceous, glabrous, ciliate, mucronate; petioles $\frac{1}{12}$ in. long, hairy. Flowers yellow, fading to pink, in axillary or extra-axillary, short, almost capitate, few-flowered racemes; crest of a single tubular appendage multifid only at the apex; pedicels very short; bracts small, membranous, oblong-ovate, acute, ciliate, persistent. Outer sepals broadly ovate, acuminate, with broad, membranous, ciliate margins.

Wings herbaceous, oblique, ovate-oblong, acuminate, with narrow, membranous margins ciliate towards the base, longer than the capsule. Capsules didymous, orbicular-oblong, strongly ciliate, obliquely obcordate at the apex, narrowly margined. Seeds hairy; strophiole glabrous or nearly so, rounded at the apex, furnished with 3 membranous basal appendages. Fl. B. I. v. 1, p. 204; Chodat, Monogr. Polygal. part 2, p. 385, t. 29, figs. 45–46; Woodr. in Journ. Bomb. Nat. v. 11 (1897) p. 124; Watt, Dict. Econ. Prod. v. 6, part 1, p. 315. *Polygala arvensis*, Willd. Sp. Pl. v. 3, p. 876; Grah. Cat. p. 11; Dalz. & Gibs. p. 12. *Polygala Rothiana*, W. & A. Prodr. p. 37; Dalz. & Gibs. p. 13.—Flowers: Oct.–Mar. VERN. *Phutáni*.

Tolerably common throughout the Presidency. KONKAN: *Stocks*!; Island of Bombay, *Dalzell & Gibson*. DECCAN: *Dalzell & Gibson*, *Stocks*!, *Jacquemont*, 1012!, *Woodrow*! GUJARAT: Surat, *Dalzell & Gibson*. S. M. COUNTRY: Belgaum, *Ritchie*, 985!; Badami, *Cooke*!—DISTRIB. Tropical Asia and Australia.

5. **Polygala irregularis,** *Boiss. Diag.* ser. 1 (1842) fasc. 1, p. 8. Perennial, 8–18 in. high, erect, branching from the base; branches elongate, twiggy. Leaves very shortly petioled; the lower obovate, very small; the upper $\frac{1}{2}$–$1\frac{1}{2}$ by $\frac{1}{8}$–$\frac{1}{4}$ in., linear-oblong, mucronate, attenuate at the base, glabrous, margins repand. Flowers in terminal, elongate lax racemes, 2–8 in. long; crest small, multifid; pedicels very short, pendulous, thickened at the apex, shorter than the flowers; bracts ovate, acute, scarious, caducous, leaving a projecting cicatrix. Outer sepals ovate, acute, margins membranous. Wings $\frac{3}{16}$ in. long, membranous, petaloid, ovate, obtuse, gibbous at the base, reticulately nerved, longer than the capsule. Capsules obliquely emarginate, glabrous, margins membranous, transversely striate, not ciliate. Seeds conical, very acute at the apex, densely clothed with short hairs; strophiole 0, its place being taken by 2 lateral inconspicuous, aculeiform, pendent appendages. Not in Fl. B. I.; Boiss. Fl. Orient. v. 1, p. 469; Oliver, Fl. Trop. Afr. v. 1, p. 131; Chodat, Monogr. Polygal. part 2, p. 392, t. 30, figs. 12–14. *Polygala abyssinica*, Woodr. in Journ. Bomb. Nat. v. 11 (1897) p. 124 (*not* of R. Br.).—Flowers: Dec.

A rare plant, found in Sind and on the coast of Kathiawar. GUJARAT: Coast of Kathiawar, *Dalzell*! SIND: *Cooke*!, *Woodrow*!—DISTRIB. Arabia, Cordofan, Beluchistan.

ORDER XVI. CARYOPHYLLACEÆ.

Annual herbs, rarely shrubby at the base; the branches often thickened and sometimes articulated at the joints. Leaves opposite, usually connate at the base; stipules scarious or 0. Inflorescence usually a dichotomous cyme, rarely racemose or solitary; flowers regular, usually hermaphrodite. Sepals 4–5, free or connate, imbricate in bud. Petals as many as the sepals (rarely 0), inserted on a hypogynous or more rarely perigynous ring, imbricate. Stamens 8 or 10, rarely fewer, inserted with the petals; anthers 2-celled, cells parallel, dehiscing longitudinally. Torus usually small and annular, or elongated into a gynophore, so that the petals, stamens, and ovary are stalked within the calyx, or expanded into an annular disk slightly adhering to the calyx, or into short glands between the stamens, or, very rarely, into staminodes opposite the sepals outside the stamens. Ovary free, 1-celled, or sometimes imperfectly 2–5-celled at the base; ovules 2 or many, on slender basal funicles which are either free or united into a column, amphitropous; styles 2–5, stigmatose within at the upper part, or rarely from the base, free or more or less united. Capsule membranous or crustaceous, rarely sub-baccate, opening by as many valves as there are styles (or twice as many), rarely indehiscent or bursting transversely. Seeds generally numerous (rarely few or solitary); testa membranous or crustaceous; albumen farinaceous, rarely fleshy; embryo usually more or less curved; cotyledons narrow, incumbent, rarely accumbent.—DISTRIB. Throughout the globe; chiefly in extratropical regions of the N. hemisphere; genera 35; species about 800.

Stipules 0.
  Sepals united into a 4–5-lobed or -toothed calyx.
    Styles 2 .... 1. SAPONARIA.
    Styles 3 .... 2. SILENE.
  Sepals separate.
    Capsule long, cylindric, twice as long as the sepals; petals 2-fid .... 3. CERASTIUM.
    Capsule short, ovoid, a little longer than the sepals; petals 2-fid .... 4. STELLARIA.
    Capsule short, about equalling the sepals; petals entire. 5. ARENARIA.
Stipules scarious.
  Valves of capsule 5; styles 5, free .... 6. SPERGULA.
  Valves of capsule 3; styles 3, combined.
    Sepals keeled .... 7. POLYCARPON.
    Sepals not keeled .... 8. POLYCARPÆA.

1. SAPONARIA, Linn.

Annual or perennial herbs. Leaves flat. Flowers in dichotomous cymes. Calyx more or less tubular, ovoid or oblong, 5-toothed, nerves obscure. Petals 5, with a narrow claw; limb entire or emarginate, with or without a basal scale. Stamens 10. Torus small or produced into a short gynophore. Ovary 1-celled or septate at the very base; ovules many; styles 2. Capsule ovoid or oblong, opening at the apex by 4 teeth or short valves. Seeds reniform or subglobose, laterally compressed, having the hilum on one of the margins; embryo hemispheric, forming nearly a circle.—DISTRIB. South Europe, the Mediterranean region, and extratropical Asia; species 30.

1. **Saponaria Vaccaria,** *Linn. Sp. Pl.* (1753) p. 409. A tall robust annual, 1–2 ft. high; branches quite glabrous. Leaves 1–2½ by ¼–¾ in., sessile, glabrous; the lower oblong, acute; the upper oblong-lanceolate, very acute or mucronate. Flowers in corymbose dichotomous cymes; pedicels slender, 1–2 in. long; bracts foliaceous. Calyx ½ in. long, ventricose in fruit, with 5 broad green nerves and scarious margins; teeth triangular. Petals rosy, obovate, slightly emarginate; claw shortly exserted; limb ½ in. long. Capsules included, broadly ovoid. Seeds globose, black, granulate. Fl. B. I. v. 1, p. 217; Boiss. Fl. Orient. v. 1, p. 525; Woodr. in Journ. Bomb. Nat. v. 11 (1897) p. 124; Watt, Dict. Econ. Prod. v. 6, part 2, p. 473.—Flowers: Feb. VERN. *Sábani.*

A weed of cultivation, met with in wheat-fields and cultivated ground throughout India. KONKAN: Panwell, *Woodrow*! DECCAN: Nasik, *Cooke*!, *Woodrow*!; Mahableshwar, *Woodrow*!—DISTRIB. A weed of cultivation throughout temperate and subtropical countries.

2. SILENE, Linn.

Annual or perennial herbs, frequently viscous in the upper parts. Flowers solitary or cymose, often forming unilateral spikes or terminal panicles. Calyx more or less inflated, ovoid, campanulate, clavate or tubular, 5-toothed or 5-fid, generally 10- (more rarely 20- or 30-) nerved, 5 of the nerves indicating the line of demarcation between the sepals. Petals 5; claw narrow; limb entire, 2-fid or rarely laciniate, frequently with 2 scales at the base. Stamens 10. Torus elongated into a more or less stalked gynophore. Ovary 1-celled or septate at the very base; ovules numerous; styles usually 3 (rarely 5). Capsule dehiscing at the apex by 6 (rarely 3) short valves. Seeds reniform, laterally compressed, tubercled, with the hilum on the inner margin; embryo peripheric, forming a semicircle or a complete circle.—DISTRIB. Europe, N. and S. Africa, N. America, extratropical Asia; species about 250.

1. **Silene noctiflora,** *Linn. Sp. Pl.* (1753) p. 419. Stem erect, 1–2 ft. high, viscous-pubescent in the upper part, usually dichotomously branched. Leaves: the lower obovate-oblong; the upper narrowly lanceolate. Flowers $\frac{7}{8}$ in. long, few, in a dichotomous cyme. Calyx hairy and viscous, cylindric, inflated, truncate at the base; teeth very long, subulate, half as long as the tube, ciliate, the points diverging before the flower opens; nerves very broad, green on a whitish membranous ground. Petals white, tinged with rose within and with yellow on the outside. Styles 3. Gynophore about $\frac{1}{6}$ the length of the capsule. Capsules $\frac{3}{4}$–1 in. long, ovoid-conical. Seeds globose-reniform, convex on the back, tubercled. Not in Fl. B. I.; Boiss. Fl. Orient. v. 1, p. 581; Woodr. in Journ. Bomb. Nat. v. 11 (1897) p. 124; Syme, Eng. Bot. v. 2, p. 66, t. 209.—Flowers: Dec.–Jan.

A weed of cultivation which (fide *Woodrow*, l. c.) is to be met with in cultivated ground about Poona.—DISTRIB. Europe, Siberia, W. Asia.

3. CERASTIUM, Linn.

Herbs, usually pubescent or hirsute. Leaves usually small, elliptic or oblong, rarely subulate. Flowers white, in terminal dichotomous cymes. Sepals 5 (rarely 4). Petals as many (rarely 0), bifid or notched at the apex, seldom entire. Stamens 10, rarely 5 or fewer. Ovary 1-celled; ovules many; styles 5, opposite the sepals (rarely 4 or 3). Capsule cylindric or conic-ovoid, often incurved, dehiscing at the apex by twice as many teeth as there are styles; teeth short, straight or more rarely recurved. Seeds numerous, brown, globose-reniform, laterally compressed, granulate or tubercled.—DISTRIB. All temperate regions; species about 40.

1. **Cerastium glomeratum,** *Thuill. Flor. Par.* ed. 2 (1824) p. 226. Annual, 6–12 in. high, the whole plant clothed with glandular and simple hairs. Leaves sessile or nearly so, $\frac{1}{3}$–1 by $\frac{1}{4}$-$\frac{3}{8}$ in., mucronate; the lower leaves obovate-spathulate; the upper elliptic-ovate, obtuse or acute, becoming gradually smaller upwards. Flowers white, less than $\frac{1}{4}$ in. across, in corymbose cymes, which are at first capitate afterwards open and spreading; pedicels as long as the calyx, at length spreading;

bracts ovate, herbaceous. Calyx less than ¼ in. long; sepals hairy, lanceolate, very acute, their margins narrowly membranous. Petals about equal in length to the sepals or a little longer, bifid to about one third of the way down. Capsules more than twice as long as the sepals, curved upwards. Seeds yellowish-brown, minute, roundish-obovoid, tuberculate. Syme, Eng. Bot. v. 2, p. 82, t. 221. *Cerastium vulgatum*, var. *glomerata*, Edgew. & Hook. f. in Fl. B. I. v. 1, p. 228; var. *glomeratum*, Trim. Fl. Ceyl. v. 1, p. 85. *Cerastium indicum*, Woodr. in Journ. Bomb. Nat. v. 11 (1897) p. 124.—Flowers: Sept.

The only locality in the Bombay Presidency from which the plant has been obtained is Purandhar, a hill fort in the Poona Collectorate, where it is doubtless an introduction.—Distrib. Throughout the world.

4. STELLARIA, Linn.

Annual or perennial herbs, usually diffusely branched. Flowers white, in terminal (rarely axillary), paniculate cymes, rarely subsolitary. Sepals 5 (very rarely 4). Petals as many, 2-partite or 2-fid, or 0. Stamens 10 (sometimes fewer), hypogynous or perigynous. Disk annular or sometimes divided into prominent glands between the stamens. Ovary 1-celled; ovules many (rarely 3); styles 3 (rarely 2–5). Capsule short, globose, ovoid or oblong, splitting to below the middle into as many simple or 2-fid valves as there are styles. Seeds numerous, more or less laterally compressed, tubercled, granulate or nearly smooth; embryo annular.—Distrib. All temperate and cold regions; species 70.

1. **Stellaria media,** *Cyrill. Charac. Comm.* (1784) p. 36. A very variable annual; stems 3–20 in. long, much branched, procumbent, with a line of hairs down one side. Leaves ½–1 in. long, usually glabrous; the lower long-petioled, ovate; the upper sessile, elliptic or lanceolate. Flowers white, numerous, in terminal dichotomous cymes; pedicels pubescent. Sepals lanceolate, subobtuse, hairy or glandular, margins scarious. Petals shorter than the sepals or 0. Stamens 10, or often fewer. Capsules ovoid, longer than the sepals. Seeds brown, acutely tubercled. Fl. B. I. v. 1, p. 230; Boiss. Fl. Orient. v. 1, p. 707; Syme, Eng. Bot. v. 2, p. 93, t. 229; Woodr. in Journ. Bomb. Nat. v. 11 (1897) p. 124; Watt, Dict. Econ. Prod. v. 6, part 3, p. 358.

The common Chickweed. Has been found at Mahableshwar (fide *Woodrow*, l. c.), where it has probably been introduced.

5. ARENARIA, Linn.

Annual or perennial, often tufted herbs. Flowers white, very rarely pink, in terminal paniculate or capitate cymes, rarely axillary and subsolitary. Sepals 5. Petals 5 (rarely 0), entire or slightly notched. Stamens 10 (rarely 5 or 8), inserted on the disk. Disk annular or of inter-staminal glands. Ovary 1-celled; ovules many (rarely few); styles 3–4. Capsule short, rarely exceeding the sepals, with as many entire or 2-fid valves as there are styles. Seeds compressed or turgid, smooth or tubercled; embryo annular.—Distrib. All temperate and cold regions; species 130.

1. **Arenaria neelgherrensis,** *Wight & Arn. Prodr.* (1834) p. 43. Annual; stems procumbent, elongate, much-branched, with an alternate line of pubescence on one side. Leaves subsessile, distant, $\frac{1}{4}$–$\frac{5}{8}$ by $\frac{1}{8}$–$\frac{1}{4}$ in., obovate or elliptic, mucronate, glabrous, dotted with minute, whitish points. Flowers in terminal, few-flowered cymes or solitary and axillary; pedicels long, slender, viscidly pubescent; bracts leafy. Sepals ovate, very acute, with a strong dorsal hairy nerve, the margins membranous. Petals usually longer than the sepals. Styles usually 3 (sometimes 2 or 4). Capsules ovoid, about equalling the sepals. Seeds compressed, transversely striate. Fl. B. I. v. 1, p. 239; Dalz. & Gibs. p. 15; Woodr. in Journ. Bomb. Nat. v. 11 (1897) p. 124.—Flowers: Feb.

Southern districts of the Presidency; not common. KANARA: Yacombi (N. Kanara), *Woodrow*. S. M. COUNTRY: Belgaum and Dharwar, *Dalzell & Gibson*.

6. SPERGULA, Linn.

Annual herbs, with forked or fascicled branches. Leaves opposite, often with abbreviated leaf-buds in their axils whence the foliage appears whorled; stipules small, scarious. Flowers white, in peduncled, panicled cymes. Sepals 5. Petals 5, entire. Stamens 10 (rarely 5). Ovary 1-celled; ovules many; styles 5, opposite the petals. Capsule 5-valved; valves entire, opposite the sepals. Seeds black, compressed, margined or winged; embryo annular.—DISTRIB. Weeds of cultivation in temperate regions; species 2 or 3.

1. **Spergula arvensis,** *Linn. Sp. Pl.* (1753) p. 440. Annual, 6–18 in. high, pubescent or glandular; stems geniculate, branched from the root. Leaves in false whorls, $\frac{1}{2}$–$1\frac{1}{2}$ in. long, linear-subulate, semiterete, grooved beneath, rather fleshy. Flowers white, $\frac{1}{8}$–$\frac{1}{4}$ in. in diam., in terminal, subumbellate cymes; pedicels slender, spreading or deflexed. Sepals ovate, obtuse, slightly shorter than the petals, with very narrow, membranous margins. Capsules longer than the sepals, subglobose. Seeds tubercled, narrowly margined. Fl. B. I. v. 1, p. 243; Boiss. Fl. Orient. v. 1, p. 731; Syme, Eng. Bot. v. 2, p. 126, t. 253; Woodr. in Journ. Bomb. Nat. v. 11 (1897) p. 125; Watt, Dict. Econ. Prod. v. 6, part 3, p. 320.

SIND: Kirthar mountains, *Woodrow*.—DISTRIB. A weed of cultivation in all temperate regions.

7. POLYCARPON, Linn.

Diffuse or dichotomously branched glabrous or pubescent herbs. Leaves flat, opposite or whorled; stipules scarious. Flowers numerous, small, in crowded, much-branched, terminal, bracteate cymes; bracts scarious. Sepals 5, keeled, entire. Petals 5, small, entire or slightly notched. Stamens 3–5. Ovary 1-celled; ovules many; style short, 3-fid. Capsule 3-valved. Seeds ovoid, not winged.—DISTRIB. Temperate and warm regions of both hemispheres; species 6.

1. **Polycarpon Lœflingiæ,** *Benth. & Hook. f., Gen. Pl.* v. 1 (1862) p. 153, *in note* (Lœflingii); *Edgew. & Hook. f. in Fl. B. I.* v. 1, p. 245. A perennial herb; branches more or less pubescent, 4–10 in. long,

numerous, spreading from a centre, diffuse, wiry, prostrate or ascending Leaves $\frac{1}{4}$–$\frac{3}{4}$ in. long, linear-oblong or spathulate, acute or obtuse, pubescent or glabrous; stipules scarious, white. Flowers small, in numerous, usually dense, dichotomous cymes, either terminal or in the forks of the branches; pedicels stout, more or less pubescent; bracts ovate, acute, penicillate at the tip. Sepals ovate-oblong, acute, keeled on the back, margins scarious. Petals small, shorter than the sepals, linear, truncate, toothed at the apex. Capsules very thin, membranous, enclosed in the sepals. Seeds numerous, subcylindric, rough, pale brown. Trim. Fl. Ceyl. v. 1, p. 87; Woodr. in Journ. Bomb. Nat. v. 11 (1897) p. 125.

Rare. DECCAN: Lanoli, *Woodrow*!; Mahableshwar, *Cooke*! S. M. COUNTRY: *Ritchie*, 1019! KANARA: Waguli, *Ritchie*!

8. POLYCARPÆA, Lamk.

Annual or perennial herbs, usually erect. Leaves linear or rarely ovate, often appearing whorled by the presence of secondary axillary fascicles; stipules scarious. Flowers in lax or contracted or capitate cymes, often showy from the white, rosy or purple, scarious sepals. Sepals 5, scarious, or rarely herbaceous and scarious at the margins only. Petals 5, entire, 2-toothed or with the margins erose. Stamens 5, slightly perigynous or subhypogynous, or cohering with the petals into a ring or tube. Ovary 1-celled; ovules many; style elongate, 3-grooved, 3-fid or 3-dentate. Capsule 3-valved. Seeds obovoid or compressed; embryo curved, rarely almost straight.—DISTRIB. In tropical or warm, extratropical countries; species 24.

Leaves linear .... 1. *P. corymbosa.*
Leaves obovate .... 2. *P. spicata.*

1. **Polycarpæa corymbosa,** *Lam. Tab. Encyc. et Méthod.* v. 2 (1800) p. 129. An erect, annual herb, 6–18 in. high, sometimes woody below, dichotomously branched; branches slender terete, the young ones hoary-pubescent. Leaves $\frac{1}{3}$–$\frac{3}{4}$ in. long, narrow-linear, mucronate; stipules lanceolate, very acute, 1-nerved. Flowers numerous, small, in dense much-branched, terminal cymes, forming flat-topped heads; pedicels hoary-pubescent; bracts $\frac{1}{8}$ in. long, silvery white, bristle-pointed. Sepals lanceolate, very acute, scarious, silvery-white or colored, much exceeding the petals and capsule. Petals less than $\frac{1}{2}$ the length of the sepals. Capsules very small, shining, brown. Fl. B. I. v. 1, p. 245; Wight, Icon. t. 712; Dalz. & Gibs. p. 16; Trim. Fl. Ceyl. v. 1, p. 88; Woodr. in Journ. Bomb. Nat. v. 11 (1897) p. 125; Watt, Dict. Econ. Prod. v. 6, part 1, p. 314.—Flowers: Oct.–Jan.

Common throughout the Presidency. KONKAN: *Dalzell & Gibson*. DECCAN: Poona, *Woodrow*; Junnar, *Woodrow*!; Kolapur, *Cooke*! S. M. COUNTRY: Belgaum, *Ritchie*, 617!; Dharwar, *Woodrow*. SIND: Jemadar ka Landa, near Karachi, *Stocks*! —DISTRIB. Tropical Asia, Africa, America and Australia.

VAR. *aurea*. A smaller plant, very much branched from a woody base; branches hoary-tomentose. Flowers smaller, orange or brownish red. Fl. B. I. v. 1, p. 245; Wight, Ill. v. 2, t. 110. *Polycarpæa diffusa*, Woodr. in Journ. Bomb. Nat. v. 11 (1897) p. 125.

KONKAN: *Stocks*! S. M. COUNTRY: Badami, *Woodrow*!, *Cooke*!

2. **Polycarpæa spicata,** *Wight, ex Arnott in Ann. Nat. Hist.* ser. 1, v. 3 (1839) p. 91. A small slender glabrous herb, 2–4 in. high; branches numerous from the root, terete, filiform. Leaves subfleshy, glaucous, ¼–1 in. long, petioled, obovate-spathulate, very much attenuated at the base, mucronate; radical leaves rosulate; cauline leaves in 1–3 whorls between the root and the apex; stipules lanceolate, very acute, prolonged to a fine point. Flowers in fascicled spikes at the apex of the peduncles; peduncles filiform, 1 or more from a whorl of leaves; bracts scarious. Sepals scarious, lanceolate, acute, with a colored, broad, herbaceous midrib. Petals very small, oblong. Capsules about ½ as long as sepals. Seeds smooth, shining, brown. Fl. B. I. v. 1, p. 246; Boiss. Fl. Orient. v. 1, p. 738; Woodr. in Journ. Bomb. Nat. v. 11 (1897) p. 125; Oliver, Fl. Trop. Afr. v. 1, p. 146.—Flowers: Nov.–Feb.

Sind and Kathiawar (Gujarat) not common. GUJARAT: Mángrol and Porbandar (Kathiawar coast), *Woodrow*! SIND: seashore, Karachi, *Dalzell*!; Tata district, *Woodrow*!; Landhi, near Karachi, *Cooke*!—DISTRIB. Abyssinia, Arabia, Egypt.

ORDER XVII. PORTULACACEÆ.

Herbs, rarely undershrubs, usually glabrous and more or less succulent. Leaves opposite or alternate, entire, often fleshy; stipules scarious or lacerate, sometimes changed into hairs or 0. Inflorescence various, usually terminal; flowers regular, hermaphrodite. Sepals fewer than the petals, usually 2, free or adnate to the ovary at the base, much imbricate. Petals 4–5, rarely more, hypogynous or perigynous, free or connate at the base, imbricate, entire, fugacious. Stamens 4–many, inserted with the petals and often adnate to them at the base; filaments filiform; anthers 2-celled, cells parallel, dehiscing longitudinally. Ovary free or semi-inferior, 1-celled; ovules 2–many on basal funicles or a central column, amphitropous; style 2–8-fid, branches longitudinally stigmatose. Capsule membranous or crustaceous, circumsciss or dehiscing by as many valves as there are styles. Seeds many or solitary, compressed; embryo curved round mealy albumen.—DISTRIB. Chiefly American; genera 15; species 125.

Ovary half-adnate .... 1. PORTULACA.
Ovary free.. 2. TALINUM.

1. PORTULACA, Linn.

Diffuse or ascending, fleshy herbs. Leaves alternate or subopposite; stipules scarious or reduced to fascicles of hairs or scales (*nodal appendages*) at the nodes, or 0. Flowers terminal, solitary or clustered, surrounded by a whorl of leaves. Sepals 2, united at the base into a tube adnate to the ovary, the free part above deciduous. Petals 4–6, distinct or a little united at the base, inserted on the top of the tube of the calyx just where it becomes free from the ovary. Stamens 8 or numerous, inserted at the base of the petals; filaments subulate or filiform. Ovary ovoid, semi-inferior, 1-celled; ovules numerous; style deeply 3–8-fid. Capsule membranous, semi-inferior, the free part circumsciss. Seeds numerous, compressed, reniform, the crustaceous and shining testa often granulate; embryo peripheric.—DISTRIB. Chiefly tropical American; species 16.

Nodes without appendages; flowers in clusters .... 1. *P. oleracea.*
Nodes with stipulary scales; flowers solitary .... 2. *P. Wightiana.*
Nodes with a ring of hairs.
Leaves opposite .... 3. *P. quadrifida.*
Leaves alternate; root tuberous .... 4. *P. tuberosa.*
Leaves terete or nearly so; root woody .... 5. *P. suffruticosa.*

1. **Portulaca oleracea,** *Linn. Sp. Pl.* (1753) p. 445. An annual succulent prostrate herb; stems 6–12 in. long, reddish, swollen at the nodes, quite glabrous. Leaves fleshy, subsessile, ¼–1 in. long, alternate or subopposite, cuneiform, rounded and truncate at the apex, spangled when fresh with glistening dots, margins reddish; stipules (or nodal appendages) 0. Flowers few together, in sessile terminal heads. Sepals unequal, obtuse. Petals 5, obovate, yellow. Stamens 8–12. Style 3–8- (often 5-) partite. Capsules ovoid, circumsciss. Seeds numerous, black, concentrically striate and granulate. Fl. B. I. v. 1, p. 246; Grah. Cat. p. 81; Dalz. & Gibs. p. 15; Boiss. Fl. Orient. v. 1, p. 757; Sprague & Gray, Ill. Gen. Fl. Amer. v. 1, t. 99; Trim. Fl. Ceyl. v. 1, p. 89; Woodr. in Journ. Bomb. Nat. v. 11 (1897) p. 125; Watt, Dict. Econ. Prod. v. 6, part 1, p. 329.—Flowers: Oct.–Dec. *The Purslane.* VERN. *Ghol.*

Very common throughout the Presidency from Sind to Kanara, as a weed in gardens and cultivated ground. The leaves are used as a potherb by the natives, and with the seeds as a domestic remedy by the Hindus.—A full account of their uses may be found in Watt's Dict. Econ. Prod. l. c.

2. **Portulaca Wightiana,** *Wall. Cat.* (1828) 6845. A small much-branched prostrate herb, 2–4 in.; stems stout, consisting of a number of short, angled, glabrous, easily separable joints about ⅜ in. long. Leaves alternate, ⅛–¼ in. long, ovate, acute, fleshy, easily detachable; stipules (or nodal appendages) in a whorl of about 6, scarious, lanceolate, very acute, persistent, silvery-white, as long as and almost concealing the leaves. Flowers terminal, sessile, solitary, surrounded by an involucre of fleshy leaves and a number of thread-like silvery scales. Sepals broadly oblong-elliptic, rounded at the apex, membranous. Petals 4, longer than the sepals, united to them at the base and coming off with them and the lid of the capsule. Stamens 8; anthers yellow. Style 4-fid to ⅓ its length. Seeds numerous, reniform, brown, granulate. Fl. B. I. v. 1, p. 247; W. & A. Prodr. p. 356; Trim. Fl. Ceyl. v. 1, p. 89; Woodr. in Journ. Bomb. Nat. v. 11 (1897) p. 125.—Flowers: July–Oct.

Rare; found in the southern districts of the Presidency. S. M. COUNTRY: Badami, *Cooke*!, *Woodrow*!; Londa, *Woodrow*; Belgaum, *Woodrow*.—DISTRIB. Ceylon.

3. **Portulaca quadrifida,** *Linn. Mant.* (1767) p. 73. A small diffuse annual; stems filiform, glabrous, rooting at the nodes. Leaves opposite, fleshy, ⅛–¼ in. long, ovate, acute; stipules (or nodal appendages) a ring of silvery hairs; petioles short. Flowers terminal, solitary, subsessile, surrounded by silvery hairs and an involucre of 4 leaves. Sepals broadly oblong, rounded at the apex. Petals 4, yellow, oblong-obovate. Stamens 8. Style slender, 4-fid to near the middle. Capsules

conical. Seeds minutely tubercled. Fl. B. I. v. 1, p. 247; Grah. Cat. p. 81; Dalz. & Gibs. p. 15; Wight, Ill. v. 2, t. 109; Boiss. Fl. Orient. v. 1, p. 757; Trim. Fl. Ceyl. v. 1, p. 90; Woodr. in Journ. Bomb. Nat. v. 11 (1897) p. 125; Watt, Dict. Econ. Prod. v. 6, part 1, p. 330.—Flowers: Nov.

A common weed. DECCAN: Poona, *Woodrow*! S. M. COUNTRY: Badami, *Cooke*!; Dharwar, *Woodrow*; Padshapur, *Ritchie*, 1765! SIND: Karachi, *Stocks*!

4. **Portulaca tuberosa,** *Roxb. Hort. Beng.* (1814) p. 91. A perennial succulent herb; root thick, fusiform; branches numerous, prostrate, glabrous, 2–4 in. long. Leaves alternate, ½–¾ in. long, fleshy, linear-oblong, obtuse or acute; stipules (or nodal appendages) a ring of long brownish hairs. Flowers terminal, solitary, sessile, surrounded by a ring of brownish hairs and an involucre of 6–8 long leaves. Petals 5, yellow. Stamens 20 or more. Style filiform, 5-cleft at the apex. Capsules ovoid, with a short conical top, smooth and polished. Seeds black, granulate. Fl. B. I. v. 1, p. 247; W. & A. Prodr. p. 356; Trim. Fl. Ceyl. v. 1, p. 90; Boiss. Fl. Orient. v. 1, p. 757; Woodr. in Journ. Bomb. Nat. v. 11 (1897) p. 125; Watt, Dict. Econ. Prod. v. 6, part 1, p. 331.—Flowers: Aug. VERN. *Jangli-gájar.*

SIND: Jemadar ka Landa, near Karachi, *Stocks*!; Malir, river-banks (near Karachi), *Woodrow*.—DISTRIB. Ceylon.

5. **Portulaca suffruticosa,** *Wight, in Wall. Cat.* (1828) 6842. Suffruticose, about 1 ft. high; root woody, much divided; branches numerous, short, terete, glabrous, ascending. Leaves alternate, ¼–½ in. long, terete, or elliptic in section, acute; stipules (or nodal appendages) a few, short, brownish hairs. Flowers large, sessile, surrounded by a ring of brownish hairs and an involucre of 6–8 leaves. Stamens about 16. Seeds minute, black, tubercled. Fl. B. I. v. 1, p. 247; W. & A. Prodr. p. 356; Trim. Fl. Ceyl. v. 1, p. 90; Woodr. in Journ. Bomb. Nat. v. 11 (1897) p. 125.—Flowers: Nov.

A rare plant. GUJARAT: Ahmedabad, *Woodrow*.—DISTRIB. Ceylon.

2. TALINUM, Adans.

Succulent glabrous herbs or shrubs. Leaves alternate or subopposite, flat; stipules 0. Flowers terminal, racemed or panicled, rarely solitary. Sepals 2, herbaceous, ovate, deciduous or rarely subpersistent. Petals 5, hypogynous. Stamens 5-many, hypogynous or adhering to the base of the petals. Ovary free; ovules many; style 3-fid or 3-furrowed at the apex. Capsule globose or ovoid, papery or thinly crustaceous, 2–3-valved. Seeds subglobose or subreniform, strophiolate; testa shining; embryo peripheric.—DISTRIB. Tropical and warm regions of the world; species 11, chiefly American.

1. **Talinum cuneifolium,** *Willd. Sp. Pl.* v. 2 (1799) p. 864. A glabrous shrub, attaining a height of several feet, with erect, slender, rod-like branches. Leaves 1–2 by ½–1 in., fleshy, obovate, cuneate, attenuated into the petiole, entire or emarginate, the uppermost mucronate. Flowers in terminal panicles, purple; pedicels curved; bracts acute, deciduous. Sepals ovate-orbicular, apiculate, veined. Ovary

subglobose; style 3-fid. Capsules crustaceous, globose, glabrous, about the size of a pea. Seeds reniform, compressed, concentrically striate. Fl. B. I. v. 1, p. 247; Oliver, Fl. Trop. Afr. v. 1, p. 150; Woodr. in Journ. Bomb. Nat. v. 11 (1897) p. 125. *Talinum indicum*, W. & A. Prodr. p. 356; Dalz. & Gibs. Suppl. p. 39.—Flowers: Nov.

Very rare. Hill Forts in the Deccan. DECCAN: Singhad, *Woodrow*; Purandhar, *Woodrow*.—DISTRIB. Arabia, Africa.

ORDER XVIII. TAMARICACEÆ.

Shrubs or small trees. Leaves alternate, small, often scale-like, quite entire, usually fleshy; stipules 0. Flowers terminal or axillary, solitary, or arranged in spicate or paniculate racemes, regular, usually hermaphrodite. Sepals 5, rarely 4, connate at the base, much imbricate. Petals as many as the sepals, inserted beneath a disk, imbricate, free or united at the base into a tube. Disk hypogynous or slightly perigynous. 10-glandular, crenate or angled, rarely obsolete. Stamens 5-many, inserted on the disk, free or variously united at the base; anthers 2-celled, versatile, usually apiculate. Ovary free, 1-celled or imperfectly septate; placentas 3–5; ovules 2–many on each placenta, anatropous; raphe ventral; micropyle inferior; styles 3–5. Capsule dehiscent, with as many valves as there are styles. Seeds erect, plumed or winged, albuminous or not; embryo straight; cotyledons flat; radicle inferior, short.—DISTRIB. Temperate and warm regions of the N. hemisphere and in S. Africa, often in maritime or sandy places; genera 5; species about 40.

1. **TAMARIX,** Linn.

Shrubs or small trees. Leaves minute, scale-like, amplexicaul or sheathing. Flowers white or rosy, spicate or densely racemose. Sepals 4–5 (rarely 6), free. Petals inserted beneath a glandular-crenate, angled or lobed disk, free or slightly connate at the base. Stamens 5–10 (rarely 4 or 11–12), inserted on the disk, free, or scarcely connate at the base into a ring. Ovary attenuated at the apex; ovules many; styles 3–4 (rarely 2–5), short, thick; placentas very short, basal. Capsule 3–4-valved. Seeds many, small, glabrous, produced at the apex into a sessile plume, the axis of which is setiform and feathered with long hairs; albumen 0; embryo ovoid-oblong.—DISTRIB. S. Europe, N. Africa, Central and tropical Asia, usually near the coast; species about 20.

Stamens 5.
- Flowers 2-sexual, in racemose panicles .... 1. *T. gallica.*
- Flowers 1-sexual, in close cylindrical spikes .... 2. *T. dioica.*
- Flowers 2-sexual, in usually interrupted spikes .... 3. *T. articulata.*

Stamens 10.
- Glands of the disk separating the filaments; axis of plume very long .... 4. *T. ericoides.*
- Glands of the disk passing into the bases of the filaments; axis of plume short .... 5. *T. stricta.*

1. **Tamarix gallica,** *Linn. Sp. Pl.* (1753) p. 270; VAR. *indica*, *Willd. in Gesel. Naturf. Fr. Berl. Neue Schr.* v. 4 (1803) p. 214 (sp.).

A shrub or small tree, with slender erect or pendulous branches. Leaves $\frac{1}{10}$–$\frac{1}{8}$ in. long, subulate-acute from a triangular semi-amplexicaul base, at first imbricate, afterwards distant. Flowers hermaphrodite, numerous, crowded, in slender lateral and terminal panicled spike-like racemes; pedicels short; bracts very acute, immediately beneath the flowers. Sepals 5, much shorter than the petals, triangular-ovate, margins minutely denticulate. Petals oblong, rounded and often notched at the top, pink. Disk 5-lobed; lobes entire or nearly so. Stamens 5, inserted at the margins of the middle of the lobes of the disk. Ovary bottle-shaped, trigonous, truncate at top; styles 3, articulated to the ovary. Capsules about $\frac{1}{8}$ in. long, conical, somewhat trigonous, tapering, pale pink, glabrous. Seeds with a plume of white hairs. Fl. B. I. v. 1, p. 248. *Tamarix gallica*, W. & A. Prodr. p. 40; Grah. Cat. p. 11; Trim. Fl. Ceyl. v. 1, p. 91; Talb. Trees, Bomb. p. 14; Woodr. in Journ. Bomb. Nat. v. 11 (1897) p. 125; Watt, Dict. Econ. Prod. v. 6, part 3, p. 411.—Flowers: Dec.–Mar. VERN. *Jhavrájhad*; *Lai*.

Abundant on the banks of the Indus and throughout Sind. SIND; *Woodrow*!, *Cooke*!

2. **Tamarix dioica,** *Roxb. Hort. Beng.* (1814) p. 22. A small diœcious tree with a short trunk; branches spreading with drooping extremities. Leaves sheathing, glabrous, obliquely truncate, abruptly acuminate. Flowers $\frac{1}{8}$ in. in diam., in dense peduncled spikes, 1–2 in. long, forming drooping, terminal panicles; peduncles about equalling the spikes; bracts lanceolate, acuminate, with membranous margins, persistent. Sepals about half as long as the petals, elliptic-obovate and with a strong midrib, margins membranous. Petals elliptic-oblong, pink. Stamens 5, inserted in the notches of the minute 5-lobed disk (in the female flowers reduced to short filaments usually without anthers); filaments ligulate. Styles 3, as long as the ovary; stigmas clavate, truncate. Fl. B. I. v. 1, p. 249; Grah. Cat. p. 11; Boiss. Fl. Orient. v. 1, p. 777; Talb. Trees, Bomb. p. 14; Woodr. in Journ. Bomb. Nat. v. 11 (1897) p. 125; Watt, Dict. Econ. Prod. v. 6, part 3, p. 410.—Flowers: Nov. VERN. *Jháu*; *Lál Jháu*; *Gaz*.

Beds of rivers throughout the Presidency, common. Forms extensive forests along the Indus. Beds of Konkan and Deccan rivers, *Graham*. GUJARAT; Broach, *Cooke*!; banks of the Nerbudda, *Woodrow*! SIND: *Cooke*!, *Woodrow*!—DISTRIB. Afghanistan, Assam, Birma.

3. **Tamarix articulata,** *Vahl, Symb.* v. 2 (1791) p. 48, t. 32. A shrub or small tree, reaching 20 ft. high; the slender ultimate branches hoary with a saline efflorescence from the impressed, punctate glands. Leaves reduced to a short sheath, the free part to a small triangular tooth. Flowers hermaphrodite, in slender, usually interrupted spikes; bracts sheathing, acute, shorter than the flowers. Sepals 5, broadly elliptic, much shorter than the petals, entire or minutely toothed. Petals oblong, conniving at the top. Stamens 5; filaments filiform, inserted in alternate notches of the 10-lobed disk. Capsules trigonous, rounded at the tip; styles 3, about half the length of the ovary; stigmas ovoid. Fl. B. I. v. 1, p. 249; Oliver, Fl. Trop. Afr. v. 1, p. 151; Boiss. Fl. Orient. v. 1, p. 777; Talb. Trees, Bomb. p. 14; Watt, Dict. Econ. Prodr. v. 6, part 3, p. 409.

Upper and middle Sind eastwards. SIND: *Stocks*!, *Cooke*!—DISTRIB. Beluchistan, Algeria, Arabia, S. Africa.

4. **Tamarix ericoides,** *Rottl. in Gesel. Naturf. Fr. Berl. Neue Schr.* v. 4 (1803) p. 214. A shrub with dark cracked bark. Leaves minute, scale-like, ovate-lanceolate, acuminate, epunctate. Flowers handsome, ¼ in. in diam. in terminal racemes; pedicels very short; bracts membranous, acuminate, from a broad base. Sepals ovate-elliptic, with white membranous margins. Petals 5, rose-colored, slightly unequal, broadly elliptic-obovate, twice as long as the sepals, with minutely denticulate margins. Stamens 10, alternately long and short, not exceeding the petals; glands of the disk separating the filaments. Styles 3, short, dilated at the apex; stigmas ellipsoid. Capsules dull yellowish-white. Plume of the seeds with a very long axis, feathered with dirty white hairs. Fl. B. I. v. 1, p. 249; Niedenzu, in Engl. & Prantl, Pflanzenf. v. 3, part 6, fig. 134, O–Q; Talb. Trees, Bomb. p. 14; Woodr. in Journ. Bomb. Nat. v. 11 (1897) p. 125; Watt, Dict. Econ. Prod. v. 6, part 3, p. 411. *Trichaurus ericoides*, W. & A. Prodr. p. 40; Grah. Cat. p. 11; Dalz. & Gibs. p. 14; Camb. in Jacquem. Voy. Bot. p. 58, t. 70.—Flowers: Nov.–Jan. VERN. *Jhdu*; *Sárub*; *Kádsherni*.

Common in the beds of Konkan and Deccan rivers. KONKAN: *Law*!, *Stocks*! DECCAN: banks of the Indrayáni river near Karli, *Graham*; banks of the Mutha river (Poona districts), *Woodrow*! GUJARAT: banks of the Narbada river near Broach, *Woodrow*! KANARA: Kála naddi, near Sulgeri (N. Kanara), *Talbot*! SIND: *Cooke*.

5. **Tamarix stricta,** *Boiss. Diag.* ser. 2 (1856) fasc. 2, p. 57. Glaucous, glabrous. Leaves closely sheathing, very narrow, shortly and abruptly mucronulate. Flowers subsessile, in slender, panicled spikes or racemes; bracts broadly triangular-ovate, cucullate, acuminate, shorter than the flowers. Sepals oblong-obovate, rounded and minutely denticulate. Petals oblong-elliptic, obtuse, minutely toothed at the apex, a little longer than the sepals. Stamens 10. Disk 10-lobed, the lobes passing into the slightly dilated bases of the filaments. Stigmas 3, subsessile. Capsules short, conical, dull white. Fl. B. I. v. 1, p. 249; Boiss. Fl. Orient. v. 1, p. 778; Talb. Trees, Bomb. p. 14.

A very rare plant. SIND: *Stocks*!—DISTRIB. Beluchistan.

ORDER XIX. ELATINACEÆ.

Semi-aquatic or terrestrial herbs or undershrubs. Leaves opposite or whorled, entire or serrate; stipules twin. Flowers hermaphrodite, small, regular, axillary, solitary or cymose. Sepals 2–5, free, imbricate. Petals as many, hypogynous, imbricate. Disk 0. Stamens equal in number to the petals or twice as many, hypogynous, free; anthers versatile, 2-celled, the cells dehiscing longitudinally. Ovary free, the cells as many as the sepals; ovules numerous, on the inner angles of the cells, horizontal or subascending, anatropous; raphe lateral or ventral; styles as many as the cells, distinct from the base; stigmas capitate. Capsule septicidal; valves flat, concave or incurved, separating from a central placentiferous and often more or less septiferous column. Seeds straight or curved; raphe on the concave side; testa often rugose or ribbed; albumen 0, or very thin; embryo conform to the seed; cotyledons short; radicle next the hilum.—DISTRIB. Throughout the world; genera 2; species about 20.

1. BERGIA, Linn.

Herbs or undershrubs, erect, decumbent or diffusely branched, often pubescent. Leaves opposite, serrate or sometimes entire. Flowers small, axillary, solitary or cymosely fascicled, usually 5-merous. Sepals acute with an herbaceous midrib, the margins usually membranous. Ovary ovoid. Capsule subcrustaceous, septicidal.—DISTRIB. Warm countries throughout the world; species about 14.

Terrestrial woody plant; stamens 10 .... 1. *B. odorata.*
Semi-aquatic plants.
  Stamens 5 .... 2. *B. ammannioides.*
  Stamens 10 .... 3. *B. capensis.*

1. **Bergia odorata,** *Edgew. in Journ. Asiat. Soc. Beng.* v. 7 (1838) p. 765. Shrubby, 6–24 in., decumbent or spreading, glandular-pubescent; the bark deciduous in cinnamon-colored flakes. Leaves subsessile, often fascicled in the axils, $\frac{1}{10}$–$\frac{3}{4}$ in. long, from oblong-lanceolate to elliptic, obtuse, crenate-serrate, hispid and often glandular on both sides, often with revolute margins; stipules linear. Flowers solitary or in axillary fascicles of 2 to 6 or 8; pedicels about as long as the sepals. Sepals ovate, acute, hairy without and on the margins. Petals obovate-oblong, entire. Stamens 10, alternately shorter or nearly equal; filaments dilated below. Ovary ovoid, sulcate, narrowed into the styles; styles 5, one half the length of the ovary. Capsules 5-celled. Seeds minute, numerous, slightly curved, dark brown, shining. Fl. B. I. v. 1, p. 251; Woodr. in Journ. Bomb. Nat. v. 11 (1897) p. 125. *Bergia æstivosa*, Woodr. in Journ. Bomb. Nat. v. 11 (1897) p. 125. *Elatine odorata*, Dalz. & Gibs. p. 14. *Bergia suffruticosa*, Fenzl, in Denks. Bot. Gesel. Regens. v. 3 (1841) p. 183; Boiss. Fl. Orient. v. 1, p. 783; Oliver, Fl. Trop. Afr. v. 1, p. 153; Niedenzu, in Engl. & Prantl, Pflanzenf. v. 3, part 6, fig. 130, A–J.—Flowers: Oct.–Nov.

The leaves vary much in size; while usually $\frac{1}{8}$–$\frac{1}{4}$ in. long, they occasionally reach nearly 1 in. I have noticed these large leaves in specimens from Baroda as also in some from Senegal.

Common in Gujarat and Sind. GUJARAT: Surat, *Dalzell*!; Baroda, *Woodrow*!; Porbandar, *Cooke*! SIND: Sibi, *Woodrow*; Jemadar ka Landa, near Karachi, *Stocks*!; Hyderabad, *Cooke*!—DISTRIB. Trop. Africa, Persia, Egypt.

2. **Bergia ammannioides,** *Roxb. Hort. Beng.* (1814) p. 34. Annual, 6–15 in. high, erect, often with many decumbent branches from the base; stem and branches glandular, pubescent. Leaves $\frac{1}{4}$–$\frac{3}{4}$ by $\frac{1}{5}$–$\frac{3}{8}$ in., oblanceolate or elliptic, acute, tapering to a long base or into the petiole, very sharply serrulate, thinly hispid or glabrescent; stipules subulate, hairy. Flowers minute, crowded in dense axillary fascicles, subsessile, or pedicelled. Sepals 5, linear-lanceolate, very acute, with ciliate, often colored margins. Petals 5, very thin, elliptic-oblong, acute. Ovary subglobose, sulcate; styles 5, short. Capsules subglobose, the margins of the valves incurved. Seeds numerous, minute, ovoid, polished. Fl. B. I. v. 1, p. 251; Dalz. & Gibs. p. 14; Boiss. Fl. Orient. v. 1, p. 782; Oliver, Fl. Trop. Afr. v. 1. p. 152 (*exclud. citation*); Woodr. in Journ. Bomb. Nat. v. 11 (1897) p. 125. *Elatine ammannoides*, W. & A. Prodr. p. 41; Grah. Cat. p. 12.—Flowers: Nov.–Dec.

On the margins of tanks and in other moist places. KONKAN: *Stocks*! DECCAN: Poona, banks of the river Mula, *Ranade*!; Kelgaon, *Cooke*!, *Woodrow*! SIND: Karachi, *Cooke*!; Bubak, *Woodrow*.—DISTRIB. Abyssinia, Nubia, Senegambia, Australia.

3. **Bergia capensis** *, *Linn. Mantiss.* (1771) p. 241. A glabrous succulent herb, ½–1 ft. high; stems pink, branched, rooting from the lower joints. Leaves 1–1½ by ¼–⅜ in., elliptic-lanceolate, narrowed at each end, acute or subobtuse, serrate, glabrous; petioles short; stipules triangular-acute, caducous. Flowers in sessile or subsessile, few or many-flowered, axillary clusters. Sepals 5, lanceolate, acuminate. Petals 5, ovate-oblong. Stamens 10. Capsules globose, valves 5, broad, apiculate. Styles short. Seeds minute, cylindric, slightly curved and transversely rugose, dark brown. *Bergia verticillata*, Willd. Sp. Pl. (1799) v. 2, p. 770; Fl. B. I. v. 1, p. 252; Dalz. & Gibs. p. 14; Oliver, Fl. Trop. Afr. v. 1, p. 152; Woodr. in Journ. Bomb. Nat. v. 11 (1897) p. 125. *Elatine verticillata*, W. & A. Prodr. p. 41; Grah. Cat. p. 12. *Bergia aquatica*, Roxb. Corom. Pl. v. 2, p. 22, t. 142; Boiss. Fl. Orient. p. 782.—Flowers: Oct.

Margins of tanks and in rice-fields in the Konkan and Deccan. KONKAN: Dasgaon, in rice-fields, *Woodrow*.—DISTRIB. Trop. Africa, Egypt.

ORDER XX. HYPERICACEÆ.

Herbs or shrubs, rarely trees. Leaves opposite (rarely verticillate), often glandular-dotted, entire or toothed, exstipulate. Flowers hermaphrodite, regular, solitary or cymose, terminal (rarely axillary). Sepals and petals 5 (rarely 4), distinct imbricate. Stamens usually indefinite, usually in bundles of 3 or 5, rarely free or all connate; anthers versatile. Ovary of 3–5 carpels, 1- or 3–5-celled; ovules few or numerous on parietal or axile placentas, anatropous; raphe lateral or superior; styles as many as the carpels, filiform, free or rarely united. Fruit capsular or baccate. Seeds straight or variously curved, exarillate; embryo straight or curved.—DISTRIB. Temperate and warm regions; species 210.

1. HYPERICUM, Linn.

Herbs or shrubs. Leaves usually sessile. Flowers yellow (rarely white), solitary, cymose or paniculate. Sepals 5. Petals 5, not hairy within. Stamens free or connate at the base into 3–8 bundles. Ovary 1-celled, with 3–5 more or less prominent parietal placentas or imperfectly or perfectly 3–5-celled; ovules many (rarely few); styles distinct (rarely united). Capsule septicidal or dehiscing at the placentas; placentas adhering to the axis or the margins of the valves. Seeds not winged; embryo straight (rarely curved), oblong or cylindric; cotyledons shorter than the radicle, sometimes very short.—DISTRIB. In temperate regions chiefly of the N. hemisphere, and in mountains in the tropics; species about 160.

A shrub; flowers large and showy .... 1. *H. mysorense*.
An herb; flowers small .... 2. *H. japonicum*.

1. **Hypericum mysorense,** *Wall. Cat.* (1828) 4808 (*Herb. Madr.*). A much-branched, glabrous shrub, 4–8 ft. high; very young branches obscurely 4-angled. Leaves numerous, decussate, 1–1½ by

* Following the 'Index Kewensis,' I have restored Linnæus's original name (*B. capensis*), which was changed by Willdenow (*l. c.*) on the ground that the plant was not a native of the Cape.

$\frac{1}{4}$–$\frac{1}{2}$ in., oblong-lanceolate, acute, entire, glabrous, with pellucid striæ, tapering to an amplexicaul base with very small auricles. Flowers bright golden-yellow, 2–2$\frac{3}{4}$ in. across, in terminal 1–3-flowered cymes; pedicels short. Sepals $\frac{1}{2}$ in. long, oblong-ovate, acute persistent. Petals 1$\frac{1}{4}$ in. long, elliptic-oblong, very oblique, twice as long as the stamens. Stamens very numerous, in 5 groups, spreading. Ovary 5-lobed, tapering into 5 long, persistent styles; ovules numerous on 5 axile placentas; styles longer than the ovary. Capsules $\frac{1}{2}$ in. long; valves 5, with long beaks. Seeds cylindric. Fl. B. I. v. 1, p. 253; Trim. Fl. Ceyl. v. 1, p. 93. *Norysca mysorensis*, Wight, Icon. t. 56.—Flowers all the year.

On hills in the Konkan; rare. KONKAN: *Stocks*!

2. **Hypericum japonicum,** *Thunb. Fl. Jap.* (1784) p. 295, t. 31. An annual herb, erect or procumbent; stem 6–12 in. long, 4-angled, dichotomously branched above. Leaves $\frac{1}{4}$–$\frac{3}{8}$ by $\frac{1}{8}$–$\frac{3}{16}$ in., amplexicaul, elliptic or ovate, obtuse at both ends, pellucido-punctate. Flowers $\frac{1}{4}$–$\frac{1}{3}$ in. across in elongate dichotomous cymes; pedicels $\frac{1}{4}$ in. long; bracts linear-lanceolate. Sepals lanceolate, acute, entire, persistent, pellucido-punctate at the margin. Petals yellow, as long as the sepals, persistent. Stamens not very numerous; filaments slightly connate at the base. Ovary 1-celled, with 3 parietal placentas; styles 3 (rarely 4), one third the length of the ovary. Capsules ovoid, equalling the persistent sepals, 3-valved. Seeds oblong, ribbed. Fl. B. I. v. 1, p. 256; Trim. Fl. Ceyl. v. 1, p. 93.—Flowers all the year.

Rare. S. M. COUNTRY: Castlerock, *Gammie*.—DISTRIB. Japan, China, Java, Australia, New Zealand.

ORDER XXI. GUTTIFERÆ.

Trees or shrubs, abounding in yellow or greenish juice. Leaves opposite, coriaceous or membranous, often decussate, rarely whorled, usually exstipulate. Flowers axillary or terminal, solitary, fascicled, subracemose or panicled, regular, diœcious, polygamous or hermaphrodite. Sepals 2–6, imbricate. Petals 2–6 (rarely more or 0), hypogynous, usually much imbricate or contorted. MALE FLOWERS: Stamens usually indefinite, hypogynous; filaments free or rarely connate, monadelphous or in as many bundles as there are petals; anthers various. FEMALE FLOWERS: Staminodes various. Ovary 2–many- or (rarely) 1-celled; ovules 1–many, axile or erect from the base of the cavity; stigmas as many as the cells of the ovary, free or connate, sometimes peltate, entire, sessile, subsessile or with a more or less elongate style. Fruit usually baccate, indehiscent, with a fleshy or pulpy pericarp. Seeds large; albumen 0; embryo with a large radicle (*tigellus*) with small or obsolete cotyledons, or of thick consolidated or free cotyledons and very short inferior radicle.—DISTRIB. Throughout the tropics, chiefly in America and Asia, rare in Africa; species 250.

Stigma sessile or subsessile; embryo of a solid tigellus with minute cotyledons or 0.
  Calyx of 4 or 5 sepals .... 1. GARCINIA.
  Calyx closed in bud, bursting into 2 valves .... 2. OCHROCARPOS.

Stigma on a slender style; embryo of two fleshy, free or consolidated cotyledons with a small radicle.
Ovary 1-celled, 1-ovuled .... 3. CALOPHYLLUM.
Ovary 2-celled, 4-ovuled .... 4. MESUA.

1. GARCINIA, Linn.

Trees, usually with yellow juice. Leaves usually coriaceous. Flowers polygamous, solitary, fascicled or panicled, axillary or terminal. Sepals 4–5. Petals 4–5, imbricate. MALE FLOWERS: Stamens many, free or united into an entire or 4-lobed mass, or tetradelphous around a rudimentary style; anthers sessile or on short filaments, 2-celled, dehiscing by slits or pores, rarely 4-celled, or peltate and dehiscing by a circular slit (*circumsciss*). FEMALE OR HERMAPHRODITE FLOWERS: Staminodes free or variously united. Ovary 2–12-celled; ovule solitary, erect, or laterally affixed; stigma sessile or subsessile, broadly peltate, entire or radiately lobed, smooth or tubercled. Berry with a coriaceous rind. Seeds with a pulpy aril; embryo a solid homogeneous mass (*tigellus*) without obvious cotyledons.—DISTRIB. Tropics of the Old World; species 50.

Flowers tetramerous.
Fruit exceeding 1 in. in diam.
Fruit globose, not grooved .... 1. *G. indica.*
Fruit ovoid, 7–8-grooved .... 2. *G. Cambogia.*
Fruit not exceeding 1 in. in diam.
Fruit globose, slightly 4-lobed.. 3. *G. Morella.*
Flowers pentamerous.
Fruit large, yellow .... 4. *G. Xanthochymus.*
Fruit small, green .... 5. *G. spicata.*

1. **Garcinia indica,** *Choiss. in DC. Prodr.* v. 1 (1824) p. 561. A small tree. Leaves $2\frac{1}{2}$–$3\frac{1}{2}$ by 1–$1\frac{1}{2}$ in., red when young, oblong-lanceolate, glabrous with entire, repand margins; petioles $\frac{1}{4}$–$\frac{3}{8}$ in. long. Flowers axillary or terminal, solitary or in spreading fascicles; pedicels gradually thickened upwards, $\frac{1}{8}$–$\frac{1}{3}$ in. long or 0; bracts scale-like, deciduous. Sepals $\frac{3}{16}$ in. long, decussate, thick and fleshy; outer smaller, oblong-ovate; inner larger obovate-orbicular. Petals 4, thick, a little longer than the sepals. MALE FLOWERS 3–8, in axillary and terminal fascicles, the pedicels of the terminal fascicles carried on a short peduncle. Stamens very numerous, on a short column; anthers 2-celled, dehiscing longitudinally; filaments very short. FEMALE FLOWERS sessile or very shortly pedicelled, solitary or 2–3 together, the fascicles not peduncled. Staminodes in 4 bundles, arranged crosswise, each bundle containing 2–7 staminodes in one or more rows; filaments short, very thick. Ovary 4–8-celled; stigma sessile, with as many lobes as the cells. Fruit globose, not furrowed, 1–$1\frac{1}{4}$ in. in diam., purple throughout. Seeds 5–8, compressed, embedded in pulp. Fl. B. I. v. 1, p. 261; Engler, in Engl. & Prantl, Pflanzenf. v. 3, part 6, fig. 109, H, J; Talb. Trees, Bomb. p. 15; Woodr. in Journ. Bomb. Nat. v. 11 (1897) p. 125; Watt, Dict. Econ. Prod. v. 3, p. 466. *Garcinia purpurea*, Roxb. Fl. Ind. v. 2, p. 624; Grah. Cat. p. 25; Dalz. & Gibs. p. 31. *Brindonia indica*, Dupetit-Thouars, in Dict. Sc. Nat. v. 5, p. 340.—Flowers: Nov.–Feb. VERN. *Kokam*; *Rátamba.*

The Konkans and Kanara; cultivated in the S. Konkan and about Goa. KONKAN: *Dalzell & Gibson, Talbot*; Bombay, *Graham*; Matheran, *Cooke*!; Ambeghát, *Ranade*!;

Bombay Ghâts, *Woodrow*!; ravines at Khandala, *Graham*. KANARA: in evergreen forests, *Talbot*; near Yellapur (N. Kanara), *Talbot*!

The fruit is eaten and used for making syrup. A concrete oil or soapy substance named *Kokam* is extracted from the seeds, which is used for healing chaps and abrasions.

The tree is largely grown in the southern districts of the Bombay Presidency; in the Ratnagiri Collectorate alone, it is estimated that upwards of 13,000 trees are in cultivation. It was known to the Portuguese at Goa under the name of *Brindon*; hence the name *Brindonia* given to it by Thouars. A considerable trade in *Kokam butter* is carried on by the Goanese. A full account of the mode of its extraction from the seeds will be found in Watt's Dictionary of Economic Products of India, v. 3, pp. 467–470.

2. **Garcinia Cambogia,** *Desrous. in Lamk. Encyc.* v. 3 (1789) p. 701. A moderate-sized tree with round head, drooping branches, and rough, dark-brown bark; young shoots glabrous. Leaves 2–5 by $\frac{3}{4}$–2 in., elliptic-lanceolate, acute or slightly acuminate, glabrous, nerves oblique; petioles $\frac{1}{2}$–$\frac{5}{8}$ in. long, stout. MALE FLOWERS in the axils of fallen leaves, 3 or 4 together; pedicels thickened upwards, variable in length. Sepals thick and fleshy, with membranous margins; outer sepals $\frac{1}{5}$ in. long, shorter than the inner, orbicular; inner elliptic-oblong. Petals more than twice as long as the sepals, obovate-oblong, concave, with narrowly membranous margins. Stamens numerous on a short, thick androphore, monadelphous, forming a globular head. FEMALE or HERMAPH. FLOWERS larger than the male, in terminal and axillary fascicles of 1–3. Sepals and petals as in the male. Staminodes 10–20, unequal, in a ring round the ovary, free or connate at the base. Ovary globular, grooved; stigma 5–12-rayed, tubercled. Fruit $2\frac{1}{2}$–3 in. in diam., yellow or reddish, more or less globular, with 7–13 (usually 8) deep, vertical furrows, not continued to the apex which is smooth, depressed, and often mammillate; pericarp very thick, fleshy. Seeds as many as the grooves of the fruit, $\frac{3}{4}$ in. long, ovoid, compressed, surrounded by a white or red aril; testa pale-brown, veined. Fl. B. I. v. 1, p. 261; Lanessan, Mem. Garcin. [Tr. Bot. (1872)] p. 36; Pierre, Fl. For. Cochinch. t. 83, H; Trim. Fl. Ceyl. v. 1, p. 95; Talb. Trees, Bomb. p. 15; Watt, Dict. Econ. Prod. v. 3, p. 464.—Flowers: Jan.–May. VERN. *Upagi-mara.*

On the Southern Ghâts. KONKAN: *Stocks*!, *Law*!; Bombay, *Law*! KANARA: *Stocks*!, *Law*!; S. Ghâts of S. Kanara in evergreen forests, *Talbot*.

3. **Garcinia Morella,** *Desrous. in Lamk. Encyc.* v. 3 (1789) p. 701, t. 405, fig. 2. A middling-sized tree, with spreading branches, quite glabrous; young branches quadrangular, smooth. Leaves 3–5 by $1\frac{1}{2}$–$2\frac{1}{2}$ in., elliptic-obovate to ovate-lanceolate, subacute or shortly and bluntly acuminate, narrowed at the base; petioles $\frac{1}{4}$ in. long. MALE FLOWERS axillary, in fascicles of 2–5, subsessile, or on pedicels $\frac{1}{6}$–$\frac{1}{4}$ in. long. Sepals 4, decussate, orbicular, concave, the outer the smaller. Petals 4, a little larger than the sepals. Stamens 25–40, monadelphous, the filaments combined into a subquadrangular central column, but free at the apex, the free portion very short; anthers orbicular, flattened, dehiscing transversely. Rudimentary ovary 0. FEMALE FLOWERS larger than the male, solitary, axillary, usually sessile. Sepals and petals as in the male, the former persistent, the latter deciduous. Staminodes 18–30, in a ring round the ovary, connate at the base. Ovary globular, smooth, 4-celled; stigma peltate, irregularly lobed and tubercled. Fruit

¾ in. in diam., subglobose, surrounded at the base by the persistent sepals, glabrous. Seeds 4, ovoid-reniform, slightly compressed; testa muriculate, dark brown. Fl. B. I. v. 1, p. 264; Bedd. Flor. Sylvat. v. 1, t. 86; Trim. Fl. Ceyl. v. 1, p. 96; Pierre, Fl. For. Cochinch. t. 85, A; Talb. Trees, Bomb. p. 15; Woodr. in Journ. Bomb. Nat. v. 11 (1897) p. 125; Watt, Dict. Econ. Prod. v. 3, p. 472. *Hebradendron cambogioides*, Grah. in Hook. Comp. Bot. Mag. v. 2 (1836) p. 199, t. 27.—Flowers: Nov. VERN. *Arsina-gurgi*; *Nardala.*

The Gamboge tree, occurring frequently in the Kanara evergreen forests. KANARA: *Stocks*!, *Law*!; Siddapur (N. Kanara), *Talbot*, *Woodrow*.—DISTRIB. Siam, Ceylon.

Although the tree is fairly abundant in India, being found in Eastern Bengal, the Khasia hills and the Western Peninsula, gamboge does not appear to have been ever collected in India as an article of commerce, most of the gamboge imported into Europe being the produce of Siam and Cochin-China. Watt's Dictionary of Economic Products of India, vol. 3, pp. 473–478, contains a very full account of its mode of collection and uses.

4. **Garcinia Xanthochymus,** *Hook. f.*, *Fl. B. I.* v. 1 (1874) p. 269. A large tree; trunk straight, covered with dark-colored, scabrous bark; branches angular, spreading, forming a large shady head. Leaves coriaceous, 8–18 by 1½–4 in., linear-oblong or oblong-lanceolate, acute or acuminate, smooth, shining; petioles ½–1 in. long, transversely rugose. MALE FLOWERS white, ¾ in. in diam., in fascicles of 4–8, from the axils of fallen leaves; pedicels thickened upwards, 1–1½ in. long. Sepals 5, fleshy, ⅛–¼ in. long, unequal, orbicular, concave, persistent. Petals 5, orbicular, spreading, ⅓ in. in diam. Stamens 15–20, in 5 bundles, alternating with 5 fleshy glands; anthers 2-celled. HERMAPH. FLOWERS similar to those of the male but with longer pedicels. Ovary ovoid, pointed, usually 5-celled; stigma 5-lobed, the lobes large, oblong, spreading, entire. Fruit as large as a middle-sized apple, smooth, very little pointed at the apex, deep yellow when ripe. Seeds 1–4, oblong. Fl. B. I. v. 1, p. 269; Talb. Trees, Bomb. p. 15; Woodr. in Journ. Bomb. Nat. v. 11 (1897) p. 125; Watt, Dict. Econ. Prod. v. 3, p. 478. *Xanthochymus pictorius*, Roxb. Cor. Pl. v. 2, p. 51, t. 196; Dalz. & Gibs. p. 31.—Flowers: Mar.–May.

Abundant in the evergreen forests of N. Kanara. KONKAN: *Law*!, *Stocks*!; W. Ghâts (widely), *Woodrow*; Island of Karanja, probably planted, *Dalzell & Gibson*. KANARA: Southern Ghâts, *Dalzell & Gibson*; N. Kanara, in evergreen forests, abundant, *Talbot*. The fruit is eaten by the poorer natives and is not unpalatable, though strongly acid, especially the fleshy pericarp.—DISTRIB. Penang and the Andamans.

5. **Garcinia spicata,** *Hook. f. in Journ. Linn. Soc.* v. 14 (1875) p. 486. A middling-sized tree with straight trunk; branches angular, striate. Leaves coriaceous, 2–4 by 1½–2½ in., broadly-elliptic or almost orbicular, obtuse or retuse, rarely subacute, reticulately veined, the veins conspicuous in dried specimens; petioles ½ in. long, stout, transversely rugose. Flowers about ¼ in. in diam. in the axils of fallen leaves, the males numerous, sometimes mixed with the females in the same fascicle, but more commonly crowded in a short spiciform raceme, the females being in fascicles of 2–5; pedicels ¼–½ in. long. Sepals 5, very unequal, ⅛–⅕ in. long, orbicular, ciliolate, the 2 outer thick and fleshy, the 3 inner larger and thinner. Petals 5, membranous, much longer than the sepals, orbicular, concave, veined. MALE FLOWERS: Stamens in 5 bundles; filaments combined into a long, somewhat spathulate, fleshy

androphore, carrying 8–10 anthers near the top, the free portion of the filament below the anther very short; anthers didymous. FEMALE FLOWERS usually fascicled. Staminodes in 5 trifid bundles; anthers sterile. Ovary ovoid, 3-celled; stigma thick, fleshy, 3-lobed. Fruit green, 1–1½ in. long, ovoid or subglobose, 1–3-seeded. Trim. Fl. Ceyl. v. 1, p. 98. *Garcinia ovalifolius*, var. *ovalifolia*, Hook. f. in Fl. B. I. v. 1, p. 269 (*not* of Oliver); Talb. Trees, Bomb. p. 15. *Xanthochymus ovalifolius*, Roxb. Fl. Ind. v. 2, p. 632.—Flowers: Mar.–May.

Evergreen forests of N. Kanara and Konkan Ghâts, *Talbot*.

VAR. *macrantha*. Leaves larger, 3½–7 by 1½–3¾ in., elliptic-oblong, obtuse or retuse. Male flowers much larger, reaching ⅜ in. in diam., fascicled (rarely spiciform). *Garcinia ovalifolius*, var. *macrantha*, Fl. B. I. v. 1, p. 269; Talb. Trees, Bomb. p. 15. *Xanthochymus ovalifolius*, Grah. Cat. p. 26; Dalz. & Gibs. p. 31; Woodr. in Journ. Bomb. Nat. v. 11 (1897) p. 125.—Flowers: Dec.–Jan. VERN. *Haldi*; *Ont*.

This variety is much the more common form in the Bombay Presidency. It flowers in the cold, while the former flowers in the hot season. It is confined to the Ghâts of the Konkan and Kanara.

KONKAN: the Ghâts, *Dalzell*!; S. of Baitsi (S. Konkan), *Ritchie*, 1648!; Matheran, *Cooke*!, *Woodrow*. DECCAN: ravines at Khandala, *Graham*; Phunda Ghât, *Ritchie*!; Párghât, *Graham*. KANARA: Gairsoppa Ghât, common, *Talbot*.

2. OCHROCARPOS, Thouars.

Trees. Leaves coriaceous, opposite, or ternately whorled. Flowers in short cymes or lateral or axillary fascicles, polygamous. Calyx closed before flowering, at length opening valvately into 2 sepals. Petals 4 or more. Stamens indefinite; filaments filiform, free or shortly connate below; anthers erect, oblong, 2-celled, dehiscing longitudinally. Ovary 2-celled; ovules 2 in each cell; style short, stout or 0; stigma 3-lobed. Berry 1–4-seeded. Seeds large, enclosed in pulp; embryo of a large fleshy tigellus with the cotyledons reduced to a small mammilla or 0.—DISTRIB. Madagascar, West Africa; species 6.

1. **Ochrocarpos longifolius,** *Benth. & Hook. f. ex T. Anders. in Fl. B. I.* v. 1 (1874) p. 270 (*Ochrocarpus*). A large tree; young shoots terete or slightly 4-gonous. Leaves thickly coriaceous, 6–8 by 2–2½ in., oblong, obtuse or shortly and bluntly pointed, quite glabrous, with slightly repand margins and prominent midrib, base rounded, veins inconspicuous in fresh, but beautifully reticulate in dried specimens; petioles ¼ in. long, stout. Flowers numerous, in short fascicles on tubercles from the axils of fallen leaves; buds globose, apiculate, orange-red; pedicels ½–¾ in. long, thickened upwards; bracts numerous, subulate. Calyx bursting into 2 valves, reflexed during flowering. Petals 4, ovate-oblong, acute, thin, deciduous, white streaked with red. Stamens many, sterile in the female flowers. Style short, stout; stigma broad, peltate. Fruit 1 in. long, obliquely ovoid, tipped by the hard, pointed style, 1-seeded. Bedd. Flor. Sylvat. t. 89; Talb. Trees, Bomb. p. 15; Woodr. in Journ. Bomb. Nat. v. 11 (1897) p. 125; Watt, Dict. Econ. Prod. v. 5, p. 439. *Calysaccion longifolium*, Wight, Ill. v. 1, p. 130; Grah. Cat. p. 27; Dalz. & Gibs. p. 32.—Flowers: Feb.–Mar. VERN. *Surangi*; *Pundga*.

In the evergreen Ghát-forests of the Konkans and Kanara. KONKAN: *Stocks*!, *Law*!; Ratnagiri Collectorate, common, *Dalzell & Gibson*; Kanheri jungles, abundant, *Graham*; Parel and Worlee hills (Bombay), *Graham*, *Dalzell*! DECCAN: Shirol, *Ritchie*, 1650! KANARA: in evergreen forests on the Ghâts, *Talbot*!; Kadgal (N. Kanara), *Woodrow*.

The flower-buds are an article of commerce and used for dyeing silk.

3. CALOPHYLLUM, Linn.

Trees. Leaves coriaceous, shining, striately penninerved. Flowers polygamous, in axillary or terminal panicles. Sepals and petals 4–12, imbricate in 2–3 series. Stamens indefinite, free or scarcely connate at the base; filaments filiform; anthers erect, ovate or oblong, 2-celled, dehiscing longitudinally. Ovary 1-celled; ovule 1, erect; style rather long; stigma peltate. Drupe indehiscent; putamen crustaceous. Seed erect, ovoid or globose; testa thin, or thick and spongy.—DISTRIB. Tropical Asia and America; species 25.

1. **Calophyllum inophyllum,** *Linn. Sp. Pl.* (1753) p. 513. A very handsome, small or middle-sized glabrous tree, with a crooked trunk; bark grey, smooth. Leaves 4–7 by 3–4 in., broadly elliptic, rounded at the apex, often emarginate, with subrepand waved margins and very close lateral nerves, giving a striate appearance to the blade, base acute; petioles $\frac{3}{8}$–$\frac{5}{8}$ in. long, stout, flat. Flowers $\frac{3}{4}$–1 in. in diam., pure white, fragrant, in lax few-flowered racemes 4–6 in. long. Sepals 4, ovate-orbicular, concave, reflexed, ciliolate, the two outer much the smaller. Petals 4, oblong, obtuse, spreading. Stamens numerous; filaments united into 4–6 bundles. Style long, twisted; stigma large, mushroom-shaped. Fruit globose, 1–1½ in. in diam., smooth, yellowish; pulp scanty. Fl. B. I. v. 1, p. 273; Grah. Cat. p. 26; Dalz. & Gibs. p. 31; Engler, in Engl. & Prantl, Pflanzenf. v. 3, part 6, fig. 105, A–F; Talb. Trees, Bomb. p. 15; Woodr. in Journ. Bomb. Nat. v. 11 (1897) p. 126; Watt, Dict. Econ. Prod. v. 2, p. 29.—Flowers: Dec.–Jan. VERN. *Undi.*

A strikingly handsome tree often called the *Alexandrian Laurel*, cultivated throughout India; indigenous in the coast districts of the Presidency; very common at Ratnagiri.

KONKAN: Salsette, *Graham*; Malwan taluka and sandy shores of the S. Konkan, *Dalzell & Gibson*; Love Grove, Bombay, *Graham*; banks of rivers near the coast, *Law*!, *Stocks*!; Ratnagiri, *Cooke*!, *Woodrow*!—DISTRIB. Ceylon, E. African islands, Malaya, Australia, Polynesia.

The timber is used for knees for boats, and an oil called *Wundi* is extracted from the seeds. For an account of the uses of the oil &c. consult Watt, Dict. Econ. Prod. l. c.

2. **Calophyllum tomentosum,** *Wight, Ill.* v. 1 (1840) p. 128. A tree, attaining a great height; young shoots, buds and panicles clothed with rusty tomentum; young branches quadrangular. Leaves coriaceous, 3–5 by 1¼–2 in., oblong-lanceolate, acuminate, acute at the base, glabrous, shining; nerves very fine equally conspicuous on both surfaces; petioles ½–¾ in. long, stout, pubescent, at length glabrous. Flowers ½–¾ in. in diam., in terminal panicles, and in racemes or panicles from the axils of the upper leaves; pedicels long, slender, tomentose. Sepals 4, the outer orbicular, much shorter than the inner, ciliolate. Petals 4, oblong, obtuse, spreading, exceeding the sepals. Stamens numerous; filaments united at the base. Style long, flexuous; stigma

peltate. Fruit obliquely ovoid, ¾ in. long, pointed, smooth. Fl. B. I. v. 1, p. 274; Wight, Icon. t. 110; Trim. Fl. Ceyl. v. 1, p. 101; Talb. Trees, Bomb. p. 16; Watt, Dict. Econ. Prod. v. 2, p. 32. *Calophyllum elatum*, Bedd. Flor. Sylvat. t. 2. *Calophyllum angustifolium*, Dalz. & Gibs. p. 32 (*not* of Roxb.).—Flowers: Mar.–May. VERN. *Pun.*

Known in W. India as the *Pun* or *Poon* tree. It furnishes the *Poon* spars of commerce, which are much used for masts.

Dalzell and Gibson (Bombay Flora, p. 32) in describing *C. angustifolium*, adopt the description given by Roxburgh (Fl. Ind. v. 2, p. 608), which is not applicable to *C. tomentosum*. As, however, Dalzell and Gibson indicate the same locality (Nilkund Ghát) in which the tree has been found by Mr. Talbot, there can be little doubt that *C. tomentosum* was intended by these botanists, and not *C. angustifolium* of Roxburgh.

KANARA: in many of the Ghát evergreen forests of N. Kanara, Nilkund and Gairsoppa Gháts, common, *Talbot*; Nilkund and Wulwi Gháts, ex *Dalzell & Gibson.*

3. **Calophyllum Wightianum,** *Wall. Cat.* (1828) 4847. A middle-sized tree, with yellowish bark; young shoots 4-gonous, glabrous. Leaves coriaceous, 2–3½ by 1–1½ in., obovate-oblong, cuneate, rounded at the apex, often emarginate, with close nerves most prominent on the lower surface; petioles ¼ in. long. Flowers ½ in. in diam., in racemes from the upper axils; bracts small, boat-shaped, caducous; pedicels slender, ½ in. long. Sepals 4, strongly veined, subequal, deflexed, the two outer orbicular, the two inner boat-shaped. Petals 0. Stamens numerous, many-seriate; anthers large. Style flexuous; stigma peltate with crenulate margin. Fruit ¾ in. long, ellipsoid, smooth, apiculate, red when ripe. Fl. B. I. v. 1, p. 274; Bedd. Flor. Sylvat. t. 90; Talb. Trees, Bomb. p. 16; Woodr. in Journ. Bomb. Nat. v. 11 (1897) p. 126; Watt, Dict. Econ. Prod. v. 2, p. 33. *Calophyllum spurium*, Chois. in DC. Prodr. v. 1, p. 563; Grah. Cat. p. 27; Dalz. & Gibs. p. 32 (*speurium*).—Flowers: Dec. VERN. *Bobbi*; *Irai.*

Western Gháts. KONKAN: *Law*!, *Stocks*! KANARA: plentiful in Honore, *Dalzell & Gibson*; very common along the banks of N. Kanara rivers, *Talbot*; Kála naddi, *Ritchie*, 1649!; Yellapur, *Talbot*!

4. MESUA, Linn.

Trees or shrubs. Leaves closely and finely penninerved. Flowers hermaphrodite or polygamous, axillary, solitary, large. Sepals 4. Petals 4. Stamens indefinite; filaments free or connate at the very base; anthers erect, oblong, 2-celled, dehiscing longitudinally. Ovary 2-celled, ovules 2 in each cell, erect; style elongate; stigma peltate. Fruit between fleshy and subwoody, 1-celled by the absorption of the septum, at length dehiscing by 4 valves; valves often finely striate without. Seeds 1–4, exarillate; testa fragile.—DISTRIB. Tropical Asia; species 3.

1. **Mesua ferrea,** *Linn. Sp. Pl.* (1753) p. 515. A middling-sized, glabrous tree; trunk straight, erect; bark smooth, ash-coloured; young branches twiggy, slender. Leaves 3–5 by 1–1⅓ in., oblong-lanceolate, acute or acuminate, red when young, afterwards shining above, glaucous and pruinose beneath, rounded or acute at the base and with close, inconspicuous nerves; petioles ¼–⅓ in. long. Flowers very fragrant,

1–3 in. in diam., axillary or terminal, solitary or in pairs, subsessile; buds subglobose; bracts 0. Sepals 4, orbicular, cupped, puberulous outside, persistent, the inner pair much longer than the outer. Petals 4, pure white, spreading, obovate-cuneate, with crisped and undulate margins often torn. Stamens very numerous, golden-yellow, much shorter than the petals, slightly united at the base into a fleshy ring; anthers oblong. Style twice as long as the stamens; stigma peltate. Fruit 1–1¼ in. long, ovoid with a conical point, surrounded by the enlarged sepals; pericarp tough, semi-woody, at length 2-valved. Seeds 1–4, angular, smooth, chestnut-brown. Fl. B. I. v. 1, p. 277; Grah. Cat. p. 26; Dalz. & Gibs. p. 31; Engler, in Engl. & Prantl, Pflanzenf. v. 3, part 6, p. 219, fig. 103; Talb. Trees, Bomb. p. 16; Woodr. in Journ. Bomb. Nat. v. 11 (1897) p. 126; Watt, Dict. Econ. Prod. v. 5, p. 236.—Flowers: Mar. VERN. *Nág-chápha.*

A very beautiful tree, often planted near temples, indigenous in the forests of S. Konkan and N. Kanara. KONKAN: *Law*!, *Stocks*!, *Woodrow*!; Bombay, *Dalzell*!; Wari (S. Konkan). *Dalzell & Gibson.* S. M. COUNTRY: Ramghát, *Ritchie*, 5! KANARA: about villages, *Ritchie*, 5!; sparingly in the evergreen forests of N. Kanara, *Talbot.*—DISTRIB. Ceylon.

ORDER XXII. TERNSTRŒMIACEÆ.

Trees or shrubs, rarely scandent. Leaves alternate (rarely opposite), simple, usually serrate, coriaceous; stipules 0. Flowers regular, usually hermaphrodite, axillary and 1 or more together, or in terminal or axillary racemes (rarely panicled). Sepals 5 (rarely 4–7), free or slightly connate, imbricate, the inner usually the larger. Petals 5 (rarely 4–9), free or often united at the base into a ring or short tube, much imbricate or contorted. Stamens indefinite, rarely equal in number to the petals or twice as many, hypogynous, free or connate at the base with one another, or adnate to the base of the petals and deciduous with them (very rarely persistent); anthers basifixed or versatile, 2-celled, dehiscing by parallel slits, rarely by terminal pores. Disk 0. Ovary free (rarely half inferior), sessile, 3–5- (rarely 2–many-) celled; ovules 2–many in each cell, rarely solitary, never orthotropous; styles as many as the cells of the ovary; stigmas usually small. Fruit baccate or capsular. Seeds few or numerous; placentas axile; albumen scanty or 0 (rarely copious); embryo straight or hippocrepiform; cotyledons various.—DISTRIB. Tropical Asia and America, Malaya, few in Africa, absent from Australia and New Zealand; genera 32; species about 270.

Styles 3; anthers basifixed; seeds not winged.......................... 1. EURYA.
Style single; anthers versatile; seeds winged .... 2. GORDONIA.

1. EURYA, Thunb.

Shrubs. Leaves usually crenate-serrate and glabrous. Flowers diœcious, small, sessile or shortly pedicelled, in axillary fascicles, rarely solitary; bracts persistent. Sepals 5, much imbricate. Petals 5, imbricate, connate at the base. Stamens 15 or less (rarely 5), adnate to the base of the corolla; anthers glabrous, basifixed. Ovary 3- (rarely 2–5-) celled; ovules many in the inner angle of each cell; styles 3 (rarely 2–5), free or connate. Fruit baccate; albumen fleshy.—DISTRIB. Warmer parts of Asia and Malaya; species about 10.

1. **Eurya japonica,** *Thunb. Nov. Gen.* (1783) p. 68, VAR. *Thunbergii*, Thw. Enum. (1858) p. 41. A shrub reaching 15 feet in height; young branches glabrous, striate. Leaves 2–4 in. long, lanceolate, acuminate serrate, acute at the base; petioles $\frac{1}{4}$ in. long. Flowers in axillary fascicles of 1–3, small; bracts 2, beneath the flowers, small, oblong, obtuse; pedicels short. Sepals unequal, the 2 outer the smaller, ovate or suborbicular, glabrous, persistent. Petals white, elliptic-oblong, about twice as long as the sepals. Stamens 5–15. Styles 3. Fruit $\frac{1}{6}$–$\frac{1}{4}$ in., ovoid or subglobose, tipped with the persistent style, glabrous. Fl. B. I. v. 1, p. 284; Trim. Fl. Ceyl. v. 1, p. 109. *Eurya japonica*, Thunb. Fl. Japon. (1784) p. 191, t. 25; Bedd. Flor. Sylvat. v. 1, t. 92; Talb. Trees, Bomb. p. 16; Watt, Dict. Econ. Prod. v. 3, p. 302.

Flowers all the year (*Trimen*).

This plant has been included on the authority of a specimen in Herb. Kew. ticketed "Konkan, Stocks," without any further information as to the locality from which it was obtained. It does not seem to have been found by any other collector.

2. GORDONIA, Ellis.

Trees. Leaves evergreen, entire or crenate. Flowers solitary and axillary, or crowded at the ends of the branches, often subsessile, bracteate. Sepals usually 5, unequal, graduating from the bracts to the petals. Petals free or slightly connate, much imbricate, the inner the larger. Stamens indefinite, usually 5-adelphous, or connate into a ring, or adnate to the base of the petals. Ovary 3–5- (rarely 6-) celled; ovules 4–8 in each cell, pendulous; style simple; stigma 5-lobed. Capsule woody, oblong, loculicidal; axis persistent. Seeds flat or compressed, prolonged upwards into an oblong wing; albumen 0; embryo generally straight, oblique; cotyledons ovate, flat or slightly crumpled; radicle small, superior.—DISTRIB. N. America, tropical Asia and Malaya; species about 10.

1. **Gordonia obtusa,** *Wall. Cat.* (1828) 1459. A tall tree. Leaves 2–4 by 1–1$\frac{1}{2}$ in., elliptic-lanceolate, obtuse, often emarginate, crenulate, acute at the base, glabrous, shining; petioles $\frac{1}{4}$ in. long. Flowers 1$\frac{1}{2}$ in. across, white; pedicels $\frac{1}{4}$ in. long. Sepals orbicular-oblong, silky outside. Petals obcordate, pubescent outside, slightly connate at the base; styles combined to the apex; stigma peltate, 4-5-lobed. Capsules 1–1$\frac{1}{4}$ in. long, oblong; valves deeply sulcate towards the apex. Seeds terminated by a leafy wing. Fl. B. I. v. 1, p. 291; Wight, Spicil. Nilgher. v. 1, t. 20; Talb. Trees, Bomb. p. 17; Watt, Dict. Econ. Prod. v. 3, p. 533.—Flowers: July–Sept.

KONKAN: *Stocks*!; Ghâts, *Talbot*.

ORDER XXIII. DIPTEROCARPACEÆ.

Resiniferous trees. Leaves alternate, entire or sinuate-crenate, penninerved; stipules usually small, deciduous or inconspicuous, sometimes larger and persistent, or caducous leaving an annular scar. Flowers regular, hermaphrodite, fragrant, in axillary or terminal panicles; bracts usually minute or 0, rarely large and persistent. Flowering calyx free and campanulate, or very short and adnate to the base of the ovary; lobes 5, usually imbricate. Fruiting calyx enlarged; tube free or adnate to the fruit; lobes unchanged, or 2–3 or all enlarged like a wing. Petals 5, contorted, connate at the very base or free. Stamens indefinite or 15, 10, or 5, hypogynous or subperigynous, free or cohering with one another at the base, or, more rarely, with the petals; filaments short, usually dilated at the base; anthers erect, 2-celled, dehiscing introrsely or laterally by a slit, valves of the cells equal or the inner smaller; connective often aristate or with an obtuse appendage. Ovary seated on or slightly immersed in the torus, usually 3-celled; ovules 2 in each cell, pendulous or affixed laterally, anatropous; raphe ventral; micropyle superior. Fruit free or enclosed in the enlarged calyx, indehiscent or 3-valved, 1- (rarely 2-) seeded. Seeds thick, equal or unequal; testa thin; albumen 0; cotyledons equal or unequal, straight or more or less plaited and crumpled; radicle directed towards the hilum, usually included between the cotyledons.—DISTRIB. All are natives of tropical East Asia, except 3 species in Africa; genera 12; species about 106.

Calyx much enlarged in fruit; lobes erect.
- Calyx in fruit with a distinct tube; 2 lobes only enlarged; stamens ∞ .... 1. DIPTEROCARPUS.
- Calyx in fruit with an obscure tube; 3 or all the lobes enlarged; stamens 15-many .... 2. SHOREA.
- Calyx with only 2 lobes enlarged; stamens 10–15 .... 3. HOPEA.

Calyx scarcely enlarged in fruit; lobes reflexed .... 4. VATERIA.

1. DIPTEROCARPUS, Gærtn.

Lofty resinous trees. Leaves coriaceous, entire or sinuate-dentate; stipules large, valvate, enclosing the terminal bud, afterwards caducous, leaving an annular scar. Flowers large, few, in axillary racemes, white or reddish. Calyx smooth, or variously ribbed or winged, or transversely lamellate; tube free; lobes slightly imbricate when young, afterwards open or subvalvate, unequal. Stamens indefinite; anthers linear; connective acuminate. Ovary 3-celled; ovules 2 in each cell; style filiform. Fruit nut-like, 1- (rarely 2-) seeded, woody, indehiscent, free, enclosed in the enlarged calyx 2 lobes of which are produced into long wings. Seed adnate to the base of the pericarp; cotyledons very large and fleshy, unequal; radicle inconspicuous.—DISTRIB. Tropical Asia and Malaya; species about 60.

1. **Dipterocarpus turbinatus,** *Gærtn. f., Fruct.* v. 3 (1805) p. 51, t. 188. A tall tree; trunk straight to the top; bark deeply cracked. Leaves 5–12 by 2½–6 in., ovate, acute or very shortly acuminate, entire or sinuate-crenate, glabrous on both surfaces, shining above, base rounded or acute; lateral nerves prominent, 14–18 pairs, oblique, parallel; petioles 1–2½ in. long; stipules oblong-ovate, acute, grey-velvety, with a tuft of soft hairs at the apex. Flowers 3 in. in diam., in axillary, 3–8-flowered racemes. Calyx: tube obconic, hoary-puberulous, the mouth contracted in fruit; the 2 enlarged lobes (wings) 5 by 1 in., oblong, obtuse, strongly 3–5-nerved and reticulately veined; the other lobes deltoid. Petals white, tinged with red, linear, obtuse, puberulous without, twisted in bud. Stamens numerous; filaments yellow, linear-subulate, terminated by a long slender bristle. Fruit 1 in. in diam.,

subglobose, pubescent. Fl. B. I. v. 1, p. 295; Roxb. Cor. Plts. v. 3, p. 10, t. 213; Talb. Trees, Bomb. p. 17; Brandis, Enum. Dipter. in Journ. Linn. Soc. v. 31 (1895) p. 27; Watt, Dict. Econ. Prod. v. 3, p. 161.—Flowers: Dec.-Jan. VERN. *Challan.*

Sparingly in the southern forests of the Presidency. KONKAN: *Stocks*! KANARA: Southern Ghâts of N. Kanara, certainly indigenous, ex *Talbot*; Gairsoppa Ghât, *Talbot*!—DISTRIB. Pegu, Singapore and the Andamans.

In Chittagong, where the tree is abundant, it attains a height of upwards of 200 feet. Roxburgh (Fl. Ind. v. 2, p. 612) says that the trunk is large enough to furnish a canoe capable of containing 100 men. It produces the celebrated *Garjan* or *Kanyin* oil, for a full description of the mode of extraction and uses of which, see Watt, Dict. Econ. Prod. l. c.

2. SHOREA, Roxb.

Resiniferous trees. Leaves entire or repand, with parallel nerves; stipules large, coriaceous and persistent, or small and deciduous, or inconspicuous. Calyx: tube very short, not enlarged in fruit, adnate to the torus; lobes ovate-lanceolate imbricate, unequally enlarged in fruit, wing-like (3 usually larger), closely embracing the fruit. Stamens 15-many; anthers ovate or oblong, rarely linear; connective subulate or cuspidate; valves obtuse, rarely cuspidate, equal, or with the exterior valve the larger. Ovary 3-celled; ovules 2 in each cell; style usually subulate; stigma entire or 3-toothed. Capsule coriaceous, indehiscent, usually 1-seeded, enclosed within the base of the calyx-lobes. Seed ovoid; cotyledons fleshy, unequal, usually enclosing the superior radicle.—DISTRIB. Tropical Asia and Malaya; species about 80.

1. **Shorea Talura,** *Roxb. Hort. Beng.* (1814) p. 93. A large tree; branches glabrous. Leaves 2½–4 by 1½–2 in., elliptic-ovate, obtuse, often emarginate, rounded at the base, glabrous; nerves 12–15 pairs; petioles ½–¾ in. long. Flowers exceeding 1 in. in diam., white, in numerous panicles 2½–3½ in. long from the axils of fallen leaves. Calyx: in flower, glabrous, small, lobes ovate, acute; in fruit, 3 lobes much more enlarged than the other 2, reaching 3 in. long, by ½–⅝ in. broad, the two less enlarged lobes 2½ by 1¼ in., all linear-oblong, obtuse, with 8–12 prominent nerves and with netted veins. Fruit smooth, obconical, ½–¾ in. long. Fl. B. I. v. 1, p. 304; Talb. Trees, Bomb. p. 18; Brandis, Enum. Dipter. in Journ. Linn. Soc. v. 31 (1895) p. 84; Woodr. in Journ. Bomb. Nat. v. 11 (1897) p. 126; Watt, Dict. Econ. Prod. v. 6, part 2, p. 678. *Vatica laccifera*, W. & A. Prodr. p. 84. *Shorea laccifera*, Bedd. Flor. Sylvat. t. 6.—Flowers: Jan.-Mar. VERN. *Jalaranda.*

Rare. KANARA: Sirsi taluka of N. Kanara, *Talbot*, *Woodrow*; Siddapur (N. Kanara), *Woodrow*.

3. HOPEA, Roxb.

Resinous tree, glabrous or hoary-tomentose. Leaves quite entire, coriaceous, usually penninerved and reticulately veined; stipules small, deciduous or inconspicuous. Flowers small, in axillary and terminal panicles, sessile or shortly pedicelled; bracts 0. Calyx: tube very short, adnate to the torus; lobes short, obtuse, imbricate, often with membranous margins, in fruit enlarged, the 2 largest wing-like, erect, the others small, all closely embracing the fruit. Stamens 15 (rarely 10); anthers ovate or orbicular, cells obtuse, valves equal; connective subulate or cuspidate. Ovary 3-celled; ovules 2 in each cell; style shortly terete or subulate. Fruit nut-like, indehiscent, usually 1-seeded, closely enclosed within the base of the calyx-lobes. Seeds ovoid; cotyledons fleshy, unequal, enclosing a superior radicle.—DISTRIB. Tropical Asia and Malaya; species about 45.

1. **Hopea Wightiana,** *Wall. Cat.* (1828) 6295. A large tree; young branches pubescent, at length glabrous. Leaves 5–8 by 2–3 in., oblong or ovate-oblong, obtuse or subacute, glabrous, rounded at the base; lateral nerves 7–10, oblique, curved; petioles $\frac{1}{2}$ in. long, velvety-pubescent. Flowers secund, in axillary panicles, the panicles 1–6 together, slender, glabrous, shorter or rarely longer than the leaves; bracts lanceolate, $\frac{1}{12}$–$\frac{1}{8}$ in. long; pedicels very short. Calyx glabrous; lobes (when flowering) ovate, obtuse, the exterior larger. Petals pink, $\frac{1}{4}$ in. long, oblong, acute, externally pubescent, ciliate. Filaments 10, dilated at the base, each alternate one carrying 2 anthers; anthers ovate, each with a long filiform appendage about 4 times its length. Nuts $\frac{1}{2}$ in. long, ovoid, apiculate, glabrous, surrounded by the accrescent calyx, 2 of the lobes of which are developed into long crimson wings 2–2$\frac{3}{4}$ by $\frac{1}{2}$–$\frac{5}{8}$ in., oblong-obovate, 7–9-nerved. Fl. B. I. v. 1, p. 309; Bedd. Flor. Sylvat. t. 96; Brandis & Gilg, in Engl. & Prantl, Pflanzenf. v. 3, part 6, p. 261, fig. 121, H–M; Talb. Trees, Bomb. p. 18; Woodr. in Journ. Bomb. Nat. v. 11 (1897) p. 126; Brandis, Enum. Dipter. in Journ. Linn. Soc. v. 31 (1895) p. 58; Watt, Dict. Econ. Prod. v. 4, p. 273.

A globular, echinate excrescence, resembling the young fruit of the horse-chestnut, probably due to some insect, often deforms the inflorescence. Roxburgh described this deformation as *Artocarpus lancæfolia* (Fl. Ind. v. 3, p. 527).

The figure K, in Engl. & Prantl, Pflanzenf. l. c., which is taken from Wight, Ill. t. 37, does not show the 2 anthers on the alternate filaments. These are well figured by Beddome, l. c.—Flowers: Mar.–June.

Common along the banks of rivers and streams in the S. Konkan and N. Kanara. KONKAN: *Stocks*!; S. Konkan, *Law*! KANARA: Supa, *Ritchie*, 83!; evergreen forests, N. Kanara, *Brandis*!; Kála naddi, *Ritchie*, 83! S. M. COUNTRY: Londa, *Woodrow*; Castlerock, *Cooke*!

4. VATERIA, Linn.

Resinous trees, glabrous, tomentose or furfuraceous. Leaves quite entire, coriaceous, penninerved, reticulately veined; stipules small, deciduous or inconspicuous (rarely large and persistent). Flowers white, in terminal panicles, or 1–3 on axillary peduncles. Calyx: tube very short, adnate to the torus; lobes imbricate, scarcely enlarged in fruit, reflexed. Stamens 15 or more; anthers linear or oblong, the exterior valves of the cells the largest with involute margins; connective rarely produced. Ovary 3-celled; ovules 2 in each cell; style subulate; stigma small. Capsule ovoid or globose, coriaceous or fleshy, 1-seeded, indehiscent or 3-valved. Seeds thick; cotyledons thick, unequal, the largest usually lobed, involute, enclosing the superior radicle.—DISTRIB. Tropical Asia, Mauritius; species 3.

1. **Vateria indica,** *Linn. Sp. Pl.* (1753) p. 515. A large and very handsome tree; bark whitish; young branches and inflorescence clothed with hoary, stellate pubescence. Leaves 5–8 by 2–4 in., elliptic-oblong,

shortly pointed or obtuse, cordate or rounded at the base, glabrous; lateral nerves 12–15 pairs, very prominent beneath; petioles 1 in. long, stout. Flowers ¾ in. in diam., remote, in large terminal panicles 6–8 in. long; bracts ovate, acute, caducous; pedicels ¼–½ in. long. Calyx divided nearly to the base; lobes oblong-lanceolate, hoary-puberulous on both surfaces, not enlarged in fruit, deflexed. Petals a little longer than the calyx, oblong, obtuse, white. Stamens numerous (about 50); anthers slightly hairy at the base, otherwise glabrous, cells linear; connective adnate to the apex of the anther, produced into a subulate point, splitting along with the anther. Ovary pubescent; style longer than the stamens, filiform, glabrous; stigma small. Capsule 2½ by 1½ in., oblong, obtuse, fleshy, 3-valved, the valves 1-seeded. Fl. B. I. v. 1, p. 313; Grah. Cat. p. 22; Brandis & Gilg, in Engl. & Prantl, Pflanzenf. v. 3, part 6, p. 271, fig. 127, A–E; Talb. Trees, Bomb. p. 18; Brandis, Enum. Dipter. in Journ. Linn. Soc. v. 31 (1895) p. 143; Woodr. in Journ. Bomb. Nat. v. 11 (1897) p. 126; Watt, Dict. Econ. Prod. v. 6, part 4, p. 222.—Flowers: Feb.–Apr. VERN. *Dhupa.*

The Indian Copal or *Piney varnish* tree; abundant in S. Kanara.—It is very handsome and often planted as an avenue tree.

KANARA: Siddapur, Sirsi, *Woodrow*; S. Ghâts of N. Kanara in evergreen forests, commonly planted along roadsides in the N. Kanara district, *Talbot.*

The tree produces the *Indian Dammar* or *Piney resin*, which makes a valuable varnish. For an account of the product consult Watt, Dict. Econ. Prod. l. c.

ORDER XXIV. ANCISTROCLADACEÆ, Planch. in Annal. Sc. Nat. ser. 3, v. 13, p. 316.

Scandent glabrous shrubs; branches hooked. Leaves alternate, shortly petioled, coriaceous, penninerved and reticulately veined, usually entire, often crowded at the ends of the branches; stipules small, deciduous or 0. Flowers regular, hermaphrodite, in axillary (or apparently terminal) racemes or panicles, soon falling off; pedicels articulated at the base of the flower. Calyx accrescent in fruit; tube very short, adnate to the base of the ovary; lobes 5, unequal, imbricate. Petals 5, alternate with the sepals, unequal, contorted in æstivation, slightly connate at the base. Stamens 5–10, 1-seriate, those alternating with the petals slightly longer; filaments short, dilated and connate at the base; anthers basifixed, introrse, dehiscing longitudinally, apiculate by the slightly produced connective or muticous. Ovary adnate to the calyx, 1-celled; ovule 1 in each cell, erect or laterally affixed; styles 3, articulated to a rounded or shortly cylindric epigynous disk, each stigmatiferous at the apex. Fruit a 1-seeded, indehiscent nut, adnate to the turbinate calyx-tube, surmounted by the enlarged unequal calyx-lobes, mucronate. Seed subglobose; embryo straight, clavate; cotyledons subfoliaceous, divergent; albumen copious, fleshy, in closely folded brain-like convolutions.—DISTRIB. Tropical Asia; genus 1; species 10.

1. ANCISTROCLADUS, Wall.

For characters see ORDER.

1. **Ancistrocladus Heyneanus,** *Wall. Cat.* (1828) 7262. A scandent shrub, with hooked branches. Leaves deep green, 4–10 by 1½–3 in., oblanceolate-oblong, subacute, glabrous, shining, reticulately

veined, narrowed at the base and with subrepand margins; petioles very short or 0. Flowers small, very caducous, in branched panicles; corolla about equalling the calyx. Calyx-lobes enlarged in fruit, unequal, 1½–2¼ in. long, obovate, cuneate, with prominently and closely reticulate veins. Petals small, white, ovate-oblong. Stamens 10, alternately shorter. Fruit small, surmounted by 5 wings (accrescent calyx-lobes). Fl. B. I. v. 1, p. 299; Grah. Cat. p. 28; Dalz. & Gibs. p. 34; Gilg, in Engl. & Prantl, Pflanzenf. v. 3, part 6, p. 275, fig. 129, A; Talb. Trees, Bomb. p. 17; Woodr. in Journ. Bomb. Nat. v. 11 (1897) p. 126.—Flowers: Mar. VERN. *Kardal.*

Pretty common on the Ghâts. KONKAN: *Stocks*!, *Law*!; Matheran, *Cooke*!, *Woodrow*!, *Macnaghten*!; Mira Donger (near Pen), *Dalzell & Gibson*; Ghâts in the Thana district, *Woodrow*. DECCAN: ravines at Khandala, *Graham*; Parghât, *Graham*. S. M. COUNTRY: Ramghât, *Dalzell & Gibson*. KANARA: in evergreen forests of N. Kanara, *Talbot*; Divimana (N. Kanara), *Woodrow*.

ORDER XXV. MALVACEÆ.

Herbs, shrubs, rarely soft-wooded trees with tenacious inner bark, often with stellate hairs. Leaves alternate, frequently palmi-nerved, entire, toothed or lobed; stipules free, sometimes caducous. Flowers irregular, hermaphrodite or very rarely diœcious or polygamous (*Kydia*), axillary, terminal, solitary, clustered or cymoso-paniculate. Involucral bracts 2 or more, connate or free (absent in *Sida*, *Abutilon*, *Bombax*, and *Eriodendron*). Sepals 5 (rarely 3–4), valvate, more or less united into a lobed or subentire calyx. Petals 5, more or less adnate to the base of the staminal-tube, twisted, imbricate. Stamens indefinite (rarely definite), usually connate into a tube adnate to the base of the petals, and divided at the apex into numerous antheriferous filaments, or into 2–many 1–many-antheriferous branches, or sometimes emitting shortly stipitate or sessile anthers from its outer surface; anthers globose, oblong or reniform, cells sinuous or twisted, linear or annular, ultimately 1-celled, bursting longitudinally. Ovary 2–many-celled, entire or lobed, of 2–5 or more carpels, whorled round a central axis; ovules 1 or more, curved, attached to the inner angle of each carpel; styles distinct or more or less connate; stigmas linear, peltate, capitate or spathulate. Fruit of dry cocci, or capsular and loculicidal, sometimes large and woody. Seeds reniform or obovoid, rarely arillate; albumen scanty, often mucilaginous or 0; embryo curved in reniform seeds, usually straight in obovoid; cotyledons leafy, usually folded or crumpled.—DISTRIB. Warm and temperate regions; genera 57; species about 700.

TRIBE I. **MALVEÆ.** Staminal-tube antheriferous at or to the apex. Involucral bracts present or 0. Branches of the style as many as the carpels. Ripe carpels separating from the axis or united into a capsule (*Kydia*). Pollen globose, echinulate.

Ovule solitary, ascending; styles longitudinally stigmatose on the inside.
  Invol. bracts 6–9, connate at the base .... 1. ALTHÆA.
  Invol. bracts 3, distinct .... 2. MALVA.
Ovule solitary, pendulous; invol. bracts 0 .... 3. SIDA.
Ovules 2–many.
  Invol. bracts 4–6; fruit capsular .... 4. KYDIA.
  Invol. bracts 0 .... 5. ABUTILON.

TRIBE II. **URENEÆ.** Staminal-tube antheriferous outside, truncate or 5-toothed at the apex. Branches of the style twice as many as the carpels. Ripe carpels separating from the axis. Pollen globose, echinulate.

Invol. bracts 4, large, leafy; flowers densely involucrato-capitate. 6. MALACHRA.
Invol. bracts 5 or more.
Ripe carpels glochidiate .... 7. URENA.
Ripe carpels 1–3-aristate or naked, not glochidiate .... 8. PAVONIA.

TRIBE III. **HIBISCEÆ.** Staminal-tube antheriferous outside, truncate or 5-toothed at the apex (very rarely antheriferous). Branches of the style as many as the cells of the ovary. Fruit capsular, loculicidally dehiscent; carpels not separating. Pollen globose, echinulate.

Branches of the style at length spreading; seeds reniform.
Invol. bracts 10; ovary 10-celled .... 9. DECASCHISTIA.
Invol. bracts 3, large, cordate .... 10. SENRA.
Invol. bracts 5 or more; ovary 5-celled .... 11. HIBISCUS.
Branches of the style coherent into a club-shaped mass; seeds obovoid or angled.
Invol. bracts 3–5, small .... 12. THESPESIA.
Invol. bracts 3, large, leafy .... 13. GOSSYPIUM.

TRIBE IV. (or SUBORDER) **BOMBACEÆ.** Staminal-tube divided at the apex (rarely to the base) into numerous 1-antheriferous or 5–8, 2–∞-antheriferous branches. Style entire or divided into as many very short branches as there are cells to the ovary. Capsule loculicidally dehiscent or indehiscent. Pollen smooth.

Calyx 5-cleft .... 14. ADANSONIA.
Calyx truncate or irregularly 3–5-lobed.
Branches of the staminal-tube 1-antheriferous .... 15. BOMBAX.
Branches of the staminal-tube 2–3-antheriferous .... 16. ERIODENDRON.

1. ALTHÆA, Linn.

Herbs pubescent or villous. Leaves lobed or partite. Flowers axillary, solitary or clustered, or arranged in a terminal raceme. Involucral bracts 6–9, connate at the base. Staminal-tube divided to the apex into numerous antheriferous linear filaments. Ovary many- (more than 5-) celled; ovule 1 in each cell; styles as many as the carpels, longitudinally stigmatose on the inside. Carpels forming a round depressed fruit, separating from each other and from the short central axis.—DISTRIB. Temperate regions of the Old World; species 32.

1. **Althæa Ludwigii,** *Linn. Mantiss.* (1767) p. 98. A prostrate, hairy annual, branched from the base. Leaves 1–1¼ in. in diam., orbicular, deeply 5–7-lobed; lobes cuneate, 3–5-fid at the apex; petioles 2–4 in. long, slender. Flowers axillary, 3–1 together; pedicels ¼–1 in. long. Involucral bracts 7–9, linear, as long as the calyx, hispid with long white and stellate hairs. Calyx-lobes ⅓ in. long, deltoid. Corolla ½–⅔ in. in diam., whitish. Anthers round. Fruit ⅓–½ in. in diam.; carpels 8–9, doubly keeled, not winged, wrinkled at the sides, glabrous. Seeds smooth, brown. Fl. B. I. v. 1, p. 319; E. Bak. in Journ. Bot. v. 28 (Lond. 1890) p. 140; Woodr. in Journ. Bomb. Nat. v. 11 (1897) p. 126. *Malwa Malwensis*, Edgew. in Hook. Journ. Bot. v. 2 (1840) p. 284.—Flowers: Mar.–July.

DECCAN: Poona, *Woodrow*; Karli, *Cooke*! SIND: *Stocks*, 681!; Shikarpur and Sukkur, *Vicary*!; Sehwan, *Woodrow*; Hyderabad, *Cooke*!—DISTRIB. Western Asia and the Mediterranean region, S. Africa.

Althæa rosea, Cav. Diss. 2 (1786) p. 91, t. 28, fig. 1, the well-known *Hollyhock*, a native of Crete and Greece (*fide* E. Baker, l. c.), is extensively cultivated as an ornamental plant in gardens throughout India. It often exceeds 6 ft. in height, with leaves 3–5 in. in diam., long-petioled, cordate-ovate, acutely 5–7-lobed, and with very shortly-pedicelled flowers in a terminal raceme 1–3 ft. long. The corolla, which is purple, rose, yellow, or white, often (in cultivation) exceeds 4 in. across. Fl. B. I. v. 1, p. 319 (*in note*); Grah. Cat. p. 12; Dalz. & Gibs. Suppl. p. 6; Firminger, Man. Gard. ed. 2, p. 406; Woodr. Gard. in Ind. p. 186; E. Bak. in Journ. Bot. v. 28 (Lond. 1890) p. 207.—Flowers: Jan.–Mar.

2. **MALVA,** Linn.

Herbs hirsute or downy. Leaves angled or lobed. Flowers axillary, solitary or clustered, pedicelled. Involucral bracts 3 (very rarely 2), distinct. Staminal-tube divided to the apex into numerous antheriferous filaments. Ovary many- (more than 5-) celled; ovule 1, in each cell; styles as many as the carpels, filiform, longitudinally stigmatose on the inside. Carpels forming a round depressed fruit, separating, when ripe, from each other and the short central axis, indehiscent, not beaked.—DISTRIB. Temperate Europe and Asia, N. Africa; species 17.

Claw of petal bearded.
  Carpels rounded on the back .... 1. *M. rotundifolia.*
  Carpels 2-keeled on the back .... 2. *M. sylvestris.*
Claw of petal glabrous .... 3. *M. parviflora.*

1. **Malva rotundifolia,** *Linn. Sp. Pl.* (1753) p. 688. A much-branched herb, sparingly pubescent and with some stellate hairs. Leaves ½–1½ in. in diam., suborbicular, cordate, crenate; petioles up to 2–4 in. long. Pedicels axillary, 1–5 together, ½–1½ in. long, deflexed in fruit. Involucral bracts half the length of the calyx, lanceolate, hairy. Calyx hairy; lobes ⅙ in. long, ovate, acute. Corolla ¾ in. in diam., pale purple or white; petals notched at the top, bearded at the claw. Fruit ¼–⅓ in. in diam., olive-brown; carpels 13–16, pubescent, not reticulated on the back, the margins of the back rounded, not keeled. Seeds brown-black, glabrous. Fl. B. I. v. 1, p. 320; E. Bak. in Journ. Bot. v. 28 (Lond. 1890) p. 341; Woodr. in Journ. Bomb. Nat. v. 11 (1897) p. 126; Watt, Dict. Econ. Prod. v. 5, p. 141.—Flowers: Jan.–Mar. VERN. *Khaparkuti*; *Chandiri*; *Khabási*. The seeds are used in native medicine as a demulcent.

SIND: *Stocks*, 234!—DISTRIB. Europe, N. Africa, N. and W. Asia.
In the list of Bombay plants given by Woodrow (*l. c.*) the localities in which this plant and *M. parviflora* occur seem to have been transposed.

2. **Malva sylvestris,** var. **mauritiana,** *Boiss. Fl. Orient.* v. 1 (1867) p. 819. A sparingly pubescent or nearly glabrate herb. Leaves 1–2½ in. in diam., round, cordate, 5-angular or shortly lobed; petioles long. Pedicels axillary, usually many together, some of them as long as the flowers. Involucral bracts ovate, shorter than the calyx. Corolla 1½ in. in diam., purple; claw of petals bearded. Fruit ⅓ in. in diam.; carpels

about 10–12, nearly glabrous, reticulated, with 2 angular margins. Seeds brown-black, glabrous. Fl. B. I. v. 1, p. 320; E. Bak. in Journ. Bot. v. 28 (Lond. 1890) p. 340; K. Schum. in Mart. Fl. Bras. v. 12, part 3, p. 265; Watt, Dict. Econ. Prod. v. 5, p. 141. *M. mauritiana*, Linn. Sp. Pl. p. 689; Grah. Cat. p. 12; Dalz. & Gibs. Suppl. p. 6.

BOMBAY: *Capt. Geburne*!; in gardens, *Graham, Dalzell & Gibson*.—DISTRIB. Europe, N. Africa, N. Asia.

3. **Malva parviflora,** *Linn. Amœn. Acad.* ed. 2, v. 3 (1787) p. 416. A spreading herb, ½–1½ ft. high, pubescent and with some stellate hairs. Leaves 1–2½ in. in diam., suborbicular, cordate, obscurely 5–7-lobed, finely crenate; petioles long, up to 2–4 in. Pedicels axillary, 1 or few together, short, rarely exceeding ¾ in. Involucral bracts short, linear, caducous, hairy at tip. Calyx in fruit accrescent, reticulately veined, glabrous; lobes ovate, mucronate. Corolla ½–¾ in. in diam., purplish or white. Fruit ¼ in. in diam.; carpels 10, glabrous, strongly reticulated on the back, the two margins of the back keeled, sometimes slightly winged, often with a few minute teeth. Seeds black, glabrous. Fl. B. I. v. 1, p. 321; E. Bak. in Journ. Bot. v. 28 (Lond. 1890) p. 341; K. Schum. in Mart. Fl. Bras. v. 12, part 3, p. 263, t. 51; Woodr. in Journ. Bomb. Nat. v. 11 (1897) p. 126; Watt, Dict. Econ. Prod. v. 5, p. 141. *M. rotundifolia*, Dalz. & Gibs. p. 21 (*not* of Linn.).—Flowers: Jan.–Mar. VERN. *Nárr*; *Gogi-Ság*.

DECCAN: common about villages, *Dalzell*; Dongergaon (near Ahmednagar), *Cooke*!; Jejuri, *Woodrow*! SIND: Karachi, *Stocks*, 582!; Gurapad, *Pierce*!—DISTRIB. Europe, N. Africa, W. Asia.

3. SIDA, Linn.

Herbs or undershrubs, hairy and with stellate hairs. Leaves toothed; stipules linear, ¼–⅓ in. long. Pedicels axillary, solitary or clustered, disarticulating in fruit at a constriction below the calyx. Involucral bracts 0. Sepals 5, valvate, connate below for ⅓–½ their length. Corolla small, yellow or white; petals connate at base and with the staminal-tube. Staminal-tube divided at the top into numerous antheriferous filaments. Ovary of 5–12 cells; ovule 1, in each cell, pendulous; styles as many as the carpels; stigmas terminal. Fruit globose, depressed, enclosed by the calyx; carpels separating from each other and from the central axis, beaked or not. Seeds black-chestnut, smooth.—DISTRIB. Throughout the warmer parts of the world, most numerous in America; species about 120.

Prostrate trailing herb .... 1. *S. veronicifolia.*
Erect or suberect herbs or undershrubs.
  Viscous-hairy .... 2. *S. glutinosa.*
  Stellately hairy.
    Petioles spiny at the base .... 3. *S. spinosa.*
    Petioles not spiny at the base.
      Awns hardly ⅛ the length of the carpels.
        Flowers white; leaves downy on both sides .... 4. *S. grewioides.*
        Flowers yellow.
          Leaves lanceolate, glabrous on both sides .... 5. *S. acuta.*
          Leaves obovate-cuneate, glabrous on the upper side. 6. *S. rhombifolia,* var. *retusa.*
      Awns nearly as long as the carpels .... 7. *S. cordifolia.*

1. **Sida veronicifolia,** *Lam. Encyc.* v. 1 (1783) p. 5. A perennial much-branched herb; branches prostrate or trailing, sometimes rooting, more or less hairy. Leaves ½–2 in. long, cordate, ovate, acute or acuminate, serrate, sparsely clothed with stellate hairs; petioles ⅜–⅞ in. long. Pedicels ½–1½ in. long, slender, axillary, solitary or twin, jointed a little above the middle. Calyx ⅙ in. long, 5-angled, hairy; lobes triangular, acute or acuminate. Corolla pale-yellow, slightly exceeding the calyx. Carpels 5, smooth, not reticulated, muticous or with a small slightly 2-lipped beak, not cuspidate. Seeds brown, glabrous. K. Schum. in Mart. Bras. v. 12, part 3, p. 319; E. Bak. in Journ. Bot. v. 30 (Lond. 1892) p. 293. *S. humilis*, Cav. Diss. p. 277; Fl. B. I. v. 1, p. 322; Dalz. & Gibs. p. 17; Trim. Fl. Ceyl. v. 1, p. 141; Woodr. in Journ. Bomb. Nat. v. 11 (1897) p. 126; Watt, Dict. Econ. Prod. v. 6, part 2, p. 681.—Flowers: Oct.–Nov.

Common throughout the Presidency on sandy soil, *Dalzell & Gibson*. KONKAN: *Law*!; Karanja, on sea sand, *Stocks*! GUJARAT: widely, *Woodrow*; Gadhavi (Dangs) and Baroda, *Cooke*! S. M. COUNTRY: Belgaum, *Ritchie*, 217!; Londa and Badami, *Cooke*! SIND: widely, *Woodrow*.—DISTRIB. In tropical and subtropical regions of the globe.

2. **Sida glutinosa,** *Cav. Diss.* 1 (1785) p. 16, t. 2, fig. 8. Suberect, more hairy than *S. veronicifolia* and glutinous-hairy. Pedicels axillary, several crowded together, nearly all less than ⅔ in. long. Carpels 5–6, smooth, grey-puberulous, not reticulated; beak consisting of 2 rounded or ovate lobes, rather longer than as in *S. veronicifolia*, but not bicuspidate. Otherwise as *S. veronicifolia*. K. Schum. in Mart. Bras. v. 12, part 3, p. 310; E. Bak. in Journ. Bot. v. 30 (Lond. 1892) p. 293. *S. mysorensis*, W. & A. Prod. p. 59; Fl. B. I. v. 1, p. 322; Trim. Fl. Ceyl. v. 1, p. 142; Woodr. in Journ. Bomb. Nat. v. 11 (1897) p. 126.—Flowers: Nov.–Jan.

DECCAN: widely, *Woodrow*. KONKAN: *Law*!, *Stocks*! KANARA: *Dalzell*! S. M. COUNTRY: Belgaum, *Ritchie*, 4!—DISTRIB. Widely spread throughout the tropics of both hemispheres.

3. **Sida spinosa,** *Linn. Sp. Pl.* (1753) p. 683. A suberect branched shrub, grey from minute stellate hairs. Leaves up to 2 in. long, elliptic, crenate, obtuse or cuneate at the base, rounded or narrowed at the top to obtuse triangular, not acuminate, ultimately glabrate above, grey beneath; petioles ½–1 in. long, with often 1–3 small recurved spines beneath the petiole. Pedicels 0–¾ in. long, clustered or solitary, jointed just below the calyx. Calyx grey, stellately hairy; lobes triangular. Corolla slightly exceeding the calyx, pale yellow. Carpels 3 (rarely 6), pubescent; awns 2, about ½ the length of the carpel from a conic base, slightly divergent, with spreading or erect hairs. Seeds smooth, black-brown. Fl. B. I. v. 1, p. 323; K. Schum. in Engl. & Prantl, Pflanzenf. v. 3, part 6, p. 42, fig. 18, J, K, & in Mart. Bras. v. 12, part 3, p. 297; E. Bak. in Journ. Bot. v. 30 (Lond. 1892) p. 237; Woodr. in Journ. Bomb. Nat. v. 11 (1897) p. 126; Watt, Dict. Econ. Prod. v. 6, part 2, p. 686. *S. alba*, Linn. Sp. Pl. ed. 2, p. 960; Dalz. & Gibs. p. 17.—Flowers: Oct.–Nov.

KONKAN: *Stocks*!; Bombay, *Capt. Geburne*! DECCAN: *Woodrow*. GUJARAT: *Woodrow*; Surat, *Dalzell & Gibson*; Ankleshwar (near Broach), *Cooke*!; Domas (near Surat), *Cooke*! SIND: *Cooke*!, *Vicary*!, *Stocks*!—DISTRIB. Tropical and subtropical regions of both hemispheres.

4. **Sida grewioides,** *Guill., Perr. et A. Rich. Fl. Senegamb.* v. 1 (1830) p. 71. A branched undershrub, grey-tomentose with stellate hairs. Leaves ½–1½ in. long, elliptic-oblong, sometimes obovate, obtuse, crenate, downy on both sides; petioles ⅛–½ in. long. Pedicels 1–2 together, 0–½ in. long, jointed close under the calyx. Calyx (in flower) much as in *S. spinosa*, in fruit somewhat enlarged, sometimes exceeding ½ in. in diam., the lobes becoming very broad. Corolla a little longer than the calyx, white. Carpels 7–8, nearly glabrous, hoary, strongly reticulated; awns 2, linear, small, hardly ⅓ the length of the carpel. Seeds black, smooth, sometimes with stellate hairs near the hilum. Fl. B. I. v. 1, p. 323; E. Bak. in Journ. Bot. v. 30 (Lond. 1892) p. 238; Woodr. in Journ. Bomb. Nat. v. 11 (1897) p. 126.—Flowers: Nov.–Dec.

SIND: common, *Dalzell*, 1!; Karachi, *Stocks*, 565!, *Cooke*!, *Woodrow*.—DISTRIB. Tropical Africa.

5. **Sida acuta,** *Burm. Fl. Ind.* (1768) p. 147. Shrubby, much-branched; branches slender, terete, minutely stellately hairy. Leaves 1–2½ in. long, lanceolate, with rounded base, sharply serrate, glabrous on both sides; petioles 0–¼ in. long, shorter than the stipules. Pedicels 1–2 in each axil, shorter or longer than the petiole, jointed about the middle. Calyx ¼–⅓ in. long; lobes triangular, acute. Corolla nearly twice as long as the calyx, yellow. Fruit ⅕–¼ in. in diam.; carpels 5–9, puberulous, not pubescent, strongly reticulated, toothed on the dorsal margins; awns 2, nearly linear, about ⅓ the length of the carpel. Seeds smooth, black. Grah. Cat. p. 16; Wight, Ic. t. 95; Dalz. & Gibs. p. 17; K. Schum. in Mart. Bras. v. 12, part 3, p. 325; E. Bak. in Journ. Bot. v. 30 (Lond. 1892) p. 238. *S. carpinifolia*, Linn. f., Suppl. (1781) p. 307; Fl. B. I. v. 1, p. 323; Woodr. in Journ. Bomb. Nat. v. 11 (1897) p. 126; Watt, Dict. Econ. Prod. v. 6, part 2, p. 679.—Flowers: Nov.–Dec. VERN. *Bála*; *Jangali-methi*; *Lahán-chikna.*

KONKAN: common, *Law*!; Bombay, *Capt. Geburne*!, *Dalzell & Gibson*, *Graham*; Marmagao, *Woodrow*. DECCAN: Poona, *Cooke*!, *Woodrow*!; Kirkee, *Woodrow*! S. M. COUNTRY: Belgaum, *Ritchie*, 1627!—DISTRIB. In tropical and subtropical regions of both hemispheres.

6. **Sida rhombifolia,** var. **retusa,** *Masters, in Fl. B. I.* v. 1 (1874) p. 324.—Shrubby, erect; branches minutely stellately hairy. Leaves on the middle of the stem obovate or truncate, sometimes retuse, cuneate at base, often coarsely toothed at top, ¾–1½ in. long, dark green and glabrous above, more or less tomentose beneath; petioles very short, ⅛ in. or less. Pedicels axillary and crowded towards the ends of the branches, jointed above the middle, longer or shorter than the petiole. Calyx angular; lobes triangular, acute. Corolla yellow, more than twice as long as the calyx. Carpels 9–10, reticulated, with 2 short awns. Seeds smooth, black. K. Schum. in Mart. Fl. Bras. v. 12, part 3, p. 339; E. Bak. in Journ. Bot. v. 30 (Lond. 1892) p. 239; Watt, Dict. Econ. Prod. v. 6, part 2, p. 682. *S. retusa*, Linn. Sp. Pl. ed. 2, p. 961; Grah. Cat. p. 16; Dalz. & Gibs. p. 17.—Flowers: Oct.–Dec. VERN. *Bála*; *Jangali-methi*; *Ati-bála.*

A common weed. KONKAN: "very common," *Dalzell*!, *Stocks*!, *Law*!; Collem (Portuguese territory), *Cooke*! DECCAN: Poona, *Woodrow*! GUJARAT: Petlad, *Woodrow*! S. M. COUNTRY: Belgaum, *Ritchie*, 62!; Dharwar, *Cooke*!

7. **Sida cordifolia,** *Linn. Sp. Pl.* (1753) p. 684. Shrubby, branched, softly hairy and with much stellate hair nearly all over and subpersistent. Leaves 1–2 in. long, cordate, ovate-oblong, crenate, obtuse or subacute, not acuminate; petioles $\frac{1}{2}$–$1\frac{1}{2}$ in. long. Pedicels solitary or few together, short, some up to $\frac{1}{2}$–$\frac{3}{4}$ in. long, jointed much above the middle. Calyx $\frac{1}{4}$–$\frac{1}{3}$ in. long; lobes ovate, acute. Corolla slightly exceeding the calyx, yellow. Fruit $\frac{1}{4}$–$\frac{1}{3}$ in. in diam.; carpels 7–10, strongly reticulated, ciliate on the upper margins, the two dorsal margins almost scabrid; awns 2, nearly as long as the carpels, linear, retrorsely scabrid-hairy. Fl. B. I. v. 1, p. 324; Grah. Cat. p. 16; Dalz. & Gibs. p. 17; K. Schum. in Mart. Bras. v. 12, part 3, p. 329, t. 62; E. Bak. in Journ. Bot. v. 30 (Lond. 1892) p. 291; Woodr. in Journ. Bomb. Nat. v. 11 (1897) p. 126; Watt, Dict. Econ. Prod. v. 6, part 2, p. 680.—Flowers: Oct.–Nov. VERN. *Búla.*

KONKAN: *Stocks*!; Malwan, *Dalzell*! GUJARAT: Godra, *Cooke*! S. M. COUNTRY: Belgaum, *Woodrow, Ritchie*, 611!; Badami, *Woodrow*!, *Cooke*!; Dharwar, *Woodrow*. —DISTRIB. Tropical and subtropical regions of both hemispheres.

All the species of *Sida* enumerated above yield valuable fibres, but the species from which the best fibre has been obtained are *S. acuta* and *S. cordifolia*. The fibre from these was, in December 1894, chemically examined in the Research Laboratory of the Imperial Institute, according to the method elaborated by Messrs. Cross and Bevan. Complete details may be found in the Imperial Institute Journal for January 1895, p. 29. See also Dr. Watt's account of *Sida* fibre in Watt, Dict. Econ. Prod. l. c.

4. KYDIA, Roxb.

Trees with stellate hairs. Leaves ovate, entire or lobed. Flowers in terminal panicles, polygamous. Involucral bracts 4–6, connate at the base, spathulate-oblong, exceeding the calyx, spreading in fruit, persistent, brown. Sepals 5, connate below the middle, ovate, incurved over the fruit. Petals 5, obcordate; filaments united in a tube a little more than half their length, then divided into 5 spreading branches, each carrying 3 subsessile anthers; variously reduced or wanting in the carpellate flowers. Style-branches 3, each carrying a large peltate stigma. Ovary 2–3-celled; ovules 2 in each cell. Capsule globose, woody, at length loculicidally dehiscent. Seed usually 1 in each cell, reniform-ellipsoid, brown-black.—DISTRIB. Species 2, in India.

1. **Kydia calycina,** *Roxb. Hort. Beng.* (1814) p. 51; *Corom. Plts.* v. 3 (1819) p. 12, t. 215. A tree. Leaves 3–6 in. long, palmately 7-nerved, cordate, usually 3–7-lobed; lobes often angular, the mid-lobe the longest, glabrous above, hoary tomentose beneath; petioles 1–2 in. long. Panicles many-flowered, clothed with dense tawny tomentum; pedicels $\frac{3}{8}$ in. long. Involucral bracts 4–6, strongly nerved, accrescent, $\frac{1}{4}$–$\frac{3}{8}$ in. long, in fruit. Corolla white or pink; petals emarginate, exceeding the calyx, clawed, with a tuft of hairs at each side of the base of the claw. Staminal-tube hairy at the base; filaments longer in the male than in the carpellate flowers. Capsule loculicidally 3-valved, about the size of a very small pea, covered with mealy tomentum, globose, top slightly umbonate. Seeds reniform, striate, brown-black.

Fl. B. I. v. 1, p. 348; Dalz. & Gibs. p. 24; Talb. Trees, Bomb. p. 20; Woodr. in Journ. Bomb. Nat. v. 11 (1897) p. 128.—Flowers: Aug.-Dec. VERN. *Várang.*

Common on the Ghâts, *Dalzell & Gibson.* KONKAN: Ghâts, *Talbot*; Amboli Ghât, *Cooke*! DECCAN: Khandala and Sattara Ghâts, *Cooke*! KANARA: North Kanara Ghâts, *Talbot.*

5. ABUTILON, Tournef.

Tomentose herbs or shrubs. Leaves cordate, ovate, toothed or slightly lobed, long-petioled. Peduncles axillary (uppermost running into a raceme in *A. polyandrum* &c.), 1-flowered (in *A. ramosum* often 2-flowered), jointed near the flower. Flowers yellow. Involucral bracts 0. Staminal-tube divided at the top into numerous, antheriferous filaments. Carpels 5–25; styles as many as the carpels, long; stigmas capitate. Ripe carpels separating from the short central axis, rounded on the back, dehiscent, truncate, pointed, apiculate or with a short oblique or horizontal mucro, 3–5-seeded. Seeds reniform, dark brown. —DISTRIB. In nearly all warm regions; species 170.

Carpels 5.
  Staminal-tube very short, densely hairy .... 1. *A. polyandrum.*
  Staminal-tube long, glabrous .... 2. *A. Ranadei.*
Carpels more than 10, usually 15–20.
  Carpels pointed or with a distinct mucro.
    Carpels ⅓–½ in. long.
      Carpels hairy, ultimately glabrate, shining .... 3. *A. indicum.*
      Carpels densely hairy, ultimately shaggy .... 4. *A. asiaticum.*
    Carpels ⅛–⅙ in. long .... 5. *A. bidentatum.*
  Carpels obtuse, without a mucro.
    Corolla 2 in. in diam.
      Fruit globose, densely silky-villous .... 6. *A. muticum.*
      Fruit roughly hairy .... 7. *A. graveolens.*
    Corolla ½ in. in diam. .... 8. *A. crispum.*
Carpels 8–10.
  Carpels ¼ in. long; fruit short, cylindric.
    Carpels beaked .... 9. *A. ramosum.*
    Carpels hardly beaked, truncate .... 10. *A. fruticosum.*
  Carpels ½ in. long; fruit ovoid .... 11. *A. cornutum.*

1. **Abutilon polyandrum,** *Wight et Arn. Prodr.* (1834) p. 55. An erect undershrub, 4 ft. high. Leaves up to 9 by 7 in., roundish or ovate, cordate, long-acuminate, irregularly toothed, tomentose beneath, the young leaves velvety; petioles 3–4 in. long. Racemes terminal, 8–15 in. long; pedicels 1–2½ in. long, jointed near the flower; bracts (at the base of the pedicels) ½–1 in. long, lanceolate, toothed. Calyx-lobes ⅜–½ in. long, lanceolate, tomentose. Corolla 1½ in. in diam., orange-yellow, purple-veined near the base. Staminal-tube very short, densely hairy; filaments long, free almost to the very base. Carpels 5, acuminate, mucronate, a little longer than the calyx. Seeds smooth, brown. Fl. B. I. v. 1, p. 325 (excluding syn. Schlecht); Grah. Cat. p. 15; Dalz. & Gibs. p. 17; E. Bak. in Journ. Bot. v. 31 (Lond. 1893) p. 270; Woodr. in Journ. Bomb. Nat. v. 11 (1897) p. 126; Watt, Dict. Econ. Prod. v. 1, p. 17.—Flowers: Nov.-Jan. VERN. *Maddm.*

Abutilon polyandrum, G. Don, Gen. Syst. v. 1 (1831) p. 500, is evidently a misprint for *Abutilon polyanthum* and was nothing more than *Sida polyantha*, Schlecht, a remote species.

Very common on the Ghâts. KONKAN: *Stocks!*, *Law!*; Par, *Graham*; W. Ghâts, widely, *Woodrow*. S. M. COUNTRY: Belgaum, *Ritchie*, 60!—DISTRIB. S. Africa, Java.

2. **Abutilon Ranadei,** *Woodr. et Stapf, in Kew Bull.* (1894) p. 99. An undershrub, 4 ft. high, densely and minutely stellately tomentose. Leaves up to 7 by 6 in., cordate, ovate, acuminate, distantly toothed; petioles stout, 2–4 in. long. Flowers axillary, solitary; pedicels $\frac{1}{4}$–$1\frac{1}{2}$ in. long, jointed near the flower. Calyx $\frac{3}{4}$–$\frac{7}{8}$ in. long; base campanulate; lobes ovate-lanceolate, acute, as long as the tube. Petals $1\frac{1}{2}$ by $\frac{1}{2}$ in. long, orange-yellow, purple-veined at base. Staminal-tube 1 in. long, glabrous; filaments exceedingly short. Carpels 5, acuminate, mucronate, $\frac{5}{8}$ in. long, densely shortly hairy all over. Seeds large, dusky-black, furfuraceous-dotted. Woodr. in Journ. Bomb. Nat. v. 11 (1897) p. 126. —Flowers: Jan.

A rare plant, named after N. B. Ranade, for many years keeper of the Herbarium at the College of Science, Poona, who died of the plague in 1897. KONKAN: Ambeghât, on the Ratnagiri and Kolhapur Road, *Ranade!*, *Woodrow!*, *Cooke!*

3. **Abutilon indicum,** *Sweet, Hort. Brit.* v. 1 (1827) p. 54. Suffrutescent, minutely hoary-tomentose. Leaves up to $3\frac{1}{2}$ by 2 in., cordate, ovate, acuminate, toothed, rarely subtrilobate; petioles $1\frac{1}{2}$–3 in. long; stipules $\frac{3}{8}$ in. long, linear, acute, deflexed. Pedicels often 1–2 in. long, axillary, solitary, jointed very near the top. Calyx $\frac{1}{2}$–$\frac{1}{3}$ in. long, divided to the middle; lobes ovate, apiculate. Corolla 1 in. in diam., yellow, opening in the evening. Staminal-tube hairy at the base; filaments long. Carpels usually 15–20, longer than the calyx, with a distinct small acute point, hairy, ultimately shining, dark brown. Seeds brown-black, densely and minutely scrobiculate. Fl. B. I. v. 1, p. 326; Wight, Ic. t. 12; Grah. Cat. p. 15; Dalz. & Gibs. p. 18; Trim. Fl. Ceyl. v. 1, p. 145; E. Bak. in Journ. Bot. v. 31 (Lond. 1893) p. 213; Woodr. in Journ. Bomb. Nat. v. 11 (1897) p. 126; Watt, Dict. Econ. Prod. v. 1, p. 16. *A. graveolens*, Grah. Cat. p. 15.—In flower most of the year. VERN. *Mudra*; *Petâri*. The seeds are used in native medicine as a demulcent.

Very common, especially in the Deccan, where it is abundant along the roadsides. KONKAN: *Law!*, *Stocks!*; Bombay, *Capt. Geburne!* DECCAN: Ahmednagar, *Cooke!* S. M. COUNTRY: Belgaum, *Ritchie*, 63! SIND: Jemadar ka Landa, near Karachi, *Stocks*, 493!

4. **Abutilon asiaticum,** *G. Don, Gen. Syst.* v. 1 (1831) p. 503. Rather more tomentose than *A. indicum*. Calyx densely clothed with long woolly hairs. Flowers 2 in. in diam., orange-yellow. Carpels acuminate, shaggy on the back when ripe. Seeds smooth. Otherwise as *A. indicum*. Fl. B. I. v. 1, p. 326; Grah. Cat. p. 15; Trim. Fl. Ceyl. v. 1, p. 144; E. Bak. in Journ. Bot. v. 31 (1893) p. 214; Watt, Dict. Econ. Prod. v. 1, p. 15.

BOMBAY: *Capt. Geburne!*; in gardens, Bombay, *Graham*.
I have only seen one specimen from Bombay marked as above, in Herb. Kew.

5. **Abutilon bidentatum,** *A. Rich. Fl. Abyss.* v. 1 (1847) p. 68. Erect. Leaves cordate, ovate, acuminate, toothed; lower petioles 4–5 in. long. Carpels about 20, $\frac{1}{4}$–$\frac{1}{3}$ in. long, black, moderately grey-woolly, tips acuminate. Otherwise as in *A. indicum*, from which it

differs chiefly in the slightly smaller fruit, a difference which might perhaps disappear if a larger number of specimens were available for examination. Fl. B. I. v. 1, p. 326. *Sida bidentata*, Hochst. l. c.

KONKAN: *Stocks*!—DISTRIB. Tropical Africa, Arabia.

6. **Abutilon muticum,** *Sweet, Hort. Brit.* ed. 2 (1830) p. 65. A tomentose undershrub. Leaves up to 3–4 in. in diam., cordate, roundish-ovate, very shortly acuminate, rarely obtuse, velvety on both surfaces, irregularly toothed; petioles 1–3 in. long; stipules lanceolate. Pedicels ½–2 in. long, axillary, solitary, stout, jointed near the flower. Calyx ½ in. long, divided to the middle, very villous; lobes broad, shortly acuminate. Corolla 2 in. in diam., orange-yellow; petals often lobed. Fruit globose, depressed at the summit, densely silky-villous. Carpels about 25, not beaked. Seeds 3 in each carpel, clothed with minute shining hairs. Fl. B. I. v. 1, p. 327; E. Bak. in Journ. Bot. v. 31 (Lond. 1893) p. 214; Trim. Fl. Ceyl. v. 1, p. 145; Woodr. Journ. Bomb. Nat. v. 11 (1897) p. 126; Watt, Dict. Econ. Prod. v. 1, p. 17. *A. tomentosum*, W. & A. Prodr. p. 56; Dalz. & Gibs. p. 18.—Flowers: Jan.–June. VERN. *Kasili*; *Karandi*.

Widely distributed throughout the Presidency. KONKAN: *Stocks*! DECCAN: widely, *Woodrow*; Poona, *Cooke*!; Nasik, *Woodrow*!; Lasalgaon, *Ranade*! GUJARAT: Surat, *Dalzell*! SIND: Karachi to Mugger Peer, *Perry*!; Karachi, *Cooke*!

7. **Abutilon graveolens,** *Wight et Arn. Prodr.* (1834) p. 56. Stems with long spreading scattered hairs, and also with a sticky covering of much shorter hairs. Leaves 2–3 in. in diam., deeply cordate, shortly acuminate; petioles 1–2 in. long. Pedicels jointed above the middle. Calyx-lobes more pointed than in *A. muticum* and not so villous. Corolla large, orange-yellow. Carpels 15–20, acute, not awned. Seeds with minute, shining, stellate hairs. Fl. B. I. v. 1, p. 327; E. Bak. in Journ. Bot. v. 31 (Lond. 1893) p. 213; Woodr. in Journ. Bomb. Nat. v. 11 (1897) p. 126; Watt, Dict. Econ. Prod. v. 1, p. 16; *not* Grah. Cat. p. 15.—Flowers in the cold season. VERN. *Barkanghi*.

SIND: Sehwan, *Woodrow*.—DISTRIB. Extends from tropical Africa to Queensland. There is no specimen of this plant from Sind or from Bombay in Herb. Kew.

8. **Abutilon crispum,** *Medik. Malv. Fam.* (1787) p. 29 (*cryspum*). A large annual, more or less hairy; young parts tomentose. Leaves 2½–3 by 2 in., ovate, cordate, acuminate, crenate-toothed; petioles ½–1½ in. long. Pedicels ½–1½ in. long, axillary, solitary, or 2 together of different lengths, filiform, jointed above the middle, bent down in fruit. Calyx ⅛ in. long, divided below the middle; lobes lanceolate. Corolla ½ in. in diam., yellow. Fruit ⅓ in. in diam., globose, bladdery, wrinkled; carpels 10–12, awnless, when ripe sparsely hairy with a silky lustre on the sides. Seeds very small, reniform, brownish-black with scattered minute glistening hairs. Fl. B. I. v. 1, p. 327; K. Schum. in Mart. Bras. v. 12, part 3, p. 382, t. 70; E. Bak. in Journ. Bot. v. 31 (Lond. 1893) p. 213; Trim. Fl. Ceyl. v. 1, p. 146; Woodr. in Journ. Bomb. Nat. v. 11 (1897) p. 127.—Flowers: Oct.–Nov.

A rare plant. S. M. COUNTRY: Dharwar, *Woodrow*; Badami, *Cooke*!—DISTRIB. In most tropical and subtropical regions.

9. **Abutilon ramosum,** *Guill., Perr. et A. Rich., Fl. Senegamb.* v. 1 (1830) p. 68. Shrubby, erect, 4–5 ft. high, with ash-colored bark, minutely hairy. Leaves 2–5 in. in diam., cordate, angular, often subtrilobate; petioles 2–4 in. long; stipules subulate, $\frac{1}{2}$ in. long. Pedicels $\frac{1}{2}$–$1\frac{1}{2}$ in. long, frequently divided into 2 branches near the top, jointed not far below the calyx. Calyx $\frac{1}{4}$–$\frac{1}{3}$ in. long, divided to the middle, viscous-pubescent; lobes ovate, cuspidate. Corolla $\frac{2}{3}$ in. in diam., yellow. Fruit short, cylindric; carpels 8–10, glutinous-pubescent, $\frac{1}{3}$ in. long, acute, mucronate. Seeds dull, furfuraceous-dotted. Fl. B. I. v. 1, p. 328; E. Bak. in Journ. Bot. v. 31 (Lond. 1893) p. 75; Woodr. in Journ. Bomb. Nat. v. 11 (1897) p. 127. *A. sidoides*, Dalz. & Gibs. p. 18.—Flowers: Dec.

A rare plant. Gujarat: Ahmedabad, *Cooke*! Cambay; *Dalzell*! Sind: Karachi, *Woodrow*.—Distrib. Tropical Africa, Arabia.

10. **Abutilon fruticosum,** *Guill., Perr. et A. Rich., Fl. Senegamb.* v. 1 (1830) p. 70. A much-branched rigid undershrub, closely hoary. Leaves $\frac{1}{2}$–2 in. long, deeply cordate, ovate-oblong, acute or obtuse, often regularly crenate, sometimes toothed; petioles $\frac{1}{2}$–$1\frac{1}{2}$ in. long. Pedicels $\frac{1}{2}$–$1\frac{1}{4}$ in. long, axillary, scattered, slender, jointed near the top. Calyx $\frac{1}{4}$ in. long, divided more than half way down; lobes ovate, acute or mucronate. Corolla $\frac{3}{4}$ in. in diam., yellow. Fruit $\frac{1}{3}$ in. long, cylindric; carpels 10, grey-tomentose, truncate, not beaked. Seeds small, brown, dotted with minute white hooked hairs. Fl. B. I. v. 1, p. 328; Boiss. Fl. Orient. v. 1, p. 836; E. Bak. in Journ. Bot. v. 31 (Lond. 1893) p. 214; Woodr. in Journ. Bomb. Nat. v. 11 (1897) p. 127.—Flowers: Aug.-Sept. Unlike other Abutilons, the flowers open at mid-day (*Dalzell* MS. in Herb. Kew.). Vern. *Pát-til.*

Sind: *Dalzell*!; Jemadar ka Landa, near Karachi, *Stocks*, 371!; Malir, near Karachi, *Woodrow*!

11. **Abutilon cornutum,** *T. Cooke.* Erect, 2 ft. high, grey-tomentose. Leaves orbicular, $2\frac{1}{2}$–3 in. in diam., cordate, very shortly acuminate, subobtuse, slightly crenate-denticulate; petioles up to $3\frac{1}{2}$ in. long; stipules $\frac{5}{16}$ in. long, densely pubescent. Pedicels $\frac{3}{4}$ in. long, slender, jointed above the middle. Calyx $\frac{1}{3}$ in. long, divided more than half way down; lobes ovate with a long mucro. Corolla spreading, flat, 9 lines in diam., expanding in the evening. Carpels 8–10, stellately hairy, $\frac{1}{2}$ in. long, truncate, with strong mucro. Seeds brown, furfuraceous-dotted. *A. cornutum*, Dalzell MS. in Herb. Kew.

Sind: *Dalzell* 8!; Karachi to Mugger Peer, *Perry*!

The following is grown as an ornamental plant and is common in gardens throughout the Presidency:—

Abutilon striatum, Dicks. in Lindl. Bot. Reg. (1839) Miscell. p. 39. A slender erect branching shrub, glabrous even as to the young parts. Leaves long-petioled, broadly ovate, 3- or obsoletely 5-lobed; lobes acuminate or subcuspidate, irregularly coarsely serrate; stipules narrowly linear, oblanceolate, acuminate, spreading, subpersistent. Flowers axillary, large, rosy with white streaks. Dalz. & Gibs. Suppl. p. 8 Gris. Fl. B. W. Ind. p. 79; K. Schum. in Mart. Fl. Bras. v. 12, part 3, p. 426; Firm. Man. Gard. Ind. ed. 3, p. 413. *Abutilon pictum*, Walp. Rep. v. 1, p. 324. *Sida picta*, Gill. in Hook. Bot. Misc. v. 3 p. 154.

Cultivated in gardens.

6. MALACHRA, Linn.

Hispid herbs. Leaves often angled or lobed. Flowers yellow of whitish, in dense heads, with foliaceous involucral bracts. Sepals 5, united into a tube below the middle. Staminal-tube short, truncate or 5-toothed at the apex; filaments numerous. Ovary 5-celled; cells 1-ovuled; styles 10; stigmas capitate. Ripe carpels separating from the axis, indehiscent, smooth. Seeds reniform, ascending.—DISTRIB. Warmer regions of America; species 5–6, of which 1 or 2 have become naturalized in Asia and Africa. The following is one of these:—

1. **Malachra capitata,** *Linn. Syst.* ed. 12, v. 2 (1767) p. 458. A coarsely hispid annual. Leaves 2–3 in. long, cordate, crenate, from orbicular more or less lobed or angled, to ovate and entire; petioles $1\frac{1}{2}$–2 in. long, jointed below the blade; stipules $\frac{1}{2}$–$\frac{7}{8}$ in. long, simple, linear or often 2–3-branched, the branches connate at or near the very base, flat at base, above filiform. Pedicels $\frac{1}{2}$–2 in. long, several of different lengths arranged on a very short stout axillary peduncle, each pedicel carrying a 4-leaved involucre, 3 of the leaves of which are equal, the fourth smaller and attached higher up than the others. Involucral leaves with stiff bristles on the margins and on the nerves beneath, variously lobed and toothed, with a white spot at the base and with 2 opposite ciliate appendages, each $\frac{3}{8}$ in. long, on the short stalk below the blade. Flowers subsessile, 4–6 within the involucre, yellow. Calyx membranous; lobes ovate, acute, prominently margined, the midrib produced into a long bristly point. Carpels 5, rounded on the back, wedge-shaped on the inner side, white when ripe, reticulated with brown veins. Seeds smooth, brown-black. Fl. B. I. v. 1, p. 329; Woodr. in Journ. Bomb. Nat. v. 11 (1897) p. 127; Watt, Dict. Econ. Prod. v. 5, p. 109. *M. rotundifolia*, Schrank, Pl. Rar. Hort. Monac. t. 56; Grah. Cat. p. 13; Dalz. & Gibs. Suppl. p. 9.—Flowers: Sept.-Dec. VERN. *Rán-bhendi*; *Ván-bhendi*.

Very common in waste places in the island of Bombay and, especially, in the marshy, low-lying tract known as the Byculla Flats. The plant, though completely naturalized and a weed in many places in India, is not indigenous. *Graham* (Cat. p. 13) states that it was introduced from Brazil into Bombay by Nimmo as a fibre-plant. The plant produces an excellent fibre, but the expectation of its being used in Bombay as a substitute for Jute has not been realized. For a full account, consult Watt, Dict. Econ. Prod. l. c.

7. URENA, Linn.

Herbaceous tomentose perennials. Leaves usually angled or lobed. Flowers clustered, sessile or shortly pedicelled. Involucral bracts 5, connate at the base, adnate to the tube of the calyx, ultimately rigid. Sepals 5, connate into a cup-shaped calyx. Petals 5, connate below, united to the staminal-tube. Staminal-tube bearing short filaments or subsessile anthers below the truncate or 5-toothed apex. Ovary 5-celled; cells 1-ovuled; branches of the style 10; stigmas capitate.

Ripe carpels 5, muticous, covered with glochidiate spines, separating from a short axis, indehiscent.—DISTRIB. Warmer regions of both hemispheres; species 4–5.

Leaves not divided below the middle.. 1. *U. lobata.*
Leaves divided below the middle.. 2. *U. sinuata.*

1. **Urena lobata,** *Linn. Sp. Pl.* (1753) p. 692. Herbaceous, erect, 2–4 ft. high. Leaves usually broader than long, up to 4½ by 6 in., cordate, serrate or toothed, stellately hairy on both surfaces, roundish, angled; lobes generally acute or acuminate varying in size and number (3–10 or more), not extending half way down, sometimes nearly obsolete; nerves 5–7, prominent beneath, with often a gland at the base of the midrib and sometimes on the 2 adjacent nerves; petioles variable in length, ½–6 in. long, hairy. Pedicels hairy, very short, clustered. Involucral bracts less than ¼ in. long, equalling or slightly exceeding the calyx and alternate with its lobes, linear-oblong, acute, united at the base into a cup, clothed with rigid hairs. Calyx deeply divided; lobes less than ¼ in. long, lanceolate, ciliate. Corolla ⅝ in. long, pink. Capsules pubescent, covered with blunt spines, each spine having 2 straight bristles pointing downwards at an angle from the apex. Seeds rounded on the back, wedge-shaped on the inner side, smooth. Fl. B. I. v. 1, p. 329; Grah. Cat. p. 13; Dalz. & Gibs. p. 18; K. Schum. in Engl. & Prantl, Pflanzenf. v. 3, part 6, p. 45, fig. 19, D, E; Guerke, in Mart. Bras. v. 12, part 3, p. 469; Trim. Fl. Ceyl. v. 1, p. 147; Woodr. in Journ. Bomb. Nat. v. 11 (1897) p. 127; Watt, Dict. Econ. Prod. v. 6, part 4, p. 212.—Flowers: Oct.–Dec. VERN. *Ván-bhendi.*

Widely distributed throughout the Presidency (except Sind); "a common weed," *Dalzell & Gibson.* KONKAN: *Stocks*!, *Law*!; Kalyan, *Woodrow.* DECCAN: Poona, *Jacquemont*, 298! S. M. COUNTRY: Gháts, 40 miles east of Belgaum, *Woodrow*!; Castlerock, *Cooke*!; Párva Ghát, *Ritchie*, 47!—DISTRIB. All tropical regions.

VAR. *scabriuscula*, Mast. in Fl. B. I. v. 1, p. 329. Herbaceous. Leaves roundish, scarcely lobed, with clustered needle-like hairs beneath, hardly tomentose. Woodr. in Journ. Bomb. Nat. v. 11 (1897) p. 127. *U. scabriuscula* (sp.), DC. Prodr. v. 1, p. 441; W. & A. Prodr. p. 46; Dalz. & Gibs. p. 18.—Flowers: Dec.

KONKAN: *Stocks*! DECCAN: Phunda Ghát, *Dalzell & Gibson.* S. M. COUNTRY: Belgaum, *Woodrow*; Ramghát, *Dalzell & Gibson.*

2. **Urena sinuata,** *Linn. Sp. Pl.* (1753) p. 692. Shrubby, 2–4 ft. high. Leaves 1–3 in. long, more or less stellately hairy on both surfaces, cordate or truncate at the base, irregularly lobed to below the middle; lobes 3–5 or more, dilated upwards, with rounded sinuses, serrate or toothed, pale beneath, with, in most cases, a gland near the base of the midrib and sometimes on one or both of the adjoining nerves; petioles ⅜–1½ in. long. Pedicels short, axillary, clustered. Involucral bracts ¼ in. long, linear-oblong, acute, as long as, or slightly longer than the calyx and alternate with its lobes. Calyx minutely pubescent; lobes lanceolate. Corolla rose-colored, ¾–1 in. in diam., handsome. Capsules and seeds as in *U. lobata.* Fl. B. I. v. 1, p. 329; Grah. Cat. p. 13; Guerke, in Mart. Bras. v. 12, part 3, p. 472; Trim. Fl. Ceyl. v. 1, p. 148; Woodr. in Journ. Bomb. Nat. v. 11 (1897) p. 127; Watt, Dict. Econ. Prod. v. 6, part 4, p. 213.—Flowers: Oct.–Nov. VERN. *Jangali-kápas*; *Lichi*; *Rán-kápas.*

Widely distributed throughout the Presidency (except Sind); a common weed, *Dalzell & Gibson.* DECCAN: Poona, *Woodrow*!; Koina Valley, *Cooke*! GUJARAT: Dabhoi, *Woodrow*!; Baroda, *Cooke*! S. M. COUNTRY: Londa, *Woodrow*; Badami, *Cooke*!—DISTRIB. All tropical regions.

8. PAVONIA, Cav.

Herbs or shrubs. Leaves often angled or lobed. Flowers axillary or clustered at the ends of the branches. Involucral bracts 5–∞, nearly or entirely free. Petals 5, connate at the base, adnate to the staminal-tube. Staminal-tube bearing numerous filaments below the truncate or 5-toothed apex. Ovary 5-celled; cells 1-ovuled; styles 10; stigmas capitate. Carpels 5, separating from the axis or more or less 2-valved, never glochidiate. Seed ascending.—*Lass*, Adans. Fam. v. 2 (1763) p. 400.—DISTRIB. Chiefly tropical American; species more than 60.

Invol. bracts 5–6, foliaceous .... 1. *P. glechomifolia.*
Invol. bracts 8–14, subulate.
  Ripe carpels downy, slightly winged; leaves entire .... 2. *P. arabica.*
  Ripe carpels glabrous, narrowly winged; leaves usually lobed.... 3. *P. zeylanica.*
  Ripe carpels unarmed, wingless.......... 4. *P. odorata.*
  Ripe carpels with 3 stout horns and 4 basal appendages......... 5. *P. ceratocarpa.*
  Ripe carpels with 2 short prickles.......... 6. *P. propinqua.*

1. **Pavonia glechomifolia,** *Garcke, in Schweinf. Beitr. Fl. Æthiop.* (1867) p. 54. Shrubby, procumbent. Leaves $1\frac{1}{2}$–$2\frac{1}{4}$ by 1–$1\frac{3}{4}$ in., ovate, cordate, acute, or roundish, more or less 3-lobed, coarsely crenate-serrate, stellately hairy or tomentose; petioles 1–2 in. long, pubescent or hairy; stipules subulate. Pedicels 1 in. long, axillary, solitary, slender, jointed near the flower, stellately hairy. Involucral bracts 5, leafy, $\frac{1}{2}$ in. long, broadly lanceolate, sometimes unequal, much longer than the calyx, connate at the base. Calyx deeply divided; lobes ovate, acute, densely downy. Corolla yellow, longer than the involucre. Carpels muricated and with a serrulate crest. Seeds chestnut-colored, reniform, smooth. Fl. B. I. v. 1, p. 330; Trim. Fl. Ceyl. v. 1, p. 148; Woodr. in Journ. Bomb. Nat. v. 11 (1897) p. 127. *Lebretonia glechomifolia*, A. Rich. Fl. Abyss. v. 1, p. 54.

SIND: *Dalzell*!, *Cooke*!; Jemadar ka Landa, near Karachi, *Stocks*, 497! GUJARAT: Mangrol (coast of Kathiawar), *Woodrow*!—DISTRIB. Arabia, tropical Africa.

2. **Pavonia arabica,** *Steud. Nom.* ed. 2, v. 2 (1841) p. 279 (name only). A much-branched undershrub, stellately downy all over; stem woody. Leaves $\frac{3}{4}$–1 in. long, ovate, cordate, prominently nerved beneath, entire or slightly toothed; petioles $\frac{1}{2}$–1 in. long. Pedicels axillary, solitary, jointed near the flower and with stellate and glandular hairs. Involucral bracts 10–13, linear, hairy, more than twice as long as the calyx, free to the base. Calyx hairy; lobes lanceolate. Corolla pink, more than twice as long as the calyx. Carpels villous, slightly winged. Seeds minutely pubescent. Mast. in Oliv. Fl. Trop. Afr. v. 1, p. 193; Fl. B. I. v. 1, p. 331; Woodr. in Journ. Bomb. Nat. v. 11 (1897) p. 127; Hochst. et Steud. in Schimp. Pl. Abyss. exsicc. 2139.—Flowers in the cold season.

A rare plant. SIND: *Dalzell*!, *Stocks*!; Karachi, *Vicary*!, *Cooke*!—DISTRIB. Abyssinia.

3. **Pavonia zeylanica,** *Cav. Diss.* 3 (1787) p. 134, t. 48, fig. 2. A perennial undershrub, 2–4 ft. high; branches slender, terete. Leaves roundish, ½–1 in. in diam., cordate or truncate at base, usually 3-lobed, the mid-lobe the longest, less commonly entire, dentate, stellately hairy; petioles ½–1¼ in. long, viscous-hairy; stipules filiform. Pedicels 1–1¼ in. long, slender, axillary, solitary, viscous-hairy, jointed about three fourths of their length from the base. Involucral bracts 8–12, free, ⅜–½ in. long, twice the length of the calyx or more. Calyx-lobes lanceolate. Corolla pink, longer than the involucre. Ripe carpels rounded on the back, wedge-shaped, slightly wrinkled, narrowly winged, glabrous, enclosed in the persistent involucre. Seeds brown-black, minutely pubescent. Fl. B. I. v. 1, p. 331; Dalz. & Gibs. p. 21; Trim. Fl. Ceyl. v. 1, p. 149; Woodr. in Journ. Bomb. Nat. v. 11 (1897) p. 127; Watt, Dict. Econ. Prod. v. 6, part 1, p. 116.—Flowers: Nov.

DECCAN: Dongergaon near Ahmednagar, *Cooke*! GUJARAT: Baroda, *Cooke*!; Broach, *Woodrow*!; Kathiawar, *Dalzell*, 11! SIND: *Dalzell*, 11!; Jemadar ka Landa, near Karachi, *Stocks*!—DISTRIB. Tropical Africa, Mauritius, Ceylon.

4. **Pavonia odorata,** *Willd. Sp. Pl.* v. 3 (1800) p. 837. Herbaceous, erect; stem and branches covered with viscous pubescence. Leaves 1–2 in. long, cordate, roundish-ovate, slightly 3–5-lobed or angled; lobes acute, distantly toothed, stellately hairy on both surfaces; petioles up to 2½ in. long, longer than the leaves. Flowers pink, rather longer than in *P. zeylanica*, solitary; pedicels 1–1½ in. long, jointed near the flower. Involucral bracts 10–12, linear, ⅜ in. long, with long white hairs. Carpels usually glabrous, not winged. Fl. B. I. v. 1, p. 331; Trim. Fl. Ceyl. v. 1, p. 149; Watt, Dict. Econ. Prod. v. 6, part 1, p. 115.—Flowers: Oct.

KONKAN: *Stocks*!, *Dalzell*! S. M. COUNTRY: Belgaum, *Ritchie*, 1082!—DISTRIB. Tropical Africa, Ceylon.

5. **Pavonia ceratocarpa,** *Mast. in Fl. B. I.* v. 1 (1874) p. 331. An undershrub, more or less stellately hairy. Leaves 1–2 by ½–1 in., rounded or subcordate at the base, oblong, obtuse, serrate; petioles ½–¾ in. long; stipules ¼ in. long, subulate. Pedicels ¼–½ in. long, jointed near the flower. Involucral bracts 8–10, ciliate, ⅜ in. long, narrow-linear, longer than the calyx, connate at the very base. Calyx densely hispid; lobes ovate, acute. Corolla yellow or red, hairy without, twice as long as the calyx. Carpels muricated, triple-crested, with 3 stout horns and 4 basal wing-like appendages, presenting somewhat the appearance of a bull's head. Woodr. in Journ. Bomb. Nat. v. 1 (1897) p. 127. *Lebretonia* ? Stocks, MS. with description and drawing in Herb. Kew. in Stocks, 482; not *Pavonia ceratocarpa*, Dalz. (!) MS. in Herb. Kew. which is *P. arabica*.—Flowers: Dec.

A very rare plant which appears to occur in Sind only. SIND: *Stocks*, 483!; near Karachi, *Cooke*!

6. **Pavonia propinqua,** *Garcke, in Schweinf. Fl. Æthiop.* v. 1 (1867) p. 55. Suffrutescent, stellately hairy. Leaves 1–4 in. long, subcordate, oblong, crenate, stellately hairy; petioles shorter than the leaves; stipules subulate. Pedicels axillary, solitary or clustered at the ends of the branches. Involucral bracts 10, free or slightly connate at the very base, closely ciliate, lanceolate, longer than the calyx. Calyx-lobes ovate-

lanceolate. Corolla yellow, longer than the involucre, 1 in. in diam., conspicuously veined. Fruit subglobose, depressed. Carpels woody, with 2 short prickles. Fl. B. I. v. 1, p. 332. *P. grewioides*, Boiss. Fl. Orient. v. 1, p. 837.

SIND: *Stocks* (*fide* Mast. in Fl. B. I. l. c.). I have not seen any specimens of this plant from Sind.—DISTRIB. Beluchistan, Abyssinia.

9. DECASCHISTIA, Wight & Arn.

Tomentose shrubs. Leaves lobed or entire. Flowers shortly pedicelled, collected in the uppermost axils or at the tops of the branches. Involucral bracts 10. Calyx 5-divided. Staminal-tube bearing numerous filaments below the apex. Ovary 10-celled; cells 1-ovuled; branches of the style 10; stigmas capitate. Capsule loculicidally 10-valved. Seeds reniform, ascending.—DISTRIB. Exclusively Indian; species 2.

1. **Decaschistia trilobata,** *Wight, Ic.* v. 1 (1840) t. 88. Shrubby, erect, tomentose and with fulvous stellate and simple hairs. Leaves up to 4½ by 3½ in., 3-lobed, the lobes of the lower broader than those of the upper, the uppermost leaves often undivided and subsessile; lobes usually oblong, mucronate, dentate, prominently nerved and veined beneath, the upper side dark-colored, the lower paler, all hairy and tomentose, often with a gland at the base of the midrib; petioles very short; stipules ¾ in. long, linear-subulate, often bi- or tri-fid. Pedicels ¼ in. long, axillary. Involucral bracts 10, linear, acute, ⅝ in. long, connate near the base into a cup, hairy. Calyx ½-⅝ in. long, divided to about the middle, clothed with fulvous hairs; lobes ovate, acute or acuminate. Corolla 2 in. in diam., yellow with purple centre, hairy outside. Capsules hispid. Seeds smooth. Fl. B. I. v. 1, p. 332; Grah. Cat. p. 14; Dalz. & Gibs. p. 21; Talb. Trees, Bomb. p. 19; Woodr. Journ. Bomb. Nat. v. 11 (1897) p. 127.—Flowers: Oct.-Nov.

KONKAN: *Talbot*; S. Konkan, *Law*!; Amboli Ghát, *Woodrow*! S. M. COUNTRY: Belgaum, *Ritchie*, 53!; Castlerock, very abundant, *Cooke*! N. KANARA: *Talbot*, 113!; Supa Gháts, *Talbot*.

10. SENRA, Cav.

A softly-canescent undershrub. Leaves cordate, orbicular, 3-lobed. Flowers axillary, shortly pedicelled; petals purple or yellow spotted with purple. Involucral bracts 3, large, cordate, free, at length membranous. Calyx 5-divided. Staminal-tube bearing numerous filaments below the apex. Ovary 5-celled; cells 2-ovuled; branches of the style 5, dilated above, obliquely truncate and stigmatose at the apex. Capsule loculicidally 5-valved. Seeds, by suppression, solitary, reniform, ascending, usually pubescent or villous. Species 1.

1. **Senra incana,** *Cav. Diss.* 2 (1786) p. 83, t. 35, fig. 3 (*Serra*) p. 104 (*Senra*). Erect or sometimes climbing, not much-branched, softly downy. Leaves toothed, 3-lobed (the mid-lobe the largest), deltoid; petioles ¾-1¾ in. long. Pedicels ⅛-½ in. long, solitary or clustered, more crowded towards the ends of the branches. Involucral bracts often ⅞ in. long, reticulately veined. Calyx ¼-⅜ in. long, campanulate, membranous, much shorter than the corolla; lobes triangular, acute. Corolla ¾-⅞ in. long, usually violet, rarely yellow. Capsules wrinkled. Seeds hairy,

brown. Fl. B. I. v. 1, p. 334; K. Schum. in Engl. & Prantl, Pflanzenf. v. 3, part 6, p. 48, fig. 20, E, F; Woodr. in Journ. Bomb. Nat. v. 11 (1897) p. 127.—Flowers: Nov.-Jan.

SIND: hills in Sind, *Stocks*, 503!, *Dalzell*, 2!, *Vicary*!; Moach, near Karachi, very abundant, *Cooke*!; Jemadar ka Landa, near Karachi, *Stocks*!

It is a mistake to suppose that this plant grows *on rocks*. Together with *Gossypium Stocksii*, it is found very plentifully near Karachi, on an extensive plain over which some boulders or outliers are sparingly scattered. It is also common on some of the Sind hills (*Stocks*).—DISTRIB. Arabia, Abyssinia, Nubia.

11. **HIBISCUS,** Linn.

Herbs or shrubs, rarely trees. Flowers axillary or solitary or in a terminal raceme. Leaves various, usually more or less palmately lobed. Involucral bracts 4–12 (rarely 0), free, or connate. Sepals 5, valvate, more or less combined into a 5-lobed calyx, sometimes spathaceous and circumsciss. Staminal-tube truncate or 5-toothed at the apex; filaments numerous. Ovary 5-celled; ovules 3 or more in each cell; styles 5, more or less connate; stigma capitate or spathulate. Capsule loculicidally 5-valved, sometimes with false dissepiments forming a spuriously 10-celled fruit. Seeds numerous, reniform, subglobose, rarely obovoid, glabrous, tomentose or woolly.—DISTRIB. Chiefly in the tropical regions of both hemispheres; species about 150.

Capsule 5-celled.
- Calyx membranous, inflated .... 1. *H. Trionum.*
- Calyx not inflated.
  - Invol. bracts distinct, 8–12, forked or provided with a leafy appendage.
    - Stipules semi-cordate, auricled .... 2. *H. surattensis.*
    - Stipules lanceolate .... 3. *H. furcatus.*
    - Stipules linear .... 4. *H. radiatus.*
  - Invol. bracts without appendages; seeds cottony.
    - Leaves long and narrow; lower often 3-lobed ...... 5. *H. hirtus.*
    - Leaves broad-ovate, not lobed .... 6. *H. micranthus.*
    - Leaves obovate, retuse or truncate, cuneate at base. 7. *H. sindicus.*
    - Leaves deeply 3–7-lobed .... 8. *H. intermedius.*
  - Invol. bracts 0; seeds smooth .... 9. *H. Solandra.*
  - Invol. bracts without appendages, sometimes adnate to the calyx-tube; seeds smooth, tubercled or hairy, not cottony.
    - Involucral bracts not adnate to the calyx-tube.
      - A tree; invol. bracts foliaceous, free; seeds glabrous .... 10. *H. collinus.*
      - An undershrub; invol. bracts flat, linear, connate at the base; seeds muricated .... 16. *H. punctatus.*
      - Herbs.
        - Invol. bracts connate at the base.
          - Invol. bracts narrow-linear; seeds with minute stellate scales .... 11. *H. lunariifolius.*
          - Invol. bracts spathulate; seeds shaggy ...... 12. *H. panduræformis.*
        - Invol. bracts free.
          - Invol. bracts linear, shorter than the calyx.
            - Calyx-lobes eglandular at base; capsule 5-winged .... 13. *H. vitifolius.*
            - Calyx-lobes with an obovate gland at base; capsule not winged .... 14. *H. cannabinus.*
          - Invol. bracts subspinous, longer than the calyx .... 15. *H. cæsius.*

Invol. bracts adnate to the calyx-tube, accrescent, thick, fleshy, purple .... 17. *H. Sabdariffa.*
Calyx elongate, spathaceous, circumsciss.
Invol. bracts 4–6, broad, leafy.
Invol. bracts 4, distinct .... 19. *H. tetraphyllus.*
Invol. bracts 4, connate for their entire length......... 20. *H. angulosus.*
Invol. bracts 5–6, fugacious .... 18. *H. ficulneus.*
Invol. bracts more than 5, linear.
Invol. bracts shorter than the calyx .... 21. *H. Abelmoschus.*
Invol. bracts equalling the calyx .... 22. *H. esculentus.*
Capsule with false dissepiments, spuriously 10-celled.
Invol. bracts connate at the base.
A tree .... 23. *H. tiliaceus.*

1. **Hibiscus Trionum,** *Linn. Sp. Pl.* (1753) p. 697. Annual, more or less clothed with stellate hairs. Leaves 1–1½ in. long, palmately divided to the base (the lower leaves sometimes orbicular and undivided); lobes usually 3, again variously lobed and toothed; petioles 1–1½ in. long; stipules subulate, clothed with long stiff hairs. Pedicels axillary, longer than the petioles, jointed near the flower. Involucral bracts 8–12, linear-subulate, less than half as long as the calyx, ciliate with long hairs rising from thickened bases. Calyx divided above the middle; lobes broadly ovate, acute, membranous, with many hispid tortuous nerves, which are green at first, afterwards turning purple. Corolla ½ in. in diam., yellow with a purple spot at base. Capsules oblong, obtuse, pubescent. Seeds rounded on the back, dotted with minute, stellate pubescence. Fl. B. I. v. 1, p. 334; K. Schum. in Engl. & Prantl, Pflanzenf. v. 3, part 6, p. 49, fig. 20, J; Woodr. in Journ. Bomb. Nat. v. 11 (1897) p. 127. *H. vesicarius,* Cav. Diss. 3, p. 171, t. 64, fig. 2; Grah. Cat. p. 13; Dalz. & Gibs. p. 19.—Flowers: Aug.–Jan.

Common during the rains, chiefly on black soil, *Dalzell & Gibson.* KONKAN: *Stocks*!; Bombay, *Capt. Geburne*! DECCAN: widely, *Woodrow*!; Poona, *Cooke*! SIND: widely, *Woodrow.*—DISTRIB. Southern Europe and the tropics of the Old World.

2. **Hibiscus surattensis,** *Linn. Sp. Pl.* (1753) p. 696. Erect or trailing; branches slender, sparsely covered with recurved prickles. Leaves up to 2 in. long, from orbicular, or ovate, acute, to palmately 3–5-lobed, with a more or less truncate base, crenate-serrate; petioles 1–1¼ in. long, prickly; stipules broad, leafy, ear-shaped, toothed, ciliate. Pedicels prickly, longer or shorter than the petioles. Involucral bracts 9–12, each consisting of a prickly stalk ⅓ in. long, carrying a spathulate apiculate leaf-like appendage $\frac{5}{16}$ in. long, prolonged downwards into a linear toothed ciliate spur ½ in. long. Calyx membranous, deeply divided; lobes ovate, acuminate, the tips often armed with stout recurved prickles, with colored mid- and marginal-nerves and hairy, sometimes prickly, margins. Corolla yellow, centre dark purple. Capsules ovoid, hairy. Fl. B. I. v. 1, p. 334; Grah. Cat. p. 13; Dalz. & Gibs. p. 20; K. Schum. in Engl. & Prantl, Pflanzenf. v. 3, part 6, p. 48, fig. 20, G; Trim. Fl. Ceyl. v. 1, p. 152; Woodr. in Journ. Bomb. Nat. v. 11 (1897) p. 127; Watt, Dict. Econ. Prod., v. 4, p. 246.—Flowers: Nov.–Dec.

A rare plant. KONKAN: Island of Salsette, *Jacquem. Voy.* 794!; Malabar Hill, Bombay, *Dalzell & Gibson.* KANARA: Kumpta, *Woodrow*!—DISTRIB. Tropical Asia, Africa, Australia.

3. **Hibiscus furcatus,** *Willd. Enum.* (1809) p. 736. Suffrutescent, rambling or climbing; stem thinly covered with recurved prickles from thickened colored bases. Leaves 2½–3 in. long, clothed with appressed hairs, palmately 3–5-lobed, cordate or truncate at the base, prickly on the nerves beneath, crenate-serrate; lobes acute or acuminate; petioles 2–4 in. long, prickly. Calyx enlarged in fruit, deeply divided; lobes lanceolate, hispid with stiff bristles from thickened bases. Involucral bracts 8–12, variable, a prevalent form consisting of a stout stalk, across the top of which is attached a small oblong leafy appendage, which is prolonged upwards into a curved horn, all densely hispid. Flower-buds with a tuft of hairs at the apex; corolla large, 3 in. in diam., yellow with purple centre. Capsules ½ in. long, ovoid, pointed, enclosed in the enlarged calyx. Fl. B. I. v. 1, p. 335; Dalz. & Gibs. p. 19; Talb. Trees, Bomb. p. 19; Trim. Fl. Ceyl. v. 1, p. 152; Woodr. in Journ. Bomb. Nat. v. 11 (1897) p. 127; Watt, Dict. Econ. Prod. v. 4, p. 241.—Flowers: Dec.–Feb.

KONKAN: *Talbot, Stocks*!, *Ritchie*, 58!; Bombay, *Law*!; Sawantwari, *Woodrow*!; Ghâts near Goa, *Cooke*! S. M. COUNTRY: Castlerock, *Cooke*! Ramghât, *Ritchie*!—DISTRIB. Tropics of the Old World.

4. **Hibiscus radiatus,** *Cav. Diss.* 3 (1787) p. 150, t. 54, fig. 2. A tall undershrub, 5–6 ft. high; branches armed with small prickles. Leaves 3 by 2 in., sometimes entire, ovate-acute, usually palmately lobed; lobes narrow- or broad-lanceolate, serrate; petioles up to 3½ in. long, armed with distant prickles; stipules linear, with stiff bristles from spinous or thickened bases. Pedicels ½–1 in. long. Involucral bracts 8–10, very often forked, linear, shorter than the calyx. Calyx-lobes ¾ in. long, ovate, acuminate, with reflexed bristle-pointed prickles on the margins. Corolla large, bell-shaped, yellow with purple base; petals spreading horizontally. Capsules ovoid, beaked, densely hairy. Seeds smooth. Fl. B. I. v. 1, p. 335; Guerke, in Mart. Fl. Bras. v. 12, part 3, p. 559; *not* Woodr. in Journ. Bomb. Nat. v. 11 (1897) p. 127.

DECCAN: Phunda Ghât, *Ritchie*!

A rare plant in the Bombay Presidency. A single fragment, marked as above in Herb. Kew. is the only Bombay specimen I have seen. The plant named *H. radiatus* by Woodrow in Journ. Bomb. Nat. is *H. cæsius*, Garcke.—DISTRIB. Malaya, Java.

5. **Hibiscus hirtus,** *Linn. Sp. Pl.* (1753) p. 694. Shrubby, hairy. Leaves 3–5 by 1–2½ in., oblong, acute or acuminate (the lower often shortly lobed) crenate, serrate, or irregularly toothed, more or less stellately hairy on both surfaces; petioles ½–1½ in. long, hairy; stipules ½ in. long, subulate. Pedicels 1–2½ in. long. Involucral bracts 6–9, subulate, shorter than the calyx. Calyx hairy, divided nearly to the base; lobes ½ in. long, narrow-lanceolate. Corolla about 1 in. in diam., white or occasionally pink. Staminal-tube toothed at the top; anthers in tufts. Capsules globose. Seeds clothed with long white hairs. Fl. B. I. v. 1, p. 335; Grah. Cat. p. 14; Dalz. & Gibs. p. 20; Woodr. in Journ. Bomb. Nat. v. 11 (1897) p. 127.—Flowers: Oct.–Jan. VERN. *Dupári.*

I cannot find the large gland on the underside of the midrib mentioned by *Masters* (Fl. B. I. l. c.).

Very common all along the lower Ghâts. KONKAN: *Stocks*, 13!; Bombay, *Capt. Geburne*!; below Matheran, *Cooke*! DECCAN: Khandala, Poona, Tulligaum, *Woodrow*!; below Phunda Ghât, *Ritchie*, 48!

6. **Hibiscus micranthus,** *Linn. f. Suppl.* (1781) p. 308. Shrubby, erect; branches slender, terete, stellately hairy. Leaves 1-2 in. long (in Sind specimens often smaller), more or less scabrid and hairy, ovate, acute or obtuse, serrate, sometimes cordate; petioles ½-1 in. long, often very short towards the top of the plant; stipules ⅛ in. long, subulate, hairy. Pedicels longer than the petioles, reaching 1¼ in. long, slender, jointed above the middle. Involucral bracts 6, filiform, hairy, longer or shorter than the calyx. Calyx short, deeply divided; lobes lanceolate, hairy. Corolla small, pink or pink and white, stellately hairy outside. Stamens in tufts on the staminal-tube. Capsules ¼-5/16 in. in diam., globose. Seeds reniform, cottony. Fl. B. I. v. 1, p. 335; Dalz. & Gibs. p. 20; Trim. Fl. Ceyl. v. 1, p. 153; Woodr. in Journ. Bomb. Nat. v. 11 (1897) p. 127.—Flowers: Oct.

Common. KONKAN: *Stocks*! DECCAN: Ahmednagar, Tulligaum, *Cooke*!; Poona, *Woodrow*! GUJARAT: Kathiawar, *Dalzell & Gibson*; Broach and Kaira, *Woodrow*! S. M. COUNTRY: *Ritchie*, 210! SIND: widely, *Woodrow*.—DISTRIB. Tropical Africa, Ceylon.

7. **Hibiscus sindicus,** *Stocks, in Hook. Ic. Plant.* (1852) t. 802. A subspinous much-branched shrub, scarcely 1 ft. high; branches terete, light-colored, stellately tomentose. Leaves ½-1 in. long, cuneate, obovate, retuse or truncate, toothed at the top, subsessile, more or less stellately hairy; stipules subulate. Pedicels short, axillary, solitary. Involucral bracts 6-8, linear-acute, connate at the base, much shorter than the calyx. Calyx-lobes lanceolate, longer than the capsule. Flowers very pale yellow; petals longer than the calyx, twisted into a tube below. Anthers in a globose head. Capsules globose, smooth. Seeds clothed with long white wool. Fl. B. I. v. 1, p. 336; Woodr. in Journ. Bomb. Nat. v. 11 (1897) p. 127.

SIND: rare, *Dalzell*, 7!; Jemadar ka Landa, near Karachi, *Stocks*, 450!—DISTRIB. Beluchistan.

8. **Hibiscus intermedius,** *A. Rich. Tent. Fl. Abyss.* v. 1 (1847) p. 58. A weak-stemmed annual; stem slender, hispid with deflexed aculeiform simple or stellate white hairs. Leaves 1-2 in. long, pellucido-punctate, deeply 3-7-lobed (lobes again more or less irregularly lobed or toothed), cordate or truncate at the base, upper surface subglabrous, lower slightly stellately-hairy; petioles 1-2½ in. long. Pedicels axillary, solitary, shorter than the petioles. Involucral bracts strap-shaped, hairy, shorter than, or equalling the calyx. Calyx-lobes lanceolate, hispid on the nerves beneath. Corolla 1 in. long, pale yellow with purple centre, exceeding the calyx. Capsules hispid, beaked. Seeds numerous, black, clothed with minute rigid unicellular shining, more or less tufted hairs. Fl. B. I. v. 1, p. 336; Woodr. in Journ. Bomb. Nat. v. 11 (1897) p. 127. *H. scandens*, Dalz. & Gibs. p. 20.

SIND: *Stocks*, 480!, *Dalzell*, 5! GUJARAT: Kathiawar, *Dalzell*, 5!—DISTRIB. Arabia, tropical Africa.

9. **Hibiscus Solandra,** *L'Hér. Stirp.* v. 1 (1784) p. 103, t. 49. Herbaceous, erect. Leaves orbicular-ovate, obtuse or acute, with a few simple and stellate hairs, crenate (upper leaves often palmately lobed); petioles ¾-1½ in. long, slender. Flowers arranged in a terminal lax raceme; pedicels 1-1½ in. long, jointed near the top. Calyx divided to about the middle, pubescent; lobes lanceolate, prominently 3-nerved. Involucral bracts 0. Corolla 3/16 in. long, white; petals obovate. Capsules

slightly hairy, ovoid, somewhat wrinkled, beaked; beak short, hairy. Seeds smooth, blackish. Fl. B. I. v. 1, p. 336; Trim. Fl. Ceyl. v. 1, p. 155; Woodr. in Journ. Bomb. Nat. v. 11 (1897) p. 127. *Lagunæa lobata*, Willd. Sp. Pl. v. 3, p. 733; Dalz. & Gibs. p. 21.—Flowers: Oct.–Nov.

KONKAN: *Stocks*! S. M. COUNTRY: Dharwar, *Cooke*!; Belgaum, *Stocks & Ritchie*, 973!; near Belgaum, *Dalzell & Gibson*. GUJARAT: *Woodrow*.—DISTRIB. Asia, tropical Africa.

10. **Hibiscus collinus,** *Roxb. Hort. Beng.* (1814) p. 51. Arboreous. Leaves 5 by 4 in., cordate, 3-lobed; lobes acute or acuminate, glabrous, except on the nerves on the upper surface, irregularly toothed; petioles 1–2¾ in. long; stipules subulate. Pedicels 2½ in. long. Involucral bracts ½ by ¼–$\frac{3}{16}$ in., leaf-like, free, lanceolate, about equalling the calyx. Calyx pubescent, divided below the middle; lobes ovate, acute, 1-nerved. Corolla 3 in. across, pink with dark centre. Capsules ¾ in. in diam., globose, slightly pointed, densely covered with fulvous hairs. Seeds smooth. Fl. B. I. v. 1, p. 338; Trim. Fl. Ceyl. v. 1, p. 152; Talb. Trees, Bomb. p. 19; Woodr. in Journ. Bomb. Nat. v. 11 (1897) p. 127; Watt, Dict. Econ. Prod. v. 4, p. 236.—Flowers: Aug.

Cultivated extensively in gardens. KONKAN: *Stocks*!—DISTRIB. Ceylon.

11. **Hibiscus lunariifolius,** *Willd. Sp. Pl.* v. 3 (1800) p. 811. Herbaceous; young parts densely clothed with appressed simple and stellate hairs. Leaves 3–4 in. in diam., orbicular, serrate, cordate with a wide sinus, glabrate when mature, shallowly 3–5-lobed; lobes acuminate; petioles as long as, or longer than the blade; stipules subulate. Flowers axillary, pedicelled, ultimately growing out into a terminal raceme 4–6 in. long; pedicels short and stout. Involucral bracts usually 5, narrow-linear, acute, generally shorter than the calyx. Calyx divided below the middle, sinuses rounded; lobes lanceolate, acuminate. Corolla yellow with a purple centre, 2 in. across. Capsules at first hairy, afterwards subglabrous, beaked. Seeds brown-black, reniform, covered with minute scattered stellate scales. Fl. B. I. v. 1, p. 338; Trim. Fl. Ceyl. v. 1, p. 153.

KANARA: *Ritchie*, 1623! I have only seen one specimen from Bombay, which is in Herb. Kew. marked as above.—DISTRIB. Tropical Africa, Ceylon.

12. **Hibiscus panduræformis,** *Burm. Fl. Ind.* (1768) p. 151, t. 47, fig. 2. Herbaceous, 6–8 ft. high, hoary; stem and branches clothed with rigid hairs. Leaves 2½–3 in. long, cordate, variously lobed, usually acute, irregularly toothed, both surfaces covered with silky hairs; petioles 1½–3½ in. long, hairy. Pedicels stout, axillary, solitary or in pairs, one of each pair much longer than the other, the short pedicel of each pair jointed in the middle. Involucral bracts 6–9, almost free, about half as long as the calyx, linear, dilated upwards, densely ciliate. Calyx ⅝ in. long, hispid; lobes lanceolate, 3-nerved. Corolla yellow with purple centre, hairy outside. Capsules ovoid, very hairy. Seeds shaggy. Fl. B. I. v. 1, p. 338; Dalz. & Gibs. p. 20; Trim. Fl. Ceyl. v. 1, p. 154; Woodr. in Journ. Bomb. Nat. v. 11 (1897) p. 127.—Flowers: Oct.

KONKAN: *Stocks*!; Bombay, *Capt. Geburne*! DECCAN: Chinchwad and Tulligaum (near Poona), *Woodrow*! GUJARAT: Surat, *Dalzell & Gibson*. S. M. COUNTRY: Belgaum, *Ritchie*, 986!, *Cooke*!—DISTRIB. Tropical Africa, Australia, Ceylon.

13. **Hibiscus vitifolius,** *Linn. Sp. Pl.* (1753) p. 696. Herbaceous, more or less hairy and tomentose. Leaves cordate (the lower 4–5 in. across), 3–7-lobed; lobes acute or acuminate, crenate, serrate or toothed, tomentose beneath; petioles 2–3 in. long, hairy. Pedicels axillary, solitary or clustered at the ends of the branches, jointed about the middle, longer (rarely shorter) than the petioles. Involucral bracts 7–12, free, ⅜ in. long, linear, acute, hairy. Calyx ¾ in. long; lobes ½ in. long, ovate, acute, 3–5-nerved. Corolla 2–2½ in. across, sulphur-yellow with a purple centre. Capsules hairy, apiculate, 5-winged, the wings reticulately veined. Seeds brown, minutely tubercled. Fl. B. I. v. 1, p. 338; Grah. Cat. p. 13; Dalz. & Gibs. p. 20; Trim. Fl. Ceyl. v. 1, p. 154; Woodr. in Journ. Bomb. Nat. v. 11 (1897) p. 127; Watt, Dict. Econ. Prod. v. 4, p. 248.—Flowers: Oct.–Dec. VERN. *Ván-kápas.*

KONKAN: *Stocks*!, *Law*!; Revdanda, *Woodrow*!; below Matheran, *Cooke*!; Malwan, *Dalzell & Gibson.* DECCAN: Bahuli (Poona districts), *Woodrow*!; hills in the Deccan, *Stocks*! S. M. COUNTRY: Belgaum, *Ritchie,* 491!—DISTRIB. Tropical Africa, Australia, Ceylon.

14. **Hibiscus cannabinus,** *Linn. Syst. Nat.* (1759) p. 1149. A shrub with prickly stems. Leaves 2 in. across, glabrous, cordate (those near the base often undivided), roundish-ovate, the upper deeply palmately 3–5-lobed; lobes usually narrow-lanceolate, serrate; petioles 1½–2 in. long, sometimes prickly; stipules ⅜ in. long, subulate. Pedicels axillary, very short. Involucral bracts 7–10, free, ⅜ in. long, linear, acute, often with prickly margins, shorter than the calyx. Calyx (in fruit) 1 in. long, divided three fourths of the way down; lobes long, lanceolate, very acute, with a strong midrib and thickened, often prickly, margins, and with an oblong-obovate gland at the base of each lobe. Corolla yellow with purple centre. Capsules ovoid, beaked, very hairy. Seeds large, brown, dotted with minute stellate scales. Fl. B. I. v. 1, p. 339; Grah. Cat. p. 13; Dalz. & Gibs. p. 20; Woodr. in Journ. Bomb. Nat. v. 11 (1897) p. 127; Watt, Dict. Econ. Prod. v. 4, p. 231.—Flowers: Jan. VERN. *Ambádi.*

Said to be found wild on the Gháts, but largely cultivated for its fibre, which is extensively employed by the natives in the manufacture of ropes, coarse sacking and other articles required for agricultural purposes. For a full account consult Watt, Dict. Econ. Prod. l. c.—DISTRIB. Cultivated in most tropical countries.

15. **Hibiscus cæsius,** *Garcke, in Oester. Bot. Zeit.* (1849) p. 850, & *in Peters, Reise Mossamb.* p. 125. Herbaceous, erect, 4–5 ft. high; stem and branches light-colored, terete, with a few, often bristle-pointed prickles. Leaves 3–5-partite; segments ½–2 in. long, lanceolate, sharply serrate, more or less stellately hairy; petioles 1½–2 in. long, with a few small prickly and scattered bristles; stipules ½ in. long, subulate, with long hairs. Pedicels up to 4 in. long, jointed near the flower, slender, with a few small prickles below, the prickles longer and more numerous above the joint. Involucral bracts usually 10, free, 1–1½ in. long, straight or very slightly curved, spreading like a ray beneath the flower, subspinous, prickly. Calyx ⅞ in. long, divided nearly to the base; lobes lanceolate, strongly nerved, distantly ciliate. Corolla large, yellow with purple centre, stellately hairy on the outside. Capsules ovoid, pointed; valves setose. Seeds pilose. *H. pentaphyllus,* Muell. Fragm. Austr. v. 2, p. 13; Oliv. Fl. Trop. Afr. v. 1, p. 198. *H. heptaphyllus,* Dalz. & Gibs.

p. 20. *H. Gibsoni*, Stocks, in Harv. et Sond. Fl. Capensis, v. 2, p. 587; Fl. B. I. v. 1, p. 339. *H. radiatus*, Woodr. in Journ. Bomb. Nat. v. 11 (1897) p. 127.—Flowers: Sept.-Oct.

DECCAN: (rare) *Stocks*!; N. Deccan, *Gibson*!; Junnar (Poona districts), *Cooke*!; Dhulia, *Woodrow*!; Mountain valleys, Eastern side of the Northern Ghâts, *Dalzell & Gibson*.—DISTRIB. Afghanistan, N. Australia, S. Africa.

16. **Hibiscus punctatus,** *Dalz. in Dalz. & Gibs. Bomb. Fl.* (1861) p. 20. Suffruticose, 3–4 ft. high, scarcely branched. Leaves 1–3½ in. long, pellucido-punctate, ovate, obtuse, unequally 3-lobed (the mid-lobe very long), sinuate-dentate, with scattered stellate hairs on both surfaces; petioles 1–3 in. long; stipules small, linear-lanceolate. Pedicels ½–2½ in. long, jointed near the flower, solitary, or clustered at the ends of the branches. Involucral bracts 8–10, flat, linear, acute, $\frac{3}{16}$ in. long, connate at the base. Calyx ⅜ in. long, covered with dense stellate tomentum, divided to the middle; lobes lanceolate. Flowers pale rose-colored. Capsules ovoid, nearly as long as the calyx, pubescent, with a short beak. Seeds muricated, black. Fl. B. I. v. 1, p. 340; Woodr. in Journ. Bomb. Nat. v. 11 (1897) p. 127.—Flowers: Aug.-Dec.

GUJARAT: Broach Collectorate (rare), *Dalzell & Gibson*; Surat, *Dalzell*! SIND: *Stocks*!; Karachi, *Woodrow*!, *Cooke*!; Jemadar ka Landa, near Karachi, *Stocks*!

17. **Hibiscus Sabdariffa,** *Linn. Sp. Pl.* (1753) p. 695. Annual, erect, glabrous, unarmed; stem and branches purple. Leaves 2–3 in. long, cuneate at the base, usually 3-5-lobed (the lower leaves sometimes entire); lobes lanceolate or oblong, the mid-lobe the longest, serrate, glandular on the midrib beneath, often blotched with purple; petioles 1½–2½ in. long, reddish-purple; stipules ½ in. long, linear, acute. Pedicels axillary, very short, stout, jointed near the base, purple. Involucral bracts 10, lanceolate, shorter than the calyx, adnate to its base, purple. Calyx fleshy; lobes lanceolate, 3-nerved, purple, and, together with the involucre, accrescent in fruit. Corolla purple with darker centre. Capsules ovoid, beaked, hairy. Seeds large, black-brown, closely covered with minute stout stellate hairs. Fl. B. I. v. 1, p. 340; Guerke, in Mart. Fl. Bras. v. 12, part 3, p. 556; Woodr. in Journ. Bomb. Nat. v. 11 (1897) p. 127; Watt, Dict. Econ. Prod. v. 4, p. 243. *H. Subdariffa*, Dalz. & Gibs. Suppl. p. 7.—Flowers: Oct.-Dec. VERN. *Lál-* or *Támbadi-ambádi.*

Cultivated throughout the Presidency, especially in Gujarat. A strong fibre may be obtained from the stems, and an agreeable acid jelly is made from the succulent calyces. The plant is known to Anglo-Indians as the *Rozelle*, and is the *Red Sorrel* of the West Indies. For a full account of its mode of cultivation and uses, see Watt, Dict. Econ. Prod. l. c.—DISTRIB. Tropics of the Old World.

18. **Hibiscus ficulneus,** *Linn. Sp. Pl.* (1753) p. 695. Annual, usually prickly. Leaves cordate, orbicular, angled or palmately 3–5-lobed; lobes with wide sinuses, slightly hairy, coarsely crenate; petioles 3 in. long; stipules ¼ in. long, narrow-linear, acute, slightly hairy. Pedicels shorter than the petioles, axillary or in a lax raceme. Involucral bracts 5–6, broadly lanceolate, villous on both surfaces, caducous. Calyx spathaceous, ¾ in. long, densely villous. Corolla 1¼ in. long. Capsules 1⅝ in. long, ovoid, hairy, with a long slightly curved beak. Seeds round, black, sulcate, faintly pubescent. Fl. B. I. v. 1, p. 340;

Woodr. in Journ. Bomb. Nat. v. 11 (1897) p. 127; Watt, Dict. Econ. Prod. v. 4, p. 240. *Abelmoschus ficulneus*, W. & A. Prodr. p. 53; Grah. Cat. p. 14.

Yields an excellent fibre, which Roxburgh considered the best fibre produced from any of the species of *Hibiscus* with which he had experimented.

Not common in the Bombay Presidency. KONKAN: *Stocks*!, *Ritchie*, 57!, *Cooke*! —DISTRIB. Tropics of the Old World.

19. **Hibiscus tetraphyllus,** *Roxb. Hort. Beng.* (1814) p. 52. A large annual erect hairy plant, 4–6 ft. high; stems with small scattered prickles. Leaves $3\frac{1}{2}$ in. long, scabrid with short stiff hairs, cordate, serrate, acutely angled or more or less palmately 5–7-lobed; lobes again variously divided, usually acuminate; petioles 2–5 in. long, prickly. Stipules $\frac{3}{8}$ in. long, linear-lanceolate, with stiff bristles on the margins. Pedicels less than 1 in. long, axillary and clustered at the ends of the branches, stout, sometimes with a few prickles. Involucral bracts 4, longer or shorter than the calyx, $\frac{1}{2}$–$\frac{3}{4}$ in. long, ovate-lanceolate. Calyx softly villous, within and without, ovoid, acuminate in bud, $\frac{7}{8}$ in. long; sepals connate to the very tip, splitting down one side. Corolla 2–3 in. across, yellow with purple centre. Capsules $1\frac{1}{2}$ in. long, ovoid, 5-angled, hispid, cuspidate. Seeds faintly pubescent. Fl. B. I. v. 1, p. 341; Woodr. in Journ. Bomb. Nat. v. 11 (1897) p. 127; Watt, Dict. Econ. Prod. v. 4, p. 246. *Abelmoschus tetraphyllus*, Grah. Cat. p. 14; Dalz. & Gibs. p. 19. *A. Warreensis*, Dalz. & Gibs. p. 19.—Flowers: Oct. VERN. *Jangali-bhendi*; *Rán-bhendi*.

Common. KONKAN: *Stocks*!, *Dalzell*!; Matheran and Sawantwari, *Cooke*!; Amboli Ghát and Jambalpada (near Pen), *Woodrow*!; Karanja and the Meera Hills, *Dalzell & Gibson*; Girgaum Woods, Bombay, *Graham*. GUJARAT: Bilapur, *Woodrow*! KANARA: *Cooke*!

20. **Hibiscus angulosus,** *Steud. Nom.* ed. 2, v. 1 (1841) p. 758. A large perennial herb; young parts hispid with long rigid simple and stellate hairs. Leaves 4 in. long, cordate, irregularly toothed, deeply 3–5-lobed, hispid when young, more or less glabrate when mature; petioles of lower leaves long, reaching 6 in., those of the upper shorter. Flowers large, 4 in. across, axillary, growing out into a terminal raceme; pedicels reaching 4 in. long, hairy. Involucral bracts 4, ovate, acute, $1\frac{1}{2}$ in. long, completely connate and enclosing the calyx and flower-bud, afterwards splitting down one or more sides, softly hairy within, more or less hispid without, especially on the sutures, generally persistent in fruit. Calyx thin, membranous, pubescent, splitting down one side, caducous. Capsules $1\frac{1}{2}$ in. long, ovoid, acuminate, hairy. Seeds reniform, with pubescent striæ. Fl. B. I. v. 1, p. 341; Trim. Fl. Ceyl. v. 1, p. 156; Woodr. in Journ. Bomb. Nat. v. 11 (1897) p. 128. *Abelmoschus angulosus*, W. & A. Prodr. p. 53.

Wight and Arnott (l. c.) in describing this plant have evidently mistaken the involucre for the calyx and described it as such.

KONKAN: *Stocks*!

The only specimens I have seen from Bombay are those marked as above in Herb. Kew. The plant does not seem to have been found by any other Bombay collectors. —DISTRIB. Ceylon.

21. **Hibiscus Abelmoschus,** *Linn. Sp. Pl.* (1753) p. 696. A tall annual; stems clothed with long deflexed hairs. Leaves polymorphous, more or less cordate, the lower ovate, acute or roundish-angled, the upper palmately 3–7-lobed divided nearly to the base; lobes narrow-acute, or oblong-ovate, crenate, serrate, or irregularly toothed, hairy on both surfaces; petioles 1 in. long, hairy; stipules ½ in. long, subulate, hairy. Pedicels stout, equalling or shorter than the petioles. Involucral bracts 8–12, fulvous-hairy, ⅝ in. long, shorter than the calyx, caducous. Calyx 1¼ in. long, hairy, ovoid, cuspidate in bud; sepals connate, except at the tips, 5-toothed at the apex, splitting down one side. Corolla 3 in. across, yellow with purple centre. Capsules fulvous-hairy, oblong-lanceolate, acute. Seeds subreniform, blackish, with a few raised striæ. Fl. B. I. v. 1, p. 342; Guerke, in Mart. Fl. Bras. v. 12, part 3, p. 570; Trim. Fl. Ceyl. v. 1, p. 156; Woodr. in Journ. Bomb. Nat. v. 11 (1897) p. 128; Watt, Dict. Econ. Prod. v. 4, p. 229. *Abelmoschus moschatus*, Medik. Malv. p. 46; K. Schum. in Engl. & Prantl, Pflanzenf. v. 3, part 6, p. 49, fig. 21, B–F; Grah. Cat. p. 14. *A. muscatus* (?), Dalz. & Gibs. Suppl. p. 7.—Flowers in the cold season. The Musk-mallow. VERN. *Kasturi-bhendi.*

The stems yield an excellent fibre. The seeds when ground are used in perfumery, possessing an odor of musk, and are known in Europe under the title "grains d'ambrette." Consult Watt, Dict. Econ. Prod. l. c.

Cultivated extensively throughout the Presidency and in most tropical countries.—DISTRIB. Tropics of the Old World.

22. **Hibiscus esculentus,** *Linn. Sp. Pl.* (1753) p. 696. Hairy, erect, not prickly. Leaves cordate, 3–5-lobed; lobes oblong, coarsely toothed, scabrous; petioles 6 in. long, hairy; stipules subulate. Pedicels about 1 in. long. Involucral bracts 8–10, deciduous, equalling the calyx. Flowers yellow with purple centre. Staminal-tube antheriferous throughout. Fruit pyramidal-oblong, 6–8-ribbed, 7–9 by 1–1¼ in. Seeds striate, hairy. Fl. B. I. v. 1, p. 343; Guerke, in Mart. Fl. Bras. v. 12, part 3, p. 569; Woodr. in Journ. Bomb. Nat. v. 11 (1897) p. 128; Watt, Dict. Econ. Prod. v. 4, p. 237. *Abelmoschus esculentus*, W. & A. Prodr. p. 53; Dalz. & Gibs. Suppl. p. 7; K. Schum. in Engl. & Prantl, Pflanzenf. v. 3, part 6, p. 48, fig. 20, K.—Flowering time depends on the time of sowing. VERN. *Bhendi*; *Rama-turai*; *Bhajichi-bhendi.*

Extensively cultivated throughout India, where the fruit and seeds are used as a vegetable, and also medicinally, as a demulcent.

The native country of the plant is doubtful, but it is probably of African origin, though naturalized in India.—DISTRIB. Naturalized or cultivated in most tropical countries.

23. **Hibiscus tiliaceus,** *Linn. Sp. Pl.* (1753) p. 694. A tree; young parts pubescent. Leaves 4–5 in. long, cordate, roundish-ovate, abruptly acuminate, finely reticulately veined, entire or crenulate; petioles 1½–2 in. long; stipules subulate. Flowers in terminal racemes; peduncles with a small linear deciduous bract at the base; pedicels short, stout. Involucral bracts 10, connate above the middle, lanceolate, acute, shorter than the calyx, tomentose. Calyx ⅜ in. long, divided nearly to the base; lobes narrow-lanceolate with a prominent mid-nerve, tomentose. Corolla 2–3 in. across, pubescent outside, yellow in the morning, turning red in the afternoon, centre dark crimson. Staminal-

tube antheriferous all the way down. Styles connate $\frac{3}{16}$ in. below the stigmas. Capsule $\frac{1}{2}$ in. in diam., globose, with a short beak, spuriously 10-celled, 5-valved, hidden in the persistent calyx, tomentose. Seeds subreniform, black, sulcate. Fl. B. I. v. 1, p. 343; K. Schum. in Engl. & Prantl, Pflanzenf. v. 3, part 6, p. 48, fig. 20, H; Trim. Fl. Ceyl. v. 1, p. 157; Woodr. in Journ. Bomb. Nat. v. 11 (1897) p. 128; Watt, Dict. Econ. Prod. v. 4, p. 247. *Paritium tiliaceum*, St.-Hil.; W. & A. Prodr. p. 52; Grah. Cat. p. 14; Dalz. & Gibs. p. 19.—Flowers: Jan. VERN. *Belapata*.

Found wild only near the sea. KONKAN: *Talbot*, *Stocks*!; Ratnagiri and banks of the Terricol river, *Dalzell & Gibson*. KANARA: along the sea-coast and banks of tidal rivers, *Talbot*. DECCAN: gardens at Dapoorie (planted), *Gibson*!; gardens in Poona (planted), *Woodrow*!—DISTRIB. All tropical regions.

The tree yields a useful, easily separable fibre, which, according to Roxburgh, gains in strength by tarring. See Watt, Dict. Econ. Prod. l. c.

The following plants of the genus are grown as ornamental plants in gardens throughout the Presidency:—

Hibiscus Rosa-sinensis, Linn. Sp. Pl. (1753) p. 694. Arborescent; stem without prickles. Leaves short-petioled, ovate or ovate-lanceolate, more or less acuminate, irregularly and coarsely serrate towards the top, entire near the base, glabrous on both sides or with a few minute stellate hairs on the nerves beneath; stipules lanceolate-subulate, glabrous. Pedicels axillary, solitary, very long, as long as, or longer than the leaves, jointed above the middle. Involucral bracts 5–7, about half as long as the calyx, lanceolate, glabrous. Calyx divided almost to the middle, puberulous with very minute stellate hairs; lobes $\frac{3}{4}$ in. long, lanceolate. Corolla 3 in. in diam., tubular below, red; petals thrice as long as the calyx. Staminal-tube exserted far beyond the petals. Fl. B. I. v. 1, p. 344; Spr. Syst. v. 3, p. 103; Don, Syst. v. 1, p. 478; Dalz. & Gibs. Suppl. p. 6; Firm. Man. Gard. ed. 3, p. 412; Woodr. Gard. Ind. p. 179, et in Journ. Bomb. Nat. v. 11 (1897) p. 128; Watt, Dict. Econ. Prod. v. 4, p. 242.—In flower during most of the year. The Shoe flower of Anglo-Indians. VERN. *Jasud*.

Cultivated in gardens everywhere throughout India. There is a variety with straw-coloured flowers.

Hibiscus mutabilis, Linn. Sp. Pl. (1753) p. 694. A small tree without prickles. Branches tomentose. Leaves cordate, long-petioled, suborbicular, 5–7-lobed or angled, irregularly crenate-dentate, often entire near the base, more or less softly pubescent or tomentose; stipules linear-lanceolate. Pedicels 4–5 in. long, jointed near the flower, axillary, solitary. Involucral bracts 7–10, linear-lanceolate, shorter than the calyx. Calyx-lobes ovate, acuminate, velvety-pubescent. Corolla 3–4 in. across, spreading, white or pink in the morning, turning red before night; petals almost twice as long as the calyx. Staminal-tube shorter than the corolla. Capsules globose, flattened, hairy. Seeds reniform, hispid. Fl. B. I. v. 1, p. 344; Spr. Syst. v. 3, p. 104; Firm. Man. Gard. ed. 3, p. 411; Woodr. in Journ. Bomb. Nat. v. 11 (1897) p. 128; Watt, Dict. Econ. Prod. v. 4, p. 242. *H. Rosa-mutabilis*, Dalz. & Gibs. Suppl. p. 7.—The Changeable Rose.

Cultivated in gardens throughout India. A native of China.

Hibiscus syriacus, Linn. Sp. Pl. (1753) p. 695. A bushy shrub, 4–5 ft. high, not prickly. Leaves ½–2 in. long, cuneate at the base, the lower ovate or rhomboid-ovate, the upper more or less 3-lobed, repand-toothed, slightly pubescent when young; petioles ½–⅔ in. long, puberulous. Pedicels axillary, shorter than or equalling the petioles. Involucral bracts 6–7, linear, 1-nerved, shorter than the calyx. Calyx scurfy-tomentose; lobes oblong, acute. Corolla lilac-blue, with dark purple eye. Capsules oblong, obtuse, slightly hairy. Seeds pilose. Fl. B. I. v. 1, p. 344; Dalz. & Gibs. Suppl. p. 7; Firm. Man. Gard. ed. 3, p. 411; Woodr. Gard. Ind. p. 181, et in Journ. Bomb. Nat. v. 11 (1897) p. 128; K. Schum. in Engl. & Prantl, Pflanzenf. v. 3, part 6, p. 49, fig. 21.

Cultivated as an ornamental plant in gardens throughout India.—DISTRIB. Warm regions of the Old World.

12. THESPESIA, Soland. ex Corr.

Trees or erect shrubs. Leaves entire, or angularly lobed. Inflorescence axillary, solitary or racemose. Involucral bracts 5, deciduous, or 0. Calyx truncate, 5-toothed. Staminal-tube toothed at the apex. Ovary 4–5-celled; cells few-ovuled; styles club-shaped at the apex, 5-furrowed, or subdivided into erect club-shaped short stigmatiferous branches. Capsule loculicidally dehiscent or almost indehiscent. Seeds glabrous or pubescent. Cotyledons much folded, usually glandular with black dots.—DISTRIB. Tropical Asia, Africa and the Pacific Islands; species about 6.

Leaves 3-lobed .... 1. *T. macrophylla.*
Leaves entire .... 2. *T. populnea.*

1. **Thespesia macrophylla,** *Blume, Bijdr.* (1825) p. 73. A shrub, 3–4 ft. high. Leaves 3–6 in. long, cordate or truncate at the base, 3-lobed; lobes triangular, acuminate, finely reticulately veined, with black glandular dots on the lower surface, subglabrous on the upper; petioles 1½–3½ in. long. Peduncles 3–4 in. long, axillary, 3-flowered; pedicels ¼–½ in. long. Involucral bracts 5, small, subulate, fugacious. Calyx cupular, truncate, persistent; teeth subulate, $\frac{1}{32}$–½ in. long. Corolla 3 in. in diam., yellow with crimson centre. Capsules 1 in. long, ovoid, pointed, 4–5-valved, pilose. Seeds glabrous. *Thespesia Lampas*, Dalz. & Gibs. Bomb. Fl. (1861) p. 19; Fl. B. I. v. 1, p. 345; Talb. Trees, Bomb. p. 19; Woodr. in Journ. Bomb. Nat. v. 11 (1897) p. 128; Watt, Dict. Econ. Prod. v. 6, part 4, p. 45.—Flowers: Aug.–Oct. VERN. *Rân-bhendi.*

The calyx-teeth vary much in length. Most of the Bombay specimens have the minute calyx-teeth described by Dalzell (*l. c.*); in a few they are longer. I have seen specimens from other parts of India with calyx-teeth exceeding ½ in. in length.

Very common along the Western Ghâts. KONKAN: *Dalzell*!, *Stocks*!, *Law*!; Ghâts and Konkan, *Ritchie*! KANARA: in forests, *Talbot.* DECCAN: Khandala, *Cooke*!—DISTRIB. Tropical Africa, Java.

2. **Thespesia populnea,** *Soland. ex Correa, in Ann. Mus.* v. 9 (1807) p. 290. A small tree. Leaves 3–6 in. long, broadly ovate, cordate, acuminate, entire, smooth, finely reticulately veined, with 5–7 prominent nerves and often a glandular pore in one or more of the

intercostal spaces beneath, sometimes with a few minute peltate scales on one or both surfaces; petioles 2–4 in. long; stipules subulate, deciduous. Pedicels 2–3 in. long, axillary, shorter or longer than the petioles. Involucral bracts 0 or 5, lanceolate, shorter than the calyx, caducous. Calyx cupular, truncate, covered with minute peltate scales; teeth minute, sometimes obscure. Corolla 2–3 in. in diam., yellow with purple base. Capsules globose, 1 in. in diam., covered with minute peltate scales, surrounded at the base by the persistent calyx. Seeds $\frac{3}{8}$ in. long, ovoid, channelled along the back, pubescent. Fl. B. I. v. 1, p. 345; Grah. Cat. p. 15; Dalz. & Gibs. p. 18; Talb. Trees, Bomb. p. 19; Woodr. in Journ. Bomb. Nat. v. 11 (1897) p. 128; Watt, Dict. Econ. Prod. v. 6, part 4, p. 45.—Flowers in the cold season. The Tulip or Portia tree; the Bhendy tree. VERN. *Bhendi-ke-jhár.*

Wild along the sea-shores of the districts south of Bombay. Often planted as a roadside tree; abundant along the road which passes through the Marine Lines, Bombay. KONKAN: *Talbot*; Bombay, *Capt. Geburne!*, *Cooke!*, Shrivardhan, *Woodrow.* N. KANARA: along the sea-shore, *Talbot.* S. M. COUNTRY: Dharwar, planted as a roadside tree, *Cooke!*

The wood is fine-grained and tough and has been used for gun-stocks and cart-wheels; the bark affords a strong fibre, which is not, however, of commercial importance. Consult Watt, Dict. Econ. Prod. l. c.—DISTRIB. Tropical Asia and Africa, the Pacific islands; maritime.

13. GOSSYPIUM, Linn.

Erect herbs or shrubs, sometimes subarboreous. Leaves 3–9-lobed, rarely entire. Involucral bracts 3, large, usually cordate, incised, toothed or entire, sprinkled with black dots. Calyx truncate or shortly 5-toothed, sprinkled with black dots. Staminal-tube bearing numerous filaments below the naked, or very rarely, antheriferous apex. Ovary 5-celled; cells many-ovuled; style club-shaped, 5-furrowed; stigmas 5. Capsule loculicidally 3–5-valved. Seeds densely clothed with cottony hairs; cotyledons much folded, sprinkled with black dots.—DISTRIB. Throughout the tropics of the Old and New World; species few.

The synonymy of the forms of *Gossypium* is much complicated from the fact that, owing to the readiness with which the plant admits of hybridisation, many of the commercial cottons are hybrids. The researches of Todaro have recently supplied important additions to our knowledge of the cultivated cottons of the world, and much valuable information, as to the history and cultivation of the Indian cottons, may be obtained from Watt's Dictionary of the Economic Products of India, v. 4, pp. 1–174.

Flowers wholly yellow, or yellow with purple base; invol. bracts laciniate.
  Cotton adherent to the seeds.
    Seeds without underlying down.................................. 1. *G. Stocksii.*
    Seeds with underlying down .... 2. *G. herbaceum.*
  Cotton easily separable from the seeds .... 3. *G. barbadense.*
Flowers wholly purple, or yellow with purple base; invol. bracts subentire or toothed, not laciniate.................................. 4. *G. arboreum.*

1. **Gossypium Stocksii,** *Mast. in Hook. f. Fl. B. I.* v. 1 (1874) p. 346. Shrubby, branching, often climbing. Leaves 1–2½ in. in diam., orbicular, cordate, 3-lobed, the lateral lobes again more or less deeply divided so as to make a 5-lobed leaf, mucronate, palmately nerved, more or less tomentose and with black glandular dots; petioles ¾–1¼ in. long,

sprinkled with black dots; stipules ¼ in. long, lanceolate. Pedicels axillary, jointed, 1-flowered. Involucral bracts up to 1 in. long, oblong-elliptic, not or scarcely cordate at base, palmately nerved, sprinkled like the calyx with black dots, deeply laciniate; segments 8–12, linear-lanceolate, with rounded sinuses. Calyx $\frac{5}{16}$ in. long; lobes short, triangular at base, very acute. Corolla 1 in. long, yellow with purple base; petals toothed. Staminal-tube antheriferous all the way down; anthers reniform. Capsules 3–5-valved; valves mucronate. Seeds wedge-shaped, cottony; cotton yellowish, adherent and close appressed to the seeds, giving them a silky appearance before being pulled out, without underlying down. Talb. Trees, Bomb. p. 20; Woodr. in Journ. Bomb. Nat. v. 11 (1897) p. 128; Watt, Dict. Econ. Prod. v. 4, p. 39. *G. obtusifolium*, Stocks, 469, in Herb. Kew.; Dalz. MS. in Herb. Kew.; Dalz. & Gibs. p. 21.' *G. herbaceum*, Todaro, Cult. Cot. p. 132.—Flowers: Dec. VERN. *Hiragundi-kápas.*

This appears to be the only species in which the involucral bracts are not distinctly cordate.

SIND: *Stocks*, 469 (labelled *G. obtusifolium*) in Herb. Kew.!; *Dalzell* (similarly labelled) in Herb. Kew.!; very abundant at Moach, near Karachi, *Cooke*!

Stocks (n. 469, Herb. Kew.) remarks that it is "*quite wild on limestone hills.*" This has been interpreted to mean that the plant grows *on rocks*, which is far from being the case. It is very abundant on an extensive plain at Moach, near Karachi. The writer, some years ago, planted in the small botanical garden attached to the College of Science at Poona, seeds of *G. Stocksii* collected by him on this plain. The plants grew luxuriantly, showing a strong tendency to become climbers, or at least ramblers.

2. **Gossypium herbaceum,** *Linn. Sp. Pl.* (1753) p. 693. Annual or perennial; stems erect, more or less hairy. Leaves divided to the middle, cordate, usually with a gland on the midrib beneath, 3–5- (sometimes 7-) lobed; lobes broadly ovate, acuminate, shortly mucronate, more or less hairy: petioles twice as long as the pedicels; stipules linear-lanceolate. Involucral bracts ovate obtuse, not gashed below the middle, slightly connate below, the entire portion subrotund. Calyx truncate or obsoletely crenulate, much shorter than the involucre. Corolla yellow with purple base; petals obovate, cuneate. Capsules ovoid-globose, mucronate; cells 6–7-seeded. Seeds 6–7, ovoid, with white cotton overlying a greyish firmly adherent down. Fl. B. I. v. 1, p. 346; Dalz. & Gibs. Suppl. p. 8; Talb. Trees, Bomb. p. 20; Todaro, Cult. Cot. p. 131, t. 4, figs. A, B, C, et t. 11, fig. 13; Watt, Dict. Econ. Prod. v. 4, p. 25.

The species *G. herbaceum* proper, according to Todaro, does not occur in India.

VAR. 1. *Wightianum.* Shrubby; stems erect, somewhat hairy. Leaves, when young, clothed with short thick closely stellate hairs, ovate-rotund, almost obsoletely cordate, 3–5- (rarely 7-) lobed; lobes ovate-oblong, acute, constricted at the base into the rounded sinus, which in the young leaves rises up as a fold; stipules on the pedicels almost ovate, the others linear-lanceolate, acuminate. Pedicels erect in flower, recurved in fruit, ¼ the length of the petioles. Involucral bracts small, slightly united at the base, ovate, cordate, acute, shortly toothed. Corolla yellow with purple base, becoming reddish on the outside after maturity. Capsules small, ovoid, acute, 4-celled with 8 seeds in each cell. Seeds small, ovoid, subrotund; velvet very short and firmly adherent; wool white or whitish-red. *G. Wightianum*, Tod. Cult. Cot. p. 141, t. 4, figs. 1–9, et t. 11, fig. 10; Woodr. in Journ. Bomb. Nat. v. 11 (1897) p. 128; Watt, Dict. Econ. Prod. v. 4, p. 28.

Hinganghat cotton, ex Woodrow l. c. This, according to Todaro, is the principal source of the Indian cotton.

The wild cotton from Badami in Woodrow's list l. c. appears to be a wild condition of *G. Wightianum*, or a hybridised form with perhaps *G. neglectum*.

VAR. 2. *religiosum*, Mast. in Fl. B. I. v. 1, p. 347. Perennial, diffuse. Leaves hairy, 3–5-lobed; lobes triangular, acute; stipules cordate, acuminate. Involucral bracts large, deeply laciniate. Corolla uniformly yellow or yellowish-white. Capsules 4–5-celled, oblong, much pointed. Seeds free, with firmly adherent tawny down; underlying cotton of the same color or white; cotton not easily separable from the seeds. *G. religiosum*, Roxb. Fl. Ind. v. 3, p. 185; Woodr. in Journ. Bomb. Nat. v. 11 (1897) p. 128; Watt, Dict. Econ. Prod. v. 4, p. 16; *not* of Grah. Cat. p. 15; *not* of Dalz. & Gibs. Suppl. p. 8.

A vigorous shrub, thriving in moist sandy soil, ex Woodrow, l. c.

Yields the cotton known as Nankin or Khaki cotton. Its cultivation has been periodically encouraged by Government officials, with a view to obtain *khaki-colored* or *nature-dyed* cotton. Roxburgh was of opinion that the plant came to India from China.

VAR. 3. *hirsutum*, Mast. in Fl. B. I. v. 1, p. 347. Shrubby; young parts hairy. Leaves divided to the middle, 3–5-lobed; lobes triangular. Involucral bracts deeply laciniate, obtuse. Flowers wholly pale yellow without purple base. Capsules ovoid, acute. Seeds free, clothed with closely adherent green or grey down underlying long white wool. *G. hirsutum*, Linn. Sp. Pl. ed. 2, p. 975; Tod. Cult. Cot. p. 210; Parl. Sp. Cot. p. 41, t. 5 (exclud. some syn.); K. Schum. in Engl. & Prantl, Pflanzenf. v. 3, part 6, p. 51, fig. 23; Watt, Dict. Econ. Prod. v. 4, p. 17. *G. barbadense*, var. *Upland Georgian*, Royle, Cot. in India, p. 148, t. 3, fig. 4.

The deeply laciniate involucral bracts resemble those of *G. barbadense*, of which R. Wight considers it to be a variety. The foliage, however, resembles that of *G. herbaceum*, while the cotton is adherent to the seeds which are furnished with underlying down. It is not improbable that it may be a hybrid.

Grown largely in the S. M. Country, especially in the Dharwar Collectorate. The cotton is known as Saw-ginned Dharwar, or Upland Georgian.

3. **Gossypium barbadense,** *Linn. Sp. Pl.* (1753) p. 693. A much-branched shrub reaching 5–8 ft. high, glabrous or the young parts more or less pubescent. Leaves cordate, black-dotted, the midrib or the two lateral nerves with a gland, deeply 3–5-lobed; lobes acuminate; petioles rather long, slender; stipules linear-lanceolate. Pedicels short, stout, often glandular at the top, axillary, solitary. Involucral bracts very large, deeply laciniate. Corolla yellow with purple base. Capsules

3–5-celled, ovoid, acuminate. Seeds free or coherent, black, covered with readily separable cotton, without any underlying down. Fl. B. I. v. 1, p. 347; K. Schum. in Engl. & Prantl, Pflanzenf. v. 3, part 6, p. 52, fig. 24; Todaro, Cult. Cot. p. 234; Guerke, in Mart. Fl. Bras. v. 12, part 3, p. 582; Watt, Dict. Econ. Prod. v. 4, p. 15.

Yields the American varieties known as Barbadoes, Bourbon and Sea Island cottons. It was introduced into Bombay in the early part of the present century, where it failed in Gujarat and all the Northern provinces of the Presidency, but was successfully established in the Dharwar Collectorate, though its yield per acre was not large. (*Dalzell & Gibson*, Bombay Flora, Suppl. p. 8.)

VAR. 1. *brasiliense*. A much-branched shrub. Leaves large, 3–7-lobed with the sinuses rising up as a fold between the lobes. Involucral bracts large, deeply laciniate. Corolla large, wholly yellow or yellow with purple base. Capsules ovoid, acuminate, shorter than the involucre; cells 7–9-seeded. Seeds firmly adhering together; cotton easily separable from the seed, without any underlying down. *G. brasiliense*, Macf. Fl. Jamaica (1837) p. 72 "chain cotton"; Tod. Cult. Cot. p. 265; Woodr. in Journ. Bomb. Nat. v. 11 (1897) p. 128; Watt, Dict. Econ. Prod. v. 4, p. 23. *G. acuminatum*, Dalz. & Gibs. Suppl. p. 8. *G. Vaupellii* (?), Grah. Cat. p. 15. *G. religiosum* (?), Grah. Cat. p. 15.

One of the varieties classed as *kidney-cottons* from the coherent seeds. Pernambuco or Brazilian cotton, an introduction by the Portuguese from Peru or Brazil. (*Dalzell & Gibson*, l. c.)

4. **Gossypium arboreum,** *Linn. Sp. Pl.* (1753) p. 693. Arborescent; branches purple, hairy. Leaves deeply palmately 5–7-lobed, with often an extra tooth in the sinus, coriaceous, subglabrous; lobes linear-oblong, contracted at the base, bristle-tipped; petioles villous, longer than the pedicels, rigid; stipules lanceolate. Pedicels axillary, 1-flowered, jointed above the middle. Involucral bracts cordate, ovate-acute, subentire. Corolla small, purple; petals spreading. Staminal-tube antheriferous for its whole length. Capsule about 1 in. long, oblong, pointed. Seeds free, covered with white cotton not readily separable from the seed, overlying dense greenish velvety down. Fl. B. I. v. 1, p. 347; K. Schum. in Engl. & Prantl, Pflanzenf. v. 3, part 6, p. 52, fig. 25; Woodr. in Journ. Bomb. Nat. v. 11 (1897) p. 128; Watt, Dict. Econ. Prod. v. 4, p. 5. *G. religiosum* and *G. vitifolium* (?), Dalz. & Gibs. Suppl. p. 8.—VERN. *Narma*; *Deva-kápas*.

In gardens and about temples; not grown as a field crop. The cotton, which is of fine quality, is used in making the sacred thread, "Munj"; hence the native name.

VAR. 1. *neglectum*. Shrubby, size dependent on soil and cultivation. Leaves 3–5–7-lobed; lobes narrower than in *G. arboreum*, acute, rarely bristle-tipped, hairy; extra tooth less distinct than in *G. arboreum*. Inflorescence on short lateral branches, 2–4-flowered; corolla yellow with purple centre. Involucral bracts much larger than in *G. arboreum*, with greatly elongate lateral ears, ovate, acute, toothed above. Capsules pointed. Seeds with green velvet down below white cotton. *G. neglectum*, Tod. Cult. Cot. p. 169; Woodr. in Journ. Bomb. Nat. v. 11 (1897) p. 128; Watt, Dict. Econ. Prod. v. 4, p. 7.—VERN. *Deshi* at Ahmednagar, ex Woodrow l. c.

Cultivated in parts of the Deccan, but more extensively in Bengal, Central India, Rajpootana and the N.W. Provinces, as a field crop. The cotton is known commercially as "Bengals."

14. ADANSONIA, Linn.

Trees with a low trunk of great diameter. Leaves digitate; leaflets 3–9; quite entire. Pedicels axillary, 1-flowered. Involucral bracts 2. Flowers large, pendulous. Calyx ovoid or oblong, deeply 5-fid, silky-villous within. Petals 5. Staminal-tube dividing above into numerous longish 1-antheriferous filaments; anthers reniform. Ovary 5–10-celled; cells many-ovuled; style shortly divided at the apex into as many spreading stigmatic branches as there are cells to the ovary. Fruit oblong, woody; cells packed with farinaceous pulp. Seeds reniform, nesting in pulp; hilum lateral; testa thick; albumen thin, membranous; embryo curved. Cotyledons much contortuplicate, enclosing a slightly curved radicle.—DISTRIB. Species 2, one of which is African, the other Australian.

1. **Adansonia digitata,** *Linn. Sp. Pl.* (1753) p. 1190. Trunk of great diameter at base, rapidly narrowing upwards. Leaves deciduous, glabrous; leaflets 2–5 in. long, obovate-oblong, acute or obtuse; petioles up to 6 in. long, villous; petiolules 0–1/8 in. long. Pedicels reaching 8 in. long, softly hairy. Calyx tawny-tomentose outside, grey silky-villous within, divided below the middle; lobes 2 in. long, oblong-lanceolate. Ovary densely villous; style up to 4 in. long, lower part villous. Fl. B. I. v. 1, p. 348; Grah. Cat. p. 16; Dalz. & Gibs. Suppl. p. 9; K. Schum. in Engl. & Prantl, Pflanzenf. v. 3, part 6, p. 59, fig. 28; Talb. Trees, Bomb. p. 20; Woodr. in Journ. Bomb. Nat. v. 11 (1897) p. 128; Watt, Dict. Econ. Prod. v. 1, p. 105.—Flowers: May–June. The Baobab or Monkey-bread tree. VERN. *Gorak-amla*; *Gorak-chinch*.

The tree is not indigenous to India, but has been planted in a few places in the Bombay Presidency. It is supposed to have been introduced from Africa by Arabian traders. The fruit is used medicinally by the natives, who esteem it cooling; the leaves are eaten with their food, and are supposed to restrain excessive perspiration (*Graham*).

There are several trees on the so-called Island of Karanja in Bombay harbour, and a tree, celebrated in Meadows Taylor's romance of Tara, as the tree under which executions used to be held when the Mahomedans were in power at Bijapur, still exists at that place.—DISTRIB. Endemic in tropical Africa.

15. BOMBAX, Linn.

Trees, often lofty. Leaves digitate; leaflets 3–9, subentire. Pedicels axillary or subterminal, solitary or clustered, 1-flowered. Petals 5, narrow or obovate, often pubescent. Calyx cup-shaped, truncate or irregularly 2–5-lobed. Stamens indefinite, inserted at the base of the calyx, adnate to the petals, united into 5 bundles opposite to the petals. Ovary 5-celled; cells many-ovuled; style clavate, 5-gonous or shortly 5-fid. Capsule loculicidally 5-valved; cells very densely woolly within. Seeds obovoid or subglobose, polished or opaque: albumen thin; cotyledons much contortuplicate covering a straight radicle.—DISTRIB. Chiefly tropical American; species about 10.

Trunk prickly; leaflets lanceolate; filaments flattened ...... 1. *B. malabaricum.*
Trunk not prickly; leaflets obovate; filaments filiform ... 2. *B. insigne.*

1. **Bombax malabaricum,** *DC. Prodr.* v. 1 (1824) p. 479. A tall deciduous tree, with straight buttressed trunk and wide-spreading branches; bark grey, covered with hard sharp conical prickles. Leaves large; leaflets 3–7, entire, 3–7 in. long, glabrous, penninerved, reticulately veined, lanceolate or oval, cuspidate, acute at the base; petioles 8 in. long, glabrous; petiolules ½–1 in. long; stipules small, triangular, caducous. Flowers numerous, near the ends of the branches, appearing before the new leaves. Calyx thick, usually 3-lobed; lobes rounded, densely silky within, glabrous without, coming away from the receptacle with the stamens and corolla. Corolla bright red, tomentose on the outside, sparingly pubescent within; petals elliptic-oblong, recurved, with close parallel veins. Stamens more than 60, arranged in 5 bundles of about 9–12 each, and an inner bundle of 15 of which the 5 innermost are longest; filaments flattened, slightly pubescent, rather more than half as long as the petals, connate only at the base of the bundles. Ovary conical, glabrous; style a little longer than the stamens; stigmas 5, linear, ¼ in. long. Capsules 4–5 in. long, ovoid, downy, 5-valved, lined within with white silky hairs. Seeds ⅜ in. long, numerous, ovoid, packed in white cotton. Fl. B. I. v. 1, p. 349; Grah. Cat. p. 16; Woodr. in Journ. Bomb. Nat. v. 11 (1897) p. 128; Watt, Dict. Econ. Prod. v. 1, p. 487. *Salmalia malabarica*, Schott. & Endl. Meletem. p. 35; Dalz. & Gibs. p. 22.—Flowers: Feb.–Mar., when the tree is bare of leaves. The Silk-cotton tree. VERN. *Káte-Sáveri*; *Sávar*; *Sáur.*

The cotton obtained from the capsules, though not well adapted for spinning, is an excellent material for filling beds, cushions and pillows, for which purpose it is extensively used in India and, under the name of *Simal*, exported to Europe. A gum called *Mocha-rus*, employed in native medicine, is also a product of the tree, while the inner bark affords a fibre which can be used in the manufacture of cordage.—See Watt, Dict. Econ. Prod. l. c.

Very common throughout the Presidency. KONKAN: hilly parts, *Graham*; widely, *Woodrow.* DECCAN: Poona, *Cooke*! S. M. COUNTRY: *Law*!

2. **Bombax insigne,** *Wall. Pl. Asiat. Rar.* v. 1 (1830) p. 71, tt. 79, 80. A tree, leafless in the hot season; trunk unarmed; branchlets sometimes prickly. Leaves glabrous; petioles longer than the leaflets; leaflets 7–9, glabrous, 5–6 in. long, obovate, shortly acuminate, attenuate at the base; petiolules ⅕–⅓ in. long. Pedicels ½ in. long, solitary, scattered on the leafless branches, stout, jointed at top. Calyx 1½ in. long, urceolate-globose, truncate or slightly 2-lobed, finally deeply 2-cleft, sometimes prickly outside, densely silky-hairy within. Corolla showy, scarlet or white; petals 5 in. long, narrowed at the base, stellately tomentose outside. Staminal-bundles consisting of 50 or more unequal filiform filaments, about ⅔ the length of the corolla. Ovary ovoid, tomentose (red, *Talbot*); stigma 5-lobed. Capsules oblong, woody, 7–10 in. long, obtusely 5-angular, glabrous. Fl. B. I. v. 1, p. 349;

Talb. Trees, Bomb. p. 21; Woodr. in Journ. Bomb. Nat. v. 11 (1897) p. 128.—Flowers: Feb.–Mar.

Appears to be var. *Wightii* of Prain in Journ. Asiat. Soc. Beng. v. 62 (1893) p. 67.

Southern districts of the Presidency, not common. KANARA: Kaiga Ghát, *Talbot*; N. Kanara, in deciduous forests, *Talbot*; below the fall on the Kála naddi, *Ritchie*, 1629!—DISTRIB. Burma and the Andaman Islands.

16. ERIODENDRON, DC.

Trees unarmed or with thorns. Leaves digitate; leaflets usually entire. Pedicels 1-flowered, axillary, solitary or clustered. Involucral bracts 0. Calyx cup-shaped, truncate or irregularly 3–5-lobed, persistent. Flowers rosy or whitish; petals 5, oblong, slightly connate at the base, pubescent or woolly. Stamens in 5 bundles opposite the petals, connate at base, each bearing 2–3 sinuous or linear anthers. Ovary 5-celled; cells many-ovuled; style cylindric, dilated; stigma obscurely 5-lobed. Capsule woody or coriaceous, oblong, dehiscent by 5 thin deciduous valves, densely woolly within. Seeds obovoid or globose, numerous, enveloped in copious silky cotton; testa crustaceous, polished; albumen thin; cotyledons contortuplicate. DISTRIB. America, tropical Africa; species about 3.

1. **Eriodendron anfractuosum,** *DC. Prodr.* v. 1 (1824) p. 479. A tall tree; trunk prickly when young; branches horizontal, in whorls of 3. Leaves glabrous; petioles 4–6 in. long; leaflets 5–8, lanceolate, 2–5 in. long, cuspidate, entire, glaucous beneath; petiolules $\frac{1}{10}$ in. long; stipules filiform, caducous. Pedicels 1–2 in. long, in clusters of 2–8. Calyx $\frac{1}{2}$–$\frac{3}{4}$ in. long, glabrous outside, hairy at the base within, 5-lobed; lobes rounded or triangular, sometimes almost obsolete. Flowers $1\frac{1}{2}$–2 in. in diam., dirty white, appearing with the young leaves at the ends of the branches; petals twice the length of the calyx, woolly outside. Ovary conical, glabrous. Capsules fusiform, blunt, lined with long white silky hairs. Seeds $\frac{1}{4}$ in. long or more, pyriform, glabrous, black, enveloped in silky wool. Fl. B. I. v. 1, p. 350; Grah. Cat. p. 17; Dalz. & Gibs. p. 22; Trim. Fl. Ceyl. v. 1, p. 161; Talb. Trees, Bomb. p. 21; Woodr. in Journ. Bomb. Nat. v. 11 (1897) p. 129; Watt, Dict. Econ. Prod. v. 3, p. 258.—Flowers: Jan. The White Silk-cotton tree. VERN. *Shameula*; *Pándhari-Sávar*.

The floss from the capsules is used for the same purposes as that of *Bombax malabaricum*, but is of greater commercial value and is largely imported into Europe, where it is known as *Kapok*. The tree is so rare in Bombay that it is not of economic importance in that Presidency.

Very rare in the Bombay Presidency. DECCAN: wild in Khandesh, *Graham*; Khandesh, *Dalzell & Gibson*; Mawal (Poona districts), planted, *Woodrow*!—DISTRIB. S. America, W. Indies, Ceylon.

ORDER XXVI. STERCULIACEÆ.

Herbs, shrubs or trees, usually with soft wood, the herbaceous parts usually with stellate often mixed with simple hairs. Leaves alternate, simple, lobed or digitate, usually stipulate. Inflorescence axillary (rarely terminal), usually cymose. Flowers regular, hermaphrodite or unisexual.

Sepals valvate, more or less combined into a calyx. Petals 5, hypogynous, free or connate at the base or 0. Stamens various; filaments (*a*), united into a column or tube, divided at the apex into 5 teeth or ligulate lobes (*staminodes*), alternating with the petals, and bearing, in the spaces between the staminodes, solitary or 2-5-nate (rarely indefinite), stalked or subsessile anthers; or (*b*), staminodes 0, the column bearing many anthers many-seriate from the middle to the top (*Eriolæna*), or 1-seriate at the top of the cup; or (*c*), the anthers adnate to the top of the column and arranged in a ring or without order (*Sterculia*): or (*d*), fertile stamens 5, almost if not entirely free and alternate with the sepals, staminodes 0 or 5 opposite the sepals. Anthers 2-celled; cells parallel or diverging, rarely confluent at the top (*Helicteres*). Ovary free, 4-5- (rarely 10-12-) celled or reduced to a single carpel; ovules 2-many (rarely 1), in each cell attached to the inner angle, ascending or horizontal, anatropous or amphitropous; raphe ventral or lateral; micropyle inferior; styles as many as the cells of the ovary, distinct or more or less connate. Fruit dry, rarely baccate; carpels sometimes united into a loculicidal or woody indehiscent capsule, sometimes dividing when ripe into cocci, which are indehiscent or dehiscing by 2 valves or follicularly. Seeds not woolly, sometimes arillate; albumen fleshy, thin, or 0; embryo straight or curved; cotyledons foliaceous, flat, folded or convolute, rarely fleshy; radicle short, pointing in different directions in different species.—DISTRIB. Throughout the tropical regions of both hemispheres and in S. Africa and extratropical Australia; genera 41; species more than 500.

Flowers unisexual or polygamous; petals 0.
- Anthers 10 or more .... 1. STERCULIA.
- Anthers 5 .... 2. HERITIERA.

Flowers hermaphrodite; petals present.
- Petals deciduous; andrœcium columnar below, dilated into a cup above; anthers on the margin of the cup, usually alternating with staminodes.
  - Capsule membranous, inflated .... 3. KLEINHOVIA.
  - Capsule woody, not inflated.
    - Anther-cells divaricate; seeds not winged. 4. HELICTERES.
    - Anther-cells parallel; seeds winged........ 5. PTEROSPERMUM.
- Petals deciduous; andrœcium tubular, conical, antheriferous for nearly its whole length; staminodes 0 ... 6. ERIOLÆNA.
- Petals persistent; andrœcium tubular, antheriferous at the margin; anthers alternating with staminodes ... 7. MELHANIA.
- Petals marcescent; andrœcium tubular at the base only; stamens 5, staminodes 0.
  - Ovary 5-celled .... 8. MELOCHIA.
  - Ovary 1-celled .... 9. WALTHERIA.

1. STERCULIA, Linn.

Trees. Leaves undivided, lobed or digitate. Inflorescence paniculate (rarely racemose), usually axillary. Flowers unisexual or polygamous. Calyx 4-5-fid or partite, usually colored. Petals 0. Staminal-column bearing at its apex 10-30 anthers arranged in a ring or without order. Carpels of the ovary 5, subdistinct; ovules 2-many in each carpel; styles connate at the base; stigmas as many as the carpels, free, radiating. Ripe carpels distinct, follicular, sessile or stalked, woody or membranous. Seeds 1-many, naked or rarely winged, sometimes arillate;

albumen bipartite, adhering to the cotyledons; cotyledons flat or slightly undulate, thin or fleshy; radicle near to, or remote from the hilum.—DISTRIB. Warmer regions of both hemispheres, especially in tropical Asia; species about 70.

Follicles coriaceous or woody; seeds not winged.
Leaves digitate .... 1. *S. fœtida.*
Leaves palmately lobed.
Follicles armed with sharp stinging hairs .... 2. *S. urens.*
Follicles rusty villous, without stinging hairs .... 3. *S. villosa.*
Leaves entire not lobed.. 4. *S. guttata.*
Follicles membranous, opening before maturity; seeds few, not winged .... 5. *S. colorata.*
Follicles very large, woody; seeds many, with a corky wing ...... 6. *S. alata.*

1. **Sterculia fœtida,** *Linn. Sp. Pl.* (1753) p. 1008. A large tree; bark whitish, flaking off; branches whorled, horizontal. Leaves digitate, crowded at the ends of the branches; leaflets 5–9, subsessile, 4–7 by 1½–2 in., oblong-lanceolate, acute or acuminate, tapering to the base, pubescent when young, glabrous on both surfaces when mature; petioles 6–9 in. long, terete, grooved; stipules caducous. Flowers 1–1½ in. in diam., in erect racemose panicles 6–8 in. long, formed immediately under the young leaves; pedicels ¾–1 in. long, jointed above the middle. Calyx deeply divided; lobes linear-oblong, subacute, spreading, much longer than the tube, slightly pubescent outside, woolly inside. MALE FLOWERS: Staminal column ⅜ in. long, curved, hairy at the base, bearing 10–15 anthers. FEMALE FLOWERS: Carpels 5, downy; gynophore stout, ¼ in. long. Staminodes subsessile, in a ring beneath the carpels. Styles deflexed, hairy. Follicles 1–5 (commonly 3), 4–5 in. long, boat-shaped, shortly beaked, thick and woody, bright red when ripe, nearly glabrous without, quite glabrous within. Seeds numerous, ¾ in. long, ovoid-oblong, the back with a small yellow caruncle on one side at the base. Fl. B. I. v. 1, p. 354; Grah. Cat. p. 18; Dalz. & Gibs. Suppl. p. 10; Wight, Icon. tt. 181, 364; Trim. Fl. Ceyl. v. 1, p. 164; Talb. Trees, Bomb. p. 22; Woodr. in Journ. Bomb. Nat. v. 11 (1897) p. 129; Watt, Dict. Econ. Prod. v. 6, part 3, p. 362.—Flowers: Mar.–May. VERN. *Jangli-badam*; *Pun.*

Not common in a wild state; often planted. KONKAN: *Law*!, *Stocks*!; Konkan (planted), *Woodrow*!; Bombay, *Capt. Gelurne*!; Mahim and Girgaum Woods (Bombay), *Graham.*

The flowers have a most offensive odor. The seeds are roasted and eaten, especially in times of scarcity.—DISTRIB. East tropical Africa, the Moluccas, North Australia, Ceylon.

2. **Sterculia urens,** *Roxb. Cor. Pl.* v. 1 (1795) p. 25, t. 24. A large tree; young parts more or less pubescent; trunk erect, straight; bark white, smooth, papery, the outer surface thin, peeling off, the inner coat fibrous and netted. Leaves 8–12 in. in diam., crowded at the ends of the branches, shallowly palmately lobed, glabrous or nearly so above, velvety beneath; lobes 5, caudate-acuminate, base cordate; petioles terete, 5–9 in. long, velvety-tomentose. Flowers yellow, numerous, small, ¼–⅜ in. in diam., the hermaphrodite or female mixed with many males, in much-branched glandular-pubescent terminal panicles appearing before the leaves at the ends of the branches. Calyx campanulate, hairy on both surfaces; lobes oblong, acute, about as long as the tube, with a small hairy gland at the base of each lobe. MALE FLOWERS:

Staminal-column short; filaments 10. HERMAPH. FLOWERS: Carpels usually 5, on a short stout gynophore; style short, thick, hairy; stigmas 5. Stamens in a ring round the carpels. Follicles 4–6, ovoid-oblong, 1 in. long, densely pubescent, the pubescence mixed with stinging hairs. Seeds 3–6, oblong, black. Fl. B. I. v. 1, p. 355; Roxb. Hort. Beng. (1814) p. 50; Grah. Cat. p. 18; Dalz. & Gibs. p. 23; Trim. Fl. Ceyl. v. 1, p. 164; Talb. Trees, Bomb. p. 22; Woodr. in Journ. Bomb. Nat. v. 11 (1897) p. 129; Watt, Dict. Econ. Prod. v. 6, part 3, p. 364.—Flowers: Dec.-Feb. VERN. *Kándol*; *Karai*; *Pándruk*.

Common throughout the Konkans. The bark of the tree is white and when the leaves have fallen the tree has the appearance of being dead and withered.

KONKAN: *Stocks*!, *Law*!, *Dalzell*!; Bombay, *Capt. Gelburne*!; Matheran Hill (not reaching the summit), *Cooke*! DECCAN: Khandesh Satpudas, *Talbot*. KANARA: Kála naddi, *Ritchie*, 73! S. M. COUNTRY: N. East of Belgaum, *Ritchie*!; Castlerock, *Woodrow*! GUJARAT: Panch Mahals, *Brandis*!; Dangs, *Woodrow*, 11!—DISTRIB. Assam, Ceylon.

A gum called *Kátila*, which has been used as an inferior substitute for tragacanth, is obtained from the tree; the seeds are roasted and eaten by the poorer natives and in some parts of India are ground and used as a kind of coffee. See Watt, Dict. Econ. Prod. l. c.

3. **Sterculia villosa,** *Roxb. Hort. Beng.* (1814) p. 50. A tree with light-colored bark; branches few, spreading. Leaves 10–18 in. in diam., palmately 5–7-lobed, glabrescent or thinly stellately hairy above, velvety and with spreading hairs intermixed with the pubescence beneath, lobes long-acuminate, base cordate; petioles 6–15 in. long, pubescent, enlarged and very downy near the top; stipules lanceolate, caducous. Flowers pinkish, $\frac{3}{4}$ in. in diam., in much-branched rusty-pubescent terminal panicles 12–14 in. long, males and females intermixed, the males much the more numerous. Calyx campanulate, downy outside, divided to the middle; lobes oblong-lanceolate, acute, nerved. MALE FLOWERS: Staminal-column $\frac{3}{16}$ in. long, recurved; stamens 10. FEMALE FLOWERS: Ovary strigose with stellate hairs; gynophore $\frac{1}{12}$ in. long, stout, cylindric; style stout, hairy, deflexed. Staminodes on a ring beneath the ovary. Follicles about 5, oblong, $1\frac{1}{2}$–2 in. long, spreading, rusty-villous. Seeds oblong, smooth, black. Fl. B. I. v. 1, p. 355; Grah. Cat. p. 18; Dalz. & Gibs. p. 22; Talb. Trees, Bomb. p. 22: Woodr. in Journ. Bomb. Nat. v. 11 (1897) p. 129; Watt, Dict. Econ. Prod. v. 6, part 3, p. 365.—Flowers: Dec.-Feb. VERN. *Sárdol*.

From Gujarat southwards to N. Kanara. KONKAN: *Stocks*!; near Goa, *Dalzell*!; S. Konkan, *Graham*; Vingorla, *Dalzell & Gibson*. KANARA: *Dalzell & Gibson*, *Talbot*; Kála naddi, *Ritchie*, 35! GUJARAT: Gadhivi (Dangs), *Woodrow*.

A valuable fibre is obtained from the *liber* which is made into ropes and bags (*Watt*).

4. **Sterculia guttata,** *Roxb. Hort. Beng.* (1814) p. 50. A tall tree; trunk straight; bark much cracked; young shoots clothed with stellate down. Leaves 5–8 by 3–$4\frac{1}{2}$ in., ovate-oblong, acute or acuminate, glabrous above, stellately pubescent, prominently nerved and reticulately veined beneath, base rounded or subcordate; petioles 1–2 in. long, terete, stout, pubescent; stipules ensiform, caducous. Flowers $\frac{3}{4}$ in. across, yellow spotted with purple, generally arranged in fascicles of 3, along the branches of short rusty-pubescent racemes, the pedicel of the

central flower of each fascicle longer than the others; bracts lanceolate, beneath each flower, that beneath the central flower of each fascicle the larger. Calyx campanulate, densely pubescent without, clothed with stellate hairs within; lobes oblong, subacute, about equalling the tube, ultimately reflexed. MALE FLOWERS: Staminal-column slender, exceeding $\frac{1}{4}$ in. long; anthers 10–12. HERMAPHRODITE FLOWERS: Ovary globose, strigose with stellate hairs; gynophore stout, round, $\frac{1}{4}$ in. long; style stout, deflexed. Follicles 1-5, obovoid, 3 in. long, deep orange-colored, villous without, smooth and pink within. Seeds large, size of a bean, oblong; testa long, brittle. Fl. B. I. v. 1, p. 355; Grah. Cat. p. 17; Dalz. & Gibs. p. 23; Bedd. Flor. Sylvat. t. 105; Trim. Fl. Ceyl. v. 1, p. 165; Talb. Trees, Bomb. p. 22; Woodr. in Journ. Bomb. Nat. v. 11 (1897) p. 129; Watt, Dict. Econ. Prod. v. 6, part 3, p. 363.—Flowers: Jan.-Feb. VERN. *Kukar*; *Goldár*.

Throughout the forests of the Konkan and S. Kanara; common on the Ghâts. KONKAN: *Dalzell!*, *Law!*, *Stocks!*; Bombay, *Capt. Geburne!*; near Ratnagiri, *Woodrow!*; W. Ghâts, *Cooke!*, *Woodrow!* KANARA: S. Kanara, *Dalzell & Gibson*.

5. **Sterculia colorata,** *Roxb. Hort. Beng.* (1814) p. 50. A tree, growing to a great size; trunk erect; bark ash-colored; branches numerous, spreading. Leaves crowded at the ends of the branches, broader than long, 4–8 by 5–9 in., deeply cordate at the base, glabrous or the young leaves pubescent, variable in shape, commonly 3-lobed; lobes triangular, acuminate; main nerves 3–5; petioles 4–12 in. long; stipules lanceolate. Flowers about 1 in. long, numerous, appearing before the leaves, in short terminal panicles densely clothed with orange-red coral-like stellate tomentum. Calyx funnel-shaped; tube very long; lobes $\frac{1}{8}$ in. long, triangular, covered outside with orange-red stellate tomentum, villous at the base inside. Staminal-column $\frac{3}{4}$–$1\frac{1}{4}$ in. long, ultimately exserted, bearing at its top about 30 sessile anthers. Styles short, recurved. Follicles stalked, glabrous, membranous, 3 in. long, opening before maturity; valves flat, leaf-like, elliptic-oblong, veined. Seeds usually 2, one adhering to each margin of the gaping follicle, $\frac{3}{8}$ in. long, ovoid, smooth, yellow. Fl. B. I. v. 1, p. 359; Grah. Cat. p. 17; Dalz. & Gibs. p. 23; Trim. Fl. Ceyl. v. 1, p. 166; Talb. Trees, Bomb. p. 22; Woodr. in Journ. Bomb. Nat. v. 11 (1897) p. 129; Watt, Dict. Econ. Prod. v. 6, part 3, p. 361.—Flowers: Mar.-April. VERN. *Kaushi*.

Throughout the Konkan and Deccan forests. KONKAN: *Stocks!*, *Law!*; Bombay, *Law!*; W. Ghâts, *Woodrow*; Elephanta Hill, *Graham*. DECCAN: jungles in the Deccan, *Dalzell & Gibson*; Lanoli, *Cooke!*, *Kanitkar!* S. M. COUNTRY: jungles north of Belgaum, *Ritchie*, 939!—DISTRIB. Pegu, Ceylon.

6. **Sterculia alata,** *Roxb. Hort. Beng.* (1814) p. 50. A tall tree; trunk straight; bark smooth, ash-colored (not white); young parts covered with dense golden stellate pubescence. Leaves crowded about the ends of the branches, falling before the flowers appear, 4–10 by 3–7 in., ovate, cordate, acute or shortly acuminate, glabrous on both surfaces, 3–7-nerved; petioles 2–$3\frac{1}{2}$ in. long, terete, subglabrous; stipules minute, subulate. Flowers about 1 in. across, in subpanicled few-flowered racemes from the old axils below the leaves; pedicels short; bracts ensiform, caducous. Calyx campanulate, divided almost to the base; lobes 5 (rarely 6), valvate, thick and fleshy, linear-lanceo-

late, coated without with dense ferruginous stellate down, striate within with red and yellow veins. MALE FLOWERS: Staminal-column slender, three-fourths the length of the lobes of the calyx, bearing 5 or 6 very small sterile ovaries at its apex, round which are arranged 4–5 phalanges of subsessile stamens; pollen smooth, yellow. FEMALE or HERMAPHRODITE FLOWERS: Ovaries 5, sessile; ovules numerous; styles very short, pilose, recurved; stigma 2-lobed. Staminodes or stamens round the base of the ovary. Follicles 5, subglobose, about 5 in. in diam., on stalks 1½ in. long, hard and woody, clothed with mealy pubescence without, corky within. Seeds about 40, oblong, compressed, furnished with a corky oblong-obovate wing, which, with the seed, is about 3 by 1½ in.; cotyledons not separable from the mealy albumen; radicle small, close to the hilum. Fl. B. I. v. 1, p. 360; Dalz. & Gibs. Suppl. p. 10; Talb. Trees, Bomb. p. 22; Woodr. in Journ. Bomb. Nat. v. 11 (1897) p. 129; Watt, Dict. Econ. Prod. v. 6, part 3, p. 360. *Sterculia Haynii*, Bedd. Flor. Sylvat. t. 230.

A very rare tree in the Bombay Presidency, the only locality from which it has been reported being the foot of the Burboli Ghát in N. Kanara, where it has been found by *Talbot* and *Woodrow*. It has been planted about Poona and Khandala.—DISTRIB. Chittagong, Pegu and the Andamans.

Sterculia populnifolia, Roxb. Hort. Beng. (1814) p. 50 (erroneously cited as *S. populifolia* in Wight & Arn. Prodr. p. 62, in Fl. B. I. v. 1, p. 361, and in Woodrow's list Journ. Bomb. Nat. v. 11 (1897) p. 129), is not indigenous. It has been planted in the old botanic garden at Hewra (*fide* Woodrow, l. c.).

Sterculia campanulata, Wall., a native of Pegu and Java, has also been planted as an ornamental tree. A tree may be found in the grounds of the hotel at Khandala (*fide* Woodrow, l. c.).

2. HERITIERA, Ait.

Trees. Leaves simple, coriaceous, scaly beneath, penninerved. Flowers small, unisexual, in axillary panicles. Calyx 5-toothed or 5-fid. Petals 0. Staminal-column slender, bearing, in a ring beneath the apex 5 adnate anthers with parallel cells. Carpels of the ovary 5, subdistinct; ovule 1 in each carpel; style short; stigmas 5, thick. Ripe carpels woody, indehiscent, keeled or winged on the back. Seeds exalbuminous; cotyledons thick; radicle next the hilum.—DISTRIB. Tropical Asia, Africa and Australia, near the coast; species 4–5.

1. **Heritiera litoralis,** *Dryand. in Ait. Hort. Kew.* ed. 1, v. 3 (1789) p. 546. A tree, attaining a considerable size; bark longitudinally furrowed; young parts scaly. Leaves 5–8 by 2–4 in., elliptic-oblong, acute or obtuse, glabrous above, entirely covered beneath with minute silvery scales, base rounded or acute; petioles ¾ in. long; stipules small, setaceous, caducous. Flowers small, the females rather larger than the males, in tomentose much-branched drooping axillary panicles in the upper axils shorter than the leaves. Calyx campanulate, 4–6-toothed, clothed on both surfaces with orange-yellow, stellate pubescence; teeth short, ovate, acute. Staminal-column shorter than the calyx; anthers 5, sessile. Carpels of the ovary glabrous; style tapering, much shorter than the calyx. Ripe carpels 1–3, spreading horizontally, 1–3 in. long, broadly ovoid, thick and woody, smooth or tubercled, the dorsal margin

with a broad keel or wing. Seeds 1 in. long. The fruit remains on the tree for a considerable time. Fl. B. I. v. 1, p. 363; Grah. Cat. p. 18; Dalz. & Gibs. p. 22; Bedd. For. Man. in Flor. Sylvat. p. lxxv, t. 11, fig. 6; Trim. Fl. Ceyl. v. 1, p. 167; K. Schum. in Engl. & Prantl, Pflanzenf. v. 3, part 6, p. 99, fig. 51; Talb. Trees, Bomb. p. 22; Watt, Dict. Econ. Prod. v. 4, p. 223.—Flowers: July–Oct. VERN. *Sundri*.

The Looking-glass plant. Rare in the Bombay Presidency. Found along the banks of the Kála naddi and near the coast of N. Kanara and at Karwar, but nowhere abundant (*Talbot*). *Nimmo* (ex *Graham*, l. c.) gives its habitat as S. Konkan, but *Dalzell & Gibson* (Bombay Flora, p. 22) have failed to find it there.—DISTRIB. Tropics of the Old World, near the coast.

3. KLEINHOVIA, Linn.

A tree. Leaves quite entire, 3–7-nerved. Flowers in large terminal panicles; bracts small or remote from the calyx. Sepals 5, at length free, deciduous. Petals unequal, the upper with longer claws, margins involute. Staminal-column elongate, adnate to the gynophore, dilated above into a 5-fid bell-shaped cup, the divisions each with 3 anthers, and alternate teeth without anthers; anthers shortly stalked, cells divaricate, distinct. Ovary inserted within the dilated apex of the staminal-column, 5-lobed, 5-celled; ovules 3–4 in each cell; style slender, at length divided. Capsule membranous, inflated, turbinately 5-lobed, loculicidally 5-valved. Seeds 1 or 2 in each cell, globose, naked, tubercled, exalbuminous; cotyledons spirally twisted; radicle next the hilum.—DISTRIB. One species, Asiatic.

1. **Kleinhovia Hospita,** *Linn. Sp. Pl.* ed. 2 (1763) p. 1365. A middle-sized tree; young shoots and panicles tomentose. Leaves 4–6 by 3–5 in., broadly ovate or suborbicular, cordate, acuminate, palmately 3–5-nerved, glabrous on both surfaces; petioles 1–4 in. long, terete; stipules linear, ¼ in. long. Flowers rosy, in large terminal panicles; pedicels jointed about the middle. Sepals ⅜ in. long, linear, acute, pubescent outside. Petals 5, unequal, shorter than the sepals. Capsules membranous, inflated. Seeds usually 1 in each cell, roundish, tubercled. Fl. B. I. v. 1, p. 364; Grah. Cat. p. 18; Dalz. & Gibs. p. 23, and Suppl. p. 10; K. Schum. in Engl. & Prantl, Pflanzenf. v. 3, part 6, p. 93, fig. 48, B–D; Bedd. For. Man. in Flor. Sylvat. p. xxxiii, t. 4, fig. 4: Talb. Trees, Bomb. p. 22; Woodr. in Journ. Bomb. Nat. v. 11 (1897) p. 129; Oliv. Fl. Trop. Afr. v. 1, p. 226; Watt, Dict. Econ. Prod. v. 4, p. 566.—Flowers: July–Aug.

A handsome tree, planted throughout the Presidency, said by *Nimmo* (ex *Graham*, l. c.) to be found in the S. Konkan. It is probable that an introduced, not an indigenous, plant is referred to. *Beddome* (l. c.) states that it has never been seen by him in any of the southern forests, and *Talbot* does not mention it as growing in the S. Konkan or Kanara. Several trees may be seen growing in the botanical garden of the College of Science at Poona.—DISTRIB. Malaya, East tropical Africa.

4. HELICTERES, Linn.

Trees or shrubs, more or less stellately pubescent. Leaves entire or serrate. Flowers axillary, solitary or fascicled. Calyx tubular, 5-fid at the apex; lobes often unequal. Petals 5, equal, or somewhat 2-lipped, with long claws which sometimes have ear-shaped appendages. Staminal-column elongate, adnate to the gynophore, 5-toothed or 5-lobed at the apex; anthers in groups at the top of the column between its teeth; cells divergent, sometimes confluent. Ovary at the top of the column, 5-lobed, 5-celled; ovules many in each cell; styles 5, subulate, more or less united, slightly thickened and stigmatose at the tips. Follicles spirally twisted or straight. Seeds tubercled; albumen scanty; cotyledons leafy, folded round the radicle which is next the hilum.—DISTRIB. Warmer regions of both hemispheres, chiefly America; species about 30.

1. **Helicteres Isora,** *Linn. Sp. Pl.* (1753) p. 963. A shrub or small tree; young shoots clothed with stellate hairs. Leaves bifarious, 3–5 by 2–4 in., oblong, obovate or roundish, cordate, suddenly and shortly acuminate, closely dotted on both surfaces with stellate hairs, more or less irregularly crenate-serrate; petioles $\frac{1}{4}$–$\frac{3}{8}$ in. long; stipules subulate, $\frac{1}{4}$ in. long. Flowers 1–1$\frac{1}{2}$ in. long, distinctly bilabiate, in axillary clusters of 2–6 together; pedicels very short, stellately tomentose; bracts small, subulate, hairy. Calyx tubular, $\frac{3}{4}$ in. long, somewhat 2-lipped, stellately pubescent without, curved, laterally compressed, mouth wide; teeth triangular, unequal. Petals red at first, fading to lead-color, very unequal, closely reflexed on the calyx, separate but with the claws closely hooked together. Staminal-column fused with the gynophore, much exserted, suddenly deflexed; anthers 10, in a ring round the ovary. Ovary conical, on a curved gynophore 1$\frac{1}{2}$ in. long; style as long as the ovary, deflexed. Follicles 5, beaked, 2–2$\frac{1}{2}$ in. long, linear, twisted together into the form of a screw, stellately tomentose. Seeds numerous, angular; testa loose, wrinkled. Fl. B. I. v. 1, p. 365; Grah. Cat. p. 16; Dalz. & Gibs. p. 22; Trim. Fl. Ceyl. v. 1, p. 168; Pierre, Fl. For. Cochinch. t. 208, B; Talb. Trees, Bomb. p. 23; Woodr. in Journ. Bomb. Nat. v. 11 (1897) p. 129; Watt, Dict. Econ. Prod. v. 4, p. 212.—Flowers: July–Dec. VERN. *Murudseng*; *Kewan*.

Abundant in hilly jungles throughout the Presidency. KONKAN: *Law*!; Salsette, *Jacquem.*, 941!; Koina valley, *Cooke*!, *Woodrow*! DECCAN: hilly parts, *Dalzell & Gibson*. GUJARAT: widely, *Woodrow*. KANARA: abundant in hilly jungles, *Talbot*. S. M. COUNTRY: Belgaum Ghâts, *Ritchie*, 69!; Londa, *Cooke*!, *Woodrow*!; Castlerock, *Cooke*!

A strong fibre has been extracted from the bark and the follicles have been employed medicinally among the natives, but are of doubtful therapeutic value.

5. PTEROSPERMUM, Schreb.

Trees or shrubs, scaly or stellately tomentose. Leaves coriaceous, often oblique, entire or more or less angled or toothed above, penninerved. Peduncles axillary, short, 1- or few-flowered. Flowers often very long; bracts usually 3, entire, laciniate, or 0. Calyx tubular, 5-fid or 5-partite, deciduous. Petals 5, obovate, oblong or linear, deciduous. Staminal-column adnate to the gynophore, bearing 15 fertile stamens and 5 staminodes, the fertile stamens in groups of 3 between the staminodes; anthers stipitate, linear, erect, cells parallel. Ovary inserted within the apex of the column, 5-celled; ovules many in each cell; style entire; stigma 5-furrowed. Capsule woody or coriaceous, ovoid or oblong, terete or angled, loculicidally 5-valved. Seeds ascending, produced above into a wing; albumen thin or 0; cotyledons corrugated or folded; radicle inferior.—DISTRIB. Tropical Asia; species 15.

Leaves deeply cordate and subpeltate........ 2. *P. acerifolium.*
Leaves not or slightly oblique at the base........ 4. *P. Heyneanum.*
Leaves distinctly oblique at the base.
 Invol. bracts entire, bi- or tri-fid........ 1. *P. suberifolium.*
 Invol. bracts pinnatisect........ 3. *P. reticulatum.*

1. **Pterospermum suberifolium,** *Lam. Tab. Encyc. et Méthod.* v. 3 (1823) p. 136, t. 576. A small tree; young parts covered with a light-buff stellate tomentum. Leaves distichous, 2½–4 by 1¼–1¾ in., oblong or obvate-oblong, acuminate, often irregularly angled towards the apex, glabrous above, clothed with a cream-colored tomentum beneath, oblique and rounded at the base; petioles ¼ in. long, tomentose; stipules small, caducous. Flowers fragrant, white, 1½–2 in. across, axillary; buds oblong, prominently 5-ribbed; pedicels thick, jointed, tomentose; involucral bracts 3, a little distant from the flower, entire, bi- or tri-fid, caducous. Calyx divided to the base; sepals linear, subacute, reflexed, stellately tomentose outside, hairy within. Petals slightly shorter than the sepals, lanceolate-oblong, distantly spangled with stellate hairs on the outside when young. Stamens connate into a short tube at the base; anthers linear. Ovary densely silky-villous; ovules 4 in each cell. Capsules 1½–2½ in. long, ovoid-oblong, tapering at both ends, covered with fine white tomentum. Seeds with a broad terminal wing, twice as long as the seed. Fl. B. I. v. 1, p. 367; Grah. Cat. p. 19; Dalz. & Gibs. p. 24; Talb. Trees, Bomb. p. 23; Woodr. in Journ. Bomb. Nat. v. 11 (1897) p. 129; Watt, Dict. Econ. Prod. v. 6, part 1, p. 362.—Flowers: Dec. VERN. *Muchukund.*

In the forests of S. Konkan and Kanara; planted in many places. KONKAN: *Dalzell & Gibson, Graham, Talbot.* DECCAN: planted in the old Botanic Garden Kirkee, *Woodrow*!; Dapudi, near Poona, *Woodrow*! KANARA: S. Ghâts of N. Kanara, *Talbot*; N. Kanara, *Woodrow.*

2. **Pterospermum acerifolium,** *Willd. Sp. Pl.* v. 3 (1800) p. 729. A large tree; bark smooth, ash-colored; young parts clothed with floccose pubescence. Leaves variable in shape and size, 10–14 by 6–12 in., orbicular or oblong, entire or variously lobed, cordate and sometimes peltate, at length glabrous above, clothed beneath with whitish floccose tomentum; petioles 4–12 in. long, terete, tomentose; stipules multifid, caducous. Flowers fragrant, white, axillary, solitary or in pairs; involucral bracts multifid, caducous. Sepals up to 4 in. long, linear-oblong, obtuse, densely tomentose outside, villous in a broad line within. Petals linear-oblong, somewhat obliquely cuneate, slightly shorter than the sepals. Staminodes club-shaped. Ovary oblong, 5-angled, 5-celled; ovules 12–20 in each cell. Capsules 4–6 in. long, oblong, 5-angled, clothed outside with furfuraceous pubescence. Seeds obliquely ovoid, compressed; wing large, thin. The ripe fruit remains for a long time on the tree. Fl. B. I. v. 1, p. 368; Grah. Cat. p. 20; Bedd. For. Man. in Flor. Sylvat. p. xxxv; K. Schum. in Engl. & Prantl, Pflanzenf. v. 3, part 6, p. 93, fig. 48, H; Talb. Trees, Bomb. p. 23; Woodr. in Journ. Bomb. Nat. v. 11 (1897) p. 129; Watt, Dict. Econ. Prod. v. 6, part 1, p. 362.—Flowers: Dec.–Mar. VERN. *Karnikár.*

The tree is extensively planted, but a doubtful native. Stocks! gives the Konkan as its habitat, and Woodrow and Talbot report that it is abundant on the Deviman Ghát in N. Kanara. Graham mentions it as growing in a garden in Kolaba and in the Girgaum woods, Bombay. Beddome (*l. c.*) says that the tree has only been seen by him in gardens.—DISTRIB. Chittagong, Birma.

3. **Pterospermum reticulatum,** *Wight & Arn. Prodr.* p. 69. A middling-sized tree. Leaves 3½–6 by 2–3 in., cuneate-oblong, acuminate, often cut at the apex into several acute lobes or coarse teeth, oblique and subcordate at the base, the underside covered with a cream-colored mealy tomentum dotted with darker minute stellate hairs, glabrous above; nerves and veins prominent beneath and covered with buff stellate tomentum; petioles ¼–½ in. long. Flowers 1–3, in the upper axils, 1¼–1¾ in. across; involucral bracts pinnatisect, a little distant from the flowers, stellately tomentose, segments filiform. Calyx rusty-pubescent outside, villous within; sepals linear-oblong, subobtuse. Petals obovate-oblong, spreading. Staminodes filiform. Ovary hairy; ovules about 6 in each cell. Capsules up to 3½ in. long, ovoid, contracted at the base, stellately pubescent. Seeds 4 in each cell, prominently veined, dark brown; wing papery, oblique, falcate. The ripe fruit remains for a long time on the tree. Fl. B. I. v. 1, p. 369; Bedd. For. Man. in Flor. Sylvat. p. xxxiv; Talb. Trees, Bomb. p. 23; Woodr. in Journ. Bomb. Nat. v. 11 (1897) p. 129. *Pterospermum Lawianum,* Nimmo, in Grah. Cat. p. 246; Dalz. & Gibs. p. 24.—Flowers: Dec.–Feb.

Western Ghâts, rare; planted in Poona (*Woodrow*). KANARA: Falls of Gairsoppa (rare), *Talbot*!; Deviman Ghát, *Talbot*!

4. **Pterospermum Heyneanum,** *Wall. Cat.* (1828) 1169. A middle-sized tree; young shoots covered with ferruginous stellate pubescence. Leaves 4–6 by 2–3 in., oblong, acuminate, more or less angled or toothed towards the apex, rounded or subcordate, not or but slightly oblique at the base, glabrous above, grey-pubescent beneath; nerves and veins prominent, clothed with ferruginous pubescence; petioles ¼–⅜ in. long, rufous-pubescent, attached a little within the margin; stipules ensiform, ½ in. long. Flowers up to 3½ in. across, white, fragrant; involucral bracts imbricate, subpersistent, foliaceous, broadly ovate, deeply and variously gashed, the segments triangular, acute. Sepals up to 2 in. long, rufous-pubescent on the outside, villous within. Petals obovate, spreading. Capsules 2 in. long, narrowed at both ends. Seeds 8–10 in each cell; wing as in the preceding species. Fl. B. I. v. 1, p. 369; Bedd. For. Man. in Flor. Sylvat. p. xxxiv; Talb. Trees, Bomb. p. 23; Woodr. in Journ. Bomb. Nat. v. 11 (1897) p. 129. —Flowers: Dec.–Feb.

I have seen no specimens of this tree from Bombay. The specimens in Herb. Kew. marked *P. Heyneanum* by Stocks and Dalzell are all referable to *P. reticulatum*. The leaves of *P. Heyneanum* are much less oblique at the base than those of *P. reticulatum* while its stipules and flowers are larger. The involucral bracts of *P. reticulatum* are pinnatisect with filiform segments, those of *P. Heyneanum* foliaceous, variously cut and gashed. The capsules of *P. Heyneanum* contain 8–10, those of *P. reticulatum* 4 seeds.

6. ERIOLÆNA, DC.

Trees. Leaves cordate, crenate or serrate, stellately pubescent or tomentose beneath. Peduncles axillary, 1-flowered. Flowers rather large; bracts multisect, laciniate or small and caducous. Calyx 5-fid, or at length 5-partite. Petals 5, deciduous, with dilated tomentose claws; blade flat, glabrous. Staminal-column bearing outside many-seriate, 1-antheriferous filaments up to the apex; anthers erect, oblong-linear, cells parallel; pollen globose, muricate. Staminodes 0. Ovary sessile, 5–10-celled; ovules many in each cell; style stigmatose at the apex, stellately 5–10-lobed. Capsule woody, dehiscing loculicidally. Seeds ascending, produced above into a wing; albumen thin; cotyledons folded or contortuplicate; radicle next the hilum.—DISTRIB. Species about 7, all Indian.

Involucral bracts multisect.
  Peduncles few-flowered .... 1. *E. Stocksii.*
  Peduncles many-flowered.
    Sepals lanceolate; style pubescent........................ 2. *E. Hookeriana.*
    Sepals linear-oblong; style glabrous .... 3. *E. Candollei.*
Involucral bracts entire or toothed, not multisect .... 4. *E. quinquelocularis.*

1. **Eriolæna Stocksii,** *Hook. f. & Thoms. in Fl. B. I.* v. 1, p. 370. A tree or shrub (?); bark purplish; young parts stellately pubescent. Leaves 3–5 by 2½–4 in., deeply cordate, orbicular, shortly and bluntly acuminate, irregularly crenate, 5–7-nerved, dotted above with stellate hairs, finely pubescent beneath; petioles 2–3 in. long, terete, clothed with dense, stellate pubescence; stipules linear-falcate, caducous. Flowers 1½–2 in. across, near the top of a long peduncle,* in few-flowered lax axillary racemose cymes; peduncles reaching 6 in. long, stellately pubescent; pedicels ½ in. long, grooved, pubescent; involucral bracts multisect, segments very numerous, linear or filiform, clothed with dense stellate pubescence so as to appear mossy. Sepals lanceolate, cuspidate, stellately pubescent outside, villous within, glandular at the base inside. Petals obovate, cuneate. Ovary 8–10-lobed, pubescent; style stout, long, pubescent. Fruit not seen. Fl. B. I. v. 1, p. 370; Talb. Trees, Bomb. p. 24; Woodr. in Journ. Bomb. Nat. v. 11 (1897) p. 129.

Scarcely if at all distinct from *E. Hookeriana*, the next species. There are two good specimens of *E. Stocksii* in Herb. Kew. ticketed "Konkan, *Stocks*," but as there is no fruit on either, it is impossible to say whether the species should be maintained as separate or united with *E. Hookeriana.*

KONKAN: fide *Stocks*!

2. **Eriolæna Hookeriana,** *Wight & Arn. Prodr.* p. 70. A small tree. Leaves 4–5 in., as broad as long, roundish, cordate, acuminate, irregularly crenate-dentate, dotted with small tufts of stellate hairs above, finely pubescent beneath; nerves prominent on the underside; petioles 1–2½ in. long. Peduncles axillary, 3–6 in. long, stellately pubescent when young, afterwards glabrous. Flowers 1½–2 in. across, in many-flowered cymes towards the extremities of the branches; involucral bracts shorter than the calyx, multisect, the segments linear. Sepals linear-lanceolate, pubescent outside, stellately-hairy and glandular at the base within. Petals obovate, claw densely pubescent within. Style pubescent; stigma 8–10-lobed. Capsules ovoid-oblong pointed, 10-valved, valves pubescent. Fl. B. I. v. 1, p. 370; Grah. Cat. p. 20;

Bedd. For. Man. in Flor. Sylvat. p. xxxv, t. 5, fig. 2; Talb. Trees, Bomb. p. 24; Watt, Dict. Econ. Prod. v. 3, p. 265.—Flowers: Mar.-April. VERN. *Bute*; *Bother*.

Along the Southern Ghâts, not common. The Konkans and the dry forests of the Satpudas, *Talbot*.

3. **Eriolæna Candollei,** *Wall. Pl. As. Rar.* v. 1 (1830) p. 51, t. 64. A tree; bark grey; young parts stellate-hairy. Leaves 5–7 by 3–5 in., broadly ovate, cordate, acute or acuminate, glabrous or with a few stellate hairs above, grey-tomentose beneath, crenate or crenate-dentate; petioles 1½–2½ in. long. Flowers 1½ in. across, in corymbose cymes at the extremities of long peduncles, yellow, showy; involucral bracts subpinnatifid, pubescent. Sepals linear-oblong, acute, pubescent on both surfaces. Petals oblong, the apex notched; claw thick, villous. Stigma 8–10-lobed; lobes revolute. Capsules 2 in. long, woody, ovoid, acute, beaked, 10-valved, the valves usually villous at the inner margins. Seeds numerous, imbricate. Fl. B. I. v. 1, p. 370; Dalz. & Gibs. p. 24; Talb. Trees, Bomb. p. 24; Woodr. in Journ. Bomb. Nat. v. 11 (1897) p. 129; Watt, Dict. Econ. Prod. v. 3, p. 265.—Flowers: Mar.-May. VERN. *Bothi*; *Hadang*.

KONKAN: *Stocks*!, *Dalzell*!, *Talbot*. S. M. COUNTRY: Belgaum, *Talbot*; Ramghát, *Dalzell*, *Talbot*. KANARA: deciduous forests of N. Kanara, *Talbot*.—DISTRIB. Birma.

4. **Eriolæna quinquelocularis,** *Wight, Icon.* t. 882* (1847). A small tree. Leaves up to 5 by 6 in., orbicular, cordate, acuminate, coarsely crenate-serrate, dotted with small tufts of stellate hairs above, softly tomentose beneath; petioles 2–5 in. long, tomentose when young, becoming at length nearly glabrous. Flowers about 2 in. across, in peduncled, few- (usually 1–3-) flowered cymes near the ends of the branches; involucral bracts a little distant from the flower, minute, entire or with toothed margins, very caducous. Sepals linear-oblong, acute, 1 in. long, pubescent on both surfaces, glandular at the base inside. Petals obovate-oblong, equalling the sepals; claw broad, thick, densely pubescent, deflexed between the sepals. Ovary pubescent; style long, the lower portion hairy; stigma 5-lobed, the lobes revolute. Capsules woody, 1¼ in. long, pointed, 5-celled, 5–10-valved; valves tubercled, more or less pubescent, usually silky-villous at the inner angle. Seeds numerous, imbricate; wing papery, falcately curved.

In Wight's figure (Icones, t. 882) the artist has made it appear that the petals are outside the calyx. The claw of the petal is in appearance like the sepals and is deflexed between them. Fl. B. I. v. 1, p. 371; Bedd. For. Man. in Flor. Sylvat. p. xxxv, t. 5, fig. 2; Talb. Trees, Bomb. p. 24; Woodr. in Journ. Bomb. Nat. v. 11 (1897) p. 129; Watt, Dict. Econ. Prod. v. 3, p. 265. *Eriolæna Hookeriana* (?), Grah. Cat. p. 20.—Flowers: July. VERN. *Badjari-dhâman*; *Bothi*.

KONKAN: *Law*!, *Stocks*,!; Bombay, *Captain Geburne*!; Forests of the Konkan, *Talbot*. DECCAN: Khandala, *Woodrow*!; Purandhar, Poona Districts, *Woodrow*! S. M. COUNTRY: Belgaum, *Ritchie*, 72!

---

* Wight, Icon. v. 3, p. 7, describes the plant under *Microchlæna*, but states that the genus ought to have been united with *Eriochlæna* (now *Eriolæna*), from which (he remarks) it does not differ in any essential point. In the Index to the Icones, page 36, he cites his Plate 882, as representing *Eriochlæna*.

7. MELHANIA, Forsk.

Herbs or undershrubs, softly tomentose. Leaves simple, ovate or cordate, crenate or serrate. Peduncles axillary, 1–few-flowered. Flowers yellow; bracts cordate or narrow, often longer than the calyx. Calyx 5-partite. Petals 5, withering round the ovary. Stamens 10, of which 5 are sterile, connate below into a short cup, the staminodes ligulate alternating with the perfect stamens; anther-cells parallel. Ovary sessile, 5-celled; ovules 1–many in each cell; style short, rarely long; branches 5, subulate, spreading, stigmatose on the inside. Capsule loculicidally dehiscent. Seeds albuminous; cotyledons plicate, 2-partite; radicle inferior.—DISTRIB. Africa, the warmer parts of Asia and tropical Australia; species 16.

Cymes axillary; invol. bracts linear.
- Petals longer than the sepals .... 1. *M. incana.*
- Petals shorter than the sepals.. 2. *M. abyssinica.*

Cymes terminal; invol. bracts ovate .... 3. *M. tomentosa.*
Cymes axillary; invol. bracts reniform, greatly enlarged in fruit.. 4. *M. Denhamii.*

1. **Melhania incana,** *Heyne, in Wall. Cat.* (1828) 1200. An undershrub, 4–15 in. high; branches terete, slender, the young ones stellately tomentose. Leaves 1–2¼ by ⅓–½ in., oblong, obtuse, rounded at the base, serrulate or subentire, glabrous above, more or less tomentose beneath, 3-nerved from the base; petioles ½–¾ in. long; stipules ¼ in. long, filiform. Flowers axillary; peduncles longer or shorter than the petiole, 1–4-flowered; pedicels short; involucral bracts 3, linear-oblong, a little shorter than the sepals, tomentose. Sepals lanceolate, acuminate, tomentose. Petals obovate, longer than the sepals. Capsules hairy, globose, shorter than the sepals. Seeds angled, tuberculate. Fl. B. I. v. 1, p. 372; Wight & Arn. Prodr. p. 68.

Rare. Specimens have been found at Badami in the S. Maratha Country, not elsewhere as far as is at present known.

2. **Melhania abyssinica,** *A. Rich. Tent. Fl. Abyss.* (1847) v. 1, p. 76. A low much-branched undershrub; branches terete, cano-tomentose. Leaves 1 by ¾ in., elliptic, obtuse, doubly serrate or sometimes sublobate, pubescent above, cano-tomentose beneath; petioles pubescent, ¼–½ in. long; stipules ¼ in. long, subulate, stellately hairy. Flowers ¾ in. across, axillary, solitary; pedicels ½ in. long; involucral bracts linear, shorter than the sepals. Sepals lanceolate, acute, pubescent. Petals obovate, shorter than the sepals. Stigma subsessile. Capsules ovoid, silky-villous, a little longer than the sepals. Fl. B. I. v. 1, p. 372; Oliv. Fl. Trop. Afr. v. 1, p. 231. *Melhania ovata,* Boiss. Fl. Orient. v. 1, p. 841, *excl. syn.*

SIND: *Stocks!*
I have seen but a single specimen which was collected by *Stocks!* in Sind.—DISTRIB. Abyssinia, Cape de Verde Islands.

3. **Melhania tomentosa,** *Stocks, ex Mast. in Hook. f. Fl. B. I.* v. 1, p. 373. A cano-tomentose branched shrub. Leaves 1–2 by ¾–1¼ in., ovate-oblong, acute, crenate-serrate, cano-tomentose on the underside, more or less pubescent above, rounded or subcordate at the base; petioles ½–¾ in. long, tomentose; stipules subulate, pubescent.

Flowers in terminal 2–3-flowered peduncled cymes; pedicels $\frac{1}{4}$–$\frac{1}{2}$ in. long, softly pubescent; involucral bracts $\frac{1}{2}$ in. long, ovate, acuminate, tomentose, shorter than the sepals. Sepals $\frac{3}{4}$ in. long, narrow-lanceolate, cuspidate, tomentose. Petals exceeding the sepals. Capsules subglobose, silky-villous, shorter than the sepals. Seeds angled, muriculate.

GUJARAT: near Deesa, *Stocks*! SIND: *Dalzell*!, *Cooke*!, *Woodrow*!

4. **Melhania Denhamii,** *R. Br. in Denh. & Clapp. Trav.* (1826) *App.* p. 232. A small shrub; young parts hoary-pubescent. Leaves $\frac{3}{4}$–$1\frac{1}{2}$ by $\frac{1}{4}$–$\frac{3}{4}$ in., elliptic, stellately hairy above, hoary-pubescent beneath, crenate-serrate, apiculate, 5-nerved at the base; petioles $\frac{1}{2}$–$\frac{3}{4}$ in. long; stipules $\frac{3}{16}$ in., subulate, hairy. Flowers in axillary peduncled racemose cymes; pedicels very short; involucral bracts greatly enlarged, up to $\frac{5}{8}$ in. broad in fruit, reniform, broader than long, membranous, veined, apiculate, completely enclosing the capsule. Sepals ovate-lanceolate, pubescent. Petals about equalling the sepals, yellow. Style as long as the ovary. Capsules globose, densely pubescent, the size of a pea. Seeds smooth, angled. *Melhania Denhami*, Masters, in Oliv. Fl. Trop. Afr. v. 1, p. 230; Fl. B. I. v. 1, p. 373; K. Schum. in Engl. & Prantl, Pflanzenf. v. 3, part 6, p. 77, fig. 40, G, H; Woodr. in Journ. Bomb. Nat. v. 11 (1897) p. 129. *Melhania bracteosa*, Boiss. Fl. Orient. v. 1, p. 841.—Flowers: Nov.–Dec.

SIND: *Stocks*!, *Cooke*!; hills near Karachi, *Strachan*!—DISTRIB. Beluchistan, tropical Africa and Arabia.

8. MELOCHIA, Linn.

Herbs or shrubs, rarely trees, stellately pubescent, the stellate mixed with simple hairs. Leaves usually serrate. Flowers usually small, clustered or panicled. Calyx 5-fid or 5-toothed, campanulate or inflated. Petals 5, spathulate or oblong, marcescent. Stamens 5, opposite the petals, connate at the base or beyond the middle; staminodes 0, or (rarely) minute and dentiform; anther-cells parallel. Ovary sessile or shortly stalked, 5-celled; ovules 2 in each cell; styles 5, free or united at the base, stigmatose and usually thickened above. Capsule loculicidally 5-valved. Seeds ascending, more or less albuminous; embryo straight; cotyledons flat; radicle next the hilum.—DISTRIB. Warmer regions of both hemispheres; species about 50.

A branched herb .... 1. *M. corchorifolia*.
A small tree .... 2. *M. velutina*.

1. **Melochia corchorifolia,** *Linn. Sp. Pl.* (1753) p. 675. An erect branched herb; stems and branches nearly glabrous. Leaves very variable in size and shape, 1–3 by $\frac{1}{2}$–$1\frac{1}{2}$ in., ovate-oblong, acute, serrate, sometimes obscurely lobed, glabrous on both surfaces or with a few scattered stellate hairs, base acute, rounded or truncate; petioles $\frac{3}{8}$–1 in. long, slender; stipules lanceolate, $\frac{1}{8}$ in. long, ciliate. Flowers small, pink, subsessile, densely crowded in terminal clusters; involucral bracts lanceolate-subulate, hairy. Sepals lanceolate, ciliate, $\frac{1}{4}$ in. long. Petals $\frac{1}{4}$ in. long, thin, oblong-cuneate, truncate. Capsules depressed-globose; valves sparingly hairy. Seeds angular, mottled black and grey. Fl. B. I. v. 1, p. 374; Trim. Fl. Ceyl. v. 1, p. 170; Woodr. in Journ.

Bomb. Nat. v. 11 (1897) p. 129; Watt, Dict. Econ. Prod. v. 5, p. 225. *Riedleia corchorifolia*, DC. Prodr. v. 1, p. 491; Grah. Cat. p. 19; Dalz. & Gibs. p. 24.—Flowers: Sept.-Nov.

GUJARAT: Godra, *Cooke!*, *Woodrow!* KANARA: *Hohenhacker!*—DISTRIB. Ceylon.

2. **Melochia velutina,** *Bedd. For. Man. in Flor. Sylvat.* p. xxxv, t. 5, fig. 3. A small ornamental tree; young parts stellately hairy. Leaves up to 7 by 6 in., broadly ovate or suborbicular, acute, cordate, truncate, or subacute at the base, serrate, velvety on both surfaces when young, both surfaces and especially the upper losing much of their pubescence when older; petioles 1½-3½ in. long, stellately pubescent; stipules ½ in. across, foliaceous, orbicular-ovate, nerved, very caducous. Flowers ¾ in. across, pale-pink, in many-flowered terminal and axillary corymbose panicles; peduncles and pedicels velvety. Calyx campanulate, velvety; lobes 5, deltoid-ovate, connate for about half their length. Petals about twice as long as the calyx, ovate-oblong, veined. Stamens inserted with the petals on a hypogynous disk; filaments glabrous, flattened, dilated at the base, more or less connate, but easily separable into 5 distinct filaments. Ovary pilose; styles 5, free. Capsules ⅜ in. long, deeply 5-lobed, oblong, pilose. Seeds black, with a thin papery wing. Fl. B. I. v. 1, p. 374; Woodr. in Journ. Bomb. Nat. v. 11 (1897) p. 129; Watt, Dict. Econ. Prod. v. 5, p. 226. *Riedleia tiliæfolia*, DC. Prodr. v. 1, p. 491; Grah. Cat. p. 19; Dalz. & Gibs. p. 24. *Glossospermum velutinum*, Wall. Cat. 1153; Dalz. & Gibs. Suppl. p. 11.—Flowers: Nov. VERN. *Methuri*.

Widely planted throughout the Presidency; a very doubtful native. KONKAN: *Stocks!*; Bombay, *Lambert!*; Bassein, *Dalzell & Gibson*. DECCAN: Poona, planted in gardens, *Cooke!*, *Woodrow!*; Khandala (planted), *Graham*. S. M. COUNTRY: Belgaum Camp, *Ritchie*, 71!; Belgaum, *Dalzell & Gibson*.—DISTRIB. Mauritius, Malaya, wild or cultivated.

9. WALTHERIA, Linn.

Herbs, shrubs (rarely trees), with stellate mixed with simple pubescence. Leaves serrate; stipules narrow. Flowers usually small, in dense axillary or terminal clusters. Calyx 5-fid. Petals 5, spathulate, marcescent. Stamens 5, connate at the base, opposite the petals; staminodes 0; anther-cells parallel. Ovary sessile, 1-celled; ovules 2; style excentric; stigma club-shaped above or fimbriate. Capsule 2-valved, 1-seeded, Seed ascending, albuminous; embryo straight; cotyledons flat; radicle next the hilum.—DISTRIB. 1 species widely diffused throughout the tropics, 2 in Africa, 2 in Oceania and the remainder natives of tropical America; species about 16.

1. **Waltheria indica,** *Linn. Sp. Pl.* (1753) p. 673. A perennial erect herb 2-3 ft. high; stems terete, softly cano-pubescent. Leaves 1-2½ by ¾-1¾ in., ovate or elliptic, obtuse, rounded or subcordate at the base, toothed or serrate, softly pubescent on both surfaces, strongly nerved, the nerves impressed on the upper surface; petioles ¼-½ in. long, densely pubescent; stipules subulate, hairy. Flowers ⅙ in. in diam., yellow, sessile, in dense axillary heads which are peduncled or not; involucral bracts narrow-lanceolate, ciliate. Calyx campanulate; teeth triangular, very acute, ciliate, about ⅓ as long as the calyx. Capsules

very small, enclosed in the calyx, membranous. Seeds solitary, smooth, black. Fl. B. I. v. 1, p. 374; Grah. Cat. p. 246; Dalz. & Gibs. p. 23; Woodr. in Journ. Bomb. Nat. v. 11 (1897) p. 130.—Flowers: Aug.-Sept.

A tolerably abundant weed. KONKAN: *Stocks*! DECCAN: Dongergaon, near Ahmednagar, *Cooke*! S. M. COUNTRY: Badami, *Woodrow*!; Bagalkot, *Graham*; Dharwar, *Woodrow*!—DISTRIB. Throughout the warmer regions of the world.

The following plants of the Order (*Sterculiaceæ*) have been introduced into the Presidency, and are extensively cultivated:—

Pentapetes phœnicea, Linn. Sp. Pl. (1753) p. 698, an annual with showy scarlet flowers 1–1½ in. in diam., which open at noon and drop next morning, a native of Bengal and the N.W. Provinces, is cultivated in gardens, especially in Sind. Fl. B. I. v. 1, p. 371; Dalz. & Gibs. Suppl. p. 11; K. Schum. in Engl. & Prantl, Pflanzenf. v. 3, part 6, p. 77, fig. 40, D, E; Watt, Dict. Econ. Prod. v. 6, part 1, p. 131.—Flowers: Aug.–Nov. VERN. *Dupdri.*

Abroma augusta, Linn. f. Suppl. (1781) p. 341 (*Ambroma*), a shrub or small tree with velvety branches and large dark-red flowers, is often cultivated as an ornamental plant in gardens. The seeds are enveloped in light cottony wool; hence its name "*Devil's Cotton.*"—It is very easily grown and the bark affords a very strong fibre, an account of which will be found in Watt's Dictionary of Economic Products of India, v. 1, pp. 8–9. Fl. B. I. v. 1, p. 375; Grah. Cat. p. 18; Dalz. & Gibs. Suppl. p. 10; K. Schum. in Engl. & Prantl, Pflanzenf. v. 3, part 6, p. 85, fig. 44, A–C; Woodr. in Journ. Bomb. Nat. v. 11 (1897) p. 130; Watt, Dict. Econ. Prod. v. 1, p. 8.—Flowers: Jan. VERN. *Ulat-kambal.*

Guazuma tomentosa, H. B. & K. Nov. Gen. Pl. (1821) v. 5, p. 320, a small tree, a native of tropical America, with obliquely cordate leaves and showy yellow flowers in large terminal and axillary panicles, is widely planted as an ornamental tree throughout the Presidency. It is sometimes called the *Bastard Cedar* and yields a fairly good fibre suitable for rope-making. Fl. B. I. v. 1, p. 375; Grah. Cat. p. 18; Dalz. & Gibs. Suppl. p. 11; Bedd. Flor. Sylvat. t. 107; Woodr. in Journ. Bomb. Nat. v. 11 (1897) p. 130; Watt, Dict. Econ. Prod. v. 4, p. 184.—Flowers: Mar.–Aug. VERN. *Rudrakshi.*

ORDER XXVII. TILIACEÆ.

Trees or shrubs, rarely herbs. Leaves usually alternate, entire, toothed or rarely lobed; stipules 2, free, usually small and deciduous, rarely persistent or 0. Flowers axillary or terminal, usually cymose, regular, hermaphrodite (rarely unisexual). Sepals 3–5, free or connate or united into a campanulate calyx, usually valvate. Petals as many or fewer or 0, alternate with the sepals, inserted round the base of the torus, contorted, or variously imbricate, induplicate or valvate. Stamens usually indefinite, sometimes distant from the petals on the top of an elevated torus, sometimes covering a small or discoid torus, or (rarely) inserted close to the petals round the edge of the torus; filaments free or rarely connate into a short ring at the base or shortly 5–10-adelphous, all antheriferous or some without anthers; anther-cells 2, parallel, contiguous, dehiscing longitudinally or by an apical pore, rarely divergent and confluent at top. Ovary free, sessile above the torus, 2–10-celled; ovules attached to the inner angle of the cells, solitary or twin, pendulous from the top or ascending from the base, sometimes few inserted at the middle of the cell, sometimes numerous, 2–many-seriate, anatropous or subanatropous; raphe ventral or lateral; style entire or divided at the apex into as many lobes or stigmas as there are cells to the ovary, rarely divided to the base, or the stigmas large, sessile, distinct or united into one. Fruit 2–10- or 1-celled by suppression, or many-celled by false septa, dry, drupaceous or baccate and indehiscent, or separating into cocci, sometimes loculicidally (rarely septicidally) dehiscent. Seeds solitary or numerous in each cell, ascending, pendulous or transverse, exarillate; testa usually coriaceous or crustaceous, sometimes pilose; albumen fleshy, copious or thin, rarely 0; embryo straight, rarely curved; cotyledons ovate or cordate-orbicular, foliaceous or slightly fleshy; radicle next the hilum, short or rarely longer than the cotyledons.—DISTRIB. Most abundant in the tropics of both hemispheres, less in the temperate, wanting in the arctic zones; genera 40; species about 350.

Anthers opening by slits.
  Petals usually foveolate or glandular at the base; stamens springing from the apex of a raised torus.
    Fruit without prickles .... 1. GREWIA.
    Fruit prickly.
      Trees; fruit large .... 2. ERINOCARPUS.
      Herbs or undershrubs; fruit small........................ 3. TRIUMFETTA.
  Petals not foveolate or glandular at the base; stamens springing from a contracted torus .... 4. CORCHORUS.
Anthers opening by a terminal pore.
  Petals sepaloid .... 5. ELÆOCARPUS.

1. GREWIA, Linn.

Trees or shrubs, usually stellately pubescent. Leaves 3–7-nerved. Flowers usually yellow, in axillary, terminal or extra-axillary cymes or panicles. Sepals 5, distinct. Petals 5, usually with a gland at the base within, generally shorter than the sepals, inserted round the base of the torus, very rarely 0. Stamens numerous, inserted on a turbinate often glandular torus. Ovary 2–4-celled; ovules 2–many in each cell; style subulate; stigma short, 2–5-lobed or laciniate. Drupes 1–4-pyrened, entire or 2–4-lobed; pyrenes 1- or 2–many-seeded and spuriously septate between the seeds. Seeds ascending or horizontal; albumen copious, fleshy or rarely scanty, or almost 0; cotyledons flat, foliaceous or fleshy.—DISTRIB. Warmer regions of the Old World; species about 60.

Inflorescence terminal and axillary (sometimes extra-axillary); flowers in umbellate cymes.
  Erect shrub or small tree .... 1. *G. columnaris.*
  Scandent shrubs.
    Torus long; drupes deeply lobed, purplish .... 2. *G. umbellifera.*
    Torus short; drupes yellow, wrinkled .... 3. *G. orientalis.*
    Torus long; drupes obscurely lobed, purple .... 4. *G. umbellata.*
Inflorescence leaf-opposed and axillary (sometimes extra-axillary).
  Leaves scabrous with stellate hairs .... 5. *G. heterotricha.*
  Leaves glabrous or nearly so .... 6. *G. populifolia.*

Inflorescence axillary (rarely extra-axillary).
Leaves usually hoary, at least beneath.
Gland of the petals minute or 0 .... 8. *G. orbiculata.*
Gland of the petals conspicuous.
Leaves 3-nerved from the base.................................. 7. *G. salvifolia.*
Leaves 5–6-nerved from the base.
Stipules leafy, auricled .... 9. *G. tiliæfolia.*
Stipules linear-lanceolate .... 10. *G. asiatica.*
Leaves not hoary beneath.
Drupes with a crustaceous rind.
Leaves ovate-oblong; anthers hairy .... 11. *G. pilosa.*
Leaves orbicular; anthers glabrous .... 12. *G. villosa.*
Drupes fleshy.
Flowers all bisexual.
A small tree; leaves lanceolate; drupes didymous ... 13. *G. lævigata.*
A straggling shrub; leaves roundish, irregularly toothed or lobed; drupes 1–4-lobed .... 14. *G. abutilifolia.*
Flowers polygamous.
A branched shrub; stamens more than 40 .... 15. *G. hirsuta.*
A small tree; stamens 16–20 .... 16. *G. polygama.*
Inflorescence terminal in panicled cymes; flowers involucrate. 17. *G. Microcos.*

1. **Grewia columnaris,** *Sm. in Rees, Cyclop.* (1811) v. 17, n. 5. A much-branched shrub or small tree; young parts stellately pubescent. Leaves 2–3½ by ¾–1½ in., elliptic-oblong, acute or acuminate, serrate, crenate or dentate, more or less rough with short, stellate hairs, at length glabrous or nearly so, rounded at the base, 3-nerved; petioles ⅛–¼ in. long, pubescent. Flowers in umbellate cymes, which are more or less corymbose when terminal; buds conical, ribbed, dilated at the base, densely pubescent; peduncles solitary or 2–3 together, axillary, extra-axillary and terminal, twice as long as the petioles; pedicels 3–5, shorter than the peduncles, supported by small lanceolate deciduous bracts. Sepals ½ in. long, linear-oblong, pubescent outside, 3-nerved. Petals white, ¼ in. long, oblong, acute, entire; gland less than half the length of the petal, densely villous on the upper margin, less so on the lateral ones. Torus nearly ¼ in. long, softly villous, 5-angled, hairy at the apex, the part beneath the gland glabrous. Stamens shorter than the sepals. Ovary densely hairy; style longer than the stamens; stigma 5-lobed, papillose. Drupes ½ in. in diam., subglobose, depressed, slightly 4-lobed, bristly with stiff hairs from glandular bases; stones 4, 2-celled. Fl. B. I. v. 1, p. 383; Grah. Cat. p. 21; Dalz. & Gibs. p. 26; Trim. Fl. Ceyl. v. 1, p. 174; Talb. Trees, Bomb. p. 25; Woodr. in Journ. Bomb. Nat. v. 11 (1897) p. 130.—Flowers: Apr.–June.

Konkan: Malabar hill, Bombay, *Graham*; Salsette, common, *Graham*. Kanara: in evergreen forests of N. Kanara, Sautaveri, *Talbot*.—Distrib. Java, East tropical Africa, Ceylon.

2. **Grewia umbellifera,** *Bedd. For. Man. in Flor. Sylvat.* p. xxxvii. A large scandent shrub; stem at the base covered with blunt protuberances; branches terete, the young ones slightly fulvous-pubescent. Leaves 3–5 by 1–2 in., elliptic-oblong, acute or acuminate, serrulate or dentate, reticulately veined, dotted with minute stellate hairs, ultimately glabrous, base rounded or subacute, 3-nerved; petioles ¼–½ in. long, pubescent; stipules ¼ in. long, lanceolate, acute. Flowers in umbellate cymes; buds oblong, grooved, pubescent; peduncles terminal and axillary, 1–1½ in. long, 1–3 together, pubescent; pedicels ⅛–¼ in. long, 10–20

crowded together in each umbel; bracts of the pedicels oblong-lanceolate. Sepals $\frac{3}{8}$ in. long, linear, acute, hairy. Petals white, $\frac{3}{8}$ in. long, oblong, acute; gland oblong, rounded at the apex, half as long as the petal, margins villous. Torus $\frac{3}{8}$ in. long, softly villous. Style glabrous; stigma 5-lobed. Drupes purplish, fleshy, $\frac{1}{2}$ in. across, deeply 2-4-lobed, subglabrous; stones 2-4, 1-seeded. Talb. Trees, Bomb. p. 26. *Grewia Ritchiei*, Mast. in Fl. B. I. v. 1, p. 389; Talb. Trees, Bomb. p. 26; Woodr. in Journ. Bomb. Nat. v. 11 (1897) p. 130.—Flowers: Dec.-Jan.

KONKAN: *Stocks*!, *Ritchie*, 991! KANARA: Yellapur and Gairsoppa, *Talbot*, 64!

3. **Grewia orientalis,** *Linn. Sp. Pl.* (1753) p. 964. A sarmentose shrub; young parts fulvous-pubescent. Leaves 2-5 by $\frac{3}{4}$-$2\frac{1}{4}$ in., ovate-elliptic, acuminate, crenate-serrate, glabrous, except on the nerves beneath which are clothed with appressed, simple hairs, rounded or subacute and more or less oblique at the base, 3-nerved; petioles $\frac{1}{8}$-$\frac{1}{4}$ in. long, rufous-pubescent. Flowers about $1\frac{1}{2}$-2 in. across, in small axillary and terminal peduncled umbellate cymes shorter than the leaves; buds ovoid-oblong, ribbed, pubescent; pedicels shorter than the flowers, each with a small deciduous lanceolate bract at the base. Sepals $\frac{3}{4}$-1 in. long, linear-oblong, acute, fulvous-pubescent outside, rugose within, with inflexed margins. Petals one third the length of the sepals, ovate-oblong, entire or very slightly emarginate; gland exceeding half the petal, the upper margin thick, very densely hairy. Torus 5-angled, villous except at the insertion of the glands, the villous portion usually longer than the glabrous part, with 5 villous teeth at the base. Ovary pilose; stigma 5-lobed. Drupes yellow, wrinkled, the size of a small cherry, hairy; stones 4, 1-2-celled. Fl. B. I. v. 1, p. 384; Dalz. & Gibs. p. 26; Trim. Fl. Ceyl. v. 1, p. 176; Talb. Trees, Bomb. p. 25; Woodr. in Journ. Bomb. Nat. v. 11 (1897) p. 130.—Flowers: June.

On the Southern Ghâts, *Dalzell & Gibson*.—DISTRIB. Ceylon.

4. **Grewia umbellata,** *Roxb. Hort. Beng.* (1814) p. 42. Shrubby, scandent; branches virgate, thinly stellate-hairy. Leaves 4-5 by $1\frac{1}{2}$-2 in., oblong, acuminate, serrulate, glabrous on both sides, reticulately veined, rounded at the base, 3-nerved; petioles $\frac{1}{4}$ in. long. Flowers in axillary, extra axillary and terminal umbellate cymes; buds narrow-oblong, striate; peduncles longer than the petioles, 1 or more together; pedicels many, from the top of the peduncle; bracts below the pedicels oblong-lanceolate. Sepals $\frac{3}{8}$-$\frac{1}{2}$ in. long, pubescent outside. Petals lanceolate, entire, about half as long as the sepals; gland about half as long as the petal, pilose at top, the lateral margins ciliate. Torus rather long, villous. Drupe the size of a cherry, stellately hairy, slightly wrinkled, obscurely lobed, purplish, 1-celled, 1-seeded. Fl. B. I. v. 1, p. 385.

Masters, in Fl. B. I. l. c. gives the Konkan as a habitat of this plant—I have seen no specimens from the Konkan.—DISTRIB. Philippines, Sumatra, Penang, Singapore.

5. **Grewia heterotricha,** *Mast. in Fl. B. I.* v. 1, p. 385. A scandent shrub; branches striate; young parts clothed with ferruginous stellate hairs. Leaves 2-4 by 1-2 in., ovate-oblong, acute, scabrous above with short stellate hairs, more densely stellately hairy beneath, finely serrate, base rounded or cordate, oblique; petioles $\frac{1}{4}$ in. long, densely stellately

hairy; stipules subulate, nearly equalling the petioles, caducous. Flowers in axillary and leaf-opposed, fulvous-pubescent, umbellate cymes; buds oblong, striate; peduncles 1–1¾ in. long; pedicels ⅜–1 in. long; bracts beneath the pedicels lanceolate. Sepals ⅝ in. long, densely fulvous-pubescent outside. Petals half as long as the sepals, oblong-lanceolate, entire; margin of gland villous. Torus elongate, villous. Style longer than the stamens, glabrous; stigma obscurely 5-lobed. Fruit not seen. Fl. B. I. v. 1, p. 385; Talb. Trees, Bomb. p. 26; Woodr. in Journ. Bomb. Nat. v. 11 (1897) p. 130.—Flowers: Nov.

KANARA: common in the evergreen forests of N. Kanara from Ainshi southwards, ex *Talbot*; Nilkund, *Talbot*; Gairsoppa Falls, *Talbot*!

6. **Grewia populifolia,** *Vahl, Symb.* v. 1 (1790) p. 33. An undershrub, 2–6 ft. high; stems and branches terete, slender. Leaves up to 1½ by 1¼ in., broadly ovate or suborbicular, sometimes obovate, acute or obtuse, coarsely dentate, glabrous or nearly so, base rounded or cuneate; petioles ¼–½ in. long, very slender; stipules small, linear, caducous. Flowers pure white, ¾–1 in. across; buds oblong, tomentose; peduncles usually solitary, leaf-opposed, thickened near the top, bearing 1 (rarely 2 or 3) flowers; bracts 2, near the middle of the pedicel, caducous, leaving a mark which has the appearance of a joint. Sepals ½–¾ in. long, linear-oblong, tomentose outside. Petals linear-oblong, usually notched, about two thirds the length of the sepals, attached along the back of the gland; gland broad, suborbicular or obscurely 3-lobed, the margin villous. Torus about $\frac{1}{12}$ in. long, the lower portion glabrous, faintly ribbed, with 5 densely villous teeth at the top beneath the ovary. Ovary 4-lobed, glabrous (rarely pilose); style longer than the stamens; stigma 4–5-lobed. Drupes smooth, orange-yellow, about ½ in. broad, usually of two separable halves, each half didymous; stones 1–4, muriculate, 1–2-celled. Fl. B. I. v. 1, p. 385; Trim. Fl. Ceyl. v. 1, p. 178; Boiss. Fl. Orient. v. 1, p. 843; Talb. Trees, Bomb. p. 26; Woodr. in Journ. Bomb. Nat. v. 11 (1897) p. 130; Watt, Dict. Econ. Prod. v. 4, p. 182.—Flowers: Aug.–Oct. VERN. *Gango*; *Gangi*.

Common in Sind. S. M. COUNTRY: Dharwar, *Talbot*, *Woodrow*; Badami, *Woodrow*!, *Cooke*! SIND: *Vicary*!, *Stocks*, 539!, *Dalzell*, 67!, *Cooke*!; Karachi, *Woodrow*!; rocky ground in Sind, *Stocks*!

The acid fruit is eaten by the natives and the wood is used for walking-sticks. —DISTRIB. Arabia, S. Persia, Afghanistan, Beluchistan, tropical Africa, Mauritius, Ceylon.

7. **Grewia salvifolia,** *Heyne, ex Roth, Nov. Pl. Sp.* p. 239 (1821). A shrub or small tree, 6–8 ft. high; branches hoary-pubescent. Leaves 1½–2 by ½–¾ in., ovate-oblong or lanceolate, rounded and oblique at the base, 3-nerved, minutely serrate or subentire, upper surface glabrous or with a few scattered hairs, the lower densely hoary-tomentose; petioles ¼ in. long, hoary-tomentose; stipules ⅓ in. long, subulate. Flowers in small umbels; buds ovoid-oblong, striate; peduncles 1–3, less than ½ in. long; pedicels ⅓–½ in. long, usually 3 on each peduncle, stellately tomentose, thickened at the top; bracts lanceolate. Sepals ½ in. long, linear-oblong, tomentose without. Petals yellow, ¼ in. long, obovate, notched; gland hairy, one third the length of the petal. Torus short, glabrous except at the apex beneath the ovary; style exceeding the stamens; stigma 4-lobed, lobes deflexed. Drupes ⅜ in. across, sparsely pubescent, 1–4- (usually 2-) lobed. Fl. B. I. v. 1, p. 386; Talb. Trees,

Bomb. p. 26; Woodr. in Journ. Bomb. Nat. v. 11 (1897) p. 130; Watt, Dict. Econ. Prod. v. 4, p. 182. *Grewia bicolor*, Juss. in Ann. Mus. v. 4, p. 90, t. 50, fig. 2; Boiss. Fl. Orient. v. 1, p. 844.—Flowers: June–Aug. VERN. *Bihul.*

Not common. S. M. COUNTRY: Badami, *Cooke*! SIND: hills in Sind, *Stocks*, 532!

8. **Grewia orbiculata,** *Rottl. in Ges. Naturf. Fr. Neue Schr.* v. 4 (1803) p. 205. A shrub reaching 6 ft. high; young branches softly pubescent. Leaves 1–2½ by ½–1½ in., ovate-oblong, suborbicular or obovate, acute or obtuse, minutely and irregularly serrate, hoary-tomentose beneath, velvety above, base rounded or cordate often oblique; petioles ⅛ in. long, densely pubescent; stipules lanceolate, caducous. Flowers in umbellate cymes; buds subglobose or ovoid; peduncles axillary, 1–3 together, reaching 1½ in. long, densely pubescent; pedicels 1–3, sometimes more, on the top of each peduncle, ⅛–½ in. long, pubescent; bracts linear-lanceolate, caducous. Sepals ¼ in. long, oblong, acute, pale-tomentose without, minutely hairy within. Petals yellow, obovate, entire, half as long as the sepals; gland minute or scarcely any. Torus very short, almost 0. Ovary villous; stigma 4-lobed, laciniate. Drupes pilose, slightly 2-lobed; stones 1–2, 2-celled. Fl. B. I. v. 1, p. 386; Talb. Trees, Bomb. p. 26. *Grewia rotundifolia*, Juss. in Ann. Mus. Par. v. 4 (1804) p. 92, t. 50; Wight, Icon. t. 45.

Rare. KONKAN: *Talbot.* DECCAN: hills at Gokak, *Ritchie*, 1634!

9. **Grewia tiliæfolia,** *Vahl, Symb.* v. 1 (1790) p. 35. A tree, 30–35 ft. high; bark pale brown; young parts densely pubescent. Leaves 3–5 by 2–3 in., ovate, acuminate with a tendency to become lobate at the apex, crenate-dentate, upper surface minutely stellately hairy or subglabrous, the nerves pubescent, lower surface hoary-tomentose, cordate and inequilateral at the base, 6-nerved, 3 nerves at the larger and two at the smaller side of the midrib; petioles ¼–¾ in. long, pubescent; stipules ⅜ in. long, leafy, somewhat falcate, auricled, with a rounded lobe on the lower side, veined. Flowers small, umbellate; buds obovoid-oblong or subglobose, tomentose; peduncles 3 or several, axillary, thick, about equalling the petioles; pedicels 3–5, divergent, shorter than the peduncles; bracts beneath the pedicels linear-lanceolate. Sepals ¼ in. long, oblong, subacute, pubescent outside, glabrous within. Petals about half as long as the sepals, oblong or spathulate, entire or notched; gland about one third the length of the petal, densely white-villous on the margin. Torus rather long, ribbed, glabrous, with 5 obscure villous teeth at the apex. Ovary villous; style longer than the stamens; stigma somewhat irregularly 5-lobed. Drupes size of a pea, black, globose or 2- (rarely 4-) lobed; stones 1–2-celled. Fl. B. I. v. 1, p. 386; Grah. Cat. p. 21; Dalz. & Gibs. p. 26; Bedd. Flor. Sylvat. t. 108; Trim. Fl. Ceyl. v. 1, p. 175; Talb. Trees, Bomb. p. 26; Woodr. in Journ. Bomb. Nat. v. 11 (1897) p. 130; Watt, Dict. Econ. Prod. v. 4, p. 183.—Flowers: May–Aug. VERN. *Dháman*; *Thadsal.*

Common throughout the Presidency in deciduous forests. KONKAN: *Stocks*!, *Law*!, *Gibson*!; Worli (Bombay), *Dalzell*!; Elephanta and Salsette, *Graham.* DECCAN: Ganesh Khind (Poona), *Woodrow*!; Koina valley below Mahableshwar, *Cooke*! KANARA: Yellapur, *Talbot*!; Kála naddi, *Ritchie*, 79!—DISTRIB. Birma, Ceylon, East tropical Africa.

VAR. *leptopetala*, Brandis (*sp.*). Branchlets and underside of the leaves varying from glabrous to densely and softly tomentose. Petals without a gland or the gland reduced to a thickened base with a few hairs.

10. **Grewia asiatica,** *Linn. Mantiss.* (1767) p. 122. A small tree; young parts stellately pubescent. Leaves 3–7 by 2½–5 in., ovate or suborbicular, acute or subacuminate, irregularly and coarsely toothed, subglabrous above, hoary-tomentose beneath, obliquely cordate or rounded at the base, 5–6-nerved; petioles ½ in. long, thickened at the top; stipules nearly as long as the petioles, linear or lanceolate, acute. Flowers slightly larger than in the preceding species, in umbellate cymes; buds obovate-oblong, ribbed, pubescent; peduncles axillary, 1–4 together, slender, ½–1½ in. long, puberulous; pedicels 2–5, shorter than the peduncles; bracts beneath the pedicels lanceolate. Sepals ⅜ in. long, linear-oblong, acute, pubescent outside. Petals yellow, oblong or ovate-oblong, subacute, notched, about two thirds the length of the sepals; gland about one third the length of the petal, the margin white-villous. Torus ⅛ in. long, glabrous below, with a villous ring at top beneath the ovary. Ovary villous. Drupe globose, 1–2-lobed, 1-celled, pilose. Fl. B. I. v. 1, p. 386; Grah. Cat. p. 21; Dalz. & Gibs. p. 26 et Suppl. p. 11; Boiss. Fl. Orient. v. 1, p. 844; Pierre, Fl. For. Cochinch. t. 155; Talb. Trees, Bomb. p. 26; Woodr. in Journ. Bomb. Nat. v. 11 (1897) p. 130; Watt, Dict. Econ. Prod. v. 4, p. 177.—Flowers: Apr.–June. VERN. *Phalsa.*

Extensively cultivated throughout the Presidency; largely in Gujarat. The fruit is gratefully acid and sherbet in made from it. KONKAN: *Law*!; Bombay, *Gibson*!, *Captain Geburne*! DECCAN: truly wild in the Poona Collectorate, ex *Dalzell & Gibson*; hills near Poona, *Woodrow*! SIND: *Woodrow*!; Jemadar ka Landa, near Karachi, *Stocks*!—DISTRIB. East tropical Africa.

11. **Grewia pilosa,** *Lam. Encyc.* v. 3 (1789) p. 43. A shrub or small tree. Leaves 2–3 by ¾–1½ in., ovate-oblong, acute, irregularly serrate, stellately hairy on both surfaces, base rounded or subcordate, more or less oblique, 3-nerved; petioles $\frac{1}{10}$–⅛ in. long, hairy; stipules linear-subulate, hairy, longer than the petioles. Flowers in short axillary umbels; buds oblong, obtuse, slightly dilated at the base, pilose, ribbed; peduncles 1–3 together, as long as, or longer than the petioles, pilose; pedicels usually 3, about as long as the peduncles, pilose; bracts beneath the pedicels ovate. Sepals ⅝ by $\frac{1}{10}$ in., linear, acute, pilose without, glabrous within, with a small pale pubescent patch at the base inside. Petals usually bifid at the apex, rounded and thickened at the base, nearly ½ in. long, linear-oblong, hairy near the base outside, and with a few small tufts of stiff, fascicled hairs about ⅔ of the way up; gland oblong, about one third the length of the petal, pilose at top, less densely so on the lateral margins. Anthers with a few simple hairs on the back. Torus short, glabrous, 5-lobed at the apex beneath the ovary, the lobes ciliate. Ovary hairy; style pilose at the base; stigma small, bifid. Drupes stellately hairy, 1–4-lobed, yellowish brown; rind crustaceous; stones 1–4, muricate, 1–3-celled; mesocarp thick, fibrous. Fl. B. I. v. 1, p. 388; Dalz. & Gibs. p. 26; Talb. Trees, Bomb. p. 26; Woodr. in Journ. Bomb. Nat. v. 11 (1897) p. 130.—Flowers: Aug.–Oct. VERN. *Khatakhati.*

Throughout the Presidency in deciduous forests. DECCAN: *Dalzell & Gibson*; Singhad hill near Poona, *Woodrow*! S. M. COUNTRY: Badami, *Cooke*!, *Woodrow*! GUJARAT: near Deesa, *Stocks*!

12. **Grewia villosa,** *Willd. in Ges. Naturf. Fr. Neue Schr.* v. 4 (1803) p. 205. A shrub reaching 6 ft. high; branches grey-puberulous. Leaves 1½–3 in., rotund-ovate, subcordate, shortly acuminate or rounded, crenate-serrate, the serratures usually with a tuft of hairs at the apex, 5-nerved, rugoso-reticulate with numerous transverse veins, rough with stellate hairs above, velvety beneath; petioles ½–1 in. long, densely villous; stipules foliaceous, ovate-oblong, acute, hairy, caducous. Flowers in axillary or leaf-opposed cymes; buds ellipsoid, pilose; peduncles very short; pedicels 2–4; bracts oblong. Sepals ¼–⅜ in. long, lanceolate, pilose. Petals dull yellow, oblong-obovate, slightly emarginate, about half the length of the sepals; gland orbicular-oblong, ciliate, a little less than half the length of the petal. Anthers glabrous. Torus very short, almost 0. Ovary densely pilose; style hairy; stigma lacerate. Drupes globose, about ½ in. in diam., yellowish-red; rind crustaceous, stellately hairy; stones 4, 1–2-seeded, smooth, in a sweet edible pulp. Fl. B. I. v. 1, p. 388; Grah. Cat. p. 21; Dalz. & Gibs. p. 25; Talb. Trees, Bomb. p. 26; Woodr. in Journ. Bomb. Nat. v. 11 (1897) p. 130; Watt, Dict. Econ. Prod. v. 4, p. 184.

Throughout the Presidency in dry districts; common in Sind. KONKAN: *Stocks*!, *Gibson*! DECCAN: Nalatwar, near Kaladgi, *Graham*; throughout the Deccan, sparingly, *Dalzell & Gibson*. GUJARAT: Porbander, *Cooke*!, *Woodrow*! SIND: *Stocks*, 510!, *Dalzell*, 84!, *Woodrow*!, *Cooke*!; Karachi, *Woodrow*!—DISTRIB. Tropical Africa. The fruit is eaten. Dalzell calls it "very delicious."

There is in Herb. Kew. a single specimen communicated by *Stocks* (n. 616)!, in which the sepals have a curious trifid appendage at their apex.

13. **Grewia lævigata,** *Vahl, Symb.* v. 1 (1790) p. 34. A small tree; branches slender, terete. Leaves thin, 2–4¼ by ⅞–1¾ in., lanceolate, acuminate, sharply serrate-dentate, sparsely stellately hairy when young, at length glabrous or nearly so, base acute, 3-nerved; petioles ¼ in. long, hairy; stipules linear-lanceolate, nearly as long as the petioles. Flowers in umbellate cymes; buds ovoid or subglobose, many-ribbed, pubescent; peduncles axillary, 1–2 together, longer than the petioles, sparsely hairy towards the apex; pedicels about equalling the peduncles, pilose; bracts beneath the pedicels linear-lanceolate. Sepals ⅜–½ in. long, linear, subacute, stellately pubescent outside, furnished with a small hairy gland at the base inside, 3-nerved. Petals small, one third the length of the sepals, triangular, often notched; gland almost as long as the petal, densely villous on the upper margin, less densely on the lateral ones. Torus rather long, ribbed, the lower part glabrous, the upper part villous, the villous portion shorter than the glabrous part, sometimes reduced to a narrow band. Ovary pilose; stigma 5-lobed, the lobes laciniate. Drupes glabrous, 1–4-lobed; stones 1-celled. Fl. B. I. v. 1, p. 389; Pierre, Fl. For. Cochinch. t. 161; Talb. Trees, Bomb. p. 26; Woodr. in Journ. Bomb. Nat. v. 11 (1897) p. 130; Watt, Dict. Econ. Prod. v. 4, p. 179.—Flowers: Aug.–Oct. VERN. *Kaori*; *Gulgollop*.

Not common. KONKAN: *Law*!, *Stocks*!; Bombay, *Captain Geburne*!; Amboli Ghát, *Cooke*! DECCAN: near Junnar, *Woodrow*! S. M. COUNTRY: Londa, *Cooke*!;

Dharwar, *Woodrow*. KANARA: Kála naddi, *Ritchie*, 78!; N. Kanara, near villages and in deciduous forests, not common, *Talbot*.—DISTRIB. Tropical Africa, Malaya, Australia.

The tree yields a fibre which is used for cordage in Kanara but is not sufficiently abundant to be of commercial importance. Consult Watt, Dict. Econ. Prod. l. c.

14. **Grewia abutilifolia,** *Vent. ex Juss. in Ann. Mus. Par.* v. 4 (1804) p. 92. A straggling shrub; young parts stellately hairy. Leaves 3–4½ by 2½–3½ in., roundish-ovate, acute or acuminate, often more or less lobed, irregularly serrate, scabrous above, stellately hairy beneath, base subcordate, 3-nerved; petioles ⅜–½ in. long, hairy; stipules ¼ in. long, lanceolate, hairy. Flowers in short, umbellate cymes; buds ovoid or oblong, pilose; peduncles axillary, 1–3 together, shorter than the petioles, hairy; pedicels usually 3, longer than the peduncles, pilose; bracts lanceolate, acute, hairy. Sepals ⅓ in. long, linear-oblong, acute, hairy outside. Petals about a quarter the length of the sepals, oblong, rounded at the apex, entire; gland a little more than half the length of the petal, margin villous. Torus short, with tufted hairs at the apex, the lower part glabrous. Ovary villous; style much longer than the stamens, glabrous; stigma laciniate. Drupes ⅓ in. across, fleshy, minutely stellately hairy, obscurely 4-lobed, wrinkled. Fl. B. I. v. 1, p. 390; Dalz. & Gibs. p. 26; Pierre, Fl. For. Cochinch. t. 165; Talb. Trees, Bomb. p. 26; Woodr. in Journ. Bomb. Nat. v. 11 (1897) p. 130. —Flowers: June.

Common in N. Kanara along nálas and in moist shady places; somewhat rare in other districts. KONKAN: *Stocks*!, *Law*!; Bombay, *Dr. Lush*! DECCAN: *Dalzell & Gibson*; Chatarsinghi hill, near Poona, *Cooke*! S. M. COUNTRY: Dharwar, *Woodrow*! KANARA: Halyal (N. Kanara), *Talbot*!—DISTRIB. Java.

15. **Grewia hirsuta,** *Vahl, Symb.* v. 1 (1790) p. 34. A branched shrub; young parts softly pubescent with (usually) fulvous hairs. Leaves distichous, 2–3 by ¾–1¼ in., ovate or lanceolate, acute, serrate, the upper surface glabrescent or with a few stellate hairs, the lower usually densely villous with fasciculate hairs, base rounded, oblique, 3-nerved; petioles $\frac{1}{12}$–¼ in. long, densely hairy; stipules subulate, longer than the petioles, linear-lanceolate, hairy. Flowers polygamous (male and bisexual), in axillary umbellate cymes; buds ovoid, densely villous; peduncles 1–3; pedicels 2–4, very short, pubescent; bracts linear-lanceolate, hairy. MALE FLOWERS: Sepals ¼–$\frac{5}{16}$ in. long, linear-lanceolate, softly hairy outside. Petals ⅛ in. long, oblong, rounded at the apex, entire, hairy at the back; gland about half the length of the petal, orbicular-oblong with a fringe of long, white, stiff hairs on the upper margin, ciliate on the lateral ones. Stamens more than 40, intermixed with white hairs. Torus short, the lower part glabrous with a ring of long soft hairs at the apex. HERMAPH. FLOWERS as in the male. Ovary densely villous, the hairs often equalling or sometimes exceeding the stamens; style glabrous; stigma 5-lobed, the lobes fringed; anthers very small. Drupes ½ in. in diam., fleshy, wrinkled, slightly 4-lobed, sparingly stellately hairy; stones 4, 2-celled. Fl. B. I. v. 1, p. 391; Grah. Cat. p. 21; Trim. Fl. Ceyl. v. 1, p. 176; Talb. Trees, Bomb. p. 26; Woodr. in Journ. Bomb. Nat. v. 11 (1897) p. 130; Pierre, Fl. For. Cochinch. t. 167.—Flowers: Aug.–Sept.

KONKAN: *Stocks*!, *Law*!; Salsette jungles and on the Gháts, *Graham*. DECCAN:

hills near Poona, *Woodrow*! ; Bowdhan, 10 miles from Poona, *Cooke*! S. M. COUNTRY Dharwar districts, in deciduous open forests, *Talbot*.

16. **Grewia polygama,** *Roxb. Hort. Beng.* (1814) p. 42.—A small much-branched tree; young parts velvety-tomentose; branches terete, slender. Leaves distichous, 2–4½ by ¾–1¼ in., oblong-lanceolate, very acute, irregularly serrate, glabrous or with a few stellate hairs on the upper surface, velvety beneath, base rounded or subacute, 3-nerved; petioles ⅛–¼ in. long, softly hairy; stipules longer than the petioles, subulate, hairy. Flowers about ⅓ in. across or less, polygamous (male and bisexual) in axillary umbellate cymes; buds oblong or subglobose, densely pubescent; peduncles axillary, 1–5 together, short, hairy; pedicels 2–6, divergent, usually shorter than the peduncles; bracts subulate, hairy. MALE FLOWERS: Sepals ⅕–¼ in. long, linear, acute, pilose outside, glabrous within. Petals white, $\frac{1}{10}$ in. long, oblong, rounded or subacute at the apex, entire, hairy on the back; gland half as long as the petal, orbicular-oblong, with a fringe of long white stiff hairs on the upper margin, ciliate on the lateral ones. Stamens 16–20, with short white hairs intermixed. Torus $\frac{1}{30}$ in. long, the lower part glabrous, with a dense ring of erect stiff white hairs at the apex and a ring of fewer and longer hairs at the base. HERMAPH. FLOWERS as in the male. Ovary very hairy, the hairs shorter than the stamens; style glabrous; stigma laciniate. Drupes ⅓ in. across, hairy, brownish, obscurely 4-lobed; stones 4, 1-seeded. Fl. B. I. v. 1, p. 391; Dalz. & Gibs. p. 26; Trim. Fl. Ceyl. v. 1, p. 177; Pierre, Fl. For. Cochinch. t. 166; Talb. Trees, Bomb. p. 26; Woodr. in Journ. Bomb. Nat. v. 11 (1897) p. 130; Watt, Dict. Econ. Prod. v. 4, p. 181. *Grewia lancæfolia*, Grah. Cat. p. 21.—Flowers: Sept.–Nov. VERN. *Gauli*; *Gavali*.

Pretty common along the Ghâts, especially those to the south. KONKAN: *Stocks*!; Kanheri jungles, *Graham*; Matheran, *Woodrow*; Amboli Ghát, *Woodrow*. S. M. COUNTRY: Dharwar, *Talbot*!—DISTRIB. Ceylon, Pegu, N. Australia.

A decoction of the leaves has been recommended as a never-failing remedy in cases of dysentery. See Watt, Dict. Econ. Prod. l. c.

17. **Grewia Microcos,** *Linn. Syst.* ed. 12, v. 2 (1767) p. 602. A shrub; young parts stellately pubescent. Leaves 4–6 by 1½–2¼ in., elliptic-oblong, acuminate, glabrous, entire or slightly and irregularly toothed, base oblique, rounded or acute, 3-nerved, the nerves and veins prominent beneath; petioles ¼–⅜ in. long; stipules ¼–½ in. long, linear, acute. Flowers in terminal panicles; buds subglobose or ovoid, grey-tomentose, 2 or 3 close together enclosed within an involucre of 6–8 oblong-lanceolate imbricate bracts; pedicels short; bracts of the pedicels subulate. Sepals ¼ in. long, obovate-oblong, tomentose on both surfaces. Petals less than ⅓ the length of the sepals, ovate, acute, pubescent at the base outside; gland half as long as the petal, slightly ciliate. Torus short, lobed at the apex. Ovary glabrous; style much longer than the stamens, glabrous; stigma minute, bifid. Fruit globose or slightly obovoid, about ⅜ in. across, purplish, glabrous, wrinkled; mesocarp fibrous; stone 1-celled. Fl. B. I. v. 1, p. 392; Grah. Cat. p. 21; Dalz. & Gibs. p. 26; Trim. Fl. Ceyl. v. 1, p. 177; Pierre, Fl. For. Cochinch. t. 152; Talb. Trees, Bomb. p. 26; Woodr. in Journ. Bomb. Nat. v. 11 (1897) p. 130; Watt, Dict. Econ. Prod. v. 4, p. 179.—Flowers: May–Oct. VERN. *Shirul*; *Asolin*.

Several stones examined by me were unmistakably 1-celled.

Common in evergreen forests throughout the Konkan and N. Kanara. The fruit is eaten by the natives. KONKAN: hilly parts, *Dalzell & Gibson*, *Graham*; Goa jungles, *Dr. Lush* (ex *Graham*); W. Ghâts, *Woodrow*. DECCAN: Fitzgerald Ghât below Mahableshwar, *Cooke*!, *H. M. Birdwood*; Koina valley, *Cooke*! S. M. COUNTRY: Londa, *Woodrow*!; Castlerock, *Woodrow*! KANARA: *Hohenhacker*, 753!; in evergreen forests, *Talbot*.

2. ERINOCARPUS, Nimmo.

A tree. Leaves broad, palminerved, toothed or lobed. Flowers large, in terminal panicles; bracts broadly ovate. Sepals 5, distinct. Petals 5, foveolate or glandular at the base, inserted round the base of the torus. Stamens indefinite, springing from a raised torus, free or the exterior very shortly connate into a ring. Ovary 3–5-celled; ovules 2 in each cell; style filiform. Fruit woody, indehiscent, triquetrous, angles somewhat winged, the cordate faces echinate, 1–4-celled. Seeds 1 in each cell, pendulous, oblong; testa coriaceous; albumen fleshy; cotyledons ovate, flat.—DISTRIB. Peninsular India; species 1.

1. **Erinocarpus Nimmonii,** *Grah. Cat. Bomb. Plts.* (1839) p. 21. A small tree. Leaves up to 8 in. in diam., orbicular, acutely 5–7-lobed, irregularly toothed, glabrous, cordate at the base, 5–9-nerved; petioles 2–4½ in. long. Flowers yellow, 1½–2½ in. across, in lax, terminal panicles; buds oblong, fulvous-pubescent, 5-pointed, 2 or 3 together enclosed in an involucre of broadly ovate acute bracts, which are velvety-tomentose on both surfaces and very caducous. Sepals up to 1½ in. long, narrow-linear, acute, deflexed, covered outside with fulvous, stellate pubescence, the inner surface glabrous. Petals a little shorter than the sepals, with a very long narrow claw; limb obovate; gland oblong, with ciliate margins. Ovary 3–5-celled, pilose with stiff hairs; style long, filiform, glabrous. Fruit 1–4-celled, triquetrous, 1½–2 in. long, acuminate, angles winged, faces cordate at the base, covered with straight or slightly curved prickles from broad bases. Seeds 1 in each cell, ¼ in. long, oblong. Dalz. & Gibs. p. 27. *Erinocarpus Nimmoanus*, M. Masters, in Hook. f. Fl. B. I. v. 1, p. 394; K. Schum. in Engl. & Prantl, Pflanzenf. v. 3, part 6, p. 26, fig. 12, E; Talb. Trees, Bomb. p. 27; Woodr. in Journ. Bomb. Nat. v. 11 (1897) p. 265; Watt, Dict. Econ. Prod. v. 3, p. 257.—Flowers: Aug.–Sept. VERN. *Chaora*; *Cher*; *Jangli-bhendi*.

I have examined several of the fruits and have invariably found them 4-celled with 1 perfect seed in each cell.

KONKAN: *Stocks*!, *Law*!; Bombay, *Graham*!, *Capt. Geburne*!; hills near Matheran, *H. M. Birdwood*, *Kanitkar*!; Wassind, *Kanitkar*!; top of Karanja Hill, *Graham*. DECCAN: hills of the Deccan, *Stocks*!, *Gibson*!; Khandala, *Woodrow*!; Koina valley, below Mahableshwar, *Cooke*! S. M. COUNTRY: Belgaum, *Ritchie*, 81! KANARA: N. Kanara forests, *Talbot*.

3. TRIUMFETTA, Linn.

Herbs or undershrubs with stellate pubescence. Leaves serrate, entire or 3–5-lobed. Flowers yellow, axillary or leaf-opposed, few or densely fasciculately cymose. Sepals 5, distinct, frequently mucronate at the apex. Petals 5 (rarely 0), glandular, thickened or foveolate at the base, inserted round the base of the torus. Stamens indefinite or rarely twice as many as the sepals, inserted on a glandular torus, free. Ovary 5-celled; ovules 2 in each cell; style filiform; stigma 2–5-toothed.

Capsule subglobose, echinate or setose, indehiscent or separating into cocci. Seeds 1–2 in each cell, pendulous, albuminous; embryo straight; cotyledons flat, foliaceous.—DISTRIB. Throughout the tropics generally; species about 40.

Leaves ovate lanceolate; basal half of the spines of the capsule hispid, the upper half glabrous; stamens 10 .... 1. *T. pilosa.*
Lower leaves more or less 3–5-lobed; spines of the capsule glabrous; stamens 8–15 .... 2. *T. rhomboidea.*
Leaves orbicular; spines of the capsule pubescent; stamens 15–25 .... 3. *T. rotundifolia.*

1. **Triumfetta pilosa,** *Roth, Nov. Pl. Sp.* (1821) p. 223. A large branched perennial herb; branches clothed with soft stellate hairs. Leaves 3–5 by 1–2 in., ovate, acute, irregularly serrate, stellately hairy above, felted with stellate hairs beneath, rounded or subcordate at the base, 5-nerved; petioles of the lower leaves 1–1½ in. long, those of the upper much shorter, all very hairy; stipules lanceolate, acute. Flowers in fascicled axillary and leaf-opposed cymes; buds narrow-oblong, slightly dilated at the base, stellately hairy; peduncles usually shorter than the petioles, hairy; pedicels many, very short, very hairy; bracts subulate, hairy. Sepals ½ in. long, with tufts of stellate hairs outside, linear-oblong, mucronate. Petals yellow, oblong-obovate, a little shorter than the sepals, the glandular base densely ciliate. Fruit (excluding the spines) about ¼ in. in diam.; spines ¼ in. long, hooked and with a transparent point, the basal half of the spine hispid, the upper half glabrous. Seeds 8, rounded on the back, ⅛ in. long, flattened on one side, dark brown, smooth, polished. Fl. B. I. v. 1, p. 394; Dalz. & Gibs. p. 25; Trim. Fl. Ceyl. v. 1, p. 179; Woodr. in Journ. Bomb. Nat. v. 11 (1897) p. 265; Watt, Dict. Econ. Prod. v. 6, part 4, p. 202.—Flowers: Nov. VERN. *Nichardi.*

KONKAN: Bombay, *Law*!; Wari, *Dalzell.* DECCAN: Panchgani, *Cooke*!, *Woodrow*! S. M. COUNTRY: Nagargali, near Dharwar, *Cooke*!; Castlerock, *Woodrow*! KANARA: Kála naddi, *Ritchie*, 988!—DISTRIB. Abyssinia, W. tropical Africa, Ceylon.

2. **Triumfetta rhomboidea,** *Jacquin, Enum. Pl. Carib.* (1760) p. 22 *& Select. Am.* (1763) p. 147, t. 90. Suffruticose, 2–5 ft. high; branches slender, more or less pubescent with simple hairs. Leaves variable, stipules subulate; lower leaves 2–3 in. in diam., usually 3-lobed, irregularly serrate, clothed with simple and stellate hairs on both surfaces and simple hairs on the nerves beneath, base cordate or cuneate, the petioles up to 1½ in. long, more or less hairy; upper leaves usually simple, with very short petioles. Flowers ¼ in. across, yellow, in dense terminal and leaf-opposed cymes; buds oblong apiculate; peduncles and pedicels very short; bracts subulate. Sepals oblong, hooded and apiculate at the apex. Petals shorter than the sepals, obovate-oblong, ciliate at the base; claw very long. Stamens 8–15. Fruit ⅙ in. in diam., the surface at the base of the spines araneously pubescent; spines glabrous, the bristle points hooked, very slender, transparent. Fl. B. I. v. 1, p. 395; Trim. Fl. Ceyl. v. 1, p. 179; K. Schum. in Engl. & Prantl, Pflanzenf. v. 3, part 6, fig. 13, A, B; Woodr. in Journ. Bomb. Nat. v. 11 (1897) p. 265; Watt, Dict. Econ. Prod. v. 6, part 4, p. 202. *Triumfetta angulata*, Lam. Encyc. v. 3, p. 421; Grah. Cat. p. 21; Dalz. & Gibs. p. 25.—Flowers: Sept.–Dec.

KONKAN: Ghotande near Jambalpada, *Kanitkar*! DECCAN, Poona, *Woodrow*. S. M. COUNTRY: Dharwar, *Cooke*!; Belgaum, *Ritchie*, 46! KANARA: *Hohenhacker*, 40!; Kála naddi, *Ritchie*, 46!—DISTRIB. Malaya, China, tropical Africa.

3. **Triumfetta rotundifolia,** *Lam. Encyc.* v. 3 (1789) p. 421. Suffruticose. Leaves $\frac{3}{4}$–$1\frac{1}{2}$ in. in diam., orbicular, irregularly toothed, glabrous or stellately hairy above, softly grey-tomentose beneath, base rounded or cuneate, 3–5-nerved; petioles $\frac{1}{2}$–$1\frac{1}{2}$ in. long, tomentose; stipules subulate. Flowers about $\frac{1}{4}$ in. across, in interrupted racemes; buds oblong, clavate, 5-pointed, grey-tomentose; peduncles and pedicels very short, tomentose. Sepals linear-oblong, apiculate, stellately pubescent outside. Petals a little shorter than the sepals, obovate, ciliate at the base. Stamens 15–25. Fruit ovoid, $\frac{1}{6}$ in. long, pubescent beneath the spines; spines dilated at the base, pubescent, the bristle points hooked, transparent. Fl. B. I. v. 1, p. 395; Dalz. & Gibs. p. 25; Woodr. in Journ. Bomb. Nat. v. 11 (1897) p. 265.—Flowers: Aug.

KONKAN: *Stocks*! DECCAN: Poona, *Jacquemont*, 964!, *Kanitkar*!; Ahmednagar, *Cooke*! GUJARAT: Surat, *Dalzell & Gibson*.

4. CORCHORUS, Linn.

Herbs or undershrubs, with simple and stellate hairs. Leaves serrate. Flowers small, yellow; peduncles very short, axillary or leaf-opposed, 1- or few-flowered, bracteate. Sepals 4–5. Petals 4–5, naked at the base. Stamens numerous or rarely twice as many as the sepals, inserted on a very short torus. Ovary 2–5-celled; ovules many in each cell; style short, the apex stigmatose, hollow, crenulate. Capsule siliquiform and naked, or subglobose and echinate or muricate, loculicidally 2–5-valved, rarely transversely septate between the seeds, many-seeded. Seeds pendulous or horizontal, albuminous; embryo usually incurved; cotyledons foliaceous.— DISTRIB. Throughout the Tropics; species about 35.

Capsule globose; beak 0 .... 1. *C. capsularis*.
Capsule elongate; beak entire.
  Capsule glabrous, cylindric, 10-ribbed; beak long, erect... 2. *C. olitorius*.
  Capsule scabrous or aculeate, 3-angled; beak short, erect. 3. *C. trilocularis*.
Capsule short; beak entire.
  Annual; capsule pubescent, 3-valved .... 4. *C. fascicularis*.
  Perennial; capsule glabrous, 4-valved .... 5. *C. Antichorus*.
Capsule elongate; beak trifid, spreading.
  Capsule cylindric, not winged .... 6. *C. tridens*.
  Capsule 6-angled, 3 of the angles winged .... 7. *C. acutangulus*.

1. **Corchorus capsularis,** *Linn. Sp. Pl.* (1753) p. 529. Annual, growing very tall under cultivation; stem and branches glabrous. Leaves 3–4 by $\frac{3}{4}$–$1\frac{1}{4}$ in., lanceolate, acute or acuminate, glabrous, serrate, the lower serrature on each side usually prolonged into a filiform appendage, base rounded or acute; petioles reaching $1\frac{1}{2}$ in. long, shorter upwards, slender, glabrous; stipules $\frac{1}{4}$–$\frac{1}{2}$ in. long, filiform. Flowers less than $\frac{1}{2}$ in. across, in short cymes; buds obovoid, shortly apiculate; peduncles short; pedicels 1–2, short. Capsules $\frac{1}{2}$ in. in diam., subglobose, not beaked, depressed, broader than long, ridged and muricated, 5-valved; valves woody, without transverse septa. Seeds few in each cell, wedge-shaped, smooth, brown. Fl. B. I. v. 1, p. 397; Grah. Cat.

p. 246; Dalz. & Gibs. p. 25; Trim. Fl. Ceyl. v. 1, p. 181; Woodr. in Journ. Bomb. Nat. v. 11 (1897) p. 265; Watt, Dict. Econ. Prod. v. 2, p. 535.—Flowers: Sept.

KONKAN: Salsette and both Konkans, *Graham*; Bombay, *Ranade*!, *Woodrow*!; Vingorla, *Woodrow*. GUJARAT: *Woodrow*.

A doubtful native. The well-known fibre *Jute* is obtained from this plant and from *Corchorus olitorius*. For a full description of the fibre, the mode of its extraction, &c., see Watt, Dict. Econ. Prod. v. 2, pp. 545–562, also v. 4, pp. 558–560.

2. **Corchorus olitorius,** *Linn. Sp. Pl.* (1753) p. 529. Annual, 3–4 ft. high, much-branched; stems glabrous. Leaves 2½–4 by 1½–2 in., elliptic-lanceolate, acute or acuminate, glabrous, serrate, the lower serratures on each side prolonged into a filiform appendage over ¼ in. long, rounded at the base, 3–5-nerved; petioles ¾–1 in. long, slightly hairy, especially towards the apex; stipules subulate, ¼–⅜ in. long. Flowers pale yellow; buds obovoid, angled, cuspidate; bracts lanceolate; peduncle shorter than the petiole; pedicels 1–3, very short. Sepals ⅛ in. long, oblong, apiculate. Petals ⅕ in. long, oblong-spathulate. Style short; stigma microscopically papillose. Capsules 1¼–2½ in. long, linear, cylindric, erect, 10-ribbed, beaked, glabrous, 5-valved; valves with transverse partitions between the seeds. Seeds trigonous, black. Fl. B. I. v. 1, p. 397; Grah. Cat. p. 20; Dalz. & Gibs. p. 25; Boiss. Fl. Orient. v. 1, p. 845; Trim. Fl. Ceyl. v. 1, p. 182; K. Schum. in Engl. & Prantl, Pflanzenf. v. 3, part 6, p. 19, fig. 8, A; Woodr. in Journ. Bomb. Nat. v. 11 (1897) p. 265; Watt, Dict. Econ. Prod. v. 2, p. 540. —Flowers: Sept. VERN. *Banpát.*

Common, springing up in gardens and cultivated ground; a doubtful native. KONKAN: Bombay, *Dalzell*, *Gaburne*! DECCAN: Poona, *Cooke*!, *Woodrow*! S. M. COUNTRY: Belgaum and Ramghát, *Ritchie*, 149! GUJARAT: *Woodrow*. SIND: *Woodrow*!—DISTRIB. All tropical regions.

The well-known fibre *Jute* is obtained from this plant as well as from *C. capsularis*, which see.

3. **Corchorus trilocularis,** *Linn. Mantiss.* (1767) p. 77. Annual; stems and branches more or less hairy. Leaves 1–4 by ¾–1¼ in., elliptic or oblong-lanceolate, acute or obtuse, serrate (the lower serratures often destitute of filiform appendages), somewhat rough below, base rounded or cuneate; petioles ¼–½ in. long, pilose; stipules lanceolate-subulate. Flowers in short cymes; buds ovoid or obovoid apiculate; bracts lanceolate-subulate; peduncles very short, leaf-opposed, hairy; pedicels very short, pubescent. Sepals ¼ in. long, linear-oblong, acuminate. Petals oblong, slightly longer than the sepals. Capsules 2–3 in. long, with a short erect beak, hairy when young with stiff stellate hairs, scabrous when old, 3–4-angled, 3–4-valved; valves with transverse partitions between the seeds. Seeds trigonous, black. Fl. B. I. v. 1, p. 397; Grah. Cat. p. 20; Dalz. & Gibs. p. 25; Boiss. Fl. Orient. v. 1, p. 845; Woodr. in Journ. Bomb. Nat. v. 11 (1897) p. 265; Watt. Dict. Econ. Prodr. v. 2, p. 544.—Flowers: Sept. VERN. *Kadu-chinch.*

DECCAN: Poona, *Cooke*!, *Woodrow*!, *Jacquemont*, 961!; Sholapore district, *Law*. GUJARAT: *Woodrow*, *Dalzell*.—DISTRIB. Tropical Africa, Afghanistan.

4. **Corchorus fascicularis,** *Lam. Encyc.* v. 2 (1786) p. 104. Annual, 6–18 in. high, much-branched from the base; stem and

branches terete, glabrous. Leaves $\frac{3}{4}$–$1\frac{1}{2}$ by $\frac{1}{4}$–$\frac{1}{2}$ in., elliptic-oblong, obtuse, serrate, the lower serratures not (or rarely) produced into filiform appendages, glabrous, base rounded or cuneate; petioles very short, pilose; stipules lanceolate-subulate. Flowers in very short (almost sessile), leaf-opposed cymes; buds obovoid apiculate; bracts long, lanceolate; peduncles 2–5-flowered. Sepals $\frac{1}{12}$ in. long, linear, apiculate. Petals oblong-obovate. Capsules $\frac{1}{2}$ in. long, shortly beaked, straight, cylindric, pubescent, 3-valved; valves slightly septate between the seeds. Seeds wedge-shaped, black, smooth. Fl. B. I. v. 1, p. 398; Dalz. & Gibs. p. 24; Trim. Fl. Ceyl. v. 1, p. 183; Woodr. in Journ. Bomb. Nat. v. 11 (1897) p. 265; Watt, Dict. Econ. Prod. v. 2, p. 539. —Flowers: Sept. VERN. *Bahuphalli.*

Tolerably common in the hotter parts of the Presidency. DECCAN: Poona, *Woodrow*!; Kolhapur, *Cooke*! GUJARAT: *Woodrow*; Surat, *Dalzell*.—DISTRIB. Tropical Africa, Australia, Ceylon.

5. **Corchorus Antichorus,** *Raeusch. Nom.* ed. 3 (1797) p. 158. Perennial, 6–9 in., prostrate, much-branched from the base; branches twisted, imbricate, woody. Leaves $\frac{1}{4}$–$\frac{3}{4}$ by $\frac{1}{4}$–$\frac{1}{2}$ in., roundish, usually wrinkled, glabrous, irregularly crenate-serrate, the serratures not appendaged, base rounded or cuneate; petioles $\frac{1}{2}$–1 in. long, very slender; stipules subulate. Flowers numerous, on leaf-opposed cymes; buds obovoid, apiculate; bracts lanceolate-subulate; peduncles and pedicels very short. Sepals $\frac{3}{16}$ in. long, linear-oblong, apiculate. Petals longer than the sepals, oblong-obovate. Capsules $\frac{3}{8}$–$\frac{5}{8}$ in. long, cylindric, beaked, glabrous, often curved upwards, 4-valved; valves scarcely, if at all, septate between the seeds. Seeds trigonous, black. Fl. B. I. v. 1, p. 398; Boiss. Fl. Orient. v. 1, p. 846; Woodr. in Journ. Bomb. Nat. v. 11 (1897) p. 265; Watt, Dict. Econ. Prod. v. 2, p. 535. *Corchorus humilis,* Munro, Hort. Agrensis, App. p. 35; Dalz. & Gibs. p. 25.— Flowers: Sept.–Oct. VERN. *Mulhiri.*

Common in dry and hot districts; a member of the Indian desert flora. DECCAN: *Dalzell.* GUJARAT: *Dalzell*; Rajkot (Kathiawar), *Cooke*!; Gogo (Kathiawar), *Dalzell*! SIND: *Stocks*!, *Dalzell*!; Hyderabad, *Strachan*!—DISTRIB. Tropical Africa, Afghanistan, Arabia, Cape de Verde Islands.

6. **Corchorus tridens,** *Linn. Mantiss., App.* (1771) p. 566. Annual, 1–2 ft. high; branches glabrous. Leaves $1\frac{1}{2}$–$3\frac{1}{2}$ by $\frac{1}{2}$–1 in., linear-oblong or lanceolate, crenate-serrate, the lower serratures on each side usually prolonged into filiform appendages, glabrous or more or less pubescent; petioles $\frac{1}{4}$–$\frac{1}{2}$ in. long; stipules subulate, $\frac{1}{4}$ in. long. Flowers 1–4 together, nearly sessile; buds obovoid, apiculate. Sepals $\frac{1}{8}$ in. long, linear-oblong, apiculate. Petals obovate-oblong, slightly longer than the sepals. Capsules 1–$1\frac{1}{2}$ in. long, slender, glabrous, terminating in 3 stellately spreading or deflexed points, 3-valved; valves without partitions. Seeds truncate at both ends, black. Fl. B. I. v. 1, p. 398; Woodr. in Journ. Bomb. Nat. v. 11 (1897) p. 265; Watt, Dict. Econ. Prod. v. 2, p. 544.

SIND: *Woodrow, Stocks*!—DISTRIB. Tropical Africa and Australia.

7. **Corchorus acutangulus,** *Lam. Encyc.* v. 2 (1786) p. 104. Annual, much-branched; branches more or less pubescent. Leaves 1–$3\frac{1}{2}$ by $\frac{1}{2}$–$1\frac{3}{4}$ in., ovate, acute, serrate, the lower serratures on each side

usually produced into filiform appendages, glabrous, base rounded; petioles $\frac{1}{2}$–1 in. long, slender, hairy; stipules lanceolate, acicular. Flowers small, in leaf-opposed cymes; buds obovoid, apiculate; bracts filiform; peduncles almost 0; pedicels 2–3, very short. Sepals $\frac{3}{16}$ in. long, linear-oblong, apiculate. Petals spathulate, a little longer than the sepals. Capsules $\frac{3}{4}$–$1\frac{1}{2}$ in. long, erect, stout, cylindric, truncate, 6-angled (3 of the angles winged); valves 3–4, slightly septate or without partitions; beak 3-fid, the tips stellately spreading or recurved. Seeds truncate, dark brown. Fl. B. I. v. 1, p. 398; Grah. Cat. p. 20; Dalz. & Gibs. p. 25; Trim. Fl. Ceyl. v. 1, p. 183; Woodr. in Journ. Bomb. Nat. v. 11 (1897) p. 265; Watt, Dict. Econ. Prod. v. 2, p. 534.—Flowers: Sept.

A common weed. KONKAN: *Law*!, *Stocks*!; Bombay, *Capt. Geburne*!; Parel (Bombay), *Woodrow*!; Neral (below Matheran), *Woodrow*! GUJARAT: Godra, *Cooke*! SIND: Jemadar ka Landa (near Karachi), *Stocks*!—DISTRIB. Ceylon.

5. ELÆOCARPUS, Linn.

Trees. Leaves simple, entire or serrate. Flowers in racemes, rarely polygamous. Sepals 4–5, valvate (rarely imbricate), distinct. Petals as many as the sepals, laciniate, lobed or rarely entire, inserted round the base of a thickened glandular torus. Stamens numerous (rarely 8–12), inserted on the torus between the glands; anthers linear, dehiscing by a transverse valve at the apex. Ovary 2–5-celled; ovules 2 in each cell; style subulate, entire. Drupe with a single bony tuberculate stone, 3–5- or (by suppression) 1-celled; cells 1-seeded. Seeds pendulous; testa crustaceous or bony; albumen fleshy; cotyledons broad, flat or undulate.—DISTRIB. Tropical Asia, islands of the Pacific and Australia; species about 50.

Anthers not terminated by an awn.
  Drupe 5-celled .... 1. *E. Ganitrus.*
  Drupe 1–3-celled.
    Anthers bearded; filaments short, straight .... 2. *E. serratus.*
    Anthers rarely bearded; filaments long, twice bent......... 3. *E. oblongus.*
Anthers terminated by a long awn.
  Leaves obovate.
    Stone much tubercled .... 4. *E. tuberculatus.*
    Stone rugose, not tubercled .... 5. *E. aristatus.*
  Leaves ovate-lanceolate...................................... 6. *E. Munroii.*

1. **Elæocarpus Ganitrus,** *Roxb. Hort. Beng.* (1814) p. 42. A tree. Leaves 4–6 by 1–$1\frac{3}{4}$ in., oblong-lanceolate, acute or acuminate (rarely obtuse), obscurely and irregularly crenate-serrate or subentire, decurrent into the petiole, glabrous; petioles $\frac{1}{4}$–$\frac{3}{8}$ in. long. Racemes 2–3 in. long, from the old wood; buds ovoid-conical, pointed; pedicels $\frac{1}{4}$ in. long. Sepals $\frac{1}{4}$ in. long, oblong, acuminate, pubescent outside. Petals $\frac{5}{16}$ in. long, oblong, laciniate about half way down, ciliolate. Stamens about 40, in groups opposite each petal; filaments very short; anthers linear, one valve tipped at the apex with a small tuft of glistening hairs. Ovary pilose, 5-celled; style longer than the stamens. Drupes $\frac{1}{2}$–$\frac{3}{4}$ in. in diam., globose or somewhat obovoid, purple; stone tubercled, 5-celled, 5-seeded. Fl. B. I. v. 1, p. 400; Grah. Cat. p. 22; Dalz. & Gibs. p. 27; Talb. Trees, Bomb. p. 27; Woodr. in Journ. Bomb. Nat. v. 11 (1897)

p. 265; Watt, Dict. Econ. Prod. v. 3, p. 205.—Flowers: Jan.-Feb. VERN. *Rudráksh.*

On the Western Gháts, but not common. KONKAN: W. Gháts, *De Crespigny*; S Konkan, *Graham*; on the higher Gháts, *Dalzell & Gibson.*—DISTRIB. Malaya.
The tubercled stones are made into rosaries and bracelets which are worn by Brahmins and Fakirs. The stones are imported from Singapore where the tree is abundant.

2. **Elæocarpus serratus,** *Linn. Sp. Pl.* (1753) p. 515. A small tree; young parts pubescent. Leaves 2–4½ by 1–2 in., oblong or obovate, obtuse, acute or shortly acuminate, irregularly crenate, glabrous, often with glandular thickenings in the nerve-axils, base acute; petioles ½–¾ in. long, glabrous. Flowers in drooping racemes 2–3 in. long, in the axils of fallen leaves; buds ovoid; pedicels ¼–⅜ in. long. Sepals ¼ in. long, lanceolate, acute. Petals 5/16 in. long, white, cuneate-obovate, laciniate half way down. Stamens about 30; filaments short; anthers linear, one valve tipped at the apex with a small tuft of glistening hairs. Ovary pilose, 3-celled; style slender, longer than the stamens, the basal part hairy. Drupes 1–1¼ in. long, oblong, narrowed at the base, bluntly pointed at the apex, greenish yellow, smooth; stone oblong, pointed, much tubercled, 1-celled, 1-seeded. Fl. B. I. v. 1, p. 401; Trim. Fl. Ceyl. v. 1, p. 184; Talb. Trees, Bomb. p. 27; Watt, Dict. Econ. Prod. v. 3, p. 206.—Flowers: Jan.-Feb. VERN. *Perinkara.*

KANARA: S. Gháts of N. Kanara in evergreen forests; common near the falls of Gairsoppa, *Talbot*; Kadgal (N. Kanara), *Talbot*, 281!—DISTRIB. Malaya, Ceylon.
The fruit is pickled in oil and salt like olives, and the outer fleshy portion eaten in curries (*Watt*).

3. **Elæocarpus oblongus,** *Gærtn. Fruct.* v. 1 (1788) p. 202, t. 43. A tree, the foliage often tinged with red. Leaves 3–4 by 1¾–2 in., elliptic, acute or acuminate, crenate-serrate with a small glandular point at each of the crenatures, quite glabrous, shining, base cuneate; petioles ¾–1¼ in. long, more or less pubescent. Flowers in racemes from the axils of fallen leaves; buds ovoid or subglobose; peduncles 3–5 in. long, red; pedicels ¼–⅜ in. long, red. Sepals ¼ in. long, ovate, acute, reddish brown. Petals ¼–5/16 in. long, white, fringed to about half way down or a little less, ciliolate. Stamens about 45, in groups of about 9 opposite each petal; filaments long, curved outwards at the base, abruptly incurved at the apex; anthers not (or rarely ?) bearded at the apex, the valves puberulous. Ovary pilose; style short, conical, hairy. Drupes 1–1¼ in. long, oblong, narrowed at both ends; stone 2-celled, 2-seeded. Fl. B. I. v. 1, p. 403; Grah. Cat. p. 21; Dalz. & Gibs. p. 27; Wight, Icon. t. 46; Talb. Trees, Bomb. p. 27; Woodr. in Journ. Bomb. Nat. v. 1, p. 265; Watt, Dict. Econ. Prod. v. 3, p. 206.—Flowers: May. VERN. *Kásav*; *Kása.*

On the higher Gháts to the south. KONKAN: *Gibson*!, *Law*! DECCAN: Wai Ghát, *Graham*!; Mahableshwar, *H. M. Birdwood*, *Cooke*!; near Satara, *Woodrow*! KANARA: *Ritchie*, 1635! N. Kanara in evergreen forests, *Talbot*.—DISTRIB. Malaya.

4. **Elæocarpus tuberculatus,** *Roxb. Hort. Beng.* (1814) p. 93; *Fl. Ind.* v. 2, p. 594. A large tree. Leaves 5–8 by 2½–4 in., obovate-cuneate, obtuse, obscurely crenate-dentate or subentire, strongly penninerved, glabrous above, fulvous-pubescent on the nerves beneath, base usually rounded; petioles 1 in. long, more or less hairy. Flowers very

numerous, in rusty-pubescent racemes 2–4 in. long; buds ovoid, acute; pedicels up to 1 in. long. Sepals $\frac{1}{2}$–$\frac{9}{16}$ in. long, oblong-lanceolate or linear-oblong, acute, fulvous-pubescent without and with a few hairs within. Petals a little longer than the sepals, wedge-shaped, hairy at the base inside, silky villous outside, laciniate one third of the way down. Stamens 40–50; filaments $\frac{1}{12}$ in. long; anthers slender, linear, each with an erect awn $\frac{1}{10}$–$\frac{1}{8}$ in. long, which is often slightly curled or twisted. Ovary conical, silky-villous, 2-celled; style silky near the base, rapidly tapering from base to apex. Drupes 1½–2 in.; stone compressed, tubercled on the flattened sides and with a thickened margin. Fl. B. I. v. 1, p. 404; K. Schum. in Engl. & Prantl, Pflanzenf. v. 3, part 6, p. 4, fig. 1, A, B; Talb. Trees, Bomb. p. 27; Woodr. in Journ. Bomb. Nat. v. 11 (1897) p. 265; Watt, Dict. Econ. Prod. v. 3, p. 206. *Monocera tuberculata*, W. & A. Prodr. p. 83; Wight, Icon. t. 62; Dalz. & Gibs. p. 27.—Flowers: Jan. VERN. *Rudrak*.

In Wight's Icon. t. 62, the style is incorrectly copied from Roxburgh's drawing.—It is shown as terete, glabrous, while it should have been shown as tapering, silky.

Southern Ghâts from Belgaum southwards ex *Talbot*. KANARA: *Stocks*!, *Hohenhacker*, 581!—DISTRIB. Malaya.

5. **Elæocarpus aristatus,** *Roxb. Hort. Beng.* (1814) p. 42; *Fl. Ind.* v. 2, p. 599. A tree. Leaves 8–11 by 3–4½ in., obovate-cuneate, obtuse, acute or somewhat acuminate, more or less irregularly crenate-serrate, glabrous on both surfaces, base acute (rarely rounded); petioles 1 in. long, usually glabrous. Flowers numerous; buds long, elliptic-lanceolate, pointed. Sepals $\frac{9}{16}$ in. long, pubescent. Petals cuneate, a little longer than the sepals, hairy at the base within, silky-villous without, somewhat more deeply and more finely divided at the apex than in the last species. Stamens 40–50; awn erect; filaments glabrous, short. Ovary 2-celled, silky-villous, conical; style tapering from a conical base, the basal portion silky. Fruit of the size and shape of an olive; stone oblong, pointed at both ends, somewhat rugose (not tuberculate), 1- or (rarely) 2-celled. Fl. B. I. v. 1, p. 405; Talb. Trees, Bomb. p. 27. *Monocera Roxburghii*, Wight, Icon. t. 63.—Flowers: Apr.

Rare. KONKAN: *Stocks*!; Talkat Ghât, *Dalzell*!

6. **Elæocarpus Munroii,** *Mast. in Hook. f. Fl. B. I.* v. 1, p. 407. A tree. Leaves 2½–4 by 1¼–2 in., crowded towards the ends of the branches, ovate-lanceolate, acuminate, crenate-serrate, glabrous on both surfaces, base rounded, acute or subcordate; petioles 1–1½ in. long, glabrous. Flowers numerous in racemes which are usually shorter than the leaves; buds ellipsoid; pedicels ¼–½ in. long. Sepals $\frac{5}{16}$ in. long, narrow-lanceolate, acute, pubescent without. Petals a little longer than the sepals, oblong, silky on both surfaces, laciniate about one third of the way down; segments 10–12. Ovary 2-celled, silky-puberulous; style straight, tapering, longer than the stamens, the basal half silky-puberulous. Drupe size of a small olive, yellowish, edible; stone 1-celled. Fl. B. I. v. 1, p. 407; Talb. Trees, Bomb. p. 27. *Monocera Munroii*, Wight, Icon. t. 952.—Flowers: Sept.–Oct.

This plant has been included on the authority of a specimen in Herb. Kew. marked "Konkan, *Stocks*!"

Order XXVIII. LINACEÆ.

Herbs or shrubs, rarely trees, usually glabrous. Leaves usually alternate, simple, entire, rarely crenate-serrate; stipules lateral or intrapetiolar or 0. Inflorescence various, normally racemose. Flowers regular, hermaphrodite. Sepals 5 (rarely 4), free or connate at the base, imbricate. Petals as many as the sepals, hypogynous or rarely slightly perigynous, imbricate, often contorted, usually fugacious, blue, yellow or white, rarely rosy. Stamens as many as the petals with as many interposed staminodes, or twice (rarely thrice) as many, united at the base into a ring or a short hypogynous or slightly perigynous tube; filaments filiform, inserted on the apex or a little below the apex of the tube, within or without; anthers versatile, 2-celled, dehiscing longitudinally; glands 5, entire or didymous, usually adnate to the staminal-tube or obsolete. Ovary free, entire, 3-5-celled; ovules 1-2 in each cell, inserted beneath the apex of the inner angle, pendulous, anatropous; raphe ventral; micropyle superior; styles 3-5, free or more or less connate; stigmas terminal. Fruit capsular, septicidally splitting into as many (or by the presence of false dissepiments), double as many valves as there are cells to the ovary, leaving no axis, less commonly a drupe. Seeds in each valve or pyrene 1-2, usually compressed; testa sometimes expanded into a membranous wing; albumen fleshy or 0; embryo almost as long as the seed, straight or rarely incurved; cotyledons flat or plano-convex, usually ovate or elliptic; radicle superior.—Distrib. Throughout the world; genera 14; species about 135.

Herbs .... 1. Linum.
An erect undershrub .... 2. Reinwardtia.
A scandent shrub, with hooked woody tendrils .... 3. Hugonia.

1. LINUM, Linn.

Herbs sometimes suffrutescent, usually glabrous. Leaves generally alternate, narrow, entire, 1-many-nerved; stipules 0 or glanduliform. Inflorescence various. Sepals 5, entire. Petals 5, contorted, fugacious. Stamens 5, connate at the base, hypogynous, alternate with the petals, often alternating with minute or setiform staminodes; glands 5, small, adnate to the staminal-tube outside, opposite to the petals. Ovary 5-celled, the cells imperfectly septate, 2-seeded, or with a perfect, fissile septum, 10-valved, 1-seeded. Seeds compressed; albumen scanty; embryo straight.—Distrib. Temperate and warm regions; species 80.

Flowers large, 1 in. in diam., blue .... 1. *L. usitatissimum.*
Flowers small, ⅓ in. in diam., yellow .... 2. *L. mysorense.*

1. **Linum usitatissimum,** *Linn. Sp. Pl.* (1753) p. 277. Annual, 2–4 ft. high; stems solitary or few, corymbosely branched; branches ascending towards the apex. Leaves up to 1½ in. long, linear-lanceolate, attenuated at both ends, acute at the apex. Flowers about 1 in. across, in corymbose panicles. Sepals: the two outer elliptic, acuminate, with entire membranous margins; the three inner broader, acuminate, with ciliate margins, all strongly 3-nerved, the middle nerve alone reaching the apex. Petals blue, slightly crenate. Capsules mucronate, the edge of the dissepiments in the interior glabrous. Seeds compressed, ellipsoid,

smooth, dark brown, shining. Fl. B. I. v. 1, p. 410; Grah. Cat. p. 34; Dalz. & Gibs. Suppl. p. 16; Woodr. in Journ. Bomb. Nat. v. 11 (1897) p. 265; Watt, Dict. Econ. Prod. v. 5, p. 2.—Flowers: Feb.-Mar. VERN. *Alsi*; *Javas*.

The well-known flax-plant. Native country unknown, but supposed to have originally been introduced from Egypt, where it was in use in the time of the Pharaohs. It is grown in India for the oil procurable from the seeds, not for the fibre. For a full account of the plant and its uses, consult Watt, Dict. Econ. Prod. l. c.—DISTRIB. All regions where flax is cultivated for oil or fibre.

2. **Linum mysorense,** *Heyne, in Wall. Cat.* (1828) 1507. Annual, 6–18 in. high, glabrous; stem erect, slender, striate, leafy. Leaves sessile, ½–¾ in. long, oblong-elliptic or obovate, mucronate, tapering at the base, 3-nerved. Flowers ⅓ in. across, on short pedicels, solitary, collectively forming a corymbose terminal panicle made up of unilateral cymes. Sepals ⅛ in. long, elliptic-lanceolate, pointed, glabrous, 3-nerved. Petals yellow, about twice as long as the sepals, obovate, rounded at the apex, acute at the base. Filaments dilated and connate below. Ovary glabrous; styles slightly connate at the base. Capsules globose, apiculate, surrounded by the persistent sepals. Seeds 10, elliptic, compressed, smooth. Fl. B. I. v. 1, p. 411; Grah. Cat. p. 33; Dalz. & Gibs. p. 16; Trim. Fl. Ceyl. v. 1, p. 188; Woodr. in Journ. Bomb. Nat. v. 11 (1897) p. 265; Watt, Dict. Econ. Prod. v. 5, p. 1.—Flowers: Oct.-Dec. VERN. *Undri*.

Very common on the Konkan and Deccan hills; abundant at Mahableshwar. DECCAN: hills at Pár, *Dalzell*!; Khandala, *Graham*; Kolhapur, *Woodrow*; Mahableshwar, *Cooke*!—DISTRIB. Ceylon.

2. REINWARDTIA, Dumort.

Undershrubs. Leaves alternate, membranous, usually serrate, penninerved; stipules minute, caducous. Flowers large, yellow or white, in very short fasciculate axillary racemes or in dense corymbs at the ends of the branches; pedicels bracteate. Sepals 5, entire. Petals 5, contorted, fugacious. Stamens 5, connate at the base, hypogynous, with as many interposed setiform staminodes. Glands 2–3, adnate to the staminal-tube. Ovary 3–5-celled, cells 2-locellate; ovule 1 in each locellus; styles 3–4 (rarely 5 or 7), filiform, stigmatose at the apex. Capsule globose, splitting into 6–8 valves; valves 1-seeded. Seeds reniform; albumen thin; embryo straight.—DISTRIB. Endemic; species 1 or 2.

1. **Reinwardtia trigyna,** *Planch. in Hook. Lond. Journ. Bot.* v. 7 (1848) p. 522. An undershrub, 2–3 ft. high; branches terete, with longitudinally wrinkled bark, glabrous. Leaves 2–4 by 1–1½ in., elliptic-lanceolate, acute, distantly serrate, decurrent into a short petiole, glabrous, mucronate; stipules minute, subulate, caducous. Flowers yellow, handsome, 1–1½ in. across. Sepals ½–⅝ in. long, oblong-lanceolate, very acute. Petals obovate, cuneate. Stamens 5, dimorphic, long stamens and short styles and short stamens and long styles occurring in different flowers; pollen grains of the short stamens larger than those of the long ones. Styles normally 3, free or connate at the base, sometimes 4, 5 or 7 of different lengths; stigmas of the long styles larger than those of the short ones. Capsules globose, shorter than the sepals. Fl. B. I. v. 1, p. 412; Woodr. in Journ. Bomb. Nat. v. 11 (1897) p. 265; Watt, Dict.

Econ. Prod. v. 6, part 1, p. 427. *Reinwardlia trigyna*, Dalz. & Gibs. p. 16. *Linum trigynum*, Roxb. in As. Res. v. 6, p. 357; Grah. Cat. p. 34.—Flowers: Jan. VERN. *Abai.*

Widely planted in gardens, but found wild in a few localities.—Dalzell notes that it occurs wild on Miradonger, near Pen in the Konkan, where it has also been found by Woodrow. I have found it in the Deccan on the banks of the Koina river below Mahableshwar far removed from any habitation.

The dimorphism of the sexual organs of *Reinwardtia trigyna* has been treated of by Alefeld in Botan. Zeit. (1863) p. 282. Sir Henry Collett in 1884 made a careful and exhaustive examination of upwards of 100 fresh specimens from the hills below Simla, and the subjoined table gives the forms which he has been able to differentiate (MS. in Herb. Kew.).

A. Long-styled forms.
   Stamens in 2 rows, 3 of the stamens being distinctly longer than the other 2.
   (*a*) Styles 3; stamens about half as long as the styles.
   (*b*) Styles 4, three long and one short, the latter equalling the longer stamens.
   (*c*) Styles 5, three long and two short, the 2 shorter equalling respectively the long and short stamens.

B. Short-styled forms.
   Stamens in 2 rows, three being distinctly longer than the other two.
   (*a*) Styles 3, equalling in length the 2 shorter stamens.
   (*b*) Styles 3, standing below the 2 shorter stamens.
   (*c*) Styles 7, standing below the 2 shorter stamens.
   (*d*) An abnormal form with all 5 stamens of slightly unequal lengths; the 3 styles on a level with the shortest stamen.

C. All the styles and stamens of the same length.

Sir H. Collett's observations make it evident that the species *R. tetragyna* can scarcely be maintained as a separate one, a fact long since suspected by Hooker (Fl. B. I. v. 1, p. 412 under *R. tetragyna*).

3. **HUGONIA,** Linn.

Scandent shrubs, often tomentose. Leaves alternate, penninerved, stipulate. Inflorescence various; flowers yellow, the 2 lowest peduncles of each branch converted into spiral hooks. Sepals 5. Petals 5, hypogynous, contorted, fugacious. Stamens 10, connate at the base into a short tube, with glandular swellings between the petals. Ovary 5-celled; ovules 2 collateral in each cell; styles 5, filiform, stigmatose at the apex. Drupe globose, fleshy or baccate. Seeds compressed, albuminous; embryo straight or slightly curved; cotyledons flat; radicle short.—DISTRIB. Tropical Asia and Africa; species 6.

1. **Hugonia Mystax,** *Linn. Sp. Pl.* (1753) p. 675. A rambling scandent shrub; branches yellow-tomentose, with short horizontal branchlets, leafless below and provided near the ends with a pair of circinate hooks. Leaves $1\frac{1}{2}$–$2\frac{1}{2}$ by 1–$1\frac{1}{2}$ in., elliptic-obovate, obtuse or subacute, entire, reticulately veined, the veins conspicuous on both surfaces, glabrous, base tapering; petioles $\frac{1}{16}$ in. long, hairy; stipules lanceolate-subulate. Flowers at the extremities of the short branchlets 1–$1\frac{1}{4}$ in. across, terminal and in the upper axils; pedicels short, 1-flowered, clothed with soft yellow hairs. Sepals $\frac{5}{16}$ in. long, ovate-lanceolate, acute, fulvous-pubescent. Petals many times longer than the sepals, thin, ovate-oblong, acute or truncate. Styles longer than the stamens; stigmas capitate. Drupes about $\frac{3}{8}$ in. in diam., globose, surrounded by the persistent sepals; pulp scanty; stone bony, grooved,

10-celled, with usually 2 or 3 seeds. Fl. B. I. v. 1, p. 413; Dalz. & Gibs. p. 17; Trim. Fl. Ceyl. v. 1, p. 189; Reiche, in Engl. & Prantl, Pflanzenf. v. 3, part 4, p. 33, fig. 29; Talb. Trees, Bomb. p. 28; Watt, Dict. Econ. Prod. v. 4, p. 302.—Flowers: Aug.

Rare. KONKAN: *Law*!, *Stocks*!; between Malwan and Vingorla, *Dalzell*! KANARA: *Stocks*!—DISTRIB. Ceylon.

ORDER XXIX. MALPHIGIACEÆ.

Trees or shrubs, often climbing. Leaves (in the Indian genera) opposite, entire; glands often present on the petiole or the bottom of the blade or margin of the leaf; stipules small or 0. Inflorescence axillary and terminal; flowers hermaphrodite, regular or irregular; pedicels articulated, bracteate. Calyx usually 5-partite; segments imbricate, very rarely valvate, 1 or more (never all) furnished with a large gland, rarely eglandular (*Aspidopterys*). Petals 5, longer than the calyx, usually equal, fimbriate or dentate, clawed or not. Disk inconspicuous. Stamens usually 10, hypogynous or subperigynous, equal, or 1 or more much longer than the others; filaments free or connate at the base; anthers short, 2-celled. Ovary 3-celled; ovules solitary in each cell; styles 1–3, straight or circinate; stigmas terminal or sublateral, inconspicuous. Fruit (in the Indian genera) of one or more winged samaras. Seeds exalbuminous; embryo straight or curved; radicle superior.—DISTRIB. Throughout Brazil and Guiana, less widely in tropical America, Africa and Asia; species about 600.

Styles 1, rarely 2; calycine gland large .... 1. HIPTAGE.
Styles 3; calycine gland 0 .... 2. ASPIDOPTERYS.

1. HIPTAGE, Gærtn.

Scandent shrubs. Leaves opposite, coriaceous, entire, petioled, eglandular, exstipulate. Racemes terminal and axillary, sometimes compound; peduncles erect, bracteate at the base, articulated with the 2-bracteate pedicels. Flowers white, fragrant, the fifth petal discolored. Calyx 5-partite, with 1 large gland partly adnate to the pedicel. Petals clawed, unequal, silky. Stamens 10, declinate, all fertile, one much larger than the others; filaments connate at the very base. Ovary 3-lobed; lobes appendiculate; styles 1–2, filiform, at first circinate, the others rudimentary; stigma capitellate. Fruit of 1–3 samaras, 2–3-winged. Seeds subglobose; cotyledons unequal, thick, curved.—DISTRIB. Tropical Asia; species 4.

1. **Hiptage Madablota,** *Gærtn. Fruct.* v. 2 (1791) p. 169, t. 116. A large woody much-branched climbing shrub; young parts silky. Leaves coriaceous, 4–7 by $1\frac{3}{4}$–3 in., elliptic-oblong, acuminate or acute, entire, glabrous, strongly nerved beneath, base acute; petioles $\frac{1}{4}$–$\frac{3}{8}$ in. long, silky-pubescent. Flowers $\frac{1}{2}$–$\frac{3}{4}$ in. across, fragrant, white, in erect finely tomentose racemes about as long as the leaves; bracts lanceolate. Calyx persistent, densely pubescent outside; lobes oblong, obtuse, one with a large oblong gland at the base outside. Petals twice as long as the sepals, orbicular, clawed, fringed on the margin, the uppermost petal broader than the rest. Carpels with a central wing between the two lateral, the inner wing 1–$1\frac{1}{2}$ in. long, the 2 lateral wings $\frac{3}{4}$ in. long.

Seed solitary, globose. Fl. B. I. v. 1, p. 418; Grah. Cat. p. 28; Trim. Fl. Ceyl. v. 1, p. 193; Niedenzu, in Engl. & Prantl, Pflanzenf. v. 3, part 4, p. 46, fig. 38, E, et p. 49, fig. 39, D; Talb. Trees, Bomb. p. 28; Woodr. in Journ. Bomb. Nat. v. 11 (1897) p. 265; Watt, Dict. Econ. Prod. v. 4, p. 252. *Heptage Madablota*, Dalz. & Gibs. p. 33.—Flowers: Jan.-Mar. VERN. *Madhumálati*; *Haladvel.*

Grows abundantly on the Western Ghâts. KONKAN: *Stocks*!, *Law*!, *Woodrow*; Bombay, in gardens, *Graham*. DECCAN: Panchgani, *H. M. Birdwood.* KANARA: Supa, on the Kála naddi, *Ritchie*, 1001!—DISTRIB. China, Java, Ceylon.

2. **ASPIDOPTERYS,** A. Juss.

Scandent shrubs. Leaves quite entire, petioled, eglandular, exstipulate. Panicles axillary or terminal, simple or compound; peduncles bracteate; pedicels usually slender. Flowers white or yellow, inodorous. Calyx short, 5-partite, eglandular. Petals clawed, entire. Stamens 10, all perfect; filaments filiform, distinct or connate at the base; anthers ovate, glabrous. Ovary 3-lobed, the lobes flattened at the back, the sides winged; styles 3, glabrous; stigmas capitate. Fruit of 1–3 samaras surrounded by a scutiform, ovate or orbicular, membranous wing, sometimes shortly crested in the middle. Seeds oblong, subterete; cotyledons straight, equal; radicle short.—DISTRIB. Tropical Asia; species 15.

Nucleus not dorsally winged.
  Leaves ovate-elliptic, glabrous beneath .... 1. *A. Roxburghiana.*
  Leaves cordate, clothed with white tomentum beneath ...... 2. *A. cordata.*
Nucleus dorsally winged .... 3. *A. canarensis.*

1. **Aspidopterys Roxburghiana,** *A. Juss. in Ann. Sc. Nat.* ser. 2, v. 13 (1840) p. 267. A climbing shrub; branches slender; young parts glabrous or tomentose. Leaves 3–4 by 1½–2 in., ovate-elliptic, acuminate, entire, glabrous on both surfaces except on the midrib which is more or less pubescent, base rounded; petioles ¼–½ in. long, rusty-pubescent. Flowers small, ⅛ in. across, in dense terminal and axillary rusty-tomentose panicles; bracts lanceolate, pubescent. Calyx persistent; lobes ovate, obtuse, tomentose. Petals obovate, concave, white. Stamens 10; filaments connate at the base, the exterior shorter. Ovary pilose; styles slightly longer than the stamens. Samara linear-oblong, 1–2 by ½–¾ in., membranous, glabrous, yellowish-brown; nucleus not winged or keeled. Fl. B. I. v. 1, p. 420; Dalz. & Gibs. p. 33; Niedenzu, in Engl. & Prantl, Pflanzenf. v. 3, part 4, p. 46, fig. 38, A; Talb. Trees, Bomb. p. 29; Woodr. in Journ. Bomb. Nat. v. 11 (1897) p. 265. *Hiræa indica*, Roxb. Hort. Beng. p. 90; Grah. Cat. p. 28.—Flowers: Dec.

Forests of the Western Ghâts; not common. KONKAN: *Dalzell & Gibson*; Ghât forests, *Talbot.* DECCAN: hills near Satara, *Woodrow*; Khandala, *Dalzell & Gibson*; Khandala Ghât, *Graham.*

2. **Aspidopterys cordata,** *A. Juss. in Ann. Sc. Nat.* ser. 2, v. 13 (1840) p. 267. A slender climber; young parts tomentose. Leaves 4–7 in. in diam., orbicular or broadly ovate, abruptly terminated by a broad acuminate tip, glabrous or nearly so above, white-tomentose beneath, base cordate; petioles 1–1¼ in. long, rusty-pubescent. Flowers ¼ in. across, in tomentose lax panicles; bracts subulate or 0. Calyx

small; lobes ovate, acute. Petals thrice as long as the lobes of the calyx, oblong-elliptic, rounded at the apex. Samara orbicular or slightly elliptic, 1-1¼ in. in diam., membranous, closely reticulately veined, glabrous, pale brown; nucleus not dorsally winged or keeled. Fl. B. I. v. 1, p. 421; Dalz. & Gibs. p. 34; Talb. Trees, Bomb. p. 29; Woodr. in Journ. Bomb. Nat. v. 11 (1897) p. 265.—Flowers: Sept.-Nov. VERN. *Buryel.*

Throughout the Konkan, Deccan and Kanara in moist forests. KONKAN: *Stocks*!; island of Salsette, *Jacquemont*, 991!; near Pen, *Dalzell & Gibson*; Matheran, *Woodrow*. DECCAN: Bowdhan jungle, near Poona, *Cooke*! S. M. COUNTRY: Belgaum, *Ritchie*, 1⁸⁄₁ !; Londa, *Woodrow*. KANARA: Yellapur (N. Kanara), *Talbot*!

3. **Aspidopterys canarensis,** *Dalz. in Hook. Kew Journ. Bot.* v. 3 (1851) p. 37. A climbing shrub; branches with wrinkled bark, glabrous. Leaves 3–4 by 1½-2 in., elliptic-lanceolate, obtusely acuminate, glabrous when adult, sparingly clothed with fusiform hairs attached by the middle when very young, margins repand, base rounded or subacute; petioles ⅛ in. long, channelled, glabrous. Flowers in long-pedicelled umbelliform racemes from a very short peduncle, which is clothed with minute rusty-tomentose bracts; pedicels filiform, ⅜-¾ in. long, glabrous. Calyx rufous-tomentose outside; lobes ovate, obtuse. Petals oblong, obtuse, 4 times as long as the calyx. Ovary glabrate. Samaras 1-1⅓ in. in diam., suborbicular, very membranous, pale yellowish-brown, the margins entire or lobed towards the apex; nucleus with a dorsal wing. Fl. B. I. v. 1, p. 420; Talb. Trees, Bomb. p. 29; Woodr. in Journ. Bomb. Nat. v. 11 (1897) p. 265.—Flowers: Feb.-Mar.

The Ghâts of the Konkan and Kanara; rare. KONKAN: *Stocks*!, *Dalzell*! KANARA: *Dalzell*; evergreen forests of the Supa Ghâts, N. Kanara (rare), *Talbot*; Kumta and Sirsi Road, *Woodrow*; Nilkund (N. Kanara), *Woodrow*.

ORDER XXX. ZYGOPHYLLACEÆ.

Herbs or shrubs, rarely trees; branches usually articulate. Leaves opposite or alternate (by suppression), stipulate, 2-3-foliolate or pinnate; leaflets entire, opunctate, sometimes connate; stipules twin, persistent, sometimes spiny. Peduncles usually 1-2 in the axils of the stipules, 1-flowered, rarely bracteate. Flowers hermaphrodite, regular or irregular, white, yellow or red, rarely blue. Sepals 5 (rarely 4), free or rarely connate at the base, imbricate (rarely valvate or open), in æstivation. Petals 5-4 rarely 0, hypogynous, free, imbricate or contorted, rarely valvate. Disk convex or depressed, rarely annular inconspicuous or 0, eglandular. Stamens as many as the petals or twice (rarely thrice) as many, inserted at the base of the disk, those opposite to the petals often connate at the base with the claw of the petals; filaments filiform, usually with a scale within at the base or the middle; anthers versatile, dehiscing longitudinally. Ovary sessile or rarely on a short gynophore, furrowed, angled or winged, 4-5- (rarely 2-12-) celled; cells very rarely with partial transverse septa; ovules 2 or more (rarely 1), often filiform, pendulous or ascending; raphe ventral; micropyle superior; style simple, terminal, angular or furrowed; stigma simple, rarely discoid, or stigmas 5. Fruit various (never baccate), coriaceous or crustaceous, sometimes dividing into 2–10 dehiscent or indehiscent (sometimes spiny) cocci cohering or free from the axis, or capsular and septicidally dehiscent. Seeds usually pendulous and solitary (rarely 2 or more) in each cell, oblong or linear; raphe adnate or free; testa membranous, crustaceous or thick and mucilaginous; albumen scanty (rarely 0); embryo as long as the seed, green, straight or rarely curved; cotyledons oblong or linear, thick or foliaceous; radicle short, straight, superior.—DISTRIB. Tropical and warm regions of both hemispheres; rare in tropical Africa; genera 17; species about 100.

Seeds exalbuminous .... 1. TRIBULUS.
Seeds albuminous.
  Petals 0 .... 2. SEETZENIA.
  Petals 4–5.
    Stamens 12–15 .... 3. PEGANUM.
    Stamens 8–10.
      Ovules axile; stipules not spiny .... 4. ZYGOPHYLLUM.
      Ovules basal; stipules spiny .... 5. FAGONIA.

1. TRIBULUS, Linn.

Branching prostrate herbs, often with silky hairs. Leaves stipulate, opposite (or sometimes alternate by suppression), usually one of the pair smaller than the other, abruptly pinnate. Flowers solitary, pseudo-axillary, white or yellow. Sepals 5, imbricate. Petals 5, spreading, imbricate, fugacious. Disk annular, 10-lobed. Stamens 10 (rarely 5), inserted on the base of the disk, the longer opposite to the petals, the 5 shorter with a small gland outside; filaments filiform, naked. Ovary sessile, hirsute, 5–12-lobed, 5–12-celled; ovules 1–5 in each cell, superposed; style short, pyramidal or filiform; stigmas 5–12. Fruit 5-angled, of 5–12 winged or spinous or tuberculate indehiscent cocci. Seeds obliquely pendulous; testa membranous; embryo exalbuminous; cotyledons oval; radicle short.—DISTRIB. Warmer regions of the globe; species about 15.

Cocci with 2 long and 2 short spines .... 1. *T. terrestris.*
Cocci broadly winged .... 2. *T. alatus.*

1. **Tribulus terrestris,** *Linn. Sp. Pl.* (1753) p. 387. A procumbent herb; stems and branches pilose; young parts silky-villous. Leaves opposite, abruptly pinnate, one of each pair usually smaller than the other, sometimes wanting; stipules lanceolate, hairy; leaflets 3–6 pairs, ¼–½ in. long, oblong, mucronate, sericeo-villous with appressed hairs beneath and more or less so on the upper surface, base rounded oblique; petiolules very short, pilose. Flowers axillary or leaf-opposed, solitary; pedicels ½–¾ in. long, slender, hairy. Sepals ¼ in. long, lanceolate, acute, hairy. Petals ⅜ in. long, oblong-obovate; claw short, hairy. Ovary bristly; style short, stout; stigmatic lobes longer than the diameter of the style. Fruit globose, consisting of (usually) 5 hairy or nearly glabrous, often muriculate, woody cocci, each with 2 pairs of hard sharp spines, one pair longer than the other. Seeds several in each coccus, with transverse partitions between them. Fl. B. I. v. 1, p. 423; Dalz. & Gibs. p. 45; Boiss. Fl. Orient. v. 1, p. 902; Trim. Fl. Ceyl. v. 1, p. 194; Woodr. in Journ. Bomb. Nat. v. 11 (1897) p. 266; Watt, Dict. Econ. Prod. v. 6, part 4, p. 78. *Tribulus lanuginosus*, Linn.

Sp. Pl. p. 387; Grah. Cat. p. 35.—Flowers throughout the year. VERN. *Gokru*; *Sarátá*.

In dry and hot parts of the Presidency, a common weed. This and the next species are members of the Desert Flora.

DECCAN: *Dalzell & Gibson*, *Graham*, *Woodrow*; Bijapur, *Cooke*!; Poona, *Cooke*! GUJARAT: *Dalzell & Gibson*; Kathiawar, *Dalzell & Gibson*; Deesa, *Stocks*! S. M. COUNTRY; Padshapur (Belgaum districts), *Ritchie*, 1606! SIND: *Woodrow*; Jemadar ka Landa, near Karachi, *Stocks*!

The plant is used medicinally throughout India and the young leaves and stems are eaten as a potherb. See Watt, Dict. Econ. Prod. l. c.

2. **Tribulus alatus,** *Delile, Flor. Ægypt. Illustr.* (1812) p. 62. Annual; branches procumbent or ascending, densely silky-villous. Leaves as in the former species; stipules broadly ovate, acute, hairy. Flowers $\frac{1}{3}$–$\frac{1}{2}$ in. in diam. Sepals $\frac{3}{16}$ in. long, ovate, acuminate, villous outside. Petals very thin, scarcely longer than the sepals, cuneate-oblong, the apex sometimes slightly dentate. Stamens 5 (or ? 10). Ovary bristly with long white hairs; style short, stout. Fruit of 5 2-seeded cocci, the cocci very hirsute, the spines confluent into toothed wings. Fl. B. I. v. 1, p. 423; Boiss. Fl. Orient. v. 1, p. 902; Woodr. in Journ. Bomb. Nat. v. 11 (1897) p. 266; Watt, Dict. Econ. Prod. v. 6, part 4, p. 78.—Flowers: Oct.–Dec. Native names *Nindo-trikund*; *Latak*.

In all the specimens examined by me the number of stamens was invariably 5 and not 10.

A member of the Desert Flora growing in Sind. SIND: *Stocks*!, *Vicary*!; Sehwan, *Cooke*!, *Woodrow*!—DISTRIB. North Africa, Arabia.

2. SEETZENIA, Br.

A small prostrate herb, frutescent at the base, usually glabrate. Leaves opposite, stipulate, trifoliolate; leaflets obovate, apiculate. Flowers small, axillary, solitary. Sepals 5, linear-oblong, valvate, incurved at the apex. Petals 0. Disk small, 5-lobed. Stamens 5, inserted on the disk; filaments filiform, glabrous, naked at the base; anthers subglobose. Ovary oblong-clavate, sessile, 5-gonous, truncate, fleshy, 5-celled; ovule 1, in each cell, pendulous; styles 5, short, spreading; stigmas small, capitate. Capsule pendulous, ovoid, pentagonal, separating into 5 1-seeded cocci with a narrow succulent exocarp on the back only; endocarp crustaceous. Seeds solitary, ovoid, compressed; testa thick with 3 skins, the outer membranous, the middle one cellular and mucilaginous, the inner coriaceous; albumen thin; cotyledons thick.—DISTRIB. Africa; species 1.

1. **Seetzenia orientalis,** *Dcne. in Ann. Sc. Nat.* ser. 2, v. 3 (1835) p. 281. A branching herb; stem and branches terete, articulate, somewhat swollen at the nodes, usually glabrous. Leaves glaucous; petioles $\frac{1}{10}$–$\frac{1}{8}$ in. long; stipules intrapetiolar, triangular, ciliate; leaflets fleshy, the terminal one the larger, $\frac{1}{8}$ in. long, obovate, the lateral oblique, all with a hard, polished, horny apiculation. Flowers solitary, axillary; pedicels exceeding the leaves, $\frac{1}{4}$–$\frac{1}{2}$ in. long, cernuous, often abruptly deflexed at the apex, glabrous. Fruit as in the genus. Seeds oblong, compressed, somewhat pointed at the ends, smooth, brown. Fl. B. I.

v. 1, p. 424; Boiss. Fl. Orient. v. 1, p. 916; Woodr. in Journ. Bomb. Nat. v. 11 (1897) p. 266.—Flowers: Oct.

SIND: rare; Sind hills, *Dalzell*!, *Stocks*, 1200!; Hala range, *Vicary*!; Laki, *Woodrow*.—DISTRIB. N. and S. Africa, Arabia.

3. PEGANUM, Linn.

Branching perennial-rooted herbs. Leaves alternate, not glandular, entire or irregularly multifid; stipules setaceous. Flowers solitary on subterminal leaf-opposed pedicels, white. Sepals 4–5, narrow, often foliaceous and pinnatifid, open in æstivation, persistent. Petals 4–5, subequal, imbricate. Disk annular or cup-shaped. Stamens 12–15, inserted at the base of the disk, some without anthers; filaments dilated below; anthers linear. Ovary globose, deeply 2–3-lobed, 2–3-celled; ovules many in each cell, suspended by short funicles from the central angle; styles basal, twisted, 2–3-keeled above the middle, the keels stigmatose. Fruit globose, 3–4-celled, dry and dehiscing with 3 valves, or baccate and indehiscent; cells many-seeded. Seeds angled; testa spongy, scrobiculate; albumen fleshy; embryo curved.—DISTRIB. Species 4, of which 1 is widely dispersed on the shores of the Mediterranean and tropical Asia, the others natives of Central Asia and Mexico.

1. **Peganum Harmala,** *Linn. Sp. Pl.* (1753) p. 444. A bush, 1–3 ft. high, dichotomously and corymbosely branched. Leaves 2–3 in. long, multifid, the segments narrow, linear, acute. Flowers $\frac{3}{4}$–1 in. across, solitary, sessile or pedicelled. Sepals narrow, linear, acute, usually exceeding the petals. Petals white, elliptic-oblong. Capsules globose, $\frac{3}{16}$–$\frac{1}{3}$ in. in diam., deeply lobed, veined, glabrous. Fl. B. I. v. 1, p. 486 (*under Rutaceæ*); Grah. Cat. p. 35; Dalz. & Gibs. p. 45; Boiss. Fl. Orient. v. 1, p. 917; Woodr. in Journ. Bomb. Nat. v. 11 (1897) p. 267; Watt, Dict. Econ. Prod. v. 6, part 1, p. 124.—Flowers: Oct.–Dec. VERN. *Harmal.*

Common in the drier parts of the Presidency. KONKAN: *Law*! DECCAN: Indapur (Poona Collectorate), *Dalzell & Gibson*; Bijapur, *Cooke*!, *Woodrow*! SIND: *Stocks*!; Hyderabad, *Woodrow*!—DISTRIB. Soongaria, Arabia, N. Africa and westward to Hungary and Spain.

The plant is of considerable repute in native medicine. See Watt, Dict. Econ. Prod. l. c.

4. ZYGOPHYLLUM, Linn.

Small shrubs or prostrate herbs; branches terete, often spinescent. Leaves opposite, 1–2-foliolate; leaflets usually fleshy; stipules 2, often spiny. Flowers from among the stipules, white or yellow, usually marked with a red or purple spot at the base. Calyx 4–5-partite, persistent or deciduous, imbricate. Petals 4–5, clawed, imbricate and contorted. Disk fleshy, angular, cup-shaped or concave. Stamens 8–10, inserted at the base of the disk, longer than the petals; filaments filiform, with a scale at the base within; anthers oblong. Ovary sessile on the disk, 4–5-gonous, 4–5- (rarely 2–3-) celled, attenuated into an angled style; stigma minute; ovules 2-many in each cell, superposed; raphe free or adnate. Fruit capsular, 4–5-gonous or 4–5-winged, indehiscent or septicidally dehiscent into 5 cocci, or loculicidally 5-valved, the endocarp sometimes separating. Seeds 1 or more in each cell, pendulous; testa crustaceous; albumen scanty; cotyledons oblong.—DISTRIB. Natives chiefly of the Cape and Australia; species about 54.

Annual; leaves simple, cylindric .... 1. *Z. simplex.*
Perennial; leaves 2-foliolate .... 2. *Z. coccineum.*

1. **Zygophyllum simplex,** *Linn. Mantiss.* v. 1 (1767) p. 68. A succulent watery much-branched procumbent herb; branches slender, reddish, striate, glabrous. Leaves small, subsessile, cylindric, oblong or obovate, obtuse, fleshy; stipules lanceolate, acute. Flowers small. Sepals obovate, cucullate at the apex. Petals yellow, spathulate, spreading, margins flat. Staminal-scale bipartite, hyaline, the segments obovate. Ovary turbinate, glabrous, ribbed; style tapering. Capsules deflexed, rugulose, separating into 5 compressed 3–5-seeded cocci. Seeds minute, oblong, attenuated at both ends, smooth. Fl. B. I. v. 1, p. 424; Boiss. Fl. Orient. v. 1, p. 912; Woodr. in Journ. Bomb. Nat. v. 11 (1897) p. 266; Watt, Dict. Econ. Prod. v. 6, part 4, p. 375.—Flowers: Nov.–Jan. VERN. *Putláni.*

Very common all over Sind. The plant is eaten by camels. SIND: *Royle!*, *Stocks!*; Hala range, *Vicary!*; Karachi, *Cooke!*, *Woodrow!*—DISTRIB. Arabia, tropical Africa, Western Asia.

2. **Zygophyllum coccineum,** *Linn. Sp. Pl.* (1753) p. 386. Suffruticose; branches woody, striate and papillose, hoary at first with a white powdery tomentum, at length glabrous. Leaves 2-foliolate, powdery; petioles stout, fleshy, grooved, longer than the leaflets; stipules triangular, scarious; leaflets oblong, cylindric or semicylindric, obtuse, minutely powdery. Flowers solitary, white or tinged with yellow. Sepals fleshy, cucullate, the margins membranous. Petals spathulate, spreading, longer than the sepals, undulate on the margin. Staminal-scale ovate-lanceolate, entire or lacerate at the apex. Ovary glabrous or velvety. Capsules $\frac{3}{8}$ in. long, oblong or obovoid, 5-ribbed, truncate at the base and the apex; cocci 3–5-seeded. Seeds small, ovoid, acute, tubercled, compressed. Fl. B. I. v. 1, p. 425; Boiss. Fl. Orient. v. 1, p. 915.

Rare. SIND: on hills, *Stocks!*

5. FAGONIA, Linn.

Branching herbs woody at the base, erect or prostrate. Leaves opposite, 1–3-foliolate, the leaflets quite entire, mucronate; stipules often spiny. Flowers solitary from among the stipules, rosy or violet, rarely yellow. Sepals 5, deciduous, imbricate. Petals 5, clawed, caducous, imbricate. Disk short, inconspicuous. Stamens 10, inserted on the disk; filaments filiform, naked: anthers shortly oblong. Ovary sessile, 5-gonous, 5-celled, narrowed into a 5-gonous subulate style; ovules 2, near the base of the cell, collateral, pendulous from ascending funicles; stigma simple. Fruit 5-gonous, of 5 1-seeded cocci which dehisce along the ventral suture and separate from a horny endocarp. Seeds erect, compressed, broadly oblong; testa mucilaginous; albumen horny; cotyledons broad, flat, ovate.—DISTRIB. Widely dispersed throughout the Mediterranean and the Eastern regions, rarer in S. Africa, California and Chili; species 2 or 3, well-defined.

1. **Fagonia cretica,** *Linn. Sp. Pl.* (1753) p. 386. A small spiny erect undershrub, more or less glandular; branches slender, terete, striate, glabrous. Leaves opposite, 1–3-foliolate; petioles very variable in length, from $\frac{1}{8}$–$1\frac{1}{4}$ in. long, deeply striate, very slender; stipules 2 pairs of sharp slender thorns sometimes exceeding $\frac{1}{2}$ in. long; leaflets $\frac{1}{2}$–$\frac{3}{4}$ by $\frac{1}{16}$–$\frac{1}{8}$ in., linear, acute (when the leaflets are 3 in number, the middle the largest), sessile or with very short petiolules. Flowers small, pale rose-colored; pedicels slender, $\frac{1}{4}$–$\frac{1}{2}$ in. long. Sepals $\frac{1}{8}$ in. long, ovate, aristate. Petals twice as long as the sepals, spathulate; claw long. Ovary hairy; style tapering. Fruit glandular-pubescent, rounded at the base, pyramidal towards the apex, deeply 5-partite almost to the axis. Seeds ovoid, acute, flattened, smooth. *Fagonia arabica*, Linn. Sp. Pl. p. 386; Fl. B. I. v. 1, p. 425; Boiss. Fl. Orient. v. 1, p. 907; Woodr. in Journ. Bomb. Nat. v. 11 (1897) p. 266; Watt, Dict. Econ. Prod. v. 3, p. 308. *Fagonia mysorensis*, Roth, Nov. Sp. p. 215; Grah. Cat. p. 35; Dalz. & Gibs. p. 45.—Flowers: Oct.–Dec. VERN. *Dhamása*.

Common in the Deccan; less common in Sind. DECCAN: *Dalzell & Gibson*; in grain fields (common), *Graham*; Bijapur, *Cooke*!, *Woodrow*! SIND: *Woodrow*!, *Cooke*!

The plant has some repute in native medicine. See Watt, Dict. Econ. Prod. l. c.

ORDER XXXI. GERANIACEÆ.

Herbs, undershrubs, rarely trees, often glandularly pubescent. Leaves opposite or alternate, rarely entire, often 2-stipulate. Flowers hermaphrodite, regular or irregular, solitary, umbelled, cymose or racemose; peduncles usually axillary. Sepals 5, rarely fewer, free or united to the middle, usually imbricate, the posticous sometimes spurred, persistent or rarely deciduous. Petals as many as the sepals or fewer (by suppression) or 0, hypogynous or subperigynous, variously imbricate, rarely contorted. Torus scarcely expanded into a disk, with 5 glands alternating with the petals, or eglandular, raised in the centre, rarely flat. Stamens as many or twice as many (rarely thrice as many) as the sepals; filaments filiform or dilated or connate into a ring; anthers versatile, 2-celled, cells parallel, dehiscing longitudinally. Ovary 3–5-(rarely 2-) lobed, 3–5-celled. Carpels united with the axis as far as the insertion of the ovules, prolonged above into a styliferous beak or into styles which are more or less united; stigmas capitate, linear or ligulate; ovules 1–2 or many in each cell, anatropous, pendulous; raphe ventral. Fruit capsular, 3–5-lobed; lobes 1-seeded, often separating from the axis, septicidal or loculicidal, rarely berried. Seeds pendulous, horizontal or ascending, usually exarillate; testa membranous, rarely subcrustaceous; albumen scanty or 0, rarely thick and fleshy; embryo straight or curved; cotyledons flat, plano-convex or variously folded, foliaceous or thick, rarely fleshy; radicle short, straight, looking towards the hilum, or longer, inflexed or usually incumbent on the cotyledons.—DISTRIB. Temperate and subtropical regions of both hemispheres; genera 20; species about 800.

Several varieties of the *Pelargonium* (commonly called *Geranium*) are cultivated in gardens, where they flourish and bloom extremely well. The genus is not indigenous to India.

Glands alternate with the petals; flowers regular or nearly so.
Perfect stamens 15 .... 1. MONSONIA.
Perfect stamens 5; staminodes 5 .... 2. ERODIUM.
Glands 0; leaves compound.
Herbs; fruit capsular.
Leaves 3-foliolate .... 3. OXALIS.
Leaves abruptly pinnate .... 4. BIOPHYTUM.
Trees; leaves pinnate .... 5. AVERRHOA.
Flowers irregular; leaves simple; sepals usually colored .... 6. IMPATIENS.

1. MONSONIA, Linn.

Herbs or undershrubs. Leaves alternate or opposite, toothed or divided. Flowers regular; peduncles axillary, bracteate about the middle, 1-flowered or umbellately many-flowered. Sepals 5, imbricate. Petals 5, hypogynous, imbricate; glands 5, alternate with the petals. Stamens 15, all antheriferous, very shortly connate at the base into a ring and higher up into 5 bundles, one bundle of 3 stamens opposite to each sepal. Ovary 5-lobed, 5-celled, beaked, the beak ending in a style bearing 5 linear branches which are stigmatose on the inside; ovules 2 in each cell, superposed. Lobes of the capsule 1-seeded, separating septifragally from the placentiferous axis, the tails rolling up elastically from the base to the apex, bearded within. Seeds exalbuminous, the radicle incumbent on convolutely folded cotyledons.—DISTRIB. Africa and tropical Asia; species about 12.

Flowers solitary; petals longer than the sepals .... 1. *M. senegalensis.*
Flowers umbelled; petals shorter than the sepals .... 2. *M. heliotropioides.*

1. **Monsonia senegalensis,** *Guill. & Perr. Fl. Seneg. Tent.* v. 1 (1830) p. 131.—A diffuse annual herb, 3–12 in. high, woody at, and divaricately-branched from the base, clothed with viscid glandular hairs. Leaves ¾–1¼ by ½–⅞ in., ovate, acute or subobtuse, mucronate, distantly toothed, glabrous above or nearly so, softly villous beneath and on the margins, base cordate or rounded; petioles reaching 1½ in. long, slender, softly hairy; stipules lanceolate-subulate, very acute, hairy. Peduncles reaching 1½ in. long, slender, hairy, usually 1-flowered, often sharply deflexed near the flower or at the bracts; bracts 2, subulate, hairy, inserted on the peduncle one fourth to one third of the way up from the base. Sepals elliptic-oblong, awned, becoming somewhat obovate in fruit, ¼–⅜ in. long (excluding the awn), densely clothed with long, soft hairs, the margins membranous; awn about $\frac{1}{12}$ in. long. Petals pink, ¾ in. long, obovate. Filaments broad and flattened at the base. Carpels stipitate, obconical, clothed with stiff hairs, obliquely truncate, with 2–3 pocket-like depressions or wrinkles beneath the apex; beak 3 in. long, finely downy outside and with long silky hairs on the inner face. Fl. B. I. v. 1, p. 427; Dalz. & Gibs. p. 41; Boiss. Fl. Orient. v. 1, p. 898; Woodr. in Journ. Bomb. Nat. v. 11 (1897) p. 266. *Geranium Lawianum*, Nimmo, in Grah. Cat. (flyleaf).—Flowers: Aug.

Throughout the dry districts of the Presidency; not common. DECCAN: hills near Ganesh Khind, Poona, *Woodrow*!; Chattersinghi hill near Poona, *Woodrow*!; Dongergaon near Ahmednagar, *Cooke*!; Indapur and N. of the Bhima river, near Khed, *Gibson*. GUJARAT: Baikar near Deesa, *Stocks*! SIND: Jemadar ka Landa, near Karachi, *Stocks*!—DISTRIB. Beluchistan, Arabia, Senegambia.

2. **Monsonia heliotropioides,** *Boiss. Fl. Orient.* v. 1 (1867) p. 897. A small hoary annual, with a woody rootstock. Leaves chiefly radical, $\frac{1}{2}$–1 by $\frac{3}{8}$–$\frac{3}{4}$ in., variable in shape, ovate, obtuse or rhomboid, softly villous with long white hairs on both surfaces, sharply denticulate; base cordate, rounded or cuneate; petioles up to $2\frac{1}{4}$ in. long, clothed with long white hairs; stipules subulate, hairy. Flowers in umbels on the summit of a very long scape which sometimes reaches 8 in. long, slender, distantly clothed with long, white hairs; bracts beneath the pedicels lanceolate; pedicels 5–8, slender, slightly hairy. Sepals $\frac{3}{16}$ in. long, elliptic-oblong, abruptly mucronate, becoming enlarged and obovate in fruit, canescent outside, the margins membranous. Petals obovate, shorter than the sepals. Filaments slightly ciliate. Carpels stipitate, densely hairy at the base, obliquely truncate, with 2–3 grooves or wrinkles beneath the apex; beak up to $3\frac{1}{2}$ in. long, slightly downy outside, clothed with silky hairs within. Fl. B. I. v. 1, p. 428; Woodr. in Journ. Bomb. Nat. v. 11 (1897) p. 266.—Flowers: Aug.

Rare. Sind: Thano-Bula-Khan road, 51 miles from Karachi, *Woodrow.*—Distrib. Westwards to Egypt.

2. ERODIUM, L'Hérit.

Herbs, rarely undershrubs; branches swollen or jointed at the nodes. Leaves usually pinnately divided. Flowers regular or irregular; peduncles axillary, umbelled at the apex, rarely 1-flowered. Sepals 5, imbricate. Petals 5, hypogynous, imbricate, with alternating glands. Stamens 5, alternating with 5 staminodes. Ovary 5-lobed, 5-celled, beaked, the beak running into a style with 5 longitudinally stigmatose branches; ovules 2 in each cell, more or less superposed. Lobes of the capsule 1-seeded, separating septifragally from the axis, the beaks rolling up elastically from the base to the apex, hairy on the inner surface, each with usually 2 pits at the top below the beak. Seeds exalbuminous; embryo incumbent on the induplicate or flexuous radicle.—Distrib. Chiefly in temperate regions in the N. hemisphere of the Old World; species about 50.

1. **Erodium cicutarium,** *L'Hérit. ex Ait. Hort. Kew.* ed. 1, v. 2 (1789) p. 414. An annual herb; branches short or long, sometimes reaching 2 ft. and upwards, more or less clothed with white hairs. Leaves oblong, pinnatisect; segments 7–11 pairs, sessile, not decurrent, ovate-oblong or obovate, deeply inciso-dentate; stipules scarious, ovate-lanceolate, acute. Peduncles many-flowered; pedicels hoary; bracts small, scarious, ovate. Sepals oblong-lanceolate, shortly mucronate, hairy outside. Petals obovate, unequal, as long as, or longer than the sepals, purple, often spotted. Filaments glabrous, without teeth. Beak 5–6 times as long as the carpels, pits with a concentric fold beneath. Seeds very smooth; cotyledons 3-lobed. Fl. B. I. v. 1, p. 434; Boiss. Fl. Orient. v. 1, p. 890; Woodr. in Journ. Bomb. Nat. v. 11 (1897) p. 266.—Flowers: Feb.–Dec.

A very rare plant, occurring in Sind. It is abundant near Quetta, which is not, however, within the limits of the Bombay Presidency.

Sind: Tata district, *Woodrow*!—Distrib. Throughout Europe and temperate N. Asia.

3. OXALIS, Linn.

Acid herbs, rarely shrubby. Leaves radical or cauline, alternate, digitately or pinnately 3-foliolate. Flowers on axillary, 1- or more-flowered peduncles, regular, yellow, rosy or white. Sepals 5, imbricate. Petals 5, hypogynous, contorted. Disk without glands. Stamens 10, free or united at the base, all antheriferous. Ovary 5-lobed, 5-celled; ovules 1–many in each cell; styles 5, distinct; stigmas terminal, capitate, 2-fid or laciniate. Capsule dehiscing loculicidally; valves persistent to the axis. Seeds with an outer fleshy coat bursting elastically; testa crustaceous; albumen fleshy; embryo straight.—Distrib. Largely distributed in S. Africa and S. America; a few species in temperate and tropical regions; species more than 200.

1. **Oxalis corniculata,** *Linn. Sp. Pl.* (1753) p. 435. A small procumbent herb; stems rooting, pubescent with appressed hairs. Leaves palmately 3-foliolate; petioles 1½–3½ in. long, very slender, pubescent; stipules small, oblong, adnate to the petiole; leaflets ½–1 in. long, obcordate, cuneate at the base, subsessile, glabrous or with a few appressed hairs and with ciliate margins. Flowers axillary, subumbellate; peduncles solitary, up to 3½ in. long, deflexed in fruit, pubescent; bracts beneath the pedicels lanceolate, hairy. Sepals ⅛–3/16 in. long, oblong, obtuse, appressedly hairy outside. Petals yellow, oblong, rounded at the apex, emarginate, twice as long as the sepals. Stigma papillose. Capsules ¾ in. long, linear-oblong, 5-angled, shortly beaked, tomentose. Seeds numerous, broadly ovoid, acute, transversely striate, brown. Fl. B. I. v. 1, p. 436; Grah. Cat. p. 35; Dalz. & Gibs. p. 42; Wight, Icon. t. 18; Boiss. Fl. Orient. v. 1, p. 866; Trim. Fl. Ceyl. v. 1, p. 196; Woodr. in Journ. Bomb. Nat. v. 11 (1897) p. 266; Watt, Dict. Econ. Prod. v. 5, p. 658.—Flowers: Oct.–May. Vern. *Ambusi.*

Common everywhere; a troublesome weed in gardens.—Distrib. Cosmopolitan.

4. BIOPHYTUM, DC.

Annual or perennial herbs. Leaves crowded at the ends of the stem and branches, abruptly pinnate; leaflets opposite, oblique. Flowers dimorphous, in small umbels; peduncles terminal. Sepals 5, imbricate, lanceolate, acuminate. Petals 5, yellow, connate into a salver-shaped corolla. Stamens 10, distinct; filaments free, the 5 inner longer. Ovary 5-celled; styles 5; stigmas notched at the apex or 2-fid. Capsule ovoid or oblong or subglobose, dehiscing loculicidally into 5 spreading valves. Seeds as in *Oxalis.*—Distrib. Tropical Asia, Africa and America; species about 20.

1. **Biophytum sensitivum,** *DC. Prod.* v. 1 (1824) p. 690. Annual; stem erect, from 1–10 in. long, stout or slender, glabrous or hairy. Leaves sensitive, crowded into a rosette on the top of the stem 1½–3 in. long; petiole short; rhachis slender, glabrous or hairy; leaflets opposite, ⅜ in. long, 6–15 pairs (the terminal pair the largest, the pairs becoming smaller downwards), oblong, obliquely rounded and apiculate at the apex, subsessile, glabrous, paler beneath. Flowers dimorphic, ⅓ in. across, yellow; peduncles many, of various lengths up to 4 in. long, slender, pubescent or glabrous; pedicels many; bracts lanceolate, small, crowded

beneath the pedicels. Sepals lanceolate, acute, with parallel nerves. Corolla much exceeding the sepals; lobes rounded, spreading. Style nearly glabrous. Capsules ellipsoid, apiculate, slightly exceeding the sepals; cells few-seeded. Seeds ovoid, transversely striate. Fl. B. I. v. 1, p. 436; Dalz. & Gibs. p. 42; Reiche, in Engl. & Prantl, Pflanzenf. v. 3, part 4, p. 16, fig. 14, G; Trim. Fl. Ceyl. v. 1, p. 197; Woodr. in Journ. Bomb. Nat. v. 11 (1897) p. 266.—Flowers: Oct.–Jan.

A common weed in the Konkan during the rains. KONKAN: Sion, near Bombay, *Woodrow*!; Neral, *Woodrow*! DECCAN: Poona, *Cooke*!, *Woodrow*! GUJARAT: Baroda, *Woodrow*. KANARA: *Talbot*!—DISTRIB. Tropical Asia, Africa and America.

5. AVERRHOA, Linn.

Trees. Leaves alternate, imparipinnate, exstipulate. Flowers regular, small, in short panicles. Sepals 5, imbricate. Petals 5, hypogynous, contorted. Glands 0. Stamens 10, very shortly connate at the base into a ring, all perfect or 5 without anthers. Ovary 5-lobed, 5-celled; ovules numerous; styles 5, distinct; stigmas capitate. Berry oblong, indehiscent. Seeds naked or arillate; albumen fleshy, scanty; embryo straight.—DISTRIB. Probably natives of the New World; species 3 or 4, of which the following are cultivated in many hot countries.

Leaflets 5–11; fruit with sharp angles; seeds arillate .... 1. *A. Carambola.*
Leaflets 11–35; fruit with obtuse angles; seeds exarillate......... 2. *A. Bilimbi.*

1. **Averrhoa Carambola,** *Linn. Sp. Pl.* (1753) p. 428. A small tree with close drooping branches. Leaves alternate; leaflets 5–11, irritable to the touch, $1\frac{1}{2}$–$2\frac{1}{2}$ by $\frac{3}{4}$–$1\frac{1}{4}$ in., ovate-oblong, acuminate, entire, glabrous or pubescent above, glaucous and glabrous beneath, base oblique, acute; petiolules short, stout, pubescent. Flowers in short racemes chiefly axillary or sometimes springing from the bark. Sepals $\frac{1}{8}$–$\frac{1}{6}$ in. long, glabrous. Petals more than twice as long as the sepals, oblong-obovate, variegated white and purple. Stamens 10, of which 5 are shorter and without anthers, or sometimes 1 or 2 of these longer and antheriferous; filaments dilated at the base. Fruit oblong, acutely angled, yellow. Seeds arillate. Fl. B. I. v. 1, p. 439; Dalz. & Gibs. Suppl. p. 16; Bedd. For. Man. in Fl. Sylvat. p. xxxix; Reiche, in Engl. & Prantl, Pflanzenf. v. 3, part 4, p. 16, fig. 14, H, and p. 22, fig. 20; Woodr. in Journ. Bomb. Nat. v. 11 (1897) p. 266; Talb. Trees, Bomb. p. 29; Watt, Dict. Econ. Prod. v. 1, p. 359.—Flowers: May–Aug. VERN. *Kamaranga.*

Cultivated in many parts of India for its fruit which is eaten. See Watt, Dict. Econ. Prod. l. c.

2. **Averrhoa Bilimbi,** *Linn. Sp. Pl.* (1753) p. 428. A small tree, 15 to 20 ft. high. Leaflets 11–35, entire, $1\frac{1}{2}$–2 by $\frac{3}{4}$ in., oblong, more or less pubescent on both surfaces, base usually rounded, somewhat oblique; petiolules $\frac{1}{12}$–$\frac{1}{8}$ in. long, pubescent. Flowers from the trunk and branches; panicles villous. Sepals $\frac{1}{8}$ in. long, ovate-lanceolate, acute, pubescent. Petals oblong-spathulate, more than twice as long as the sepals. Fruit oblong, obtusely lobed. Seeds exarillate. Fl. B. I. v. 1, p. 439; Dalz. & Gibs. Suppl. p. 16; Bedd. Flor. Sylvat. t. 117; Reiche, in Engl. & Prantl, Pflanzenf. v. 3, part 4, p. 22, fig. 19; Talb. Trees, Bomb. p. 29; Woodr. in Journ. Bomb. Nat. v. 11 (1897) p. 266;

Watt, Dict. Econ. Prod. v. 1, p. 359.—Flowers: Mar.-May. VERN. *Bilimbi.*

Cultivated throughout the plains of India. The fruit is very acid when green, and is made into pickles, &c. See Watt, Dict. Econ. Prod. l. c.

6. IMPATIENS, Linn.

Annual or perennial herbs, rarely shrubby at the base, usually glabrous. Leaves simple, variously arranged, exstipulate or with stipular glands at the base of the petiole. Flowers irregular, often handsome, axillary, solitary or in racemes (less commonly in scapes), resupinate. Sepals 3 (very rarely 5), colored, imbricate; 2 anterior when present minute; 2 lateral small, flat, usually green; posterior (*lip*) (anterior in flower owing to inversion of the flower) large, petaloid, usually produced into a hollow spur. Petals 3 (or 5); anterior (*standard*) (posterior in flower, outer in bud) erect; lateral (*wings*) 2-lobed or composed of 2 united together. Stamens 5; filaments short, broad; anthers cohering. Disk 0. Ovary oblong, 5-celled; ovules many in each cell, 1-seriate; stigma sessile, 5-toothed. Capsule short or long, loculicidally dehiscent; valves 5, elastically springing away from a placentiferous axis. Seeds smooth or tubercled, glabrous or hairy; albumen 0; embryo straight.—DISTRIB. A genus of about 135 species, the greater number natives of the mountains of tropical Asia and Africa; rare in temperate Europe, N. America, N. Asia and S. Africa.

Scapigerous; rootstock tuberous, perennial; flowers racemed.
  Spur shorter than the flower or 0.
    Spur clavate, obtuse .... 1. *I. Beddomei.*
    Spur 0 .... 2. *I. Stocksii.*
  Spur longer than the flower.
    Wings 2-partite .... 3. *I. acaulis.*
    Wings 3-partite .... 4. *I. rivalis.*
Annual; leaves all opposite or the upper (rarely all) whorled in threes (never alternate).
    Spur as long as, or longer than the flower; leaves all opposite.
      Flowers ½–1 in. across; wings auricled at the base... 5. *I. chinensis.*
      Flowers ⅓ in. across; wings with long claws .... 6. *I. Kleinii.*
    Spur shorter than the flower or 0.
      Flowers purple or rosy.
        Pedicels with a line of pubescence.
          Lip saccate; leaves reaching 4 in............ 7. *I. inconspicua.*
          Lip boat-shaped; leaves not exceeding 1 in. ... 9. *I. Lawii.*
        Pedicels glabrous .... 8. *I. oppositifolia.*
        Pedicels rufous-hairy all over .... 11. *I. tomentosa.*
      Flowers yellow............ 10. *I. Dalzellii.*
Annual; leaves subopposite and whorled.
  Tall, 2–3 ft. high; flowers 1–1½ in. across .... 12. *I. latifolia.*
  Short, 4–8 in. high; flowers ½ in. across .... 13. *I. lucida.*
Mostly annual; leaves alternate, usually distant.
  Spur long.
    Capsule tomentose .... 14. *I. Balsamina.*
    Capsule glabrous .... 16. *I. pulcherrima.*
  Spur 0; capsule villous .... 15. *I. scabriuscula.*

1. **Impatiens Beddomei,** *Hook. f. in Fl. B. I.* v. 1, p. 442. Rootstock tuberous, perennial; scape about 1 ft. high. Leaves 1½–3 in. in diam., all radical, fleshy, orbicular and reniform, cordate, with distant

short teeth on the margins; nerves flabellate, conspicuous beneath; petioles 1–2 in. long. Flowers ½ in. in diam., 6–15 in each raceme; racemes 1–4 in. long; bracts broadly ovate, obtuse or acute; pedicels slender, ½–1 in. long. Sepals obliquely ovate. Standard short, broader than long. Wings 3-lobed, the lobes subequal or the inner the smaller. Spur rather shorter than the flower, ⅜ in. long, incurved, clavate, rounded at the apex. Capsules ⅓ in. long, ellipsoid. Seeds minute, granulate. Fl. B. I. v. 1, p. 442; Woodr. in Journ. Bomb. Nat. v. 11 (1897) p. 266. *Impatiens scapiflora*, W. & A. Prodr. p. 137; Wight, Icon. t. 967; Grah. Cat. p. 34 (*not* of Heyne).

KONKAN: Western Ghâts, *De Crespigny* ex *Woodrow*; S. Konkan, *Graham*.

2. **Impatiens Stocksii,** *Hook. f. & Thoms. in Journ. Linn. Soc.* v. 4 (1860) p. 119. A small glabrous plant scarcely reaching 5 in. high. Rootstock tuberous, perennial. Leaves ½–1 in. in diam., orbicular-oblong or broadly ovate, crenate, usually with a small tooth between the crenatures; petioles ½–1½ in. long. Flowers few, 3–6 together; racemes 1–1¼ in. long; bracts small, ovate, acute; pedicels ⅜–½ in. long, rather stout for the size of the plant. Sepals $\frac{1}{12}$ in. long, ovate, obtuse. Standard somewhat rhomboidal, as broad as long. Wings with 3 obtuse lobes, the lower the longest. Spur 0. Capsules ⅛–¼ in. long, ellipsoid. Seeds minute, linear-oblong. Fl. B. I. v. 1, p. 442; Dalz. & Gibs. p. 42; Woodr. in Journ. Bomb. Nat. v. 1 (1897) p. 266.

KONKAN: *Stocks*!; mountains of the Konkan, *Woodrow*. KANARA: *Law*!

3. **Impatiens acaulis,** *Arn. in Hook. Comp. Bot. Mag.* v. 1 (1835) p. 325. Rootstock tuberous, perennial; scape 3–12 in. high. Leaves all radical, variable in size and shape, 1½–5 in. in diam., suborbicular, ovate or oblong, obtuse or subacute, glabrous, subentire or crenate, often with irregular short teeth, base subcordate or rounded, truncate or subacute; petioles 1–2½ in. long. Flowers pink, 1–1¼ in. across, in racemes 1–4 in. long; bracts ovate; pedicels ¾–1 in. long. Sepals ovate, obtuse. Standard short, obovate, concave, broader upwards. Wings 2-partite, the terminal lobe the largest. Spur long, very slender, curved. Capsules ¾ in. long, ellipsoid, acute at both ends. Fl. B. I. v. 1, p. 443; Dalz. & Gibs. p. 42; Trim. Fl. Ceyl. v. 1, p. 201; Woodr. in Journ. Bomb. Nat. v. 11 (1897) p. 266. *Impatiens scapiflora*, Hook. in Bot. Mag. v. 64 (1837) t. 3587 (*not* of Heyne).—Flowers: Sept.–Nov.

A very beautiful plant found on wet rocks on many of the Konkan and Deccan hills. It is very common at Mahableshwar, often out of reach on the summit of rocks over which water trickles. It may be found in similar places at Khandala.

KONKAN: mountains of the Konkan, *Stocks*!; the Ghâts, *Dalzell & Gibson*; Matheran, *H. M. Birdwood*. DECCAN: Mahableshwar, *Cooke*!; Khandala, *Woodrow*!; Lanoli, *Woodrow*!; Fitzgerald Ghât, below Mahableshwar, *Cooke*!, *H. M. Birdwood*.

4. **Impatiens rivalis,** *Wight, in Madr. Journ.* v. 5 (1837) p. 13, t. 8. Rootstock tuberous; scape 6–18 in. high. Leaves very variable in form and pubescence, 2–7 in. long, ovate-oblong or elliptic, glabrous or more or less hairy above, irregularly, sometimes obscurely, crenate-serrate with distant short stout teeth, base cordate, rounded or acute; petioles reaching 7 in. long. Flowers as in the preceding species; bracts ovate. Standard broader than long, vaulted. Wings 3-partite. Spur very long, curved. Capsules as in *I. acaulis*. Fl. B. I. v. 1, p. 444; Wight,

Icon. t. 751; Dalz. & Gibs. p. 42; Woodr. in Journ. Bomb. Nat. v. 11 (1897) p. 266.—Flowers: Aug.–Jan.

The only specific distinction between this species and *I. acaulis* seems to be in the wings, which are tripartite in *I. rivalis* and bipartite in *I. acaulis*. The specimens of Stocks from the Konkan (*var.* 2, Fl. B. I.) have very large leaves, attenuated and somewhat oblique at the base, with very long petioles.

KONKAN: *Stocks*! S. M. COUNTRY: Ramghât, *Dalzell*!

5. **Impatiens chinensis,** *Linn. Sp. Pl.* (1753) p. 937. Stem 4–20 in. high, erect, angled, from a rooting prostrate base, glabrous. Leaves all opposite, subsessile, ½–4 in. long, the breadth very variable, linear-oblong or obovate, sharply serrate, the serratures usually terminating in a stiff bristle, the upper surface more or less hairy, the lower silvery-grey, glabrous, base rounded or subcordate; petioles usually almost 0, or, if present, short and broad; stipules linear-lanceolate, recurved. Flowers ½–1 in. across, rose-purple or white; pedicels slender, axillary, solitary or fascicled, shorter or longer than the leaves, deflexed in fruit. Sepals ⅓ in. long, linear-acute, with a callous point. Standard orbicular, acuminate or horned. Wings semi-obovate, auricled at the base. Spur long, slender, incurved. Capsules ½–¾ in. long, ellipsoid, tapering at both ends, turgid in the middle. Seeds numerous, shortly oblong, smooth, black, shining. Fl. B. I. v. 1, p. 444; Dalz. & Gibs. p. 42; Woodr. in Journ. Bomb. Nat. v. 11 (1897) p. 266. *Impatiens fasciculata*, Lam. Encyc. v. 1, p. 363; Wight, Icon. t. 748.

KONKAN: *Dalzell & Gibson*. KANARA: Sampkhand, Yacombi (N. Kanara), *Woodrow*.

6. **Impatiens Kleinii,** *Wight & Arn. Prodr.* (1834) p. 140. A slender branched annual, 6–15 in. high. Leaves all opposite, usually petioled, 1–2½ by ¾–1 in., elliptic, lanceolate or obovate, acute or obtuse, distantly serrulate, more or less hairy on the veins above, glabrous and glaucous beneath, base narrowed into a short petiole; stipules 0, or of 2 small glands. Flowers very small, ¼–⅓ in. across, violet-purple; pedicels ½–¾ in. long, axillary, filiform, solitary or twin, deflexed in fruit, glabrous. Sepals $\frac{1}{10}$ in. long, linear, acute. Standard small, orbicular-oblong, horned. Wings with long claws, broadly obovate, almost entire. Spur slender, usually longer than the flower, straight or curved. Capsules narrow, ½ in. long, fusiform. Seeds few, globose, black, shining. Fl. B. I. v. 1, p. 445; Grah. Cat. p. 34; Dalz. & Gibs. p. 43; Woodr. in Journ. Bomb. Nat. v. 11 (1897) p. 266.

Common in the rains. KONKAN: *Stocks*!; Miradonger, *Dalzell*! S. M. COUNTRY: Castlerock, *Cooke*! KANARA: Sampkhand (N. Kanara), *Woodrow*!

7. **Impatiens inconspicua,** *Benth. in Wall. Cat.* (1828) 4741. A small plant, 4–12 in. high, much-branched from the base. Leaves variable, the lower usually petioled, the upper sessile or nearly so, ½–4 in. long, ovate, oblong or linear, serrate, glabrous or pubescent above, pale beneath, base rounded or acute; stipules setaceous or 0. Flowers pink, small; pedicels with a line of pubescence, axillary, solitary or twin, very slender, shorter than the leaves. Sepals linear-subulate. Wings with a broad rhomboid-obovate terminal lobe and a small linear lateral one. Lip saccate, acuminate, not spurred or with a

very minute spur. Capsules $\frac{3}{8}$ in. long, ellipsoid, shortly pointed, turgid in the middle. Seeds few, subglobose, black, shining. Fl. B. I. v. 1, p. 447; Dalz. & Gibs. p. 43; Woodr. in Journ. Bomb. Nat. v. 11 (1897) p. 266.—Flowers: Aug.-Oct. VERN. *Terda.*

A very variable plant whose different forms are numerous.

The following varieties are given by Sir J. Hooker in the Fl. B. I. (l. c.):—

VAR. *inconspicua* proper, of which the plate 970 in Wight's Icones is taken as the type.

Stem 4–8 in. high, somewhat robust, branched. Leaves ovate or ovate-lanceolate, petioled, strongly serrate. Pedicels usually short. Spur 0.

VAR. 2. *pusilla.* Smaller. Lower leaves more or less petioled, lanceolate, serrate; the upper longer, narrow, subsessile, remotely serrate. *I. pusilla*, Heyne, in Wall. Cat. 4745.

VAR. 3. *filiformis.* Slender, much-branched. Leaves subsessile, very long, slender, remotely serrate, the lower sometimes petioled and lanceolate. Flowers few. *I. filiformis*, W. & A. Prod. p. 140; Grah. Cat. p. 34.

Khandala, *Graham.*

VAR. 4. *ramosissima.* Robust, much-branched. Leaves short, sessile, oblong, obtuse or subacute, subcordate or rounded at the base. Flowers reddish-purple. Standard keeled, with a row of hairs along the keel and with a short greenish horn. Wings tinged with darker purple at the base. Lip veined within. Spur minute. *I. ramosissima*, Dalz. in Hook. Kew Journ. Bot. v. 3, p. 230.

This variety is very common throughout the Presidency. It is abundant on many of the Konkan and Deccan hills during September and October.
KONKAN: *Law!*, *Stocks!*

8. **Impatiens oppositifolia,** *Linn. Sp. Pl.* (1753) p. 937. Erect, 1–1½ ft. high, glabrous, flaccid. Leaves 1–3 in. long, opposite, subsessile or the lower petioled, linear or linear-lanceolate, oblong or obovate, obtuse or acute, remotely spinous-serrate, glabrous or with a few short hairs above, pale beneath; stipules small, subulate. Flowers about $\frac{1}{2}$ in. across, purple or purple with an orange tinge; pedicels elongate, slender, quite glabrous, axillary, solitary or 2–3 together. Sepals linear, with a callous point. Standard orbicular. Wings with a broadly obovate clawed terminal lobe and a small falcate lateral one. Lip somewhat conical. Spur short, stout, usually curved like a hook. Capsules $\frac{5}{16}$–$\frac{1}{2}$ in. long, ellipsoid, attenuated at both ends. Seeds subglobose, glabrous, black, shining. Fl. B. I. v. 1, p. 448; Grah. Cat. p. 34; Trim. Fl. Ceyl. v. 1, p. 202; Woodr. in Journ. Bomb. Nat. v. 11 (1897) p. 266.

Very common in the Konkans. KONKAN: *Stocks!*, *Dalzell!*; Vingorla, *Dalzell!*; Ghát road, Wadi to Poladpur, *Woodrow!* DECCAN: Parghát, *Dalzell!* S. M. COUNTRY: Belgaum hills to the North, *Ritchie*, 120! KANARA: Tinai (N. Kanara), *Talbot!*; Halyal (N. Kanara), *Talbot!*

9. **Impatiens Lawii,** *Hook. f. & Thoms. in Journ. Linn. Soc.* v. 4 (1860) p. 122. Erect, much-branched, 8–12 in. high; stem stout,

glabrous. Leaves sessile or nearly so, $\frac{3}{4}$–1 by $\frac{1}{2}$–$\frac{5}{8}$ in., smaller upwards, oblong or ovate, obtuse or acute, distantly spinous-toothed or subserrate, upper surface scabrid, the lower glabrous and paler, base rounded or cuneate, the upper leaves sometimes cordate; stipules 0. Flowers $\frac{3}{4}$ in. across; pedicels equalling the leaves, deflexed in fruit and with a line of pubescence. Sepals linear-lanceolate. Standard orbicular, cuspidate. Wings with very broad obovate subsessile terminal, and small lateral lobes. Lip boat-shaped. Spur 0, or rudimentary. Capsules $\frac{1}{3}$ in. long, ellipsoid, acute at both ends. Fl. B. I. v. 1, p. 448; Dalz. & Gibs. p. 43; Woodr. in Journ. Bomb. Nat. v. 11 (1897) p. 266.—Flowers: Oct.

KONKAN: S. Konkan, *Dalzell & Gibson*; W. Ghâts, *Woodrow*; S. Konkan, *Law*! S. M. COUNTRY: Castlerock, *Woodrow*.

10. **Impatiens Dalzellii,** *Hook. f. & Thoms. in Journ. Linn. Soc.* v. 4 (1860) p. 123. Smooth, erect, branched, 10–18 in. high. Leaves 2–5 by $\frac{5}{8}$–1$\frac{1}{2}$ in., lanceolate or oblong (the upper often linear), acute or acuminate, spinous-serrate (the basal serratures often with long cilia), glabrous or with short hairs above, pale beneath, base cordate, truncate or acute; the lower leaves with short petioles, the upper sessile or subsessile; stipules 0. Flowers yellow, about $\frac{3}{4}$ in. across; pedicels shorter than the leaves, solitary or sometimes fascicled on the very short peduncle, not, or rarely, deflexed in fruit. Sepals long, linear-lanceolate, somewhat falcate, acuminate, exceeding the lip in length when in bud. Standard orbicular, hooded, winged on the back and horned. Wings with an obovate lateral lobe, slightly incumbent on a clawed obovate terminal one. Lip boat-shaped, acuminate, streaked inside with red veins. Spur very short. Capsules about $\frac{1}{2}$ in. long, ellipsoid, turgid in the middle, tapering at both ends, smooth. Seeds few (rarely as many as 5), large, black. Fl. B. I. v. 1, p. 449; Dalz. & Gibs. p. 43; Woodr. in Journ. Bomb. Nat. v. 11 (1897) p. 266.—Flowers: Sept.–Oct.

KONKAN: Ghâts, *Dalzell*!, *Stocks*! DECCAN: Purandhar, *Woodrow*!; Mahableshwar, *Cooke*!

Very common at Mahableshwar in the early part of October.—It may be at once recognized by its yellow flowers.

11. **Impatiens tomentosa,** *Heyne, in Wall. Cat.* (1828) 4751. Stem erect, not much branched, the upper part more or less clothed with rufescent hairs. Leaves $\frac{1}{2}$–1 by $\frac{1}{4}$–$\frac{1}{2}$ in., elliptic- or ovate-oblong, the uppermost sometimes linear, acute or subobtuse, all distantly spinous-serrate, more or less hispid or tomentose above, pale and tomentose beneath, the nerves often clothed with rufous hairs, base usually rounded; petioles short, more or less rufous-hairy. Flowers $\frac{1}{3}$–$\frac{1}{2}$ in. across; pedicels solitary, rufous-hairy, deflexed in fruit. Sepals linear-lanceolate, ciliate. Standard orbicular-oblong, slightly keeled, apiculate. Wings with a small ovate acute lateral lobe incumbent on a large, sessile terminal one. Lip saccate, acuminate, hairy outside. Spur short, stout, hooked or 0. Capsules $\frac{1}{2}$ in. long, turgid in the middle, acute at both ends. Fl. B. I. v. 1, p. 449; Dalz. & Gibs. p. 43 (exclud. syn. *I. ramosissima*).—Flowers: Sept.

DECCAN: Phunda Ghát, *Dalzell & Gibson*.

This appears to be a rare plant in the Bombay Presidency. Dalzell gives Phunda Ghát in the Kolhapur State as its habitat, but I have seen no specimens from thence.

12. **Impatiens latifolia,** *Linn. Sp. Pl.* (1753) p. 937. A robust branched glabrous annual, 2–3 ft. high; branches alternate. Leaves membranous, 2–5 by ¾–2 in., alternate, subopposite or subverticillate, often crowded at the ends of the branches, ovate-lanceolate, acuminate, crenate-serrate (the crenatures often setose), glabrous or pubescent above, glabrous beneath, base cuneate; petioles 1–2 in. long, glabrous. Flowers 1–1½ in. across, rose-purple or violet, in axillary fascicles; pedicels very slender, usually recurved in fruit. Sepals ovate, cuspidate. Standard broad, 2-lobed, winged and spurred behind. Wings 2-lobed. Lip greenish-white or reddish, boat-shaped, acuminate. Spur green, long, slender, straight or incurved. Capsules ellipsoid, turgid. Fl. B. I. v. 1, p. 450; Grah. Cat. p. 34; Dalz. & Gibs. p. 44.

Common on the Konkan hills. KONKAN: *Stocks!*, *Law!*, *Dalzell & Gibson.*

13. **Impatiens lucida,** *Heyne, in Wall. Cat.* (1828) 4738. A slender glabrous annual, 4–8 in. high. Leaves subopposite or whorled, 1½–4 by ¾–2 in., ovate or ovate-lanceolate, acuminate, crenate-serrate (the crenatures sometimes setose), glabrous or with a few scattered hairs above, paler beneath, base cuneate; petioles ½–1½ in. long, very slender, glabrous. Flowers small, ⅓ in. across, solitary or fascicled. Sepals small, ovate, acute. Standard orbicular-oblong, horned and keeled at the back. Wings with broad (nearly orbicular) terminal lobes and scarcely any lateral ones. Spur very long, 3 or 4 times as long as the flower, slender, incurved. Capsules ½ in. long, ellipsoid, turgid in the middle, attenuated at both ends, glabrous. Fl. B. I. v. 1, p. 451.

KONKAN: *Stocks!*

14. **Impatiens Balsamina,** *Linn. Sp. Pl.* (1753) p. 938. Annual, erect, 1–3 ft. high; stem glabrous or pubescent, slightly branched. Leaves alternate, up to 6 in. long, lanceolate, acuminate, deeply serrate, glabrous, decurrent into a glandular petiole. Flowers rose-colored, showy; pedicels 1–3, axillary, slender, pubescent, shorter than the leaves. Sepals minute, ovate. Standard small, orbicular, retuse, horned. Wings broad, the lateral lobes rounded, the terminal sessile, very large. Lip small, boat-shaped, mucronate. Spur short or long, incurved. Capsules tomentose. Seeds reticulate. Fl. B. I. v. 1, p. 453; Trim. Fl. Ceyl. v. 1, p. 203; Watt, Dict. Econ. Prod. v. 4, p. 334.

VAR. 1. *coccinea.* Leaves very deeply serrate. Flowers medium-sized. Spur long and slender. *I. Balsamina*, Dalz. & Gibs. p. 44; Grah. Cat. p. 34; Woodr. in Journ. Bomb. Nat. v. 11 (1897) p. 266; *I. cornuta*, Linn. This is the common form in the Bombay Presidency.

Western Gháts widely, *Woodrow*; Párva Ghát, *Ritchie*, 123!; hills north of Belgaum, *Ritchie!*; Konkan: *Dalzell!*, *Stocks!*

VAR. 2. *brevicalcarata*, T. Cooke. Leaves reaching 6 in. long, narrow-lanceolate. Flowers smaller. Standard winged at the back, horned at the apex. Spur very short, stout, incurved.

This variety occurs at Mahableshwar and does not agree with any of the varieties given in the Flora of British India. It agrees with a specimen in Herb. Kew. from Rottler's Herbarium, marked *I. cornuta* from Samulcott.

15. **Impatiens scabriuscula,** *Heyne, in Roxb. Fl. Ind. (ed. Carey)* v. 2 (1824) p. 464. Low, erect, 4–10 in. high, usually much-branched,

pubescent and tomentose. Leaves 1–2 in. long, elliptic-lanceolate or obovate, serrate, glabrous or with a few hairs above, more or less hairy on the nerves beneath, base narrowed into the petiole, which is sometimes slightly glandular. Flowers rose-colored, $\frac{1}{2}$ in. across, axillary, fascicled; pedicels short, scabrid. Sepals small, linear-lanceolate, hairy. Standard somewhat rhomboidal, hairy outside, produced into a long hairy beak. Wings with long oblong-obovate terminal, and small rounded lateral lobes. Lip boat-shaped, acuminate, hairy. Spur 0. Capsules $\frac{1}{3}$ in. long, ellipsoid, mucronate, villous. Seeds globose, minutely tubercled, dark brown. Fl. B. I. v. 1, p. 454; Dalz. & Gibs. p. 44; Bedd. Ic. t. 144.

Very rare. KONKAN: *Stocks*!; S. Konkan, *Dalzell & Gibson*.

16. **Impatiens pulcherrima,** *Dalz. in Hook. Kew Journ. Bot.* v. 2 (1850) p. 37. Stem erect, $1\frac{1}{2}$–2 ft. high, glabrous, simple or branched. Leaves alternate, membranous, 3–5 by $1\frac{1}{4}$–2 in., elliptic-oblong, acuminate, glabrous or with a few scattered hairs above, glabrous and glaucous beneath, crenate-serrate, the crenatures setose, base acute; petioles $\frac{1}{2}$–$1\frac{1}{2}$ in. long, the upper part often with stipitate glands. Flowers violet-purple, $1\frac{1}{2}$–2 in. across; pedicels 2–3 in. long, 2–3 together, curved in fruit. Sepals small, lanceolate. Standard orbicular, notched, spurred and keeled at the back. Wings broad, the terminal lobes obovate, the lateral lobes large, oblong-elliptic. Lip short, deeply boat-shaped, mucronate. Spur long, curved. Capsules $\frac{5}{8}$ in. long, very turgid in the middle, at first puberulous, at length glabrous, obtusely beaked. Seeds subglobose, rugose. Fl. B. I. v. 1, p. 458; Dalz. & Gibs. p. 44; Woodr. in Journ. Bomb. Nat. v. 11 (1897) p. 266.—Flowers: Sept.–Oct.

In the Flora of British India l. c. the sepals are described as bifid. In all the specimens I have examined, I have found the sepals entire at the apex.

Rather rare. KONKAN: shady jungles in the Wari country, *Dalzell & Gibson*; road from Wadi to Poladpur, *Woodrow*! DECCAN: Fitzgerald Ghát below Mahableshwar, *Cooke*! S. M. COUNTRY: Londa, *Woodrow*.

A very handsome plant which has been successfully grown at Kew from seeds supplied by Dalzell. There is an excellent figure in the Botanical Magazine for 1851, t. 4615.

ORDER XXXII. RUTACEÆ.

Trees or shrubs, rarely herbs, abounding in pellucid glands filled with essential oil. Leaves exstipulate. Flowers regular, usually hermaphrodite, in axillary or terminal cymes or panicles, never spiked. Calyx of 4–5 small lobes or sepals. Petals 4–5, hypogynous, valvate or imbricate. Stamens 4–5 or 8 or 10, rarely more (*Citrus, Ægle*); filaments usually free, hypogynous; anthers 2-celled, introrse. Disk within the stamens, crenate or lobed, sometimes large and long. Ovary of 4–5 free or connate carpels; ovules usually 2 in each cell; styles as many as the carpels, free or variously united; stigmas terminal, entire or lobed. Fruit a capsule, berry or drupe, or of 1–4 capsular cocci. Seeds usually solitary in the cells; testa various, often crustaceous and shining; albumen fleshy or 0; embryo straight or curved; radicle always superior. —DISTRIB. Throughout the warm and temperate regions of the world;

the greatest number occur in S. Africa and Australia; genera 82; species about 650.

Ovary deeply 2–5-lobed; fruit capsular or 3–5-coccous.
  Herbs, sometimes shrubby at the base; flowers hermaphrodite. 1. **Ruta.**
  Shrubs or trees; flowers polygamous.
    Leaves opposite .... 2. **Evodia.**
    Leaves alternate .... 3. **Zanthoxylum.**
Ovary entire or slightly 2–5-lobed; fruit drupaceous or baccate, usually indehiscent.
  Flowers polygamous; seeds albuminous.
    Stamens 2–5 .... 4. **Toddalia.**
    Stamens 8 .... 5. **Acronychia.**
  Flowers hermaphrodite; seeds exalbuminous.
    Ovules solitary or twin in each cell.
      Unarmed.
        Style very short, persistent .... 6. **Glycosmis.**
        Style jointed on the top of the ovary, deciduous; leaves pinnate.
          Filaments not dilated at the base .... 7. **Murraya.**
          Filaments dilated at the base .... 8. **Clausena.**
      Armed; leaves 3–8-foliolate.
        Stamens 6; calyx 3-lobed .... 9. **Triphasia.**
        Stamens 8 or 10.
          Calyx 4–5-lobed .... 10. **Limonia.**
          Calyx cupular, obscurely lobed .... 11. **Luvunga.**
      Unarmed or armed; leaves 1-foliolate.
        Anthers linear-oblong; disk elongate .... 12. **Paramignya.**
        Anthers ovate or cordate (except in *A. missionis*); disk cupular .... 13. **Atalantia.**
    Ovules many in each cell.
      Stamens 20–60; leaves 1-foliolate.................... 14. **Citrus.**
      Stamens 10–12; leaves pinnate .... 15. **Feronia.**
      Stamens 30–60; leaves 3-foliolate .... 16. **Ægle.**

1. RUTA, Linn.

Strong-smelling glanduloso-punctate herbs, often shrubby below. Leaves alternate. Flowers numerous, in terminal corymbs, cymes or panicles, greenish or yellow. Calyx short, 4–5-lobed or -partite, persistent. Petals 4–5, concave, often toothed or ciliate, imbricate. Disk thick, urceolate, 8–10-glandular or 8–10-foveolate. Stamens 8–10, inserted round the base of the disk, the alternate shorter; filaments dilated at the base. Ovary sessile, deeply 3–5-lobed, 3–5-celled; ovules pendulous from the axis of the cells; style central, stigmatose at the apex. Capsule 4–5-lobed; lobes indehiscent or dehiscing at the apex, many-seeded. Seeds angled; testa pitted; albumen fleshy; embryo slightly curved; cotyledons sometimes 2-partite.—Distrib. Chiefly Mediterranean, Western and Central Asian; species about 40.

Flowers 4-merous; filaments glabrous .... 1. *R. graveolens.*
Flowers 5-merous; filaments pilose .... 2. *R. tuberculata.*

1. **Ruta graveolens,** *Linn. Sp. Pl.* (1753) p. 383, var. *angustifolia*, Hook. f. in Fl. B. I. v. 1, p. 485. Leaves petioled, decompound; segments cuneate, spathulate-oblong or linear-oblong. Flowers in divaricately spreading corymbs; pedicels longer than the capsule; bracts lanceolate. Sepals triangular, acute. Petals oblong-obovate, pectinate, abruptly clawed. Capsules obtuse, shortly pedicelled. Seeds angled. *Ruta graveolens*, Grah. Cat. p. 36; Dalz. & Gibs. Suppl.

p. 17; Woodr. in Journ. Bomb. Nat. v. 11 (1897) p. 267.—VERN. *Satáp.*

Cultivated for its medicinal properties in gardens throughout India. Below the Ghâts it is largely grown, "being much used by the Konkan people as a fumigation in infant catarrh" (Dalzell & Gibson). Consult Watt, Dictionary of Economic Products of India, v. 6, part 1, p. 593.—DISTRIB. Westward to the Canary Islands.

2. **Ruta tuberculata,** *Forsk. Fl. Ægypt.-Arab.* (1775) p. 86. Stem erect or ascending, terete, branched, woody, minutely glandular, glaucous, glabrous. Leaves ½–1 in. long, linear-oblong or somewhat spathulate, obtuse or subacute, pustular and pubescent, base narrowed into the petiole. Cymes dichotomously branched; flowers ¼ in. across, the central one of each cyme sessile, the others shortly pedicelled. Sepals small, broadly elliptic, about $\frac{1}{10}$ in. long. Petals $\frac{1}{8}$–$\frac{1}{6}$ in. long, yellow, elliptic-oblong, obtuse, concave, entire, glabrous. Filaments dilated and hairy at the base. Capsules 5-lobed, 5-celled, tubercled, often with 2 seeds in each cell. Fl. B. I. v. 1, p. 485; Woodr. in Journ. Bomb. Nat. v. 11 (1897) p. 267; Watt, Dict. Econ. Prod. v. 6, part 1, p. 594. *Haplophyllum tuberculatum*, Boiss. Fl. Orient. v. 1, p. 939.—Flowers: Dec.

SIND: Boogta hills, *Vicary*!; Sibi, *Cooke*!, *Woodrow*!—DISTRIB. Egypt and Algeria.

2. EVODIA, Forst.

Trees or shrubs, unarmed. Leaves opposite, simple or 1–3-foliolate or imparipinnate; leaflets pellucido-punctate, quite entire. Flowers small, in axillary paniculate cymes, unisexual. Sepals 4–5, imbricate. Petals 4–5, sessile, valvate or slightly imbricate. Disk 4–5-lobed. Stamens 4–5, inserted at the base of the disk; filaments subulate; anthers oblong. Ovary deeply 4-lobed, 4-celled; ovules 2 in each cell, collateral or superposed; style basilar. Fruit of 4 coriaceous 2-valved 1-seeded cocci; endocarp horny, elastically separable, 2-lobed. Seeds oblong; testa bony or crustaceous, shining; hilum linear; albumen fleshy; embryo straight; cotyledons ovate.—DISTRIB. Tropical Asia, Malaya, the Mascarene and Pacific Islands and Australia; species 22.

1. **Evodia Roxburghiana,** *Benth. Fl. Hongk.* (1861) p. 59. A small soft-wooded tree, about 30 ft. high; bark corky; branches opposite. Leaves 3-foliolate; petioles 1½–4 in. long, terete, glabrous; leaflets 2–5 by 1¼–2½ in., oblong, acuminate, closely pellucid-dotted, with slightly repand margins, glabrous on both surfaces, shining above, base narrowed, the lobes sometimes unequal; petiolules ¼–½ in. long. Flowers diœcious, small, in dense axillary bracteate cymes; pedicels short, more or less glandular-pubescent; bracts minute, broadly ovate, acute. Sepals minute, broadly elliptic or suborbicular. Petals white, $\frac{1}{12}$ in. long, ovate, acute, reflexed. MALE FLOWERS: Stamens 4; filaments glabrous; anthers elliptic. Disk pulvinate, pubescent. FEMALE FLOWERS: Ovary pubescent; style short, thick; stigma obsoletely 4-lobed. Staminodes 4, with small barren anthers. Cocci the size of a peppercorn, 2-valved. Seeds black, globose, polished, shining. Fl. B. I. v. 1, p. 487; Trim. Fl. Ceyl. v. 1, p. 214; Talb. Trees, Bomb. p. 30; Woodr. in Journ. Bomb. Nat. v. 11 (1897) p. 267; Watt, Dict. Econ. Prod. v. 3, p. 305. *Xanthoxylon triphyllum*, Wight, Icon. t. 204; Grah. Cat. p. 36; Dalz. & Gibs. p. 45.—Flowers: May.

Tolerably abundant along the line of the Ghâts. KONKAN: *Stocks*!, *Law*! DECCAN: Pargbát, *Graham*; Mahableshwar, *Cooke*!, *Woodrow*!, *H. M. Birdwood*; ravines at Khandala, *Graham*. S. M. COUNTRY: Ramghát, *Ritchie*, 200! KANARA: throughout the Ghâts of N. Kanara in moist situations; forests near Yellapur, N. Kanara, *Talbot*.—DISTRIB. Sumatra, Java, Ceylon.

3. ZANTHOXYLUM, Linn.

Shrubs or trees, often armed. Leaves alternate, 3-foliolate or pinnate; leaflets opposite or alternate, entire or crenate, often oblique, pellucido-punctate. Flowers polygamous, small, in axillary or terminal, usually paniculate cymes. Calyx 3–8-fid, imbricate, rarely 0. Petals 3–5, rarely 0. MALE FLOWERS: Disk inconspicuous. Stamens 3–5, hypogynous. Ovary rudimentary. FEMALE FLOWERS: Stamens 0 or squamiform. Disk very short. Carpels 1–5, oblique, 1-celled; ovules 2 in each cell, usually collateral; styles sublateral, short or long, free or connate above; stigmas capitate. Fruit of 1–5 globose coriaceous or fleshy 1-seeded carpels dehiscing ventrally; endocarp horny, separating or not. Seeds globose or oblong, often hanging out of the carpel; hilum broad; testa bony or crustaceous, blue or black, shining; albumen fleshy; embryo straight or curved; cotyledons flat; radicle very short.—DISTRIB. Throughout the tropical and warm regions of the world; species 80.

Leaves 3-foliolate; branches of the cyme alternate.................. 1. *Z. ovalifolium*.
Leaves 5-many-foliolate; branches of the cyme opposite .... 2. *Z. Rhetsa*.

1. **Zanthoxylum ovalifolium,** *Wight*, *Ill.* v. 1 (1840) p. 169. A shrub about 6 ft. high, glabrous, armed with short straight or slightly curved prickles from thickened bases. Leaves 3-foliolate; petioles $\frac{3}{8}$–1 in. long; leaflets coriaceous, 3–4 by $1\frac{1}{2}$–$1\frac{3}{4}$ in., elliptic-oblong or obovate, bluntly acuminate, tip rounded, emarginate, glabrous on both surfaces, obscurely crenate, base acute; petiolules $\frac{1}{8}$ in. long. Flowers $\frac{3}{16}$ in. across, in dense paniculate cymes with alternate branches; peduncles and pedicels glabrous, the latter very short. Calyx small; lobes minute, fleshy, triangular. Petals $\frac{1}{10}$ in. long, ovate, obtuse, valvate. Ripe carpels solitary, spherical, size of a pea, slightly pitted, glabrous. Seed globose, smooth, shining, black. Fl. B. I. v. 1, p. 492; Bedd. For. Man. in Flor. Sylvat. p. xlii, et Anal. Gen. t. 6, fig. 3; Talb. Trees, Bomb. p. 30; Woodr. in Journ. Bomb. Nat. v. 11 (1897) p. 267; Watt, Dict. Econ. Prod. v. 6, part 4, p. 325.—Flowers: Nov.–Dec.

Rare; the only specimens I have seen have been collected in Kanara. KANARA: *Hohenhacker*, 763 *a*!, *Stocks*!, *Woodrow*!; Yacombi, *Woodrow*!—DISTRIB. Singapore.

2. **Zanthoxylum Rhetsa,** *DC. Prod.* v. 1 (1824) p. 728.—A middle-sized tree, covered all over (even occasionally the petioles and peduncles) with sharp curved or straight prickles, those from the old wood with a solid conical base; bark corky, deeply cracked; branches numerous, spreading. Leaves crowded at the ends of the branches, equally or unequally pinnate, 12–20 in. long; leaflets 8–20 pairs, 3–5 by $1\frac{3}{4}$–$2\frac{1}{4}$ in., opposite, ovate-oblong or oblong-lanceolate, caudate-acuminate, entire, glabrous, the upper side of each leaflet rounded at the base, the lower side narrowed into the costa; nerves 10–12 on the upper side, 2 fewer on the lower; petiolules very short. Flowers in large terminal paniculate cymes often more than 12 in. broad, the branches

opposite, angled; bracts minute, caducous; peduncles very long, sometimes prickly. Calyx-lobes minute, triangular. Petals 4, elliptic, $\frac{1}{10}$ in. long, yellow, valvate. Ripe carpels $\frac{1}{4}$ in. in diam., spherical, rugose. Seeds globose, bluish-black, smooth, shining. Fl. B. I. v. 1, p. 495; Grah. Cat. p. 36; Dalz. & Gibs. p. 45; Bedd. For. Man. in Flor. Sylvat. p. xli, et Anal. Gen. t. 6; Talb. Trees, Bomb. p. 30; Woodr. in Journ. Bomb. Nat. v. 11 (1897) p. 267; Watt, Dict. Econ. Prod. v. 6, part 4, p. 325.—Flowers: July–Oct. VERN. *Tisal*; *Chirphal*; *Kokli.*

KONKAN: Vingorla, *Dalzell*!; Waral (Ratnagiri districts), *Woodrow*; Banda in the Wari country, *Dalzell*. DECCAN; Khandala, *Graham*; Khandesh, *Graham*; Pár village, *Graham*. S. M. COUNTRY: Párva Ghát (Belgaum districts), *Ritchie*, 1187! KANARA: Karwar, *Talbot*; throughout N. Kanara in moist, evergreen forests, *Talbot*.

The unripe carpels are gratefully aromatic and have the flavor of orange peel. The seeds taste exactly like black pepper. Both are employed in Southern India as condiments. The essential oil obtained from the fruit is used medicinally. See Watt, Dict. Econ. Prod. l. c.

4. TODDALIA, Juss.

Subscandent or sarmentose shrubs, usually prickly. Leaves alternate, 1–3-foliolate; leaflets sessile. Flowers small, in axillary or terminal cymes or panicles, unisexual. Calyx short, 2–5-toothed -lobed or -partite. Petals 2–5, imbricate or valvate. Disk inconspicuous or slightly elongate. MALE FLOWERS: Stamens 2–4–5 (or 8, the alternate ones opposite the petals, short and imperfect), inserted at the base of the disk; filaments subulate or filiform. Ovary rudimentary, simple or 4-partite. FEMALE FLOWERS: Ovary ovoid, oblong or globose, sessile or inserted on a short torus, 2–7- (very rarely 1-) celled; ovules 2 in each cell, superposed or collateral; style short or 0; stigma capitate. Fruit pisiform, subglobose or lobed, coriaceous or fleshy, punctate, 2–7-celled; cells 1- (rarely 2-) seeded. Seeds angled, reniform; testa coriaceous; cotyledons oblong or linear.—DISTRIB. Tropical and subtropical Asia, Africa and Australia; species about 8.

Prickly shrub; fruit 3–7-celled; petals 5 .... 1. *T. aculeata.*
Unarmed tree; fruit 2-celled; petals 2–3 .... 2. *T. bilocularis.*

1. **Toddalia aculeata,** *Pers. Syn.* v. 1 (1805) p. 249. A large sarmentose shrub, usually armed with sharp curved or straight prickles (sometimes unarmed). Leaves 3-foliolate; leaflets coriaceous, sessile, $1\frac{1}{2}$–$3\frac{1}{2}$ by $\frac{3}{4}$–$1\frac{1}{2}$ in., lanceolate-oblong or obovate, usually with a long blunt acumen, notched at the apex, crenulate or subentire, glabrous, many-nerved, the midrib often prickly, base acute. Flowers white, $\frac{1}{6}$–$\frac{1}{3}$ in. across, in axillary cymes. Calyx small, glandular; lobes triangular. Petals 5, oblong, thickened at the apex, imbricate. MALE FLOWERS: Petals shorter than the stamens; buds globose. Ovary (rudimentary) cylindric-oblong, grooved, seated on a lobed disk. FEMALE FLOWERS: Petals longer than in the male; buds oblong. Stigma sessile, 5–7-lobed. Fruit globose, size of a large pea, 3–5-grooved, orange-colored, pitted on the rind, 3–7-celled. Seed solitary in each cell, smooth, reniform, rounded on the back. Fl. B. I. v. 1, p. 497; Grah. Cat. p. 37 (*Toddelia*); Dalz. & Gibs. p. 46; Trim. Fl. Ceyl. v. 1, p. 215; Engler, in Engl. & Prantl, Pflanzenf. v. 3, part 4, p. 176, fig. 101, A–K; Talb. Trees, Bomb. p. 31; Woodr. in Journ. Bomb. Nat. v. 11 (1897) p. 267; Watt, Dict. Econ. Prod. v. 6, part 4, p. 67. *Limonia oligandra*, Dalz. in Kew Journ. Bot. v. 2 (1850) p. 258; Dalz. & Gibs. p. 28.—Flowers: Sept.–Dec. VERN. *Jangli-káli-mirchi.*

KONKAN: *Law!*, *Stocks!*, *Dalzell!*; S. Konkan, *Graham*. DECCAN: Khandala, *Dalzell & Gibson*; Mahableshwar, *Cooke!*, *H. M. Birdwood*. S. M. COUNTRY: Ramghát, *Ritchie*, 91! KANARA: plentiful, *Dalzell & Gibson*; Sirsi (N. Kanara), *Talbot*, 338!—DISTRIB. Sumatra, Java, China, the Philippines, Ceylon.

A valuable medicinal plant, the root-bark especially possessing high therapeutic properties. See Watt, Dict. Econ. Prod. l. c.

2. **Toddalia bilocularis,** *Wight & Arn. Prod.* (1834) p. 149. A handsome, middle-sized tree with dark green foliage, unarmed. Leaves 3-foliolate; petioles 1½–3 in. long, terete, glabrous; leaflets 3–7½ by 1½–3 in., elliptic-lanceolate, bluntly acuminate, notched at the tip, entire, glabrous, base acute; lateral nerves numerous, parallel and uniting into one that is parallel to and close to the margin; petiolules ¼–⅜ in. long. Flowers terminal and from the upper axils. Calyx cupular. Petals usually 2 (sometimes 3), orbicular-oblong. Stigma large, peltate. Fruit as large as a small cherry, 2-celled. Fl. B. I. v. 1, p. 497; Dalz. & Gibs. p. 46; Bedd. For. Man. in Flor. Sylvat. p. xliii, et Icon. t. 167; Talb. Trees, Bomb. p. 31. *Dipetalum biloculare*, Dalz. in Kew Journ. Bot. v. 2 (1850) p. 38.

A very rare plant, of which but few specimens have been available for examination. KANARA: *Dalzell & Gibson*.

5. ACRONYCHIA, Forst.

Trees. Leaves opposite or alternate, very rarely 3-foliolate; leaflets large, quite entire, pellucido-punctate. Flowers in axillary and terminal corymbs, polygamous. Calyx short, 4-lobed, imbricate, sometimes enlarged after flowering. Petals 4, much longer than the calyx, spreading or revolute, valvate. Disk thick, 8-gonous, tomentose or pubescent. Stamens 8, inserted beneath the disk; filaments subulate, the alternate longer. Ovary inserted in the hollowed apex of the disk, pubescent or tomentose, 4-celled; ovules 2 in each cell, superposed; style terminal, short or long; stigma 4-grooved. Fruit 4-celled, the cells 1–2-seeded, or drupaceous with a coriaceous or bony putamen, or capsular and loculicidally 4-valved. Seeds usually exserted and dependent from a slender funicle; testa black; albumen copious; embryo straight; cotyledons oblong, flat.—DISTRIB. Tropical Asia, Australia and the Pacific Islands; species 15.

1. **Acronychia laurifolia,** *Blume, Cat. Gew. Buitenz.* (1823) p. 63; *Bijdr.* p. 245. A small tree with pale smooth bark; young twigs glabrous. Leaves 1-foliolate; leaflets 3–5 by 1¼–2 in., oblong-lanceolate or somewhat obovate, usually shortly and obtusely acuminate, entire, glabrous and shining above, base acute; petioles ¼–¾ in. long. Flowers fragrant, in paniculately corymbose cymes; buds linear-oblong; peduncles long, straight, terete; pedicels glabrous. Calyx small; lobes broadly ovate, ciliolate. Petals ¼ in. long, yellowish-white, strap-shaped, cucullate, inflexed at the apex, hairy at the base inside. Stamens shorter than the petals; filaments dilated and hairy at the base; anthers versatile. Disk 8-ribbed, softly pubescent towards the apex. Ovary conical, softly hairy; style shorter than the stamens. Capsules ¼–½ in. in diam., subglobose, 3–5-celled, glabrous, rough with immersed glands, more or less lobed, tip angled or grooved. Fl. B. I. v. 1, p. 498; Trim. Fl. Ceyl. v. 1, p. 216; Engler, in Engl. & Prantl, Pflanzenf. v. 3, part 4, p. 180,

g. 104; Talb. Trees, Bomb. p. 31; Woodr. in Journ. Bomb. Nat. v. 11 (1897) p. 267. *Cyminosma pedunculata*, DC. Prod. v. 1, p. 722; Dalz. & Gibs. Suppl. p. 17. *Clausena simplicifolia*, Dalz. in Kew Journ. Bot. v. 3 (1851) p. 180; Dalz. & Gibs. p. 30.—Flowers: Aug.–Sept.

KONKAN: *Law*!, *Stocks*! KANARA: *Dalzell*!; Godhuli (N. Kanara), *Talbot* ex *Woodrow*, l. c.; Karwar, *Talbot*!, *Woodrow*.—DISTRIB. Sumatra, Java, Cochinchina.

6. GLYCOSMIS, Corr.

Unarmed trees or shrubs. Leaves 1-foliolate or imparipinnate; leaflets usually alternate. Flowers small, in axillary, rarely terminal panicles. Calyx 5-partite; lobes broad, imbricate. Petals 4–5, imbricate. Stamens 8–10, free, inserted round a disk; filaments subulate, dilated below; anthers small, often furnished with a dorsal or apical gland. Ovary seated on the disk, 2–5-celled; ovule solitary in each cell, pendulous. Berry pulpy or somewhat dry, 1–3-seeded. Seeds oblong; testa membranous; cotyledons equal; radicle very short.—DISTRIB. Tropical Asia and Australia; species 5.

1. **Glycosmis pentaphylla,** *Corr. in Ann. Mus. Hist. Nat.* v. 6 (1805) p. 386. An erect shrub or small tree. Leaves 3–5- (rarely 1-) foliolate; leaflets 2–8 by $\frac{3}{4}$–$2\frac{1}{4}$ in., subsessile, alternate and subopposite, polymorphous, usually oblong-lanceolate, obtuse, acute or acuminate, entire or obscurely crenulate, glabrous, base acute. Flowers small, less than $\frac{1}{2}$ in. across, crowded in small clusters in erect axillary panicles 1–4 in. long; pedicels very short; bracts beneath the calyx triangular. Calyx small; lobes ovate-orbicular, margins membranous, ciliolate, with a gland on the outside of each lobe a little below its apex. Petals imbricate, white, very broadly obovate or suborbicular, the margins membranous. Filaments flattened; anthers with a gland at the apex and sometimes with another smaller gland at the back of the anther. Ovary on a short thick disk, covered all over, as is the style, with mammillate glands; style as wide as the ovary in bud. Berry globose, $\frac{3}{8}$ in. in diam., apiculate, smooth, pinkish-white or cream-colored. Fl. B. I. v. 1, p. 499; Grah. Cat. p. 23; Dalz. & Gibs. p. 29; Bedd. For. Man. in Flor. Sylvat. p. xliii, et Anal. Gen. t. 6; Trim. Fl. Ceyl. v. 1, p. 217; Talb. Trees, Bomb. p. 31; Woodr. in Journ. Bomb. Nat. v. 11 (1897) p. 267; Watt, Dict. Econ. Prod. v. 3, p. 512.

Common throughout the moist evergreen forests of the Konkan and N. Kanara. KONKAN: *Law*!, *Stocks*!; Wada, *Woodrow*!; jungles in the Konkan, *Dalzell & Gibson*. DECCAN: Khandala, *Woodrow*. KANARA: Kála naddi, *Ritchie*, 87! S. M. COUNTRY: Castlerock, *Woodrow*!; Belgaum Ghâts, *Ritchie*, 87!—DISTRIB. Malaya, China, Borneo, Australia, Ceylon.

7. MURRAYA, Linn.

Shrubs or small trees, unarmed. Leaves pinnate; leaflets alternate, petioluled, cuneate or oblique at the base. Flowers solitary, axillary, or in terminal corymbs or axillary cymes. Calyx 5-fid or 5-partite. Petals 5, free, imbricate. Stamens 10, free, the alternate shorter; filaments linear-subulate; anthers small, short. Disk stipitiform. Ovary seated on the disk, 2–5-celled, narrowed into the style; ovules 1–2 in each cell, superposed or collateral; style elongate, at length deciduous; stigma capitate.

Berry small, 1–2-celled, oblong or ovoid, 1–2-seeded. Seeds with a woolly or glabrous testa; cotyledons equal.—DISTRIB. Tropical Asia; species about 5.

Flowers few; leaflets 3–7 .... 1. *M. exotica.*
Flowers numerous; leaflets 11–25 .... 2. *M. Kœnigii.*

1. **Murraya exotica,** *Linn. Mantiss.* v. 2 (1771) p. 563 (*Murræa*); VAR. 2, *Fl. B. I.* v. 1, p. 503. A small evergreen tree; bark smooth, yellowish-white; branches slender. Leaves imparipinnate, 4–7 in. long; petioles glabrous; leaflets 3–7, alternate, $1\frac{1}{2}$–3 by $\frac{3}{4}$–$1\frac{1}{2}$ in. (the terminal leaflet the largest), ovate-elliptic, obovate or rhomboid, usually acuminate with a notched tip, entire, glabrous and shining, base acute, oblique; petiolules $\frac{1}{8}$–$\frac{1}{4}$ in. long. Flowers very fragrant, campanulate, solitary or in terminal and axillary corymbs. Sepals small, glandular, oblong, obtuse. Petals white, $\frac{1}{2}$–$\frac{3}{4}$ in. long, oblong-lanceolate, subobtuse, erect at the base, the upper half spreading. Filaments flat, linear, tapering beneath the anther. Ovary 2-celled. Berry $\frac{1}{2}$–$\frac{3}{4}$ in. in diam., oblong or ovoid, pointed, smooth, 1-celled, 2-seeded, red when ripe. Grah. Cat. p. 24; Bedd. For. Man. in Flor. Sylvat. p. xliv, et Anal. Gen. t. 7, fig. 2; Trim. Fl. Ceyl. v. 1, p. 219; Engler, in Engl. & Prantl, Pflanzenf. v. 3, part 4, p. 187, fig. 108, A–G; Talb. Trees, Bomb. p. 31; Woodr. in Journ. Bomb. Nat. v. 11 (1897) p. 267; Watt, Dict. Econ. Prod. v. 5, p. 288. *Murraya paniculata*, Jack, in Mal. Misc. v. 1, p. 31; Dalz. & Gibs. p. 29.—Flowers: June–Oct. VERN. *Kunti*; *Chula-juti.*

Pretty common on the higher Gháts; frequently grown in gardens throughout the Presidency. KONKAN: *Stocks*!; Gháts, *Talbot*; Rohe, *Dalzell & Gibson.* DECCAN: Khandala, *Woodrow*; Mahableshwar and Matheran, *H. M. Birdwood*; Lanoli, *Kanitkar*! S. M. COUNTRY: Ramghát, *Ritchie*, 89! KANARA: Kála naddi, *Ritchie*, 89!; Gháts of N. Kanara, *Talbot.*—DISTRIB. China, Australia and the Pacific Islands, Ceylon.

2. **Murraya Kœnigii,** *Spreng. Syst. Veg.* v. 2 (1825) p. 315. A small tree with dark grey bark. Leaves imparipinnate, up to 12 in. long; petioles terete, pubescent; leaflets 11–25, alternate, $\frac{3}{4}$–2 by $\frac{3}{8}$–1 in., obliquely ovate or somewhat rhomboid, acuminate, obtuse or acute, tip usually notched (the lower leaflets often suborbicular or obovate, much smaller than the upper), irregularly crenate-dentate, glabrous or nearly so above, pubescent beneath, sprinkled with black dots; petiolules very short. Flowers white, in much-branched terminal peduncled corymbose cymes; peduncles and pedicels pubescent. Calyx pubescent; lobes subacute, triangular. Petals $\frac{1}{4}$ in. long, linear-oblong, rounded at the apex, gland-dotted. Filaments dilated at the base. Ovary 2-celled; ovules solitary (rarely 2), in each cell. Fruit ovoid or subglobose, $\frac{1}{4}$–$\frac{3}{8}$ in. in diam., apiculate, rough with glands, black, 2-seeded. Fl. B. I. v. 1, p. 503; Bedd. For. Man. in Flor. Sylvat. p. xliv; Trim. Fl. Ceyl. v. 1, p. 220; Talb. Trees, Bomb. p. 31; Woodr. in Journ. Bomb. Nat. v. 11 (1897) p. 267; Watt, Dict. Econ. Prod. v. 5, p. 288. *Bergera Kœnigii*, Linn. Mantiss. p. 563; Grah. Cat. p. 24; Dalz. & Gibs. p. 29. —Flowers: Feb.–Apr. VERN. *Kadhi-nim.*

Common all along the line of the Gháts. KONKAN: *Law*!, *Stocks*!; on the Gháts, common, *Dalzell & Gibson.* DECCAN: Mahableshwar, common, *Cooke*!; hills near Poona, *Woodrow*! S. M. COUNTRY: Hill of Backur, 5 miles west of Belgaum, *Ritchie*,

105! KANARA: *Ritchie*!; common in the Supa district of N. Kanara, *Talbot*.—DISTRIB. Ceylon.

The leaves under the name of *Karripák* are used to flavor curries, and the leaves, bark, and root are employed in native medicine. See Watt, Dict. Econ. Prod. l. c.

8. CLAUSENA, Burm.

Trees or shrubs, unarmed. Leaves imparipinnate, usually deciduous; leaflets membranous. Flowers small, in terminal or axillary cymes, panicles or lax racemes. Calyx 4–5-lobed or -partite. Petals 4–5, free, usually tender, elliptic or rotund, imbricate. Stamens 8–10, free, the alternate a little shorter; filaments dilated in the middle or below the middle, subulate at the apex; anthers short. Disk stipitiform. Ovary 4–5-(rarely 2–3-) celled, stalked; ovules 2 in each cell, collateral or superposed; style usually distinct, at length deciduous; stigma obtuse, entire or 2–5-lobed. Berry ovoid, oblong or globose, 2–5-celled. Seeds oblong; testa membranous; cotyledons equal, plano-convex.—DISTRIB. Chiefly tropical Asia, a few in tropical Africa and Australia; species 14.

Flowers in terminal panicles, usually 5-merous; ovules collateral .... 1. *C. indica.*
Flowers in axillary racemes, usually 4-merous; ovules superposed .... 2. *C. Wildenowii.*

1. **Clausena indica,** *Oliver, in Journ. Linn. Soc.* v. 5 (1861), *Suppl.* 2, p. 36. A shrub or small tree. Leaves 4–10 in. long; petioles slender, terete, glabrous; leaflets 7–13, alternate, $1\frac{1}{2}$–3 by $\frac{3}{4}$–$1\frac{1}{2}$ in., ovate-oblong or lanceolate, obtusely acuminate, acute or rounded, notched at the tip, crenulate, glabrous, shining, base very oblique; petiolules $\frac{1}{8}$ in. long. Flowers small, in terminal corymbosely branched peduncled panicles; pedicels short. Sepals ovate, acute, ciliolate. Petals white, elliptic, $\frac{1}{8}$ in. long. Ovary 2–5-celled, glabrous, papillose; ovules 2 in each cell, collateral. Fruit nearly globular, $\frac{1}{2}$ in. in diam., salmon- or cream-colored; pulp abundant, edible. Fl. B. I. v. 1, p. 505; Bedd. For. Man. in Flor. Sylvat. p. xlv; Trim. Fl. Ceyl. v. 1, p. 221; Engler, in Engl. & Prantl, Pflanzenf. v. 3, part 4, p. 187, fig. 108, L–O; Talb. Trees, Bomb. p. 32; Woodr. in Journ. Bomb. Nat. v. 11 (1897) p. 267; Watt, Dict. Econ. Prod. v. 2, p. 358. *Piptostylis indica*, Dalz. in Kew Journ. Bot. v. 3 (1851) p. 33, t. 2; Dalz. & Gibs. p. 29.—Flowers: Apr.–May.

S. M. COUNTRY: Párva Ghát, *Dalzell*! KANARA: common in the evergreen forests on the Gháts of N. Kanara from Ainshi southwards, *Talbot*.—DISTRIB. Ceylon.

2. **Clausena Wildenowii,** *Wight & Arn. Prodr.* (1834) p. 96. A large shrub; young parts more or less pubescent. Leaves 6–16 in. long; rhachis slender, terete; leaflets 5–15, membranous, distant, 2–4 by $\frac{3}{4}$–$1\frac{3}{4}$ in., ovate-oblong or ovate-lanceolate, acute, obtuse or acuminate, more or less emarginate, crenulate, finely reticulately veined and gland-dotted, glabrous, base very oblique; petiolules $\frac{1}{8}$ in. long, pubescent. Flowers fragrant, in slender racemes 3–10 in. long, from the axils of the young leaves and shorter than them. Sepals ovate, acute, ciliate. Petals white, $\frac{1}{8}$ in. long, ovate, concave, reticulately veined. Filaments dilated at the base. Ovary 4-angled or grooved, cylindric, 4-celled; ovules 2 in each cell, superposed; style short; stigma 4-lobed. Fruit size of a large pea, ovoid, smooth, greenish-white, 1–2-seeded.

Fl. B. I. v. 1, p. 506; Dalz. & Gibs. p. 30; Bedd. For. Man. in Flor. Sylvat. p. xlv, et Anal. Gen. t. 7, fig. 3; Trim. Fl. Ceyl. v. 1, p. 222; Talb. Trees, Bomb. p. 32; Woodr. in Journ. Bomb. Nat. v. 11 (1897) p. 267.—Flowers: Feb.

KONKAN: *Stocks*! S. M. COUNTRY: Ramghát, *Ritchie*, 1644!; Chorla Ghát, *Dalzell & Gibson*. KANARA: *Stocks*!; Hatkumba (N. Kanara), *Ritchie*, 1644!; Gháts of N. Kanara in evergreen forests, *Talbot*.—DISTRIB. Moluccas, Ceylon.

Clausena Wampi, Oliver (*Cookia punctata*, Sonnerat), a native probably of China, is often grown in gardens. Its fruit is about as large as a marble and is used for tarts and preserves. *Grah. Cat.* p. 24; *Dalz. & Gibs. Suppl.* p. 12.

9. **TRIPHASIA,** Lour.

A spiny shrub. Leaves alternate, 3-foliolate; leaflets ovate, obtuse, usually crenate, the lateral smaller. Flowers solitary or in 2–3-flowered cymes, axillary, white, odorous. Calyx 3-lobed. Petals 3, free, imbricate. Stamens 6, free, subequal; filaments subulate, dilated at the base; anthers linear. Disk fleshy, annular or stipitiform. Ovary seated on the disk, ovoid, 3-celled, narrowed into the style; ovule 1 in each cell; style slender, at length deciduous; stigma obtuse or capitate and 3-lobed. Berry small, ovoid, 1–3-celled, 1–3-seeded. Seeds oblong, immersed in mucilage; testa coriaceous; cotyledons plano-convex, often unequal and lobed.—DISTRIB. A native of China, cultivated in the tropics; species 1.

1. **Triphasia Aurantiola,** *Lour. Fl. Cochinch.* v. 1 (1790) p. 153. A spinous straggling shrub; branches terete; spines axillary, straight, slender. Leaves 3-foliolate; leaflets thick and soft, $\frac{3}{4}$–$1\frac{1}{2}$ by $\frac{1}{2}$–$\frac{7}{8}$ in. (the terminal leaflet much the largest, the lateral ones more rounded and oblique), ovate-elliptic, tip rounded, notched, crenulate, closely gland-dotted, glabrous, base cuneate; petiolules short. Flowers fragrant, solitary or in 2–3-flowered peduncled cymes; pedicels very short. Calyx 3-lobed; lobes broadly ovate or suborbicular, ciliolate. Petals 3, linear-oblong, rounded at the tip, $\frac{1}{2}$ in. long, white. Fruit ellipsoid, $\frac{1}{2}$ in. long, fleshy, apiculate, gland-dotted. *Triphasia trifoliata*, DC. Prod. v. 1 (1824) p. 536; Fl. B. I. v. 1, p. 507; Grah. Cat. p. 23; Dalz. & Gibs. Suppl. p. 12; Talb. Trees, Bomb. p. 32; Woodr. in Journ. Bomb. Nat. v. 11 (1897) p. 267; Watt, Dict. Econ. Prod. v. 6, part 4, p. 88.—VERN. *Chin-ke-limbu.*

A native probably of China, grown in gardens throughout India. The fruit is used in preserves and pickles, being a common ingredient in Chinese preserved fruits.

Graham is in error in stating that the plant is a native of the S. Konkan. Dalzell and Gibson (Suppl. to Bo. Fl. p. 12) correct a similar error.

10. **LIMONIA,** Linn.

Shrubs or small trees, often spiny. Leaves alternate, 3-foliolate or imparipinnate; petiole winged; leaflets opposite or alternate. Flowers paniculate, racemose or fascicled. Calyx 4–5-lobed or -partite; lobes equal. Petals 4–5, imbricate. Disk annular or stipitiform. Stamens 8–10, free, subequal; filaments subulate; anthers cordate or linear-oblong. Ovary oblong, 4–5-celled; ovules 1–2 in each cell; style short, thick, at length deciduous; stigma obtuse or capitate. Berry globose, 1–4-celled, 1–4-seeded. Seeds imbedded in mucilage; cotyledons fleshy. —DISTRIB. Tropical Asia; species 2–3.

1. **Limonia acidissima,** *Linn. Sp. Pl.* ed. 2 (1762) p. 554. A spinous glabrous shrub or small tree; spines sharp, ½–1 in. long. Leaves pinnate, 1–4 in. long; petiole and rhachis jointed, the former narrowly, the latter very broadly winged; leaflets 2–4 pairs, 1–2 by ½ 1 in., trapezoid-ovate, obtuse, rarely acute, notched at the tip, crenulate, glabrous, base cuneate; joints of rhachis obovate-oblong, crenulate. Flowers in umbelliform, often leafy racemes; peduncles 2–3 together from the axils of fallen leaves; pedicels slender. Calyx small, glandular; lobes 4, broadly-ovate, acute. Petals 4, glandular, ¼ in. long, elliptic-oblong. Stamens 8, free, subequal; filaments linear-subulate. Disk stipitiform. Ovary papillose, 4-celled; style stout. Berry ½ in. in diam., globose, 1–4-seeded, very acid. Fl. B. I. v. 1, p. 507; Grah. Cat. p. 23; Dalz. & Gibs. p. 29; Bedd. For. Man. in Flor. Sylvat. p. xlv; Talb. Trees, Bomb. p. 32; Watt, Dict. Econ. Prod. v. 4, p. 641.—Flowers: Apr.–May.

S. M. COUNTRY: Falls of Gokak, *Dalzell & Gibson, Graham*; hills at Padshapur, *Graham*.

11. LUVUNGA, Ham.

Scandent glabrous shrubs, usually armed with axillary spines. Leaves 3-foliolate; leaflets coriaceous, quite entire. Flowers in axillary, fascicled or panicled racemes. Calyx cupular, entire or obscurely 4–6-lobed. Petals 4–5, free, thick, oblong or lanceolate, imbricate. Stamens 8–10, equal or subequal; filaments linear-subulate, free or connate below; anthers linear or linear-oblong. Disk elevated, annular or cupular. Ovary 2–4-celled; ovules 2 in each cell, superposed; style short, continuous, stout, at length deciduous; stigma capitate. Berry large, ellipsoid, with a thick rind, 1–3-seeded. Seeds large, ovoid; testa membranous, nerved; cotyledons equal, oblong, fleshy.—DISTRIB. Tropical Asia; species about 4.

1. **Luvunga eleutherandra,** *Dalz. in Kew Journ. Bot.* v. 2 (1850) p. 258. Shrubby, scandent, with long, flexuose branches armed with sharp axillary somewhat deflexed or scarcely curved spines ½–¾ in. long. Leaves large, 3-foliolate; petiole 1–3 in. long; leaflets nearly equal, 2–5 by 1–2½ in., coriaceous, elliptic-oblong or obovate, shortly acuminate, entire, glabrous, base usually acute; petiolules short. Flowers in axillary glabrous racemes or panicles shorter than the petioles. Calyx cupular, truncate, entire or obscurely lobed, glandular. Petals ¼ in. long, thick, glandular, elliptic-oblong, subacute. Stamens 8, shorter than the petals; filaments all free, longer than the style. Ovary 3-celled, glandular; style short, stout. Berry ½–1 in. long, ellipsoid, pitted. Fl. B. I. v. 1, p. 509; Dalz. & Gibs. p. 30; Engler, in Engl. & Prantl, Pflanzenf. v. 3, part 4, p. 189, fig. 109, M–R; Trim. Fl. Ceyl. v. 1, p. 224; Talb. Trees, Bomb. p. 32; Woodr. in Journ. Bomb. Nat. v. 11 (1897) p. 267.—Flowers: Jan.

KONKAN: *Stocks*!, *Dalzell*!; the Ghâts, common, *Dalzell & Gibson*. KANARA: in moist, evergreen forests, *Talbot*; Mundele, *Ritchie*, 1647!; Divimana Ghât, *Woodrow*! —DISTRIB. Java, Ceylon.

12. PARAMIGNYA, Wight.

Erect or climbing shrubs, unarmed or with axillary spines. Leaves 1-foliolate (the articulation often obscure), subcoriaceous, persistent. Flowers rather large, axillary, solitary or fascicled. Calyx cupular or small and 4-5-lobed. Petals 4–5, free, imbricate or very rarely induplicato-valvate. Stamens 8–10, free, equal or subequal; filaments linear; anthers linear-oblong. Disk thick, columnar. Ovary 3–5-celled; ovules 1 or 2, obliquely superposed in each cell; style elongate, continuous with the ovary, finally deciduous; stigma capitate. Berry ovoid or subglobose, often contracted at the base, 1–5-seeded; rind thick. Seeds large, oblong, compressed; testa membranous; cotyledons fleshy, equal.—DISTRIB. Tropical India; species 4.

1. **Paramignya monophylla,** *Wight, Ill.* v. 1 (1840) p. 109. A climbing evergreen shrub, the older branches armed with sharp recurved axillary spines $\frac{1}{2}$–$\frac{3}{4}$ in. long. Leaves numerous, 1-foliolate, gland-dotted; petioles $\frac{1}{4}$–$\frac{1}{2}$ in. long, usually twisted; leaflets 2–4 by 1–2$\frac{1}{2}$ in., ovate-oblong, acute, obtuse or acuminate, entire or nearly so, glabrous, base rounded often oblique. Flowers white; pedicels axillary, 1–3 together, pubescent. Calyx softly woolly; lobes 5, shallow, rounded. Petals 5, linear-oblong, $\frac{3}{4}$ in. long, recurved. Filaments flat, linear, hairy, suddenly tapering beneath the anthers. Ovary hairy, 3–5-celled; style long, stout, the lower part hairy. Berry obovoid or ellipsoid, 1 in. long, smooth. Seeds numerous, large, compressed. Fl. B. I. v. 1, p. 510; Grah. Cat. p. 25; Dalz. & Gibs. p. 30; Engler, in Engl. & Prantl, Pflanzenf. v. 3, part 4, p. 191, fig. 111, A–B; Trim. Fl. Ceyl. v. 1, p. 224; Talb. Trees, Bomb. p. 33; Woodr. in Journ. Bomb. Nat. v. 11 (1897) p. 267; Watt, Dict. Econ. Prod. v. 6, part 1, p. 110.—Flowers: Nov.–Jan.

KONKAN: *Law*!; Ghâts, *Stocks*!; Amboli Ghât, *Kanitkar*!; 23 miles west of Ratnagiri, *Woodrow*!; jungles at Virdi and throughout the S. Konkan as far as the Savitri river, *Dalzell & Gibson*. DECCAN: Phunda Ghât, *Ritchie*, 903!; Parghât, *Dalzell & Gibson*. S. M. COUNTRY: Ramghât, *Ritchie*, 993! KANARA: evergreen forests of N. Kanara, *Talbot*; Chandawar (N. Kanara), *Woodrow*!—DISTRIB. Ceylon.

13. ATALANTIA, Corr.

Shrubs or small trees, spinous or unarmed. Leaves alternate, 1-foliolate, coriaceous, persistent; stipule-like scales which belong to undeveloped leaf-buds are often present at the base of the petioles and spines. Flowers in axillary (rarely terminal) fascicles, racemes or panicles, rarely solitary. Calyx 3–5-lobed, or -partite, sometimes irregularly split. Petals 3–5, free or adnate to the stamens and united with them into a tube, imbricate. Stamens 6–8 (rarely 15–20), free or irregularly connate into a tube, subequal or the alternate shorter; anthers ovate-oblong or with a cordate base (linear-oblong in *A. missionis*). Ovary 2–4- (rarely 3–5-) celled; ovules 1 or 2, collateral; style at length deciduous; stigma capitate. Berry large, subglobose, 1–5-celled, 1–5-seeded. Seeds oblong; cotyledons fleshy, plano-convex.—DISTRIB. Tropical Asia and China, 1 in Australia; species 10.

Stamens usually combined into a tube.
  Calyx irregularly split to the base; cymes contracted .... 1. *A. monophylla.*
  Calyx regularly or subregularly lobed; cymes long, racemose. 2. *A. racemosa.*
Stamens not combined into a tube.
  Ovary sunk in the annular disk; anthers cordate .... 3. *A. ceylanica.*
  Ovary stipitate; anthers linear-oblong .... 4. *A. missionis.*

1. **Atalantia monophylla,** *DC. Prod.* v. 1 (1824) p. 535. A shrub or small tree with numerous rigid branches, the older ones armed with short sharp axillary spines. Leaves 1-foliolate; petioles $\frac{1}{4}$ in. long, with 1 or 2 stipulary scales at the base; leaflet coriaceous, 1–3 by $\frac{1}{2}$–$1\frac{1}{2}$ in., ovate-oblong or elliptic, obtuse, emarginate, bright green, entire, glabrous, reticulately veined. Flowers crowded in axillary fascicles or in racemose much-contracted cymes; buds oblong or slightly clavate; pedicels $\frac{1}{4}$–$\frac{1}{2}$ in. long; bracts minute. Calyx, at the time of flowering or after it, irregularly split at the base. Petals white, $\frac{3}{8}$ in. long, cuneate-obovate, rounded or subacute, clawed, adnate to the staminal-tube. Stamens 8; filaments united into a tube almost throughout their entire length; anthers small, elliptic, inserted on the triangular teeth of the staminal-tube. Disk inconspicuous. Ovary conical, gradually sloping into the style, 3–5-celled; style long, cylindric, equalling the staminal-tube. Berry globular, very like a lime, about as large as a nutmeg, usually 4-celled; cells 1-seeded. Fl. B. I. v. 1, p. 511; Grah. Cat. p. 23; Dalz. & Gibs. p. 28; Bedd. For. Man. in Flor. Sylvat. p. xlvi, et Anal. Gen. t. 7, fig. 5; Engler, in Engl. & Prantl, Pflanzenf. v. 3, part 4, p. 191, fig. 111, C–D; Trim. Fl. Ceyl. v. 1, p. 226; Talb. Trees, Bomb. p. 33; Watt, Dict. Econ. Prod. v. 1, p. 349. *Atalantia floribunda*, Wight, Icon. t. 1611.

KONKAN: on the Ghâts, ex *Dalzell & Gibson*, and ex *Graham*. KANARA: moist forests of N. Kanara, ex *Talbot*. S. M. COUNTRY: Belgaum Ghâts, ex *Talbot*.—DISTRIB. Ceylon.

2. **Atalantia racemosa,** *Wight & Arn. Prodr.* (1834) p. 91. A shrub or small tree; spines strong and sharp, sometimes absent. Leaves 1-foliolate; leaflet 2–4 by 1–$1\frac{1}{2}$ in., elliptic, rounded at the apex, emarginate, entire or crenulate, glabrous, reticulately veined, base acute; petioles $\frac{1}{4}$ in. long. Flowers in axillary racemose cymes; pedicels short; bracts minute, subulate. Calyx usually 4- sometimes 3–5-lobed; lobes rounded or subacute, ciliolate. Petals white, $\frac{3}{8}$ in. long, broadly elliptic or obovate, very concave in bud, not adnate to the staminal-tube, glandular. Stamens 8; filaments usually united into a tube throughout nearly their entire length, sometimes united at the base only when they are linear and flattened; anthers large, cordate, attached at the back near the base on the triangular teeth of the staminal-tube or the triangular apex of the filaments. Disk cupular. Ovary ovoid, oblong, or obovoid; style short, stout, somewhat clavate. Berry globular, $\frac{3}{4}$ in. in diam. Fl. B. I. v. 1, p. 512; Bedd. For. Man. in Flor. Sylvat. p. xlvi; Trim. Fl. Ceyl. v. 1, p. 226; Talb. Trees, Bomb. p. 33. *Atalantia monophylla*, Woodr. in Journ. Bomb. Nat. v. 11 (1897) p. 267. *Sclerostylis atalantioides*, W. & A. in Wight, Icon. t. 71 (in textu *S. parviflora*); Dalz. & Gibs. p. 29.—Flowers: Nov.–Dec. VERN. *Makad-limbu*; *Rán-limbu*.

KONKAN: *Law*!, *Stocks*!, *Dalzell*!, *Capt. Geburne*!; Amboli Ghát, *Woodrow*. DECCAN: Khandala, *Cooke*!; Raighar, *Dalzell*!; Pár, *Dalzell*.—DISTRIB. Ceylon.

Much more common than the preceding species, which is rare. *Atalantia racemosa* has been frequently mistaken for *A. monophylla* and ticketed as such by collectors. In a recent communication from Mr. Gammie of the College of Science at Poona, that gentleman informed me that there was not, when he wrote, a single specimen of *A. monophylla* in the College Herbarium, all the specimens there preserved being specimens of *A. racemosa*, though some had been erroneously labelled as *A. monophylla*. *A. racemosa* is tolerably abundant at Mahableshwar and Matheran, but I have seen no specimen of *A. monophylla* from either locality.

3. **Atalantia ceylanica,** *Oliver, in Journ. Linn. Soc.* v. 5 (1861), *Suppl.* 2, p. 25. A much-branched shrub, usually armed with sharp stout spines ¼–1 in. long; bark smooth; young parts glabrous. Leaves 1-foliolate; petioles ¼ in. long; leaflets very variable, coriaceous, 1–4 in. long, ovate-oblong, elliptic-oblong or ovate-lanceolate, rounded at the apex or with an emarginate or 2-lobed tip (rarely obtusely acuminate), entire, glabrous. Flowers crowded in short finely pubescent corymbose or racemose cymes much shorter than the leaves; bracts minute; pedicels short. Calyx 4-lobed; lobes shallow, rounded, ciliate, sometimes obscure. Petals 4 (rarely 3 or 5), ⅓ in. long, elliptic-oblong, obtuse, slightly concave, glandular. Stamens 8, the alternate ones longer; filaments flat, free, or 2 to 3 of them more or less combined; anthers cordate. Disk annular, subcupular. Ovary sunk in the disk, 2-celled; ovules 2 in each cell, collateral; style short, stout; stigma clavate. Berry ½–¾ in. in diam., globose or ovoid, 2-4-seeded. Fl. B. I. v. 1, p. 512; Trim. Fl. Ceyl. v. 1, p. 227; Talb. Trees, Bomb. p. 33.

DECCAN: Phunda Ghát, *Ritchie*!

This species has been included on the authority of a single imperfect specimen in Herb. Kew. marked "Phoondah Ghát, *Ritchie*"; it does not seem to have been found by any other collector.—DISTRIB. Ceylon.

4. **Atalantia missionis,** *Oliver, in Journ. Linn. Soc.* v. 5 (1861), *Suppl.* 2, p. 25. A small much-branched tree, armed with long sharp spines which are solitary or in pairs; branchlets smooth, often angled. Leaves 1-foliolate; petioles ¼–½ in. long; leaflets thick and coriaceous, 2–3 by 1–1½ in., broadly oblong-obovate or elliptic, obtuse or rounded, entire or crenulate, undulate, glabrous, glaucous when dry, base acute; nerves and veins obscure. Flowers small, white, in glabrous racemes 1–2½ in. long. Calyx usually 4- (rarely 5-) lobed; lobes ovate-triangular. Petals 5, lanceolate-oblong. Stamens 8, equal; filaments free, broader and flattened near the base; anthers narrow-linear. Ovary seated on a gynophore, 4–5-celled; ovules 2 in each cell; style stout, thickened upwards. Berry 1 in. in diam., globose, with a thick rind, 4-5-celled; cells 1–2-seeded. Seeds globose, embedded in glutinous mucilage. Fl. B. I. v. 1, p. 513; Bedd. For. Man. in Fl. Sylvat. p. xlvi; Talb. Trees, Bomb. p. 33; Watt, Dict. Econ. Prod. v. 1, p. 349.

KANARA: N. Kanara in evergreen forests, near Karwar, ex *Talbot*.

14. CITRUS, Linn.

Trees or shrubs, usually spinous. Leaves 1-foliolate; petiole often winged; leaflets entire or crenulate, coriaceous, persistent. Flowers white or pinkish, sweet-scented, solitary, fascicled or in small cymes. Calyx cupular or urceolate, 3-5-fid. Petals 4–8, linear-oblong, thick, imbricate. Stamens 20–60; filaments variously connate, compressed at the base; anthers oblong. Disk large, cupular or annular. Ovary many-celled; ovules 4–8 in each cell, 2-seriate; style deciduous; stigma capitate. Berry globose or oblong, fleshy, many-celled; septa membranous; cells few-seeded, filled with horizontal or fusiform cellules replete with juice. Seeds horizontal or pendulous; testa coriaceous or membranous; embryos sometimes 2 or more in one seed; cotyledons plano-convex, often unequal; radicle small, superior.—DISTRIB. Tropical Asia, 5 species; Australia, 2 species.

Young shoots and leaves glabrous; transverse vesicles of pulp concrete.
Young shoots purple; petals tinged with red; flowers often unisexual; fruit often mammillate at the apex... 1. *C. medica.*
Young shoots greenish-white; petals white; flowers bisexual; fruit not mammillate .... 2. *C. Aurantium.*
Young shoots and underside of leaves pubescent; transverse vesicles of pulp distinct .... 3. *C. decumana.*

1. **Citrus medica,** *Linn. Sp. Pl.* (1753) p. 782. A shrub or small tree flowering and fruiting almost the whole year; young shoots glabrous, purple. Leaves 1-foliolate; petioles naked or winged; leaflets 3–6 in. long, elliptic-ovate or ovate-lanceolate, usually obtuse, crenate-serrate, base acute. Flowers white, usually tinged with red, small or medium sized, often unisexual, 5–10 in a raceme. Stamens 20–40. Fruit globose or oblong, often mammillate at the apex, usually yellow when ripe; rind thick or thin. Fl. B. I. v. 1, p. 514; Brandis, For. Fl. p. 51; Talb. Trees, Bomb. p. 33; Woodr. in Journ. Bomb. Nat. v. 11 (1897) p. 267; Watt, Dict. Econ. Prod. v. 2, p. 349.

Cultivated throughout the Presidency; said to be wild on the Western Ghâts. *Graham* (Cat. Bo. Pl. p. 25) mentions the occurrence of a plant called by the natives *Malunga*, apparently wild near Pár and on the level part of the Rotunda Ghát (below Mahableshwar), which, however, *Dalzell & Gibson* (Bo. Fl. Suppl. p. 13) failed to find. *Mr. Nairne* (Flowering Plants of W. India, p. 48) mentions that he had himself found the plant on the Parpoli Ghát (Wari Country).

The varieties of *Citrus medica* cultivated in the Bombay Presidency are the following:—

VAR. 1. *Citrus medica* proper. The Citron. Fruit large, oblong, obovoid or somewhat irregularly shaped; mammilla obtuse; rind thick, very aromatic; pulp scanty, subacid. Fl. B. I. v. 1, p. 514; Brandis, For. Fl. p. 52. *Citrus medica*, Linn.; Dalz. & Gibs. Suppl. p. 13.—VERN. *Mahálungi.*

VAR. 2. *Limonum.* The Lemon. Petiole margined or winged. Fruit ovoid, yellow, mammillate; rind thin; pulp abundant, very acid. Fl. B. I. v. 1, p. 515; Brandis, For. Fl. p. 52. *Citrus Limonum*, Risso, in Ann. Mus. Par. v. 20, p. 201; Grah. Cat. p. 25; Dalz. & Gibs. Suppl. p. 13.

VAR. 3. *acida.* The Sour Limo of India. Leaflets elliptic-oblong. Racemes short; flowers small; petals usually 4. Fruit usually small, globose or ovoid; rind thick or thin; pulp pale, very acid. Fl. B. I. v. 1, p. 515; Brandis, For. Fl. p. 52. ? *Citrus Bergamia*, Dalz. & Gibs. Suppl. p. 13.—VERN. *Limbu.* Very widely cultivated.

VAR. 4. *Limetta.* The Sweet Lime of India. Fruit globose, 3–5 in. in diam.; rind thin, smooth, adhering to the pulp; juice abundant, sweet, not aromatic. Fl. B. I. v. 1, p. 515; Brandis, For. Fl. p. 52. *Citrus Limetta*, Risso; Dalz. & Gibs. Suppl. p. 13.—VERN. *Mitha limbu.* Widely cultivated.

2. **Citrus Aurantium,** *Linn. Sp. Pl.* (1753) p. 782. A tree, rarely a shrub; young shoots glabrous, greenish-white. Leaves 1-foliolate; leaflets 3–6 in. long, elliptic or ovate, obtuse, acute or acuminate; petioles naked or winged, the wing often obovate and nearly as large as the blade. Flowers bisexual, pure white. Stamens 20–30. Fruit globose, generally oblate, not mammillate, usually orange-colored; rind loose or adherent; pulp sweet, yellow, rarely red. Fl. B. I. v. 1, p. 515; Grah. Cat. p. 25; Dalz. & Gibs. Suppl. p. 12; Talb. Trees, Bomb. p. 34; Woodr. in Journ. Bomb. Nat. v. 11 (1897) p. 268; Watt, Dict. Econ. Prod. v. 2, p. 335.—VERN. *Náringi.*

The sweet and bitter orange; widely cultivated. Of the former (*C. aurantium* proper, Fl. B. I. l. c.) many kinds are cultivated in India, one of the best of which is probably that known as the "Cintra" Orange, the name of which was supposed to denote its Portuguese origin. Dr. Bonavia is of opinion that the term is a corruption of a Sanskrit name *Santara*, and has nothing to do with the Portuguese town Cintra.

This orange is cultivated in many places in the Bombay Presidency (*e. g.* about Poona), but Nagpur in the Central Provinces is the great source of supply for the Bombay market. The tree is capable of producing 2 crops of fruit annually, but as such excessive production would naturally result in deterioration, the Nagpur orange-growers, by allowing one plantation to rest while the other is bearing, obtain a yield of fruit at two different seasons, from two distinct plots.

The fruit of the Cintra Orange weighs from 7 to 10 ounces, has a smooth loose skin in one variety, tight in another, with pulp of a deep orange color and excellent flavor.

The *Ládu* Orange of the Deccan comes next to the "Cintra" among the cultivated oranges of the Presidency. The fruit weighs 7 to 8 ounces, but the color of its skin is not attractive. Woodrow (Gardening in India) mentions a remarkable malformation which occurs in many of the fruits, viz., that at the stigmatic end, enclosed within the skin, a small completely formed orange, as large as a marble, with 5 or 7 carpels, may often be found. The tree grows to a large size. Woodrow mentions one in Sir A. Sassoon's garden (Garden Reach, Poona) which, planted 20 years previously, had covered an area of 400 square feet.

The *Mandarin* Orange (*Lál Ládu* of the Deccan) produces a handsome fruit, which is in season from November to January. The appearance of the fruit is attractive, but in flavor the pulp is inferior to that of the *Ládu*.

A variety of the *Mozambique* Orange, named *Khâguzi*, is also grown in the Deccan. The fruit attains a large size, sometimes weighing as much as 13 ounces. The skin is tight and the endocarp so strong that the uit can only be sucked (*Woodrow*).

An orange, called in the vernacular *Resemi-náringi*, is cultivated about Poona. It produces a small fruit weighing about 3 ounces, with very little juice and a great number of seeds (about 20). It is a very poor orange and hardly worth cultivating.

The *Bitter* or *Seville* Orange (var. 2, *Bigaradia*, Fl. B. I. l. c.) does not appear to be largely cultivated in India.—It is grown sparingly on the hills about Panchgani and used for making marmalade.

A full description of the several species and varieties of *Citrus* grown in India may be found in Watt's Dictionary of Economic Products of India, vol. 2, pp. 333–358. Woodrow (Gardening in India, p. 202 *et seq.*) gives a concise account of the mode of growing, budding and pruning the orange.

3. **Citrus decumana,** *Murr. Syst.* ed. 13 (1774) p. 580. A tree 30–40 ft. high; young shoots pubescent. Leaflets large, 6–9 in. long, ovate-oblong, frequently emarginate, pubescent beneath; petioles broadly winged. Flowers large, white. Stamens 16–24. Fruit large, pale yellow, globose or pyriform; rind thick; pulp varying in color from crimson to pale pink or yellow; vesicles distinct. Fl. B. I. v. 1, p. 516; Grah. Cat. p. 25; Dalz. & Gibs. Suppl. p. 12; Brandis, For. Fl. p. 55; Talb. Trees, Bomb. p. 34; Woodr. in Journ. Bomb. Nat. v. 11 (1897) p. 268; Watt, Dict. Econ. Prod. v. 2, p. 348.—Vern. *Papanas*.

The *Pummelo*, or *Shaddock* of the W. Indies, a native of the Malayan and Polynesian Islands, largely cultivated in the Presidency and arriving at great perfection along the coast of Kanara and the Konkan.

Dr. Bonavia (Cultivated Oranges and Lemons of India and Ceylon, p. 167) says "The best pummelos I have ever seen are the thin-skinned red pummelos of Bombay. All the other varieties of pummelo I have seen in India and Ceylon are not to be compared with this and hardly worth propagating to any extent."

15. FERONIA, Corr.

A spinous tree. Leaves alternate, imparipinnate; petioles simple or winged; leaflets opposite, subsessile. Flowers white, in lax racemes or panicles, polygamous. Calyx small, flat, 5-toothed, deciduous. Petals 5 (rarely 4–6), spreading, imbricate. Stamens 10-12 (some of them often imperfect); filaments dilated, villous in front and on the margins, subulate at the apex; anthers linear-oblong. Disk short. Ovary oblong, 5–6- at length 1-celled; ovules many, crowded, in many series, on 5–6 at length parietal placentas; style 0; stigma oblong, fusiform, deciduous. Berry globose, 1-celled, many-seeded, filled with pulp; rind woody. Seeds oblong, compressed; cotyledons thick, fleshy.—Distrib. Tropical India and Java; species 1.

1. **Feronia Elephantum,** *Corr. in Trans. Linn. Soc.* v. 5 (1800) p. 225. A moderate-sized tree with straight sharp strong spines ½–1½ in. long. Leaves smelling of aniseed, alternate, imparipinnate; petiole and rhachis flat, often narrowly winged; leaflets 3–9, opposite, 1–2 by ½–1 in., cuneate or obovate, tip often crenulate. Flowers small, numerous, dull red, in lateral or terminal pubescent panicles, male and female flowers often in the same panicle. Calyx small, 5–6-lobed; lobes triangular. Petals 5–6, free, elliptic-oblong, ⅕ in. long, spreading or deflexed. Stamens 10–12, 1-seriate; filaments equal, subulate, densely hairy at the base within; anthers large, linear-oblong. Ovary glabrous, sessile. Fruit 2–2½ in. in diam., globose, hard; pericarp woody, rough, grey-colored. Seeds embedded in an edible pulp. Fl. B.

I. v. 1, p. 516; Grah. Cat. p. 24; Dalz. & Gibs. p. 30; Bedd. Flor. Sylvat. t. 121; Trim. Fl. Ceyl. v. 1, p. 228; Engler, in Eng. & Prantl, Pflanzenf. v. 3, part 4, p. 193, fig. 112; Talb. Trees, Bomb. p. 34; Woodr. in Journ. Bomb. Nat. v. 11 (1897) p. 268; Watt, Dict. Econ. Prod. v. 3, p. 324.—Flowers: Mar. VERN. *Kavath.*

The Elephant- or Wood-apple; often cultivated. KONKAN: *Stocks*!, *Capt. Geburne*!; in gardens, Bombay, *Graham*. DECCAN: cultivated, *Jacquemont*, 984!; Ahmednagar, *Graham*; gardens, Poona, *Cooke*! KANARA: Halyal, *Ritchie*, 1643! GUJARAT: *Dalzell & Gibson*; valley of the Tapti, common, *Graham*.—DISTRIB. Java, Ceylon.

16. ÆGLE, Corr.

Spinous trees. Leaves 3- (rarely 5-) foliolate; leaflets membranous, subcrenulate, pellucido-punctate. Flowers hermaphrodite, rather large, white, in axillary panicles. Calyx small, 4-5-lobed, deciduous. Petals 4-5, oblong, spreading, imbricate. Stamens numerous; filaments short, subulate; anthers elongate, erect. Disk inconspicuous. Ovary ovoid, attenuated into the style; cells 8-20 peripheral; ovules numerous, 2-seriate; style short; stigma capitate or fusiform, deciduous. Berry globose or ovoid, 8-15-celled; cells many-seeded; rind woody. Seeds numerous, oblong, compressed, in an aromatic pulp; testa woolly and mucous.—DISTRIB. Java and tropical Africa; species 2-3.

1. **Ægle Marmelos,** *Corr. in Trans. Linn. Soc.* v. 5 (1800) p. 223. A small tree, armed with strong straight sharp spines ½-1 in. long. Leaves 3- (rarely 5-) foliolate; petioles puberulous, 1-1½ in. long; leaflets lanceolate or elliptic-lanceolate, 1½-3 by ¾-1½ in., glabrous, the lateral leaflets subsessile, the terminal leaflet long-petioluled. Flowers bisexual, greenish-white, scented; buds globose; pedicels pubescent. Calyx flat, pubescent, 4-lobed; lobes rounded, sometimes obscure, ciliolate. Petals 4, much imbricate, ½ in. long, free, oblong, coriaceous. Stamens numerous, sometimes 50 or more; filaments subulate, glabrous, free or sometimes 2 or 3 of them more or less united or subfascicled; anthers linear-oblong, apiculate. Ovary 11-celled, glabrous, ovoid-oblong, faintly ribbed, seated on an elevated disk; cells many-ovuled; ovules biseriate. Fruit 2-5 in. in diam., globose; rind grey or yellowish; pulp sweet, thick, orange-colored. Fl. B. I. v. 1, p. 516; Grah. Cat. p. 24; Dalz. & Gibs. p. 31; Engler, in Engl. & Prantl, Pflanzenf. v. 3, part 4, p. 194, fig. 113; Talb. Trees, Bomb. p. 34; Woodr. in Journ. Bomb. Nat. v. 11 (1897) p. 268; Watt, Dict. Econ. Prod. v. 1, p. 117.—Flowers: Apr.-May. VERN. *Bel.*

Cultivated in many places and found wild occasionally in the Deccan. KONKAN: *Stocks*!, *Law*!; Bombay, *Capt. Gelnurne*! Elephanta, *Graham*. DECCAN: wild in many parts, ex *Dalzell & Gibson*; widely planted, *Woodrow*; about temples in the Deccan, *Graham*. S. M. COUNTRY: Gatpraba river N. of Belgaum, *Ritchie*, 994!

The *Bael* tree, known commonly as the *Bengal Quince*. Many parts of the tree possess highly valuable medicinal properties, and the dried unripe fruit has been long used as a remedy for diarrhœa and dysentery. See Watt, Dict. Econ. Prod. l. c.

ORDER XXXIII. SIMARUBACEÆ.

Trees or shrubs, usually with bitter bark. Leaves usually alternate, pinnate, rarely simple; stipules 0, or deciduous. Inflorescence mostly axillary, paniculate or racemose, rarely spicate; flowers regular, usually small, diclinous or polygamous, rarely hermaphrodite. Calyx 3–5-lobed or -partite. Petals 3–5, very rarely 0, imbricate or valvate. Disk annular, cupular, or elongated into a gynophore, rarely 0. Stamens inserted at the base of the disk, equal in number to the petals or twice as many; filaments free, naked, often with a scale at the base; anthers oblong, usually introrse, 2-celled, dehiscing longitudinally. Ovary often deeply 2–5-lobed, 1–6-celled; ovules usually solitary (rarely many) in each cell; raphe ventral; micropyle superior; styles 2–5, free at the base and apex or at the base only, or connate by the usually capitellate stigmas. Fruit drupaceous or capsular or sometimes samaroid. Seeds usually solitary, pendulous; testa membranous; albumen copious, fleshy, scanty or 0; embryo straight or curved; cotyledons usually plano-convex or flat, rarely contorted or rugose; radicle superior.—DISTRIB. Tropical and warm regions; species about 120.

Ovary deeply divided.
  Leaves pinnate; fruit samaroid .... 1. AILANTHUS.
  Leaves simple; fruit drupaceous, winged .... 2. SAMADERA.
Ovary entire; leaves 2-foliolate .... 3. BALANITES.

1. AILANTHUS, Desf.

Lofty trees. Leaves alternate, pinnate; leaflets alternate or sub-opposite. Flowers in terminal or axillary branched panicles, small; pedicels bracteate. Calyx short, 5-fid; lobes equal, imbricate. Petals 5, spreading, induplicato-valvate. Disk 10-lobed. Stamens 10 in the male, 2–3 in the hermaphrodite and 0 in the female flowers, inserted at the base of the disk; filaments very short or filiform, without scales. Ovary 2–5-partite (rudimentary in the male flowers); ovule 1 in each cell, semianatropous; styles connate. Samaras 1–5, large, membranous, linear-oblong, veined, 1-seeded in the middle. Seed compressed; testa membranous; albumen scanty, adhering to the testa; cotyledons flat, foliaceous, suborbicular.—DISTRIB. India, Australia, China; species 3–4.

Leaflets coarsely toothed; filaments shorter than the anthers . 1. *A. excelsa.*
Leaflets entire; filaments longer than the anthers .... 2. *A. malabarica.*

1. **Ailanthus excelsa,** *Roxb. Cor. Pl.* v. 1 (1795) p. 24, t. 23. A tree 60–80 ft. high. Leaves unequally or equally pinnate, usually 8–12 in. but sometimes reaching 2–3 ft. long, the younger tomentose, the older more or less so or glabrous; leaflets 8–14 pairs, alternate or subopposite, very variable in shape, 4–6 in. long, coarsely and irregularly toothed or sublobate, very unequal at the base; petiolules $\frac{3}{4}$–2 in. long. Flowers in large lax often much-branched panicles; pedicels long, slender. Calyx-lobes ovate triangular. Petals $\frac{1}{8}$ in. long, ovate-lanceolate, glabrous, reflexed. Filaments glabrous, about half as long as the anthers. Samara $1\frac{1}{2}$–$2\frac{1}{4}$ in. long by $\frac{3}{8}$–$\frac{1}{2}$ in. broad, lanceolate, acute at both ends, reddish-brown, twisted near the base, many-nerved, the nerves reticulate above the seed, otherwise nearly parallel. Seed solitary in the centre of the samara. Fl. B. I. v. 1, p. 518; Grah. Cat.

p. 37; Dalz. & Gibs. p. 46; Pierre, Flor. For. Cochinch. t. 295, A; Talb. Trees, Bomb. p. 35; Woodr. in Journ. Bomb. Nat. v. 11 (1897) p. 268; Watt, Dict. Econ. Prod. v. 1, p. 148.—Flowers: Jan.-Mar. VERN. *Mahdruk.*

KONKAN: *Dalzell*!, *Stocks*! DECCAN: *Gibson, Woodrow.* GUJARAT: English burial-ground, Surat, *Geburne*; common about Broach and Baroda, *Dr. Lush.*—DISTRIB. India (N.W. Prov., W. Peninsula, Behar); Queensland (var. *imberbiflora*).

2. **Ailanthus malabarica,** *DC. Prod.* v. 2 (1825) p. 89. A large tree. Leaves very large, 1½–2 ft. long, crowded, spreading, glabrous; leaflets 8–10 pairs, 3–6 by 1¼–2¼ in., alternate or subopposite, ovate-oblong or oblong-lanceolate, tapering, acute or acuminate, entire, glabrous, glaucous beneath, unequal-sided at the base, the upper side the larger and rounded, the lower smaller and acute; petiolules $\frac{3}{16}$–$\frac{3}{4}$ in. long. Flowers white (the bisexual rather larger than the male), in lax axillary panicles; pedicels short. Calyx-lobes triangular, acute. Petals about ⅛ in. long, oblong-lanceolate. Stamens longer than the petals; filaments filiform, much longer than the anthers. Samara 2–2½ by ⅝–¾ in., linear-oblong, rounded at both ends, reddish-brown, not or very rarely twisted. Fl. B. I. v. 1, p. 518; Grah. Cat. p. 37; Dalz. & Gibs. p. 46; Trim. Fl. Ceyl. v. 1, p. 230; Talb. Trees, Bomb. p. 35; Woodr. in Journ. Bomb. Nat. v. 11 (1897) p. 268.—Flowers: Feb.-Mar.

KONKAN: *Stocks*!, *Law*!, *Gibson, Dalzell*!; Nagotna, *Dalzell & Gibson, Woodrow.* DECCAN: Pant Sachiv's country at Udhár, Ranishwár, *Dalzell & Gibson.* KANARA: N. Kanara, in evergreen forests, *Talbot*; Kumpta-Sirsi Road, *Woodrow.*—DISTRIB. India (W. Peninsula); Ceylon, Cochinchina.

2. SAMADERA, Gærtn.

Small glabrous trees. Leaves alternate, simple, short-petioled, oblong, coriaceous, shining. Flowers hermaphrodite, few, in axillary and terminal umbels. Calyx small, 3–5-partite, glandular at the base outside, imbricate. Petals 3–5, coriaceous, much longer than the calyx, imbricate. Disk large. Stamens 6–10, with small basilar scales, included. Carpels 4–5, distinct, free; ovule solitary, pendulous; styles free at the base, more or less united above; stigmas acute. Drupes 1–5, large, dry, compressed, rigid, winged. Seed solitary; testa membranous; cotyledons plano-convex, fleshy; radicle very short.—DISTRIB. Tropical Asia and Madagascar; species 3.

1. **Samadera indica,** *Gærtn. Fruct.* v. 2 (1791) p. 352, t. 156. A small tree 30–35 ft. high, with stout branches. Leaves large, sometimes reaching 10 by 3½ in., elliptic-oblong, usually shortly acuminate, entire, reticulately veined, glabrous, shining, base rounded rarely subacute: petioles ½–¾ in. long, stout. Flowers in few- or many-flowered umbels; peduncles axillary, glabrous, often longer than the leaves; pedicels ⅝–¾ in. long, glabrous, red. Calyx small, glabrous, persistent; lobes broad, thick, ciliate. Petals ¾–1 in. long, oblong, obtuse. Stamens twice as many as the petals and slightly shorter than them; filaments long, with a hairy scale at the base. Ovary shortly stalked, glabrous, usually 4-celled; style glabrous, a little longer than the stamens. Ripe carpels 2–2½ in. long, nearly semicircular, much compressed, smooth, reticulate. Seed large. Fl. B. I. v. 1, p. 519; Grah.

Cat. p. 37; Engler, in Engl. & Prantl, Pflanzenf. v. 3, part 4, p. 211, fig. 120; Trim. Fl. Ceyl. v. 1, p. 231; Talb. Trees, Bomb. p. 35; Watt, Dict. Econ. Prod. v. 6, part 2, p. 451.

KONKAN: throughout the S. Konkan jungle, *Nimmo ex Graham*; jungles near Goa, *Dr. Lush*; along river-banks, *Talbot*.—DISTRIB. India (W. Peninsula); Ceylon.

The tree furnishes the *Niepa* bark of commerce.—See Watt, Dict. Econ. Prod. l. c.

3. BALANITES, Delile.

Spiny shrubs or trees. Leaves alternate, 2-foliolate; leaflets coriaceous, entire. Flowers greenish, in axillary cymes, fragrant. Sepals 5, concave, imbricate. Petals 5, oblong, spreading, glabrous or villous, imbricate. Stamens 10, inserted in the furrows at the base of the disk; filaments naked, filiform, subulate; anthers inserted at the back. Disk thick, depressed-conic or pulvinate, 10-grooved, hollowed at the apex. Ovary globose, half-immersed in the disk, villous, 5-celled; ovule solitary in each cell, linear, pendulous below the apex of the cell; style short, subulate, terete or 5-furrowed; stigmas 1 or 5, simple, minute. Drupe fleshy, oily; putamen bony, 5-angled, 1-celled, 1-seeded. Seed pendulous, ovoid; testa subfibrous; albumen 0, embryo green, ovoid; cotyledons thick, oblong, plano-convex, sometimes corrugated or 2-lobed; radicle superior.—DISTRIB. Northern and Tropical Africa, Tropical and Western Asia; species 2.

1. **Balanites Roxburghii**, *Planch. in Ann. Sc. Nat.* ser. 4, v. 2 (1854) p. 258. A small tree rarely reaching 30 ft. high; young parts pubescent or tomentose; branches yellowish-green, glabrous or puberulous; spines 1–1¼ in. long, axillary, straight, strong, very sharp. Leaves 2-foliolate; petioles ⅛–¼ in. long; leaflets elliptic or obovate, obtuse or subacute, sometimes slightly mucronate, base usually acute; petiolules very short. Flowers small, greenish-white, fragrant, in axillary few- or many-flowered short-peduncled cymes or fascicles. Sepals ovate, ⅛ in. long, pubescent outside, silky within. Petals oblong-obovate, glabrous outside, silky villous within, very little longer than the sepals. Filaments subulate, glabrous; anthers attached at the back. Disk cupular, with a 10-lobed glandular margin. Ovary silky-villous; style short, conical. Drupes large, ovoid, woody, angular, 1–2 in. long, 5-grooved. Fl. B. I. v. 1, p. 522; Talb. Trees, Bomb. p. 35; Woodr. in Journ. Bomb. Nat. v. 11 (1897) p. 268; Watt, Dict. Econ. Prod. v. 1, p. 363.—Flowers: Mar.–May. VERN. *Hingu*; *Hinganbet*.

Engler & Prantl (Pflanzenf. v. 3, part 4, p. 355, fig. 189) unite this with *B. ægyptiaca*, Delile, a species growing in N. and Tropical Africa which is distinguished from *B. Roxburghii* by its glabrous petals.

KONKAN: Bombay, *Capt. Geburne*! DECCAN: widely, *Woodrow*; Ahmednagar, *Cooke*!, *Woodrow*! S. M. COUNTRY: Dharwar, *Cooke*!, *Woodrow*! GUJARAT: Ahmedabad, *Cooke*!—DISTRIB. Drier parts of India.

ORDER XXXIV. OCHNACEÆ.

Trees or shrubs with watery juice. Leaves alternate, glabrous, simple (very rarely pinnate), coriaceous, stipulate. Flowers hermaphrodite, usually paniculate, rarely solitary. Sepals 4–5, free, imbricate. Petals 4–12 (usually 5), free, deciduous, spreading, imbricate. Disk enlarged after flowering, sometimes 0. Stamens inserted at the base of or on the disk, 4, 5, 8, 10 or indefinite; filaments usually short, persistent; anthers linear, dehiscing longitudinally or by terminal pores. Ovary short and 2–10-lobed, or terete, elongate and 1–10-celled; placentas axile or parietal; ovules 1–2 in each cell or indefinite, ascending or rarely pendulous; raphe ventral; micropyle superior; style simple, subulate, acute, straight or incurved; stigma simple, terminal. Fruit indehiscent, drupaceous or baccate, compound, each drupe or pyrene 1–4-seeded, or capsular and 1–5-celled with septicidal dehiscence.—Distrib. Tropical regions of the world, very many in America; genera 12; species about 150.

Stamens indefinite .... 1. Ochna.
Stamens 10 .... 2. Gomphia.

1. OCHNA, Linn.

Glabrous trees or shrubs. Leaves alternate, usually serrate, shining, many-nerved; stipules 2. Flowers yellow, in panicles or umbels, springing from a scaly bud beneath the last year's leaves, bracteate. Sepals 5, imbricate, persistent, colored. Petals 5–12, deciduous, imbricate. Disk thick, lobed. Stamens indefinite, inserted at the base of the disk, shorter than the petals; anthers dehiscing longitudinally, deciduous. Ovary 1-celled, deeply 3–10-lobed; lobes obtuse; ovule solitary in each cell, axile; styles connate or sometimes free at the apex; stigmas simple or capitate. Drupes 3–10, seated on the enlarged disk. Seed erect, oblong; testa membranous; cotyledons thick, plano-convex; radicle minute.—Distrib. Tropical Asia and Africa; species 25.

A small tree; flowers in short racemes .... 1. *O. squarrosa.*
A low undershrub; flowers in long-peduncled umbels .... 2. *O. pumila.*

1. **Ochna squarrosa,** *Linn. Sp. Pl.* ed. 2 (1762) p. 731. A shrub or small tree. Leaves 2–5 in. long, oblong-lanceolate, elliptic or obovate, usually acute, finely serrulate, quite glabrous, base narrowed into a short petiole; stipules lanceolate, $\frac{1}{8}$–$\frac{1}{4}$ in. long. Flowers fragrant, in umbellate panicles on the old wood, or sometimes on short leafless branchlets; pedicels jointed. Sepals coriaceous, $\frac{1}{2}$–$\frac{3}{4}$ in. long, elliptic-oblong, with close parallel veins. Petals 5–12, a little longer than the sepals. Stamens indefinite, deciduous; filaments very short; anthers long, linear. Styles completely combined, longer than the stamens. Fruit of 3–6 drupes, $\frac{1}{4}$ in. long, oblong-ovoid, sessile, black, surrounded by the persistent calyx. Fl. B. I. v. 1, p. 523; Grah. Cat. p. 37; Dalz. & Gibs. Suppl. p. 17; Trim. Fl. Ceyl. v. 1, p. 233; Talb. Trees, Bomb. p. 36; Woodr. in Journ. Bomb. Nat. v. 11 (1897) p. 268; Watt, Dict. Econ. Prod. v. 5, p. 439.—Flowers: Feb.–April. Vern. *Kanak-champa.*

Konkan: *Law*!; S. Konkan, on hills near the sea, *Talbot*; Parel road, Bombay, planted, *Graham*. Deccan: gardens about Poona, *Cooke*!, *Woodrow*! S. M. Country: Castlerock, *Woodrow*. Kanara: *Dalzell*!, *Stocks*!; near Karwar, *Talbot*, 116!; Chandawár, *Ritchie*, 1667!—Distrib. India (E. & W. Peninsulas, Birma); Ceylon.

2. **Ochna pumila,** *Buch.-Ham. ex D. Don, Prodr. Fl. Nep.* (1825) p. 224. A low undershrub about 2 ft. high. Leaves 4–6$\frac{1}{2}$ by 1$\frac{1}{2}$–2 in., oblanceolate, spinous-serrate, glabrous, base acute; petioles short;

stipules lanceolate, $\frac{1}{4}$-$\frac{3}{8}$ in. long. Flowers 3-6, in axillary umbels; peduncles 2-3 in. long, with 2 lanceolate bracts $1\frac{1}{2}$ in. long at the base; pedicels 1-$1\frac{1}{2}$ in. long, slender, jointed below the middle; bracts below the pedicels $\frac{1}{4}$-$\frac{1}{3}$ in. long, lanceolate. Sepals $\frac{5}{8}$ in. long, coriaceous, elliptic-oblong. Petals upwards of 1 in. long by $\frac{5}{8}$ in. broad, obovate, with a very short narrow claw, tender. Stamens indefinite; filaments short; anthers elongate. Styles connate throughout their entire length, shortly 4-divided at the apex. Drupes reticulately rugose, $\frac{1}{3}$-$\frac{1}{2}$ in. long, ellipsoid. Fl. B. I. v. 1, p. 524; Woodr. in Journ. Bomb. Nat. v. 11 (1897) p. 268. *Ochna nana*, Buch.-Ham. in Wall. Cat. 3761; Dalz. & Gibs. p. 46.

KONKAN: *Dalzell & Gibson.*—DISTRIB. India (at the foot of the Himalayas, Pegu).

2. GOMPHIA, Schreb.

Glabrous trees or shrubs. Leaves alternate, simple, coriaceous, shining, narrowly serrate, many-nerved; stipules 2. Flowers yellow, in axillary or terminal bracteate racemes; pedicels jointed near the base. Sepals 5, usually colored. Petals 5, imbricate. Disk thick, lobed. Stamens 10, inserted at the base of the disk; filaments short; anthers opening by terminal pores. Ovary 5-6-lobed; lobes 1-celled; ovule solitary in each cell; styles connate; stigma simple. Drupes 5 or fewer, seated on the enlarged disk. Seed erect; testa membranous; cotyledons fleshy, plano-convex; radicle very short.—DISTRIB. Chiefly Tropical American, a few species in Africa, fewer in Asia; species about 80.

1. **Gomphia angustifolia,** *Vahl, Symb.* v. 2 (1791) p. 49. A small much-branched tree; young parts glabrous. Leaves 3-6 by 1-2 in., distichous, oblong-lanceolate, acute, finely serrate, glabrous, closely reticulately veined, base acute; petioles very short; stipules deciduous. Flowers in pyramidal terminal and axillary panicles; buds globose; pedicels slender, jointed near the base. Sepals $\frac{1}{6}$ in. long, elliptic. Petals $\frac{1}{4}$ in. long, obovate, shortly clawed. Stamens 10; filaments short; anthers rugose. Ovary glabrous, 4-5-lobed; lobes obovoid; style much exceeding the stamens. Drupes 5 or fewer, $\frac{1}{4}$-$\frac{3}{8}$ in. in diam., usually obovoid, smooth, reticulately veined, surrounded by the persistent sepals. Fl. B. I. v. 1, p. 525; Grah. Cat. p. 38; Trim. Fl. Ceyl. v. 1, p. 235; Talb. Trees, Bomb. p. 36; Watt, Dict. Econ. Prod. v. 3, p. 533.

KONKAN: on the Ghâts of the S. Konkan, *Talbot*; S. Konkan, *Nimmo* ex *Graham.*—DISTRIB. S. India; Singapore, Ceylon, Philippines.

ORDER XXXV. BURSERACEÆ.

Balsamiferous trees or shrubs. Leaves alternate (very rarely opposite), 3- (rarely 1-) foliolate or imparipinnate, without or rarely with stipules. Flowers hermaphrodite or polygamous, usually small, racemose or panicled. Calyx 3-5-fid or -partite, imbricate or valvate. Petals 3-5, free or rarely connate, deciduous, imbricate or valvate. Disk annular or cupular, rarely inconspicuous, free or adnate to the calyx-tube. Stamens as many or twice as many as the petals, inserted at the base or margin of the disk, equal or unequal; filaments free, rarely connate at the base; staminodes 0; anthers usually versatile, 2-celled. Ovary free, 2–5- (rarely 1-) celled, usually attenuated into a short style; ovules 2 (very rarely 1) in each cell, axile, usually pendulous, rarely ascending; micropyle superior; raphe ventral; stigma undivided or 2–5-lobed. Fruit drupaceous, usually indehiscent, containing 2–5 pyrenes, or rarely pseudo-capsular and dehiscent. Seeds pendulous; testa membranous; albumen 0.—DISTRIB. Tropics of both hemispheres; genera 18; species about 160.

Drupe dehiscent; pyrenes separating .... 1. BOSWELLIA.
Drupe indehiscent; pyrenes not separating.
  Calyx 5-fid; disk lining the calyx-tube .... 2. GARUGA.
  Calyx 4-toothed; disk cupular .... 3. COMMIPHORA.
  Calyx usually 3-fid; disk annular .... 4. CANARIUM.

1. BOSWELLIA, Roxb.

Trees usually with papery bark. Leaves alternate, crowded at the ends of the branches, deciduous, imparipinnate; leaflets opposite, usually serrate. Flowers hermaphrodite, small, white, in axillary racemes or panicles. Calyx small, 5-toothed, persistent. Petals 5, narrowed at the base, imbricate. Disk annular, crenate. Stamens 10, alternately long and short, inserted at the base of the disk. Ovary sessile, 3-celled; ovules 2 in each cell, pendulous; style short; stigma 3-lobed. Drupe trigonous, 3-valved, valves separating from the pyrenes; pyrenes bony, 1-seeded, finally separating from the trigonous axis. Seeds compressed, pendulous; cotyledons contortuplicate, multifid; radicle superior.—DISTRIB. India; Tropical Africa; species about 6.

1. **Boswellia serrata,** *Roxb. ex Coleb. As. Res.* v. 9 (1807) p. 379, t. 5. A deciduous middle-sized tree; bark ash-colored, peeling off in thin flakes; young shoots and leaves pubescent. Leaves 8–15 in. long; leaflets opposite, 1–2½ by ½–1¼ in., sessile, 8–15 pairs and an odd one (the pair at the base of the leaf often much smaller than the others), variable in shape, ovate or ovate-lanceolate, usually inequilateral and obtuse, crenate-serrate, more or less pubescent; base acute, rounded, or somewhat truncate. Flowers in axillary racemes, shorter than the leaves. Calyx pubescent outside; lobes broadly triangular-ovate. Petals ⅕ in. long, ovate, pubescent outside, tips inflexed. Stamens inserted at the base of an annular crenate disk; anthers slightly pubescent. Ovary surrounded by the disk; style grooved. Drupe trigonous; pyrenes heart-shaped; cotyledons trifid. Fl. B. I. v. 1, p. 528; Talb. Trees, Bomb. p. 36; Woodr. in Journ. Bomb. Nat. v. 11 (1897) p. 268; Watt, Dict. Econ. Prod. v. 1, p. 515. *Boswellia thurifera*, Roxb. ex Fleming, in Asiat. Res. v. 11, p. 158; Grah. Cat. p. 42.—Flowers: Feb.–Apr. VERN. *Sálai*; *Sálphali*.

KONKAN: *Stocks*!, *Nimmo* ex *Graham*. DECCAN: Sátpudas of the Khandesh district, *Talbot*; hills in the Deccan, widely, *Woodrow*; Kartriz and Kamatki Ghâts on the road to Mahableshwar, *H. M. Birdwood*; hill-sides, Poona districts, *Woodrow*; Pál jungles, Khandesh district, *Kanitkar*! S. M. COUNTRY: hill of Shendur in the Chichuri taluka, Belgaum Collectorate, *Law* ex *Graham*.—DISTRIB. Throughout India.

VAR. *glabra*, Hook. f. Fl. B. I. *l.c.* Glabrous; leaflets entire or nearly so, rounded at the apex. *Boswellia glaber*, Roxb. Hort. Beng. p. 90; Grah. Cat. p. 42.

Padshapur (Belgaum districts), *Ritchie*, 1009!—DISTRIB. N.W. India.

2. GARUGA, Roxb.

Trees more or less tomentose. Leaves crowded towards the ends of the branches, alternate, imparipinnate; leaflets opposite, subsessile, serrate. Flowers in dense panicles, polygamous. Calyx campanulate, 5-fid, valvate. Petals 5, inserted on the tube of the calyx, induplicato-valvate. Disk thin with a crenate margin, lining the calyx-tube. Stamens 10, equal, free, inserted in the tube of the calyx at the margin of the disk. Ovary ovoid, sessile, 4–5-celled, attenuated into an erect style; ovules 2 in each cell; stigma capitate, 4–5-lobed. Drupe without valves, globose, fleshy, containing 1–5 bony rugose pyrenes. Seed conform to the cell; testa membranous; cotyledons thin, contortuplicate; radicle short, superior.—DISTRIB. Tropical Asia, America, and Australia; species 8–10.

1. **Garuga pinnata,** *Roxb. Hort. Beng.* (1814) p. 33; *Cor. Pl.* v. 3, p. 5, t. 208. A tree sometimes reaching 50 ft. in height; bark furrowed, the outer layers peeling off in flakes. Leaves 6–18 in. long, deciduous in the cold season; leaflets 6–10 pairs and an odd one, opposite or nearly so, subsessile, sometimes 6 in. long, lanceolate or ovate-lanceolate, usually acuminate, oblique, crenate, pubescent when young, at length glabrous. Flowers yellow, in much-branched axillary tomentose panicles, several together at the ends of the branches; bracts deciduous. Calyx ¼ in. long, campanulate, cleft a little less than half way down, densely tomentose outside; lobes ovate-oblong, subobtuse. Petals ⅙ in. long, linear-oblong, tomentose outside, sparsely pubescent within, attached to the tube of the calyx beneath the margin of the disk, tip thickened, inflexed. Disk thin, lining the calyx-tube, crenate. Stamens inserted on the tube of the calyx at the margin of the disk between the crenatures; filaments slightly hairy. Style long, stout, hairy; stigma capitate, 5-lobed. Drupes black, fleshy, size of a gooseberry, edible; pyrenes 1–3 (commonly 2), bony, rugose. Seed with a membranous wing. Fl. B. I. v. 1, p. 528; Grah. Cat. p. 43; Talb. Trees, Bomb. p. 37; Engler, in Engl. & Prantl, Pflanzenf. v. 3, part 4, p. 257, fig. 150; Woodr. in Journ. Bomb. Nat. v. 11 (1897) p. 268; Watt, Dict. Econ. Prod. v. 3, p. 483.—Flowers: Feb.–Mar. VERN. *Kákad.*

KONKAN: *Law*!; hilly parts of the Konkan, *Graham*; Bombay, *Capt. Gebarne*!; Matheran Ghát, *H. M. Birdwood.* DECCAN: Ganesh Khind (Poona), *Woodrow*!; Deccan hills, *Woodrow.* S. M. COUNTRY: Belgaum, *Ritchie*, 1016! KANARA: Honore, *Hohenhacker*, 726! GUJARAT: hills, *Woodrow.*—DISTRIB. Throughout India; Malaya, Philippines.

The drupe is eaten raw, pickled or cooked, and the young shoots and leaves are used as fodder, especially for elephants. See Watt, Dict. Econ. Prod. l. c.

3. COMMIPHORA, Jacquin, Hort. Schœnbr. v. 2 (1797) p. 66, t. 249.

(BALSAMODENDRON, Kunth.)

Balsamiferous trees or shrubs; branches often spinescent. Leaves membranous, 3-foliolate, sometimes with very small lateral leaflets, or imparipinnate; leaflets sessile or shortly petioluled, small, crenate or serrate, rarely entire. Flowers polygamous, small, fascicled, shortly pedicelled. Calyx cupular, urceolate or tubular, 4 (rarely 5–6)-toothed or -lobed, persistent. Petals 4 (rarely 5–6), inserted on the margin of a more or less concave disk, oblong, erect, spreading or reflexed at the apex, valvate or induplicato-valvate. Stamens 8–10, inserted on the margin of the disk, the alternate usually longer, rarely equal; filaments dilated at the base; anthers ovate. Disk cupular. Ovary ovoid, sessile, 3- rarely 2–4-celled; ovules 2 in each cell; style short; stigma obtusely 3–4-lobed. Drupe ovoid or subglobose; epicarp 2–6-valved; pyrenes crustaceous or woody, connate into a compound pyrene, one cell seed-bearing, the rest barren.—DISTRIB. Africa; species 35.

Calyx-lobes equalling the tube .... 1. *C. Mukul.*
Calyx-lobes shorter than the tube.
 Unarmed; stamens equal .... 2. *C. Stocksiana.*
 Armed; stamens alternately long and short .... 3. *C. Berryi.*

1. **Commiphora Mukul,** *Engl. in DC. Monogr. Phan.* v. 4 (1883) p. 12. Shrubby, 4–6 feet high; young parts glandular-pubescent; branches knotty and crooked, divaricate, usually ending in a sharp spine. Leaves 1–3-foliolate; leaflets subsessile (the terminal up to ¾ by ⅓ in.), rhomboid-ovate, serrate-toothed in the upper part (the tapering base entire), smooth, and shining, the lateral leaflets when present less than half the size of the terminal ones. Flowers in fascicles of 2–3; pedicels very short. Calyx campanulate, glandular-hairy; lobes 4–5, triangular, as long as the tube. Petals brownish-red, broadly linear, nearly thrice the length of the calyx, reflexed at the apex. Stamens 8–10, alternately long and short, half the length of the petals. Disk 8–10-lobed, the alternate sinuses deeper and in these are inserted the shorter stamens. Ovary oblong-ovoid, attenuated into the style. Drupes red when ripe, ¼–½ in. in diam., ovoid, acute; epicarp 4-valved; pyrenes ovate, acute, readily splitting into 2. *Balsamodendron Mukul*, Hook. ex Stocks, in Hook. Kew Journ. Bot. v. 1 (1849) p. 259, t. 8; Fl. B. I. v. 1, p. 529; Boiss. Fl. Orient. v. 2, p. 3; Talb. Trees, Bomb. p. 37; Woodr. in Journ. Bomb. Nat. v. 11 (1897) p. 268; Watt, Dict. Econ. Prod. v. 1, p. 366. *Balsamodendron Roxburghii*, Stocks, in Journ. As. Soc. Bomb. v. 2 (1848) p. 391 (*not* of Arnott); Dalz. & Gibs. Suppl. p. 19; Aitch. Pb. & Sind Pl. p. 30.—Flowers: Mar.–Apr. VERN. *Gugal.*

Dry regions of Sind and Khandesh. DECCAN: Peit, 30 miles north of Poona, *Woodrow*!, *Dalzell & Gibson*; between Salher and Abowna (Khandesh), *Dalzell & Gibson*. SIND: hills in Sind, *Stocks*, 440!

The gum-resin known as *Gugal* or *Indian Bdellium* is obtained from the tree. It is extensively used in native medicine. See Watt, Dict. Econ. Prod. l. c.—DISTRIB. India (Rajputana); Beluchistan, Arabia.

2. **Commiphora Stocksiana,** *Engl. in DC. Monogr.* v. 4 (1883) p. 17. An unarmed shrub, much resembling *C. Mukul* in general habit; branches not tipped with a spine; young shoots and leaves rusty-pubescent. Leaves 2–3 pairs with an odd one; leaflets entire, the terminal obovate, petioluled, the lateral subsessile, usually oblong-obovate. Flowers fascicled, 1–3 together, subsessile. Calyx urceolate; teeth short. Petals red or white, obovate, acute, spreading at the apex, not reflexed. Stamens equal in height. Disk equally toothed. Drupes red, subglobose, shortly pointed, marked by 4 conspicuous white sutures,

the alternate ones not reaching to the apex, 2-valved, the valves semi-bifid. *Balsamodendron pubescens*, Stocks, in Journ. As. Soc. Bomb. v. 2 (1848) p. 395, t. 26; Hook. Kew Journ. Bot. v. 1 (1849) p. 264, t. 9; Aitch. Pb. & Sind Pl. p. 30; Fl. B. I. v. 1, p. 529; Boiss. Fl. Orient. v. 2, p. 2; Talb. Trees, Bomb. p. 37; Woodr. in Journ. Bomb. Nat. v. 11 (1897) p. 268; Watt, Dict. Econ. Prod. v. 1, p. 369.—Flowers: Mar.-Apr. VERN. *Bayi.*

Protium pubescens, W. & A. Prodr. (1834) p. 176, having been transferred to the genus *Commiphora* becomes *Commiphora pubescens* by right of priority, and *Balsamodendron* (now *Commiphora*) *pubescens* of Stocks (1848) has been called *Commiphora Stocksiana* by Engler.

SIND: hills and rocky places, *Stocks*, 439!—DISTRIB. Beluchistan.

3. **Commiphora Berryi,** *Engl. in DC. Monogr. Phan.* v. 4 (1883) p. 17. A much-branched small tree or bush; branches spiny, the lateral ones ending in sharp spines. Leaves 3-foliolate; petioles slender; leaflets obovate, sessile, the terminal ½-¾ in. long, twice as large as the lateral ones, all entire or the upper part obsoletely crenate, glabrous, cuneate at the base. Flowers small, about ⅓ in. long, subsessile, solitary or fascicled. Calyx campanulate; teeth 3-4, short, triangular. Petals 3-4, twice as long as the calyx, with a recurved apex which terminates in an incurved tip. Stamens 6-8, alternately long and short, those of the male flowers longer than those of the female or hermaphrodite flowers. Disk small, 6-8-crenate. Drupes oblong, apiculate. *Balsamodendron Berryi*, Arn. in Ann. Nat. Hist. v. 3 (1839) p. 86; Fl. B. I. v. 1, p. 529; Bedd. Flor. Sylvat. t. 126; Trim. Fl. Ceyl. v. 1, p. 237; Talb. Trees, Bomb. p. 37; Woodr. in Journ. Bomb. Nat. v. 11 (1897) p. 268; Watt, Dict. Econ. Prod. v. 1, p. 366. *Balsamodendron gileadense*, Grah. Cat. p. 43 (*not* of Kunth).—Flowers: Feb.-Mar.

Cultivated, but not apparently wild, in the Bombay Presidency. Graham (*l. c.*) says that it was introduced into Bombay in 1837 by Mr. Watson from Mecca. It is abundant in the dry jungles to the east of the Nilghiris (*Beddome*) and is largely used for hedges throughout the Madras Presidency.

4. CANARIUM, Linn.

Tall balsamiferous trees. Leaves large, alternate, distant, imparipinnate (rarely 1-3-foliolate); leaflets usually petioluled, often very unequal, the lowest rotund, remote from the base, or sessile at the base of the leaf and stipuliform. Flowers hermaphrodite or polygamous, in axillary branched panicles. Calyx cupular or urceolate, 3- (rarely 5-) lobed or -fid, valvate, persistent. Petals 3-5, thick, usually longer than the calyx, valvate or slightly imbricate. Disk annular, entire or lobed. Stamens 6-10, inserted outside the disk or at the base of the disk; filaments free or connate at the base with one another and with the disk. Ovary ovoid (rudimentary in the male flowers), 3- (rarely 2-4-) celled; ovules 2 in each cell; style short or equalling the ovary in length; stigma capitate, 2-4-lobed. Drupe ovoid or ellipsoid, often trigonous, with a 1-3-celled, 1-3-seeded stone. Seed conform to the cell; testa membranous; cotyledons sometimes partite, contortuplicate; radicle short, straight, superior.—DISTRIB. Tropical Asia, Africa, Malaya; species about 70.

1. **Canarium strictum,** *Roxb. Hort. Beng.* (1814) p. 49. A large tree; young branches and leaves beneath densely rufous-tomentose. Leaves coriaceous, shining and glabrous above, reaching 2 feet (*Beddome*, Flor. Sylvat. l. c. says 4 feet) in length; leaflets 3–7 pairs and an odd one, 4–8 by $1\frac{1}{4}$–$3\frac{1}{2}$ in., ovate-oblong or ovate, to ovate-lanceolate, acuminate, opposite or alternate, finely serrate, with 10–15 pairs of lateral nerves very prominent beneath; petiolules $\frac{1}{10}$–$\frac{1}{3}$ in. long. Flowers in short-branched axillary panicles shorter than the leaves; pedicels very short. Calyx usually 3-lobed, cupular, rusty tomentose outside; tube $\frac{1}{8}$ in. long; lobes triangular, $\frac{1}{24}$ in. long. Petals $\frac{1}{4}$ in. long by $\frac{1}{12}$ in. broad, oblong-obovate, slightly hairy on the outside towards the rounded apex. Ovary ovoid, attenuated into a style as long as the ovary, glabrous, rudimentary in the male flowers. Drupes $1\frac{1}{2}$–2 in. long, ellipsoid or ovoid, tapering at both ends; stone hard, bony. Fl. B. I. v. 1, p. 534; Dalz. & Gibs. p. 52; Engler, in DC. Monogr. Phan. v. 4, p. 118; Bedd. Flor. Sylvat. t. 128; Talb. Trees, Bomb. p. 37; Woodr. in Journ. Bomb. Nat. v. 11 (1897) p. 268; Watt, Dict. Econ. Prod. v. 2, p. 96.—Flowers: Feb.–Apr. VERN. *Raldhup.*

KONKAN: *Law* !, *Dalzell*, 1679 !; Mira hills near Pen, *Dalzell & Gibson*; Matheran, near the Chauki, *H. M. Birdwood.* KANARA: *Law* !; Ainshi Ghát (N. Kanara), common, *Talbot.*—DISTRIB. India (W. Peninsula).

The tree is known as "*the black dammar tree*" and yields a brilliant resin. For particulars as to its uses, consult Watt, Dict. Econ. Prod. l. c.

ORDER XXXVI. MELIACEÆ.

Trees or shrubs. Leaves alternate, exstipulate, usually pinnate; leaves or leaflets usually entire. Flowers regular, usually hermaphrodite, in terminal or axillary panicles. Calyx usually small, 4–5-fid or -partite, imbricate, rarely valvate. Petals 4–5 (rarely 3–7), sometimes free and contorted or imbricate, sometimes connate or adnate to the staminal-tube and valvate. Stamens 4–10, generally 8–10 (very rarely more), inserted with the petals outside of the base of a hypogynous disk; filaments united by their margins into a more or less complete tube which is entire, toothed or variously laciniate, rarely free; anthers introrse or versatile, erect, usually sessile on the staminal-tube, included or exserted, 2-celled, dehiscing longitudinally; connective sometimes produced. Disk various, usually annular, or tubular and sheathing, free or adnate to the ovary or staminal-tube, or 0. Ovary usually free, 2–5-celled; ovules 1–2 (rarely more) in each cell, collateral or superposed; raphe ventral, micropyle superior; style simple; stigma disciform or capitate. Fruit capsular, baccate or drupaceous. Seeds exalbuminous or with fleshy albumen, winged or not; embryo flat; hilum usually ventral; cotyledons fleshy.—DISTRIB. Frequent in the warm regions of Asia and America, rarer in Africa; genera 37; species about 300.

Seeds not winged; filaments united into a tube.
  Seeds albuminous; cotyledons foliaceous.
    Leaves simple .... 1. TURRÆA.
    Leaves compound.
      Common petiole winged .... 2. NAREGAMIA.
      Common petiole not winged.
        Flowers elongate; fruit drupaceous........... 3. MELIA.
        Flowers globose; fruit baccate .... 4. CIPADESSA.

Seeds exalbuminous; cotyledons thick.
Flowers and staminal-tube oblong; style long.
Disk 0; petals 5 .... 5. AZADIRACHTA.
Disk large, usually sheathing the ovary; petals 4 .... 6. DYSOXYLUM.
Flowers and staminal-tube globose or turbinate; style short or obsolete.
Anthers included in the staminal-tube or the tips only exserted.
Fruit baccate.
Anthers 5; seeds exarillate .... 7. AGLAIA.
Anthers 10, in 2 series; seeds arillate .... 8. LANSIUM.
Fruit capsular.
Seeds arillate .... 9. AMOORA.
Seeds exarillate .... 10. CARAPA.
Anthers wholly exserted from the staminal-tube.
Fruit baccate, indehiscent................. 11. WALSURA.
Fruit capsular, loculicidal................. 12. HEYNEA.
Seeds winged.
Filaments united into a tube.
Staminal-tube cup-shaped; disk conspicuous........... 13. SOYMIDA.
Staminal-tube cylindric; disk 0 .... 14. CHUKRASSIA.
Filaments distinct.
Stamens 4–6 .... 15. CEDRELA.
Stamens 10........ .... 16. CHLOROXYLON.

1. TURRÆA, Linn.

Trees or shrubs. Leaves alternate, petioled, entire or obtusely lobed. Flowers in axillary clusters or short racemes, bracteate. Calyx 5–4-toothed or -partite. Petals 5–4, elongate, free, contorted. Staminal-tube cylindric, toothed at the apex; anthers 10 or 8, short, included or exserted, inserted just within the mouth, alternating with the teeth. Disk annular or obsolete. Ovary 5 (or more) -celled; ovules 2 in each cell, superposed; style filiform, thickened at the apex; stigma discoid or capitate. Capsule 4 (or more) -celled, cells 1–2-seeded, 5- or many-valved; valves woody or coriaceous, separating from the winged axis. Seeds oblong, with a broad ventral hilum, the margins sometimes winged; albumen fleshy; embryo curved; cotyledons foliaceous; radicle terete. DISTRIB. Tropical Asia and Tropical and South Africa; species about 23.

Teeth of staminal-tube subulate; anthers shorter than the teeth; style just exserted .... 1. *T. virens.*
Teeth of staminal-tube short; anthers longer than the teeth; style far-exserted .... 2. *T. villosa.*

1. **Turræa virens,** *Linn. Mantiss. alt.* (1771) p. 237. A shrub 3–4 ft. high. Leaves coriaceous, alternate, elliptic-lanceolate, sub-acuminate, emarginate, quite entire, glabrous, paler beneath; petioles very short. Flowers in axillary or lateral clusters, yellow; bracts small, linear, villous. Calyx small, shortly 5-fid, persistent, sericeo-villous. Petals lanceolate or spathulate. Staminal-tube about 1 in. long, with 10 lanceolate teeth; anthers alternate with the teeth and shorter than them; style just exserted. Ovary 5-celled. Capsule $\frac{1}{3}$ in. long, hairy. Fl. B. I. v. 1, p. 541.

Dalzell & Gibson (Bomb. Fl. p. 36) state that the plant is "common on the Ghâts."

The only specimen in Herb. Kew., marked *T. virens* in Dalzell's handwriting, is without flowers, but the leaves and capsules are unmistakably those of *T. villosa*. Graham (Cat. Bomb. Plts. l. c.) gives as the habitat of *T. virens*, Khandala and the bottom of Parghát, where it is, he states, abundant, flowering in April and May. I have myself collected specimens on the hills not far from Parghát in the month of May in full flower, but these were all *Turræa villosa*, and were, as Graham describes, destitute of leaves when the flowers appeared. There can be little doubt that both Graham and Dalzell have mistaken *T. villosa* for *T. virens*. Neither author mentions *T. villosa* at all, while *T. virens* has not, as far as I am aware, been found by any botanical collector. It seems more than doubtful therefore if *T. virens* really occurs in the Bombay Presidency.

There are but 2 authentic specimens of the species in existence, one in the Linnean Herbarium in the Linnean Society, and the other in the British Museum, both of which I have seen. Kœnig the collector states that they were found on heaps of scoriæ from extinct volcanoes in the East Indies, but gives no precise locality.

2. **Turræa villosa,** *Benn. Pl. Jav. Rar.* (1840) p. 182. A large shrub. Leaves membranous, appearing after the flowers, 2–4 by $1\frac{1}{4}$–$2\frac{1}{4}$ (when mature), elliptic or ovate, acuminate, entire, softly villous when young, becoming more or less glabrous when old, base acute or rounded; petioles $\frac{1}{4}$–$\frac{3}{8}$ in. long, pubescent. Flowers axillary, $1\frac{1}{2}$–2 in. long, solitary or in fascicles of 2–6, or in short-peduncled umbels; buds clavate. Calyx campanulate, pubescent outside, 5-toothed; teeth triangular. Petals yellow, linear-spathulate. Staminal-tube reaching 1 in. in length, glabrous; teeth very short; anthers longer than the teeth of the staminal-tube. Ovary 5-celled; style long, far-exserted; stigma large, ovoid. Capsule subglobose, about $\frac{1}{2}$ in. in diam., glabrous. Fl. B. I. v. 1, p. 542; Wight, Icon. t. 1593; Talb. Trees, Bomb. p. 38; Woodr. in Journ. Bomb. Nat. v. 11 (1897) p. 268.—Flowers: Apr.–June.

Konkan: *Law*!; Ghâts in S. Konkan, *Capt. Geburne*!; near Pen, *Woodrow*. Deccan: Mahableshwar hills, *Ralph*, 213!; Koina Valley, below Mahableshwar, *Cooke*! Kanara: moist forests of the Supa subdivision of N. Kanara, *Talbot*.—Distrib. India (Anamallay hills); Java.

2. NAREGAMIA, W. & A.

A glabrous branching undershrub. Leaves alternate, 3-foliolate. Flowers axillary, solitary. Calyx 5-fid, deciduous, imbricate. Petals 5, elongate-spathulate, free, contorted. Staminal-tube elongate, cylindric, inflated at the apex; anthers 10, appendaged at the apex. Disk annular. Ovary ovoid, 3-celled; ovules 2 in each cell, collateral, pendulous; style filiform; stigma capitate. Capsule ovoid-globose, 3-lobed, 3-celled, loculicidally 3-valved; valves separating from the 3-winged axis, cells 2-seeded. Seeds pendulous, curved, truncate at both ends, with a short double membrane along the side next the axis; albumen fleshy; cotyledons foliaceous.—Distrib. India; Angola (W. Tropical Africa).

1. **Naregamia alata,** *Wight & Arn. Prodr.* (1834) p. 117. Suffruticose, about 1 ft. high. Leaves 3-foliolate, 1–3 in. long (including the winged petiole); petiole $\frac{7}{8}$–$1\frac{1}{2}$ in. long; leaflets $\frac{3}{4}$–2 in. long, sessile (the terminal slightly the largest), cuneate-obovate, sometimes obtusely lobed, entire, glabrous. Flowers 1–$1\frac{1}{4}$ in. long, longer than the pedicels, white, axillary, solitary. Calyx hairy outside; lobes oblong-lanceolate. Petals linear-spathulate. Capsule somewhat membranous, 3-lobed, 3-valved, valves orbicular. Seeds muriculate, chestnut-brown, terete, curved,

truncate at both ends. Fl. B. I. v. 1, p. 542; Grah. Cat. p. 30; Dalz. & Gibs. p. 36; Harms, in Engl. & Prantl, Pflanzenf. v. 3, part 4, p. 281, fig. 158, G–H; Woodr. in Journ. Bomb. Nat. v. 11 (1897) p. 269; Watt, Dict. Econ. Prod. v. 5, p. 342.—Flowers: Nov.–Dec. VERN. *Kápur-bhendi.*

KONKAN: *Dalzell*!; east of Panwell, rare, *Nimmo* ex *Graham*; plentiful on the sides of nalas near Vingorla, *Dalzell & Gibson*; Sawantwari, *Kanitkar*!; Vingorla, *Kanitkar*! KANARA: *Thomson*!; Karwar, *Woodrow*!—DISTRIB. India (W. Peninsula); Angola (a pubescent form).

3. **MELIA,** Linn.

Trees or shrubs. Leaves alternate, simply or 2–3-pinnate with an odd one, the young ones often stellately tomentose; leaflets toothed, serrate or entire. Flowers hermaphrodite, elongate, in large many-flowered axillary much-branched panicles. Calyx 5–6-partite, imbricate. Petals 5–6, free, much exceeding the calyx. Staminal-tube a little shorter than the petals, laciniate, the mouth dilated; anthers 10, within the staminal-tube at its apex, sessile between its laciniæ, erect. Disk annular. Ovary 5–8-celled; cells opposite the sepals; ovules 2 in each cell, superposed; style cylindric, much exceeding the ovary; stigma capitate. Drupe subfleshy; endocarp woody; cells 1-seeded. Seeds pendulous, elliptic; testa crustaceous; albumen fleshy or scanty; cotyledons foliaceous; radicle terete, superior.—DISTRIB. Tropical Asia and Australia; species about 12.

Flowers lilac; anthers nearly equalling the teeth of the purple staminal-tube .... 1. *M. Azedarach.*
Flowers white; anthers exceeding the teeth of the white staminal-tube .... 2. *M. composita.*

1. **Melia Azedarach,** *Linn. Sp. Pl.* (1753) p. 384. A tree reaching 40 ft. Leaves impari- bi- (or sometimes tri-) pinnate, 9–18 in. long; pinnæ opposite or alternate; ultimate leaflets 3–11, opposite or nearly so, ½–2 by ¼–1 in., ovate or lanceolate, acuminate, obtusely serrate, sometimes lobed, glabrous on both surfaces, slightly inequilateral at the base; petiolules short, slender. Flowers fragrant, lilac, in long-peduncled, axillary panicles which are shorter than the leaves and glabrous or sparsely puberulous; pedicels slender. Calyx pubescent outside, divided nearly to the base; lobes ovate-oblong acute, ciliolate. Petals ⅜ in. long, oblong-lanceolate. Staminal-tube purple, $\frac{5}{16}$ in. long, glabrous, slightly ribbed outside, faintly pubescent within, acutely 20-toothed; anthers sessile, glabrous, apiculate, 1 between each pair of teeth. Ovary glabrous, 5-celled. Drupe ellipsoid-globose, 4-seeded. Fl. B. I. v. 1, p. 544; Grah. Cat. p. 30; Harms, in Engl. & Prantl, Pflanzenf. v. 3, part 4, p. 287, fig. 160, A–L; Boiss. Fl. Orient. v. 1, p. 954; Talb. Trees, Bomb. p. 39; Woodr. in Journ. Bomb. Nat. v. 11 (1897) p. 269; Watt, Dict. Econ. Prod. v. 5, p. 221. *Melia sempervirens*, Sw. Prodr. Veg. p. 67; Dalz. & Gibs. Suppl. p. 15.—Flowers: Apr.–May. VERN. *Bakán-nimb*; *Bakáyan.*

Cultivated throughout the Presidency; common about villages in the Konkan and Deccan. The tree is known to Anglo-Indians as the *Persian lilac* the *bead-tree* or *bastard cedar* and has some medicinal value. See Watt, Dict. Econ. Prod. l. c.—DISTRIB. India (Sub-Himalayas); Persia, China.

2. **Melia composita,** *Willd. Sp. Pl.* (1799) v. 2, p. 559. A tall handsome tree; young branches densely clothed with stellate pubescence, ultimately smooth. Leaves bi- sometimes tri-pinnate, 9–30 in. long; ultimate leaflets 5–11, opposite, ¾–3 by ¼–1½ in. (the terminal the largest), from ovate-lanceolate to ovate-rotund, acute or acuminate, entire or crenulate, thinly stellately pubescent on both surfaces when young, at length glabrous, base acute or rounded, more or less oblique; main nerves 7–8 pairs; petiolules ⅛–¼ in. long. Flowers greenish-white, ⅓ in. long, fragrant, in stellately pubescent many-flowered branched panicles shorter than the leaves; peduncles long; pedicels short. Calyx stellately tomentose outside, deeply divided; lobes ovate, erect, ciliate. Petals ¼ in. long, linear-spathulate, concave, pubescent outside, puberulous within, ciliate. Staminal-tube scarcely ¼ in. long, slightly expanded at the mouth, 10-toothed (the teeth bifid), silky puberulous on both surfaces; anthers exserted, pubescent, longer than the teeth. Ovary glabrous, 5-celled; style a little longer than the staminal-tube, overtopped by the apiculate anthers; stigma cylindric, 5-toothed, teeth erect. Drupes ovoid or ellipsoid, 1–1½ in. long, smooth, yellowish. Seed 1 in each cell, smooth, pointed. Grah. Cat. p. 30; Dalz. & Gibs. p. 36; Bedd. Flor. Sylvat. t. 12; Brandis, For. Fl. p. 69; King, in Journ. As. Soc. Beng. v. 64, p. 18. *Melia dubia*, Hiern (*not* of Cav.), Fl. B. I. v. 1, p. 545; DC. Monogr. Phan. v. 1, p. 453; Watt, Dict. Econ. Prod. v. 5, p. 223 (excluding from all three the syn. *M. superba*, Roxb.); Talb. Trees, Bomb. p. 39; Woodr. in Journ. Bomb. Nat. v. 11 (1897) p. 269. *Melia robusta*, Roxb. Hort. Beng. p. 33.—Flowers: Mar. VERN. *Kadu-khajur*; *Kála-khajur*.

I have followed Sir G. King in the separation of this species from *M. dubia*, Cav., with which it had been united by Mr. Hiern, Fl. B. I. *l. c.* The reasons given by Sir G. King (*l. c.*) for its separation appear quite conclusive.

KONKAN: hilly parts of the Konkan, *Graham*. DECCAN: Málshiras, Purandar taluka, *Kanitkar*!; Parghát, *Dalzell & Gibson*. S. M. COUNTRY: on the Gatparba river, *Ritchie*, 1021! KANARA: common on the Supa Ghâts, *Talbot*; Harihar and Yacombi, *Woodrow*.—DISTRIB. India generally; Australia, Angola.

4. CIPADESSA, Blume.

Shrubs or small trees. Leaves alternate or subopposite, imparipinnate or 3-foliolate; leaflets entire or coarsely serrate. Flowers hermaphrodite, in axillary panicles. Calyx 5-toothed. Petals 5, valvate. Stamens 5–10; filaments united below into a short tube, free above, 2-toothed at the apex, antheriferous between the teeth; anthers short. Disk cupular, adnate to the base of the staminal-tube. Ovary 5-celled; ovules 2 in each cell, collateral; style short; stigma capitate. Fruit baccate, subfleshy, 5-ribbed, 5-celled; cells 1–2-seeded. Seeds angled; albumen fleshy; embryo curved; cotyledons oblong; radicle superior.—DISTRIB. India, Java; species 4.

1. **Cipadessa fruticosa,** *Blume, Bijdr.* (1825) p. 162. A small much-branched shrub; young parts silky. Leaves imparipinnate, 4–9 in. long; leaflets 3–6 pairs and an odd one, opposite, 1½–2½ by ⅝–1¼ in., elliptic-lanceolate, acute at both ends, very coarsely serrate, rarely subentire, glabrous except the nerves which are more or less hairy;

petiolules very short, slender. Flowers small, white, in axillary corymbose panicles which are shorter than the leaves; peduncles long, slender; pedicels short. Calyx pubescent outside, 5-toothed; teeth short, triangular. Petals $\frac{1}{8}$ in. long, membranous, oblong, acute, pubescent outside. Stamens a little shorter than the petals; filaments hairy inside, the teeth sharp and as long as the anthers. Ovary glabrous; style short; stigma capitate, shortly 5-lobed. Berry $\frac{1}{5}$–$\frac{1}{4}$ in. in diam., globose, 5-lobed, scarlet. Seeds angular. Fl. B. I. v. 1, p. 545; Harms, in Engl. & Prantl, Pflanzenf. v. 3, part 4, p. 281, fig. 158, A–D; Trim. Fl. Ceyl. v. 1, p. 215; Talb. Trees, Bomb. p. 39; Woodr. in Journ. Bomb. Nat. v. 11 (1897) p. 269. *Mallea Rothii*, A. Juss. in Mém. Mus. Par. v. 19 (1830) p. 222, t. 13, fig. 6; Grah. Cat. p. 31; Dalz. & Gibs. p. 37.—Flowers: Sept. VERN. *Gudmei.*

KONKAN: *Stocks!* DECCAN: abundant on the Kartrix Ghát near Poona, *Graham*; Kadakvasla near Poona, *Cooke!*; Khandala, *Woodrow.* S. M. COUNTRY: Belgaum hills, *Ritchie*, 110!—DISTRIB. India (W. Peninsula); Ceylon, Java.

5. **AZADIRACHTA,** A. Juss. Mém. Mél. (1830) p. 68, t. 2, n. 5; C. De Candolle, in DC. Monogr. Phan. v. 1, p. 459, t. 6, fig. 10.

Trees. Leaves alternate, imparipinnate; leaflets serrate. Flowers hermaphrodite, in axillary panicles. Calyx 5-partite. Petals 5, much exceeding the calyx, free, imbricate. Staminal-tube a little shorter than the petals, laciniate at the apex; anthers within the tube at its apex, sessile, opposite to the laciniæ. Disk 0. Ovary 3-celled, the cells opposite the petals; ovules 2 in each cell, collateral; style much exceeding the ovary; stigma shortly cylindric, 3-toothed. Drupe 1-seeded; endocarp woody. Seed exalbuminous, ellipsoid; cotyledons very thick and fleshy, acutely 2-lobed at the base; radicle exserted from the cotyledons, superior.—DISTRIB. India, Ceylon, Java; species 1.

1. **Azadirachta indica,** *A. Juss. in Mém. Mus. Par.* v. 19 (1830) p. 221. A large tree 40–50 ft. high, with a straight trunk. Leaves simply pinnate, 8–15 in. long, crowded near the ends of the branches; leaflets 9–12, subopposite, 1–3 by $\frac{1}{2}$–$1\frac{1}{2}$ in., obliquely lanceolate, sometimes falcate, acuminate, serrate, glabrous on both surfaces, base inequilateral, acute; petiolules very short. Flowers white, fragrant, in branched glabrous panicles shorter than the leaves; bracts minute, lanceolate, caducous. Calyx puberulous outside, divided almost to the base; lobes rotund-ovate, minutely ciliolate. Petals $\frac{1}{4}$ in. long, obovate-oblong, faintly puberulous outside, ciliolate. Staminal-tube glabrous, a little shorter than the petals, obconic, the laciniæ truncate and toothed at the apex; anthers 10, opposite the laciniæ and a little shorter than them, apiculate. Disk 0. Ovary glabrous, 3-celled, the cells opposite to the petals; ovules 2 in each cell, collateral; stigma 3-toothed, included in the tube. Drupes the shape of an olive, $\frac{1}{2}$–$\frac{3}{4}$ in. long, glabrous, 1-seeded. Grah. Cat. p. 30; Dalz. & Gibs. p. 36; Trim. Fl. Ceyl. v. 1, p. 244; DC. Monogr. Phan. v. 1, p. 459, t. 6, fig. 10; Harms, in Engl. & Prantl, Pflanzenf. v. 3, part 4, p. 287, fig. 160, M–S. *Melia Azadirachta*, Linn. Sp. Pl. p. 385; Fl. B. I. v. 1, p. 544; Talb. Trees, Bomb. p. 38; Woodr. in Journ. Bomb. Nat. v. 11 (1897) p. 269; Watt, Dict. Econ. Prod. v. 5, p. 211.—Flowers: Mar.–May. VERN. *Nim.*

Cultivated throughout the Presidency and self-planted, but nowhere really wild; common about villages. KONKAN: *Stocks*! DECCAN: Poona, *Cooke*!; Hubli, *Hohenhacker*, 765!—DISTRIB. Cultivated throughout India and in many hot climates.

The well-known *Nim* or *Margosa* tree. Its valuable properties attracted the notice of the Mohammedans on their arrival in India and it was named by them *Azad-daracht-i-hindi* from its resemblance to the Persian lilac (*Melia Azedarach*). For a full description of the valuable products of the tree, consult Watt, Dict. Econ. Prod. l. c.

6. DYSOXYLUM, Blume.

Glabrous often fœtid trees. Leaves large, alternate (rarely opposite), impari- or abruptly-pinnate; leaflets usually quite entire, oblique at the base. Flowers hermaphrodite, in axillary or supra-axillary lax panicles. Calyx short, 4–5-fid or -partite, imbricate, caducous. Petals 4–5, valvate or slightly imbricate, free or connate below with the staminal-tube (never with the ovary). Stamens united into a tube which is a little shorter than the petals and usually laciniate or crenate; anthers 8–10, inserted beneath the apex of the staminal-tube, glabrous, included or half exserted. Disk tubular, crenulate or entire at the mouth, glabrous or ciliate, usually sheathing and exceeding the ovary. Ovary free, 3–5-celled, attenuated into a style much longer than the ovary; ovules 1–2 in each cell, superposed or collateral; stigma discoid. Capsule thickly coriaceous, globose or pyriform, 1–5-celled, loculicidally 2–5-valved; cells 1–2-seeded. Seeds exarillate (rarely arillate); cotyledons thick, plumule often hirsute; albumen 0.—DISTRIB. Malaya, Australia, New Zealand, Polynesia; species 85.

Leaves imparipinnate; calyx nearly half as long as the flower, lobes obscure .... 1. *D. binectariferum.*
Leaves abruptly-pinnate; calyx short, lobes acute .... 2. *D. malabaricum.*

1. **Dysoxylum binectariferum,** *Hook. f. ex Bedd. in Trans. Linn. Soc.* v. 25 (1866) p. 212. A tree 30 ft. high or more; young parts finely puberulous. Leaves imparipinnate, pale, 6–10 in. long; rhachis angular; leaflets 5–9, alternate, 4–7 by 1½–3 in., oblong-elliptic, acuminate, glabrous on both surfaces, entire or obscurely and distantly toothed, base acute often inequilateral; nerves about 14 pairs, prominent beneath; petiolules ⅛–⅓ in. long. Flowers ⅜ in. long, in axillary or supra-axillary subglabrous panicles which are shorter than the leaves; pedicels short, articulated. Calyx cupular, nearly half as long as the flower, coriaceous, truncate, entire or obscurely lobed, glabrous. Petals 4, greenish-yellow, valvate except at the apex, tomentose outside. Staminal-tube cylindric, toothed, glabrous; anthers 8, included. Disk surrounding and twice as long as the ovary, irregularly 8-toothed, the teeth again dentate. Ovary ribbed, villous, attenuated into the style, 4-celled; ovules 2 in each cell; stigma hemispheric, truncate. Capsules 2–2½ in. long, obovoid or subglobose, grooved, glabrous, orange-colored when ripe, 4-celled, 4-seeded. Seeds large, nearly 1 in. long, purplish-brown, shining. Fl. B. I. v. 1, p. 546; DC. Monogr. Phan. v. 1, p. 493; Trim. Fl. Ceyl. v. 1, p. 247; Talb. Trees, Bomb. p. 39; Woodr. in Journ. Bomb. Nat. v. 11 (1897) p. 269; Watt, Dict. Econ. Prod. v. 3, p. 199. *Epicharis exarillata*, Arn. ex W. & A. Prodr. p. 120 (*not* of Nimmo); Dalz. & Gibs. p. 37. *Guarea binectarifera*, Roxb. Hort. Beng. p. 28; Grah. Cat. p. 31.—Flowers: Aug.–Sept. VERN. *Yerindi.*

KONKAN: near Vingorla, *Dalzell & Gibson.* DECCAN: Lanoli Grove, *Graham*;

Khandala, *Woodrow*; Phunda Ghát, *Ritchie*, 675! KANARA: common near the Falls of Gairsoppa, *Talbot*.—DISTRIB. India (W. Peninsula, Assam and Khasia hills); Ceylon, the Andamans.

2. **Dysoxylum malabaricum,** *Bedd. ex Hiern, in Hook. f. Fl. B. I.* v. 1 (1875) p. 548. A very large tree; young shoots slightly puberulous. Leaves up to 18 in. long, abruptly-pinnate; rhachis angular; leaflets alternate or subopposite, 4–5 pairs, 4–9 in. long, pale green, elliptic-oblong, acuminate, entire, puberulous when young; lateral nerves 12–20 pairs, prominent beneath; petiolules $\frac{1}{4}$–$\frac{1}{3}$ in. long. Flowers $\frac{1}{3}$ in. long, in axillary racemiform panicles shorter than the leaves; buds oblong; pedicels $\frac{1}{8}$ in. long. Calyx short, finely pubescent outside, deeply 4-lobed; lobes ovate, acute. Petals 4, linear-oblong, subacute, imbricate. Staminal-tube urceolate, with 8 deep emarginate crenatures, contracted about $\frac{2}{3}$ of the way up; anthers 8, alternate with the crenatures, included. Disk cupular, truncate, subentire or irregularly toothed, not concealing the ovary, pubescent within. Ovary densely pubescent, tapering into the style, 4-celled; ovules 2 in each cell; stigma capitate, 4-lobed. Fruit 2 in. in diam., pyriform, verrucose, bright yellow when ripe, 3–4-seeded. Seeds bluntly trigonous; testa reddish brown; cotyledons green. Fl. B. I. v. 1, p. 548. *Dysoxylum glandulosum* *, Talb. Trees, Bomb. p. 39.—Flowers: Feb.

KANARA: evergreen forests of N. Kanara, *Talbot*, 228!—DISTRIB. India (W. Peninsula).

7. **AGLAIA,** Lour.

Trees or shrubs, glabrous, lepidote, or stellately-pubescent. Leaves alternate, pinnate; leaflets opposite, often oblique at the base, quite entire. Flowers polygamo-diœcious, minute, in axillary branching panicles. Calyx 5-toothed or 5-partite, imbricate. Petals 5, free, or more or less connate at the base, imbricate. Staminal-tube urceolate or subglobose, 5-toothed or quite entire at the apex; anthers usually 5, or 4 or 10, included or half exserted, erect. Disk inconspicuous. Ovary 1–2- (rarely 3-) celled, short; ovules 1–2 in each cell; style thick, very short or 0; stigma scarcely broader than the style, 1–3-toothed. Berry 1- or few-seeded; pericarp coriaceous. Seeds with a fleshy integument.—DISTRIB. Tropical and subtropical Asia and Polynesia; rare in temperate climates; species more than 50.

1. **Aglaia odoratissima,** *Blume, Bijdr.* (1825) p. 171. A tree reaching 40 ft. high; young branches, petiolules and inflorescence covered with minute brown deciduous scales. Leaves 3–7 in. long, imparipinnate; leaflets opposite, usually 5 (rarely 3 or 7), thinly coriaceous, 2–4$\frac{1}{2}$ by 1–2 in., elliptic-oblong or obovate, usually shortly acuminate, upper surface glabrous, the lower and especially the nerves more or less lepidote, base cuneate; petiolules $\frac{1}{8}$–$\frac{1}{2}$ in. long (those of the terminal leaflets the longest). Flowers globular, in axillary or supra-axillary pyramidally-branched elongate lepidote panicles 3–8 in. long. Calyx appressedly lepidote-pubescent outside; lobes 5, short, rounded, ciliolate. Petals yellow, $\frac{1}{8}$ in. long, much longer than the calyx, unequal,

* The glands in the axils of the lateral nerves noted by Mr. Talbot (*l. c.*) appear to be the work of insects.

broadly elliptic-oblong, rounded at the apex, glabrous. Staminal-tube urceolate-globose, shorter than the petals, truncate, the mouth open, obscurely 5-lobed; anthers 5, concealed in the tube, inserted below its mouth. Ovary small, stellately lepidote; style half as long as the staminal-tube; stigma small, broadly ovoid. Berry $\frac{1}{2}$–$\frac{3}{4}$ in. long, pyriform or subglobose, velvety-tomentose, buff-colored, usually 1-seeded. Seeds ellipsoid. King, in Journ. Asiat. Soc. Beng. v. 64 (1895) p. 67; Harms, in Engl. & Prantl, Pflanzenf. v. 3, part 4, p. 299, fig. 163, G. *Aglaia Roxburghiana*, Hiern, in Hook. f. Fl. B. I. v. 1, p. 555 (*not* of Miquel); DC. Monogr. Phan. v. 1, p. 604; Trim. Fl. Ceyl. v. 1, p. 246; Talb. Trees, Bomb. p. 40; Watt, Dict. Econ. Prod. v. 1, p. 145.—Flowers: Nov.–Dec.

KONKAN: *Stocks*!, *Law*! S. M. COUNTRY: Ramghát, *Ritchie*, 1858! KANARA: Kumpta, *Talbot*, 2955!; Falls of Gairsoppa, *Talbot*, 2673!; Karwar (near the coast), *Talbot*, 499!; evergreen forests of N. Kanara, from Ainshi southwards, *Talbot*.—DISTRIB. India (W. Peninsula and Birma); Singapore, Ceylon, Java, Sumatra.

8. LANSIUM, Rumph.

Trees or shrubs. Leaves imparipinnate. Inflorescence axillary; flowers small, diœcious, the male usually in lax branching panicles, the female spicate or racemose. Sepals 5, rounded, imbricate. Petals 5, rounded, connivent, imbricate. Staminal-tube globose, mouth crenulate; anthers 10, subacute, usually in 2 rows, the shorter one included, the longer semi-exserted. Disk inconspicuous. Ovary globose, 3–5-celled; ovules 1–2 in each cell, attached to the axis; style very short, thick; stigma truncate, 3–5-lobed. Berry 3–5-celled, corky or fleshy. Seeds solitary or twin, collateral, oblong, exalbuminous, embedded in a pulpy aril; hilum ventral; cotyledons transverse; radicle superior.—DISTRIB. India, Malaya; species 4–6.

1. **Lansium anamallayanum,** *Bedd. in Trans. Linn. Soc.* v. 25 (1866) p. 212. A moderate-sized tree. Leaves imparipinnate, 6–9 in. long; leaflets 3–5, alternate, 3–6 by $1\frac{1}{4}$–$2\frac{1}{4}$ in., elliptic-lanceolate, acuminate, glabrous on both surfaces, base acute, subequilateral; petiolules $\frac{1}{8}$–$\frac{3}{8}$ in. long. Flowers in panicles, spikes or racemes shorter than the leaves, 2–3-fasciculate, the hermaphrodite flowers sessile; buds globose. Calyx rugose outside; lobes orbicular, ciliate. Petals $\frac{1}{8}$ in. long, elliptic-obovate, veined. Staminal-tube irregularly crenate, striate inside; anthers 2-seriate, the upper row slightly exserted. Ovary densely hairy, 3-lobed, 3-celled; ovules usually 2 (sometimes 1 *Beddome*) in each cell; style very short; stigma large, 3-lobed. Fruit oblong, size of a grape, 2-celled, 2-seeded. Fl. B. I. v. 1, p. 558; Bedd. Flor. Sylvat. t. 131; DC. Monogr. Phan. v. 1, p. 597; Talb. Trees, Bomb. p. 40; Woodr. in Journ. Bomb. Nat. v. 11 (1897) p. 269.—Flowers: Apr.–May. VERN. *Telya*.

KANARA: abundant on the S. Gháts of N. Kanara in evergreen forests, *Talbot*; Hulical, *Woodrow*!—DISTRIB. India (W. Peninsula).

9. AMOORA, Roxb.

Trees, often tall; young parts sometimes lepidote. Leaves usually imparipinnate; leaflets few- or multi-jugate, entire. Flowers polygamo-diœcious, small, the male in axillary panicles, the female usually in spikes or racemes. Calyx 3-5-partite or -fid. Petals 3-5, thick, concave, free or rarely slightly united at the base, imbricate or rarely valvate. Staminal-tube a little shorter than the petals, subglobose or campanulate, obsoletely 6-10-crenate; anthers 6-10, included, sessile or subsessile. Disk obsolete. Ovary sessile, depressed, 3-5-celled; ovules 1-2 in each cell; style 0 or short or elongate; stigma entire or toothed. Capsule subglobose, coriaceous or woody, 3-4-celled; cells 1-seeded, loculicidally 3-5-valved. Seeds in a fleshy aril, with ventral hilum; cotyledons often conferruminate; radicle superior.—DISTRIB. Tropical and Subtropical Asia, Polynesia and Australia; species about 25.

Leaves imparipinnate.
  Petals 3; anthers 6.
    Seeds with a scarlet aril .... 1. *A. Rohituka.*
    Seeds with an orange-colored aril .... 2. *A. cucullata.*
  Petals 4; anthers 8 .... 3. *A. Lawii.*
Leaves abruptly-pinnate .... 4. *A. canarana.*

1. **Amoora Rohituka,** *Wight & Arn. Prodr.* (1834) p. 119. An evergreen tree 30-60 ft. high; young parts finely silky. Leaves large, imparipinnate, 1-2½ ft. long; leaflets opposite, 4-8 pairs and an odd one, 3-9 by 1½-4 in., elliptic-oblong or oblong-lanceolate, acuminate, glabrous on both surfaces, very inequilateral, obtuse or acute at the base; petiolules ¼-⅓ in. long. MALE FLOWERS numerous, erect, ⅛ in. long, subglobular, in solitary axillary panicles more than half as long as the leaves, the branches of the panicle about 3 in. long spreading at right angles or slightly drooping; bracts beneath each flower small, scale-like; pedicels short. Calyx glabrous, 5-partite; lobes orbicular, ciliate. Petals 3, orbicular, concave, thick, glabrous, much larger than the calyx-lobes. Staminal-tube nearly as long as the petals, subglobular, with a small opening at the apex; anthers 6, subsessile, elliptic-oblong, attached near the base of the tube, the tips just exserted. FEMALE OF HERMAPHRODITE FLOWERS larger than the male, in axillary or supra-axillary solitary spikes much shorter than the leaves. Calyx and petals as in the male, the anthers narrower. Ovary hairy, globular or ellipsoid; stigma 3-lobed. Fruit 1-1½ in. in diam., globular, yellow when ripe; pericarp coriaceous, smooth, 3-celled, opening by 3 valves. Seed oblong with a scarlet aril. Fl. B. I. v. 1, p. 559; Trim. Fl. Ceyl. v. 1, p. 249; DC. Monogr. Phan. v. 1, p. 581; Talb. Trees, Bomb. p. 41; Woodr. in Journ. Bomb. Nat. v. 11 (1897) p. 269; King, in Journ. As. Soc. Beng. v. 64 (1895) p. 53; Watt, Dict. Econ. Prod. v. 1, p. 224. *Amoora macrophylla*, Nimmo, in Grah. Cat. p. 31. *Aphanamixis Rohituka*, Pierre, Fl. For. Cochinch. t. 344; Harms, in Engl. & Prantl, Pflanzenf. v. 3, part 4, p. 292, fig. 162, Q.—Flowers: July.

KONKAN: *Law!*, *Stocks!*; S. Konkan Ghâts, *Talbot.* DECCAN: Khandala, *Graham*; planted in gardens, *Woodrow.* KANARA: abundant in the forests of Yellapur (N. Kanara), *Talbot.*—DISTRIB. India (W. Peninsula, Assam, Oude); Ceylon, Malaya, Philippines.

2. **Amoora cucullata,** *Roxb. Cor. Pl.* v. 3 (1819) p. 51, t. 258. A tree 30-40 ft. high. Leaves imparipinnate, 12-15 in. long; leaflets 2-4 pairs and an odd one, opposite or subopposite, 3-7 by 1¼-2½ in., oblong-elliptic, subfalcate, subacute, glabrous on both surfaces, base rounded very inequilateral except that of the terminal leaflet; petiolules

$\frac{1}{4}$–$\frac{1}{2}$ in. long. MALE FLOWERS about $\frac{1}{8}$ in. long, in axillary lax branched sparingly lepidote panicles about equalling the leaves; peduncles long; pedicels short. Calyx lepidote outside, 3-lobed; lobes rounded, ciliolate. Petals 3, longer than the calyx, broadly elliptic, concave, glabrous. Staminal-tube scarcely shorter than the petals, obovoid, irregularly and obtusely 5–7-toothed; anthers 6, attached half way up the tube. Rudimentary ovary stalked, ovoid-oblong, truncate, obscurely grooved. FEMALE OR HERMAPHRODITE FLOWERS a little larger than the male, in few-flowered supra-axillary racemes about 2 in. long. Calyx, petals and staminal-tube as in the male. Ovary lepidote, ovate, 3-angled, 3-celled; stigma sessile, large, 3-lobed. Fruit depressed, globular, 2–5 in. in diam., dehiscing by 3 valves; pericarp coriaceous. Seeds 3, rounded, trigonous, with an orange-colored aril. Fl. B. I. v. 1, p. 560; Dalz. & Gibs. p. 37; DC. Monogr. Phan. v. 1, p. 583; Talb. Trees, Bomb. p. 41; King, in Journ. As. Soc. Beng. v. 64 (1895) p. 55; Watt, Dict. Econ. Prod. v. 1, p. 224.

S. M. COUNTRY: Párva Ghát (Belgaum Collectorate), *Dalzell & Gibson*.—DISTRIB. India, Lower Bengal and the Andamans.

3. **Amoora Lawii,** *Hiern, in Hook. f. Fl. B. I.* (1875) v. 1, p. 561. A moderate-sized tree; young branches lepidote with yellowish-brown scales, at length glabrous. Leaves imparipinnate, 6–9 in. long; common petiole short; leaflets 1–2 pairs and an odd one, opposite or subalternate, 2$\frac{1}{2}$–4$\frac{1}{2}$ by 1–1$\frac{3}{4}$ in., elliptic or oblong-lanceolate, acuminate, glabrous, base rounded or acute, subequilateral; petiolules $\frac{1}{8}$–$\frac{1}{2}$ in. long. Flowers white, in axillary much-branched panicles clothed with yellowish-brown scales. Calyx lepidote, truncate, more or less obscurely 4-toothed. Petals usually 4, glabrous, $\frac{1}{8}$ in. long, broadly elliptic-oblong. Staminal-tube subentire at the apex, glabrous outside, slightly ribbed inside; anthers 8 (rarely 7), long, triangular-oblong, attached near the base of the staminal-tube, the tips just level with its apex. Ovary conical, 3-celled, lepidote; style almost 0: stigma 3-toothed. Fruit buff-coloured, pyriform, densely lepidote, 1 in. long. Fl. B. I. v. 1, p. 561; Talb. Trees, Bomb. p. 41; DC. Monogr. Phan. v. 1, p. 585. *Epicharis exarillata*, Nimmo, in Grah. Cat. p. 31. *Nemedra Nimmonii*, Dalz. in Dalz. & Gibs. p. 37.—Flowers: Dec.–Jan. VERN. *Burumb*.

KONKAN: *Stocks*!, *Law*!, *Dalzell*!; hills about Nagotna, *Graham*; Karjat, *Woodrow*!; Amboli Ghát, *Kanitkar*! DECCAN: Khandala, *Graham*; Párghát, *Graham*. KANARA: throughout the evergreen forests of N. Kanara; very common in the Ainshi Ghát forests, *Talbot*.—DISTRIB. India (W. Peninsula).

4. **Amoora canarana,** *Hiern, in Hook. f. Fl. B. I.* v. 1 (1875) p. 560. A tree; young parts, inflorescence and calyx lepidote. Leaves abruptly-pinnate, 6–15 in. long; leaflets 4–6 pairs, subalternate, 3–7 by 1$\frac{1}{4}$–2$\frac{3}{4}$ in., oblong, acute or acuminate, glabrous above, lepidote beneath, narrowed at the base; petiolules $\frac{1}{4}$–$\frac{1}{2}$ in. long. Flowers small, in dense divaricately-branched panicles much shorter than the leaves; buds globose; pedicels short. Calyx obtusely 3–5-toothed, lepidote outside. Petals 3–4, orbicular, glabrous, $\frac{1}{10}$ in. long. Staminal-tube obovoid, glabrous, truncate or very faintly and obscurely toothed at the apex, the mouth open; anthers 6, sessile, attached near the mouth of the tube, the tips just exserted. Ovary lepidote; style 0; stigma 3-toothed. Fruit

(immature) obovoid. Fl. B. I. v. 1, p. 560; DC. Monogr. Phan. v 1, p. 586; Talb. Trees, Bomb. p. 41; Woodr. in Journ. Bomb. Nat. v. 11 (1897) p. 269.—Flowers: Mar.–April.

KANARA: *Stocks*!; Goond, *Talbot*, 2730! ; throughout the evergreen forests of N. Kanara, from Goond southwards, *Talbot*.—DISTRIB. India (W. Peninsula).

10. CARAPA, Aubl.

Glabrous littoral trees. Leaves impari- or abruptly-pinnate; leaflets opposite, entire. Flowers hermaphrodite, in lax axillary cymose panicles. Calyx 4–5-fid or -partite. Petals 4–5, free, reflexed. Staminal-tube urceolate-globose, 8–10-dentate, the teeth entire or bipartite; anthers 8–10, alternate with the teeth of the staminal-tube. Disk fleshy, cup-shaped, adherent to the base of the ovary. Ovary 4–5-ribbed or sulcate, 4–5-celled; ovules 2–8 in each cell; style short; stigma discoid. Fruit capsular, subglobose, large, 6–12-seeded; pericarp fleshy, dehiscing by 4 valves. Seeds exarillate, large, thick, angular; testa hard, spongy; hilum large, ventral; cotyledons amygdaloidal.—DISTRIB. Tropical countries, usually littoral; species 6.

1. **Carapa obovata,** *Blume, Bijdr.* (1825) p. 179. A small tree. Leaves abruptly-pinnate, 3–6 in. long; leaflets coriaceous, 1–2 pairs, 3–4 by 1½–1¾ in., oblong-obovate or elliptic, obtuse or shortly acuminate, rarely subacute or notched, glabrous, base narrowed, subequilateral; petioles ⅛–⅓ in. long. Flowers in axillary few-flowered cymose panicles 1½–2½ in. long; pedicels ⅓–½ in. long. Calyx-teeth broad, rounded. Petals ¼ in. long, broadly elliptic-oblong, rounded at the apex. Staminal-tube shorter than the petals; anthers included. Ovary broadly ovoid; style conical; stigma large, discoid. Fruit the size of an orange, 3–4 in. in diam., apiculate when young, not so when ripe. Seeds angular; testa hard, spongy. King, in Journ. As. Soc. Beng. v. 64 (1895) p. 87; DC. Monogr. Phan. v. 1, p. 718. *Carapa moluccensis*, Fl. B. I. v. 1, p. 567 (*in part*); Bedd. Flor. Sylvat. t. 136; Trim. Fl. Ceyl. v. 1, p. 251; Talb. Trees, Bomb. p. 42; Watt, Dict. Econ. Prod. v. 2, p. 141.

Sea-coasts of the Konkan, *Talbot*.—DISTRIB. Muddy sea-coasts of India and Ceylon, Tropical Africa, Malaya, N. Australia.

11. WALSURA, Roxb.

Trees. Leaves 1–5-foliolate; leaflets usually opposite, entire. Flowers small, hermaphrodite, in axillary and terminal many-flowered panicles. Calyx short, 5-fid or 5-partite, imbricate. Petals 5, free, imbricate or subvalvate. Stamens 10 or 8; filaments linear or flattened, free or connate into a tube; anthers terminal, or inserted in the notch at the apex of the filament. Disk usually annular, fleshy. Ovary short, 2–3-celled, sunk in the disk; ovules 2 in each cell, collateral; style short; stigma turbinate-capitate, 2–3-toothed. Fruit baccate, shortly tomentose, indehiscent, 1- (rarely 2-) celled, 1–2-seeded. Seeds enclosed in a fleshy aril, exalbuminous.—DISTRIB. India, Malaya; species about 12.

1. **Walsura piscidia,** *Roxb. Hort. Beng.* (1814) p. 32. A small tree; young parts glabrous. Leaves 3-foliolate; leaflets subcoriaceous, 2–3½ by ¾–1¼ in., oblong-elliptic, obtuse, sometimes retuse, glabrous on

both surfaces, shining above, paler beneath (the lateral leaflets opposite, very shortly-petioluled, the terminal with a longer petiolule), base subacute. Flowers yellowish-white, in corymbosely-branched axillary or terminal panicles about equalling the leaves; buds globose; peduncles long, pubescent; bracts minute, triangular, caducous. Calyx small, pubescent outside; lobes ovate, acute. Petals $\frac{1}{10}$ in. long, ovate-oblong, acute, glabrous or puberulous outside, imbricate. Staminal-tube half as long as the petals, hairy inside, equally 10-cleft for about two-thirds of its length, the divisions 2-toothed at the apex; anthers 10, acuminate, slightly hairy, inserted between the teeth and exceeding them. Disk large, annular. Ovary sunk in the disk; stigma 2-dentate. Berry $\frac{3}{8}$–$\frac{5}{8}$ in. long, ovoid, oblong or subglobose, bright orange-yellow when ripe, finely tomentose, minutely apiculate. Seed usually solitary, completely enveloped in a white juicy aril. Fl. B. I. v. 1, p. 564; DC. Monogr. Phan. v. 1, p. 634; Trim. Fl. Ceyl. v. 1, p. 250; Talb. Trees, Bomb. p. 41; Woodr. in Journ. Bomb. Nat. v. 11 (1897) p. 269; Watt, Dict. Econ. Prod. v. 6, part 4, p. 299.—Flowers: Nov. VERN. *Wálsura*; *Walursi*.

F. M. COUNTRY: Ramghát, plentiful, *Dalzell*! KANARA: evergreen forests of N. Kanara, common in the Devimana Ghát forests, *Talbot*.—DISTRIB. India (W. Peninsula); Ceylon.

The bark of the tree is used for poisoning fish; hence the specific name.

12. HEYNEA, Roxb.

Trees, rarely shrubs. Leaves imparipinnate; leaflets opposite, petioluled, entire. Flowers small, hermaphrodite, in axillary and terminal corymbosely-branched long-peduncled panicles. Calyx 4–5-fid, imbricate. Petals 4–5, free, oblong, suberect, subimbricate, much longer than the calyx. Staminal-tube deeply 8–10-fid, the lobes linear, 2-toothed at the apex, bearing the anthers between the linear teeth. Disk annular, fleshy. Ovary sunk in the disk, 2–3-celled, narrowing into the style; ovules 2 in each cell; style as long as or longer than the ovary; stigma discoid, 2–3-dentate. Fruit capsular, 1-celled, 2-valved, 1-seeded. Seeds exalbuminous, with a thin white aril; cotyledons hemispheric; radicle superior.—DISTRIB. India, Malaya; species 3.

1. **Heynea trijuga,** *Roxb. Hort. Beng.* (1814) p. 33. A small tree reaching 30 ft. Leaves 6–15 in. long; common petiole with a thickened base; rhachis slender, glabrous; leaflets 2–6 pairs and an odd one, $2\frac{1}{2}$–$5\frac{1}{2}$ by 1–$2\frac{1}{2}$ in., ovate-oblong or oblong-lanceolate, acuminate, glabrous above, glaucous and pubescent or glabrous beneath, base rounded or acute; petiolules $\frac{1}{8}$–$\frac{7}{8}$ in. long, the terminal ones the longer. Flowers about $\frac{1}{6}$ in. long, white, in corymbosely-branched panicles nearly as long as the leaves; peduncles very long, slender, glabrous; bracts linear-lanceolate, caducous. Calyx with a few scattered hairs on the outside; lobes ovate, subacute. Petals much longer than the calyx with a thickened midrib and membranous finely ciliolate margins. Staminal-tube shorter than the petals, split for about two-thirds of its length, the lobes linear, 2-dentate, slightly hairy outside, densely so within; anthers between the teeth of the lobes, about equal to them in length or a little longer, slightly mucronate. Ovary glabrous; style slightly obconical; stigma 2-dentate, with a thickened ring at the base. Capsules $\frac{1}{3}$–$\frac{1}{2}$ in. long, ovoid or subglobose. Fl. B. I. v. 1,

p. 565; Grah. Cat. p. 31; Dalz. & Gibs. p. 38; DC. Monogr. Phan. v. 1, p. 713; Talb. Trees, Bomb. p. 42; Woodr. in Journ. Bomb. Nat. v. 11 (1897) p. 269.—Flowers: Feb.-Mar. VERN. *Limbára.*

KONKAN: *Stocks*!; common all along the Ghâts, *Dalzell & Gibson.* DECCAN: Khandala, *Graham, Woodrow*; Párghât, *Graham.* KANARA: common along the banks of rivers and in evergreen forests in N. Kanara, *Talbot*; Kasarli, *Ritchie*, 1190!; Yacombi, *Woodrow*!—DISTRIB. Throughout India generally.

13. SOYMIDA, Adr. Juss.

A lofty tree with bitter bark and hard wood. Leaves abruptly-pinnate; leaflets opposite, obtuse, entire. Flowers hermaphrodite, in axillary and terminal panicles. Sepals 5, short, imbricate. Petals 5, spreading, clawed, contorted. Staminal-tube short, cup-shaped, 10-lobed, lobes 2-dentate; anthers inserted between the teeth. Disk conspicuous. Ovary ovoid, 5-celled; ovules many in each cell, biseriate, pendulous; style short; stigma thick, discoid, 5-angled. Capsule woody, 5-celled, septifragally 5-valved, the valves consisting of 2 plates separating from the 5-winged axis. Seeds pendulous from the top of the axis, imbricate in two series, compressed, winged at both ends; cotyledons foliaceous, 2-auricled at the base; radicle very short, superior.—DISTRIB. One species, endemic in India.

1. **Soymida febrifuga,** *Adr. Juss. Mém. Mus. Par.* v. 19 (1830) p. 251, t. 22, fig. 26. A tall tree. Leaves 9–18 in. long, crowded towards the ends of the branches; leaflets 3–6 pairs, opposite, 2–4½ by 1–2½ in., elliptic or oblong, obtuse, glabrous, penninerved, the nerves numerous and conspicuous beneath, base rounded, inequilateral, the lower side generally extending further down the petiolule than the upper; petiolules ⅛–¼ in. long. Flowers in large terminal or axillary divaricately branched panicles often equalling the leaves, the branches of the panicle alternate; pedicels very short; bracts minute, triangular, acute. Sepals 5, rotund, the margins membranous, slightly lacerate. Petals 5, obovate, ¼ in. long, clawed, often notched at the apex. Staminal-tube about half as long as the petals, slightly urceolate; anthers attached by the middle of the back. Ovary glabrous; stigma large, discoid, $\frac{1}{16}$ in. in diam., 5-lobed, the lobes radiating to the centre. Capsules 1–2½ in. long, obovoid, 5-celled, 5-valved. Seeds winged. Fl. B. I. v. 1, p. 567; Dalz. & Gibs. p. 38; Bedd. Flor. Sylvat. t. 8; DC. Monogr. Phan. v. 1, p. 722; Harms, in Engl. & Prantl, Pflanzenf. v. 3, part 4, p. 271, fig. 152, K–M; Talb. Trees, Bomb. p. 42; Woodr. in Journ. Bomb. Nat. v. 11 (1897) p. 269; Watt, Dict. Econ. Prod. v. 6, part 3, p. 318. *Swietenia febrifuga*, Roxb. Hort. Beng. p. 33; Cor. Pl. v. 1, p. 18, t. 17; Grah. Cat. p. 32.—Flowers: Mar. VERN. *Ruhin*; *Rohan.*

KONKAN: *Stocks*!; Thana districts, *Woodrow.* DECCAN: Khandesh and Jowar jungles, *Dalzell & Gibson.* GUJARAT: *Graham.* S. M. COUNTRY: in dry forests and on stony hills, *Talbot.*

The bark of the tree has been recommended as a substitute for Peruvian bark. The heart wood is heavy and close-grained and well adapted for ornamental furniture. See Watt, Dict. Econ. Prod. l. c.

14. **CHUKRASSIA,** Adr. Juss. Mém. Mus. Par. v. 19 (1830) p. 251.

CHICKRASSIA, Wight & Arn. Prodr. p. 122; Hook. f. & Benth. Gen. Plant.

A tree. Leaves abruptly-pinnate; leaflets alternate or opposite. Flowers hermaphrodite, rather large, in terminal panicles, 4–5-merous. Calyx short, dentate. Petals oblong, free, erect, contorted. Staminal-tube cylindric, its mouth with 10 short blunt teeth; anthers 10, erect, inserted within the teeth, entirely exserted. Disk obsolete. Ovary shortly stalked, cylindric, 3–5-celled; ovules numerous, 2-seriate; style short, stout; stigma discoid. Capsule woody, 1–5- (usually 3-) celled, 3-5-valved. Seeds numerous, winged below, exalbuminous; cotyledons orbicular, inequilateral.—DISTRIB. India, Ceylon; species 1.

The name originally given to this genus by Adr. Juss. (Mém. Mus. Par. v. 19 [1830] p. 21) was *Chukrassia*, derived from the Bengali name of a tree of the genus which Roxburgh (Hort. Beng. [1814] p. 33) gave as *Chukrasi*. Subsequent to the publication of the name as *Chukrassia* by Adr. Juss., Roxburgh (Fl. Ind. [1832] p. 399) corrected the Bengali name to *Chickrassee*, and Wight and Arnott (Prodr. [1834] p. 122) adopted the spelling *Chickrassia*, as agreeing better with the more recent vernacular synonym given by Roxburgh. This mode of spelling the name of the genus has been adopted in the 'Genera Plantarum' of Hooker and Bentham and in Fl. B. I. v. 1, p. 568. Continental and other foreign botanists are however reverting to the original mode of spelling the name (*e. g.* DC. Monogr. Phan. and Harms in Engl. & Prantl, Pflanzenf.), and, as there can be no question as to its correctness, the spelling of the name as *Chukrassia* and not *Chickrassia* is certain to be ultimately adopted universally.—The change has therefore been made above.

1. **Chukrassia tabularis,** *Adr. Juss. in Mém. Mus. Par.* v. 19 (1830) p. 251, t. 22, fig. 27. A tall tree; young branches lenticellate, glabrous. Leaves abruptly-pinnate, 12–18 in. long; leaflets 5–8 pairs, 2–5 by 1–2½ in. (the upper leaflets often larger than the lower), ovate or ovate-oblong, acute or acuminate, glabrous above, more or less velvety beneath, base inequilateral, the upper side the larger and usually rounded, the lower side usually acute; petiolules ⅙–⅓ in. long. Flowers in terminal panicles which are shorter than the leaves, the branches of the panicles spreading, many-flowered; buds oblong. Calyx pubescent outside, obtusely 5-toothed. Petals dirty-white, ⅝ in. long by ⅛ in. broad, linear-oblong, spathulate. Staminal-tube cylindric, glabrous. Ovary hairy, attenuated into the style; stigma 4-lobed, just appearing above the apex of the staminal-tube. Capsules ovoid or obovoid, 1¾–2¼ in. long, by about ⅞ in. in diam. Seeds winged, 1½ by ½ in. (including the wing). Fl. B. I. v. 1, p. 568; Grah. Cat. p. 32; Harms, in Engl. & Prantl, Pflanzenf. v. 3, part 4, p. 271, fig. 152, S–T; DC. Monogr. Phan. v. 1, p. 726; Talb. Trees, Bomb. p. 43; Woodr. in Journ. Bomb. Nat. v. 11 (1897) p. 269; Watt, Dict. Econ. Prod. v. 2, p. 268.—Flowers: Feb.–Apr. VERN. *Ddl-devdár*; *Dalmara.*

KONKAN: *Law*!, *Stocks*!; Matheran, *H. M. Birdwood.* DECCAN: Hewra botanical garden, *Dalzell*! KANARA: evergreen forests of N. Kanara, *Talbot*; Yellapur, *Woodrow.*—DISTRIB. India (W. Peninsula).

VAR. *velutina*, King, in Journ. As. Soc. Beng. v. 64 (1895) p. 88. Leaflets tomentose or pubescent on both surfaces. Panicles tomentose. Petals puberulous on the outside. Capsules often 4-valved. Trim. Fl. Ceyl. v. 1, p. 252; Talb. Trees, Bomb. p. 43. *C. velutina* (sp.), Wight & Arn.

Prodr. p. 123; Rœm. Synop. fasc. 1, p. 135; DC. Monogr. Phan. v. 1, p. 727; Trim. Fl. Ceyl. v. 1, p. 252. *C. Nimmonii*, Grah. in Wight, Ill. v. 1, p. 148; Dalz. & Gibs. p. 38.

KONKAN: *Woodrow*!, *Talbot*; Tungar hill, *Graham*; jungles at Bohe, *Dalzell & Gibson*. KANARA: N. Kanara, *Talbot*.—DISTRIB. India (W. Peninsula); Ceylon.

15. CEDRELA, Linn.

Tall trees with colored wood. Leaves pinnate; leaflets numerous, usually quite entire. Flowers hermaphrodite, small, in terminal and subterminal panicles. Calyx short, 5-partite. Petals 5, suberect, free, imbricate. Stamens 4–6, free, inserted at the top of the disk, sometimes alternating with staminodes; filaments subulate; anthers broadly oblong, versatile. Ovary sessile on the top of the disk, ovoid, 5-celled, the cells opposite the petals; ovules 8–12, biseriate, pendulous; stigma discoid. Capsule coriaceous, 5-celled septifragally; valves 2-lamellate. Seeds pendulous, compressed, imbricate, winged; albumen thin, fleshy; cotyledons flat, subfoliaceous; radicle short, superior.—DISTRIB. Tropical Asia, Australia, America; species about 16.

1. **Cedrela Toona,** *Roxb. ex Rottl. & Willd. in Ges. Naturf. Fr. Neue Schr.* v. 4 (1803) p. 198. A tall tree reaching 60 ft.: branches numerous, forming a shady head. Leaves abruptly-pinnate, 12–18 in. long or more; leaflets opposite or alternate, 4–15 pairs, 2–6 by $\frac{3}{4}$–$2\frac{1}{2}$ in., lanceolate or ovate-lanceolate, acuminate, entire or slightly undulate, glabrous, base inequilateral, the upper side usually larger rounded, the lower smaller acute; petiolules $\frac{1}{4}$–$\frac{1}{2}$ in. long. Flowers white, honey-scented, in large drooping terminal more or less pubescent panicles nearly as long as the leaves; buds ovoid or oblong; pedicels short, slender. Calyx divided nearly to the base; lobes orbicular-ovate, ciliate. Petals $\frac{1}{5}$ in. long, broadly elliptic, obscurely veined, ciliate, keeled at the base inside. Stamens 5, each inserted on one of the orange-colored hairy lobes of the disk; staminodes 0; filaments subulate; anthers oblong, cordate, rounded and apiculate at the apex. Ovary hairy, ovoid or subglobose; stigma $\frac{1}{20}$ in. in diam. Capsules oblong, $\frac{3}{4}$–1 in. long. Seeds with a membranous wing at each end, about $\frac{3}{4}$ in. long including the wings. Fl. B. I. v. 1, p. 568; Grah. Cat. p. 246; Dalz. & Gibs. p. 38; DC. Monogr. Phan. v. 1, p. 745; Talb. Trees, Bomb. p. 43; Woodr. in Journ. Bomb. Nat. v. 11 (1897) p. 269; Watt, Dict. Econ. Prod. v. 2, p. 233.—Flowers: Jan. VERN. *Mahá-nim*; *Kudak*; *Tuni*.

KONKAN: road to Matheran, *Kanitkar*!, *Cooke*!; Rambág, Matheran, *H. M. Birdwood*. DECCAN: ravines at Khandala, *Graham*, *Woodrow*; Panchgani, *Woodrow*; Khandala, *Dalzell & Gibson*. KANARA: abundant in the forests of N. Kanara; immense trees common at Yellapur, *Talbot*.—DISTRIB. India (Central and Southern and Birma); Java, Australia.

The tree is known as the *Toon*, the *Indian Mahogany* tree and the *Moulmein Cedar*. The wood is valuable for furniture, the flowers yield a dye and the bark has some repute in native medicine. See Watt, Dict. Econ. Prod. l. c.

16. CHLOROXYLON, DC.

A lofty tree; wood yellow, hard. Leaves abruptly-pinnate; leaflets numerous, very oblique, entire. Flowers small, in axillary and terminal pubescent panicles. Calyx short, 5-partite. Petals 5, clawed, imbricate.

Disk thick, 10-lobed, pubescent. Stamens 10, inserted in the sinuses at the base of the disk; filaments subulate, the alternate somewhat longer; anthers cordate, apiculate, versatile. Ovary immersed in the disk, pubescent, depressed, 3-lobed, 3-celled; ovules about 8 in each cell, attached to the axis, ascending; style short; stigma obscurely 3-lobed. Capsule oblong, coriaceous, 3-celled, loculicidally 3-valved. Seeds compressed, exalbuminous, margins angular, winged above; cotyledons plano-convex.—DISTRIB. India and Ceylon; species 1.

1. **Chloroxylon Swietenia,** *DC. Prodr.* v. 1 (1824) p. 625. A tree 30–40 ft. high; bark corky, rough, deeply furrowed, yellowish. Leaves 6–9 in. long, abruptly-pinnate; leaflets subopposite or alternate, 10–20 pairs, $\frac{3}{4}$–$1\frac{1}{4}$ by $\frac{1}{3}$–$\frac{1}{2}$ in., oblong, obtuse, glabrous, glaucous, very inequilateral, the upper side of the leaflet larger than the lower and rounded, the lower side acute at the base; petiolules $\frac{1}{16}$–$\frac{1}{8}$ in. long. Flowers in branched many-flowered terminal and axillary panicles shorter than the leaves; buds globose; bracts minute, caducous. Calyx pubescent, deeply divided; lobes ovate. Petals $\frac{3}{16}$ in. long, ovate, acute, sagittate at the base, abruptly and shortly clawed, externally pubescent. Disk fleshy, pubescent. Stamens inserted between the lobes of the disk, shorter than the petals. Ovary immersed in the disk, 3-lobed, pubescent. Capsules oblong, acute, glabrous. Seeds $\frac{3}{4}$–$\frac{7}{8}$ in. long (including the membranous, somewhat falcate wing), $\frac{1}{16}$ in. broad. Fl. B. I. v. 1, p. 569; Grah. Cat. p. 32; Dalz. & Gibs. p. 39; Engler, in Engl. & Prantl, Pflanzenf. v. 3, part 4, p. 171, fig. 99, A–H (under *Rutaceæ*); DC. Monogr. Phan. v. 1, p. 748; Trim. Fl. Ceyl. v. 1, p. 253; Talb. Trees, Bomb. p. 43; Woodr. in Journ. Bomb. Nat. v. 11 (1897) p. 269; Watt, Dict. Econ. Prod. v. 2, p. 270.—Flowers: Mar.–Apr. VERN. *Halda*; *Billu*.

KONKAN: *Law*!, *Stocks*!, *Dalzell*!, *Woodrow*! S. M. COUNTRY: abundant in the dry deciduous forests of the Dharwar and Belgaum districts, *Talbot*; Falls of Gokak, *Graham*, *Woodrow*; hills N. of Belgaum, *Ritchie*, 104!—DISTRIB. India (W. Peninsula); Ceylon.

The Indian Satinwood tree. The wood is hard and durable, beautifully mottled and excellent for the manufacture of furniture, for which purpose it is much used in Ceylon. See Watt, Dict. Econ. Prod. l. c.

ORDER XXXVII. CHAILLETIACEÆ.

Small trees or shrubs. Leaves alternate, quite entire; stipules 2, deciduous. Flowers small, unisexual or polygamous, in corymbose cymes. Sepals 5, free or connate, imbricate. Petals 5, free, subperigynous, notched or 2-fid, with often an inflexed lamina which is adnate to the face of the petal. Stamens 5, subperigynous, all or some only fertile, free or adnate to the corolla; anthers oblong; connective often thickened at the back. Disk of 5 glands or scales or a 5-glandular or lobed cup. Ovary free, 2–3-celled; ovules anatropous, in pairs from the top of each cell, pendulous; styles 1–3, free or more or less connate; stigmas simple or capitate. Drupe pubescent or hispid, transversely oblong or didymous, compressed; epicarp entire or splitting and disclosing the putamen; putamen 1–3-celled, the cells 1-seeded.

Seeds pendulous, hilum broad; testa membranous; albumen 0; embryo large; cotyledons thick; radicle small, superior.—DISTRIB. Tropics of the Old and New World; genera 3; species about 40.

1. CHAILLETIA, DC.

Flowers polygamo-monœcious. Sepals 5, unequal, united at the base or above it, obtuse. Petals 5, 2-fid. Stamens 5, sometimes slightly adnate at the base to the petals. Disk of 5 quadrate scales placed opposite the petals. Ovary 2–3-celled.—DISTRIB. Tropical Asia, Africa and especially America; species about 30.

1. **Chailletia sumatrana,** *Miq. Fl. Ind. Bat. Suppl.* (1860) p. 328. A bush or small tree. Leaves 2–4 by 1–1¾ in., elliptic or oblong-elliptic, acuminate, entire, glabrous, base acute; petioles $\frac{1}{16}$–$\frac{1}{8}$ in. long; stipules pubescent. Flowers small, in axillary or extra-axillary clusters. Sepals $\frac{1}{10}$ in. long, elliptic-oblong, obtuse, densely pubescent. Petals as long as the sepals or a little longer, linear-oblong, deeply notched at the apex. Connective of anthers broad. Ovary (in the female flowers only) downy; styles 2, recurved. Fruit transversely oblong or obcordate, didymous, compressed, covered with soft greyish down; epicarp coriaceous, 2-valved, dehiscing along the edge; stone thin, hard, rugose, covered by a soft scarlet mesocarp. Trim. Fl. Ceyl. v. 1, p. 254. *Chailletia gelonioides*, Bedd. For. Man. in Flor. Sylvat. (1871) p. lix, t. 9, fig. 1; Fl. B. I. v. 1 (1875) p. 570; Talb. Trees, Bomb. p. 43; Woodr. in Journ. Bomb. Nat. v. 11 (1897) p. 269; Watt, Dict. Econ. Prod. v. 2, p. 263. *Moacurra gelonioides*, Roxb. Fl. Ind. v. 2, p. 69; Dalz. & Gibs. p. 52.—Flowers: Apr.–June.

KONKAN: *Stocks*!; edge of the Ghâts in lat. 16°, *Dalzell*! S. M. COUNTRY: Ramghât, *Ritchie*, 1855!, plentiful, *Dalzell & Gibson*. KANARA: very common in N. Kanara near the Falls of Gairsoppa, *Talbot*.—DISTRIB. India widely; Ceylon, Sumatra.

ORDER XXXVIII. OLACACEÆ.

Trees or shrubs, erect, scandent or twining. Leaves alternate (rarely opposite), simple or lobed, exstipulate. Inflorescence cymose or racemose (rarely capitate), terminal, axillary or extra-axillary; flowers usually small, regular, hermaphrodite, polygamo-diœcious or diœcious. Calyx 4–5-toothed, sometimes accrescent, free or adherent to the fruit, valvate or imbricate. Petals 3–6, valvate or imbricate, free or more or less coherent. Stamens 3–15, inserted with the petals and more or less adnate to them, all antheriferous or rarely some without anthers; filaments free or rarely monadelphous; anthers erect, 2-celled, dehiscing longitudinally. Disk hypogynous or perigynous, cup-shaped or 0. Ovary free or half-inferior, 1-celled or imperfectly 2–3–5-celled (from the dissepiments not reaching the apex of the cavity); ovules 1–5, pendulous from the apex of a minute free central placenta, or from the side or apex of the ovarian cavity, the funicle (or ? placenta) often dilated into a thickened process above the ovule; style simple or 0; stigmas 1 (rarely 2), entire or lobed. Fruit drupaceous or dry, indehiscent, 1- (rarely 2-) celled, 1- (rarely 2-) seeded, free or more or less adnate to the calyx-tube and disk. Seed pendulous; albumen fleshy, entire or lobed, rarely wanting; radicle superior; cotyledons leafy, flat or folded, rarely fleshy.—DISTRIB. Tropics of both hemispheres; genera about 45; species about 220.

Stamens 10; calyx not accrescent .... 1. XIMENIA.
Stamens 3; calyx accrescent .... 2. OLAX.
Stamens usually 5 (rarely 4).
  Stamens opposite the petals or the lobes of the calyx when petals are absent.
    Stamens 5; ovary 3–5-celled .... 3. STROMBOSIA.
    Stamens 4–5; ovary 1-celled; petals 0 .... 4. CANSJERA.
  Stamens 5, alternate with the petals.
    Trees or erect shrubs.
      Petals glabrous within.
        Petals connate .... 5. GOMPHANDRA.
        Petals free .... 6. APODYTES.
      Petals villous within .... 7. MAPPIA.
    A climbing shrub .... 8. SARCOSTIGMA.

1. XIMENIA, Linn.

Shrubs or low trees; branches spiny. Leaves alternate, quite entire. Flowers rather large, racemose, usually hermaphrodite. Calyx small, 4–5-toothed or -lobed, not altered in fruit. Petals 4–5, hypogynous, valvate, hairy within. Stamens twice as many as the petals, hypogynous; anthers innate, linear, erect. Staminodes 0. Ovary superior, 3–4-celled; ovule solitary in each cell, pendulous, anatropous; style columnar: stigma simple. Drupe ovoid, 1-celled; stone solitary.—DISTRIB. Throughout the Tropics of both hemispheres; species 4–5.

1. **Ximenia americana,** *Linn. Sp. Pl.* (1753) p. 1193. A small much-branched spiny shrub; young parts glabrous; branches often ending in a spine. Leaves coriaceous, 1–2 by $\frac{1}{2}$–$1\frac{1}{2}$ in., elliptic, obtuse at both ends, the apex sometimes emarginate; petioles scarcely $\frac{1}{4}$ in. long. Flowers white, fragrant, bisexual or sometimes polygamous, $\frac{3}{8}$ in. long, in short racemes which are axillary or on the ends of lateral twigs; buds oblong, subacute; pedicels short; bracts minute, subulate. Calyx small, glabrous, deeply divided; lobes 5, ovate, acute, ultimately reflexed. Petals much longer than the calyx, $\frac{7}{16}$ in. long, equalling the stamens in length, linear-oblong, acute, shaggy inside. Ovary glabrous, ovoid-conical, longitudinally sulcate, rugose. Fruit ovoid or ellipsoid, $\frac{3}{4}$–1 in. long, deep orange when ripe; pericarp pulpy; endocarp 1-celled, 1-seeded. Fl. B. I. v. 1, p. 574; Trim. Fl. Ceyl. v. 1, p. 255; Talb. Trees, Bomb. p. 44; Woodr. in Journ. Bomb. Nat. v. 11 (1897) p. 269; Watt, Dict. Econ. Prod. v. 6, part 4, p. 319.—Flowers: Jan.–Feb.

S. M. COUNTRY: Kedur, near Badámi, *Woodrow*!; north-east of Belgaum, *Ritchie*, 994!—DISTRIB. India (E. & W. Peninsulas); Malaya, Tropical Africa, America.

2. OLAX, Linn.

Trees or shrubs often scandent, sometimes armed. Leaves alternate. Flowers small, in axillary simple or branched racemes. Calyx minute, cup-shaped, truncate or obscurely toothed, much enlarged in fruit, enclosing the drupe, but free. Petals 4–6, hypogynous, free or more or less coherent, valvate. Stamens (fertile) usually 3, generally opposite the edges of the petals and attached to their bases, rarely opposite their centres; anthers adnate to the filaments, oblong, 2-celled, dehiscing longitudinally. Staminodes 5–6, bifid, usually opposite the petals. Ovary free, more or less 3-celled below, 1-celled above, usually surrounded by a cup-shaped hypogynous disk; ovules 3, linear, pendulous from the apex of a central placenta; style simple; stigma 3-lobed. Drupe globose or oblong, more or less covered by the accrescent calyx; stone crustaceous, 1-celled, 1-seeded. Seed spuriously erect, albuminous; embryo minute in the apex of fleshy albumen; radicle superior.—DISTRIB. Chiefly in the Tropics of the Old World, a few in Australia; species 25–30.

Climbing shrubs.
  Armed; drupe ⅝ in. .... 1. *O. scandens.*
  Unarmed; drupe ¾ in. .... 2. *O. Wightiana.*
A low undershrub; pedicels solitary .... 3. *O. nana.*

1. **Olax scandens,** *Roxb. Cor. Pl.* v. 2 (1798) p. 2, t. 102. A climbing, much-branched shrub, armed with slightly curved stout prickles on the old wood; branches terete, more or less pubescent. Leaves 2–3½ by 1–1½ in., elliptic or oblong-elliptic, usually obtuse, glabrous above, glabrous or pubescent beneath, entire, base rounded or subacute; petioles ⅛–¼ in. long, pubescent. Flowers white, fragrant, about ¼ in. long, in axillary racemes which are shorter than the leaves; buds oblong, somewhat clavate; pedicels short, pubescent; bracts ovate-oblong, as long as the pedicels, pubescent, ciliate, caducous. Calyx cup-shaped, truncate, ciliate. Petals linear, acute, more or less connate. Stamens about half as long as the petals. Ovary ovoid, glabrous; style about half as long as the petals; stigma 3-lobed. Drupes globose, ⅝ in. in diam., apiculate, covered, except the top, by the accrescent calyx. Fl. B. I. v. 1, p. 575; Grah. Cat. p. 22; Trim. Fl. Ceyl. v. 1, p. 256; Engler, in Engl. & Prantl, Pflanzenf. v. 3, part 1, p. 240, fig. 153; Talb. Trees, Bomb. p. 44; Woodr. in Journ. Bomb. Nat. v. 11 (1897) p. 270; Watt, Dict. Econ. Prod. v. 5, p. 479.—Flowers: Feb.

Along the Ghâts, *Graham.* DECCAN: Khandala, *Woodrow, Graham.* KANARA: Nilkund (N. Kanara), *Woodrow.*—DISTRIB. Throughout Tropical India and Birma; Ceylon.

2. **Olax Wightiana,** *Wall. Cat.* (1828) 6779. A large much-branched unarmed scandent shrub or small tree; young parts glabrous. Leaves 3–5 by 1¼–2¼ in., oblong-elliptic, acuminate, subacute or obtuse, glabrous and shining, entire, base acute or rounded; petioles ¼ in. long. Flowers about ⅜ in. long, white, in axillary solitary or clustered racemes about 1 in. long; buds clavate; pedicels puberulous or subglabrous; bracts minute, much shorter than the pedicels, caducous. Calyx externally puberulous, truncate or obscurely lobed. Petals puberulous on the outside near the apex, linear, acute. Stamens 3, each inserted at the edge of a petal and about half its length. Staminodes 5, opposite the petals and nearly as long as them. Ovary ovoid, glabrous; style a little shorter than the petals; stigma deeply 3-lobed. Drupes ¾ in. long, oblong or subglobose, covered, except at the top, by the accrescent calyx. Fl. B. I. v. 1, p. 575; Dalz. & Gibs. p. 27; Trim. Fl. Ceyl. v. 1, p. 256; Talb. Trees, Bomb. p. 44; Woodr. in Journ. Bomb. Nat. v. 11 (1897) p. 270.—Flowers: Dec.–Feb.

KONKAN: high hills, *Dalzell*!, *Law*!; Campuli, *Woodrow*! DECCAN: Dabili, near Poona, *Woodrow*! KANARA: common in the evergreen forests of the Ghâts of N. Kanara, from Ainshi southwards, *Talbot*; Falls of Gairsoppa, *Talbot*!—DISTRIB. India (W. Peninsula); Ceylon, Malacca.

3. **Olax nana,** *Wall. Cat.* (1828) 6783. A low undershrub; branches from a woody rootstock, twiggy. Leaves subsessile, 1–2$\frac{1}{4}$ by $\frac{1}{4}$–$\frac{5}{8}$ in., oblong-lanceolate, obtuse, glabrous, base usually acute; midrib strong. Flowers $\frac{1}{4}$–$\frac{5}{16}$ in. long, white, solitary, axillary; pedicels slender, $\frac{1}{4}$–$\frac{1}{2}$ in. long. Calyx free, minute, cup-shaped, truncate or obscurely lobed. Petals 3, oblong-obovate, rounded at the apex, the tip inflexed, cohering about half way up but readily separable. Stamens 3, one in the centre of each petal, a little more than half the length of the petal and adnate to it about half way up; anthers yellow. Staminodes 6, one at each edge of each petal and a little shorter than it. Ovary ovoid; style shorter than the stamens. Fruit globose, $\frac{1}{4}$ in. long, apiculate, deep yellow when ripe, nearly covered by the accrescent calyx, 1-seeded. Fl. B. I. v. 1, p. 576; Woodr. in Journ. Bomb. Nat. v. 11 (1897) p. 270; Watt, Dict. Econ. Prod. v. 5, p. 479.

GUJARAT: Rajkot (Kathiawar), *C. Macnaghten*!—DISTRIB. India (W. Himalaya, Punjab, Nipal).

3. STROMBOSIA, Blume.

Trees or shrubs, usually glabrous. Leaves alternate, coriaceous, quite entire. Flowers small, in axillary cymes, regular, hermaphrodite. Calyx: a shallow cup, more or less 5-lobed. Petals 5, free, hairy within, valvate. Stamens 5, opposite the petals and adnate to them; anthers 2-celled. Staminodes 0. Ovary inferior or superior, more or less imperfectly 4–5-celled, surrounded by a lobed disk; ovules 4–5, pendulous from a central placenta. Fruit drupaceous; stone crustaceous. Seed pendulous; embryo minute, within fleshy albumen.—DISTRIB. Species 6, one in Tropical Africa, the others Tropical Asiatic.

1. **Strombosia ceylanica,** *Gard. in Calc. Journ. Nat. Hist.* v. 6 (1846) p. 350. A large tree with greyish bark. Leaves coriaceous, 3$\frac{1}{2}$–6$\frac{1}{2}$ by 1$\frac{1}{2}$–2$\frac{1}{4}$ in., oblong-lanceolate, shortly acuminate, acute or obtuse, glabrous, base inequilateral, usually acute; petioles $\frac{1}{2}$ in. long, glabrous. Flowers subsessile, crowded in heads on axillary scaly tubercles. Calyx minute; lobes very short, suborbicular. Petals longer than the calyx, linear-oblong, acute, externally glabrous, hairy within, recurved at the apex. Filaments opposite the petals and adnate to them throughout their whole length, the anthers appearing as if sessile in the centre of the petals about one-third the way below their apex. Disk large, fleshy. Ovary inferior, adnate to the calyx-tube, 5-celled. Fruit pyriform when young, more or less globose when old, apiculate, rugose, deep purple, tuberculate when ripe. Fl. B. I. v. 1, p. 579; Trim. Fl. Ceyl. v. 1, p. 257; Talb. Trees, Bomb. p. 45; Woodr. in Journ. Bomb. Nat. v. 11 (1897) p. 270. *Sphærocarya leprosa*, Dalz. in Hook. Kew Journ. v. 3 (1851) p. 34; Dalz. & Gibs. p. 223.—Flowers: Dec.

KONKAN: *Law*!; in the Wari Country, *Dalzell & Gibson*; Konkan Ghâts, *Talbot*. KANARA: *Dalzell*!; Poteli (N. Kanara), *Woodrow*; N. Kanara Ghâts, *Talbot*.—DISTRIB. India (W. Peninsula); Ceylon.

4. CANSJERA, Juss.

Climbing shrubs, sometimes spiny. Leaves alternate, entire, penninerved. Flowers in short axillary spikes, hermaphrodite, monochlamydeous. Perianth tubular or urceolate, regular, 4–5-lobed. Stamens as many as the lobes of the perianth and opposite to them; filaments glabrous, free, or attached between the thick fleshy lobes of the disk; anthers small, oblong, adnate, 2-celled, dehiscing longitudinally. Ovary superior, ovoid-conical, glabrous; ovule solitary, pendulous from a short placenta; style cylindric; stigma capitate, 4-lobed. Fruit superior, drupaceous, surrounded at the base by the marcescent perianth; mesocarp thin; endocarp bony. Seed solitary, erect, roundish; embryo in the upper part of fleshy albumen; radicle superior; cotyledons sometimes 3, very long, plano-convex.—DISTRIB. Tropical Asia and Australia; species 4.

1. **Cansjera Rheedii,** *J. F. Gmel. Linn. Syst. Nat.* ed. 13, v. 2 (1791) p. 280. A climbing shrub, sometimes spiny; young branches yellowish-green, pubescent. Leaves $1\frac{1}{2}$–$3\frac{3}{4}$ by $\frac{5}{8}$–$1\frac{5}{8}$ in., thinly coriaceous, oblong-lanceolate or ovate, glabrous on both surfaces, base narrowed or rounded, often slightly inequilateral; main nerves 3–5 pairs, curved, ascending; petioles $\frac{1}{16}$–$\frac{1}{8}$ in. long. Flowers $\frac{1}{10}$ in. long, in pubescent axillary spikes $\frac{1}{2}$–1 in. long, one or two spikes from an axil; bracts minute, linear-lanceolate, one at the base of each flower. Perianth pubescent externally, urceolate, 4–5-toothed, the apices of the teeth recurved. Fruit about $\frac{1}{2}$ in. long, ovoid or ellipsoid, orange-red, surmounted by the remains of the style, glabrous. Fl. B. I. v. 1, p. 582; Bedd. For. Man. in Flor. Sylvat. p. clxxix, t. 26, fig. 6; Trim. Fl. Ceyl. v. 1, p. 259; Talb. Trees, Bomb. p. 45; Woodr. in Journ. Bomb. Nat. v. 11 (1897) p. 270.—Flowers: Nov.–Dec.

KONKAN: *Law*!; Elephanta, *Graham*; Salsette, *Graham*. DECCAN: valley of the Koina, *Cooke*! S. M. COUNTRY: Párva Ghát (Belgaum districts), *Ritchie*!; hills east of Belgaum, *Ritchie*, 926! KANARA: on the Ghâts in evergreen moist forests, *Talbot*; Yellapur, *Woodrow*.—DISTRIB. Throughout India; Indian Archipelago, Hongkong, N. Australia.

5. GOMPHANDRA, Wall.

Shrubs or trees. Leaves alternate, entire, penninerved (rarely 3-nerved at the base). Flowers small, polygamo-diœcious, cymose. Calyx cup-shaped, minutely 4–5-toothed. Petals 4 or 5, inserted on a short hypogynous disk, more or less connate into a corolla, free at the apex, valvate, often absent in the female flowers. Stamens 4 or 5, hypogynous, alternate with the petals; filaments fleshy, flattened, usually with a small tuft of gland-tipped hairs at the top on the back, hollowed in front; anthers small, pendulous from the apices of the filaments, 2-lobed, dehiscing longitudinally. MALE FLOWERS with rudimentary ovary sunk in the fleshy disk; stigma minute. FEMALE FLOWERS with long cylindric 1-celled ovary and large discoid stigma; ovules 2, collateral, pendulous from the apex, the funicle dilated. Fruit elongate, drupe-like, surmounted by the remains of the stigma; pericarp smooth, thin; endocarp leathery. Seed solitary, pendulous; albumen fleshy, bipartite; embryo minute.—DISTRIB. Tropical Asia; species 5 or 6.

Leaves thin; inflorescence axillary; hairs on the filaments usually very long .... 1. *G. axillaris.*
Leaves coriaceous; inflorescence extra-axillary or leaf-opposed; hairs on the filaments short or 0.. 2. *G. polymorpha.*

1. **Gomphandra axillaris,** *Wall. Cat.* (1828) 3718. A shrub or small tree; branches terete, glabrous or puberulous. Leaves thin, reaching 6 in. in length, very variable in breadth, from broadly elliptic-oblong to narrow-lanceolate, acuminate, entire, glabrous on both surfaces, paler beneath, base acute, rarely rounded; petioles $\frac{1}{4}$–$\frac{1}{2}$ in. long. Flowers practically unisexual, rarely polygamous, very small, 2–10 (usually 3) together, in puberulous paniculate axillary cymes a little longer than the petioles. Calyx minute, cup-shaped, 4–5-toothed, ciliolate. Petals connate into a tubular corolla; lobes 4–5, ovate, acuminate, ultimately spreading, the tips inflexed. Stamens exserted, the hairs usually 3 or 4 times as long as the anthers; pollen-grains acutely trigonous. Ovary small, oblong, 4–5-gonous. Style conical; stigma sessile, 4–5-toothed. Drupes $\frac{1}{2}$–$\frac{5}{8}$ in. long, oblong, blunt at both ends, smooth, white. Seeds large. Fl. B. I. v. 1, p. 586; Bedd. For. Man. in Flor. Sylvat. p. lxi; Trim. Fl. Ceyl. v. 1, p. 261; Talb. Trees, Bomb. p. 45. *Platea axillaris*, Thw. Enum. Pl. Zeyl. p. 44; Dalz. & Gibs. p. 28.—Flowers: Apr.–May.

KONKAN: Gháts, *Talbot.* S. M. COUNTRY: Chorla and Párva Gháts (Belgaum districts), *Dalzell & Gibson.* KANARA: common in the evergreen forests of the Kanara Gháts, *Talbot.*—DISTRIB. India (Silhet and W. Peninsula); Ceylon.

2. **Gomphandra polymorpha,** *Wight, Ill.* (1840) p. 103; *Wight, Icon.* t. 953. A shrub. Leaves coriaceous, otherwise as in the preceding; petioles rather longer than in *G. axillaris.* Flowers more numerous than in that species, rather larger, sessile; panicle leaf-opposed * or extra-axillary, rarely axillary. Corolla more deeply lobed than in *G. axillaris.* Stamens exserted; hairs on the filaments about the length of the anther, sometimes absent. Drupes as in *G. axillaris.* Fl. B. I. v. 1, p. 586; Woodr. in Journ. Bomb. Nat. v. 11 (1897) p. 270. *G. coriacea*, Wight, Ill. p. 103; Bedd. For. Man. in Flor. Sylvat. p. lxi, t. 9, fig. 4; Trim. Fl. Ceyl. v. 1, p. 261.—Flowers: Dec.

KONKAN: *Law!*, *Dalzell!* KANARA: Santaveri, *Woodrow.*—DISTRIB. India (W. Peninsula); Ceylon.

6. APODYTES, E. Meyer.

Shrubs or trees. Leaves entire. Flowers hermaphrodite, small, in corymbose cymes or terminal or axillary panicles. Calyx small, 5-toothed. Petals 5, hypogynous, free, valvate. Stamens 5, alternate with the petals and slightly coherent with them at the base; filaments dilated; anthers 2-lobed. Ovary 1-celled, obliquely gibbous; ovules 2, pendulous, superposed; style excentric, more or less incurved; stigma small. Drupe obliquely ovoid, compressed; stone crustaceous, 1-celled, 1-seeded. Seed pendulous; embryo small, in the apex of fleshy albumen; cotyledons narrow.—DISTRIB. Tropical Asia, Tropical and Subtropical Africa; species 9.

* "The peduncle is at first axillary, but a leaf being most commonly produced upon it at about its middle, its upper part, of course, appears opposite to this new leaf and more strikingly so when a leaf-bud has been developed in the axil of the latter."—*Thwaites, Enum.* p. 44.

1. **Apodytes Beddomei**, *Masters, in Hook. f. Fl. B. I.* v. 1 (1875) p. 588. A shrub. Leaves membranous, 3–5 by 1½–2½ in., turning black in drying, ovate, acute or acuminate, glabrous, base rounded or acute more or less inequilateral; petioles ¼–½ in. long. Flowers ⅛ in. long, in branched terminal panicles; buds ellipsoid; pedicels pubescent, the ultimate ones very short. Calyx small, cup-shaped; lobes obscure, ciliolate. Petals oblong-elliptic, obtuse at the apex. Anthers elongate, linear-oblong. Drupes obliquely ovoid, ⅜ in. long, rugose. *Apodytes Benthamiana*, Var. β, Bedd. Flor. Sylvat. t. 140.—Flowers: Mar.

A very rare plant. I have seen but a single specimen from the Bombay Presidency, collected by *Mr. Talbot* from Dadmune, N. Kanara!—Distrib. India (W. Peninsula).

7. MAPPIA, Jacq.

Trees. Leaves alternate. Flowers small, polygamous, in terminal corymbose cymes, pubescent outside, rarely glabrate. Calyx small, 5-toothed. Petals hypogynous, valvate, villous within. Stamens 5, hypogynous, alternate with the petals; anthers oblong, dorsifixed; connective often mucronate. Disk cup-shaped, surrounding the ovary, sometimes inconspicuous. Ovary 1-celled; ovules 2, pendulous; style short; stigma thickened. Drupe with a slender crustaceous or subwoody putamen. Seed pendulous; embryo large, in fleshy albumen; cotyledons foliaceous; radicle superior.—Distrib. India; Ceylon, Tropical S. America; species 8–10.

1. **Mappia fœtida**, *Miers, Contrib.* v. 1 (1851) p. 64. A small tree with a shady head; young branches pale and with wrinkled bark. Leaves crowded towards the ends of the branches, 3–6 by 1½–3 in., ovate-oblong, acuminate, dark green and glabrous above, paler and pubescent on the nerves beneath, reticulately veined, base rounded or acute more or less inequilateral; petioles ½–1¼ in. long, glabrous or faintly pubescent. Flowers in terminal panicles 2–4 in. long; pedicels stout, densely pubescent. Calyx small, pubescent externally, 5-toothed; teeth triangular, very acute. Petals yellow, ¼ in. long, linear-oblong, acute, densely sericeo-villous on both surfaces, tip inflexed. Stamens 5, a little shorter than the petals and alternate with them; filaments flattened and dilated below, attached to the edges of the petals at the base; anthers elliptic-oblong, not apiculate. Disk shallow, cup-shaped, villous within. Ovary ovoid, densely clothed with silky hairs, free, attenuated into a stout slightly conical style. Drupes ellipsoid or somewhat obovoid, ⅜–⅝ in. long, pubescent when young, glabrous and purple when ripe. Fl. B. I. v. 1, p. 589; Bedd. Flor. Sylvat. t. 141; Talb. Trees, Bomb. p. 45; Woodr. in Journ. Bomb. Nat. v. 11 (1897) p. 270. *Mappia oblonga*, Dalz. & Gibs. p. 28.—Flowers: Oct.–Nov. Vern. *Kálgur*; *Ghánera*.

Common along the Gháts, abundant at Mahableshwar. The flowers are very fetid. Konkan: *Law*!, *Dalzell*!; Western Gháts, widely, *Woodrow*; Gháts opposite Goa, *Dalzell & Gibson*. Deccan: Mahableshwar, abundant, *Cooke*!, *H. M. Birdwood*. S. M. Country: Belgaum, *Ritchie*, 1012!; near Belgaum, *Cooke*! Kanara: Gháts of N. Kanara, *Talbot*.—Distrib. India (W. Peninsula).

8. SARCOSTIGMA, Wight & Arn.

Scandent shrubs. Leaves alternate. Flowers diœcious, minute, in distant sessile fascicles arranged on elongate interrupted spikes. Calyx cup-shaped, unequally 4–5-toothed. Petals 4–5, united into a short tube which is adnate to a stipitiform torus, free above, valvate, slender, flat. MALE FLOWERS: Stamens hypogynous, alternate with the petals and scarcely cohering with them at the base; filaments filiform; anthers versatile. FEMALE FLOWERS: Ovary sessile, 1-celled, superior; ovules 2, pendulous from the apex of the cell, funicle thick; stigma subsessile. Drupe oblong; epicarp coriaceous; putamen woody. Seeds pendulous; albumen 0; cotyledons fleshy, cordate at the base, wrapping round the short superior radicle.—DISTRIB. Tropical Asia; species 3 or 4.

1. **Sarcostigma Kleinii,** *Wight & Arn. in Edin. New Phil. Journ.* (1832–33) p. 299. A large climbing shrub; young branches terete, glabrous. Leaves coriaceous, 4–12 by 2–4 in., oblong, oblong-lanceolate or ovate, acuminate or acute, glabrous, shining, closely reticulately veined (the reticulations prominent on both surfaces), base acute, rarely rounded; petioles $\frac{1}{4}$–$\frac{3}{4}$ in. long. Inflorescence axillary or extra-axillary, in spicate racemes which are solitary or fascicled and longer than the leaves; flowers minute, in fascicles of 1–4, subsessile along a woody rhachis. MALE FLOWERS: Calyx small, cup-shaped, pubescent outside, 5-toothed; teeth short, triangular. Petals $\frac{1}{10}$ in. long, oblong, acute, reflexed. Stamens a little shorter than the petals. Ovary rudimentary, small, conical. FEMALE FLOWERS slightly larger than the male. Calyx and petals as in the male. Stamens small, about half as long as the ovary, hypogynous. Ovary large, oblong or somewhat obovoid, pubescent; stigma large, subsessile, conical. Fruit 1–1$\frac{1}{2}$ in. long, the shape of an olive, bright orange-red, externally rugose. Fl. B. I. v. 1, p. 594; Dalz. & Gibs. p. 221; Miers, Contrib. v. 1, p. 103, t. 18 (female flowers only); Talb. Trees, Bomb. p. 46; Watt, Dict. Econ. Prod. v. 6, part 2, p. 478.—Flowers: Nov.

KANARA: in evergreen forests along the N. Kanara Ghâts; common near the Falls of Gairsoppa, *Talbot*. S. M. COUNTRY: Chorla Ghât (Belgaum districts), *Dalzell & Gibson*.—DISTRIB. India (E. & W. Peninsulas).

ORDER XXXIX. ILICACEÆ.

Trees or shrubs. Leaves usually coriaceous and evergreen, alternate, simple, exstipulate or with 2 minute stipules. Flowers small, usually diœcious, in axillary cymes, fascicles or umbels, the male flowers with an imperfect ovary, the female with imperfect stamens. Calyx persistent, 3–6-partite or -lobed; segments or lobes imbricate. Petals 4–5, rarely 6–8, connate at the base (or connate in the male and free in the female), deciduous, imbricate. Stamens isomerous with the petals, inserted on the base of the corolla; filaments subulate; anthers shortly oblong, dorsifixed. Disk 0. Ovary free, 3–6- (rarely many-) celled; ovules 1 or 2, collateral, pendulous; style very short or 0; stigma capitate or discoid. Drupe with 2 or more 1-seeded free (rarely connate) stones. Seed pendulous; testa membranous; albumen copious, fleshy; embryo minute.—DISTRIB. Chiefly tropical; genera 3; species about 220.

1. ILEX, Linn.

Trees or shrubs. Leaves alternate, often shining. Flowers axillary, white. Calyx small, persistent, 4–6-lobed or 4–6-partite. Corolla rotate, 4–6-partite; lobes obtuse. Stamens isomerous with the corolla-lobes, slightly adherent to the short tube; anthers oblong. Ovary sessile, subglobose, 2–12-celled; ovules 1–2 in each cell; style short, thick, or 0; stigmas free or confluent. Drupe globose, rarely ovoid, with 2–16 stones.—DISTRIB. Tropical and temperate regions of the world, most numerous in N. America, rare in Africa and Australia; species more than 200.

1. **Ilex malabarica,** *Bedd. Flor. Sylvat.* (1871) t. 143. A large tree quite glabrous. Leaves 2–4 by $\frac{7}{8}$–1$\frac{5}{8}$ in., elliptic or lanceolate, acute or acuminate, often mucronate, usually entire but sometimes with one or two spinulose teeth towards the tip, glabrous on both surfaces, dark green and shining above, very pale beneath, base acute; petioles $\frac{1}{8}$–$\frac{1}{4}$ in. long. Flowers in axillary fascicles or very shortly peduncled umbellate cymes, rarely solitary; pedicels 3–8, slender. Calyx puberulous outside; lobes usually 6, broadly ovate, acute, ciliate. Petals white, united at the base into a deciduous corolla about $\frac{1}{10}$ in. long; lobes 4–6, oblong, rounded at the apex. Stamens 4–6, inserted at the base of the corolla; filaments short. Ovary in the female globose; style short, thick; stigma large, obsoletely 6-lobed. Ovary in the male imperfect, with 4 minute stigmas. Drupes small, globose, $\frac{1}{8}$ in. in diam., usually 6-celled, crowned by the thick style and supported by the persistent calyx. Fl. B. I. v. 1, p. 600; Talb. Trees, Bomb. p. 46; Woodr. in Journ. Bomb. Nat. v. 11 (1897) p. 270; Watt, Dict. Econ. Prod. v. 4, p. 328. *Ilex Wightiana,* Dalz. & Gibs. p. 143 (*not* of Wall.).—Flowers: Feb.–Apr.

KONKAN: Ghâts, *Dalzell & Gibson, Stocks!, De Crespigny* ex *Woodrow*; in evergreen forests, *Talbot*; Ghâts near Sivapur (Wari country), *Dalzell!* KANARA: along the banks of streams near Amod, Supa subdivision of N. Kanara, *Talbot.*—DISTRIB. India (W. Peninsula).

ORDER XL. CELASTRACEÆ.

Trees or erect or climbing shrubs, sometimes spinescent. Leaves opposite and alternate, usually coriaceous, simple, never lobed; stipules very caducous or 0. Flowers small, hermaphrodite or polygamous, usually cymose. Calyx small, 4–5-lobed or -partite, imbricate, persistent. Petals 4–5 (rarely 0), inserted under the edge of the disk or continuous with its margin, imbricate. Stamens 5, 4 or 3 (rarely 2), inserted under, on, or within the edge of the disk; filaments subulate, usually short; anthers short, muticous, 2-celled. Disk usually conspicuous, pulvinate or flattened, lobed or entire, rarely 0. Ovary sessile on the disk, free or adherent at the base, 2–5-celled; ovules 1–2 in each cell, anatropous, erect, rarely 1 and pendulous, or many ascending and attached to the axis; raphe ventral in the ascending, dorsal in the pendulous; style short, thick or 0; stigma simple or lobed. Fruit capsular, baccate, drupaceous or samaroid. Seeds usually arillate, sometimes winged; albumen fleshy or 0; embryo usually large; cotyledons flat, foliaceous; radicle almost always inferior.—DISTRIB. Throughout tropical and temperate regions of the world; genera 39; species about 400.

Stamens 4–5 (rarely 10); filaments usually incurved; seeds albuminous.
  Leaves opposite (sometimes alternate in *Lophopetalum*).
    Fruit capsular, dehiscent.
      Ovules 1–2 in each cell.
        Petals free .... 1. EUONYMUS.
        Petals connate .... 2. MICROTROPIS.
      Ovules 4 or more in each cell .... 3. LOPHOPETALUM.
    Fruit indehiscent, coriaceous .... 4. PLEUROSTYLIA.
  Leaves alternate; fruit capsular and dehiscent.
    Cells 2-ovuled.
      Shrubs, usually scandent; ovary free .... 5. CELASTRUS.
      Erect often spinous shrubs; ovary confluent with the disk .... 6. GYMNOSPORIA.
  Leaves alternate and opposite; fruit drupaceous and indehiscent .... 7. ELÆODENDRON.
Stamens 3; filaments recurved; seeds exalbuminous.
  Fruit dry; seeds winged .... 8. HIPPOCRATEA.
  Fruit baccate; seeds not winged .... 9. SALACIA.

1. EUONYMUS, Linn.

Trees or shrubs, usually glabrous. Leaves opposite; stipules caducous. Flowers axillary, small. Calyx 4–5-fid, persistent. Petals 4–5, inserted on the disk; filaments usually very short; anthers broad, 2-celled. Disk large, fleshy, 4–5-lobed. Ovary sunk in the disk, 3–5-celled; ovules 2 in each cell; style short or 0; stigma 3–5-lobed. Capsule 3–5-celled, 3–5-lobed, angled, or winged, sometimes echinate, loculicidally 3–5-valved, cells 1–2-seeded. Seeds enclosed in a fleshy aril, albuminous; cotyledons broad, foliaceous.—DISTRIB. India, China, Japan, Malaya, Europe and N. America; species about 40.

1. **Euonymus indicus,** *Heyne, ex Wall. in Roxb. Fl. Ind. (ed. Carey)* v. 2 (1824) p. 409. A small tree. Leaves coriaceous, 2¼–4 by 1–2¼ in., elliptic or oblong-lanceolate, acute or sometimes shortly acuminate, entire or with a few obscure serrations towards the apex, glabrous on both surfaces, smooth and shining above, base acute; petioles ⅛–⅜ in. long; stipules linear-subulate, very caducous. Flowers about ½ in. across, axillary, solitary or in peduncled umbellate cymes; peduncles 1–2, variable in length, from 0–1¼ in. long; pedicels 1–3, glabrous, when more than 1 and on the top of a peduncle about ¼ in. long, when not peduncled reaching 1 in. long. Calyx glabrous, fleshy, deeply divided; lobes semicircular, entire. Petals reddish, orbicular-oblong, fringed at the apex. Stamens inserted on the disk near its margin; filaments short, flattened. Disk ⅛ in. in diam., 5-lobed, fleshy. Ovary sunk in the disk. Fruit ⅝ in. long, obovoid-clavate, 5-winged. Fl. B. I. v. 1, p. 608; Talb. Trees, Bomb. p. 47; Woodr. in Journ. Bomb. Nat. v. 11 (1897) p. 270. *Euonymus Goughii*, Wight, Ill. v. 1, p. 178; Dalz. & Gibs. p. 47; Wight, Icon. t. 215.—Flowers: Dec.–Feb.

S. M. COUNTRY: Castlerock, *Woodrow, Kanitkar!* KANARA: evergreen forests of N. Kanara Ghâts; common on the S. Ghâts of N. Kanara, *Talbot*; Devimane Ghât, N. Kanara, *Woodrow!*—DISTRIB. India (W. Peninsula).

2. MICROTROPIS, Wall.

Glabrous trees or shrubs. Leaves opposite, persistent, exstipulate, entire. Flowers in sessile clusters or peduncled cymes, axillary or supra-axillary, sometimes unisexual. Sepals 5, imbricate. Petals 5 (rarely 0), connate at the base. Stamens 5, inserted on the disk or the tube of the corolla; filaments very short; anthers broadly ovate. Disk 0 or annular, free or connate with the petals. Ovary free, ovoid, perfectly or imperfectly 2-3-celled; ovules 2 in each cell, collateral at the inner angle; style thick; stigma minute, 2-4-lobed. Capsule oblong, coriaceous, 1-celled, 2-valved, 1-seeded, tardily dehiscent, surrounded at the base by the calyx. Seed erect, exarillate; testa polished.—DISTRIB. Singapore, Nepal, Ceylon, Malaya, Java; species 9.

Flowers in sessile clusters .... 1. *M. latifolia.*
Flowers in peduncled cymes .... 2. *M. microcarpa.*

1. **Microtropis latifolia,** *Wight, MSS. ex Laws. in Fl. B. I.* v. 1 (1875) p. 613. A small tree. Leaves coriaceous, opposite, 3½-5 by 1¾-3 in., elliptic, acute or shortly acuminate, glabrous, light green above, very pale beneath, reticulately veined, base acute, margins repand; petioles ¼-½ in. long, rugose. Flowers sessile, in axillary or extra-axillary clusters. Calyx 5-lobed, externally rugose, the upper margin membranous, lacerate. Petals $\frac{1}{10}$-⅛ in. long, obovate-cuneate, united at the base into a ring. Stamens inserted on the ring, erect; filaments short, flat. Ovary somewhat flask-shaped, furrowed. Fruit ½-¾ in. long, oblong-ellipsoid, narrowed at both ends. Seeds rugose. Fl. B. I. v. 1, p. 613; Talb. Trees, Bomb. p. 47.

KONKAN: without locality, *Stocks*!—DISTRIB. India (W. Peninsula).

2. **Microtropis microcarpa,** *Wight, Icon.* (1845) t. 975. An erect shrub. Leaves coriaceous, opposite, 1½-2 by ¾-1 in., elliptic or oblong-lanceolate, subobtuse, glabrous above, pale beneath, base acute, margins repand; petioles ¼ in. long. Flowers in peduncled cymes, shorter than the leaves. Calyx large, 5-lobed, persistent in fruit, much imbricate, the lower part thick and fleshy and externally rugose, the upper part membranous, petal-like, lacerate. Petals about ⅛ in. long, obovate, clawed, veined, soon falling off. Stamens inserted at the base of the petals; filaments very short; anthers large. Ovary ovoid-conical, ribbed; style very short. Fruit ½ in. long, narrow-oblong, subcylindric or ellipsoid, pointed, apiculate, longitudinally rugose. Seed 1; testa reddish-brown, shining. Fl. B. I. v. 1, p. 614; Talb. Trees, Bomb. p. 47.

KONKAN: without locality, *Stocks*!—DISTRIB. India (W. Peninsula).

3. LOPHOPETALUM, Wight.

Glabrous trees or shrubs. Leaves opposite or alternate, exstipulate. Flowers rather large, in axillary or terminal cymes. Calyx 5-lobed; lobes short, rounded. Petals 4-5, continuous with the disk, persistent, the inner side cristate or lamellate, the margins usually fimbriate. Stamens 5-6, inserted on the disk; filaments subulate; anthers oblong. Disk large, usually 4-5-lobed. Ovary small, continuous with the disk and immersed in it, trigonal or pyramidal, 3–4-celled, contracted into the style; ovules 4 or more in each cell, 2-seriate; style short; stigma capitate. Capsule coriaceous, 3–4-angled, 3–4-celled, loculicidally dehiscent. Seeds few or many, rarely winged, arillate; albumen fleshy.—DISTRIB. India, Malaya, Java; species about 9.

1. **Lophopetalum Wightianum,** *Arn. in Ann. Nat. Hist.* ser. 1, v. 3 (1839) p. 151. A large tree. Leaves 3–6 by 1¼–2¼ in., coriaceous, ovate-oblong or oblong-lanceolate, acute or shortly and bluntly acuminate, glabrous, entire, reticulately veined, base rounded or subacute; petioles ½–⅝ in. long, striate. Flowers nearly ¾ in. across, in branched terminal and axillary panicled cymes. Calyx 5-lobed, adhering to the disk; lobes orbicular. Petals obovate, continuous with the lobes of the disk, with a membranous laciniate crest on the inner face, minutely denticulate at the apex. Disk fleshy, more than ¼ in. in diam., 5-lobed, adherent to the calyx. Ovary glabrous, triangular in cross section at the base, sunk in the disk; style short, conical. Fruit sharply triangular in cross section, 4 in. long, 3-celled. Seeds oblong, compressed, surrounded by a long linear wing (*fide* Dalzell & Gibson l. c.). Fl. B. I. v. 1, p. 615; Dalz. & Gibs. p. 48; Wight, Icon. t. 162; Bedd. Flor. Sylvat. t. 145; Talb. Trees, Bomb. p. 47; Woodr. in Journ. Bomb. Nat. v. 11 (1897) p. 270; Watt, Dict. Econ. Prod. v. 5, p. 92.—Flowers: Mar.–May. VERN. *Balpale.*

KONKAN: *Dalzell*, 1669!; Wari, *Stocks*!; S. Konkan, *Woodrow*!; evergreen forests of the Konkan Ghâts, *Talbot*. KANARA: in evergreen forests of the Ghâts, *Talbot*; Sampkhand, *Woodrow*.—DISTRIB. India (W. Peninsula).

4. PLEUROSTYLIA, Wight & Arn.

Trees or shrubs. Leaves opposite, exstipulate. Cymes axillary, short, few-flowered. Calyx small, 4-lobed. Petals 5, exceeding the calyx. Stamens 5, inserted below the disk; filaments short, flat; connective of the anthers dilated at the back. Disk thick, crenulate. Ovary half-immersed in the disk and confluent with it, 1–2-celled; ovules 2 in each cell, erect; style short, thick; stigma broad, peltate. Fruit coriaceous, indehiscent, 1–2-celled. Seed 1 (rarely 2), erect, covered by an arilliform endocarp; testa coriaceous; albumen copious, fleshy; cotyledons large, orbicular.—DISTRIB. Mountains of the Indian Peninsula, Ceylon, Mauritius, and Madagascar; species 2.

1. **Pleurostylia Wightii,** *Wight & Arn. Prodr.* (1834) p. 157. A shrub or small much-branched tree; young parts glabrous; bark rough, pale. Leaves 1½–2½ by ¾–1¼ in., elliptic-oblong, oblong-lanceolate or somewhat obovate, usually rounded at the apex, sometimes emarginate, pale, glabrous, reticulately veined, entire, acutely tapering at the base; petioles very short, scarcely ⅛ in. long. Flowers ⅛–⅙ in. across, in small axillary paniculate cymes; peduncles short, more or less pubescent; pedicels usually shorter than the peduncles. Calyx glabrous; lobes short, rounded. Petals elliptic-oblong, rounded at the apex, concave. Stamens shorter than the petals. Drupes ⅜ in. long, ovoid, supported on the persistent calyx, white, smooth. Fl. B. I. v. 1, p. 617; Dalz. & Gibs. p. 47; Bedd. For. Man. in Flor. Sylvat. p. lxvi, t. 10, fig. 1; Trim. Fl. Ceyl.

v. 1, p. 271; Talb. Trees, Bomb. p. 48; Woodr. in Journ. Bomb. Nat. v. 11 (1897) p. 270.

The Ghâts, *Dalzell & Gibson*.—DISTRIB. India (mountains of the W. Peninsula); Ceylon, Mauritius, Madagascar.

5. CELASTRUS, Linn.

Shrubs usually scandent, unarmed. Leaves alternate; stipules minute or 0. Flowers in axillary and terminal racemes or panicles, sometimes unisexual. Calyx urceolate at the base, 5-fid. Petals 5, inserted below the disk, spreading at the apex. Stamens 5, inserted on the margin of the disk. Disk cup-shaped or concave, 5-lobed. Ovary seated on the disk (not immersed), 2-4-lobed, 2-4-celled; ovules 2 from the base of the cell, collateral, erect; style thick; stigma 3-4-lobed. Capsule terete, globose or oblong, coriaceous, 2-4-celled, dehiscing loculicidally, the cells 1-2-seeded. Seeds erect, enclosed in a fleshy aril; testa membranous; albumen copious, fleshy; cotyledons foliaceous.—DISTRIB. Tropical Asia, China, Japan, Australia, N. America, and Madagascar; species about 15.

1. **Celastrus paniculata,** *Willd. Sp. Pl.* v. 1 (1797) p. 1125. A climbing unarmed shrub; young branches usually covered with pale lenticular warts. Leaves alternate, $2\frac{1}{2}$–4 by $1\frac{1}{4}$–$2\frac{1}{4}$ in., broadly elliptic, ovate, or obovate, shortly acuminate, crenate-serrate in the upper part, usually entire near the base, glabrous, base rounded or acute; petioles $\frac{1}{4}$–$\frac{1}{2}$ in. long. Flowers yellowish- or greenish-white, unisexual, in terminal pyramidal panicles 2–6 in. long; pedicels pubescent; bracts small, lanceolate. Calyx pubescent outside; lobes semiorbicular, ciliate. Petals $\frac{1}{8}$ in. long, oblong, rounded at the apex. MALE FLOWERS: Stamens inserted on the margin of the disk; filaments short; anthers oblong, about $\frac{1}{12}$ in. long. Rudimentary ovary small, subconical, slightly 3-toothed at the apex. FEMALE FLOWERS: Ovary globose, narrowed into a short stout style, glabrous; stigma large, 3-lobed. Stamens inserted on the edge of the disk which is larger than the disk in the male flowers; anthers small, without pollen, ovate, acute or subtriangular, about $\frac{1}{32}$ in. long. Capsules $\frac{3}{8}$–$\frac{1}{2}$ in. in diam., subglobose, bright yellow, transversely wrinkled, 3-valved, the valves spreading after dehiscence remaining united at the base exposing the seeds. Seeds 1–6, often solitary, ovoid, cinnamon-brown, striate, completely enveloped in a scarlet fleshy aril. Fl. B. I. v. 1, p. 617; Grah. Cat. p. 38; Dalz. & Gibs. p. 47; Trim. Fl. Ceyl. v. 1, p. 272; Lösener, in Engl. & Prantl, Pflanzenf. v. 3, part 5, p. 194, fig. 120, E–H; Talb. Trees, Bomb. p. 48; Woodr. in Journ. Bomb. Nat. v. 11 (1897) p. 270; Watt, Dict. Econ. Prod. v. 2, p. 237.—Flowers: Nov.–Feb. VERN. *Mál-kángoni*; *Karad-kángoni*.

KONKAN: throughout the hilly parts, *Graham*, *Dalzell & Gibson*; Matheran, *H. M. Birdwood*. DECCAN: hills near Alandi (Poona districts), *Kanitkar*!; Deccan, widely, ex *Woodrow*. GUJARAT: widely, ex *Woodrow*. S. M. COUNTRY: Belgaum, *Ritchie*, 1668!

An oil of some therapeutic value is extracted from the seeds and known as Black Oil (*Oleum nigrum*). Consult Watt, Dict. Econ. Prod. l. c.—DISTRIB. Throughout India in hilly districts; Ceylon, Malaya, Philippines.

6. GYMNOSPORIA, Wight & Arn.

Shrubs or small trees often spinous. Leaves alternate, exstipulate. Flowers small, greenish or yellow, in axillary solitary or fascicled cymes. Calyx 4–5-fid or 4–5-partite. Petals 4–5, spreading. Stamens 4–5, inserted on the margin of, or beneath the disk; anthers broadly didymous. Disk broad, lobed or sinuate. Ovary usually with a broad base, confluent with the disk, trigonal or pyramidal, 2–3-celled; ovules 2 in each cell; style short; stigmas 3. Capsule obovoid or rarely globose, 3-gonous, 2–3-celled, 1–4-seeded. Seeds with a perfect or imperfect aril or exarillate; testa coriaceous; albumen fleshy; cotyledons foliaceous.—DISTRIB. Dry and hot parts of Asia, Africa, Australia, and Malaya; less common in the Pacific and Mascarene Islands; species about 55.

Branches unarmed.
Cymes dichotomous, 1–2 in. long .... 1. *G. puberula.*
Branches armed.
Cymes reduced to subsessile clusters from tubercles on the old wood; ripe capsules bright red .... 2. *G. Rothiana.*
Cymes axillary; ripe capsules dark purple .... 3. *G. montana.*

1. **Gymnosporia puberula,** *Laws. in Hook. f. Fl. B. I.* v. 1 (1875) p. 619. A shrub; branches unarmed. Leaves 2–2⅞ by 1–1⅜ in., obovate, acute or acuminate, serrate-crenate, reticulately veined, glabrous or nearly so above, hispid on the nerves and veins beneath, base tapering, acute; petioles ⅛–¼ in. long. Flowers in slender, dichotomous cymes 1–2 in. long, which are axillary or fascicled at the ends of short branches; pedicels slender; bracts lanceolate, acute. Calyx deeply divided; lobes suborbicular. Petals $\frac{1}{10}$ in. long, elliptic, obtuse. Fruit obovoid, ⅓ in. long. Talb. Trees, Bomb. p. 48.

KONKAN: *Law!* KANARA: forests near the Ainshi Ghát (N. Kanara), ex *Talbot.*—DISTRIB. Apparently endemic in the Bombay Presidency.

2. **Gymnosporia Rothiana,** *Laws. in Hook. f. Fl. B. I.* v. 1 (1875) p. 620. A large shrub, sometimes a small tree, usually armed with long straight thorns. Leaves coriaceous, 3–4½ by 1¾–2½, broadly obovate-cuneate, rounded or very shortly and bluntly acuminate at the apex, crenulate, dark green, glabrous and polished above, pale beneath, reticulately veined, the veins not prominent on the underside; petioles ¼–⅜ in. long, stout. Flowers greenish-white, in short-peduncled or subsessile cymes or fascicles from the tubercles of the older branches. Calyx glabrous, divided nearly to the base; lobes broadly ovate or triangular, with membranous ciliolate margins. Petals ⅛ in. long, ovate-oblong, obtuse, the margin entire or faintly denticulate. Stamens shorter than the petals; filaments flattened, inserted below the 10-lobed fleshy disk at alternate sinuses. Ovary glabrous; style stout, short, subcylindric; stigmas 3, as long as the style, spreading. Capsules 3-lobed, bright red when ripe, the valves turning back in dehiscence shewing their white inner surfaces. Seeds 6, ellipsoid, ¼ in. long, with a small basal aril, brownish-orange, smooth, shining. Talb. Trees, Bomb. p. 48; Woodr. in Journ. Bomb. Nat. v. 11 (1897) p. 270. *Celastrus Rothiana*, Wight & Arn. Prodr. p. 159; Dalz. & Gibs. p. 47 and p. 318. *Celastrus emarginata*, Grah. Cat. p. 39 (*not* of Roth).—Flowers: Apr.–June. VERN. *Yenkli.*

KONKAN: hills in the Konkan, common, *Dalzell & Gibson*; Matheran, *Kanitkar*! S. M. COUNTRY: Ramghát, *Ritchie*, 141! DECCAN: Panchgani, *Woodrow*; Mahableshwar, *Cooke*!, *Graham*. KANARA: *Ward*!; Katgal (N. Kanara), *Talbot*.—DISTRIB. Apparently endemic.

3. **Gymnosporia montana,** *Benth. Fl. Austral.* v. 1 (1863) p. 400. A tall shrub or sometimes a small tree; young branches often spinescent at the extremities and bearing leaves and flowers. Leaves turning very pale in drying, coriaceous, about $1\frac{1}{4}$–2 by $\frac{3}{4}$–$1\frac{1}{2}$, variable in size and shape, elliptic or obovate, usually rounded at the apex, entire or crenulate, tapering at the base into the petiole; petioles $\frac{1}{8}$–$\frac{3}{8}$ in. long. Flowers in axillary usually furcately-branched cymes; peduncles slender, solitary or fascicled; pedicels filiform, jointed below the middle; bracts small, lanceolate, acute. Calyx-lobes broadly elliptic-oblong, rounded at the apex, ciliate. Petals $\frac{1}{8}$ in. long, elliptic-oblong. Filaments flattened and dilated at the base. Disk fleshy, 10-lobed. Ovary glabrous, orbicular; style in the fertile flowers deeply 2–3-cleft. Capsules about as large as a good-sized peppercorn or small pea, purple when ripe. Seeds glabrous, chestnut-brown, rugose, arillate. Fl. B. I. v. 1, p. 621; Talb. Trees, Bomb. p. 48; Woodr. in Journ. Bomb. Nat. v. 11 (1897) p. 270. *Celastrus montana*, Roth, Nov. Pl. Sp. (1821) p. 154; Roxb. Fl. Ind. v. 1, p. 620; Grah. Cat. p. 38; Dalz. & Gibs. p. 48. *Celastrus senegalensis*, Lam. Encyc. v. 1, p. 661; Bedd. For. Man. in Flor. Sylvat. p. lxvi, t. 10, fig. 2; Watt, Dict. Econ. Prod. v. 2, p. 239.—Flowers: Oct. VERN. *Hekel*; *Mál-kánguni*.

KONKAN: *Law*!, *Stocks*! DECCAN: hills near Alandi (Poona districts), *Kanitkar*!; Kamatki Ghát, abundant, *Woodrow*; Kartriz hills (Poona districts), *Kanitkar*!; Dongergaon (near Ahmednagar), *Cooke*!; Khandesh, *Edgeworth*! GUJARAT: Koodiana, *Dalzell & Gibson*. KANARA: Sirsi, *Hohenhacker*, 734! SIND: *Dalzell & Gibson*.—DISTRIB. India (Central, South-western, and North-western parts); Afghanistan, Central Africa, Malaya, Australia.

7. ELÆODENDRON, Jacq. f.

Trees and shrubs, usually glabrous. Leaves opposite and alternate; stipules minute, caducous. Flowers in axillary cymes, small, sometimes polygamous, usually white or green; peduncles solitary or fascicled. Calyx 4–5-partite. Petals 4–5, spreading. Stamens 4–5, inserted beneath the margin of the disk; filaments short, subulate; anthers subglobose. Disk thick, 4–5-sinuate, -angled or -lobed. Ovary pyramidal, confluent with the disk, usually 3-gonous, 2–5-celled; ovules 2 in each cell; style very short; stigma 2–5-lobed. Drupes dry or succulent; stone 1–3-celled, cells 1- (rarely 2-) seeded. Seeds erect, exarillate; albumen fleshy; cotyledons flat.—DISTRIB. Tropical Asia, America and Australia, S. Africa; species 30.

1. **Elæodendron glaucum,** *Pers. Syn.* v. 1 (1805) p. 241. A small tree. Leaves $2\frac{1}{2}$–6 by 1–$2\frac{1}{2}$ in., extremely variable, elliptic, acute or acuminate, often twisted at the apex, crenate-serrate or subentire, glabrous, base acute or rounded; petioles $\frac{1}{2}$–$\frac{3}{4}$ in. long. Flowers numerous, in divaricate axillary or extra-axillary paniculate dichotomously branched cymes; pedicels slender, glabrous; bracts small, ovate, acute. Calyx very deeply divided; lobes unequal, orbicular, with membranous margins. Petals $\frac{1}{8}$ in. long, oblong, obtuse, distant. Stamens much shorter than the petals; anthers roundish. Disk thick

and fleshy. Drupes obovoid, $\frac{1}{3}$–$\frac{1}{2}$ in. long, apiculate. Fl. B. I. v. 1, p. 623; Talb. Trees, Bomb. p. 49; Woodr. in Journ. Bomb. Nat. v. 11 (1897) p. 270; Watt, Dict. Econ. Prod. v. 3, p. 207. *Elæodendron Roxburghii*, W. & A. Prodr. p. 157; Grah. Cat. p. 38; Dalz. & Gibs. p. 48.—Flowers: Feb.–Aug. VERN. *Bhutkes*; *Tâmruj*.

KONKAN: *Law*!, *Stocks*! DECCAN: Dapudi, near Poona, *Woodrow*!; Harishchandragad, *Graham*; Sattara and Kamatki Ghâts, *Dalzell & Gibson*; Peint taluka, *Woodrow*; Bhimashankar, *Gibson*. S. M. COUNTRY: Belgaum, *Ritchie*, 1006!; Duddi, *Ritchie*!; Padshapur, *Ritchie*!; Dharwar forests near Devilkope, *Talbot*. KANARA; Ghâts of N. Kanara; common in the Goond forests, *Talbot*.—DISTRIB. India (the hotter parts); Malaya.

8. HIPPOCRATEA, Linn.

Small trees or scandent shrubs. Leaves opposite, petioled, the petioles articulated at the base; stipules caducous. Flowers in axillary (rarely terminal) cymes or panicles, small, green or white. Calyx small, 5-partite. Petals 5, spreading. Stamens 3; filaments free or adnate to the ovary, dilated at the base, recurved or reflexed at the apex; anthers didymous. Disk conical or cup-shaped. Ovary free or confluent with the disk, 3-celled; ovules 2–6 in each cell; style short. Fruit of 1–3 distinct carpels, each 2-valved or indehiscent; cells few-seeded. Seeds* compressed, usually winged below, exarillate; albumen 0.—DISTRIB. Tropical Asia, Australia, Africa, and America; species about 60.

Style overtopping the stamens; ripe carpels reaching 2 in. in length .... 1. *H. obtusifolia.*
Style shorter than the stamens.
  Ripe carpels reaching 4 in. in length; anthers subsessile ...... 2. *H. Grahami.*
  Ripe carpels reaching $1\frac{1}{2}$ in. in length; filaments longer than the anthers .... 3. *H. indica.*

1. **Hippocratea obtusifolia,** *Roxb. Fl. Ind.* v. 1 (1832) p. 166. A climbing shrub; young parts glabrous. Leaves coriaceous, 3–5 by $1\frac{3}{4}$–$2\frac{3}{4}$ in., elliptic, ovate or lanceolate, rounded, acute or very shortly acuminate, entire or shallowly crenate-serrate, reticulately veined, glabrous, base rounded or acute; petioles $\frac{1}{8}$–$\frac{1}{4}$ in. long. Flowers in axillary paniculate dichotomous cymes usually shorter than the leaves; buds conical. Calyx small, puberulous, deeply divided; lobes triangular-ovate. Petals $\frac{1}{8}$ in. long, triangular, acute, subfleshy, puberulous outside, 1-nerved. Stamens 3; filaments short, flat, broad. Style overtopping the stamens, conical-subulate. Carpels $1\frac{1}{2}$–2 by $\frac{3}{4}$–$1\frac{1}{4}$ in., oblong-obovoid, compressed, emarginate, prominently nerved and veined, 4–6-seeded. Seeds $\frac{1}{2}$ in. long, subfalcate, compressed, the funicle developing into a large membranous wing $\frac{7}{8}$ by $\frac{1}{2}$ in. at the base of the seed, the funicle conspicuous in the middle of the wing. Fl. B. I. v. 1, p. 623; Grah. Cat. p. 27; Wight, Icon. t. 963; Trim. Fl. Ceyl. v. 1, p. 275;

---

* After the opening of the flower, a fold is produced on the back of the ovary which grows rapidly and attains a great size, compared with the rest of the ovary. The fold is hollow and its cavity communicates with that of the cell, on the back of which it is inserted. For a long time the cavity of the fold remains empty, but a short time before maturity the funicle which supports each ovule elongates greatly, and forces the ovule to pass out of the cell and into the fold. See *Payer*, Organog. Comp. p. 163, t. 35.

Lösener in Engl. & Prantl, Pflanzenf. v. 3, part 5, p. 227, fig. 130, E-G; Talb. Trees, Bomb. p. 49; Woodr. in Journ. Bomb. Nat. v. 11 (1897) p. 270.—Flowers: Jan. VERN. *Daushir.*

Not common. KONKAN: *Stocks*!, *Dalzell*!, *Talbot*. DECCAN: Lanoli Grove and Khandala, *Graham*; about Pár, *Graham*. KANARA: Ainshi (N. Kanara), *Talbot*.—DISTRIB. India (E. & W. Peninsulas); Ceylon, Malaya, China, Australia, Tropical Africa.

2. **Hippocratea Grahami,** *Wight, Ill.* v. 1 (1840) p. 134. A climbing glabrous shrub. Leaves coriaceous, entire, $2\frac{1}{2}$–5 by $1\frac{3}{4}$–$2\frac{3}{4}$, ovate-elliptic, acute or subacuminate; petioles $\frac{1}{4}$ in. long. Flowers white, in dense branched panicles longer than the leaves; buds globose; peduncles several, crowded towards the ends of the branches; bracts minute, lanceolate. Calyx divided to the base or nearly so; lobes orbicular, with laciniate or ciliate margins. Petals $\frac{1}{12}$–$\frac{1}{10}$ in. long, oblong, membranous. Anthers subsessile. Style shorter than the stamens. Carpels linear-oblong, reaching nearly 4 in. long, striate, rounded and emarginate at the apex. Seeds about 1 in. long, ovoid-oblong; basal wing $1\frac{3}{4}$ by $\frac{3}{4}$, the funicle conspicuous in its centre. Fl. B. I. v. 1, p. 624; Wight, Icon. t. 380; Dalz. & Gibs. p. 32; Talb. Trees, Bomb. p. 49; Woodr. in Journ. Bomb. Nat. v. 11 (1897) p. 270.—Flowers: Jan.–Apr. VERN. *Lokandi*; *Yesti.*

KONKAN: *Law*!; common at Matheran, *H. M. Birdwood*. DECCAN: Phunda Ghát, *Ritchie*, 1651! S. M. COUNTRY: near Dharwar, *Hohenhacker*, 754! KANARA: Katgal (N. Kanara), *Talbot*!—DISTRIB. India (W. Peninsula).

3. **Hippocratea indica,** *Willd. Sp. Pl.* v. 1 (1797) p. 193. A climbing shrub; young parts glabrous. Leaves opposite, $1\frac{1}{2}$–3 by $\frac{3}{4}$–$1\frac{1}{2}$ in., elliptic, usually bluntly acuminate, pale, glabrous, finely serrate, tapering at the base; petioles $\frac{1}{8}$–$\frac{1}{2}$ in. long. Flowers yellow, minute; cymes corymbosely branched, paniculate, shorter than the leaves, in opposite leaf-axils; buds oblong or obovoid; bracts small, ovate, acute. Calyx glabrous; lobes triangular-ovate. Petals $\frac{1}{20}$ in. long, subfleshy, elliptic-oblong, acute; filaments longer than the anthers. Style shorter than the stamens. Carpels ellipsoid, 1–$1\frac{1}{2}$ by $\frac{3}{8}$–$\frac{1}{2}$, rounded at the apex, not emarginate, striate. Seeds $\frac{3}{16}$ in. long; basal wing $\frac{3}{4}$ by $\frac{3}{8}$ in., with conspicuous funicle in its middle. Fl. B. I. v. 1, p. 624; Roxb. Cor. Pl. v. 2, p. 16, t. 130; Grah. Cat. p. 27; Dalz. & Gibs. p. 32; Trim. Fl. Ceyl. v. 1, p. 276; Talb. Trees, Bomb. p. 49; Woodr. in Journ. Bomb. Nat. v. 11 (1897) p. 270.—Flowers: Apr. VERN. *Kazurdti*; *Turruli.*

KONKAN: moist forests, *Talbot*; along the Ghâts, pretty common, *Dalzell & Gibson*. DECCAN: banks of the Koina river above Pár bridge, *Graham*. KANARA: Divimana, *Woodrow*!; moist forests of N. Kanara, *Talbot*.—DISTRIB. India (hotter parts); Ceylon, Malaya, Africa.

9. SALACIA, Linn.

Scandent or sarmentose shrubs or small trees. Leaves usually opposite, petioled, coriaceous, shining above, exstipulate. Flowers small, axillary or extra-axillary, fascicled or cymose, rarely solitary or 2-nate. Calyx small, 5-partite. Petals 5, spreading, imbricate. Stamens 3 (very rarely 2 or 4), inserted on the disk, free or connate with the ovary; filaments conniving at the apex, recurved; anthers small, dehiscing extrorsely (on account of the recurved filaments), adnate, 2-celled, lobes divaricating at the base. Disk thick, sinuate. Ovary sunk in the disk, conical, 3-celled; ovules 2, 4 or more in each cell, affixed to the axis, 1- or 2-seriate; style usually very short; stigma simple or 3-lobed. Fruit baccate, edible, 1–3-celled; cells 1–4-seeded; rind coriaceous or subwoody; pulp mucilaginous. Seeds large, angular; testa rather thick, coriaceous or fibrous; cotyledons thick, usually conferruminate.—DISTRIB. Tropical and subtropical regions of Asia, Africa, and America; species about 130.

Flowers from axillary or extra-axillary tubercles.
  Flowers few.
    Flowers 3-6 .... 1. *S. prinoides.*
    Flowers 1-2 .... 2. *S. Brunoniana.*
  Flowers numerous .... 3. *S. macrosperma.*
Flowers in short-peduncled cymes, not from axillary tubercles. 4. *S. oblonga.*

1. **Salacia prinoides,** *DC. Prodr.* v. 1 (1824) p. 571. A large straggling or climbing shrub; branches divaricate; young twigs angular, glabrous. Leaves thinly coriaceous, $1\frac{3}{4}$–$3\frac{1}{2}$ by 1–$1\frac{1}{2}$ in., elliptic-oblong, shortly acuminate, subobtuse, crenate-serrate or entire, glabrous, base acute; petioles $\frac{1}{8}$–$\frac{1}{4}$ in. long. Flowers yellow, $\frac{1}{4}$ in. in diam., 3–6 (rarely more), from small tubercles in the axils of the leaves or from the smaller branches below the leaves; pedicels slender, $\frac{1}{4}$–$\frac{1}{3}$ in. long. Calyx cupular, persistent; lobes 5, rounded, concave, pubescent outside, ciliate. Petals much larger than the calyx-lobes, oblong or obovate, clawed, rounded at the apex and with membranous margins. Disk convex, fleshy. Stamens 3 from the face of the disk, inserted at a little distance from the ovary; filaments narrow, flat, erect; anthers small, transversely oblong, 2-celled. Ovary conical, trigonous. Fruit $\frac{1}{2}$ in. in diam., subglobose, minutely apiculate, fleshy, red when ripe, 1-celled, 1-seeded. Fl. B. I. v. 1, p. 626; Grah. Cat. p. 27; Dalz. & Gibs. p. 33; Trim. Fl. Ceyl. v. 1, p. 276; Talb. Trees, Bomb. p. 50; Woodr. in Journ. Bomb. Nat. v. 11 (1897) p. 270.—Flowers: Dec.–Feb. VERN. *Nisul-bondi.*

KONKAN: *Stocks*!, *Law*!; Atgaon, *Woodrow*!; Malbar and Amboli (Salsette), *Nimmo* ex *Graham*; Wari Country, not common, *Dalzell & Gibson.* DECCAN: Khandala, *Graham*; Phunda Ghát, *Ritchie*, 1603! S. M. COUNTRY: Párva Ghát (Belgaum districts), *Ritchie*, 1652! KANARA: near Sirsi, *Hohenhacker*, 749!; Dehalli (N. Kanara), *Talbot* ex *Woodrow.*

The scandent form is often found on river-banks in N. Kanara (Kála naddi, &c.), the erect shrubby form is abundant in the evergreen forests of the S. Ghâts of N. Kanara, *Talbot.*—DISTRIB. India (Silhet, Khasia mountains, and the E. & W. Peninsulas); Ceylon, Java, Philippines.

2. **Salacia Brunoniana,** *Wight & Arn. Prodr.* (1834) p. 105. A scandent shrub (?); branches terete. Leaves coriaceous, oblong or elliptic, acuminate, subobtuse, minutely serrate, glabrous, base acute; petioles $\frac{1}{4}$ in. long. Flowers few (1–2), from an axillary tubercle; pedicels about equalling the petioles. Calyx with 5 short blunt teeth. Petals ovate from a broad base, sessile, coriaceous, with incurved margins (when dried), entire, somewhat persistent. Torus cup-shaped, thick and fleshy, at first nearly enclosing the ovary. Stamens short, from the inner side of the torus. Ovules 2, superposed. Fl. B. I. v. 1,

p. 626; Dalz. & Gibs. p. 33; Talb. Trees, Bomb. p. 50; Woodr. in Journ. Bomb. Nat. v. 11 (1897) p. 270.

This has been included on the authority of *Dalzell & Gibson* (Bo. Fl. p. 33), who give its habitat as Ramghát (*S. M. Country*), but there is no specimen from that locality in Dalzell's Herbarium in Herb. Kew., and the plant does not seem to have been found by any other collector. There is but one specimen in Herb. Kew. which is from Wight's Herbarium, and this specimen is destitute of fruit and has but a single flower on it. The description above is taken from *Wight & Arnott*, Prodr. l. c. *Woodrow & Talbot* simply quote *Dalzell & Gibson*.

3. **Salacia macrosperma,** *Wight, Icon.* t. 962. A scandent shrub; branches not lenticellate. Leaves coriaceous, 3½–5 by 1½–2 in., elliptic-oblong, acuminate, subobtuse, entire, glabrous, cuneate at the base; petioles ¼–⅓ in. long. Flowers in dense fascicles from axillary or extra-axillary tubercles. Calyx-lobes much shorter than the petals, oblong, fringed with rust-colored hairs. Petals elliptic-oblong, $\frac{1}{12}$ in. long. Disk convex, slightly depressed in the centre, margined at the edge. Stamens inserted close to the ovary; filaments very short, broad. Ovary almost entirely sunk in the disk; style very short. Fruit 1½ in. in diam., globose, verrucose, orange when ripe. Fl. B. I. v. 1, p. 628; Talb. Trees, Bomb. p. 50; Woodr. in Journ. Bomb. Nat. v. 11 (1897) p. 270. *S. Roxburghii* (?), Dalz. & Gibs. p. 33.—Flowers: Jan.

KONKAN: N. & S. Konkan, *Law*! S. M. COUNTRY: Ramghát, *Ritchie*, 99! KANARA: *Gibson*!; Yacombi (N. Kanara), *Woodrow*!; Ainshi Ghát, *Talbot*!—DISTRIB. India (W. Peninsula).

4. **Salacia oblonga,** *Wall. Cat.* (1828) 4226. A scandent shrub; young parts glabrous; branches lenticellate. Leaves numerous, 3–6 by 1¼–2 in., elliptic-oblong, rounded or sometimes obtusely acuminate at the apex, crenate-serrate, glabrous, tapering into the petiole, prominently reticulately veined beneath; petioles ¼ in. long, rugose. Flowers greenish-yellow, axillary, usually 3 together, with or without a short common peduncle. Calyx persistent, glabrous outside, deeply divided; lobes orbicular, finely ciliate, about half as long as the petals. Petals ⅛ in. long, oblong, rounded at the apex, spreading. Stamens inserted on the disk close up to the ovary; filaments erect, dilated at the base, the triangular dilated base embracing the ovary; anthers suborbicular-oblong, 2-celled. Ovary about half immersed in the disk, conical, attenuated into the style which is slightly shorter than the stamens. Fruit reaching 2 in. in diam., globose or somewhat pyriform, orange when ripe. Seeds 1–8, angular, large, immersed in pulp. Fl. B. I. v. 1, p. 628; Wight, Ill. t. 47, B; Dalz. & Gibs. p. 33; Trim. Fl. Ceyl. v. 1, p. 277; Talb. Trees, Bomb. p. 50; Woodr. in Journ. Bomb. Nat. v. 11 (1897) p. 270.—Flowers: Dec.–Feb.

KONKAN: N. & S. Konkan, *Law*! S. M. COUNTRY: Chorla Ghát, *Dalzell & Gibson*. KANARA: evergreen forests of the N. Kanara Gháts from Ainshi southwards, *Talbot*; Ainshi Ghát, *Talbot*, 1378!—DISTRIB. India (W. Peninsula); Ceylon.

ORDER XLI. RHAMNACEÆ.

Trees or shrubs, erect or scandent; branches sometimes spinescent, sometimes climbing by their extremity which is bare of leaves (*Gouania*). Leaves alternate (opposite in *Scutia* and *Sageretia*), usually coriaceous;

stipules small or 0, sometimes transformed into prickles. Flowers hermaphrodite or polygamous, small, greenish, usually axillary, solitary or variously fascicled. Calyx 4-5-fid; lobes shortly triangular, erect or recurved, usually keeled within, valvate. Petals 4–5 (rarely 0), inserted on the throat of the calyx-tube, usually less than its lobes, cucullate or involute, sessile or clawed. Stamens 4-5, opposite to and inserted with the petals, often enclosed within their folds; anthers versatile, 2-celled, sometimes ovoid and dehiscing longitudinally, sometimes reniform and 1-celled, by the confluence of the cells at top, and opening into 2 valves by an arched slit. Disk fleshy and filling the calyx-tube, or thin and lining it, entire or lobed. Ovary sessile, free or immersed in the disk, wholly free from, or more or less adnate to the calyx-tube, 3- (rarely 2-4-) celled; ovule 1 (rarely 2) in each cell, erect, anatropous; raphe dorsal; style erect, short, usually 2–4-fid. Fruit superior or inferior, 3- (more rarely 1–4-) celled, capsular and often winged, or drupaceous. Seeds with fleshy albumen (rarely exalbuminous); embryo large, straight; cotyledons flat, fleshy.—DISTRIB. Warm regions and tropics of both hemispheres; genera 37; species about 420.

Fruit dry, indehiscent, 1-celled; ovary ½-inferior .... 1. VENTILAGO.
Fruit drupaceous; stone 1–4-celled; ovary ½-inferior .... 2. ZIZYPHUS.
Fruit baccate; pyrenes 2–4; ovary superior.
  Disk thin, lining the calyx-tube .... 3. RHAMNUS.
  Disk fleshy, filling the calyx-tube.
    Flowers pedicelled, in axillary umbels .... 4. SCUTIA.
    Flowers sessile, in long spicate panicles... .... 5. SAGERETIA.
Fruit capsular.
  Fruit globose; ovary ½-inferior .... 6. COLUBRINA.
  Fruit boldly angled; ovary quite inferior........................... 7. GOUANIA.

1. VENTILAGO, Gærtn.

Scandent shrubs. Leaves subdistichous, alternate, petioled; stipules very minute, caducous. Flowers small, in terminal and axillary panicles (rarely fascicles). Calyx 5-fid; tube obconic; lobes spreading, acute, keeled within. Petals 5, deltoid or obcordate, cucullate, involute. Stamens 5, adnate to the base of the petals and a little longer than them. Disk 5-gonous, naked or pubescent, its margin free. Ovary immersed in the disk, subglobose, 2-celled; style very short, compressed; stigmas 2, short. Ripe fruit subglobose, 1-celled, 1-seeded, surrounded at its base or middle by the adherent calyx-tube, the fruit prolonged into a linear or linear-oblong coriaceous apical wing. Seed subglobose, exalbuminous.—DISTRIB. Tropics; species about 16.

Flowers in terminal panicles.
  Nut girt at the base by the persistent calyx .... 1. *V. madraspatana.*
  Nut girt round the middle by the persistent calyx .... 2. *V. calyculata.*
Flowers in axillary fascicles .... 3. *V. bombaiensis.*

1. **Ventilago madraspatana,** *Gærtn. Fruct.* v. 1 (1788) p. 223, t. 49, fig. 2. A large much-branched woody climber; young branches and panicles pubescent. Leaves 2–4 by 1–1½ in., oblong-lanceolate or elliptic-ovate, subacute, entire or more or less crenate, glabrous above, glabrous or puberulous beneath, base rounded or acute; main nerves 4–8 pairs, alternate, ascending; petioles ⅛–⅜ in. long; stipules small, subulate. Flowers greenish, with an offensive odor, ⅛ in. in diam.,

in large spreading and drooping leafless pubescent terminal panicles; buds 5-angled; pedicels very short. Calyx pubescent or puberulous outside, glabescent within; lobes erect, triangular, very acute, keeled on the inner face and with a hard incurved point at the apex within. Petals much smaller than the calyx-lobes, enveloping the stamens and shorter than them. Disk softly pubescent. Ovary pubescent; styles more or less divergent. Nuts about ⅛ in. in diam., yellowish, globular, supported by the persistent calyx which forms a flat disk at the base of the fruit; wing 1½–2 in. long by ⅓–⅜ in. broad, linear-oblong, 1-nerved, rounded at the apex and terminated by the remains of the bifid style. Fl. B. I. v. 1, p. 631; Dalz. & Gibs. p. 48; Talb. Trees, Bomb. p. 51; Woodr. in Journ. Bomb. Nat. v. 11 (1897) p. 271; Watt, Dict. Econ. Prod. v. 6, part 4, p. 227. *V. maderaspatana*, Wight, Icon. t. 163; Grah. Cat. p. 40; Trim. Fl. Ceyl. v. 1, p. 279.—Flowers: Dec.–Jan. VERN. *Lokandi*; *Kánvel.*

KONKAN: *Stocks*!; common at Matheran, *H. M. Birdwood*; 23 miles east of Ratnagiri, *Woodrow.* DECCAN: Khandala, *Dalzell & Gibson, Graham*; Lanoli Grove, *Graham.* S. M. COUNTRY: Rámghát, *Ritchie*, 1685!; Padshapur, *Dr. Lush.* – DISTRIB. India (W. Peninsula, Tenasserim); Ceylon.

The root bark produces a valuable dye which is well adapted for *tasar* silk. See Watt, Dict. Econ. Prod. l. c.

2. **Ventilago calyculata,** *Tulasne in Ann. Sc. Nat.* ser. 4, v. 8 (1857) p. 124. An extensive climber. Leaves 2–5½ by 1–2½ in., elliptic-oblong, subacute, crenate-serrate, pubescent when young (especially the lower surface), base oblique, rounded or acute; nerves 4–6 pairs; petioles ¼ in. long. Flowers with an offensive odor, numerous, greenish, in densely pubescent paniculate spikes. Ovary pubescent. Fruit 1½–2 in. long (including the wing), girt about the middle by the persistent calyx; wing pubescent, ⅜ in. broad, rounded at the apex, terminated by the remains of the bifid style. Fl. B. I. v. 1, p. 631; Talb. Trees, Bomb. p. 51; Woodr. in Journ. Bomb. Nat. v. 11 (1897) p. 271; Watt, Dict. Econ. Prod. v. 6, part 4, p. 226.

KONKAN, *Law*!, *Stocks*!; in deciduous forests, *Talbot.* S. M. COUNTRY: Belgaum Gháts, *Ritchie*!; Dharwar, *Woodrow*; Badami, *Bhiva*! KANARA: Yellapur (N. Kanara), *Woodrow.*—DISTRIB. India (throughout the hotter parts); Java.

3. **Ventilago bombaiensis,** *Dalz. in Hook. Kew Journ. Bot.* v. 3 (1851) p. 36. Branches, petioles and inflorescence fulvous-pubescent. Leaves 3–4 by 1–1½ in., lanceolate, acute or subacuminate, crenate (the crenatures with callous points), glabrous, shining, base oblique, acute; main nerves 3–4 (rarely 5) pairs, furnished with rufous-villous glands in the axils; petioles ¼ in. long; stipules subulate. Flowers (15–20), fascicled in the axils of the leaves; pedicels shorter than the petioles, fulvous-pubescent. Calyx strongly fulvous-pubescent outside, cleft about half way down; lobes triangular, very conspicuously keeled on the inner face. Petals truncate at the apex, cuneate at the base, shorter than the stamens. Disk filling the calyx-tube. Filaments flattened; anthers subglobose, enveloped by the petals; connective shortly excurrent. Ovary sunk in the disk, 2-celled; ovule 1 in each cell; style bifid, fleshy, slightly recurved at the apex. Fruit not seen. Fl. B. I. v. 1, p. 631; Dalz. & Gibs. p. 48; Woodr. in Journ. Bomb. Nat. v. 11 (1897) p. 271. —Flowers: Feb.

In the absence of fruit it is impossible to determine this plant with certainty. Bentham (Journ. Linn. Soc. v. 5 [1861] p. 77) says that he suspects Dalzell's specimens to be side-shoots from *V. calyculata* with the inflorescence abnormally axillary. The shape and nervation of the leaves are, however, opposed to this view. In addition to the specimens obtained by Dalzell from Chorla Ghât, there is one other specimen in Herb. Kew. marked "Konkan, *Stocks*," while I have in my own Herbarium 4 good specimens, in full flower, collected from Devimana Ghát (N. Kanara) in the month of February. Unfortunately none of these specimens are in fruit. Woodrow in his list of Bombay plants (l. c.) gives Tinai (N. Kanara) as a habitat of the plant, while Mr. Talbot (Trees, Bomb. p. 51) says he has no knowledge whatever of it. Beddome (Icon. t. 114) figures a plant which he has named *Zizyphus wynadensis*, but of which no specimens exist either at Kew or in the British Museum. The figure exactly represents this plant. In the Index to his Icon. (p. iii), Beddome withdraws the name *Zizyphus wynadensis* in favor of *Ventilago bombaiensis*, Dalz. The general appearance of the plant is in favor of its being a *Ventilago* rather than a *Zizyphus*. No fruit has been figured by Beddome, but he describes the plant as a *lofty tree*, while Dalzell allows it to be inferred that it is (as are all the species of *Ventilago*) a *climber*. Lawson in Hook. f. Fl. B. I. v. 1, p. 631 & p. 633, retains both plants under the same citation from Bedd. Icon. One of these must of course disappear.—Local botanists would render a service by obtaining the fruit and so clearing up the question.—Distrib. Apparently endemic.

2. ZIZYPHUS, Juss.

Trees or shrubs often decumbent or sarmentose, usually armed with sharp straight or hooked thorns (transformed stipules). Leaves subdistichous, alternate, 3–5-nerved, usually coriaceous. Flowers axillary, fascicled or in sessile or peduncled cymes, small, greenish. Calyx 5-fid; tube broadly obconic; lobes triangular-ovate, acute, spreading, keeled within. Petals 5 (rarely 0), cucullate, deflexed. Disk 5–10-lobed, flat or pitted, the margin free. Stamens 5, enclosed by the petals and longer than them. Ovary immersed in the disk and confluent with it at the base, 2–4-celled; styles 2–3, conical, free or connate, divergent; stigmas small, papillose. Drupe globose or oblong, with a woody or bony 1–4-celled 1–4-seeded stone. Seed plano-convex; albumen 0 or scanty; cotyledons thick; radicle short.—Distrib. Tropical Asia and America and in temperate regions of both hemispheres; species about 60.

Petals 5.
  Styles connate to the middle.
    Fruit exceeding $\frac{1}{2}$ in. in diam.; leaves tomentose beneath... 1. *Z. Jujuba.*
    Fruit under $\frac{1}{2}$ in. in diam.
      Leaves glabrous .... 2. *Z. trinervia.*
      Leaves tomentose on both sides .... 3. *Z. rotundifolia.*
      Leaves clothed with silky hairs beneath .... 4. *Z. Œnoplia.*
  Styles distinct or nearly so.
    Fruit $\frac{3}{4}$–1 in. in diam. .... 5. *Z. xylopyra.*
    Fruit $\frac{1}{2}$–$\frac{5}{8}$ in. in diam. .... 6. *Z. horrida.*
Petals 0 .... 7. *Z. rugosa.*

1. **Zizyphus Jujuba,** *Lamk. Encyc.* v. 3 (1789) p. 318. A small much-branched tree or large shrub; young branches softly pubescent. Leaves 1–2$\frac{1}{2}$ by $\frac{3}{4}$–1$\frac{1}{2}$ in., bifarious, ovate-elliptic, rounded at both ends, slightly inequilateral at the base, faintly and irregularly denticulate, glabrous above, covered beneath with a dense whitish or buff tomentum, strongly 3-nerved from the base; petioles $\frac{1}{4}$–$\frac{1}{2}$ in. long; prickles solitary or in pairs, when twin 1 often straight, the other bent. Flowers greenish-yellow, in small axillary clusters or short-peduncled axillary cymes. Calyx pubescent or woolly outside, glabrous within, cleft about half way down; lobes triangular, prominently keeled on the inner face

for about half their length. Petals cucullate, rounded at the apex, deflexed with the stamens between the calyx-lobes; pedicels short, hairy. Stamens enclosed in the petals, but not exserted beyond them; filaments $\frac{1}{24}$ in. long, slightly dilated at the base. Disk with 10 grooved lobes. Ovary about half sunk in the disk, ovoid; styles 2, connate for about half their length. Drupes edible, $\frac{1}{2}$-$\frac{5}{8}$ in. in diam., globose, fleshy, smooth, yellow or orange when ripe; stone 1-2-celled. Fl. B. I. v. 1, p. 632; Grah. Cat. p. 39; Dalz. & Gibs. p. 49; Weberbauer, in Engl. & Prantl, Pflanzenf. v. 3, part 5, p. 403, fig. 198, A-D; Talb. Trees, Bomb. p. 52; Woodr. in Journ. Bomb. Nat. v. 11 (1897) p. 271; Watt, Dict. Econ. Prod. v. 6, part 4, p. 367.—Flowers: Sept.-Oct. VERN. *Bor*; *Bor*.

Not abundant in a truly wild state, but plentiful near sites of former villages throughout the Presidency.—Dr. Gibson (fide Graham l. c.) states that it is abundant in the Khandesh jungles, particularly towards the Tapti. It is extensively cultivated throughout India for its edible fruit and for its timber, which, though small, is much valued for certain purposes. See Watt, Dict. Econ. Prod. l. c.—DISTRIB. Throughout India; Afghanistan, Ceylon, China, Australia, Africa.

2. **Zizyphus trinervia,** *Roxb. Hort. Beng.* (1814) p. 17 (*not* of Poir.); *Fl. Ind.* v. 1, p. 606. A small unarmed tree. Leaves 1-3 by $\frac{5}{8}$-$1\frac{1}{2}$ in., elliptic, subobtuse, often mucronate, serrate (the serratures with short callous points), prominently 3-nerved from the base, glabrous, shining, base more or less oblique, rounded or subacute; petioles $\frac{1}{8}$-$\frac{1}{2}$ in. long; stipules filiform, caducous. Flowers greenish-yellow, in axillary peduncled cymes scarcely $\frac{1}{2}$ in. long. Calyx finely pubescent outside; lobes triangular, keeled within, deflexed. Petals small, shorter than the recurved stamens, obtriangular, cuneate. Disk 10-lobed, not grooved. Filaments flattened. Ovary 2-celled; styles 2, united to the middle. Fruit $\frac{3}{8}$ in. in diam., globose or obovoid, somewhat rugose, 1-2-celled, yellow when ripe. *Z. trinervius*, var. *glabratus*, Heyne, in Roth, Nov. Sp. (1821) p. 159. *Z. glabrata*, Wight, Icon. t. 282; Laws. in Hook. f. Fl. B. I. v. 1, p. 633; Woodr. in Journ. Bomb. Nat. v. 11 (1897) p. 271; Watt, Dict. Econ. Prod. v. 6, part 4, p. 367.—Flowers: Nov.-Dec.

GUJARAT: Surat, *Woodrow*; Ahmedabad, *Cooke* !, *Woodrow*.

This species was named *Z. trinervia* by *Roxburgh* (Hort. Beng. p. 17) in 1814, and Wallich (Roxb. Fl. Ind. v. 2 [1824] p. 354) after a comparison of Roxburgh's plant with that named *Z. glabratus* by *Heyne* (Roth, Nov. Sp. [1821] p. 159), found them to be identical. The older name given by *Roxburgh* is therefore retained.—DISTRIB. India (E. Bengal, Bhotan, W. Peninsula).

3. **Zizyphus rotundifolia,** *Lamk. Encyc.* v. 3 (1789) p. 319. A small shrub branched from near the root; branches divaricate, slender, zigzag; bark light-colored. Leaves $\frac{1}{2}$-$\frac{3}{4}$ in., orbicular or ovate, spinous-dentate, clothed beneath with a whitish or buff tomentum, less densely tomentose above; petioles $\frac{1}{8}$-$\frac{1}{4}$ in. long, tomentose; stipular thorns usually in pairs, one straight, sharp and slender, nearly as long as the leaf, the other short, hooked. Flowers in axillary sessile pubescent cymes; buds globose; pedicels short. Calyx pubescent outside, cleft about half way down; lobes triangular-ovate, keeled on the inner face for about half their length. Petals cuneate, rounded or truncate at the apex, longer than the stamens. Filaments deflexed together with the enclosing petals. Disk 10-lobed, with a pit opposite to each lobe. Ovary 2-celled; styles 2, united to above the middle. Drupes globose, $\frac{1}{3}$ in. in diam., glabrous, red when ripe, edible. *Zizyphus nummularia*,

DC. Prodr. v. 2 (1825) p. 21 (*in syn.*); W. & A. Prodr. (1834) p. 162; Fl. B. I. v. 1, p. 633; Grah. Cat. p. 247; Dalz. & Gibs. p. 49; Talb. Trees, Bomb. p. 52; Woodr. in Journ. Bomb. Nat. v. 11 (1897) p. 271; Watt, Dict. Econ. Prod. v. 6, part 4, p. 370.—Flowers: Oct.-Dec. VERN. *Jangra*; *Gangr.*

Very common in Gujarat, where it is often very troublesome to sportsmen from its hooked thorns. GUJARAT: Broach, *Woodrow*! Porbandar (Kathiawar), *Cooke*! S. M. COUNTRY: Belgaum, *Ritchie*, 211!—DISTRIB. India (Punjab, W. Peninsula); Persia.

The fruit has a pleasant acid flavor and is eaten during times of scarcity. See Watt, Dict. Econ. Prod. l. c.

4. **Zizyphus Œnoplia,** *Mill. Gard. Dict.* ed. 8 (1768) n. 3. A straggling shrub often semi-scandent by its prickles; young branches rusty-tomentose. Leaves numerous, distichous, 1–2½ by ¾-1 in., ovate or ovate-lanceolate, acute or subacuminate, with pubescent or tomentose tips, minutely denticulate, glabrous or pubescent above, densely silky with appressed rufous hairs beneath, base very oblique; main basal nerves usually 3, with numerous ascending branches, the lowest branch on the large side of the leaf starting almost, but usually not quite, from the base; petioles ¼–⅓ in. long; stipular prickle 1, stout, short, hooked, pubescent except the tip. Flowers 12–20, in subsessile pubescent paniculate cymes which are slightly longer than the petioles. Calyx hairy outside; lobes ovate, acute, keeled to the middle or a little below it. Petals obovate, cuneate, shorter than the calyx-lobes, exceeding the stamens. Disk with 10 short deeply pitted lobes, glabrous. Styles united almost to the apex. Drupe edible, ¼ in. in diam., globose or obovoid, 1- (rarely 2-) celled, black, shining; pulp scanty; stone woody or bony. Fl. B. I. v. 1, p. 634; Grah. Cat. p. 39; Dalz. & Gibs. p. 49; Trim. Fl. Ceyl. v. 1, p. 280; Talb. Trees, Bomb. p. 52; Woodr. in Journ. Bomb. Nat. v. 11 (1897) p. 271; Watt, Dict. Econ. Prod. v. 6, part 4, p. 371.—Flowers: Aug.-Sept. VERN. *Burgi.*

KONKAN: *Graham, Dalzell & Gibson*; in moist forests, *Talbot*. DECCAN: *Dalzell & Gibson*. S. M. COUNTRY: Belgaum jungles, *Ritchie*, 132!; Badami, *Cooke*!; Dharwar, *Woodrow*! KANARA: in moist forests of N. Kanara, *Talbot*; Kála naddi, *Ritchie*, 132!—DISTRIB. Throughout the hotter parts of India; Tropical Asia, Australia.

5. **Zizyphus xylopyra,** *Willd. Sp. Pl.* v. 1 (1797) p. 1104. A straggling shrub, or in favorable situations, a tree; branches armed or not, covered when young with a short grey tomentum. Leaves 1½–3 in. long, elliptic-oblong or suborbicular, crenate-serrate, often mucronate, glabrous above, covered with white or yellowish tomentum beneath, very oblique and sometimes cordate at the base; petioles ¼ in. long; stipular prickles frequently absent (when present, twin, one straight, the other curved). Flowers sometimes 4-merous, in small dense pubescent paniculate cymes; peduncles ¼ in. long; pedicels short. Calyx pubescent outside; lobes ovate, acute or acuminate, keeled about half way down. Petals spathulate, with long claws. Disk thin, 5-angled. Ovary 3- (rarely 2-) celled; styles 3 or 2, distinct or nearly so. Fruit hard and woody, ¾-1 in. in diam., globose, covered with close dense grey tomentum; stone large, very thick and hard, 2–3-celled, 2–3-seeded. Fl. B. I. v. 1, p. 634; Grah. Cat. p. 39; Dalz. & Gibs. p. 49; Trim. Fl. Ceyl. v. 1, p. 282; Woodr. in Journ. Bomb. Nat. v. 11 (1897) p. 271; Watt,

Dict. Econ. Prod. v. 6, part 4, p. 374.—Flowers: May-July. VERN. *Guti.*

KONKAN: *Law!*, *Stocks!*; the Ghâts pretty common, *Graham*; Matheran near Garbat Point, *C. Macnaghten!*; Hart Point, *H. M. Birdwood.* DECCAN: Bowdhan, near Poona, *Cooke!*, *Woodrow!*; Lanoli, *Woodrow!* S. M. COUNTRY: near Belgaum, *Ritchie!* KANARA: in moist forests growing to a tree, a straggling shrub in drier parts of the Presidency, *Talbot*; Kála naddi, *Ritchie*, 138!—DISTRIB. India (N.W. Prov., Oude, Rajputana, W. Peninsula); Ceylon.

6. **Zizyphus horrida,** *Roth, Nov. Pl. Sp.* (1821) p. 159. A shrub with slender divaricate branches. Leaves $\frac{3}{4}$-$1\frac{1}{4}$ by $\frac{1}{2}$-1 in., broadly elliptic or suborbicular, often mucronate, crenate, glabrous; petioles $\frac{1}{8}$-$\frac{1}{4}$ in. long; stipular prickles from broad triangular bases, twin, one straight and the other hooked, $\frac{1}{4}$-$\frac{1}{2}$ in. long, glabrous, shining, hard and sharp. Flowers in dense much-branched pubescent cymes; peduncles stout, $\frac{1}{4}$ in. long; pedicels shorter than the peduncles. Calyx pubescent outside; lobes ovate, acuminate, keeled about half way down. Petals broadly obovate with a very long claw. Disk 5-angled, not pitted. Styles 3, distinct or nearly so. Fruit $\frac{1}{2}$-$\frac{5}{8}$ in. in diam., globose, woody, 3-celled, 3-seeded. Fl. B. I. v. 1, p. 636; Talb. Trees, Bomb. p. 52.

KONKAN: *Stocks!*

I have seen only one Bombay specimen which is in Herb. Kew. marked as above, without more precise information as to locality.—DISTRIB. India (W. Peninsula).

7. **Zizyphus rugosa,** *Lamk. Encyc.* v. 3 (1789) p. 319. A large straggling armed shrub sometimes climbing: young branches clothed with fulvous tomentum. Leaves 2-5 in. long, broadly elliptic, shortly acuminate, denticulate, glabrous above, fulvous-tomentose beneath, base oblique, often cordate; petioles $\frac{1}{4}$-$\frac{1}{2}$ in. long, tomentose; prickles from a broad base, solitary, short, recurved, tomentose except the tips. Flowers in long-peduncled tomentose cymes arranged along usually leafless spinous branches forming a panicle (the cymes sometimes turned to one side); buds globose and as well as the peduncles and pedicels densely tomentose. Calyx pubescent outside; lobes ovate acute, the keel on the inner face reduced to a line. Petals 0. Disk 5-lobed. Ovary 2-celled. Styles 2, connate below the middle. Drupe $\frac{1}{4}$-$\frac{1}{3}$ in. in diam., globose or pyriform, white when ripe; stone thin, 1-celled, 1-seeded. Fl. B. I. v. 1, p. 636; Grah. Cat. p. 39; Dalz. & Gibs. p. 49; Trim. Fl. Ceyl. v. 1, p. 282; Talb. Trees, Bomb. p. 52; Woodr. in Journ. Bomb. Nat. v. 11 (1897) p. 271; Watt, Dict. Econ. Prod. v. 6, part 4, p. 372.—Flowers: Dec.-Feb. VERN. *Turan.*

Very common throughout the Ghâts of the Presidency. KONKAN: *Stocks!*; Konkan, and Ghâts, *Ritchie*, 135!; Bombay, *Capt. Geburne!* DECCAN: Mahableshwar, *Cooke!*; Khandala, *Woodrow!*; Ganesh Khind (Poona), *Woodrow!*; Igatpuri, *Kanitkar!* KANARA: N. Kanara Ghâts, *Talbot.* SIND: Hyderabad, *Cooke!* The fruit is eaten largely by the hill tribes in April and May. Dalzell & Gibson (*l. c.*) consider it palatable, but I have always thought it mawkish.—DISTRIB. India generally; Ceylon.

3. RHAMNUS, Linn.

Shrubs or trees. Leaves alternate (rarely subopposite), petioled, penninerved; stipules small, deciduous. Flowers hermaphrodite or polygamous, axillary, racemose or cymose, the cymes fasciculate. Calyx 4-5-fid; tube urceolate; lobes keeled within. Petals 4-5 or 0, inserted on the edge of the disk. Disk lining the calyx-tube, the margin thin.

Stamens 4–5; filaments very short. Ovary free, ovoid, 3–4-celled, attenuated into a 3–4-fid style; stigmas obtuse, papillose. Fruit a berry-like drupe, oblong or globose, girt at the base by the small calyx-tube; pyrenes 2–4, dehiscent or indehiscent, 1-seeded. Seeds obovoid; testa membranous or crustaceous; albumen fleshy; cotyledons flat, recurved at the margins; radicle short.—DISTRIB. Warm and temperate regions of both hemispheres; species about 60.

1. **Rhamnus Wightii,** *Wight & Arn. Prodr.* (1834) p. 164. A large glabrous, unarmed shrub. Leaves alternate (rarely a few sub-opposite), $2\frac{1}{2}$–4 by $\frac{7}{8}$–$1\frac{7}{8}$ in., ovate-oblong, acuminate, finely serrate, glabrous, base rounded or subacute; petioles $\frac{3}{8}$–$\frac{5}{8}$ in. long, puberulous. Flowers in axillary fascicles, or in fascicles along an elongate, axillary rhachis; pedicels shorter than the petioles. Calyx pubescent outside, cleft about half way down; lobes triangular, keeled on the inner face. Petals minute, lanceolate, flat. Stamens 5. Ovary 3- or 4-celled; styles 3 or 4, connate half way up. Berry $\frac{1}{5}$ in. in diam., globose, supported by the persistent calyx and tipped with the remains of the styles, smooth, reddish-purple when ripe. Fl. B. I. v. 1, p. 639; Dalz. & Gibs. p. 50; Trim. Fl. Ceyl. v. 1, p. 283; Talb. Trees, Bomb. p. 52; Watt, Dict. Econ. Prod. v. 6, part 1, p. 442.—VERN. *Ragt-roda.*

Rare. Found only on the highest hills of the Northern Ghâts (*Dalzell & Gibson*). There is one specimen in Herb. Kew. from Dalzell (!) from Hewra botanical garden, but no specimen from a plant truly wild. Mr. Woodrow informs me that he has searched for the plant himself and sent collectors to search for it, but has failed to find it.—DISTRIB. India (W. Peninsula): Ceylon.

Rhamnus triqueter, Laws. in Hook. f. Fl. B. I. v. 1 (1875) p. 639, has been found by N. B. Ranade, late herbarium-keeper in the College of Science, Poona, on the hill fort of *Kori* about 12 miles S. of Lanoli. It has also been found at the hill fort of Purandhar about 25 miles from Poona. The plant is a native of the Western Himalaya and the Salt range in the Panjab, and has not been found wild in Western or Southern India. It seems highly probable that the ancestors of the plants in the two Deccan hill forts were introduced, perhaps as medicinal plants. Mr. Woodrow informs me that they were abundant on the highest parts of the walls of the Kori fort.

4. SCUTIA, Commers.

Glabrous shrubs, spinous or unarmed; branches often angular. Leaves opposite or subopposite, coriaceous, penninerved. Flowers hermaphrodite, in axillary fascicles, or subumbellate. Calyx 5-fid; tube hemispheric or turbinate; lobes ovate, acute, thickened at the apex. Petals 5, clawed, erect, flat or cucullate. Disk filling the calyx-tube, the margin free, undulate. Stamens 5, as long as the petals, free. Ovary ovoid or globose, immersed in the disk, free, 2–4-celled, narrowed into a short 2–3-fid style; stigmas obtuse, papillose. Fruit obovoid or subglobose, dry or slightly fleshy, girt at the base by the persistent calyx-tube; pyrenes 2–4, crustaceous, angular or compressed. Seeds compressed; testa membranous; albumen 0 or thin.—DISTRIB. Asia, Africa and Tropical America; species 8.

1. **Scutia indica,** *Brongn. in Ann. Sc. Nat.* ser. 1, v. 10 (1827) p. 363. A straggling shrub, sometimes scandent; branches often decussate, armed

with recurved prickles. Leaves subopposite, subbifarious, ¾–1½ in. long, orbicular, elliptic or obovate, entire, glabrous, dark green and shining above; petioles ⅛ in. long; stipules subulate. Prickles hooked, usually inserted a little higher up than the petiole and a little to one side of it. Flowers small, in axillary umbels which are as long as, or sometimes slightly longer than, the petioles; peduncles and pedicels glabrous. Calyx glabrous; lobes ovate, acute, keeled below the thickened apex. Petals deeply bifid, clawed, as long as the stamens. Stamens inserted on the mouth of the calyx-tube and enclosed by the petals. Fruit ¼ in. in diam., globose, smooth; pyrenes crustaceous, compressed. Fl. B. I. v. 1, p. 640; Grah. Cat. p. 39; Dalz. & Gibs. p. 50; Trim. Fl. Ceyl. v. 1, p. 284; Talb. Trees, Bomb. p. 53; Woodr. in Journ. Bomb. Nat. v. 11 (1897) p. 271.—Flowers: Feb.–Apr. VERN. *Chimat.*

Very common on the higher Ghâts; abundant at Mahableshwar, where it is known as the "*wait-a-bit*" thorn. KONKAN: *Stocks*!, *Law*!, *Dalzell*, 80! DECCAN: Phunda Ghât, *Ritchie*, $\frac{80}{2}$!; Mahableshwar, *H. M. Birdwood*, *Cooke*!, *Woodrow*! KANARA: *Ritchie*, 80!; Supa Ghâts of N. Kanara, *Talbot*.—DISTRIB. India (W. Peninsula); Mauritius.

5. SAGERETIA, Brongn.

Shrubs unarmed or spinous; branches often decussate. Leaves subopposite; stipules minute, deciduous. Flowers hermaphrodite, very small, fascicled along terminal or axillary leafless paniculate branches. Calyx 5-fid; tube hemispheric or urceolate; lobes ovate, acute, keeled within. Petals 5, clawed, cucullate. Stamens 5, equalling the petals or nearly so. Disk cupular, filling the calyx-tube, the margin free, 5-lobed. Ovary ovoid, sunk in the disk, free, 3-celled; style short, 3-furrowed; stigmas 3, capitate or obtuse. Fruit globose, coriaceous, indehiscent; pyrenes 3. Seeds oblong; albumen thin; cotyledons flat.—DISTRIB. Central and E. Asia, Java and the warmer parts of N. America; species about 11.

1. **Sageretia oppositifolia,** *Brongn. Ann. Sc. Nat.* ser. 1, v. 10 (1827) p. 360. A shrub or small tree; branches slender, spinous, tomentose when young. Leaves 1½–4 by ¾–1½ in., ovate-oblong, acute or acuminate, serrate, clothed beneath when young with a dense woolly tomentum, base rounded or cordate; petioles ¼ in. long. Flowers in sessile clusters along the branches of terminal and axillary tomentose panicles; buds globose; bracts ovate, acute. Calyx pubescent outside; lobes triangular, thickened at the apex, keeled on the inner face. Petals obovate, clawed, longer than the stamens, keeled on the back. Disk in the form of a deep cup with free margin. Fruit obovoid, ⅓ in. long, not lobed, black when ripe, edible. Fl. B. I. v. 1, p. 641; Brandis, For. Fl. p. 95; Talb. Trees, Bomb. p. 53.

KONKAN: *Stocks*! and ex *Brandis* l. c. There is only one specimen in Herb Kew from Bombay marked "Konkan, *Stocks*."—DISTRIB. Throughout the greater part of India; Java.

6. COLUBRINA, *Rich.*

Erect or sarmentose shrubs. Leaves alternate; stipules small, deciduous. Flowers axillary, cymose or paniculate. Calyx 5-fid; tube hemispheric. Petals 5, inserted below the disk, clawed, cucullate.

Stamens 5, enclosed within the petals; filaments filiform. Disk thick, filling the calyx-tube, annular, 5-angled or 5-10-lobed. Ovary sunk in the disk and confluent with it, subglobose, 3-celled, attenuated into a 3-fid or 3-partite style; stigmas obtuse, papillose. Fruit subglobose, girt below the middle by the tube of the calyx, 3-celled; cells 1-seeded, tardily dehiscent. Seeds obovoid, compressed, 3-gonous; albumen thin, fleshy; cotyledons orbicular.—DISTRIB. Chiefly in the Tropical and warmer parts of N. America; species about 10.

1. **Colubrina asiatica,** *Brongn. in Ann. Sc. Nat.* ser. 1, v. 10 (1827) p. 369. A glabrous much-branched unarmed shrub. Leaves membranous, 1½–3 by 1–2¼ in., broadly ovate, acute or acuminate, crenate-serrate or subentire, glabrous, rounded or subcordate at the base; petioles ⅜–⅝ in. long. Flowers yellowish, in small axillary shortly peduncled pubescent cymes which are shorter than the petioles. Calyx-lobes broadly and acutely triangular, keeled on the inner face, scarcely thickened at the apex. Petals as long as the calyx, enveloping the stamens and longer than them, broadly obovate or orbicular, cucullate, the claw short and very slender. Ovary 3-celled; style 3-fid. Capsule globose, quite smooth, ⅜ in. in diam. Seeds chocolate-brown, rounded on the back, angled on the ventral side, slightly emarginate at the base, smooth. Fl. B. I. v. 1, p. 642; Grah. Cat. p. 39; Dalz. & Gibs. p. 50; Trim. Fl. Ceyl. v. 1, p. 285; Talb. Trees, Bomb. p. 53.—VERN. *Guti.*

KONKAN: Ghâts of the Konkan, *Talbot*; Elephanta, *Dalzell & Gibson*, *Graham*; near the sea at Ratnagiri, *Stocks*!, *Dalzell*!—DISTRIB. India (E. & W. Peninsulas); Java, Borneo, Australia, S.E. Africa, Ceylon.

7. GOUANIA, Linn.

Unarmed climbing shrubs, cirrhiferous. Leaves alternate, petiolate; stipules oblong, deciduous. Flowers polygamous, small, in axillary or terminal spikes or racemes; rhachis often cirrhose. Calyx superior, 5-fid; tube short, obconic; lobes 5. Petals 5, inserted below the margin of the disk, cucullate. Stamens 5, enclosed within the petals; anthers dehiscing longitudinally. Disk glabrous or pilose, epigynous and filling the calyx-tube, 5-gonous, or produced into 5 horns. Ovary sunk in the disk, 3-celled; style 3-partite or 3-fid; stigmas minute. Fruit coriaceous, inferior, crowned by the persistent limb of the calyx, 3-winged or boldly 3-angled. Seeds plano-convex, obovate; albumen scanty.—DISTRIB. Chiefly Tropical American; species about 50.

1. **Gouania microcarpa,** *DC. Prodr.* v. 2 (1825) p. 40. A shrub climbing by circinate axillary or sometimes extra-axillary tendrils. Leaves 2–4 by 1–2¼ in., ovate or elliptic, acute or acuminate, entire, glabrous, penninerved, rounded or subcordate at the base; secondary nerves 4–6 pairs, the pairs near the base often opposite; petioles ¼–⅝ in. long. Flowers in distant pubescent clusters, on the long branches of spicate terminal and axillary panicles. Calyx pubescent outside; lobes triangular, thickened at the apex, keeled on the inner face. Petals spathulate, clawed, truncate or slightly emarginate at the tip. Disk pubescent, the angles truncate. Fruit ¼ in. long by ½ in. broad, pubescent at first, afterwards glabrous and polished, with 3 large lobes

(scarcely wings) which are rounded at top and bottom. Fl. B. I. v. 1, p. 643; Trim. Fl. Ceyl. v. 1, p. 286; Talb. Trees, Bomb. p. 53. *G. leptostachya*, Dalz. & Gibs. p. 50; Talb. Trees, Bomb. p. 53 (*not* of DC.).—Flowers: Nov.-Dec.

KONKAN: *Stocks*!; Wari, *Dalzell*, 1684!; Banda, *Dalzell & Gibson*. S. M. COUNTRY: Ramghát, *Ritchie*, 1684! KANARA: very common on the N. Kanara Gháts, *Talbot*; Divimana (N. Kanara), *Woodrow*!; Supa, *Ritchie*, 1684!; Kumpta, *Cooke*!—DISTRIB. India (W. Peninsula); Ceylon, Java.

ORDER XLII. VITACEÆ, Lindl.

(*AMPELIDEÆ*, Endl.; Hook. f. & Benth. Gen. Pl.)

Small trees or shrubs which are usually climbers (except *Leea*); juice copious, watery; stems and branches nodose. Leaves alternate (the lower sometimes opposite), simple or digitately or pedately 3-11-foliolate, rarely pinnate. Flowers regular, hermaphrodite (rarely unisexual), usually small, generally greenish, in cymes, racemes, panicles or thyrsi usually opposite the leaves; peduncles often transformed into simple or compound tendrils. Calyx small, entire, or 4-5-toothed or -lobed. Petals 4-5, free or variously cohering, valvate, usually caducous. Stamens 4-5, opposite to the petals, inserted at the base of the disk or between its lobes; filaments subulate. Anthers free or connate, short, 2-celled, introrse. Disk between the stamens and ovary, various in form, free or connate with the petals and stamens or the ovary, urceolate, annular or widely expanded, rarely entirely confluent with the ovary. Ovary usually sunk in the disk, 2-6-celled; ovules 1-2 in each cell, ascending, anatropous; raphe ventral; style short, conical, subulate, or 0; stigma capitate or discoid, sublobate. Fruit baccate, often watery, 1-6-celled; cells 1-2-seeded. Seeds erect, rugulose; testa bony; embryo short, at the base of cartilaginous (often ruminate) albumen; cotyledons oval; radicle inferior.—DISTRIB. Throughout the tropical and temperate regions of the whole world; genera 3; species about 375.

Shrubs, usually scandent and cirrhose; stamens distinct, free; ovary 2-celled .... 1. VITIS.
Erect shrubs, ecirrhose; stamens connate with the disk; ovary 3-6-celled .... 2. LEEA.

1. VITIS, Linn.

Shrubs usually cirrhose, sarmentose, often climbing to a great height, very rarely erect. Leaves simple or compound (very rarely 2-pinnate). Flowers small, sometimes polygamous, umbellate, cymose, paniculate, racemose or spicate; peduncles leaf-opposed (very rarely axillary), usually towards the ends of the branches. Calyx short, entire or 4-5-toothed or -lobed. Petals 4-5, free or calyptrately cohering at the apex. Disk various or obsolete. Stamens 4-5, inserted below the margin of the disk; anthers free. Ovary 2-celled (sometimes imperfectly), very rarely 3-4-celled; ovules 2 in each cell; style 0 or short. Berry ovoid or globose, 1-2-celled; cells 1-2-seeded.—DISTRIB. Chiefly Tropical and Subtropical; not common in Tropical America; species about 320.

Leaves simple.
Flowers 4-merous.
An erect shrub; tendrils 0 .... 1. *V. Woodrowii.*
Scandent shrubs; tendrils leaf-opposed.
Leaves quite glabrous.
Stems terete or obscurely angled.
Leaves pale green.
Stems woody below .... 2. *V. pallida.*
Stems weak, trailing .... 3. *V. repens.*
Leaves blotched with white above, bright red beneath .... 4. *V. discolor.*
Stems and branches acutely angled or winged ...... 5. *V. quadrangularis.*
Leaves pubescent or tomentose beneath.
Leaves ovate.
Leaves subtomentose beneath; flowers green ... 6. *V. gigantea.*
Leaves when young densely tomentose beneath; flowers pink .... 7. *V. repanda.*
Leaves with orange-red pubescence beneath; flowers greenish-yellow .... 8. *V. adnata.*
Leaves 3-5-lobed, grey tomentose beneath .... 9. *V. Linnæi.*
Flowers 5-merous; peduncles cirrhiferous.
Leaves 3-5-lobed, floccose on both sides; flowers scarlet. 10. *V. tomentosa.*
Leaves ovate, glabrous above; flowers greenish-purple. 11. *V. indica.*
Leaves 3-7-lobed, at length glabrous; flowers reddish-brown .... 12. *V. latifolia.*
Leaves 3-foliolate (sometimes simple in *V. Rheedei*).
Flowers 4-merous.
Leaflets sessile or subsessile.
Berry black, smooth, 1-seeded; leaflets subsessile ... 13. *V. Rheedei.*
Berry scarlet, hispid, 1-seeded; leaflets quite sessile. 14. *V. setosa.*
Leaflets stalked.
Berry black, smooth, 2-4-seeded .... 15. *V. trifolia.*
Berry yellow, afterwards turning red, smooth, 1-seeded .... 16. *V. canarensis.*
Flowers 5-merous .... 17. *V. araneosa.*
Leaves digitate, usually 5-foliolate; flowers 4-merous.
Stipules small, cordate; berry black .... 18. *V. elongata.*
Stipules large, ear-shaped; berry red .... 19. *V. auriculata.*
Leaves usually pedate (sometimes 3-foliolate in *V. lanceolaria*).
Flowers bisexual.
Leaves 5-7-foliolate; stems glabrous .... 20. *V. tenuifolia.*
Leaves 7-11-foliolate; stems pubescent or hairy ...... 21. *V. pedata.*
Flowers diœcious .... 22. *V. lanceolaria.*

1. **Vitis Woodrowii,** *Stapf, MS.* An erect shrub 5-6 ft. high; trunk 3-4 in. thick at the base; bark rough, grey; lower branches 2-3 ft. long, annual, ecirrhose, slightly tomentose at the apex. Leaves up to 9 in. long and broad, pale green, cordate-ovate or cordate-rotund (with a broad sinus), usually shortly (rarely obscurely) 3-lobed, acute or acuminate, repand-crenate (the crenatures recurved), at first sparingly tomentose, at length glabrate, rather firm, palmi-nerved; petioles nearly equalling the blade, more or less tomentose when young; stipules triangular-ovate, reddish, caducous. Flowers tetramerous, in compound umbels; peduncles 1 in. or afterwards 2 in. long; primary rays usually 4, about $\frac{1}{2}$-$\frac{3}{4}$ in. long at time of flowering, afterwards up to $1\frac{1}{2}$ in. long; pedicels at time of flowering $\frac{1}{8}$ in., afterwards $\frac{1}{2}$ in. long, thick, straight. Calyx saucer-shaped: limb membranous, truncate or very obscurely lobed. Petals 4, calyptrately deciduous, hooded and thickened at the apex. Disk 4-lobed. Style short, stout, conical. Berry obovoid-globose,

about $\frac{1}{4}$ in. in diam. Seed solitary. ? *Cissus vitiginea*, Dalz. & Gibs. p. 40 (*not* of Roxb.); *Cissus* ——, Grah. Cat. p. 33 (n. 244).—Flowers: June. VERN. *Girnul.*

Very closely allied to *V. pallida*, W. & A., from which it differs in the absence of tendrils, an erect thick trunk and larger leaves which are almost invariably 3-lobed. The root contains starch-granules in abundance, of variable form, also raphides which are pointed at one end and 2–3-furcate at the other (*Woodrow*).

KONKAN: Bombay, *Capt. Geburne*! DECCAN: common in the Poona districts, *Woodrow*!; a roadside bush, *Nairne*; Bowdban forest near Poona, *Woodrow*!—DISTRIB. Apparently endemic in the Bombay Presidency.

2. **Vitis pallida,** *Wight & Arn. Prodr.* (1834) p. 125. A climbing shrub; stems woody below, terete or nearly so; tendrils simple. Leaves 3–6 in. in diam., pale green, cordate (with a wide sinus), ovate or orbicular, shortly acuminate, glabrous, the margins with shallow distant glandular incurved serratures; petioles 2–5 in. long; stipules membranous, broadly oblong, obtuse, caducous. Flowers in compound umbellate cymes; peduncle 1–2 in. long, thick and fleshy. Calyx saucer-shaped, the margins membranous. Petals 4, calyptrately deciduous but free at the apex, triangular-ovate. Style rather long, slender. Disk 4-lobed. Berry 1- (rarely 2-) seeded, size of a pea, pyriform or subglobose, mucronate, supported on an incurved pedicel. Fl. B. I. v. 1, p. 647; Trim. Fl. Ceyl. v. 1, p. 291; Talb. Trees, Bomb. p. 55; Woodr. in Journ. Bomb. Nat. v. 11 (1897) p. 271. *Cissus pallida*, Planch. in DC. Monogr. Phan. v. 5, part 2, p. 477.—Flowers: June–July.

Rare in the Bombay Presidency. S. M. COUNTRY: Padshapur, *Ritchie*; near Dharwar, *Talbot*.

3. **Vitis repens,** *Wight & Arn. Prodr.* (1834) p. 125. Scandent, quite glabrous; branches subterete when fresh, angled when dry; young shoots glaucous; tendrils weak, leaf-opposed, forked. Leaves membranous, pale green, 3–6 by 1–3½ in., broadly ovate, acuminate, glabrous, the margins undulate and distinctly spinous-toothed, base deeply cordate; main nerves about 4 pairs, the lower pair branching outwards; petioles 1–2¼ in. long; stipules rounded. Flowers in compound umbellate cymes; buds conical; peduncles leaf-opposed, solitary or rarely fascicled, 1–2½ in. long; pedicels slender. Calyx membranous, truncate. Petals 4, triangular-ovate, subacute, $\frac{1}{10}$ in. long, free. Berry subglobose or pyriform, $\frac{1}{8}$–$\frac{1}{4}$ in. in diam., usually 1-seeded. Fl. B. I. v. 1, p. 646; Talb. Trees, Bomb. p. 55; Woodr. in Journ. Bomb. Nat. v. 11 (1897) p. 271. *V. glauca*, W. & A. Prodr. p. 126. *Cissus repens*, Lam. Encyc. v. 1, p. 31; Dalz. & Gibs. p. 39; Planch. in DC. Monogr. Phan. v. 5, part 2, p. 504. *Cissus cordata*, Roxb. Fl. Ind. v. 1, p. 407; Grah. Cat. p. 32.—Flowers: Feb.–Mar.

I have followed Planchon (*l. c.*) in uniting this species with *V. glauca*. Although Lawson (Fl. B. I. l. c.) makes *Cissus cordata* Roxb. a synonym of both *V. repens* and *V. glauca*, he still retains these as separate species.

KONKAN: *Dalzell & Gibson*, *Graham*, *Talbot*. S. M. COUNTRY: Belgaum, *Ritchie*, 114! KANARA: in evergreen forests, not common; Ghâts near Supa, *Talbot*, 20!; Nilkund (N. Kanara), *Woodrow*.—DISTRIB. India (E. Tropical Himalaya, Assam, Chittagong, W. Peninsula); Java, Amboyna.

4. **Vitis discolor,** *Dalz. in Hook. Kew Journ. Bot.* v. 2 (1850) p. 39. Scandent; stem woody at the base only; young shoots and branches more or less 5–6-angled, deep red; tendrils leaf-opposed, forked. Leaves 3–5 by 1¼–2½ in., ovate-oblong, acuminate, usually irregularly blotched with white above, deep red and shining beneath, remotely bristle-serrate, glabrous, base more or less oblique, cordate, truncate or rounded, sometimes cuneate; main nerves 5–7 pairs; petioles red, those of the lower leaves reaching 2 in., those of the upper leaves about ¼ in. long or less; stipules ovate-oblong, rounded at the apex. Flowers 4-merous, in umbellate cymes on umbellately arranged branches; buds oblong; peduncles leaf-opposed, slender, short or long, and as well as the pedicels deep red. Calyx glandular, fleshy, truncate. Petals red outside, glabrous, $\frac{1}{12}$ in. long, thickened at the apex. Disk 4-lobed. Style long, glabrous. Fruit subglobose or pyriform, about ¼ in. long, red when ripe. Seed solitary. Fl. B. I. v. 1, p. 647; Talb. Trees, Bomb. p. 55; Woodr. in Journ. Bomb. Nat. v. 11 (1897) p. 271; Watt, Dict. Econ. Prod. v. 6, part 4, p. 253. *Cissus discolor*, Blume, Bijdr. p. 181; Dalz. & Gibs. p. 40; Planch. in DC. Monogr. Phan. v. 5, part 2, p. 496.—Flowers: Aug.–Oct. Vern. *Telitsayel.*

A very handsome plant, often grown in gardens in India and in conservatories in England. According to Watt (*l. c.*) depth of color and breadth of leaf are obtained when the plant is grown in shade.

Konkan: *Law!*, *Stocks!*, *Dalzell!*, *Talbot*; W. Ghâts, *Woodrow!* Deccan: below Mahableshwar near Wada bungalow, *Cooke!* Kanara: moist forests of N. Kanara, Yellapur, *Talbot!*—Distrib. Throughout India, Java.

5. **Vitis quadrangularis,** *Wall. Cat.* (1828) 5992. Stems leafless when old, very long, fleshy, glabrous, much contracted at the nodes, quadrangular, the angles of the young branches winged; tendrils long, slender, simple. Leaves 1–2 in. long, broadly ovate or reniform, sometimes 3–7-lobed, denticulate, glabrous, cordate, rounded, truncate or cuneate at the base; petioles ¼–½ in. long; stipules small, broadly ovate, obtuse. Flowers in shortly peduncled cymes with spreading umbellate branches. Calyx cup-shaped, truncate or very obscurely lobed. Petals 4, ovate-oblong, acute, ⅛ in. long, hooded at the apex. Disk erect, 4-lobed. Style short, stout. Berry obovoid or globose, scarcely ¼ in. long, apiculate, red when ripe, 1- (very rarely 2-) seeded. Fl. B. I. v. 1, p. 645; Trim. Fl. Ceyl. v. 1, p. 289; Talb. Trees, Bomb. p. 54; Woodr. in Journ. Bomb. Nat. v. 11 (1897) p. 271; Wight, Icon. t. 51; Watt, Dict. Econ. Prod. v. 6, part 4, p. 256. *Cissus quadrangularis*, Linn. Mantiss. p. 39; Planch. in DC. Monogr. Phan. v. 5, part 2, p. 509; Grah. Cat. p. 33; Dalz. & Gibs. p. 39. *Cissus edulis*, Dalz. in Hook. Kew Journ. Bot. v. 9 (1857) p. 248; Dalz. & Gibs. p. 40.—Flowers: July. Vern. *Chaudári*; *Kándvel*; *Harsankar.*

Throughout the driest districts of the Presidency, *Talbot.* Konkan: in gardens Bombay, *Graham.* Gujarat: in hedges, *Dalzell & Gibson*; Bhavnagar (Kathiawar), *Woodrow.*

The succulent stems are eaten in curries when young. Graham says that the Arabs, when suffering from affections of the spine, make beds of them. See Watt. Dict. Econ. Prod. l. c.—Distrib. Throughout India; Java, E. Africa, Malaya, Ceylon.

6. **Vitis gigantea,** *Bedd. in Trans. Linn. Soc.* v. 25 (1866) p. 212. An enormous climber; trunk 4–5 in. in diam.; bark corky; branches

terete, glabrous; tendrils bifid. Leaves 6–8 by 5–6 in., exactly cordate with a deep sinus, long-acuminate and mucronate, glabrous above, subtomentose beneath, bristle-crenate, 5-nerved from the base, much reticulate; petioles 2–5 in. long; stipules glandular. Flowers minute, green, cymose; peduncles shorter than the petioles; branches of the cymes 3–5, umbellate or bearing 2–3 umbellate branches at the apex. Fruit not seen. Fl. B. I. v. 1, p. 648. *Cissus gigantea*, Planch. in DC. Monogr. Phan. v. 5, part 2, p. 622.—Flowers: Aug.

There is but one specimen in Herb. Kew. communicated by Mr. Talbot.—It is without fruit. KANARA: Karwar, *Talbot*, 229!, *Woodrow*.

7. **Vitis repanda,** *Wight & Arn. Prodr.* (1834) p. 125. Scandent; branches terete, covered with appressed rufous tomentum when young, at length more or less glabrate; tendrils forked or 0. Leaves 3–7 by 2–6 in. (the lower sometimes opposite), broadly ovate, cordate, acuminate, coarsely crenate-dentate, inciso-serrate or sublobed, often repand, densely tomentose when young, particularly on the underside, at length glabrous above; petioles 1–3½ in. long; stipules oblong, rounded at the apex. Peduncles leaf-opposed, solitary or sometimes 1–4, each bearing 1–4 compound umbellately branched cymes; buds oblong-globose, hairy at the tips. Calyx truncate, hairy outside. Petals 4, pink, triangular-oblong, $\frac{1}{12}$ in. long, free or scarcely cohering at the apex. Berry pyriform, mucronate, 1-seeded. Seed obovoid, smooth. Fl. B. I. v. 1, p. 648 (exclud. syn. *Cissus vitiginea*, L.); Trim. Fl. Ceyl. v. 1, p. 292; Talb. Trees, Bomb. p. 55; Woodr. in Journ. Bomb. Nat. v. 11 (1897) p. 271. *Cissus repanda*, Vahl, Symb. v. 3, p. 18; Grah. Cat. p. 32; Dalz. & Gibs. p. 39; Planch. in DC. Monogr. Phan. v. 5, part 2, p. 474.—Flowers: Mar.–Apr. VERN. *Gendal*.

Common throughout the Presidency on the border of the heavy rainfall zone, *Talbot*. KONKAN: *Law*!, *Stocks*!; Malabar Hill, Bombay, *Graham*; Elephanta Island, *Graham*. DECCAN: Bowdhan Forest near Poona, *Woodrow*!—DISTRIB. Throughout India; Ceylon.

8. **Vitis adnata,** *Wall. Cat.* (1828) 5998. Scandent; stems and inflorescence clothed with orange-red pubescence, at length glabrate; tendrils forked. Leaves 3–5 by 2–3½ in., broadly ovate, abruptly and shortly acuminate or cuspidate, bristle-serrate, densely clothed with orange-red pubescence beneath, pubescent (at length glabrate) above; main nerves 4–5 pairs, prominent beneath; petioles 1–3 in. long, pubescent; stipules suborbicular, hairy, caducous. Flowers greenish-yellow, in much-branched peduncled compound umbellate cymes; buds oblong; fruiting pedicels more or less recurved. Calyx truncate or obscurely lobed. Petals 4, sometimes cohering at the apex and calyptrately deciduous. Berry ¼ in. in diam., obovoid or subglobose, glabrous, apiculate, 1- (rarely 2-) seeded, black when ripe. Seeds with angular pits on the surface. Fl. B. I. v. 1, p. 649; Trim. Fl. Ceyl. v. 1, p. 290; Talb. Trees, Bomb. p. 55; Woodr. in Journ. Bomb. Nat. v. 11 (1897) p. 271; Watt, Dict. Econ. Prod. v. 6, part 4, p. 251. *Cissus adnata*, Roxb. Fl. Ind. v. 1, p. 405; Wight, Icon. t. 144; Planch. in DC. Monogr. Phan. v. 5, part 2, p. 494.—Flowers: Dec.

Roxburgh (*l. c.*) says that the stipules are adnate, but I have not found them so, nor has Planchon (Monogr. l. c.). In Roxburgh's figure

(Icon. 1787), which has been copied by Wight (Icon. 144), the stipules are shown with a deep green centre, which cannot be distinguished in dried specimens.

KONKAN: *Stocks*! DECCAN: Bowdhan near Poona, *Woodrow*, *Bhiva*! KANARA: *Law*!; moist forests near Goond (N. Kanara), *Talbot*.—DISTRIB. Throughout India; Java, Borneo, Philippines, Ceylon.

9. **Vitis Linnæi,** *Wall. Cat.* (1828) 5987. Scandent, clothed with short grey or fulvous pubescence; branches terete; tendrils stout, simple, woody, pubescent near the base, glabrous upwards. Leaves 2–5¼ by 1¾–5 in., rotund-ovate, cordate or truncate at the base, shallowly or deeply palmately 3–5-lobed, sharply and irregularly dentate, softly glandular-pubescent and grey beneath (generally like the leaves of *Malva*); petioles ½–1⅝ in. long, pubescent; stipules membranous, ovate, obtuse, pubescent outside. Flowers 4-merous, in pedunculate cymes of 5–6 unequal branches; pedicels umbellate, slender, pubescent; buds oblong or subglobose, pubescent. Calyx truncate, pubescent outside. Petals $\frac{1}{18}$–$\frac{1}{12}$ in. long, pubescent outside, oblong, hooded, often calyptrately deciduous, usually free at the apex. Disk fleshy, 4-lobed. Style as long as the ovary. Berry ⅜ in. long, pyriform, blue and with a glaucous bloom on the surface, drooping, apiculate, 1-seeded. Seed obovoid, rugulose. Fl. B. I. v. 1, p. 649; Trim. Fl. Ceyl. v. 1, p. 291; Woodr. in Journ. Bomb. Nat. v. 11 (1897) p. 271; Watt, Dict. Econ. Prod. v. 6, part 4, p. 255. *Cissus vitiginea*, Linn. Sp. Pl. p. 117; Planch. in DC. Monogr. Phan. v. 5, part 2, p. 472.—Flowers: Aug.

There can be no doubt that this plant is the true *Cissus vitiginea* of Linnæus, the original type of his genus *Cissus*. Linnæus (Flor. Zeyl. [1747] p. 24) describes the leaves as subrotund, obsoletely pentagonal (as of *Malva*), tomentose, and the berry as blue, descriptions which are quite characteristic, that which compares the leaves to those of *Malva* especially so. In Amœn. Acad. ed. 1, v. 1 (1749) p. 390, Linnæus amplifies the description, and in Sp. Pl. (1753) p. 117 he gives the name *C. vitiginea* to the plant which he again describes therein.

DECCAN: near Wadi Station, G. I. P. Railway, *Cooke*! S. M. COUNTRY: Badami, *Woodrow*!—DISTRIB. India (W. Peninsula); Ceylon.

10. **Vitis tomentosa,** *Heyne, in Roth, Nov. Pl. Sp.* (1821) p. 157. Scandent; stems stout, covered with a dense reddish or white detergible tomentum; tendrils long, forked, woody. Leaves 4–8 in. long, as broad as, or sometimes broader than long, palmately 3–5-angled, -lobed or -partite, closely serrate-dentate, floccose with whitish cobwebby wool, base cordate with a wide sinus, less commonly truncate; petioles 1½–3 in. long; stipules short, truncate. Flowers 5-merous, scarlet, small, sessile, in shortly peduncled compact densely woolly cymes 1–2 in. long, at the ends of stiff leaf-opposed peduncles; peduncles bearing a long 1–3-forked tendril below the cyme; buds broadly oblong, truncate, araneously woolly. Calyx thin, membranous, woolly outside, covering over the petals in bud, 5-lobed; lobes short, triangular. Petals 5, ovate-oblong, not cohering at the apex, glabrous. Ovary conical, 10-furrowed at the apex; style 0; stigma foveolate. Berry subglobose, ⅓ in. in diam., 2–3-seeded. Seeds ovoid-oblong, coarsely and irregularly rugose. Fl. B. I. v. 1, p. 650; Trim. Fl. Ceyl. v. 1, p. 288; Talb. Trees, Bomb. p. 55; Watt, Dict. Econ. Prod. v. 6, part 4, p. 258. *Ampelocissus tomentosa*, Planch. in Journn. Vigne Amer. (Dec. 1884) p. 375 & in

DC. Monogr. Phan. v. 5, part 2, p. 376.—Flowers: Mar. VERN. *Shend-vel.*

S. M. COUNTRY: common in the forests of the Dharwar districts along the banks of streams and rivers, *Talbot*; Belgaum, *Ritchie*, 116! KANARA: dry forests on the N. Kanara border, *Talbot*; Mándgod (N. Kanara), *Talbot*, 144!—DISTRIB. India (W. Peninsula); Ceylon.

11. **Vitis indica,** *Linn. Sp. Pl.* (1753) p. 202. Scandent; stems stout, hollow, cylindric, more or less floccose-woolly, striate; tendrils simple, 6 in. long or more, floccose-woolly. Leaves 4–9 by 3–8 in., broadly ovate, deeply cordate with a narrow sinus and rounded lobes, acute or acuminate, coarsely glandular-dentate, glabrous at length above, rufous- or grey-tomentose on the nerves beneath; nerves 6–8 pairs, prominent beneath, the two lower pairs much branched on the lower side; petioles 3 in. long, densely floccose-woolly. Flowers 5-merous, greenish-purple, almost hidden in a reddish woolly tomentum, nearly sessile, in dense clusters on the thick branches of a racemose or paniculate cyme 2–3 in. long; buds oblong-obovoid, flattened at the top; peduncles 2–7 in. long, usually bearing a simple tendril below the cyme. Calyx small, truncate. Petals oblong, $\frac{1}{12}$ in. long. Ovary grooved; stigma foveolate. Berry $\frac{3}{4}$ in. long, ovoid-oblong, smooth, purple. Grah. Cat. p. 33; Dalz. & Gibs. p. 41; Trim. Fl. Ceyl. v. 1, p. 288; Talb. Trees, Bomb. p. 55; King, in Journ. As. Soc. Beng. v. 65 (1897) p. 112. *Vitis erioclada*, W. & A. Prodr. p. 130; Laws. in Fl. B. I. v. 1, p. 651; Woodr. in Journ. Bomb. Nat. v. 11 (1897) p. 271. *Schembra Valli*, Rheede, Hort. Mal. v. 7, p. 11, t. 6. *Ampelocissus erioclada* (?), Planch. in DC. Monogr. Phan. v. 5, part 2, p. 380.

KONKAN: *Graham*; evergreen forests, *Talbot*. KANARA: Kadgal, *Woodrow*; evergreen forests, *Talbot*.—DISTRIB. India (W. Peninsula); Ceylon.

12. **Vitis latifolia,** *Roxb. Hort. Beng.* (1814) p. 18. An extensive climber; stems weak, finely striate, glabrous; tendrils forked. Leaves 4–7 in. long, as broad as long, orbicular, cordate, 3–7-angled or -lobed (sometimes palmately), sharply and irregularly toothed, reticulately veined, tomentose beneath when young, at length glabrous; main nerves 5–7 pairs, the lowest pair almost horizontal, branched on the lower side; petioles $2\frac{1}{2}$–4 in. long. Flowers small, 5-merous, deep reddish-brown, in compact thyrsoid cymes; buds ovoid-oblong, glabrous; peduncles bearing a slender forked tendril below the cyme. Calyx small, truncate. Petals $\frac{1}{10}$ in. long, oblong, not cohering at the apex. Style 0; stigma foveolate. Berry edible, $\frac{1}{4}$–$\frac{3}{8}$ in. long, globose, glabrous, usually 2- (rarely 3-) seeded, black. Seeds ellipsoid, $\frac{1}{4}$–$\frac{1}{3}$ in. long, rounded and transversely grooved on the back, flattened on, and with a raised ridge in the middle of the face, smooth, polished. Fl. B. I. v. 1, p. 652; Talb. Trees, Bomb. p. 55; Woodr. in Journ. Bomb. Nat. v. 11 (1897) p. 271. *Cissus latifolia*, Vahl, Symb. v. 3, p. 18; Grah. Cat. p. 32; Dalz. & Gibs. p. 39. *Ampelocissus latifolia*, Planch. in Journ. Vigne Amer. (Dec. 1884) p. 374 & in DC. Monogr. Phan. v. 5, part 2, p. 370.—Flowers: June–Aug. VERN. *Nadena.*

KONKAN: common, *Dalzell & Gibson*; Malabar Hill (Bombay), *Graham*; W. Gháts, *Kanitkar*!, *Woodrow*!; Ratnagiri, *Nairne*. DECCAN: Bowdhan near Poona, *Woodrow*! KANARA: moist forests near the coast; common near Karwar and on the N. Kanara Gháts, *Talbot*. GUJARAT: Godra, *Cooke*!—DISTRIB. India (N.W. Prov., Assam, W. Peninsula).

13. **Vitis Rheedei,** *Wight & Arn. Prodr.* p. 127. Quite glabrous; stem stout, cylindric or tetragonous. Leaves variable, usually 3-foliolate (with very shortly stalked or sessile leaflets), sometimes 3-partite or 3-lobed or simple (often all 3 kinds of leaves on one and the same plant); leaflets or segments unequal, the middle one lanceolate, the lateral ones very obliquely ovate or oblong, all acuminate or acute, bristle-serrate, glabrous on both sides; petioles 1–2 in. long; stipules ovate-orbicular. Flowers 4-merous, in subumbellate divaricate cymes which are usually shorter than the petioles, numerous near the end of the branch and the last cyme terminating it; pedicels short. Calyx saucer-shaped, subtruncate. Petals 4, free. Style long. Berry $\frac{3}{8}$ in. long, obovoid, 1-seeded, black. Seed $\frac{1}{8}$–$\frac{3}{16}$ in. in diam., girt with a ring round the middle, smooth, yellowish-white. Fl. B. I. v. 1, p. 653; Trim. Fl. Ceyl. v. 1, p. 293; Talb. Trees, Bomb. p. 55. *Cissus trilobata,* Lam. Encyc. v. 1, p. 31; Grah. Cat. p. 33; Dalz. & Gibs. p. 39; Planch. in DC. Monogr. Phan. v. 5, part 2, p. 503.

KONKAN: ex *Dalzell & Gibson* l. c.—DISTRIB. India (W. Peninsula); Ceylon.

14. **Vitis setosa,** *Wall. Cat.* (1828) 6009. Whole plant clothed with scattered glandular bristly hairs; stem herbaceous, prostrate, weak, succulent, striate and sulcate; tendrils leaf-opposed, forked, long. Leaves succulent, sessile, 3-foliolate (the lower sometimes simple); leaflets subfleshy, 2–3 by 1$\frac{1}{2}$–2 in., shortly petioluled (the petiolule of the terminal leaflet the longest), elliptic or obovate-oblong, obtuse, irregularly bristle-toothed or laciniate, glabrous or nearly so above, glandular-hispid on the nerves beneath, pale green; stipules broadly ovate, acute. Flowers $\frac{1}{12}$ in. long, contracted in the middle, arranged in leaf-opposed or apparently terminal dichotomous or trichotomous lax divaricate glandular cymes; peduncles 1$\frac{1}{2}$–3 in. long, glandular-hispid; pedicels short. Calyx cup-shaped, subtruncate. Petals hooded at the apex, ultimately reflexed. Style subulate. Berry $\frac{1}{4}$–$\frac{5}{16}$ in. in diam., ovoid, glandular-hispid, scarlet. Fl. B. I. v. 1, p. 654; Trim. Fl. Ceyl. v. 1, p. 296; Talb. Trees, Bomb. p. 55; Woodr. in Journ. Bomb. Nat. v. 11 (1897) p. 271; Watt, Dict. Econ. Prod. v. 6, part 4, p. 257. *Cissus setosa,* Roxb. Fl. Ind. v. 1, p. 410; Dalz. & Gibs. p. 41; Planch. in DC. Monogr. Phan. v. 5, part 2, p. 608. VERN. *Khájagolicha-vel.*

Planchon is, I think, in error in calling the cymes axillary.

DECCAN: *Woodrow*!; Alandi, near Poona, *Bhiva*!; Poona districts, *Cooke*!; about Junnar, *Dalzell & Gibson*. S. M. COUNTRY: Kuput hills of Dharwar in dry rocky situations, *Talbot*.—DISTRIB. India (W. Peninsula); Ceylon.

Every part of the plant is acrid. It has some repute in native medicine, being used to promote suppuration and assist in the extraction of Guinea-worms.—See Watt, Dict. Econ. Prod. l. c.

15. **Vitis trifolia,** *Linn. Sp. Pl.* (1753) p. 203. Scandent; stems herbaceous or woody at the base only, compressed, densely pubescent when young; tendrils short, slender, usually branched. Leaves 3-foliolate; common petioles $\frac{3}{4}$–1$\frac{3}{4}$ in. long; leaflets thick, 1$\frac{1}{2}$–2$\frac{1}{4}$ by $\frac{7}{8}$–1$\frac{1}{4}$ (the middle one the largest), rotund-ovate, ovate-lanceolate or obovate, acute or obtuse, crenate-serrate or subinciso-dentate, more or less pubescent on both surfaces; main nerves 5–6 pairs; petiolules of the lateral leaflets $\frac{1}{8}$–$\frac{1}{4}$ in. long, those of the terminal leaflets twice as long; stipules small, ovate, acute. Flowers in branched divaricate pubescent

long-peduncled cymes; buds globose; pedicels about $\frac{1}{8}$ in. long. Calyx pubescent outside, funnel-shaped, truncate or obscurely 4-lobed. Petals 4, oblong, rounded at the apex, $\frac{1}{10}$ in. long, hooded, pubescent outside. Disk cup-shaped with a plicate margin. Style conical. Berry turbinate, fleshy, $\frac{1}{2}$-$\frac{3}{4}$ in. long, 2-4-seeded. Seeds triangular, rounded and rugose on the back, cuneate on the face. King, in Journ. As. Soc. Beng. v. 65 (1897) p. 402. *Vitis carnosa*, Wall. Cat. 6018; Laws. in Fl. B. I. v. 1, p. 654 (*exclud. syn.* Cissus auriculata, *Roxb.*); Trim. Fl. Ceyl. v. 1, p. 294; Talb. Trees, Bomb. p. 56; Woodr. in Journ. Bomb. Nat. v. 11 (1897) p. 271; Watt, Dict. Econ. Prod. v. 6, part 4, p. 252. *Cissus carnosa*, Lam. Encyc. v. 1, p. 31; Roxb. Fl. Ind. v. 1, p. 409; Grah. Cat. p. 33; Dalz. & Gibs. p. 40; Planch. in DC. Monogr. Phan. v. 5, part 2, p. 570.—Flowers: Aug. VERN. *A'mbat-vel.*

There is no doubt as to the identity of this plant with *Vitis trifolia*, Linn. That Linnæus included under the genus *Vitis* a plant with 4-merous flowers is easily accounted for by the fact that he never saw the plant. There is no specimen in the Linnean Herbarium in the Linnean Society, and Linnæus merely copied a portion of the very meagre description given by Ray, Hist. Pl. v. 3 (1704) lib. 28, p. 68, who calls the plant *Vitis pearmedoorica*, a synonym quoted by Linnæus. Ray, however, merely quotes Pettiver, who first described the plant in Phil. Trans. v. 22 (1700-1701) p. 707. I have personally examined Pettiver's actual specimens which are in the British Museum. Rheede (Hort. Mal. v. 7, t. 9) gives a good figure of the plant.

KONKAN: Ghâts, *Talbot.* DECCAN: widely, *Woodrow*; Bhadgaon near Poona, *Bhiva*!; below Mahableshwar, *Cooke*!; hills near Bowdhan (Poona district), *Woodrow*! S. M. COUNTRY: Badami, *Woodrow*!; common in the Dharwar district bordering on N. Kanara, *Talbot.* KANARA: Ghâts of N. Kanara, *Talbot.*—DISTRIB. Throughout India; Ceylon, Malacca.

16. **Vitis canarensis,** *Dalz. in Hook. Kew Journ. Bot.* v. 3 (1851) p. 123. Whole plant except the inflorescence at length glabrous; branches terete, striate. Leaves 3-foliolate, long-petioled; leaflets 3-4 by $1\frac{1}{2}$-$2\frac{1}{2}$ in., elliptic-obovate or lanceolate, suddenly and shortly acuminate, pubescent on both surfaces, at length glabrous, distantly serrate, reticulately veined, base inequilateral, somewhat cuneate; petiolules of the lower leaflets $\frac{1}{2}$ in. long, those of the terminal leaflets twice as long. Flowers in axillary or leaf-opposed puberulous cymes; peduncles shorter than the petioles. Calyx small, truncate or obscurely lobed. Petals 4, oblong, subacute, hooded at the apex, $\frac{1}{12}$-$\frac{1}{10}$ in. long, faintly puberulous outside. Style short; stigma acute. Berry $\frac{5}{16}$ in. in diam., globose, almost smooth, yellow, afterwards turning red, dry, 1-seeded. Seeds $\frac{1}{4}$ in. long, ellipsoid or subglobose, smooth, speckled and faintly transversely striate. Fl. B. I. v. 1, p. 655; Talb. Trees, Bomb. p. 56. *Cissus canarensis*, Planch. in DC. Monogr. Phan. v. 5, part 2, p. 620.—Flowers: Apr.

KANARA: Supa Ghâts of N. Kanara in evergreen forests, common, *Talbot*; Kanara, *Dalzell*!; Ainshi (N. Kanara), *Talbot*, 2700!—DISTRIB. Apparently endemic.

17. **Vitis araneosa,** *Laws. in Hook. f. Fl. B. I.* v. 1 (1875) p. 657. Scandent, the whole plant covered with floccose down which is deciduous except on the underside of the leaves; tendrils forked. Leaves 3-foliolate, ultimately glabrous above, clothed beneath with persistent floccose

down, the common petiole 1–2¼ in. long; terminal leaflets 3–4 by 1½–2 in., elliptic or lanceolate, acute, crenate-serrate, attenuated or rounded and nearly equilateral at the base, on petiolules about ½–¾ in. long; lateral leaflets scarcely smaller, very inequilateral at the base (the lower side much the larger and rounded, the upper side smaller and acute), on petiolules about ½ as long as those of the terminal leaflets. Flowers 5-merous, in leaf-opposed small umbellate cymes; peduncles reaching 3 in. long, bearing a forked tendril below the cyme; pedicels very short. Calyx small, membranous, 5-lobed or truncate. Petals 5, oblong, rounded at the apex, $\frac{1}{12}$ in. long. Ovary ribbed at the apex; style short, stout; stigma foveolate. Berry globose, size of a pea, 1–4-seeded. Seeds ellipsoid, ¼ by ⅙ in., rugose, pointed at one end, longitudinally grooved on the back and with a deep circular depression on the face. Talb. Trees, Bomb. p. 56; Planch. in DC. Monogr. Phan. v. 5, part 2, p. 405; Watt, Dict. Econ. Prod. v. 6, part 4, p. 252. *Cissus araneosus*, Dalz. & Gibs. p. 41.—Flowers: Sept.

Rare. DECCAN: highest Ghâts west of Junnar, *Dalzell & Gibson*.

This plant has been included on the authority of Dalzell and Gibson (Bomb. Fl. p. 41), who give its habitat as the highest Ghâts west of Junnar. I have seen no specimens from the Bombay Presidency, those in Herb. Kew. being from the Pulney Hills *ex* Herb. Wight.—DISTRIB. India (W. Peninsula).

18. **Vitis elongata,** *Wall. Cat.* (1828) 6016. A large glabrous climber; stems very long, somewhat compressed, succulent, smooth, branching only near the top; tendrils long, simple, leaf-opposed. Leaves digitately usually 5- (less commonly 3-) foliolate, the common petiole 2–4 in. long, sulcate; stipules small, cordate; leaflets 4–6 by 1–2 in., oblong-lanceolate or elliptic-lanceolate, acuminate, serrate, narrowed into a very short petiolule. Flowers greenish-purple, 4-merous, in di- or di-trichotomous leaf-opposed cymes, the ultimate branches short, umbellate. Calyx membranous, cup-shaped, truncate. Petals 4, oblong, subacute, $\frac{1}{10}$–⅛ in. long. Disk 4-lobed. Ovary ovoid; style slender; stigma simple. Berry about the size of a cherry, ellipsoid, 1-seeded, black when ripe. Seed ¾ in. long, ellipsoid, pointed at one end, rugose on the back and with a large elliptic pit on the face. Fl. B. I. v. 1, p. 658; Talb. Trees, Bomb. p. 56; Woodr. in Journ. Bomb. Nat. v. 11 (1897) p. 272. *Cissus elongata*, Roxb. Fl. Ind. v. 1, p. 411; Planch. in DC. Monogr. Phan. v. 5, part 2, p. 621.—Flowers: May–Oct.

KONKAN: *Law*! DECCAN: Lanoli, *Dalzell*!; Khandala, *Bhiva*!; Panchgani, *Cooke*!; Mahableshwar, *Cooke*! KANARA: in the forests on the coast near Karwar, *Talbot*; Sirsi-Kumpta road, *Woodrow*!—DISTRIB. India (Sikkim Himalaya, Bengal, Silhet, Coromandel).

19. **Vitis auriculata,** *Wall. Cat.* (1828) 6031. An extensive climber; branches succulent; young parts softly pubescent; tendrils leaf-opposed, 2–3-cleft. Leaves 5-foliolate, common petioles 3–6 in. long, stipules large, ear-shaped; leaflets membranous, 2–6 by 1–4 in., obovate or rhomboidal, acute or shortly acuminate, serrate, glabrous above, more or less pubescent beneath; petiolules ½–1½ in. long, those of the terminal leaflet nearly twice as long as those of the lateral ones. Flowers 4-merous, small, in much-branched divaricate cymes longer than the petioles; peduncles weak, striate, pubescent; pedicels very short. Calyx membranous, truncate, pubescent outside. Petals 4, oblong, obtuse, hooded at the apex, pubescent outside. Fruit the size

of a cherry, globose, smooth, shining, red when ripe, 1-seeded. Seed ellipsoid or subglobose, concave on the face. Fl. B. I. v. 1, p. 658; Talb. Trees, Bomb. p. 56; Woodr. in Journ. Bomb. Nat. v. 11 (1897) p. 272. *Cissus auriculata*, Roxb. Fl. Ind. (ed. Carey) v. 1 (1820) p. 430; DC. Prodr. v. 1, p. 632; Grah. Cat. p. 246; Dalz. & Gibs. p. 40; Wight, Icon. t. 145; Planch. in DC. Monogr. Phan. v. 5, part 2, p. 565. —Flowers: Mar.–June. VERN. *Kali-vel*; *Jangli-kájorni.*

KONKAN: on rocks by the seashore, Bombay, *Woodrow*; Vingorla, *Dalzell & Gibson*. DECCAN: Sindewadi, top of Kartriz Ghát (Poona districts), *Woodrow*! S. M. COUNTRY: about Dharwar, *Law ex Graham*; Belgaum and Dharwar districts, *Talbot*.—DISTRIB. Throughout India.

20. **Vitis tenuifolia,** *Wight & Arn. Prodr.* (1834) p. 129. Scandent; stems slender, striate, glabrous; tendrils leaf-opposed, slender, usually forked. Leaves compound, petioled, the petioles 1–3 in. long; leaflets 5–7, 1–3 by $\frac{3}{4}$–2 in. long, the lateral pedately arranged, the terminal leaflet slightly larger and with a longer petiolule than the lateral ones, all lanceolate, acuminate, mucronate, cuneate at the base, shallowly repand-serrate, glabrous. Flowers bisexual, 4-merous, in axillary dichotomously branched lax divaricate cymes. Calyx funnel-shaped, truncate. Petals 4, ovate-oblong, obtuse, hooded at the apex, $\frac{1}{12}$ in. long. Disk 4-lobed. Style short, conical. Berry $\frac{3}{8}$–$\frac{1}{2}$ in. long, turbinate-globose, cream-colored when ripe, 1–4-seeded. Seeds $\frac{3}{16}$ in. long, pointed, cuneate on the face and with a prominent longitudinal midrib down the centre of the rounded back, transversely rugose at each side of the midrib. Fl. B. I. v. 1, p. 660; Trim. Fl. Ceyl. v. 1, p. 295; Talb. Trees, Bomb. p. 56; Woodr. in Journ. Bomb. Nat. v. 11 (1897) p. 272. *Cissus tenuifolia*, Heyne, in Wall. Cat. 6022; Planch. in DC. Monogr. v. 5, part 2, p. 563.—Flowers: May–Aug.

KANARA: moist forests of the N. Kanara Ghâts from Ainshi southwards, *Talbot*; Gudehalli near Karwar, *Woodrow*.—DISTRIB. India generally; China, Japan.

21. **Vitis pedata,** *Vahl, ex Wall. Cat.* (1828) 6027. Scandent, softly pubescent, sometimes hairy, rarely glabrate; tendrils long, slender, forked. Leaves 7–11-foliolate, the lateral leaflets pedately arranged; common petioles 2–3 in. long, hairy or glabrate; leaflets 2–5 by 1–2$\frac{1}{2}$ in., oblong-lanceolate, acuminate, serrate, pubescent or glabrous, often oblique at the base; petiolules variable in length, those of the terminal leaflets usually much longer than those of the lateral ones. Flowers bisexual, white, in axillary divaricate shortly pedunculate corymbose cymes. Calyx shallow, 4-lobed; lobes triangular. Petals 4 (rarely 5), triangular, calyptrately deciduous, cohering at the apex. Disk large, cup-shaped, exceeding the ovary. Berry about the size of a pea, subglobose or often 4-lobed, 2–4-seeded, cream-colored when ripe. Seeds hemispheric, smooth, with a deep circular pit closed by a thin membrane on the flat lower face. Fl. B. I. v. 1, p. 661; Trim. Fl. Ceyl. v. 1, p. 295; Talb. Trees, Bomb. p. 56; Watt, Dict. Econ. Prod. v. 6, part 4, p. 256. *Cissus pedata*, Lamk. Encyc. v. 1, p. 31; Grah. Cat. p. 33; Dalz. & Gibs. p. 40; Planch. in DC. Monogr. Phan. v. 5, part 2, p. 558.

KONKAN: *Stocks*!, *Dalzell*!, *Graham*, *Talbot*. KANARA: not common, *Talbot*; Shiroli (N. Kanara), *Talbot*, 2687!—DISTRIB. India generally; Malaya, Ceylon.

22. **Vitis lanceolaria,** *Wall. Cat.* (1828) 6013. Scandent, glabrous except the inflorescence; stem woody; branches with lenticellate bark; tendrils long, slender, simple. Leaves 3- or 5-foliolate (in the latter case the leaflets pedately arranged); petioles 1–2½ in. long; leaflets stalked, 3–5 by 1–2 in., oblong-lanceolate, irregularly serrate, glabrous. Flowers 4-merous, diœcious, axillary; male cymes paniculate, longer than the petiole; female cymes denser, corymbose, shorter than the petiole; branches of the inflorescence pubescent. Calyx funnel-shaped, truncate at the apex. Petals ovate-oblong, obtuse, hooded at the apex, $\frac{1}{12}$ in. long. Stigma large, 4-lobed. Berry about ½ in. in diam., globose, 2–4-seeded, cream-colored when ripe. Seeds ellipsoid, obtusely angular on the face, rounded and with a single deep groove on the back, smooth. Fl. B. I. v. 1, p. 660; Trim. Fl. Ceyl. v. 1, p. 296; Talb. Trees, Bomb. p. 56; Woodr. in Journ. Bomb. Nat. v. 11 (1897) p. 272. *Cissus lanceolaria*, Roxb. Hort. Beng. p. 11; Grah. Cat. p. 33. *Cissus muricata*, Dalz. & Gibs. p. 40. *Tetrastigma lanceolarium*, Planch. in DC. Monogr. Phan. v. 5, part 2, p. 423.—Flowers: Dec.–Mar. Vern. *Kazorlicha-yel.*

Konkan: *Graham*; Matheran, *Woodrow.* Kanara: plentiful, *Dalzell & Gibson*; N. Kanara Ghâts in evergreen forests, *Talbot.*—Distrib. India (Assam, E. & W. Peninsulas); Ceylon.

Vitis vinifera, Linn. The grape vine (Vern. *Angur*) is cultivated in several parts of the Presidency. The moist climate of the Konkan is not suitable for vine-growing, but in parts of the Deccan, *e.g.* Ahmednagar, and especially Nasik, grapes of fairly good quality are grown for the Bombay market. The vines are usually trained on live posts cut from *Erythrina indica*, a tree known in the vernacular as the *Pángara.*

The vine is largely cultivated in Sind, the climate of which province seems highly favorable to its growth. Woodrow (Gardening in India) speaks in terms of high approbation of the system of growing the vine at Hyderabad which was introduced by Mr. Strachan.

For an exhaustive account of the culture of the vine in India consult Watt's Dict. Econ. Prod. v. 6, part 4, pp. 258–296. Woodrow (Gardening in India, ed. 5 (1889) pp. 218–230) gives a full account of the mode of culture adopted in the Bombay Presidency.

2. LEEA, Linn.

Small trees, shrubs or herbs; branches usually striate or sulcate. Leaves alternate, usually large, simple or 1–2–3-pinnate; petioles often dilated at the base; stipules sheathing. Peduncles leaf-opposed or subterminal. Tendrils 0. Inflorescence corymbosely cymose. Flowers small, red, yellow, white or green. Calyx 5-toothed. Petals 5, connate at the base and adhering to the staminal tube, revolute. Stamens united at the base into a 5-lobed tube; filaments inserted between the lobes of the tube, inflexed; anthers either free and exserted or connate and enclosed in the tube. Ovary inserted on the disk, 3–8-celled; ovules 1–2 in each cell, erect: style short; stigma thickened. Fruit 3–8-celled, baccate, usually succulent, depressed-globular and lobed. Pyrenes wedge-shaped. Seed compressed.—Distrib. Tropical Asia, Africa, a few species in Australia; species about 50.

Leaves simple .... 1. *L. macrophylla.*
Leaves usually simply pinnate.
  Main nerves of leaflets close; bracts subpersistent.
    Stems with crisp wings .... 2. *L. crispa.*
    Stems without crisp wings .... 3. *L. aspera.*
  Main nerves of leaflets not close; bracts caducous .... 4. *L. latifolia.*
Leaves 2–3-pinnate.
  Leaves glabrous .... 5. *L. sambucina.*
  Leaves hairy beneath.
    Lobes of staminal-tube entire .... 6. *L. robusta.*
    Lobes of staminal-tube notched.
      Leaves with scattered glandular discs beneath .... 7. *L. æquata.*
      Leaves without glandular discs .... 8. *L. setuligera.*

1. **Leea macrophylla,** *Roxb. ex Hornem. Hort. Hafn.* v. 1 (1813) p. 231. Herbaceous, erect, 1–3 ft. high; root tuberous, perennial, red. Leaves simple, broadly ovate, cordate, acute or acuminate, coarsely serrate or sublobed, nearly as broad as long, the lower leaves up to 2 ft., the upper 6–9 in. long, dark green and glabrous above, cano-pubescent beneath; main nerves opposite, 8–10 pairs, very prominent; petioles 2–5 in. long, deeply striate, glabrous. Flowers white, in terminal much-branched puberulous corymbose cymes often 1 ft. long; buds oblong; peduncles deeply grooved; pedicels short. Calyx divided about $\frac{1}{3}$ of the way down; lobes triangular-ovate, tipped with a small hard point. Petals oblong. Staminal-tube deeply divided; lobes oblong, entire or emarginate; anthers laterally united in bud. Berry $\frac{1}{4}$–$\frac{1}{3}$ in. in diam., black, 3–6-celled, depressed-globose, usually 3–6-lobed. Fl. B. I. v. 1, p. 664 (excluding syn. *L. latifolia*); Grah. Cat. p. 247; Dalz. & Gibs. p. 41; Wight, Icon. t. 1154; C. B. Clarke, in Trim. Journ. Bot. (1881) p. 137; Talb. Trees, Bomb. p. 57; Woodr. in Journ. Bomb. Nat. v. 11 (1897) p. 272; Watt, Dict. Econ. Prod. v. 4, p. 617.—Flowers: July–Sept. Vern. *Dinda.*

Konkan: *Nimmo* ex *Graham*; Neral, *Woodrow*!; W. Ghâts, *Woodrow*. Deccan: Singhad near Poona, *Bhiva*! Kanara: common in the forests near Yellapur (N. Kanara), *Talbot*.

The root is employed in native medicine, being used for the cure of Guinea-worm. See Watt, Dict. Econ. Prod. l. c.—Distrib. Throughout the hotter parts of India.

2. **Leea crispa,** *Linn. Mantiss.* v. 1 (1767) p. 124. An erect shrub, 4–8 ft. high; stems somewhat woody, jointed, swollen above the joints, and together with the branches, peduncles, and petioles, furnished with 6–8 short crisp wings. Leaves usually simply pinnate (the lower pair of leaflets rarely with one (or both?) of the pair compound); leaflets oblong, very parallel-sided, 4–7 by $1\frac{1}{2}$–3 in., acute or shortly acuminate, sharply serrate, glabrous above, pubescent on the nerves and veins beneath, usually rounded at the base; main nerves 12–20 pairs, prominent, parallel, nearly straight, one running into each serrature; veins transverse, nearly parallel, close, conspicuous beneath; petiolules of the lateral leaflets $\frac{1}{8}$–$\frac{1}{2}$ in. long, those of the terminal much longer. Flowers greenish-white, in small terminal slightly pubescent cymes; bracts subpersistent, linear-subulate, $\frac{1}{4}$–$\frac{1}{3}$ in. long; bracteoles $\frac{1}{8}$ in. long, lanceolate. Calyx shortly divided; lobes triangular, gland-tipped. Petals oblong. Lobes of the staminal-tube linear-oblong, bifid; anthers not united in bud. Style grooved. Berry $\frac{1}{3}$ in. in diam., depressed-globular, usually 2–6 (or more) -lobed, black when ripe. Fl. B. I. v. 1,

p. 665; C. B. Clarke, in Trim. Journ. Bot. (1881) p. 135; Talb. Trees, Bomb. p. 57; Watt, Dict. Econ. Prod. v. 4, p. 616.—Flowers: Aug.

KONKAN: from the sea-level upwards in moist forests, *Talbot*. KANARA: Karwar, *Talbot*!—DISTRIB. India (W. Trop. Himalaya, Oude, W. Peninsula).

3. **Leea aspera,** *Edgew. in Trans. Linn. Soc.* v. 20 (1841) p. 36 (*not* of Wall.). A shrub 6–10 ft. high; stems terete, not crisply winged. Leaves usually simply pinnate (one or both the leaflets of the lowest pair sometimes compound); leaflets 5–7, elliptic, not parallel-sided, 5–8 by 2½–4 in., more or less acuminate, glabrous or with short stiff hairs above, finely pubescent beneath, irregularly serrate, cordate at the base; main nerves 12–18 pairs carried nearly to the margin, then curved and bifurcate so that the crenatures of the margin are often nearly twice as many as the nerves; petiolules ¼–¾ in. long, those of the terminal leaflets twice as long as those of the lateral ones. Flowers white, in much-branched trichotomous pubescent cymes, which are shorter than the leaves; bracts linear-subulate, ¼–⅜ in. long, subpersistent. Calyx shallowly lobed; lobes gland-tipped and with membranous margins. Petals ovate-oblong, subacute. Staminal-tube divided about ½ way down; lobes bifid, sloping towards the apex; anthers not united in bud. Berry size of a pea, depressed-globular, often 2–6-lobed, smooth, black when ripe. Fl. B. I. v. 1, p. 665; C. B. Clarke, in Trim. Journ. Bot. (1881) p. 136; Talb. Trees, Bomb. p. 57; Woodr. in Journ. Bomb. Nat. v. 11 (1897) p. 272; Watt, Dict. Econ. Prod. v. 4, p. 616.—Flowers: July–Aug.

KONKAN: *Law*!; Bombay, *Capt. Geburne*! DECCAN: Khandala, *Cooke*!; Karli, *Woodrow*! Kartriz hills near Poona, *Kanitkar*! KANARA: throughout N. Kanara in moist forests, *Talbot*; Karwar, *Talbot*!, *Woodrow*!—DISTRIB. India (W. Tropical Himalaya, Oude, W. Peninsula).

4. **Leea latifolia,** *Wall. Cat.* 1828, 6821. A shrub; young branches rusty-puberulous. Leaves simply pinnate; leaflets 3–5, elliptic-oblong, 9–12 by 6–11 in., subacute or obtuse, distantly serrate, glabrous above, mealy-white pubescent beneath, base cordate; main nerves opposite, 8–10 pairs; veins transverse and distinct; petiolules of terminal leaflets ¾–1 in. long, the upper pair of lateral leaflets sessile or nearly so, the lower pair (when present) shortly stalked. Flowers in long-peduncled pubescent umbellate cymes; bracts caducous. Calyx pubescent outside; lobes short, triangular, with membranous margins. Petals oblong. Lobes of the staminal-tube notched; anthers united in bud. Style angled and ribbed; stigma concave. Berry size of a pea, depressed-globular, usually 2–6-lobed. C. B. Clarke, in Trim. Journ. Bot. (1881) p. 138; King, in Journ. As. Soc. Beng. v. 65 (1897) p. 410. *L. coriacea*, Laws. in Fl. B. I. v. 1, p. 665; Talb. Trees, Bomb. p. 57. *L. cinerea*, Laws. in Fl. B. I. v. 1, p. 665.

There is but one specimen (in fruit only) from Bombay in Herb. Kew. labelled "Konkan, *Stocks*"!—DISTRIB. India (W. Peninsula); Malaya.

5. **Leea sambucina,** *Willd. Sp. Pl.* v. 1 (1797) p. 1177. A shrub 4–10 ft. high; branches numerous, straight, tough, the young ones green, glabrous. Leaves 15–20 in. long, 2- (rarely 3-) pinnate; leaflets 3–8 by 1½–3½ in., oblong or elliptic-oblong, acuminate, coarsely and irregularly serrate, glabrous, base acute or cuneate; main nerves 7–12 pairs,

prominent beneath, arched; petiolules of the lateral leaflets $\frac{1}{4}$-$\frac{3}{8}$ in. long, those of the terminal much longer. Flowers white, in large branched corymbose cymes; bracts inconspicuous, caducous. Calyx shortly divided; lobes subacute or rounded and with membranous margins. Lobes of the staminal-tube rounded at the apex, notched; anthers united in bud. Berry $\frac{1}{4}$-$\frac{1}{3}$ in., depressed-globular, often 2-6-lobed, smooth, shining, purple-black. Fl. B. I. v. 1, p. 666 (excluding some synonyms); C. B. Clarke, in Trim. Journ. Bot. (1881) p. 139; Talb. Trees, Bomb. p. 57; Woodr. in Journ. Bomb. Nat. v. 11 (1897) p. 272; Watt, Dict. Econ. Prod. v. 4, p. 618. *L. Staphylea*, Roxb. Hort. Beng. p. 18; Grah. Cat. p. 33; Dalz. & Gibs. p. 41; Trim. Fl. Ceyl. v. 1, p. 297.—Flowers: July-Oct. VERN. *Karkani*; *Dinda*.

Where there is a heavy rainfall short aerial roots are developed abundantly from the branches (*Talbot* l. c.).

Widely distributed throughout the Presidency. KONKAN: *Stocks*!, *Law*!; W. Ghâts, *Woodrow*; Konkan and Ghât jungles, common, *Dalzell*!; Salsette, *Graham*; Matheran, *Cooke*!, *H. M. Birdwood*. DECCAN: Khandala, *Cooke*!; Lanoli, *Woodrow*!; Kartria Ghât near Poona, *Kanitkar*!; Karli, *Woodrow*!; Mahableshwar, *Cooke*!, *H. M. Birdwood*.—DISTRIB. Throughout India; Malay islands, Ceylon.

6. **Leea robusta,** *Roxb. Hort. Beng.* (1814) p. 18. A shrub 5-6 ft. high; young branches rusty-pubescent. Leaves simply pinnate to tripinnate; rhachis and petioles angled, not winged; leaflets 3-9 by 1-3$\frac{3}{4}$ in. (the terminal leaflets very much larger than the lateral ones, acute at the base while the lateral leaflets are rounded), oblong or elliptic-oblong, acuminate, irregularly serrate, sparsely strigose above, pubescent and with the nerves sparsely strigose beneath; main nerves 8-12 pairs, ascending; petiolules of the terminal leaflets often reaching 2 in., those of the lateral leaflets $\frac{1}{8}$-$\frac{1}{2}$ in. long. Flowers greenish-white in long-peduncled much-branched compound cymes; bracts caducous. Calyx divided about $\frac{1}{3}$ of the way down. Lobes of the staminal-tube rounded or truncate, not bifid at the apex; anthers slightly united in bud. Berry $\frac{1}{4}$ in., depressed-globular, black when ripe; pyrenes 6-4. C. B. Clarke, in Trim. Journ. Bot. (1881) p. 164; King, in Journ. As. Soc. Beng. v. 65 (1897) p. 417; Talb. Trees, Bomb. p. 57. *L. diffusa*, Laws. in Fl. B. I. v. 1, p. 667.—Flowers: Aug.

KONKAN: Mira Donger near Pen, *Dalzell*! KANARA: Ghâts of N. Kanara and sea-level near Kadra, *Talbot*.—DISTRIB. India (Nipal, Khasia mountains, Andamans); Malaya.

7. **Leea æquata,** *Linn. Mantiss.* v. 1 (1767) p. 124. A shrub 4-10 ft. high; young shoots more or less pubescent. Leaves 2-pinnate (the upper often simply pinnate or rarely simple); rhachis angled but hardly winged, pubescent; petioles not dilated at the base; leaflets 3-7 by 1-1$\frac{3}{4}$ in., oblong or ovate-oblong, acuminate, irregularly serrate, more or less hairy on both surfaces, covered beneath with numerous flat circular discs; main nerves 7-12 pairs, ascending, curved; petioles of the lateral leaflets $\frac{1}{8}$-$\frac{1}{4}$ in., those of the terminal reaching 1 in. long. Flowers white, very shortly pedicelled, in short compact pubescent cymes; bracts large, broadly ovate, obtuse, caducous. Calyx pubescent and sparsely covered with glandular discs outside, cleft about $\frac{1}{4}$ the way down; lobes ovate, subacute. Lobes of the staminal tube oblong, bifid; anthers united in bud. Berry $\frac{1}{4}$ in. in diam., depressed-globular, usually 2-6-

lobed, black when ripe. C. B. Clarke, in Trim. Journ. Bot. (1881) p. 163; King, in Journ. As. Soc. Beng. v. 65 (1897) p. 418. *L. hirta*, Roxb. ex Hornem. Hort. Hafn. v. 1, p. 231; Laws. in Fl. B. I. v. 1, p. 668; Talb. Trees, Bomb. p. 57; Watt, Dict. Econ. Prod. v. 4, p. 617.—Flowers in the rains (*Talbot*).

The circular discs on the underside of the leaves furnish an excellent specific character. They are found on no other Indian *Leea* and are always present in this species.

KANARA: evergreen forests near Karwar, *Talbot* l. c.—DISTRIB. India (Sikkim Himalaya, Assam, East Bengal, Silhet, the Andamans).

8. **Leea setuligera,** *C. B. Clarke, in Trim. Journ. Bot.* (1881) p. 105. Leaves compound, 2–3-pinnate; leaflets elliptic or elliptic-lanceolate, acuminate, sharply and closely serrate, clothed with stiff bristles between the nerves above, bristly on the nerves beneath, base rounded or sub-acute; main nerves about 7–12 pairs; petiolules of lateral leaflets 0–$\frac{1}{8}$ in. long. Flowers in small compact umbellate cymes; bracts linear-subulate, caducous; peduncles $1\frac{1}{2}$–$1\frac{3}{4}$ in. long; pedicels very short. Lobes of the staminal-tube bifid; anthers united in bud. Fruit not seen.

The flowers are, as far as it is possible to judge from a dried specimen, red.

There is but one specimen in Herb. Kew. labelled "Konkan, *Stocks*" (!) which matches with no other specimen of *Leea* in the Herbarium.

ORDER XLIII. SAPINDACEÆ.

Trees or shrubs, rarely climbing herbs. Leaves alternate (rarely opposite), generally compound; stipules caducous or 0. Flowers usually polygamo-diœcious, often irregular. Calyx usually 4–5-lobed or 4–5-sepalous; lobes or sepals often unequal, imbricate or rarely valvate. Petals 4–5 or 0, free, equal or unequal, often bearded or squamate at the base within. Disk annular or unilateral, rarely wanting in the male flowers. Stamens 5–10 (usually 8), inserted inside the disk at the base of the ovary, or outside, or on the disk, sometimes unilateral; filaments often pubescent, usually free; anthers 2-celled, basifixed or versatile. Ovary centric or excentric, entire, lobed or partite nearly to the base, 1–4-celled; ovule 1 (rarely 2 or more) in each cell, affixed to the axis of the ovary, ascending; style simple or divided, usually terminal; stigma usually simple. Fruit capsular or indehiscent, entire or lobed, sometimes winged. Seeds globose or compressed, arillate or naked, usually exalbuminous; embryo usually thick, sometimes plicate or spirally convolute.—DISTRIB. Throughout the world, especially in the Tropics; genera 73; species 500–800.

Erioglossum edule, Blume, Bijdr. p. 229, a tree which occurs in the Sikkim Himalaya, Assam, Birma, the Indian Archipelago, and North-western Australia, has been planted in the Girgaum Woods, Bombay, but is certainly not indigenous. It has sweet-scented flowers in panicled racemes, and the wood is useful, strong, and durable, chocolate-colored in the centre.

Blighia sapida, Konig, in Kon. & Sims, Ann. Bot. v. 2, p. 571, the *Akee* tree of Jamaica, a native of Africa and the West Indies, has been planted in Parel and Dapuri gardens and in Lanoli Wood. It has abruptly-pinnate leaves, 3 or 4 pairs of pale-green glabrous leaflets, small white flowers and a bright-red pear-like fruit about

4 inches long, which is edible, but (*fide* Dalzell & Gibson) can only be eaten fried and is insipid (see Dalz. & Gibs. Suppl. p. 13).

Filicium decipiens, Thwaites, Enum. p. 408, a very ornamental tree, rather slow of growth, with bright-green fern-like leaves, narrow leaflets and a winged rhachis, has been grown at Poona from seeds procured from the botanical gardens at Peradeniya, Ceylon (see Woodrow, Gardening in India, ed. 5, p. 232).

Leaves alternate, exstipulate; seeds exalbuminous.
  Stamens inserted within the disk.
    Flowers irregular; disk unilateral.
      Herbs; fruit an inflated capsule .... 1. CARDIOSPERMUM.
      Trees or shrubs; fruit indehiscent.
        Leaves pinnate .... 2. HEMIGYROSA.
        Leaves 1–3-foliolate .... 3. ALLOPHYLUS.
    Flowers regular; disk annular.
      Fruit not inflated, indehiscent; flowers small.
        Fruit not breaking up into cocci; petals 0. 4. SCHLEICHERA.
        Fruit of 1–3 indehiscent cocci.
          Sepals free, much imbricate .... 5. SAPINDUS.
          Sepals connate, valvate or nearly so . 6. NEPHELIUM.
      Fruit an inflated capsule; flowers large .... 7. HARPULLIA.
  Stamens inserted outside the disk; fruit 3-winged ...... 8. DODONÆA.
Leaves opposite, stipulate; seeds albuminous .... 9. TURPINIA.

1. CARDIOSPERMUM, Linn.

Climbing tendril-bearing herbs with wiry stems. Leaves alternate, exstipulate, 2-ternate; leaflets coarsely crenate or serrate. Flowers irregular, polygamo-diœcious, in axillary racemes or corymbs, the common peduncle 2-cirrhose. Sepals 4, much imbricate, the 2 exterior small. Petals 4, arranged in pairs, the two upper furnished with a large scale below the base of each, the 2 lower smaller, distant, each furnished with a small crested scale. Disk unilateral, undulate, of 2 glands opposite the lower petals. Stamens 8, excentric; filaments unequal, free or connate at the base. Ovary sessile or subsessile, 3-celled; ovule solitary, ascending; style short, 3-fid. Capsule membranous, trigonous, 3-celled, 3-valved, inflated, loculicidal. Seeds globose, usually arillate at the base; testa crustaceous; cotyledons large, transversely conduplicate.—DISTRIB. Chiefly in Tropical America and Africa; species about 30.

Capsules winged at the angles .... 1. *C. Halicacabum*.
Capsules not winged at the angles .... 2. *C. canescens*.

1. **Cardiospermum Halicacabum,** *Linn. Sp. Pl.* (1753) p. 366. Annual and perennial; branches slender, striate, pubescent or glabrous. Leaves deltoid, 2-ternate; petioles $\frac{3}{4}$–$1\frac{1}{2}$ in. long; ultimate segments of the leaves lanceolate, glabrous or sparsely pubescent, inciso-serrate, very acute at the apex and narrowed at the base. Flowers white, $\frac{1}{8}$–$\frac{1}{6}$ in. long, in few-flowered umbellate cymes; peduncles slender, stiff, axillary, $1\frac{1}{2}$–4 in. long, provided beneath the cyme with 2 opposite usually circinate tendrils; pedicels very slender, $\frac{1}{8}$–$\frac{1}{2}$ in. long. Outer sepals rounded, obovate, usually with a few scattered hairs on the back just below the apical margin; inner sepals larger than the outer, rounded, membranous. Petals rounded at the apex. Style very short. Capsules shortly stalked, subglobose or more commonly depressed-pyriform, trigonous, truncate at top, winged at the angles, bladdery, veined. Seeds globose, $\frac{1}{6}$–$\frac{1}{4}$ in. in diam., smooth, black, with a small white heart-shaped aril. Fl. B. I. v. 1, p. 670; Grah. Cat. p. 28; Dalz. & Gibs. p. 34; Aitch. Pb. & Sind Pl. p. 34; Trim. Fl. Ceyl. v. 1, p. 299; Radlk. in

Engl. & Prantl, Pflanzenf. v. 3, part 5, p. 308, fig. 159, A–C; Woodr. in Journ. Bomb. Nat. v. 11 (1897) p. 272; Watt, Dict. Econ. Prod. v. 2, p. 155.—Flowers: Dec. VERN. *Tejovati*; *Kapal-phodi.*

Known as the *Heart-pea* or *Balloon-vine.* Common in hedges throughout the Presidency, *Graham*, *Dalzell & Gibson.* DECCAN: hills, *Woodrow*; Poona, *Raoji*!, *Cooke*!, *Jacquemont*, 443! SIND: *Stocks.*

The root, leaves and seeds are extensively employed in native medicine. See Watt, Dict. Econ. Prod. l. c.—DISTRIB. Most warm countries.

2. **Cardiospermum canescens,** *Wall. Pl. As. Rar.* v. 1 (1830) p. 14. Scandent; stem shrubby, deeply 5-furrowed, more or less pubescent. Leaves 2-ternate, pubescent on both sides; ultimate segments smaller than in the preceding species and blunter, the terminal segment mucronate or cuspidate. Flowers larger than in the preceding species, $\frac{3}{8}$–$\frac{5}{8}$ in. long, in long-peduncled umbellate cymes. Tendrils as in *C. Halicacabum.* Capsules 1–1$\frac{1}{2}$ in. long, inflated, subglobose, 3-angled, not winged. Seeds as in the preceding species. Fl. B. I. v. 1, p. 670; Wight, Icon. t. 74. *C. Corindum*, Trim. Fl. Ceyl. v. 1, p. 300.

I have seen only one specimen from Bombay in Herb. Kew. marked "Konkan, *Stocks*!"—DISTRIB. India (Birma, W. Peninsula); Ceylon, Abyssinia.

2. HEMIGYROSA, Blume.

Trees. Leaves alternate, exstipulate, pinnate, pale; leaflets opposite or nearly so, 2–3 pairs, petioluled, entire, coriaceous, oblong, reticulately veined. Flowers polygamo-monœcious, irregular, in axillary many-flowered paniculately arranged spicate racemes. Sepals 5, unequal, erect, concave, the 2 outer smaller. Petals 4–5, unequal (the 5th often deficient or scale-like), erect, clawed, with a jagged hooded scale near the base. Disk pulvinate, unilateral. Stamens usually 8, unequal, unilateral; filaments pilose; anthers not or scarcely exserted. Ovary excentric, turbinately trigonous, 3-celled; ovule solitary in each cell; stigma trigonous, obtuse. Fruit indehiscent, thickly coriaceous, fleshy or woody, trigonous or globose, velvety or tomentose, 3-celled, the cells hirsute within. Seeds oblong, exarillate; testa coriaceous; cotyledons fleshy, equal.—DISTRIB. Tropical Asia; species 3–4.

1. **Hemigyrosa canescens,** *Thwaites, Enum.* (1858) p. 56 & p. 408. A middle-sized tree with a crooked trunk of considerable girth; bark ash-colored. Leaves variable in length; rhachis smooth; leaflets 2–3 pairs, opposite or subopposite, oblong-lanceolate, obtuse, acute or emarginate, 3–5 by 1–1$\frac{3}{4}$ in., entire, glabrous, shining, ashy green; petiolules $\frac{1}{8}$–$\frac{1}{4}$ in. long. Flowers about $\frac{1}{5}$–$\frac{1}{4}$ in. long, in simple or panicled velvety-pubescent racemes which are axillary or scattered over the branches; bracts minute, triangular. Sepals unequal, the 2 outer ovate-orbicular, ciliate, the 3 inner larger, orbicular, concave, with ciliate or laciniate margins. Petals white, oblong-spathulate, shortly clawed, slightly laciniate; scale about $\frac{1}{2}$ as long as the petal, hairy at the base, 2-lobed at the apex, the lobes laciniate. Stamens slightly longer than the petals; filaments hairy. Fruit $\frac{1}{2}$–1 in. in diam., subglobose or trigonous, velvety-tomentose, apiculate, yellow. Fl. B. I. v. 1, p. 671; Bedd. Flor. Sylvat. t. 151; Trim. Fl. Ceyl. v. 1, p. 301; Talb. Trees, Bomb. p. 58; Woodr. in Journ. Bomb. Nat. v. 11 (1897) p. 272; Watt, Dict. Econ. Prod.

v. 4, p. 221. *Cupania canescens*, Pers. Syn. v. 1 (1805) p. 413; Grah. Cat. p. 29; Dalz. & Gibs. p. 35.—Flowers: Feb.–May. VERN. *Karpa*; *Lokhandi*.

KONKAN: Parel, *Woodrow*; Matheran, *Kanitkar*!, *H. M. Birdwood*. DECCAN: Palasdari, *Woodrow*!; Bimashankar, *Gibson*; Khandala, *Graham*. S. M. COUNTRY: Ramghât, *Dalzell & Gibson*.—DISTRIB. India (Birma, Madras, W. Peninsula); Ceylon.

3. ALLOPHYLUS, Linn.

Shrubs or small trees, ecirrhose. Leaves alternate, exstipulate, 1–3-foliolate; leaflets usually large, entire or serrate. Racemes simple or laxly paniculate, axillary. Flowers irregular, small, polygamo-diœcious. Sepals 4, in opposite pairs, cucullate, membranous, widely imbricate, the 2 outer smaller. Petals 4 (the place of the 5th vacant), usually small, naked inside or with a shaggy scale above the claw. Disk unilateral, lobed or swollen into 4 glands opposite the petals, very rarely obsolete. Stamens excentric or scarcely centric, included or shortly exserted. Ovary usually 2-celled; ovule 1 in each cell, ascending from its base. Fruit indehiscent, usually 1–2-lobed; lobes subglobose, fleshy or dry. Seeds erect, usually with a very short fleshy aril; embryo curved; cotyledons plicate. DISTRIB. Chiefly Tropical America; less frequent in Tropical and S. Africa, the Pacific Islands and Australia; species about 80.

1. **Allophylus Cobbe,** *Blume, Rumph.* v. 3 (1847) p. 131. A small tree, or a shrub often climbing to a considerable height. Leaves 3-foliolate, 3–5½ by 1¾–2¾ in., alternate, crowded at the extremities of the branchlets, drooping; common petioles 2–2½ in. long, ferrugineo-pubescent; leaflets ovate or elliptic, acute or acuminate, sharply and distantly serrate-dentate, more or less hairy or pubescent on both surfaces, the terminal leaflet usually acute at the base, the lateral leaflets usually rounded and more or less oblique; petiolules of the lateral leaflets ¼–⅓ in., those of the terminal leaflets sometimes reaching 1 in. long. Flowers small, white, shortly pedicelled, in fascicles along the branches of spicate axillary 2–4-branched racemes. Sepals glabrous. Petals cuneate, with a fringed scale above the claw. Stamens 8. Ovary 2-lobed, hairy. Fruit globose, smooth, size of a pea, red when ripe. Fl. B. I. v. 1, p. 673; Trim. Fl. Ceyl. v. 1, p. 303; Talb. Trees, Bomb. p. 58; Woodr. in Journ. Bomb. Nat. v. 11 (1897) p. 272; Watt, Dict. Econ. Prod. v. 1, p. 175. *Schmidelia Kobbe*, Lamk. Tab. v. 2, p. 443, t. 312, f. 2. *S. Cobbe*, DC. Prodr. v. 1, p. 610; Grah. Cat. p. 29. *Cardiospermum Schmidelia* & *Cardiospermum villosa*, Dalz. & Gibs. p. 34. —Flowers: May–Aug. VERN. *Tipan*.

KONKAN: Mira hills near Pen, *Dalzell & Gibson*. DECCAN: Lanoli, *Woodrow*, *Kanitkar*! Mahableshwar, very common, *Cooke*!, *H. M. Birdwood*. KANARA: in moist forests and along the banks of rivers and streams in N. Kanara, usually a scandent shrub, *Talbot*.—DISTRIB. India (Assam, Silhet, Birma, E. & W. Peninsulas); Ceylon, Malaya, N. Australia.

4. SCHLEICHERA, *Willd.*

Trees. Leaves alternate, exstipulate, pinnate; leaflets opposite or alternate. Flowers regular, polygamo-diœcious, small, fascicled on slender simple racemes or panicles; pedicels slender. Calyx small, 4–6-fid;

lobes valvate or obscurely imbricate. Petals 0. Disk complete, with waved margin. Stamens 5–8 inserted within the disk; filaments more or less pubescent. Ovary 3–4-celled, attenuated into a rigid style; ovule 1 in each cell, erect; stigma 3-4-lobed. Fruit dry, subcrustaceous, indehiscent, ovoid, cuspidate with the style, 1–3-celled. Seeds with a fleshy aril, erect; embryo conduplicate; cotyledons connate, unequal.—DISTRIB. Tropical Asia and the Philippines; species 2.

1. **Schleichera trijuga,** *Willd. Sp. Pl.* v. 4 (1805) p. 1096. A large tree 40–60 ft. high, with smooth grey bark. Leaves abruptly pinnate; petioles and rhachis terete, pubescent; leaflets 2–4 pairs (the leaflets of the lowest pair 2–3½ by 1–2½ in., those of the terminal pair 4–9 by 1½–4 in.) opposite or nearly so, usually very obtuse (rarely shortly acuminate), entire, glabrous, base rounded or tapering; lateral nerves 12–20 pairs with reticulate veins between; petiolules very short, articulated with the rhachis. Flowers white or yellowish, fascicled, on interrupted often branched racemes which are axillary or below the leaves, often several on short branchlets. Calyx-lobes acute. Fruit size of a small plum, pointed, often echinate with stout rather blunt prickles. Seeds 1 or 2, enclosed in a pulpy edible aril which has a pleasant acid taste; testa smooth brown. Fl. B. I. v. 1, p. 681; Grah. Cat. p. 29; Dalz. & Gibs. p. 35; Trim. Fl. Ceyl. v. 1, p. 304; Talb. Trees, Bomb. p. 59; Woodr. in Journ. Bomb. Nat. v. 11 (1897) p. 272; Watt, Dict. Econ. Prod. v. 6, part 2, p. 487. *Sapindus trifoliata*, Linn. Sp. Pl. (1753) p. 367.—Flowers: Feb.-May. VERN. *Kosimb.*

KONKAN: *Stocks*!; Bombay, *Law*!; Kanheri forests and Salsette, *Graham*; Thana districts, *Cooke*!; Matheran Ghát, *H. M. Birdwood.* DECCAN: Khandala, *Woodrow.* KANARA: Mandgod (N. Kanara), *Talbot*, 364!; Sirsi, *Woodrow*; Kála naddi (below fall), *Ritchie*, 1657!—DISTRIB. Throughout India; Ceylon, Java, Timor.

The tree is sometimes known as the *Lac tree*, the lac which is produced on it being the most highly prized quality. The wood is hard and durable and the oil obtained from the seeds has been employed for the cure of itch. See Watt, Dict. Econ. Prod. l. c.

5. **SAPINDUS,** Tournef. ex Linn.

Trees or shrubs. Leaves alternate, exstipulate, simple, 1-foliolate or abruptly pinnate; leaflets usually entire. Flowers polygamous, regular, in terminal or axillary racemes or panicles. Sepals 4–5, in 2 series, much imbricate. Petals 4–5, naked or with scales above the claw. Disk complete, annular or fleshy, usually lobed. Stamens usually 8–10, inserted within the disk; filaments free, usually pilose; anthers versatile. Ovary entire or 2–4-lobed, 2–4-celled; ovule 1 in each cell; style terminal; stigma 2–4-lobed. Fruit fleshy or coriaceous, 1–2 (rarely 3–4-) coccous, the cocci oblong or globose, indehiscent. Seeds usually globose, usually exarillate; testa crustaceous or membranous; cotyledons thick; radicle short.—DISTRIB. Tropical regions of the world; species about 40.

1. **Sapindus laurifolius,** *Vahl, Symb.* v. 3 (1794) p. 54. A handsome tree. Leaves abruptly-pinnate; leaflets subopposite, 2–3 pairs, 3–7 by 1–4 in., lanceolate or elliptic-lanceolate, acute or acuminate, entire, glabrous above, more or less pubescent beneath, base acute; main nerves about 8–12 pairs; petioles ⅛ in. long, pubescent. Flowers

dingy white, in terminal rusty-pubescent panicles, the males numerous, the bisexual flowers few. Sepals 5, rotund-ovate, ciliolate, fulvous-pubescent outside, glabrous within, $\frac{1}{8}$ in. long. Petals 4–5, shortly clawed, narrower than the sepals, lanceolate, villous outside and more or less so within, usually furnished with 2 villous scales attached at each side of the petal about half way up. Disk concave with a fleshy hirsute margin. Stamens 8; filaments villous; anthers oblong, apiculate. Ovary densely hairy. Fruit fleshy, 2- (usually 3-) lobed, clothed with fulvous hairs when young, glabrous and wrinkled when ripe, with 1 seed in each lobe. Seeds blackish, smooth, about the size of a large pea, very hard. Grah. Cat. p. 29; Dalz. & Gibs. p. 34; Brandis, For. Flor. p. 106; Trim. Fl. Ceyl. v. 1, p. 306. *S. trifoliatus*, Fl. B. I. v. 1, p. 682, in part (*not* of Linn.); Talb. Trees, Bomb. p. 59; Woodr. in Journ. Bomb. Nat. v. 11 (1897) p. 272; Watt, Dict. Econ. Prod. v. 6, part 2, p. 468.—Flowers: Oct.-Dec. VERN. *Ritha.*

Generally to be met with about villages in the Konkan, *Graham.* KONKAN: *Stocks*!, *Dalzell*!; Rambág (Matheran), *H. M. Birdwood.* S. M. COUNTRY: Ramghát, *Ritchie*, 1000!; Londa, *Bhiva*! KANARA: Kála naddi, *Ritchie*, 1000!; indigenous on the Ghâts of N. Kanara in evergreen forests, *Talbot.*—DISTRIB. Cultivated in Bengal and in S. & W. India.

VAR. *emarginatus.* Leaflets ovate-oblong or obovate-oblong, glabrous above, softly tomentose beneath, rounded or emarginate at the apex. *Sapindus emarginatus* (sp.), Vahl, Symb. v. 3 (1794) p. 54; Wight & Arn. Prodr. p. 111; Grah. Cat. p. 29; Dalz. & Gibs. p. 35; Bedd. Flor. Sylvat. t. 154; Trim. Fl. Ceyl. v. 1, p. 307. *S. trifoliatus*, Hiern, in Hook. f. Fl. B. I. v. 1, p. 682, in part (*not* of Linn.); Watt, Dict. Econ. Prod. v. 6, part 2, p. 468.

Found in the same localities as the preceding.

The berries of both trees are used as a substitute for soap; hence the name *Soap-nut* tree which is given to them by Anglo-Indians. The fruit is also employed in native medicine, while the wood is hard and useful for many purposes. See Watt, Dict. Econ. Prod. l. c.

6. NEPHELIUM, Linn.

Trees or shrubs. Leaves alternate, exstipulate, pinnate; leaflets subopposite, entire (rarely serrate). Flowers numerous, regular, small, polygamo-diœcious, in terminal and axillary racemes or panicles. Calyx small, 4-6-lobed, usually cupular; lobes short, valvate or slightly imbricate in bud. Petals 4–6 or 0, villous, rarely with 2 scales. Disk annular or swollen, glabrous or pubescent. Stamens 6–8, inserted within the disk, long-exserted; filaments filiform, usually pubescent. Ovary pubescent, often verrucose, 2–3-lobed; lobes 1-celled, 1-ovulate; style 2–3-fid or -partite, the lobes recurved. Fruit 1–3-coccous, indehiscent, globose or ovoid, echinate, tubercled or smooth. Seeds ellipsoid or globose, exalbuminous, covered with a pulpy aril; cotyledons fleshy but not plicate.—DISTRIB. Chiefly Malayan; species about 20.

1. **Nephelium Longana,** *Camb. in Mém. Mus. Par.* v. 18 (1829) p. 30. A tree 30–40 ft. high; bark smooth, flaking off in small pieces; young parts clothed with rufous stellate pubescence. Leaves 4–18 in. long, equally or unequally pinnate; rhachis rusty-puberulous when young, afterwards glabrous; leaflets 2-5 pairs, reddish when young,

coriaceous, 2½-8 by 1-2 in., oblong or ovate-lanceolate, more or less oblique, shortly acuminate, glabrous and reticulately veined, base cuneate; main nerves 10-15 pairs, prominent beneath; petiolules ¼-½ in. long. Flowers small, white, in clusters on the branches of terminal and axillary large much-branched puberulous panicles; pedicels short, pubescent. Calyx 5-6-lobed; lobes obtuse, densely pubescent. Petals 5-6, linear-spathulate, pubescent, about as long as the calyx. Disk pubescent. Stamens 6-10, included in the female, exserted in the male flowers; filaments hairy at the base. Ovary 2-3-lobed; style long; stigmas 2, recurved. Fruit supported on the persistent calyx, edible when young, globose, reddish, tubercled. Seed solitary, enveloped in a fleshy pale subacid aril, black, shining. Fl. B. I. v. 1, p. 688; Grah. Cat. p. 29; Dalz. & Gibs. p. 35; Trim. Fl. Ceyl. v. 1, p. 309; Talb. Trees, Bomb. p. 59; Woodr. in Journ. Bomb. Nat. v. 11 (1897) p. 272; Watt, Dict. Econ. Prod. v. 5, p. 348.—Flowers: Feb.-Apr. VERN. *Umb*; *Vumb*.

KONKAN: *Law*!, *Stocks*!; evergreen forests of Konkan Ghâts, *Talbot*. DECCAN: Mahableshwar, *Cooke*!; Koina valley, *H. M. Birdwood*; Pár in a ravine near which there is a forest chiefly of *Vumb* trees, ex *Graham* l. c. S. M. COUNTRY: Ramghát, *Dalzell & Gibson*. KANARA: *Ritchie*, 1656!; evergreen forests of N. Kanara Ghâts, *Talbot*; Ainshi (N. Kanara), *Talbot*, 952!—DISTRIB. India (E. Bengal, W. Peninsula); Ceylon. Often cultivated in tropical countries.

The fruit is about the size of a cherry and the pulpy aril is eaten. See Watt, Dict. Econ. Prod. l. c.

Nephelium Lit-chi, Camb., the *Litchi* introduced from S. China has been occasionally, though rarely, cultivated in Bombay. See Watt, Dict. Econ. Prod. v. 5, p. 346.

7. HARPULLIA, Roxb.

Erect trees. Leaves alternate, exstipulate, pinnate; leaflets alternate, entire. Flowers regular, diœcious or polygamous, racemose or paniculate, pedicelled. Sepals 4-5, erect, equal. Petals 4-5, linear-obovate, sometimes clawed, but without either glands or scales. Disk obscure. Stamens 5-8, elongate, centric. Ovary oblong, 2-lobed, 2-celled; ovules 2 in each cell; style usually elongate; stigma linear, usually more or less twisted. Capsule coriaceous, inflated, 2-lobed, 2-celled, loculicidally 2-valved, cells 1-2-seeded. Seeds subglobose, exalbuminous, usually arillate; embryo thick.—DISTRIB. Tropical Asia, Australia and Madagascar; species about 6.

1. **Harpullia imbricata,** *Thwaites, Enum.* (1858) p. 56. A large tree with an erect straight trunk; young parts finely fulvous-pubescent. Leaves imparipinnate; rhachis cylindric, 6-10 in. long, pubescent; leaflets 4-5 pairs, opposite or alternate, 3-6 by 1-2 in., oblong-lanceolate, obtusely acuminate, entire, glabrous and shining, bright light green, thin; main nerves 8-12 pairs; petiolules ⅛-¼ in. long. Flowers ⅝ in. long, in lax drooping axillary panicles; pedicels long, slender, puberulous. Sepals 5, free, oblong, obtuse, fulvous-pubescent, subpersistent. Petals much exceeding the sepals, spathulate, veined, and with a long claw which is pubescent within. Stamens in bisexual flowers shorter than the petals, in male flowers exserted beyond them. Ovary ovoid, hairy; style 3 or 4 times as long as the ovary, much exserted; stigma oblong,

usually more or less spirally twisted. Capsules inflated, broadly reniform, compressed, broader than long, about 1 by 1½–4¾, bright orange, ultimately glabrous, tipped with the long persistent style. Seeds ovoid, black, smooth, with a small disciform aril. Trim. Fl. Ceyl. v. 1, p. 311; Bedd. Flor. Sylvat. t. 158. *H. cupanioides*, Hiern, in Hook. f. Fl. B. I. v. 1, p. 692 (*not* of Roxb.); Talb. Trees, Bomb. p. 59; Woodr. in Journ. Bomb. Nat. v. 11 (1897) p. 272. *Streptostigma viridiflorum*, Thwaites, in Kew Journ. Bot. v. 6 (1854) p. 298, t. 9.—Flowers: Nov.–Jan.

There is no doubt that this plant is perfectly distinct from *H. cupanioides* of Roxburgh.

Roxburgh, Fl. Ind. (1824) p. 442, describes *H. cupanioides*, a native of Chittagong, as having a somewhat 2-lobed ovary, a short style, a 2-lobed stigma with reflexed lobes, a semi-oval seed, of which the inner side is straight, with a deep orange aril covering the whole seed. The Bombay plant agrees exactly with the description given by Thwaites (Kew Journ. Bot. l. c.) and Trimen (Fl. Ceyl. l. c.) and with the plate (t. 158) given by Beddome. The aril of the Bombay plant is small and disciform, the seed is ovoid, black, the style is long and the stigma oblong and spirally twisted.

KONKAN: *Stocks*!, *Law*! KANARA: in the evergreen forests of N. Kanara; very common in the forests near Goond, *Talbot*.—DISTRIB. India (Chittagong, Birma, S. Andamans, W. Peninsula); Ceylon, Sumatra, Borneo, Java.

8. DODONÆA, Linn.

Shrubs, rarely trees, often viscous. Leaves alternate, exstipulate, simple or abruptly-pinnate. Flowers unisexual or polygamo-diœcious in axillary or terminal racemes, corymbs or panicles, inconspicuous. Sepals 2–5, imbricate or valvate. Petals 0. Disk obsolete in the male, small in the female flowers. Stamens 5–10 (usually 8), inserted on the outer side of the disk; filaments very short; anthers linear-oblong, obtusely 4-gonous. Ovary sessile, 3–6-gonous, 3–6-celled; ovules 2 in each cell, collateral or superposed. Capsule membranous or coriaceous, 2–6-gonous, septicidally 2–6-valved, valves winged at the back, cells 1–2-seeded. Seeds lenticular or subglobose, compressed, exalbuminous, exarillate; funicle thickened; testa crustaceous or coriaceous; embryo spirally convolute.—DISTRIB. Chiefly Australian; species about 65.

1. **Dodonæa viscosa,** *Linn. Mantiss.* v. 2 (1771) p. 149. A shrub, rarely a small tree, with erect twiggy branches often angled; young parts scurfy-puberulous. Leaves subsessile, simple, more or less viscid with a yellowish resinous exudation, 1½–4 by ¼–1½ in. (the breadth very variable), oblanceolate, subacute or shortly apiculate, glabrous, shining, tapering much towards the base. Flowers greenish-yellow, small, in short few-flowered axillary spreading cymes; pedicels slender, nodding. Sepals oblong, $\frac{1}{10}$–⅛ in. long, about equalling the stamens. Anthers oblong-linear, very large. Ovary pilose; style long. Capsules membranous, compressed, ½–¾ in. long and slightly broader, with a wide marginal wing notched at the base and apex, viscid, orange-brown. Seeds black. Fl. B. I. v. 1, p. 697; Trim. Fl. Ceyl. v. 1, p. 312; Talb. Trees, Bomb. p. 60; Woodr. in Journ. Bomb. Nat. v. 11 (1897) p. 272; Watt, Dict. Econ. Prod. v. 3, p. 172. *D. Burmanniana*, DC. Prodr. v. 1, p. 616; Grah. Cat. p. 30; Dalz. & Gibs. p. 36; Aitch. Pb. & Sind Pl. p. 34.

D. angustifolia, Linn. f. Suppl. Pl. p. 218.—Flowers: Nov. VERN. *Jakhmi.*

Throughout the Presidency, chiefly in dry open situations. KONKAN: *Stocks*!, *Law*! DECCAN: Khandala Ghát, *Graham*. S. M. COUNTRY: Badami, *Kanitkar*!, *Woodrow*, *Cooke*!; Dharwar, *Woodrow*; very common on sandstone hills north and east of Belgaum, *Graham*, *Dalzell & Gibson*. SIND: *Stocks*, 573!, *Cooke*!

The specimens from Sind are usually very narrow-leaved.—DISTRIB. Throughout India, Ceylon and in most warm countries.

9. TURPINIA, Vent.

Glabrous trees or shrubs with terete branches. Leaves opposite, stipulate, usually imparipinnate; leaflets opposite, serrulate, sometimes with coriaceous stipules. Flowers white, small, regular, hermaphrodite, in terminal and axillary panicles with opposite branches. Calyx 5-fid, imbricate, persistent. Petals 5, sessile, imbricate. Disk raised, crenate or lobed. Stamens 5, inserted outside the disk between the lobes; filaments flattened. Ovary sessile, 3-lobed, 3-celled; ovules few or very many and then 2-seriate, ascending, anatropous; styles 3, united or free; stigmas subcapitate. Fruit subglobose, indehiscent, fleshy or coriaceous, 3-celled; cells few- or many-seeded. Seeds angular, compressed, exarillate; testa crustaceous or bony; hilum large; albumen fleshy; embryo straight; cotyledons plano-convex.—DISTRIB. East and West Indies, Malaya, China and the northern provinces of S. America; species about 8.

1. **Turpinia pomifera,** *DC. Prodr.* v. 2 (1825) p. 3. A large tree; young parts glabrous. Leaves 6–15 in. long, opposite, stipulate, usually imparipinnate; rhachis glabrous; stipules intrapetiolar, triangular, caducous; leaflets 3–9, opposite, $2\frac{1}{2}$–8 by 1–3 in., oblong-lanceolate, shortly acuminate, finely serrate, glabrous and shining; main nerves 5–6 pairs, distant, ascending; petiolules of the lateral leaflets $\frac{1}{4}$–$\frac{1}{3}$ in., of the terminal ones up to 2 in. long; stipels lanceolate-subulate, caducous. Flowers numerous, near the ends of the branches, in lax axillary and terminal panicles shorter than the leaves; pedicels glabrous. Calyx-lobes oblong, obtuse, ciliate. Petals white, oblong, obtuse, slightly exceeding the calyx, ciliate. Stamens about equalling the petals or a little shorter; filaments glabrous. Ovary broadly ovoid, glabrous, furrowed, tapering into a stout style. Fruit globose, smooth, purplish-black, $\frac{1}{2}$–1 in. in diam.; pericarp fleshy. Seeds angular, shining, dark brown. Fl. B. I. v. 1, p. 698; Trim. Fl. Ceyl. v. 1, p. 313; Talb. Trees, Bomb. p. 60; Woodr. in Journ. Bomb. Nat. v. 11 (1897) p. 272; Watt, Dict. Econ. Prod. v. 6, part 4, p. 203. *T. nepalensis*, Wall. Cat. 4277; Dalz. & Gibs. p. 47.—Flowers: Jan.

KONKAN: *Law*!, *Stocks*!, *De Crespigny* ex *Woodrow*; evergreen forests, *Talbot*. S. M. COUNTRY: Párva Ghát, *Dalzell & Gibson*. KANARA: evergreen forests, *Talbot*.—DISTRIB. India generally; Ceylon, Yunan, China.

ORDER XLIV. SABIACEÆ.

Trees or erect or climbing shrubs, glabrous or with simple hairs. Leaves alternate, simple or compound, exstipulate. Flowers hermaphrodite or polygamous, usually panicled. Calyx 4–5-partite, imbricate.

Petals 4–5, imbricate. Disk usually small, annular. Stamens 4–5, opposite the petals, inserted at the base of or on the disk, free or coherent with the petals, all perfect or 2 only perfect and 3 without anthers; filaments clavate, flattened or subulate; anthers didymous, the cells separated by a thick connective and bursting transversely by a deciduous cap. Ovary sessile, 2–3-celled, compressed or 2–3-lobed; ovules 1–2 in each cell; styles 2–3, free or connate or 0; stigmas punctiform. Ripe carpels 1–2, dry or fleshy, indehiscent. Seeds compressed or globose, basilar; hilum broad; testa membranous or coriaceous; albumen 0; cotyledons often contorted; radicle deflexed.—Distrib. Tropical and subtropical regions chiefly of the N. hemisphere; genera 4; species about 35.

1. MELIOSMA, Blume.

Trees or shrubs, usually pubescent. Leaves alternate, simple or imparipinnate; leaflets subopposite, the terminal one rarely wanting. Flowers small, hermaphrodite, in branched terminal, or terminal and axillary panicles; bracts caducous. Bracteoles and sepals 5–9, persistent, forming an uninterrupted whorl round the petals. Petals 5: 3 large nearly orbicular, valvate; 2 smaller, interior, placed behind the fertile stamens, either membranous and nearly free, or reduced to a bifid scale adnate to the filament. Stamens 5: 2 fertile, opposite the smaller petals, the filaments short, flattened incurved, expanded at the top into a cup which bears 2 globose cells that burst transversely, springing back elastically; 3 deformed, broad, opposite the larger petals, 2-fid, with 2 empty cells together forming a cup over the pistil. Disk cupular or annular with 2–5 simple or dentate teeth. Ovary sessile, 2- (rarely 3-) celled, contracted into a simple or 2-partite style; ovules 2 in each cell; stigma simple. Drupe small, oblique, subglobose; stone crustaceous, 1-celled, with usually a basilar rounded projection over which the seed is curved. Seeds globose; testa membranous; cotyledons conduplicate; radicle incurved.—Distrib. Tropical Asia, Malaya, a few in S. America; species about 32.

1. **Meliosma Wightii,** *Planch. ex Brand. For. Fl.* (1874) p. 116. A small tree; branches, petioles and panicles clothed with ferruginous pubescence. Leaves 3½–7 by 1¼–2½ in., coriaceous, oblong-elliptic or lanceolate, acute or acuminate, usually entire, glabrous above except on the nerves, prominently reticulately veined and more or less pubescent beneath; petioles about ½ in. long. Flowers small, in rigid pyramidal rufous-hairy panicles. Sepals and bracteoles about 7–9, all suborbicular, ciliate, the outer ones pubescent outside. Petals membranous, the 3 larger ones rounded, obtuse, the 2 smaller bifid. Ovary flask-shaped, glabrous. Drupes ¼–⅓ in. in diam., nearly globular, supported on the persistent sepals. Fl. B. I. v. 2, p. 4; Trim. Fl. Ceyl. v. 1, p. 314; Talb. Trees, Bomb. p. 60. *Millingtonia pungens*, Wight, Icon. t. 964.

Konkan: *Dalzell*!

I have seen only one specimen from Bombay which was collected by Dalzell. The plant appears to be tolerably common on the Nilgherries.—Distrib. India (W. Peninsula); Ceylon.

ORDER XLV. ANACARDIACEÆ.

Trees or shrubs usually with oleo-resinous often acrid juice. Leaves alternate, simple or compound, exstipulate. Flowers small, regular, 1-sexual, polygamous, or 2-sexual, usually panicled. Calyx 3-5-partite, sometimes accrescent. Disk flat, cupular or annular, entire or lobed, rarely obsolete. Stamens equal in number to the petals, rarely more, inserted under (rarely on) the disk; filaments usually subulate; anthers 2-celled, basi- or dorsi-fixed. Ovary superior (half inferior in *Holigarna*), 1- or 2-6-celled, rudimentary or 2-3-fid in the male (of 5-6 carpels in *Buchanania*); ovule solitary in each cell, pendulous from the top or side of the cell or from an ascending basal funicle. Fruit superior (except in *Holigarna*), usually a 1-5-celled, 1-5-seeded drupe; stone sometimes dehiscent. Seed exalbuminous; embryo straight or curved; cotyledons plano-convex; radicle short.—DISTRIB. Chiefly tropical; genera 55; species about 450.

Ovary 1-celled or if 2-celled with 1 cell early suppressed.
  Ovules pendulous from a basal funicle.
    Leaves pinnate or 3-foliolate (sometimes simple in *R. Cotinus*) .... 1. RHUS.
    Leaves simple.
      Flowers polygamous.
        Stamens 1-5; fruit a fleshy drupe........ 2. MANGIFERA.
        Stamens 8-10; fruit a reniform nut .... 3. ANACARDIUM.
      Flowers hermaphrodite; stamens 10; fruit a drupe .... 4. BUCHANANIA.
  Ovules pendulous from the top or above the middle of the cell.
    Leaves pinnate.
      Petals valvate; style 1 .... 5. SOLENOCARPUS.
      Petals imbricate; styles 3-4 .... 6. ODINA.
    Leaves simple.
      Stamens 5-6; styles 3.
        Petals imbricate; drupe superior .... 7. SEMECARPUS.
        Petals valvate; drupe inferior........ 8. HOLIGARNA.
      Stamens 4; style 1 .... 9. NOTHOPEGIA.
Ovary 4-5-celled; leaves pinnate .... 10. SPONDIAS.

1. RHUS, Linn.

Trees or shrubs often with acrid juice. Leaves alternate, 3-foliolate or imparipinnate (simple in *R. Cotinus*). Flowers small, in terminal and axillary panicles, polygamous. Calyx small, 4-6-partite, persistent; segments subequal. Petals 4-6, equal, spreading, imbricate. Stamens 4, 5, 6 or 10, inserted at the base of the disk, free; filaments subulate; anthers short, imperfect in the female flower. Ovary sessile, ovoid or globose, 1-celled; ovule pendulous from a basal funicle; styles 3, free or connate, short or long; stigmas simple or capitate. Drupe small, dry, compressed; stone coriaceous, crustaceous or bony. Seed pendulous from the funicle; testa membranous; cotyledons flattish; radicle hooked, short, superior.—DISTRIB. Chiefly in warm extratropical regions of both hemispheres; species about 120.

1. **Rhus mysurensis,** *Heyne, ex Wight & Arn. Prodr.* (1834) p. 172. A shrub or small tree; branches woody, often spiny, the younger pubescent. Leaves 3-foliolate; leaflets obovate, cuneate, sinuate-toothed or sublobed,

with a few scattered hairs above, softly pubescent beneath; terminal leaflet sessile or shortly petioluled, much larger than the lateral ones, reaching 1–1½ in. long; lateral leaflets sessile, sometimes very small. Flowers in terminal and axillary branched pubescent panicles; pedicels short; bracts minute, linear, pubescent. Calyx pubescent outside, much shorter than the petals; lobes ovate. Petals $\frac{1}{12}$ in. long, oblong, subacute, glabrous. Disk 5-lobed, the lobes often notched. Drupes $\frac{1}{8}$–$\frac{1}{6}$ in. in diam., subglobose, brown, glabrous, shining. Engler, in DC. Monogr. Phan. v. 4, p. 420. *Rhus mysorensis*, Hook. f. in Fl. B. I. v. 2, p. 9; Aitch. Pb. & Sind Pl. p. 35; Talb. Trees, Bomb. p. 61; Woodr. in Journ. Bomb. Nat. v. 11 (1897) p. 272; Watt, Dict. Econ. Prod. v. 6, part 1, p. 497.—Flowers: June. VERN. *Amani*.

DECCAN: Ghát between Wai and Wathár, *Cooke*!; hills near Poona, *Woodrow*! Chattarsinghi hill near Poona, *Kanitkar*! S. M. COUNTRY: common in the Dharwar forests, *Talbot*. SIND: on the hills, *Stocks*, 475!—DISTRIB. India generally.

Graham states that the bark is used for tanning, and in Rajputana, where the shrub is common, it is largely employed for this purpose and is said to give a fine brown color to leather.—See Watt, Dict. Econ. Prod. l. c.

2. MANGIFERA, Linn.

Trees. Leaves alternate, petioled, simple, entire, coriaceous. Flowers small, polygamous, in terminal panicles. Calyx 4–5-partite; segments imbricate, deciduous. Petals 4–5, free or adnate to the disk, imbricate; nerves thickened, sometimes ending in excrescences. Stamens 1–5, inserted just within the disk or on it, 1 usually more perfect and much longer than the others, the others with imperfect or smaller anthers, or reduced to teeth, or absent. Ovary sessile, 1-celled, oblique; ovule pendulous, funicle basal or inserted on the side of the cell above its base (rarely horizontal). Drupe large, fleshy; stone compressed, fibrous. Seed large, compressed; testa papery; cotyledons plano-convex, often unequal and lobed.—DISTRIB. Tropical Asia, chiefly Malaya; species about 30.

1. **Mangifera indica**, *Linn. Sp. Pl.* (1753) p. 200. A large spreading evergreen tree reaching 50 ft. in height, all parts glabrous except the inflorescence. Leaves crowded at the ends of the branches, coriaceous, 5–10 by 1½–3 in., oblong, or oblong-lanceolate, acute, acuminate or subobtuse, shining, entire, the margins often undulate, base narrowed; petioles ½–2½ in. long. Flowers monœcious, $\frac{1}{6}$ in. long, with a somewhat disagreeable odor, arranged in large many-flowered pubescent panicles longer than the leaves; pedicels short, thick; bracteoles ovate, small. Sepals ovate, concave, pubescent outside, shorter than the petals. Petals oblong, subacute, reflexed, glabrous, with 3 strong orange-colored ridges on the inner face. Disk fleshy, 5-lobed. Stamen 1; filament subulate; anther purple. Ovary glabrous. Drupes large, fleshy, obliquely pyriform or subovoid, subcompressed, 3–8 in. long; stone compressed, fibrous, very hard. Fl. B. I. v. 2, p. 13; Grah. Cat. p. 41; Dalz. & Gibs, p. 51; Talb. Trees, Bomb. p. 61; Woodr. in Journ. Bomb. Nat. v. 11 (1897) p. 273; Engler, in DC. Monogr. v. 4, p. 198; Watt, Dict. Econ. Prod. v. 5, p. 146.—Flowers: Jan.–Feb. VERN. *A'mb*.

The well-known *Mango* tree, cultivated throughout India and in the Tropics generally. It is said to be wild in the Western Peninsula from Khandesh southwards, but in the case of a tree so widely cultivated as is the Mango, the fruit of which is eaten largely by the natives and its stones dropped everywhere throughout the jungles, it is difficult to determine in what localities the tree may be considered truly wild. It is planted everywhere throughout the Presidency, and its dense shady foliage renders it valuable as a roadside tree as well as for planting near main roads in *topes*, whose shade at midday is valuable to wayfarers and their cattle. The fruit varies much in quality, in some cases being graphically described as a mixture of tow with turpentine, while in the case of some of the more highly cultivated trees the fruit is very delicious.

Bombay has been long celebrated for its cultivated mangoes, of which those grown in the island of Bombay are undoubtedly the best, perhaps from the care bestowed on their cultivation. Most of the mangoes grown throughout the country are raised from seedlings, with the result that the quality of the fruit is extremely variable. To secure good fruit, grafting is essential, and was apparently introduced into Bombay by the Portuguese, to propagate the valuable kinds known as the Mazagon (Bombay) and Goa mangoes. Of the Bombay mangoes, the best kinds are those known as the *Aphoos* (probably a native corruption of the Portuguese name *Alphonse*) and the *Pirie*. The fruit of both weighs on an average about 8 ounces, that of the *Aphoos* is greenish-yellow on the unexposed, red on the exposed side, without any stigmatic point or beak. The flavor of the fruit is indescribably delicious and it commands the highest price in the market. The *Pirie* mango has less of a yellowish tinge on the unexposed side than the *Aphoos*, the exposed side being red, and the fruit is furnished with a distinct beak. The ripe fruit does not keep as well as that of the *Aphoos* and the flavor is not quite so good, so that its market price is lower. The midrib of the leaves and the branches of the inflorescence of the best variety of the *Aphoos* are of a rich rosy color, while the corresponding parts of the *Pirie* are white or greenish-white. Woodrow ('Gardening in India,' edition 5 [1889] pp. 69–72 & pp. 240–260) gives a full description of the best modes of growing and grafting the mango, as well as a list of the most celebrated trees in the Bombay Presidency and the localities in which they are to be found. Watt, Dict. Econ. Prod. v. 5, pp. 146–156, also gives valuable information.

3. ANACARDIUM, Rottb.

Shrubs or trees. Leaves alternate, petioled, simple, coriaceous, quite entire. Flowers polygamous, in terminal bracteate panicles. Calyx 5-partite, deciduous, erect, imbricate. Disk filling the base of the calyx, erect. Stamens 8–10, all or some fertile; filaments connate and adnate to the disk. Ovary obovoid or obcordate; ovule 1, ascending from a very short lateral funicle. Nut reniform, seated on a large pyriform fleshy body, formed of the enlarged disk and top of the peduncle; pericarp cellular and full of oil. Seed reniform, ascending; testa membranous, adherent; cotyledons semi-lunar; radicle short, hooked.—Distrib. Tropical America; species 6, of which 1, the following, has been naturalized in Asia.

1. **Anacardium occidentale,** *Linn. Sp. Pl.* (1753) p. 383. A small tree with a short thick crooked trunk; branches terete, glabrous. Leaves coriaceous, 4–6 by $2\frac{1}{2}$–3 in., obovate or elliptic, rounded at the apex, glabrous, finely reticulately veined, base cuneate; main nerves 10–12 pairs, prominent beneath; petioles $\frac{3}{8}$–$\frac{5}{8}$ in. long. Panicles terminal, longer than the leaves, the branches cymose; peduncles lengthening with age; bract $\frac{1}{5}$–$\frac{2}{5}$ in. long, ovate, very acute, nerved, puberulous outside. Sepals $\frac{1}{8}$ in. long, lanceolate, puberulous outside. Petals $\frac{1}{3}$–$\frac{1}{2}$ in. long, linear-lanceolate, deflexed from the middle, minutely puberulous outside. Stamens about 9, one longer than the others, the longer one exserted beyond the recurved petals. Ovary about $\frac{1}{12}$ in. long, glabrescent, attenuated into a subulate style $\frac{1}{8}$ in. long. Fruit reniform, 1 in. long, its pedicel large, fleshy, dark-colored. Fl. B. I. v. 2, p. 20; Grah. Cat. p. 40; Dalz. & Gibs. Suppl. p. 18; Talb. Trees, Bomb. p. 61; Woodr. in Journ. Bomb. Nat. v. 11 (1897) p. 273;

Engler, in DC. Monogr. Phan. v. 4, p. 219; Watt, Dict. Econ. Prod. v. 1, p. 232.—Flowers: Jan.–Mar. VERN. *Kâju*; *Hijuli-badam*; *Geru mavu*.

The *Cashew-nut* tree, a native of Tropical America, naturalized and cultivated in India, especially near the coast. KONKAN: *Stocks*!; Malabar and Parel hills (Bombay), *Graham*; Salsette, common, *Graham*; Southern Konkan, *Dalzell & Gibson*; Ratnagiri, *Cooke*!, *Kanitkar*!; Vingorla, *Ritchie*, 142!; Wari Country, *Dalzell & Gibson*. S. M. COUNTRY: Dharwar, *Talbot*.

The nuts are eaten roasted and are much esteemed. The plant is also used in native medicine. See Watt, Dict. Econ. Prod. l. c.

The fruit is very curious, the nut appearing to be outside it, an error into which Graham and Dalzell & Gibson have fallen. What is regarded by them as the fruit is, however, the enlarged pedicel and disk on which the nut is seated.

4. BUCHANANIA, Spreng. in Schrader, Journ. v. 4 (1801) p. 234.

Trees. Leaves alternate, petioled, simple, coriaceous, quite entire. Flowers hermaphrodite, small, white, in terminal and axillary branched panicles. Calyx short, obtusely 3–5-toothed or -lobed, persistent, imbricate. Petals 4–5, oblong, imbricate, at length recurved. Disk orbicular, 5-crenate. Stamens 8–10, free, inserted at the base of the disk. Carpels 5–6, free, seated in the cavity of the disk, one fertile, the others imperfect; ovule 1, pendulous from a basal funicle; style short; stigma truncate. Drupe small, scantily fleshy; stone crustaceous or bony, 2-valved. Seed gibbous, acute at one end; cotyledons thick; radicle superior.—DISTRIB. Tropical Asia, Australia and the Pacific Islands; species about 25.

Leaves broadly oblong, more or less villous beneath; panicles pilose .... 1. *B. Lanzan.*
Leaves narrowly oblong, glabrous beneath; panicles glabrous . 2. *B. angustifolia.*

1. **Buchanania Lanzan,** *Spreng. in Schrader, Journ.* v. 4 (1801) p. 234. A tree 40–50 ft. high, with straight trunk; young branches clothed with silky hairs. Leaves thickly coriaceous, 5–10 by $2\frac{1}{2}$–5 in., broadly oblong, obtuse, sometimes emarginate, glabrescent above, more or less villous beneath, reticulately veined, the nerves and veins impressed on the upper surface, base rounded; main nerves 10–20 pairs; petioles about $\frac{1}{2}$ in. long. Flowers small, sessile, greenish white, in terminal and axillary pyramidal ferrugineo-pilose panicles which are shorter than the leaves; bracts small, caducous. Calyx-lobes short, broadly ovate, ciliate. Petals $\frac{1}{10}$ in. long, ovate-oblong, subacute. Disk fleshy. Stamens 10, a little shorter than the petals; filaments flattened; anthers about as long as the filaments. Ovaries: 1 perfect, conical, villous, the other 4 reduced to cylindrical filaments. Drupes obliquely lentiform, $\frac{1}{3}$–$\frac{1}{2}$ in. in the long diameter, black; stone hard, 2-valved. *Buchanania latifolia*, Roxb. Hort. Beng. (1814) p. 32; Hook. f. Fl. B. I. v. 2, p. 23; Grah. Cat. p. 41; Dalz. & Gibs. p. 52; Bedd. Flor. Sylvat. t. 165; Talb. Trees, Bomb. p. 62; Woodr. in Journ. Bomb. Nat. v. 11 (1897) p. 273; Engler, in DC. Monogr. Phan. v. 4, p. 182; Watt, Dict. Econ. Prod. v. 1, p. 544.—Flowers: Jan.–Mar. VERN. *Châr*; *Piyal*.

The specific name *Lanzan* is derived from the native Birmese name, and was given to the plant by Sprengel in 1800–1801. The name is therefore prior to that given by Roxburgh (1814), and though not as characteristic as Roxburgh's name (*latifolia*), must necessarily be adopted. See note under *B. angustifolia*, the next species.

KONKAN: *Stocks*!; Bombay, *Lambert*!; Wari, *Cooke*!; Baitsi (Wari Country), *Dalzell & Gibson*. DECCAN: Kartriz Ghát (near Poona), *Woodrow*!; Singhad hill, *Woodrow*! GUJARAT: Barria jungles east of Baroda, *Gibson*; Dangs, *Woodrow*. S. M. COUNTRY: Belgaum, *Law*!, *Ritchie*, 1010!—DISTRIB. Hot and drier parts of India.

The fruit is eaten and an oil is extracted from the kernels. See Watt, Dict. Econ. Prod. l. c.

2. **Buchanania angustifolia,** *Roxb. Hort. Beng.* (1814) p. 32; *Fl. Ind.* v. 2 (1832) p. 386. A glabrous tree. Leaves thinly coriaceous, 3–6 by 1¼–2 in., linear-oblong, elliptic or elliptic-lanceolate, obtuse or rounded, very often emarginate, quite glabrous, reticulately veined, the nerves and veins slightly prominent on the upper surface, base rounded or acute; main nerves 12–15 pairs; petioles ¾–1¼ in. long, slender. Flowers in glabrous branched panicles about equalling the leaves; pedicels $\frac{1}{25}$–$\frac{1}{12}$ in. long. Calyx-lobes semiorbicular. Petals $\frac{1}{10}$ in. long, oblong. Fertile ovary pilose. Drupes ½ in. in diam., obliquely globose, slightly compressed. Fl. B. I. v. 2, p. 23; Grah. Cat. p. 41; Wight, Icon. t. 101; Trim. Fl. Ceyl. v. 1, p. 316; Talb. Trees, Bomb. p. 62; Engler, in DC. Monogr. Phan. v. 4, p. 184.

This tree has been included on the authority of *Graham* (l. c.), who gives the Ajanta jungles as its habitat. It has not apparently been found in the Bombay Presidency by any other collector. *Dalzell & Gibson* do not include the plant in their Bombay Flora, and *Talbot* (l. c.) merely quotes *Graham*. There are no specimens in Herb. Kew. from the Bombay Presidency. *Wight's* specimens and those in Herb. Rottl. are from Southern India. *Roxburgh* states (*l. c.*) that it is a native of the south end of India. On the other hand, *Duthie* (9350 in Herb. Kew.!) has found the plant in the Chanda district of the Central Provinces.—DISTRIB. India from the Central Provinces southward.

Note.—Steudel, Nom. v. 1, p. 233, and, following him, Daydon Jackson, in 'Index Kewensis,' give *B. Lanzan*, Spreng. in Schrader, Journ. v. 4 (1801), as a synonym for *B. angustifolia*.—The plant to which the name *B. Lanzan* was given by Sprengel was first described by Buchanan in Asiat. Res. v. 5 (1798) p. 123, but was not named in that publication. Sprengel, two years later, named the plant *B. Lanzan* from the native Birmese name communicated by Buchanan, and at the same time founded the genus *Buchanania* (1800–1801). Roxburgh (Hort. Beng. [1814] p. 32), no doubt in ignorance of Sprengel's work which had appeared in a journal printed in Göttingen in 1801, gave the *same* name to the genus. That the plant described by Buchanan could not possibly have been *B. angustifolia* of Roxburgh is evident from the fact that *B. angustifolia* is not a native of Birma, but is confined to S. India, whereas, from Buchanan's notes, it is clear that the plant described by him was abundant on the mountainous districts of Upper Birma and that its seeds were widely distributed commercially and used for the same purposes as almonds. Moreover, Roxburgh (Fl. Ind. v. 2, p 385) makes it quite clear that the *B. Lanzan* of Sprengel was the same plant that he described as *B. latifolia*. Roxburgh quotes Buchanan in Asiat. Res. (*l. c.*) as the original author, and gives the native name of the plant as *Larmzon*, which is doubtless a misprint for *Launzan*. See remarks under the preceding species.

5. SOLENOCARPUS, Wight & Arn.

A tree. Leaves alternate, crowded towards the ends of the branches, imparipinnate; leaflets opposite, glabrous, crenulate. Flowers hermaphrodite, small, in terminal branched panicles. Calyx minute, 5-toothed, imbricate, deciduous. Petals 5, spreading, valvate. Disk broad, annular. Stamens 10, inserted at the base of the disk. Ovary free, sessile, 1-celled; ovule 1, pendulous from the top of the cell; style clavate; stigma obliquely truncate. Drupe small, obliquely oblong truncate, compressed; pericarp cellular, full of oil; stone bony. Seed linear, compressed; cotyledons linear, plano-convex; radicle very short, thick, superior.—DISTRIB. Peninsular India; species 1.

1. **Solenocarpus indica,** *Wight & Arn. Prodr.* (1834) p. 171. A tree. Leaves imparipinnate; rhachis slender, angled; leaflets sessile (except the terminal one, which has a petiolule about ½ in. long), 2–3½ by ⅜–1¼ in., oblong, acuminate, slightly crenate, glabrous on both surfaces, pale beneath, base oblique, the upper side of the leaflet shorter than the lower and suddenly contracted at the base; main nerves 8–10 pairs, faint. Flowers white, in much-branched panicles, the branches puberulous, angled; pedicels solitary or 2–3 together, short. Calyx-lobes scarcely $\frac{1}{50}$ in. long, deltoid. Petals oblong-lanceolate, about ⅛ in. long and about $\frac{1}{24}$ in. broad. Drupes ¼ in. long, pedicelled. Fl. B. I. v. 2, p. 27; Bedd. Flor. Sylvat. t. 233; Engler, in DC. Monogr. Phan. v. 4, p. 250; Talb. Trees, Bomb. p. 62.—Flowers: Jan.

Rare in the Bombay Presidency. *Dalzell* in Herb. Kew. without locality! KONKAN: *Stocks*! KANARA: in the evergreen forests of the Yellapur taluka in N. Kanara, rare, *Talbot*.—DISTRIB. As the genus.

6. ODINA, Roxb.

Trees with stout soft branches. Leaves few at the ends of the branches, alternate, usually imparipinnate, deciduous; leaflets opposite, quite entire. Flowers small, monœcious or diœcious, fascicled, shortly pedicelled, in simple and panicled terminal fascicled racemes. Calyx 4–5-lobed, persistent; lobes rounded, imbricate. Disk annular, crenate. MALE FLOWERS: Stamens 8–10 inserted below the disk. Ovary 4–5-partite. FEMALE FLOWERS: Ovary sessile, oblong, 1-celled; ovule 1 in each cell, pendulous from near its apex by a long funicle, often abortive in 3 of the cells; styles 3–4, stout; stigmas simple or capitellate. Drupe small, compressed, oblong, subreniform, crowned by the distant styles; stone hard. Seed compressed; embryo curved; cotyledons flat, fleshy; radicle superior.—DISTRIB. Africa and Tropical Asia; species about 13.

1. **Odina Woodier,** *Roxb. Hort. Beng.* (1814) p. 29; **Odina Wodier,** *Roxb. Fl. Ind.* v. 2 (1832) p. 293. A large tree 40–50 ft. high; trunk thick; bark ash-colored, smooth, exfoliating; young parts more or less stellately puberulous. Leaves crowded about the ends of the branches, 10–18 in. long; leaflets membranous, green above, brown beneath (when dry), 3–5 pairs and an odd one, 3–6 by 1–2 in., ovate-oblong, acuminate, glabrous, shining, tinged with pink when young, base acute or rounded, often oblique; main nerves 6–8 pairs; petiolules of the lateral leaflets 0–⅛ in. long, those of the terminal leaflets much longer. Flowers purplish, appearing when the tree is bare of leaves, crowded in cymose fascicles, the male racemes compound, the female simple; pedicels very short, fulvous-pubescent; bracts ovate, acute, pubescent outside, ciliate. Calyx-lobes about $\frac{1}{20}$ in. long, ovate-orbicular, ciliate. Petals 4, ovate-oblong, acute, ⅛–⅙ in. long. Stamens in the male flowers equalling the petals. Ovary in the female ovoid-oblong, in the male rudimentary, 4-lobed. Drupes reniform,

compressed, red. Fl. B. I. v. 2, p. 29; Grah. Cat. p. 42; Dalz. & Gibs. p. 51; Bedd. Flor. Sylvat. t. 123; Engler, in DC. Monogr. Phan. v. 4, p. 267; Trim. Fl. Ceyl. v. 1, p. 318; Talb. Trees, Bomb. p. 62; Woodr. in Journ. Bomb. Nat. v. 11 (1897) p. 273; Watt, Dict. Econ. Prod. v. 5, p. 445.—Flowers: Feb.-May. VERN. *Shimti*; *Moya*.

Common throughout the Presidency in deciduous forests. KONKAN: *Law*!, *Stocks*!; Malabar hill and Elephanta (Bombay), *Graham*. DECCAN: Khandala, *Bhiva*!; Bowdhan near Poona, *Woodrow*. GUJARAT: Rajkot, *Woodrow*. KANARA: Kála naddi, *Ritchie*, 140!—DISTRIB. India; Ceylon.

Often planted as a roadside tree, especially in the Madras Presidency, a purpose for which it is by no means suitable, as it is bare of leaves in the hot weather when shade is required. It grows very readily from cuttings, which is perhaps the reason of its being so often planted. The tree exudes a gum which is not of much value, and the bark is employed in native medicine. See Watt, Dict. Econ. Prod. l. c.

7. SEMECARPUS, Linn. f.

Trees. Leaves alternate, simple, quite entire, coriaceous. Flowers small, polygamous or diœcious, in terminal (rarely axillary) panicles. Calyx 5-6-fid; segments deciduous. Petals 5-6, imbricate. Disk broad, annular. Stamens 5-6, inserted at the base of the disk, imperfect in the female flowers. Ovary very rudimentary or 0 in the male flowers; in the female superior, 1-celled; ovule pendulous from the apex of the cell, funicle short; styles 3; stigmas subclavate. Drupe fleshy, oblong, subglobose or reniform, oblique, seated on a fleshy receptacle formed of the thickened disk and calyx-base; pericarp charged with acrid resin. Seed pendulous; testa coriaceous, the inner coat somewhat fleshy; embryo thick; cotyledons plano-convex; radicle superior.—DISTRIB. Tropical Asia and Australia; species about 38.

1. **Semecarpus Anacardium,** *Linn. f. Suppl.* (1781) p. 182. A moderate-sized tree. Leaves 7–24 by 4–12 in., obovate-oblong, rounded at the apex, coriaceous, glabrous above, ashy grey or buff and more or less pubescent beneath and with cartilaginous margins, base rounded, cordate or cuneate, sometimes shortly auricled; main nerves 15–25 pairs making a large angle with the costa, sometimes nearly horizontal, prominent on both surfaces; petioles $\frac{1}{2}$–$1\frac{1}{2}$ in. long. Flowers greenish-white, subsessile, fascicled in pubescent panicles which are equal to or shorter than the leaves, the female panicles shorter than the male; pedicels short; bracts lanceolate, pilose. Calyx-segments about $\frac{1}{24}$ in. long, pilose outside. Petals $\frac{1}{8}$–$\frac{1}{6}$ in. long by $\frac{1}{12}$ in. broad, ovate, acute. Ovary in the male flowers rudimentary, hairy; in the female subglobose, densely pilose, crowned with the 3 styles. Drupes 1 in. long, obliquely ovoid or oblong, smooth and shining, black when ripe, seated on a fleshy receptacle or hypocarp about $\frac{3}{4}$ in. long, smooth and yellow when ripe. Fl. B. I. v. 2, p. 30; Grah. Cat. p. 41; Dalz. & Gibs. p. 52; Bedd. Flor. Sylvat. t. 163; Engler, in DC. Monogr. Phan. v. 4, p. 478, & in Engl. & Prantl, Pflanzenf. v. 3, part 5, p. 175, fig. 110, H–N; Talb. Trees, Bomb. p. 62; Woodr. in Journ. Bomb. Nat. v. 11 (1897) p. 273; Watt, Dict. Econ. Prod. v. 6, part 2, p. 498.—Flowers: May-July. VERN. *Bibba*; *Bhildvá*.

Throughout the Presidency in dry forests. KONKAN: common, *Dalzell & Gibson*, *Law*!, *Stocks*!, *Graham*; Wari Country, *Dalzell & Gibson*. DECCAN: common, *Dalzell & Gibson*; Singhad, *Woodrow*. S. M. COUNTRY: Belgaum, *Ritchie*, 1014!

GUJARAT: *Graham.* KANARA: Kála naddi, *Ritchie,* $\frac{1014}{3}$!— DISTRIB. India; E. Archipelago, N. Australia.

The tree is known to Anglo-Indians as the *marking-nut* tree, the juice of the pericarp being used for marking cotton cloths. An acrid viscid juice is extracted from it which is used in making a kind of varnish, while the fleshy receptacles on which the drupes rest are roasted and eaten. See Watt, Dict. Econ. Prod. l. c.

VAR. *cuneifolia*, DC. Prodr. v. 2, p. 62. Leaves cuneate at the base, often tomentose beneath. *S. cuneifolia* (sp.), Roxb. Fl. Ind. v. 2, p. 86; Grah. Cat. p. 41.—Flowers: Dec. VERN. *Bibu.*

Dalzell, without locality, in Herb. Kew.! DECCAN: Lanoli Grove, Khandala and jungles about Pár, *Graham.*—DISTRIB. Tropical Himalaya, Khasia mountains and Behar.

This is included on the authority of Graham (*l. c.*).

8. HOLIGARNA, Ham.

Lofty trees. Leaves alternate, simple, quite entire, coriaceous; petiole furnished with 2 or 4 spur-like deciduous appendages. Flowers small, crowded, in axillary and terminal racemes or panicles. Calyx superior; tube cup-shaped; teeth 5, imbricate. Petals 5, densely villous in front, cohering at the base and with the edge of the disk, persistent, valvate. Disk lining the calyx-tube, obscure in the female flowers. Stamens 5, inserted at the edge of the disk, coherent at the base with the petals; filaments subulate, glabrous; anthers small, subglobose. Ovary in the male flowers 0, in the female flowers inferior, 1-celled; ovule pendulous from near the top of the cell; styles 3–5, terminal; stigmas capitate or clavate. Drupe inferior, subcompressed, oblong or ovoid, resinous, acrid; stone coriaceous. Seed parietal; testa membranous; embryo thick; cotyledons plano-convex; radicle minute, next the hilum.—DISTRIB. Throughout India; species 5 or 6.

Leaves quite glabrous beneath; drupe almost entirely included in the torus .... 1. *H. Arnottiana.*
Leaves rusty-pubescent beneath; drupe $\frac{1}{4}$–$\frac{1}{3}$ exserted from the torus .... 2. *H. Grahamii.*

1. **Holigarna Arnottiana,** *Hook. f. in Fl. B. I.* v. 2 (1876) p. 36. A tall tree; branches densely leafy at the apex. Leaves 6–12 by 2–4 in., obovate or oblanceolate, decurrent into the petiole, acute or rounded at the apex, glabrous on both surfaces, paler beneath; main nerves 12–20 pairs, prominent on both surfaces, nearly straight, making a large angle with the costa; petioles $\frac{1}{4}$–1 in. long, with 2 petiolar spurs or tubercles at the top, which are early deciduous. Flowers minute, crowded, in rufous-tomentose panicles which are shorter or longer than the leaves. Calyx-teeth very short. Petals $\frac{1}{10}$ in. long, oblong, acute. Drupes reaching 1 in. long, obliquely ovoid, rounded at the top, quite glabrous, long-pedicelled, almost entirely included in the torus. Talb. Trees, Bomb. p. 63; Woodr. in Journ. Bomb. Nat. v. 11 (1897) p. 273; Engler, in DC. Monogr. Phan. v. 4, p. 497; Watt, Dict. Econ. Prod. v. 4, p. 259. *Holigarna longifolia*, W. & A. Prodr. p. 169 (*not* of Roxb.); Grah. Cat. p. 41; Dalz. & Gibs. p. 51.—Flowers: Jan.–Feb. VERN. *Hulyeri.*

Common in the evergreen forests of the Konkan and N. Kanara. *Dalzell* in Herb. Kew. without any locality! KONKAN: *Stocks*!; hilly and wooded parts, *Graham.* S. M. COUNTRY: *Woodrow*! KANARA: Nilkund (N. Kanara), *Talbot*!; Divimana, *Woodrow.*—DISTRIB. India (Western and Southern Ghâts).

2. **Holigarna Grahamii,** *Hook. f. in Fl. B. I.* v. 2 (1876) p. 37. A tree 20–30 ft. high; young branches ferrugineo-tomentose. Leaves 12–16 by 4–6 in., rigidly coriaceous, oblanceolate, triangular above the middle, acute or acuminate, glabrous and shining above, ferrugineo-pubescent beneath, base cuneate; main nerves 20–30 pairs, prominent and pilose beneath; petioles $\frac{1}{2}$–$\frac{5}{8}$ in. long, stout, with 1 or 2 spurs on each side $\frac{1}{4}$–$\frac{1}{3}$ in. long. Flowers in rusty-tomentose terminal panicles, clustered, the male panicle about 1 ft. long, the female shorter. Calyx cup-shaped; lobes minute. Petals $\frac{1}{10}$ in. long, $\frac{1}{20}$ in. broad. Drupes about $\frac{3}{4}$ in. long, enclosed in the cup-shaped torus, except one-sixth or one-fourth of the upper part which is exserted. Fl. B. I. v. 2, p. 37; Talb. Trees, Bomb. p. 63; Woodr. in Journ. Bomb. Nat. v. 11 (1897) p. 273; Engler, in DC. Monogr. Phan. v. 4, p. 499; Watt, Dict. Econ. Prod. v. 4, p. 260. *Semecarpus Grahamii,* Wight, Icon. t. 235; Dalz. & Gibs. p. 52.

KONKAN: *Law*!, *Stocks*!; Mira hills near Pen, *Dalzell & Gibson.* DECCAN: Khandala, *Woodrow.* S. M. COUNTRY: Ramghát, *Ritchie,* 1677! KANARA: common on the N. Kanara Gháts from Ainshi southwards, *Talbot.*—DISTRIB. India (W. Peninsula).

9. NOTHOPEGIA, Blume.

Trees. Leaves alternate or opposite, coriaceous, quite entire. Flowers small, bracteate, polygamous, in short axillary racemes. Calyx small, 4–5-lobed, persistent. Petals 4–5, spreading, imbricate. Disk annular, 4–5-lobed. Stamens 4–5, inserted on the margin of the disk; filaments free, pilose. Ovary free, sessile, ovoid, 1-celled; ovule 1, pendulous from near the top of the cell; style short. Drupe depressed-globose, striate, apiculate with the style, seated on the slightly thickened torus. Seed pendulous; testa membranous; cotyledons thick, plano-convex; radicle very short, sublateral.—DISTRIB. India (W. Peninsula); species 3.

1. **Nothopegia Colebrookiana,** *Blume, Mus. Bot.* v. 1 (1849) p. 203. A small tree about 15 ft. high, with acrid milky juice. Leaves 3–8$\frac{1}{2}$ by 1$\frac{1}{4}$–2$\frac{1}{2}$ in., elliptic-oblong, acute or acuminate (rarely subobtuse), glabrous and shining above, pale beneath, base decurrent into the petiole; main nerves 15–20 pairs; petioles $\frac{1}{2}$–$\frac{3}{4}$ in. long. Flowers small, white; the female sessile or nearly so, in more or less rufous-pubescent racemes which are much shorter than the leaves, solitary and fascicled; the male racemes much longer and more branched than the female. Calyx-lobes 4, about $\frac{1}{30}$ in. long. Petals 4, hairy on the back, linear-oblong, obtuse, $\frac{1}{10}$ in. long and about $\frac{1}{25}$ in. broad, with recurved tips. Stamens 4. Drupes seated on the slightly enlarged torus, the shape of a fig, about $\frac{1}{2}$ in. long, longitudinally striate, purple; pulp copious, edible. Fl. B. I. v. 1, p. 40; Trim. Fl. Ceyl. v. 1, p. 325; Talb. Trees, Bomb. p. 63; Woodr. in Journ. Bomb. Nat. v. 11 (1897) p. 273; Engler, in DC. Monogr. Phan. v. 4, p. 467, & in Engl. & Prantl, Pflanzenf. v. 3, part 5, p. 175, fig. 110, A–D; Watt, Dict. Econ. Prod. v. 5, p. 430. *Glycycarpus racemosa,* Dalz. in Kew Journ. Bot. v. 2 (1850) p. 39; Dalz. & Gibs. p. 51 (exclud. syn.).—Flowers: Jan.–Mar. VERN. *A'mbari.*

KONKAN: *Stocks*!, *Law*!; Baitai (Wari Country), *Ritchie,* 422! DECCAN: Phunda Ghát, *Ritchie,* 422! S. M. COUNTRY: Ramghát, *Ritchie,* 422! KANARA: evergreen forests of N. Kanara Gháts, common, *Talbot*; Divimana Ghát, *Woodrow*!; Sampkhand (N. Kanara), *Woodrow*!—DISTRIB. India (W. Peninsula); Ceylon.

10. SPONDIAS, Linn.

Deciduous glabrous trees. Leaves usually crowded at the ends of the branches, alternate, imparipinnate; leaflets subopposite, usually caudate-acuminate. Flowers small, shortly pedicelled, polygamous, in terminal spreading panicles. Calyx small, deciduous, 4–5-fid; lobes slightly imbricate. Petals 4–5, spreading, subvalvate. Disk cup-shaped, broad, crenate. Stamens 8–10, inserted beneath the disk. Ovary sessile, free, 4–5-celled; ovule 1 in each cell, pendulous; styles 4–5, conniving above. Drupe fleshy; stone hard, thick, 1–5-celled, the cells erect or diverging and opening by canals through the top of the stone. Seed pendulous; testa membranous; embryo straight; cotyledons elongate, plano-convex; radicle short, superior.—Distrib. Tropical regions; species about 8.

Panicle 12–15 in. long; stone rough .... 1. *S. mangifera.*
Panicle 6–8 in. long; stone smooth .... 2. *S. acuminata.*

1. **Spondias mangifera,** *Willd. Sp. Pl.* v. 2 (1799) p. 751. A glabrous tree 30–35 ft. high; trunk straight; bark smooth, ash-colored; branches nearly horizontal. Leaves 12–18 in. long, the common petioles slender, terete, smooth, striate; leaflets 3–5 pairs and a terminal one, 3–7 by 1½–3 in. oblong or elliptic-oblong, acuminate, quite entire, more or less oblique; main nerves numerous, horizontal, straight, joined by a strong intramarginal one; petiolules ⅛–¼ in. long. Flowers 1- or 2-sexual, sessile, numerous, pinkish-green, in sparingly-branched glabrous terminal panicles 10–15 in. long. Calyx-teeth minute, triangular. Petals $\frac{1}{10}$–⅛ in. long, ovate-oblong, acute. Disk 10-crenate. Stamens 10, about half as long as the petals. Drupes ovoid, yellow, about 1½ in. long; stone woody, hard, rough with irregular furrows and cavities, fibrous outside. Seeds usually 1, more rarely 2 or 3. Fl. B. I. v. 2, p. 42; Grah. Cat. p. 42; Dalz. & Gibs. Suppl. p. 19; Trim. Fl. Ceyl. v. 1, p. 327; Talb. Trees, Bomb. p. 63; Engler, in DC. Monogr. Phan. v. 4, p. 248, & in Engl. & Prantl, Pflanzenf. v. 3, part 5, p. 149, fig. 97, B–D; Watt, Dict. Econ. Prod. v. 6, part 3, p. 338.—Flowers: Feb.–Apr. Vern. *A'mbádá.*

Often planted throughout the Presidency. Konkan: *Stocks*!; Girgaum and Mahim woods (Bombay), probably planted, *Graham*. Gujarat: widely planted, *Woodrow*. S. M. Country: Ramghât, *Ritchie*, 1008!; Belgaum (planted), *Ritchie*, 1008! Kanara: Usheli jungles, *Ritchie*, 1008!—Distrib. Throughout tropical Asia.

The ripe fruit is eaten, but is not very palatable, having an astringent terebinthaceous taste. It is known to Anglo-Indians as the *hog-plum*. It is not, however, the *hog-plum* of the W. Indies, which is *Spondias dulcis*, Willd.

2. **Spondias acuminata,** *Roxb. Hort. Beng.* (1814) p. 34. An elegant middle-sized tree with a dense crown; trunk perfectly straight; bark smooth, olive-grey; branches spreading in all directions, from erecto-patent above to divaricate below. Leaflets 5–8 pairs, subopposite, elliptic, caudate-acuminate, entire, obscurely crenulate, polished. Panicles 6–8 in. long. Drupes ovoid, yellow when ripe, the size of a pullet's egg; stone smooth, fibrous outside. Fl. B. I. v. 2, p. 42; Roxb. Fl. Ind. v. 2, p. 451; Grah. Cat. p. 42; Talb. Trees, Bomb. p. 63; Watt, Dict. Econ. Prod. v. 6, part 3, p. 338.

Konkan: hills near Kanheri, *Graham*, l. c. Kanara: *Talbot*.

The existence of the plant in the Bombay Presidency is somewhat doubtful. I have seen one *imperfect* specimen from the hills near Kanheri which does not appear to differ from *S. mangifera*. Engler, in DC. Monogr. Phan. v. 4, p. 249, considers the species a doubtful one. The specimens in Herb. Kew. are very imperfect.

ORDER XLVI. MORINGACEÆ.

Unarmed trees with soft wood. Leaves alternate, 2–3-pinnate, the pinnæ and pinnules imparipinnate, opposite; leaflets opposite, quite entire, obovate, caducous, and, as well as the pinnæ and pinnules, with glands at the base; stipules 0. Flowers large, white, or white streaked with red, hermaphrodite, irregular, in axillary panicles. Calyx cup-shaped, 5-cleft; segments unequal, petaloid, deciduous from above the base, imbricate. Petals 5, unequal, the upper smaller, the lateral ascending, the anterior the larger. Disk lining the calyx-tube. Stamens inserted on the edge of the disk, declinate, 5 perfect opposite the petals alternating with 5 (or 7) which are reduced to antherless filaments; anthers dorsifixed, 1-celled. Ovary stipitate; ovules numerous, in 2 series, on parietal placentas; style slender, tubular; stigma perforated. Capsule elongate, beaked, 3–6-angled, 1-celled, loculicidally 3-valved. Seeds many, in pits of the valves; testa corky, winged or not; albumen 0; embryo straight; cotyledons plano-convex; radicle very short, superior; plumule many-leaved.—DISTRIB. W. Asia and N. Africa.

A Natural Order of doubtful affinity, containing 1 genus (*Moringa*) and 3 species.

1. MORINGA, Lamk.

Character of the Order.

Leaves usually 3-pinnate; leaflets $\frac{1}{2}$–$\frac{3}{4}$ in. long, nerves obscure; flowers white .... 1. *M. pterygosperma.*
Leaves usually 2-pinnate; leaflets $\frac{3}{4}$–$1\frac{1}{2}$ in. long, nerves distinct; flowers yellow, streaked with red .... 2. *M. concanensis.*

1. **Moringa pterygosperma,** *Gærtn. Fruct.* v. 2 (1791) p. 314. A small or middle-sized tree; bark corky; wood soft; root pungent; young parts tomentose. Leaves usually 3-pinnate, sometimes $1\frac{1}{2}$ ft. long; rhachis slender, thickened and articulated at the base; pinnæ and pinnules opposite, deciduous, their rhachides very slender, articulated and with a gland at the articulations; ultimate leaflets $\frac{1}{2}$–$\frac{3}{4}$ by $\frac{1}{4}$–$\frac{3}{8}$ in., the lateral elliptic, the terminal obovate and slightly larger than the lateral ones; nerves obscure; petiolules of the lateral leaflets $\frac{1}{16}$–$\frac{1}{10}$ in., those of the terminal $\frac{1}{8}$–$\frac{1}{4}$ in. long. Flowers white, in large puberulous panicles. Calyx-lobes linear-lanceolate reflexed, puberulous outside. Petals spathulate, veined. Stamens 5 fertile, alternating with 5–7 antherless ones; filaments villous at the base. Ovary oblong, villous; style cylindric. Pods reaching 18 in. long, 9-ribbed. Seeds 3-angled, the angles winged. Fl. B. I. v. 2, p. 45; Grah. Cat. p. 43; Dalz. & Gibs. p. 311; Ait. Pb. & Sind Pl. p. 36; Bedd. Flor. Sylvat. t. 80; Talb. Trees, Bomb. p. 64; Woodr. in Journ. Bomb. Nat. v. 11 (1897) p. 273; Watt, Dict. Econ. Prod. v. 5, p. 276.—Flowers: Jan.–Apr. VERN. *Shevga.*

The *horseradish* tree or *drumstick* tree of Anglo-Indians. It is found wild in the forests of the Western Himalaya and Oudh, but is cultivated throughout India and in many other tropical countries. The scraped root furnishes an excellent substitute for horseradish, while the long immature pods are used in making what is known to Europeans as drumstick-curry. Several parts of the tree are used in native medicine and an oil called *Ben oil* is extracted from the seeds. The oil is highly valued by watchmakers and generally as a lubricant for fine machinery, while perfumers hold it in high esteem from the property it possesses of absorbing and retaining fugitive odors. It seems surprising that a greater trade is not done in this oil considering the number of trees that are planted throughout India.—Consult Watt, Dict. Econ. Prod. l. c.

2. **Moringa concanensis,** *Nimmo, in Grah. Cat. Bo. Pl.* (1839) p. 43. A tree, glabrous except the young parts and the inflorescence. Leaves 2- (very rarely 3-) pinnate, reaching 1½ ft. long; primary pairs 5–6, distant, 4–8 in. long, the primary rhachis thickened at the base and as well as the secondary articulated, and with a gland at the articulations; leaflets 4–6 pairs and an odd one, broadly elliptic or suborbicular, obtuse at both ends, often retuse at the apex, of variable size, sometimes ⅝–1⅓ by ½–1 in., pale beneath, articulated with a slender petiolule $\frac{1}{12}$–⅛ in. long; nerves 4–8 pairs, slender, distinct. Flowers in lax divaricate thinly pubescent panicles reaching 1½ ft. long; pedicels ¼–½ in. long, articulated with the flower; bracts minute, caducous. Calyx thinly tomentose, about ⅓–½ in. long; segments white, oblong, reflexed. Petals yellow, veined with red, oblong or oblong-spathulate, the lower about ⅝ in. long. Stamens 5 fertile and 4–5 staminodes; filaments hairy at the base. Capsules straight, acutely triquetrous, slightly constricted between the seeds, 1–1½ ft. long; valves hard, ½–⅗ in. broad. Seeds white or pale yellow, 3-angled, ⅞–¾ in. long, 3-winged; wings very thin, hyaline. Fl. B. I. v. 2, p. 45; Dalz. & Gibs. p. 311; Talb. Trees, Bomb. p. 64; Hook. Icon. Plant. ser. 4, v. 6 (1899) t. 2596; Watt, Dict. Econ. Prod. v. 5, p. 275.—Flowers: Oct.–Dec. Vern. *Mhua* (in Sind).

A somewhat rare plant. Konkan: *Law*!, *Dalzell*!, *Capt. Geburne*!; jungles near Pen, *Dalzell*! Sind: *Stocks*, 584!, *Dalzell*, 58!; Sind hills, *Dalzell*!—Distrib. India (Rajputana); Beluchistan.

Order XLVII. CONNARACEÆ.

Trees or shrubs erect or scandent. Leaves alternate, exstipulate, 1–3-foliolate or imparipinnate; leaflets quite entire. Flowers usually hermaphrodite, racemose or paniculate, regular or subregular. Calyx 5-lobed or -partite, usually persistent, imbricate or valvate. Petals 5, usually narrow, free or slightly cohering, very rarely valvate. Stamens perigynous or hypogynous, sometimes declinate, 5 or 10, those opposite the petals usually shorter and often imperfect; filaments filiform, often connate at the base. Disk 0 or small, annular or incomplete. Carpels 5, rarely 1–3 or 6–7, globose-ovoid, hirsute, 1-celled; ovules 2, collateral, ascending, orthotropous; styles subulate or filiform; stigmas capitellate, simple or 2-lobed. Fruit usually of 1 (rarely 2–3), sessile or stalked 1- (rarely 2-) seeded follicles. Seed erect, often arillate; testa thick, sometimes arilliform below the middle, the aril various; cotyledons fleshy in the exalbuminous, leafy in the albuminous seeds; radicle superior, rarely ventral.—Distrib. Tropics; genera 14; species about 140.

Calyx enlarged after flowering; follicles sessile .... 1. Rourea.
Calyx not enlarged after flowering; follicles stipitate .... 2. Connarus.

1. ROUREA, Aubl.

Trees or shrubs sometimes scandent. Leaves imparipinnate; leaflets opposite or alternate. Flowers small, numerous, in axillary panicles; pedicels usually slender. Sepals 5, broadly ovate or orbicular, imbricate, enlarged and clasping the base of the ripe follicle. Petals 5, usually linear-oblong. Stamens 10; filaments connate at the base. Ovaries 5, of which 4 are usually imperfect; styles slender. Follicle sessile, curved. Seed erect, arillate, exalbuminous.—DISTRIB. Species about 52, all tropical.

1. **Rourea santaloides,** *Wight & Arn. Prodr.* (1834) p. 144. A climbing or sarmentose shrub; branches slender. Leaflets 2–4 pairs and a terminal one, 1½–3½ by ¾–1½ in., coriaceous, elliptic or lanceolate, caudate-acuminate, shining above, prominently reticulately veined beneath, base rounded, less commonly acute; petioles ⅛–½ in. long. Flowers small, in glabrous racemose panicles, several of which spring from leaf-axils; pedicels short, slender; bracts minute. Sepals $\frac{1}{10}$ in. long, broadly ovate or suborbicular, more or less minutely ciliolate. Petals $\frac{3}{16}$ in. long, spathulate-oblong. Ovaries ovoid, glabrous; styles shorter than the stamens; stigmas 2-lobed. Follicles ¾ in. long, conical-ovoid, tapering to a point, falcately curved, chestnut-brown, finely striate, supported on the enlarged calyx, dehiscing ventrally. Seeds about ⅜ in. long, ovoid-oblong, arillate. Fl. B. I. v. 2, p. 47; Dalz. & Gibs. p. 53; Trim. Fl. Ceyl. v. 2, p. 1; Gilg, in Engl. & Prantl, Pflanzenf. v. 3, part 3, p. 63, fig. 34, F–H; Talb. Trees, Bomb. p. 64; Woodr. in Journ. Bomb. Nat. v. 11 (1897) p. 420; Watt, Dict. Econ. Prod. v. 6, part 1, p. 570.—Flowers: Oct. VERN. *Vardhárá.*

KONKAN: *Stocks*!; Wari Country, *Dalzell & Gibson*; Miradonger near Pen, *Kanitkar*!, *Woodrow*. S. M. COUNTRY: Belgaum districts, *Cooke*!; Ramghát, *Ritchie*, 126!; Castlerock, *Cooke*!, *Woodrow*! KANARA: Yellapur, *Woodrow*; abundant on the hills near Karwar, *Talbot*.—DISTRIB. India (Konkan to Travancore).

Mr. Talbot reports a variety with ciliate sepals and small follicles at Ainshi Ghát (N. Kanara). I have generally found the sepals of the species above described to be, if not ciliate, at all events almost invariably minutely ciliolate. I have examined specimens from the Konkan, Castlerock, Belgaum districts, and Ramghát, with the above result.—I have not seen any specimens of the variety noted by Mr. Talbot.

2. CONNARUS, Linn.

Trees or shrubs often scandent. Leaves imparipinnate; leaflets usually 5, quite entire. Flowers small, in axillary and terminal branched panicles. Sepals 5, not enlarged after flowering, imbricate, embracing the pedicel of the fruit. Petals 5, linear or ligulate, slightly dilated upwards. Stamens 10, those opposite the sepals long, with perfect anthers, those opposite the petals shorter and sometimes antherless. Ovaries 5, densely pubescent, 4 usually imperfect or obsolete, the fifth with a slender style; stigma capitellate. Follicle oblique, stipitate, inflated, glabrous or pubescent within. Seed arillate; testa shining; albumen 0; cotyledons amygdaloid.—DISTRIB. Species about 80, all tropical.

A branched shrub; follicles not striate nor shining, contracted into the stalk .... 1. *C. monocarpus.*
A climbing shrub; follicles chestnut-brown, strongly striate, shortly narrowed into the stalk .... 2. *C. Wightii.*
A small tree; follicles dark brown, striate, cordate at the base... 3. *C. Ritchei.*

1. **Connarus monocarpus,** *Linn. Sp. Pl.* (1753) p. 675. A much-branched shrub. Leaflets 1 or 2 pairs with a terminal one, 3–4 by 1¼–1¾ in., glabrous, shining, elliptic or elliptic-lanceolate, obtusely acumi-

nate, rounded or acute at the base; nerves 3–5 pairs; petiolules of the lateral leaflets $\frac{1}{8}$–$\frac{1}{4}$ in., those of the terminal leaflets longer. Flowers about $\frac{1}{4}$ in. long, crowded, in erect pyramidal densely pubescent terminal panicles; pedicels short, stout, articulated with the flower. Sepals ovate-oblong, subacute, densely pubescent. Petals much longer than the calyx, linear-oblong, more or less pubescent outside. Follicles glabrous within, at first bright scarlet, afterwards dark brown outside, $1\frac{1}{2}$–$2\frac{1}{4}$ in. long, fusiform, slightly falcate, tapering into a narrow stalk surrounded at the base by the persistent (non-accrescent) calyx, smooth, not striate nor shining. Seeds 1 in. long, ovoid, slightly compressed, surrounded at the base by a large pulpy yellow aril; testa black, shining. Fl. B. I. v. 2, p. 50; Dalz. & Gibs. p. 53; Grah. Cat. p. 35; Trim. Fl. Ceyl. v. 2, p. 2; Talb. Trees, Bomb. p. 65; Woodr. in Journ. Bomb. Nat. v. 11 (1897) p. 420; Watt, Dict. Econ. Prod. v. 2, p. 517. *Connarus pinnatus*, Lamk. Encyc. v. 2, p. 95; Grah. Cat. p. 35.—Flowers: Feb. VERN. *Sundar*.

KONKAN: *Stocks*!; S. Konkan, *Nimmo* ex *Graham*; Southern Ghâts, *Dalzell & Gibson*; Goa jungles, *Graham*. KANARA: Ghât forests of N. Kanara, *Talbot*.—DISTRIB. India (from the Konkan to Travancore); Ceylon.

2. **Connarus Wightii,** *Hook. f. in Fl. B. I.* v. 2 (1876) p. 51. An extensive climber. Leaflets 3–$3\frac{1}{2}$ by $1\frac{1}{4}$–$1\frac{3}{4}$ in., elliptic-ovate, obtusely pointed, coriaceous, hardly shining, reticulately veined, glabrous; nerves 5–6 pairs, arched, slender. Follicles $1\frac{1}{2}$ by $\frac{3}{4}$ in., compressed, bright red, afterwards chestnut-brown, strongly striate on the faces, narrowly keeled at the sutures, slightly pointed at the apex, base shortly narrowed into the stalk, quite glabrous within. Seeds obovoid-oblong, compressed, arillate at the base; testa black, shining. Talb. Trees, Bomb. p. 65; Woodr. in Journ. Bomb. Nat. v. 11 (1897) p. 420.—Flowers: Feb.

KONKAN: Amboli Ghât, *Kanitkar*! S. M. COUNTRY: Castlerock, *Woodrow*!, *Cooke*! KANARA: Potelli (N. Kanara), *Talbot*, 2733!; Karwar, *Talbot*, 89!—DISTRIB. India (Western Peninsula).

3. **Connarus Ritchei,** *Hook. f. in Fl. B. I.* v. 2 (1876) p. 51. A small tree (?). Leaflets 3–4 by $1\frac{1}{4}$–$1\frac{3}{4}$ in., elliptic-lanceolate, obtusely acuminate, finely reticulated, quite glabrous. Flowers $\frac{1}{8}$ in. long, in rusty-pubescent panicles. Sepals ovate-oblong. Petals about twice as long as the sepals. Follicles $\frac{3}{4}$ by $\frac{1}{2}$ in., turgidly oblong, rounded at the top, cordate at the base, as broad from suture to suture as across, dark brown, striate. Talb. Trees, Bomb. p. 65.—Flowers: Apr.

A rare plant. S. M. COUNTRY: Ramghât, *Ritchie*, 931! KANARA: *Law*!, *Stocks*!; Supa Ghâts of N. Kanara, *Talbot*.—DISTRIB. India (W. Peninsula).

ORDER XLVIII. LEGUMINOSÆ.

Herbs, shrubs or trees. Leaves alternate (very rarely opposite), usually stipulate, compound (rarely simple); leaflets sometimes stipellate. Flowers usually irregular and hermaphrodite. Sepals 5, combined or free, often unequal, sometimes combined into 2 lips. Petals 5 (rarely fewer), usually irregular and imbricate in SUBORDERS 1 and 2, regular and valvate in 3. Stamens normally 10 (rarely fewer) or indefinite, perigynous or subhypogynous; filaments free or variously combined; anthers 2-celled. Ovary free, with 1 or more ovules on the ventral suture; style simple, cylindric, often declinate. Fruit a legume more rarely follicular or indehiscent or breaking up into 1-seeded joints, very rarely fleshy and drupe-like. Seed usually exalbuminous; cotyledons foliaceous or amygdaloid with a straight or inflexed accumbent radicle.—DISTRIB. The second largest Natural Order of flowering plants. Of the three Suborders into which it has been subdivided, the first is distributed throughout the globe, the second and third confined to tropical and warm regions; genera about 400; species 6000 or 7000.

SUBORDER I. PAPILIONACEÆ.

Herbs, shrubs or trees. Leaves alternate, digitate or pinnate, rarely 1-foliolate or simple, often terminating in tendrils. Flowers irregular (rarely subregular), hermaphrodite. Calyx gamosepalous, 5-toothed or -lobed or the upper lobes more or less connate, or bilabiate, the 2 upper lobes opposed to the 3 lower, rarely closed in bud and spathaceous. Corolla papilionaceous; petals 5, free or adnate to the staminal tube, the posterior (standard) outside in bud, the 2 lateral (wings) intermediate, the 2 lower inside and usually cohering by their lower margins (keel). Stamens 10, diadelphous, monadelphous or free. Ovary free. Embryo with an inflexed radicle. Cotyledons accumbent.

TRIBE I. **GENISTEÆ.** Herbs or shrubs. Leaves simple or digitately 3–∞-foliolate. Stamens monadelphous. Pod dehiscent, not jointed.

Anthers uniform; keel-petals scarcely cohering .... 1. ROTHIA.
Anthers dimorphous; keel-petals firmly cohering.
  Keel obtuse.
    Calyx 2-lipped .... 2. ARGYROLOBIUM.
    Calyx subequally 5-toothed .... 3. LOTONONIS.
  Keel beaked.
    Pod flattened .... 4. HEYLANDIA.
    Pod turgid .... 5. CROTALARIA.

TRIBE II. **TRIFOLIÆ.** Herbs. Leaves pinnately 3-foliolate, the veins of the leaflets usually excurrent into teeth; stipules usually adnate to the petiole. Stamens diadelphous; filaments usually dilated at the apex. Pod usually dehiscent, not jointed.

Pod elongate, straight or recurved .... 6. TRIGONELLA.
Pod short, globose or ovoid .... 7. MELILOTUS.
Pod spirally falcate, circinate or cochleate .... 8. MEDICAGO.

TRIBE III. **LOTEÆ.** Herbs. Leaves pinnately 5-foliolate; leaflets entire. Stamens diadelphous; filaments all or the alternate ones dilated at the apex. Pod dehiscent, not jointed.

Lowest pair of leaflets stipule-like.................................. 9. LOTUS.

TRIBE IV. **GALEGEÆ.** Herbs or shrubs. Leaves pinnate, usually many- (rarely 3–1-) foliolate; petiole not cirrhiferous. Stamens usually diadelphous; filaments filiform at the apex. Pod not jointed, usually dehiscent, but if indehiscent, usually small, 1–2-seeded, or membranous-inflated.

Anthers apiculate; hairs medifixed.
 Stamens monadelphous .... 10. CYAMOPSIS.
 Stamens diadelphous .... 11. INDIGOFERA.
Anthers muticous; hairs basifixed.
 Pod 1-seeded, indehiscent.
  Herbaceous plant (the Bombay species).................. 12. PSORALEA.
 Pod few- or many-seeded, tardily dehiscent.
  Filaments not dilated.
   A climbing shrub (the Bombay species) .... 13. MILLETTIA.
  Filaments dilated; pod 6–8-seeded.
   An erect shrub .. .. 14. MUNDULEA.
 Pod many-seeded, soon dehiscing.
  Flowers generally in leaf-opposed racemes; pods flattened, continuous or scarcely septate .... 15. TEPHROSIA.
  Flowers in axillary racemes.
   Pod very long, distinctly septate .... 16. SESBANIA.
   Pod short, not transversely septate, often longitudinally 2-celled .... 17. ASTRAGALUS.

TRIBE V. **HEDYSAREÆ.** Herbs or shrubs sometimes twining or scandent. Leaves impari- or less commonly abruptly-pinnate (rarely simple); petiole not cirrhiferous. Stamens diadelphous or monadelphous. Pod jointed if more than 1-seeded.

Leaflets exstipellate.
 Stamens monadelphous; anthers uniform.
  Leaflets 1–3 .... 18. TAVERNIERA.
  Leaflets 4 .... 19. GEISSASPIS.
 Stamens diadelphous (9 and 1); anthers uniform.
  Spiny shrub with simple leaves .... 20. ALHAGI.
 Stamens monadelphous; anthers dimorphous.
  Joints of pod 2-6, echinate; calyx-tube short......... 21. ZORNIA.
  Joints of pod 1–2, rugose; calyx-tube long .... 22. STYLOSANTHES.
 Stamens in 2 bundles of 5 each; anthers uniform.
  Pod twisted, enclosed in the calyx........................ 23. SMITHIA.
  Pod straight, exserted from the calyx .... 24. ÆSCHYNOMENE.
Leaflets stipellate.
 Stamens diadelphous (9 and 1); anthers uniform.
  Seed solitary; pod boat-shaped .... 25. ELEIOTIS.
  Seeds many; pod not distinctly jointed.
   Pod turgid .... 26. PYCNOSPORA.
   Pod flat.. 27. PSEUDARTHRIA.
  Seeds 2 or more; pod distinctly jointed.
   Joints of pod folded on one another .... 28. URARIA.
   Joints of pod not folded on one another.
    Joints of pod turgid .... 29. ALYSICARPUS.
    Joints of pod flattened.
     A tree; racemes fascicled from the old wood .... 30. OUGEINIA.
     Herbs or shrubs; racemes simple or panicled from the year's shoots ...... 31. DESMODIUM.

TRIBE VI. **VICIÆ.** Herbs (except *Abrus*) low or climbing. Leaves usually abruptly-pinnate; petiole ending in a tendril or bristle (very rarely in an odd leaflet); stipules usually foliaceous. Leaflets exstipellate. Stamens diadelphous (the tenth suppressed in *Abrus*); anthers uniform. Pod dehiscent, not jointed.

Shrubs with the tenth stamen absent .... 32. ABRUS.
Herbs with diadelphous stamens (9 and 1) .... 33. LATHYRUS.

TRIBE VII. **PHASEOLEÆ.** Climbing or prostrate herbs, rarely erect or shrubby, very rarely trees. Leaves pinnately 3-foliolate (rarely

1- or 5-7-foliolate). Bracts 2, opposite, persistent, stipular or caducous. Stamens monadelphous or diadelphous. Pod dehiscent, not jointed.

Leaves not gland-dotted; leaflets stipellate.
 Style beardless.
  Nodes of raceme not tumid; petals about equal in length.
   Stamens diadelphous; stipules and bracts conspicuous, persistent.
    Style filiform; calyx-teeth distinct .... 34. Shuteria.
    Style flattened upwards; calyx truncate ... 35. Dumasia.
   Stamens monadelphous; stipules and bracts minute, caducous.
    Anthers uniform, all fertile .... 36. Glycine.
    Alternate anthers sterile........................ 37. Teramnus.
  Nodes of raceme more or less tumid.
   Petals very unequal.
    Climbing shrubs .... 38. Mucuna.
    Armed trees .... 39. Erythrina.
   Petals equal.
    Stamens diadelphous.
     Herbs.
      Two upper calyx-teeth not fused into one............................ 40. Grona.
      Two upper calyx-teeth fused into one.................................. 41. Galactia.
     Shrubs or trees.
      Flowers small, panicled .... 42. Spatholobus.
      Flowers large, racemose .... 43. Butea.
    Stamens monadelphous.
     Upper lip of calyx projecting........... 44. Canavalia.
     Upper lip of calyx not projecting ...... 45. Pueraria.
 Style bearded below the stigma.
  Stamens diadelphous.
   Stigma oblique.
    Keel spiral .... 46. Phaseolus.
    Keel not spiral .... 47. Vigna.
   Stigma terminal.
    Petals very unequal in length .... 48. Clitoria.
    Petals equal in length .... 49. Dolichos.
Leaves gland-dotted beneath; stipellæ often abortive; nodes of raceme not tumid.
 Style not bearded.
  Ovules 3 or more.
   Pod with deep lines between the seeds; seeds with a large strophiole .... 50. Atylosia.
   Pod with faint lines between the seeds; seeds with a small strophiole .... 51. Dunbaria.
  Ovules 1–2.
   Calyx-teeth accrescent .... 52. Cylista.
   Calyx-teeth not accrescent.
    Leaves pinnate; pod compressed .... 53. Rhynchosia.
    Leaves digitate; pod turgid .... 54. Flemingia.

Tribe VIII. **DALBERGIÆ.** Trees or shrubs. Leaves imparipinnate; leaflets usually exstipellate. Stamens monadelphous or diadelphous; anthers usually uniform. Pod longer than the calyx, continuous, indehiscent.

Leaflets distinctly alternate.
 Flowers small, whitish or reddish .... 55. Dalbergia.
 Flowers large, yellow .... 56. Pterocarpus.
Leaflets opposite.
 Pod flat, almost woody, not winged .... 57. Pongamia.
 Pod flat, thin, winged down one or both sides.............. 58. Derris.

TRIBE IX. **SOPHOREÆ.** Trees or shrubs (rarely herbs). Leaves imparipinnate. Stamens free or very slightly connate at the base. Pod not jointed, indehiscent or 2-valved.

Pod moniliform .... 59. SOPHORA.

1. ROTHIA, Pers.

Annual diffuse herbs. Leaves digitately 3-foliolate. Flowers numerous, minute, axillary, solitary or in very short racemes. Calyx-tube turbinate; calyx-lobes as long as the tube, the two upper broader and arched. Corolla scarcely exserted; petals nearly equal, narrow, clawed, those of the keel very slightly cohering. Stamens monadelphous, the staminal-tube split at the top; anthers uniform, minute. Ovary sessile, linear: ovules numerous; style short, straight, filiform; stigma capitate. Pod linear, slender, nearly straight, compressed, many-seeded, continuous within, dehiscing by the upper suture.—DISTRIB. Species 2, of which one is a native of Tropical Asia, the other of India and N. Australia.

1. **Rothia trifoliata,** *Pers. Syn. Pl.* v. 2 (1807) p. 302 & p. 659. A much-branched hairy prostrate herb growing in sandy soil; stem slightly woody at the base. Leaflets somewhat fleshy, $\frac{3}{8}$-$\frac{7}{8}$ in. long, oblong-lanceolate or oblanceolate, obtuse or acute, mucronate, clothed with silky hairs; petioles shorter than the leaves; stipules elliptic-oblong, acute, sometimes slightly falcate, hairy, $\frac{3}{16}$ in. long; petiolules very short. Flowers on very short pedicels, solitary or 2–4 together, in very short axillary racemes. Calyx silky-hairy, $\frac{1}{6}$-$\frac{1}{4}$ in. long; segments lanceolate, very acute. Corolla yellow, fugacious; standard clawed, pink. Pods $1\frac{1}{2}$-2 in. long, silky, narrow-linear, flattened, straight or nearly so, pointed by the style. Seeds numerous, 20 or more. Fl. B. I. v. 2, p. 63; Trim. Fl. Ceyl. v. 2, p. 7; Woodr. in Journ. Bomb. Nat. v. 11 (1897) p. 420; Watt, Dict. Econ. Prod. v. 6, part 1, p. 569.—Flowers: Aug.-Oct.

DECCAN: Bijapur, *Woodrow*!; Burhanpur (S. M. Railway), *Woodrow*!; Hotgi, *Bhiva*! S. M. COUNTRY: Badami, *Cooke*!, *Woodrow*; Belgaum, *Ritchie*, 1727!—DISTRIB. India and Ceylon in sandy soil, N. Australia.

2. ARGYROLOBIUM, Eckl. & Zeyh.

Herbs or shrubs. Leaves digitately 3-foliolate; stipules free. Flowers in terminal or leaf-opposed racemes or umbels. Calyx 2-lipped, deeply divided; teeth 5, distinct (in the Indian species), 2 teeth forming the upper, and 3 the lower lip. Corolla scarcely exserted; standard suborbicular; wings oblong. Keel-petals broad, joined down the back to the obtuse incurved tip. Stamens monadelphous; anthers dimorphous. Ovary linear, sessile; ovules numerous; style curved gradually upwards; stigma terminal, often oblique. Pod linear, compressed, silky or villous, continuous within or septate between the seeds, subtorulose.—DISTRIB. Species 40–50, chiefly South-African.

1. **Argyrolobium roseum,** *Jaub. & Spach. Illustr.* v. 1 (1842) p. 116. A small diffuse annual; stems many from the root, reaching 6 in. long, very slender, terete, clothed with short appressed silky hairs.

Leaves 3-foliolate; petioles $\frac{3}{16}$–$\frac{3}{8}$ in. long, silky; stipules minute, triangular, acute, persistent. Leaflets $\frac{1}{4}$–$\frac{3}{8}$ by $\frac{3}{16}$–$\frac{1}{4}$ in., broadly obovate-cuneate, occasionally retuse (the lateral leaflets more or less oblique), silky on both sides with appressed hairs; petiolules very short. Peduncles reaching 1–2 in. long, very slender, 1–4-flowered. Calyx pubescent outside; upper lip shorter than the lower; teeth all triangular, acute. Corolla rose-colored or purplish; standard longer than the upper lip of the calyx. Pods $\frac{1}{2}$–$\frac{3}{4}$ in. long by $\frac{1}{8}$ in. broad, silky-pubescent. Seeds 10–15. Fl. B. I. v. 2, p. 64; Ait. Pb. & Sind Pl. p. 38. *A. Kotschyi*, Boiss. Diag. ser. 1, fasc. 6, p. 32.

A very rare plant. SIND: *Stocks*!; Boogta hills, *Vicary* ex *Aitchison* (l. c.).—DISTRIB. India (N.W. Provinces); Beluchistan, Persia.

3. LOTONONIS, DC.

Herbs, rarely shrubs. Leaves digitately 3-foliolate; stipules connate or free. Flowers in terminal or leaf-opposed racemes or umbels. Calyx-tube narrow, turbinate, the 4 upper teeth more or less connate, the lowest deeper and narrower than the others. Corolla slightly exserted; standard oblong; wings shorter and narrower; keel longer, suddenly incurved at the tip, its petals firmly united along the back. Stamens united in a tube slit along the top; anthers dimorphous. Ovary sessile or scarcely stalked; ovules many; style abruptly incurved at the base; stigma terminal, often oblique. Pod linear, usually compressed, but in the species below turgid.—DISTRIB. Chiefly inhabitants of S. Africa; species about 60.

1. **Lotononis Leobordea,** *Benth. in Lond. Journ. Bot.* v. 2 (1843) p. 607. A diffuse much-branched herb; stems less than 6 in. long, clothed as is the rest of the plant with fulvous silky hairs. Leaves somewhat fleshy; petioles as long as the leaves. Leaflets subsessile, $\frac{1}{8}$–$\frac{3}{8}$ in. long, obovate or oblanceolate, sometimes mucronate; stipules ovate-lanceolate, $\frac{1}{8}$ in. long, hairy. Flowers in subsessile clusters of 1–5, in the axils of most of the leaves. Calyx $\frac{1}{8}$–$\frac{1}{4}$ in. long. Corolla pale yellow or red, scarcely exserted. Pods linear-oblong, turgid, scarcely longer than the calyx, 4–8-seeded. Fl. B. I. v. 2, p. 64; Aitch. Pb. & Sind Pl. p. 36; Oliver, Fl. Trop. Afr. v. 2, p. 5; Woodr. in Journ. Bomb. Nat. v. 11 (1897) p. 420.

A very rare plant. SIND: cultivated land between the plains and the Rohill pass, *Stocks*, 698!; Sehwan, *Woodrow*!—DISTRIB. India (Panjab), Arabia, Perim, Syria, Abyssinia, Egypt, Beluchistan.

4. HEYLANDIA, DC.

A prostrate herb. Leaves simple, entire. Flowers small, axillary, solitary. Calyx-tube turbinate, the 2 upper lobes slightly connate, the lower much deeper cleft. Corolla much exserted; standard large, suborbicular; wings obovate-oblong, much smaller; keel-petals joined along the back, narrowed into an incurved beak. Stamens all united in a tube slit above; anthers dimorphous. Ovary sessile; ovules 2; style abruptly inflexed above the ovary; stigma terminal. Pod small, oblong, flat, 1–2-seeded.—DISTRIB. Endemic in India and Ceylon; species 1.

1. **Heylandia latebrosa,** *DC. Mém. Leg.* (1825) p. 201. A prostrate much-branched herb; branches sometimes reaching 20 in. long, slender, wiry, clothed with long hairs. Leaves numerous, simple, $\frac{1}{4}$–$\frac{1}{2}$ by $\frac{1}{8}$–$\frac{1}{4}$ in., subsessile, ovate, subacute, hairy on both surfaces, obliquely cordate at the base. Flowers in the axils of most of the leaves, solitary, subsessile. Calyx-segments acute. Corolla yellow, much exserted, $\frac{1}{8}$–$\frac{1}{4}$ in. long. Pods silky, $\frac{1}{8}$–$\frac{1}{6}$ in. long, surrounded at the base by the persistent calyx and tipped by the style, smooth or slightly hairy, flattened, pale brown. Fl. B. I. v. 2, p. 65; Grah. Cat. p. 44; Dalz. & Gibs. p. 54; Aitch. Pb. & Sind Pl. p. 36; Trim. Fl. Ceyl. v. 2, p. 8; Woodr. in Journ. Bomb. Nat. v. 11 (1897) p. 420.—Flowers: Feb.-June. VERN. *Godhadi.*

Very common, especially throughout the Deccan; abundant at Poona.—DISTRIB. Throughout Tropical India and Ceylon.

5. CROTALARIA, Linn.

Herbs or shrubs. Leaves simple or 3-foliolate, rarely imparipinnate, with or without stipules. Flowers in terminal or leaf-opposed racemes, usually yellow, often showy. Calyx-tube short; teeth linear or lanceolate, subequal or shortly connate into 2 lips. Corolla equalling or exceeding the calyx; standard orbicular (rarely ovate), shortly clawed; wings obovate or oblong, shorter than the standard; keel broad, equalling the wings, its petals joined down the back, much incurved, distinctly beaked. Stamens monadelphous; anthers dimorphous. Ovary sessile (rarely stalked), usually many- (rarely 2-) ovulate; style long, abruptly incurved at the base, more or less bearded upwards; stigma minute, oblique. Pod sessile or stalked, straight, linear-oblong, turgid or inflated, continuous within, usually many-seeded.—DISTRIB. Tropical and subtropical regions of the globe; species about 300.

- Leaves simple.
  - A rigid copiously stiffly-branched undershrub with small exstipulate deciduous leaves; pod slightly longer than the calyx, pubescent .... 1. *C. Burhia.*
  - Diffuse herbs; stems prostrate or ascending; racemes all lateral, few-flowered.
    - Stipules 0.
      - Corolla exserted .... 2. *C. filipes.*
      - Corolla not exserted.
        - Bracts minute, subulate .... 3. *C. prostrata.*
        - Bracts leafy, lanceolate .... 4. *C. vestita.*
    - Stipules present.
      - Leaves linear-oblong; wings of corolla yellow .... 5. *C. Stocksii.*
      - Leaves rotund-ovate; wings of corolla purple .... 6. *C. bifaria.*
  - Diffuse annuals or low shrubs with slender branches; racemes all terminal or a few also lateral.
    - Pod distinctly exserted; racemes lax.
      - Stipules present.
        - Branches terete; pods glabrous .... 7. *C. mysorensis.*
        - Branches triquetrous; pods hairy .... 8. *C. triquetra.*
      - Stipules 0.
        - Plant exceeding 1 ft. in height .... 9. *C. albida.*
        - Plant less than 6 in. high .... 10. *C. pusilla.*
    - Pod included or scarcely exserted.
      - Racemes capitate.
        - Stipules 0.
          - Upper teeth of calyx connate .... 11. *C. nana.*
          - Upper teeth of calyx long, lanceolate.
            - Leaves much longer than broad, silky beneath . 12. *C. chinensis.*

Leaves nearly as broad as long, shaggy beneath. 13. *C. priestleyoides.*
Stipules present .... 14. *C. dubia.*
Racemes lax.
Stipules 0; upper teeth of calyx connate .... 15. *C. linifolia.*
Stipules minute, subulate; upper teeth of calyx oblanceolate .... 16. *C. calycina.*
Erect herbs or shrubs; racemes usually terminal; pod glabrous, much longer than the calyx.
Stipules 0 .... 17. *C. lutescens.*
Stipules and bracts subulate .... 18. *C. retusa.*
Stipules and bracts foliaceous .... 19. *C. sericea.*
Erect shrubs; leaves usually large, not deciduous; flowers in terminal or terminal and lateral racemes; pod silky or velvety.
Branches angled.
Stipules foliaceous; corolla blue and white .... 20. *C. verrucosa.*
Stipules 0 or minute; corolla yellow .... 21. *C. leptostachya.*
Branches terete.
Stipules ½-lunate; wings of corolla often pale blue in the upper part .... 22. *C. Heyneana.*
Stipules 0 or minute; wings of corolla yellow .... 23. *C. juncea.*
Erect shrubs; pods silky or velvety; flowers panicled.
Pod 10–12-seeded .... 24. *C. madurensis.*
Pod 2 seeded .... 25. *C. fulva.*
Pod 1-seeded .... 26. *C. ramosissima.*
Leaves trifoliolate.
Perennial herbs or undershrubs.
Pod 2-seeded.
Calyx-teeth exceeding the tube; pod subglobose .... 27. *C. medicaginea.*
Calyx-teeth equalling the tube; pod subquadrangular... 28. *C. Notonii.*
Pod many-seeded.
Stipules present.
Bracts large, ovate; pod 8–10-seeded..................... 29. *C. orixensis.*
Bracts minute, setaceous; pod 20–30-seeded............ 30. *C. striata.*
Stipules 0. Pod with a stalk ¾–1 in. long.................. 31. *C. laburnifolia.*
Leaves usually 5- but varying from 3- to 7-foliolate; pod glabrous, 30–40-seeded.
An erect annual; stipules linear-lanceolate; bracts foliaceous .... 32. *C. quinquefolia.*

1. **Crotalaria Burhia,** *Ham. in Wall. Cat.* (1828) 5386. A low undershrub; branches numerous, stiff, close, entangled, striate, hoary with appressed pubescence. Leaves few, inconspicuous, deciduous, subsessile, ¼–1 by ⅛–⅜ in., oblong, usually rounded, sometimes mucronate at the apex, pale-green, silky; stipules 0. Flowers 6–12, in elongate terminal racemes; pedicels very short, bibracteolate. Calyx ⅛ in. long, hairy; segments lanceolate, acute. Corolla slightly exserted, yellow; standard veined. Style long, slightly bearded at the top. Pods scarcely longer than the calyx, hairy. Seeds 3–4. Fl. B. I. v. 2, p. 66; Benth. in Hook. Lond. Journ. v. 2 (1843) p. 474; Dalz. & Gibs. p. 54; Aitch. Pb. & Sind Pl. p. 37; Talb. Trees, Bomb. p. 67; Woodr. in Journ. Bomb. Nat. v. 11 (1897) p. 420; Watt, Dict. Econ. Prod. v. 2, p. 595.—Flowers: Dec.–Feb. VERN. *Ghágri.*

A member of the desert Flora. GUJARAT: Ahmedabad, *Kanitkar*!; Cambay, *Dalzell & Gibson.* SIND: *Cooke*!, *Stocks*, 379!; Mirpur-Khas, *Woodrow*; Jemadar ka Landa, near Karachi, *Stocks*!; Shikarpur, *Cooke*!—DISTRIB. N.W. India; Afghanistan, Beluchistan.

2. **Crotalaria filipes,** *Benth. in Hook. Lond. Journ.* v. 2 (1843) p. 475. A prostrate herb; stems 6–15 in. long, many from a woody

root, very slender, terete, clo'hed with spreading deciduous silky hairs. Leaves $\frac{1}{4}$–$\frac{3}{8}$ by $\frac{1}{8}$–$\frac{5}{16}$ in., ovate-oblong, obtuse or acute, mucronulate, prominently veined, subsessile, clothed with scattered silky hairs, obliquely cordate at the base; stipules 0. Flowers distant, in leaf-opposed or extra-axillary 1–3-flowered racemes, which are much longer than the leaves; peduncles and pedicels very slender, the latter $\frac{1}{8}$–$\frac{1}{4}$ in. long; bracts $\frac{1}{12}$ in. long, linear-lanceolate, hairy, persistent. Calyx $\frac{1}{8}$ in. long, hairy; teeth long, lanceolate. Corolla yellow, exserted; standard erect, orbicular, veined, $\frac{1}{5}$ in. broad. Pods $\frac{1}{4}$ in. long, shortly stalked, glabrous. Seeds 8–10. Fl. B. I. v. 2, p. 68; Dalz. & Gibs. p. 56; Woodr. in Journ. Bomb. Nat. v. 11 (1897) p. 420.—Flowers: Oct.–Dec.

KONKAN: common about Bombay and Salsette, *Dalzell & Gibson*; Bombay, *Ritchie*, 153!, *Law*!, *Capt. Geburne*!; Andheri, *Cooke*! DECCAN: between Nasik and Igatpuri, *Edgeworth*!; Ghát between Wai and Wathár, *Cooke*!; Phunda Ghát, *Ritchie*, 153!; Mahableshwar, *Cooke*!; Dongergaon, near Ahmednagar, *Cooke*! KANARA: *Mrs. Ward*!; near Honore, *Hohenhacker*, 731!—DISTRIB. India (W. side of the W. Peninsula).

VAR. *trichophora*. Somewhat larger and coarser, clothed with silky yellow-brown hairs. Leaves $\frac{1}{2}$–1 in. long. Peduncles 1–2-flowered. Corolla scarcely exserted. *Benth. ex Baker in Fl. B. I.* v. 2, p. 67 (sp.).

Except the hairiness and somewhat larger leaves, I find nothing to separate this from *C. filipes*, of which I think it should be considered a variety.

KONKAN: *Stocks*!

3. **Crotalaria prostrata,** *Roxb. Hort. Beng.* (1814) p. 54. Annual, 6–15 in. high; branches many, ascending, slender, clothed with silky yellowish hairs. Leaves subsessile, $\frac{3}{4}$–1$\frac{1}{2}$ by $\frac{3}{8}$–$\frac{3}{4}$ in., oblong or oblong-obovate, rounded at the apex, clothed on both surfaces with silky yellowish or yellowish-brown hairs, paler beneath, usually oblique or subcordate at the base; stipules 0. Flowers small, pedicelled, in 2–4-flowered racemes; peduncles slender, hairy, longer than the leaves; bracts and bracteoles minute, subulate. Calyx $\frac{1}{8}$–$\frac{1}{6}$ in. long, densely hairy; segments linear. Corolla yellow, not exserted; standard broadly oblong, $\frac{1}{12}$ in. in breadth. Pods $\frac{1}{2}$–$\frac{5}{8}$ in. long, inflated, glabrous. Seeds 12–15, highly polished. Fl. B. I. v. 2, p. 67; Trim. Fl. Ceyl. v. 2, p. 9; Woodr. in Journ. Bomb. Nat. v. 11 (1897) p. 420; Watt, Dict. Econ. Prod. v. 2, p. 613.—Flowers: Oct.–Nov.

Stocks, without locality! S. M. COUNTRY: Halyal, near Dharwar, *Ritchie*, 1023! KANARA: Kála naddi, *Ritchie*, 1023!; Yellapur, *Talbot*.—DISTRIB. Drier parts of India; Ceylon, Java.

4. **Crotalaria vestita,** *Baker, in Hook. f. Fl. B. I.* v. 2 (1876) p. 67. An erect usually much-branched herb 9–24 in. high; stems and branches slender, terete, clothed with long silky hairs. Leaves firm, subsessile, $\frac{3}{4}$–1$\frac{1}{2}$ by $\frac{1}{4}$–$\frac{5}{8}$ in., oblong or oblong-obovate, obtuse or subacute, densely clothed with white or yellowish hairs, base usually rounded, equal-sided; stipules 0. Flowers in densely silky 4–5-flowered racemes; peduncles much longer than the leaves; bracts $\frac{1}{4}$–$\frac{3}{4}$ in. long, persistent, leafy, lanceolate, silky; pedicels shorter than the calyx; bracteoles 2 beneath the calyx, $\frac{1}{4}$ in. long, linear, very hairy. Calyx shaggy, $\frac{1}{4}$–$\frac{7}{16}$ in. long; the 2 upper segments lanceolate, acute; the 3 lower linear.

Corolla not exserted; standard suborbicular-oblong, veined; wings linear-oblong, rounded at the tip. Pods oblong, turgid, glabrous, ½–¾ in. long, subsessile. Seeds 15–20. Woodr. in Journ. Bomb. Nat. v. 11 (1897) p. 420.

Stocks and *Dalzell*, without localities! DECCAN: Khandala, *Bhiva*!; Mahableshwar, *Cooke*!—DISTRIB. Apparently endemic in Bombay.

5. **Crotalaria Stocksii,** *Benth. ex Baker, in Hook. f. Fl. B. I.* v. 2 (1876) p. 67. A much-branched annual 1–1½ ft. high; stems and branches pale, slender, terete, glabrous. Leaves ¾–1¼ by $\frac{3}{16}$–¼ in., subsessile, linear-oblong, tip rounded, tomentose on both surfaces, equally narrowed at both sides at the base; stipules minute, subulate, deciduous. Flowers very small, yellow; pedicels filiform, 2 or 3 times as long as the leaves, solitary, leaf-opposed, with 2 subulate bracts about $\frac{1}{16}$ in. long below the flower and with 2 small subulate bracteoles beneath the calyx. Calyx $\frac{1}{12}$ in. long, pubescent outside; segments very acute. Corolla slightly exserted; standard obovate-oblong. Pods sessile, ¼–⅜ in. long, linear-oblong, glabrous, finally black. Seeds 12–16, reniform, compressed. Woodr. in Journ. Bomb. Nat. v. 11 (1897) p. 420.

Rare. KONKAN: *Stocks*!; Jambalpada, Colaba district, *Kanitkar*!—DISTRIB. Tenasserim and the Andamans.

6. **Crotalaria bifaria,** *Linn. f. Suppl.* (1781) p. 322. A much-branched herb; branches terete, more or less pubescent. Leaves ⅝–1¼ by ½–1 in., rotund-ovate or a few of the upper oblong, rounded at the apex, mucronulate, more or less hairy on both surfaces, oblique or rounded at the base; petioles $\frac{1}{16}$ in. long; stipules ⅛ in. long, lanceolate, reflexed. Racemes 1–2-flowered; peduncles stout, usually exceeding the leaves; bracts 2, about ¼ in. below the calyx, foliaceous, persistent, lanceolate or ovate-lanceolate, ¼–⅜ in. long. Calyx reaching ¾ in. long, hairy outside; segments linear-lanceolate, very acute. Corolla slightly exserted: standard orbicular, reaching ¾ in. long, yellow, veined with bluish-purple; wings ½–⅝ in. long, oblong, rounded at the tip, bluish-purple. Keel with a long beak, veined with purple. Pods shortly stalked, much inflated, ¾–1¼ in. long, usually mottled with purple, at first pubescent, becoming nearly glabrous before splitting. Seeds 10–12. Fl. B. I. v. 2, p. 69; Grah. Cat. p. 45; Dalz. & Gibs. p. 55; Wight, Icon. t. 30; Woodr. in Journ. Bomb. Nat. v. 11 (1897) p. 420.—Flowers: Aug.–Oct.

S. M. COUNTRY: Ramghát, *Law* ex *Graham, Dalzell & Gibson*; Badami, *Cooke*!, *Woodrow*!—DISTRIB. India (W. Peninsula).

The measurements have been taken from a well-grown specimen from Badami (S. M. Country), where the plant is tolerably abundant.—The flowers are handsome, the purple wings contrasting well with the yellow standard.

7. **Crotalaria mysorensis,** *Roth, Nov. Pl. Sp.* (1821) p. 338. An erect herb 1–2 ft. high, with numerous ascending branches clothed with long spreading hairs. Leaves subsessile, 1–2½ by $\frac{3}{16}$–½ in., linear-oblong, rounded at both ends, apiculate, clothed (especially beneath) with long spreading silky hairs; stipules linear-lanceolate, ¼–⅜ in. long, persistent. Flowers yellow, in lax erect terminal 6–9-flowered racemes; bracts foliaceous, lanceolate, hairy; bracteoles beneath the calyx ¼ in. long, lanceolate, hairy. Calyx ½–⅝ in. long, the upper segments lanceolate,

the lower linear, all clothed with long spreading hairs. Corolla not exserted; standard ovate, acute; wings narrow-oblong, rounded at the tip. Pods ¾–1¼ in. long, scarcely stalked, truncate at the apex, much inflated, glabrous when ripe, pale brown. Seeds 20–30. Fl. B. I. v. 2, p. 70; Trim. Fl. Ceyl. v. 2, p. 12; Woodr. in Journ. Bomb. Nat. v. 11 (1897) p. 420.—Flowers: Oct.

KONKAN: *Stocks!* DECCAN: Poona, *Woodrow!*; Nasik hills, *Dalzell!*; Wada Ghát below Mahableshwar, *Cooke!*; Dongergaon near Ahmednagar, *Cooke!* GUJARAT: Dakor, *Kanitkar!*—DISTRIB. Throughout India; Ceylon.

8. **Crotalaria triquetra,** *Dalz. in Hook. Kew Journ. Bot.* v. 2 (1850) p. 34. Suffruticose, 12–20 in. high, branched from the base; branches acutely triquetrous, glabrous or with a few scattered spreading hairs. Leaves subsessile, 1–1¾ by ½–⅞ in., elliptic-oblong, glabrous above, glabrous or with a few scattered hairs beneath, rounded or subcordate at the base; stipules small, ovate, acute, reflexed. Flowers pale yellow, in long very lax 2–3-flowered terminal and lateral racemes 6 or 7 times as long as the leaves; pedicels about as long as the calyx; bracts ovate, acute; bracteoles beneath the calyx minute, setaceous. Calyx ¼–⅓ in. long; segments subequal, triangular, acute, silky. Corolla slightly exserted; standard broadly ovate, subacute, with a tuft of hairs at the back below the apex; wings oblong, rounded at the tip. Pods ¾–⅞ in. long, oblong, cylindrical, with appressed silky hairs. Seeds 15–20. Fl. B. I. v. 2, p. 71; Dalz. & Gibs. p. 56; Trim. Fl. Ceyl. v. 2, p. 12; Woodr. in Journ. Bomb. Nat. v. 11 (1897) p. 420.—Flowers: Oct. VERN. *Ghâti.*

KONKAN: *Law!, Stocks!, Dalzell!*; Malwan, *Dalzell & Gibson*; Vingorla, *Woodrow.* DECCAN: Poona, *Woodrow,* 191!, also 235!; Mahableshwar, *Cooke!*—DISTRIB. India (Rajputana to Tinnevelly).

9. **Crotalaria albida,** *Heyne, ex Roth, Nov. Pl. Sp.* (1821) p. 333. A much-branched undershrub 1–2 ft. high; branches slender, terete, more or less silky-pubescent. Leaves 1–2 by $\frac{3}{16}$–½ in., linear-oblong or oblanceolate, obtuse, apiculate, pellucido-punctate, more or less silky-pubescent (especially beneath), base acute; petioles $\frac{1}{16}$–$\frac{1}{10}$ in. long; stipules 0. Flowers in terminal (rarely lateral) 6–20-flowered racemes, 2–5 in. long; pedicels ⅛–⅙ in. long; bracts and bracteoles linear. Calyx ¼ in. (finally ⅜ in.) long; teeth long, the 3 lower linear, acuminate, the 2 upper broader, sometimes subobtuse. Corolla ⅓ in. long, pale yellow; standard suborbicular, with a few hairs on the back; wings obovate-oblong. Pods glabrous, sessile, ½–⅝ in. long, oblong-cylindric. Seeds 6–12. Fl. B. I. v. 2, p. 71; Trim. Fl. Ceyl. v. 2, p. 12; Woodr. in Journ. Bomb. Nat. v. 11 (1897) p. 420. *Crotalaria punctata*, Grah. in Wall. Cat. 5401. *Crotalaria epunctata*, Dalz. in Hook. Kew Journ. v. 3 (1851) p. 210; Dalz. & Gibs. p. 56.—Flowers: Dec.–Feb.

KONKAN: *Stocks!, Law!*; Ratnagiri, *Kanitkar!* DECCAN: Fitzgerald Ghát below Mahableshwar, *Cooke!* KANARA: near Honore, *Hohenhacker*, 731!; N. Kanara, *Talbot*, 119! GUJARAT: *Kanitkar!*—DISTRIB. Throughout the plains of India; Malaya, Ceylon, China, Philippines.

I have examined a large number of specimens from Bombay, but have not found the leaves of any of them to be epunctate. In a specimen in Herb. Kew. labelled *C. epunctata* in Dalzell's own handwriting, the leaves are pellucid-dotted.—It sometimes happens, when the leaves are densely pubescent, that the dots are not readily distinguishable, but careful examination will reveal them. I have not therefore retained the var. *epunctata*.

10. **Crotalaria pusilla,** *Heyne, ex Roth, Nov. Pl. Sp.* (1821) p. 335. A much-branched leafy herb 2–5 in. high; branches ascending, clothed with appressed brownish silky hairs. Leaves $\frac{1}{4}$–$\frac{3}{4}$ by $\frac{1}{10}$–$\frac{3}{16}$ in., subsessile, linear-oblong, densely silky, obtuse or subacute, narrowed at the base; stipules 0. Racemes terminal and lateral, numerous, $\frac{1}{2}$–1 in. long, 3–10-flowered; pedicels short; bracts minute, lanceolate. Calyx hairy outside; teeth $\frac{1}{10}$ in. long, linear, acute. Corolla yellow, slightly exserted. Pods $\frac{1}{8}$–$\frac{1}{4}$ in. long, oblong, densely silky-villous. Seeds 4–8. This is the smallest species of *Crotalaria* in India. Fl. B. I. v. 2, p. 70; Woodr. in Journ. Bomb. Nat. v. 11 (1897) p. 420.—Flowers: Sept.-Oct.

Konkan: Bombay, *Capt. Geburne*! Deccan: near Wadi Junction, G. I. P. Railway, *Vaidya*! S. M. Country: Dharwar, *Woodrow*; Badami, *Woodrow*!; Padshapur, *Ritchie*, 1171!—Distrib. From the Bombay Presidency southwards.

11. **Crotalaria nana,** *Burm. Fl. Ind.* (1768) p. 156, t. 48, fig. 2. Annual, 9–18 in. high, sometimes erect and without branches, sometimes branched from the base or from above the base; stem and branches clothed with long spreading hairs. Leaves $\frac{3}{4}$–2 by $\frac{1}{4}$–$\frac{5}{8}$ in., subsessile, closely and minutely pellucido-punctate, oblong or oblanceolate, subacute, apiculate, silky-hairy on both surfaces, base subcuneate; stipules 0. Flowers small, usually in crowded capitate or quasiumbellate terminal racemes, sometimes a few solitary or 2–3 together in some of the upper leaf-axils; pedicels short, hairy; bracts and bracteoles small, linear-subulate, very hairy. Calyx densely hairy outside, the 2 upper teeth connate for nearly their entire length very shortly divided at the apex, the 3 lower teeth triangular, acute. Corolla not exserted; standard oblong, rounded, with a tuft of hairs at the back below the apex. Pods $\frac{1}{4}$ in. long, globose-ovoid, glabrous, black when ripe, scarcely exceeding the calyx. Seeds 6–10. Fl. B. I. v. 2, p. 71; Dalz. & Gibs. p. 56; Trim. Fl. Ceyl. v. 2, p. 13; Woodr. in Journ. Bomb. Nat. v. 11 (1897) p. 420. *Crotalaria umbellata*, Wight, in Wall. Cat. 5383; Grah. Cat. p. 45; Dalz. & Gibs. p. 56.—Flowers: Sept.-Oct.

Konkan: *Stocks*!; Vingorla and Malwan, *Dalzell & Gibson*. Deccan: Mahableshwar, *Cooke*!, *Woodrow*! S. M. Country: Ramghát, *Law* ex *Graham*.—Distrib. India (W. Peninsula); Ceylon.

12. **Crotalaria chinensis,** *Linn. Syst.* ed. 10 (1759) p. 1158. Annual, 1–2 ft. high, usually much-branched; stems and branches clothed with long spreading brown silky hairs. Leaves subsessile, 1–$2\frac{1}{2}$ by $\frac{1}{4}$–$\frac{3}{4}$ in., oblong or oblanceolate, rounded at the base and apex, pellucido-punctate, apiculate, more or less silky-hairy; stipules 0. Flowers in terminal capitate racemes, 3–6 in a head; bracts and bracteoles linear, persistent. Calyx $\frac{3}{8}$–$\frac{1}{2}$ in. long, densely hairy; lower teeth linear, the upper lanceolate. Corolla pale yellow, not exserted; standard orbicular-oblong, subacute, with a dense tuft of long hairs at the back below the apex. Pods sessile, as long as the calyx, glabrous. Seeds 15–20. Fl. B. I. v. 2, p. 73; Benth. in Hook. Lond. Journ. v. 2 (1843) p. 566 (*not* of Roxb.).—Flowers: Oct.

Rare. Konkan: *Stocks*!; Severndroog taluka, *Stocks*!—Distrib. Throughout India; Sumatra, China, Philippines.

13. **Crotalaria priestleyoides,** *Baker, in Hook. f. Fl. B. I.* v. 2 (1876) p. 74. A low undershrub; branches ascending, densely clothed with spreading brown silky hairs. Leaves nearly as broad as long, subsessile, $\frac{1}{2}$–$\frac{7}{8}$ by $\frac{3}{8}$–$\frac{5}{8}$ in., broadly obovate or oblanceolate, mucronate, the upper surface sparsely clothed with long hairs, the lower shaggy, base rounded or acute; stipules 0. Flowers 4–8, in dense terminal heads; bracts $\frac{1}{2}$ in. long, lanceolate, acuminate, persistent, shaggy outside, glabrous or nearly so within. Calyx shaggy; lower teeth linear, acute, the upper lanceolate and $\frac{1}{8}$–$\frac{1}{6}$ in. broad. Corolla as long as the calyx; standard $\frac{5}{8}$ by $\frac{3}{8}$ in., obovate-oblong, rounded at the apex and with a small tuft of hairs at the back. Pods sessile, $\frac{1}{2}$ in. long, dark brown, glabrous, smooth and polished. Seeds 10–16, chestnut-brown, smooth, polished.

Rare. KONKAN: *Law*!, *Stocks*!, *Dalzell*!—DISTRIB. India, Anamallay hills (*Beddome*).

14. **Crotalaria dubia,** *Grah. in Wall. Cat.* (1828) 5404. Annual, 1–2 ft. high, simple or branched; stems and branches silky with appressed hairs. Leaves membranous, 2–3 by 1–1$\frac{1}{4}$ in., obovate, subacute, mucronate, more or less silky above, densely so beneath, base cuneate; main nerves 6–9 pairs, prominent on the under surface, hairy; petioles $\frac{1}{16}$–$\frac{1}{8}$ in. long; stipules minute, setaceous. Flowers 12–20 in dense, silky-villous, usually oblong terminal heads, sometimes reaching 2 in. long, with often a leaf just below the head; bracts and bracteoles ovate-lanceolate, acute, about $\frac{1}{4}$ in. long, hairy on both surfaces. Calyx densely fulvous-silky outside, glabrous within; segments all long, acuminate, the 2 upper slightly broader and less deeply divided than the 3 lower. Corolla as long as the calyx; standard broadly oblong, emarginate, with 2 or 3 long hairs at the back near the apex. Pods sessile, as long as the calyx, glabrous, $\frac{1}{4}$ in. long, oblong. Seeds 6–8, pale brown, polished. Fl. B. I. v. 2, p. 73; Benth. in Hook. Lond. Journ. v. 2 (1843) p. 568.—Flowers: Nov.–Dec.

A rare plant in the Bombay Presidency. KONKAN: *Stocks*! KANARA: common on the banks of the Kála naddi near Lálguli, Yellapur taluka, *Talbot*, 120!—DISTRIB. India (W. Peninsula, Chittagong, Tenasserim).

15. **Crotalaria linifolia,** *Linn. f. Suppl.* (1781) p. 322. Suffruticose, 9–20 in. high, usually much-branched; branches terete, clothed with appressed silky hairs. Leaves 1–2 by $\frac{1}{4}$–$\frac{1}{2}$ in., oblanceolate or oblong, rounded at the apex, apiculate, densely silky with appressed hairs beneath, more or less hairy above, base subcuneate; petioles very short, silky; stipules 0. Flowers in terminal elongate silky 6–20-flowered racemes reaching 1 ft. long; pedicels $\frac{1}{16}$–$\frac{1}{8}$ in. long; bracts and bracteoles subulate. Calyx densely silky; the 2 upper segments connate except at the very apex, forming a broadly ovate upper lip $\frac{1}{4}$ by $\frac{1}{6}$ in., the 3 lower segments triangular, acuminate. Corolla scarcely longer than the calyx; standard oblong, rounded, truncate or sometimes slightly emarginate, with a very few minute hairs at the back below the apex. Pods ovoid-oblong, sessile, as long as the calyx, obliquely truncate at the apex, glabrous, black when ripe. Seeds 4–10. Fl. B. I. v. 2, p. 72; Grah. Cat. p. 45; Dalz. & Gibs. p. 56; Trim. Fl. Ceyl. v. 2, p. 13; Woodr. in Journ. Bomb. Nat. v. 11 (1897) p. 420. *C. sobolifera*, Grah. in Wall. Cat. 5420 A.—Flowers: Sept.

I have examined many living specimens in which there were only 4 seeds.

KONKAN: *Stocks*! DECCAN: Poona, *Cooke*!, *Woodrow*!; Khed, *Kanitkar*!; Khandala, *Graham*. GUJARAT: Surat, *Dalzell & Gibson*.—DISTRIB. E. tropical regions.

16. **Crotalaria calycina,** *Schrank, Pl. Rar. Monac.* (1819) t. 12. An erect herb 1–2 ft. high; stem simple or branched, densely clothed with appressed silky hairs. Leaves variable, dimorphous, in one form narrow-linear, acute, reaching 5–6 in. long, in the other and more common form lanceolate, acute or subobtuse, $1\frac{1}{2}$–$3\frac{1}{2}$ by $\frac{1}{2}$–$\frac{7}{8}$ in., mucronate, glabrous or nearly so above, more or less silky with appressed hairs beneath, base acute; petioles $\frac{1}{20}$–$\frac{1}{10}$ in. long; stipules minute, subulate, hairy. Flowers large, in terminal 2–12-flowered racemes; pedicels stout, $\frac{1}{4}$ in. long, deflexed in fruit; bracts and bracteoles large, foliaceous, lanceolate, very acute, shaggy with long hair. Calyx $\frac{3}{4}$–1 in. long, densely clothed with long fulvous persistent hairs; lower teeth lanceolate, acuminate, the upper obovate-oblong, $\frac{1}{4}$–$\frac{3}{8}$ in. wide. Corolla pale yellow, shorter than the calyx; standard obovate-oblong, rounded at the apex and with a small tuft of long hairs at the back. Pods sessile, shorter than the calyx, glabrous, dark brown. Seeds 20–30. Fl. B. I. v. 2, p. 72; Trim. Fl. Ceyl. v. 2, p. 14; Woodr. in Journ. Bomb. Nat. v. 11 (1897) p. 420. *C. anthylloides*, Don, Prodr. p. 241; Grah. Cat. p. 44; Dalz. & Gibs. p. 54 (*not* of Lamk.).—Flowers: Oct.

Pretty common in the rains, *Graham*. KONKAN: *Stocks*!; S. Konkan, *Dalzell & Gibson*. DECCAN: Poona, *Woodrow*!; Soos, Poona Collectorate, *Bhiva*!—DISTRIB. E. tropical regions, Tropical Africa.

17. **Crotalaria lutescens,** *Dalz. in Hook. Kew Journ.* v. 2 (1850) p. 34. Annual, erect, 1–3 ft. high, sparingly branched; branches terete or obscurely angled, striate, glabrous. Leaves membranous, pale, subsessile, variable, in one form reaching 8 in. long by $\frac{1}{8}$–$\frac{1}{4}$ in. in breadth, linear, in another 3–5 by $\frac{3}{8}$–$\frac{3}{4}$ in., elliptic-lanceolate, all acute (rarely rounded) at the apex, apiculate, glabrous except the young leaves; stipules 0. Flowers distant, in long slender lax 6–15-flowered racemes; pedicels $\frac{1}{2}$ in. long, slender; bracts and bracteoles small, subulate, persistent. Calyx glabrous outside, about $\frac{1}{2}$ in. long; upper teeth connate at the base only, the 3 lower teeth connate for about half their length, all linear, very acute. Corolla yellow, twice as long as the calyx; standard 1 in. long, conspicuously veined, ovate-oblong, acute, reflexed in flowering; keel with a hairy line on its back. Pods quite glabrous, cylindric, oblong, 1–$1\frac{1}{4}$ in. long. Seeds numerous.—Fl. B. I. v. 2, p. 74; Woodr. in Journ. Bomb. Nat. v. 11 (1897) p. 420. *C. peduncularis*, Dalz. & Gibs. p. 55 (*not* of Graham).—Flowers: Aug.-Oct.

KONKAN: *Law*!, *Stocks*!, *Dalzell*!; Vingorla, *Dalzell & Gibson*; Malwan, *Dalzell*. S. M. COUNTRY: Castlerock, abundant, *Cooke*! KANARA: on the Ghâts near the Yena temple (N. Kanara), *Talbot*, 280!—DISTRIB. Apparently endemic.

18. **Crotalaria retusa,** *Linn. Sp. Pl.* (1753) p. 715. A robust undershrub 2–4 ft. high; branches striate, glabrous or appressedly pubescent. Leaves $1\frac{1}{2}$–$3\frac{1}{2}$ by $\frac{3}{8}$–$\frac{7}{8}$ in., oblanceolate-oblong, obtuse or retuse, sometimes mucronate, rarely subacute, glabrous above, silky-pubescent beneath, base cuneate; petioles very short; stipules subulate. Flowers numerous, large and showy, in erect terminal racemes 6–12 in. long;

pedicels $\frac{1}{4}$–$\frac{5}{16}$ in. long; bracts subulate, 1 at the base of each pedicel and 2 much smaller about half way up. Calyx $\frac{3}{8}$–$\frac{1}{2}$ in. long, glabrous or nearly so outside; tube campanulate; upper teeth ovate, acute, divaricate, connate near the base only, the 3 lower teeth much narrower, triangular, acuminate, connate about half the way up. Corolla much exserted, about 1 in. long, yellow with a purple tinge; standard suborbicular, conspicuously veined, with a strong rib down the middle of the back. Pods 1–1$\frac{1}{2}$ in. long, stalked, linear-oblong, slightly broader upwards. Seeds 15–20. Fl. B. I. v. 2, p. 75 (*exclud. syn.* Dalz. & Gibs.); Bot. Mag. t. 2561; Trim. Fl. Ceyl. v. 2, p. 15; Watt, Dict. Econ. Prod. v. 2, p. 613. *C. Leschenaultii*, Grah. Cat. p. 44; Dalz. & Gibs. p. 54; Woodr. in Journ. Bomb. Nat. v. 11 (1897) p. 420.—Flowers: Sept.–Nov. VERN. *Dingala.*

KONKAN: *Law*!, *Stocks*!, *Capt. Geburne*! DECCAN: Mahableshwar, *Cooke*!, *Woodrow*!; Khandala, *Woodrow*! S. M. COUNTRY: Ramghát, *Ritchie*, 150!—DISTRIB. India generally; Ceylon, China, Malaya, N. Australia, Tropical Africa.

Very common at Mahableshwar, where it has been erroneously referred to *C. Leschenaultii*, DC. *Crotalaria Leschenaultii* [DC. Prodr. v. 2, p. 125; Benth. in Hook. Lond. Journ. v. 2 (1843) p. 481; Wight & Arn. Prodr. p. 186: *C. lupiniflora*, Grah. in Wall. Cat. 5407] has foliaceous ovate bracts, by which it may be readily distinguished from *C. retusa*. *C. Leschenaultii* seems to be a rare plant, confined apparently to the Nilghiris. There are only 2 specimens in Herb. Kew., one from Wight's Herbarium and the other from McIvor's (n. 80). There is every reason to believe that it is not a Bombay plant at all. It has not been found in that Presidency by Law, Stocks or Ritchie or by more recent collectors. Ritchie's specimen (n. 150) from Ramghát mentioned by Baker in Fl. B. I. v. 2, p. 76, is *C. retusa*. What *C. retusa* of Graham (Cat. p. 45) is, which he says grows in compounds on the Esplanade in Bombay and flowers in the cold season, or what *C. retusa* of Dalzell & Gibson (Bo. Fl. p. 55) is, which is said to be common in sandy soil in company with *C. verrucosa* and to flower in February and March, when all the Bombay Crotalarias are practically out of bloom, I can form no idea.

19. **Crotalaria sericea,** *Retz. Obs.* fasc. 5 (1789) p. 26. A short undershrub 3–4 ft. high; branches stout, striate, subglabrous. Leaves 2–6 in. long, very variable in breadth, oblong-lanceolate, acute or subacute, mucronate, glabrous above, finely silky beneath, base cuneate; petioles $\frac{1}{16}$–$\frac{1}{8}$ in. long; stipules large, leafy, persistent. Flowers in elongate terminal 20–50-flowered racemes 10–12 in. long; pedicels longer than the calyx, with 1 large foliaceous ovate-acute bract at the base of each pedicel and a pair of minute subulate bracts on each pedicel below the middle. Calyx $\frac{1}{2}$ in. long, almost glabrous outside; tube campanulate, half as long as the teeth; upper teeth large, triangular, acute, about $\frac{1}{4}$ in. broad at the base, the 3 lower teeth smaller and less deeply cut than the upper, linear-lanceolate, acute. Corolla yellow with a purplish tinge; standard broadly ovate, with a strong midrib at the back. Pods glabrous, linear-oblong, stalked, 1–2 in. long. Seeds 20–30. Fl. B. I. v. 2, p. 75; Grah. Cat. p. 45; Dalz. & Gibs. p. 55; Woodr. in Journ. Bomb. Nat. v. 11 (1897) p. 420; Watt, Dict. Econ. Prod. v. 2, p. 614.—Flowers: Oct.–Dec.

KONKAN: *Law*!, *Stocks*!; Bombay, in pasture grounds, *Dalzell & Gibson*, *Graham*. KANARA: Gund (N. Kanara), *Woodrow*.—DISTRIB. Throughout India generally; Malaya, Andamans.

20. **Crotalaria verrucosa,** *Linn. Sp. Pl.* (1753) p. 715. A much-branched herb 2–3 ft. high; branches acutely angled, at first puberulous,

afterwards glabrescent. Leaves 2–6 by 1¼–3 in., ovate-rhomboid or ovate-deltoid, obtuse or occasionally acute at the apex, tapering to the base, subglabrous above, more or less downy and paler beneath; nerves prominent; petioles $\frac{1}{10}$–⅛ in.; stipules large, foliaceous, semilunate, persistent. Flowers in terminal or lateral 12–20-flowered racemes 6–8 in. long; pedicels $\frac{3}{16}$ in. long; bracts at the base of the pedicels linear-lanceolate, ⅛ in. long, those on the pedicels much smaller, subulate. Calyx membranous, ⅓ in. long, faintly pubescent; tube short, campanulate; teeth subequal, triangular, acute. Corolla ¾ in. long, exserted, bluish-purple and white, rarely entirely white. Pods densely villous when young, softly pubescent when ripe, 1–1½ in. long, oblong-cylindric, stalked. Seeds 10–15, yellow, ⅛ in. long, polished. Fl. B. I. v. 2, p. 77; Grah. Cat. p. 45; Dalz. & Gibs. p. 55; Trim. Fl. Ceyl. v. 2, p. 15; Woodr. in Journ. Bomb. Nat. v. 11 (1897) p. 420; Watt, Dict. Econ. Prod. v. 2, p. 614.—Flowers: Oct.–Nov.

KONKAN: *Law*!, *Stocks*!; Vingorla, *Woodrow*; near Goa, *Cooke*! DECCAN: Sholapur districts, *Law* ex *Graham*.—DISTRIB. Tropical India; Ceylon, China, Tropical Africa, Mauritius, Tropical America.

21. **Crotalaria leptostachya,** *Benth. in Hook. Lond. Journ. Bot.* v. 2 (1843) p. 562. A stiff erect shrub; stems and branches tetragonous, fulvous-pubescent at the angles. Leaves membranous, 3½–5½ by ¾–1 in., oblong-lanceolate or linear-oblong, acute, apiculate (sometimes very narrow in proportion to their length), thinly clothed on both sides with fulvous appressed silky hairs, base usually rounded; nerves numerous, conspicuous, fulvous-hairy; petioles very short; stipules minute, deciduous. Flowers in elongate many-flowered racemes 6–12 in. long; pedicels short, fulvous-hairy; bracts small, subulate, hairy. Calyx ¾ in. long, clothed with fulvous silky glistening hairs on the outside; tube very short; teeth long, triangular, acute, the 2 upper divaricate, slightly broader and a little more deeply cleft than the 3 lower ones. Corolla yellow, not exserted; standard suborbicular, glabrous on the back. Pods densely fulvous-silky, ⅝–⅞ in. long. Seeds 4–6. Fl. B. I. v. 2, p. 78; Woodr. in Journ. Bomb. Nat. v. 11 (1897) p. 420.—Flowers: Oct.

KONKAN: *Stocks*!, *Law*! DECCAN: Ambenala Ghát, *Kanitkar*!; Khandala, *Cooke*!, *Woodrow*. KANARA: Yellapur, *Talbot*, 80!—DISTRIB. Apparently endemic in Bombay.

22. **Crotalaria Heyneana,** *Grah. in Wall. Cat.* (1828) 5414. A sparingly-branched undershrub 1–2 ft. high; branches slender, terete, the young ones pubescent. Leaves membranous, subsessile, 3–5 by 1¼–2 in., elliptic-lanceolate, very acute (sometimes acuminate), mucronate, glabrous above, sparsely and minutely puberulous beneath, base acute; nerves slender, conspicuous; petioles $\frac{1}{20}$–$\frac{1}{10}$ in. long, pubescent; stipules small, semilunate, reflexed. Flowers in terminal and lateral many-flowered racemes; pedicels ¼–⅜ in. long; bracts linear-subulate, those beneath the pedicels ⅛–$\frac{3}{16}$ in. long, those on the pedicels smaller. Calyx ½ in. long, pubescent outside; tube campanulate; segments long, linear-lanceolate, very acute, the 2 upper slightly broader and more deeply cut than the lower. Corolla about ¾ in. long; standard erect, suborbicular, pale yellow or nearly white, with blue streaks at the base; wings usually pale blue in the upper part. Pods 1½ in. long, linear-oblong, broader towards the apex, softly pubescent. Seeds 10–12,

yellow. Fl. B. I. v. 2, p. 78; Benth. in Hook. Lond. Journ. v. 2 (1843) p. 560; Bot. Mag. t. 5974.—Flowers: Nov.-Jan.

Rare. KANARA: Kadgal (N. Kanara), *Woodrow*!; Lalguli, near Yellapur, *Talbot*, 33! and 223!—DISTRIB. India (Kanara to Travancore).

23. **Crotalaria juncea,** *Linn. Sp. Pl.* (1753) p. 714. Annual, 2–8 ft. high; branches numerous, ascending, slender, terete, striate, silky-pubescent. Leaves 1–4 by $\frac{1}{4}$–$\frac{3}{4}$ in., linear or oblong, obtuse or subacute, apiculate, clothed on both sides with appressed silky shining hairs, base usually acute; petioles $\frac{1}{10}$–$\frac{1}{10}$ in. long; stipules 0 or very minute. Flowers large, in erect terminal and lateral 12–20-flowered racemes often reaching 1 ft. long; pedicels $\frac{1}{8}$–$\frac{1}{4}$ in. long, pubescent; bracts minute, linear-subulate; bracteoles 2 beneath the calyx, minute, linear-subulate. Calyx $\frac{3}{4}$ in. long, clothed with fulvous hairs; teeth linear-lanceolate, very deep. Corolla bright yellow, slightly exserted; standard ovate-oblong, subacute. Pods 1–1$\frac{1}{4}$ in. long, sessile, clothed with short fulvous silky hair. Seeds 10–15. Fl. B. I. v. 2, p. 79.

Doubtfully wild, but often found as an escape from cultivation. The plant is cultivated throughout India, extensively so in the Bombay Presidency, for the sake of its fibre, which furnishes the *Sunn Hemp* of commerce and which is largely exported from Bombay. Consult Watt, Dict. Econ. Prod. v. 2, p. 595, where will be found an exhaustive description of the mode of cultivation of the plant and of the extraction and uses of its fibre.—DISTRIB. Malay islands, Australia.

24. **Crotalaria madurensis,** *Wight, in Wall. Cat.* (1828) 5376. A much-branched erect undershrub; branches terete, clothed with short yellowish-brown silky hairs. Leaves 1$\frac{1}{2}$–3$\frac{1}{2}$ by 1–2 in., ovate-oblong, obtuse (rarely subacute), mucronate or not, closely covered with shining yellowish-brown silky hairs, base usually rounded; main nerves numerous, conspicuous; petioles $\frac{1}{8}$ in. long, densely silky; stipules 0. Flowers often large and showy, more than twice as long as the calyx, in panicled racemes; bracts and bracteoles $\frac{3}{16}$–$\frac{5}{16}$ in. long, ovate-lanceolate, acute or acuminate. Calyx $\frac{3}{8}$–$\frac{5}{8}$ in. long, densely silky, deeply bilabiate; tube short; the 2 upper teeth triangular-acute, divaricate, scarcely connate at the very base; the 3 lower about half as broad as the upper, linear-lanceolate, very acute, connate for about one-third of their length. Corolla yellow, exserted; standard orbicular, slightly mucronate, silky on the back; wings often rugose or presenting a honeycombed appearance on the upper side near the base. Pods 1–1$\frac{1}{4}$ in. long, shortly stalked, sparsely hairy, turgid. Seeds 10–12. Fl. B. I. v. 2, p. 79; Benth. in Hook. Lond. Journ. v. 2 (1843) p. 563; Woodr. in Journ. Bomb. Nat. v. 11 (1897) p. 421.—Flowers: Dec.

Very rare in the Bombay Presidency. KANARA: Kumpta-Sirsi road, *Woodrow*.—DISTRIB. India (Nilghiri and Madura hills).

25. **Crotalaria fulva,** *Roxb. Fl. Ind.* v. 3 (1832) p. 266. An erect much-branched undershrub 3–5 ft. high; branches densely clothed with short brown silky hairs. Leaves 2$\frac{1}{2}$–4 by $\frac{3}{4}$–1 in., oblong or oblanceolate, obtuse or subacute, often apiculate, clothed on both sides with yellowish-brown shining silky hairs, base cuneate; petioles $\frac{1}{16}$ in. long, silky-hairy; stipules 0 or minute. Flowers numerous, in panicled racemes; bract 1 beneath the pedicel, ovate, acute or acuminate, hairy, reflexed; bracteoles 2 beneath the calyx, similar, but a little smaller, all persistent. Calyx

$\frac{1}{2}$-$\frac{5}{8}$ in. long, silky-hairy; teeth lanceolate, about equally cleft, the 2 upper oblong, broader than the 3 lower lanceolate ones. Corolla $\frac{3}{4}$-1 in. long, exserted; standard elliptic, acute, silky on the back. Pods included, clothed with appressed silky yellowish-brown hairs. Seeds 2, light brown, polished. Fl. B. I. v. 2, p. 80; Grah. Cat. p. 44; Dalz. & Gibs. p. 54; Woodr. in Journ. Bomb. Nat. v. 11 (1897) p. 421.—Flowers: Feb.

KONKAN: *Law*!; *Dalzell*, without locality! S. M. COUNTRY: Ramghát, *Dalzell & Gibson*, common, *Graham*. KANARA: Kumpta-Sirsi road, *Woodrow*!—DISTRIB. India (W. Peninsula); Java, Sumatra, Seychelles and Mauritius.

26. **Crotalaria ramosissima,** *Roxb. Fl. Ind.* v. 3 (1832) p. 268. A very much-branched woody herb scarcely reaching 1 ft. high; branches densely clothed with silky hairs. Leaves $\frac{1}{2}$-1 by $\frac{1}{8}$-$\frac{3}{16}$ in., crowded, subsessile, linear or oblanceolate, usually obtuse, apiculate, densely silky-hairy on both surfaces, base cuneate; stipules 0. Flowers in panicled racemes; bracts lanceolate, recurved. Calyx $\frac{1}{3}$ in. long, hairy outside; teeth linear, acute, the margins reflexed. Corolla $\frac{3}{8}$ in. long; standard pointed, silky on the back. Pods sessile, $\frac{3}{8}$ in. long, oblong, densely silky. Seed 1, brownish-black, polished. Fl. B. I. v. 2, p. 80; Grah. Cat. p. 44; Woodr. in Journ. Bomb. Nat. v. 11 (1897) p. 421; Oliver, Flor. Trop. Afr. v. 2, p. 26.—Flowers: Dec.

Rare. S. M. COUNTRY: Badami, *Cooke*!, *Woodrow*!—DISTRIB. India (W. Peninsula); Tropical Africa.

27. **Crotalaria medicaginea,** *Lamk. Encyc. Méthod.* v. 2 (1786) p. 201. A perennial herb scarcely reaching 1 ft.; rootstock woody, branched; stems and branches numerous, diffuse, filiform, terete, sparsely clothed with appressed hairs. Leaves 3-foliolate; common petioles $\frac{1}{10}$-$\frac{1}{6}$ in. long; stipules minute, filiform. Leaflets $\frac{1}{4}$-$\frac{3}{8}$ by $\frac{1}{10}$-$\frac{1}{6}$ in., oblanceolate, rounded, apiculate, glabrous, more or less silky beneath; petiolules distinct, very short. Flowers in terminal and leaf-opposed 2-6-flowered racemes; peduncles longer than the leaves, filiform; bracts minute, linear-subulate. Calyx $\frac{1}{10}$ in. long, silky outside with appressed hairs; teeth triangular, acute, exceeding the campanulate tube, all about equally long, the two upper a little broader. Corolla yellow, twice as long as the calyx; standard silky on the back. Pods obliquely subglobose, $\frac{1}{8}$ in. long, sparingly silky, beaked. Seeds 2. Fl. B. I. v. 2, p. 81; Trim. Fl. Ceyl. v. 2, p. 18; Watt, Dict. Econ. Prod. v. 2, p. 613.

I have seen no specimens of the true *C. medicaginea* from Bombay. The var. *neglecta* is plentiful and the var. *luxurians* is occasionally met with.—DISTRIB. Tropical India; Ceylon, Malaya, Afghanistan, China, Australia.

VAR. 1. *neglecta*, Baker, in Fl. B. I. v. 2, p. 81. Branches more ascending than in the type. Leaflets larger, retuse or rounded, apiculate or not. Racemes 6-9-flowered. *C. neglecta* (sp.), Wight & Arn. Prod. p. 192.

KONKAN: Bombay, *Capt. Geburne*!; Revadanda, *Gungaram*! GUJARAT: Baroda, *Kanitkar*!, *Woodrow*! SIND: *Dalzell*!; Umrak, *Cooke*!

VAR. 2. *luxurians*, Baker, in Fl. B. I. v. 2, p. 81. A much stouter and stronger plant, 2-3 ft. high. Leaflets larger, usually retuse, the terminal leaflet $\frac{3}{4}$-1 in. long. Petioles up to $\frac{1}{2}$ in. long. Racemes

6–12-flowered. *C. luxurians* (sp.), Benth. in Hook. Lond. Journ. v. 2 (1843) p. 578.

KONKAN: *Stocks*!; Salsette, *Jacquemont*, 718! DECCAN: near Talegaon, Poona districts, *Bhiva*!

28. **Crotalaria Notonii,** *Wight & Arn. Prodr.* p. 192. Suffruticose, erect; branches divaricate, more or less silky. Leaves approximated; petioles slightly shorter than the leaves; stipules $\frac{1}{8}$–$\frac{1}{6}$ in. long, linear, acute, persistent. Leaflets $\frac{5}{8}$–1 by $\frac{1}{4}$–$\frac{5}{8}$ in., obovate-cuneate, rounded, truncate or retuse at the apex, apiculate or not; petiolules $\frac{1}{16}$ in. long, pubescent. Flowers 12–20, close, in terminal or leaf-opposed racemes 2–3 in. long; pedicels $\frac{1}{12}$–$\frac{1}{8}$ in. long, pubescent; bracts $\frac{1}{8}$–$\frac{1}{6}$ in. long, linear, acute, persistent. Calyx $\frac{1}{6}$–$\frac{1}{4}$ in. long, sparsely silky; teeth lanceolate, acute, equalling the tube. Corolla more than twice as long as the calyx, yellow; keel with a very long beak. Pods $\frac{3}{4}$ in. long, subquadrangular, thinly silky. Fl. B. I. v. 2, p. 82; Wight, Icon. t. 752. *C. rostrata*, Wight & Arn. Prodr. p. 191; Dalz. & Gibs. p. 57.

Rare. GUJARAT: sandy soil at Domas near Surat, also in Kathiawar, ex *Dalzell & Gibson*, l. c.—DISTRIB. India (Nilghiri and Pulney hills).

29. **Crotalaria orixensis,** *Willd. in Ges. Naturf. Fr. Neue Schr.* v. 4 (1803) p. 217. Perennial, herbaceous, diffuse; stems slender, copiously branched, 1–1$\frac{1}{2}$ ft. long, sparingly clothed with spreading brownish hairs. Leaves glabrous above, clothed with appressed hairs beneath; petioles $\frac{1}{2}$–1$\frac{1}{4}$ in. long, hairy; stipules $\frac{1}{8}$ in. long, foliaceous, lanceolate, persistent. Leaflets $\frac{3}{8}$–1 by $\frac{1}{4}$–$\frac{5}{8}$ in., obovate-oblong, obtuse; petiolules very short. Flowers small, in very lax lateral or terminal 3–12-flowered racemes; pedicels $\frac{1}{4}$–$\frac{1}{2}$ in. long, filiform; bracts large, foliaceous, ovate, acute, deflexed. Calyx $\frac{1}{8}$–$\frac{1}{4}$ in. long, silky outside; teeth lanceolate, acute. Corolla scarcely exserted, yellow. Pods $\frac{1}{2}$–$\frac{5}{8}$ in. long, glabrous, with a stalk as long as the calyx. Seeds 8–10. Fl. B. I. v. 2, p. 83; Dalz. & Gibs. p. 57; Oliver, Fl. Trop. Afr. v. 2, p. 27; Woodr. in Journ. Bomb. Nat. v. 11 (1897) p. 421.—Flowers: Sept.–Oct. VERN. *Andabel*; *Jenaru*.

KONKAN: *Stocks*! DECCAN: Poona, *Col. Sykes*!, *Woodrow*!; Ghát between Wathár and Wai, *Cooke*! S. M. COUNTRY: Dharwar, *Cooke*!—DISTRIB. India (W. Peninsula); Tropical Africa.

30. **Crotalaria striata,** *DC. Prodr.* v. 2 (1825) p. 131. Suffruticose, 2–3 ft. high; stem stout, more or less striate; branches puberulous, the very young ones silky. Leaves membranous; petioles 1$\frac{1}{2}$–3 in. long, stout, slightly pubescent; stipules minute, deciduous or 0. Leaflets 2–3 by 1–1$\frac{1}{2}$ in., elliptic, obtuse or acute, sometimes emarginate, glabrous above, minutely puberulous and glaucous beneath. Flowers numerous, in erect terminal and lateral elongate spicate 20–50-flowered racemes which sometimes reach 1 ft. long; pedicels very short; bracts setaceous, minute. Calyx $\frac{1}{4}$ in. long, slightly pubescent outside; teeth as long as the tube, lanceolate. Corolla dull yellow, veined with purple, twice as long as the calyx. Pods 1$\frac{1}{2}$–2 in. long, much deflexed, oblong, cylindric, glabrous, shortly stalked. Seeds 20–30, dark brown. Fl. B. I. v. 2, p. 84; Oliver, Fl. Trop. Afr. v. 2, p. 38; Trim. Fl. Ceyl. v. 2, p. 18; Woodr. in Journ. Bomb. Nat. v. 11 (1897) p. 421; Watt, Dict. Econ. Prod. v. 2, p. 614.—Flowers: Nov.

DECCAN: Poona, *Woodrow*!; Ganesh Khind, *Woodrow*!—DISTRIB. Throughout India; Ceylon, Malaya, Tropical America and Africa.

31. **Crotalaria laburnifolia,** *Linn. Sp. Pl.* (1753) p. 715. An erect shrub 2–4 ft. high; branches slender, terete, glabrous. Leaves 3-foliolate; petioles 1½–2½ in. long; stipules 0. Leaflets membranous, 1–1¾ by ¾–1½ in., elliptic-oblong, acute or subacute at both ends; petiolules $\frac{1}{16}$–⅛ in. long. Flowers in terminal and lateral few-flowered lax racemes ½–1 ft. long; pedicels about ¼ in. long; bracts minute, deciduous. Calyx ⅓–⅜ in. long, glabrous, turbinate; teeth lanceolate, as long as the tube. Corolla 1 in. long, much exserted, yellow, glabrous; keel broad, with a long incurved beak. Pods cylindric, 1½–2 in. long, glabrous, with a very long stalk ¾–1 in. long, much exceeding that of any other species. Seeds 20–30. Fl. B. I. v. 2, p. 84; Dalz. & Gibs. p. 57; Trim. Fl. Ceyl. v. 2, p. 19; Watt, Dict. Econ. Prod. v. 2, p. 613.

SOUTHERN KONKAN: *Nimmo* ex *Dalzell & Gibson*. This has been included on the authority of Dalzell and Gibson (Bo. Fl. p. 57), who cite Nimmo as above.

It has not apparently been found by any other Bombay collector, and there are no specimens from Bombay in Herb. Kew. Woodrow does not include the plant in his list published in Journ. Bomb. Nat.—DISTRIB. India (W. Peninsula); Ceylon, Malaya, Philippines.

32. **Crotalaria quinquefolia,** *Linn. Sp. Pl.* (1753) p. 716. An erect annual 1–3 ft. high; stem and branches pale, furrowed, glabrous or the young ones more or less thinly silky. Leaves 5- (rarely 3-) foliolate; petioles variable in length, from ½–3 in., channelled, glabrous or sparsely pubescent; stipules linear-lanceolate, acute, subpersistent. Leaflets subsessile, usually narrow-linear, 1–4½ by ¼–½ in. (rarely oblanceolate or elliptic-oblong when they are shorter and broader), obtuse or subacute, glabrous above, pale beneath, base acute. Flowers in lax usually terminal 10–20-flowered racemes reaching 8 in. long; pedicels ¼–⅜ in. long; bracts ¼–½ in. long, foliaceous, lanceolate, very acute, persistent. Calyx campanulate, ½ in. long, glabrous or nearly so; teeth triangular, acute, as long as the tube. Corolla glabrous, twice as long as the calyx. Pods 1½–2 by ¾–1 in., oblong, glabrous, slightly tapering at the base. Seeds 30–40. Fl. B. I. v. 1, p. 84; Grah. Cat. p. 45; Dalz. & Gibs. p. 57; Trim. Fl. Ceyl. v. 2, p. 19.

KONKAN: margins of rice-fields in Salsette, *Graham*, *Dalzell & Gibson*; Wari Country, *Stocks*!—DISTRIB. India (W. Peninsula, Birma); Ceylon, Malaya, Philippines.

6. TRIGONELLA, Linn.

Annual herbs. Leaves pinnately 3-foliolate, toothed; stipules adnate to the petiole. Flowers lemon-yellow, in axillary racemes. Calyx-tube campanulate; teeth distant, subequal. Petals free from the staminal-tube; standard obovate or oblong; wings oblong; keel shorter than the wings, obtuse. Stamens diadelphous; filaments not dilated; anthers uniform. Ovary sessile or shortly stalked; ovules usually many; style glabrous; stigma terminal. Pod linear or linear-oblong, compressed or subterete (not spiral), usually exserted, continuous within. Seeds few or many.—DISTRIB. Europe, Asia, N. and S. Africa, with 1 species in Australia; species about 50.

1. **Trigonella occulta,** *Delile, Fl. Ægypt. Illustr.* (1812) p. 71. A low densely cæspitose diffuse annual; stems not more than a few inches long, pale, glabrous or with a few scattered silky hairs. Leaves pinnately 3-foliolate; petioles $\frac{1}{4}$-$\frac{3}{8}$ in. long, striate, silky-hairy when young; stipules $\frac{1}{4}$ in. long, leafy, deeply lancinate-toothed, strongly nerved. Leaflets $\frac{3}{16}$-$\frac{1}{4}$ in. long, oblanceolate-cuneate, sharply toothed, subglabrous above, sparsely silky beneath; nerves strong, conspicuous; lateral petiolules short, the terminal ones $\frac{1}{16}$-$\frac{1}{12}$ in. long. Flowers 2-4 together, in sessile axillary clusters. Calyx $\frac{1}{8}$ in. long, membranous, hairy; teeth longer than the tube, subulate. Corolla scarcely exserted; standard obovate-oblong; wings oblanceolate. Pods membranous, slightly longer than the calyx, oblong-ellipsoid, strongly veined, sparsely clothed with spreading white hairs. Seeds 1-2, oblong, $\frac{1}{16}$-$\frac{1}{12}$ in. long, smooth, yellowish-brown or sometimes mottled. Fl. B. I. v. 2, p. 87; Boiss. Fl. Orient. v. 2, p. 84; Aitch. Pb. & Sind Pl. p. 38; Woodr. in Journ. Bomb. Nat. v. 11 (1897) p. 421; Watt, Dict. Econ. Prod. v. 6, part 4, p. 88.—Flowers: Jan.

Very rare except in Sind. DECCAN: Lanoli, *Woodrow*. SIND: *Stocks*!—DISTRIB. India (Upper Gangetic plain); Egypt, Nubia.

7. MELILOTUS, Juss.

Annual or biennial herbs. Leaves pinnately 3-foliolate; stipules adnate to the petiole; leaflets toothed. Flowers small, yellow or white, in slender or abbreviated axillary racemes; bracts minute or 0; bracteoles 0. Calyx short; teeth subequal. Corolla free from the staminal-tube, deciduous; standard obovate or oblong, contracted at the base, subsessile; wings obtuse; keel shorter than the wings, obtuse. Stamens diadelphous; filaments not dilated; anthers uniform. Ovary sessile or stalked; ovules few; style filiform, incurved; stigma terminal. Pod subglobose or ovoid, longer than the calyx, indehiscent or tardily dehiscent. Seeds 1 or few.—DISTRIB. Temperate and subtropical regions of the Old World; species 10 or 12.

1. **Melilotus indica,** *All. Fl. Pedem.* v. 1 (1785) p. 308. An erect annual herb, 1-1$\frac{1}{2}$ ft. high; stem and branches pale, slightly striate, glabrous or nearly so. Leaves 3-foliolate; petioles $\frac{3}{4}$-1$\frac{1}{2}$ in. long, very slender; stipules $\frac{1}{4}$ in. long, lanceolate, very acute, adnate to the petiole. Leaflets $\frac{1}{2}$-$\frac{5}{8}$ by $\frac{5}{16}$-$\frac{3}{8}$ in., toothed, oblanceolate or obovate-cuneate (sometimes a few casually linear-oblong), rounded, truncate, or retuse at the apex, glabrous or with a few scattered hairs on both sides; petiolules of the lateral leaflets very short, those of the terminal leaflets $\frac{1}{10}$-$\frac{1}{4}$ in. long. Flowers small, in slender spicate close racemes; pedicels short, deflexed; bracts subulate. Calyx $\frac{1}{24}$-$\frac{1}{16}$ in. long; teeth triangular. Corolla twice the calyx. Pods ellipsoid, compressed, tapering at both ends, reticulato-venose, glabrous. Seed 1, oblong-ellipsoid, compressed, $\frac{1}{10}$ in. long, brown. *Melilotus parviflora*, Desf. Fl. Atlant. v. 2 (1800) p. 192; Fl. B. I. v. 2, p. 89; Grah. Cat. p. 46; Dalz. & Gibs. Suppl. p. 21; Boiss. Fl. Orient. v. 2, p. 108; Watt, Dict. Econ. Prod. v. 5, p. 225.—Flowers: Jan. VERN. *Vánmethiká*; *Rán-methi*.

In pasture grounds, *Graham, Dalzell & Gibson*. DECCAN: Poona, *Woodrow*. SIND: *Woodrow*!, *Cooke*!—DISTRIB. India (tropical zone): Europe, S. Persia, Afghanistan, and introduced in many other regions.

8. MEDICAGO, Linn.

Herbs, rarely shrubs. Leaves pinnately 3-foliolate; stipules adnate to the petiole; leaflets toothed. Calyx-tube campanulate; teeth 5, subequal. Corolla free from the staminal-tube; standard obovate or oblong, contracted at the base, subsessile; wings oblong; keel shorter than the wings, obtuse. Stamens diadelphous; filaments not dilated at the apex; anthers uniform. Ovary sessile, usually many-ovulate; style subulate, glabrous; stigma oblique. Pod spirally twisted (rarely falcate), reticulately veined, scarcely dehiscent.—DISTRIB. Europe, W. Asia, N. Africa; species about 40.

Pod unarmed, 1-seeded .... 1. *M. lupulina.*
Pod armed, many-seeded.
  Pod covered with spines on the exterior faces as well as on the margins .... 2. *M. laciniata.*
  Pod covered with spines on the margins but not on the exterior faces .... 3. *M. denticulata.*

1. **Medicago lupulina,** *Linn. Sp. Pl.* (1753) p. 779. Annual or biennial, more or less pubescent; stem 1 ft. or more, finely downy, grooved. Leaves 3-foliolate; petioles ½–1 in. long, slender, more or less pubescent; stipules subentire or subdentate at the base, lanceolate and acuminate at the apex. Leaflets ¼–⅜ in. long, nearly as broad as long, obovate-cuneate, faintly inciso-crenate, slightly retuse and apiculate with a triangular tooth at the apex. Flowers 10–20, in dense spicate axillary racemes; peduncles 1–1½ in. long, filiform; pedicels $\frac{1}{16}$ in. long in fruit; bracts minute, subulate. Calyx $\frac{1}{10}$ in. long, hairy outside; teeth linear-lanceolate, very acute. Corolla scarcely longer than the calyx. Pods indehiscent, unarmed, $\frac{1}{10}$ in. long, glabrous or pubescent, subglobose, arcuately reticulato-venose, black when ripe. Seed 1, ovoid-oblong, ⅛ in. long, yellowish-brown, smooth. Fl. B. I. v. 2, p. 90; Boiss. Fl. Orient. v. 2, p. 105; Woodr. in Journ. Bomb. Nat. v. 11 (1897) p. 421; Watt, Dict. Econ. Prod. v. 5, p. 199.—Flowers: Mar.

SIND: Sehwan, *Kanitkar*!, *Woodrow*.—DISTRIB. India (N.W.); Orient, Mediterranean, Abyssinia, Afghanistan.

2. **Medicago laciniata,** *All. Fl. Pedem.* v. 1 (1785) p. 316. Annual; stems glabrous, slender, reaching 1 ft. long. Leaves 3-foliolate; petioles ½–1 in. long, slender; stipules laciniate. Leaflets ¼–⅜ in. long, obovate-cuneate, truncate or retuse, sharply dentate or sometimes pinnatifid. Peduncles ½–1 in. long, produced into an awn, 2-flowered; pedicels $\frac{1}{12}$ in. long; bracts minute, subulate. Calyx ⅛ in. long, campanulate, faintly pubescent or glabrous outside; teeth about as long as the tube, triangular, acute. Corolla exserted. Pod globose, of 4–5 spirals, which are armed with long sharp close spines on the margins as well as on the exterior faces. Seeds usually 8–10, about $\frac{1}{6}$–$\frac{1}{8}$ in. long. Fl. B. I. v. 2, p. 90; Aitch. Pb. & Sind Pl. p. 39; Boiss. Fl. Orient. v. 2, p. 104.

SIND: *Stocks*, fide *Aitchison*, Pb. & Sind Pl. p. 39.

This plant has been included on the authority of Aitchison (*l. c.*), who gives it in his list as having been found in Sind by Stocks.—I have seen no specimens from Sind. —DISTRIB. India (Panjab and Salt range); Beluchistan, Egypt, Abyssinia.

3. **Medicago denticulata,** *Willd. Sp. Pl.* v. 3 (1800) p. 1414. Annual. Leaves 3-foliolate; petioles ½–1¾ in. long; stipules laciniate. Leaflets ½–¾ by ⅜–½ in., obovate-cuneate, slightly toothed, somewhat deeply emarginate, mucronate. Peduncles ¼–½ in. long, closely 2–6-flowered, awned; pedicels short. Calyx $\frac{1}{10}$ in. long, glabrous or nearly so outside; teeth lanceolate, slightly shorter than the tube. Corolla twice as long as the calyx. Pods of 2–4 spirals, with spiny margins, the outer face reticulato-venose, ⅛–¼ in. across, not spiny. Seeds about 4–8. Fl. B. I. v. 2, p. 90; Boiss. Fl. Orient. v. 2, p. 102; Woodr. in Journ. Bomb. Nat. v. 11 (1897) p. 421; Watt, Dict. Econ. Prod. v. 5, p. 199.

SIND: Bhubak, *Cooke*!; Sehwan, *Woodrow*.—DISTRIB. India (tropical zone of the North-west); Orient, Abyssinia, Europe, Japan, China, Siberia.

Medicago sativa, Linn., *Lucerne*, is commonly grown throughout the Bombay Presidency, and indeed throughout the greater part of India, as fodder. The flowers are usually purple and the pod forms a double spiral.—VERN. *Vilayti-ghás*; *Lasan-ghás*. See Watt, Dict. Econ. Prod. v. 5, p. 199.

9. LOTUS, Linn.

Herbs. Leaves usually 5- (sometimes 3-) foliolate, the lowest pair of leaflets arising from the base of the petioles like stipules; stipules minute, tuberculiform or 0. Flowers axillary, umbellate or rarely solitary; bracts 3-foliolate, usually stalked. Calyx-lobes subequal or the lowest longest, very rarely more or less connate into 2 lips. Corolla free from the staminal-tube; standard obovate, suborbicular or ovate-acuminate, contracted at the base into a claw; wings obovate; keel incurved, beaked. Stamens diadelphous; alternate filaments dilated at the apex; anthers uniform. Ovary sessile, many-ovulate: style inflexed above the ovary; stigma terminal or lateral. Pod linear, turgid, dehiscent, septate (very rarely continuous) between the seeds.—DISTRIB. Europe, temperate Asia, N. & S. Africa, N. & S.W. America and Australia; species about 50.

Flowers peduncled; corolla twice as long as the calyx .... 1. *L. corniculatus.*
Flowers sessile; corolla scarcely exceeding the calyx .... 2. *L. Garcini.*

1. **Lotus corniculatus,** var. **minor,** *Baker, in Hook. f. Fl. B. I.* v. 2 (1876) p. 91. A perennial herb; rootstock short, cæspitosely branched; stems decumbent, 2–6 in. long, glabrous or slightly pubescent. Leaves 5-foliolate, somewhat fleshy, ⅛–⅜ by $\frac{1}{16}$–⅛ in., sessile, obovate or oblong, subacute, the lower pair of leaflets stipule-like and distant from the other three. Flowers solitary, on a long slender peduncle, each flower subtended by a 3-foliolate leaf or bract. Calyx ⅛ in. long, glabrous or faintly pubescent; teeth equal, linear-subulate from a triangular base, equalling the tube. Corolla twice as long as the calyx. Pods ¾–1 in. long, cylindric, straight. Seeds 20–30. Aitch. Pb. & Sind Pl. p. 39; Woodr. in Journ. Bomb. Nat. v. 11 (1897) p. 421.—Flowers: Jan.–Mar.

SIND: *Stocks*, 680!, *Bhola*!, *Woodrow*.
The variety with solitary flowers seems to be confined to Sind.

2. **Lotus Garcini,** *DC. Prodr.* v. 2 (1825) p. 212. Suffruticose, reaching scarcely 1 ft. high; branches many from a little above the base, covered with short grey silky hairs. Leaves 3- or 5-foliolate; leaflets $\frac{1}{4}$–$\frac{5}{16}$ by $\frac{3}{16}$ in., sessile (3 when the stipule-like pair is absent or 5 when that pair is present), fleshy, pale, obovate-cuneate, obtuse or retuse, clothed on both sides with grey hairs. Flowers sessile, axillary, solitary. Calyx $\frac{1}{4}$–$\frac{5}{16}$ in. long, clothed with long white hairs; teeth linear or linear-lanceolate, twice as long as the tube. Corolla a little longer than the calyx; standard orbicular, clawed. Pods $\frac{3}{8}$–$\frac{7}{16}$ in. long, 1½ times as long as the calyx, glabrous or pubescent, linear, straight, compressed, black when ripe. Seeds about 6. Fl. B. I. v. 2, p. 91; Aitch. Pb. & Sind Pl. p. 40; Woodr. in Journ. Bomb. Nat. v. 11 (1897) p. 421. *Lotus Stocksii*, Boiss. Fl. Orient. v. 2, p. 174.—Flowers: Nov.–Dec.

Gujarat: Porbandar, *Cooke*!, *Woodrow*. Sind: *Vicary*, *Stocks*, 563!; sandy ground near the sea, *Dalzell*, 22!; Jemadar ka Landa (near Karachi), *Stocks*!—Distrib. Through Persia to Nubia.

10. CYAMOPSIS, DC.

Erect herbs with appressed medifixed hairs. Leaves imparipinnate; stipules small, setaceous; leaflets usually 3 (rarely many), exstipellate. Flowers small, purplish, in axillary racemes. Calyx oblique; teeth unequal, the lowest the longest. Corolla caducous; standard obovate, sessile; wings oblong, free from the keel; keel erect, subincurved, obtuse. Stamens monadelphous; anthers uniform, apiculate. Ovary sessile, many-ovulate; style incurved at the apex; stigma capitate. Pod linear, subtetragonous, acuminate, 2-valved, septate between the seeds. Seeds square, compressed.—Distrib. Species 2, one Indian, the other Arabian and Tropical African.

1. **Cyamopsis psoralioides,** *DC. Prodr.* v. 2 (1825) p. 216. An erect annual, 2–3 ft. high, more or less clothed with appressed medifixed greyish hairs; stem grooved. Leaves 3-foliolate; petioles 1–1½ in. long, sparsely hairy; stipules $\frac{1}{4}$–$\frac{3}{8}$ in. long, linear-subulate, persistent. Leaflets 1½–3 by ½–2 in., elliptic, acute, sharply dentate (the teeth usually ending in a weak spine), clothed on both sides with appressed medifixed hairs, base acute; main nerves prominent; petiolules of the lateral leaflets $\frac{1}{8}$ in., those of the terminal one $\frac{1}{4}$–$\frac{1}{2}$ in. long. Flowers small, purplish, in axillary 6–30-flowered close racemes; peduncles and pedicels short, hairy; bracts linear-subulate, persistent, $\frac{3}{16}$ in. long. Calyx hairy outside, $\frac{1}{5}$–$\frac{1}{4}$ in. long to the extremity of the longest tooth; teeth very unequal, the 2 lowest the longest, linear-subulate, the 3 upper shorter, triangular-acute. Corolla slightly longer than the calyx; standard orbicular, shortly clawed. Pods thick, fleshy, subtetragonal, 1½–2 in. long, slightly pubescent. Seeds 5 or 6, square, slightly compressed. Fl. B. I. v. 2, p. 92; Grah. Cat. p. 46; Dalz. & Gibs. Suppl. p. 21; Wight, Icon. t. 248; Woodr. in Journ. Bomb. Nat. v. 11 (1897) p. 421; Watt, Dict. Econ. Prod. v. 2, p. 673.—Flowering time depends on the time of planting. Vern. *Gavdri*; *Matki*.

Cultivated in many parts of India from the Himalayas to Cape Comorin. It is grown as a vegetable for human consumption, the cooked pods being used as food, or as food for cattle when the grain is used as dry, and the whole plant as green fodder. Consult Watt, Dict. Econ. Prod. l. c.—Distrib. Afghanistan.

11. INDIGOFERA, Linn.

Herbs, shrubs or undershrubs often silvery-canescent, more or less densely clothed with appressed medifixed hairs (sometimes mixed with tomentum and laxer hairs). Leaves imparipinnate or simple; stipules usually small, setaceous, very shortly adnate to the petiole; leaflets quite entire, sometimes stipellate. Flowers in axillary racemes or spikes, each flower pedicelled or sessile in the axil of a caducous bract; bracteoles 0. Calyx minute; teeth subequal or the lowest longest. Corolla usually rosy or purple; standard ovate or orbicular, sessile or clawed, often persistent for a long time; wings oblong, slightly adherent to the keel, caducous; keel erect, obtuse or acuminate, spurred on each side near the base, caducous. Stamens diadelphous; anthers uniform, apiculate. Ovary sessile or subsessile, usually many-ovulate; style glabrous; stigma capitate, often penicillate. Pod septate between the seeds, usually linear-cylindric (rarely oblong or globose), turgid, rarely flattish (in *I. echinata* sickle-shaped).—Distrib. Throughout the warmer regions of both hemispheres, abundant in Southern and Tropical Africa; species 250–300.

Leaves simple.
  Pod 1-seeded.
    Pod sickle-shaped, spiny .... 1. *I. echinata.*
    Pod globose, not spiny .... 2. *I. linifolia.*
  Pod 2 (or more) -seeded.
    Pod 2-seeded; leaves ovate, cordate .... 3. *I. cordifolia.*
    Pod 4–6-seeded; leaves oblong, not cordate .... 4. *I. Dalzellii.*
Leaves imparipinnate.
  Flowers in axillary sessile or short-peduncled heads.
    Leaves 3-foliolate; pod 1–2-seeded .... 5. *I. glandulosa.*
    Leaves 5–11-foliolate.
      Pod 3–4-seeded .... 6. *I. trigonelloides.*
      Pod 2-seeded .... 7. *I. enneaphylla.*
  Flowers solitary.
    Herbaceous; stems prostrate .... 8. *I. uniflora.*
    Shrubby; stems erect, rigid .... 9. *I. aspalathoides.*
  Flowers in axillary racemes.
    Pod quite flat and papery .... 10. *I. anabaptista.*
    Pod not flat and not papery.
      Leaflets alternate.
        Leaves argenteo-canescent; pod curved .... 11. *I. paucifolia.*
        Leaves not argenteo-canescent; pod straight .... 12. *I. hendecaphylla.*
      Leaflets opposite.
        Leaflets 3–5.
          Leaflets 3; racemes 6–12-flowered.
            Terminal leaflet sessile .... 13. *I. trifoliata.*
            Terminal leaflet stalked .... 14. *I. trita.*
          Lower leaflets 3, the middle and upper leaflets 5; racemes 12–20-flowered .... 15. *I. articulata.*
          Leaflets 5.
            Pod deflexed .... 16. *I. marginulata.*
            Pod not deflexed .... 17. *I. glabra.*
        Leaflets 7, 9 or 11 (sometimes 13 in *I. tinctoria*).
          Racemes few-flowered.
            Racemes 3–6-flowered; seeds 8–12; pod torulose; hairs of stem not gland-tipped .... 18. *I. tenuifolia.*
          Racemes many-flowered.
            Racemes 6–12-flowered.
              Hairs of stem gland-tipped.
                Seeds 10–12; pod faintly torulose .... 19. *I. viscosa.*

Hairs of stem not gland-tipped.
Seeds 3–8; pod straight, not torulose ... 20. *I. argentea.*
Seeds 15–20; pod recurved at the tip ... 21. *I. parviflora.*
Racemes more than 12-flowered.
Pod cylindric.
Pod thinly hairy, torulose .... 22. *I. Houer.*
Pod glabrous, not torulose .... 23. *I. tinctoria.*
Pod 4-gonous.
Pod densely pubescent, not torulose, deflexed .... 24. *I. hirsuta.*
Pod thinly hairy, torulose, not deflexed ... 25. *I. constricta.*
Leaflets 13–21.
Standard and keel-petals hairy outside .... 26. *I. Wightii.*
Standard and keel-petals glabrous .... 27. *I. pulchella.*

1. **Indigofera echinata,** *Willd. Sp. Pl.* v. 3 (1800) p. 1222. A diffuse annual; stems many, spreading from the base, 1-2 ft. long, 2-edged, glabrous or nearly so. Leaves simple, $\frac{1}{2}$–1 by $\frac{3}{8}$–$\frac{3}{4}$ in., rotund-ovate, very obtuse and usually apiculate at the apex, with a few scattered hairs on both sides; petioles $\frac{1}{16}$–$\frac{1}{12}$ in. long; stipules $\frac{1}{10}$ in. long, linear-subulate. Flowers in axillary 6–10-flowered racemes; peduncles $\frac{3}{8}$–$\frac{7}{8}$ in. long. Calyx hairy, $\frac{1}{10}$ in. long; teeth lanceolate, acute, many times longer than the tube. Corolla pink, slightly longer than the calyx. Pods $\frac{1}{4}$ in. long, semilunate, compressed, beaked with the persistent style, furnished with several rows of divaricate hooked bristles along the ventral suture. Seed 1. Fl. B. I. v. 2, p. 92; Dalz. & Gibs. p. 57; Trim. Fl. Ceyl. v. 2, p. 21; Wight, Icon. t. 316; Woodr. in Journ. Bomb. Nat. v. 11 (1897) p. 421.—Flowers: Aug.-Dec.

Dalzell characterises the plant as "*very common,*" but I have not found it so. My experience is that it is rare. KONKAN: *Law*!, *Stocks*!—DISTRIB. India (W. Peninsula); Ceylon, Guinea.

2. **Indigofera linifolia,** *Retz. Obs. Bot.* fasc. 4 (1786) p. 29 & fasc. 6 (1791) t. 2. Annual; stems numerous, much-branched, 6-18 in. long, somewhat 2-edged, silvery-white with appressed hairs. Leaves numerous, simple, $\frac{1}{2}$–1 by $\frac{1}{16}$–$\frac{1}{10}$ in., linear, acute at both ends, mucronate, silvery on both surfaces with appressed hairs; petioles 0–$\frac{1}{16}$ in. long; stipules minute, setaceous. Flowers 6–12, in dense sessile or very shortly peduncled axillary racemes. Calyx $\frac{1}{10}$ in. long, very deeply cut, clothed with silvery hairs; teeth linear-subulate, many times longer than the tube. Corolla bright red, 2–3 times as long as the calyx. Pod $\frac{1}{16}$–$\frac{1}{12}$ in. long, globose, apiculate, glistening-white with appressed silky hairs. Seed 1. Fl. B. I. v. 2, p. 92; Grah. Cat. p. 46; Dalz. & Gibs. p. 58; Wight, Icon. t. 313; Trim. Fl. Ceyl. v. 2, p. 22; Woodr. in Journ. Bomb. Nat. v. 11 (1897) p. 421; Watt, Dict. Econ. Prod. v. 4, p. 386.—Flowers: July-Oct. VERN. *Pandarphalli.*

KONKAN: Oorun, *Stocks*! DECCAN: Poona, *Cooke*!; Ahmednagar, *Cooke*! S. M. COUNTRY: Belgaum, *Ritchie*, 640!—DISTRIB. Throughout India; Ceylon, Afghanistan, Abyssinia, N. Australia.

VAR. *Campbellii*, Wight. Leaves ovate-elliptic, subacute, or obovate, obtuse, $\frac{1}{4}$–$\frac{1}{2}$ by $\frac{3}{16}$–$\frac{1}{4}$ in.

DECCAN: Poona, *Woodrow*, 317!; Ahmednagar, *Cooke*! GUJARAT: Ankleshwar. *Kanitkar*!

3. **Indigofera cordifolia,** *Heyne, ex Roth. Nov. Pl. Sp.* (1821) p. 357. A diffuse copiously branched annual, usually more or less clothed with long white hairs; stems 3–9 in. long, the young ones pubescent, the older nearly glabrous. Leaves simple, $\frac{1}{4}$–$\frac{5}{8}$ by $\frac{1}{8}$–$\frac{1}{2}$ in., subsessile, broadly ovate-cordate, subobtuse, mucronate, hairy on both sides, very densely so beneath; stipules minute, setaceous. Flowers in dense subsessile 4-8-flowered heads. Calyx $\frac{1}{8}$ in. long, hairy outside; tube very short; teeth linear, acute, very hairy. Corolla bright red, not exserted; standard spathulate. Pods cylindric, oblong, straight, $\frac{1}{4}$ in. long (including the straight beak), densely pubescent. Seeds 2, yellow. Fl. B. I. v. 2, p. 93; Dalz. & Gibs. p. 58; Aitch. Pb. & Sind Pl. p. 40; Woodr. in Journ. Bomb. Nat. v. 11 (1897) p. 421; Watt, Dict. Econ. Prod. v. 4, p. 385.—Flowers: Aug.–Dec. VERN. *Godadi*; *Bechka.*

Common. KONKAN: *Law*!, *Stocks*!; Oorun, *Stocks*! DECCAN: Poona, *Woodrow*!, *Cooke*! S. M. COUNTRY: Padshapur, *Ritchie*, 1692!; Badami, *Cooke*! SIND: *Woodrow*; Karachi, *Stocks*!—DISTRIB. Throughout India; Afghanistan, Beluchistan, N. Australia.

4. **Indigofera Dalzellii,** *T. Cooke.* Perennial, more or less silvery-canescent; stems many from a woody root, prostrate, ascending at the apex, flexuous, acutely triquetrous. Leaves simple, subsessile, $\frac{1}{2}$–$\frac{3}{4}$ by $\frac{3}{16}$–$\frac{3}{8}$ in., elliptic-oblong, subacute, mucronate, glabrous above, hairy beneath, base acute; stipules subulate from a triangular base, persistent. Flowers in axillary 12–20-flowered racemes which are 3 to 4 times as long as the leaves; rhachis acutely triquetrous, glabrous; pedicels deflexed in fruit; bracts minute, ovate, acuminate. Calyx $\frac{1}{10}$–$\frac{1}{8}$ in. long; tube scarcely any; teeth triangular, very acute. Corolla purple, twice as long as the calyx; standard orbicular, hairy on the back. Pods $\frac{1}{2}$–$\frac{7}{8}$ by $\frac{1}{10}$ in., linear, 4-gonous, beaked, glabrous, shortly 4-winged. Seeds 4–6. *Indigofera triquetra*, Dalz. in Hook. Kew Journ. v. 2 (1850) p. 36; Fl. B. I. v. 2, p. 93; Dalz. & Gibs. p. 58; Woodr. in Journ. Bomb. Nat. v. 11 (1897) p. 421.—Flowers: July–Sept.

The name *I. triquetra* was given to a wholly different species (a S. African plant) by E. Meyer in 1836 (Comm. p. 95), and, as Dalzell named his species in 1850, the other has priority.—I have therefore named this *I. Dalzellii.*

A rare plant, apparently endemic in the Bombay Presidency. KONKAN: *Stocks*!; rocky hills in the Malwan district, *Dalzell & Gibson.* DECCAN: Panchgani, *Woodrow*!, *Cooke*!, *Raoji*!

The plant is abundant on the rocky table-land above the traveller's bungalow at Panchgani, where it grows all over the bare rocks. Dalzell found it growing on rocks near Malwan, so that it apparently flourishes on rocky ground.

5. **Indigofera glandulosa,** *Willd. Sp. Pl.* v. 3 (1800) p. 1227. Annual, 9–20 in. high, much-branched; branches long, slender, clothed with spreading hairs when young, not at all argenteo-canescent. Leaves 3-foliolate; petioles $\frac{3}{8}$–$\frac{1}{2}$ in. long, slender, hairy; stipules setaceous, minute. Leaflets $\frac{1}{2}$–1 by $\frac{1}{4}$–$\frac{1}{2}$ in., oblanceolate, rounded or slightly retuse, apiculate, green and with a few appressed hairs above, glaucous, appressedly hairy and copiously nigro-punctate beneath; petiolules of the lateral leaflets $\frac{1}{20}$–$\frac{1}{16}$ in. long, those of the terminal leaflets longer. Flowers in short axillary sessile heads $\frac{1}{4}$–$\frac{3}{8}$ in. long. Calyx $\frac{1}{12}$–$\frac{1}{10}$ in. long, hairy outside; teeth long, setaceous. Corolla 2–3 times as long

as the calyx. Pods $\frac{1}{5}$ in. long, pubescent, angled, the angles slightly winged and often toothed. Seeds 1–2, spherical, smooth and polished, sometimes mottled. Fl. B. I. v. 2, p. 94; Dalz. & Gibs. p. 58; Woodr. in Journ. Bomb. Nat. v. 11 (1897) p. 421; Watt, Dict. Econ. Prod. v. 4, p. 386.—Flowers: Aug.-Dec. VERN. *Barbadá.*

A common weed. KONKAN: *Stocks*!; Elephanta (Bombay), *Stocks*! DECCAN: *Woodrow*; Poona, *Cooke*!, *Woodrow*! S. M. COUNTRY: Belgaum, *Ritchie*, 1038!—DISTRIB. India (W. Peninsula and Bandelkhand).

6. **Indigofera trigonelloides,** *Jaub. & Spach. Illustr.* v. 5 (1857) p. 92, t. 482. Annual, densely silvery; stems many, cæspitose, trailing, much-branched, 6–15 in. long, trigonous, clothed with appressed silvery hairs and a few spreading ones. Leaves 5–7-foliolate; petioles $\frac{3}{16}$–$\frac{3}{8}$ in. long, hairy; stipules linear, acute, hairy. Leaflets alternate, $\frac{1}{4}$–$\frac{3}{8}$ by $\frac{1}{8}$–$\frac{3}{16}$ in., oblanceolate or elliptic, rounded at the apex, densely clothed on both sides with silvery appressed hairs, base acute; petiolules of the lateral leaflets 0–$\frac{1}{16}$ in., those of the terminal leaflets $\frac{1}{8}$ in. long. Flowers in dense sessile villous heads, each consisting of 12–20 sessile flowers; bract minute, ovate-lanceolate, acute, hairy. Calyx $\frac{1}{8}$–$\frac{3}{16}$ in. long; teeth long, linear, acute, hairy. Corolla red, scarcely exserted. Pods $\frac{1}{4}$ in. long, linear-cylindric, straight, silvery-hairy, torulose. Seeds 3–4. Fl. B. I. v. 2, p. 94; Woodr. in Journ. Bomb. Nat. v. 11 (1897) p. 421.

Confined to Sind; a rare plant. SIND: *Cooke*!, *Woodrow*!; Jemadar ka Landa (near Karachi), *Stocks*!; Boogta hills, *Vicary*!; Karachi to Mugger Peer, *Perry*!—DISTRIB. India (Panjab); Afghanistan, Abyssinia, Aden.

7. **Indigofera enneaphylla,** *Linn. Mantiss.* v. 2 (1771) p. 571. Annual or biennial; rootstock woody; stems densely cæspitose, 1–1$\frac{1}{2}$ ft. long, trailing, prostrate but not rooting, much-branched, terete or somewhat angled, sparsely clothed with white appressed hair. Leaves $\frac{1}{2}$–$\frac{3}{4}$ in. long, 7–9- (rarely 11-) foliolate, nearly sessile; stipules scarious, $\frac{1}{5}$–$\frac{1}{4}$ in. long, ovate, long-cuspidate. Flowers small, in short-peduncled 10–20-flowered spicate heads about $\frac{1}{2}$ in. long; pedicels almost 0; bracts scarious, $\frac{1}{10}$ in. long, ovate, acuminate, persistent. Calyx $\frac{1}{8}$–$\frac{1}{6}$ in. long, hairy outside; teeth long, setaceous. Corolla bright red, slightly exserted. Pods $\frac{1}{8}$–$\frac{1}{6}$ in. long, cylindric, oblong, more or less clothed with white appressed hair. Seeds 2, globose. Fl. B. I. v. 2, p. 94; Dalz. & Gibs. p. 58; Trim. Fl. Ceyl. v. 2, p. 22; Woodr. in Journ. Bomb. Nat. v. 11 (1897) p. 421; Watt, Dict. Econ. Prod. v. 4, p. 385. *I. semitrijuga*, Forsk. Fl. Ægypt.-Arab. p. 137 (*not* of Baker, in Hook. f. Fl. B. I.).—Flowers: Oct. VERN. *Bhuiguli.*

KONKAN: *Stocks*! DECCAN: Bijapur, *Woodrow*. S. M. COUNTRY: Badami, *Woodrow*!, *Bhiva*! GUJARAT: Baroda, *Kanitkar*!; Surat, *Dalzell & Gibson*.—DISTRIB. Throughout the plains of India; Ceylon, Angola, Malay Islands, N. Australia.

8. **Indigofera uniflora,** *Buch.-Ham.* ex *Roxb. Hort. Beng.* (1814) p. 57: *Fl. Ind.* v. 3, p. 374. Perennial; stems herbaceous, very slender, much-branched, prostrate, terete, glabrous or with a few appressed hairs, purple. Leaves sessile, 3–7- (rarely 1-) foliolate, usually digitate; stipules very minute, caducous. Leaflets $\frac{1}{8}$–$\frac{3}{8}$ in. long, pale green, narrow-linear, subacute and with a few appressed hairs. Flowers solitary, on long filiform pedicels which are longer than the leaves and equal in length to the pods; bracts on the pedicel a little below the flower,

minute. Calyx $\frac{1}{16}$ in. long; teeth long, linear, acute. Corolla red, $\frac{1}{8}$ in. long. Pods $\frac{3}{8}$–$\frac{1}{2}$ in. long, linear, straight, glabrous. Seeds 4–7, cubical, yellowish-brown, smooth. Fl. B. I. v. 2, p. 94; Dalz. & Gibs. p. 58; Wight, Icon. t. 333; Woodr. in Journ. Bomb. Nat. v. 11 (1897) p. 421.—Flowers: Oct.

A rare plant in the Bombay Presidency. S. M. COUNTRY: *Law ex Dalzell & Gibson*; Belgaum hills, *Ritchie*, 1028! KANARA: *Stocks*!—DISTRIB. India (W. Peninsula and Carnatic).

9. **Indigofera aspalathoides,** *Vahl, ex DC. Prodr.* v. 2 (1825) p. 231. A low much-branched erect undershrub; branches rigid, terete, divaricately spreading, the young ones argenteo-canescent, the hairs soon falling off, the older ones purple and nearly glabrous. Leaves 1–5-(often 3-) foliolate, digitate, sessile, crowded on the young branches, but soon deciduous; stipules minute, subulate. Leaflets $\frac{1}{10}$–$\frac{1}{4}$ in. long, sessile, linear or oblanceolate, apiculate, rather fleshy, with a few white appressed hairs. Flowers solitary, axillary; pedicels filiform, longer than the leaves, but shorter than the pods. Calyx $\frac{1}{16}$ in. long; teeth linear-subulate. Corolla dark pink, exserted. Pods $\frac{1}{2}$–$\frac{5}{8}$ in. long, somewhat turgid, straight, glabrous or with a few scattered hairs. Seeds 6–8. Fl. B. I. v. 2, p. 94; Dalz. & Gibs. p. 58; Trim. Fl. Ceyl. v. 2, p. 23; Wight, Icon. t. 332; Watt, Dict. Econ. Prod. v. 4, p. 384.

S. M. COUNTRY: near Belgaum, *Dalzell & Gibson*.—DISTRIB. India (plains of the Carnatic); Ceylon.

This plant has been included on the authority of Dalzell & Gibson (Bo. Fl. l. c.). Dalzell & Gibson, who describe the plant accurately, say that it is "common in the Deccan," which must, I think, be a mistake. I have lived in the Deccan for 25 years and have largely collected plants therein, but I have never found it, nor, as far as I know, has it been found in the Bombay Presidency by any other collectors. It does not appear in Woodrow's list in the Journal of the Bombay Natural History Society, nor are there any specimens from the Bombay Presidency in Herb. Kew.

10. **Indigofera anabaptista,** *Steud. Nom.* ed. 2 (1840) p. 805. A diffuse annual; stems 12–15 in. long; branches numerous, slender, grooved, glabrous or nearly so. Leaves 1–1$\frac{1}{2}$ in. long; petioles $\frac{1}{4}$–$\frac{1}{2}$ in. long; stipules $\frac{1}{6}$ in. long, filiform, persistent. Leaflets 5, opposite, $\frac{1}{2}$–$\frac{3}{4}$ by $\frac{3}{16}$–$\frac{5}{16}$ in., oblanceolate, rounded, apiculate, clothed with white appressed hairs on both surfaces, base acute; petiolules of the lateral leaflets $\frac{1}{20}$ in., those of the terminal ones $\frac{3}{16}$ in. long. Flowers in short-peduncled 12–20-flowered racemes, which are shorter than the leaves; pedicels short; bracts lanceolate. Calyx $\frac{1}{8}$ in. long, densely hairy; tube very short; teeth long, linear-subulate. Corolla slightly exserted; standard oblong, hairy on the back. Pods linear, quite flat, $\frac{1}{2}$–$\frac{3}{4}$ in. long by $\frac{1}{8}$ in. broad, much recurved, deflexed, clothed with white appressed hairs, with a raised longitudinal ridge along the centre of each of the flattened faces and a transverse ridge between each of the seeds. Seeds $\frac{1}{12}$ in. in diam., discoid, pale brown. Fl. B. I. v. 2, p. 102; Woodr. in Journ. Bomb. Nat. v. 11 (1897) p. 421.—Flowers: Aug.–Oct.

A very rare plant, confined (in India) to Sind and the Panjab. SIND: *Cooke*!, *Puran*!; Mulir near Karachi, *Woodrow*!—DISTRIB. Afghanistan, Arabia.

11. **Indigofera paucifolia,** *Delile, Fl. d'Egypte* (1812) p. 251. A shrub 3–6 ft. high; branches numerous, stout, woody, argenteo-canescent. Leaves imparipinnate; petioles $\frac{1}{4}$–$\frac{1}{3}$ in. long; stipules $\frac{1}{8}$ in. long, lanceolate,

acuminate. Leaflets 3-5, alternate, $\frac{5}{8}$-1 by $\frac{1}{4}$-$\frac{1}{2}$ in., oblanceolate or elliptic-oblong, more or less hairy above, hoary with dense fine white hairs beneath, base acute; petiolules of lateral leaflets $\frac{1}{20}$ in., those of the terminal $\frac{1}{4}$ in. long. Flowers small, in long spicate 20-50-flowered racemes reaching 4 in. long, rather close, longer than the leaves; pedicels short. Calyx $\frac{1}{12}$ in. long, silvery outside; teeth as long as the tube, triangular, acute. Corolla red, thrice as long as the calyx; standard $\frac{3}{8}$ in. long, densely hairy on the back. Pods numerous, along the whole length of the rhachis, $\frac{1}{2}$-$\frac{3}{4}$ in. long, slightly curved outwards, torulose, hoary when young with a fine appressed pubescence. Seeds 6-8, oblong, obtusely 4-gonous, truncate at one end. Fl. B. I. v. 2, p. 97; Aitch. Pb. & Sind Pl. p. 41; Trim. Fl. Ceyl. v. 2, p. 25; Talb. Trees, Bomb. p. 67; Woodr. in Journ. Bomb. Nat. v. 11 (1897) p. 421; Watt, Dict. Econ. Prod. v. 4, p. 386.—Flowers: Sept.-Nov.

Tolerably common in Gujarat and Sind. GUJARAT: Surat, *Dalzell & Gibson*; Baroda, *Kanitkar*!; Dakor, *Woodrow*. SIND: *Cooke*!, *Vicary*!, *Woodrow*, *Puran*!; Karachi to Mugger Peer, *Perry*!—DISTRIB. Throughout the plains of India; Ceylon, Beluchistan, Arabia, Java, Tropical Africa.

12. **Indigofera hendecaphylla,** *Jacquin, Collect.* v. 2 (1788) p. 358, & *Icon. Plant. Rar.* t. 570. Herbaceous, procumbent; stems 1-2 ft. long, trailing, glabrous or with a few appressed hairs. Leaves nearly sessile, 1-2$\frac{1}{2}$ in. long; stipules scarious, $\frac{1}{4}$-$\frac{1}{3}$ in. long, lanceolate, cuspidate. Leaflets 5-11, alternate, $\frac{1}{2}$-1 by $\frac{1}{16}$-$\frac{3}{8}$ in., oblanceolate, rounded, apiculate, with appressed grey hairs on both surfaces, glaucous beneath, base acute; petiolules of lateral leaflets $\frac{1}{20}$-$\frac{1}{16}$ in., those of the terminal $\frac{1}{12}$-$\frac{1}{8}$ in. long. Flowers in close many-flowered usually peduncled racemes 1-4$\frac{1}{2}$ in. long; pedicels very short. Calyx $\frac{1}{8}$ in. long, hairy; teeth lanceolate-subulate, very long. Corolla twice as long as the calyx. Pods numerous, imbricately deflexed, $\frac{3}{4}$-1$\frac{1}{4}$ in. long, 4-gonous, straight, pointed, not reflexed at the tip, nearly sessile, with a few appressed white hairs, not torulose. Seeds 6-10, oblong, 4-gonous, truncate at both ends. *Indigofera endecaphylla*, Bot. Reg. t. 789; DC. Prodr. v. 2, p. 228; Fl. B. I. v. 2, p. 98; Woodr. in Journ. Bomb. Nat. v. 11 (1897) p. 421. *I. Kleinii*, W. & A. Prodr. p. 204; Dalz. & Gibs. p. 60.—Flowers: Oct.-Nov.

KONKAN: *Stocks*! DECCAN: Panchgani Ghát, *Cooke*!, *Woodrow*; Ambhil Odha, *Kanitkar*! S. M. COUNTRY: Belgaum, *Ritchie*, 167!, *Dalzell & Gibson*; Dharwar, *Ritchie*, 167! KANARA: *Stocks*!—DISTRIB. India (W. Peninsula, Birma); Tropical Africa, Cape, China.

13. **Indigofera trifoliata,** *Linn. Amœn. Acad.* v. 4 (1759) p. 327. Perennial, somewhat shrubby; stems much branched, 1-2 ft. long; young branches with scattered white appressed hairs, soon glabrescent. Leaves membranous, subdigitately 3-foliolate; petioles $\frac{1}{4}$-$\frac{1}{2}$ in. long, slender; stipules small, setaceous. Leaflets $\frac{3}{8}$-1 by $\frac{1}{4}$-$\frac{3}{8}$ in., oblanceolate, rounded and minutely apiculate at the apex, sparingly clothed with white appressed hairs above, more densely hairy, nigro-punctate and glaucous beneath; petiolules of the lateral leaflets $\frac{1}{16}$ in. long, the terminal leaflets sessile or nearly so. Flowers small, in congested sessile, 6-12-flowered racemes, which are usually shorter than the leaves; pedicels very short. Calyx $\frac{1}{8}$ in. long, hairy outside; teeth lanceolate-subulate. Corolla dark pink, nearly twice as long as the calyx; standard

$\frac{1}{4}$ by $\frac{1}{10}$ in., oblong-obovate, densely hairy on the back. Pods deflexed, $\frac{1}{2}$-$\frac{3}{4}$ in. long, straight, somewhat 4-gonous, thinly hairy, with 4 narrow wings one at each side of the suture, and with a few scattered white hairs, not torulose. Seeds 6-8. Fl. B. I. v. 2, p. 96; Dalz. & Gibs. p. 59; Trim. Fl. Ceyl. v. 2, p. 24; Wight, Icon. t. 314; Woodr. in Journ. Bomb. Nat. v. 11 (1897) p. 421.—Flowers: Aug.-Oct.

Konkan: *Stocks*!; Parel (Bombay), *Ranade*!, *Woodrow*!; Chiplun, *Woodrow*; Ambeghát, *Bhiva*! Deccan: Poona, *Cooke*! S. M. Country: Belgaum, *Ritchie*, 168! Gujarat: Domas, *Dalzell*!—Distrib. Throughout India; Ceylon, Java, China, Philippines, N. Australia.

14. **Indigofera trita,** *Linn. f. Suppl. Pl.* (1781) p. 335. An undershrub 2-3 ft. high; branches hoary with fine appressed hairs. Leaves 3-foliolate; petioles $\frac{1}{4}$-$\frac{1}{2}$ in. long; stipules small, setaceous. Leaflets: the lateral ones opposite, nearly sessile, $\frac{1}{2}$-$\frac{7}{8}$ by $\frac{1}{4}$-$\frac{1}{2}$ in.; the terminal stalked, $\frac{3}{4}$-$1\frac{1}{2}$ by $\frac{3}{8}$-$\frac{7}{8}$ in., all obovate-oblong, slightly emarginate, clothed with fine appressed grey hairs, base acute. Flowers small, in short sessile or stalked 6-12-flowered spicate racemes, which are shorter than the leaves. Calyx $\frac{1}{8}$ in. long, hairy outside; teeth linear-lanceolate. Corolla salmon-colored, $\frac{1}{4}$ in. long; standard orbicular, hairy on the back. Pods divaricate or sometimes deflexed, rigid, straight, 4-gonous, spine-pointed, not torulose, silvery with fine appressed hairs. Seeds 6-10, oblong, truncate at both ends. Fl. B. I. v. 2, p. 96: Grah. Cat. p. 46; Dalz. & Gibs. p. 60; Wight, Icon. tt. 315, 386; Trim. Fl. Ceyl. v. 2, p. 25; Woodr. in Journ. Bomb. Nat. v. 11 (1897) p. 421.—Flowers: Feb.-Mar.

Deccan: Poona, *Cooke*!, *Woodrow*!; Talegaon (Poona dists.), *Bhiva*! Gujarat: Nausári, *Kanitkar*! S. M. Country: Belgaum hills, *Ritchie*, 1165!—Distrib. Throughout India; Ceylon, Tropical Africa, Malay Islands, N. Australia.

15. **Indigofera articulata,** *Goüan, Illustr. et Obs.* (1773) p. 49. A shrub 2-3 ft. high; stem and branches argenteo-canescent, more or less angled. Leaves 1-2 in. long; petioles $\frac{1}{4}$-$\frac{1}{2}$ in. long; stipules minute, subulate. Leaflets 3-5, very rarely 7 (those of the lower leaves usually 3, those of the middle and upper leaves usually 5, the terminal leaflet the largest), $\frac{1}{2}$-1 by $\frac{3}{8}$-$\frac{5}{8}$ in., obovate, rounded and apiculate at the apex, argenteo-canescent on both surfaces, base cuneate; petiolules of the lateral leaflets $\frac{1}{30}$ in., those of the terminal $\frac{1}{8}$-$\frac{1}{4}$ in. long. Flowers in short-peduncled or subsessile 12-20-flowered racemes shorter than the leaves; pedicels short, slender. Calyx $\frac{1}{20}$ in. long, silvery-hairy; teeth triangular, acute, rather shorter than the tube. Corolla $\frac{1}{6}$ in. long; standard pubescent on the back. Pods $\frac{3}{8}$ in. long, thick, turgid, recurved, shortly mucronate, silvery-canescent when young, finally glabrescent, torulose. Seeds 2-4 (commonly 3). *Indigofera argentea*, Linn. Mantiss. p. 273; Fl. B. I. v. 2, p. 98; Aitch. Pb. & Sind Pl. p. 40; Boiss. Fl. Orient. v. 2, p. 190; Talb. Trees, Bomb. p. 67; Woodr. in Journ. Bomb. Nat. v. 11 (1897) p. 421; Watt, Dict. Econ. Prod. v. 4, p. 383. *I. spicata*, Forsk. Fl. Ægypt.-Arab. p. 138.—Flowers: Nov.-Dec. Vern. *Karumili*.

The name *I. argentea* was given in 1768 by Burmann (Fl. Ind. p. 171) to a Persian plant and is therefore earlier than that of Linnæus (1771) As to the plant intended by Burmann, De Candolle indentifies it with *I. semitrijuga*, var. β, *tetrasperma*, DC., and the actual specimen in Herb.

Burm. has been seen and verified by him (Prodr. v. 2, p. 230). There is no doubt whatever that the plant described above is *I. articulata* of Goüan, whose description is full and accurate, while the figure by Zanoni (Rar. Stirp. Hist. [1742] p. 18, t. 12), quoted by Goüan, correctly represents it.

Chiefly confined to Sind, rare in the Deccan. DECCAN: Poona, *Woodrow*. SIND: *Stocks*, 488!, *Puran*!—DISTRIB. Arabia, Egypt, Abyssinia, cultivated for the indigo it produces.

16. **Indigofera marginulata,** *Grah. in Wall. Cat.* (1828) 5467. Suffruticose; stem and branches angled, thinly clothed with appressed grey hairs. Leaves imparipinnate; stipules setaceous, $\frac{1}{16}$ in. long. Leaflets 5, opposite, $\frac{3}{8}$-$\frac{5}{8}$ by $\frac{3}{16}$-$\frac{5}{16}$, elliptic or oblanceolate, apiculate, sparsely clothed on both surfaces with appressed white hairs; petiolules of lateral leaflets $\frac{1}{32}$ in., those of the terminal $\frac{1}{8}$ in. long. Flowers in elongate lax racemes reaching 4 in. long, exceeding the leaves. Calyx $\frac{1}{8}$ in. long, hairy outside; teeth much longer than the tube, lanceolate-subulate. Corolla twice as long as the calyx. Pods straight, pointed, deflexed, $\frac{3}{4}$-1 in. long, sparsely clothed with appressed white hairs, sutures margined, valves rounded, not torulose. Seeds 5-6, oblong, obtusely 4-gonous, truncate at one end, rounded at the other. Fl. B. I. v. 2, p. 97.

Very rare. I have seen only one specimen marked KONKAN: *Stocks*!—DISTRIB. India (Carnatic, Dindigul hills).

17. **Indigofera glabra,** *Linn. Sp. Pl.* (1753) p. 751. Annual, 1-3 ft. high; branches numerous, ascending, glabrous or with a few spreading deciduous eglandular hairs. Leaves $\frac{3}{4}$-$1\frac{1}{4}$ in. long; stipules $\frac{3}{16}$ in. long, lanceolate, very acute, hairy, persistent. Leaflets 5, opposite, thin, $\frac{3}{16}$-$\frac{1}{2}$ by $\frac{1}{8}$-$\frac{3}{8}$, obovate-elliptic, obtuse, apiculate, more or less appressedly hairy on both surfaces, the lateral leaflets shortly petioluled, the terminal with a petiolule $\frac{1}{8}$-$\frac{1}{4}$ in. long. Flowers small, in 2-4-flowered short axillary racemes; peduncles slender; pedicels short. Calyx $\frac{1}{10}$ in. long, hairy outside; teeth subulate. Corolla red, $\frac{1}{8}$ in. long. Pods $\frac{3}{4}$-1 in. long, straight, subcylindric or obscurely 4-gonous, glabrous, not torulose. Seeds 10-12, cubical. Trim. Fl. Ceyl. v. 2, p. 23. *I. pentaphylla*, Murr. Syst. Veg. ed. 13 (1774) p. 564 (*not* of Burch.); Fl. B. I. v. 2, p. 95; Wight, Icon. t. 385; Woodr. in Journ. Bomb. Nat. v. 11 (1897) p. 421.—Flowers: Oct.

A rare plant. The only specimens from the Bombay Presidency that I have seen were collected by Woodrow at Badami in the S. M. Country, where it seems to be fairly abundant.—DISTRIB. Throughout India; Tropical Africa.

18. **Indigofera tenuifolia,** *Rottl. ex Wight & Arn. Prodr.* (1834) p. 200. Herbaceous, diffuse, 6-8 in. high; branches numerous, spreading or ascending, slender, glabrous or more or less clothed with appressed hairs. Leaves short-petioled, $\frac{3}{4}$-1 in. long; stipules setaceous, very minute. Leaflets 7-9, opposite, oblanceolate or linear-obovate, $\frac{1}{4}$-$\frac{3}{8}$ by $\frac{1}{8}$ in., apiculate, clothed with appressed white hairs on both surfaces; petiolules of the lateral leaflets $\frac{1}{20}$-$\frac{1}{16}$ in. long, those of the terminal slightly longer. Flowers small, in short 3-6-flowered racemes usually longer than the leaves; peduncles filiform; pedicels short. Calyx $\frac{1}{12}$ in. long, hairy: teeth setaceous, scarcely longer than the tube. Corolla

$\frac{1}{8}$ in. long, bright red. Pods $\frac{3}{4}$-1 in. long, straight, linear, subcylindric or compressed, distinctly torulose. Seeds 10–12, oblong, truncate at both ends, punctate, black when ripe. Fl. B. I. v. 2, p. 95; Dalz. & Gibs. p. 58; Trim. Fl. Ceyl. v. 2, p. 24.—Flowers: Sept.–Oct.

KONKAN: *Stocks*! S. M. COUNTRY: Padshapur, *Ritchie*, 1097!; Badami, *Cooke*!, *Woodrow*! GUJARAT: Ankleshwar near Broach, *Dalzell & Gibson*. SIND: *Bhola*!—DISTRIB. India (W. Peninsula); Ceylon.

19. **Indigofera viscosa,** *Lamk. Encyc. Méthod.* v. 3 (1789) p. 247. Annual, 1–3 ft. high; branches numerous, densely clothed with minute viscous gland-tipped hairs. Leaves $\frac{3}{4}$-1$\frac{3}{4}$ in. long; petioles $\frac{1}{2}$ in. long, glandular-hairy; stipules $\frac{1}{8}$-$\frac{3}{16}$ in. long, filiform. Leaflets 7–11 (usually 11), $\frac{5}{16}$-$\frac{3}{8}$ by $\frac{1}{8}$ in., opposite, obovate-elliptic, obtuse, apiculate, sparsely clothed with white appressed hairs above, more densely so beneath. Flowers small, in glandular 6–12-flowered racemes nearly as long as the leaves. Calyx $\frac{1}{10}$ in. long, hairy; teeth setaceous, about equalling the tube. Corolla pink, $\frac{1}{8}$ in. long. Pods $\frac{3}{4}$-1 in. long, straight, subcylindric, faintly torulose, clothed with gland-tipped as well as with appressed white hairs. Fl. B. I. v. 2, p. 95; Trim. Fl. Ceyl. v. 2, p. 24; Aitch. Pb. & Sind Pl. p. 41.

A rare plant in the Bombay Presidency. SIND: *Dalzell*!, *Vicary* ex *Aitch.* l. c.—DISTRIB. Sparingly throughout India; Ceylon.

20. **Indigofera argentea,** *Burm. Fl. Ind.* (1768) p. 171 (*not* of Linn.). A low diffusely-branched argenteo-canescent undershrub reaching 2 ft. high; branches numerous, slender, terete, silvery-canescent. Leaves $\frac{3}{8}$-1 in. long; petioles $\frac{3}{16}$-$\frac{3}{8}$ in. long; stipules minute, setaceous. Leaflets 7–9 (rarely 11), subsessile (except the terminal one), broadly obovate, rounded at the apex, densely clothed with long silvery appressed hairs, base cuneate. Flowers in lax 6–12-flowered peduncled racemes which are usually longer than the leaves; pedicels very short. Calyx $\frac{1}{12}$ in. long, canescent; teeth linear-lanceolate, as long as the tube. Corolla rather more than twice as long as the calyx; standard orbicular, $\frac{1}{6}$ in. long, silvery-pubescent on the back. Pods $\frac{3}{8}$-$\frac{1}{2}$ in. long, turgid, clothed with white appressed hairs, shortly mucronate, not torulose. Seeds 4–6. *Indigofera semitrijuga*, var. *tetrasperma*, DC. Prodr. v. 2, p. 230. *I. semitrijuga*, Baker, in Hook. f. Fl. B. I. v. 2, p. 98 (*not* of Forsk.); Aitch. Pb. & Sind Pl. p. 41.

The name *I. argentea* was given by Burmann in 1768, and is therefore prior to the name *I. argentea* given by Linnæus (Mantiss. [1771] p. 273) to a different plant. The plant described by Burmann has been identified by De Candolle, from actual examination of Burmann's specimens, as *I. semitrijuga*, var. *tetrasperma*, DC. (See under n. 15, *I. articulata* preceding.) *I. semitrijuga*, Forsk., is *I. enneaphylla*, Linn.

A rare plant. SIND: Jemadar ka Landa near Karachi, *Stocks*!; sandy soil near the sea, *Stocks*, 562!—DISTRIB. Egypt, Arabia, Abyssinia.

21. **Indigofera parviflora,** *Heyne, in Wall. Cat.* (1828) 5457. A much-branched annual, 1–2$\frac{1}{2}$ ft. high; stems and branches slender, grooved or angled, more or less argenteo-canescent. Leaves 1$\frac{1}{2}$-2 in. long; petioles $\frac{1}{4}$-$\frac{1}{2}$ in. long; stipules minute, setaceous. Leaflets opposite, 7–9, membranous, $\frac{3}{4}$-1 by $\frac{1}{8}$-$\frac{3}{8}$ in., linear-oblong, elliptic-oblong or oblanceolate, rounded or subacute, shortly apiculate, thinly argenteo-

canescent; petiolules of lateral leaflets about $\frac{1}{20}$ in., those of the terminal about $\frac{1}{8}$ in. long. Flowers in short close sessile 6–12-flowered racemes shorter than the leaves; pedicels very short. Calyx $\frac{1}{12}$–$\frac{1}{8}$ in. long, hairy; teeth linear-lanceolate, longer than the tube. Corolla lilac, $\frac{1}{4}$ in. long. Pods linear, 1–1$\frac{3}{8}$ in. long, clothed with appressed white hairs, straight, pointed, recurved at the tip, deflexed, not torulose. Seeds 15–20, truncate at both ends. Fl. B. I. v. 2, p. 97; W. & A. Prodr. p. 201.—Flowers: Nov.

Rare. KONKAN: *Stocks*! S. M. COUNTRY: Padshapur, *Ritchie*, 1693!—DISTRIB. India (W. Peninsula and Carnatic); Arabia, Tropical Africa, N. Australia.

22. **Indigofera Houer,** *Forsk. Fl. Ægypt.-Arab.* (1775) p. 137. An erect shrub about 3 ft., when cultivated reaching 5–6 ft. high; stem woody, argenteo-canescent, more or less angled, striate. Leaves 2–3 in. long; petioles $\frac{1}{2}$–$\frac{3}{4}$ in. long; stipules minute, subulate. Leaflets 7–11, opposite, $\frac{3}{4}$–1$\frac{1}{4}$ by $\frac{1}{2}$–1 in., obovate, usually emarginate, sparingly clothed with short appressed white hairs above, not or scarcely argenteo-canescent, the lower surface pale, glabrous or nearly so; petiolules of the lateral leaflets $\frac{1}{16}$–$\frac{1}{8}$ in., those of the terminal $\frac{1}{4}$–$\frac{1}{2}$ in. long. Flowers 15–30, in axillary subsessile racemes 1–2 in. long, usually shorter than the leaves; pedicels short, slender. Calyx $\frac{1}{20}$ in. long; teeth triangular. Corolla reddish-yellow, $\frac{1}{6}$ in. long; standard and keel hairy. Pods $\frac{5}{8}$ in. long, thick, turgid, recurved, shortly mucronate, silvery-hairy when young, finally glabrescent, slightly torulose. Seeds 2–4 (usually 3). *I. cærulea*, Roxb. Fl. Ind. v. 3, p. 377; Dalz. & Gibs. p. 59; Aitch. Pb. & Sind Pl. p. 40. *I. argentea*, var. *cærulea*, Baker, in Hook. f. Fl. B. I. v. 2, p. 99; Watt, Dict. Econ. Prod. v. 4, p. 383.—Flowers: Nov.–Dec.

The name *I. Houer* given to this plant by Forskåhl is many years earlier than *I. cærulea* given to it by Roxburgh. Steudel (Nom. Bot. ed. 2, p. 807), under the name *I. Hover*, gives as a synonym *I. lateritia*, Willd., which is *I. viscosa*, Lamk. The 'Index Kewensis' also, under the name *I. Hover*, gives as a synonym *I. lateritia*, Bertol., a native of the Cape of Good Hope. *I. lateritia*, Bertol., is described in Bertol. Nov. Comm. Bonon. v. 2 (1836) p. 215, and figured in tab. 8, fig. 1. The description and figure show that it is very remote from *I. Houer*, Forsk.

GUJARAT: Dhej near Broach, *Dalzell*! SIND: *Stocks*! Cultivated extensively in Egypt as a source of indigo (see Forsk. *l. c.*). Roxburgh (*l. c.*) says that he has extracted better indigo from it than from *I. tinctoria*.—DISTRIB. India (W. Peninsula and plains of Banda); Arabia, Egypt, Abyssinia.

23. **Indigofera tinctoria,** *Linn. Sp. Pl.* (1753) p. 751. A shrub 4–6 ft. high; branches terete or more or less angular, slightly silvery from fine appressed hairs. Leaves 1–3 in. long; petioles $\frac{1}{2}$–1 in. long; stipules small, subulate. Leaflets 9–13, opposite, membranous, green but drying a greyish-black, $\frac{1}{2}$–1 by $\frac{1}{4}$–$\frac{1}{2}$ in., oblong or oblanceolate, rounded, apiculate, glabrous above or nearly so, thinly clothed with appressed hairs beneath, base acute; petiolules of lateral leaflets $\frac{1}{20}$–$\frac{1}{12}$ in., those of the terminal reaching $\frac{1}{4}$ in. long. Flowers numerous, in nearly sessile lax spicate racemes 2–4 in. long. Calyx $\frac{1}{20}$–$\frac{1}{16}$ in. long, hairy outside; teeth triangular, acute, as long as the tube. Corolla pink, $\frac{1}{6}$ in. long; standard pubescent at the back. Pods $\frac{3}{4}$–1$\frac{1}{4}$ in. long,

linear, straight or slightly curved, apiculate, thickened at the sutures, glabrous, not torulose. Seeds 8–12. Fl. B. I. v. 2, p. 99; Grah. Cat. p. 46; Dalz. & Gibs. p. 59; Trim. Fl. Ceyl. v. 2, p. 26; Woodr. in Journ. Bomb. Nat. v. 11 (1897) p. 421; Watt, Dict. Econ. Prod. v. 4, p. 387.—Flowers: Nov.-Dec. VERN. *Nil*; *Guli*.

The *Indigo-plant*, widely cultivated in many parts of India, doubtfully wild, but found as an escape in localities not far removed from human influence. Indigo was at one time cultivated extensively in Gujarat and Sind, but its cultivation has greatly fallen off in late years.—For a full description see Watt, Dict. Econ. Prod. l. c.

24. **Indigofera hirsuta,** *Linn. Sp. Pl.* (1753) p. 751. Annual or biennial, erect, 2–4 ft. high; stems and branches covered with soft spreading reddish-brown hairs. Leaves 2–5 in. long; petioles $\frac{1}{4}$–2 in. long; stipules $\frac{1}{2}$ in. long, filiform, plumose, conspicuous. Leaflets 5–11, opposite, membranous, 1–2 by $\frac{3}{8}$–1 in., elliptic-oblong or sometimes obovate, clothed on both sides with appressed hairs, glaucous beneath; petiolules of lateral leaflets $\frac{1}{8}$–$\frac{1}{10}$ in., those of the terminal sometimes reaching $\frac{1}{2}$ in. long, clothed (as is the rhachis) with spreading hairs. Flowers in dense many-flowered peduncled racemes 2–6 in. long, longer or shorter than the leaves; pedicels very short. Calyx $\frac{1}{4}$ in. long, densely hairy; teeth very long, subulate, plumose. Corolla pink, scarcely exserted. Pods $\frac{1}{2}$–$\frac{3}{4}$ in. long, imbricately deflexed, straight, 4-gonous, pointed, densely clothed with soft spreading hairs. Seeds 6–8, cubical. Fl. B. I. v. 2, p. 98; Dalz. & Gibs. p. 60; W. & A. Prodr. p. 204; Jacquin, Icon. Plant. Rar. t. 569; Trim. Fl. Ceyl. v. 2, p. 26; Woodr. in Journ. Bomb. Nat. v. 11 (1897) p. 421.—Flowers: Aug.-Oct.

KONKAN: S. Konkan, common, *Dalzell & Gibson*; Neral, *Woodrow*!; Poladpur, *Woodrow*!; Pen, *Stocks*! S. M. COUNTRY: Badami, *Bhiva*!; Belgaum, *Ritchie*, 1026!—DISTRIB. Throughout the plains of India; Ceylon, Tropical Africa, Tropical America, Java, Philippines, N. Australia.

25. **Indigofera constricta,** *Trim. Cat. Ceyl. Pl.* (1885) p. 23. An erect shrub 3–4 ft. high; branches divaricate, terete or obscurely angled, and with a few appressed hairs. Leaves about 2 inches long; petioles $\frac{1}{2}$–$\frac{3}{4}$ in. long, slender; stipules minute, subulate. Leaflets 7–11, opposite, soon deciduous, dark green above, glaucous beneath, thin, $\frac{3}{4}$–1 by $\frac{3}{8}$–$\frac{1}{2}$ in., elliptic-oblong, rounded or faintly emarginate and apiculate at the apex, sparingly clothed on both surfaces with appressed white hairs, base rounded; petiolules of lateral leaflets $\frac{1}{20}$ in. long, those of the terminal $\frac{1}{8}$ in. long. Flowers numerous, in racemes about as long as the leaves. Calyx silky; tube campanulate; teeth short, triangular, acute. Pods $1\frac{1}{2}$–$2\frac{1}{4}$ in. long, linear, pointed, slightly curved, somewhat 4-gonous, much constricted between the seeds, sparingly silky with white appressed hairs. Seeds 8–12. Trim. Fl. Ceyl. v. 2, p. 27; Talb. Trees, Bomb. p. 67; Woodr. in Journ. Bomb. Nat. v. 11 (1897) p. 421. *I. flaccida*, var. *constricta*, Thw. Enum. p. 411.—Flowers: Oct.-Nov.

A rare plant, confined to Kanara. KANARA: common on the Nilkund Ghát, *Talbot*, 259!; moist forests of N. Kanara, common on the Supa Gháts, *Talbot*.—DISTRIB. Ceylon.

26. **Indigofera Wightii,** *Grah. in Wall. Cat.* (1828) 5458. A small erect shrub; branches numerous, furrowed, silvery-grey with appressed hairs. Leaves $1\frac{1}{2}$–$2\frac{1}{4}$ in. long; petioles $\frac{1}{4}$–$\frac{1}{2}$ in. long; stipules

minute, subulate. Leaflets 13–21, opposite, ¼–½ in. long, elliptic or oblanceolate, rounded and mucronate at the apex, densely clothed on both sides with persistent appressed white hairs, base acute; petiolules of the lateral leaflets $\frac{1}{20}$ in. long, those of the terminal ones a little longer. Flowers in dense subsessile racemes, shorter than the leaves; pedicels short. Calyx $\frac{1}{15}$ in. long, silvery outside; teeth triangular, acute. Corolla red, ⅙–¼ in. long; standard broadly ovate, shortly acuminate, hairy on the back; keel-petals hairy outside. Pods 1–1¼ in. long, straight, cylindric, mucronate, clothed with appressed white hairs, not deflexed nor torulose. Seeds 8–12. Fl. B. I. v. 2, p. 99; Dalz. & Gibs. p. 59; Trim. Fl. Ceyl. v. 2, p. 27; Talb. Trees, Bomb. p. 67.

A rare plant. KONKAN: *Stocks*! S. M. COUNTRY: Belgaum, *Ritchie*, 166!, *Dalzell*!, *Stocks*!, *Talbot*.—DISTRIB. India (W. Peninsula); Ceylon.

27. **Indigofera pulchella,** *Roxb. Hort. Beng.* (1814) p. 57; *Fl. Ind.* v. 3, p. 382. An erect ramous shrub 4–6 ft. high; branches striate, glabrous or more or less hairy. Leaves 3–6 in. long; petioles ¾–⅞ in. long; stipules very minute, subulate, caducous. Leaflets 13–21, opposite or a few casually alternate, ½–1 by $\frac{5}{16}$–⅝ in., elliptic-oblong, rounded, truncate or emarginate, apiculate, thinly clothed with short grey appressed hairs, base acute; main nerves prominent on the under surface; petiolules of the lateral leaflets $\frac{1}{12}$–⅛ in., those of the terminal ones ¼–⅜ in. long. Flowers the largest of the genus, numerous, in moderately close short-peduncled racemes shorter than the leaves; pedicels short, slender, hairy; bracts large, boat-shaped, long-cuspidate, exceeding the buds, silky-hairy, caducous. Calyx $\frac{1}{12}$–⅛ in. long, appressedly hairy outside; teeth short, triangular. Corolla purple, ½–¾ in. long; standard orbicular, as broad as long, glabrous on the back; keel-petals glabrous outside. Pods 1–1¾ in. long, straight, turgid, cylindric, glabrous. Seeds 8–12. Fl. B. I. v. 2, p. 101; Dalz. & Gibs. p. 60; Talb. Trees, Bomb. p. 67; Woodr. in Journ. Bomb. Nat. v. 11 (1897) p. 421; Watt, Dict. Econ. Prod. v. 4, p. 387. *I. Gibsonii*, Grah. Cat. p. 46.—Flowers: Oct.–Jan. VERN. *Baroli*; *Chimnati*.

DECCAN: Mahableshwar, *Cooke*!, *H. M. Birdwood*, *Woodrow*!; Kartriz hills, *Kanitkar*!; hills about Hewra, *Graham*. S. M. COUNTRY: Nagargali near Dharwar, *Kanitkar*!; near Hubli, *Hohenhacker*, 774!; Belgaum, *Ritchie*, 165! KANARA: N. Kanara in moist forests along the ghâts, *Talbot*.—DISTRIB. Throughout the hills of India.

12. PSORALEA, Linn.

Herbs or undershrubs punctate with black or pellucid glands. Leaves simple or imparipinnate, stipulate. Inflorescence capitate, spicate, subracemose or fasciculate. Calyx-lobes subequal, or the lowest the larger, the two upper often connate. Petals all with distinct claws; keel obtuse, the tip slightly incurved. Upper stamen free or more or less connate with the others, the tube often closed at the commencement of flowering; anthers small, uniform or slightly dimorphous. Ovary sessile or shortly stalked; ovule 1; style filiform or dilated at the base, curved above; stigma terminal. Pod ovoid or oblong, 1-seeded, indehiscent, the pericarp usually adhering to the seed.—DISTRIB. Chiefly the Cape and North America; species about 100.

Leaves simple .... 1. *P. corylifolia*.
Leaves 3-foliolate .... 2. *P. plicata*.

1. **Psoralea corylifolia,** *Linn. Sp. Pl.* (1753) p. 764. An erect annual 2–4 ft. high; stem and branches grooved, studded with conspicuous glands and with a few appressed and spreading white hairs. Leaves simple, $1\frac{1}{2}$–3 by 1–2 in., broadly elliptic, inciso-dentate, rounded and mucronate at the apex, sparingly clothed with white hairs on both surfaces, closely nigro-punctate, base cuneate, rarely rounded; main nerves 5, springing from the base, and 4–6 pairs of lateral nerves higher up from the midrib; petioles $\frac{1}{4}$–1 in. long, hairy and gland-dotted; stipules lanceolate, persistent. Flowers close, in dense axillary solitary 10–30-flowered racemes; peduncles 1–2 in. long, hairy; pedicels very short. Calyx $\frac{1}{8}$–$\frac{1}{6}$ in. long, hairy outside; the upper teeth linear-lanceolate, the lower ovate, twice as long as the upper. Corolla bluish-purple, nearly twice as long as the calyx; standard orbicular, $\frac{1}{4}$ in. long, clawed, glabrous. Pods $\frac{1}{6}$ in. long, ovoid-oblong, somewhat compressed, closely pitted, mucronate, black, glabrous. Seed 1, smooth, adhering to the pericarp. Fl. B. I. v. 2, p. 103; Grah. Cat. p. 46; Dalz. & Gibs. p. 60; Trim. Fl. Ceyl. v. 2, p. 28; Woodr. in Journ. Bomb. Nat. v. 11 (1897) p. 422; Watt, Dict. Econ. Prod. v. 6, part 1, p. 353.—Flowers: Aug.–Dec. VERN. *Bávchi*.

A common weed in waste places. KONKAN: *Stocks*! DECCAN: Nasik, *Woodrow*!, *Vadekar*!; Kolhapur, *Cooke*! S. M. COUNTRY: Belgaum, *Ritchie*, 1039!—DISTRIB. Throughout India; Ceylon.

The seeds have some repute in native medicine as a remedy for certain skin diseases. A preparation made therefrom is stated to be valuable for restoring the hair in the case of broken knees in horses, and its use for this purpose is advocated in the agricultural publication 'Farm and Home' of April 8th, 1890, recipe no. 2777.

2. **Psoralea plicata,** *Delile, Fl. d'Egypte* (1812) p. 252, t. 37, fig. 3. A low much-branched undershrub 1–2 ft. high; stems whitish, terete, striate, glabrous or nearly so, sparingly gland-dotted. Leaves 3-foliolate; petioles $\frac{3}{16}$–$\frac{1}{2}$ in. long; stipules linear-oblong, acute, nerved. Leaflets oblanceolate (the lateral $\frac{1}{4}$–$\frac{1}{2}$ by $\frac{1}{8}$–$\frac{3}{16}$ in., the terminal $\frac{1}{2}$–$\frac{7}{8}$ by $\frac{1}{4}$–$\frac{5}{16}$ in.), rounded at the apex, apiculate or not, both surfaces clothed with closely appressed hairs, gland-dotted on the lower, but not on the upper surface, the margins irregularly sinuate or subserrate, base acute; petiolules of the lateral leaflets 0–$\frac{1}{30}$, those of the terminal ones reaching $\frac{3}{16}$ in. long. Flowers solitary or in fascicles of 2 or 3 along a striate axillary rhachis 2–4 in. long; pedicels short, deflexed; bracts small, ovate, acute. Calyx accrescent in fruit, in flower $\frac{1}{8}$–$\frac{1}{6}$ in. long, silvery-hairy outside; teeth triangular, shorter than the tube, the lowest the largest. Corolla yellow, slightly exserted. Pods $\frac{1}{6}$ in. long, ellipsoid, densely hairy, completely enclosed in the accrescent persistent calyx, which becomes membranous and many-nerved. Seed 1, adherent to the pericarp, smooth. Fl. B. I. v. 2, p. 103; Watt, Dict. Econ. Prod. v. 6, part 1, p. 354.

A very rare plant. SIND: *Stocks*!, *Woodrow*!—DISTRIB. India (Panjab); Arabia, Egypt, Tropical Africa.

13. MILLETTIA, Wight & Arn.

Trees or shrubs, often climbing. Leaves imparipinnate; stipules small. Leaflets often stipellate. Flowers in axillary and terminal racemes or panicles, often fascicled, rarely scattered along the rhachis. Calyx-tube truncate, or with very short teeth. Corolla much exserted;

standard broad; keel not beaked. Stamens monadelphous or diadelphous; filaments filiform; anthers uniform. Ovary sessile or rarely stalked, usually girt at the base by an annular disk or by a short sheath; ovules usually few; style inflexed, terete, glabrous; stigma small, terminal. Pod linear or oblong, 1- or few-seeded, flat or turgid, coriaceous or woody, small, tardily or scarcely dehiscent.—DISTRIB. Tropics of the Old World; species 40–50.

1. **Millettia racemosa,** *Benth. Pl. Jungh.* (1851-55) p. 249. A large woody climber; branches glabrous or thinly silky. Leaves reaching 1 ft. long; petioles 2–4 in. long; stipules subulate, $\frac{3}{8}$ in. long. Leaflets 11–15, membranous, opposite, 2–3 by 1–1½ in., oblong or obovate-oblong, suddenly and obtusely acuminate, glabrous above, pale and more or less silky or glabrescent beneath, base cuneate; petiolules $\frac{1}{8}$–$\frac{3}{16}$ in. long; stipels $\frac{1}{4}$ in. long, filiform. Flowers close, not fascicled, in axillary and terminal silky-brown racemes 3–9 in. long shorter than the leaves; pedicels $\frac{1}{10}$–$\frac{1}{4}$ in. long; bracts conspicuous, linear-cuspidate, $\frac{1}{2}$ in. long. Calyx $\frac{1}{8}$ in. long, clothed with fine silky-brown hairs; teeth very short, triangular, the two on the upper side often obsolete. Corolla yellowish-white, about twice as long as the calyx; standard $\frac{3}{8}$–$\frac{1}{2}$ in. long, quite glabrous, exappendiculate, shortly clawed. Ovary glabrous, shortly stalked; ovules 6. Pods compressed between the seeds, linear, coriaceous, 4–8 in. long, $\frac{1}{2}$–$\frac{5}{8}$ in. broad, scarcely at length dehiscent. Seeds 3–5, ovoid. Fl. B. I. v. 2, p. 105; Talb. Trees, Bomb. p. 68; Woodr. in Journ. Bomb. Nat. v. 11 (1897) p. 422. *Millettia pallida*, Dalz. in Journ. Linn. Soc. v. 13 (1873) p. 187. *Wisteria racemosa*, Dalz. & Gibs. p. 61. *Wisteria pallida*, Dalz. & Gibs. p. 61.—Flowers: Apr.–May.

KONKAN: *Law*!, *Stocks*!, *Dalzell*!; Dasgaon, *Woodrow*. GUJARAT: Dangs, rare, *Dalzell & Gibson*. S. M. COUNTRY: near Belgaum, *Dalzell & Gibson*.—DISTRIB. India (Behar, Central India).

14. MUNDULEA, DC.

Shrubs usually sericeo-pubescent. Leaves imparipinnate; stipules small. Flowers in terminal racemes; pedicels fascicled along the rhachis; bracts small; bracteoles 0. Calyx campanulate; teeth short, the 2 upper often subconnate. Corolla rosy, exserted; standard large, clawed; wings falcate-oblong; keel incurved and obtuse at the apex. Stamens monadelphous; alternate filaments slightly dilated; anthers uniform. Ovary sessile; ovules many; style incurved, subterete, glabrous, inflexed at the very apex; stigma capitate. Pod subindehiscent, linear, flat, the sutures much thickened. Seeds reniform.—DISTRIB. Species 3, of which 1 (the following) is an inhabitant of Tropical Asia and S. & W. Africa, the 2 others of Madagascar.

1. **Mundulea suberosa,** *Benth. Pl. Jungh.* (1851-55) p. 248. A small tree 10–15 ft. high; bark pale, corky; branches sericeous. Leaves numerous; petioles $\frac{1}{2}$–$\frac{3}{4}$ in. long; stipules small. Leaflets 17–23, opposite or alternate, $\frac{1}{2}$–1$\frac{3}{4}$ by $\frac{1}{4}$–$\frac{5}{8}$ in., coriaceous, oblong-lanceolate, obtuse, glabrous and bright green above, silvery-silky beneath; petiolules of the lateral leaflets $\frac{1}{16}$ in., those of the terminal $\frac{1}{4}$ in. long. Flowers in close terminal racemes; pedicels $\frac{3}{8}$–$\frac{5}{8}$ in. long, slender. Calyx $\frac{1}{4}$ in. long, clothed with silky hairs; teeth short deltoid. Corolla $\frac{3}{4}$–$\frac{7}{8}$ in.

long, pinkish-violet; standard silky outside. Pods 3–4 by $\frac{5}{16}$–$\frac{3}{8}$ in., flattened, densely velvety with short golden-brown hairs, thickened at the sutures. Seeds 3–8, about $\frac{1}{8}$ in. long, yellowish-brown. Fl. B. I. v. 2, p. 110; Trim. Fl. Ceyl. v. 2, p. 29; Talb. Trees, Bomb. p. 68; Woodr. in. Journ. Bomb. Nat. v. 11 (1897) p. 422; Watt, Dict. Econ. Prod. v. 5, p. 288. *Tephrosia suberosa*, DC. Prodr. v. 2, p. 249; Grah. Cat. p. 47; Dalz. & Gibs. p. 60.—Flowers: Aug.-Oct. VERN. *Supti.*

KONKAN: *Stocks*!, *Dalzell*! DECCAN: Gokak, *Cooke*!, *Woodrow*. S. M. COUNTRY: rocky hills east of Belgaum, *Graham & Gibson*; S. of Padshapur, *Ritchie*, 1173!; Badami, *Cooke*!, *Woodrow*!, *Talbot*.—DISTRIB. India (W. Peninsula); Ceylon, Tropical Africa, Natal.

The seeds are said to be used for poisoning fish. See Watt, Dict. Econ. Prod. l. c.

15. TEPHROSIA, Pers.

Herbs or undershrubs. Leaves usually imparipinnate, sometimes simple, stipulate; leaflets opposite, usually numerous (rarely 1–3), parallel-veined, often silky beneath. Flowers in terminal or leaf-opposed racemes which are often leafy at the base, or solitary, or in pairs in the axils of the leaves. Calyx-teeth or -lobes subequal, or the 2 upper more deeply connate, or the lower longer. Petals clawed; standard suborbicular; wings obliquely obovate or oblong. Stamens diadelphous when the flower is fully open; anthers obtuse, uniform. Ovary sessile; ovules many (rarely 2); style incurved, often flattened, glabrous or bearded; stigma terminal, often penicillate. Pod usually linear, flattened, many-seeded, 2-valved, continuous within or obscurely septate between the seeds. Seeds sometimes with a small strophiole.—DISTRIB. Tropics of both hemispheres; species about 100.

Leaves simple.
  Flowers 1–2 in the axils of the leaves .... 1. *T. tenuis.*
Leaves compound (sometimes a few casually simple in *T. tinctoria* and *T. coccinea*).
  Flowers in elongated racemes.
    Pod slightly pilose or silky.
      Style bearded throughout.
        Leaflets 7–13, elliptic-oblong .... 2. *T. tinctoria.*
        Leaflets 5, obovate .... 3. *T. coccinea.*
      Style not bearded throughout.
        Leaflets 11–21 .... 4. *T. purpurea.*
        Leaflets 5–9 .... 5. *T. Appollinea.*
    Pod densely hairy .... 6. *T. villosa.*
  Flowers 1–2 in the axils of the leaves.
    Pod much recurved .... 7. *T. senticosa.*
    Pod nearly straight .... 8. *T. pauciflora.*

1. **Tephrosia tenuis,** *Wall. Cat.* (1828) 5970. Annual; stems slender, terete, densely cæspitose, reaching 1 ft. long; branches filiform, and as well as the stems more or less clothed with closely appressed hairs. Leaves simple, 1–$1\frac{1}{2}$ by $\frac{3}{16}$–$\frac{5}{16}$ in., linear, suddenly or gradually narrowed at the apex, long-apiculate, slightly hairy above, silky beneath, narrowed at the base; midrib prominent on the under surface; nerves obscure; petioles $\frac{1}{16}$–$\frac{1}{12}$ in. long; stipules $\frac{1}{10}$–$\frac{1}{8}$ in. long, subulate. Flowers solitary or 2 together in the axils of the leaves; pedicels $\frac{1}{4}$–$\frac{1}{2}$ in. long, filiform. Calyx $\frac{1}{10}$ in. long, silky; teeth lanceolate-subulate. Corolla $\frac{1}{6}$ in. long, at first bluish, afterwards turning yellow (*Ritchie*);

standard long-clawed, pubescent at the back. Pods $\frac{1}{2}$–1 by $\frac{1}{8}$–$\frac{3}{16}$ in., thinly clothed with appressed hairs. Seeds 6–10. Fl. B. I. v. 2, p. 111; Dalz. & Gibs. p. 61; Aitch. Ph. & Sind Pl. p. 42; Woodr. in Journ. Bomb. Nat. v. 11 (1897) p. 422; Watt, Dict. Econ. Prod. v. 6, part 4, p. 15. *Macronyx strigosus*, Dalz. in Hook. Kew Journ. v. 2 (1850) p. 35. —Flowers: Sept.–Oct.

Tolerably common. KONKAN: *Stocks*!, *Dalzell*!, *Capt. Geburne*!, *Woodrow*. DECCAN: Poona, along the railway line near the Bamburda crossing, abundant, *Cooke*! S. M. COUNTRY: Belgaum hills, *Ritchie*, 134! SIND: *Stocks*!; Jemadar ka Landa near Karachi, *Stocks*, 1185!—DISTRIB. India (Panjab, Birma); Laccadives.

The twigs are used by natives for cleaning the teeth (*Murray*). See Watt, Dict. Econ. Prod. l. c.

2. **Tephrosia tinctoria,** *Pers. Syn. Pl.* v. 2 (1807) p. 329. A perennial undershrub 1$\frac{1}{2}$–3 ft. high; stems and branches more or less angled, densely velvety with yellowish-brown pubescence. Leaves subcoriaceous, very variable, 1–4 in. long, subsessile; stipules small, triangular, acuminate, hairy. Leaflets usually 7–13 (sometimes reduced to the terminal one), decreasing in size towards the base of the leaf (the terminal leaflet much larger than the others and varying from 1–3 by $\frac{3}{8}$–$\frac{7}{8}$), elliptic-oblong, usually mucronate, glabrous above, more or less densely silvery-silky beneath; lateral nerves numerous, slender, conspicuous on the under surface; petiolules of lateral leaflets $\frac{1}{30}$–$\frac{1}{12}$ in., those of terminal $\frac{1}{8}$–$\frac{1}{4}$ in. long. Flowers in short erect densely fulvous-silky 3–12-flowered close racemes; peduncles usually longer than the leaves; pedicels short, densely silky; bracts lanceolate, very hairy. Calyx $\frac{1}{6}$ in. long, hairy; teeth longer than the tube, subulate from a triangular base. Corolla bright pink, about twice as long as the calyx; standard $\frac{1}{3}$ in. long, broadly obovate, silky-hairy on the back, the claw cuneate; keel glabrous. Style flattened, bearded throughout its entire length. Pods 2–2$\frac{1}{2}$ by $\frac{3}{16}$–$\frac{1}{4}$ in., linear, flattened, mucronate, slightly curved upwards at the apex, more or less clothed with soft silky hair. Seeds 8–12, distant, $\frac{1}{8}$ in. long, ellipsoid, compressed, smooth, dark brown. Fl. B. I. v. 2, p. 111; Wight, Icon. t. 388; Trim. Fl. Ceyl. v. 2, p. 31; Woodr. in Journ. Bomb. Nat. v. 11 (1897) p. 422; Watt, Dict. Econ. Prod. v. 6, part 4, p. 15.—Flowers: Oct. VERN. *Nil*; *Guli*.

KONKAN: widely, *Woodrow*; near Poladpur, *Woodrow*! DECCAN: below Mahableshwar, *Cooke*! KANARA: Yellapur, *Talbot*!—DISTRIB. India (W. Peninsula); Ceylon.

A blue dye similar to Indigo is sometimes extracted from this plant in Mysore. See Watt, Dict. Econ. Prod. l. c. and v. 4, pp. 410, 412, 451.

VAR. *intermedia*, Baker, in Hook. f. Fl. B. I. v. 2, p. 112. Branches velvety. Leaflets 9–13, much smaller than the type, $\frac{1}{4}$–$\frac{1}{2}$ in. broad, the terminal leaflets about equalling the lateral ones in size; nerves less prominent. Racemes not so close as in the type. Trim. Fl. Ceyl. v. 2, p. 31. *T. intermedia* (sp.), Grah. in Wall. Cat. 5632.

KONKAN: Miradonger near Pen, *Stocks*!

3. **Tephrosia coccinea,** *Wall. Cat.* (1828) 5633. An erect branched shrub 2–3 ft. high; branches terete, flexuous, closely argenteo-canescent with soft appressed hairs. Leaves somewhat membranous, nearly sessile, 2–3 in. long; stipules scarious, lanceolate, acute, nerved,

persistent. Leaflets usually 5, opposite or casually alternate, gradually decreasing in size downwards (the terminal leaflet 1½–2 by ¾–1¼ in.), all obovate, cuneate, rounded and mucronate at the apex, quite glabrous above, clothed with appressed silvery hairs beneath, base acute; lateral nerves very numerous, close, slender, conspicuous; petiolules of the lateral leaflets $\frac{1}{16}$ in., those of the terminal ⅛ in. long. Flowers in erect lax racemes; peduncles much longer than the leaves, silvery-hairy; pedicels short, hairy; bracts scarious, lanceolate, very acute. Calyx ⅛–⅙ in. long, hairy outside; teeth subulate from a triangular base, longer than the tube. Corolla thrice as long as the calyx, bright red, handsome; standard suborbicular, hairy on the back. Style flattened, bearded throughout its entire length. Pods 2–2½ by $\frac{3}{16}$–¼ in., linear, flattened, mucronate, slightly curved upwards at the apex, more or less silky-hairy. Seeds 8–12. Wall. Pl. As. Rar. t. 60. *T. tinctoria*, var. *coccinea*, Baker, in Hook. f. Fl. B. I. v. 2, p. 112.—Flowers: Oct.

I have adopted Dr. Prain's suggestion, founded on a recent examination of a large number of specimens (Journ. As. Soc. Beng. v. 66 (1898) p. 365), as to the propriety of recognizing this as a distinct species instead of a variety of *T. tinctoria*.

KONKAN: road from Poladpur to Mahableshwar, *Woodrow*!; Neral, *Woodrow*!—DISTRIB. India (W. Peninsula and Birma).

4. **Tephrosia purpurea,** *Pers. Syn. Pl.* v. 2 (1807) p. 329. A copiously branched herbaceous perennial 1–2 ft. high; branches spreading, glabrous or sparsely pilose. Leaves 2–4 in. long; petioles ¼–½ in. long; stipules linear-subulate, nerved, erect or sometimes reflexed. Leaflets 11–21, oblanceolate, obtuse or retuse, mucronate, ¾–1⅛ by $\frac{5}{16}$–½ in., glabrous above, clothed with fine appressed silky hairs beneath, base cuneate; nerves close, ascending, slender, conspicuous on both surfaces; petiolules of lateral leaflets $\frac{1}{16}$–$\frac{1}{10}$ in., those of the terminal ⅛–$\frac{3}{16}$ in. long. Flowers in leaf-opposed lax racemes 3–5 in. long, the lower flowers of the racemes fascicled; pedicels slender; bracts subulate. Calyx ⅙ in. long, thinly silky; teeth triangular-subulate, as long as the tube. Corolla twice as long as the calyx; standard pubescent on the back. Style flattened, glabrescent; stigma penicillate. Pods 1¼–1¾ in. long, linear, slightly curved, mucronate, at first thinly hairy, finally glabrescent. Seeds 5–6. Fl. B. I. v. 2, p. 112; Grah. Cat. p. 47; Dalz. & Gibs. p. 61; Trim. Fl. Ceyl. v. 2, p. 31; Woodr. in Journ. Bomb. Nat. v. 11 (1897) p. 422; Watt, Dict. Econ. Prod. v. 6, part 4, p. 14.—Flowers: Oct.–Jan. VERN. *Unhdli*; *Sarpunká*.

KONKAN: *Stocks*! DECCAN: Ahmednagar, *Cooke*! GUJARAT: Chandod, *Woodrow*; Baroda, *Woodrow*!; Deesa, *Graham* (abundant). S. M. COUNTRY: Badami, *Cooke*!; Kuput hills, *Talbot*!

The odor of the decaying plant is very offensive.

VAR. *pumila*, Baker, in Hook. f. Fl. B. I. v. 2, p. 113. Not more than 18 in. high, more diffuse, persistently finely downy, sometimes canescent. Stipules lanceolate, deflexed or not. Leaflets 9–15, smaller, densely hairy beneath. Racemes densely hairy; flowers smaller. Pods 1–1½ in. long, finely downy, curved. Seeds 8–10. *Tephrosia pumila*, Pers. (*sp.*) l. c. p. 330. *T. diffusa*, Wight & Arn. (*sp.*) Prodr. p. 213.

GUJARAT: Ankleshwar near Broach, *Dalzell*! S. M. COUNTRY: Belgaum, *Ritchie*, 103!

5. **Tephrosia Apollinea,** *Link, Enum. Hort. Berol.* v. 2 (1822) p. 252. Suffruticose, 12–18 in. high, diffusely branched from the base; branches glabrous or sparsely hairy. Leaves 1½–2¼ in. long; petioles ¼–½ in. long; stipules ⅛–⅙ in. long, linear-subulate, deflexed or spreading, rigid, conspicuous. Leaflets 5–9, oblong or oblanceolate, ¾–1½ by ¼–½ in., emarginate, mucronate, glabrous above, more or less silky beneath. Flowers in leaf-opposed lax 6–12-flowered racemes longer than the leaves; pedicels ⅛ in. long; bracts rigid, subulate. Calyx ⅙ in. long, silky; teeth triangular, acute, equalling the tube. Corolla violet, about twice as long as the tube. Standard downy on the back. Style glabrous; stigma penicillate. Pods 1½–1¾ in. long, curved upwards, mucronate, appressedly thinly hairy. Seeds 6–9. Not in Fl. B. I.; Baker, in Fl. Trop. Afr. v. 2, p. 124; Aitch. Pb. & Sind Pl. p. 42; Boiss. Fl. Orient. v. 2, p. 192.

A very rare plant in the Bombay Presidency. SIND: *Stocks* ex *Aitchison* l. c. and fide *Baker*, in Fl. Trop. Afr. l. c. I have seen no specimens. The plant has been included on the authority of Aitchison.—DISTRIB. Beluchistan, Aden, Nubia, Abyssinia, Egypt.

6. **Tephrosia villosa,** *Pers. Syn. Pl.* v. 2 (1807) p. 329. Perennial; branches numerous, spreading, clothed with white appressed hairs. Leaves nearly sessile, 2–3 in. long; stipules linear-lanceolate, acute, sometimes reaching ⅜ in. long, deflexed or spreading (rarely ascending). Leaflets 11–19, grey-green, ½–⅞ by 3/16–6/16, narrowly oblanceolate, usually emarginate and mucronate, nearly glabrous above, silky beneath, base cuneate; petiolules of lateral leaflets 1/16 in., those of the terminal ⅛ in. long. Flowers large, few, in lax elongate racemes 6 in. or more in length, the lower flowers in distant fascicles, the lowest often in the axils of the leaves; pedicels very short; bracts linear-subulate, plumose. Calyx 7/16 in. long, hairy outside; teeth thrice as long as the tube, linear-subulate, densely hairy. Corolla red; standard equalling the calyx, suborbicular, silky on the back. Style flattened, glabrous; stigma penicillate. Pods 1–1½ in. long by ⅛–⅙ in. broad, persistently velvety with dense spreading fulvous hairs, very shortly mucronate, falcately curved upwards. Seeds 6–8. Fl. B. I. v. 2, p. 113; Trim. Fl. Ceyl. v. 2, p. 33; Woodr. in Journ. Bomb. Nat. v. 11 (1897) p. 422; Watt, Dict. Econ. Prod. v. 6, part 4, p. 15.—Flowers: July–Sept.

GUJARAT: Godra, *Cooke*! S. M. COUNTRY: Badami, *Woodrow*; abundant in the compound of the Engineer's bungalow, *Cooke*!—DISTRIB. Throughout the plains of India; Mauritius, Tropical Africa.

VAR. *incana*, Baker, in Hook. f. Fl. B. I. v. 2, p. 113. Stems clothed with short spreading pubescence. Leaflets somewhat broader, sometimes reaching ½ in. broad. Pods more densely velvety and somewhat broader than in the type. *Tephrosia incana*, Grah. in Wall. Cat. 5644 (*sp.*); Wight & Arn. Prodr. p. 212; Grah. Cat. p. 47.

S. M. COUNTRY: Padshapur jungles (near Belgaum), *Ritchie*, 1167! GUJARAT: *Law* ex *Graham*.

7. **Tephrosia senticosa,** *Pers. Syn. Pl.* v. 2 (1807) p. 330. A low much-branched shrub; branches divaricate, slender, terete, argenteo-canescent. Leaves 1–1½ in. long; petioles 1/16–⅛ in. long; stipules ⅛ in. long, subulate, hairy. Leaflets ½–1⅛ by ¼–5/16 in., light-green and glabrous

above, argenteo-canescent with appressed hairs beneath, oblanceolate, deeply emarginate, cuneate at the base; petiolules of lateral leaflets $\frac{1}{20}-\frac{1}{16}$ in., those of the terminal $\frac{1}{16}-\frac{1}{8}$ in. long. Flowers usually 1-2, in the axils of the leaves; pedicels $\frac{1}{8}-\frac{1}{4}$ in. long, silky-hairy. Calyx silky outside, $\frac{1}{6}-\frac{1}{5}$ in. long; teeth subulate from a triangular base, a little longer than the tube. Corolla a little more than twice as long as the calyx; standard orbicular, densely hairy on the back. Ovary densely hairy; style much flattened, not bearded throughout its entire length. Pods $1\frac{1}{2}$-2 by $\frac{3}{16}$ in., linear, flattened, much curved upwards, densely hairy, apiculate, the sutures not much thickened. Seeds 6-8, oblong-ellipsoid, $\frac{1}{8}-\frac{1}{6}$ in. long, smooth. Fl. B. I. v. 2, p. 112; Dalz. & Gibs. p. 61; Trim. Fl. Ceyl. v. 2, p. 30; Woodr. in Journ. Bomb. Nat. v. 11 (1897) p. 422.—Flowers: Sept.-Oct.

KONKAN: *Dalzell & Gibson.* DECCAN: Wadi, *Cooke*!, Jeur (Sholapur districts), *Woodrow.*—DISTRIB. India (W. Peninsula and Birma); Ceylon.

8. **Tephrosia pauciflora,** *Grah. in Wall. Cat.* (1828) 5635. Herbaceous; stems densely cæspitose, 9-20 in. long, terete, slender, clothed with spreading hairs. Leaves 2-4 in. long; petioles $\frac{1}{2}$ in. long; stipules lanceolate-subulate. Leaflets 5-9, lanceolate-oblong or narrowly oblanceolate, rounded or sometimes subacute at the apex, often emarginate, usually apiculate, $\frac{1}{2}-1\frac{1}{4}$ by $\frac{1}{8}-\frac{1}{2}$ in., glabrous or nearly so above, finely silky with appressed hairs beneath; petiolules of lateral leaflets $\frac{1}{24}$ in., those of the terminal $\frac{1}{8}-\frac{3}{16}$ in. long. Flowers geminate in the leaf-axils; pedicels short. Calyx $\frac{1}{8}-\frac{1}{6}$ in. long, silky with spreading hairs: teeth about equalling the tube, subulate from a triangular base. Corolla less than twice as long as the calyx; standard $\frac{3}{16}-\frac{1}{4}$ in. long, suborbicular, densely silky on the back. Style flattened, glabrous; stigma penicillate. Pods 1-$1\frac{3}{4}$ in. long, by $\frac{1}{8}-\frac{3}{16}$ in. broad, linear, very shortly mucronate, very slightly curved, thinly silky. Seeds 6-9. Fl. B. I. v. 2, p. 114; Woodr. in Journ. Bomb. Nat. v. 11 (1897) p. 422.

A rare plant in the Bombay Presidency. SIND: *Stocks*!, *Dalzell*!, *Puran*!; Jemadar ka Landa near Karachi, *Stocks*, 454!—DISTRIB. India (Panjab, Birma); Afghanistan.

Tephrosia candida, DC. Prodr. v. 2, p. 249, a native of the Himalayas, W. Indo-China, and the Malay Archipelago, is occasionally planted in gardens. Its flowers are white or rose-colored, about 1 in. long, showy. Fl. B. I. v. 2, p. 111; Grah. Cat. p. 47; Dalz. & Gibs. Suppl. p. 25.

According to Dr. Lush (Grah. Cat. l. c.) the plant was introduced into the botanical garden at Dápuri from Bengal.

16. SESBANIA *, Scop. Introd. (1777) p. 308.

Herbs or soft-wooded trees or shrubs. Leaves abruptly pinnate; leaflets numerous, linear-oblong, obtuse, quite entire, mucronate, deciduous. Flowers in axillary lax racemes. Calyx campanulate, shallowly 2-lipped or 5-toothed. Corolla much exserted; petals all with long claws; standard orbicular or ovate, spreading or reflexed; wings falcate-oblong; keel obtuse and straight, or subrostrate and recurved. Stamens diadelphous; anthers uniform. Ovary usually stalked, many-

* The oldest name of the genus was "*Sesban*," which was given to it by Adanson in 1763 (Fam. v. 2, p. 327) and which was simply the Egyptian name of *S. ægyptiaca*. The name *Sesbania* has, however, been universally adopted.

ovulate; style incurved, glabrous; stigma small, capitate. Pod very long and narrow, dehiscent, septate transversely between the seeds. Seeds numerous, oblong or subquadrate.—DISTRIB. Throughout the Tropics; species about 40.

Pod 6-9 in. long.
Unarmed; pod twisted, torulose .... 1. *S. ægyptiaca.*
Armed; pod not twisted, not torulose .... 2. *S. aculeata.*
Pod 2-3 in. long .... 3. *S. procumbens.*

1. **Sesbania ægyptiaca,** *Poir. Encyc.* v. 7 (1806) p. 128 (*Sesban ægyptiacus*); *Pers. Syn.* v. 2 (1807) p. 316; var. **picta,** *Prain, in Journ. As. Soc. Beng.* v. 66 (1898) p. 367. A soft-wooded short-lived unarmed shrub 6–15 ft. high; branches pale, terete or obscurely angled, striate, glabrous or nearly so. Leaves 2–4 in. long; petioles $\frac{1}{4}$–$\frac{3}{4}$ in. long; stipules scarious, linear, acute, caducous. Leaflets 20–30, shortly petioluled, $\frac{1}{2}$-1 by $\frac{1}{8}$–$\frac{1}{4}$ in., pale-green, linear-oblong, obtuse, faintly apiculate, glabrous. Flowers in lax slender pendulous 6–10-flowered racemes; buds straight; pedicels filiform, $\frac{1}{4}$–$\frac{1}{2}$ in. long. Calyx $\frac{1}{4}$ in. long, glabrous, membranous; teeth deltoid, much shorter than the tube. Corolla $\frac{1}{2}$–$\frac{3}{4}$ in. long; standard as broad as long, mottled with purple on the outside, glabrous on the back, furnished at the base with 2 keel-like appendages which are free and falcate above, running down wing-like into the claw. Pods pendulous, 6–9 in. long, twisted, weak, slightly torulose, sharply beaked, the sutures not much thickened. Seeds 20–30. *S. picta* (sp.), Pers. Syn. v. 2, p. 316. *S. ægyptiaca*, Fl. B. I. v. 2, p. 114 in part (*not* of Pers.); Grah. Cat. p. 47; Dalz. & Gibs. Suppl. p. 21; Wight, Icon. t. 32; Trim. Fl. Ceyl. v. 2, p. 34; Talb. Trees, Bomb. p. 68; Woodr. in Journn. Bomb. Nat. v. 11 (1897) p. 422; Watt, Dict. Econ. Prod. v. 6, part 2, p. 543. *Colutea exotica*, Pluk. Phytogr. t. 164, f. 5.—Flowers: Aug.–Dec. VERN. *Sevari*; *Jayanti*.

VAR. *bicolor*, Wight & Arn. Prodr. p. 214. Standard maroon-colored or dark purple (not mottled) outside. Prain, in Journ. As. Soc. Beng. l. c.

According to Prain (*l. c.*) the typical *S. ægyptiaca* has uniformly yellow flowers and is a native of India. It does not, however, appear to occur in the Bombay Presidency either wild or cultivated. Both the above-named varieties are cultivated and more or less naturalized in Bombay. The wood is used to supply poles as substitutes for bamboos and furnishes excellent charcoal for gunpowder. The seeds and leaves are employed in native medicine, being considered a valuable remedy in cutaneous diseases. See Watt, Dict. Econ. Prod. l. c.—DISTRIB. Throughout the Tropics of the Old World.

2. **Sesbania aculeata,** *Poir. Encyc.* v. 7 (1806) p. 128 (*Sesban aculeatus*); *Pers. Syn.* v. 2 (1807) p. 316. A sparingly-branched annual of rapid growth, sometimes reaching 8 ft. or more in height; stems semiwoody; branches and leaf-rhachises more or less prickly. Leaves abruptly pinnate, sometimes reaching 1 ft. in length; stipules membranous, acuminate, caducous. Leaflets 20-50 pairs, close, $\frac{3}{8}$–$\frac{3}{4}$ by $\frac{1}{8}$ in., linear-oblong, obtuse, strongly mucronate, glabrous, base acute; petiolules very short. Flowers in lax axillary 3-6-flowered drooping racemes; peduncles slender; pedicels $\frac{1}{4}$ in. long, filiform. Calyx $\frac{1}{8}$–$\frac{1}{6}$ in. long, membranous, glabrous; teeth deltoid, much shorter than the tube. Corolla $\frac{3}{8}$–$\frac{1}{2}$ in. long, yellow, usually with red dots on the back of the

glabrous standard. Pods 6–9 in. long, not twisted, slightly falcate, beaked, not torulose. Fl. B. I. v. 2, p. 114; Grah. Cat. p. 48; Dalz. & Gibs. p. 62; Trim. Fl. Ceyl. v. 2, p. 34; Woodr. in Journ. Bomb. Nat. v. 11 (1897) p. 422; Watt, Dict. Econ. Prod. v. 6, part 2, p. 542.—Flowers: Sept.–Oct. VERN. *Rána-sevari*; *Chuncha*.

Very common in wet places throughout the Konkan and the Deccan.—DISTRIB. Cosmopolitan in the Tropics of the Old World.

3. **Sesbania procumbens,** *Wight & Arn. Prodr.* (1834) p. 215. Annual, diffuse, more or less armed with inoffensive prickles; branches glabrous, subterete, striate. Leaves $1\frac{1}{2}$–$2\frac{1}{2}$ in. long; petioles $\frac{1}{8}$–$\frac{1}{4}$ in. long; stipules $\frac{1}{8}$ in. long, membranous, very acute from a triangular base. Leaflets 15–20 pairs, linear-oblong, $\frac{1}{4}$ by $\frac{1}{12}$ in., obtuse, apiculate, glabrous, base rounded; petiolules about $\frac{1}{20}$ in. long. Flowers in short 2–4-flowered racemes. Calyx $\frac{1}{10}$–$\frac{1}{8}$ in. long, membranous, glabrous; teeth short, deltoid. Corolla $\frac{1}{4}$–$\frac{1}{3}$ in. long. Pods straight, erect, 2–$3\frac{1}{2}$ in. long, not twisted, beaked, torulose. Seeds 12–20. Fl. B. I. v. 2, p. 115; Grah. Cat. p. 48; Dalz. & Gibs. p. 62. *Æschynomene procumbens*, Roxb. Fl. Ind. v. 3, p. 337.

Abundant in rice-fields in Bombay during the rains, *Dalzell & Gibson*; eaten by cattle, *Graham*.—DISTRIB. India (W. Peninsula).

Sesbania grandiflora, Pers. Syn. v. 2 (1807) p. 316, a soft-wooded tree reaching 20–30 ft. high, with large white or red flowers, is often grown about temples and villages, but is nowhere indigenous. Its flowers are 2–3 inches long and very showy. Pods often reach a foot long. Fl. B. I. v. 2, p. 115; Woodr. in Journ. Bomb. Nat. v. 11 (1897) p. 422. *Agati grandiflora*, Desv. Journ. Bot. v. 1 (1813) p. 120; Grah. Cat. p. 48; Dalz. & Gibs. Suppl. p. 22; Watt, Dict. Econ. Prod. v. 6, part 2, p. 544.—Flowers at various times. VERN. *Agastá*; *Hadgá*.

The tender leaves, flowers and pods are eaten. Certain parts of the tree have repute in native medicine. See Watt, Dict. Econ. Prod. l. c.

17. ASTRAGALUS, Linn.

Herbs or undershrubs. Leaves pinnate, the rhachis terminating either in a leaflet or a spine; stipules free or adnate to the petiole or united into one leaf-opposed one. Calyx tubular or companulate; teeth 5, subequal. Petals usually with rather long claws; standard erect, ovate-oblong or panduriform; wings oblong; keel equalling the wings or a little shorter, obtuse. Stamens diadelphous; anthers uniform. Ovary sessile or stalked, many-ovulate; style filiform, straight or incurved, not bearded; stigma small, terminal. Pod linear or oblong, usually turgid, continuous within or more or less completely longitudinally 2-celled from the introversion of the inferior suture. Seeds usually reniform.—DISTRIB. Chiefly throughout the N. temperate zone; species 1100–1200.

Leaves imparipinnate.
  Pod straight .... 1. *A. prolixus*.
  Pod contortuplicate .... 2. *A. contortuplicatus*.
Leaves abruptly pinnate .... 3. *A. Stocksii*.

1. **Astragalus prolixus,** *Sieb. Pl. Ægypt. exsicc. ex Bunge, Monogr. Astr.* (1868–69) part 1, p. 9; part 2, p. 6. Stems cæspitose, 3–12 in.

long, slender, terete, clothed with appressed white hairs. Leaves petioled, $\frac{3}{4}$–$1\frac{1}{2}$ in. long, with a terminal leaflet; stipules lanceolate, hairy, free. Leaflets 11–21, elliptic-oblong, obtuse, $\frac{1}{8}$–$\frac{1}{4}$ in. long, clothed on both sides with appressed white hairs, base rounded or subacute; petiolules very short. Flowers 6–12, sessile, in dense heads; peduncles axillary, $\frac{1}{4}$–$\frac{5}{8}$ in. long, appressedly hairy. Calyx $\frac{1}{12}$–$\frac{1}{10}$ in. long, densely hairy; teeth linear-subulate, about as long as the tube. Corolla $\frac{1}{8}$ in. long; standard orbicular, with a very long claw. Pods $\frac{1}{4}$–$\frac{3}{8}$ in. long, linear-oblong, membranous when ripe, straight, mucronate, turgid, densely silky-pubescent, nearly bilocular. Seeds 4–6, reniform, dark-brown. Fl. B. I. v. 2, p. 121; Aitch. Pb. & Sind Pl. p. 43; Bunge, Monogr. Astr. (1868–69) part 1, p. 9; part 2, p. 6.

A very rare plant. SIND: *Stocks* ex *Aitch.* l. c.

I have seen no specimens from the Bombay Presidency.—DISTRIB. India (Panjab); Egypt, Arabia, Cape Verde Islands.

2. **Astragalus contortuplicatus,** *Linn. Sp. Pl.* (1753) p. 758. Annual; stems numerous, 6–18 in. long, suberect or procumbent, obscurely angled, clothed with soft spreading white hairs. Leaves $2\frac{1}{2}$–4 in. long, imparipinnate, distinctly petioled; stipules large, broadly ovate, acute, free. Leaflets 13–17, oblanceolate, elliptic or oblong, $\frac{1}{4}$–$\frac{1}{2}$ in. long, densely pilose on both surfaces; petiolules short. Flowers numerous, in dense heads; peduncles axillary, much shorter than the leaves, clothed with long soft spreading hairs; bracts linear-subulate, plumose. Calyx $\frac{1}{6}$–$\frac{1}{5}$ in. long, densely pilose; teeth longer than the tube, linear-subulate, plumose, the 3 lower the longer. Corolla yellow, slightly exserted, deciduous; standard oblong, obcordate; wings narrow, much shorter than the standard; keel broader and longer than the wings. Pods $\frac{1}{2}$ in. long, completely bilocular except at the apex, quite contortuplicate, membranous, rugose, densely pilose. Seeds 20–30, reniform. Fl. B. I. v. 2, p. 122; Aitch. Pb. & Sind Pl. p. 43; Bunge, Monogr. Astr. part 1, p. 18; part 2, p. 20; Woodr. in Journ. Bomb. Nat. v. 11 (1897) p. 422.

Rare. SIND: *Stocks*, 406!; Hyderabad, *Woodrow.*—DISTRIB. India (Panjab); E. Europe, Orient, W. Siberia.

3. **Astragalus Stocksii,** *Benth. ex Bunge, Monogr. Astr.* (1868–69) part 1, p. 6; part 2, p. 4. Shrubby, much-branched; branches elongate, hairy with appressed soft hairs, armed with yellow spreading spines (really the persistent rhachises of fallen leaflets), $\frac{1}{2}$–$\frac{5}{8}$ in. long. Leaves abruptly-pinnate, the rhachis ending in a spine, the leaves on the young shoots with a strong spiny fulvous persistent rhachis with a resting bud in its axil which develops in the second season, the leaflets deciduous, leaving scars on the spiny rhachis; leaves of the second season with slender rhachises fascicled in the axils of the naked old ones, which then appear as spines; stipules minute, caducous. Leaflets 2–3 pairs, obovate, oblong or oblanceolate, $\frac{1}{8}$–$\frac{1}{4}$ by $\frac{1}{16}$–$\frac{1}{8}$ in., clothed with closely appressed medifixed hairs, base usually acute; petiolules short. Flowers in lax short or elongate, 5–7-flowered racemes; bracts minute. Calyx shortly campanulate, $\frac{1}{6}$–$\frac{1}{5}$ in. long, hairy; teeth short, triangular. Corolla $\frac{3}{8}$–$\frac{7}{16}$ in. long, yellow; standard broadly obovate-oblong, retuse. Pods stalked, $\frac{1}{2}$–$\frac{3}{4}$ in. long, glabrous, completely bilocular, attenuated at both ends, sulcate and very convex on the dorsal, straight on the ventral side.

Seeds 2–5. Not in Fl. B. I.; Boiss. Fl. Orient. v. 2, p. 492; Woodr. in Journ. Bomb. Nat. v. 11 (1897) p. 422.

SIND: Kirthár mountains, *James*!

The plant had not hitherto been reported from Sind, though very common in Beluchistan. The specimens found on the Kirthár mountains were sent to Poona by Mr. James, Chief Commissioner in Sind.—DISTRIB. Beluchistan, Afghanistan.

18. TAVERNIERA, DC.

Much-branched undershrubs. Leaves few, 1- or pinnately 3-foliolate; stipules scarious; leaflets usually obovate or orbicular, exstipellate. Flowers rosy or white, in axillary lax racemes. Calyx-teeth subequal or the 2 upper more remote. Corolla much-exserted; standard broadly obovate, narrowed at the base, scarcely clawed; wings small; keel about equal to the standard, obliquely truncate at the apex. Stamens monadelphous; anthers uniform. Ovary stalked; ovules usually 2; style filiform, inflexed; stigma small, terminal. Pod of 1–3 flattened indehiscent densely muricated joints. Seeds reniform.—DISTRIB. India and the Orient; species 6–8.

1. **Taverniera nummularia,** *DC. Mém. Légum.* (1825) p. 340, t. 52. A much-branched undershrub, 1–2 ft. high; branches twiggy, terete, minutely velvety-canescent. Leaves 1-foliolate; stipules scarious, triangular, acute, free, united into one deciduous one which is opposite the leaf. Leaflets very variable in size, $\frac{1}{4}$–1 in. across, orbicular or obovate, thick, glaucous, mucronulate, much longer than the petiolules; petiolules $\frac{1}{16}$–$\frac{1}{8}$ in. long. Flowers in axillary lax 2–6-flowered racemes longer than the leaves. Calyx $\frac{1}{8}$ in. long, finely pubescent; teeth triangular, acute, about equalling the tube, the 2 upper larger and more remote than the 3 lower. Corolla red, $\frac{3}{8}$–$\frac{1}{2}$ in. long; standard obovate-orbicular, slightly longer than the keel, glabrous, veined with dark purple parallel veins, emarginate. Pods with 1–2 one-seeded joints; joints ovoid, transversely and subreticulately rugose and echinate. Fl. B. I. v. 2, p. 140; Boiss. Fl. Orient. v. 2, p. 508; Aitch. Pb. & Sind Pl. p. 44; Woodr. in Journ. Bomb. Nat. v. 11 (1897) p. 422; Watt, Dict. Econ. Prod. v. 6, part 3, p. 414. *T. cuneifolia*, Arn. in Wight, Icon. t. 1055; Dalz. & Gibs. p. 67. *Hedysarum Gibsonii*, Grah. Cat. Bo. Pl. p. 49.—Flowers: Dec. VERN. *Jethmad.*

DECCAN: waste places, *Dalzell & Gibson*; Chattersinghi hill near Poona, *Ranade*!; Nasik, *Bhiva*!; S. Deccan, *Cleghorn* ex *Prain*. GUJARAT: near Gogo in Kathiawar (plentiful), *Dalzell & Gibson*. SIND: *Stocks* ex *Aitchison*.—DISTRIB. India (Panjab); Afghanistan, Orient.

The root is sweet, hence the Maratha name, which is also the name of liquorice.

19. GEISSASPIS, Wight & Arn.

Slender diffuse herbs. Leaves abruptly-pinnate; stipules membranous, produced below the insertion. Leaflets few, obovate, exstipellate. Flowers very small, yellow or purplish, in long-peduncled axillary racemes; bracts large, obliquely reniform, veined, imbricate, persistent, usually concealing the flowers and fruit, ciliate or not; bracteoles 0. Calyx deeply 2-lipped, the upper lip entire, the lower obscurely 3-toothed. Corolla exceeding the calyx; standard broadly suborbicular, with a short claw; wings obliquely obovate or oblong; keel incurved, obtuse, a little shorter than the standard. Stamens monadelphous; anthers uniform. Ovary shortly stipitate; ovules 2; style incurved; stigma minute, terminal. Pods with 1–2 joints; joints turgid in the middle with a flat border, reticulately veined, 1-seeded, indehiscent.—DISTRIB. India, Tropical Africa; species about 5.

Flowers not more than one-third as long as the long-bristled bracts. 1. *G. cristata.*
Flowers nearly or quite as long as the short-bristled bracts .... 2. *G. tenella.*

1. **Geissaspis cristata,** *Wight & Arn. Prodr.* (1834) p. 218. A procumbent trailing annual, with densely cæspitose terete glabrous stems $\frac{1}{2}$–2 ft. long. Leaves abruptly-pinnate; petioles $\frac{3}{16}$–$\frac{1}{4}$ in. long; stipules scarious, lanceolate, $\frac{3}{16}$ in. long, continued below the insertion, spurred at the base, strongly nerved, ciliate. Leaflets 4, obovate, $\frac{1}{4}$–$\frac{1}{2}$ by $\frac{1}{8}$–$\frac{1}{4}$ in., slightly oblique, obtuse, glabrous on both surfaces, narrowed at the base; nerves prominent beneath; petiolules very short. Heads of flowers dense, 1 in. or more long; peduncles axillary; pedicels short, slender, curved; bracts reniform, reaching $\frac{1}{2}$ in. or even more in breadth, much imbricate, reticulately veined, ciliate with stiff yellow bristles $\frac{1}{12}$–$\frac{1}{10}$ in. long, each bract about 3 times as long the single flower it encloses. Calyx membranous, glabrous, $\frac{1}{10}$ in. long; lobes lanceolate, acute. Corolla $\frac{1}{6}$ in. long; standard broadly obovate, glabrous, veined. Pods 1- (rarely 2-) jointed; joints about $\frac{1}{6}$ in. long, reticulately veined, nearly straight on the upper, much rounded (sometimes almost semicircular) on the lower side, long-beaked and with a flat margin, glabrous. Seed 1 in each joint, chestnut-brown when ripe. Fl. B. I. v. 2, p. 141; Dalz. & Gibs. p. 62; Taubert, in Engl. & Prantl, Pflanzenf. v. 3, part 3, p. 82, fig. 45, B; Woodr. in Journ. Bomb. Nat. v. 11 (1897) p. 422.—Flowers: Oct. VERN. *Barki.*

In grass during the rains, tolerably common. KONKAN: *Stocks*!, *Law*!, *Dalzell*! DECCAN: Khandala, *Cooke*! S. M. COUNTRY: Belgaum, *Ritchie*, 181! KANARA: Kála naddi, *Ritchie*, 181!—DISTRIB. India (W. Peninsula, Birma); China.

2. **Geissaspis tenella,** *Benth. in Flora*, v. 32 (1849) p. 559. A weak trailing annual 3–12 in. long; stems and branches from a thick root, slender, terete. Leaves abruptly-pinnate; petioles $\frac{1}{8}$–$\frac{3}{16}$ in. long; stipules membranous, oblong or oblanceolate, ciliate, not spurred. Leaflets 4, sessile, $\frac{3}{16}$–$\frac{1}{4}$ by $\frac{1}{10}$–$\frac{1}{8}$ in., all starting almost from the same point, somewhat oblique, obovate, rounded or truncate at the apex, glabrous on both surfaces, base cuneate; nerves prominent beneath. Flowers in copious axillary racemes; bracts obliquely oblong, $\frac{1}{8}$–$\frac{1}{6}$ in. broad, ciliate-toothed with short stiff hairs (almost spinous); peduncles very slender; pedicels short, curved. Calyx $\frac{1}{12}$ in. long, membranous. Corolla yellow, nearly as long as the enclosing bracts and sometimes even slightly longer. Pods 1–2-jointed; joints $\frac{1}{8}$ in. in diam., orbicular, reticulately veined, shortly pointed and with a flat margin, turgid in the middle. Seed 1 in each joint, dark-brown when ripe. Fl. B. I. v. 2, p. 141.—Flowers: Oct. VERN. *Lahán-barki.*

A rare plant. KONKAN: *Stocks*! KANARA: Siddapur in rice-fields, *Talbot*!—DISTRIB. India (W. Peninsula).

20. ALHAGI, Tourn. ex Adans. Fam. v. 2 (1763) p. 328.

Much-branched rigid shrubs armed with axillary spines (abortive branches or peduncles). Leaves simple, quite entire, usually small;

stipules small. Flowers red, usually few, in axillary racemes. Calyx campanulate; teeth short, subequal. Corolla exserted; standard obovate, with a short claw; wings falcate-oblong, free; keel incurved, obtuse, about equalling the standard and the wings. Stamens diadelphous; anthers uniform. Ovary stalked; ovules many; style filiform, incurved, glabrous; stigma small, terminal. Pod linear, jointed, somewhat thick, subterete or compressed, smooth, indehiscent, usually contracted between the seeds; joints not separating. Seed reniform.—DISTRIB. From Greece and Egypt to Soongaria and the Himalayas; species 3.

1. **Alhagi camelorum,** *Fisch. Ind. Hort. Gorenk.* ed. 2 (1812) p. 72. A low erect shrub, armed with copious hard sharp spines reaching sometimes 1½ in. long; branches terete, striate, glabrous or nearly so. Leaves simple, coriaceous, ¼–⅝ by ⅛–$\frac{3}{16}$ in., obovate-oblong, obtuse, apiculate, glabrous or puberulous, base cuneate; petioles very short; stipules minute, subulate. Flowers 5–8 on a spine; pedicels short, slender. Calyx glabrous, ⅛ in. long; teeth short, triangular. Corolla a little more than twice as long as the calyx; standard ⅓ in. long by ¼ in. broad, obovate-oblong, auricled at the base above the claw, glabrous. Ovary glabrous. Pods ¾–1¼ in. long, usually falcate, more or less contracted between the seeds, glabrous. Seeds blackish-brown, smooth, polished. Boiss. Fl. Orient. v. 2, p. 559; Prain, in Journ. As. Soc. Beng. v. 66 (1898) p. 377. *Alhagi Maurorum*, Baker, in Hook. Fl. B. I. v. 2, p. 145 (*vix* Tournef.); Grah. Cat. p. 50; Dalz. & Gibs. p. 67; Talb. Trees, Bomb. p. 68; Woodr. in Journ. Bomb. Nat. v. 11 (1897) p. 422; Watt, Dict. Econ. Prod. v. 1, p. 164.—Flowers: Mar. VERN. *Javasa.*

I have followed Prain (*l. c.*) in naming the Indian species with a glabrous ovary *A. camelorum*, as distinct from *A. Maurorum*, which has a silky one.

GUJARAT: common, *Graham, Dalzell & Gibson*; abundant about Broach, *Cooke*! S. M. COUNTRY: *Graham, Law.* SIND: *Cooke*!, *Vicary*!, *Woodrow*!; Hyderabad, *Strachan*!; Sehwan, *Kanitkar*!—DISTRIB. India (N. & N.W. Prov.); Beluchistan, Egypt, Arabia.

The *camel-thorn* or *Persian manna* plant. The freshly-cut plants are used largely in Gujarat for making *tatties* in the hot season. The plant comes into leaf in the hot season and is used as a fodder for camels; hence its name. Some of its parts supply medicine which is considered valuable by the natives. See Watt, Dict. Econ. Prod. l. c.

21. ZORNIA, Gmel.

Herbs. Leaves digitately 2–4-foliolate; stipules subfoliaceous, often punctate. Leaflets usually dotted, exstipellate. Flowers in lax racemes; peduncles terminal and axillary; bracts twin, lateral, nerved, of the same form as the stipules but larger and broader, each pair enclosing a sessile flower. Calyx small, membranous; the 2 upper teeth connate. Corolla much exserted; standard suborbicular, clawed; wings obliquely obovate or oblong; keel incurved, subrostrate. Stamens monadelphous; anthers dimorphous. Ovary sessile; ovules many; style filiform; stigma small, terminal. Pod jointed, compressed, the upper suture nearly straight, the lower deeply sinuate; joints easily separable, smooth or echinate, indehiscent, flattened, 1-seeded.—DISTRIB. Species 10, all but 2 American.

1. **Zornia diphylla,** *Pers. Syn. Pl.* v. 2 (1807) p. 318. Annual, much-branched, 8–15 in.; branches prostrate or ascending, glabrous or puberulous. Leaves 2-foliolate; petioles $\frac{1}{4}$–$\frac{3}{4}$ in. long; stipules $\frac{3}{8}$ in. long, lanceolate, acute, strongly nerved, produced below the insertion into a triangular spur. Leaflets variable in size and shape, $\frac{1}{2}$–$1\frac{1}{8}$ by $\frac{1}{8}$–$\frac{3}{8}$ in., sessile, often unequal-sided, lanceolate, linear-lanceolate or occasionally linear, dotted with black glands beneath, glabrous, rigid. Flowers small, in 3–12-flowered spicate racemes 1–4 in. long; peduncles slender, terete; bracts foliaceous, reaching $\frac{1}{2}$ in. long, ovate-lanceolate, acute, ciliate, sprinkled with black dots, produced below the insertion into a triangular spur, strongly nerved from the base, completely enclosing the flower and often the entire pod. Calyx membranous, $\frac{1}{8}$ in. long, the 2 upper teeth broad, obtuse, deeply connate, ciliate at the apex, the 2 lateral teeth smaller, deltoid, the lowest tooth the longest, lanceolate, acute, ciliate. Corolla twice as long as the calyx; standard orbicular, with a long claw. Pods 1–6-jointed, either quite enclosed by the bracts or exserted; joints about $\frac{1}{12}$ in. long, compressed, indehiscent, covered with numerous short straight fulvous spines. Fl. B. I. v. 2, p. 147; Benth. in Mart. Fl. Bras. v. 15, part 1, p. 80, t. 21–22; Taubert, in Engl. & Prantl, Pflanzenf. v. 3, part 3, p. 325, fig. 125, D (fruit); Trim. Fl. Ceyl. v. 2, p. 35; Woodr. in Journ. Bomb. Nat. v. 11 (1897) p. 422; Watt, Dict. Econ. Prod. v. 6, part 4, p. 374. *Zornia angustifolia*, Sm.; Grah. Cat. p. 48; Dalz. & Gibs. p. 62.—Flowers: Aug.–Sept. VERN. *Lándgu*.

Tolerably common. DECCAN: Poona, *Woodrow*; Chattersinghi hill near Poona, *Ranade*! S. M. COUNTRY: Badami, *Woodrow*!

VAR. *zeylonensis*, Baker, in Hook. f. Fl. B. I. v. 2, p. 148. Leaflets ovate. Pod much longer than the bracts; joints longer than in the type. Var. *conjugata*, Trim. Fl. Ceyl. v. 2, p. 35. *Zornia zeylonensis* (sp.), Pers. Syn. Pl. v. 2 (1807) p. 318; Dalz. & Gibs. p. 62. *Z. zeylonica* (sp.), Grah. Cat. p. 48. *Z. conjugata* (sp.), Sm. in Rees, Cyclop. v. 39 (1819).

22. STYLOSANTHES, Swartz.

Rigid undershrubs. Leaves pinnately 3-foliolate; stipules adnate to the base of the petiole. Leaflets exstipellate. Flowers small, in dense spikes or terminal heads. Calyx tubular; tube filiform; lobes membranous, the 4 upper connate, the lowest narrow, distinct. Petals inserted at the throat of the calyx-tube; standard orbicular; wings oblong, free; keel incurved, obtuse, about equalling the standard. Stamens monadelphous; anthers dimorphous. Ovary subsessile at the base of the calyx-tube; ovules 2–3; style elongate, filiform, the lower part persistent; stigma minute, terminal. Pod sessile, compressed, hooked at the apex with the persistent base of the style; joints 1–2, reticulate or muricate. Seed compressed, ovate or lenticular.—DISTRIB. Cosmopolitan in the Tropics; species about 15.

1. **Stylosanthes mucronata,** *Willd. Sp. Pl.* v. 3 (1800) p. 1166. A much-branched dwarf woody perennial; branches stiff, wiry, ascending, more or less hairy. Leaves 3-foliolate; petioles $\frac{1}{8}$–$\frac{3}{16}$ in. long; stipules scarious, strongly nerved, adnate downwards to the petiole for half their length, terminating above in 2 spreading teeth. Leaflets elliptic-oblong,

$\frac{3}{16}$–$\frac{3}{8}$ by $\frac{1}{8}$–$\frac{3}{16}$ in., the terminal leaflet a little larger than the lateral ones, all acute and mucronate at the apex, glabrous above, silky-pubescent, strongly nerved and gland-dotted beneath, base subacute or rounded; lateral leaflets subsessile, the terminal with a petiolule about $\frac{1}{16}$ in. long. Flowers small, 1 or few, sessile in the axils of leaf-like stipulate bracts and forming close terminal heads or spikes. Calyx $\frac{1}{10}$ in. long, membranous, the upper connate lobes ciliate at the apex. Corolla twice the length of the calyx. Pods very short, concealed by the persistent bracts, tipped with the curved lower portion of the style; joints pubescent with raised veins. Fl. B. I. v. 2, p. 148; Trim. Fl. Ceyl. v. 2, p. 36; Talb. Trees, Bomb. p. 69.

Common on the dry hills near Dharwár, ex *Talbot*.—DISTRIB. India (W. Peninsula); Ceylon, Cape, Tropical Africa, Malay Islands.

28. SMITHIA, Ait.

Herbs or undershrubs. Leaves impari- or abruptly-pinnate; stipules scarious, persistent. Leaflets small, sensitive, often falcate, exstipellate. Flowers usually arranged in unilateral axillary racemes; bracts and bracteoles scarious or striate, persistent. Calyx deeply 2-lipped, the upper lip entire or emarginate, the lower entire, 3-toothed or 3-fid. Corolla exserted; standard suborbicular, shortly clawed; wings obliquely oblong or subrostrate, about equalling the standard. Stamens in 2 bundles of 5 each; anthers uniform. Ovary sessile or stalked; ovules many; style filiform, incurved; stigma small, terminal. Pod of few or many flattened or turgid joints folded inside the calyx.—DISTRIB. Tropics of the Old World; species 20–30.

Calyx rigid; veins close, parallel, simple.
  Stems not bristly.
    Flowers yellow.
      Flowers in short simple racemes .... 1. *S. sensitiva.*
      Flowers 1 or 2 in the axils of leaves which are crowded at the ends of the branches .... 2. *S. conferta.*
    Flowers purple .... 3. *S. purpurea.*
  Stems densely bristly .... 4. *S. setulosa.*
Calyx membranous; veins distinctly anastomosing.
  Flowers in globose terminal heads.
    Leaflets 9–15 pairs .... 5. *S. capitata.*
    Leaflets 3–4 pairs .... 6. *S. pycnantha.*
  Flowers in racemes.
    Lower lip of calyx 3-lobed.
      Leaflets 2 pairs .... 7. *S. bigemina.*
      Leaflets 3–4 pairs .... 8. *S. blanda,* var. *racemosa.*
    Lower lip of calyx entire.
      Upper lip larger than the lower .... 9. *S. hirsuta.*
      Lower lip larger than the upper .... 10. *S. salsuginea.*

1. **Smithia sensitiva,** *Ait. Hort. Kew.* v. 3 (1789) p. 496. Annual, diffuse, much-branched; stems 1–3 ft. long, slender, not bristly. Leaves abruptly-pinnate; rhachis $\frac{1}{2}$–1 in. long, bristly and ending in a long bristle; petioles short; stipules scarious, lanceolate, prolonged below the insertion into long cuspidate or lacerate auricles. Leaflets 3–10 pairs, $\frac{1}{4}$–$\frac{1}{2}$ in. long, linear-oblong, obtuse, bristle-pointed, glabrous above and with strong bristles on the midrib and somewhat straight margins beneath, base rounded, somewhat unequal-sided. Flowers 2–6, in simple

racemes from the axils of the upper leaves; peduncles ½ in. long, slender, glabrous or with a few scattered bristles; pedicels filiform, ascending; bracteoles scarious, ⅙–⅕ in. long, ovate, acute, bristle-pointed. Calyx ¼–⅓ in. long, with a few scattered bristles, rigid; veins close, parallel, simple; lips equal, entire, acute. Corolla yellow, ⅜ in. long. Pods flattened; joints 4–6, orbicular, margined, densely papillose on the faces. Fl. B. I. v. 2, p. 148; Grah. Cat. p. 48; Dalz. & Gibs. p. 63; Trim. Fl. Ceyl. v. 2, p. 37; Woodr. in Journ. Bomb. Nat. v. 11 (1897) p. 422; Watt, Dict. Econ. Prod. v. 6, part 3, p. 255.—Flowers: Sept.–Oct. VERN. *Kavla.*

Common in Bombay towards the close of the rains, *Graham*. KONKAN: *Stocks*!, *Law*! DECCAN: Khandala, *Cooke*!; Matheran, *Woodrow*. S. M. COUNTRY: Nagargali near Dharwar, *Cooke*!; Belgaum, *Cooke*!—DISTRIB. Throughout India; Andamans and Nicobars, Tropical Africa, Madagascar, Java, China.

The leaves are used as a pot-herb, and cattle eat the plant greedily.

VAR. *flava.* General habit of *S. sensitiva* with stouter stems and larger flowers. *S. flava* (sp.), Dalz. MS. ex Prain, in Journ. As. Soc. Beng. v. 66 (1898) p. 378; *S. sensitiva*, var. *flore majore*, Herb. Ind. Or. Hook. f. & T. in Herb. Kew.

Except the slightly larger flowers (about ½ in. long) there does not seem any distinctive character to separate this from the type, certainly none to raise it to the rank of a species.

KONKAN: *Stocks*!, *Law*! KANARA: *Talbot* ex *Prain* l. c.

2. **Smithia conferta,** *Sm. in Rees, Cyclop.* v. 33 (1819) n. 2. Annual, 2–4 ft. high; stems not bristly; branches long, virgate, straggling, smooth, with long internodes below. Leaves small, nearly sessile, abruptly-pinnate; rhachis ¼–½ in. long; stipules very large, scarious, lanceolate, acute, with very long acuminate or lacerate auricles. Leaflets subsessile, 2–8 pairs, those of the stem-leaves ¼–⅜ by ⅛ in., those of the upper or floral leaves narrower, about $\frac{1}{16}$ in. broad, all linear-oblong, obtuse or subacute, densely bristly on the margins and on the midrib beneath. Flowers solitary or 2, in the axils of the upper leaves which are crowded at the ends of the branches so as to form a congested head; pedicels very short, hairy; bracteoles scarious, ⅛ in. long, elliptic-oblong, acute, with a long bristle at the apex and a few long bristles at the back. Calyx ⅕–¼ in. long, veins close, parallel; lips equal, oblong, acute, with a few long bristles at the apex and on the back. Corolla yellow, ⅓–$\frac{7}{16}$ in. long. Pods 3-6-jointed; joints small, turgid, papillose. Trim. Fl. Ceyl. v. 2, p. 37. *S. geminiflora*, Roth, Nov. Pl. Sp. (1821) p. 352; Woodr. in Journ. Bomb. Nat. v. 11 (1897) p. 422. *S. geminiflora*, var. *conferta*, Baker, in Hook. f. Fl. B. I. v. 2, p. 149.—Flowers: Nov.–Dec.

The name *S. conferta* given by Smith is 2 years prior to the name *S. geminiflora* given by Roth.

KONKAN: *Stocks*!; Malwan, *Woodrow*. S. M. COUNTRY: Belgaum, *Ritchie*, 1034! KANARA: Kála naddi, *Ritchie*, 1034!—DISTRIB. Throughout India; Ceylon, Java, N. Australia.

VAR. *geminiflora.* A somewhat more slender plant. Leaves and calyx much less hairy. Flowers in the heads much fewer, often reduced to a single pair.

KONKAN: *Stocks*!, *Capt. Geburne*!

3. **Smithia purpurea,** *Hook. Bot. Mag.* v. 73 (1847) t. 4283. Herbaceous, erect, branched, ½–2 ft. high; stems and branches slender, not bristly. Leaves nearly sessile; rhachis 1–2¼ in. long, slightly bristly, ending in a long bristle-point; stipules scarious, ovate-oblong, acute, prolonged below their insertion into acuminate or lacerate auricles. Leaflets 6–15 pairs, sessile, ¼–⅜ in. long, elliptic-oblong, subacute, terminated by a very long bristle, glabrous above, with long bristles on the oblique midrib and the margins beneath, base rounded. Flowers 6–12, in copious secund racemes from the axils of the upper leaves; peduncles filiform, more or less bristly, ascending; pedicels filiform, drooping; bracteoles ⅛–¼ in. long, ovate-oblong, subacute, parallel-veined, sometimes with a few bristles on the margin. Calyx ⅓ in. long, rigid, parallel-veined, glabrous; lips subequal, the upper obtuse, rounded, the lower acute. Corolla ½ in. long, purple, with a white spot at the base of the standard. Joints of pod 10–12, orbicular-oblong, about $\frac{1}{12}$ in. long, reticulato-venose, not papillose. Fl. B. I. v. 2, p. 149; Dalz. & Gibs. p. 64; Woodr. in Journ. Bomb. Nat. v. 11 (1897) p. 422.—Flowers: Sept.–Dec. VERN. *Burkar.*

Not common. KONKAN: *Stocks*!; Thána, *Law*! DECCAN: Mahableshwar, *Cooke*!; Lanoli (plentiful), *Cooke*!, *Woodrow*!; Khandala, *Cooke*!—DISTRIB. Appears to be endemic in the Bombay Presidency.

4. **Smithia setulosa,** *Dalz. in Kew Journ. Bot.* v. 3 (1851) p. 208. Erect, dichotomously branched, 3–4 ft. high; stems and branches bristly with deflexed yellowish hairs. Leaves abruptly-pinnate; rhachis 2–4 in. long, bristly, ending in a long bristle; petioles ¼–⅜ in. long; stipules scarious, striate, lanceolate, cuspidate, glabrous or with a few long bristles near the apex, prolonged below their insertion into acuminate or lacerate auricles. Leaflets 4–7 pairs, subsessile, ¾–1½ by ¼–⅜ in., oblong, obtuse, terminated by a long bristle, somewhat unequal-sided, glabrous, ciliate. Flowers in dichotomously forked racemes forming a thyrsoid panicle, only the lowest subtended by a leaf; peduncles terete, bristly; pedicels short, ascending; bracts ⅓ in. long, elliptic, subacute, striate. Calyx ⅓ in. long, rigid, parallel-veined, densely bristly; upper lip obtuse, slightly recurved; lower smaller, elliptic-lanceolate, acute. Corolla ⅔ in. long, bright yellow. Pods 10–12-jointed; joints reticulato-venose, not papillose. Fl. B. I. v. 2, p. 149; Dalz. & Gibs. p. 63; Bedd. Icon. t. 243; Woodr. in Journ. Bomb. Nat. v. 11 (1897) p. 422.—Flowers: Sept.–Dec.

KONKAN: *Stocks*!; W. Ghâts, *Woodrow*; Mandangarh (Dapoli taluka), *Nairne*. DECCAN: Mahableshwar (abundant), *Cooke*!, *Woodrow*! S. M. COUNTRY: Párva Ghát, *Dalzell*!; Belgaum districts, *Cooke*!—DISTRIB. India (W. Peninsula).

5. **Smithia capitata,** *Dalz. in Kew Journ. Bot.* v. 3 (1851) p. 208 (*not* of Desv.). Annual, 1–2 ft. high; stems and branches terete, not bristly. Leaves abruptly-pinnate; rhachis bristly, 1–2 in. long, ending in a bristle; petioles short; stipules scarious, lanceolate, acute, prolonged below their insertion into acute or lacerate auricles. Leaflets subsessile, 9–15 pairs, ¼–⅜ by ⅛–$\frac{3}{16}$ in. long, linear-oblong, obtuse, bristly on the midrib beneath, ciliate. Flowers in globose terminal (usually solitary) many-flowered heads; peduncles glabrous; pedicels very short; bracteoles membranous, oblanceolate, about ⅔ the length of the calyx, bristle-tipped. Calyx ⅜ in. long, membranous, reticulately

veined; lips orbicular, truncate, toothed, the teeth ending in stiff bristles. Corolla much exserted. Pods 5–7-jointed; joints neither venose nor papillose. Fl. B. I. v. 2, p. 150; Dalz. & Gibs. p. 63 (*not* Desv.); Bedd. Icon. t. 244; Woodr. in Journ. Bomb. Nat. v. 11 (1897) p. 422.—Flowers: Sept.–Oct.

KONKAN: *Law*!, *Stocks*! S. M. COUNTRY: Párva Ghát, *Dalzell*!—DISTRIB. India (W. Peninsula).

6. **Smithia pycnantha,** *Benth. ex Baker, in Hook. f. Fl. B. I.* v. 2 (1876) p. 150. An erect annual ½–2 ft. high; stems and branches bristly with bulbous hairs. Leaves abruptly-pinnate; rhachis ½–¾ in. long, bristly and bristle-pointed; stipules lanceolate, acute, very hairy, prolonged below their insertion into acuminate or lacerate auricles. Leaflets subsessile, 3–4 pairs, ⅜–⅝ by ⅛–¼ in., linear-oblong, rounded at the apex, not or slightly bristle-pointed, glabrous above, with a few scattered bristles on the midrib beneath, ciliate. Flowers in dense globose heads 1 in. or more in diam., formed of congested racemes; pedicels shorter than the calyx, bristly; bracteoles oblong or oblanceolate-oblong, about half as long as the calyx. Calyx ⅛–⅙ in. long, densely ciliate on the margins with yellow bristles rising from black glandular bases; lips subequal, the upper truncate or emarginate, the lower 3-lobed. Corolla twice as long as the calyx. Pods 5–9-jointed; joints venose. Woodr. in Journ. Bomb. Nat. v. 11 (1897) p. 422.

Rare. KONKAN: *Stocks*!, *Law*! KANARA: *Woodrow*.—DISTRIB. Apparently endemic.

7. **Smithia bigemina,** *Dalz. in Kew Journ. Bot.* v. 3 (1851) p. 208. Annual, diffuse, 6–12 in. high; stems and branches very slender, bristly with yellowish hairs. Leaves abruptly-pinnate; rhachis ⅛ in. long, hairy and bristle-pointed; petioles very short; stipules scarious, lanceolate-cuspidate, prolonged below their insertion into acuminate or lacerate auricles. Leaflets 2 pairs, subsessile, ⅜–$\frac{7}{16}$ by $\frac{3}{16}$–⅜ in., oblanceolate, cuneate, obtuse and bristle-pointed at the apex, glabrous above, more or less strigose beneath, ciliate. Flowers 2–8, in copious axillary racemes crowded towards the tops of the peduncles; peduncles glabrous, longer than the leaves; pedicels very short, hairy; bracts beneath the raceme thinly membranous, oblong, bristle-pointed, glabrous; bracteoles beneath the calyx scarious, ovate-lanceolate, bristle-pointed and bristly along the midrib at the back, half as long as the calyx. Calyx ⅛ in. long, membranous, with dichotomously branched (not parallel) veins; lips equal, bristly outside, strongly bristle-ciliate on the margins, the upper lip truncate or slightly emarginate, the lower acutely 3-toothed, the middle tooth the longest. Corolla yellow, twice as long as the calyx. Pods 6–8-jointed: joints tubercled. Fl. B. I. v. 2, p. 149; Dalz. & Gibs. p. 64; Woodr. in Journ. Bomb. Nat. v. 11 (1897) p. 422.—Flowers: Sept.–Dec. VERN. *Berki*.

KONKAN: *Stocks*! DECCAN: Poona, *Woodrow*!; Mahableshwar, *Cooke*! S. M. COUNTRY: Párva Ghát, *Dalzell*! SIND: *Stocks* ex *Prain*.—DISTRIB. India (W. Peninsula).

8. **Smithia blanda,** var. **racemosa,** *Baker, in Hook. f. Fl. B. I.* v. 2 (1876) p. 151. Annual, erect, 1–1½ ft. high; stems slender, bristly with spreading fulvous hairs. Leaves abruptly-pinnate; rhachis ½–¾ in. long, bristly and bristle-pointed; stipules scarious, more or less

hairy, lanceolate, prolonged below their insertion into acuminate or lacerate auricles. Leaflets subsessile, 3–4 pairs, $\frac{3}{8}$–$\frac{3}{4}$ by $\frac{3}{16}$–$\frac{1}{5}$ in., oblanceolate-oblong, rounded at the apex, not or minutely bristle-pointed, ciliate, glabrous above, glabrous or with a few scattered hairs beneath, the lowest pair of leaflets cuneate and nearly equal-sided, the others more or less inequilateral at the base. Flowers in capitate subsecund racemes; peduncles 6–12-flowered, longer than the leaves, bristly; pedicels short, hairy; bracteoles $\frac{1}{10}$ in. long, elliptic-oblong or oblanceolate-oblong, hairy, ciliate at the apex. Calyx $\frac{1}{6}$ in. long, bristly and densely ciliate with yellowish hairs; veins branched, not parallel; upper lip slightly larger than the lower, truncate, retuse or emarginate, cuneate; lower lip 3-lobed, the mid-lobe acute and longer than the lateral ones. Corolla $\frac{1}{3}$ in. long. Pods 4–7-jointed; joints reticulato-venose. Woodr. in Journ. Bomb. Nat. v. 11 (1897) p. 423. *Smithia racemosa* (sp.), Heyne, in Wall. Cat. 5670; Dalz. & Gibs. p. 63.—Flowers: Sept.

KONKAN: *Law*!, *Dalzell*! S. M. COUNTRY: Belgaum, *Stocks*, 315!, *Dalzell*. KANARA: *Dalzell*!; Sirsi (N. Kanara), *Woodrow*.—DISTRIB. India (W. Peninsula).

9. **Smithia hirsuta,** *Dalz. in Kew Journ. Bot.* v. 3 (1851) p. 135 (*not* of Baker). Annual, erect, 1–1½ ft. high, sparingly branched; stems and branches bristly with fulvous spreading hairs. Leaves abruptly-pinnate; rhachis bristly and ending in a bristle, $\frac{1}{2}$–$\frac{3}{4}$ in. long; petioles $\frac{1}{8}$–$\frac{1}{4}$ in. long; stipules scarious, lanceolate, slightly hairy on the back, prolonged below their insertion into acuminate or lacerate auricles. Leaflets subsessile, 3–4 pairs, $\frac{3}{8}$–$\frac{5}{8}$ by $\frac{1}{16}$–$\frac{1}{4}$ in., oblanceolate, cuneate, rounded and finely bristle-tipped at the apex, unequal-sided, ciliate on the margins and with a few hairs beneath. Flowers in somewhat capitate 4–10-flowered racemes; peduncles longer than the leaves, bristly: pedicels short, hairy; bracteoles $\frac{1}{5}$ in. long, somewhat oblique, oblong, acute and with a long bristle-point, glabrous. Calyx $\frac{1}{3}$ in. long, bristly on the outside and strongly ciliate on the margins with fulvous hairs which spring from black bulbous bases; upper lip much larger than the lower, $\frac{1}{3}$ in. long by $\frac{5}{16}$ in. broad, truncate and emarginate at the apex; lower lip $\frac{1}{4}$ in. long by $\frac{1}{6}$ in. broad, obovate, cuneate, acute and bristle-pointed at the apex not lobed. Corolla $\frac{5}{8}$ in. long, bright yellow; standard large, orbicular. Pods 4–7-jointed; joints reticulato-venose. Dalz. & Gibs. p. 63. *Smithia humilis*, Benth. MS. in Herb. Ind. Or. H. f. & T. *Smithia blanda*, Woodr. in Journ. Bomb. Nat. v. 11 (1897) p. 423. *S. blanda* var. *humilis*, Prain, in Journ. As. Soc. Beng. v. 66 (1898) p. 379.—Flowers: Sept.

As I think that this plant is entitled to rank as a separate species rather than as a variety of *S. blanda*, I have restored its status under the original name given to it by Dalzell. The lips of the calyx are very unequal and the bristles thereon spring from black bulbous glands, while the lower lip is *quite entire* and not 3-lobed, as it is in the case of *S. blanda*. Moreover, the flowers are much larger than they are in that plant. Dalzell (*l. c.*) calls attention to the distinctive characters afforded by the calyx.

Dalzell says that the plant is very rare and has been found by him in one locality only, viz. Phunda Ghát near Kolhapur in the Deccan. I have found it abundantly on the road from Panchgani to Mahableshwar, and on the roadside, close to the half-way house, it used to form large brilliant patches of bright yellow.

10. **Smithia salsuginea,** *Hance, Journ. Bot.* v. 7 (1869) p. 164. An erect annual 1–1½ ft. high; stems reddish-brown, slender, terete, glabrous or with very few scattered inconspicuous bristles; branches few, very slender, terete. Leaves abruptly-pinnate; rhachis ⅜–⅝ in. long, bristly and shortly bristle-pointed; petioles ⅛–¼ in. long; stipules oblong-lanceolate, acute, prolonged below their insertion into auricles which usually lie close to the stem or branch. Leaflets 2–4 pairs, oblanceolate-oblong, obtuse, not or rarely apiculate, glabrous on both sides with occasionally a few small bristles on the margins; petiolules $\frac{1}{30}$–$\frac{1}{20}$ in. long. Flowers in dichotomously-branched lax few-flowered corymbose panicles; peduncles slender; pedicels ⅛–¼ in. long, filiform; bracts ovate-lanceolate; bracteoles ⅛–⅙ in. long, ovate-oblong or lanceolate-oblong, acute. Calyx closely reticulately veined, becoming enlarged in fruit, the upper lip somewhat more so than the lower; upper lip (*in flower*) ⅙ by ⅛ in., cuneate oblong, deeply 2-lobed at the apex, ciliate; lower lip (*in flower*) ¼ in. long by ⅙ in. broad at its widest part, broadly ovate, acute, mucronate, ciliate and with a few bristles on the back; upper lip (*in fruit*) $\frac{7}{16}$ by ⅜ in.; lower lip (*in fruit*) ½ by $\frac{5}{16}$ in. Corolla yellow, ⅜–$\frac{7}{16}$ in. long. Pods 10–15-jointed; joints orbicular, papillose. *Smithia dichotoma*, Dalz. MS. ex Baker, in Hook. f. Fl. B. I. v. 2, p. 150.

As pointed out by Prain (Journ. As. Soc. Beng. v. 66 [1898] p. 379), the name *S. salsuginea* was published by Hance in 1869, while the name *S. dichotoma*, though given to the plant by Dalzell many years previously, was not published till 1876. Hence the name *S. salsuginea* must necessarily be adopted.

Hance (*l. c.*) describes the leaves as odd-pinnate, which is evidently a slip. His specimen n. 15113, collected by Sampson in 1868, is in Herb. Kew.

Rare. KONKAN: *Stocks*!, *Law*!—DISTRIB. China.

24. ÆSCHYNOMENE, Linn.

Herbs, undershrubs or shrubs, not twining. Leaves pinnate; stipules setaceous or lanceolate. Leaflets numerous, small, entire, exstipellate. Flowers in axillary (rarely terminal) racemes; bracts usually stipuliform; bracteoles appressed to the calyx. Calyx 2-lipped; lips entire or toothed. Corolla fugacious; standard orbicular, shortly clawed; wings obliquely obovate or oblong, equalling the standard; keel not beaked. Stamens in 2 bundles of 5 each; anthers uniform. Ovary stalked, 2–∞-ovulate; style incurved, not bearded; stigma terminal. Pod stalked, jointed; joints 4–10, flattened or turgid in the middle, 1-seeded, easily separable.—DISTRIB. Throughout the Tropics; species about 30.

Stems woody; calyx glabrous; joints of pod smooth .... 1. *Æ. indica.*
Stems pith-like; calyx hispid; joints of pod echinulate .... 2. *Æ. aspera.*

1. **Æschynomene indica,** *Linn. Sp. Pl.* (1753) p. 713. A much-branched annual undershrub 1–3 ft. high. Stem slender, scarcely ¼ in. in diam. at the base, glabrous, pale-green; branches twiggy, terete, glabrous. Leaves imparipinnate; rhachis 1½–3½ in. long, studded with minute glandular excrescences almost amounting to prickles; stipules

scarious, lanceolate, acuminate, prolonged below their insertion into acute auricles. Leaflets alternate, 21–71, subsessile, $\frac{1}{10}$–$\frac{1}{4}$ by $\frac{1}{20}$–$\frac{1}{16}$ in., set obliquely on the rhachis and overlapping, linear, obtuse, apiculate, glabrous, unequal-sided, thin, 1-nerved, the uppermost much the smallest. Flowers in 1–4-flowered axillary racemes; peduncles about 1 in. long, and as well as the pedicels, glandular, often viscid; pedicels $\frac{1}{4}$–$\frac{1}{3}$ in. long, filiform; bracts foliaceous, bristle-toothed; bracteoles $\frac{1}{8}$–$\frac{1}{6}$ in. long, linear-oblong, acute. Calyx $\frac{1}{4}$ in. long, thinly membranous, glabrous; upper lip bifid; lower lip minutely 3-toothed. Corolla $\frac{3}{8}$ in. long, yellow; standard veined with purple. Pods 1–1$\frac{1}{2}$ by $\frac{1}{8}$ in., slightly curved or nearly straight; upper sutures straight, the lower more or less indented; joints 6–10, readily separating, smooth or slightly papillose. Fl. B. I. v. 2, p. 151; Grah. Cat. p. 48; Dalz. & Gibs. p. 62; Trim. Fl. Ceyl. v. 2, p. 38; Woodr. in Journ. Bomb. Nat. v. 11 (1897) p. 423; Watt, Dict. Econ. Prod. v. 1, p. 126.—Flowers: Aug.–Dec.

KONKAN: *Stocks*!; hills near Matheran, *Kanitkar*! DECCAN: Poona, *Cooke*!, *Woodrow*!, *Kanitkar*!; Kolhapur, *Woodrow*. GUJARAT: common about Surat, *Dalzell & Gibson*.—DISTRIB. Throughout the Tropics of the Old World.

2. **Æschynomene aspera,** *Linn. Sp. Pl.* (1753) p. 713. An erect perennial shrub reaching 10 ft. in height; stem pith-like, 3 in. or more in diam., often horizontal below and floating, then erect, full of light spongy white pith, glabrous; branches few or none. Leaves sessile or nearly so, imparipinnate; stipules $\frac{1}{2}$ in. long, lanceolate, prolonged below their insertion into short auricles, deciduous. Leaflets 61–101, alternate or opposite, sessile, $\frac{1}{8}$–$\frac{1}{2}$ by $\frac{1}{16}$–$\frac{1}{8}$ in., linear-oblong, obtuse, apiculate, 1-nerved, glabrous. Flowers in axillary 2–4-flowered corymbose racemes shorter than the leaves; peduncles and pedicels hairy; bracts $\frac{1}{8}$ in. long, ovate, acute; bracteoles 2, broadly ovate, acute, mucronate, ciliate, $\frac{1}{8}$–$\frac{1}{6}$ in. long. Calyx $\frac{3}{8}$ in. long, hispid; upper lip rounded; the lower 3-lobed. Corolla $\frac{3}{4}$ in. long, fugacious; standard glabrous; keel-petals hairy outside. Pods woody, nearly straight, 2–3 by $\frac{1}{4}$–$\frac{3}{8}$ in., often indented on both sutures, always on the lower one; joints 4–8, echinulate or smooth on the faces. Fl. B. I. v. 2, p. 152; Trim. Fl. Ceyl. v. 2, p. 39; Woodr. in Journ. Bomb. Nat. v. 11 (1897) p. 423; Watt, Dict. Econ. Prod. v. 1, p. 125.

A swamp-species, not very common in the Bombay Presidency. S. M. COUNTRY: Dharwar districts, *Woodrow*! KANARA: *Woodrow*!—DISTRIB. India (Bengal, Assam, Silhet, Birma); Malay Isles, Tropical Africa.

The soft spongy pith-like stems, known as *Sola*, are used for a variety of purposes. Owing to its lightness fishermen use *Sola* for floats, while the light helmets worn by Europeans (*Sola-topis*) are made from it. It is also employed as a surgical lint. See Watt, Dict. Econ. Prod. l. c.

25. ELEIOTIS, DC.

Annual diffuse slender herbs. Leaves 1–3-foliolate; stipules striate. Leaflets 2-stipellate. Flowers in axillary and terminal racemes. Floral bracts large, ovate, striate, deciduous, each enclosing 2 flowers in bud; bracteoles 0. Calyx small, 5-toothed. Corolla small; standard suborbicular, clawed, emarginate; wings oblong; keel obtuse. Stamens diadelphous; anthers uniform. Ovary subsessile or shortly stalked: ovules 1–2; style inflexed above, somewhat thickened at the flexure;

stigma capitate, terminal. Pod of a single boat-shaped membranous joint, compressed, reticulate, indehiscent, channelled along the back. Seed oblong, subreniform.—DISTRIB. India; species 2.

Leaves 1-foliolate; calyx-teeth very short .... 1. *E. sororia.*
Leaves 3-foliolate; calyx-teeth nearly equalling the tube ...... 2. *E. trifoliolata.*

1. **Eleiotis sororia,** *DC. Mém. Légum.* (1825) *Mém.* 7, p. 350; *Prodr.* v. 2, p. 348. A prostrate annual; stems densely cæspitose, trailing, 1–2½ ft. long, triquetrous, glabrous. Leaves 1-foliolate; petioles ⅜–¾ in. long, slender, with a few scattered hairs and with a tuft of hairs at the base; stipules scarious, ovate-lanceolate, acuminate, striate. Leaflets often mottled with brown spots, reniform, retuse or rounded at the apex, usually broader than long, ⅝–1¼ by ¾–1½ in. (the lower leaflets near the base of the stem often much smaller), glabrous above, with a few scattered appressed hairs beneath, base cordate; nerves and veins conspicuous on the underside; petiolules about $\frac{1}{16}$ in. long, densely hairy; stipels 2 at the base of each petiolule, subulate. Flowers in lax 6–30-flowered axillary racemes; peduncles filiform, hairy; pedicels filiform, hairy, usually in opposite pairs; floral bracts broadly ovate, acute, striate, ciliate. Calyx $\frac{1}{25}$ in. long, truncate; teeth very short, rounded, ciliate. Corolla $\frac{1}{12}$ in. long; standard emarginate. Ovary pubescent, subsessile. Pods subsessile, ¼ by ⅛ in., boat-shaped, pointed, reticulately veined, glabrous when ripe. Seed ⅛ by $\frac{1}{16}$ in., dark-brown, polished. Fl. B. I. v. 2, p. 153; Wall. Cat. 5741; Wight & Arn. Prodr. p. 231; Trim. Fl. Ceyl. v. 2, p. 40; Woodr. in Journ. Bomb. Nat. v. 11 (1897) p. 423. *E. monophylla*, DC. (*l. c.*). *Glycine monophyllos*, Burm. Fl. Ind. p. 161, t. 50, fig. 2. *Hedysarum sororium*, Linn. Mantiss. p. 270.—Flowers: July–Aug.

Sometimes there is present a very small pair of stipule-like leaflets at the base of the petiole, above the true stipules. These were noticed by Linnæus (*l. c.*) and were considered by DC. to be a character of sufficient importance to found a species on. Wight & Arn., however, declare (*l. c.*) that these leaflets are not constant on the same plant, but that some stems, even from the same root, have them, others not.

A very rare plant in the Bombay Presidency. It is abundant at Badami, a station on the S. M. Railway, where it has been found by Mr. Woodrow! and myself. I have not heard of it from any other locality in the Presidency.—DISTRIB. India (plains of Bandelkhand and W. Peninsula); Ceylon.

2. **Eleiotis trifoliolata,** *T. Cooke.* Prostrate; stems many, cæspitose, reaching 18 in. long, obscurely triquetrous, striate, glabrous. Leaves 3-foliolate; petioles filiform, ½–1 in. long, glabrous; stipules $\frac{3}{16}$ in. long, linear-lanceolate, cuspidate, striate. Leaflets nearly equal, or the terminal one a little longer, ⅜–⅝ by ⅜–¾ in., not broader than long, broadly obovate, rounded, truncate or retuse at the apex, glabrous above, with a few appressed hairs beneath, base narrowed (not cordate); nerves and veins conspicuous on the underside; stipels 2 beneath each leaflet, subulate. Flowers at first aggregated at the tops of the peduncles, elongating in fruit in a lax few-flowered raceme; peduncles hairy, axillary or terminal, with 1 or 2 scarious bracts on the naked portion; pedicels filiform; floral bracts large, striate, ovate-orbicular, shortly acuminate, ciliate, each bract enclosing 2 flowers. Calyx $\frac{1}{16}$ in. long; teeth triangular, almost as long as the tube. Corolla ⅛ in. long; standard emarginate.

Ovary pubescent, shortly stalked, 1 (rarely 2) -ovulate; style inflexed, thickened at the flexure. Pods $\frac{1}{4}$–$\frac{5}{16}$ in. long, boat-shaped, pointed, shortly stalked, pubescent and reticulate on the faces, channelled at the back.

Very rare. S. M. COUNTRY: Badami, *Woodrow*!, *Cooke*!, *Bhiva*!—DISTRIB. Apparently endemic.

26. PYCNOSPORA, R. Br.

A low shrub. Leaves pinnately 3-foliolate; stipules free, membranous, striate. Leaflets stipellate. Flowers minute, in terminal racemes; bracts membranous, caducous; bracteoles 0. Calyx deeply cleft, the 2 upper teeth subconnate. Corolla much exserted; standard suborbicular, narrowed at the base: wings obliquely oblong, adhering to the keel; keel slightly curved, obtuse. Stamens diadelphous; anthers uniform. Ovary sessile; ovules many; style inflexed, filiform; stigma terminal. Pod oblong, turgid, not jointed, 2-valved, continuous within, valves thin, transversely veined. Seeds small, subreniform.—DISTRIB. India, Ceylon, China, Philippines, N. Australia; species 1, combining the habit and flowers of *Desmodium* with the pod of *Crotalaria*.

1. **Pycnospora hedysaroides,** *R. Br. ex Wight & Arn. Prodr.* (1834) p. 197. Perennial; stems and branches numerous from a woody base, appressedly pubescent. Leaves 3-foliolate, sometimes with a few small casually simple ones near the base of the stems; petioles $\frac{1}{4}$–$\frac{3}{8}$ in. long; stipules scarious, lanceolate-cuspidate, striate, hairy. Leaflets $\frac{1}{4}$–1 by $\frac{3}{16}$–$\frac{7}{8}$ (the terminal much the larger), obovate, obtuse, rounded or slightly emarginate, finely pubescent on both surfaces especially the lower one, reticulately veined, base narrowed; main nerves 5–6 pairs, prominent and pubescent beneath; stipels filiform. Flowers small, in terminal and axillary lax racemes; peduncles hairy; pedicels filiform, pubescent. Calyx $\frac{1}{8}$ in. long, pubescent; teeth longer than the tube, linear, acute. Corolla $\frac{3}{16}$ in. long, purplish. Pods $\frac{3}{8}$–$\frac{1}{2}$ by $\frac{3}{16}$ in., black when ripe, oblong-ellipsoid, turgid, apiculate, veined, pubescent, the upper suture straight, the lower curved. Seeds 6–10. Fl. B. I. v. 2, p. 153; Trim. Fl. Ceyl. v. 2, p. 41; Woodr. in Journ. Bomb. Nat. v. 11 (1897) p. 423. *Pycnospora nervosa*, Wight & Arn. Prodr. p. 197; Dalz. & Gibs. p. 75.—Flowers: Dec.

KONKAN: *Stocks*!; near Vingorla, *Dalzell*!—DISTRIB. Throughout India; China, Philippines, N. Australia.

27. PSEUDARTHRIA, Wight & Arn.

Herbs or undershrubs, villous or viscidly-pubescent. Leaves pinnately 3-foliolate; stipules free, membranous or striate. Leaflets large, stipellate. Flowers small, twin or fascicled along the rhachis of a terminal or axillary raceme or panicle; bracts narrow. Calyx-teeth as long as the tube, the 2 upper subconnate. Corolla much exserted; standard suborbicular; wings oblique, oblong; keel obtuse. Stamens diadelphous; anthers uniform. Ovary subsessile; ovules many; style inflexed, subulate; stigma small, terminal. Pod linear-oblong, flat, continuous within, not jointed, the faces transversely veined. Seeds compressed, subreniform. Habit of *Desmodium*, from which it differs in pod.—DISTRIB. Species 5, of which 1 is Tropical Asian, the other 4 African.

1. **Pseudarthria viscida,** *Wight & Arn. Prodr.* (1834) p. 209. Perennial, diffuse, prostrate; stems 2–4 ft. long, slender, more or less clothed with soft whitish hairs. Leaves 3-foliolate; petioles $\frac{1}{2}$–1 in. long, densely hairy; stipules $\frac{3}{16}$–$\frac{1}{4}$ in. long, lanceolate-cuspidate, hairy. Leaflets stipellate, the terminal $1\frac{3}{4}$–$3\frac{1}{2}$ by $1\frac{1}{2}$–2 in., rhomboid-ovate, the lateral $1\frac{1}{4}$–$1\frac{3}{4}$ by $\frac{7}{8}$–$1\frac{1}{4}$ in., obliquely ovate-oblong or subrhomboid, all more or less hairy above, densely grey-silky beneath; stipels filiform, often $\frac{1}{8}$ in. long. Flowers small, numerous, in distant fascicles along the rhachis of terminal and axillary racemes or panicles; peduncles 1–3; pedicels filiform, spreading, much longer than the calyx; bracts lanceolate-subulate, shorter than the pedicels. Calyx $\frac{1}{16}$ in. long, hairy; teeth as long as the tube, the 3 lower linear-subulate, the 2 upper shorter, subconnate. Corolla $\frac{1}{4}$ in. long. Pods $\frac{5}{8}$–$\frac{7}{8}$ by $\frac{1}{4}$–$\frac{5}{16}$ in., linear-oblong, flattened, clothed on the faces with fine hooked viscous hairs, densely ciliate on the margins, one or both sutures often slightly indented between the seeds. Seeds 4–6, subreniform, compressed, brownish-black. Fl. B. I. v. 2, p. 154; Dalz. & Gibs. p. 74; Trim. Fl. Ceyl. v. 2, p. 41; Woodr. in Journ. Bomb. Nat. v. 11 (1897) p. 423.—Flowers: Aug.-Sept.

KONKAN: *Stocks*!; Vingorla, *Kanitkar*!, *Woodrow*. KANARA: Kála naddi, *Ritchie*, 1030!—DISTRIB. India (tropical zone, W. Peninsula); Ceylon, Timor.

28. URARIA, Desv.

Herbs or undershrubs. Leaves pinnately 3–9-foliolate or the lower rarely 1-foliolate; stipules free, acuminate, striate at the base. Leaflets often large, stipellate. Flowers in terminal racemes; bracts ovate or lanceolate, acuminate; bracteoles 0. Calyx-tube very short; the upper teeth short, the 3 lower elongated. Corolla purple or yellow; standard orbicular or obovate, narrowed into a claw; wings falcate-oblong, adhering to the keel; keel slightly incurved, obtuse. Stamens diadelphous; anthers uniform. Ovary sessile or shortly stalked; ovules 2–∞; style filiform, inflexed above; stigma capitate, terminal. Pod of 2–6 small turgid 1-seeded joints folded on one another within the calyx. Seeds orbicular or subglobose.—DISTRIB. Tropical Asia, Africa, and Australia; species 8.

1. **Uraria picta,** *Desv. Journ. Bot.* v. 1 (1813) p. 123, t. 5, fig. 19. A suffruticose sparingly branched perennial 3–6 ft. high; stems stout, reaching $\frac{1}{2}$ in. in diam. at the base, finely downy with hooked hairs. Leaves imparipinnate, 8–12 in. long (including the petiole); petioles $1\frac{1}{2}$–$2\frac{1}{2}$ in. long, striate, downy; stipules $\frac{1}{2}$ in. long, triangular, long-acuminate, striate. Leaflets on the upper part of the stem 5–7 (rarely 9), rigidly subcoriaceous, 4–8 by $\frac{3}{8}$–$\frac{3}{4}$ in., linear-oblong, acute, blotched with white and glabrous above, finely reticulately veined and minutely pubescent beneath, base rounded; stipels subulate, $\frac{3}{16}$ in. long; leaflets on the lower part of the stem 1–3-foliolate, suborbicular or oblong. Flowers in close fascicles along the rhachis of spicate cylindric racemes 6–12 in. long, $\frac{5}{8}$–$\frac{3}{4}$ in. broad; rhachis and pedicels downy with hooked hairs; pedicels $\frac{1}{4}$–$\frac{3}{8}$ in. long, curved upwards after flowering so that the pods are in contact with the rhachis; bracts large, scarious, striate, strongly ciliate, the upper lanceolate-acuminate, the lower ovate-acuminate, completely concealing the buds, soon deciduous. Calyx $\frac{1}{6}$ in. long; teeth

plumose, subulate, much longer than the tube. Corolla $\frac{1}{4}$ in. long, purple. Pods glabrous, pale lead-colored; joints 3–6, smooth, polished, seed-like, $\frac{1}{8}$ by $\frac{1}{12}$ in., folded on one another. Fl. B. I. v. 2, p. 155; Dalz. & Gibs. p. 65; Trim. Fl. Ceyl. v. 2, p. 42; Woodr. in Journ. Bomb. Nat. v. 11 (1897) p. 423; Watt, Dict. Econ. Prod. v. 6, part 4, p. 212. *Hedysarum pictum*, Jacquin, Collect. v. 2, p. 262; Icon. t. 567.—Flowers: Aug.–Sept. VERN. *Prishnaparni*; *Pithvan.*

Rare. KONKAN: Island of Bombay, *Woodrow*!; Parel, *Ranade*!; near Pen, *Dalzell & Gibson*; Salsette, *Nairne.*—DISTRIB. Throughout India; Ceylon, Tropical Africa, Malay Islands, Philippines.

29. ALYSICARPUS, Neck.

Diffuse or erect herbs. Leaves 1- (rarely 3-) foliolate; stipules scarious, acuminate, free or connate. Leaflets 2-stipellate. Flowers in leaf-opposed, terminal, or axillary racemes; pedicels often twin; bracts scarious, generally deciduous. Calyx glumaceous; teeth deep, the 2 upper often connate. Corolla not or hardly exserted; standard obovate or orbicular, narrowed into the claw; wings obliquely oblong, adhering to the keel, slightly curved, obtuse, usually appendiculate. Stamens diadelphous; anthers uniform. Ovary sessile or shortly stalked; ovules numerous; style incurved; stigma capitate. Pod terete or turgid, composed of several indehiscent 1-seeded joints.—DISTRIB. Tropics of the Old World and Australia; species 15.

Calyx shorter or very slightly longer than the first joint of the pod.
- Pod moniliform, veinless .... 1. *A. monilifer.*
- Pod not moniliform, veined.
  - Calyx shorter than the first joint of the pod .... 2. *A. hamosus.*
  - Calyx equalling or slightly longer than the first joint of the pod .... 3. *A. vaginalis.*

Calyx much longer than the first joint of the pod.
- Teeth of calyx imbricate in the fruiting stage.
  - Pod slightly moniliform, neither veined nor rugose ... 4. *A. bupleurifolius.*
  - Pod moniliform, reticulately veined .... 5. *A. longifolius.*
  - Pod transversely ribbed.
    - Pod 2-edged, not exserted .... 6. *A. rugosus.*
    - Pod 4-angled, exserted .... 7. *A. tetragonolobus.*
- Teeth of calyx not imbricate in the fruiting stage.
  - Flowers sessile .... 8. *A. pubescens.*
  - Flowers pedicelled .... 9. *A. belgaumensis.*

1. **Alysicarpus monilifer,** *DC. Prodr.* v. 2 (1825) p. 353. Stems $\frac{1}{2}$–2 ft. long, slender, tufted, prostrate, much-branched; young branches clothed with deciduous bristly hairs. Leaves 1-foliolate; petioles $\frac{3}{16}$–$\frac{5}{16}$ in. long, more or less hairy; stipules scarious, about as long as the petioles, lanceolate, very acute, striate. Leaflets $\frac{1}{2}$–1 by $\frac{3}{8}$–$\frac{5}{8}$, oblong-elliptic, rounded and mucronulate at the apex, glabrous above, slightly hairy on the nerves and prominently reticulately veined beneath, base rounded, often cordate: petiolules very short; stipels minute, filiform. Flowers erect, close, in 4–10-flowered axillary racemes; pedicels very short. Calyx obscurely hairy, $\frac{1}{12}$–$\frac{1}{8}$ in. long, about equalling or rather less than the first joint of the pod; tube very short; teeth narrow-lanceolate, very acute, striate. Pods $\frac{1}{2}$–1 in. long by $\frac{1}{12}$–$\frac{1}{8}$ in. thick, erect, moniliform; joints 4–8, turgid, subglobose, finely downy with minute hooked hairs, not reticulately veined. Fl. B. I. v. 2, p. 157;

Wight & Arn. Prodr. p. 232; Trim. Fl. Ceyl. v. 2, p. 43; Woodr. in Journ. Bomb. Nat. v. 11 (1897) p. 423.—Flowers: Sept.-Oct.

S. M. COUNTRY: Badami, *Cooke*!, *Woodrow*!; Dharwar, *Woodrow*. — DISTRIB. Throughout India; Nubia, Abyssinia.

2. **Alysicarpus hamosus,** *Edgew. in Journ. Asiat. Soc. Beng.* v. 21 (1853) p. 171. Diffuse; stems 6–30 in. long; branches numerous, ascending, slender, clothed with long spreading hairs. Leaves 1-foliolate; petioles $\frac{1}{8}$–$\frac{1}{4}$ in. long, hairy; stipules scarious, reaching $\frac{5}{16}$ in. long, linear, very acute, striate. Leaflets $\frac{1}{2}$–$1\frac{1}{4}$ by $\frac{3}{8}$–1 in., broadly ovate or suborbicular, rounded or mucronate at the apex, more or less hairy on both surfaces and on the nerves beneath, base rounded or slightly cordate; petiolules short, hairy; stipels minute, subulate. Flowers usually in pairs along the rhachis, in axillary 4–8-flowered racemes; rhachis filiform, hirsute; pedicels as long as the calyx; bracts scarious, ovate, acute, ciliate. Calyx $\frac{1}{8}$ in. long, shorter than the first joint of the pod, the 3 lower teeth linear-lanceolate, acute, ciliate. Pods $\frac{1}{2}$–$\frac{3}{4}$ by $\frac{1}{8}$ in., compressed, clothed with both straight and hooked hairs, linear, mucronate; joints 3–7. Fl. B. I. v. 2, p. 157; Woodr. in Journ. Bomb. Nat. v. 11 (1897) p. 423. *Hedysarum procumbens*, Roxb. Hort. Beng. p. 56; Fl. Ind. v. 3, p. 345.—Flowers: Sept.-Oct.

Rare. KONKAN: Parel (island of Bombay), *Woodrow*!; Bombay, *Capt. Geburne*! S. M. COUNTRY: Badami, *Cooke*!, *Woodrow*!—DISTRIB. India (Plains of Banda, W. Peninsula).

3. **Alysicarpus vaginalis,** *DC. Prodr.* v. 2 (1825) p. 353. Suffruticose, diffuse; stems numerous, robust, ascending, 1–3 ft. long, glabrescent or with a few scattered hairs. Leaves 1-foliolate; petioles $\frac{1}{4}$–$\frac{1}{3}$ in. long; stipules scarious, often exceeding $\frac{1}{2}$ in. long, ovate, acuminate, striate, closely appressed to the stem, straw-colored, persistent. Leaflets very variable in form on one and the same plant, $\frac{1}{2}$–$2\frac{1}{2}$ by $\frac{1}{4}$–1 in., lanceolate, oblong, or ovate-oblong, rounded or acute, or sometimes truncate at the apex, apiculate, glabrous, closely reticulately veined, base usually cordate; petiolules very short; stipels minute, caducous. Flowers in elongated 6–12-flowered racemes 1–3 in. long; pedicels about $\frac{1}{12}$ in. long. Calyx $\frac{1}{8}$ in. long, glabrescent, equalling or slightly longer than the first joint of the pod; teeth longer than the tube, linear, very acute, striate. Corolla pinkish, small, included. Pods $\frac{1}{2}$–$\frac{3}{4}$ by $\frac{1}{12}$ in., subterete, not or very rarely obscurely moniliform, apiculate, glabrous or nearly so, reticulately veined; joints 4–8, longer than broad. Fl. B. I. v. 2, p. 158; Dalz. & Gibs. p. 64; Wight & Arn. Prodr. p. 233; Trim. Fl. Ceyl. v. 2, p. 44; Woodr. in Journ. Bomb. Nat. v. 11 (1897) p. 423.—Flowers: Oct.

KONKAN: *Stocks*!, *Law*!; Neral, *Cooke*! DECCAN: *Woodrow*. GUJARAT: *Woodrow*; Surat, *Kanitkar*!, *Dalzell & Gibson*.—DISTRIB. Throughout India; Ceylon, Afghanistan, and generally throughout the Tropics of the Old World.

VAR. 1. *nummularifolius*, Baker, in Hook. f. Fl. B. I. v. 2, p. 158. Procumbent, diffusely branched; stems 8–12 in. long, slender. Leaflets elliptic-oblong or roundish, obtuse. Racemes dense, congested, often under 1 in. long. Watt, Dict. Econ. Prod. v. 1, p. 204. *A. nummularifolius* (sp.), DC. Prodr. v. 2, p. 353; Wight & Arn. Prodr. p. 232; Grah. Cat. p. 50; Dalz. & Gibs. p. 64.

KONKAN: *Dalzell!* DECCAN: *Woodrow!*—DISTRIB. As common and widely distributed as the type.

VAR. 2. *Stocksii*, Baker, in Hook. f. Fl. B. I. v. 2, p. 158. Stems clothed with fine spreading hairs. Leaflets much thinner than in the type, elliptic or oblong-elliptic, more or less hairy beneath. Racemes elongated.

I have seen but one specimen in Herb. Kew. marked "Konkan, *Stocks*."—DISTRIB. Apparently endemic.

VAR. 3. *heterophyllus*, Baker, in Hook. f. Fl. B. I. v. 2, p. 158. Stems many, slender, 4–10 in. long. Upper leaves 3-foliolate; the lower 1- and 3-foliolate intermixed. Leaflets thin, lanceolate or oblong-lanceolate, acute or subobtuse, the upper sometimes very narrow. Racemes 6–20-flowered, reaching 5 in. long; flowers in distant pairs along a filiform rhachis. *Alysicarpus heterophyllus*, Benth. MS. in Herb. Kew.

Rare. SIND: *Stocks!*; Jemadar ka Landa near Karachi, *Stocks*, 1181!—DISTRIB. Apparently endemic.

4. **Alysicarpus bupleurifolius,** *DC. Prodr.* v. 2 (1825) p. 352. Stems 1–2 ft. long, slender, terete, ascending, glabrous. Leaves 1-foliolate; petioles $\frac{1}{16}$–$\frac{1}{10}$ in. long, glabrous; stipules $\frac{1}{3}$–$\frac{5}{8}$ in. long, linear, very acute, glabrous. Leaflets rigid, variable, usually linear, linear-oblong or lanceolate, acute, $\frac{3}{4}$–$2\frac{1}{2}$ by $\frac{1}{8}$–$\frac{1}{4}$ in. (the lower leaflets sometimes broadly elliptic), all glabrous, reticulately veined; petiolules very short; stipels minute, caducous. Flowers in 10–20 distant pairs, in rigid erect spicate lax racemes; pedicels very short. Calyx $\frac{1}{4}$ in. long, much longer than the first joint of the pod; tube funnel-shaped, glabrous; teeth acute, ciliate, imbricate. Corolla red. Pods $\frac{3}{8}$–$\frac{1}{2}$ in. long, stalked, strongly apiculate, cylindric, glabrous, smooth, scarcely moniliform; joints 4–8, as broad as long, not veined nor rugose. Fl. B. I. v. 2, p. 158; Grah. Cat. p. 50; Dalz. & Gibs. p. 64; Trim. Fl. Ceyl. v. 2, p. 44; Woodr. in Journ. Bomb. Nat. v. 11 (1897) p. 423. *Hedysarum bupleurifolium*, Roxb. Cor. Pl. t. 194.—Flowers: June–Sept.

KONKAN: *Stocks!*; Island of Bombay, *Cooke!*; Neral, *Bhiva!* GUJARAT: Nausari, *Kanitkar!* S. M. COUNTRY: Karlimatti near Badami, *Woodrow!*; Belgaum, *Ritchie*, 164!—DISTRIB. Throughout India; Ceylon, Malay Isles, China, Philippines, Mauritius, Polynesia.

5. **Alysicarpus longifolius,** *Wight & Arn. Prodr.* (1834) p. 233. Stem stout, 4–5 ft. high, ascending, terete, slightly striate, glabrous. Leaves 1-foliolate; petioles $\frac{1}{8}$–$\frac{3}{8}$ in. long; stipules scarious, $\frac{5}{8}$–$\frac{3}{4}$ in. long, lanceolate, very acute. Leaflets 2–6 by $\frac{3}{8}$–$\frac{3}{4}$ in., oblong or lanceolate, obtuse or subacute, glabrous above, appressedly hairy on the nerves beneath, closely reticulately veined, the reticulations conspicuous on both surfaces, base subcordate; petiolules very short; stipels linear, acute. Flowers erect, appressed to a more or less hairy rhachis, in dense spicate racemes $\frac{1}{2}$–1 ft. long; pedicels $\frac{1}{10}$ in. long, hairy; bracts conspicuous, often exceeding $\frac{1}{2}$ in. long, ovate, acuminate, more or less silky outside, ciliate, concealing the buds and falling before the flowers open. Calyx $\frac{1}{4}$–$\frac{3}{8}$ in. long, pubescent, ciliate, striate, as long as or longer than the two lower joints of the pod; tube funnel-shaped, plicate; teeth much longer than the tube, imbricate in the fruiting stage. Pods

usually exserted, $\frac{3}{8}$–$\frac{1}{2}$ by $\frac{1}{12}$ in., very shortly stalked, glabrous, terete-compressed, apiculate, slightly moniliform; joints 4–6, glabrous, reticulately veined, the veins not very conspicuous. Fl. B. I. v. 2, p. 159; Dalz. & Gibs. p. 65; Trim. Fl. Ceyl. v. 2, p. 45; Woodr. in Journ. Bomb. Nat. v. 11 (1897) p. 423.—Flowers: Sept. VERN. *Savard.*

KONKAN: *Stocks!*; Matunga, *Woodrow!* DECCAN: Poona, *Woodrow!* GUJARAT: Surat, *Cooke!*, *Kanitkar!*, *Capt. Geburne!*, *Dalzell!*; Dakor, *Kanitkar!*
The root is like liquorice, *Dalzell & Gibson.*—DISTRIB. Throughout the plains of India.

6. **Alysicarpus rugosus,** *DC. Prodr.* v. 2 (1825) p. 353. Stems 1–2 ft. long, ascending, glabrous except for a decurrent line of hairs. Leaves 1-foliolate; petioles $\frac{1}{8}$–$\frac{1}{6}$ in. long; stipules scarious, $\frac{1}{4}$–$\frac{3}{8}$ in. long, linear-lanceolate, very acute, striate. Leaflets 1–3 by $\frac{3}{8}$–1 in., usually oblong, rarely orbicular or linear-lanceolate, obtuse, apiculate, glabrous above, slightly appressedly hairy and reticulately veined beneath, base often cordate; petiolules extremely short; stipels minute, caducous. Flowers appressed to the subglabrous rhachis, crowded in dense spicate racemes 1–4 in. long; pedicels $\frac{1}{8}$–$\frac{1}{6}$ in. long, slender, glabrous; bracts large, chaffy, ovate, acuminate, glabrous. Calyx glabrous on the back, $\frac{1}{4}$–$\frac{3}{8}$ in. long, deeply divided; teeth lanceolate, much imbricate, minutely ciliate. Pods $\frac{1}{12}$ in. broad, turgid, very shortly stalked, apiculate, moniliform, included in the calyx; joints 3–6, broader than long, closely transversely ribbed, glabrous. Fl. B. I. v. 2, p. 159. *A. Wallichii*, Wight & Arn. Prodr. p. 234.

Not nearly as common as the varieties. S. M. COUNTRY: Belgaum, *Ritchie*, 180!—DISTRIB. Throughout India; Tropics of the Old World, Ceylon, Cape, W. Indies.

VAR. 1. *Heyneanus*, Baker, in Hook. f. Fl. B. I. v. 2, p. 159. A larger plant 3–4 ft. high. Stems more robust, pubescent or villous. Leaflets large, obovate-oblong, obtuse, permanently pubescent beneath. Racemes longer, 4–6 in. long; flowers more distant. Calyx shorter. Pods $\frac{1}{8}$ in. broad, often exserted. *A. Heyneanus* (sp.), Wight & Arn. Prodr. p. 234. *A. obovatus*, Edgew. Cat. Banda Pl. p. 45. *A. rugosus*, Woodr. in Journ. Bomb. Nat. v. 11 (1897) p. 423.

Common in the Bombay Presidency. KONKAN: *Stocks!*; Matunga, *Woodrow!* DECCAN: Poona, *Woodrow!*, *Kanitkar!* GUJARAT: Dabhoi, *Kanitkar*; Dakor, *Kanitkar!*—DISTRIB. India (Bandelkhand, W. Peninsula); Ceylon.

VAR. 2. *styracifolius*, Baker, in Hook. f. Fl. B. I. v. 2, p. 159. A smaller plant; stems diffuse, rarely reaching 18 in. long, finely pubescent. Leaflets small, elliptic-oblong, obtuse, hairy beneath. Racemes short, dense; flowers subsessile along a very hairy rhachis. Calyx hairy on the back, strongly ciliate on the margins. Pods $\frac{1}{12}$ in. broad, included or rarely exserted. Trim. Fl. Ceyl. v. 2, p. 45. *A. styracifolius* (sp.), DC. Prodr. v. 2. p. 353 (*exclud. syn.*); Wight & Arn. Prodr. p. 234; Grah. Cat. p. 50; Dalz. & Gibs. p. 65. *A. lupulinus*, Stocks, ex Baker in Hook. f. Fl. B. I. v. 2, p. 159. *A. scariosus*, Grah. in Wall. Cat. 5766; Aitch. Pb. & Sind Pl. p. 45.

KONKAN: *Stocks!*, *Law!* GUJARAT: Surat, *Dalzell & Gibson*; Ankleshwar, *Kanitkar!*; Dakor, *Kanitkar!* SIND: *Stocks!*; Jemadar ka Landa near Karachi, *Stocks*, 1180!—DISTRIB. Throughout India; Ceylon.

VAR. 3. *minor*, Prain, in Journ. As. Soc. Beng. v. 66 (1898) p. 384.

Dwarf, diffuse; stems glabrous. Leaflets small, oblong, ovate or orbicular, obtuse or subacute. Racemes short, dense; bracts and calyx glabrous.

Western India, *Gibson* ex *Prain* (*l. c.*). DECCAN: *Woodrow*! GUJARAT: Rajkote (Kathiawar), *C. Macnaghten* ex *Prain* (*l. c.*).

7. **Alysicarpus tetragonolobus,** *Edgew. in Journ. As. Soc. Beng.* v. 21 (1853) p. 169. Procumbent, cæspitose; stems numerous, slender, $\frac{1}{2}$–1 ft. long, marked with a line of hairs. Leaves 1-foliolate; petioles $\frac{1}{12}$–$\frac{1}{8}$ in. long; stipules scarious, $\frac{1}{6}$–$\frac{1}{5}$ in. long, lanceolate with a broad base, acute, ciliate, striate. Leaflets $\frac{3}{4}$–$1\frac{1}{4}$ by $\frac{1}{8}$–$\frac{3}{8}$ in., elliptic-oblong or lanceolate, obtuse or subacute, glabrous above, hairy beneath, base rounded or slightly cordate; petiolules very short; stipels minute, caducous. Flowers in lax racemes 2–3 in. long, the lower flowers in distant pairs along a slender rhachis, the upper approximated; pedicels $\frac{1}{32}$–$\frac{1}{16}$ in long, filiform; bracts $\frac{1}{5}$ in. long, ovate-lanceolate, acute, caducous. Calyx $\frac{1}{6}$–$\frac{1}{5}$ in. long, deeply divided, puberulous outside; teeth lanceolate, acute, ciliate with long white hairs, imbricate in the early fruiting stage, afterwards spreading. Pods $\frac{3}{8}$–$\frac{1}{2}$ in. long, moniliform, furnished with a projecting ridge down the middle of each face making the pod quadrangular, distinctly exserted; joints 2–6, transversely ribbed, glabrous. Fl. B. I. v. 2, p. 159; Edgew. Cat. Banda Pl. p. 45; Woodr. in Journ. Bomb. Nat. v. 11 (1897) p. 423. *A. quadrangularis*, Edgew. MS. ex Baker, in Hook. f. Fl. B. I. v. 2, p. 159.—Flowers: Aug.

KONKAN: *Stocks*! DECCAN: Poona, *Herb. Mus. Par.*, 393! and 498!, *Woodrow*, 49!, *Cooke*!; Ahmednagar, *Woodrow*. S. M. COUNTRY: Badami, *Cooke*!, *Woodrow*! SIND: *Stocks*, 1181!—DISTRIB. India (Plains of Bandelkhand).

8. **Alysicarpus pubescens,** *Law, in Wight, Icon.* (1840) t. 250. An erect herbaceous plant 3–4 ft. high; stems and branches terete, softly hairy. Leaves 1-foliolate; petioles $\frac{1}{16}$–$\frac{1}{8}$ in. long, softly hairy; stipules reaching $\frac{1}{2}$ in. long, linear-lanceolate, prolonged to a fine acicular point, clothed with long white hairs. Leaflets linear-oblong or oblong-lanceolate, acute, mucronate, slightly hairy or subglabrous above, clothed beneath and on the nerves and margins with soft white hairs; base rounded, subacute or slightly cordate; main nerves 3, starting from the base, conspicuous; petiolules very short; stipels minute, caducous. Flowers sessile, in dense spikes 2–6 in. long; rhachis plumose; bracts broadly ovate, acuminate, silky-villous outside. Calyx $\frac{1}{3}$ in. long, divided nearly to the base; teeth narrowly lanceolate-subulate, densely plumose, not imbricate. Corolla included or scarcely exserted. Pods $\frac{1}{12}$ in. broad, moniliform, with a long mucro, included in the calyx; joints 3–4, globose, reticulate, the reticulations somewhat honeycombed. Fl. B. I. v. 2, p. 160; Dalz. & Gibs. p. 65; Woodr. in Journ. Bomb. Nat. v. 11 (1897) p. 423.—Flowers: Sept.–Nov.

A very common plant. KONKAN: *Stocks*! DECCAN: Poona, *Cooke*!, *Woodrow*!; Chattersinghi hill near Poona, *Kanitkar*!; Kolapur, *Cooke*! S. M. COUNTRY: Belgaum, common, *Dalzell & Gibson*, *Ritchie*, 177!, *Cooke*!, *Wight*! KANARA: *Dalzell*! GUJARAT: about Broach, *Cooke*!—DISTRIB. Apparently endemic.

9. **Alysicarpus belgaumensis,** *Wight, Icon.* (1840) t. 92. Erect, 1–$2\frac{1}{2}$ ft. high; stems stout, terete, hairy. Leaves 1- or the upper often

3-foliolate; petioles $\frac{1}{4}$–$\frac{1}{2}$ in. long, appressedly hairy; stipules $\frac{1}{2}$ in. long, oblong-lanceolate, prolonged to a long acicular point, ciliate. Leaflets $1\frac{1}{2}$–$3\frac{3}{4}$ by $\frac{5}{8}$–1 in., oblong or oblong-lanceolate, acute, mucronate, subcordate (those near the base of the stem often smaller and sometimes broadly elliptic), all glabrous and reticulately veined above, densely appressedly-silky beneath, ciliate; petiolules very short, hairy; stipels subulate. Flowers at first in dense close terminal and axillary racemes which afterwards elongate, sometimes reaching 9 in. long; pedicels elongating after flowering to $\frac{1}{2}$–$\frac{5}{8}$ in., slender, hairy, in pairs along a hairy rhachis; bracts $\frac{1}{3}$ in. long, broadly ovate, acuminate, strongly nerved, slightly hairy on the back, ciliate, concealing the flowers when in bud, soon falling. Calyx scarious, $\frac{3}{8}$–$\frac{1}{2}$ in. long, divided nearly to the base, slightly hairy on the back; teeth oblong-lanceolate, acute, not imbricate, strongly and closely nerved, ciliate with long, stiff hairs, the 2 upper teeth connate for about $\frac{1}{2}$ their length. Corolla rosy; standard $\frac{1}{3}$ by $\frac{1}{4}$ in. suborbicular or obovate. Pods $\frac{1}{8}$–$\frac{1}{6}$ in. broad, included or slightly exserted, subcompressed, finely pubescent, slightly moniliform; joints 3–4, reticulately veined, the reticulations honeycombed. Fl. B. I. v. 2, p. 160; Dalz. & Gibs. p. 65; Woodr. in Journ. Bomb. Nat. v. 11 (1897) p. 423.—Flowers: Sept.–Oct.

Konkan: *Stocks*! Deccan: Ambenali near Lanoli, *Kanitkar*!; Mahableshwar, abundant, *Cooke*! S. M. Country: Belgaum Districts, *Cooke*!; Párva Ghát, *Ritchie*, 1189!; Ramghát, *Dalzell & Gibson*. Kanara: *Dalzell*!—Distrib. Apparently endemic.

Var. *racemosus*, Baker, in Hook. f. Fl. B. I. v. 2, p. 160. Dwarf, 4–12 in. high. Leaflets 1-foliolate, broadly-elliptic, obovate or suborbicular, under 1 in. long, rounded or subacute. Racemes shorter, with fewer and more distant flowers. Calyx $\frac{1}{4}$–$\frac{5}{16}$ in. long. Pods included or slightly exserted. *A. racemosus* (sp.), Benth. in Hohen. Pl. Ind. Or. n. 1212; Bedd. Icon. t. 292.

Deccan: Mahableshwar, *Cooke*!, *Woodrow*!.

30. OUGEINIA, Benth.

A tree. Leaves pinnately 3-foliolate; stipules free, deciduous. Leaflets large, stipellate. Flowers in fascicled axillary racemes; pedicels filiform, usually fascicled along the rhachis; bracts small, squamiform; bracteoles beneath the calyx minute, persistent. Calyx-tube campanulate; teeth obtuse, the two upper connate into a broad emarginate lip, the lowest tooth longer than the lateral ones. Corolla much exserted; standard suborbicular or obovate, clawed; keel obtuse. Stamens diadelphous; anthers uniform. Ovary sessile; ovules many; style incurved, subulate; stigma terminal, capitate. Pod linear, elongate, flat, smooth, formed of 2–5 large, more or less distinct, scarcely dehiscent joints.—Distrib. East Indies; species 1.

1. **Ougeinia dalbergioides,** *Benth. Pl. Jungh.* (1851–55) p. 216. A tree 20–40 ft. high, with a short crooked trunk; bark dark brown, deeply cracked; branches slender, terete. Leaves pinnately 3-foliolate, often reaching 12 in. long (including the petiole); common petioles $1\frac{1}{2}$–2 in. long; stipules $\frac{1}{4}$ in. long, lanceolate, acute, caducous. Leaflets rigidly coriaceous, the terminal broadly elliptic or roundish, sometimes

trapezoidal, 3-6 by 2-4 in., the lateral leaflets opposite, obliquely ovate, cordate, 3-4 by $1\frac{1}{2}$-3 in., on petiolules $\frac{1}{8}$ in. long, all glabrous above, glabrous or more or less downy beneath, distantly and shallowly crenate, bluntly pointed; main nerves 4-8 pairs, prominent; stipules subulate. Flowers numerous, in short fascicled racemes from the nodes of old branches; pedicels colored, $\frac{1}{2}$-$\frac{3}{4}$ in. long, filiform; bracts $\frac{1}{20}$ in. long, ovate, acuminate, broader than long, villous outside; bracteole 1 beneath the calyx, minute, villous. Calyx $\frac{1}{6}$-$\frac{1}{4}$ in. long, pubescent; teeth short, triangular. Corolla $\frac{3}{8}$-$\frac{1}{2}$ in. long, white or rose-colored, somewhat fragrant. Pods 2-3 in. long; joints reticulately veined, 2-3 times as long as broad. Fl. B. I. v. 2, p. 161; Bedd. Flor. Sylvat. t. 36; Talb. Trees, Bomb. p. 69; Woodr. in Journ. Bomb. Nat. v. 11 (1897) p. 423; Watt, Dict. Econ. Prod. v. 5, p. 657. *Dalbergia ougeinensis*, Roxb. Hort. Beng. p. 53; Wight, Icon. t. 391; Dalz. & Gibs. p. 78.—Flowers: Feb.-May. VERN. *Tivas*; *Kálá-palas*.

KONKAN: *Dalzell & Gibson*. DECCAN: hills near Poona, *Woodrow*!; Kartriz Ghát, *Gaba*!; Khandesh, *Talbot*; Dapuri garden, *Dalzell*! GUJARAT: Dang jungles, *Dalzell & Gibson*. KANARA: Yellapur forests of N. Kanara, common, *Talbot*.—DISTRIB. India (Northern Provinces).

The bark affords a fine *Kino* and is used medicinally (*Dalzell & Gibson*). The wood is highly valued for its toughness. See Watt, Dict. Econ. Prod. l. c.

31. DESMODIUM, Desv.

Herbs or shrubs (rarely small trees). Leaves pinnately 1-3- (rarely 5-) foliolate; stipules usually striate, dry, free or united into 1 leaf-opposed one. Leaflets stipellate, often large. Flowers usually small, in copious usually dense racemes, bracteate. Calyx-tube short, the 2 upper teeth more or less connate, the 3 lower acute or acuminate. Corolla exserted; standard oblong, obovate or orbicular; wings obliquely oblong, more or less adhering to the keel; keel obtuse. Vexillary stamen entirely or partially free, the other 9 united; anthers uniform. Ovary sessile or stalked; ovules 2-∞; style incurved; stigma terminal, minute, capitate. Pod exserted from the calyx, sessile or stalked, usually formed of several 1-seeded indehiscent joints, the faces compressed, the upper suture rarely splitting open, the joints usually separating.—DISTRIB. Throughout the Tropics of both hemispheres, a few in N. America and temperate S. Africa; species about 150.

Leaves 3-foliolate.
  Shrubs or undershrubs.
    Flowers in axillary peduncled umbels.
      Branches terete .... 1. *D. umbellatum*.
      Branches triquetrous .... 2. *D. Cephalotes*.
    Flowers in terminal and axillary racemes.
      Pod indehiscent.
        Bracts large, leafy, concealing the flowers .... 3. *D. pulchellum*.
        Bracts small, scarious, not concealing the flowers ... 4. *D. laxiflorum*.
      Pod dehiscent .... 5. *D. polycarpum*.
  Herbs.
    Erect; stipules foliaceous, auricled .... 6. *D. diffusum*.
    Trailing; stipules scarious, not auricled .... 7. *D. triflorum*.
Leaves 1-foliolate.
  Shrubs or undershrubs.
    Petiole winged.. 8. *D. triquetrum*.

Petiole not winged.
Branches angled; joints of pod longer than broad...... 9. *D. gangeticum.*
Branches terete; joints of pod as broad as long......... 10. *D. latifolium.*
Herbs.
Leaflets broader than long .... 11. *D. reniforme.*
Leaflets as broad as long .... 12. *D. rotundifolium.*
Leaves 1- and 3-foliolate intermixed.
Herbaceous; pod indehiscent.. 13. *D. parviflorum.*
An erect undershrub; pod dehiscent .... 14. *D. gyrans.*

1. **Desmodium umbellatum,** *DC. Prodr.* v. 2 (1825) p. 325. A bushy shrub (occasionally growing into a small tree) 5–15 ft. high; young branches terete, downy with appressed pubescence. Leaves 3-foliolate, 3–6 in. long (including the petiole); common petioles $\frac{3}{4}$–1 in. long, thickened at the base, channelled, rusty-puberulous; stipules $\frac{1}{3}$ in. long, closely parallel-striate, caducous. Leaflets subcoriaceous, ovate-oblong, obtuse or subacute, glabrous above, canescent beneath (the terminal 2–3 by $1\frac{1}{2}$–2 in., the lateral $1\frac{1}{2}$–2 by 1–$1\frac{1}{2}$ in.); petiolules $\frac{1}{8}$–$\frac{3}{16}$ in. long; main nerves 4–8 pairs, slender, parallel, curved; stipels $\frac{1}{8}$ in. long, subulate. Flowers in axillary peduncled 6–12-flowered umbels; peduncles $\frac{1}{3}$–$\frac{1}{2}$ in. long; pedicels $\frac{1}{8}$–$\frac{1}{6}$ in. long; bracts deciduous; bracteoles broadly ovate-oblong, acuminate. Calyx $\frac{1}{8}$–$\frac{1}{6}$ in. long; teeth triangular, as long as the tube. Corolla $\frac{1}{2}$ in. long, white. Pods $1\frac{1}{2}$–2 in. long, sparsely silky when young, glabrous when ripe, thick and coriaceous, almost turgid, not reticulately veined, indented on both sutures; joints 4–5 (usually 4) $\frac{1}{3}$ by $\frac{1}{4}$ in. Fl. B. I. v. 2, p. 161; Grah. Cat. p. 49; Dalz. & Gibs. p. 66; Trim. Fl. Ceyl. v. 2, p. 47; Talb. Trees, Bomb. p. 69; Woodr. in Journ. Bomb. Nat. v. 11 (1897) p. 423.

Rare. GUJARAT: S.E. of Surat, *Dalzell & Gibson*. S. M. COUNTRY: near Belgaum, always growing on the banks of streams, *Law* ex *Graham* l. c.—DISTRIB. India near the coast; Ceylon, Mascarene Islands, Malaya, Philippines, Polynesia. Prain says (Journ. As. Soc. Beng. v. 66 (1898) p. 137) that all the specimens in the Calcutta Herbarium were invariably sent from the sea-coast or the shores of tidal rivers.

2. **Desmodium Cephalotes,** *Wall. Cat.* (1828) 5721; var. **congestum,** *Prain, in Journ. As. Soc. Beng.* v. 66 (1898) p. 389. A shrub 4–5 ft. high; branches appressedly silky, triquetrous. Leaves 3-foliolate, 4–6 in. long; petioles $\frac{3}{4}$–1 in. long, appressedly silky; stipules $\frac{1}{2}$ in. long, linear-lanceolate, bristle-pointed, striate, glabrous. Leaflets elliptic-oblong, obovate-oblong, or lanceolate, acuminate, grey-silky and finely reticulately veined beneath (the terminal $2\frac{3}{4}$–4 by $1\frac{1}{8}$–2 in., the lateral 2–$3\frac{1}{2}$ by $\frac{7}{8}$–$1\frac{1}{2}$ in.); petiolules $\frac{1}{8}$ in. long; main nerves 12–16 pairs, prominently slender; stipels $\frac{1}{3}$ in. long, filiform, conspicuous. Flowers 20 or more, crowded in dense axillary peduncled umbellate heads; peduncles $\frac{1}{8}$–$\frac{1}{6}$ in. long, stout, silky; pedicels 0–$\frac{1}{10}$ in. long (when present, silky, cup-shaped and fringed with white silky hairs at the apex); bracts $\frac{1}{8}$–$\frac{1}{6}$ in. long, linear-subulate, ciliate, caducous; bracteoles $\frac{1}{6}$ in. long, linear-subulate, ciliate, caducous. Calyx $\frac{1}{8}$ in. long, campanulate, densely silky; teeth lanceolate, acute, about as long as the tube. Corolla $\frac{1}{3}$ in. long, red. Pods $\frac{3}{4}$–1 in. long, slightly curved, indented on both sutures, more deeply on the lower one; joints 3–6, as broad as long, slightly pubescent. *D. congestum* (sp.), Wall. Cat. 5723; Dalz. & Gibs. p. 66. *D. Cephalotes*, Fl. B. I. v. 2, p. 161 (in part); Wight, Icon. t. 373; Trim. Fl. Ceyl. v. 2, p. 47; Talb. Trees, Bomb. p. 69; Woodr. in Journ. Bomb. Nat. v. 11 (1897)

p. 423; Watt, Dict. Econ. Prod. v. 3, p. 81.—Flowers: Aug.-Oct. VERN. *Lapoti.*

D. Cephalotes (typical) is Subhimalayan, rare in India proper.

KONKAN: *Law*!, *Stocks*!; Island of Caranja, *Dalzell & Gibson*; hills near Matheran, *Kanitkar*!; Matheran Ghât, *H. M. Birdwood.* S. M. COUNTRY: Belgaum, *Ritchie*, 188!; Castlerock, *Cooke*! KANARA: Yellapur (N. Kanara), *Talbot*!—DISTRIB. Throughout the plains of India; Ceylon.

3. **Desmodium pulchellum,** *Benth. ex Baker, in Hook. f. Fl. B. I.* v. 2 (1876) p. 162. A shrub 4–5 ft. high; branches slender, terete or sometimes slightly angled, grey-downy. Leaves 3-foliolate, 3–7 in. long; petioles $\frac{1}{8}$–$\frac{5}{8}$ in. long, channelled above, densely downy; stipules $\frac{1}{6}$ in. long, ovate, long-acuminate. Leaflets coriaceous, ovate-elliptic, obtuse or subacute, subglabrous and subrugose above, finely downy, reticulately veined and pale beneath, repand or undulate on the margins, base rounded or subcordate (the terminal 2–5 by 1–2$\frac{1}{2}$ in., equilateral, the lateral 1–3 by $\frac{5}{8}$–1$\frac{1}{2}$ in. oblique); main nerves 8–10 pairs, oblique, prominent beneath; petiolules $\frac{1}{16}$–$\frac{1}{8}$ in. long; stipels subulate. Inflorescence axillary or terminal; flowers in racemes 3–10 in. long, composed of solitary, fascicled or umbellate flowers in the axils of 12–40 compound leafy bracts; bracts 2-foliolate, their leaflets orbicular, stipellate, $\frac{1}{2}$ in. across, glabrous on the upper, finely downy on the lower side, placed back to back on a very short densely villous common petiole which is stipulate at the base. Calyx $\frac{1}{12}$ in. long, puberulous; teeth lanceolate, shorter than the tube. Corolla $\frac{1}{4}$ in. long, yellow. Pods $\frac{1}{8}$–$\frac{1}{4}$ in. long, indented on both sutures; joints usually 2 (rarely 1 or 3), slightly longer than broad, reticulately veined, pubescent. Trim. Fl. Ceyl. v. 2, p. 48; Talb. Trees, Bomb. p. 69; Woodr. in Journ. Bomb. Nat. v. 11 (1897) p. 123; Watt, Dict. Econ. Prod. v. 3, p. 83. *Dicerma pulchellum*, DC. Prodr. v. 2, p. 339; Wight, Icon. t. 418.—Flowers: Aug.-Oct.

KONKAN: *Stocks*! KANARA: common in N. Kanara as undergrowth in the high timber deciduous forests of the Yellapur Ghâts, *Talbot.*—DISTRIB. Throughout India; Ceylon, Malaya.

4. **Desmodium laxiflorum,** *DC. Prodr.* v. 2 (1825) p. 335. An erect undershrub 2–5 ft. high; stems slender, woody, obtusely angled, clothed when young with short white subappressed hairs, at length glabrescent. Leaves 3-foliolate; petioles 1–2$\frac{1}{2}$ in. long, channelled above, pubescent with appressed hairs; stipules $\frac{3}{8}$ in. long, linear-lanceolate, very acute, striate. Leaflets membranous, ovate-elliptic or sometimes broadly lanceolate, acute or subobtuse, green and glabrous above, appressedly hairy, reticulately veined and paler beneath, base rounded or acute (the terminal 3–6 by 1$\frac{1}{2}$–2$\frac{3}{4}$ in., the lateral 1$\frac{3}{4}$–4 by 1–1$\frac{1}{2}$ in.); main nerves 7–12 pairs, slender, prominent beneath; petiolules $\frac{1}{12}$ in. long; stipels $\frac{1}{4}$ in. long, linear-subulate. Flowers in terminal and axillary racemes 6–10 in. long, usually arranged in distant few-flowered fascicles (rarely solitary) along a slender hairy rhachis; pedicels filiform, pubescent, ultimately $\frac{1}{8}$–$\frac{1}{4}$ in. long, finally spreading; bracts and bracteoles linear-acute, hairy. Calyx $\frac{1}{10}$–$\frac{1}{8}$ in. long, campanulate, strigose; teeth lanceolate, slightly longer than the tube. Corolla $\frac{1}{4}$ in. long; standard white; wings and keel blue. Pods 1–1$\frac{3}{4}$ in. long, scarcely constricted between the seeds, clothed with minute hooked

hairs; joints 6–10, flat, $\frac{1}{8}$ in. long, by $\frac{1}{16}$–$\frac{1}{10}$ in. broad. Fl. B. I. v. 2, p. 164; Talb. Trees, Bomb. p. 70; Woodr. in Journ. Bomb. Nat. v. 11 (1897) p. 423. *D. recurvatum*, Wall. Cat. 5717; Grah. Cat. p. 49; Wight, Icon. t. 374.—Flowers: Aug.-Oct. VERN. *Jangli-gánjá*.

KONKAN: *Law*!; near Poladpur, *Woodrow*!; Matheran, *Cooke*! DECCAN: Koosgaon near Karkala, *Kanitkar*! S. M. COUNTRY: Castlerock, *Cooke*! KANARA: common in the forests along the Supa Ghâts of N. Kanara, *Talbot*.—DISTRIB. India generally; Java, Borneo, Philippines.

5. **Desmodium polycarpum,** *DC. Prodr.* v. 2 (1825) p. 334. An erect or suberect undershrub 2–5 ft. high; branches woody, slightly angular, slender, clothed upwards with short grey appressed hairs. Leaves 3-foliolate; petioles $\frac{5}{8}$–1 in. long, angular, more or less appressedly hairy; stipules $\frac{1}{3}$–$\frac{1}{2}$ in. long, lanceolate-subulate. Leaflets subcoriaceous, 1–2$\frac{1}{2}$ by $\frac{3}{4}$–1 in. (the terminal the largest), obovate-cuneate, rounded at the apex, glabrous above, paler, closely reticulately veined and with a few appressed hairs beneath; main nerves 6–8 pairs, inconspicuous; petiolules $\frac{1}{16}$–$\frac{1}{12}$ in. long; stipels $\frac{1}{8}$–$\frac{1}{4}$ in. long, filiform. Flowers in dense axillary and terminal subsessile racemes 1–3 in. long; pedicels $\frac{1}{8}$–$\frac{3}{16}$ in. long, filiform, ascending; bracts ovate-cuspidate, $\frac{1}{8}$–$\frac{1}{6}$ in. long, ciliate with white hairs. Calyx $\frac{1}{10}$ in. long, glabrescent; teeth triangular, acute, about as long as the tube. Corolla $\frac{1}{6}$ in. long, purple. Pods $\frac{1}{2}$–$\frac{3}{4}$ by $\frac{1}{8}$–$\frac{1}{6}$ in., ciliate on both edges, densely pubescent when young, glabrescent or more or less hairy when ripe, indented and dehiscing along the lower suture; joints 5–8, faintly reticulately veined, as broad as long, the upper edge straight, the lower rounded. Fl. B. I. v. 2, p. 171; Grah. Cat. p. 49; Dalz. & Gibs. p. 66; Wight, Icon. t. 406; Talb. Trees, Bomb. p. 70; Woodr. in Journ. Bomb. Nat. v. 11 (1897) p. 423; Watt, Dict. Econ. Prod. v. 3, p. 83. *Desmodium heterocarpum*, DC. Prodr. v. 2, p. 337; Trim. Fl. Ceyl. v. 2, p. 53.—Flowers: Aug.-Oct.

Common throughout the Presidency. KONKAN: *Jacquemont*, 684!; hills north-east of Pen, *Dalzell & Gibson*; Dapoli, *Nairne*. S. M. COUNTRY: Castlerock, *Bhiva*!, *Cooke*!; Ramghât, *Law* ex *Graham*; Londa, *Cooke*! KANARA: Kumpta and Yellapur, *Woodrow*!—DISTRIB. Throughout India; Ceylon, Malaya, E. Africa, China, Japan, Philippines, Polynesia.

6. **Desmodium diffusum,** *DC. Prodr.* v. 2 (1825) p. 336, n. 106 (*not* p. 335, n. 88). Herbaceous, 1–2 ft. high; stems stout, angular, deeply grooved, clothed with long spreading soft white hairs. Leaves 3-foliolate; petioles $\frac{1}{2}$–1$\frac{1}{2}$ in. long, densely hairy; stipules large, foliaceous, amplexicaul, auricled. Leaflets subcoriaceous, 1–3$\frac{1}{4}$ by $\frac{1}{2}$–2 in., ovate-oblong, elliptic-oblong, or obovate (the terminal the largest), obtuse, apiculate, hairy on both surfaces, ciliate with long white hairs, reticulately veined beneath, base acute or rounded; main nerves 10–12 pairs, conspicuous beneath; petiolules $\frac{1}{16}$ in. long; stipels linear-lanceolate, $\frac{1}{8}$–$\frac{3}{16}$ in. long. Flowers in terminal and axillary racemes or panicles reaching 1 ft. long, laxly arranged in few- (usually 2–3-) flowered fascicles along a grooved and hairy rhachis; pedicels filiform, $\frac{1}{8}$–$\frac{1}{4}$ in. long; bracts $\frac{1}{10}$–$\frac{1}{8}$ in. long, lanceolate, acute, ciliate. Calyx $\frac{1}{10}$ in. long, hairy; teeth about as long as the tube, linear, acute, ciliate. Corolla $\frac{1}{8}$–$\frac{1}{6}$ in. long. Pods $\frac{5}{8}$–$\frac{3}{4}$ by $\frac{1}{10}$–$\frac{1}{6}$ in., straight, indented on both sutures, more so on the lower; joints 3–6, rounded on both edges, as

broad as long, clothed with hooked hairs, faintly reticulately veined. Fl. B. I. v. 2, p. 169; Wight, Icon. t. 298; Woodr. in Journ. Bomb. Nat. v. 11 (1897) p. 423; Watt, Dict. Econ. Prod. v. 3, p. 82. *Hedysarum diffusum*, Willd. Sp. Pl. v. 3, p. 1180.—Flowers: Sept. VERN. *Chikta.*

Bombay Presidency, without locality, *Dalzell*! KONKAN: *Stocks*!; Bombay, *Capt. Geburne*! DECCAN: Poona, *Woodrow*; Nasik, *Nairne*.—DISTRIB. Throughout the greater part of India.

7. **Desmodium triflorum,** *DC. Prodr.* v. 2 (1825) p. 334. A small perennial trailing herb; stems slender, 6–18 in. long; branches numerous, prostrate, rooting at the nodes, sparsely hirsute with white spreading hairs. Leaves 3-foliolate (the lower sometimes 1-foliolate); petioles $\frac{1}{5}$–$\frac{1}{4}$ in. long; stipules ovate, acuminate, $\frac{1}{8}$–$\frac{1}{6}$ in. long, persistent. Leaflets membranous, obovate, cuneate, $\frac{1}{5}$–$\frac{1}{4}$ by $\frac{1}{6}$–$\frac{1}{5}$ in. (the terminal slightly larger than the lateral), truncate or emarginate, rarely rounded, glabrous above, more or less hairy beneath; petiolules $\frac{1}{16}$–$\frac{1}{12}$ in. long. Flowers 1–5 (usually 3), fascicled in the axils of the leaves; pedicels $\frac{1}{4}$ in. long, hairy; bracts ovate, acute, ciliate; bracteoles minute. Calyx $\frac{1}{8}$–$\frac{1}{6}$ in. long, clothed with long white hairs; teeth lanceolate, longer than the campanulate tube, ciliate with long white hairs. Corolla $\frac{1}{5}$ in. long, pink or occasionally white; standard $\frac{1}{10}$ in. broad, broadly obovate, cuneate, produced into a long slender claw. Pods $\frac{3}{8}$–$\frac{5}{8}$ by $\frac{1}{8}$–$\frac{1}{6}$ in., the upper edge straight, the lower indented; joints 3–5, as broad as long, reticulately veined, more or less puberulous, the upper edge straight, the lower rounded. Fl. B. I. v. 2, p. 173; Grah. Cat. p. 49; Dalz. & Gibs. p. 67; Trim. Fl. Ceyl. v. 2, p. 54; Woodr. in Journ. Bomb. Nat. v. 11 (1897) p. 423; Watt, Dict. Econ. Prod. v. 3, p. 84.—Flowers: Oct. VERN. *Rán-methi.*

A very common plant throughout the Presidency. KONKAN: *Stocks*! DECCAN: widely, *Woodrow*; Mahableshwar, *Cooke*!; Koina valley, *Cooke*! S. M. COUNTRY: Belgaum, *Ritchie*, 187!; Castlerock, *Cooke*!—DISTRIB. Common throughout India; cosmopolitan in the Tropics.

8. **Desmodium triquetrum,** *DC. Prodr.* v. 2 (1825) p. 326. An erect shrub; branches triquetrous, grooved, glabrescent. Leaves 1-foliolate; petioles $\frac{3}{4}$–$1\frac{1}{4}$ in. long, hairy, furnished on each side with a leaf-like reticulately veined glabrous wing of variable breadth; stipules scarious, $\frac{1}{2}$–$\frac{3}{4}$ in. long, linear-lanceolate, acute, closely parallel-striate, persistent. Leaflets 4–6 by 1–2 in., ovate-oblong or oblong-lanceolate, acute, glabrous above, slightly hairy on the nerves and reticulately veined beneath, base rounded or subcordate; main nerves 12–20 pairs; petiolules very short; stipels adnate to the top of the petiolar wing, curved, acute, nerved. Flowers in axillary and terminal racemes 6–9 in. long, in fascicles of 1–3 in the axils of subulate bracts $\frac{1}{4}$–$\frac{3}{8}$ in. long; pedicels filiform, short; bracteoles linear-subulate, ciliate. Calyx $\frac{1}{8}$ in. long, hairy; teeth unequal, the upper deltoid, the lower linear, acute. Corolla $\frac{1}{3}$ in. long, violet. Pods 1–2 by $\frac{1}{4}$ in., linear-oblong, with a long apiculation, flat, continuous, scarcely indented, densely and persistently strigose with appressed grey hairs; joints 4–8, rather broader than long. Fl. B. I. v. 2, p. 163 (exclud. syn. *D. auriculatum*, *D. pseudotriquetrum*, and *D. alatum*, DC.); Grah. Cat. p. 49; Dalz. & Gibs. p. 66; Trim. Fl. Ceyl. v. 2, p. 49; King, in Journ. As. Soc. Beng. v. 66

(1898) p. 143; Talb. Trees, Bomb. p. 70; Woodr. in Journ. Bomb. Nat. v. 11 (1897) p. 423. *Hedysarum triquetrum*, Linn. Sp. Pl. p. 746. *Hedysarum alatum*, Roxb. Fl. Ind. v. 3, p. 348.—Flowers: Sept.-Dec. VERN. *Kákgangá*.

KONKAN: *Stocks*!; Malabar Hill (Bombay), *Graham*; Salsette, *Graham*; Matheran, *Cooke*!; Poladpur, *Woodrow*! DECCAN: Koosgaon near Karkala, *Woodrow*!; Panchgani, *Woodrow*! S. M. COUNTRY: Castlerock, *Cooke*! KANARA: moist forests of N. Kanara from the coast inwards, *Talbot*.

9. **Desmodium gangeticum,** *DC. Prodr.* v. 2 (1825) p. 327. An undershrub 2–4 ft. high; stems irregularly angled, glabrescent; branches angled, clothed with appressed white hairs. Leaves 1-foliolate; petioles 3/8–3/4 in. long; stipules scarious, 1/4–1/3 in. long, linear-subulate, striate at the base. Leaflets membranous, 3½–5 by 1⅜–2½ in., ovate-oblong, acute or slightly acuminate, the margins somewhat waved, glabrous and green above, paler and clothed with dense soft whitish appressed hairs beneath, reticulately veined, base rounded, truncate or subcordate; main nerves 8–12 pairs; petiolules 1/16 in. long, hairy; stipels 1/8 in. long, subulate. Flowers in copious ascending terminal and axillary racemes 6–12 in. long, arranged in few-flowered fascicles along a slender pubescent somewhat angular rhachis; pedicels 1/6–1/4 in. long, filiform, pubescent; bracts subulate, 1/16–1/8 in. long; bracteoles minute. Calyx 1/12 in. long, hairy; teeth triangular, longer than the campanulate tube. Corolla 1/6 in. long, violet or white; standard 1/8 in. broad, cuneate at the base. Pods subfalcate, 1/2–3/4 by 1/12 in., deeply indented on the lower, slightly indented on the upper edge; joints 6–8, longer than broad, indehiscent, sparsely clothed with minute hooked hairs, the lower edge rounded, the upper straight. Fl. B. I. v. 2, p. 168; Grah. Cat. p. 49; Dalz. & Gibs. p. 66; Trim. Fl. Ceyl. v. 2, p. 51; Talb. Trees, Bomb. p. 70; Woodr. in Journ. Bomb. Nat. v. 11 (1897) p. 423; Watt, Dict. Econ. Prod. v. 3, p. 82.—Flowers: May–July. VERN. *Sálvan*; *Sálparni*.

KONKAN: *Stocks*!; Malabar Hill (Bombay), *Graham*; near Pen, *Dalzell & Gibson*. DECCAN: Bowdhan near Poona, *Woodrow*, *Kanitkar*!; Kolapur, *Cooke*! S. M. COUNTRY: Belgaum, *Ritchie*, 1033! KANARA: moist forests of N. Kanara, *Talbot*.—DISTRIB. India (Himalayas to Pegu); Ceylon, Tropical Africa, Malay Islands, Philippines, China.

VAR. *maculatum*, Baker, in Hook. f. Fl. B. I. v. 2, p. 168. Dwarf, a few inches (rarely 1 ft.) high. Leaflets rounded, cordate, 3/4–1¼ in. long, green blotched with paler spots. *D. maculatum* (sp.), DC. Prodr. v. 2, p. 327. *Hedysarum maculatum*, Linn. Sp. Pl. (1753) p. 746. *Hedysarum humile* (*capparidis folio maculato*), Dill. Hort. Elth. (1732) p. 170, t. 141, fig. 168.

Rare. Belgaum, *Ritchie*, 1033!—DISTRIB. India (Rohilkhand, Upper Bengal).

10. **Desmodium latifolium,** *DC. Prodr.* v. 2 (1825) p. 328. An erect undershrub 3–6 ft. high; branches terete, spreading, densely clothed with short fulvous hairs. Leaves 1-foliolate; petioles 3/8–5/8 in. long, densely fulvous-hairy; stipules cordate-ovate at the base, long-acuminate, hairy, ciliate. Leaflets 1½–4 by 1¼–3½ in., broadly ovate or suborbicular, obtuse or subacute, mucronate, densely ciliate with short fulvous hairs, finely hairy above, densely so and reticulately veined beneath, base cordate or truncate; main nerves 6–8 pairs, conspicuous

and densely fulvous-hairy beneath; petiolules 1/12–1/8 in. long, densely fulvous-hairy; stipels subulate, hairy. Flowers in terminal and axillary racemes sometimes reaching 1 ft. long, arranged in (usually) 2-flowered fascicles along a hairy rhachis; pedicels shorter than the calyx, hairy; bracts linear-subulate, hairy, longer than the calyx; bracteoles minute, hairy. Calyx 1/8 in. long, densely hairy; teeth triangular, as long as the tube. Corolla 1/6 in. long, purple. Pods 1/2–3/4 by 1/12–1/8 in., straight, slightly indented on the upper, more deeply so on the lower suture; joints 4–6, about as broad as long, densely clothed with hooked hairs, the upper edge straight, the lower rounded. Fl. B. I. v. 2, p. 168 (exclud. syn. *D. virgatum*, Zoll.); Grah. Cat. p. 40; Dalz. & Gibs. p. 66; Trim. Fl. Ceyl. v. 2, p. 51; Talb. Trees, Bomb. p. 70; Woodr. in Journ. Bomb. Nat. v. 11 (1897) p. 423; Watt, Dict. Econ. Prod. v. 3, p. 82.—Flowers: July–Sept.

KONKAN: hilly places, *Graham*; moist forests, *Talbot*; Mira hills near Pen, *Dalzell & Gibson*. DECCAN: Bowdhan, 8 miles W. of Poona, *Kanitkar*! KANARA: moist forests of N. Kanara, *Talbot*.—DISTRIB. Throughout India; Ceylon, Tropical Africa, Malay Islands, Philippines.

11. **Desmodium reniforme,** *DC. Prodr.* v. 2 (1825) p. 327. A slender plant; stem reaching 18 in. long, very slender, pale, glabrous. Leaves 1-foliolate; petioles 3/8–3/4 in. long, slender, glabrous; stipules scarious, 1/6 in. long, lanceolate, striate. Leaflets broader than long, 1/2–3/4 by 3/4–1 1/4 in., reniform, glabrous on both surfaces, reticulately veined; main nerves 3–4 pairs; petiolule 1/20 in. long, slightly thickened; stipels subulate. Flowers in racemes which are usually terminal, or a few flowers solitary or 2 together fascicled in the axils of the leaves; pedicels filiform; bracts scarious, lanceolate, striate. Calyx 1/10 in. long, glabrous; teeth triangular, acute, as long as the tube. Corolla 1/8–1/6 in. long. Pods 1/2–3/4 by 1/8 in., the upper suture straight, the lower slightly indented; joints 3–5, longer than broad, glabrous, reticulately veined. Fl. B. I. v. 2, p. 173; Dalz. & Gibs. p. 67. *Hedysarum reniforme*, Linn. Sp. Pl. ed. 2 (1763) p. 1051; Burm. Fl. Ind. t. 52, fig. 1.

This has been included on the authority of *Dalzell & Gibson* (Bomb. Fl. l. c.), who state that it is common in subalpine jungles. It does not seem, however, to have been found by any other collectors and there are no specimens from the Bombay Presidency in Herb. Kew.—DISTRIB. India (E. Himalayas, Prome, Ava, W. Peninsula); Java.

12. **Desmodium rotundifolium,** *Baker, in Hook. f. Fl. B. I.* v. 2 (1876) p. 172 (*not* of Wall.). An erect much-branched herb 6–18 in. high; stem and branches terete, slender. Leaves 1-foliolate; petioles 1/4–1/3 in. long, filiform; stipules 1/8 in. long, lanceolate-cuspidate. Leaflets orbicular, 1/2–1 in. long, as broad as long, very shortly acuminate, glabrous above, appressedly hairy beneath; nerves inconspicuous; petiolules 1/20 in. long; stipels subulate. Flowers in terminal and axillary lax racemes, at first short, afterwards elongating and reaching 3–5 in. long, the lower flowers in distant pairs, the upper solitary, along a slender rhachis; pedicels ascending, 1/4–3/8 in. long, filiform; bracts ovate, acuminate, striate, at first concealing the buds, falling after the flowers develop. Calyx 1/8 in. long, hairy; tube very short; teeth subulate, 3 times as long as the tube, ciliate with long hairs. Corolla exserted, 1/3 in. long, pink. Pods 1/4–1/2 by 1/16 in., falcate, the lower suture slightly indented; joints 3–6, as broad as long, somewhat turgid, re-

ticulately veined, the upper suture straight, the lower rounded. Woodr. in Journ. Bomb. Nat. v. 11 (1897) p. 423.

Dalzell (MS. in Herb. Kew.) places this plant in the genus *Alysicarpus*, but though the pods are somewhat turgid and resemble the pods of that genus, the calyx is not glumaceous and the corolla is considerably exserted.

DECCAN: Mahableshwar, very common, *Cooke*!; Koosgaon near Karkala, *Kanitkar*! S. M. COUNTRY: Belgaum districts, *Ritchie*, 288!—DISTRIB. Apparently endemic.

13. **Desmodium parviflorum,** *Baker, in Hook. f. Fl. B. I.* v. 2 (1876) p. 172. Herbaceous, erect, much-branched; stems numerous, pale, 1–2 ft. long, glabrous at the base, clothed with spreading fulvous hairs in the upper part. Leaves 1- and 3-foliolate intermixed; petioles of the 1-foliolate leaves $\frac{1}{2}$–$\frac{3}{4}$ in., those of the 3-foliolate ones $\frac{1}{4}$–$\frac{3}{8}$ in. long; stipules $\frac{1}{4}$ in. long, ovate, produced into a long acicular point. Leaflets elliptic-oblong, obtuse or subacute, mucronate, glabrous above, appressedly hairy beneath, base subcordate (the terminal 1–2 by $\frac{1}{2}$–$\frac{3}{4}$ in., the lateral when present $\frac{1}{2}$–$\frac{3}{4}$ by $\frac{1}{4}$–$\frac{3}{8}$ in.); petiolules short. Flowers in lax, usually terminal racemes, the lower flowers in pairs, the upper solitary along a slender hairy rhachis; pedicels filiform, $\frac{1}{2}$–$\frac{3}{4}$ in. long, hairy; bracts $\frac{1}{4}$ in. long, lanceolate-cuspidate. Calyx $\frac{1}{6}$ in. long, hairy, divided almost to the base; teeth subulate, ciliate. Corolla not or very slightly exserted. Pods falcate, $\frac{3}{8}$–$\frac{1}{2}$ by $\frac{1}{12}$ in., both sutures indented, the lower the deeper; joints 4–6, rounded on both edges, reticulately veined, glabrescent. Woodr. in Journ. Bomb. Nat. v. 11 (1897) p. 423. *Alysicarpus parviflorus*, Dalz. in Kew Journ. Bot. v. 3 (1851) p. 211; Dalz. & Gibs. p. 65.

This plant forms a connecting link between the genera *Alysicarpus* and *Desmodium* and might with equal reason be placed in either. The corolla is scarcely if at all exserted and the calyx is not glumaceous.

Rare. KONKAN: *Stocks*!, *Dalzell*! DECCAN: Phunda Ghát near Kolhapur, *Dalzell & Gibson*. S. M. COUNTRY: Belgaum, *Ritchie*, 184!—DISTRIB. India (Anamallay hills).

14. **Desmodium gyrans,** *DC. Prodr.* v. 2 (1825) p. 326. An erect undershrub 2–4 ft. high; branches slender, grooved, the young ones pubescent. Leaves 1–3-foliolate; petioles $\frac{3}{8}$–1 in. long, sparsely hairy; stipules scarious, $\frac{1}{4}$ in. long, lanceolate, caducous. Leaflets subcoriaceous, oblong-lanceolate, obtuse, glabrous above, more or less silky-pubescent beneath (the terminal 1–2$\frac{1}{2}$ by $\frac{1}{4}$–$\frac{1}{2}$ in., the lateral $\frac{3}{8}$–$\frac{3}{4}$ by $\frac{1}{8}$–$\frac{1}{6}$ in.); petiolules $\frac{1}{8}$ in. long; stipels linear-subulate. Flowers in lax terminal and axillary racemes (the terminal often panicled), elongating after flowering; pedicels $\frac{1}{8}$–$\frac{1}{4}$ in. long, downy; bracts large, ovate, acuminate, striate, completely concealing the flowers in bud, falling as the flowers develop. Calyx membranous, campanulate, $\frac{1}{10}$ in. long, glabrous; teeth deltoid, shorter than the tube. Corolla $\frac{1}{3}$ in. long, pink; standard broadly obovate or suborbicular, $\frac{5}{16}$ in. broad, with a short claw. Pods 1$\frac{1}{4}$–1$\frac{3}{4}$ by $\frac{3}{16}$ in., slightly falcate, dehiscing along the ventral suture which is slightly indented; joints 5–10, inconspicuous, rather broader than long, hairy, reticulately veined, the upper suture straight, the lower rounded. The two lateral leaflets move spontaneously by jerks; hence the name. Fl. B. I. v. 2, p. 174; Grah. Cat. p. 49; Wight, Icon. t. 294; Taubert, in Engl. & Prantl, Pflanzenf.

v. 3, part 3, p. 74, fig. 39; Trim. Fl. Ceyl. v. 2, p. 56; Talb. Trees, Bomb. p. 70.

Apparently confined to the Southern districts of the Presidency. KONKAN: *Stocks*! KANARA: moist forests of N. Kanara, common, *Talbot*.—DISTRIB. India (along the Himalayas from Hazara to Assam, Ava, Pegu, Tenasserim, W. Peninsula); Ceylon, Malay Islands, Philippines.

32. ABRUS, Linn.

Climbing shrubs. Leaves abruptly-pinnate. Leaflets numerous; petiole terminated by a bristle. Flowers small, in dense racemes, on axillary peduncles or short branches. Calyx small, campanulate, truncate; teeth very short, the 2 upper subconnate. Corolla much exserted; standard broadly obovate or suborbicular, narrowed into a short claw, more or less adherent to the staminal-tube; wings narrow, oblong-falcate; keel longer and broader than the wings, arcuate. Stamens 9 (the tenth stamen absent), united into a tube slit above; anthers uniform. Ovary subsessile; ovules ∞; style short, incurved, beardless; stigma capitate. Pod oblong or linear, flat or turgid, thinly septate between the seeds.—DISTRIB. Cosmopolitan in the Tropics; species 5.

Pod turgid, 3–5-seeded .... 1. *A. precatorius*.
Pod flat, 8–12-seeded .... 2. *A. pulchellus*.

1. **Abrus precatorius**, *Linn. Syst. Nat.* ed. 12 (1767) p. 472. A perennial twiner; stems numerous, scarcely woody, slender, glabrous; branches terete, slender, glabrous or sparsely silky. Leaves 2–4 in. long; petioles $\frac{1}{4}$–$\frac{1}{2}$ in. long, thickened and hairy at the base; stipules $\frac{1}{8}$–$\frac{3}{16}$ in. long, linear-subulate, pubescent, deciduous. Leaflets 10–20 pairs, $\frac{1}{3}$–$\frac{5}{8}$ by $\frac{1}{8}$–$\frac{1}{3}$ in. (those near the base of the rhachis smaller), opposite, very deciduous, thinly membranous, ligulate-oblong, rounded, minutely apiculate, glabrous above, slightly hairy beneath, base rounded; petiolules very short; stipels 0. Flowers crowded in many-flowered racemes shorter than the leaves; rhachis usually thickened in fruit; pedicels short. Calyx $\frac{1}{12}$–$\frac{1}{8}$ in. long, glabrous or sparsely silky; teeth very short. Corolla $\frac{3}{8}$ in. long, pink, or white with a pink tinge. Pods oblong, turgid, 1–1$\frac{1}{2}$ by $\frac{3}{8}$–$\frac{1}{2}$ in., truncate, with a sharp deflexed beak, silky-pubescent. Seeds 3–5, as large as a pea, usually bright scarlet with a black spot, sometimes white with a black spot, or uniformly white, polished, shining. In cultivated forms, the seeds are sometimes wholly black. Fl. B. I. v. 2, p. 175; Grah. Cat. p. 51; Dalz. & Gibs. p. 76; Taubert, in Engl. & Prantl, Pflanzenf. v. 3, part 3, p. 356, fig. 130; Trim. Fl. Ceyl. v. 2, p. 57; Talb. Trees, Bomb. p. 70; Woodr. in Journ. Bomb. Nat. v. 11 (1897) p. 424; Watt, Dict. Econ. Prod. v. 1, p. 10.—Flowers: Sept.–Oct. VERN. *Gunj*.

KONKAN: *Stocks*!, *Woodrow*! DECCAN: near Poona, *Woodrow*!, *Cooke*!; Gokak, *Cooke*! GUJARAT: *Woodrow*. KANARA: moist forests of N. Kanara common, *Talbot*. —DISTRIB. Throughout India; Ceylon and throughout the Tropics, often planted.

The roots have been used as a substitute for liquorice. The seeds are used as weights by jewellers and for making rosaries and ornaments. They contain an acrid poison and have been employed to kill cattle, the seeds being powdered, made into a paste and introduced beneath the skin. See Watt, Dict. Econ. Prod. l. c.

2. **Abrus pulchellus**, *Wall. Cat.* (1828) 5819. A much-branched climber. Stems slender; branches slender, glabrous or thinly silky. Leaves 3–5 in. long; petioles $\frac{1}{2}$–$\frac{3}{4}$ in. long, thickened at the base,

pubescent; stipules $\frac{1}{8}$–$\frac{3}{16}$ in. long, linear-lanceolate. Leaflets membranous 12–16 pairs, opposite, $\frac{3}{4}$–$1\frac{1}{4}$ by $\frac{1}{4}$–$\frac{1}{3}$ in., ligulate-oblong, rounded, apiculate, glabrous above, thinly silky beneath, base rounded; petiolules very short; stipels 0. Flowers in many-flowered long-peduncled lax racemes equalling or exceeding the leaves; rhachis thickened in fruit; pedicels very short. Calyx $\frac{1}{8}$ in. long, thinly silky. Corolla $\frac{3}{8}$ in. long, pink or pale blue. Pods 2–$2\frac{1}{2}$ by $\frac{3}{8}$–$\frac{1}{2}$ in., linear, flat, incurved; valves mooth, thin. Seeds 8–12, oblong, $\frac{3}{16}$ by $\frac{1}{8}$ in., compressed, black. Fl. B. I. v. 2, p. 175; Trim. Fl. Ceyl. v. 2, p. 57; Talb. Trees, Bomb. p. 70; Watt, Dict. Econ. Prod. v. 1, p. 10.

Confined to the southern districts of the Presidency. KANARA: moist forests of N. Kanara, very common near Karwar and along the coast southwards, *Talbot*.—DISTRIB. India (E. Bengal, Birma, Sikkim); Ceylon, Malaya, Tropical & S. Africa, S.E. Asia.

33. LATHYRUS, Linn.

Annual or perennial herbs. Leaves abruptly-pinnate, the rhachis ending in a tendril or bristle; stipules foliaceous. Flowers solitary or racemose; bracts caducous, usually minute; bracteoles 0. Calyx-tube usually oblique at the base; teeth subequal or the upper shorter. Corolla more or less exserted; standard broadly ovate or orbicular, emarginate, narrowed into a short claw; keel shorter than the wings, incurved, obtuse. Stamens diadelphous, the mouth of the staminal-tube not oblique; anthers uniform. Ovary subsessile or stalked; ovules many; style inflexed, bearded on the inner (by the twisting of the style often the outer) face, otherwise glabrous; stigma capitate. Pod compressed or subterete, 2-valved, continuous within, many-seeded.—DISTRIB. Species about 170, spread chiefly throughout the north temperate zone.

1. **Lathyrus inconspicuus,** *Linn. Sp. Pl.* (1753) p. 730. An erect branched herb 4–9 in. high; stems slender, angled, glabrous. Leaves abruptly-pinnate; petioles short, not winged, produced at the apex into a short straight linear or lanceolate bristle; stipules $\frac{1}{5}$–$\frac{1}{3}$ in. long, linear-lanceolate, caudate at the base, veined. Leaflets 2 (rarely 1), subsessile, $\frac{3}{4}$–$1\frac{3}{8}$ by $\frac{1}{8}$–$\frac{1}{5}$ in., linear-lanceolate, acute, glabrous, conspicuously nerved beneath. Flowers solitary in the axils of the leaves; pedicels short. Calyx $\frac{1}{5}$ in. long, glabrous; teeth as long as the tube, linear-lanceolate. Corolla $\frac{1}{3}$ in. long, lilac. Pods 1–2 by $\frac{1}{5}$ in. linear, compressed, slightly incurved at the apex, thickened at the margins, reticulately veined, glabrous. Fl. B. I. v. 2, p. 180. *L. erectus*, Boiss. Fl. Orient. v. 2, p. 613.

Rare. SIND: *Stocks*, 897!—DISTRIB. India (Kashmir, Rawalpindi); Beluchistan, Afghanistan, Syria, Mesopotamia.

Lathyrus sativus, Linn. Sp. Pl. (1753) p. 730, *Chickling-vetch*, *Jarosse*, *Gesse*, is not indigenous, but is sometimes cultivated in the Presidency, more especially in Gujarat and Sind, where it is grown as a cold-season crop. The use of the grain as a food continuously for some months is often found to produce in human beings incurable paralysis of the lower extremities. Fl. B. I. v. 2, p. 179; Dalz. & Gibs. Suppl. p. 22; Watt, Dict. Econ. Prod. v. 4, p. 590.—VERN. *Kasdri*; *Láng*.

34. SHUTERIA, Wight & Arn.

Climbing slender herbs. Leaves pinnately 3-foliolate; stipules striate. Leaflets stipellate. Flowers small, in axillary racemes, often twin or fascicled along the rhachis; bracts persistent, striate; bracteoles small. Calyx-tube gibbous; teeth short, the 2 upper connate at the apex. Corolla exserted; standard obovate, narrowed at the base, not auricled; wings narrow, oblique, adhering to the keel; keel shorter than the wings, obtuse. Stamens diadelphous; anthers uniform. Ovary subsessile; ovules many; style incurved, filiform, beardless; stigma capitate. Pod linear, 2-valved, obscurely septate within between the seeds.—DISTRIB. Species 5, of which 4 are Indian, the other Tropical African.

1. **Shuteria vestita,** *Wight & Arn. Prodr.* (1834) p. 207. Herbaceous, twining; stems woody, slender, hairy. Leaves pinnately 3-foliolate; petioles 1½–2¾ in. long, more or less hairy; stipules ⅛ in. long, lanceolate, acute. Leaflets membranous or subcoriaceous, 1¼–1½ by ¾–1 in., the terminal rhomboid-obovate, the lateral slightly smaller, ovate-oblong or elliptic, all more or less hairy on both sides, rounded at both ends, minutely apiculate; stipels ⅛ in. long, linear-subulate. Racemes dense, 1–4 in. long, 2 or 3 sometimes starting from the same node, the lower flowers often twin; pedicels short, densely hairy; bracts rigid, ovate-lanceolate, hairy, persistent, about as long as the pedicels. Calyx ⅛ in. long, very hairy outside; teeth lanceolate-subulate, shorter than the tube. Corolla ½ in. long, purplish-red. Pods 1–1¼ by ⅛ in., linear, hairy, slightly recurved. Seeds 5–7, ellipsoid, compressed, brownish-black. Fl. B. I. v. 2, p. 181; Dalz. & Gibs. p. 68; Wight, Icon. t. 165; Trim. Fl. Ceyl. v. 2, p. 58; Woodr. in Journ. Bomb. Nat. v. 11 (1897) p. 424.—Flowers: Oct.

KONKAN: *Stocks*!; hills near Matheran, *Kanitkar*! DECCAN: Bowdhan near Poona, *Kanitkar*!; hills near Poona, *Woodrow*!; Pál jungles, Khandesh, *Kanitkar*! S. M. COUNTRY: Dharwar, *Cooke*!; between Párva Ghát and Talaveri, *Dalzell*!—DISTRIB. India (E. Himalayas, Khasia, Sikkim, W. Peninsula); Ceylon.

35. DUMASIA, DC.

Twining slender herbs. Leaves pinnately 3-foliolate, stipulate. Leaflets stipellate. Flowers solitary or twin along the rhachis of axillary racemes; bracts small, narrow; bracteoles minute. Calyx-tube cylindric, gibbous, with a very oblique subtruncate mouth; teeth obsolete. Corolla exserted; standard obovate, erect, the margins slightly inflexed, the claw auricled; wings and keel adherent, with small blades and long claws. Stamens diadelphous; anthers uniform. Ovary substipitate; ovules many; style flattened above the middle, beardless; stigma capitate. Pod subsessile, linear, compressed, torulose, 2-valved, continuous within.—DISTRIB. Tropical and Subtropical Asia; species 3.

1. **Dumasia villosa,** *DC. Mém. Légum.* (1825) p. 257, t. 44. A twining herb; stems slender, terete, more or less fulvous-hairy. Leaves 3-foliolate; petioles ¾–1½ in. long, fulvous-hairy; stipules ⅛ in. long, linear-lanceolate, hairy. Leaflets membranous, 1½–2½ by 1–1½ in. (the terminal leaflets not much larger than the lateral ones), ovate, subobtuse, apiculate, glabrous above, more or less hairy beneath, the margins of the young leaves ciliate, base shortly cuneate,

Flowers in axillary 6–20-flowered racemes 2–4 in. long; rhachis slender, hairy; pedicels $\frac{1}{16}$ in. long; bracts subulate, hairy, $\frac{1}{10}$ in. long. Calyx $\frac{1}{3}$ in. long, clothed when young with silky hairs, soon glabrescent, the mouth obliquely truncate, the base saccate. Corolla $\frac{1}{2}$–$\frac{5}{8}$ in. long, pale yellow. Pods $1\frac{1}{2}$ in. long, linear, straight, torulose, velvety. Seeds 3–4, ellipsoid, $\frac{3}{16}$ in. long, black, shining. Fl. B. I. v. 2, p. 183; Trim. Fl. Ceyl. v. 2, p. 58; Woodr. in Journ. Bomb. Nat. v. 11 (1897) p. 424. *D. congesta*, Grah. in Wall. Cat. 5524; Wight, Icon. t. 445.—Flowers: Oct.–Nov.

A rare plant. I have found it only at Mahableshwar along one of the paths close to Bombay Point, and it has never been brought to me by any of the plant collectors. —DISTRIB. India (Himalayas and hills of the Western Peninsula); Ceylon, Java, Madagascar, Natal.

36. GLYCINE, Linn.

Twining or prostrate herbs, rarely suberect. Leaves pinnately 3–7-foliolate; stipules small. Leaflets stipellate. Flowers small, in axillary racemes, solitary or fascicled along the rhachis; bracts and bracteoles small. Calyx-tube campanulate; teeth distinct, long or short. Corolla usually but little exserted; standard subauricled at the base; wings narrow, adhering to the keel; keel shorter than the wings, obtuse. Stamens monadelphous, or the vexillary stamen at length free; anthers uniform. Ovary subsessile; ovules many; style slightly incurved, usually short, beardless; stigma capitate. Pod linear or linear-oblong, 2-valved. Seeds few.—DISTRIB. Tropical Asia and Africa, Australia; species about 12.

Leaves 3-foliolate .... 1. *G. javanica.*
Leaves 5–7-foliolate .... 2. *G. pentaphylla.*

1. **Glycine javanica,** *Linn. Sp. Pl.* (1753) p. 754. An extensive herbaceous twiner; stems somewhat angular, slender, densely clothed with deflexed grey or fulvous hairs; young shoots silky. Leaves 3-foliolate; petioles $1\frac{1}{2}$–$3\frac{1}{2}$ in. long, hairy; stipules $\frac{1}{8}$ in. long, triangular, nerved, densely hairy. Leaflets 2–$4\frac{1}{2}$ by $1\frac{1}{4}$–3 (the terminal slightly larger than the lateral, the lateral unequal-sided, the lower side the largest), broadly ovate, subacute, mucronate, glabrous or nearly so above, appressedly hairy and pale beneath; stipels linear-subulate. Flowers numerous, crowded in narrow (usually dense) axillary racemes 1–6 in. long; pedicels short, slender, hairy; bracts $\frac{1}{8}$ in. long, linear-subulate, persistent, hairy. Calyx $\frac{1}{8}$–$\frac{1}{6}$ in. long, densely silky; teeth longer than the tube, subulate, plumose. Corolla $\frac{1}{6}$ in. long, reddish. Pods 1 by $\frac{1}{6}$ in., linear, compressed, straight, densely appressedly hairy. Seeds 4–5. Fl. B. I. v. 2, p. 183; Trim. Fl. Ceyl. v. 2, p. 59; Woodr. in Journ. Bomb. Nat. v. 11 (1897) p. 424.—Flowers: Nov.

KONKAN: *Stocks*! S. M. COUNTRY: Belgaum, *Ritchie*, 213! KANARA: Kála naddi, *Ritchie*!—DISTRIB. India (Western Peninsula); Ceylon, Tropical Africa, Natal, Java.

2. **Glycine pentaphylla,** *Dalz. in Kew Journ. Bot.* v. 4 (1852) p. 344. A large twining herb; stems slender, with a few appressed silky hairs. Leaves reaching 9 in. long, 5–7-foliolate; petioles $\frac{3}{4}$–$2\frac{1}{2}$ in. long, appressedly silky; stipules small, linear-subulate, caducous. Leaflets 1–4 by $\frac{3}{8}$–$1\frac{1}{2}$ in., opposite (the terminal the longer), oblong-lanceolate, acute, mucronate, glabrous above, appressedly silky beneath, closely reticulately

veined, base rounded; stipels minute, caducous. Flowers in axillary lax racemes 6–9 in. long, in few-flowered fascicles along an appressedly silky rhachis; pedicels very short; bracts and bracteoles minute, subulate, caducous. Calyx $\frac{1}{8}$ in. long, densely silky; teeth deltoid, shorter than the tube. Corolla $\frac{3}{4}$ in. long, reddish; standard silky on the back, inconspicuously spurred at the base. Pods $1\frac{1}{2}$ by $\frac{1}{4}$–$\frac{1}{3}$ in., linear, flat, very slightly recurved, more or less appressedly silky. Seeds 4–5. Fl. B. I. v. 2, p. 184; Dalz. & Gibs. p. 68; Woodr. in Journ. Bomb. Nat. v. 11 (1897) p. 424.—Flowers: Aug.-Oct.

KONKAN: *Stocks*!; Wari country, *Dalzell*! KANARA: Yellapur, *Talbot*!—DISTRIB. India (Khasia).

37. TERAMNUS, Sw.

Twining slender herbs. Leaves pinnately 3-foliolate; stipules small. Leaflets stipellate. Flowers very small, in few-flowered fascicles in the axils of the leaves, or in axillary racemes, the flowers twin or fascicled along the rhachis; bracts and bracteoles small. Calyx-tube campanulate; the 2 upper teeth connate or distinct. Corolla little exserted; standard obovate, narrowed at the base, not spurred; wings narrow, adhering to the keel; keel shorter than the wings, almost straight, obtuse. Stamens monadelphous; alternate anthers very small, abortive. Ovary sessile; ovules many; style short, thick, beardless; stigma capitate. Pod linear, 2-valved, septate within between the seeds, hooked with the persistent style at the tip.—DISTRIB. Tropical Asia, Africa and America; species 4.

1. **Teramnus labialis,** *Spreng. Syst.* v. 3 (1826) p. 235. A widely spreading twining herb; stems slender, more or less appressedly hairy. Leaves 3-foliolate; petioles $\frac{1}{2}$–$1\frac{1}{2}$ in.; stipules $\frac{1}{8}$ in. long, ovate-lanceolate, acute, deciduous. Leaflets membranous or subcoriaceous, $1\frac{1}{2}$–$2\frac{1}{2}$ by $\frac{3}{4}$–1 in. (the terminal slightly the largest), ovate-oblong or oblong-lanceolate, subacute, apiculate, glabrous above, slightly appressedly hairy beneath, base rounded or acute; stipels subulate, $\frac{1}{16}$–$\frac{1}{10}$ in. long. Flowers in axillary few-flowered lax racemes 2–6 in. long, solitary or fascicled along a slender more or less hairy rhachis; pedicels $\frac{1}{8}$ in. long; bracts $\frac{1}{12}$ in. long, linear-lanceolate; bracteoles $\frac{1}{16}$ in. long, subulate. Calyx $\frac{1}{8}$–$\frac{1}{6}$ in. long, silky; teeth lanceolate, as long as the campanulate tube. Corolla $\frac{3}{16}$–$\frac{1}{4}$ in. long, reddish. Pods $1\frac{1}{2}$–2 by $\frac{1}{10}$ in., narrowly linear, straight or slightly incurved, hairy when young, nearly glabrous when mature, with a short stout beak bent upwards so as to form nearly a right angle with the pod. Seeds 8–12, oblong, truncate or slightly rounded at the ends, smooth, dark brown. Fl. B. I. v. 2, p. 184; Woodr. in Journ. Bomb. Nat. v. 11 (1897) p. 424; Trim. Fl. Ceyl. v. 2, p. 60. *Glycine labialis*, Linn. f. Suppl. p. 325; Dalz. & Gibs. p. 68; Wight, Icon. t. 168. *Glycine warreensis*, Dalz. in Kew Journ. Bot. v. 3 (1851) p. 210; Dalz. & Gibs. p. 68.—Flowers: Aug.-Oct. VERN. *Rán-udid.*

Very common throughout the Presidency. KONKAN: *Law*!, *Stocks*!, *Dalzell*!; Wari country, *Dalzell & Gibson*; Bombay, *Capt. Geburne*! DECCAN: widely, *Woodrow*; Bowdhan, *Kanitkar*!; Poona, *Woodrow*!; Bhor, *Bhiva*! GUJARAT: Surat, *Kanitkar*! S. M. COUNTRY: Castlerock, *Cooke*!; Belgaum, *Ritchie*, 182!—DISTRIB. Throughout India, Ceylon and the Tropics generally, Natal.

VAR. *mollis*, Baker, in Hook. f. Fl. B. I. v. 2, p. 184. Stems with longer and more spreading hairs. Leaflets densely pubescent beneath. Calyx-teeth shorter than the tube. Pods densely hairy. *Glycine mollis* (sp.), Wight & Arn. Prodr. p. 209. *Teramnus mollis* (sp.), Benth. in Journ. Linn. Soc. v. 8 (1865) p. 265.

KONKAN: *Dalzell*! S. M. COUNTRY: Párva Ghát, *Ritchie*, 1043!

38. MUCUNA, Adans.

Twining perennials and annuals. Leaves pinnately 3-foliolate; stipules deciduous. Leaflets usually stipellate. Flowers racemose or corymbose, purple or greenish-yellow, turning black when dried; bracts small or caducous. Calyx-tube campanulate, the 2 upper teeth entirely connate, the lowest tooth longer than the others. Corolla much exserted; standard more than half as long as the rostrate keel, which usually slightly exceeds the wings. Stamens diadelphous; anthers dimorphous. Ovary sessile; ovules many; style filiform, beardless; stigma capitate. Pod very variable in shape and sculpture, usually clothed with brittle irritant fine bristles.—DISTRIB. Throughout the Tropics; species about 30.

Perennials.
  Pod winged on the sutures.
    Pod transversely plaited on the faces.
      Pod nearly as broad as long, 1-seeded .... 1. *M. monosperma.*
      Pod twice as long as broad, 2-seeded .... 2. *M. atropurpurea.*
    Pod not transversely plaited on the faces .... 3. *M. gigantea.*
Annual. Pod neither winged nor transversely plaited......... 4. *M. pruriens.*

1. **Mucuna monosperma,** *DC. Prodr.* v. 2 (1825) p. 406. A large woody perennial twiner; young branches clothed with rusty brown deciduous tomentum. Leaves 6–9 in. long; petioles 3–4½ in. long; stipules ⅛ in. long, linear, deciduous. Leaflets 2¾–4 by 2–3 in., thinly coriaceous, ovate-oblong or elliptic, shortly acuminate (the lateral leaflets inequilateral, the lower side the largest), glabrous above, more or less pubescent beneath, base rounded. Flowers in 6–12-flowered corymbose axillary racemes shorter than the leaves; peduncles variable in length, ½–2½ in. long: pedicels ¼–½ in. long; bracts small, triangular, ⅛ in. long, deciduous; bracteoles ⅜ in. long, linear-lanceolate. Calyx ⅜ in. long, clothed with irritant bristles; teeth about half as long as the tube, the upper truncate, the lateral deltoid, the lower linear. Corolla 1¼ in. long, purple; keel abruptly inflexed at the tip. Pods 2–3 by 2¼ in. (nearly as broad as long), winged on both sutures and obliquely plaited on the faces, covered with brown deciduous irritant bristles. Seed solitary, nearly circular in horizontal cross section, slightly compressed, dark brown, smooth, shining; hilum linear, extending round three-fourths of the edge. Fl. B. I. v. 2, p. 185; Grah. Cat. p. 53; Dalz. & Gibs. p. 70; Trim. Fl. Ceyl. v. 2, p. 61; Talb. Trees, Bomb. p. 70; Woodr. in Journ. Bomb. Nat. v. 11 (1897) p. 424; Watt, Dict. Econ. Prod. v. 5, p. 285.—Flowers: Nov.–Jan.

KONKAN: *Law*!, *Stocks*! S. M. COUNTRY: Kala náddi, *Ritchie*, 1714!; Ramghát, *Dalzell & Gibson*.—DISTRIB. India (E. Himalayas, Khasia, Assam, Chittagong, W. Peninsula); Ceylon.

The seed is known as the *Negro Bean* and is said to be used by the Brahmins as a restorative. See Watt, Dict. Econ. Prod. l. c.

2. **Mucuna atropurpurea,** *DC. Prodr.* v. 2 (1825) p. 406. A woody perennial twiner; young branches slender, glabrous. Leaves reaching 7 in. long; petioles 3–4 in. long; stipules 1/12 in. long, lanceolate, caducous. Leaflets 2½–5 by 1⅛–3 in., thinly coriaceous, elliptic-oblong or ovate-oblong, acuminate (the terminal equal-sided and narrowed, the lateral inequilateral and rounded at the base), glabrous above, with a few scattered hairs beneath, reticulately veined; stipels 1/16 in. long, subulate. Flowers in short 10–15-flowered racemes or panicles; pedicels ½–¾ in. long; bracts triangular. Calyx ½–⅝ in. long, downy and with a few orange-colored bristles, deeply bilabiate; upper lip about half as long as the tube, the 3 lower segments triangular, equal. Corolla dark purple, large, 2–2½ in. long; keel abruptly curved upwards at the tip; standard 1 in. broad. Pods more than double as long as broad, 3–5 by 1¼–1¾ in., winged along both sutures with 10–14 parallel plaits running obliquely across the faces from the winged margins, clothed with copious orange-colored irritant bristles. Seeds usually 2 (rarely 1), broadly ellipsoid, slightly compressed; hilum extending half round the edge. Fl. B. I. v. 2, p. 186; Grah. Cat. p. 53; Trim. Fl. Ceyl. v. 2, p. 61.

KONKAN: S. Konkan, *Nimmo*, fide *Graham* l. c.

This plant has been included on the authority of Graham who cites Nimmo. I have seen no specimens from Bombay.—DISTRIB. India (W. Peninsula); Ceylon.

3. **Mucuna gigantea,** *DC. Prodr.* v. 2 (1825) p. 405. A large woody perennial twiner; stems reaching a great length; branches slender, glabrous. Leaves 5–9 in. long; petioles 4–5 in. long, glabrous; stipules linear, ⅙ in. long. Leaflets 4–5 by 2–2½ in., ovate or elliptic, acuminate (terminal leaflets equal-sided and cuneate, lateral leaflets inequilateral and rounded at the base), glabrous on both surfaces; stipels ⅙ in. long, subulate. Flowers in umbelliform corymbs; peduncles 4–18 in. long; pedicels ¾ in. long; bracts and bracteoles minute, deciduous. Calyx ⅜–½ in. long, with a few irritant bristles; tube cylindric; upper lip subtruncate, the 3 lower teeth very small and triangular in bud, afterwards obsolete. Corolla 1–1½ in. long, greenish yellow; keel not abruptly inflexed at the tip. Pods 3–6 by 2 in., broadly winged down both sutures, but not plaited across the face, clothed with deciduous yellowish-brown irritant bristles. Seeds 2–6; hilum extending round more than half the edge. Fl. B. I. v. 2, p. 186; Grah. Cat. p. 53; Trim. Fl. Ceyl. v. 2, p. 62.

KONKAN: *Nimmo*, fide *Graham* l. c.

A littoral species found on the Indian and Malayan coasts. It is included, as the last species has been, on the authority of Graham who gives Nimmo as his authority. I have seen no specimens from the Bombay Presidency.

4. **Mucuna pruriens,** *DC. Prodr.* v. 2 (1825) p. 405. An annual twiner; branches slender, more or less hairy at first, at length glabrescent. Leaves 3-foliolate; petioles 2½–4½ in. long, appressedly silky; stipules lanceolate, ⅙ in. long. Leaflets membranous, 3–5 by 2–3 in. (the terminal leaflets slightly the smaller, rhomboid-ovate with cuneate base, the lateral leaflets with truncate base, very inequilateral, the lower side greatly dilated), all subacute, mucronate, pubescent above, densely clothed with silvery-grey hairs beneath. Flowers in elongate 6–30-flowered racemes 6–12 in. long, the flowers solitary or 2–3 together

along a slender silky rhachis; pedicels $\frac{1}{8}$–$\frac{1}{4}$ in. long, hairy; bracts $\frac{1}{2}$ in. long, lanceolate, hairy, caducous; bracteoles $\frac{1}{3}$ in. long, hairy, caducous. Calyx $\frac{3}{8}$ in. long, silky and with a few irritant bristles outside; tube campanulate; upper teeth completely connate into a triangular lip equalling the tube, lateral teeth lanceolate as long as the tube, the lower tooth lanceolate and slightly longer. Corolla 1–1$\frac{1}{2}$ in. long, purple; keel slightly incurved. Pods 2–3 by $\frac{1}{2}$ in., turgid, with a longitudinal rib running the length of each valve, not winged on the margins nor transversely plaited on the faces, falcately curved on both ends, somewhat like the letter S, densely clothed with persistent irritant bristles which are at first pale-brown, afterwards steel-grey. Seeds 5–6, small; hilum not half the length of the circumference of the seed. Fl. B. I. v. 2, p. 187; Trim. Fl. Ceyl. v. 2, p. 62; Talb. Trees, Bomb. p. 71; Woodr. in Journ. Bomb. Nat. v. 11 (1897) p. 424; Watt, Dict. Econ. Prod. v. 5, p. 286. *M. prurita*, Hook. Bot. Misc. v. 2, p. 348; Grah. Cat. p. 53; Dalz. & Gibs. p. 70.—Flowers: Aug.–Dec. Vern. *Khág-kuiri*; *Kivách*.

Common in hedges throughout the Presidency in the rains. Konkan: *Stocks*!; Bassein, *Cooke*! Deccan: Khandala, *Cooke*! Gujarat: Surat, *Kanitkar*!

The fine bristles on the pods cause much irritation to those who venture to pull them with bare hands. The name "*Cowitch*," by which the plant is known to Anglo-Indians, is a corruption of the native name *Kivách*. The plant has considerable repute in native medicine and the hairs were introduced into European pharmacy more than a century ago as a vermifuge.—See Watt, Dict. Econ. Prod. l. c.

39. ERYTHRINA, Linn.

Trees; branches usually prickly. Leaves pinnately 3-foliolate; stipules small. Leaflets furnished with glanduliform stipels. Flowers in axillary and terminal racemes, handsome, usually bright red, twin or fascicled along the rhachis; bracts and bracteoles small or 0. Calyx with an oblique mouth, splitting down to the base, or campanulately-bilabiate. Petals unequal; standard much exserted, considerably exceeding the keel and wings. Vexillary stamen free nearly to the base or connate with the others half-way up the filaments; anthers uniform. Ovary stalked; ovules many; style incurved, subulate at the apex, beardless; stigma small, terminal. Pod stalked, falcate, turgid, attenuated at the base and apex, compressed, torulose.—Distrib. Tropics and warmer regions of both hemispheres; species 25–30.

Calyx not at all 2-lipped, splitting down the back to the base.
  Calyx minutely 5-toothed at the tip; seeds 6–8 .... 1. *E. indica*.
  Calyx entire at the tip; seeds 2–3 .... 2. *E. stricta*.
Calyx more or less 2-lipped, not splitting down the back to the base. 3. *E. suberosa*.

1. **Erythrina indica,** *Lamk. Encyc. Méthod.* v. 2 (1786) p. 391. A tree reaching 60 ft. in height; bark thin, smooth, grey, armed with small conical dark-colored prickles. Leaves 6–12 in. long, deciduous; petioles 4–6 in. long, unarmed, readily disarticulating; stipules lanceolate, $\frac{3}{8}$ in. long, very caducous. Leaflets 4–6 by 3$\frac{1}{2}$–5 in. (the terminal leaflet the largest), membranous, broadly rhomboid-ovate, acute or acuminate, more or less stellately pubescent when young, glabrous when mature, base truncate or rhomboidal; petiolules $\frac{1}{3}$–$\frac{1}{2}$ in. long; stipels thick, roundish, gland-like, persistent. Flowers appearing before the leaves, in dense racemes, 4–9 in. long, arranged in clusters of 1–3

on a puberulous or tomentose rhachis; peduncles stout, woody, reaching 6 in. long; pedicels ¼ in. long; bracts small, triangular, tomentose, deciduous; bracteoles ⅛ in. long, subulate, tomentose. Calyx (before the expansion of the flower) tubular, 5-toothed at the tip, 1–1¼ in. long, clothed with deciduous tomentum, mouth very oblique, the upper segment subulate, the 2 lateral similar but smaller, the lowest one longer and doubled over the others so as to form a blunt point to the bud, the calyx soon splitting down the back to the base and appearing like a spathe. Corolla bright red, 2–2½ in. long; standard 1–1½ in. broad; wings and keel-petals subequal, ½–¾ in. long. Stamens much exserted. Pods 5–12 in. long, stalked, subcylindric, distinctly torulose, glabrescent. Seeds 4–8, subreniform, ¾ by ⅜ in., brown. Fl. B. I. v. 2, p. 188; Grah. Cat. p. 54; Dalz. & Gibs. p. 70; Trim. Fl. Ceyl. v. 2, p. 63; Wight, Icon. t. 58; Talb. Trees, Bomb. p. 71; Woodr. in Journ. Bomb. Nat. v. 11 (1897) p. 424; Watt, Dict. Econ. Prod. v. 3, p. 269.—Flowers: Mar. VERN. *Pángara*.

The *Coral-tree* of Anglo-Indians.—As a wild species it is probably wholly littoral, although it is stated by *Graham* to grow commonly throughout the Konkans, while *Talbot* gives as its habitat the deciduous forests of the Konkan and N. Kanara.—It is largely grown throughout the Bombay Presidency as a support for vines or pepper plants. Cuttings strike readily and grow quickly. The wood is used for sword-sheaths and in the manufacture of light boxes, toys, and the like.—DISTRIB. Sea-coasts of India; Java, Polynesia.

2. **Erythrina stricta,** *Roxb. Hort. Beng.* (1814) p. 53. A large tree; branches armed with numerous whitish prickles. Leaves unarmed; petioles reaching 6 in. long, sometimes prickly; stipules falcate. Leaflets 3–5 in. long, nearly as broad as long (the terminal reniform-cordate, the lateral unequal-sided, ovate-cordate or subacute at the base), all shortly acuminate, glabrous; petiolules ¼–½ in. long; stipels rounded, gland-like, persistent. Flowers in terminal horizontal racemes, arranged in fascicles of 1–3 along the rhachis; peduncles stout, woody; pedicels ¼–⅜ in. long; bracts minute, caducous. Calyx spathiform, ½ in. long, subglabrous, entire at the tip, splitting to the base down the back. Corolla bright scarlet; standard 1½ in. long, oblong-lanceolate; keel half as long as the standard, four times as long as the wings. Pods 3–6 in. long, narrowed at both ends, slightly torulose, compressed, stalked, the stalk longer than the calyx. Seeds 1–3, light brown. Fl. B. I. v. 2, p. 189; Grah. Cat. p. 54; Dalz. & Gibs. p. 70; Bedd. Fl. Sylvat. t. 175; Talb. Trees, Bomb. p. 71; Woodr. in Journ. Bomb. Nat. v. 11 (1897) p. 424; Watt, Dict. Econ. Prod. v. 3, p. 270.——Flowers: Feb.–May.

KONKAN: Elephanta, *Graham*, *Woodrow*; Matheran, *H. M. Birdwood*; deciduous forests, *Talbot*; S. Konkan, common, *Dalzell & Gibson*. DECCAN: Singhad hill near Poona, *Woodrow*. KANARA: deciduous forests of N. Kanara, *Talbot*.—DISTRIB. India (Western Peninsula).

3. **Erythrina suberosa,** *Roxb. Hort. Beng.* (1814) p. 53. A tree reaching 40–50 ft. high; bark corky, deeply cracked; branches numerous, crooked, spreading, armed with yellowish-white prickles ⅛–¼ in. long, which fall off after the third year. Leaves usually unarmed, but sometimes with a few scattered prickles; petioles 4–8 in. long, often prickly; stipules linear-lanceolate, caducous. Leaflets pale, 4–6 in. long and broad (sometimes broader than long), the terminal rhomboid-ovate,

the lateral obliquely and broadly ovate-cordate, all more or less glabrous above, densely downy with matted pubescence beneath; petiolules ¼ in. long; stipels rounded, glanduliform, persistent. Racemes 1-4, near the ends of the branchlets, densely capitate, 2-4 in. long; peduncles short; pedicels ½ in. long, in fascicles of 1-3, slender; bracts caducous; bracteoles minute, subulate. Calyx ¼-⅜ in. long, more or less pubescent, soon becoming bilabiate. Corolla scarlet; standard 1½-2 by ½-⅝ in.; keel-petals less than half as long as the standard, connate, much longer than the minute falcate wings. Pods stalked, 5-6 in. long, subterete, distinctly torulose. Seeds 2-5. Fl. B. I. v. 2, p. 189; Grah. Cat. p. 54; Dalz. & Gibs. p. 70; Talb. Trees, Bomb. p. 71; Woodr. in Journ. Bomb. Nat. v. 11 (1897) p. 424; Watt, Dict. Econ. Prod. v. 3, p. 270.—Flowers: Apr.-May.

DECCAN: Chákan (Poona districts), *Woodrow*!; Poona, *Woodrow*!; Máwal districts, *Dalzell & Gibson*; Khandesh, *Graham*. GUJARAT: *Gibson* ex *Graham*.—DISTRIB. Throughout India.

40. GRONA, Lour.

Prostrate or twining herbs. Leaves 1-foliolate; stipules very caducous. Leaflets stipellate. Flowers in axillary or subterminal racemes, solitary or fascicled along an obscurely nodiform rhachis; bracts and bracteoles caducous. Calyx-tube campanulate; teeth longer than the tube, the 2 upper connate at the base or beyond the middle. Corolla exserted, its petals nearly equal in length; standard obovate or suborbicular, with 2 small auricles at the base; wings falcate, slightly adhering to the keel; keel obtuse, nearly straight. Stamens diadelphous; anthers uniform. Ovary subsessile; ovules numerous; style long, filiform, beardless; stigma capitate. Pod linear, turgid, septate between the seeds.—DISTRIB. 4 species, of which 3 are Asiatic, the other a native of Cochin-China.

1. **Grona Dalzellii,** *Baker, in Hook. f. Fl. B. I.* v. 2 (1876) p. 191. Herbaceous twiner; stems filiform, hispid with brown retrorse hairs. Leaves 1-foliolate; petioles ½-1½ in. long, hairy; stipules ovate, acute, hairy, very caducous. Leaflets 3-4½ by 2-3 in., ovate, acute, mucronate, green and nearly glabrous above, glaucous and more or less hairy beneath, ciliate, base cordate; stipels ⅙ in. long, linear-subulate, hairy, persistent. Flowers in elongate dense racemes, arranged in clusters along a very hairy rhachis; bracts ¼ in. long, ovate, acuminate, deciduous, clothed on the back and margins with long reddish stiff hairs and enclosing in bud a small head of 1-3 subsessile flowers; bracteoles ⅙ in. long, narrowly ovate-lanceolate, densely hairy. Calyx ¼-⅓ in. long, densely clothed with long reddish-brown hairs; teeth longer than the tube, the 2 upper connate for half their length, the 3 lower lanceolate, subequal. Corolla ½ in. long, blue; standard ⅜ in. broad, clawed and with 2 small auricles at the base. Pods 2-3 by ⅙ in., linear, straight, acuminate, clothed with brownish hairs. Seeds 8-10, orbicular, compressed. Woodr. in Journ. Bomb. Nat. v. 11 (1897) p. 424. *Galactia simplicifolia*, Dalz. in Kew Journ. Bot. v. 3 (1851) p. 209; Dalz. & Gibs. p. 69.—Flowers: Sept.-Oct.

A rare plant, confined to the hills. DECCAN: Harishchandragad, *Dalzell & Gibson*;

Panchgani, *Cooke*!, *Woodrow*!; Mahableshwar, *Cooke*! S. M. COUNTRY: hills near Telavari, *Dalzell*!; Párva Ghát, *Stocks*!—DISTRIB. India (Bengal).

In the Flora of B. I. (*l. c.*) the plant is said to occur in the *plains* of the Konkan. This is an error. *Stocks, Dalzell, Woodrow*, and I have found it only at a considerable height above the level of the Konkan plains.

41. GALACTIA, P. Br.

Prostrate or twining herbs or erect shrubs. Leaves pinnately 3-foliolate (rarely 1–5- or 7-foliolate); stipules small, deciduous. Leaflets stipellate. Flowers small or moderate-sized, in axillary racemes with slightly tumid nodes; bracts and bracteoles minute. Calyx-tube short; teeth linear or lanceolate, entirely fused into one. Corolla slightly exserted, its petals nearly equal; keel obtuse, nearly straight. Stamens diadelphous; anthers uniform. Ovary subsessile; ovules many; style filiform, beardless; stigma capitate. Pod linear, flattened.—DISTRIB. Chiefly American; species about 45.

1. **Galactia tenuiflora,** *Wight & Arn. Prodr.* (1834) p. 206. An herbaceous twiner; stems very slender, slightly pubescent or subglabrous. Leaves 3-foliolate; petioles $\frac{3}{4}$–1$\frac{1}{4}$ in. long; stipules small, lanceolate, acute, caducous. Leaflets membranous, 1–1$\frac{3}{4}$ by $\frac{5}{8}$–$\frac{7}{8}$ in., elliptic-oblong or oblong-lanceolate, obtuse or sometimes retuse, minutely apiculate, glabrous above, paler and more or less silky-pubescent beneath; stipels minute, subulate. Flowers in elongate racemes, 3–6 in. long, in pairs from the slightly tumid nodes of the rhachis; pedicels short, filiform; bracts small, caducous. Calyx $\frac{1}{6}$–$\frac{1}{8}$ in. long, slightly hairy; teeth longer than the tube, lanceolate, acute. Corolla $\frac{3}{8}$–$\frac{1}{2}$ in. long, bluish-purple. Pods 1$\frac{1}{2}$–2 in. by $\frac{1}{4}$–$\frac{1}{3}$ in., slightly incurved, pubescent at first, afterwards glabrescent. Seeds 6–9. Fl. B. I. v. 2, p. 192.

Throughout the lower Deccan hills, not common.

VAR. 1. *minor*, Baker, in Hook. f. Fl. B. I. v. 2, p. 192. Stems filiform. Leaflets $\frac{1}{2}$–1 by $\frac{1}{4}$–$\frac{1}{2}$ in., oblong, obtuse, apiculate, reticulated with whitish veins, glabrous above, thinly grey-silky beneath. Flowers smaller, in axillary short-peduncled racemes, solitary or twin on a filiform rhachis. Corolla $\frac{1}{4}$–$\frac{1}{3}$ in. long, purple. Pods 1–1$\frac{1}{4}$ in. long, glabrous or faintly puberulous, obliquely constricted between the seeds. Seeds 4–5. *G. tenuiflora*, var. *β*, W. & A. Prodr. p. 206. *Leucodictyon malvensis*, Dalz. & Gibs. p. 73.

KONKAN: *Stocks*!, *Dalzell*!; rocky ground in the Malwan district, *Dalzell & Gibson*.

VAR. 2. *villosa*, Baker, in Hook. f. Fl. B. I. v. 2, p. 192. Stems, leaves and pods densely grey-downy. Leaflets 1–1$\frac{1}{2}$ by $\frac{5}{8}$–$\frac{7}{8}$ in., elliptic-oblong, obtuse, base rounded or subcordate. Flowers fewer and smaller than in the type. Pods 1$\frac{1}{2}$ in. long, densely grey-downy. *Galactia villosa* (sp.), W. & A. Prodr. p. 207.

S. M. COUNTRY: hills N. of Belgaum, *Ritchie*, 143!

VAR. 3. *latifolia*, Baker, in Hook. f. Fl. B. I. v. 2, p. 192. Stems and the leaves beneath densely pubescent. Leaflets subcoriaceous, roundish, 1$\frac{1}{2}$–2 by 1$\frac{1}{4}$–1$\frac{1}{2}$ in. Racemes elongate. Calyx hoary, more deeply cleft.

KONKAN: *Stocks*!

42. SPATHOLOBUS, Hassk.

Large scandent shrubs, often tomentose. Leaves pinnately 3-foliolate; stipules small. Leaflets stipellate. Flowers small, in ample terminal panicles extending into the axils of the upper leaves; pedicels densely fascicled at the tumid nodes; bracts and bracteoles small. Calyx campanulate, the 2 upper teeth connate into 1 entire or emarginate tooth. Corolla exserted; petals subequal; keel obtuse, nearly straight. Stamens diadelphous; anthers uniform. Ovary sessile or stalked; ovules 2; style incurved, beardless; stigma capitate. Pod sessile or stalked, broadly linear, often falcate, splitting round the single apical seed, the lowest part indehiscent.—DISTRIB. Tropical Asia; 1 species in Tropical Africa; species 10.

Pod tomentose, stalked .... 1. *S. Roxburghii.*
Pod glabrous, sessile .... 2. *S. purpureus.*

1. **Spatholobus Roxburghii,** *Benth. Pl. Jungh.* (1851–55) p. 238. A large climber; stem as thick as a man's leg; young branches clothed with soft downy pubescence. Leaves 3-foliolate; petioles 3–6 in. long, puberulous; stipules small, deciduous. Leaflets subcoriaceous, 6–8 by 4–5½ in. (the terminal equal-sided, broadly elliptic or rhomboid-obovate narrowed at the base, the lateral leaflets inequilateral, the lower side much the larger and obtuse or truncate at the base, the upper side acute at the base), obtuse, subacute or shortly acuminate, glabrous above, finely silky or subglabrous beneath; main nerves 6–8 pairs, slender, conspicuous on the underside; petiolules ¼ in. long; stipels minute subulate. Flowers in large terminal densely pubescent panicles often reaching 12–18 in. long; pedicels $\frac{1}{25}$ in. long, in close fascicles along the rhachis; bracteoles ⅛ in. long, linear, velvety. Calyx ¼ in. long, velvety; teeth subequal in length, about equalling the tube, the 2 upper connate (except at the tip) into an oblong-triangular tooth, the 3 lower teeth lanceolate. Corolla bright red, exserted. Pods stalked, 3–6 in. long, usually 1–1¼ in. (sometimes reaching 2 in.) broad, equal in breadth or narrowed towards the top, the lower side more or less curved, clothed with ferruginous tomentum (which is thickest at the apex above the solitary seed), reticulately veined; stalk about ½ in. long. Fl. B. I. v. 2, p. 193; Talb. Trees, Bomb. p. 71; Woodr. in Journ. Bomb. Nat. v. 11 (1897) p. 424; Watt, Dict. Econ. Prod. v. 6, part 3, p. 319. *Butea parviflora,* Roxb. Hort. Beng. p. 53; Grah. Cat. p. 54; Dalz. & Gibs. p. 71; Wight, Icon. t. 210.—Flowers: Jan.–Feb. VERN. *Phalsan.*

KONKAN: *Stocks*!; Mira hills near Pen and hilly places S. of Panwell, *Dalzell & Gibson*; Nagotna, *Graham.* DECCAN: Peint and Phaltan, *Woodrow.* KANARA: throughout the forests of N. Kanara, *Talbot.*

This climber does much damage to teak and other timber-trees in N. Kanara (*Talbot*).

The variety *platycarpus* (Baker, in Fl. B. I. l. c.) with broad pods conspicuously narrowed at the apex cannot be maintained. Prain (Journ. As. Soc. Beng. v. 66 [1898] p. 412) points out that there is no difference between the plants bearing the broad and the narrower pods and that it is, at times, possible to collect both "varieties" on different parts of one plant.

2. **Spatholobus purpureus,** *Benth. ex Baker, in Hook. f. Fl. B. I.* v. 2 (1876) p. 194. A lofty climber. Leaves 3-foliolate; petioles 1½–3 in. long; stipules small, caducous. Leaflets subcoriaceous, 3–5 by 1½–2½ in. (the terminal the largest and equilateral, the lateral unequal-

sided), oblong-elliptic, shortly acuminate, glabrous on both surfaces, base rounded; main nerves 6–8 pairs; petiolules $\frac{3}{16}$–$\frac{1}{4}$ in. long. Flowers numerous, in terminal and axillary leafy much-branched panicles; pedicels $\frac{1}{10}$ in. long, filiform; bracts and bracteoles linear, caducous. Calyx $\frac{1}{10}$–$\frac{1}{8}$ in. long, finely pubescent; teeth about $\frac{1}{5}$ as long as the tube, oblong, obtuse, the 2 upper connate, except at the tip. Corolla $\frac{1}{8}$–$\frac{1}{5}$ in. long, purple; standard $\frac{1}{8}$ in. broad, broadly obovate, veined and with a long claw. Pods sessile, 4 in. long, $\frac{3}{4}$ in. broad at the widest part, $\frac{1}{2}$–$\frac{5}{8}$ in. broad at the thickened apex, reticulately veined, glabrous. Fl. B. I. v. 2, p. 194; Talb. Trees, Bomb. p. 71; Woodr. in Journ. Bomb. Nat. v. 11 (1897) p. 424; Prain, in Journ. As. Soc. Beng. v. 66 (1898) p. 414.—Flowers: Dec.-Feb.

Rare. KONKAN: *Stocks*! KANARA: Supa Ghâts, *Talbot*; Diggi (N. Kanara), *Talbot*, 1630!; Kanara, *Stocks*.—DISTRIB. Apparently endemic.

43. BUTEA, Roxb.

Trees or large climbing shrubs. Leaves pinnately 3-foliolate; stipules small, caducous. Leaflets stipellate. Flowers large, showy, in axillary or terminal racemes or panicles; pedicels densely fascicled from the nodes of the rhachis; bracts and bracteoles narrow, caducous. Calyx broadly campanulate; teeth short, deltoid. Corolla much exserted; standard ovate, acute, recurved, inappendiculate; keel much curved, acute, equalling the standard. Stamens diadelphous; anthers uniform. Ovary sessile or shortly stalked; ovules 2; style elongate, incurved, beardless; stigma terminal, very small or truncate. Pod firm, oblong or broadly linear, splitting round the single apical seed, the lowest part indehiscent.—DISTRIB. Tropical Asia; species 3.

An erect tree .... 1. *B. frondosa.*
A climbing shrub .... 2. *B. superba.*

1. **Butea frondosa,** *Konig, ex Roxb. As. Res.* v. 3 (1792) p. 469; *Cor. Pl.* v. 1, p. 21, t. 21. An erect tree 40–50 ft. high, with crooked trunk and irregular branches; bark rough, ash-colored; young parts tomentose or downy. Leaves 3-foliolate; petioles 4–6 in. long; stipules linear-lanceolate, deciduous. Leaflets coriaceous (the terminal 4–8 in. long and about as broad as long, broadly obovate from a cuneate base, the lateral smaller, 4–6 by 3–4 in., obliquely rounded at the base, inequilateral, the lower side the larger), all obtuse, glabrous above when old, finely silky and conspicuously reticulately veined beneath; petiolules $\frac{1}{4}$ in. long, stout; stipels subulate, deciduous. Flowers large, in rigid racemes 6 in. long, 3 flowers together from the tumid nodes of the dark olive-green velvety rhachis; pedicels about twice as long as the calyx, densely brown-velvety; bracts and bracteoles small, deciduous. Calyx $\frac{1}{2}$ in. long, dark olive green, densely velvety outside, clothed with silky hairs within; teeth short, the 2 upper connate, the 3 lower equal, deltoid. Corolla $1\frac{1}{2}$–2 in. long, clothed outside with silky silvery hairs, orange or salmon-colored; standard 1 in. broad; keel semicircular, beaked, veined. Pods stalked, 5–8 by 1–2 in., thickened at the sutures, reticulately veined, argenteo-canescent; stalk $\frac{3}{4}$ in. long. Fl. B. I. v. 2, p. 194; Grah. Cat. p. 54; Dalz. & Gibs. p. 71; Bedd. Flor. Sylvat. t. 176; Trim. Fl. Ceyl. v. 2, p. 66; Talb. Trees, Bomb. p. 72; Woodr. in Journ.

Bomb. Nat. v. 11 (1897) p. 424; Watt, Dict. Econ. Prod. v. 1, p. 548. —Flowers: Feb.-Mar. VERN. *Palas.*

Throughout the Presidency, common. KONKAN: *Graham*; Tansa, *Cooke*! DECCAN: Khandesh, *Graham*; Khandala, *Stocks*! GUJARAT: *Graham, Dalzell & Gibson.*—DISTRIB. Throughout India; Ceylon.

When in full flower this tree is a conspicuous and handsome object throughout the Indian jungles. A gum called *Bengal Kino* is obtained from the bark and the flowers furnish a brilliant but fleeting dye. See Watt, Dict. Econ. Prod. l. c.

2. **Butea superba,** *Roxb. Cor. Pl.* v. 1 (1795) p. 23, t. 22. A gigantic climber; stem as thick as a man's leg. Trminal leaflet 6–15 in. long. Flowers bright orange, rather larger than those in the preceding species; pedicels thrice as long as the calyx. In other respects exactly resembles *Butea frondosa.* Fl. B. I. v. 2, p. 195; Grah. Cat. p. 54; Dalz. & Gibs. p. 71; Talb. Trees, Bomb. p. 72; Woodr. in Journ. Bomb. Nat. v. 11 (1897) p. 424; Watt, Dict. Econ. Prod. v. 1, p. 556. —Flowers: Feb.-Mar. VERN. *Palas-vel.*

KONKAN: forests of N. Konkan, *Dalzell & Gibson, Talbot.* KANARA: *Woodrow.*

Butea Gibsonii, Grah. Cat. Bo. Pl. p. 55, which, under the vernacular name of *Tewees,* Graham describes as having white flowers like the *Karanj* (*Pongamia glabra*) and as being common about Junar and to be met with at Yelloo on the road from Poona to Mahableshwar, I can find no record of. It may possibly be *Ougeinia dalbergioides,* Benth.

44. CANAVALIA, Adans.

Climbing or prostrate herbs. Leaves pinnately 3-foliolate; stipules usually small. Leaflets stipellate. Flowers rather large and showy, in axillary racemes; rhachis nodiform; bracts minute; bracteoles small, caducous. Calyx deep, the limb 2-lipped, the upper lip projecting, entire or emarginate, the lower lip shortly 3-toothed. Corolla much exserted; standard large, suborbicular; wings narrow, equalling the incurved obtuse or obtusely-rostrate keel. Stamens monadelphous; anthers uniform. Ovary obscurely stalked; ovules many; style incurved, beardless; stigma terminal. Pod large, linear or oblong, compressed or turgid, with a distinct rib on each valve near the upper suture.—DISTRIB. Warmer regions of both hemispheres; species about 12.

Stipules large, oblong, obtuse; bracteoles large .... 1. *C. Stocksii.*
Stipules small, triangular; bracteoles minute.
  Racemes many-flowered; pods many-seeded, 1½–2 in. broad ... 2. *C. ensiformis.*
  Racemes few-flowered; pods few-seeded, ½–¾ in. broad .... 3. *C. lineata.*

1. **Canavalia Stocksii,** *Dalzell, in Dalz. & Gibs. Bo. Fl.* (1861) p. 69. A large twiner; stems very long, terete, smooth. Leaves large; petioles 6–8 in. long; stipules ⅜–½ in. long, oblong, obtuse, nerved. Leaflets thinly membranous, 5–8 in. long, nearly as broad as long (the terminal rhomboid-obovate, the lateral broadly ovate or suborbicular), glabrous, reticulately veined; the 2 basal nerves opposite, conspicuous; petiolules ¼ in. long, hairy; stipels lanceolate. Flowers several at the apex of an angular naked peduncle 12–15 in. long; pedicels short; bracteoles elliptic-oblong, ⅜ by ¼ in., veined, concealing the flowers in bud. Calyx $\frac{5}{16}$–⅜ in. long, veined, glabrous; teeth a little shorter than the tube, the upper notched, the 3 lower deltoid, ciliate. Corolla 1¼ in.

long, bluish-purple, veined. Pods not seen. Woodr. in Journ. Bomb. Nat. v. 11 (1897) p. 424. *C. ensiformis*, var. *turgida*, Baker, in Hook. f. Fl. B. I. v. 2, p. 196.—Flowers: Oct.

This is certainly a distinct species and not a variety of *C. ensiformis* as Baker has it in Fl. B. I. (*l. c.*). The var. *turgida* to which it is there referred has been restored to the rank of a species by Prain (Journ. As. Soc. Beng. v. 66 [1898] p. 417) and is a littoral species, whereas *C. Stocksii* is apparently confined to the hills.

Very rare. DECCAN: Badgi hill, Brahminwara range, *Dalzell & Gibson*; hills near Lanoli, *Krishna!*; Mahableshwar, western slope, *Cooke!*, *Woodrow!*—DISTRIB. Apparently endemic.

2. **Canavalia ensiformis,** *DC. Prodr.* v. 2 (1825) p. 404. A stout perennial or biennial twiner; stems and branches glabrous. Leaves 10–12 in. long; petioles 6 in. long, glabrous; stipules triangular, deciduous. Leaflets membranous, 3–6 by 2–4 in., ovate, acute or shortly acuminate, apiculate, glabrous on both surfaces or nearly so, base rounded; petiolules $\frac{1}{4}$ in. long; stipels $\frac{1}{8}$–$\frac{1}{6}$ in. long, subulate, caducous. Flowers in lax 12–20-flowered curved axillary racemes 3–8 in. long; pedicels $\frac{1}{8}$ in. long, usually in pairs from the swollen nodes; bracteoles minute, ovate, caducous. Calyx $\frac{3}{8}$–$\frac{5}{8}$ in. long, glabrous or faintly pubescent, the upper lip oblong, notched, $\frac{1}{3}$ the length of the tube. Corolla 1–1$\frac{1}{2}$ in. long, lilac or white. Pods 6–12 in. (or more) long, 1–2 in. wide, slightly incurved, shortly pointed, glabrescent, strongly 3-keeled. Seeds 8–20, reddish-brown or white, about 1 in. long. Fl. B. I. v. 2, p. 195; Trim. Fl. Ceyl. v. 2, p. 67; Talb. Trees, Bomb. p. 72; Woodr. in Journ. Bomb. Nat. v. 11 (1897) p. 424; Watt, Dict. Econ. Prod. v. 2, p. 97. *C. gladiata*, DC. Prodr. v. 2, p. 404; Grah. Cat. p. 52; Dalz. & Gibs. Suppl. p. 23.—Flowers: Aug.–Oct. VERN. *Abai.*

Commonly cultivated, but doubtfully wild. KONKAN: near Bhewndy, *Edgeworth!* DECCAN: Bowdhan near Poona, *Bhiva!*; Deccan hills widely, *Woodrow.*

The tender pods are used as a vegetable and the seeds are largely eaten. The plant is commonly known as the *Sword-bean* or *Patagonian bean.* See Watt, Dict. Econ. Prod. l. c.

VAR. *virosa*, Baker, in Hook. f. Fl. B. I. v. 2, p. 196. Leaflets smaller, obovate or obovate-oblong, glabrous. Flowers smaller; rhachis of raceme more densely pubescent. Pods 2–4 by 1–1$\frac{1}{2}$ in. Seeds 4–6. *C. virosa* (sp.), W. & A. Prodr. p. 253; Dalz. & Gibs. p. 69.—VERN. *Gowara.*

KONKAN: *Stocks!* S. M. COUNTRY: Belgaum districts, *Ritchie*, 201!

The seeds are regarded as poisonous by the natives, who say that they produce insanity if eaten.

3. **Canavalia lineata,** *DC. Prodr.* v. 2 (1825) p. 404. Perennial; stems spreading, prostrate, sometimes twining, glabrous. Leaves 3-foliolate; petioles 3–5 in. long; stipules $\frac{1}{10}$ in. long, triangular, caducous. Leaflets subcoriaceous or thickly membranous, 2–3 in. long, nearly as broad as long, broadly ovate, obovate or orbicular, sometimes emarginate, glabrous, base cuneate; petiolules $\frac{1}{4}$ in. long; stipels $\frac{1}{8}$–$\frac{1}{6}$ in. long, soon deciduous. Flowers in 4–8-flowered racemes; peduncles 10–15 in. long; pedicels $\frac{1}{10}$–$\frac{1}{6}$ in. long, solitary or twin from the tumid nodes of the rhachis; bracteoles minute, ovate, caducous. Calyx $\frac{5}{8}$ in.

long, pubescent, reticulately veined; upper lip subentire, ¼ the length of the tube. Corolla 1 in. long, violet; standard orbicular, emarginate. Pods few, 3–5 by ½–¾ in., linear-oblong, shortly beaked, nearly straight, glabrous. Seeds 4–6, dark-brown, over ½ in. long. King, in Journ. As. Soc. Beng. v. 66 (1898) p. 63; Prain, in Journ. As. Soc. Beng. v. 66 (1898) p. 418. *C. obtusifolia*, Baker, in Hook. f. Fl. B. I. v. 2, p. 196 (*not* of DC.); Cleghorn, Madr. Journ. new series, v. 1, t. 4; Trim. Fl. Ceyl. v. 2, p. 68; Talb. Trees, Bomb. p. 72; Watt, Dict. Econ. Prod. v. 2, p. 98.—Flowers: Mar.

A littoral species found sparingly along the sandy shores of the Konkan and N. Kanara.—Distrib. India (sea-coasts); Malaya, Ceylon, China, Japan, Polynesia, Australia.

45. PUERARIA, DC.

Twining herbs or shrubs. Leaves pinnately 3-foliolate; stipules herbaceous, produced below their insertion in some species. Leaflets entire or sinuately 3-lobed, stipellate. Flowers in long often compound racemes; pedicels densely fascicled along a nodiform rhachis; bracts and bracteoles small. Calyx-teeth long or short, the 2 upper connate into one, which is entire or 2-dentate. Corolla exserted; standard obovate or suborbicular with inflexed auricles at the base, equalling in length the obtuse wings and keel. Stamens monadelphous; anthers uniform. Ovary subsessile; ovules many; style filiform, inflexed above, beardless; stigma small capitate. Pod linear, more or less flattened.—Distrib. Tropical Asia and Japan; species 10.

1. **Pueraria tuberosa,** *DC. Prodr.* v. 2 (1825) p. 240. A large twiner; root tuberous; stems shrubby. Leaves 3-foliolate; petioles 4–6 in. long, more or less pubescent; stipules ⅛ in. long, ovate-oblong, cordate. Leaflets subcoriaceous, 5–8 by 4½–7 in. (the terminal broadly ovate, acuminate, equal-sided, cuneate at the base, the lateral ovate-oblong, inequilateral, truncate at the base), glabrescent above, silky beneath; petiolules 3/16–¼ in. long; stipels small, subulate. Flowers in lax (sometimes panicled) leafless racemes, 6–12 in. long; pedicels 1/12–⅛ in. long, silky-pubescent, fascicled along a more or less pubescent rhachis; bracteoles 1/16 in. long, oblong, silky. Calyx ¼–⅓ in. long, densely silky; teeth shorter than the tube, oblong, obtuse, ciliate. Corolla bluish; standard ½ in. long and as broad as long, spurred. Pods 2–3 in. long, membranous, flat, constricted between the seeds, clothed with long silky bristly brown hairs. Seeds 3–6. Fl. B. I. v. 2, p. 197; Dalz. & Gibs. p. 67; Wight, Icon. t. 412; Talb. Trees, Bomb. p. 72; Woodr. in Journ. Bomb. Nat. v. 11 (1897) p. 425; Watt, Dict. Econ. Prod. v. 6, part 1, p. 363.—Flowers: Feb.–Apr. Vern. *Dári.*

Konkan: *Law*!; Oorun, *Stocks*!; Karanja hill, *Dalzell & Gibson*; Vingorla, *Nairne*. Gujarat: Dang jungles, *Woodrow*. Kanara: N. Kanara in open situations, *Talbot*.

46. PHASEOLUS, Linn.

Herbs rarely woody at the base, twining, prostrate or suberect. Leaves pinnately 3-foliolate (very rarely 1-foliolate); stipules persistent, striate. Leaflets stipellate. Flowers in axillary racemes; rhachis nodiform; bracts usually caducous; bracteoles often broader than the bracts and more persistent. Calyx campanulate, the 2 upper connate or free. Corolla much exserted; standard suborbicular; wings obovate (rarely oblong); keel produced into a very long beak which forms a complete or nearly complete spiral. Stamens diadelphous; anthers uniform. Ovary subsessile; ovules many; style within the beak of the keel and twisted with it, usually bearded down the side below the very oblique stigma. Pod linear or falcate, subterete or compressed, 2-valved, more or less septate between the seeds.—DISTRIB. Throughout the warmer regions of the globe, many species widely cultivated; species about 60.

Stipules basifixed.
  A shrubby suberect plant .... 1. *P. semierectus.*
Stipules inserted above the base.
  An erect herb with thick stems .... 2. *P. grandis.*
  Prostrate or twining herbs with slender stems.
    Terminal leaflet deeply 3-lobed, the middle lobe obtuse ... 3. *P. trilobus.*
    Terminal leaflet not or obscurely lobed, acute or acuminate.
      Stems and pod glabrous .... 4. *P. Dalzellii.*
      Stems and pod densely hairy .... 5. *P. sublobatus.*

1. **Phaseolus semierectus,** *Linn. Mantiss.* (1767) p. 100. Annual, 2–3 ft. high, suberect, somewhat shrubby; stems terete; branches clothed with long deflexed deciduous hairs. Leaves 3-foliolate; petioles 1–1½ in. long, hairy; stipules basifixed, conspicuous, ⅜–½ in. long, lanceolate-subulate. Leaflets membranous, 1½–2¾ by ½–1¾ in., oblong-lanceolate, acute, minutely apiculate, glabrous on both surfaces when mature, readily disarticulating (the terminal leaflets slightly larger than the lateral), base cuneate; petiolules $\frac{1}{16}$–⅛ in. long; stipels $\frac{1}{10}$ in. long, subulate. Flowers in spicate racemes reaching 6 in. long; peduncles 6–12 in. long, terete, pubescent; pedicels very short, usually in pairs along a pubescent rhachis; bracts ¼ in. long, linear-subulate; bracteoles lanceolate, rather more than half as long as the calyx. Calyx split open by the pod, ⅛ in. long, pubescent outside; teeth shorter than the tube, triangular at the base, cristate. Corolla ½ in. long, purple. Pods 3–4 by ⅛ in., nearly cylindric, sharply beaked, silvery-pubescent when young, nearly glabrous when mature. Seeds about 20, truncate at the ends, dark-brown. Fl. B. I. v. 2, p. 201; Trim. Fl. Ceyl. v. 2, p. 70; Woodr. in Journ. Bomb. Nat. v. 11 (1897) p. 425. *P. psoraleoides*, W. & A. Prodr. p. 244; Wight, Icon. t. 249.—Flowers: Oct.

SIND: Hyderabad, *Woodrow*, doubtfully wild. The plant is a native of Central and South America and of the West Indies.—It has no doubt been introduced.

2. **Phaseolus grandis,** *Dalzell, in Dalz. & Gibs. Bo. Fl.* (1861) p. 72. Erect, 2–5 ft. high; stem herbaceous, as thick as the finger, 5-angled, glabrous or with a few appressed bristly hairs. Leaves 3-foliolate; petioles 1–2 in. long; stipules large, foliaceous, variable in size, sometimes reaching 2 by 1¼ in., attached above the base, obovate or obovate-oblong, obtuse, ciliate, cordate at the base. Leaflets variable in shape, 3–4 in. long (the terminal often 3-lobed and as broad as long, the lateral frequently 2-lobed the lower lobe the smaller, or sometimes 3-lobed or entire), all sparsely strigose on both surfaces with appressed bristly hairs, base cuneate; petiolules $\frac{1}{16}$–⅛ in. long; stipels ⅛–¼ in. long, ovate-cuspidate. Flowers in copious close racemes; peduncles

6–9 in. long, clothed with brownish-black retrorse appressed bristly hairs; pedicels short; bracts broadly ovate, acute, deciduous; bracteoles $\frac{1}{3}$ in. long, oblong or obovate-oblong, obtuse, ciliate, veined, concealing the flower in bud. Calyx $\frac{1}{8}$ in. long, clothed outside with small blackish hairs; teeth short, deltoid. Corolla $\frac{1}{3}$ in. long, pale-yellow. Pods 2–3 in. long, cylindric, about as thick as a goose-quill, septate between the seeds, clothed with appressed black or grey bristles. Seeds 8–10, subcylindric, truncate at the ends, $\frac{1}{6}$ in. long, dark-brown, rusty-pubescent. Fl. B. I. v. 2, p. 202; Woodr. in Journ. Bomb. Nat. v. 11 (1897) p. 425.

A very rare plant, found only on Konkan and Deccan hills. KONKAN: highest Ghâts east of Bombay, *Dalzell*! DECCAN: hills, *Stocks*!; Panchgani, *Woodrow*!; hills near Poona, *Cooke*!

3 **Phaseolus trilobus,** *Ait. Hort. Kew.* ed. 1, v. 3 (1789) p. 30. Annual or perennial; stems numerous from a woody rootstock, 2–3 ft. long, prostrate, wiry, slender, not at all twining, glabrous or more or less hairy. Leaves 3-foliolate, petioles $1\frac{1}{2}$–3 in. long, grooved, glabrous or with a few scattered hairs; stipules variable in length, $\frac{1}{8}$–$\frac{3}{8}$ in. long, ovate-oblong, subacute, attached above the base, ciliate. Leaflets $\frac{1}{2}$–1 in. long, usually as broad as long, commonly 3-lobed (the middle lobe the largest and oblong, broadly spathulate, obtuse, the lateral lobes often oblong or more or less spathulate, obtuse or subacute), all pale-green, membranous, glabrous or with a few hairs on the nerves, base subacute; petiolules $\frac{1}{16}$–$\frac{1}{10}$ in. long, hairy; stipels small, lanceolate, acute. Flowers in subcapitate few-flowered racemes; peduncles 4–9 in. long, glabrous or sparsely hairy; pedicels $\frac{1}{10}$ in. long; bracts ovate, acute, deciduous; bracteoles beneath the calyx $\frac{1}{8}$ in. long, linear-lanceolate, ciliate, deciduous. Calyx $\frac{1}{10}$ in. long, glabrous; teeth minute, deltoid. Corolla $\frac{1}{6}$–$\frac{1}{4}$ in. long, yellow. Pods 1–2 in. long by $\frac{1}{8}$ in. in diam., straight, subcylindric, glabrous or sparingly hairy, slightly recurved. Seeds 6–12. Fl. B. I. v. 2, p. 201; Grah. Cat. p. 52; Dalz. & Gibs. p. 71; Wight, Icon. t. 94; Trim. Fl. Ceyl. v. 2, p. 71; Woodr. in Journ. Bomb. Nat. v. 11 (1897) p. 425; Watt, Dict. Econ. Prod. v. 6, part 1, p. 194.—Flowers: Oct. VERN. *Mukni*; *Jangli-math*.

The leaflets vary much in form and size. The wild perennial form has much more deeply lobed leaflets than the annual cultivated one. Lobed and entire leaflets may, in the latter, often be found on the same plant.

Very common throughout the Presidency, especially on the borders of cultivated fields. KONKAN: *Stocks*! DECCAN: Poona, *Cooke*!, *Woodrow*!; Dongergaon near Ahmednagar, *Cooke*! GUJARAT: *Woodrow*! SIND: *Stocks*!; Jemadar ka Landa near Karachi, *Stocks*!

Occasionally cultivated as a mixed crop for fodder purposes. See Watt, Dict. Econ. Prod. l. c.

4. **Phaseolus Dalzellii,** *T. Cooke.* Herbaceous, twining or creeping and rooting in the absence of support; stems filiform, striate, glabrous. Leaves 3-foliolate; petioles $\frac{1}{2}$–$1\frac{1}{2}$ in. long, glabrous; stipules $\frac{1}{8}$ in. long, attached above the base. Leaflets membranous, $\frac{3}{4}$–2 by $\frac{1}{2}$–$1\frac{1}{2}$ in., ovate or rhomboid-ovate with a tendency to become lobate (the terminal the largest, equal-sided, the lateral inequilateral), all acuminate, more or less hairy on both surfaces, green above, pale beneath; petiolules $\frac{1}{16}$ in. long; stipels minute, lanceolate. Flowers in capitate

2–3-flowered racemes; peduncles filiform, 1–2 in. long; pedicels short; bracteoles $\frac{1}{5}$ in. long, linear-subulate. Calyx $\frac{1}{10}$ in. long, glabrous; teeth shorter than the tube, the 2 upper connate except at the tip, the 2 lateral triangular, obtuse, the lowest longer, lanceolate. Corolla $\frac{1}{2}$ in. long, yellow. Pods $1\frac{1}{4}$–$2\frac{1}{4}$ in. long, subcylindric, slightly recurved, beaked, quite glabrous. Seeds 8–10, subcylindric, truncate, smooth, dark-brown. *Phaseolus pauciflorus*, Dalz. in Kew Journ. v. 3 (1851) p. 209; Fl. B. I. v. 2, p. 202; Dalz. & Gibs. p. 72; Woodr. in Journ. Bomb. Nat. v. 11 (1897) p. 425.—Flowers: Sept.

The name *P. pauciflorus* having been given in 1838 by Bentham (Ann. Wien. Mus. v. 2 [1840] p. 140) to a Texan plant, has priority over that given to a different plant in 1851 by Dalzell. I have therefore changed the name to *P. Dalzellii*.

KONKAN: *Stocks*!, *Dalzell*!

5. **Phaseolus sublobatus,** *Roxb. Hort. Beng.* (1814) p. 54. A perennial herb, twining when it meets support, sometimes suberect; stems slender, clothed with spreading or deflexed reddish-brown hairs. Leaves 3-foliolate; petioles 2–3 in. long; stipules $\frac{1}{5}$ in. long, ovate-oblong, acute, hairy, ciliate, attached a little below the middle. Leaflets $1\frac{1}{2}$–3 by $\frac{3}{4}$–2 in. (the terminal the larger and ovate or rhomboid-ovate, equal-sided with cuneate base, the lateral ovate-acute, inequilateral, with rounded or truncate base), all acute, silky-hairy on both sides, occasionally somewhat 3-lobed, conspicuously 3-nerved from the base; petioles $\frac{1}{10}$ in. long, hairy; stipels linear-subulate. Flowers in short close 6–12-flowered racemes with swollen nodes; peduncles 2–5 in. long, hairy; pedicels very short; bracts $\frac{1}{6}$ in. long, ovate-oblong, acute, deciduous; bracteoles $\frac{1}{4}$ in. long, linear-subulate, ciliate. Calyx $\frac{1}{8}$–$\frac{1}{6}$ in. long, glabrous; teeth shorter than the tube, deltoid. Corolla $\frac{3}{8}$–$\frac{1}{2}$ in. long, yellow. Pods $1\frac{1}{2}$–$2\frac{1}{2}$ in. long, cylindric, straight, densely clothed with reddish-brown hair. Seeds 8–12, oblong with truncate ends, about $\frac{1}{8}$ in. long, dark-brown. Prain, in Journ. As. Soc. Beng. v. 66 (1898) p. 423. *P. trinervius*, Heyne, in Wall. Cat. (1828) 5603; Fl. B. I. v. 2, p. 203; Grah. Cat. p. 51; Dalz. & Gibs. p. 71; Trim. Fl. Ceyl. v. 2, p. 72; Woodr. in Journ. Bomb. Nat. v. 11 (1897) p. 425; Watt, Dict. Econ. Prod. v. 6, part 1, p. 194.—Flowers: Aug.–Oct.

KONKAN: Neral, *Bhiva*! DECCAN: hills in the Deccan, *Woodrow*!; Mahableshwar, *Cooke*!, *Woodrow*!; Bowdhan near Poona, *Cooke*! S. M. COUNTRY: Londa, *Cooke*!—DISTRIB. India (from Behar to S. India); Ceylon.

Very closely allied to *P. radiatus*, Linn., the cultivated *Mug*, of which it may be the wild form.

VAR. *setulosus*, Prain, in Journ. As. Soc. Beng. v. 66 (1898) p. 423. Hairs on the stems and pods grey. Flowers small. *P. setulosus* (sp.), Dalz. in Kew Journ. v. 2 (1850) p. 33; Dalz. & Gibs. p. 72.

Konkan and Western Deccan only.

The following plants of the genus are cultivated throughout the Presidency:—

Phaseolus lunulatus, Linn. Sp. Pl. (1753) p. 724. The *Lima Bean*, widely cultivated as a vegetable. A tall, twining biennial with greenish-yellow flowers and pods 2–3 by about $\frac{3}{4}$ in., a native of Brazil. The seeds of the best kinds are pure ivory-white and have, when boiled, somewhat the flavor of a roasted chestnut. Fl. B. I. v. 2, p. 200; Grah. Cat. p. 51; Firminger, Man. Gard. ed. 3, p. 153; Woodr. in Journ. Bomb. Nat. v. 11 (1897) p. 425; Watt, Dict. Econ. Prod. v. 6, part 1, p. 186.—VERN. *Lobiya.*

Phaseolus vulgaris, Linn. Sp. Pl. (1753) p. 723. The *French Bean*, supposed by DeCandolle to be a native of S. America, largely grown in gardens throughout India. The dwarf kinds (*P. nanus*, Linn.) grow and yield well, particularly if irrigation is available, but I have never found the runner (*P. multiflorus*, Willd.), though flowering profusely, to fruit satisfactorily in the Deccan. Fl. B. I. v. 2, p. 200; Grah. Cat. p. 51; Dalz. & Gibs. Suppl. p. 22; Firminger, Man. Gard. ed. 3, p. 152; Woodr. in Journ. Bomb. Nat. v. 11 (1897) p. 425; Watt, Dict. Econ. Prod. v. 6, part 1, p. 187.—VERN. *Loba.*

Phaseolus radiatus, Linn. Sp. Pl. (1753) p. 725. The *Mug*, widely cultivated, but not distinctly wild in the Bombay Presidency. The crop is sown in June and harvested in September. Stems annual, 1–2 ft. high, clothed with brownish silky hairs. Leaflets dark-green, membranous, 2–4 in. long. Flowers yellow. Pods subcylindric, 1½–2½ in. long. Seeds 10–15, green. This is the kind most commonly grown and is largely cultivated in Sattara, Bijapur, Belgaum and Dharwar. *P. radiatus*, var. *typicus*, Prain, in Journ. As. Soc. Beng. v. 66 (1898) p. 422. *P. Mungo*, Roxb. Hort. Beng. p. 55; Roxb. Fl. Ind. v. 3, p. 292 (*not* of Linn.); Fl. B. I. v. 2, p. 203 (in part); Grah. Cat. p. 51; Dalz. & Gibs. Suppl. p. 23; Woodr. in Journ. Bomb. Nat. v. 11 (1897) p. 425; Watt, Dict. Econ. Prod. v. 6, part 1, p. 187.

VAR. 1. *aureus*, Prain, in Journ. As. Soc. Beng. v. 66 (1898) p. 422. Foliage paler. Pods reflexed. Seeds yellow. *P. aureus* (sp.), Roxb. Hort. Beng. p. 55; Roxb. Fl. Ind. v. 3, p. 297; Watt, Dict. Econ. Prod. v. 6, part 1, p. 188. *P. Mungo* (*aureus*), Fl. B. I. v. 2, p. 203 (in part). This is the most esteemed form and known as the *Sona-Mug.*

VAR. 2. *grandis*, Prain, in Journ. As. Soc. Beng. v. 66 (1898) p. 422. Foliage medium-green. Pods longer, spreading. Seeds black. *P. Max*, Roxb. Hort. Beng. p. 55; Roxb. Fl. Ind. v. 3, p. 295 (*vix* Linn.); Fl. B. I. v. 2, p. 203 (in part); Watt, Dict Econ. Prod. v. 6, part 1, p. 188. The least esteemed variety, introduced probably from China.

Phaseolus Mungo, Linn. Mantiss. p. 101; var. *Roxburghii*, Prain, in Journ. As. Soc. Beng. v. 66 (1898) p. 423. Stems hirsute, elongate, diffusely spreading, but not scandent. Flowers bright yellow. Seeds grey. *P. radiatus* (sp.), Roxb. Fl. Ind. v. 3, p. 296 (*not* of Linn.). *P. Roxburghii* (sp.), W. & A. Prodr. p. 246. *P. Mungo*, var. *radiatus*, Fl. B. I. v. 2, p. 203; Watt, Dict. Econ. Prod. v. 6, part 1, p. 191. One of the most important of the pulses cultivated in India.—VERN. *Udid.*

There has been some confusion as to the nomenclature of *P. Mungo* and *P. radiatus*, owing chiefly to Roxburgh having transposed the original Linnean names. Prain (Journ. As. Soc. Beng. v. 66 [1898] p. 422) has quite cleared up the matter.

Phaseolus aconitifolius, Jacquin, Obs. Bot. pars 3 (1768) p. 2, t. 52. The *Mat* or *Matki*, extensively cultivated throughout the Presidency, especially in the Deccan and Gujarat. Stems slender, 1–2 ft. long. Leaflets cut into 3 narrow lobes. Flowers yellow, in short capitate long-peduncled racemes. Pods 1–2 in. long. Fl. B. I. v. 2, p. 202; Grah. Cat. p. 52; Woodr. in Journ. Bomb. Nat. v. 11 (1897) p. 425; Watt, Dict. Econ. Prod. v. 6, part 1, p. 182.

This, though a native of India, cannot be called wild in the Bombay Presidency. It is very like *P. trilobus*, Ait., from which it is hardly separable as a species. It is a very important crop in Bombay, and is sown in June or July and harvested in November. See Watt, Dict. Econ. Prod. l. c.

47. VIGNA, Savi.

Twining or prostrate, rarely suberect herbs. Leaves pinnately 3-foliolate; stipules basifixed, or rarely produced below their insertion. Leaflets stipellate. Flowers in racemes at the upper part of an axillary peduncle; pedicels fascicled on the nodiform rhachis; bracts and bracteoles small, caducous. Calyx-teeth distinct or the 2 upper connate. Corolla much exserted; standard orbicular, auricled at the base; wings shorter than the standard; keel equalling the wings, incurved, not beaked, or prolonged into an incurved beak not making a perfect spiral. Stamens diadelphous; anthers uniform. Ovary sessile; ovules many; style filiform or thickened or dilated above, bearded along the inner face; stigma very oblique. Pod linear, straight or incurved, subterete, septate between the seeds.—Distrib. Warm regions of the world; species 40–50.

1. **Vigna capensis,** *Walp. in Linnæa*, v. 13 (1839) p. 533. Perennial, twining; stems subglabrous when mature; root fusiform. Leaves 3-foliolate; petioles 1–2 in. long, clothed with brownish deflexed hairs; stipules $\frac{1}{5}$ in. long, basifixed, oblong-lanceolate, acute, hairy. Leaflets 2–4 by $\frac{7}{8}$–$1\frac{3}{4}$ in., 3-nerved from the base, ovate, acute or acuminate, mucronate (the lateral unequal-sided and subtruncate at the base), sparsely clothed on both sides with short appressed hairs; petiolules $\frac{1}{16}$ in. long, hairy; stipules filiform. Flowers 2–4, crowded at the ends of axillary peduncles which are longer than the leaves; pedicels very short; bracteoles beneath the calyx linear, acute. Calyx nearly $\frac{1}{2}$ in. long, pubescent, nerved; teeth longer than the tube, linear, acute, from a triangular base, the 2 upper connate below the middle. Corolla $\frac{7}{8}$–1 in. long, rose-colored; standard more than 1 in. broad, emarginate, auricled, veined; keel obliquely curved into $\frac{3}{4}$ of a circle, beaked. Pods 3–4 by $\frac{1}{5}$–$\frac{1}{4}$ in., subterete, straight, clothed when young with brown shining hairs. Seeds 10–15, subreniform, compressed, $\frac{1}{8}$ in. long, black. *Vigna vexillata*, A. Rich. in Sagra, Hist. Cub. Bot. (1845) p. 440; Fl. B. I. v. 2, p. 206; Trim. Fl. Ceyl. v. 2, p. 74; Woodr. in Journ. Bomb. Nat. v. 11 (1897) p. 425. *Phaseolus sepiarius*, Dalz. in Kew Journ. v. 2 (1850) p. 33; Dalz. & Gibs. p. 72.—Flowers: Sept.-Oct. Vern. *Halunda.*

The name *V. capensis* was published by Walpers in 1839 and is prior to that of *V. vexillata* which dates from 1845.

Konkan: *Stocks*!, *Dalzell*! Deccan: Mahableshwar, *Cooke*!, *Woodrow*!; Panchgani, *Cooke*!

Very common at Mahableshwar, where it is, though not fragrant, called the *Indian Sweet Pea*.—Distrib. India (Himalayas and hills of W. Peninsula); Ceylon, Cape, Australia and the Tropics generally.

Vigna Catjang, Walp. in Linnæa, v. 13 (1839) p. 533, a suberect annual, cultivated, though not very extensively, in the Bombay Presidency, but not found wild. Its pods vary from 4 in. to 2 ft. in length, and are less than ½ in. broad. The variety *sinensis* (Vigna sinensis [sp.] *Endl.*) is a twining plant with larger leaves. Fl. B. I. v. 2, p. 205; Woodr. in Journ. Bomb. Nat. v. 11 (1897) p. 425; Watt, Dict. Econ. Prod. v. 6, part 4, p. 236.—VERN. *Chavli.*

48. CLITORIA, Linn.

Herbs or shrubs erect or climbing. Leaves pinnate, 3-many-foliolate; stipules persistent, striate. Leaflets stipellate. Flowers showy, axillary, solitary, fascicled or racemose; bracts persistent, stipule-like; bracteoles usually larger, striate, persistent. Calyx tubular; the 2 upper teeth subconnate. Corolla much exserted; standard large, erect, emarginate, narrowed and not appendiculate at the base; wings falcate-oblong, spreading, adhering to the middle of the keel; keel shorter than the wings, incurved, acute. Stamens monadelphous or diadelphous; anthers uniform. Ovary stalked; ovules many; style elongate, incurved, more or less flattened, bearded along the inner side. Pod stalked, linear, compressed or turgid.—DISTRIB. Warmer regions of the world; species 27.

Twining; stems terete; flowers solitary .... 1. *C. Ternatea.*
Erect; stems angular; flowers in pairs .... 2. *C. biflora.*

1. **Clitoria Ternatea,** *Linn. Sp. Pl.* (1753) p. 753. A perennial twining herb; stems terete, more or less pubescent. Leaves imparipinnate; petioles ¾-1 in. long; stipules ⅛ in. long, linear, acute. Leaflets 5-7, subcoriaceous, 1-2 by ¾-1¼ in., elliptic-oblong, obtuse, glabrous or with a few short appressed hairs, base obtuse or acute; stipels filiform. Flowers axillary, solitary; pedicels ⅓-½ in. long; bracts small, linear; bracteoles ¼-½ in. long, roundish, obtuse. Calyx ½-¾ in. long; teeth lanceolate, shorter than the tube. Corolla 1½-2 in. long; standard bright-blue or sometimes white, with an orange centre. Pods 2-4 by ¼-½ in., flattened, nearly straight, sharply beaked, sparsely appressedly hairy. Seeds 6-10, yellowish-brown, smooth. Fl. B. I. v. 2, p. 208; Grah. Cat. p. 47; Dalz. & Gibs. p. 68; Trim. Fl. Ceyl. v. 2, p. 75; Woodr. in Journ. Bomb. Nat. v. 11 (1897) p. 425; Watt, Dict. Econ. Prod. v. 2, p. 375.—Flowers: June-Jan. VERN. *Gokran*; *Supli.*

Very common in hedges everywhere throughout the Presidency. The root is used in medicine, being a powerful cathartic like jalap. See Watt, Dict. Econ. Prod. l. c.—DISTRIB. Cosmopolitan in the Tropics.

VAR. *pilosula*, Baker, in Hook. f. Fl. B. I. v. 2, p. 208. Leaflets much smaller, ½-¾ in. long. Flowers white; standard 1 in. long. Pods smaller. *C. pilosula*, Wall. Cat. 5347 (sp.).

GUJARAT: Dewar near Kaira, *Stocks!*

2. **Clitoria biflora,** *Dalz. in Kew Journ. Bot.* v. 2 (1850) p. 35. Herbaceous, erect, 15-20 in. high; stems angular, striate with lines of hairs. Leaves imparipinnate; petioles ⅜-½ in. long, hairy; stipules ⅛ in. long, subulate. Leaflets 5, membranous (the terminal the largest and the lowest pair of lateral leaflets smaller than the rest), 1-3 by ½-1½ in., variable in shape, from broadly elliptic-oblong, subobtuse, to lanceolate,

acute, sparingly strigose above, more densely so beneath; petiolules $\frac{1}{10}$ in. long; stipels filiform. Flowers in axillary 2-flowered racemes; peduncles and pedicels very short; bracts linear-lanceolate, subulate; bracteoles $\frac{1}{4}$–$\frac{1}{3}$ in. long, ovate or lanceolate, aristate. Calyx tubular, $\frac{1}{2}$–$\frac{5}{8}$ in. long, hairy, nerved; teeth shorter than the tube, lanceolate, aristate. Corolla 1 in. long, blue. Pods 1–2 by $\frac{1}{4}$ in., flat, reticulately veined, pubescent. Seeds 5–6. Fl. B. I. v. 2, p. 208; Dalz. & Gibs. p. 68; Woodr. in Journ. Bomb. Nat. v. 11 (1897) p. 425.—Flowers: Aug.–Sept.

KONKAN: *Dalzell*!, *Capt. Geburne*!; Salsette, *Stocks*!; near Kalyan, *Bhiva*!; Neral, *Kanitkar*!—DISTRIB. Apparently endemic.

49. DOLICHOS, Linn.

Twining prostrate or suberect herbs. Leaves pinnately 3-foliolate; stipules small. Leaflets stipellate. Flowers axillary, racemose or fascicled; bracts and bracteoles striate, very caducous. Calyx campanulate; teeth usually short, the 2 upper connate into one entire or emarginate one. Corolla much exserted, its petals usually equal in length; standard orbicular, with inflexed auricles at the base; keel obtuse or rostrate, not spiral. Stamens diadelphous; anthers uniform. Ovary subsessile; ovules many; style filiform or thickened upwards, bearded down the inner face or penicillate at the apex; stigma terminal. Pod flat, linear or oblong, recurved.—DISTRIB. Tropics of both hemispheres; species about 20.

1. **Dolichos bracteatus,** *Baker, in Hook. f. Fl. B. I.* v. 2 (1876) p. 210. A robust glabrous perennial twiner. Leaves 3-foliolate; petioles 5–9 in. long, deeply grooved, glabrous; stipules basifixed, $\frac{1}{2}$ in. long, oblong, acute or subobtuse, glabrous. Leaflets membranous, 6 in. long, as broad as long, broadly obovate, cuneate, conspicuously 3-nerved from the base; petiolules $\frac{1}{4}$ in. long; stipels $\frac{1}{2}$–$\frac{5}{8}$ in. long, linear-oblong, acute. Flowers in long-peduncled racemes reaching 1 ft. or more in length; peduncles deeply grooved, glabrous; pedicels $\frac{1}{4}$–$\frac{1}{2}$ in. long; bracts linear, acute, deciduous; bracteoles $\frac{3}{8}$ in. long, elliptic, obtuse, veined. Calyx $\frac{1}{4}$–$\frac{5}{16}$ in. long, glabrous, conspicuously veined; teeth short, deltoid, obtuse or subacute, ciliate. Corolla 1 in. long. Pods 5–6 by $\frac{3}{8}$ in., linear, much recurved, flattened, obscurely veined, glabrous. Seeds 10–12. Woodr. in Journ. Bomb. Nat. v. 11 (1897) p. 425.

A very rare plant, the only specimens seen being those in Herb. Kew. marked "Konkan, *Stocks*."—DISTRIB. Apparently endemic in the Konkan.

Dolichos Lablab, Linn. A large twining perennial or (under cultivation) annual herb with pods about $1\frac{1}{2}$–2 by $\frac{1}{2}$–$\frac{3}{4}$ in., each containing 2–4 seeds. King (Journ. As. Soc. Beng. v. 66 [1898] p. 55) recognizes as a variety *Dolichos lignosus*, Linn., with much shorter and broader pods, which Baker (Fl. B. I. v. 2, p. 209) unites with *D. Lablab*. (See also Prain, in Journ. As. Soc. Beng. v. 66 [1898] p. 430.) Woodr. in Journ. Bomb. Nat. v. 11 (1897) p. 425; Watt, Dict. Econ. Prod. v. 3, p. 183. *Lablab vulgaris*, Savi, Thw. Enum. p. 90; Grah. Cat. p. 52; Dalz. & Gibs. Suppl. p. 23.—VERN. *Vâl-pápadi*; *Pavtá*.

Cultivated largely, but not wild, in the Bombay Presidency, where it often follows rice as a second crop and is cut in February and March. It is a favorite crop on the sloping lands along the banks of rivers, as well as in river-beds. See Watt, Dict. Econ. Prod. l. c.—DISTRIB. Tropics of the Old World.

Dolichos biflorus, Linn. Sp. Pl. (1753) p. 727. A suberect (*D. uniflorus*, Lamk.) or twining (*D. biflorus*, Linn.) annual with yellow flowers and much recurved 5–6-seeded pods. Fl. B. I. v. 2, p. 210; Woodr. in Journ. Bomb. Nat. v. 11 (1897) p. 425; Watt, Dict. Econ. Prod. v. 3, p. 175. *Dolichos uniflorus*, Lamk. Encyc. Méthod. v. 2, p. 299; Grah. Cat. p. 52; Dalz. & Gibs. Suppl. p. 23. *Johnia congesta*, Dalz. & Gibs. Bo. Fl. (1861) p. 69 & Suppl. p. 23.—VERN. *Kulith*; *Hulga*.

Extensively cultivated, especially throughout the Deccan, but not wild. In the Deccan it is usually sown in June and cut in November, but in districts with a heavy rainfall (*e. g.* Thana) it is sometimes sown as a cold-season crop in November, after the rice-crops have been cut, and reaped in March. The grain, which is known as *horse-gram* or *Madras gram*, when boiled and mixed with the ordinary gram (*Cicer arietinum*), is a good food for horses, and the leaves and stalks furnish good fodder. See Watt, Dict. Econ. Prod. l. c.—DISTRIB. Tropics of the Old World.

50. **ATYLOSIA,** Wight & Arn.

Herbs or shrubs erect or twining. Leaves pinnately or (rarely) digitately 3-foliolate. Leaflets usually exstipellate, dotted with resinous glands beneath. Flowers usually yellow, fascicled in the leaf-axils, or irregularly fasciculato-racemose at the apex of an axillary peduncle, or the upper panicled; bracts usually broad, membranous, deciduous long before flowering. Calyx-teeth distinct, the lowest the longest, the 2 upper connate into one entire or bifid tooth. Corolla more or less exserted; standard orbicular, with inflexed auricles at the base; keel obtuse. Stamens diadelphous; anthers uniform. Ovary sessile; ovules 3 or more; style filiform, incurved, glabrous; stigma capitate. Pod linear or oblong, usually obtuse, more or less compressed, marked with transverse lines beneath the seeds outside, septate within. Seeds with a conspicuous divided strophiole.—DISTRIB. Tropical Asia, Australia, Mauritius; species about 25.

Erect shrubs.
  Leaflets obovate-oblong, 2–2½ times as long as broad .... 1. *A. lineata.*
  Leaflets oblanceolate, 5–6 times as long as broad .... 2. *A. sericea.*
Climbing or trailing herbs.
  Leaflets stipellate.
    Pod rounded at both ends .... 3. *A. crassa.*
    Pod narrowed at both ends .... 4. *A. goensis.*
  Leaflets exstipellate.
    Pod ¼ in. broad, with deep lines between the seeds .... 5. *A. scarabæoides.*
    Pod ½ in. broad, with sharply-defined (not deep) lines between the seeds .... 6. *A. platycarpa.*

1. **Atylosia lineata,** *Wight & Arn. Prodr.* (1834) p. 258. An erect shrub about 2 ft. high; stem and branches sulcate, densely clothed with soft hairs. Leaves 3-foliolate; petioles ¼–½ in. long, terete, pubescent; stipules ¼ in. long, linear-subulate, hairy. Leaflets ½–1¼ by ¼–½ in., obovate, acute or subobtuse, faintly mucronate, densely silky-villous when young on both surfaces (more so on the lower), becoming nearly glabrous when mature, cuneate at the base, 3-nerved and reticulately veined (the reticulations visible after the hairs fall); petiolules very

short; stipels 0. Flowers axillary, solitary or in pairs, without a common peduncle; pedicels less than ¼ in. long, hairy. Calyx ⅕ in. long, hairy; teeth (except the lowest one) shorter than the tube, deltoid, cuspidate. Corolla ½ in. long, yellow. Pods ½–⅝ by ¼ in., linear, turgid, depressed, but not very deeply so, between the seeds, clothed with long whitish hairs. Seeds 2 (rarely 3), with a conspicuous divided strophiole, black. Fl. B. I. v. 2, p. 213; Talb. Trees, Bomb. p. 73; Woodr. in Journ. Bomb. Nat. v. 11 (1897) p. 425. *A. Lawii*, Wight, Icon. t. 93; Grah. Cat. p. 53; Dalz. & Gibs. p. 74.—Flowers: Oct.–Dec. Vern. *Rán-tur*; *Jangli-tur*.

Common in the hills of the Konkan and Deccan. Konkan: Bombay Ghâts, *Dalzell*!; Matheran, *Woodrow*. Deccan: Mahableshwar, *Cooke*!, *Woodrow*!; hills at Pár, *Stocks*! S. M. Country: Belgaum hill south, *Ritchie*, 156!; Ramghát, *Ritchie*, 156! Kanara: Hathkumba (Kála naddi), *Ritchie*, 156!; N. Kanara Ghâts, *Talbot*.—Distrib. India (hills of the W. Peninsula).

2. **Atylosia sericea,** *Benth. MS. ex Baker, in Hook. f. Fl. B. I.* v. 2 (1876) p. 213. An erect shrub; stems much grooved, silky-hairy. Leaves 3-foliolate, subdigitate; petioles ¼–⅜ in. long, pubescent; stipules ¼–⅜ in. long, filiform. Leaflets 1–1¾ by ⅙–¼ in., oblanceolate, obtuse or subacute, apiculate, densely and persistently silky, 3-nerved from an acute base; petiolules scarcely any; stipels 0. Flowers axillary, solitary or in pairs, without a common peduncle; pedicels $\frac{1}{16}$ in. long. Calyx ¼ in. long, softly silky; teeth triangular, acute, as long as the tube. Corolla ⅜–½ in. long. Pods ⅜–½ by ¼–$\frac{5}{16}$ in., linear-oblong, turgid, oblique at the apex, depressed between the seeds, densely silky. Seeds 2, subcylindric, compressed, rounded at the apex, with a divided strophiole, smooth, black. Talb. Trees, Bomb. p. 73; Woodr. in Journ. Bomb. Nat. v. 11 (1897) p. 425.

Konkan: *Dalzell*!, *Stocks*!, *Law*!, *Woodrow*! Deccan: near Talegaon along the railway line, *Bhiva*!; Mahableshwar, *Woodrow*.

3. **Atylosia crassa,** *Prain, Journ. As. Soc. Beng.* v. 66 (1898) p. 45 & p. 432. Twining; stems and branches striate, tomentose. Leaves pinnately 3-foliolate; rhachis more or less elongated between the insertion of the lateral leaflets and the stipels of the terminal one; petioles 1½–2½ in. long, pubescent; stipules minute, caducous. Leaflets 2–3 by 1¼–2¼ in., rhomboid-obovate, acute, acuminate or subobtuse (the lateral leaflets smaller than the terminal and very oblique), dark-green and puberulous (especially on the nerves) above, fulvous-pubescent and reticulately veined beneath; petiolules ⅛ in. long; stipels $\frac{1}{12}$ in. long, subulate. Flowers in lax racemes 2–3 in. long; peduncles short; pedicels twin, ⅓–½ in. long; bracts ½–⅝ in. long, broadly elliptic, concealing the buds before the flowers expand. Calyx ⅜ in. long, finely grey-downy, the lowest tooth lanceolate, as long as the campanulate tube. Corolla ¾ in. long, yellow. Pods 1–1½ by ⅜ in., straight, rounded at both ends, clothed with close greenish-brown pubescence, obliquely depressed between the seeds. Seeds 3–5. *Atylosia mollis*, Benth. in Pl. Jungh. p. 243 (exclud. syn. *Collæa mollis*, Grah.); Baker, in Fl. B. I. v. 2, p. 213 (exclud. syn. *Collæa mollis*, Grah., *Cajanus glandulosus*, Dalz. & Gibs., and *Atylosia glandulosa*, Dalz.); Talb. Trees, Bomb. p. 73; Woodr. in Journ. Bomb. Nat. v. 11 (1897) p. 425.

Rare. Konkan: *Stocks*!

4. **Atylosia goensis,** *Dalz. in Journ. Linn. Soc.* v. 13 (1873) p. 186. A woody twiner, the whole plant, except the corolla, clothed with long soft fulvous hairs. Leaves pinnately 3-foliolate; rhachis elongated to $\frac{1}{2}$–$\frac{7}{8}$ in. between the insertion of the lateral leaflets and the stipels of the terminal leaflet; petioles $1\frac{1}{2}$–2 in. long; stipules $\frac{1}{6}$ in. long, ovate-oblong, acute, ciliate. Leaflets 2–3 by $1\frac{3}{4}$–$2\frac{1}{4}$ in., broadly ovate, acuminate (the lateral smaller than the terminal and very unequal-sided); petiolules $\frac{1}{16}$ in. long; stipels $\frac{1}{10}$ in. long, filiform. Flowers in many-flowered racemes which are at first close, afterwards elongating to 4–6 in.; bracts broadly ovate-cuspidate, exceeding the buds, deciduous. Calyx $\frac{1}{2}$ in. long, shaggy; teeth lanceolate, exceeding the tube. Corolla $\frac{3}{4}$ in. long, golden yellow; standard $\frac{1}{2}$ in. broad, with 2 callosities above the base and 2 small auricles below; keel $\frac{1}{2}$ in. long. Pods $1\frac{1}{2}$–2 by $\frac{3}{8}$ in., straight, cuspidate, densely clothed with long yellowish or greyish spreading soft viscid hairs, narrowed at both ends, obliquely depressed between the seeds. Seeds 4–6, strophiolate, $\frac{1}{8}$–$\frac{1}{6}$ in. long, black. *Atylosia barbata*, Baker, in Hook. f. Fl. B. I. v. 2 (1876) p. 216; Talb. Trees, Bomb. p. 73. *Cajanus goensis*, Dalz. in Kew Journ. Bot. v. 2 (1850) p. 265; Dalz. & Gibs. p. 73.

Rare. KONKAN: *Dalzell*! S. M. COUNTRY: Chorla Ghât, *Dalzell & Gibson*.—DISTRIB. India (Assam, Birma, W. Peninsula); Java.

5. **Atylosia scarabæoides,** *Benth. Pl. Jungh.* v. 3 (1851–55) p. 243. An herbaceous twiner; stem and branches slender, striate, clothed with pale-yellow or grey pubescence. Leaves 3-foliolate; petioles $\frac{1}{2}$–1 in. long, clothed with yellowish pubescence; stipules $\frac{1}{16}$ in. long, triangular, acute. Leaflets $\frac{3}{4}$–$1\frac{3}{4}$ by $\frac{5}{8}$–1 in., subcoriaceous, elliptic or elliptic-obovate, subacute, thinly pubescent above, densely grey-pubescent and reticulately veined (but not very closely) beneath; petiolules very short; stipels 0. Flowers pedicelled, 2–6 on short densely pubescent axillary peduncles; pedicels $\frac{1}{4}$ in. long, densely hairy. Calyx $\frac{1}{4}$ in. long, fulvous-pubescent; teeth linear, acute, the lowest twice as long as the tube. Corolla $\frac{5}{16}$ in. long, yellow. Pods $\frac{5}{8}$–$\frac{7}{8}$ by $\frac{1}{4}$ in., straight, apiculate, clothed with long soft brownish hair, with deep obliquely-transverse lines between the seeds. Seeds 4–6. Fl. B. I. v. 2, p. 215; Trim. Fl. Ceyl. v. 2, p. 79; Woodr. in Journ. Bomb. Nat. v. 11 (1897) p. 425. *Cantharospermum pauciflorum*, W. & A. Prodr. p. 255; Dalz. & Gibs. p. 73.—Flowers: June–Oct.

KONKAN: common, *Dalzell & Gibson*. DECCAN: Chattersinghi hill (Poona districts), *Kanitkar*!; hills near Poona, *Ranade*!, *Woodrow*!; between Shelarwadi and Talegaon, *Bhiva*!—DISTRIB. Throughout India; Ceylon, Malaya, China, Mauritius, Madagascar.

6. **Atylosia platycarpa,** *Benth. Pl. Jungh.* (1851–55) p. 243. A twining or sometimes a trailing herb; stem and branches slender, clothed with spreading fulvous or grey hairs. Leaves 3-foliolate; rhachis prolonged $\frac{1}{2}$–$\frac{5}{8}$ in. beyond the insertion of the lateral leaflets; petioles $1\frac{1}{2}$–$4\frac{1}{2}$ in. long, grooved, hairy; stipules $\frac{1}{8}$ in. long, ovate, acute. Leaflets membranous, $1\frac{1}{4}$–$2\frac{1}{2}$ in. long, as broad as long, orbicular, acute or acuminate (the lateral oblique), sparingly hairy on both surfaces, 3-nerved from the base; petiolules of the lateral leaflets $\frac{1}{8}$ in. long, very hairy; stipels 0. Flowers solitary or in 2-flowered racemes; peduncles axillary, usually short at the time of flowering, elongating afterwards; pedicels as long as the calyx, curved in fruit. Calyx $\frac{3}{8}$ in. long, densely hairy;

teeth lanceolate-subulate, longer than the tube. Corolla $\frac{1}{2}$ in. long. Pods 1–1$\frac{1}{2}$ by $\frac{1}{2}$ in., linear-oblong, flattened, mucronate, marked with sharply defined but not very deep lines between the seeds, reticulately veined, clothed with long grey hairs. Seeds 5–7, oblong, compressed, rounded at the ends, $\frac{1}{4}$ by $\frac{1}{8}$ in., furnished with a large divided strophiole, smooth, black. Fl. B. I. v. 2, p. 216. *Atylosia geminiflora*, Dalz. in Journ. Linn. Soc. v. 13 (1873) p. 185; Baker, in Hook. f. Fl. B. I. v. 2, p. 212; Talb. Trees, Bomb. p. 73; Woodr. in Journ. Bomb. Nat. v. 11 (1897) p. 425.

Dalzell (*l. c.*) describes the leaflets as stipellate, but I have not found them so.

KONKAN: *Dalzell*!; near Tulsi lake, *Woodrow*.—DISTRIB. India (Central Himalayas, Behar, Central India, Jubbulpore).

51. **DUNBARIA,** Wight & Arn.

Prostrate or twining herbs. Leaves pinnately 3-foliolate. Leaflets dotted with resinous glands beneath, rarely stipellate. Flowers in axillary peduncled racemes, solitary or twin along a not nodose rhachis, rarely solitary in the axils of the leaves; bracts usually membranous, deciduous long before flowering; bracteoles 0. Calyx-teeth long and narrow, the lowest the longest, the 2 upper connate into one entire or emarginate tooth. Corolla more or less exserted, usually yellow; standard orbicular, erect or spreading, auricled at the base; keel usually not beaked. Stamens diadelphous; anthers uniform. Ovary sessile; ovules many; style inflexed, filiform, beardless; stigma capitate. Pod linear, straight or falcate, acuminate, flat-compressed, not or faintly depressed between the seeds. Seeds suborbicular, the funicle expanded into a somewhat thickened membrane, but scarcely strophiolate.—DISTRIB. Eastern Asia, Japan, N. Australia; species about 12.

Leaflets exstipellate; hairs on the pod glandular .... 1. *D. glandulosa.*
Leaflets stipellate; hairs on the pod not glandular .... 2. *D. Heynei.*

1. **Dunbaria glandulosa,** *Prain, in Journ. As. Soc. Beng.* v. 66 (1898) p. 433. A woody twiner; young parts more or less clothed with yellowish or grey tomentum; stems terete. Leaves pinnately 3-foliolate; rhachis prolonged $\frac{1}{2}$–$\frac{7}{8}$ in. beyond the insertion of the lateral leaflets; petioles 1$\frac{1}{4}$–3 in. long, pubescent; stipules $\frac{1}{4}$ in. long, ovate-lanceolate, cuspidate. Leaflets 1$\frac{3}{4}$–3 by 1$\frac{7}{8}$–3$\frac{1}{2}$ in., usually broader than long (the terminal rhomboid-ovate, acute or acuminate, the lateral obliquely ovate, acute), subcoriaceous, glabrous or with a few scattered hairs; petiolules of lateral leaflets $\frac{1}{8}$ in. long, hairy; stipels 0. Flowers in long-peduncled lax racemes, usually in pairs along a glabrous terete rhachis; pedicels $\frac{1}{2}$–$\frac{5}{8}$ in. long, retrofracted in fruit. Calyx $\frac{1}{4}$–$\frac{3}{8}$ in. long, sparingly bristly with hairs rising from bulbous bases; teeth all shorter than the tube, the upper and lateral very short, obtuse, ciliate, the lower longer, acuminate. Corolla 1 in. long, yellow with brown lines, showy; standard 1$\frac{1}{4}$ in. broad with 2 callosities above the base. Pods faintly depressed between the seeds, 2$\frac{1}{2}$–3 by $\frac{3}{8}$ in., nearly straight, narrowed at the tip, shortly beaked, thinly clothed with stiff yellowish bristles from bulbous bases. Seeds 8–10, with a thickened funicle, scarcely strophiolate. *Atylosia glandulosa*, Dalz. in Journ. Linn. Soc. v. 13 (1873) p. 185. *Atylosia rostrata*, Baker, in Hook. f. Fl. B. I. v. 2 (1876) p. 216; Talb.

Trees, Bomb. p. 73; Woodr. in Journ. Bomb. Nat. v. 11 (1897) p. 425. *Cajanus glandulosus*, Dalz. & Gibs. p. 73.

Rare. KONKAN: *Stocks*!, *Dalzell*!; Malwan and Wagotan (S. Konkan), *Dalzell & Gibson*.—DISTRIB. India (Central India, Bengal, Birma, W. Peninsula).

2. **Dunbaria Heynei,** *Wight & Arn. Prodr.* (1834) p. 258. A woody twiner; stems stout, much-branched, more or less clothed with spreading hairs. Leaves 3-foliolate; petioles 1–2½ in. long, with a few scattered hairs; stipules ¼–⅜ in. long, ovate-oblong, acuminate, ciliate. Leaflets membranous, 2–3 by 1¼–2 in. (the terminal rhomboid or obovate, acuminate, cuneate, with a rounded base, the lateral very unequal-sided, obliquely ovate, acuminate), more or less hairy on both surfaces; petiolules very short, hairy; stipels ⅛ in. long, subulate. Flowers in peduncled few-flowered axillary lax racemes; pedicels ⅛–½ in. long, slender, hairy; bracts broadly ovate, caducous. Calyx ⅓–⅜ in. long, roughly puberulous, the lowest tooth much the longest and exceeding the tube. Corolla ⅝–1 in. long, purple or yellow. Pods 1½–2 by ⅜–½ in., straight, cuspidate, narrowed at the base, clothed with weak spreading hairs, slightly lineate between the seeds. Seeds 4–5, ovoid-reniform, mottled black and brown. Fl. B. I. v. 2, p. 217; Trim. Fl. Ceyl. v. 2, p. 80. *Cajanus kulnensis*, Dalz. in Journ. Linn. Soc. v. 13 (1873) p. 186; Fl. B. I. v. 2, p. 214; Talb. Trees, Bomb. p. 73; Woodr. in Journ. Bomb. Nat. v. 11 (1897) p. 425.—Flowers: Dec.-Mar.

KONKAN: evergreen forests, *Talbot*; Kulnawari (Wari country), *Dalzell & Gibson*, *Woodrow*. KANARA: Potelli, *Talbot*; Wadi Ghát, *Talbot*.—DISTRIB. India (Mysore hills); Ceylon.

52. CYLISTA, Ait.

A twining shrub. Leaves pinnately 3-foliolate. Leaflets stipellate, dotted beneath with resinous glands. Flowers in axillary sometimes panicled racemes; bracts membranous, hyaline, caducous; bracteoles 0. Calyx-tube campanulate; teeth obtuse, scarious, persistent, accrescent, the 2 upper connate into one emarginate tooth, the 2 lateral shorter, the lowest the largest, concave. Corolla enclosed in the calyx; standard suborbicular, with inflexed auricles at the base; wings narrow; keel incurved, obtuse. Stamens diadelphous; anthers uniform. Ovary subsessile; ovules 1–2; style filiform; stigma terminal. Pod small, oblique, oblong, enclosed in the calyx. Seed without a strophiole.—DISTRIB. India; species 1.

1. **Cylista scariosa,** *Roxb. Cor. Pl.* v. 1 (1795) p. 64, t. 92. A woody twiner; stems and branches finely downy. Leaves 3-foliolate; rhachis prolonged ¼–½ in. between the insertion of the lateral leaflets and the stipels of the terminal one; petioles ½–2 in. long, downy; stipules ⅛–³⁄₁₆ in. long, triangular, acute, downy. Leaflets 2–4 by 1½–2¼ in. (the terminal rhomboid-ovate, the lateral slightly smaller, very obliquely ovate), acute, clothed with soft velvety pubescence above, densely downy and prominently reticulately veined beneath, base subcordate; petiolules ⅛ in. long, densely downy; stipels ⅛ in. long, subulate. Flowers in copious axillary peduncled racemes or panicles; pedicels very short, downy; bracts large, ovate, caducous. Calyx finally 1–1¼ in. long; tube downy; lower lip ¾ in. broad, boat-shaped, conspicuously veined. Corolla yellow, concealed in the calyx. Pods small, oblique, downy,

enclosed in the calyx, 1-seeded. Fl. B. I. v. 2, p. 219; Grah. Cat. p. 54; Dalz. & Gibs. p. 74; Talb. Trees, Bomb. p. 73; Woodr. in Journ. Bomb. Nat. v. 11 (1897) p. 425.—Flowers: Nov.-Feb. VERN. *Rán-ghevdá.*

Roxburgh (*l. c.*) and not Aiton was the first to describe *C. scariosa.*

A very common plant. KONKAN: *Stocks*!, *Capt. Geburne*! Matheran, *Cooke*!, *Woodrow*!; Kanheri jungles, *Graham.* DECCAN: hills near Poona, *Woodrow*!; Mahableshwar, *Cooke*!; Talegaon, *Bhiva*!; Igatpuri, *Edgeworth*! S. M. COUNTRY: hills north of Belgaum, *Ritchie*, 206! KANARA: Yellu (N. Kanara), *Ritchie*, 206!—DISTRIB. India (Central Provinces, Birma, W. Peninsula); Socotra.

53. RHYNCHOSIA, Lour.

Herbs or undershrubs, twining or prostrate, rarely erect. Leaves pinnately (rarely digitately) 3-foliolate; stipules ovate or lanceolate. Leaflets dotted beneath with resinous glands, exstipellate or minutely stipellate. Flowers in axillary racemes, solitary or twin along the rhachis, rarely solitary in the axils of the leaves; bracts caducous; bracteoles 0. Calyx-teeth not accrescent, the 2 upper more or less connate. Corolla included or exserted; standard obovate or orbicular with inflexed auricles at the base; wings narrow; keel incurved at the apex. Stamens diadelphous; anthers uniform. Ovary subsessile; ovules 2 (very rarely 1); style long, filiform, much incurved; stigma capitate. Pod round or oblong, compressed or turgid, usually continuous (rarely septate) within. Seeds 2 (rarely 1), the hilum parallel to the sutures and the funicle centrical upon it; strophiole thick, small, or 0.—DISTRIB. Throughout the tropical regions of both hemispheres, some extratropical in N. America and S. Africa; species about 80.

Seeds with a waxy strophiole .... 1. *R. aurea.*
Seeds without a strophiole.
  Calyx-teeth 3 times as long as the tube; seeds blue .... 2. *R. cyanosperma.*
  Calyx-teeth twice as long as the tube; seeds black .... 3. *R. minima.*
  Calyx-teeth shorter than, or equalling, the tube .... 4. *R. bracteata.*

1. **Rhynchosia aurea,** *DC. Prodr.* v. 2 (1825) p. 386. Annual, trailing; stems sparingly clothed with fine spreading hairs. Leaves 3-foliolate; rhachis prolonged $\frac{1}{4}$–$\frac{3}{8}$ in. beyond the insertion of the lateral leaflets; petioles $1\frac{1}{2}$–3 in. long, slender, grooved, thinly hairy; stipules $\frac{1}{8}$ in. long, ovate, acuminate. Leaflets $\frac{1}{2}$–$1\frac{1}{2}$ in. long, nearly as broad as long, rhomboid-ovate or rhomboid-obovate (the lateral very unequal-sided), acute or subobtuse, with a few short scattered hairs on both surfaces, reticulately veined; stipels 0. Flowers in close 6–20-flowered racemes longer or shorter than the leaves; peduncles slender, hairy; pedicels $\frac{1}{8}$–$\frac{1}{4}$ in. long, densely pubescent. Calyx $\frac{1}{3}$ in. long, hairy; teeth linear-subulate, 3–4 times as long as the tube, the 2 upper connate, except at the tip. Corolla a little longer than the lowest tooth of the calyx, yellow; standard $\frac{7}{16}$ in. broad, with 2 callosities at the base. Pods orbicular, $\frac{1}{2}$ in. in diam., slightly compressed, transversely striate with nearly parallel lines, mucronate, mottled, sparsely clothed with long fine hairs. Seeds 2, oblong, compressed, rounded at the ends, $\frac{1}{6}$ by $\frac{1}{8}$ in., with a waxy strophiole, dark brown. Wight and Aitchison say that the plant buries its seed in the ground. Fl. B. I. v. 2, p. 221; Woodr. in Journ. Bomb. Nat. v. 11 (1897) p. 425. *Nomismia aurea*,

W. & A. Prodr. p. 237. *Nomismia capitata*, W. & A. Prodr. p. 237; Wight, Icon. t. 295.—Flowers: Sept.–Nov.

Rare. S. M. COUNTRY: Badami, *Woodrow*!, *Cooke*!; hills 8 miles north-east of Belgaum, *Ritchie*, 612!—DISTRIB. Throughout India.

2. **Rhynchosia cyanosperma,** *Benth. in Oliv. Fl. Trop. Africa*, v. 2 (1871) p. 218. A stout woody twiner; stems and branches densely clothed with velvety fulvous or rufous pubescence. Leaves 3-foliolate; rhachis prolonged $\frac{1}{4}$–$\frac{3}{4}$ in. between the insertion of the lateral leaflets and the stipels of the terminal one; petioles 1–2$\frac{1}{4}$ in. long, softly rufous-hairy; stipules $\frac{1}{4}$ in. long, ovate, acute. Leaflets 2–4$\frac{1}{2}$ by 1$\frac{1}{4}$–3$\frac{1}{2}$ in., rhomboid-ovate, acuminate (the lateral oblique), velvety-pubescent on both sides, base rounded; petiolules $\frac{1}{6}$ in. long, hairy; stipels $\frac{1}{8}$–$\frac{1}{4}$ in. long, subulate, very hairy. Flowers in close softly pubescent peduncled racemes longer than the leaves; pedicels $\frac{1}{4}$–$\frac{3}{8}$ in. long, softly downy; bracts large, ovate, acute, velvety, caducous. Calyx $\frac{5}{8}$–$\frac{3}{4}$ in. long, densely grey-downy; teeth 3 times as long as the tube, linear, obtuse, $\frac{1}{8}$–$\frac{1}{6}$ in. broad. Corolla pale yellowish-white; standard $\frac{1}{2}$ by $\frac{3}{8}$ in., emarginate. Pods $\frac{1}{2}$ by $\frac{1}{4}$ in., deeply torulose, densely velvety. Seeds 2, estrophiolate, subglobose, dark-blue, shining. Fl. B. I. v. 2, p. 222; Trim. Fl. Ceyl. v. 2, p. 84; Talb. Trees, Bomb. p. 73; Woodr. in Journ. Bomb. Nat. v. 11 (1897) p. 425. *Cyanospermum tomentosum*, W. & A. Prodr. p. 260; Wight, Ill. v. 1, p. 198, t. 81 (incorrectly numbered 84); Dalz. & Gibs. p. 75. *Cylista tomentosa*, Roxb. Fl. Ind. v. 3, p. 319; Cor. Pl. t. 221.—Flowers: Oct.–Dec.

KONKAN: evergreen forests of S. Konkan, *Talbot*. S. M. COUNTRY: Párva Ghát, *Dalzell*!; Chorla Ghát, *Stocks*!; Belgaum jungles, *Dalzell & Gibson*; Kanapur (near Belgaum), *Ritchie*, 204! KANARA: Hirdosi and Anmode (N. Kanara), *Woodrow*.—DISTRIB. India (W. Peninsula); Ceylon.

3. **Rhynchosia minima,** *DC. Prodr.* v. 2 (1825) p. 385. A twining or trailing annual; stems numerous, slender, much branched, pubescent when young. Leaves 3-foliolate; petioles $\frac{1}{4}$–$\frac{3}{4}$ in. long, more or less pubescent, striate; stipules $\frac{1}{6}$ in. long, linear-lanceolate. Leaflets $\frac{3}{8}$–1 in. long, as broad as long (the terminal sometimes broader than long), rhomboid-ovate or rhomboid-obovate, obtuse, apiculate, glabrous above, pubescent on the veins and conspicuously dotted beneath, base cuneate; stipels sometimes present, and when so, minute, subulate. Flowers in axillary 6–12-flowered lax racemes usually exceeding the leaves; pedicels very short. Calyx $\frac{1}{8}$–$\frac{1}{6}$ in. long, pubescent; teeth about twice as long as the tube, linear-subulate. Corolla yellow, $\frac{1}{6}$–$\frac{1}{4}$ in. long. Pods $\frac{1}{2}$–$\frac{5}{8}$ by $\frac{1}{4}$ in., somewhat compressed, turgid, slightly recurved, glabrescent. Seeds 2 (very rarely 1), compressed, $\frac{1}{8}$ by $\frac{1}{12}$ in., black, estrophiolate. Fl. B. I. v. 2, p. 223; Aitch. Pb. & Sind Pl. p. 49; Trim. Fl. Ceyl. v. 2, p. 84; Woodr. in Journ. Bomb. Nat. v. 11 (1897) p. 425. *Rhynchosia medicaginea*, DC. Prodr. v. 2, p. 386; Dalz. & Gibs. p. 74.—Flowers: Sept.–Jan.

KONKAN: *Stocks*!, *Dalzell*!, *Capt. Geburne*! DECCAN: widely, *Woodrow*; Poona, *Cooke*!, *Woodrow*! GUJARAT: widely, *Woodrow*. S. M. COUNTRY: Dharwar, *Cooke*!; Padshapur hills, *Ritchie*, 1705! SIND: *Stocks*.—DISTRIB. Throughout India; Ceylon, Tropics generally, Cape, United States.

VAR. 1. *laxiflora*, Baker, in Hook. f. Fl. B. I. v. 2, p. 223. Stems and branches glabrous. Petioles longer. Leaflets larger, sometimes reaching or even exceeding 2 in. long, acute at the apex, the upper and lower halves subdeltoid. Racemes more lax, sometimes reaching 6 in. long. Woodr. in Journ. Bomb. Nat. v. 11 (1897) p. 426. *R. laxiflora* (sp.), Camb. in Jacquem. Voy. Bot. p. 44, t. 54.

DECCAN: Poona, *Woodrow*! S. M. COUNTRY: Badami, *Woodrow*!, *Cooke*! SIND: *Puran*!; near Karachi, *Stocks*!

VAR. 2. *Memnonia*. Whole plant canescent with short white velvety persistent pubescence. *R. Memnonia* (sp.), DC. Prodr. v. 2, p. 386; Fl. B. I. v. 2, p. 224; Boiss. Fl. Orient. v. 2, p. 625; Woodr. in Journ. Bomb. Nat. v. 11 (1897) p. 426. *R. pulverulenta*, Stocks, in Kew Journ. Bot. v. 4 (1852) p. 147; Aitch. Pb. & Sind Pl. p. 50.—Flowers: Jan.

Except the pubescence, which is conspicuous and persistent, I can find, after a close examination of several specimens from Sind, no character to separate this as a distinct species from *R. minima*, of which I have felt constrained to make it a variety. Mr. Baker, in Fl. B. I. (*l. c.*), remarks that the plant differs from *R. minima* in vestiture only.

A rare plant, confined, in the Bombay Presidency, to Sind. SIND: *Stocks*!; Jemadar ka Landa near Karachi, *Stocks*!; hills at the Hub near Karachi, *Puran*!; Karachi districts, *Cooke*!—DISTRIB. Arabia, Tropical and S. Africa.

4. **Rhynchosia bracteata,** *Benth. MS. ex Baker, in Hook. f. Fl. B. I.* v. 2 (1876) p. 225. Sarmentose or twining; stems and branches finely striate, clothed with velvety pubescence. Leaves 3-foliolate; petioles ¾–1½ in. long, grooved, pubescent; stipules ⅙ in. long, ovate, acuminate. Leaflets 1½–3 in. long, as broad as long (the terminal rhomboid-orbicular, the lateral obliquely ovate), shortly acuminate, thinly downy above, densely so beneath; stipels 0. Flowers in axillary many-flowered simple or branched peduncled racemes much longer than the leaves; pedicels short; bracts 3/16–¼ in. long, exceeding the pedicels, ovate, acuminate, softly pubescent. Calyx ¼–⅓ in. long, softly downy; teeth triangular, the upper about equalling or slightly shorter than the tube, the lowest longer. Corolla ½ in. long, yellow; standard ⅓–⅜ in. broad, finely pubescent on the back, without callosities at the base, auricled. Pods 1–1½ by ⅜ in., turgid, mucronate, narrowed at the base, slightly recurved, minutely pubescent. Seeds estrophiolate, dark-brown. *R. mollissima*, Dalz. in Journ. Linn. Soc. v. 13 (1873) p. 186. *Dolichos bracteatus*, Wall. Cat. 5554.

A very rare plant. DECCAN: Khandesh, banks of the Girnar, *Dalzell*!—DISTRIB. India (upper Gangetic plain, Birma).

The plant was first described by Dalzell (Journ. Linn. Soc. l. c.) who named it *R. mollissima*. Unfortunately there are two different plants named *R. mollissima*, one in Tropical Africa and the other in Java, both of which were described much earlier in point of time than Dalzell's plant.

54. FLEMINGIA, Roxb.

Shrubs (rarely herbs) erect or rarely climbing. Leaves 1-foliolate or digitately 3-foliolate; stipules striate, usually caducous. Leaflets usually with prominent veins and gland-dotted beneath (except *F. tuberosa*), usually exstipellate. Inflorescence densely spicato-racemose, capitate, or paniculate; bracts various; bracteoles usually 0. Calyx-tube short; teeth subequal or the lowest the longest, free, usually falcate. Corolla slightly exserted or included; standard elliptic, obovate, or orbicular, auricled; wings obliquely obovate or oblong, usually adhering to the keel; keel straight or incurved, obtuse or acute. Stamens diadelphous; anthers uniform. Ovary subsessile, short; ovules 2; style filiform or slightly thickened above; stigma small, capitate. Pod small, oblique, turgid, continuous within. Seeds thick, not strophiolate; the funicle centric. —DISTRIB. Chiefly natives of Tropical Asia and Australia, a few in Tropical Africa; species about 26.

Leaves 1-foliolate.
  Branches terete; bracts acuminate, glabrescent; corolla white. 1. *F. strobilifera.*
  Branches angular; bracts rounded or emarginate, hirsute; corolla rosy or purple .... 2. *F. bracteata.*
Leaves 3-foliolate.
  Erect shrubs or undershrubs.
    Flowers in panicles .... 3. *F. lineata.*
    Flowers in axillary racemes; bracts small.
      A low undershrub 6–8 in. high, with woody subterranean stem .... 4. *F. nana.*
      Woody undershrubs with tall stems.
        Corolla exserted; calyx with a distinct tube, the lowest tooth the longest .... 5. *F. congesta.*
        Corolla included; calyx divided nearly to the base, the teeth subequal .... 6. *F. Wallichii.*
    Flowers in dense globose heads surrounded by large bracts. 7. *F. involucrata.*
  Trailing herbs with tuberous roots.
    Inflorescence capitate, terminal .... 8. *F. nilgiriensis.*
    Inflorescence lax, axillary .... 9. *F. tuberosa.*

1. **Flemingia strobilifera,** *R. Br. in Ait. Hort. Kew.* ed. 2, v. 4 (1812) p. 350. An erect much-branched shrub 4–10 ft. high; branches slender, terete, pubescent towards their tips. Leaves 1-foliolate; petioles $\frac{1}{4}$–1 in. long, pubescent; stipules scarious, $\frac{1}{4}$–$\frac{1}{3}$ in. long, lanceolate, caducous. Leaflets subcoriaceous, minutely gland-dotted, $3\frac{1}{2}$–$5\frac{1}{2}$ by $1\frac{5}{8}$–2 in., ovate-oblong, acute, green and glabrous or nearly so above, paler and more or less silky-pubescent (especially on the nerves) beneath, base rounded or truncate; main nerves 8–10 pairs, very conspicuous on the lower side; stipels 0. Flowers in axillary and terminal simple or branched racemes 3–6 in. long, closely arranged along a slender pubescent zigzag rhachis; bracts large, membranous, persistent, glabrescent, broadly orbicular-ovate, shortly acuminate, $\frac{1}{2}$–1 in. long, usually broader than long, cordate at the base, conspicuously nerved and reticulately veined, stalked, each bract folded over and enclosing 2 or more small flowers. Calyx $\frac{1}{8}$ in. long, pubescent; teeth linear, acute, veined, longer than the tube. Corolla white, $\frac{3}{8}$ in. long; standard $\frac{5}{16}$ in. broad, auricled. Pods $\frac{3}{8}$ by $\frac{3}{16}$ in., oblong, turgid, mucronate, densely pubescent, completely concealed by the bracts. Seeds 2 (rarely 1), dark-brown, marbled. Fl. B. I. v. 2, p. 227 (*exclud.* vars.); Grah. Cat. p. 51; Dalz. & Gibs. p. 75; Talb. Trees, Bomb. p. 74; Woodr. in Journ. Bomb. Nat. v. 11 (1897) p. 426; Watt, Dict. Econ. Prod. v. 3, p. 403. —Flowers: Nov.–Jan. VERN. *Kánphuti.*

Common in hilly parts of the Konkan, usually growing in patches. KONKAN: *Stocks*!, *Graham*; Matheran, *Cooke*!, *Woodrow*!; Mahableshwar, *Cooke*!—DISTRIB. Throughout India; S.E. Asia.

2. **Flemingia bracteata,** *Wight, Icon.* (1840) t. 268. An erect shrub 4–10 ft. high; branches more or less angular, softly downy when young. Leaves 1-foliolate; petioles $\frac{1}{8}$–$\frac{3}{4}$ in. long, downy; stipules $\frac{1}{3}$–$\frac{5}{8}$ in. long, linear, bristle-pointed, subpersistent. Leaflets 3–5$\frac{1}{2}$ by 1$\frac{1}{2}$–2$\frac{1}{2}$ in., ovate, acute, glabrous above, slightly hairy (especially on the nerves) beneath, base rounded or cordate; main nerves 4–6 pairs; stipels 0. Flowers in axillary and terminal branched racemes, closely arranged along a pubescent and nearly straight rhachis; bracts membranous, $\frac{3}{4}$ in. long, usually broader than long, rounded or emarginate at the apex, cordate at the base, stalked (with linear subulate stipules $\frac{3}{8}$ in. long below the stalks), softly hirsute and ciliate with long hairs, reticulately veined, the flowers hidden within the folded bracts. Calyx $\frac{1}{5}$ in. long, hirsute; teeth triangular, acute, longer than the tube. Corolla $\frac{1}{4}$ in. long, purple or rosy. Pods $\frac{1}{4}$–$\frac{1}{3}$ in. long, oblong, turgid, rounded and mucronate at the apex, entirely concealed by the persistent bracts. Seeds 2 (rarely 1). Prain, in Journ. As. Soc. Beng. v. 66 (1898) p. 437. *F. strobilifera,* var. *bracteata,* Baker, in Fl. B. I. v. 2, p. 227. *Hedysarum bracteatum,* Roxb. Fl. Ind. v. 3, p. 351.

KONKAN: *Ritchie.* S. M. COUNTRY: Castlerock, *Cooke*!, *Bhiva*! KANARA: *Talbot* (fide *Prain*).—DISTRIB. India (Oude, Behar, C. India, Sikkim, Birma, W. Peninsula).

3. **Flemingia lineata,** *Roxb. Hort. Beng.* (1814) p. 56. A small erect branched shrub; young branches angular, appressedly pubescent. Leaves 3-foliolate; petioles $\frac{3}{8}$–1 in. long, quadrangular, not winged, pubescent; stipules conspicuous, $\frac{1}{4}$ in. long, linear-oblong, cuspidate, subpersistent. Leaflets 1$\frac{1}{4}$–2 by $\frac{3}{8}$–$\frac{3}{4}$ in., rigidly subcoriaceous, plicate, obovate or oblanceolate, cuneate (the lateral smaller than the terminal and slightly oblique), rounded or subacute, nearly glabrous above, silky-hairy (especially on the very oblique conspicuous nerves), closely reticulately veined and inconspicuously dotted with yellowish glands beneath; stipels 0. Flowers in axillary peduncled spreading lax panicles; rhachis slender, pubescent; pedicels short; bracts linear, acute, caducous. Calyx $\frac{1}{8}$–$\frac{1}{6}$ in. long, softly downy; teeth subequal, linear-lanceolate, a little longer than the tube. Corolla $\frac{3}{16}$ in. long. Pods $\frac{3}{8}$–$\frac{1}{2}$ by $\frac{3}{16}$ in., oblong, rounded at both ends, minutely apiculate, glandular (sometimes viscidly so), pubescent. Seeds 2, orbicular-oblong, black. Fl. B. I. v. 2, p. 228; Grah. Cat. p. 51; Wight, Icon. t. 327; Trim. Fl. Ceyl. v. 2, p. 87.—Flowers: Dec.–Jan.

KONKAN: *Stocks*! DECCAN: between Nasik and Igatpuri, *Edgeworth*! GUJARAT: common, *Dr. Lush* ex *Graham*; Panch Mahals, *Dalzell*!—DISTRIB. Throughout India; Malay Islands, N. Australia.

4. **Flemingia nana,** *Roxb. Hort. Beng.* (1814) p. 56; *Fl. Ind.* v. 3, p. 339. Suffruticose, 6–8 in. high; stem scarcely any, about 1 in. above ground, woody, perennial; branches few, short, subherbaceous. Leaves 3-foliolate; petioles 1–3 in. long, winged; stipules $\frac{1}{4}$–$\frac{1}{2}$ in. long, linear-lanceolate, acute. Leaflets 1–3 by $\frac{3}{4}$–1$\frac{5}{8}$ in. (the terminal obovate, narrowed, the lateral obliquely elliptic, rounded at the base), acute at the apex, more or less downy, 3-nerved; petiolules short; stipels 0. Flowers numerous, in axillary elongate slender racemes 3–4 in. long, which are solitary or fasciculate; pedicels $\frac{1}{8}$–$\frac{1}{6}$ in. long, slender, pubescent and glandular; bracts $\frac{1}{10}$ in. long, lanceolate, caducous. Calyx $\frac{1}{6}$ in. long, pubescent and covered with ferruginous glands; teeth

lanceolate, longer than the tube, the lowest the longest. Corolla $\frac{1}{5}$ in. long, greenish-pink with darker stripes. Pods $\frac{1}{3}$–$\frac{1}{6}$ in. long, oblong, turgid, clothed with a greenish-grey tomentum and covered with viscid reddish glands. Seeds 2, round. Wight, Icon. t. 389; Prain, in Journ. As. Soc. Beng. v. 66 (1898) p. 441.

Baker, in Fl. B. I. v. 2, p. 229, makes this a variety of *F. congesta*, a shrub reaching 6 ft. high. There is evidently some mistake as to the plant which Mr. Baker took to be *F. nana* of Roxburgh. The species is very badly represented in Herb. Kew., but Roxburgh has in his 'Icones' an excellent colored drawing of the plant which has been copied by Wight (Icon. l. c.).

A very rare plant in the Bombay Presidency. *Talbot* n. 960 in Calcutta Herb. (*fide* Prain) reports the plant from Dongi (N. Kanara).

5. **Flemingia congesta,** *Roxb. Hort. Beng.* (1814) p. 56. An erect shrub 3–6 ft. high; young branches angular, sulcate, appressedly pubescent. Leaves 3-foliolate; petioles $1\frac{3}{4}$–3 in. long with angular but not winged margins, pubescent. Leaflets 4–7 by 2–$2\frac{3}{4}$ in., subcoriaceous, ovate-oblong, acute (the terminal cuneate, the lateral obliquely rounded at the base), dark green, glabrous or nearly so above, sparingly silky (especially on the nerves) beneath, strongly 3-nerved from the base; petiolules $\frac{1}{6}$–$\frac{1}{4}$ in. long, densely fulvous-pubescent. Flowers in dense axillary velvety congested racemes shorter than the petioles, the racemes sometimes solitary in the higher, usually fasciculate in the lower axils; pedicels very short, hairy; bracts lanceolate, $\frac{1}{4}$ in. long, densely velvety. Calyx $\frac{3}{8}$ in. long, softly pilose, dotted with small black glands; tube distinct; teeth linear, acute, ciliate, much exceeding the tube, the lowest the longest. Corolla $\frac{7}{16}$ in. long; standard $\frac{1}{6}$–$\frac{1}{5}$ in. broad, white streaked with pink; wings purplish. Pods $\frac{1}{8}$–$\frac{1}{2}$ by $\frac{1}{4}$ in., oblong, turgid, apiculate, finely pubescent, not glandular. Seeds 2. Fl. B. I. v. 2, p. 228 (*exclud.* varieties); Dalz. & Gibs. p. 75; Wight, Icon. t. 390; Trim. Fl. Ceyl. v. 2, p. 87 (*exclud.* var.); Talb. Trees, Bomb. p. 74; Woodr. in Journ. Bomb. Nat. v. 11 (1897) p. 426; Watt, Dict. Econ. Prod. v. 3, p. 400.—Flowers: Nov.–Dec. VERN. *Daudaula.*

KONKAN: *Dalzell*!, *Stocks*!; Wari jungles, *Dalzell*!

VAR. *viridis*, Prain, in Journ. As. Soc. Beng. v. 66 (1898) p. 440. Racemes more lax and slender, but always shorter than the petioles. Petioles distinctly winged. Leaflets thinner and paler. *Flemingia semialata* (sp.), Wall. Cat. 5746 D (*not* at all of Roxb.). *F. semialata*, var. *viridis*, Kurz, in Journ. As. Soc. Beng. v. 45, part 2 (1876) p. 261. —Flowers: Sept.–Oct.

I have followed Prain (*l. c.*) as to this variety. Prain has restored *F. semialata*, Roxb. (which Baker in Fl. B. I. v. 2, p. 229, had made a variety of *F. congesta*), to its pristine specific rank; and as the original plants from which Roxburgh described his species were grown in the Botanic Gardens, Calcutta, from seed sent by Buchanan from Nipal, Dr. Prain is in a position to know exactly what plant Roxburgh meant. The racemes of *F. semialata* exceed the petioles, those of *F. congesta* and its variety (*viridis*) are shorter than them.

KONKAN: *Stocks*!, *Gibson*; Vingorla, *Woodrow*, *Cooke*! KANARA: very common in the moist forests of N. Kanara, *Talbot*; Kumpta, *Talbot*, 249!; Yellapur, *Talbot*, 908! —DISTRIB. India (Behar, Birma, W. Peninsula).

6. **Flemingia Wallichii,** *Wight & Arn. Prodr.* (1834) p. 242. An erect shrub 3 ft. high; branches obscurely angled, clothed with spreading hairs. Leaves 3-foliolate; petioles 1–1¾ in. long, grooved, faintly winged, clothed with long spreading hairs; stipules ¼ in. long, ovate-oblong, acute. Leaflets 1½–4½ by ⅝–2 in. (the terminal obovate, cuneate, the lateral obliquely ovate-oblong, rounded at the base), acute, glabrous above, more or less hairy, dotted with black glands, prominently nerved and reticulately veined beneath; stipels 0. Flowers sessile, in dense axillary often condensed racemes 1–3 in. long, solitary or fasciculate; bracts ¼ in. long, obovate-oblong, acute, shaggy. Calyx ⅜–½ in. long, shaggy, divided almost to the very base; teeth subequal, linear, acute, plumose. Corolla included. Pods as long as the calyx, ¼ in. broad, turgid, obtuse at both ends, finely pubescent, not glandular. Seeds 2, subglobose, black. Fl. B. I. v. 2, p. 229 (exclud. syn. *F. nana* and *F. sericans*); Woodr. in Journ. Bomb. Nat. v. 11 (1897) p. 426.—Flowers: Oct.–Feb.

KONKAN: *Stocks*! S. M. COUNTRY: Belgaum, *Ritchie*, 202! KANARA: *Woodrow*!; Hulical, *Bhiva*!; Yacombi, *Bhiva*!—DISTRIB. India (W. Peninsula).

7. **Flemingia involucrata,** *Benth. Pl. Jungh.* (1851–55) p. 246. An erect shrub 2–6 ft. high; stems and branches terete, clothed with spreading fulvous hairs. Leaves 3-foliolate; petioles ⅛–⅝ in. long, densely hairy; stipules ⅝ in. long, oblong-lanceolate, acute. Leaflets 2–4 by ⅞–1¾ in., oblong or lanceolate, narrowed at both ends (the lateral oblique), subcoriaceous, glabrous above, softly hairy, paler and dotted with brownish glands beneath; main nerves 10–14 pairs, close, prominent; stipels rarely present, when present minute, filiform. Flowers in dense globose terminal and axillary heads often exceeding 1 in. in diam., surrounded by a number of bracts (like the capitula of *Compositæ*); peduncles very short, stout, densely hairy; bracts reaching ¾ by ¼ in., ovate, acuminate, pubescent on the back, ciliate on the margins with long soft hairs. Calyx ½–⅝ in. long, divided nearly to the base, densely silky-hairy; teeth subequal, lanceolate, cuspidate, plumose, the 2 upper subconnate. Corolla ⅜–½ in. long. Pods ¼ by ⅛ in., thin, oblong, turgid, apiculate, keeled on the ventral suture, downy. Seed 1, quite filling the pod, ellipsoid, black. Fl. B. I. v. 2, p. 229; Talb. Trees, Bomb. p. 74; Woodr. in Journ. Bomb. Nat. v. 11 (1897) p. 426.—Flowers: Nov.–Feb.

Rare. KONKAN: *Stocks*! KANARA: open glades in the deciduous forests of N. Kanara, *Talbot*; Dandeli (N. Kanara), *Woodrow*.—DISTRIB. India (E. Himalayas, Bengal, Assam, C. Provinces, W. Peninsula); Java.

8. **Flemingia nilgiriensis,** *Wight, MS. in Herb. Kew.* Herbaceous, diffuse, pubescent; stems many, terete, clothed with long spreading hairs. Leaves 3-foliolate; petioles ¼–⅝ in. long, hairy; stipules ⅜ by ⅛ in., ovate-oblong, acute, hairy. Leaflets ½–1 by ⅜–½ in., ovate-oblong or oblong-elliptic (the terminal sometimes obovate), mucronate, hairy on both surfaces, dotted with reddish glands beneath, base rounded (obliquely so in the lateral leaflets); stipels 0. Flowers in terminal heads ½–⅞ in. in diam.; peduncles ½–1½ in. long, densely hairy; bracts ⅛ by $\frac{1}{10}$ in., lanceolate, acute, hairy. Calyx ⅜–$\frac{7}{16}$ in. long, densely fulvous-

hairy, the hairs often rising from large yellowish bulbous bases; teeth subequal, more than twice as long as the tube, linear-lanceolate, plumose. Corolla scarcely longer than the calyx, dull-purple; standard $\frac{1}{4}$ in. broad, obovate-oblong, hairy on the back, auricled. Pods $\frac{1}{6}$ in. long, thin, obliquely ovoid or subglobose, pointed, glabrous, veined. Seed 1, ellipsoid, quite filling the pod, dark-brown, smooth. *Flemingia procumbens*, Wight, Icon. t. 987 (*not* of Roxb.); Dalz. & Gibs. p. 75. *Flemingia vestita*, var. *nilgheriensis*, Benth. ex Baker, in Fl. B. I. v. 2, p. 230; Woodr. in Journ. Bomb. Nat. v. 11 (1897) p. 426.—Flowers: Aug.–Oct.

I have restored this to the rank of a species accorded to it by Wight. It is quite impossible to consider it a variety of *F. procumbens*, Roxb., which, as Prain points out (Journ. As. Soc. Beng. v. 66 [1898] p. 442), is the same as *F. vestita*, Benth. Wight made a slip in naming the plant *F. procumbens* (Icon. 987), when he had already figured *F. procumbens*, Roxb. in t. 408. He corrected the error, however, in a note attached to a specimen in his Herbarium, which is now in Herb. Kew., in which he named the plant *F. neilgherrensis*.

Rare. KONKAN: *Stocks*! DECCAN: Phunda Ghát, *Dalzell*!—DISTRIB. Apparently endemic.

9. **Flemingia tuberosa,** *Dalz. in Kew Journ. Bot.* v. 2 (1850) p. 34. Perennial, prostrate; root tuberous, 2 in. long, edible; stems 2–3 ft. long, copiously branched; branches terete, glabrous or with a few spreading hairs, faintly striate. Leaves 3-foliolate; petioles $\frac{3}{4}$–$1\frac{1}{2}$ in. long, clothed with spreading hairs; stipules $\frac{1}{8}$ in. long, oblong, acute, caducous. Leaflets $1\frac{1}{4}$–2 by $\frac{3}{8}$–$\frac{7}{16}$ in., oblong-lanceolate, acute, sparsely hairy above, more strongly so on the nerves beneath, not or obscurely gland-dotted; midrib very conspicuous on the underside. Flowers in few-flowered lax axillary racemose cymes longer than the leaves, the branches very slender; bracts and bracteoles rigid, ovate, acute. Calyx $\frac{1}{4}$–$\frac{3}{8}$ in. long, densely hairy; teeth subequal, longer than the tube, linear, acute, strongly 3-nerved. Corolla lilac, slightly longer than the calyx; standard hairy on the back. Pods oblong, as long as or slightly exceeding the calyx, glabrous, transversely reticulate towards the apex. Seeds 1–2. Fl. B. I. v. 2, p. 230; Dalz. & Gibs. p. 75; Woodr. in Journ. Bomb. Nat. v. 11 (1897) p. 426.—Flowers: Sept.

KONKAN: *Stocks*!, *Dalzell*!, *Law*!; Malwan, *Dalzell & Gibson*; Dapoli, *Nairne*.—DISTRIB. Apparently endemic.

55. DALBERGIA, Linn. f.

Trees or shrubs often climbing. Leaves alternate, imparipinnate or rarely 1-foliolate. Leaflets usually alternate, exstipellate. Flowers small, copious, in terminal or lateral panicles; bracts small subpersistent; bracteoles usually minute. Calyx campanulate; teeth short, distinct, the lowest usually the longest. Corolla exserted; standard broad; wings oblong; keel obtuse, its petals joined at the tip. Stamens 9–10, all connate into a tube split down the upper side, or the tube split into 2 equal bundles; anthers minute, basifixed, with the cells back to back, dehiscing usually by an apical (rarely a longitudinal) slit. Ovary stalked; ovules few; style incurved, short; stigma small, terminal. Pod oblong or strap-shaped, usually thin and flat, indehiscent, not thickened or winged at the sutures. Seeds 1–4, reniform, flat-compressed.—Distrib. America, Africa, Tropical Asia, Australia; species 60–70.

An older name for the genus is *Amerimnon*, Browne (Hist. Jamaica, [1789] p. 288, t. 31, f. 3).

Stamens 9 (less commonly 10), monadelphous; staminal-tube slit along the upper side only.
  Tall trees unarmed.
    Leaflets acuminate .... 1. *D. Sissoo.*
    Leaflets obtuse .... 2. *D. latifolia.*
  A small tree armed with spines .... 3. *D. Melanoxylon.*
  Scandent shrubs.
    Leaflets 5–7.
      Pod straight .... 4. *D. rubiginosa.*
      Pod crescent-shaped .... 5. *D. torta.*
    Leaflets 11–15 .... 6. *D. sympathetica.*
    Leaflets 25–41 .... 7. *D. tamarindifolia.*
Stamens 10; staminal-tube slit on the upper and lower sides, so that the stamens are in 2 bundles of 5 each.
  Trees.
    Standard $\frac{1}{4}$ in. broad, with a callosity at the base of the limb .... 8. *D. lanceolaria.*
    Standard $\frac{3}{8}$ in. broad, without a callosity at the base of the limb .... 9. *D. paniculata.*
  An erect shrub with spine-tipped branchlets .... 10. *D. spinosa.*
  A climbing shrub; leaflets 11–15 .... 11. *D. volubilis.*

1. **Dalbergia Sissoo,** *Roxb. Hort. Beng.* (1814) p. 53; *Fl. Ind.* v. 3, p. 223. A tree reaching 60 ft. high; young parts pubescent or tomentose; branches numerous, spreading. Leaves alternate, bifarious, imparipinnate; leaf-rhachis zigzag; petioles terete, very downy when young; stipules lanceolate, caducous. Leaflets 3–5, firm, $1\frac{1}{2}$-$2\frac{1}{2}$ by $1\frac{1}{4}$–$2\frac{1}{8}$ (the terminal the largest and the lowest the smallest), distant, alternate, suborbicular, conspicuously and abruptly acuminate, puberulous when young, soon glabrescent, base narrowed or cuneate; petiolules $\frac{1}{8}$–$\frac{1}{4}$ in. long. Flowers sessile or nearly so, in axillary panicles shorter than the leaves and composed of several short subsecund spikes; rhachis and branches of the panicle densely hairy; bracts linear-subulate hairy. Calyx $\frac{1}{8}$–$\frac{1}{6}$ in. long, hairy; teeth short, ciliate, the 2 upper connate except at the tip, the lateral linear, obtuse, the lowest the longest, subacute. Corolla pale-yellow, $\frac{1}{4}$–$\frac{1}{3}$ in. long; standard $\frac{1}{8}$ in. broad, with a long claw, the limb obovate-orbicular. Stamens 9 in one bundle, the sheath of the filaments slit only at the top. Ovary pubescent; ovules 2–4. Pods $1\frac{1}{2}$–4 by $\frac{1}{4}$–$\frac{1}{2}$ in., narrowed at the base into a long stalk which is twice as long as the calyx, thin, strap-shaped, glabrous, slightly reticulate. Seeds 1–4. Fl. B. I. v. 2, p. 231; Grah. Cat. p. 55; Dalz. & Gibs. Suppl. p. 24; Benth. in Journ. Linn. Soc. v. 4 (1860) Suppl. p. 40; Bedd. Fl. Sylvat. t. 25; Talb. Trees, Bomb. p. 74; Woodr. in Journ. Bomb. Nat. v. 11 (1897) p. 426; Watt, Dict. Econ. Prod. v. 3, p. 13.—Flowers: Mar.–June. Vern. *Sisvi.*

Planted, but not extensively, in the Bombay Presidency; said to be wild in Gujarat. *Graham* (l. c.) says that it is common in the Kanheri jungles and the hills about Nagotna, but no doubt self-planted.

The wood is valuable and is largely employed in Bengal for boat-building, carts, and furniture. See Watt, Dict. Econ. Prod. l. c.—DISTRIB. India (planted throughout the plains, indigenous in the Sub-Himalayas from the Indus to Assam).

2. **Dalbergia latifolia,** *Roxb. Cor. Pl.* v. 2 (1798) p. 7, t. 113. A large glabrous tree reaching 80 ft. high; branches numerous, spreading, forming a shady head. Leaves imparipinnate, 4–6 in. long; rhachis straight, glabrous, much produced beyond the insertion of the uppermost pair of leaflets. Leaflets 5–7 (usually 5), firm, 1¼–2½ in. long, nearly as broad as long (the terminal slightly the largest), broadly ovate or sub-orbicular, rounded, sometimes emarginate at the apex, glabrous on both sides, pale beneath, base shortly cuneate; petiolules ¼–⅓ in. long. Flowers in axillary or extra-axillary lax divaricate panicles usually shorter than the leaves; pedicels 1/16–⅛ in. long, filiform; bracts minute; bracteoles membranous, very caducous. Calyx ⅛–⅙ in. long, glabrous; teeth linear-oblong, obtuse, rather shorter than the tube. Corolla ¼ in. long, greenish- or yellowish-white, the petals with long claws. Stamens 9 in one bundle. Ovary glabrous; ovules 3–5. Pods 1½–3 by ½–¾ in., strap-shaped, slightly reticulated, glabrous. Seeds 1–3 (rarely 4). Fl. B. I. v. 2, p. 231; Grah. Cat. p. 55; Dalz. & Gibs. p. 77; Bedd. Flor. Sylvat. t. 24; Benth. in Journ. Linn. Soc. v. 4 (1860) Suppl. p. 38; Talb. Trees, Bomb. p. 74; Woodr. in Journ. Bomb. Nat. v. 11 (1897) p. 426; Watt, Dict. Econ. Prod. v. 3, p. 7.—Flowers: Aug. VERN. *Shisham*; *Sissu*; *Biti*.

The *Blackwood* or *Rosewood* tree of S. India. KONKAN: *Stocks*!, *Law*!, *Capt. Geburne*!, *Dalzell & Gibson*. DECCAN: hills, *Woodrow*. S. M. COUNTRY: *Dalzell & Gibson*. KANARA: associated with teak in the high timber forests of N. Kanara, *Talbot*; banks of Kála naddi river, *Law* ex *Graham*.—DISTRIB. India (Oude, E. Bengal, Behar, Sikkim, Bandelkhand, C. India, W. Peninsula).

The tree furnishes a valuable hard and heavy wood which sinks in water before seasoning. It is the wood from which the well-known Bombay blackwood furniture is made and commands a very high price in the market. See Watt, Dict. Econ. Prod. l. c.

3. **Dalbergia Melanoxylon,** *Guill. & Per. Flor. Seneg.* v. 1 (1830) p. 227, t. 53. A small tree 15–20 ft. high; branches more or less armed with stout spines; bark white. Leaves 4–5 in. long; stipules very caducous. Leaflets 9–15, thinly subcoriaceous, ⅜–⅞ by ¼–⅝ in. (the terminal the largest, obovate, cuneate, the lateral oblong), obtuse emarginate, glabrous above and nearly so beneath; petiolules 1/16 in. long. Flowers numerous, in axillary panicles about equalling the leaves; pedicels 1/20–1/16 in. long; bracts and bracteoles minute, linear. Calyx 1/10–⅛ in. long, pubescent; teeth ciliolate, the 2 upper obtuse, the 2 lateral smaller, linear-oblong, obtuse, the lowest twice as long as the lateral, linear, acute. Corolla ⅕ in. long, yellow; standard ⅛ in. broad, oblong-obovate, emarginate. Stamens 9 (in all that I have examined), monadelphous, the central stamen longer than the others. Ovary glabrous; style short. Pods 1–2½ in. long, 1-seeded and then short, broadly elliptic-lanceolate, acute (sometimes 2-seeded and then oblong, elongate), quite glabrous, reticulately veined, narrowed into a stalk ⅓–½ in. long. Dalz. & Gibs. Suppl. p. 24; Prain, in Journ. As. Soc. Beng. v. 66 (1898) p. 446. *D. Stocksii*, Benth. in Journ. Linn. Soc. v. 4 (1860) Suppl. p. 42; Baker, in Hook. f. Fl. B. I. v. 2, p. 234; Talb. Trees, Bomb. p. 75; Woodr. in Journ. Bomb. Nat. v. 11 (1897) p. 426.

Guill. & Per. in their description say stamens 10, sometimes 9. In their figure, however, 9 stamens are shown. I have found only 9 in all the specimens I have examined and they are monadelphous, though the staminal-tube is slit some way down on the lower side.

Very doubtfully wild in the Bombay Presidency.—The tree occurs in Kanara, where it goes by the name of "Chinese blackwood." It has been planted as a roadside tree in Dharwar and also at Ganesh Khind near Poona. Dalzell (*l. c.*) says it was raised in the Botanic Gardens at Hewra and Dapuri from seed furnished by Mr. Nimmo and was called "Senaar Ebony."

The wood is remarkably hard and is used in Senegambia for many of the purposes served by ebony and according to Guill. & Per. has been imported into Europe.

4. **Dalbergia rubiginosa,** *Roxb. Cor. Pl.* v. 2 (1798) p. 9, t. 115. Scandent; branches terete, glabrous. Leaves imparipinnate, 3–4 in. long; rhachis appressedly pubescent. Leaflets 5–7, coriaceous, 1–2½ by ½–1¼ in. (the terminal much the largest), elliptic-oblong, obtuse, emarginate, glabrous and shining above, pale, minutely puberulous and inconspicuously reticulately veined beneath, base rounded or subacute; midrib prominent on the underside; petiolules $\frac{1}{10}$ in. long, pubescent. Flowers in short crowded axillary panicles 1–2 in. long, with finely pubescent branches; pedicels $\frac{1}{12}$ in. long; bracts ovate-oblong, subacute, pubescent on both sides, ciliolate; bracteoles suborbicular-oblong, concave, rounded at the apex, pubescent on both sides, ciliolate. Calyx $\frac{1}{8}$ in. long, finely brown-silky; teeth obtuse, about ¼ the length of the tube, ciliolate. Corolla $\frac{1}{5}$ in. long; standard obovate-oblong, $\frac{1}{10}$ in. broad. Stamens 9 or 10 in one bundle. Ovary stalked; ovules 2–4 Pods strongly veined, 1–2-seeded (*fide* Talbot, l. c.). Fl. B. I. v. 2, p. 232; Benth. in Journ. Linn. Soc. v. 4 (1860) Suppl. p. 43; Talb. Trees, Bomb. p. 75.

I have found the number of stamens to be usually 10, though I have found 9, but very rarely.

Rare. KONKAN: *Stocks*! KANARA: N. Kanara, *Talbot*, 431!; in the evergreen forests from the Ainshi Ghát southward, *Talbot*.—DISTRIB. India (W. Peninsula); S. China.

5. **Dalbergia torta,** *Grah. in Wall. Cat.* (1828) 5873. A stout scandent shrub, climbing by means of its divaricate lateral twigs often hooked at the ends; bark purplish-black, smooth. Leaves 2–3 in. long; rhachis finely pubescent. Leaflets 5–7 (usually 5), ¾–1 by ½–⅝ in., elliptic-oblong, obtuse, usually emarginate, quite glabrous above, glaucescent and more or less minutely puberulous beneath, base usually rounded (that of the terminal leaflet cuneate); petiolules $\frac{1}{16}$ in. long, pubescent. Flowers in axillary solitary or twin racemose or subcymose panicles shorter than the leaves; pedicels $\frac{1}{20}$–$\frac{1}{12}$ in. long; bracts and bracteoles minute, persistent, the former ovate-oblong, subacute, the latter orbicular, concave. Calyx ⅛ in. long, glabrous; teeth about ¼ the length of the tube, subequal, obtuse. Corolla ¼ in. long, white; standard $\frac{1}{12}$–$\frac{1}{10}$ in. broad, narrowly oblong, obtuse, with a very slender claw as long as the tube of the calyx, and without any callosity at the base. Stamens 10 in one bundle. Ovary glabrous; ovules usually 2. Pods 1 by ½ in., brown, shortly stalked, crescent-shaped (the upper suture recurved), polished. Seed 1. *Dalbergia monosperma*, Dalz. in Kew Journ. v. 2 (1850) p. 36; Fl. B. I. v. 2, p. 237; Dalz. & Gibs.

p. 78; Benth. in Journ. Linn. Soc. v. 4 (1860) Suppl. p. 48; Trim. Fl. Ceyl. v. 2, p. 89; Talb. Trees, Bomb. p. 75; Woodr. in Journ. Bomb. Nat. v. 11 (1897) p. 426.—Flowers: June. VERN. *Garud-yel.*

Mr. Baker has made a slip in placing this plant (Fl. B. I. l. c.) in the section with isadelphous stamens. Trimen (Fl. Ceyl. l. c.) has made a similar mistake. The stamens are distinctly monadelphous, a fact which Dalzell had noted in his original description and Mr. Bentham in Journ. Linn. Soc. (*l. c.*).

KONKAN: *Law*!; Malwan, *Dalzell & Gibson*, *Woodrow*; Vingorla, *Dalzell*!; Matheran (Chowk Plateau), *H. M. Birdwood*.—DISTRIB. India (Bengal in the Sunderbans, W. Peninsula near the coast); Ceylon, Malaya, Philippines, China, N. Australia.

6. **Dalbergia sympathetica,** *Nimmo, ex Grah. Cat. Bo. Pl.* (1839) p. 55. A large scandent shrub running over high trees; branches often twisted, the young ones pubescent; trunk armed with strong blunt often fantastically curved clustered spines 6–10 in. long. Leaves 4–6 in. long; rhachis softly pubescent. Leaflets 11–15, moderately firm, $\frac{1}{2}$–$1\frac{1}{4}$ by $\frac{1}{4}$–$\frac{3}{4}$ in., oblong, obtuse, emarginate (the terminal obovate, cuneate), softly pubescent on both surfaces, reticulately veined; petiolules $\frac{1}{20}$ in. long. Flowers numerous, in dense short axillary cymose panicles, with rusty-pubescent corymbose branches; pedicels very short; bracts and bracteoles minute, oblong, obtuse. Calyx $\frac{1}{8}$ in. long, pubescent; teeth about equalling the tube, the 2 upper broad, obtuse, the 2 lateral smaller and narrower, subacute, the lowest the longest, lanceolate, acute. Corolla $\frac{1}{5}$ in. long; standard $\frac{1}{8}$ in. broad, obovate-oblong, emarginate, without any callosity at the base, the claw shorter than the tube of the calyx. Stamens 10 in one bundle. Ovary pubescent. Pods when 1-seeded $1\frac{1}{2}$–2 by $\frac{5}{8}$–$\frac{3}{4}$ in., when (less commonly) 2-seeded reaching 3 by 1 in., narrowed to the point and at the base into a very short stalk, glabrescent, reticulate. Seeds 1–2. Fl. B. I. v. 2, p. 234; Dalz. & Gibs. p. 78; Benth. in Journ. Linn. Soc. v. 4 (1860) Suppl. p. 42; Talb. Trees, Bomb. p. 75; Woodr. in Journ. Bomb. Nat. v. 11 (1897) p. 426; Watt, Dict. Econ. Prod. v. 3, p. 16.—Flowers: Feb.–Mar. VERN. *Pendgul*; *Yekyel.*

KONKAN: *Dalzell*!, *Law*!; *Stocks*!; Matheran, *Cooke*!, *H. M. Birdwood*. DECCAN: near Pár, *Graham*; Khandala, *Woodrow*! KANARA: *Hohenhacker*, 343!; from the coast inward in the deciduous forests of N. Kanara, *Talbot*.—DISTRIB. India (hills of the W. Peninsula).

7. **Dalbergia tamarindifolia,** *Roxb. Hort. Beng.* (1814) p. 53. A scandent shrub 15–40 ft.; young branches densely rufous-pubescent. Leaves 4–6 in. long; rhachis densely puberulous; stipules lanceolate, $\frac{1}{4}$ in. long. Leaflets 25–41, moderately firm, caducous, $\frac{3}{8}$–$\frac{3}{4}$ by $\frac{3}{16}$–$\frac{3}{8}$, trapezoid-oblong, truncate, rounded, sometimes emarginate at the apex, thinly pubescent on both surfaces, paler beneath; petioles very short. Flowers in congested sessile corymbosely-branched axillary panicles $\frac{3}{4}$–2 in. long, the branches of the panicle densely brown-pubescent; pedicels $\frac{1}{16}$ in. long; bracts $\frac{1}{16}$ in. long, ovate, subacute, pubescent, persistent; bracteoles $\frac{1}{12}$ in. long, broadly oblong, obtuse, pubescent, persistent. Calyx $\frac{1}{8}$ in. long, glabrous; teeth one-third as long as the tube, short, subequal, subobtuse. Corolla $\frac{3}{8}$ in. long, white; standard $\frac{1}{10}$ in. broad, not thickened above the claw which is as long as the tube of the calyx. Stamens usually 9 (rarely 10), monadelphous. Ovary glabrous; ovules

2-3. Pods $1\frac{1}{2}$-3 by $\frac{1}{3}$-$\frac{1}{2}$ in., thin, greenish, drying bright reddish-brown, strap-shaped, glabrous, shining, slightly reticulate. Fl. B. I. v. 2, p. 234; Benth. in Journ. Linn. Soc. v. 4 (1860) p. 44; Talb. Trees, Bomb. p. 75; Woodr. in Journ. Bomb. Nat. v. 11 (1897) p. 426; Watt, Dict. Econ. Prod. v. 3, p. 16.—Flowers: Mar.-May.

KONKAN: *Law*!, *Stocks*! KANARA: in evergreen forests on the S. Ghâts of N. Kanara, common, *Talbot*; Nilkund (N. Kanara), *Woodrow*.—DISTRIB. India (Himalayas from Nipal eastwards, W. Peninsula); Indo-China, Malaya.

VAR. 1. *pubescens*, Baker, in Hook. f. Fl. B. I. v. 2, p. 235. Branches and underside of leaves clothed with persistent thick ferruginous pubescence.

KONKAN: *Stocks*!, *Law*!

VAR. 2. *acaciæfolia*, Baker, in Hook. f. Fl. B. I. v. 2, p. 235. Leaflets thicker, rigidly coriaceous, dark-green and shining above, glaucous and more or less hairy beneath. *D. acaciæfolia* (sp.), Dalz. in Kew Journ. Bot. v. 2 (1850) p. 37.—Flowers: Apr.

KONKAN: *Law*!, *Dalzell*! KANARA: *Dalzell*.
This would appear to deserve the rank of a separate species.

8. **Dalbergia lanceolaria,** *Linn. f. Suppl. Pl.* (1781) p. 316. A large tree 30–40 ft. high; bark grey. Leaves 3–7 in. long; stipules minute, caducous. Leaflets $\frac{3}{4}$-$1\frac{1}{2}$ by $\frac{3}{8}$-$\frac{3}{4}$ in., elliptic or oblong, obtuse, emarginate, glabrous above, pale and more or less puberulous beneath, base rounded or subacute; main nerves very oblique, numerous, parallel, conspicuous; petiolules $\frac{1}{8}$-$\frac{1}{6}$ in. long. Flowers in copious axillary and terminal leafless panicles clothed with rufous pubescence; pedicels $\frac{1}{12}$ in. long, rufous-hairy; bracts and bracteoles minute, caducous. Calyx $\frac{1}{6}$ in. long, silky-hairy; teeth half as long as the tube, ciliate, the 2 upper obtuse, the 2 lateral equalling the upper, subacute, the lowest the longest, linear-lanceolate, acute. Corolla $\frac{3}{8}$ in. long; standard broadly obovate, $\frac{1}{4}$ in. broad, with a large callosity above the claw. Stamens in 2 bundles of 5 each. Ovary stalked, usually hairy at the base; ovules 3. Pods $\frac{1}{2}$-$\frac{3}{4}$ in. broad and when 1-seeded $1\frac{1}{2}$-2 in. long (when 2-seeded sometimes reaching 4 in. long), thin, flexible, narrowed to the point and gradually at the base into a long stalk, glabrous or nearly so, reticulately veined. Fl. B. I. v. 2, p. 235; Dalz. & Gibs. p. 78; Benth. in Journ. Linn. Soc. v. 4 (1860) Suppl. p. 45; Trim. Fl. Ceyl. v. 2, p. 88; Talb. Trees, Bomb. p. 75; Woodr. in Journ. Bomb. Nat. v. 11 (1897) p. 426; Watt, Dict. Econ. Prod. v. 3, p. 6. *D. frondosa*, Roxb. Hort. Beng. p. 53; Wight, Icon. t. 266; Grah. Cat. p. 55.—Flowers: Mar.-May. VERN. *Dandus*; *Harrâni*.

KONKAN: rare, *Dalzell & Gibson*. DECCAN: Lalling Ghât, Khandesh, *Graham*; Alandi, *Woodrow*. KANARA: deciduous forests of N. Kanara from Mandgod to Siddapur, common, *Talbot*.—DISTRIB. Throughout India; Ceylon.

9. **Dalbergia paniculata,** *Roxb. Cor. Pl.* v. 2 (1789) p. 8, t. 114. A tree sometimes reaching 50 feet high; young branches clothed with greyish-brown pubescence; bark smooth, greenish-white. Leaves 4–6 in. long; rhachis glabrous. Leaflets 9–13, rigidly subcoriaceous, $\frac{3}{4}$-1 by $\frac{3}{8}$-$\frac{3}{4}$ in., obovate, oblong or elliptic, obtuse, emarginate, glabrous; petiolules $\frac{1}{16}$-$\frac{1}{12}$ in. long. Flowers subsessile, in copious terminal (less commonly axillary) subcymose panicles, the branches densely clothed with ferruginous pubescence; bracts oblong, hairy, caducous.

Calyx $\frac{1}{8}$–$\frac{1}{6}$ in. long, densely silky; teeth ciliate, a little more than half as long as the tube, subdeltoid, the lowest slightly the longest. Corolla $\frac{1}{3}$ in. long, bluish-white; standard oblong, emarginate, $\frac{1}{8}$–$\frac{1}{6}$ in. broad, veined, with a claw about as long as the tube of the calyx and without any callosity at the base. Stamens in 2 bundles of 5 each. Pods $1\frac{1}{2}$–$2\frac{1}{2}$ by $\frac{1}{2}$–$\frac{3}{4}$ in., narrowed at the base and apex, long-stalked, glabrous, reticulately veined. Seeds 1–2. Fl. B. I. v. 2, p. 236; Grah. Cat. p. 55; Dalz. & Gibs. p. 78; Benth. in Journ. Linn. Soc. v. 4 (1860) Suppl. p. 45; Talb. Trees, Bomb. p. 75; Woodr. in Journ. Bomb. Nat. v. 11 (1897) p. 426; Watt, Dict. Econ. Prod. v. 3, p. 11.—Flowers: Apr.–May. VERN. *Phansi.*

KONKAN: *Stocks*!, *Dalzell*!; Matheran Ghát, *H. M. Birdwood.* DECCAN: Mawal districts above the Gháts, *Graham.* S. M. COUNTRY: Kalghatgi taluka of Dharwar, *Talbot.* KANARA: deciduous forests of N. Kanara, *Talbot.*—DISTRIB. India (W. Peninsula, Birma).

10. **Dalbergia spinosa,** *Roxb. Fl. Ind.* v. 3 (1832) p. 233. A stiff erect glabrous shrub; lateral branchlets short, horizontal, ending in a hard spine. Leaves crowded in fascicles from the nodes of the spinous branchlets; rhachis slender, rusty-pubescent. Leaflets 7–11, firm, $\frac{1}{4}$–$\frac{1}{2}$ by $\frac{1}{8}$–$\frac{1}{4}$ in., oblong, obtuse, glabrous; petiolules very short. Flowers in congested corymbose axillary panicles; pedicels short. Calyx $\frac{1}{10}$ in. long, puberulous; teeth about equalling the tube, the 2 upper obtuse, the 2 lateral smaller and narrower, subacute, the lowest slightly the longest, lanceolate, acute. Corolla $\frac{1}{5}$ in. long; standard $\frac{1}{10}$ in. broad, elliptic oblong, without any callosity at the base. Stamens in 2 bundles of 5 each. Ovary glabrous. Pod 1 in. long, reniform, flat, glabrous, brown. Fl. B. I. v. 2, p. 238; Talb. Trees, Bomb. p. 75; Watt, Dict. Econ. Prod. v. 3, p. 15.

This plant has been included on the authority of Talbot (*l. c.*) who has noted it as occurring on the coast of the Konkan. I have seen no specimens from the Konkan coast nor from any part of the Presidency of Bombay.—DISTRIB. India (shores of the E. & W. Peninsulas, Chittagong).

Watt mentions a curious property which the powdered roots are reputed to possess, viz. that of absorbing alcohol. Kurz states that "a spoonful of the powdered root in a glass of water is said to destroy in less than half an hour the effects of alcohol, even in cases bordering on delirium tremens." It seems next to impossible that any substance should be possessed of such a property, but I quote the statement as given. See Watt, Dict. Econ. Prod. l. c.

11. **Dalbergia volubilis,** *Roxb. Cor. Pl.* v. 2 (1798) p. 48, t. 191. A large woody climber reaching 40–50 ft. high; branches glabrescent, thickened in places and twisted into spiral hooks. Leaves 4–6 in. long; rhachis pubescent. Leaflets 11–13, thickly coriaceous, 1–2 by $\frac{3}{4}$–1 in. (the terminal the largest), oblong or obovate-oblong, obtuse or truncate, sometimes emarginate, apiculate, dark green above, paler beneath, glabrous; petiolules $\frac{1}{8}$ in. long, glabrous. Flowers in copious axillary and terminal leafless panicles 8–12 in long, with numerous lateral branches 1–3 in. long, bearing dense corymbose cymes; pedicels very short; bracts at the base of the panicle small, ovate, subpersistent, those at the base of the pedicels $\frac{1}{16}$ in. long, oblong, obtuse, pubescent on both sides, ciliolate; bracteoles beneath the calyx 2, oblong-obtuse, $\frac{1}{16}$ in. long, pubescent on both sides, ciliolate. Calyx $\frac{1}{8}$ in. long, densely puberulous; teeth about one-third the length of the tube, the 4 upper oblong, obtuse, the lower longer, triangular, subacute. Corolla $\frac{1}{5}$–$\frac{1}{4}$ in.

long, pale blue; standard $\frac{1}{8}$ in. broad, suborbicular-oblong. Stamens 10, in 2 bundles of 5 each. Pods 2–3 by $\frac{3}{4}$–1 in., stalked, linear-oblong, obtuse, conspicuously veined, glabrous. Seeds 1–2. Fl. B. I. v. 2, p. 235; Grah. Cat. p. 55; Dalz. & Gibs. p. 78; Benth. in Journ. Linn. Soc. v. 4 (1860) Suppl. p. 46; Talb. Trees, Bomb. p. 75; Woodr. in Journ. Bomb. Nat. v. 11 (1897) p. 426; Watt, Dict. Econ. Prod. v. 3, p. 16.—Flowers: Feb.-Mar. VERN. *Alai*.

KONKAN: *Dalzell & Gibson*; Matheran, *Kanitkar*!; hills about Nagotna, *Graham*. DECCAN: Khandala hills, *Dalzell & Gibson*, *Woodrow*.—DISTRIB. India generally.

This plant is often confounded with *D. confertiflora*, Benth., but may easily be distinguished by its monadelphous stamens. The latter does not appear to be a Bombay plant at all, the specimens from the Western Ghâts named thus by Dalzell being *D. volubilis*. *Vide* Prain, Journ. As. Soc. Beng. v. 66 (1898) p. 445 & p. 449.

56. PTEROCARPUS, Linn.

Erect unarmed trees. Leaves alternate, imparipinnate. Leaflets usually alternate, exstipellate. Flowers generally yellow, in axillary and terminal racemes or panicles; bracts and bracteoles small, caducous. Calyx turbinate, usually curved before expansion; teeth short. Corolla exserted, the petals with long claws, glabrous; standard orbicular or broadly ovate; keel-petals free or slightly cohering. Staminal-tube slit both above and below or above only, the vexillary stamen often nearly or quite free; anthers versatile. Ovary sessile or stalked; ovules 2–6; style filiform, slightly incurved; stigma small, terminal. Pod orbicular or broadly ovate, with a broad rigid wing, the point turned down to opposite the base or near it. Seed 1 (rarely 2), oblong or subreniform; radicle short, incurved.—DISTRIB. Cosmopolitan in the Tropics; species about 15.

1. **Pterocarpus Marsupium,** *Roxb. Cor. Pl.* v. 2 (1798) p. 9, t. 116. A large deciduous tree with a stout crooked stem and widely spreading branches; bark thick, yellowish-grey, the outer layer corky. Leaves 6–9 in. long; rhachis glabrous, prolonged $\frac{3}{4}$–1 in. beyond the insertion of the upper lateral leaflet. Leaflets 5–7, coriaceous, $2\frac{1}{2}$–4 by $1\frac{1}{2}$–2 in., oblong, obtuse, rounded, truncate or more or less retuse at the apex, glabrous on both surfaces, shining above, base subacute; main nerves numerous, close, prominent; petiolules $\frac{1}{4}$–$\frac{3}{8}$ in. long. Flowers in short lateral and terminal fusco-pubescent paniculate racemes, usually shorter than the leaves; pedicels short, articulated beneath the flower. Calyx $\frac{1}{4}$ in. long, veined, brown-pubescent; teeth very short, broadly triangular, the upper the largest. Corolla $\frac{1}{2}$ in. long, pale-yellow, with crisped margins; standard $\frac{7}{16}$ in. broad, with a long claw. Stamens monadelphous or the staminal-tube often finally slit on both sides making them isadelphous. Ovary shortly stalked; ovules 2. Pods 1–2 in. in diam., nearly circular, glabrous or nearly so, the wing veined. Seed small. Fl. B. I. v. 2, p. 239; Grah. Cat. p. 56; Dalz. & Gibs. p. 76; Benth. in Journ. Linn. Soc. v. 4 (1860) Suppl. p. 76; Trim. Fl. Ceyl. v. 2, p. 90; Talb. Trees, Bomb. p. 76; Woodr. in Journ. Bomb. Nat. v. 11 (1897) p. 426; Watt, Dict. Econ. Prod. v. 6, part 1, p. 357.—Flowers: May–June. VERN. *Bibla*.

KONKAN: *Dalzell & Gibson*, *Stocks*!; Ghorabandar, *Nairne*. GUJARAT: Dangs, *Dalzell & Gibson*; Rajpipla hills, *Graham*. KANARA: common in N. Kanara, *Talbot*; Yellapur, *Woodrow*.—DISTRIB. India (W. Peninsula and S. India); Ceylon.

The tree supplies the gum *Kino* of European pharmacy and the timber is hard and durable. It makes excellent sleepers for railway purposes. See Watt, Dict. Econ. Prod. l. c.

VAR. *acuminatus*, Prain, in Journ. As. Soc. Beng. v. 66 (1898) p. 455. Leaflets ovate, cuspidately acuminate; pods larger. *P. Wallichii* (sp.), Wight & Arn. Prodr. p. 267; *P. indicus*, Woodr. in Journ. Bomb. Nat. v. 11 (1897) p. 426 (*not* of Willd.).

This is apparently the variety alluded to by Bentham in Journ. Linn. Soc. v. 4 (1860) Suppl. p. 77. As Dr. Prain points out (*l. c.*), the true *Pterocarpus indicus* is not indigenous in Peninsular India.

KONKAN: *Stocks*!, *Law*! DECCAN: Kartris Ghát near Poona, *Woodrow*. KANARA: Yellapur, *Talbot* ex *Prain* (*l. c.*).—DISTRIB. India (Rajmahal hills, Rajputana).

57. PONGAMIA, Vent.

A tree. Leaves imparipinnate. Leaflets opposite, exstipellate. Flowers in axillary lax racemes; pedicels 2–4-nate along the rhachis; bracts very caducous; bracteoles minute or 0. Calyx campanulate, nearly truncate; teeth obsolete. Corolla much exserted; standard suborbicular; wings obliquely oblong, slightly adhering to the keel; keel obtuse, the petals cohering at the tip. Stamens monadelphous, the vexillary stamen free at the base, connate with the others in the middle; anthers versatile. Ovary subsessile; ovules 2; style filiform, incurved; stigma small, terminal. Pod woody, obliquely oblong, flattened, not winged at the sutures, indehiscent. Seed 1, reniform.—DISTRIB. Tropical Asia and Australia; species 1.

There is considerable diversity of opinion as to the name which should be borne by this genus. Adanson (Fam. Pl. p. 322) proposed the name *Pongam* (which is the Tamil name of the only species) in 1763. Lamarck (Encyc. Méthod. v. 2, p. 594) gave it the name of *Galedupa* in 1786. Roxburgh (Fl. Ind. v. 3, p. 239) and more recently Taubert (Engl. & Prantl, Pflanzenf.) adopted this name. Lamarck (Illustr. t. 603) transformed Adanson's name into *Pungamia* in 1797, which Ventenat in 1803 altered into *Pongamia*.

1. **Pongamia glabra,** *Vent. Jard. Malm.* (1803) p. 28. A tree reaching 40–60 ft. high; branches spreading, glabrous; bark soft, greyish-green. Leaves 5–9 in. long, pale-green; petioles $1\frac{1}{2}$–2 in. long; stipules small, oblong, obtuse, caducous. Leaflets opposite, 5–9 (usually 5), $2\frac{1}{4}$–5 by $1\frac{1}{2}$–3 in., ovate-oblong or elliptic, acute or (usually) shortly acuminate, glabrous, base acute or rounded; main nerves 6–8 pairs, prominent beneath; petiolules $\frac{1}{4}$ in. long. Flowers in short axillary racemes shorter than the leaves; pedicels $\frac{3}{16}$–$\frac{5}{16}$ in. long, in fascicles of 2–4 along a glabrous or puberulous rhachis; bracteoles ovate, acute, $\frac{1}{16}$ in. long. Calyx $\frac{1}{8}$ in. long, purplish, brown-pubescent, truncate or obscurely toothed. Corolla $\frac{1}{2}$ in. long, pinkish-white; standard suborbicular, $\frac{3}{8}$–$\frac{7}{16}$ in. broad, emarginate, appendiculate at the base, the claw very short. Pods $1\frac{1}{2}$–2 by $\frac{3}{4}$–1 in., about $\frac{1}{4}$ in. thick, oblong or slightly obovoid, compressed, narrowed at the base and with a short decurved mucro at the apex, glabrous. Fl. B. I. v. 2, p. 240; Grah. Cat. p. 55; Dalz. & Gibs. p. 77; Wight, Icon. t. 59; Trim. Fl. Ceyl. v. 2, p. 91; Talb. Trees, Bomb. p. 76; Woodr. in Journ. Bomb. Nat. v. 11 (1897) p. 426; Watt, Dict. Econ. Prod. v. 6, part 1, p. 322. *Galedupa indica*, Lamk. Encyc. v. 2 (1786) p. 594; Roxb. Fl. Ind. v. 3, p. 239.—Flowers: Apr.–June. VERN. *Karanj*.

Along the banks of rivers in the Konkan and Deccan not far from the sea-coast; often planted inland. KONKAN: widely planted, *Woodrow*! DECCAN: near rivers, *Gibson* ex *Graham*; along the valley of the Koina river, *Cooke*!; Mahableshwar (planted at the Terraces), *H. M. Birdwood*.—DISTRIB. India (banks of rivers and streams especially near the coast); throughout Tropical Asia and the Seychelles.

The seeds yield an oil which is employed as a remedy in skin-diseases. See Watt, Dict. Econ. Prod. l. c.

58. DERRIS, Lour.

Climbing shrubs (rarely erect trees). Leaves alternate, imparipinnate. Leaflets opposite, usually exstipellate. Flowers copious, showy, in axillary or terminal racemes or panicles; pedicels usually fascicled along the rhachis; bracts small, caducous; bracteoles ovate or orbicular, usually small and caducous. Calyx in flower usually cyathiform, truncate or obscurely toothed. Corolla much exserted; standard broad; keel obtuse, its petals slightly cohering. Stamens usually monadelphous; anthers versatile. Ovary sessile; ovules few; style incurved, filiform; stigma capitate. Pod rigid, thin, flat, indehiscent, obliquely orbicular, oblong or elongate, distinctly winged down the upper or both sutures.—DISTRIB. Tropics generally; chiefly in Tropical Asia; species about 40.

An older name for this genus is *Deguelia* which was given to it in 1775 (Aubl. Pl. Gui. v. 2 [1775] p. 750, t. 300). This name has been adopted by Taubert in Engl. & Prantl, Pflanzenfamilien. The name *Derris* dates from 1790 and was given to the genus by Loureiro (Fl. Cochinch. v. 2 [1790] p. 432).

An erect tree .... 1. *D. robusta*.
Climbing shrubs.
  Stamens monadelphous.
    Pod winged down the upper suture only.
      Pod not exceeding ½ in. broad .... 2. *D. scandens*.
      Pod exceeding ½ in. broad.
        Standard without callosities at the base of the limb ... 3. *D. uliginosa*.
        Standard with 2 callosities at the base of the limb ... 4. *D. oblonga*.
    Pod winged down both sutures.
      Standard without callosities at the base of the limb.
        Pod glabrous, polished .... 5. *D. Heyneana*.
        Pod persistently brown-silky .... 6. *D. brevipes*.
      Standard with 2 callosities at the base of the limb ...... 7. *D. canarensis*.
  Stamens diadelphous .... 8. *D. platyptera*.

1. **Derris robusta,** *Benth. in Journ. Linn. Soc.* v. 4 (1860) *Suppl.* p. 104. An erect tree 30–40 ft. high; young parts more or less pubescent; older branches glabrous, striate. Leaves 3–6 in. long; rhachis deeply channelled; petioles $\frac{1}{2}$–1 in. long. Leaflets 9–21, opposite, 1–1½ by ½ in. (the pair at the base of the leaf the smallest), elliptic-oblong or oblong-lanceolate, apiculate, glabrous above, pale and more or less pubescent beneath, closely reticulately veined, base acute or rounded; petiolules $\frac{1}{10}$–$\frac{1}{8}$ in. long. Flowers in elongate simple racemes usually shorter than or equalling (rarely longer than) the leaves; pedicels filiform, unequal, fascicled along a more or less pubescent rhachis; bracteoles beneath the calyx minute, oblong, obtuse. Calyx $\frac{1}{12}$–$\frac{1}{10}$ in. long; teeth minute, deltoid. Corolla $\frac{1}{3}$ in. long; standard $\frac{1}{4}$–$\frac{1}{3}$ in. broad; wings not ciliate above the claw. Stamens monadelphous. Ovary pubescent. Pods $\frac{1}{4}$–$\frac{5}{16}$ in. broad, when 1-seeded 1½ in. long, when more-seeded up to 3 in. long, tapering at both ends,

strap-shaped, narrowly winged on the upper suture, fuscous-pubescent. Seeds 1–8. Fl. B. I. v. 2, p. 241; Talb. Trees, Bomb. p. 76; Watt, Dict. Econ. Prod. v. 3, p. 81. *Brachypterum robustum*, Dalz. & Gibs. Bo. Fl. p. 77. *Dalbergia robusta*, Roxb. Hort. Beng. p. 53; Wight, Icon. t. 244.

Rare. KONKAN: *Stocks*!, *Dalzell*!

2. **Derris scandens,** *Benth. in. Journ. Linn. Soc.* v. 4 (1860) *Suppl.* p. 103. A very large climber often reaching 100 ft. in length; stems smooth, dark-purple; young parts pubescent. Leaves 3–6 in. long; rhachis deeply channelled, glabrous; stipules small, caducous. Leaflets opposite, 9–19, rigidly subcoriaceous, 1½–2 by ¾ in. (the lowest pair the smallest), elliptic-oblong or obovate-oblong, subacute or very shortly acuminate, often slightly emarginate, glabrous and shining above, more or less pubescent beneath, reticulately veined, base rounded or subacute; petiolules ⅛ in. long. Flowers numerous, in short-peduncled axillary racemes 10–18 in. long, arranged in fascicles from the nodes of a puberulous rhachis, the flowers from the same node expanding at different times; pedicels filiform, ⅛–¼ in. long; bracteoles beneath the calyx 2, orbicular, $\frac{1}{30}$ in. long, ciliolate. Calyx $\frac{1}{10}$–⅛ in. long, thinly grey-silky; teeth obscure. Corolla ⅜ in. long, white or pale pink; standard ¼ in. broad, the claw long; wings ciliate at the base above a long slender claw. Stamens monadelphous. Ovary pubescent. Pods 1–3 by ⅜–½ in., tapering to both ends, pointed, straight, narrowly winged on the upper suture, finely appressedly pubescent, somewhat turgid opposite the seeds. Seeds 1–4. Fl. B. I. v. 2, p. 240; Trim. Fl. Ceyl. v. 2, p. 91; Talb. Trees, Bomb. p. 76; Woodr. in Journ. Bomb. Nat. v. 11 (1897) p. 426; Watt, Dict. Econ. Prod. v. 3, p. 81. *Dalbergia scandens*, Roxb. Cor. Pl. v. 2, t. 192; Grah. Cat. p. 55. *Brachypterum scandens*, Benth. in Ann. Wien. Mus. v. 2 (1840) p. 101; Dalz. & Gibs. p. 76.—Flowers: June–Aug. VERN. *Mota-sirili*.

KONKAN: *Dalzell & Gibson*, *Stocks*!, *Capt. Geburne*!; Wassind, *Cooke*! DECCAN: Mawal districts, *Graham*. KANARA: Karwar, *Woodrow*; N. Kanara, from the sea-coast inland, nowhere common, *Talbot*.—DISTRIB. India (Bengal, C. India, Chittagong, Birma, W. Peninsula); Ceylon, S.E. Asia to N. Australia.

3. **Derris uliginosa,** *Benth. in Pl. Jungh.* (1851–55) p. 252. A large climber; branches glabrous; bark dark-grey, covered with scattered lenticels. Leaves 5–8 in. long; rhachis striate, glabrous. Leaflets 3–7 (usually 5), 2¼–4 by 1¼–2 in. (the terminal the largest), subcoriaceous, ovate or ovate-oblong, acute or acuminate, sometimes slightly emarginate, glabrous on both surfaces, highly polished on the upper, minutely reticulately veined, base rounded or cordate; petiolules ⅛–¼ in. long. Flowers in axillary racemes 3–6 in. long, the nodes of the rhachis produced into short stalks about ⅛ in. long, each bearing 1 or more subequal slender pedicels ⅙ in. long; bracts and bracteoles minute, ovate-oblong, subacute. Calyx $\frac{1}{10}$ in. long, glabrous or nearly so, with truncate or obscurely toothed ciliolate margin. Corolla ⅓ in. long, rose-colored; standard ½ in. broad (broader than long), reniform, emarginate, without callosities at the base. Stamens monadelphous. Ovary pubescent. Pods 1–1½ in. long, variable in shape, sometimes orbicular and as broad as long, or oblong and about ⅔ as broad as long, thin, flat, reticulately veined, shortly apiculate, glabrous, narrowly

winged on the upper suture, pale-yellow when ripe. Seed 1, reniform, compressed. Fl. B. I. v. 2, p. 241; Dalz. & Gibs. p. 77; Benth. in Journ. Linn. Soc. v. 4 (1860) Suppl. p. 107; Trim. Fl. Ceyl. v. 2, p. 92; Talb. Trees, Bomb. p. 76; Woodr. in Journ. Bomb. Nat. v. 11 (1897) p. 426. *Pongamia uliginosa*, DC. Prodr. v. 2, p. 416; Grah. Cat. p. 55. *Galedupa uliginosa*, Roxb. Hort. Beng. p. 53; Fl. Ind. v. 3, p. 243.—Flowers: Feb.–Mar. VERN. *Kajarvel.*

Found along the sea-coast and on the edge of muddy saltwater creeks. KONKAN: *Law*!, *Stocks*!, *Dalzell*!; Bombay on the verge of high-water mark, *Graham*; east side of Neat's tongue, Salsette, *Graham*; Mumbra (Tanna districts), *Raoji*!—DISTRIB. India (muddy sea-coasts and creeks of the W. Peninsula); Ceylon, China, N. Australia, Polynesia, Madagascar, Zambesi-land.

4. **Derris oblonga,** *Benth. in Journ. Linn. Soc.* v. 4 (1860) *Suppl.* p. 112. A woody climber; young parts puberulous; bark dark-grey, lenticellate. Leaves 4–8 in. long; rhachis glabrous, striate; petioles 1–2½ in. long; stipules ⅕ in. long, ovate, acute, densely pubescent. Leaflets 9–15, subcoriaceous, 1¼–2½ by ⅜–¾ in., oblong-lanceolate (the terminal often oblanceolate), subobtuse, often emarginate, glabrous on both surfaces, paler beneath, base acute; petiolules ⅛ in. long. Flowers in lateral short lax racemes 3–4 in. long, the nodes prolonged into stalks ¼ in. long, each bearing 2–3 filiform pubescent pedicels as long as, or slightly shorter than the stalks; bracts minute, ovate, acute, pubescent; bracteoles 2, a little below the base of the calyx, minute, ovate-oblong, subobtuse, silky-hairy. Calyx ⅛–⅙ in. long, silky-pubescent; teeth minute, triangular, the upper often wanting. Corolla ½ in. long, white tipped with pink, or entirely plain pink; standard ⅜ in. broad, oblong, emarginate, with 2 callosities at the base. Stamens monadelphous. Ovary pubescent. Pods 1½–2 by ¼–⅜, oblong, compressed, with a decurved point, narrowed at the base, winged on the upper suture, reticulately veined, glabrous. Seed 1. Fl. B. I. v. 2, p. 242; Talb. Trees, Bomb. p. 76; Woodr. in Journ. Bomb. Nat. v. 11 (1897) p. 426.

A rare plant. KONKAN: *Stocks*!

5. **Derris Heyneana,** *Benth. Pl. Jungh.* (1851–55) p. 252 (in adnot.). A woody climber; branches glabrous. Leaves 5–8 in. long; rhachis glabrous, striate; petioles 1–2½ in. long. Leaflets 5–7, subcoriaceous, 2–3½ by 1¼–2, elliptic-oblong or obovate-oblong, usually bluntly acuminate, reticulately veined, glabrous, base rounded or subacute; main nerves 6–8 pairs; petiolules ¼ in. long. Flowers in axillary panicles 6–15 in. long, arranged in alternate rather distant corymbs of 3–10 flowers, along a rufous-pubescent rhachis and its branches; pedicels slender, rufous-pubescent, usually longer than the calyx; bracteoles 2 on the pedicel a little below the calyx, alternate, about $\frac{1}{32}$ in. long, ovate-oblong, subacute. Calyx ⅛ in. long, clothed with reddish-brown pubescence, the mouth ciliate; teeth obscure. Corolla ⅛ in. long, pale pink; standard ¼ in. broad, suborbicular, emarginate, without callosities at the base. Stamens monadelphous. Ovary silky; ovules usually 4. Pods 2–4 by 1–1½ in. (including the wing), reticulately veined (when 1-seeded ovoid or obovoid, when 2–3-seeded strap-shaped), glabrous and polished, winged on both sutures, the wing of the upper suture ¼–⅜, that of the lower ⅛ in. broad. Fl. B. I. v. 2, p. 244; Dalz. & Gibs. p. 77; Benth. in Journ. Linn. Soc.

v. 4 (1860) Suppl. p. 110; Talb. Trees, Bomb. p. 77; Woodr. in Journ. Bomb. Nat. v. 11 (1897) p. 426.—Flowers: Dec.-Mar.

KONKAN: *Stocks*!, *Law*!, *Woodrow*. KANARA: moist forests of N. Kanara, *Talbot*; Ainshi Ghát, *Talbot*, 1223!—DISTRIB. India (W. Peninsula).

6. **Derris brevipes,** *Baker, in Hook. f. Fl. B. I.* v. 2 (1878) p. 244. A climber; branches glabrous, lenticellate. Leaves 6–8 in. long; rhachis glabrous; petioles 1–2 in. long. Leaflets 5–7, moderately firm, 2–3¼ by $\frac{7}{8}$–1½ in., elliptic-oblong or oblong-lanceolate (the terminal sometimes obovate-oblong), subacute or bluntly acuminate, quite glabrous on both surfaces, the upper surface shining; petiolules $\frac{1}{8}$–$\frac{3}{16}$ in. long. Flowers in copious fastigiate axillary and terminal panicles, in short few-flowered racemes along a densely rufous-pubescent rhachis; pedicels usually shorter than the calyx, densely rufous-pubescent; bracteoles 2, close beneath the calyx, minute, broadly ovate or suborbicular, obtuse, hairy. Calyx $\frac{1}{10}$–$\frac{1}{8}$ in. long, densely silky with rufous pubescence; teeth very short, broadly triangular. Corolla $\frac{7}{16}$ in. long; standard ⅓ in. broad, obovate-oblong, emarginate, without callosities at the base. Stamens monadelphous. Ovary silky. Pods broad, oblong, 1-seeded, 1¼–1½ by 1 in., persistently brown-silky, with a narrow wing down the upper and a very obscure one down the lower suture (*Baker*). Talb. Trees, Bomb. p. 76. *Derris Heyneana*, var. *brevipes*, Benth. in Journ. Linn. Soc. v. 4 (1860) Suppl. p. 110.—Flowers: Feb.

The description of the pod is that given by Mr. Baker in Fl. B. I. l. c. I have not seen the fruit. There is no fruiting specimen in Herb. Kew.

KONKAN: *Law*!, *Stocks*!; higher Ghâts of the Konkan, *Talbot*. KANARA: on the top of Dursing the highest peak of the N. Kanara Ghâts, 3400 ft. high, *Talbot*.—DISTRIB. India (Mysore, *fide* Baker l. c.)

7. **Derris canarensis,** *Baker, in Hook. f. Fl. B. I.* v. 2 (1878) p. 246. A scandent shrub. Leaves nearly 1 ft. long; rhachis channelled; stipules semiovate, broad, clothed with ferruginous hairs. Leaflets 15–21, oblong-lanceolate, 2–2½ by ½ in., glabrous above, strigose beneath; petiolules short. Flowers in terminal rusty-tomentose racemes shorter than the leaves, the nodes of the rhachis prolonged into short stalks, each bearing 3 pedicels of equal length with the stalks. Calyx bibracteolate, wide, cup-shaped, with a ring of hairs inside the mouth. Corolla pink; standard with 2 callosities at the base which run down the short claw. Stamens monadelphous. Ovary hirsute; ovules 2–3. Pods 1–1½ in. long, flat, elliptic, pointed at both ends and winged on both sides. Talb. Trees, Bomb. p. 77; Woodr. in Journ. Bomb. Nat. v. 11 (1897) p. 426. *Pongamia canarensis*, Dalz. in Hook. Kew Journ. v. 2 (1850) p. 37. *Brachypterum canarense*, Dalz. & Gibs. Bo. Fl. p. 76.—Flowers: Apr.-May.

The above description has been taken from those by Dalzell & Gibson in the works cited.

A rare plant. KANARA: Gairsoppa Falls, *Dalzell & Gibson*; along the Ghâts of N. Kanara from the Ainshi Ghât to the Mysore frontier in moist forests, locally common, *Talbot*.

There are no specimens of this plant in Herb. Kew. nor have I seen any. The description by Mr. Baker in Fl. B. I. was, as well as mine, taken from Dalzell's published ones. Dr. Prain says (Journ. As. Soc. Beng. v. 66 [1898] p. 462) that he is unable to separate the authentic specimens of *Brachypterum canarense*, Dalzell, from the Konkan specimens of Stocks referred by Bentham (Journ. Linn. Soc. v. 4 [1860] Suppl. p. 113) to *Derris oblonga*. It is not improbable, therefore, that *Derris oblonga* may belong to this species which is the older of the two.

8. **Derris platyptera,** *Baker, in Hook. f. Fl. B. I.* v. 2 (1878) p. 245. A robust climber; branches glabrous, lenticellate. Leaves 8–14 in. long; rhachis glabrous, striate. Leaflets 5-9, subcoriaceous, 3-5 by $1\frac{1}{4}$-$2\frac{1}{4}$ in., oblong or oblong-lanceolate, subacute or obtusely acuminate, reticulately veined, glabrous, base subacute or rounded; main nerves 5-8 pairs; petiolules $\frac{1}{4}$ in. long. Flowers in copious thyrsoid axillary and terminal panicles reaching 12 in. long, with numerous ascending silky branches; pedicels $\frac{1}{8}$-$\frac{1}{4}$ in. long, silky-hairy, closely arranged, but not fascicled, usually in opposite pairs along the branches of the panicle; bracts at the base of the pedicels $\frac{1}{10}$ in. long, broadly ovate, hairy, falling before the opening of the flower; bracteoles closely appressed to the base of the calyx, minute, not exceeding $\frac{1}{32}$ in. long, broadly ovate, acute, ciliate. Calyx $\frac{1}{8}$-$\frac{1}{6}$ in. long, silky; teeth obscure, or very short and broadly deltoid. Corolla $\frac{1}{3}$ in. long; standard $\frac{1}{3}$ in. broad, without callosities at the base, the claw short. Stamens diadelphous, the vexillary stamen quite free. Ovary pubescent; ovules 4. Pods 2-4 by $1\frac{1}{4}$-$1\frac{1}{2}$ in., oblong, acute at both ends, thin, flat, glabrous, reticulately veined, not sinuate between the seeds, distinctly winged along both sutures. *Derris thyrsiflora*, Talb. Trees, Bomb. p. 77 (*not* of Benth.). *D. Wallichii*, Prain, in Journ. As. Soc. Beng. v. 66 (1891) p. 99.—Flowers: Dec.

Mr. Baker (*l. c.*) places this plant in the section with monadelphous stamens, but these are unmistakably diadelphous. The distinct pedicels and short bracts place it under *D. Wallichii*, Prain, but the name *D. platyptera* has the claim of priority.

A rare plant. Kanara: on the Ghâts, *Talbot*; Gairsoppa Ghâts, *Talbot*, 268!—Distrib. India (Silhet, Khasia, Assam, Andamans, W. Peninsula).

59. SOPHORA, Linn.

Trees or shrubs (rarely perennial herbs). Leaves imparipinnate. Leaflets usually exstipellate. Flowers showy, in terminal racemes or panicles; bracts and bracteoles minute or 0. Calyx-teeth short. Corolla much exserted; standard broadly obovate or orbicular, usually shorter than the keel; wings oblong, oblique; keel oblong, obtuse, nearly straight, the petals cohering. Stamens free, or rarely subconnate at the base into a ring; anthers versatile. Ovary shortly stalked; ovules many; style incurved; stigma minute, terminal. Pod moniliform, woody or membranous, terete or slightly compressed, usually indehiscent; joints turgid. Seeds obovoid or globose, estrophiolate. —Distrib. Throughout the warmer regions of the globe; species about 22.

1. **Sophora Wightii,** *Baker, in Hook. f. Fl. B. I.* v. 2 (1878) p. 250. A shrub; young branches clothed with persistent velvety-brown pubescence. Leaves 6-8 in. long; rhachis brown-pubescent; stipules $\frac{1}{2}$ in. long, rigid, subulate. Leaflets 11-15, alternate, subcoriaceous, $1\frac{1}{2}$-3 by $\frac{1}{2}$-$\frac{7}{8}$ in. (those near the base of the rhachis the smaller), lanceolate, acuminate, green and glabrous above, softly

pubescent and glaucous beneath, reticulately veined; main nerves numerous, fine, branched towards the apex, the midrib prominent, fulvous-hairy; petiolules $\frac{1}{16}$ in. long. Flowers in leaf-opposed racemes about as long as the leaves; pedicels $\frac{1}{4}$–$\frac{1}{2}$ in. long, slender, brown-pubescent; bracts $\frac{1}{4}$ in. long, subulate. Calyx $\frac{1}{4}$–$\frac{5}{16}$ in. long, brown-velvety; mouth oblique, truncate or obscurely toothed. Corolla $\frac{5}{8}$ in. long, yellow; standard $\frac{1}{4}$ in. broad, narrowly oblong. Pods stalked, 3–4 in. long, indehiscent, deeply constricted between the seeds and with a long point at the apex, glabrous: joints ellipsoid-oblong, veined on the faces. Seeds bright-red, shining. Talb. Trees, Bomb. p. 77. *S. heptaphylla*, Wight, Icon. t. 1155 (*not* of Linn.); Dalz. & Gibs. p. 79.

Rare. KONKAN: *Stocks*! S. M. COUNTRY: near Belgaum, *Stocks*!; hills E. of Belgaum, *Dalzell*!—DISTRIB. India (hills of W. Peninsula and Mysore).

Sophora tomentosa, Linn., is often grown as an ornamental shrub in gardens throughout the Presidency. Leaflets 15–17, alternate or sometimes opposite, broadly elliptic. Corolla nearly 1 in. long, yellow. Pods 3–6 in. long, clothed with grey velvety down, 3–8-jointed. Fl. B. I. v. 2, p. 249; Grah. Cat. p. 44; Dalz. & Gibs. Suppl. p. 20; Woodr. in Journ. Bomb. Nat. v. 11 (1897) p. 426.

The following non-indigenous plants, not belonging to any of the foregoing genera of the Suborder, are cultivated (often largely) throughout the Bombay Presidency:—

Arachis hypogæa, Linn.; Fl. B. I. v. 2, p. 161. *The Ground-nut* or *Pea-nut.* A native of S. America, largely cultivated throughout India. After the flowers wither, the pod is forced underground by the plant and ripens beneath the soil; hence its specific name. The parched seeds are eaten and furnish a very valuable oil resembling olive-oil, for which it is used as a substitute. The pods are exported to Europe in considerable quantities. See Watt, Dict. Econ. Prod. v. 1, p. 282.—VERN. *Bhui-mug.*

Cajanus indicus, Spreng.; Fl. B. I. v. 2, p. 217. *The Pigeon* or *Cadjan pea*, known also as *Dhál.* This pulse is very largely grown and consumed throughout India. There are 2 varieties, one (*C. flavus*) with the standard wholly yellow and the other (*C. bicolor*) in which it is veined with red. Its native country is uncertain. DeCandolle considers it to be a native of Tropical Africa. The stalks are used for making charcoal for gunpowder. See Watt, Dict. Econ. Prod. v. 2, p. 12.—VERN. *Tur.*

Cicer arietinum, Linn.; Fl. B. I. v. 2, p. 176. *The Gram* or *Chick-pea.* Widely cultivated throughout India, where it is, in most Provinces, the chief food of horses. The parched seeds are largely eaten by the poorer natives. It should not be confounded with the horse-gram of Madras, which is the seed of *Dolichos biflorus.* An acid liquid is obtained by collecting the dew from the leaves (see Watt, Dict. Econ. Prod. v. 2, p. 274). The native country of the plant is uncertain. It is not improbable that it is indigenous in the south-east of Europe.—VERN. *Harbara*; *Chenna.*

Lens esculenta, Mœnch.; *Ervum Lens*, Linn. *The lentil*, widely cultivated throughout India, but not very largely in the Bombay Presidency, where it would not perhaps occupy in all 20,000 acres. Its native country is uncertain. DeCandolle says that it appears to have existed in W. Temperate Asia, Greece, and Italy from early prehistoric times. See Watt, Dict. Econ. Prod. v. 4, p. 621.—VERN. *Masur.*

Pachyrhizus angulatus, Rich.; Fl. B. I. v. 2, p. 207. *The Yam bean.* Occasionally, though not commonly, grown in gardens, for its tuberous root which is eaten boiled. It is not known in a wild state, but is cultivated more or less widely throughout the Tropics. See Watt, Dict. Econ. Prod. v. 6, part 1, p. 1.

Psophocarpus tetragonolobus, DC.; Fl. B. I. v. 2, p. 211; Woodr. Gard. in Ind. ed. 5, p. 267. *The Chevaux de frise bean.* A twining plant with square pods 6–9 in. long, with much crisped and toothed wings on the angles. The young fruit is sliced and boiled as a vegetable. —VERN. *Chaudhári*; *Ghevda.*

Pisum sativum, Linn.; Fl. B. I. v. 2, p. 181; Woodr. Gard. in Ind. ed. 5, p. 263. *The cultivated pea.* The white round-seeded variety is cultivated, but not largely, in Bombay as a field-crop. The garden varieties are grown, as a rule, only in the gardens of Europeans. In the Deccan, if sown after the first rain has fallen, they produce excellent crops of well-flavored peas. The native country of the cultivated pea is uncertain, but the species seems to have existed in W. Asia before it was cultivated. See Watt, Dict. Econ. Prod. v. 6, part 1, p. 277. —VERN. *Matár.*

Pisum arvense, Linn.; Fl. B. I. v. 2, p. 181. *The grey or field-pea.* This is also grown as a cold-weather field-crop, and the small marbled seeds used by the natives in the same way as *Dhál.* See Watt, Dict. Econ. Prod. v. 6, part 1, p. 276.

SUBORDER II. CÆSALPINEÆ.

Trees or shrubs, rarely herbs. Leaves 1–2 pinnate, simple or 3-foliolate, usually stipulate. Leaflets usually many; stipels 0, or very rarely present and very minute. Flowers various in size and color, irregular (rarely regular), usually hermaphrodite, racemose, rarely cymose, very rarely spicate, the racemes axillary, lateral, or panicled at the apices of the branches. Calyx usually 5-, sometimes 4-merous from the fusion of the 2 upper lobes, divided to the summit of the disk that lines the short or long calyx-tube, very rarely (some *Bauhinias*) gamosepalous; sepals imbricate, rarely valvate. Petals usually 5 (rarely fewer or 0), the upper innermost in bud, the others variously imbricate. Stamens 10 or fewer (very rarely ∞); filaments usually free, rarely coherent, more or less unequal; anthers various. Ovary free or supported on a stalk which is more or less adnate to the disk-bearing calyx-tube. Pod dehiscent or indehiscent, sometimes divided by many transverse septa. Seeds various; albumen copious, scanty, or 0; radicle straight or slightly oblique, hidden between the cotyledons or shortly exserted.

Leaves 2-pinnate.
  Flowers in racemes or panicles.
    Sepals imbricate.
      Pod not winged (except slightly in *C. sepiaria*)...... 60. CÆSALPINIA.
      Pod broadly winged along the upper suture .... 61. MEZONEURUM.
    Sepals valvate.
      Pod thin, flat .... 62. POINCIANA.
      Pod turgid, moniliform.. 63. PARKINSONIA.
  Flowers in elongate spikes .... 64. WAGATEA.
Leaves simply pinnate (sometimes 2-foliolate in *Cynometra*).
  Corolla with 5 perfect petals.
    Pod many-seeded; seeds albuminous .... 65. CASSIA.
    Pod 1-seeded; seeds exalbuminous .... 66. CYNOMETRA.
  Petals 0.
    Calyx-tube short; ovary sessile, 2-ovulate .... 67. HARDWICKIA.
    Calyx-tube elongate; ovary stalked, ∞-ovulate........... 68. SARACA.
  Petals 3 perfect, the other 3 reduced to scales .... 69. TAMARINDUS.
Leaves 1- (rarely by fission 2-) foliolate; seeds more than 1, albuminous.. 70. BAUHINIA.
Leaves 2 (or more) -foliolate; seed 1, exalbuminous .... 66. CYNOMETRA.

60. CÆSALPINIA, Linn.

Trees or climbing shrubs, unarmed or armed. Leaves large, abruptly-pinnate; stipules various. Flowers yellow or red, in axillary or terminal racemes or panicles. Calyx deeply cleft, with the disk confined to its base; segments 5, imbricate, the lowest concave or boat-shaped. Petals distinctly clawed, orbicular (rarely oblong), spreading, imbricate, subequal or the uppermost (the inner) smaller than the others. Stamens 10, free, declinate; filaments often villous or glandular at the base: anthers uniform, dehiscing longitudinally. Ovary sessile or subsessile; ovules few; style filiform, sometimes clavate at the apex; stigma terminal. Pod oblong or ligulate, flat or turgid, indehiscent or dehiscent, smooth or prickly.—DISTRIB. Tropics of both hemispheres; species about 40.

Pod armed on the face with wiry prickles .... 1. *C. Bonducella*.
Pod not armed with prickles.
  Leaflets 2–3 pairs.. 2. *C. Nuga*.
  Leaflets 8–20 pairs.
    Pod 3–8-seeded.
      A small tree .... 3. *C. Sappan*.
      A climbing shrub .... 4. *C. sepiaria*.
    Pod 2-seeded.. 5. *C. mimosoides*.

1. **Cæsalpinia Bonducella,** *Fleming, in Asiat. Res.* v. 11 (1810) p. 159. An extensive climber; branches finely grey-downy, armed with hooked and straight hard yellow prickles. Leaves 1–2 ft. long; petioles prickly; stipules a pair of reduced pinnæ at the base of the leaf each furnished with a long mucronate point; pinnæ 6–8 pairs, 2–3 in. long, with a pair of hooked stipulary spines at the base. Leaflets 6–9 pairs, $\frac{3}{4}$–$1\frac{1}{2}$ by $\frac{1}{2}$–$\frac{7}{8}$ in., membranous, elliptic-oblong, obtuse, strongly mucronate, glabrous above, more or less puberulous beneath; petiolules very short; stipels of short hooked spines. Flowers in dense (usually spicate) long-peduncled terminal and supra-axillary racemes dense at the top, lax downwards, 6–10 in. long; pedicels very short in bud, elongating to $\frac{1}{5}$ in. in flower and $\frac{1}{4}$ in. in fruit, brown-downy; bracts squarrose, linear, acute, reaching $\frac{3}{8}$ in. long, fulvous-hairy. Calyx $\frac{1}{4}$–

$\frac{1}{3}$ in. long, fulvous-hairy; lobes obovate-oblong, obtuse. Petals oblanceolate, yellow. Filaments declinate, flattened at the base, clothed with long white silky hairs. Pods shortly stalked, oblong, 2–3 by $1\frac{3}{4}$ in., densely armed on the faces with wiry prickles. Seeds 1–2, oblong, lead-colored, $\frac{1}{2}$ in. long. Fl. B. I. v. 2, p. 254; Talb. Trees, Bomb. ed. 2, p. 141; Woodr. in Journ. Bomb. Nat. v. 11 (1898) p. 426; Watt, Dict. Econ. Prod. v. 2, p. 3. *Guilandina Bonducella*, Linn. Sp. Pl. ed. 2, p. 545. *Guilandina Bonduc*, Wight & Arn. Prodr. p. 280 (in part); Grah. Cat. p. 60; Dalz. & Gibs. p. 79.—Flowers: July–Sept. VERN. *Ságargota*; *Gajá.*

Pretty common throughout the Presidency. Common in hedges, *Graham, Dalzell & Gibson.* DECCAN: hills, *Woodrow!*; Poona, *Woodrow!* KANARA: common in the forests near Karwar, *Talbot.* SIND: *Stocks*, 546!—DISTRIB. Throughout India; Tropics generally.

The seeds, known as *Fever-nuts* or *Physic-nuts*, have a high repute in native medicine as a bitter tonic. See Watt, Dict. Econ. Prod. l. c.

2. **Cæsalpinia Nuga,** *Ait. Hort. Kew.* ed. 2, v. 3 (1811) p. 32. An extensive climber; bark rough, yellowish-grey; branches glabrous, dark green, armed with hard sharp hooked blackish distant prickles. Leaves 6–12 in. long; main rhachis terete, glabrous, armed with distant hooked prickles; pinnæ 3–4 pairs, 2–3 in. long, with a pair of hooked prickles at the base of each. Leaflets 2–3 (often 3) pairs, 1–2 by $\frac{1}{2}$–1 in., ovate or elliptic, subacute, glabrous and shining above, dull beneath, base rounded or sometimes more or less cuneate; petioles $\frac{1}{8}$ in. long. Flowers in long-peduncled terminal racemes 10–15 in. long; pedicels $\frac{1}{4}$ in. long, elongating to $\frac{1}{2}$ in. in fruit, articulated above the middle, slender, glabrous. Calyx $\frac{1}{4}$–$\frac{3}{8}$ in. long, leathery, glabrous. Corolla $\frac{1}{2}$ in. across, yellow, fragrant. Stamens declinate; filaments woolly at the base. Pods 2–$2\frac{1}{4}$ by $1\frac{3}{8}$ in., obliquely oblong-ellipsoid, beaked, narrowed at the base into a short stalk, compressed, glabrous, subrugose. Seed 1, black, 1 by $1\frac{3}{4}$ in., rotund-ovoid, smooth. Fl. B. I. v. 2, p. 255; Trim. Fl. Ceyl. v. 2, p. 99; Talb. Trees, Bomb. ed. 2, p. 141; Woodr. in Journ. Bomb. Nat. v. 11 (1898) p. 426; Watt, Dict. Econ. Prod. v. 2, p. 10. *Cæsalpinia paniculata*, Roxb. Hort. Beng. (1814) p. 32; Grah. Cat. p. 60; Dalz. & Gibs. p. 79; Wight, Icon. t. 36.—Flowers: Jan.

A littoral species found on the banks of rivers near the coast. KONKAN: pretty common, *Dalzell & Gibson*; Ratnagiri, *Woodrow*; banks of the Savitri between Dasgaon and Mahar, *Graham.*—DISTRIB. India (Chittagong, Silhet, E. & W. Peninsulas); Ceylon, Malaya, Philippines, China, N. Australia, Polynesia.

3. **Cæsalpinia Sappan,** *Linn. Sp. Pl.* (1753) p. 381. A tree 20–30 ft. high; stem prickly, 6–10 in. in diam.; branches rufous-pubescent, armed with a few small prickles. Leaves 8–15 in. long; pinnæ 8–12 pairs, 4–6 in. long, subsessile, with small prickles at the base. Leaflets 10–18 pairs, $\frac{1}{2}$–$\frac{3}{4}$ by $\frac{3}{8}$ in., subsessile, close, oblong, rounded at the apex, attached at the lowest corner, very inequilateral (the upper side much the largest), glabrous above, more or less puberulous beneath. Flowers in panicles, which are terminal and in the axils of the upper leaves, 12–16 in. long; pedicels $\frac{1}{2}$–$\frac{5}{8}$ in. long; bracts lanceolate, $\frac{1}{3}$ in. long, caducous. Calyx $\frac{7}{16}$ in. long, leathery, glabrous. Corolla $\frac{3}{4}$ in. across; petals orbicular, subequal, yellow, the upper with

a red spot at the base. Stamens declinate, waxy-white; filaments densely woolly at the base. Ovary grey-velvety. Pods 3–4 by $1\frac{1}{2}$–2 in., woody, obliquely oblong, subcompressed, polished, indehiscent, with a hard recurved short beak at the upper angle of the obtuse apex. Seeds 3–4. Fl. B. I. v. 2, p. 255; Grah. Cat. p. 60; Bedd. For. Man. in Flor. Sylvat. p. xc, t. 13, fig. 1; Woodr. in Journ. Bomb. Nat. v. 11 (1898) p. 426; Watt, Dict. Econ. Prod. v. 2, p. 10.—Flowers: Sept.-Oct. VERN. *Patang.*

A doubtful native in the Bombay Presidency; often planted in gardens in Bombay and the Deccan. DECCAN: Poona (planted), *Woodrow*; Kolhapur (cultivated), *Ritchie*, 1689!—DISTRIB. India (E. & W. Peninsulas, Pegu); Malaya.

The wood yields a valuable red dye which is largely exported and which is used in Pegu for dyeing silk, and in Madras for dyeing straw-plait for hat-making. See Watt, Dict. Econ. Prod. l. c.

4. **Cæsalpinia sepiaria,** *Roxb. Hort. Beng.* (1814) p. 32. A climbing shrub; stem stout, woody, and, as well as the finely downy branches, armed with strong sharp yellowish hooked prickles. Leaves 9–15 in. long; main rhachis prickly; stipules $\frac{1}{2}$ by $\frac{1}{3}$ in., obliquely ovate, with crisped margins, acuminate, auricled at the lower angle of the base, deciduous; pinnæ 5–10 pairs, subequal, 2–3 in. long, with a slender pubescent rhachis. Leaflets subsessile, 8–12 pairs, $\frac{1}{2}$–$\frac{3}{4}$ by $\frac{3}{16}$–$\frac{6}{16}$ in., oblong, rounded at the apex, pale green, glabrous or faintly puberulous above, glaucous and slightly pubescent beneath, base rounded, a little oblique. Flowers in simple terminal and axillary racemes 6–12 in. long; pedicels $\frac{1}{2}$–$\frac{3}{4}$ in. long, densely pubescent, articulate near the flower; bracts $\frac{3}{8}$ in. long, ovate-lanceolate, densely pubescent, caducous. Calyx $\frac{3}{8}$–$\frac{1}{2}$ in. long, densely pubescent; the upper sepals oblong, very obtuse, pubescent on both sides. Corolla $\frac{1}{2}$–$\frac{7}{8}$ in. across; petals suborbicular, bright yellow, the lower about $\frac{1}{2}$ in., the upper $\frac{1}{4}$ in. in diam. Stamens declinate; filaments densely woolly in the lower half. Pods 3–$4\frac{1}{2}$ by 1–$1\frac{1}{8}$ in., straight or slightly recurved, linear-oblong, with a long beak, not stalked, somewhat turgid, reticulately veined, especially on the lower half, narrowly winged, the faces depressed between the seeds. Seeds 6–8, greenish, mottled. Fl. B. I. v. 2, p. 256; Grah. Cat. p. 61; Dalz. & Gibs. p. 80; Wight, Icon. t. 37; Trim. Fl. Ceyl. v. 2, p. 100; Talb. Trees, Bomb. ed. 2, p. 141; Woodr. in Journ. Bomb. Nat. v. 11 (1898) p. 426; Watt, Dict. Econ. Prod. v. 2, p. 12.—Flowers: Feb.-May. VERN. *Chilhar.*

Common, often used in the Deccan as a fence, which is quite impenetrable to men and cattle. It is sometimes called the *Mysore Thorn.* KONKAN: *Stocks*! DECCAN: plentiful, *Dalzell & Gibson*; along the roadside near Wai, *Cooke*! S. M. COUNTRY: very common, *Talbot.*—DISTRIB. Throughout India; Ceylon, Malaya, China, Japan.

5. **Cæsalpinia mimosoides,** *Lamk. Encyc. Méthod.* v. 1 (1783) p. 462. A climbing shrub; stem and branches armed with short sharp usually straight prickles; young parts colored, armed with prickles and stiff bristles from glandular bases. Leaves 1–2 ft. long; main rhachis reddish, armed with distant curved prickles; stipules $\frac{3}{8}$ in. long, linear, acute, ciliate; pinnæ 10–30 pairs 2–3 in. long, the secondary rhachis slender, reddish. Leaflets subsessile, membranous, sensitive, 10–20 pairs, $\frac{1}{4}$–$\frac{3}{8}$ by $\frac{1}{8}$ in., linear-oblong, inequilateral, rounded at both ends, apiculate at the apex, glabrous above, glaucous beneath, the margins

usually colored. Flowers in terminal and leaf-opposed racemes 12–30 in. long; rhachis densely clothed with straight prickles and minute hairs rising from hard glandular bases; pedicels $\frac{3}{4}$–1 in. long, covered with minute hairs from hard glandular bases, intermixed with a few slender eglandular bristles. Calyx reddish, $\frac{3}{8}$ in. long; tube clothed with minute hairs fascicled from glandular bases; lobes obtuse, downy and gland-dotted. Corolla $\frac{7}{8}$–1 in. across, yellow, dotted with black glands. Filaments flattened at the base, the lower half densely ciliate with white woolly hairs. Pods $1\frac{1}{2}$–2 in. long, oblong-obovoid, more turgid than in any other species, $\frac{1}{2}$ in. thick, narrowed to the base, obliquely truncate and with a short recurved beak at the apex, clothed with minute bristles, finally glabrescent, the sutures not thickened. Seeds 2. Fl. B. I. v. 2, p. 256; Grah. Cat. p. 60 & p. 248; Dalz. & Gibs. p. 80; Wight, Icon. t. 392; Talb. Trees, Bomb. ed. 2, p. 141; Woodr. in Journ. Bomb. Nat. v. 11 (1898) p. 426.—Flowers: Oct.–Jan.

KONKAN: *Stocks*!; Wari country, plentiful, *Dalzell & Gibson*; Mahim woods (Bombay), *Graham*. S. M. COUNTRY: Castlerock, *Woodrow*; Belgaum, *Ritchie*, 253!; Ramghát, *Ritchie*, 253! KANARA: moist forests, *Talbot*; Kála naddi, *Ritchie*, 253! —DISTRIB. India (Birma, W. Peninsula).

Cæsalpinia pulcherrima, Swartz, Obs. p. 166. A glabrous shrub or small tree unarmed or with a few weak prickles, cultivated in gardens in the Bombay Presidency and generally throughout India. Leaves 4–6 in. long; pinnæ 6–8 pairs. Leaflets 8–12 pairs. Corolla $1\frac{1}{2}$ in. across, yellow or red. Filaments very long, bright red. Pods 2–3 by $\frac{3}{4}$ in., narrower and thinner than those of any of the genus.—Its native country is uncertain. It is not apparently wild in S.E. Asia, and may have come from America. Fl. B. I. v. 2, p. 255; Woodr. in Journ. Bomb. Nat. v. 11 (1898) p. 426; Watt, Dict. Econ. Prod. v. 2, p. 10. *Poinciana pulcherrima*, Linn. Sp. Pl. p. 380; Grah. Cat. p. 61; Dalz. & Gibs. Suppl. p. 27.—Flowers more or less throughout the year. VERN. *Sankásur*.

Cæsalpinia coriaria, Willd. *The American Sumach*. A small tree, native of S. America, which has been introduced and is rapidly becoming established in Southern India. It is cultivated in Poona, Dharwar, Belgaum, and Kanara. The sinuous pods contain a large quantity of tannin, but owing to the oil contained in the seeds discoloring the leather during the tanning process, it is necessary that these should be removed before exportation. Woodr. in Journ. Bomb. Nat. v. 11 (1898) p. 426; Watt, Dict. Econ. Prod. v. 2, p. 6.—Flowers: Oct. VERN. *Libi-dibi*. For a full account of the tanning power of the pods &c. consult Watt, Dict. Econ. Prod. l. c.

61. MEZONEURUM, Desf.

Scandent usually prickly shrubs (rarely trees). Leaves abruptly 2-pinnate; stipules small or inconspicuous. Flowers in ample panicled racemes; bracts narrow, rarely persistent; bracteoles 0. Calyx very oblique; tube short; segments 5, imbricate, the lowest the longest, covering the others in bud like a hood. Petals 5, subequal or the upper the shortest, obovate or orbicular, imbricate. Stamens 10, free, declinate, usually exserted; anthers uniform. Ovary sessile or shortly stalked; ovules few or many; style filiform; stigma small, capitate. Pod oblong, flat, thin, indehiscent, broadly winged along the upper suture. Seeds transverse, compressed, orbicular or reniform; cotyledons flat; radicle short, straight.—DISTRIB. Tropics of the eastern hemisphere; species 15.

1. **Mezoneurum cucullatum,** *Wight & Arn. Prodr.* (1834) p. 283. A large climber; branches glabrous, armed with small dark sharp recurved prickles. Leaves 6–12 in. long; pinnæ 2–5 pairs, 5–8 in. long, the rhachis slender, armed with small recurved prickles. Leaflets 4–5 pairs, 2–3½ by 1–1½ in., opposite or less commonly alternate, ovate, acute, glabrous, dark green and shining above, paler beneath, base rounded, slightly oblique; petiolules stout, ⅛–¼ in. long. Flowers in terminal and axillary panicles of simple or sometimes branched rigid racemes; main rhachis terete, glabrous; pedicels ¼–⅓ in. long, slender, jointed above the middle. Calyx ½ in. long, yellow, deeply cleft, glabrous, leathery, the lowest sepal cucullate, obtuse, ⅓ in. long, the other sepals smaller, oblong, rounded at the apex; the tube shallow. Corolla nearly ½ in. across, greenish-yellow, the upper petal 2-lobed, shorter but wider than the others. Stamens much exserted; filaments pubescent at the base. Ovary shortly stalked; ovules 1–2. Pods thin, 3–3½ by 1¼ in. (excluding the wing which is ¼–⅜ in. broad), glabrous, faintly reticulately veined. Seed 1 (rarely 2) in the middle of the pod. Fl. B. I. v. 2, p. 258; Grah. Cat. p. 61; Dalz & Gibs. p. 80; Talb. Trees, Bomb. ed. 2, p. 142; Woodr. in Journ. Bomb. Nat. v. 11 (1898) p. 427.—Flowers: Dec.–Mar. VERN. *Rági.*

KONKAN: *Stocks*!; higher Gháts, common, *Dalzell & Gibson*; moist evergreen forests, *Talbot*; Matheran, *Cooke*! DECCAN: Lanoli, *Woodrow, Graham*; Khandala, *Graham*; ravines about Pár, *Graham*. KANARA: abundant in evergreen forests in the extreme south of N. Konkan, *Talbot*.—DISTRIB. India (E. Himalayas, Behar, W. Peninsula); Indo-China, Malaya.

62. POINCIANA, Linn.

Unarmed trees. Leaves 2-pinnate; stipules inconspicuous. Leaflets numerous, small, exstipellate. Flowers handsome, in corymbose racemes; bracts small, very caducous; bracteoles 0. Calyx deeply cleft; tube short; segments valvate, subequal. Petals 5, orbicular, imbricate, subequal, the blade crisply fimbriate. Stamens 10, free, declinate, much exserted; filaments villous at the base; anthers uniform. Ovary subsessile; ovules many; style filiform or abbreviated, slightly clavate at the apex; stigma truncate, ciliolate. Pod elongate, flat, thin, dehiscent, the sutures neither thickened nor winged. Seeds transverse, oblong, albuminous; cotyledons rather thick; radicle short, straight, exserted. —DISTRIB. Tropical Asia and Africa; species 3.

1. **Poinciana elata,** *Linn. Cent. Pl.* ii. (1756) p. 16; *Amœn. Acad.* v. 4, p. 313. An erect tree, 20–30 ft. high; bark tolerably smooth, ash-colored. Leaves abruptly 2-pinnate, 4–8 in. long; main rhachis slender; pinnæ 4–8 pairs, opposite. Leaflets 10–20 pairs, subsessile, ⅜ by ⅛ in., closely set along the rhachis, linear-oblong, rounded and usually

apiculate at the apex, glabrous, caducous. Flowers in terminal few-flowered corymbiform racemes; pedicels stout, finely pubescent. Calyx ¾–1 in. long, coriaceous, silky-pubescent outside; segments linear-oblong, acute. Petals suborbicular, yellow, scarcely exserted, the upper a little smaller and of a deeper color than the others, the margins of all much curled. Filaments often 2½ in. long, villous and thickened at the base. Pods 5–7 by ¾–1¼ in., attenuated at both ends, reticulately veined, glabrous. Seeds 4–8. Fl. B. I. v. 2, p. 260; Grah. Cat. p. 61; Dalz. & Gibs. Suppl. p. 28; Bedd. Flor. Sylvat. t. 178; Brandis, For. Fl. p. 157; Talb. Trees, Bomb. ed. 2, p. 142; Woodr. in Journ. Bomb. Nat. v. 11 (1898) p. 427; Watt, Dict. Econ. Prod. v. 6, part 1, p. 309.—Flowers: June–Sept.

Doubtfully wild in the Bombay Presidency, but often planted in gardens and along roadsides. Common in Poona and in Bijapur near Mahomedan tombs. *Dalzell* (l. c.) considers it to have come from Abyssinia. *Brandis* (l. c.) says that it is indigenous in the forests as far north as Gujarat.

Poinciana regia, Bojer, ex Bot. Mag. (1829) t. 2884. *The Royal Gul-Mohor*, a native of Madagascar, has within the last 80 years been introduced into and is now grown everywhere in gardens in the Bombay Presidency, and more or less throughout India. The young leaves are exceedingly beautiful, reaching 2 ft. in length, with 11–18 pairs of pinnæ. Flowers bright scarlet, in terminal and axillary lax racemes. Fl. B. I. v. 2, p. 260; Dalz. & Gibs. Suppl. p. 27; Talb. Trees, Bomb. ed. 2, p. 142; Woodr. in Journ. Bomb. Nat. v. 11 (1898) p. 427; Watt, Dict. Econ. Prod. v. 6, part 1, p. 309.—Flowers: Apr.–June. VERN. *Gul-Mohor.*

63. PARKINSONIA, Linn.

Trees. Leaves at first sight apparently simply pinnate and fascicled, but in reality 2-pinnate from a very short rhachis; stipules usually short, spinescent; pinnæ 2–6, very long, flattened. Leaflets numerous, very small. Flowers in short axillary lax racemes; bracts small, very caducous; bracteoles 0. Calyx deeply cleft; tube short; segments 5, membranous, slightly unequal, narrowly imbricate or subvalvate. Petals 5, spreading, somewhat unequal, the upper the broadest. Stamens 10, free; filaments villous at the base; anthers uniform, versatile. Ovary shortly stalked; ovules many; style filiform; stigma small, terminal. Pod turgid, moniliform, finally dehiscent.—DISTRIB. Species 3, of which 2 are American, the other a native of the Cape.

1. **Parkinsonia aculeata,** *Linn. Sp. Pl.* (1753) p. 375. A glabrous bush or small tree armed with sharp woody spines which represent the rhachises of the 2-pinnate leaves. Pinnæ 1–3 pairs, 6–12 in. long, the rhachis much flattened, striate. Leaflets numerous, minute, oblanceolate, obtuse; petiolules distinct, short. Flowers in lax axillary racemes shorter than the leaves; pedicels ⅜–⅝ in. long, slender, jointed near the top, erecto-patent. Calyx ¼ in. long, divided nearly to the base; segments oblong, obtuse. Corolla yellow; petals ⅜–¾ in. long, broadly obovate or suborbicular, with a short stout villous claw, veined. Filaments flattened and densely villous at the base. Ovary silky-villous; ovules many.

Pods 3–4 by $\frac{1}{4}$–$\frac{3}{8}$ in., moniliform, attenuated at both ends, finely veined, glabrous. Seeds 1–6. Fl. B. I. v. 2, p. 260; Grah. Cat. p. 61; Dalz. & Gibs. Suppl. p. 28; Bedd. For. Man. in Flor. Sylvat. p. 91 & Anal. Gen. t. 13, fig. 2; Talb. Trees, Bomb. ed. 2, p. 142; Woodr. in Journ. Bomb. Nat. v. 11 (1898) p. 427; Watt, Dict. Econ. Prod. v. 6, part 1, p. 110.—Flowers: Jan.–Mar. VERN. *Vedi-bábhal*; *Viláyati-kikar.*

A native of Tropical America, often grown as a hedge plant, almost naturalized in the Bombay Presidency and more or less so throughout India.

64. **WAGATEA,** Dalz.

A climbing shrub armed with scattered prickles. Leaves abruptly 2-pinnate; stipules inconspicuous. Flowers subsessile, in long simple or panicled spicate racemes. Calyx-tube campanulate; calyx-segments about as long as the tube, slightly imbricate, the lower concave, slightly larger than the others. Petals 5, subequal, oblong, erect, imbricate, not spreading in æstivation. Stamens 10, free, slightly declinate; filaments short, pilose at the base; anthers uniform. Ovary subsessile, free; ovules many; style slightly clavate at the apex; stigma oblique. Pod ligulate-oblong, indehiscent, few-seeded, subtorulose, with thickened sutures (not winged).—DISTRIB. Western Peninsula of India; species 1.

1. **Wagatea spicata,** *Dalz. in Kew Journ. Bot.* v. 3 (1851) p. 89. A robust woody climber; branches armed with numerous recurved prickles. Leaves 2-pinnate, 9–12 in. long; main rhachis armed with recurved prickles; pinnæ 4–6 pairs, 3–5 in. long, the rhachis terete, puberulous. Leaflets 5–7 pairs, 1–1$\frac{3}{4}$ by $\frac{1}{2}$–$\frac{7}{8}$ in., coriaceous, oblong, obtuse or subacute, dark green, glabrous and shining above, paler beneath, base rounded or cordate; petiolules very short. Flowers nearly sessile, in dense spicate racemes sometimes reaching 2 ft. long; rhachis stout, more or less grooved, clothed with soft brown pubescence, often armed with recurved prickles. Calyx densely puberulous, $\frac{7}{16}$–$\frac{1}{2}$ in. long, scarlet; segments oblong or subspathulate, obtuse, equalling the campanulate tube. Petals $\frac{3}{8}$–$\frac{1}{2}$ in. long, inserted on the top of the calyx-tube, obovate-spathulate, reticulately veined, dark orange. Stamens equalling the petals, alternately long and short; filaments flattened and densely pilose at the base. Ovary densely pubescent; ovules 4–6; style as long as the filaments and the petals; stigma 2-lobed, oblique. Pods 1$\frac{1}{2}$–2$\frac{1}{2}$ by $\frac{1}{2}$–$\frac{5}{8}$ in., linear-oblong, swollen above the seeds and constricted between them, and with thickened sutures. Seeds 3–4, obovate-oblong, transverse; testa hard, thick, bony. Fl. B. I. v. 2, p. 261; Dalz. & Gibs. p. 80; Wight, Icon. t. 1995; Talb. Trees, Bomb. ed. 2, p. 143; Woodr. in Journ. Bomb. Nat. v. 11 (1898) p. 427; Watt, Dict. Econ. Prod. v. 6, part 4, p. 297. *Cæsalpinia digyna*, Grah. Cat. p. 60.—Flowers: Jan.–Feb. VERN. *Vágáti*; *Vákeri.*

KONKAN: Konkan jungles, *Dalzell & Gibson*; south of Panwell, *Dalzell*!; Bombay, *Capt. Geburne*!; pretty common on the Ghâts, *Graham*. DECCAN: Ghât near Wada below Mahableshwar, *Cooke*! KANARA: *Stocks*!—DISTRIB. Hills of the Western Peninsula.

65. CASSIA, Linn.

Trees, shrubs, or herbs. Leaves abruptly-pinnate; rhachis often furnished with glands either between the leaflets or on the petiole below them; stipules various. Flowers usually yellow, in axillary or terminal racemes or in terminal panicles, or subsolitary axillary; bracts and bracteoles various. Calyx deeply divided; tube very short; segments 5, imbricate. Petals 5, imbricate, subequal or the lower the largest. Stamens normally 10, all perfect and subequal or the upper the smaller, or 3–5 imperfect or altogether absent; anthers uniform or those of the lower stamens the larger, dehiscing by terminal pores or by a short slit. Ovary sessile or stalked, free, at the bottom of the calyx; ovules many; style short or elongate; stigma terminal. Pod variable, terete or flat, usually septate between the seeds, dehiscent or indehiscent. Seeds transverse (rarely longitudinal), horizontally or vertically compressed, albuminous.—DISTRIB. Throughout the Tropics; a few extra-tropical; species 340.

Pod 1–2 ft. long, terete .... 1. *C. Fistula.*
Pod less than 1 ft. long, more or less flattened.
  Fertile stamens 7 (sometimes 7–10 in *C. nigricans*), the others reduced to staminodes.
    Gland of the leaf-rhachis solitary, inserted beneath (not between) the leaflets.
      Leaflets 3–5 pairs .... 2. *C. occidentalis.*
      Leaflets 6–10 pairs; gland conspicuous, conical. 3. *C. Sophera.*
      Leaflets 8–18 pairs; gland obscure, flat, sessile... 4. *C. nigricans* (in part).
    Glands inserted between 1 or more pairs of leaflets.
      Leaflets 3 pairs.
        Gland between each of the 2 lowest pairs of leaflets; plant fetid .... 5. *C. Tora.*
        Gland between the lowest pair of leaflets only; plant not fetid .... 6. *C. obtusifolia.*
      Leaflets 8–12 pairs .... 7. *C. auriculata.*
    Glands of the leaf-rhachis 0.
      Pod not above 2 in. long.
        Pod with a longitudinal crest down the middle over the seeds .... 8. *C. obtusa.*
        Pod not crested over the seeds .... 9. *C. holosericea.*
      Pod 3–6 in. long.
        Stipules minute, caducous .... 10. *C. montana.*
        Stipules large, foliaceous, subpersistent .... 11. *C. timoriensis.*
  Fertile stamens 5; staminodes 0.
    Leaflets 2 pairs .... 12. *C. Absus.*
    Leaflets 10–20 pairs .... 13. *C. pumila.*
  Fertile stamens 10 (1–3 sometimes reduced to staminodes in *C. nigricans*).
    Gland solitary, inserted beneath the leaflets, stalked, peltate; leaflets 8–20 pairs .... 14. *C. Kleinii.*
    Gland inserted between each of the 2–3 lowest pairs of leaflets; leaflets 4–6 pairs .... 15. *C. glauca.*
    Gland solitary, inserted beneath the leaflets, flat, sessile.
      Leaflets 40–60 pairs .... 16. *C. mimosoides.*
      Leaflets 8–18 pairs .... 4. *C. nigricans* (in part).

1. **Cassia Fistula,** *Linn. Sp. Pl.* (1753) p. 377. A tree 20–30 ft. high; trunk straight; bark smooth and pale-grey when young, rough and dark-brown when old; branches spreading, slender. Leaves 9–16 in. long; main rhachis pubescent; stipules minute, linear-oblong, obtuse,

pubescent. Leaflets 4–8 pairs, ovate or ovate-oblong, acute, 2–5 by 1½–3¾ in., bright green and glabrous above, paler and silvery-pubescent beneath when young, the midrib densely pubescent on the underside, base cuneate; main nerves numerous, close, conspicuous beneath; petiolules ¼–⅜ in. long, pubescent or glabrous. Flowers in lax racemes 12–20 in. long; pedicels 1½–2¼ in. long, slender, pubescent or glabrous. Calyx ⅜ in. long, divided to the base, pubescent; segments oblong, obtuse. Corolla 1½ in. across, yellow; petals 5, subequal, obovate, shortly clawed, veined. Stamens all antheriferous, the 3 lowest the longest with very long curved filaments and oblong anthers dehiscing longitudinally, the 4 lateral with short straight filaments and versatile anthers opening by pores at the base, the remaining 3 much smaller, erect with indehiscent anthers. Pods 1–2 ft. long, ¾–1 in. in diam., pendulous, cylindric, nearly straight, smooth, shining, brown-black, not torulose, indehiscent, with numerous (40–100) horizontal seeds immersed in a dark-colored sweetish pulp, and completely separated by transverse dissepiments. Seeds broadly ovate, ⅓ in. long, slightly less in breadth, and ⅙ in. thick. Fl. B. I. v. 2, p. 261; Grah. Cat. p. 62; Dalz. & Gibs. p. 80; Trim. Fl. Ceyl. v. 2, p. 103; Talb. Trees, Bomb. ed. 2, p. 143; Woodr. in Journ. Bomb. Nat. v. 11 (1898) p. 427; Watt, Dict. Econ. Prod. v. 2, p. 217. *Cassia rhombifolia*, Roxb. Hort. Beng. p. 31; Wight, Icon. t. 269.—Flowers: Mar.–May. VERN. *Bává*; *Garmál*; *Chimkáni* (Sind).

Common throughout the Presidency in deciduous forests. KONKAN: *Stocks*!; Ghâts and hilly parts, *Graham*. DECCAN: hills about Poona, *Cooke*!, *Woodrow*!; Deccan hills, *Woodrow*.—DISTRIB. Throughout India; Ceylon, Malaya, China.

The tree is known to Anglo-Indians as the *Indian Laburnum*. The pulp of the fruit furnishes an excellent and safe purgative. The wood is also hard and durable but is not of sufficient size for timber. See Watt, Dict. Econ. Prod. l. c.

2. **Cassia occidentalis,** *Linn. Sp. Pl.* (1753) p. 377. A diffuse (usually annual) undershrub 2–5 ft. high; branches subglabrous, furrowed, often purplish. Leaves very fetid when bruised, 6–8 in. long; rhachis glabrous, with a single sessile gland near its base. Leaflets 3–5 pairs, 1–4 by ½–1½ in., membranous, glaucous, ovate-lanceolate, gradually attenuated to a very acute apex, glabrous above, glabrous or finely pubescent beneath, base usually rounded and somewhat oblique; petiolules very short. Flowers in short-peduncled few-flowered racemes, corymbose, axillary and forming a terminal panicle; pedicels spreading, ⅕ in. long, elongating to ½ in. in fruit; bracts ½ in. long, ovate, acuminate, caducous, white with a pink tinge. Calyx ⅜ in. long, divided to the base, glabrous; segments white, slightly tinged with pink, oblong, obtuse, membranous. Petals 5, subequal, ½ in. long, ovate-oblong, obtuse, yellow, faintly veined with orange. Stamens 10, of which the 3 upper are reduced to staminodes, the anthers of the remaining 7 perfect, the 3 lower longer and with larger anthers than the 4 lateral ones. Pods 4–5 by ⅓ in. and about ⅙ in. thick, recurved, glabrous, compressed, transversely septate, distinctly torulose. Seeds 20–30, ovoid, compressed, acute at one end and rounded at the other, ¼ in. long by ⅙ in. broad, hard, smooth, shining, dark olive-green. Fl. B. I. v. 2, p. 262; Grah. Cat. p. 63; Dalz. & Gibs. p. 81; Benth. in Trans. Linn. Soc. v. 27 (1871) p. 532; Trim. Fl. Ceyl. v. 2, p. 105; Woodr. in Journ. Bomb. Nat. v. 11 (1898) p. 427; Watt, Dict. Econ. Prod. v. 2, p. 221.—Flowers: Jan.–Mar. VERN. *Rán-táklá*: *Kasivdá*.

Abundant throughout the Presidency in the rains, especially among rubbish near villages.—DISTRIB. Throughout India and the Tropics generally.

The leaves, roots, and seeds are used medicinally, the latter also in Africa as a substitute for coffee. See Watt, Dict. Econ. Prod. l. c.

3. **Cassia Sophera,** *Linn. Sp. Pl.* (1753) p. 379. A shrub or undershrub 8–10 ft. high, annual or perennial. Leaves 7–9 in. long; rhachis grooved, glabrous or nearly so, with a solitary conical gland near the base. Leaflets 6–10 pairs $1\frac{1}{2}$–$2\frac{1}{2}$ by $\frac{1}{2}$–$\frac{3}{4}$ in., opposite, membranous, glaucous, lanceolate, acute or acuminate, glabrous, base usually rounded; main nerves 10–12 pairs; petiolules $\frac{1}{16}$–$\frac{1}{12}$ in. long, glabrous. Flowers in axillary, short, few-flowered, corymbose racemes; pedicels $\frac{1}{4}$ in. (in fruit reaching $\frac{1}{2}$ in.) long, pubescent; bracts $\frac{1}{8}$ in. long, green, ovate, acute, caducous. Calyx $\frac{1}{4}$ in. long, divided to the base; segments membranous, obtuse, green. Petals 5, subequal, $\frac{1}{2}$ in. long, ovate, obtuse, yellow. Stamens 10, of which the 3 upper are reduced to staminodes, the remaining 7 usually perfect, the 3 lower longer and with larger anthers than the 4 lateral ones, of which one is sometimes reduced to a staminode. Pods 3–4 by $\frac{3}{8}$ in. and about $\frac{1}{6}$ in. thick, slightly recurved, somewhat turgid, septate between the seeds, not or scarcely torulose. Seeds 30–40, broadly ovoid, acute, compressed, dark-brown, $\frac{1}{4}$ by $\frac{1}{8}$ in. Fl. B. I. v. 2, p. 262; Grah. Cat. p. 62; Dalz. & Gibs. p. 81; Benth. in Trans. Linn. Soc. v. 27 (1871) p. 532; Trim. Fl. Ceyl. v. 2, p. 105; Woodr. in Journ. Bomb. Nat. v. 11 (1898) p. 427; Watt, Dict. Econ. Prod. v. 2, p. 223.—Flowers: Nov.-Jan. VERN. *Jangli-táklá*; *Rán-táklá*.

A common weed in uncultivated places throughout the rains.—DISTRIB. Throughout India and in most Tropical countries.

The bark, leaves, and seeds are used medicinally. See Watt, Dict. Econ. Prod. l. c.

4. **Cassia nigricans,** *Vahl, Symb.* v. 1 (1790) p. 30. A shrub or undershrub 5 ft. high; young branches pubescent. Leaves 2–4 in. long; rhachis hairy; petioles $\frac{1}{8}$ in. long, hairy, furnished with an obscure sessile gland below the lowest pair of leaflets; stipules $\frac{1}{4}$ in. long, triangular, acute, hairy, nerved, closely appressed to the stem. Leaflets sessile, 8–18 pairs, $\frac{1}{2}$–1 by $\frac{1}{8}$–$\frac{3}{16}$ in., linear-oblong, obtuse, mucronate, unequal-sided, hairy on both sides. Flowers $\frac{1}{4}$–$\frac{1}{3}$ in. across, solitary or 2–5 together, supra-axillary; pedicels short, bracteolate. Calyx divided to the base, villous, $\frac{1}{6}$ in. long; segments oblong-lanceolate. Petals yellowish-red, scarcely exserted, the upper the smallest. Stamens 10, all perfect or 1–3 rudimentary, the 3 lowest the largest; filaments short. Ovary sessile, densely villous; style short, hooked. Pods $\frac{3}{4}$–$1\frac{1}{4}$ by $\frac{1}{8}$–$\frac{3}{16}$ in., linear-oblong, straight, compressed, marked with transverse oblique lines between the seeds, clothed with appressed hairs. Seeds 6–11, trapezoid-ovoid, compressed, brown, shining. Benth. in Trans. Linn. Soc. v. 27 (1871) p. 577; Prain, in Journ. As. Soc. Beng. v. 66 (1898) p. 477. *C. Arnottiana*, Wight, MS. in Herb. Kew (1835) n. 2410. *C. micrantha*, Guill. & Perr. Fl. Senegamb. (1830–33) p. 262.—Flowers: Nov.-Dec.

Rare, apparently confined in the Bombay Presidency to N. Kanara. KANARA: *Hohenhacker*, 730!; Kumpta on the coast of Kanara, *Talbot*, 72!; N. Kanara, *Stocks*, *Woodrow* (fide Prain).—DISTRIB. India (W. Peninsula); Tropical Africa.

5. **Cassia Tora,** *Linn. Sp. Pl.* (1753) p. 376. An annual fetid herb 1–3 ft. high. Leaves 3–4 in. long; rhachis grooved, more or less pubescent, with a conical gland between each of the 2 lowest pairs of leaflets; stipules ½–¾ in. long, linear-subulate, caducous. Leaflets 3 pairs, opposite, 1–1¾ by ½–1 in. (the lowest pair the smallest), obovate-oblong, glaucous, membranous, glabrous or more or less pubescent, base somewhat oblique, usually rounded; main nerves 8–10 pairs; petiolules $\frac{1}{10}$ in. long, pubescent. Flowers usually in subsessile pairs in the axils of the leaves, the upper crowded; common peduncle in fruit not exceeding ⅛ in. long; pedicels in fruit rarely exceeding ⅓ in. long. Calyx glabrous, divided to the base; segments ⅕ in. long, ovate, acute, spreading. Petals 5, pale yellow, subequal, ⅓ by $\frac{1}{10}$ in., oblong, obtuse, spreading, the upper petal (standard) 2-lobed, the others entire. Stamens 10, the 3 upper reduced to minute staminodes, the remaining 7 perfect, subequal. Pods 5–8 by ⅛–⅙ in., subtetragonous, much curved when young, obliquely septate, puberulous, not reticulate, the sutures very broad. Seeds 25–30, rhombohedral, with the long axis in the direction of the pod. Linn. Sp. Pl. ed. 2, p. 538 (exclud. syn. *Roy. Lugd.* & exclud. *var.* β); Baker, in Hook. f. Fl. B. I. v. 2, p. 263 (partly); Dalz. & Gibs. p. 81 (partly); Benth. in Trans. Linn. Soc. v. 27 (1871) p. 535 (partly); Grah. Cat. p. 63; Trim. Fl. Ceyl. v. 2, p. 106; Woodr. in Journ. Bomb. Nat. v. 11 (1898) p. 427; Watt, Dict. Econ. Prod. v. 2, p. 224. *Senna Tora,* Roxb. Fl. Ind. v. 2, p. 340.—Flowers: Nov.–Dec. VERN. *Tákla.*

A very common weed throughout the Presidency, where it may be found along roadsides and in waste ground.—DISTRIB. Throughout India, Ceylon, and the Tropics generally, probably native in Asia only.

6. **Cassia obtusifolia,** *Linn. Sp. Pl.* (1753) p. 377. An annual herb 2–7 ft. high, not fetid. Leaves 3–4 in. long; rhachis grooved, more or less pubescent, with a conical gland between the lowest pair of leaflets only; stipules ½–¾ in. long, linear-subulate, caducous. Leaflets 3 pairs, opposite, 1–1¾ by ½–¾ in. (the lowest pair the smallest), obovate-oblong, green, membranous, glabrous or more or less pubescent, base somewhat oblique, usually rounded; main nerves 8–10 pairs; petiolules $\frac{1}{10}$ in. long, pubescent. Flowers usually in subsessile pairs in the axils of the leaves, the upper crowded; common peduncle in fruit not exceeding ⅛ in. long; pedicels in flower 1–1¼ in. long. Calyx glabrous, divided to the base; segments ¼ in. long, ovate, acute, spreading. Petals 5, bright yellow, subequal, ½ by ⅓ in., oblong, obtuse, the upper petal (standard) truncate. Stamens 10, the 3 upper reduced to minute staminodes, the remaining 7 perfect, subequal. Pods 8–10 by ⅕ in., subterete, obliquely septate, glabrous, transversely reticulate, the sutures broad. Seeds 30–35, rhombohedral, ⅙ in. long. Linn. Sp. Pl. ed. 2, p. 539 (as to the plant, but exclud. references to Dillenius and Rumphius). *Cassia Tora*, Baker, in Hook. f. Fl. B. I. v. 2, p. 263 (in part), *not* of Linn. *Cassia Tora*, var. β, W. & A. Prod. p. 291 (exclud. references to Rheede and Lamarck). *Senna toroides*, Roxb. Fl. Ind. v. 2, p. 341.

The plant may be distinguished from *Cassia Tora* to which it is closely allied, by its greater size, longer pedicels and larger flowers, by its odor which is bland and not fetid (as in *C. Tora*), by the presence of a gland between the lowest pair of leaflets only, and by its reticulate and subterete pods. Roxburgh (*l. c.*) very clearly points out the specific differences between the 2 plants. See also Prain, Journ. As. Soc. Beng. v. 66 (1898) p. 475.

The plant is a native of Tropical America, but has become more or less naturalized in India.

7. **Cassia auriculata,** *Linn. Sp. Pl.* (1753) p. 379. A tall much-branched shrub; bark smooth, reddish-brown; branchlets finely pubescent. Leaves 3–4 in. long; rhachis densely fulvous-pubescent with an erect linear gland between each pair of leaflets; stipules foliaceous, reflexed, very large, rotundato-reniform, produced at the base on the side next the petiole into a long subulate point, persistent. Leaflets 8–12 pairs, $\frac{3}{4}$–1 by $\frac{3}{8}$–$\frac{1}{2}$ in., slightly overlapping, oblong-obovate, obtuse or emarginate, mucronate, glabrous or finely downy, dull green above, paler beneath, base usually rounded; petiolules $\frac{1}{20}$ in. long. Flowers large, reaching 2 in. across, in terminal and axillary corymbose racemes; pedicels $\frac{3}{4}$–1 in. long; bracts ovate, acuminate, caducous. Calyx glabrous; segments leathery, concave, the 2 outer much smaller than the other 3. Petals with long claws, crisped on the margin, bright yellow, veined with orange. Stamens 10, of which the 3 upper are reduced to staminodes, the remaining 7 perfect, of which the 3 lower are larger than the 4 lateral ones. Pods 3–5 by $\frac{1}{2}$–$\frac{5}{8}$ in., flat, thin, papery, oblong, obtuse, mucronate, pale brown, deeply depressed between the seeds, having a crumpled appearance, transversely veined, pubescent. Seeds 10–20. Fl. B. I. v. 2, p. 263; Grah. Cat. p. 63; Dalz. & Gibs. p. 81; Benth. in Trans. Linn. Soc. v. 27 (1871) p. 547; Trim. Fl. Ceyl. v. 2, p. 106; Talb. Trees, Bomb. ed. 2, p. 144; Woodr. in Journ. Bomb. Nat. v. 11 (1898) p. 427; Watt, Dict. Econ. Prod. v. 2, p. 215.—Flowers: Jan.–July. VERN. *Tarvad*; *Aval*.

KONKAN: *Capt. Geburne*!: DECCAN: abundant in sterile tracts, *Graham*, *Cooke*!, *Woodrow*!; Poona, *Cooke*!; Khandesh, *Edgeworth*! GUJARAT: very common, *Dalzell & Gibson*, *Graham*. S. M. COUNTRY: Dharwar, *Cooke*!—DISTRIB. India (dry regions in the Central Provinces and the W. Peninsula); Ceylon.

The bark is a most valuable tanning material and the seeds are used medicinally. Trimen says that the leaves are used in Ceylon as a substitute for tea.

8. **Cassia obtusa,** *Roxb. Hort. Beng.* (1814) p. 31. A diffuse perennial herb 1–3 ft. high; stems glabrous, pale green, obtusely angular, striate, somewhat woody below; branches spreading, glabrous except the very young parts. Leaves 2–4 in. long; rhachis glabrous, striate, without glands between the leaflets; petioles $\frac{1}{2}$–$\frac{3}{4}$ in. long; stipules $\frac{1}{4}$ in. long, obliquely lanceolate, very acute. Leaflets 3–6 (rarely 7) pairs, $\frac{3}{4}$–1 by $\frac{3}{8}$–$\frac{1}{2}$ in., broadly oblong or obovate-oblong, obtuse, mucronate, pale green and glabrous above, glaucous and glabrous or puberulous beneath, base obtuse. Flowers in axillary peduncled racemes which elongate in fruit and are ultimately longer than the leaves; pedicels very short. Calyx $\frac{3}{8}$ in. long, divided to the base; segments oblong, obtuse, membranous, veined. Petals $\frac{1}{2}$ in. long, obovate-oblong, shortly clawed, yellow, reticulate with darker veins. Perfect stamens 7, very unequal, the 2 or 3 lowest much the largest, the staminodes minute; filaments short. Ovary densely pubescent. Pods 1–1$\frac{3}{4}$ by $\frac{1}{2}$–$\frac{3}{4}$ in., flat, thin, papery, glabrous, rounded at both ends, much recurved, transversely veined and with a line of prominent longitudinal crests down the middle of the pod over the seeds, the

sutures very thin, and the persistent base of the style near the apex of the shorter side of the pod. Seeds 6–12, wedge-shaped, $\frac{1}{4}$ by $\frac{1}{8}$ in., truncate or retuse at the apex, finely reticulato-rugose, and with a transverse ridge across the middle of each face, dark-brown, shining. Wight, Icon. t. 757; Wight & Arn. Prodr. p. 288; Aitch. Pb. & Sind Pl. p. 52; Trim. Fl. Ceyl. v. 2, p. 107. *Cassia obovata*, Collad. Hist. Cass. (1816) p. 92, t. 15, A; Benth. in Trans. Linn. Soc. v. 27 (1871) p. 553; Baker, in Hook. f. Fl. B. I. v. 2, p. 264; Grah. Cat. p. 62; Woodr. in Journ. Bomb. Nat. v. 11 (1898) p. 427; Watt, Dict. Econ. Prod. v. 2, p. 220. *Cassia Senna*, Linn. Sp. Pl. (1753) p. 377 (in part); Dalz. & Gibs. p. 81.—Flowers: Nov.–Feb. VERN. *Bhui-tarvad.*

Roxburgh named the plant *C. obtusa* in 1814 (Hort. Beng. p. 31). Colladon named it *C. obovata* in 1816, two years later. There seems no reason why Roxburgh's earlier name should be set aside.

DECCAN: Bhimthuri district, *Dalzell & Gibson*; Bijapur, *Woodrow*. GUJARAT: abundant, *Graham*. S. M. COUNTRY: *Dalzell & Gibson*. SIND: *Stocks*, 482!, *Vicary*!; Hyderabad, *Kanitkar*!; Mirpur, *Kanitkar*!—DISTRIB. India (Panjab, W. Peninsula); Arabia, Egypt, Abyssinia, Nubia.

A certain amount of trade is done in the leaves in Sind, where the plant grows abundantly. It was the first kind of Senna known, and was introduced by the Moors into Europe, where 2 or 3 centuries ago it was largely cultivated in N. Italy, Spain, and the south of France.

9. **Cassia holosericea,** *Fresen. in Flora* (1839) v. 1, p. 54. Suffruticose, 1–4 ft. high; branches subterete, more or less pubescent. Leaves 2–5 in. long; rhachis densely pubescent, without glands between the leaflets; petioles $\frac{1}{2}$–$\frac{3}{4}$ in. long; stipules $\frac{1}{4}$ in. long, linear-lanceolate, very acute, with a small auricle at the base on the side remote from the petiole, rigid, densely pubescent. Leaflets 5–8 pairs, $\frac{5}{8}$–1 by $\frac{5}{16}$–$\frac{1}{2}$ in. (the upper pair the largest), obovate-oblong, obtuse or retuse, mucronate, clothed on both surfaces with soft velvety pubescence, base obliquely rounded or subacute; petiolules very short. Flowers in narrow axillary racemes shorter than the leaves; pedicels very short, densely pubescent. Calyx $\frac{3}{8}$ in. long, divided to the base; segments oblong, obtuse, membranous, veined. Petals $\frac{1}{2}$ in. long, obovate-oblong, cuneate, shortly clawed, yellow, conspicuously reticulate with darker veins. Stamens 10, of which the 3 upper are reduced to small staminodes, the remaining 7 perfect, of which the 2 or 3 lower are much the largest. Ovary densely pubescent. Pods 1–1$\frac{1}{2}$ by $\frac{1}{2}$–$\frac{3}{4}$ in., flat, thin and papery, recurved, rounded at both ends, velvety-pubescent, slightly turgid, but not longitudinally crested above the seeds, transversely veined and with the persistent base of the style on the shorter side of the pod somewhat remote from its apex. Seeds 4–10, obovoid-cuneate, $\frac{1}{4}$ by $\frac{1}{8}$ in., retuse at the apex, reticulato-rugose, flattened, glabrous, yellow. Benth. in Trans. Linn. Soc. v. 27 (1871) p. 553; Oliver, Fl. Trop. Afr. v. 2, p. 278; Prain, in Journ. As. Soc. Beng. v. 66 (1898) p. 476. *Senna ovalifolia*, Batka, Monogr. Senn. t. 4.—Flowers: Nov.–Jan.

Very closely allied to *C. obovata*, for which it is often mistaken and from which it may be distinguished by the pods, which have no longitudinal crest down the middle above the seeds, and by the greater amount of pubescence.

Common in Sind. SIND: Hyderabad, *Cooke*!, *Woodrow*!—DISTRIB. Tropical Africa, Arabia.

The leaves of this are sold as Senna in the same way as those of the former species.

Cassia angustifolia, Vahl, Symb., a plant with pods very similar to those of *Cassia holosericea* but with narrow lanceolate leaflets, is a native of Tropical Africa and has no claim to be considered indigenous in India. It was (*fide* Dalzell & Gibson) first grown at Hura from seed supplied from Aden by Captain Haines, and was subsequently grown extensively at Hura and at Ganesh Khind near Poona to supply senna leaves to the Bombay Medical Stores. Its cultivation in these localities has been discontinued for many years, as it was found that leaves could be supplied at a cheaper rate from Tinnevelly in S. India, where the plant is still very largely grown, than they could be supplied from Poona.

10. **Cassia montana,** *Heyne, ex Roth, Nov. Pl. Sp.* (1821) p. 214. A shrub or small tree; branches clothed with yellowish pubescence. Leaves 4–8 in. long; rhachis without glands, channelled, clothed with dense yellowish pubescence; stipules minute, very caducous. Leaflets 10–16 pairs, 1–1½ by ⅜–½ in., oblong, obtuse, with a long conspicuous mucro, glabrous or nearly so above, paler and sparsely clothed with yellowish hairs (more abundantly on the midrib) beneath; petiolules $\frac{1}{10}$ in. long, clothed with yellowish hairs. Flowers in corymbose racemes, axillary and forming terminal panicles; pedicels long, clothed with yellowish hairs. Calyx divided to the base, finely puberulous outside; segments broadly oblong, concave, the 3 outer much smaller than the 2 inner. Petals ½ ⅝ in. long, subequal, oblong, obtuse, very shortly clawed, yellow, not conspicuously veined. Stamens 10, the 3 upper reduced to staminodes, the remaining 7 perfect, subequal. Pods 3–5 by ½ in., straight or slightly curved, flat, stalked, tapering towards the base and pointed at the apex with the base of the style, thin, glabrous. Seeds 12–20. Fl. B. I. v. 2, p. 264; Dalz. & Gibs. p. 81; Benth. in Trans. Linn. Soc. v. 27 (1871) p. 550; Talb. Trees, Bomb. ed. 2, p. 144; Woodr. in Journ. Bomb. Nat. v. 11 (1898) p. 427.—Flowers: Aug.–Oct.

S. M. COUNTRY: Chorla Ghât (near Belgaum), *Dalzell & Gibson*; Belgaum Ghâts, *Talbot*; Castlerock, *Cooke*! KANARA: moist forests of the N. Kanara Ghâts, *Talbot*.

11. **Cassia timoriensis,** *DC. Prodr.* v. 2 (1825) p. 499. A large shrub or small tree; branches slender, finely pubescent. Leaves 6–9 in. long; rhachis fulvous-hairy without glands; stipules foliaceous, broad, with a filiform tail, subpersistent. Leaflets 10–20 pairs, ⅞–1½ by ⅓–½ in., oblong, obtuse, mucronate, clothed with appressed hairs above, densely villous beneath, base rounded; petiolules $\frac{1}{12}$ in. long, pubescent. Flowers in corymbose racemes from the axils of the young leaves, the whole forming a terminal panicle; pedicels ¾–1 in. long, fulvous-pubescent. Calyx divided to the base, pubescent; segments broadly oblong, obtuse, concave, the 3 outer smaller than the 2 inner. Petals ⅝ by ⅓ in., oblong, bright yellow, faintly veined with orange. Stamens 10, the 3 upper reduced to staminodes, the remaining 7 perfect, subequal. Pods 5–7 by ½ in., stalked, slightly tapering to both ends, straight, flat, thin, glabrous and shining, the sutures thin. Seeds 16–20, obovoid-cuneate, much compressed, ¼ by ⅙ in., with an oblong shallow pit on each face. Fl. B. I. v. 2, p. 265; Benth. in Trans. Linn. Soc. v. 27 (1871) p. 550; Trim. Fl. Ceyl. v. 2, p. 108; Talb. Trees, Bomb. ed. 2, p. 144; Watt, Dict. Econ. Prod. v. 2, p. 224. *Cassia goensis*, Dalz. in Kew Journ. Bot. v. 4 (1852) p. 112.—Flowers: Oct.

About Goa rare, *Dalzell*. KANARA: from the Goa Ghâts southwards; common in the forests of the Ankola and Kumpta talukas in N. Kanara, *Talbot*.

12. **Cassia Absus,** *Linn. Sp. Pl.* (1753) p. 376. An erect, sparingly branched annual 6–18 in. high; stems and branches clothed with spreading viscous glandular hairs. Leaves long-petioled; rhachis viscous-hairy, grooved; petioles $\frac{3}{4}$–1 in. long; stipules $\frac{1}{8}$ in. long, subulate. Leaflets 2 pairs, very oblique, $\frac{5}{8}$–$1\frac{1}{2}$ by $\frac{1}{3}$–1 in. (the terminal pair the largest), elliptic-oblong or elliptic-obovate, obtuse or subacute, minutely mucronate, glabrous or nearly so above, slightly hairy but not glandular beneath; petiolules $\frac{1}{20}$ in. long, densely hairy. Flowers in terminal or leaf-opposed erect narrow few-flowered racemes; pedicels short, viscous-hairy; bracts beneath the pedicels ovate, acute; bracteole 1 about the middle of each pedicel, small, ovate. Calyx hairy, $\frac{1}{8}$ in. long; segments oblong, obtuse, subequal. Petals $\frac{1}{4}$ in. long, obovate-cuneate, reddish-yellow, tender, veined. Stamens 5, all perfect, equal. Ovary densely bristly with long hairs. Pods 1–$1\frac{3}{4}$ by $\frac{1}{4}$–$\frac{1}{3}$ in., ligulate, nearly straight, oblique, compressed, thin, clothed with bristly hairs. Seeds 4–6, trapezoid-ovoid, $\frac{3}{16}$ by $\frac{1}{8}$ in., black, shining. Fl. B. I. v. 2, p. 265; Wight & Arn. Prodr. p. 291; Benth. in Trans. Linn. Soc. v. 27 (1871) p. 558; Trim. Fl. Ceyl. v. 2, p. 109; Woodr. in Journ. Bomb. Nat. v. 11 (1898) p. 427; Watt, Dict. Econ. Prod. v. 2, p. 210.—Flowers: Sept. VERN. *Chákan*; *Chimar.*

Pretty common throughout the Presidency. KONKAN: *Stocks*!, *Law*!; Parel, *Woodrow*!; Bandora, *Nairne*; Dapoli, *Nairne*; Vingorla, *Woodrow*! DECCAN: Poona, *Woodrow*!; Bowdhan hill near Poona, *Cooke*!—DISTRIB. Throughout India; Ceylon, Tropical Africa, Asia, and Australia.

The seeds are largely employed in native medicine in the treatment of ophthalmia and also as a cathartic. See Watt, Dict. Econ. Prod. l. c.

13. **Cassia pumila,** *Lamk. Encyc. Méthod.* v. 1, p. 651 (1784). Suffruticose, diffuse or procumbent; stems numerous, spreading, about 1 ft. long; branches slender, clothed with weak spreading white hairs. Leaves 1–2 in. long; rhachis hairy; common petiole $\frac{1}{8}$–$\frac{1}{6}$ in. long, with a peltate stalked gland on the petiole below the leaflets; stipules $\frac{1}{5}$ in. long, lanceolate, very acute, nerved. Leaflets subsessile, 10–20 pairs, $\frac{1}{4}$–$\frac{1}{2}$ by $\frac{1}{10}$–$\frac{1}{8}$ in. (the upper and lower smaller than the middle ones), linear-oblong, very unequal-sided, rounded and apiculate at the apex, usually glabrous; nerves conspicuous beneath. Flowers usually solitary or 2–3 together, supra-axillary; pedicels very short, slender; bracts beneath the pedicels lanceolate; bracteoles 2 above the middle of the pedicel, lanceolate. Calyx divided to the base, $\frac{1}{10}$–$\frac{1}{8}$ in. long, pubescent; segments oblong lanceolate, acute, subequal. Petals $\frac{1}{8}$ in. long, yellow, obovate-cuneate, tender, veined. Stamens 5; anthers equal. Ovary densely pubescent; style short; stigma peltate, concave, fringed. Pods 1–$1\frac{1}{2}$ by $\frac{1}{6}$–$\frac{1}{5}$ in., with oblique partitions between the seeds, linear, straight, or very slightly curved, flat, glabrous or with a few scattered hairs. Seeds 6–12, obovoid-cuneate, compressed, brown. Fl. B. I. v. 2, p. 266; Dalz. & Gibs. p. 82; Benth. in Trans. Linn. Soc. v. 27 (1871) p. 570; Woodr. in Journ. Bomb. Nat. v. 11 (1898) p. 427.—Flowers: Aug. VERN. *Sarmal.*

Tolerably common in pastures during the rains. KONKAN: *Stocks*! DECCAN: Poona, *Cooke*!; Bowdhan near Poona, *Cooke*!; Dhulia, *Woodrow*. S. M. COUNTRY: Badami, *Woodrow*. KANARA: Yellapur (N. Kanara), *Talbot*!—DISTRIB. Throughout India; Tropical Asia and Australia.

14. **Cassia Kleinii,** *Wight & Arn. Prodr.* (1834) p. 293. Perennial 1–3 ft. high, diffuse, much branched from a woody base; branches pubescent. Leaves abruptly-pinnate, 1–1½ in. long; rhachis more or less pilose, furnished with a small peltate stalked gland just below the lowest pair of leaflets; petioles ⅛ in. long; stipules ¼ in. long, erect, linear-lanceolate, very acute, strongly nerved. Leaflets 8–20 pairs (reduced to 4–6 pairs on the lower leaves), ⅜–½ by $\frac{1}{12}$–⅛ in., sessile, linear, subacute, obliquely mucronate, rigidly coriaceous, very unequal-sided, the midrib being quite close to the upper edge, strongly nerved on the lower side, base rounded or truncate. Flowers 1–3 together in the axils of the leaves; pedicels ⅜–⅝ in. long, slender, downy; bracts at the base of the pedicel lanceolate; bracteoles 2 near the top of the pedicel, lanceolate-subulate. Calyx divided to the base; segments membranous, lanceolate, very acute. Petals obovate, little exserted, yellow. Stamens 10, all perfect, alternately short and long; anthers equal. Ovary densely pubescent on the sutures, nearly glabrous on the flat faces. Pods 1¼–1¾ by ⅛ in., linear-oblong, flat, slightly recurved, more or less pubescent on the sutures, scarcely if at all so on the faces. Seeds 10–15, dark brown. Fl. B. I. v. 2, p. 266; Benth. in Trans. Linn. Soc. v. 27 (1871) p. 581; Trim. Fl. Ceyl. v. 2, p. 110; Woodr. in Journ. Bomb. Nat. v. 11 (1898) p. 427.—Flowers: Oct.

Rare. KONKAN: Jambhalpada (Colaba), *Woodrow.*—DISTRIB. India (W. Peninsula); Ceylon, Java.

15. **Cassia glauca,** *Lamk. Encyc. Méthod.* v. 1 (1784) p. 647. A small tree; branches numerous, spreading, glabrous. Leaves 5–9 in. long; rhachis pale, puberulous, with a clavate gland between each of the 2–3 lower pairs of leaflets; stipules ⅓ in. long, linear, acute, falcately curved, caducous. Leaflets 4–6 pairs, 1½–3 by 1–1½ in. (the lower pair the smallest), elliptic-oblong, subacute, pale green and glabrous above, glaucous and slightly pubescent or glabrous beneath, base usually rounded; petiolules ⅛ in. long, pubescent. Flowers in axillary corymbose racemes shorter than the leaves; pedicels grooved and angled, more or less pubescent; bracts ovate, acuminate, pubescent, reflexed, caducous. Calyx divided to the base, yellow, glabrous, membranous, reticulately veined; segments broadly oblong or suborbicular, the 3 outer smaller than the 2 inner. Petals ¾ by ⅝ in., broadly oblong, obtuse, shortly clawed, yellow. Stamens 10, all perfect, subequal. Pods stalked, 6–8 by ½–¾ in., straight, flat, thin, tapering to both ends, marked with raised lines between the seeds, veined, glabrous. Seeds 20–30, oblong, rounded at one end, narrowed at the other, ¼ by ⅛ in., compressed, smooth, dark-brown, shining, with a shallow oblong pit on each of the flat faces. Fl. B. I. v. 2, p. 265; Grah. Cat. p. 63; Dalz. & Gibs. Suppl. p. 30; Benth. in Trans. Linn. Soc. v. 27 (1871) p. 555; Talb. Trees, Bomb. ed. 2, p. 144; Woodr. in Journ. Bomb. Nat. v. 11 (1898) p. 427; Watt, Dict. Econ. Prod. v. 2, p. 219.—Flowers: Sept.–Mar. VERN. *Motha-tarvad.*

KONKAN: *Law!*, *Stocks!*, *Capt. Geburne!* DECCAN: Poona in gardens, *Woodrow!* S. M. COUNTRY: common in the forests of the Dharwar districts near the N. Kanara border at Devikope, *Talbot.* KANARA: forests of N. Kanara, *Talbot.*—DISTRIB. Throughout India; Tropical Asia and Australia generally but usually cultivated.

16. **Cassia mimosoides,** *Linn. Sp. Pl.* (1753) p. 379. A diffuse perennial 1–3 ft. high, usually erect, but sometimes spreading; stems and branches terete, more or less hairy. Leaves abruptly-pinnate, 2–4 in. long; rhachis very slender, curved, glabrous or pubescent, with a flat sessile gland on the very short petiole close below the lower pair of leaflets; stipules $\frac{1}{8}$–$\frac{1}{4}$ in., ovate, lanceolate, cuspidate. Leaflets very numerous (40–60 pairs), crowded and overlapping, sessile, $\frac{1}{8}$–$\frac{1}{4}$ by $\frac{1}{20}$–$\frac{1}{16}$ in., linear, subacute, obliquely mucronate, very unequal-sided, glabrous, base oblique, rounded; nerves strong, prominent beneath. Flowers axillary, solitary or 2–3 together; pedicels unequal, $\frac{1}{2}$–1 in. long, slender, pubescent; bracts beneath the pedicels lanceolate-cuspidate; bracteoles 2 a little below the calyx, linear-lanceolate, very acute. Calyx $\frac{1}{8}$–$\frac{1}{4}$ in. long, sparingly pilose; segments unequal, membranous, oblong-lanceolate, very acute. Petals $\frac{3}{16}$–$\frac{1}{4}$ in. long, elliptic, obtuse, with a longish claw, yellow. Stamens 10, all perfect, alternately long and short. Ovary silky-pubescent more especially on the sutures. Pods $1\frac{1}{2}$–2 by $\frac{1}{8}$ in., linear, nearly straight, flat, marked with oblique transverse depressions between the seeds, sparsely clothed with short hairs. Seeds 15–25, obliquely obovoid, compressed, brown, shining. Fl. B. I. v. 2, p. 266; Benth. in Trans. Linn. Soc. v. 27 (1871) p. 579; Trim. Fl. Ceyl. v. 2, p. 110; Woodr. in Journ. Bomb. Nat. v. 11 (1898) p. 427; Watt, Dict. Econ. Prod. v. 2, p. 220.—Flowers: Oct.–Dec.

KONKAN: *Stocks*!; Asre near Jambhalpada, *Kanitkar*!; Kapád near Poladpur, *Woodrow*! DECCAN: Panchgani, *Cooke*!; Poona, *Woodrow*.—DISTRIB. Throughout India; Ceylon, Tropics generally.

Cassia marginata, Roxb. Hort. Beng. p. 31. A tree with 30–40 pairs of leaflets, pink flowers and cylindric pods nearly 1 ft. long. It was introduced from Ceylon, where it is common, into the Botanic Garden at Calcutta in 1802. A tree may be seen in the Bund Gardens and one in the College of Science Botanic Garden at Poona. Fl. B. I. v. 2, p. 262; Talb. Trees, Bomb. ed. 2, p. 144; Woodr. in Journ. Bomb. Nat. v. 11 (1898) p. 427, & Gard. in Ind. ed. 5, p. 274; Watt, Dict. Econ. Prod. v. 2, p. 220.—Flowers in the rains. VERN. *Urimedi*; *Uskiamen*.

Cassia grandis, Linn. f. Suppl. p. 230. A small tree with pods $1\frac{1}{2}$–2 ft. long, a native of Tropical and Central America and the W. Indies, has been introduced into gardens at Poona, where a plant may be seen at Garden Reach. Dalz. & Gibs. Suppl. p. 29; Woodr. in Journ. Bomb. Nat. v. 11 (1898) p. 427.—Flowers: Apr.–May.

Cassia tomentosa, Linn. f. Suppl. p. 231. A tall shrub with 6–8 pairs of leaflets, bright yellow flowers in corymbose panicles, and finely downy pods 4–5 in. long, a native of Tropical America, is frequently planted in gardens. Fl. B. I. v. 2, p. 263; Wight & Arn. Prodr. p. 286; Woodr. in Journ. Bomb. Nat. v. 11 (1898) p. 427.—Flowers: Jan.–Mar.

Cassia bicapsularis, Linn. Sp. Pl. (1753) p. 376. A shrub with 3–4 pairs of leaflets, bright yellow flowers and a sausage-shaped pod

6 in. long, a native of Tropical and Subtropical S. America, is often planted in gardens and is occasionally found as an escape. Fl. B. I. v. 2, p. 263; Dalz. & Gibs. Suppl. p. 29.

Cassia alata, Linn. Sp. Pl. (1753) p. 378. A shrub with 8–14 pairs of leaflets, large yellow flowers, and a pod 4–8 in. long furnished with a wing down the middle of each valve, has been introduced into the Presidency, perhaps from the W. Indies, and is occasionally planted for the sake of its leaves which have a high repute as a remedy in skin-diseases, notably ringworm. It is not indigenous in the W. Peninsula (see Wight & Arn. *l. c.*). Fl. B. I. v. 2, p. 264; Wight & Arn. Prod. p. 287; Dalz. & Gibs. Suppl. p. 29; Talb. Trees, Bomb. ed. 2, p. 144; Woodr. in Journ. Bomb. Nat. v. 11 (1898) p. 427; Watt, Dict. Econ. Prod. v. 2, p. 211.—Flowers: Oct. VERN. *Shimai-agase.*

Cassia siamea, Lamk. Encyc. Méthod. v. 1, p. 648. A moderate-sized robust tree of quick growth with 6–14 pairs of leaflets, large panicles of yellow flowers and flat pods nearly 1 ft. long, is extensively planted as a roadside tree. It is indigenous in Ceylon, the Malayan Peninsula, Siam and South India, but not in the Bombay Presidency. Fl. B. I. v. 2, p. 264; Trim. Fl. Ceyl. v. 2, p. 108; Talb. Trees, Bomb. ed. 2, p. 144; Woodr. in Journ. Bomb. Nat. v. 11 (1898) p. 427, & Gard. in Ind. ed. 5, p. 274; Watt, Dict. Econ. Prod. v. 2, p. 223. *Cassia sumatrana*, Roxb. Hort. Beng. p. 31; Dalz. & Gibs. Suppl. p. 29.—Flowers: Aug.-May. VERN. *Kassod.*

66. CYNOMETRA, Linn.

Erect unarmed trees or shrubs. Leaves abruptly-pinnate; stipules caducous. Leaflets few pairs, coriaceous, oblique. Flowers small, in axillary corymbs or racemes. Calyx with a very short tube and subbasal disk; segments 4–5, imbricate, reflexed during flowering. Petals 5, subequal or the lowest minute, imbricate. Stamens 10, free; filaments filiform; anthers small, uniform, dehiscing longitudinally. Ovary sessile or shortly stalked; ovules 2; style filiform; stigma capitate. Pod arcuate-ovoid or subreniform (rarely straight) with thick turgid or subcompressed usually rugose tough somewhat fleshy indehiscent valves. Seed filling the cavity, exalbuminous; cotyledons thick, fleshy; radicle very short, straight, included.—DISTRIB. Throughout the Tropics; species 20.

1. **Cynometra ramiflora,** *Linn.*, VAR. **mimosoides,** *Baker, in Hook. f. Fl. B. I.* v. 2 (1878) p. 267. A shrub or small tree growing near the sea-coast. Leaves 3–5 in. long; rhachis grooved, glabrous or puberulous. Leaflets 2 pairs, $1\frac{1}{2}$–$3\frac{1}{2}$ by $\frac{3}{4}$–$1\frac{1}{2}$ in., coriaceous, obliquely obovate-oblong, often emarginate, subsessile, dark green, glabrous, shining above, base obliquely cuneate; main nerves numerous, distinct. Flowers in small axillary corymbose racemes; pedicels slender, $\frac{1}{4}$–$\frac{3}{8}$ in. long; bracts broadly ovate, deciduous; bracteoles small, lanceolate. Calyx-tube very short; segments ovate-lanceolate, $\frac{1}{10}$–$\frac{1}{8}$ in. long. Petals white, linear-lanceolate, $\frac{1}{8}$ in. long. Pods fleshy, much wrinkled, turgid, $\frac{1}{2}$–1 in. long, irregularly oblong or ovoid, with a thick fleshy pointed tip. *C. ramiflora*, Grah. Cat. p. 63; Dalz. & Gibs. p. 83; Talb. Trees, Bomb.

ed. 2, p. 144; Woodr. in Journ. Bomb. Nat. v. 11 (1898) p. 427; Watt, Dict. Econ. Prod. v. 2, p. 682.—Flowers: Mar.–May. VERN. *Irapu.*

KONKAN: S. Konkan, very rare, *Dalzell & Gibson, Nimmo ex Graham.* KANARA: forests of N. Kanara, *Talbot, Woodrow.* Talbot says (*l. c.*) that the characteristic fruit is carried down the Kála naddi during the rainy season and thrown up on the seashore near Karwar.—DISTRIB. India (W. Peninsula, the Sunderbans and Birma); Malaya.

67. HARDWICKIA, Roxb.

Unarmed trees. Leaves abruptly-pinnate. Leaflets 1–3 pairs, coriaceous. Flowers numerous, small, in panicled racemes. Calyx with scarcely any tube and a subbasal disk; segments usually 5, oblong or suborbicular, petaloid, subequal, imbricate. Petals 0. Stamens 10, the alternate ones slightly shorter; anthers dehiscing longitudinally. Ovary sessile, free; ovules 2. Pod subindehiscent, dry, with only the upper seed perfect. Seeds exalbuminous.—DISTRIB. Species 3, of which 2 are Asiatic, the other African.

1. **Hardwickia binata,** *Roxb. Cor. Pl.* v. 3 (1819) p. 6, t. 209. A tree 50–60 ft. high; branches numerous, spreading. Leaves alternate; rhachis tipped with a minute deciduous bristle; petioles $\frac{1}{2}$–1 in. long, glabrous; stipules small, caducous. Leaflets 1 pair, like those of *Bauhinia,* subsessile, 1–3 by $\frac{1}{2}$–1$\frac{1}{2}$ in., obtuse, 3–6-nerved from the base, tinged with red when young, glabrous. Flowers in axillary and terminal panicles; pedicels filiform. Calyx $\frac{1}{8}$–$\frac{1}{6}$ in. long; segments oblong, obtuse, membranous, veined, often dotted. Stamens usually 10; filaments very slender. Stigma peltate. Pods 2–3 by $\frac{3}{8}$–$\frac{7}{8}$ in., strap-shaped, veined, glabrous, narrowed at both ends, thin, flexible, opening at the apex. Seed 1, near the tip of the pod. Fl. B. I. v. 2, p. 270; Grah. Cat. p. 61; Dalz. & Gibs. p. 83; Bedd. Flor. Sylvat. t. 26; Talb. Trees, Bomb. ed. 2, p. 145; Woodr. in Journ. Bomb. Nat. v. 11 (1898) p. 427; Watt, Dict. Econ. Prod. v. 4, p. 200.—Flowers: Oct.–Jan. VERN. *Anjan.*

DECCAN: Lalling Pass between Malligaon and Dhulia (Khandesh), *Graham, Dalzell & Gibson, Woodrow*; common on the trap of the Sátpudas in Khandesh, *Talbot.* S. M. COUNTRY: Ranebennur taluka of Dharwar, locally abundant, *Talbot.*—DISTRIB. India (Behar, N.W. Provinces, W. Peninsula).

The leaves are given as fodder to cattle, who eat them greedily. The wood is extremely durable and makes excellent piles for bridge-foundations. See Watt, Dict. Econ. Prod. l. c.

68. SARACA, Linn.

Erect trees. Leaves abruptly pinnate; stipules large, intrapetiolar, completely united, or rarely foliaceous and partially free. Leaflets usually of few pairs, coriaceous. Flowers in dense sessile paniculate (rarely simple) corymbs on old nodes, or rarely axillary; bracts small, deciduous; bracteoles persistent, colored, shorter than the tube of the calyx. Calyx petaloid; tube elongate, cylindric, crowned by a lobed disk; segments 4, oblong, subequal, imbricate. Petals 0. Stamens 2–9, free, exserted; filaments long, filiform; anthers oblong, versatile, dehiscing longitudinally. Ovary stalked, the stalk attached to and produced beyond the disk; ovules many; style filiform; stigma minute, capitate. Pod flat, dehiscent, rigidly coriaceous. Seeds exalbuminous.—DISTRIB. S.E. Asia; species 16 or more.

1. **Saraca indica,** *Linn. Mantiss.* (1767) p. 98. A tree 20–30 ft. high; branches glabrous. Leaves 6–10 in. long; rhachis glabrous, corky at the base; petioles very short; stipules intrapetiolar, completely united, $\frac{3}{8}$–$\frac{1}{2}$ by $\frac{1}{4}$ in., scarious, ovate-oblong, obtuse, parallel-nerved. Leaflets 4–6 pairs, 4–8 by $1\frac{1}{4}$–$2\frac{1}{4}$ in., oblong-lanceolate, obtuse or acute, quite glabrous, base rounded or cuneate, slightly oblique; petiolules $\frac{3}{16}$–$\frac{1}{4}$ in. long, stout, wrinkled; stipels deciduous. Flowers fragrant, numerous, in dense axillary corymbs 3–4 in. across; peduncles stout; pedicels $\frac{1}{3}$–$\frac{1}{2}$ in. long, red, glabrous; bracts ovate, subacute; bracteoles 2, appearing like a calyx, $\frac{1}{6}$ in. long, spathulate-oblong, subacute, ciliolate, amplexicaul, colored. Calyx passing from yellow to orange and finally red; tube $\frac{1}{2}$–$\frac{3}{4}$ in. long, cylindric, solid at the base; segments 4, oblong or obovate-oblong, $\frac{3}{8}$ in. long. Petals 0. Stamens 7 or 8, much exserted; filaments filiform, thrice as long as the calyx-segments; anthers purple. Ovary pubescent, especially on the sutures; style curved into a ring. Pods black, 4–10 by $1\frac{3}{4}$–2 in., linear-oblong, tapering to both ends, compressed, glabrous, veined. Seeds 4–8, ellipsoid-oblong, $1\frac{1}{2}$ in. long, slightly compressed. Fl. B. I. v. 2, p. 271; Bedd. Flor. Sylvat. t. 57; Trim. Fl. Ceyl. v. 2, p. 114; Talb. Trees, Bomb. ed. 2, p. 145; Woodr. in Journ. Bomb. Nat. v. 11 (1898) p. 427; Watt, Dict. Econ. Prod. v. 6, part 2, p. 475. *Jonesia Asoka,* Roxb. in As. Res. v. 4 (1795) p. 355; Grah. Cat. p. 62; Dalz. & Gibs. p. 82.—Flowers: Dec.–May. VERN. *A'shok*; *Jásvant.*

A very handsome tree when in full flower. KONKAN: *Stocks*!, *Law*!; S. Konkan Ghâts, common, *Dalzell & Gibson*; W. Ghâts, widely, *Woodrow*; Salsette, *Graham*. DECCAN: Lanoli grove, *Graham*, *Woodrow*! S. M. COUNTRY: bottom of Ramghât, *Ritchie*, 256! KANARA: evergreen forests of N. Kanara, sometimes planted, *Talbot*; Kála naddi jungles, *Ritchie*, 256!—DISTRIB. India (Central and Eastern Himalaya, East Bengal, Birma, W. Peninsula); Ceylon, Malaya.

The bark is used in native medicine. See Watt, Dict. Econ. Prod. l. c.

VAR. *puberula,* Prain, in Journ. As. Soc. Beng. v. 66 (1898) p. 489. Leaf-rhachis, peduncles and pedicels puberulous to pubescent.

KANARA: *fide* Prain *l. c.*

69. TAMARINDUS, Linn.

An unarmed tree. Leaves abruptly-pinnate; stipules minute, caducous. Leaflets small, multijugate. Flowers in racemes at the apices of the branches; bracts and bracteoles ovate-oblong, colored, caducous. Calyx-tube turbinate; segments 4, much imbricate, membranous. Petals: the 3 upper only developed, the 2 lower reduced to scales. Stamens monadelphous, only 3 developed, the others reduced to mere bristles at the top of the sheath; anthers oblong, dehiscing longitudinally. Ovary stalked, the stalk adnate to the calyx-tube; ovules many; style elongate; stigma capitate. Pod linear-oblong, incurved, subcompressed, indehiscent, with a brittle crustaceous epicarp and thick pulpy mesocarp. Seeds exalbuminous.—DISTRIB. Species 1, now planted everywhere throughout the Tropics.

1. **Tamarindus indica,** *Linn. Sp. Pl.* (1753) p. 34. A large tree 40–60 ft. high; branches spreading, glabrous. Leaves 2–5 in. long; rhachis slender, channelled; stipules linear, caducous. Leaflets subsessile, 10–20 pairs, tolerably closely set on the rhachis, $\frac{1}{3}$–$1\frac{1}{4}$ by $\frac{1}{6}$–$\frac{1}{3}$ in.,

oblong, obtuse, glabrous, reticulately veined. Flowers in lax few-flowered racemes at the ends of the branchlets; pedicels $\frac{1}{4}$–$\frac{3}{8}$ in. long, slender, articulated below the calyx, glabrous; bracts concave, $\frac{1}{4}$–$\frac{1}{3}$ in. long, enclosing the buds, caducous; bracteoles small. Calyx $\frac{1}{2}$ in. long; tube narrowly turbinate, $\frac{1}{8}$ in. long; segments $\frac{1}{3}$ in. long, subequal, oblong, somewhat oblique, obtuse or subacute. Petals 3 (an upper and 2 lateral), $\frac{3}{8}$ in. long, subequal, obovate-oblong, yellowish with pink stripes. Stamens 3 fertile, connate nearly half their length; filaments pubescent at the base; anthers oblong. Ovary stalked; ovules 8–12 or more; style pubescent, equalling the stamens. Pods 3–8 in. long by 1 in. broad and about $\frac{3}{8}$ in. thick, slightly curved, subcompressed, scurfy. Seeds 3–12, obovate-oblong, truncate at the ends, $\frac{5}{8}$ by $\frac{5}{16}$ in., compressed, with a shallow oblong pit on each of the flat faces, smooth, brown, shining. Fl. B. I. v. 2, p. 273; Grah. Cat. p. 62; Dalz. & Gibs. p. 82; Bedd. Flor. Sylvat. t. 184; Aitch. Pb. & Sind Pl. p. 53; Talb. Trees, Bomb. ed. 2, p. 146; Woodr. in Journ. Bomb. Nat. v. 11 (1898) p. 428; Watt, Dict. Econ. Prod. v. 6, part 3, p. 404.—Flowers: May–June. VERN. *Amli*; *Chinch.*

The well-known *Tamarind tree* cultivated and self-sown throughout India and the Tropics generally, probably indigenous in Africa. The tree is of great value, almost all its parts being useful. Two different kinds of fruit are recognized, distinguished by their color, viz., the red and brown tamarind, of which the former is the most valued. Some fine specimens of the red-fruited variety grow at Bijapur in the Deccan. See Watt, Dict. Econ. Prod. l. c.

70. BAUHINIA, Linn.

Unarmed erect trees, or climbing shrubs with circinate tendrils. Leaves usually simple, more or less deeply cleft from the apex, rarely entire, or fully divided into 2 leaflets; stipules various, usually small, caducous. Flowers usually white, in simple terminal or rarely axillary racemes, or arranged in a large terminal or corymbose panicle. Calyx-tube with the disk produced to the top, sometimes long and cylindric, sometimes short and turbinate or campanulate; limb entire and spathaceous, or cleft into 2 or 5 teeth. Petals 5, subequal, erect or spreading, imbricate, the upper the inner. Stamens 10, or reduced to 5 or 3, if fewer than 10 with or without sterile filaments; filaments free, filiform; anthers versatile, dehiscing longitudinally. Ovary stalked (rarely subsessile); ovules many; style long or short; stigma small, or large and peltate, subterminal or oblique. Pod linear or oblong, flat, continuous within, dehiscent or indehiscent. Seeds albuminous.—DISTRIB. Throughout the Tropics; species 150.

Fertile stamens 10.
  Leaflets distinct .... 1. *B. diphylla.*
  Leaflets connate.
    Calyx spathaceous.
      Flowers large, 1–3, on short peduncles .... 2. *B. tomentosa.*
      Flowers small, numerous, in copious racemes .... 3. *B. racemosa.*
    Calyx-limb divided into 5 segments.
      Leaves 7–9-nerved.. 4. *B. malabarica.*
      Leaves 15–17-nerved.. 5. *B. foveolata.*
Fertile stamens 3–5.
  A large climber .... 6. *B. Vahlii.*
  An erect tree .... 7. *B. purpurea.*

1. **Bauhinia diphylla,** *Buch.-Ham.*, *in Symes, Embass.* ed. 2 (1800) v. 3, p. 311, t. 24. A large climber with circinate tendrils. Leaves of 2 distinct leaflets; petioles ¾–1½ in. long, slightly thickened at both ends, glabrous, striate. Leaflets sessile, 2½ by 1½ in., semiorbicular or subreniform, rounded at both ends, glabrous; nerves 5–6. Flowers very large, in lax terminal racemes; pedicels 1¼–1¾ in. long, glabrous, ascending; buds fusiform. Calyx thick, glabrous; tube ⅞–1 in. long, narrowly turbinate; limb divided to the base, segments lanceolate, 1–1¼ in. long, reflexed. Petals exserted, oblong-lanceolate, white, with a long claw. Stamens 10, all fertile, equal; filaments glabrous. Ovary stalked, glabrous. Pods stalked, 9–12 by 1½–2½ in., flat, thin, reticulately veined; stalk 1½–2 in. long. Seeds 30–40 along the middle of the pod, ovoid, slightly compressed, ½ by ⅓ in., pale brown, shining. Fl. B. I. v. 2, p. 278; Talb. Trees, Bomb. ed. 2, p. 147; Woodr. in Journ. Bomb. Nat. v. 11 (1898) p. 428.

KONKAN: *Stocks!*

This is included on the authority of specimens in Herb. Kew labelled as above, but no other collectors appear to have found the plant in the Konkan. *B. corymbosa* in Dalzell and Gibson's Bombay Flora, Suppl. p. 31, may probably be this species. The leaves are there said to be cleft to the base, which is not the case in *B. corymbosa*, Roxb.—DISTRIB. Birma.

2. **Bauhinia tomentosa,** *Linn. Sp. Pl.* (1753) p. 375. An erect shrub; branches slender, terete, zigzag, downy. Leaves broader than long, 1½–2 by 1½–2½ in., divided a little less than ½ way down into 2 rounded lobes, glabrous above, pubescent beneath, base truncate or rarely subcordate; main nerves 7 (rarely 9) from the base; petioles ½–⅞ in. long, pubescent, thickened at both ends. Flowers usually in pairs (rarely 1 or 3), on short axillary or leaf-opposed peduncles; bracts linear, ¼–⅓ in. long; pedicels ⅓ in. long, 2-bracteolate. Calyx ¾ in. long, velvety-pubescent; tube ⅙ in. long; limb ⅝ in. long, broadly ovate, spathaceous. Petals 1½–2 in. long, much imbricated, obovate-spathulate, yellow, the upper with a purple blotch on the face. Stamens 10, all fertile, subequal. Ovary distinctly stalked, densely tomentose; style ½–⅝ in. long; stigma peltate. Pods stalked, 4–5 by ½–⅝ in., flat, pointed, slightly puberulous when fully ripe, veined. Seeds 8–12, oblong, rounded at the apex, $\frac{5}{16}$ by $\frac{3}{16}$ in. Fl. B. I. v. 2, p. 275; Grah. Cat. p. 63; Dalz. & Gibs. Suppl. p. 31; Bedd. For. Man. p. xcii; Trim. Fl. Ceyl. v. 2, p. 116; Woodr. in Journ. Bomb. Nat. v. 11 (1898) p. 428; Watt, Dict. Econ. Prod. v. 1, p. 423.—Flowers: Nov.–Jan.

A very ornamental shrub, often cultivated in gardens, but very doubtfully wild in the Bombay Presidency. *Nimmo* (fide *Graham*, l. c.) states that it is wild in the Konkan, but no other collector seems to have found it there. *Dalzell & Gibson* say that it is a native of Malabar, and *Woodrow* in his list of plants considers it as doubtfully indigenous.—DISTRIB. India (N.W. Provinces, W. Peninsula); Ceylon, China, Tropical Africa.

3. **Bauhinia racemosa,** *Lamk. Encyc. Méthod.* v. 1 (1783) p. 390 (*not* of Vahl). A small crooked tree with dark scabrous bark; branches numerous, drooping. Leaves broader than long, ¾–2 by 1–2½ in., divided a little less than ½ way down into 2 rounded lobes, green and glabrous above, white and more or less tomentose beneath, base usually cordate; main nerves 7–9; petioles ¼–⅝ in. long, pubescent. Flowers

in terminal or leaf-opposed racemes 2–5 in. long; rhachis densely pubescent; buds pointed; pedicels $\frac{1}{8}$–$\frac{3}{16}$ in. long; bracts beneath the pedicels linear, acute. Calyx pubescent; tube very short; limb $\frac{1}{4}$–$\frac{1}{3}$ in. long, spathaceous, at length reflexed. Petals narrowly oblanceolate, acute, $\frac{3}{8}$–$\frac{7}{16}$ in. long, white or pale-yellow. Stamens 10, all fertile; filaments densely hairy at the base. Ovary pubescent; stigma sessile. Pods stalked, 6–10 by $\frac{1}{2}$–$\frac{7}{8}$ in., blunt at the apex, tapering to the base, somewhat falcate, glabrous, turgid, not or scarcely veined; stalk $\frac{3}{4}$–1 in. long. Seeds 12–20, oblong, compressed, rounded at the apex, $\frac{1}{4}$–$\frac{3}{8}$ by $\frac{3}{16}$–$\frac{1}{4}$ in., black. Fl. B. I. v. 2, p. 276; Grah. Cat. p. 64; Dalz. & Gibs. p. 82; Hook. Icon. t. 141; Trim. Fl. Ceyl. v. 2, p. 116; Talb. Trees, Bomb. ed. 2, p. 146; Woodr. in Journ. Bomb. Nat. v. 11 (1898) p. 428; Watt, Dict. Econ. Prod. v. 1, p. 422.—Flowers: Mar.–June. VERN. *A'ptá*; *Vánu-rája*.

Common throughout the Presidency in deciduous forests. KONKAN: *Stocks*!, *Dalzell*!; Ghâts and hilly parts of the Konkan, *Graham*. DECCAN: widely, *Woodrow*!, *Bhiva*!; Poona districts, *Cooke*!, *Woodrow*!—DISTRIB. Throughout India; Ceylon, China, Timor.

A sacred plant of the Hindus, worshipped at the Dasera festival. The leaves are sold in the market to wrap tobacco in and make cigarettes which are called *bidis*.

4. **Bauhinia malabarica,** *Roxb. Hort. Beng.* (1814) p. 31. An erect low bushy tree, sometimes diœcious (*Talbot*). Leaves broader than long, $1\frac{1}{2}$–5 by $1\frac{3}{4}$–6 in., divided about $\frac{1}{4}$ the way down into 2 rounded lobes, glabrous above, pale and more or less pubescent beneath, finely reticulately veined, base cordate; main nerves 7–11 (commonly 9), conspicuous; petioles 1 in. long, thickened at both ends, channelled, glabrous or pubescent. Flowers in dense axillary subsessile racemes; pedicels $\frac{1}{2}$–1 in. long, slender, ascending, brown-puberulous. Calyx clothed with brown pubescence; tube $\frac{1}{8}$–$\frac{1}{4}$ in. long, narrowly turbinate; limb $\frac{1}{4}$–$\frac{5}{16}$ in. long, divided into 5 linear subacute segments. Petals obovate-spathulate, little exserted. Stamens 10, all fertile, alternately long and short. Ovary pubescent. Pods stalked, 10–12 by $\frac{3}{4}$–1 in., nearly straight, somewhat turgid, glabrous, conspicuously reticulately veined with longitudinal wavy lines, rostrate with the style; stalk 1 in. long. Seeds 20–30, globose-ovoid, $\frac{3}{16}$ in. in diam., dark brown, polished. Fl. B. I. v. 2, p. 277; Dalz. & Gibs. p. 82; Bedd. For. Man. p. xcii; Talb. Trees, Bomb. ed. 2, p. 147; Woodr. in Journ. Bomb. Nat. v. 11 (1898) p. 428; Watt, Dict. Econ. Prod. v. 1, p. 420.—Flowers: Oct.–Nov. VERN. *Amli*.

Moist forests of the Konkan and N. Kanara, *Talbot*.—DISTRIB. Throughout India.

5. **Bauhinia foveolata,** *Dalz. in Journ. Linn. Soc.* v. 13 (1873) p. 188. A large diœcious tree reaching 100 ft. high; stem straight, 9–10 ft. in girth. Leaves suborbicular, 5–9 in. long, about as broad as long, divided about $\frac{1}{3}$ of the way down into 2 subacute lobes, glabrous above, more or less pubescent or tomentose beneath, closely reticulately veined and with numerous small pits between the veins on the lower side, base cordate with a deep sinus; main nerves 15–17, very conspicuous beneath; petioles $1\frac{3}{4}$–2 in. long, pubescent, thickened at both ends. Flowers subsessile, in dense racemes forming a terminal much-branched panicle. Calyx ferrugineo-tomentose; tube $\frac{1}{8}$–$\frac{1}{6}$ in. long, narrowly turbinate; limb $\frac{1}{4}$–$\frac{1}{3}$ in. long, splitting into 5 linear-oblong

subacute segments. Petals not much exserted, obovate-oblong, obtuse, with a long claw. Stamens in the male flowers 10, all fertile, alternately long and short; in the female flowers reduced to minute hairy staminodes. Ovary rudimentary in the male, densely hairy and without stigma; in the female clothed with long hairs and with a peltate stigma. Pods 6–9 by ⅝–1 in., stalked, linear-oblong, twisted, red, tomentose, rostrate with the style. Prain, in Journ. As. Soc. Beng. v. 66 (1898) p. 496. *Bauhinia Lawii*, Benth. ex Baker, in Hook. f. Fl. B. I. v. 2, p. 277; Talb. Trees, Bomb. ed. 2, p. 147; Woodr. in Journ. Bomb. Nat. v. 11 (1898) p. 428.—Flowers: Sept.-Oct. VERN. *Chamoli*; *Buswanpad.*

KONKAN: *Law*!; road to Matheran near 3rd milestone from Neral, *Woodrow*. DECCAN: Peint taluka, *Woodrow*. KANARA: moist forests of N. Kanara, *Talbot*; Yellapur, *Talbot*!—DISTRIB. Apparently endemic.

6. **Bauhinia Vahlii,** *Wight & Arn. Prodr.* (1834) p. 297. An immense climber with opposite circinate tendrils; young parts clothed with fulvous or rusty tomentum. Leaves 4–10 in., suborbicular, scarcely broader than long, divided about ⅓ of the way down into 2 obtuse lobes with a broad sinus, reticulately veined, glabrous or nearly so above, densely tomentose beneath, base deeply cordate; main nerves 11–15, fulvous hairy on the underside; petioles 3–6 in. long, densely tomentose. Flowers in long-peduncled terminal corymbose racemes; bracts beneath the pedicels ⅛–¼ in. long, linear-spathulate, ferruginous-hairy; pedicels variable in length, the lower often reaching 2 in., 2-bracteolate, the bracteoles linear, subopposite, densely ferruginous-hairy, persistent. Calyx densely villous with fulvous or rufous hairs; tube very slender, ¼–⅓ in. long; limb ⅜–$\frac{7}{16}$ in. long, splitting into 2 broadly ovate lobes. Petals white, ¾–1 in. long, obovate-cuneate, clothed along the middle of the back with appressed silky hairs and with crisped margins. Fertile stamens 3; filaments densely villous at the base. Staminodes 2–7. Ovary densely villous; style long, hairy; stigma capitate. Pods woody, rusty-downy, 9–12 by 2–2¼ in., shortly stalked, flat, finally splitting open. Seeds 6–12, oblong-ellipsoid, 1¼ by ¾ in., compressed, dark-brown, polished. Fl. B. I. v. 2, p. 279; Grah. Cat. p. 64; Dalz. & Gibs. p. 83; Talb. Trees, Bomb. ed. 2, p. 147; Woodr. in Journ. Bomb. Nat. v. 11 (1898) p. 428; Watt, Dict. Econ. Prod. v. 1, p. 424.—Flowers: Apr. VERN. *Chambul.*

Tolerably common throughout the Presidency. KONKAN: *Stocks*!; Konkan Ghâts, *Woodrow*!; moist forests of the Konkân Ghâts, *Talbot*; Thal Ghât, *Graham*; near Goa, *Dalzell*! DECCAN: Khandala, *Graham*.—DISTRIB. Throughout India in hilly districts.

A strong cordage is obtained from the bark. The seeds are eaten raw and roasted, and the young pods are used as a vegetable by the hill tribes. The large leaves are used as plates by the poorer natives. See Watt, Dict. Econ. Prod. l. c.

7. **Bauhinia purpurea,** *Linn. Sp. Pl.* (1753) p. 375. An erect tree 20–30 ft. high; branches stout, glabrescent. Leaves 4–5 in. in diam., roundish, about as broad as long, divided ⅓–½ the way down into 2 obtuse or subacute lobes, glabrous above, glabrous or faintly puberulous beneath, base cordate; main nerves 9–11; petioles 1–1½ in. long, glabrous; stipules $\frac{1}{10}$ in. long, triangular-oblong, acute, pubescent, deciduous. Flowers fragrant, in terminal and axillary few-flowered

corymbose racemes; bracts beneath the pedicels triangular, acute, pubescent; pedicels pubescent, 2-bracteolate below the middle; buds fusiform, pubescent. Calyx fulvous-pubescent; tube $\frac{1}{4}$–$\frac{1}{16}$ in. long, slightly dilated upwards; limb $\frac{7}{8}$ in. long, splitting into 2 coriaceous segments slightly divided at the apex into 5 short teeth. Petals $1\frac{3}{4}$ by $\frac{1}{2}$ in., oblanceolate, acute, with a long claw, white, rose or purple. Fertile stamens 3–4; filaments as long as the petals. Ovary with a very long stalk, puberulous; ovules 16–20; style $\frac{5}{8}$ in. long; stigma oblique, peltate. Pods 6–12 by $\frac{3}{4}$ in., subwoody, flat, pointed at both ends, glabrous; stalk $\frac{1}{2}$–1 in. long. Seeds 12–16, oblong-ellipsoid, compressed, $\frac{5}{8}$ by $\frac{1}{2}$ in., brown. Fl. B. I. v. 2, p. 284; Grah. Cat. p. 64; Dalz. & Gibs. Suppl. p. 30; Bedd. For. Man. p. xcii; Talb. Trees, Bomb. ed. 2, p. 147; Woodr. in Journ. Bomb. Nat. v. 11 (1898) p. 428; Watt, Dict. Econ. Prod. v. 1, p. 421.—Flowers: Sept.–Nov. VERN. *Rakta-kánchan*; *Deva-kánchan*.

Cultivated throughout the Presidency, said by *Talbot* and *Woodrow* to be wild in the dry forests of the Konkan and Deccan. Graham and Dalzell & Gibson say that it is only found in gardens, and Trimen makes the same statement as regards Ceylon. —DISTRIB. Sparingly throughout India; China.

Bauhinia acuminata, Linn. Sp. Pl. (1753) p. 375, an erect shrub, 8 ft. high with leaves divided less than $\frac{1}{2}$ way down into 2 usually subacute lobes, pure white fragrant flowers and a pod 4–5 in. long with a rib at each side of the upper suture, is often cultivated in gardens but is not indigenous in the Bombay Presidency, although indigenous in other Provinces of India. Fl. B. I. v. 2, p. 276; Grah. Cat. p. 63; Dalz. & Gibs. Suppl. p. 30; Trim. Fl. Ceyl. v. 2, p. 116; Woodr. in Journ. Bomb. Nat. v. 11 (1898) p. 428; Watt, Dict. Econ. Prod. v. 1, p. 419. —Flowers: June. VERN. *Kánchan*.

Bauhinia variegata, Linn. Sp. Pl. (1753) p. 375, a middle-sized tree with leaves divided $\frac{1}{4}$–$\frac{1}{3}$ the way down into 2 obtuse lobes, flowers beautifully variegated with red and yellow, or sometimes pure white (var. *candida*) and flat pods which are frequently variegated with reddish-brown streaks, is cultivated throughout the Presidency, often as a roadside tree, but is not indigenous in Bombay. Fl. B. I. v. 2, p. 284; Grah. Cat. p. 64; Dalz. & Gibs. Suppl. p. 30; Talb. Trees, Bomb. ed. 2, p. 147; Woodr. in Journ. Bomb. Nat. v. 11 (1898) p. 428; Watt, Dict. Econ. Prod. v. 1, p. 425.—Flowers: Nov. VERN. *Kachnár*; *Kovidara*; *Kánchan*.

Bauhinia monandra, Kurz, in Journ. As. Soc. Beng. v. 42 (1873) part 2, p. 73, which may be found in the old botanic gardens at Dapodi and at Ganesh Khind near Poona, has been mistaken for this, but has only 1 fertile stamen, whereas the fertile stamens of *B. variegata* are 3–5. The pods of the Dapodi tree are about 6 by $\frac{3}{4}$ in., flat and densely pubescent. See Prain, Journ. As. Soc. Beng. v. 66 (1898) p. 505.

SUBORDER III. MIMOSEÆ.

Trees, shrubs, or very rarely herbs. Leaves 2-pinnate or less commonly simply pinnate. Flowers small, regular, usually 5-merous, sessile, in globose heads or cylindric spikes rarely shortly pedicelled and in slender racemes or globose umbels. Sepals valvate, connate into a 5-toothed or 5-lobed calyx, rarely free. Petals valvate, equal in number to the sepals, free or connate into a lobed corolla, hypogynous or obscurely perigynous. Stamens usually exserted, equal in number to the sepals or twice or thrice as many, or indefinite, free or monadelphous, or adnate to the base of the tube of the corolla; anthers dehiscing longitudinally. Ovary free, in the bottom of the calyx. Seeds exalbuminous or with scanty albumen; cotyledons flat; radicle straight, shortly exserted or included.

Stamens definite, 5–10 (usually 10).
  Anthers gland-crested, at least in an early stage.
    Flowers in globose heads.
      Herbs .... 71. NEPTUNIA.
      A tree .... 72. XYLIA.
    Flowers in elongate spikes.
      A large cirrhiferous climber .... 73. ENTADA.
      Erect trees or shrubs.
        Not prickly .... 74. ADENANTHERA.
        Prickly.
          Pod turgid, straight .... 75. PROSOPIS.
          Pod thin, finally twisted .... 76. DICHROSTACHYS.
  Anthers not gland-crested.
    Pod straight, with continuous valves, dehiscing through the sutures .... 77. LEUCÆNA.
    Pod slightly curved, with segmented valves, with persistent indehiscent sutures .... 78. MIMOSA.
Stamens indefinite.
  Stamens free .... 79. ACACIA.
  Stamens monadelphous.
    Pod straight, flat .... 80. ALBIZZIA.
    Pod circinate, often twisted .... 81. PITHECOLOBIUM.

71. NEPTUNIA, Lour.

Herbs without prickles, diffuse, prostrate or floating. Leaves 2-pinnate; stipules membranous, obliquely cordate, persistent. Leaflets numerous, small. Flowers 5-merous, sessile, in dense heads on axillary solitary peduncles, polygamous, the upper flowers in each head hermaphrodite, the lower usually male or barren. Calyx small, campanulate, 5-toothed. Petals 5, strap shaped, connate near the base. Stamens 10 (rarely 5), free, exserted; anthers gland-crested. Ovary stalked; ovules many; style filiform; stigma terminal, small, concave. Pod coriaceous, flattened, ligulate or oblong, 2-valved, subseptate between the seeds.—DISTRIB. Cosmopolitan in the Tropics; species 8.

Annual, aquatic .... 1. *N. oleracea.*
Perennial, terrestrial .... 2. *N. triquetra.*

1. **Neptunia oleracea,** *Lour. Fl. Cochinch.* (1790) p. 654. Annual, floating; stem elongate, soft, swollen, not much branched, emitting slender fibrous roots in abundance from the leaf- and flower-bearing nodes. Leaves abruptly 2-pinnate; stipules obliquely ovate-cordate, acute; common petioles $1\frac{1}{4}$–$1\frac{3}{4}$ in. long; pinnæ 2–3 pairs, opposite, shortly stalked. Leaflets 8–15 pairs, sessile, $\frac{1}{3}$–$\frac{1}{2}$ by $\frac{1}{10}$–$\frac{1}{8}$ in., narrow-oblong, obtuse, glabrous. Flowers minute, sessile, in oblong heads $\frac{1}{2}$–$\frac{3}{4}$ in. long, the lower flowers replaced by numerous yellow staminodes $\frac{1}{4}$–$\frac{1}{3}$ in. long; peduncles 3–6 in. long, stout, erect, tapering, glabrous,

with frequently a membranous ovate acute bract about the middle. Calyx $\frac{1}{16}$ in. long, membranous; lobes acute. Corolla $\frac{1}{8}$ in. long, the lobes linear-oblong, acute. Stamens 10, much exserted; anthers gland-crested. Pods stalked, deflexed, $\frac{1}{2}$–1 by $\frac{1}{3}$ in., slightly curved, oblique at the base, depressed between the seeds, beaked, dry, dehiscing soon by the upper suture. Seeds 6–9, obovoid-oblong, slightly compressed, $\frac{1}{8}$ by $\frac{1}{8}$ in., brown. Fl. B. I. v. 2, p. 285; Dalz. & Gibs. p. 84; Trim. Fl. Ceyl. v. 2, p. 118; Woodr. in Journ. Bomb. Nat. v. 11 (1898) p. 428; Watt, Dict. Econ. Prod. v. 5, p. 348. *Desmanthus natans*, Willd. Sp. Pl. v. 4 (1805) p. 1044; Grah. Cat. p. 57.—Flowers: Oct.–Dec.

KONKAN: in tanks, *Graham, Dalzell & Gibson*. GUJARAT: Nausari, *Kanitkar*! KANARA: Halyal (N. Kanara), *Ritchie*, 1035!, *Talbot, Woodrow*.—DISTRIB. Throughout India in tanks; Ceylon and the Tropics generally.

2. **Neptunia triquetra,** *Benth. in Hook. Journ. Bot.* v. 4 (1842) p. 355. A low prostrate perennial; stems ascending, slender, compressed, more or less angular. Leaves abruptly 2-pinnate; main rhachis grooved; petioles $\frac{1}{4}$–$\frac{1}{2}$ in. long; stipules obliquely ovate, acuminate, persistent; pinnæ 2–3 pairs, shortly stalked. Leaflets 10–15 pairs, sessile, $\frac{1}{8}$–$\frac{1}{4}$ by $\frac{1}{16}$ in., glabrous. Flowers yellow (the sterile flowers few or absent) in globose heads; peduncles solitary, axillary, slender, with 1 or 2 large ovate distant bracts on the peduncle. Calyx minute, 5-toothed. Stamens 10; anthers gland-crested. Pods oblong, $\frac{1}{2}$–1 in. long, straight, nearly equal-sided and tapering at the base, rounded and with a minute beak at the apex, veined, glabrous, black when ripe. Seeds 4–8, oblong, rounded at the apex, compressed, $\frac{1}{8}$ by $\frac{1}{8}$ in., dark brown, polished. Fl. B. I. v. 2, p. 286; Dalz. & Gibs. p. 84; Woodr. in Journ. Bomb. Nat. v. 11 (1898) p. 428. *Desmanthus triquetrus*, Willd. Sp. Pl. v. 4 (1805) p. 1045; Grah. Cat. p. 57; Wight, Icon. t. 756.—Flowers: Aug.–Oct.

KONKAN: Bombay, *Capt. Geburne*! DECCAN: Ahmednagar, *Cooke*!, *Woodrow*. GUJARAT: common in pastures about Surat, *Graham, Dalzell & Gibson*; Surat, *Woodrow*. S. M. COUNTRY: Padshapur, near Belgaum, *Ritchie*, 1729!—DISTRIB. India (W. Peninsula, Bandelkhand).

72. XYLIA, Benth.

A tall unarmed tree with hard wood. Leaves 2-pinnate. Leaflets large, of few pairs. Flowers in globose heads, mostly perfect. Calyx tubular, 5-toothed at the tip. Petals 5, valvate, slightly cohering at the base. Stamens 10, free, exserted; anthers gland-crested in an early stage. Ovary sessile; ovules many; style filiform; stigma minute, terminal. Pod large, woody, flat, broadly falcate, finally dehiscent, septate between the seeds. Seeds oblong, compressed, with a short fleshy funicle.—DISTRIB. Tropical Asia; species 1.

1. **Xylia dolabriformis,** *Benth. in Hook. Journ. Bot.* v. 4 (1842) p. 417. A tall tree; young parts tomentose. Leaves 2-pinnate; pinnæ 2, terminal on a petiole 1–$2\frac{1}{4}$ in. long which is furnished with a gland at the apex between the pinnæ. Leaflets 2–4 pairs, diminishing downwards, with often a small unopposed leaflet on the outside below the lowest pair of leaflets, the terminal leaflets 3–6 by $1\frac{1}{4}$–$2\frac{1}{2}$ in., the lowest pair $1\frac{1}{4}$–$1\frac{1}{2}$ in. long, all oblong, acute, with rounded base, subcoriaceous, glabrous; petiolules $\frac{1}{10}$ in. long. Flowers sessile, in dense

globose heads $\frac{1}{2}$–$\frac{3}{4}$ in. in diam.; peduncles 3 in. long, slender, thickening in fruit, crowded on short puberulous branchlets developed with the young leaves. Calyx tubular, $\frac{1}{8}$ in. long; teeth 5, valvate. Corolla yellowish white, $\frac{1}{4}$ in. long; petals lanceolate, valvate. Stamens 10; filaments free, $\frac{1}{2}$ in. long, exserted; anthers crested when young with a stalked deciduous gland. Ovary sessile; ovules many. Pods 4–6 by 1–2$\frac{1}{2}$ in., large, woody, oblong, falcate, flat, rusty-tomentose, septate between the seeds, finally dehiscent. Seeds 6–10, oblong-ellipsoid, compressed, $\frac{1}{2}$–$\frac{5}{8}$ by $\frac{1}{4}$–$\frac{3}{8}$ in., brown, smooth, polished. Fl. B. I. v. 2, p. 286; Dalz. & Gibs. p. 85; Bedd. Flor. Sylvat. t. 186; Talb. Trees, Bomb. ed. 2, p. 148; Woodr. in Journ. Bomb. Nat. v. 11 (1898) p. 428; Watt, Dict. Econ. Prod. v. 6, part 4, p. 320. *Inga xylocarpa*, DC. Prodr. v. 2, p. 439; Grah. Cat. p. 57.—Flowers: Mar.-Apr. VERN. *Jámbhá*; *Yerul*.

KONKAN: *Stocks*!, *Law*!, *Dalzell*!; Savantvadi, *Dalzell & Gibson*, *Kanitkar*! DECCAN: Párghát, *Graham*. S. M. COUNTRY: Ramghát, *Ritchie*, 239! KANARA: N. Kanara, *Woodrow*; Kála naddi, *Ritchie*, 239!—DISTRIB. India (W. Peninsula, Birma); Singapore, Philippines, Indo-China.

The wood is very hard and durable and especially adapted for railway sleepers and telegraph posts as it resists the attacks of white ants. See Watt, Dict. Econ. Prod. l. c.

73. ENTADA, Adams.

Lofty climbing shrubs, cirrhiferous, unarmed. Leaves 2-pinnate; stipules small, setaceous. Flowers 5-merous, in long narrow spikes, minute, polygamous. Calyx campanulate, very shortly and equally 5-toothed. Petals free or slightly cohering, valvate. Stamens 10, free, shortly exserted; anthers crested with a deciduous gland. Ovary subsessile; ovules numerous; style filiform; stigma concave, terminal. Pod flat, woody, very large, composed of many discoid 1-seeded joints, the endocarp persistent round the seeds. Seeds orbicular, compressed. —DISTRIB. Species 10, of which 1, the following, is widely spread throughout the Tropics; of the others 6 are African and 3 American.

1. **Entada scandens,** *Benth. in Hook. Journ. Bot.* v. 4 (1842) p. 332. An immense woody climber with a thick trunk; branches terete, glabrous. Leaves 2-pinnate; main rhachis glabrous, grooved, usually ending in a bifid tendril; petioles 2–3$\frac{1}{2}$ in. long, glabrous; pinnæ 2–3 pairs, stalked. Leaflets 1$\frac{1}{2}$–3 by $\frac{3}{4}$–1$\frac{1}{4}$, oblong or obovate-oblong, obtuse, often emarginate, rigidly coriaceous, dark green, glabrous, reticulately veined, base acute; petiolules $\frac{1}{10}$ in. long. Flowers in peduncled, panicled, or simple spikes 6–10 in. long, axillary or from the nodes of old leafless branches. Calyx about $\frac{1}{20}$ in. long, minutely 5-toothed. Corolla $\frac{1}{10}$–$\frac{1}{8}$ in. long, yellow. Pods 1–3 ft. long by 3–4 in. wide and 1$\frac{1}{2}$ in. thick, slightly curved, woody, the sutures very thick, indented between the seeds. Seeds 6–15, orbicular or orbicular-oblong, 1$\frac{3}{4}$–2$\frac{1}{4}$ in. in diam., compressed, smooth and shining, brown. The joints of the pod break away from the thickened sutures which remain as an empty frame. Fl. B. I. v. 2, p. 287; Trim. Fl. Ceyl. v. 2, p. 119; Talb. Trees, Bomb. ed. 2, p. 148; Woodr. in Journ. Bomb. Nat. v. 11 (1898) p. 428; Watt, Dict. Econ. Prod. v. 3, p. 245. *Entada pusætha*, DC. Prod. v. 2, p. 425; Grah. Cat. p. 56; Dalz. & Gibs. p. 83.—Flowers: Mar.-May. VERN. *Gárdul*; *Gárambi*; *Gárbi*.

In the forests along the Ghâts, *Dalzell & Gibson*. KONKAN: *Stocks*!; Konkan near Mahableshwar, *Ralph*! DECCAN: Lanoli wood, *Woodrow*. KANARA: forests of the N. Kanara Ghâts, often along river banks, *Talbot*; Sirsi-Kumpta road (N. Kanara), *Woodrow*; Kála naddi, *Ritchie*, 236!—DISTRIB. India (Central and Eastern Himalayas, Nipal, W. Peninsula); Ceylon, and the Tropics generally.

74. ADENANTHERA, Linn.

Unarmed trees. Leaves 2-pinnate. Leaflets numerous, small. Flowers usually 5-merous, in elongate spiciform racemes, axillary or panicled at the tops of the branches, usually hermaphrodite. Calyx campanulate, shortly and equally toothed. Petals valvate, cohering below the middle or at length free. Stamens 10, free, scarcely exserted; anthers crested with a deciduous gland. Ovary sessile; ovules numerous; style filiform; stigma small, terminal. Pod strap-shaped, torulose, falcate, compressed or turgid above the seeds, the coriaceous valves much twisted after they separate. Seeds small, bright-colored.—DISTRIB. Tropics of the Old World; species 4.

1. **Adenanthera pavonina,** *Linn. Sp. Pl.* (1753) p. 384. A small unarmed tree 20–50 ft. high; young parts glabrous. Leaves 2-pinnate, 8–12 in. long; petioles 2–4 in. long; pinnæ 3–6 pairs, opposite, 3–6 in. long, with a stalk $\frac{1}{2}$–$\frac{3}{4}$ in. long. Leaflets alternate, 4–8 pairs, 1–1$\frac{1}{2}$ by $\frac{1}{3}$–$\frac{3}{4}$ in., papery, elliptic-oblong, obtuse, glabrous, dark green above, glaucous beneath, base shortly cuneate, unequal-sided; petiolules $\frac{1}{8}$ in. long. Flowers in short-peduncled racemes 2–6 in long, axillary or panicled at the ends of the branches; pedicels $\frac{1}{10}$–$\frac{1}{8}$ in. long, slender. Calyx minute; lobes short, triangular. Corolla pale yellow, about $\frac{1}{8}$ in. long; segments united at the base only, linear-lanceolate, acute, valvate. Stamens 10, free, hardly exserted; anthers gland-crested. Pods 6–9 by $\frac{5}{8}$–$\frac{3}{4}$ in., flat, falcately curved, pointed, tapering to the base, the valves spirally twisted after dehiscence. Seeds 8–15, lenticular-globose, with a blunt keel, smooth, shining, usually brilliant scarlet, $\frac{1}{3}$ in. in diam. Fl. B. I. v. 2, p. 287; Grah. Cat. p. 57; Dalz. & Gibs. Suppl. p. 26; Bedd. Flor. Sylvat. t. 46; Trim. Fl. Ceyl. v. 2, p. 120; Talb. Trees, Bomb. ed. 2, p. 149; Woodr. in Journ. Bomb. Nat. v. 11 (1898) p. 428; Watt, Dict. Econ. Prod. v. 1, p. 107.—Flowers: Mar.–May. VERN. *Thorla-gunj*, *Ratan-gunj*.

Often planted; rare in the wild state. In gardens at Kolaba, Byculla, and Girgaum, wild in some parts of Gujarat and Khandesh, *Graham*. Native of S. India, in gardens Bombay, *Dalzell & Gibson*. Moist forests of the Konkan and N. Kanara, nowhere abundant, *Talbot*.—DISTRIB. India (Bengal, Birma, W. Peninsula); Ceylon; Malay Islands, Timor, China, Philippines.

The timber is used as a substitute for red sandalwood (*Pterocarpus santalinus*) and the bright-red polished seeds are used as weights and are also strung as beads. See Watt, Dict. Econ. Prod. l. c.

75. PROSOPIS, Linn.

Erect prickly trees or shrubs. Leaves 2-pinnate; stipules small or 0. Leaflets small, narrow. Flowers 5-merous, usually sessile, in narrow spikes or subspicate racemes. Calyx campanulate, shortly toothed or subentire. Petals connate below the middle or at length free, valvate. Stamens 10, free, shortly exserted; anthers crested with a deciduous gland. Ovary sessile or stalked; ovules many; style filiform; stigma minute, terminal. Pod turgid, cylindric or oblong, straight, falcate or variously twisted, septate between the seeds; mesocarp thick, spongy. Seeds usually ovoid, compressed.—DISTRIB. Tropical and subtropical regions of the world; species 18.

Pinnæ 1–2 pairs; pod 4–8 in. long .... 1. *P. spicigera.*
Pinnæ 3–5 pairs; pod ½–1 in. long .... 2. *P. Stephaniana.*

1. **Prosopis spicigera,** *Linn. Mantiss.* (1767) p. 68. A tree, 30–60 ft. high, sending its roots many feet into the ground; branches slender, glabrous, armed with nearly straight, scattered, somewhat compressed prickles ⅛–¼ in. long (very rarely unarmed). Leaves 2-pinnate; main rhachis glabrous or puberulous; pinnæ usually 2 pairs, opposite, 1–3 in. long, often with round insect-galls on their rhachises. Leaflets 7–12 pairs, ⅜–⅝ by ⅛–$\frac{3}{16}$ in., subsessile, oblong, obliquely rounded and mucronate at the apex, very unequal-sided, the upper side much the smaller, reticulately veined, grey, glabrous, base rounded and very oblique. Flowers sessile or nearly so, in short-peduncled axillary spikes and terminal panicles; bracts small, membranous. Calyx $\frac{1}{16}$ in. long, membranous, cup-shaped, faintly 5-toothed or truncate. Corolla yellow, ⅛ in. long. Pods 4–8 in. long, turgid, straight, slender, cylindric, torulose, glabrous, narrowed gradually into a short stalk and filled with a brown farinaceous edible substance. Seeds 10–15, dull-brown, oblong, Fl. B. I. v. 2, p. 288; Grah. Cat. p. 57; Dalz. & Gibs. p. 84; Bedd. Flor. Sylvat. t. 56; Aitch. Pb. & Sind Pl. p. 53; Talb. Trees, Bomb. ed. 2, p. 149; Woodr. in Journ. Bomb. Nat. v. 11 (1898) p. 428; Watt, Dict. Econ. Prod. v. 6, part 1, p. 340.—Flowers: Dec.–Mar. VERN. *Shemi*; *Saundad*; *Sumri*; *Kandi.*

GUJARAT: *Law, Woodrow.* SIND: *Stocks!, Woodrow!*; Karachi to Mugger Peer, *Perry!*; Shikarpur, *Cooke!*; Ruk, *Cooke!*—DISTRIB. India (Panjáb, Rajputana, Bandelkhand, and dry regions of W. Peninsula); Beluchistan, Afghanistan, Persia.

The farinaceous substance which the pods contain is largely consumed as food by the poorer classes; the pods are also an excellent fodder for camels and goats. The wood is not durable, but furnishes good fuel. See Watt, Dict. Econ. Prod. l. c.

2. **Prosopis Stephaniana,** *Kunth, in Spreng. Syst.* v. 2 (1825) p. 326. A shrub or small tree; branches puberulous, whitish when young, armed with numerous sharp slender pale-yellow prickles. Leaves 2-pinnate, 1–2 in. long; main rhachis finely downy; petioles short; pinnæ 3–5 pairs, their rhachises finely downy. Leaflets 8–12 pairs, ⅛–¼ by $\frac{1}{30}$–$\frac{1}{16}$ in., subsessile, oblong, very oblique, closely downy beneath and with ciliate margins. Flowers in axillary spikes which are much longer than the leaves. Calyx cup-shaped, $\frac{1}{20}$ in. long, membranous, obscurely 5-toothed. Petals ⅛–⅙ in. long, ovate-oblong, acute, yellow. Stamens 10. Ovary glabrous. Pods stalked, ½–1 by ⅜–½ in., oblong, obtuse, black, filled with a soft pulp. Fl. B. I. v. 2, p. 288; Benth. in Hook. Journ. Bot. v. 4 (1842) p. 347; Woodr. in Journ. Bomb. Nat. v. 11 (1898) p. 428; Watt, Dict. Econ. Prod. v. 6, part 1, p. 342.

Very rare in the Bombay Presidency. GUJARAT: Goga, *Woodrow.*—DISTRIB. India (Panjáb); Caucasus, Orient, Afghanistan.

The pods are often infested with insects and become large and irregular in form. They are employed for tanning in Afghanistan.

76. DICHROSTACHYS, DC.

Shrubs. Leaves 2-pinnate. Leaflets usually small, multijugate. Flowers 5-merous, minute, polygamous, in solitary or twin peduncled spikes, perfect in the upper half of the spike, those of the lower half bearing long filiform staminodes. Calyx campanulate, shortly toothed. Petals cohering below the middle, valvate. Stamens in the hermaphrodite flowers 10, free, shortly exserted; anthers gland-crested. Ovary subsessile; ovules many; style filiform; stigma terminal, truncate. Pod linear, compressed, twisted up when ripe, continuous within, indehiscent, or the valves separating irregularly from the sutures. Seeds obovoid, compressed.—DISTRIB. Tropical Asia, Africa, and Australia; species 5.

1. **Dichrostachys cinerea,** *Wight & Arn. Prodr.* (1834) p. 271. A much-branched thorny shrub, sometimes a small tree; bark light-colored, furrowed; branchlets ending in spines. Leaves 2-pinnate, $1\frac{1}{4}$–$2\frac{1}{2}$ in. long; main rhachis more or less softly pubescent, with a small erect gland between each pair of pinnæ; stipules $\frac{3}{16}$ in. long, subulate from a triangular base; pinnæ 8–14 pairs, $\frac{3}{8}$–$\frac{5}{8}$ in. long, sessile or nearly so. Leaflets minute, sessile, 12–20 pairs, close, linear, oblique, subacute. Flowers numerous, crowded in dense axillary or extra-axillary spikes 1–$1\frac{1}{2}$ in. long, the upper half of the spike yellow, the lower red. Calyx $\frac{1}{30}$ in. long, membranous. Corolla $\frac{1}{12}$–$\frac{1}{10}$ in. long. Stamens of the perfect flowers in the upper half of the spike yellow. Staminodes in the lower half of the spike $\frac{1}{2}$ in. long, much longer than the stamens, red. Pods 2–3 by $\frac{1}{4}$–$\frac{3}{8}$ in., glabrous, flat, subarticulated, dark brown, twisted up when ripe. Seeds 6–10. Fl. B. I. v. 2, p. 288; Grah. Cat. p. 57; Dalz. & Gibs. p. 84; Wight, Icon. t. 357; Trim. Fl. Ceyl. v. 2, p. 121; Talb. Trees, Bomb. ed. 2, p. 149; Woodr. in Journ. Bomb. Nat. v. 11 (1898) p. 428; Watt, Dict. Econ. Prod. v. 3, p. 109.—Flowers: Sep.–Oct. VERN. *Sigam Káti.*

DECCAN: common on dry stony hills; Poona, *Cooke*!, *Woodrow*!; Badami, Jeur, *Woodrow*. S. M. COUNTRY: Pádshapur, *Ritchie*, 1055! KANARA: cultivated in N. Kanara, *Talbot*.—DISTRIB. India (N.W. Provinces, Central India, Rajputana, W. Peninsula); Ceylon, Malay Islands, N. Australia.

77. LEUCÆNA, Benth.

Unarmed trees or shrubs. Leaves 2-pinnate; stipules setaceous or small. Flowers 5-merous, sessile, usually hermaphrodite, in globose heads; peduncles axillary, subfasciculate, or the upper arranged in a terminal leafless raceme; bracts usually 2. Calyx tubuloso-campanulate, shortly toothed. Petals free or nearly so, valvate. Stamens 10, free, much exserted; anthers not gland-crested. Ovary stalked; ovules many; style filiform; stigma small, terminal. Pod stalked, strap-shaped, flat, coriaceous, continuous within, dehiscent. Seeds transverse, ovoid, compressed.—DISTRIB. Species 8, chiefly American.

1. **Leucæna glauca,** *Benth. in Hook. Journ. Bot.* v. 4 (1842) p. 416. A large erect shrub or small tree 6–20 ft. high, unarmed. Leaves 2-pinnate, 3–7 in. long; main rhachis slender, channelled, pubescent, ending in a weak spine; petioles 1–2 in. long; pinnæ 3–6 pairs, 2–$3\frac{1}{2}$ in.

long, shortly stalked, their rhachises pubescent, ending in a weak spine. Leaflets 10–15 pairs, rather distant, ⅜ by ⅛ in., membranous, glaucous, linear-oblong, acute, glabrous or nearly so above, finely pubescent beneath, base oblique. Flowers in dense globose heads; peduncles often geminate, 1–1½ in. long, slender, pubescent, elongate and slightly thickened in fruit. Calyx $\frac{1}{10}$–⅛ in. long, tubuloso-campanulate, membranous; teeth short, triangular. Petals ⅛ in. long, spathulate-oblong, indurated at the tip, whitish. Stamens 10, much exserted; anthers not gland-crested. Ovary shortly stalked, slightly pubescent. Pods 5–6 by ½–¾ in., straight, flat, obliquely triangular at the apex, narrowed at the base into a stalk ¼–½ in. long, glabrous. Seeds 15–20. Fl. B. I. v. 2, p. 290; Talb. Trees, Bomb. ed. 2, p. 150; Woodr. in Journ. Bomb. Nat. v. 11 (1898) p. 428; Watt, Dict. Econ. Prod. v. 4, p. 632. *Acacia glauca*, Willd. Sp. Pl. v. 4, p. 1075; Grah. Cat. p. 58. *Acacia leucocephala*, Link, Enum. v. 2, p. 444; Dalz. & Gibs. Suppl. p. 26.—Flowers: July–Oct. VERN. *Kubábhal*.

A native of Tropical America naturalized in the Bombay Presidency and more or less throughout India. It is common in gardens, where, owing to its spreading roots, it is difficult to eradicate.—DISTRIB. Tropical Asia and Africa, but probably indigenous only in Tropical America.

78. **MIMOSA,** Linn.

Herbs, shrubs, or small trees with or without prickles. Leaves 2-pinnate. Leaflets small, usually sensitive. Flowers polygamous, minute, in dense globose heads or cylindric spikes, often tetramerous; peduncles axillary, solitary or fascicled, the upper often forming a raceme. Calyx usually minute, almost inconspicuous. Petals more or less connate, valvate. Stamens equal in number to the petals or twice as many, free, exserted; anthers small, not gland-crested. Ovary sessile or stalked; ovules many; style filiform; stigma small, terminal. Pods flat, made up of 1-seeded joints that separate when ripe from the persistent sutures. Seeds ovoid or orbicular, flat.—DISTRIB. Chiefly Tropical American; species about 230.

Pinnæ of the leaves 1–2 pairs .... 1. *M. pudica*.
Pinnæ of the leaves more than 2 pairs.
  Pod glabrous, the sutures not prickly .... 2. *M. rubicaulis*.
  Pod pubescent, the sutures prickly .... 3. *M. hamata*.

1. **Mimosa pudica,** *Linn. Sp. Pl.* (1753) p. 518. A diffuse undershrub 1½–3 ft. high; stems and branches sparingly prickly and clothed with long weak bristles from bulbous bases. Leaves sensitive, digitate; petioles 1–2 in. long, bristly; stipules ⅓ in. long, linear-lanceolate, acute, bristly; pinnæ 1–2 pairs, 2–3 in. long, sessile or nearly so, their rhachises clothed with ascending bristles. Leaflets 12–20 pairs, ¼–⅓ by ⅛ in., sessile, coriaceous, linear-oblong, acute, glabrous above, clothed with appressed bristles beneath, base obliquely rounded. Flowers 4-merous, pink, in globose heads, ¼–⅓ in. in diam.; peduncles ¾–1 in. long, prickly, usually in axillary pairs all along the branches; bracteole solitary, linear, acute, ciliolate. Calyx very minute. Corolla pink, $\frac{1}{12}$–$\frac{1}{10}$ in. long, divided about ⅓ the way down; lobes 4, ovate-oblong, obtuse. Stamens 4, much exserted; anthers not gland-crested. Pods ½–¾ by ⅛–⅙ in., flat, slightly recurved, consisting of 3–5 one-seeded joints which fall away from the persistent sutures which are clothed with spreading yellowish

weak bristles $\frac{1}{8}$ in. long, the faces of the pods glabrous. Fl. B. I. v. 2, p. 291; Grah. Cat. p. 56; Dalz. & Gibs. Suppl. p. 25; Benth. in Mart. Fl. Bras. v. 15, part 2, p. 316; Talb. Trees, Bomb. ed. 2, p. 150; Woodr. in Journ. Bomb. Nat. v. 11 (1898) p. 428; Watt, Dict. Econ. Prod. v. 5, p. 248.—Flowers: Sept.-Oct. VERN. *Lájálu.*

The calyx is so minute that it is often overlooked. Linnæus (*l. c.*) describes the corolla as the calyx and says there is no corolla.

The *Sensitive Plant*, naturalized more or less throughout India, probab'y introduced from Tropical America.

2. **Mimosa rubicaulis,** *Lamk. Encyc. Méth.* v. 1 (1783) p. 20. A large straggling shrub; branches yellowish, grooved, furnished with numerous straw-colored hooked prickles. Leaves 2-pinnate, 5–7 in. long; main rhachis slender, grooved, closely set with numerous straw-colored hooked prickles; stipules $\frac{1}{4}$ in. long, subulate; pinnæ 5–11 pairs, $1\frac{1}{2}$–$2\frac{1}{2}$ in. long, shortly stalked, the rhachises without prickles. Leaflets 8–15 pairs, $\frac{1}{4}$–$\frac{5}{16}$ by $\frac{1}{8}$ in., linear-oblong, obtuse, mucronate, unequal-sided, glabrous above, slightly pubescent beneath, base obliquely rounded or truncate; petiolules very short. Flowers 4-merous, in globose heads; peduncles slender, axillary and crowded at the ends of the branchlets, 1–$1\frac{1}{2}$ in. long, densely pubescent; bracteole solitary, $\frac{1}{16}$ in. long, linear-spathulate, ciliate at the apex. Calyx minute, $\frac{1}{80}$ in. long; teeth very short, ciliolate. Corolla $\frac{1}{8}$ in. long, divided about $\frac{1}{3}$ of the way down; lobes 4, ovate-oblong, acute. Stamens 8. Ovary shortly stalked, glabrous. Pods 3–4 by $\frac{3}{8}$–$\frac{5}{8}$ in., flat, falcate, glabrous, consisting of 4–10 one-seeded joints which fall away from the persistent sutures which are not (except very rarely) spiny or bristly on the margins. Fl. B. I. v. 2, p. 291; Grah. Cat. p. 56; Dalz. & Gibs. p. 85; Aitch. Pb. & Sind Pl. p. 53; Talb. Trees, Bomb. ed. 2, p. 150; Woodr. in Journ. Bomb. Nat. v. 11 (1898) p. 428; Watt, Dict. Econ. Prod. v. 5, p. 249. *Mimosa octandra*, Roxb. Cor. Pl. v. 2, p. 55, t. 200.—Flowers: Aug.-Oct. VERN. *Ardi.*

In the dry districts of the Presidency. DECCAN: Poona, *Woodrow*! SIND: *Stocks*! —DISTRIB. Throughout India; Afghanistan.

3. **Mimosa hamata,** *Willd. Sp. Pl.* v. 4 (1805) p. 1033. A much-branched armed shrub; branches downy, furnished with numerous straw-colored curved or straight prickles. Leaves 2-pinnate, $\frac{1}{2}$–2 in. long; main rhachis pubescent, sometimes prickly; stipules $\frac{1}{8}$ in. long, subulate, hairy; pinnæ 3–6 pairs, $\frac{1}{2}$–1 in. long, shortly stalked, their rhachises downy, sometimes prickly. Leaflets 6–10 pairs, $\frac{1}{10}$–$\frac{1}{4}$ in. long, ovate-oblong, acute, mucronate, glabrous or nearly so above, more or less pubescent beneath, base oblique, rounded; petiolules very short. Flowers 4-merous, in globose heads; peduncles axillary and crowded at the ends of the branchlets, $\frac{3}{8}$–1 in. long, slender, downy, often with a few prickles; bracteole solitary, linear-spathulate, ciliate at the apex. Calyx $\frac{1}{20}$ in. long, shortly toothed. Corolla pink, $\frac{1}{8}$ in. long, divided nearly $\frac{1}{2}$ way down; lobes ovate-oblong, acute. Stamens 8. Ovary stalked, pubescent. Pods 2–3 by $\frac{1}{2}$ in., flat, falcate, pubescent on the faces, consisting of 4–8 one-seeded joints which fall away from the persistent sutures which are furnished with hooked or straight prickles. Seeds $\frac{1}{4}$ by $\frac{1}{6}$ in., chestnut-brown. Fl. B. I. v. 2, p. 291; Grah. Cat.

p. 56; Dalz. & Gibs. p. 85; Talb. Trees, Bomb. ed. 2, p. 150; Woodr. in Journ. Bomb. Nat. v. 11 (1898) p. 428.—Flowers: Sept. VERN. *Arkar*; *Aráti*.

KONKAN: *Capt. Geburne*! DECCAN: widely, *Woodrow*; Poona, *Cooke*!; Chandri, *Otto Kuntze*, 7443!; ravines near Hewra, *Dalzell*!; Chattersinghi hill near Poona, *Kanitkar*! GUJARAT: Surat, *Graham*, *Dalzell*!; Porbandar (Kathiawar), *Cooke*! S. M. COUNTRY: common on the Kuput range of hills, Dharwar district, *Talbot*.—DISTRIB. India (W. Peninsula).

79. **ACACIA,** Willd.

Trees or shrubs erect or climbing, usually armed. Leaves 2-pinnate; stipules spinescent or inconspicuous, rarely membranous. Leaflets usually small, multijugate or reduced to a leaf-like petiole (phyllode), Flowers small, hermaphrodite or polygamous, usually 5-merous, in globose heads or cylindric spikes; peduncles axillary, solitary or fascicled or panicled at the ends of the branches. Calyx campanulate or funnel-shaped, shortly toothed. Petals exserted, more or less united, rarely free. Stamens indefinite, much exserted, free; anthers small, not gland-crested. Ovary sessile or stalked; ovules many; style filiform; stigma small, terminal. Pod ligulate or oblong, not jointed, usually compressed and dry, dehiscent or indehiscent, rarely turgid and subcylindric, the sutures straight or wavy, not thickened.—DISTRIB. The leaf-bearing groups cosmopolitan in the Tropics, the great phyllodineous series, which comprises two-thirds of the genus, almost restricted to Australia; species 430.

Erect trees or shrubs.
  Flowers in globose heads.
    Heads on axillary peduncles.
      Pod moniliform .... 1. *A. arabica*.
      Pod cylindric, turgid, not moniliform.
        Pod nearly straight; petiole glandular .... 2. *A. Farnesiana*.
        Pod circinate; petiole eglandular .... 3. *A. planifrons*.
      Pod flat.
        Leaflets 5–8 pairs, glabrous.
          A small tree with ill-smelling flowers; pod longitudinally veined .... 4. *A. eburnea*.
          A bushy shrub with very fragrant flowers; pod transversely or reticulately veined .... 5. *A. Jacquemonti*.
        Leaflets 20–30 pairs, tomentose .... 6. *A. tomentosa*.
    Heads in panicles .... 7. *A. leucophlæa*.
  Flowers in spikes.
    Pinnæ 10–20 pairs; bark white .... 8. *A. Suma*.
    Pinnæ 20–40 pairs; bark dark-brown .... 9. *A. Catechu*.
    Pinnæ 3–6 pairs.
      Stipular spines short, hooked.
        Stipular spines in pairs .... 10. *A. ferruginea*.
        Stipular spines ternate .... 11. *A. Senegal*.
      Stipular spines long, straight .... 12. *A. latronum*.
Climbing shrubs.
  Leaflets 12–30 pairs.
    Pod thick, wrinkled when dry .... 13. *A. concinna*.
    Pod thin, not wrinkled when dry.
      Leaflets $\frac{1}{8}$–$\frac{1}{4}$ in. broad .... 14. *A. Intsia*.
      Leaflets $\frac{1}{10}$ in. broad .... 15. *A. cæsia*.
  Leaflets 40–50 pairs .... 16. *A. pennata*.

1. **Acacia arabica,** *Willd. Sp. Pl.* v. 4 (1805) p. 1085. A small

tree with dark brown or black longitudinally-fissured bark; branchlets slender, terete, pubescent when young. Leaves 2-pinnate, 2–4 in. long; main rhachis downy, often furnished with glands; petioles 1–2 in. long; stipular spines very variable, $\frac{1}{4}$–2 in. long, smooth, usually whitish, straight, sharp, often absent; pinnæ 4–9 pairs, $\frac{3}{4}$–2 in. long, shortly stalked. Leaflets subsessile, 10–25 pairs, $\frac{1}{8}$–$\frac{1}{4}$ by $\frac{1}{20}$–$\frac{1}{12}$ in., linear-oblong, subobtuse, glabrous or nearly so. Flowers yellow, in globose heads; peduncles axillary, in fascicles of 2–6, terete, pubescent; bracteoles 2 above the middle of the peduncle, broadly ovate, acute, pubescent. Calyx campanulate, $\frac{1}{20}$ in. long; teeth very short. Corolla $\frac{1}{8}$ in. long; lobes short, triangular. Pods stalked, 3–6 by $\frac{1}{2}$–$\frac{5}{8}$ in., moniliform, compressed, constricted at the sutures between the seeds, densely and persistently grey downy. Seeds 8–12. Fl. B. I. v. 2, p. 293; Grah. Cat. p. 59; Dalz. & Gibs. p. 86; Bedd. Flor. Sylvat. t. 47; Trim. Fl. Ceyl. v. 2, p. 122; Talb. Trees, Bomb. ed. 2, p. 152; Woodr. in Journ. Bomb. Nat. v. 11 (1898) p. 429; Watt, Dict. Econ. Prod. v. 1, p. 18.—Flowers: June–Jan. VERN. *Bábhal.*

Throughout the Presidency, except in moist regions near the coast. Widely planted in the Deccan, Gujarat, and Sind.—DISTRIB. Throughout the greater part of India; Ceylon, Arabia, Egypt, Tropical Africa, Natal.

The well-known *Bábhal* or *Indian Gum-Arabic* tree. The gum is used medicinally and by the calico-printer, and also forms an inferior substitute for true *Gum-Arabic.* The bark and the pods supply a valuable tanning material. The green pods, young shoots and leaves form an excellent fodder, and are especially valuable during seasons of drought. The timber is hard and durable and extensively used for wheels, well-curbs, and very largely as fuel. See Watt, Dict. Econ. Prod. l. c.

VAR. 1. *cupressiformis*, Stewart, Pb. Pl. (1869) p. 51; branches closing up to the trunk like a cypress. VAR. *cupressina*, Aitch. Pb. & Sind Pl. p. 54. VAR. *Rámkánta*, Grah. Cat. p. 59; Dalz. & Gibs. p. 86; Woodr. in Journ. Bomb. Nat. v. 11 (1898) p. 429.—VERN. *Rámkánta.*

This is rather a doubtful variety. The peculiar growth of the branches may, as Stewart remarks, have been caused by ages of ruthless lopping of the side branches. Edgeworth states that near Multán the variety is sometimes seen on the same tree with the ordinary form. It is common in the Deccan and Gujarat as well as in Sind.

Var. 2. *vediana*; bark more deeply cracked and exfoliating; crown formed of twisted angular interlacing branches; spines usually white, stout, up to 2½ in. long; pods flat, shortly stalked, $\frac{3}{4}$ in. broad, little constricted between the seeds.

Note.—In the 'Indian Forester,' v. 23 (1898) p. 359, Sir D. Brandis called attention to a variety of bábhal called in the vernacular in Berar, where he had collected the plant, "Kaulia bábhal." The variety is also common in the Deccan (Poona, Sholapur, &c.), where it is called "Vedi (*i. e.* mad) bábhal." See Gleadow and also Fagan in 'Indian Forester,' v. 23 (1898) p. 415. The ordinary form with moniliform pods is called "Telia bábhal" in Berar as well as in Khandesh on the confines of Berar, but is known as "Godi (sweet) bábhal" in the Deccan further south. The wood of the "Kaulia or Vedi bábhal" is considered useless for building or agricultural implements and fit only for firewood, while the wood of the "Telia or Godi bábhal" is used for every purpose for which a strong timber is needed. The pods of both are considered equally valuable as food for sheep and goats. Mr. Fagan (*l. c.*) states that the prices of large logs of the two kinds of bábhal would be as 1 : 5.

The tree (Vedi bábhal) is called "Eree bábhal" by *Dalzell & Gibson* (Bo. Fl. p. 86) as well as by *Woodrow* in Journ. Bomb. Nat. v. 11 (1898) p. 429. Fuller information may be obtained by consulting Mr. Fagan's paper in the 'Indian Forester' (*l. c.*). I have transformed the Deccan name "vedi" into a varietal name *vediana.*

2. **Acacia Farnesiana,** *Willd. Sp. Pl.* v. 4 (1805) p. 1083. A shrub or low tree; branches slender, zigzag, marked with grey or pale-brown dots; spines stipular only. Leaves 2-pinnate, 1–2 in. long; main rhachis more or less pubescent; petioles usually furnished with a minute gland about the middle; stipules spinescent, $\frac{1}{6}$–$\frac{1}{3}$ in. long, hard and sharp, divaricate; pinnæ 4–8 pairs, $\frac{3}{4}$–1 in. long. Leaflets 10–20 pairs, $\frac{3}{16}$–$\frac{1}{4}$ by $\frac{1}{20}$–$\frac{1}{18}$ in., sessile, rigidly coriaceous, linear-oblong, acute, green, subglabrous, base oblique, rounded. Flowers in globose heads, $\frac{1}{4}$–$\frac{1}{3}$ in. in diam., fragrant, deep yellow; peduncles $\frac{3}{4}$–1 in. long, crowded on axillary nodes, slender, terete, pubescent, with a ring of small deflexed ciliate bracts at or near the apex; bracteole solitary, deltoid, on a long slender stalk, ciliolate. Calyx $\frac{1}{16}$ in. long, membranous; teeth short, triangular, acute. Corolla $\frac{1}{10}$ in. long; lobes very short, obtuse. Ovary glabrous. Pods 2–3½ by ½ in., subcylindric, turgid, slightly curved, conspicuously striately veined, glabrous, brown; mesocarp pulpy. Seeds biseriate. Fl. B. I. v. 2, p. 292; Bedd. Flor. Sylvat. t. 52; Aitch. Pb. & Sind Pl. p. 54; Talb. Trees, Bomb. ed. 2, p. 151; Woodr. in Journ. Bomb. Nat. v. 11 (1898) p. 429; Watt, Dict. Econ. Prod. v. 1, p. 48. *Vachellia Farnesiana*, Wight & Arn. Prodr. p. 272; Grah. Cat. p. 58; Dalz. & Gibs. Suppl. p. 26.—Flowers: Aug.–Mar. Vern. *Devbdbhal*; *Kankri*.

Naturalized but not indigenous in the Bombay Presidency, where it is often planted. Deccan: eastern parts, common, *Graham*; common in the black soil nálas of the Deccan, *Dalzell & Gibson*; Kirkee, *Woodrow*. Sind: *Stocks*!—Distrib. Cosmopolitan in the Tropics, often planted.

3. **Acacia planifrons,** *Wight & Arn. Prodr.* (1834) p. 276. A small armed tree with an erect stem; branches spreading so as to form an umbrella-like head; bark thick, dark grey on the older, purplish on the younger branches. Leaves 2-pinnate, small; petioles without glands; stipular spines of two kinds, either very short and curved downwards or 1½–2 in. long, straight, divaricate, white with a brown point; pinnæ 3–6 pairs, $\frac{1}{4}$–$\frac{3}{8}$ in. long, closely placed near the end of the rhachis. Leaflets 5–10 pairs, $\frac{1}{12}$–$\frac{1}{8}$ in. long, linear, obtuse. Flowers in globular heads, $\frac{1}{4}$–$\frac{3}{8}$ in. in diam.; peduncles in axillary fascicles, filiform, ½–1 in. long; bracteoles erect, below the middle of the peduncle. Calyx $\frac{1}{20}$ in. long, funnel-shaped; teeth very short. Corolla $\frac{1}{10}$–$\frac{1}{8}$ in. long; lobes short, obtuse. Ovary glabrous. Pods about 2 in. long and $\frac{1}{4}$–$\frac{3}{8}$ in. wide, subcylindric, turgid, acute, circinate, glabrous. Fl. B. I. v. 2, p. 293 (in part); Bedd. For. Man. in Flor. Sylvat. p. xcv; Trim. Fl. Ceyl. v. 2, p. 123; Woodr. in Journ. Bomb. Nat. v. 11 (1898) p. 429; Watt, Dict. Econ. Prod. v. 1, p. 54.—Flowers: Nov. Vern. *Salé*.

Though abundant in S. India the tree can scarcely be considered indigenous in the Bombay Presidency, where it is however often planted. It is known to Anglo-Indians as the *Umbrella Tree*, from the umbrella-like appearance of its head.—Distrib. India (W. Peninsula); Ceylon.

4. **Acacia eburnea,** *Willd. Sp. Pl.* v. 4 (1805) p. 1081. A small tree; bark of the young branches purplish-brown. Leaves $\frac{3}{4}$–1 in. long; stipular spines straight, varying from $\frac{1}{8}$–2¼ in. long, gradually tapering from a broad base to a very sharp point, ivory-white, polished; pinnæ 2–7 pairs, $\frac{1}{4}$–$\frac{1}{2}$ in. long, sessile or nearly so. Leaflets 5–8 pairs, $\frac{1}{10}$–$\frac{1}{8}$ in. long, linear, subobtuse, glabrous. Flowers bright-yellow, with

a disagreeable odor, in globose heads ⅝ in. in diam.; peduncles axillary, pubescent; bracts about the middle of the peduncle. Calyx $\frac{1}{16}$ in. long, campanulate; teeth short, deltoid. Corolla ⅛ in. long; lobes ovate-oblong, acute. Ovary stalked, glabrous. Pods stalked, 3–6 by ¼–⅜ in., flat, slightly curved, indented on both sutures, longitudinally veined, glabrous. Seeds 6–10. Fl. B. I. v. 2, p. 293; Dalz. & Gibs. p. 85; Bedd. For. Man. in Flor. Sylvat. p. xcv; Trim. Fl. Ceyl. v. 2, p. 124; Talb. Trees, Bomb. ed. 2, p. 152; Woodr. in Journ. Bomb. Nat. v. 11 (1898) p. 429; Watt, Dict. Econ. Prod. v. 1, p. 48.—Flowers: Nov.–Feb. VERN. *Marmat.*

DECCAN: *Stocks*!, *Dalzell*!; Poona, *Woodrow*, 944! S. M. COUNTRY: *Woodrow*; common in stony places, *Talbot*. SIND: *Dalzell*!—DISTRIB. Throughout India in dry districts; Ceylon, Arabia, Afghanistan.

5. **Acacia Jacquemonti,** *Benth. in Hook. Lond. Journ. Bot.* v. 1 (1842) p. 499. A bushy shrub 4–8 ft. high; branches stiff, smooth, brown. Leaves 2-pinnate; stipular spines straight, slender, 1–2 in. long, ivory-white, connate at the base; pinnæ 2–4 pairs, ¼–½ in. long. Leaflets 5–10 pairs, $\frac{1}{10}$–⅛ in. long, linear-oblong, grey-green, rigidly coriaceous, glabrous. Flowers yellow, delightfully fragrant, in globose heads ½ in. in diam.; peduncles slender, in axillary fascicles of 2 or more; bracts 2, about the middle of the peduncle. Calyx campanulate, $\frac{1}{20}$–$\frac{1}{16}$ in. long; teeth very short, deltoid. Corolla ⅛ in. long; lobes ovate-oblong, acute. Ovary stalked, glabrous. Pods stalked, 2–3 by ½–⅝ in., flat, straight, reticulately or transversely veined. Seeds 5–6. Fl. B. I. v. 2, p. 293; Talb. Trees, Bomb. ed. 2, p. 152; Woodr. in Journ. Bomb. Nat. v. 11 (1898) p. 429; Watt, Dict. Econ. Prod. v. 1, p. 51.—Flowers: Feb.–May. VERN. *Rátobáwal.*

GUJARAT: *Talbot*; Ahmedabad, *Woodrow*; Baroda, *Brandis*! SIND: *Talbot*.—DISTRIB. India (Panjáb, Rajputana).

6. **Acacia tomentosa,** *Willd. Sp. Pl.* v. 4 (1805) p. 1087. A small tree; bark yellowish, with large lenticels; young parts tomentose. Leaves 2-pinnate, 1½–3½ in. long; main rhachis densely pubescent or tomentose; stipular spines straight, rapidly tapering from a broad base, brown; pinnæ 6–12 pairs, 1–2 in. long, sessile, their rhachises densely pubescent. Leaflets 20–30 pairs, ⅛–⅙ by $\frac{1}{20}$–$\frac{1}{16}$ in., linear-oblong, obtuse, sessile, pubescent on both sides. Flowers in globose heads, ½–⅝ in. in diam.; peduncles axillary, ¾–1¼ in. long, stout, densely downy; bracts a little above the middle of the peduncle. Calyx $\frac{1}{10}$ in. long, pubescent; teeth rounded, ciliolate. Corolla ⅛ in. long, greenish-white, oblong, sub-acute, ciliolate. Ovary very shortly stalked, glabrous. Pods 4–6 by ½ in., ligulate, compressed, falcate, at first pubescent, afterwards glabrous. Seeds 5–8, ellipsoid, compressed, with an areole on each face. Fl. B. I. v. 2, p. 294; Grah. Cat. p. 59; Dalz. & Gibs. p. 86; Bedd. For. Man. in Flor. Sylvat. p. xcv; Trim. Fl. Ceyl. v. 2, p. 124; Talb. Trees, Bomb. ed. 2, p. 152; Woodr. in Journ. Bomb. Nat. v. 11 (1898) p. 429; Watt, Dict. Econ. Prod. v. 1, p. 61.—VERN. *Anjar.*

DECCAN: Sholapur districts, *Law* ex *Graham*. GUJARAT: Dang jungles, *Woodrow*; Panch Mahála, *Watt*.

Dalzell & Gibson (Bo. Fl. p. 85) describe the plant as rare and occurring in the Deccan and Khandesh jungles. In the table of Addenda and Corrigenda, p. 318, this statement has been withdrawn, as the plants from which their specimens were taken were afterwards found by these botanists to have been raised in the Dapudi botanical garden from seed obtained, probably, from Nipál.—DISTRIB. India (W. Peninsula); Ceylon.

7. **Acacia leucophlœa,** *Willd. Sp. Pl.* v. 4 (1805) p. 1083. A tree with yellowish bark; branches dense, spreading, the young ones pubescent. Leaflets 2-pinnate, subsessile, 1–2 in. long; main rhachis pubescent, usually with a cup-shaped gland between each pair of pinnæ; spines variable in length, the stipular ones short, straight; pinnæ 5–15 pairs, subsessile, $\frac{3}{4}$–$1\frac{1}{2}$ in. long. Leaflets 12–30 pairs, crowded, $\frac{1}{8}$–$\frac{1}{4}$ in. long, subsessile, linear-oblong, obtuse, glabrous or nearly so. Flowers in large terminal tomentose panicles; heads numerous, globose, $\frac{1}{4}$–$\frac{3}{8}$ in. in diam.; pedicels stout, downy, with a toothed ring of bracts above the middle. Calyx $\frac{1}{20}$ in. long; teeth short. Corolla twice as long as the calyx; lobes subacute. Pods 4–8 by $\frac{1}{4}$–$\frac{1}{3}$ in., sessile, thin, flat, subindehiscent, slightly curved, clothed with pale brown tomentum. Seeds 10–20. Fl. B. I. v. 2, p. 294; Grah. Cat. p. 59; Dalz. & Gibs. p. 86; Trim. Fl. Ceyl. v. 2, p. 125; Talb. Trees, Bomb. ed. 2, p. 152; Woodr. in Journ. Bomb. Nat. v. 11 (1898) p. 429; Watt, Dict. Econ. Prod. v. 1, p. 52. *Mimosa leucophlœa*, Roxb. Cor. Pl. t. 150.—Flowers: Jan.–Feb. VERN. *Hivar.*

DECCAN: widely, *Woodrow*; Alandi, near Railway Station, *Kanitkar!*; Sholapur districts between the Kistna and Bhima rivers, *Graham*; Khandesh, *Brandis!* S. M. COUNTRY: common, *Talbot, Dalzell & Gibson.*

In the S. M. Country the bark is used in the distillation of spirit and the trees have been farmed on account of Government. See Watt, Dict. Econ. Prod. l. c.

8. **Acacia Suma,** *Buch.-Ham. in Wall. Cat.* (1828) 5227 C. A middle-sized tree; bark white; young shoots downy. Leaves 2-pinnate, 4–6 in. long; main rhachis pubescent, with glands between many of the pairs of pinnæ and a large conspicuous gland at or near the middle of the petiole; petioles 1–$1\frac{1}{4}$ in. long; stipular spines short, straight or slightly hooked, from a broad triangular base, polished; pinnæ 10–30 pairs, $1\frac{1}{2}$–$2\frac{1}{2}$ in. long, shortly stalked. Leaflets 30–50 pairs, $\frac{3}{16}$–$\frac{1}{4}$ by $\frac{1}{20}$ in., closely set on the rhachis, linear, subacute, sessile, pale green, rigidly coriaceous, glabrous or nearly so. Flowers sessile, whitish, in peduncled 1–4-nate spikes 3–4 in. long, the rhachis densely pubescent. Calyx campanulate, downy, $\frac{1}{12}$ in. long; teeth short, deltoid, ciliate. Corolla $\frac{1}{10}$–$\frac{1}{8}$ in. long, divided about $\frac{1}{2}$ way down; lobes narrow-oblong, subacute. Pods 3–5 by $\frac{1}{2}$–$\frac{3}{4}$ in., flat, with a triangular beak at the apex, tapering at the base into a stalk $\frac{1}{2}$–$\frac{3}{4}$ in. long, reticulately veined, glabrous. Seeds 6–8. Fl. B. I. v. 2, p. 294; Kurz, ex Brandis, For. Fl. (1874) p. 187; Talb. Trees, Bomb. ed. 2, p. 152; Woodr. in Journ. Bomb. Nat. v. 11 (1898) p. 429; Watt, Dict. Econ. Pron. v. 1, p. 60. *Acacia Catechu*, Wight & Arn. Prodr. p. 272 (exclud. syn.); Dalz. & Gibs. p. 86; Bedd. Flor. Sylvat. t. 49.—Flowers: May–July. VERN. *Kumtia*; *Son-khairi.*

S. M. COUNTRY: in moist places and along nálas, but not common, *Talbot*; near Belgaum, *Ritchie*, 1056! KANARA: N. Kanara, near the Dharwar frontier, *Talbot.*—DISTRIB. India (Bengal, Behar, W. Peninsula).

The extract Catechu may be obtained from the heartwood of the tree and the bark is used as a tan. See Watt, Dict. Econ. Prod. l. c.

9. **Acacia Catechu,** *Willd. Sp. Pl.* v. 4 (1805) p. 1079. A moderate-sized tree 30–40 ft. high; bark dark-colored, rough; young shoots dark-brown or purple, glabrous. Leaves 2-pinnate, 4–6 in. long; main rhachis pubescent, with glands between many of the pairs of pinnæ and a large conspicuous gland at or near the middle of the petiole; stipular spines short, hooked, from a broad triangular base, polished; pinnæ 10–30 pairs, $1\frac{1}{2}$–2 in. long, nearly sessile, their rhachises pubescent. Leaflets 30–50 pairs, $\frac{3}{16}$–$\frac{1}{4}$ by $\frac{1}{20}$ in., linear, subacute, sessile, often ciliate. Flowers sessile, pale-yellow, in peduncled 1–4-nate axillary spikes 2–4 in. long. Calyx campanulate, $\frac{1}{20}$–$\frac{1}{16}$ in. long, hairy outside; teeth deltoid, ciliate. Corolla 2–3 times as long as the calyx; lobes ovate-oblong, subacute, pubescent. Pods stalked, 2–3 by $\frac{3}{8}$–$\frac{5}{8}$ in., flat, thin, brown, shining, with a triangular beak at the apex and narrowed at the base into a stalk $\frac{1}{8}$–$\frac{1}{4}$ in. long. Seeds 3–10. Fl. B. I. v. 2, p. 295; Talb. Trees, Bomb. ed. 2, p. 153; Woodr. in Journ. Bomb. Nat. v. 11 (1898) p. 429; Watt, Dict. Econ. Prod. v. 1, p. 27. *Mimosa Catechu*, Roxb. Cor. Pl. t. 175.—Flowers: Aug.–Sept. VERN. *Khair*; *Khair-bâbhal.*

Along the coasts of the Konkan and of N. Kanara, often on laterite, *Talbot.* DECCAN: *Woodrow.* S. M. COUNTRY: *Woodrow.* GUJARAT: *Woodrow.*—DISTRIB. India (Panjáb, N.W. Himalayas, Central India, Behar, Gánjám, Birma).

I have cited the localities given by the several authors named, but have seen no specimens from any. I am therefore unable to say if the true *A. Catechu* or its variety *A. Sundra* is intended. All the specimens I have seen from the Bombay Presidency, some of which were labelled *A. Catechu*, have proved to be the variety *A. Sundra.* Consult Prain, Journ. As. Soc. Beng. v. 66 (1898) pp. 508–510.

VAR. *Sundra*, Prain, in Journ. As. Soc. Beng. v. 66 (1898) pp. 508–510. Pinnæ 15–20 pairs. Calyx, petals and rhachises all glabrous. *Acacia Sundra* (sp.), DC. Prodr. v. 2 (1825) p. 458; Fl. B. I. v. 2, p. 295; Dalz. & Gibs. p. 86; Bedd. Flor. Sylvat. t. 50; Trim. Fl. Ceyl. v. 2, p. 125; Talb. Trees, Bomb. ed. 2, p. 153; Woodr. in Journ. Bomb. Nat. v. 11 (1898) p. 429; Watt, Dict. Econ. Prod. v. 1, p. 60. *Mimosa Sundra*, Roxb. Cor. Pl. t. 225.—Flowers: Aug.–Sept. VERN. *Khair*; *Lál-khair.*

Common throughout the Presidency. KONKAN: *Law*!, *Dalzell*! DECCAN: *Dalzell & Gibson*, *Woodrow*; Karlimatti near Bagalkot, *Cooke*! GUJARAT: Godra, *Cooke*!; Rajkot (Kathiawar), *Macnaghten.* S. M. COUNTRY: *Raoji*!

This variety is the most common in the Bombay Presidency and has often been recorded as *A. Catechu* proper, which is of somewhat doubtful occurrence. Prain (*l. c.*) says that *A. Catechu* proper has never been reported to the Calcutta Herbarium from Rajputana, the Konkan, or the Deccan, whereas *A. Sundra* occurs from Coimbatore northwards to the Deccan and is common in Kanara and the Konkan.—DISTRIB. India (Rajputana, W. Peninsula, Birma); Ceylon.

10. **Acacia ferruginea,** *DC. Prodr.* v. 2 (1825) p. 458. A moderate-sized tree; bark rough, rusty-brown; young parts glabrous; prickles sometimes suppressed. Leaves 2-pinnate, 2–$4\frac{1}{2}$ in. long; main rhachis slender, glabrous, with a large gland on the petiole and another between the uppermost pair of pinnæ; petioles 1–2 in. long, thickened at the base; stipular spines short, hooked, in pairs; pinnæ 3–6 pairs, 2–3 in. long, distant, shortly stalked, the stalks thickened at the base, and the rhachis slender, glabrous. Leaflets 10–20 pairs, $\frac{1}{4}$–$\frac{1}{3}$ by $\frac{1}{10}$–$\frac{1}{8}$ in., linear-oblong, obtuse, unequal-sided, glaucous above, paler beneath, rigidly sub-coriaceous, glabrous; petiolules very short. Flowers pale-yellow, sessile, in slender axillary spikes 3–4 in. long; peduncles often numerous, glabrous. Calyx campanulate, $\frac{1}{16}$ in. long, glabrous; teeth distinct,

deltoid. Corolla $\frac{1}{8}$-$\frac{1}{6}$ in. long, divided about $\frac{1}{2}$ way down; lobes oblong-lanceolate, acute. Pods stalked, 3-5 by $\frac{3}{4}$-1 in., straight, flat, thin, brown, reticulately veined, glabrous, indehiscent, the upper suture narrowly winged. Seeds 4-8. Fl. B. I. v. 2, p. 295; Bedd. Flor. Sylvat. t. 51; Trim. Fl. Ceyl. v. 2, p. 126; Talb. Trees, Bomb. ed. 2, p. 153; Woodr. in Journ. Bomb. Nat. v. 11 (1898) p. 429; Watt, Dict. Econ. Prod. v. 1, p. 50.—Flowers: Jan.-Feb. VERN. *Pándhard-khair.*

KONKAN: *Stocks!*, *Dalzell!*, *Talbot.* DECCAN: Phalsan (Peint taluka), *Woodrow.* GUJARAT: Dangs, *Woodrow*; Panch Mahals, *Talbot*, *Brandis!*

11. **Acacia Senegal,** *Willd. Sp. Pl.* v. 4 (1805) p. 1077. A small tree 10-20 ft. high; stem prickly; branches flexuose, glaucous-grey; young shoots pubescent. Leaves 2-pinnate, $\frac{3}{4}$-1$\frac{1}{4}$ in. long; main rhachis pubescent, with a gland on the petiole below the lowest pair and one between the uppermost pair of pinnæ; stipular spines usually 3, the 2 lateral nearly straight or slightly curved upwards, the middle one curved downwards, all dark-brown, polished; pinnæ 3-5 pairs, $\frac{1}{2}$-$\frac{3}{4}$ in. long, very shortly stalked, their rhachises pubescent. Leaflets 8-15 pairs, $\frac{1}{12}$-$\frac{1}{8}$ by $\frac{1}{20}$ in., linear, subobtuse, glabrous, pale glaucous-green; petiolules very short. Flowers fragrant, in spikes 2-4 in. long; peduncles axillary, 1-3-nate. Calyx campanulate, $\frac{1}{12}$ in. long, divided about $\frac{1}{3}$ of the way down; teeth distinct, deltoid. Corolla white, twice as long as the calyx, divided about $\frac{1}{2}$ way down; lobes lanceolate, acute. Filaments white. Anthers yellow. Pods shortly stalked, 3 by $\frac{3}{4}$ in., linear-oblong, thin, flat, flexible, attenuated at both ends, reticulately veined, pale-brown and glabrous when ripe. Seeds 5-6. Fl. B. I. v. 2, p. 295; Taubert, in Engl. & Prantl, Pflanzenf. v. 3, part 3, p. 112, fig. 68; Talb. Trees, Bomb. ed. 2, p. 153; Woodr. in Journ. Bomb. Nat. v. 11 (1898) p. 429; Watt, Dict. Econ. Prod. v. 1, p. 55. *Acacia Verek,* Guill. & Perr. Fl. Seneg. (1830-33) p. 245, t. 56. *Acacia rupestris,* Stocks, ex Boiss. Fl. Orient. v. 2 (1872) p. 638.—Flowers: Nov.-Mar.

SIND: *Stocks!*—DISTRIB. India (Panjáb, Rajputana); Beluchistan, Arabia, Tropical Africa.

The tree furnishes the true gum-arabic of commerce which is largely exported from the French colony of Senegal on the West Coast of Africa. It is collected in Sind and Rajputana, but is not kept separate, being mixed with the gums from other species of *Acacia*. See Watt, Dict. Econ. Prod. l. c.

12. **Acacia latronum,** *Willd. Sp. Pl.* v. 4 (1805) p. 1077. A glabrous shrub or small tree forming an umbrella-like top when old; branches brown, glabrous. Leaves 2-pinnate, often fasciculate, 1-1$\frac{1}{2}$ in. long; main rhachis slightly pubescent; petiole with a gland about the middle; stipular spines in pairs, of two kinds, the smaller $\frac{1}{2}$-1 in. long, the larger 2-2$\frac{1}{2}$ in. long, connate at the base, conical, hollow inside, straight, sharp, ivory-white or rarely brown, polished; pinnæ 2-5 pairs, $\frac{3}{4}$-1 in. long. Leaflets 6-15 pairs, $\frac{1}{8}$-$\frac{1}{4}$ by $\frac{1}{30}$-$\frac{1}{20}$ in., linear, rigidly sub-coriaceous, glabrous. Flowers at first white, afterwards turning yellow, fragrant, in lax subsessile often fasciculate spikes 1-1$\frac{1}{2}$ in. long. Calyx campanulate, $\frac{1}{32}$ in. long, glabrous; teeth short, ciliolate. Corolla $\frac{1}{10}$ in. long, divided $\frac{1}{4}$ the way down; lobes triangular. Pods shortly stalked, 1-1$\frac{1}{2}$ by $\frac{1}{2}$-$\frac{3}{4}$ in., flat, obtuse at both ends, falcate, reticulately veined, dark-brown or nearly black, finally dehiscent. Seeds 2-4, orbicular, compressed, yellowish-brown. Fl. B. I. v. 2, p. 296; Grah. Cat. p. 58;

Dalz. & Gibs. p. 87; Wight, Icon. t. 1157; Talb. Trees, Bomb. ed. 2, p. 153; Woodr. in Journ. Bomb. Nat. v. 11 (1898) p. 429; Watt, Dict. Econ. Prod. v. 1, p. 51.—Flowers: Oct.-Mar. VERN. *Dev-bábhal*; *Tambuti*; *Bhesa*.

DECCAN: widely, *Woodrow*; Eastern Deccan, common, *Dalzell & Gibson*; common in barren tracts of the Deccan, *Graham*; Gokak, *Bhiva*!

13. **Acacia concinna,** *DC. Prodr.* v. 2 (1825) p. 464. An extensive climbing shrub armed with numerous small hooked prickles; branches brown, dotted with white. Leaves 2-pinnate, 2–4 in. long; main rhachis armed with sharp hooked prickles, with a large gland at or below the middle of the petiole, and one between the uppermost or the two uppermost pairs of pinnæ; stipules ovate, cordate; pinnæ 4–8 pairs, 1–2$\frac{1}{2}$ in. long, their rhachises slender, grooved, ending in a weak spine. Leaflets subsessile, sensitive, 12–25 pairs, $\frac{1}{4}$–$\frac{1}{2}$ by $\frac{1}{20}$–$\frac{1}{10}$ in., linear, acute or mucronate, unequal-sided, glabrous, base rounded or truncate. Flowers in globose heads, on peduncles 1–1$\frac{1}{2}$ in. long which are fascicled at the nodes or forming racemose panicles at the ends of the branches; bracts oblique, membranous, conspicuous. Calyx funnel-shaped, $\frac{1}{10}$ in. long, divided nearly $\frac{1}{4}$ way down; teeth lanceolate. Corolla $\frac{1}{8}$–$\frac{1}{6}$ in. long; lobes lanceolate. Pods shortly stalked, 3–5 by $\frac{3}{4}$–1$\frac{1}{8}$ in., linear-oblong, thick and fleshy when immature, becoming wrinkled when dry, somewhat depressed between the seeds, and with broad sutures which are sometimes more or less deeply indented. Seeds 6–10. Fl. B. I. v. 2, p. 296; Grah. Cat. p. 59; Dalz. & Gibs. p. 87; Talb. Trees, Bomb. ed. 2, p. 153; Woodr. in Journ. Bomb. Nat. v. 11 (1898) p. 429; Watt, Dict. Econ. Prod. v. 1, p. 44.—Flowers: Mar.-July. VERN. *Sikakai*.

Common in the Konkan and Ghát jungles. KONKAN: *Law*!, *Dalzell & Gibson*, *Talbot*. Matheran, *Cooke*! DECCAN: hills, *Woodrow*. S. M. COUNTRY: near Belgaum, *Ritchie*, 246! KANARA: *Woodrow*; moist forests, *Talbot*.—DISTRIB. Throughout India; Malay Isles, China.

The pods are used for washing the hair and a considerable trade is carried on in them in Kanara and Kolaba. See Watt, Dict. Econ. Prod. l. c.

14. **Acacia Intsia,** *Willd. Sp. Pl.* v. 4 (1805) p. 1091. A large climbing or sarmentose shrub; branches grooved, dark-brown, armed with small hooked prickles. Leaves 2-pinnate, 4–8 in. long (including a stout petiole which often reaches 1$\frac{1}{2}$ in. long); main rhachis pubescent, usually armed with hooked prickles on the underside, with a gland on the petiole below the lowest pair and a gland between each of the 1–4 uppermost pairs of pinnæ; pinnæ 5–10 pairs, 2–3 in. long, subsessile, their rhachises more or less pubescent. Leaflets 10–25 pairs, not closely crowded, subsessile, $\frac{1}{4}$–$\frac{3}{8}$ by $\frac{1}{8}$–$\frac{1}{6}$ in., linear-oblong, very unequal-sided, the midrib near the upper edge, shortly and obliquely mucronate, dark green and shining above, paler beneath, glabrous on both surfaces, base truncate. Flowers white or yellowish-white, in terminal panicles; heads globose, $\frac{3}{8}$–$\frac{1}{2}$ in. in diam.; peduncles 1–4-nate, finely downy; bracts at the base of the peduncles linear-oblong, acute, falcate, $\frac{1}{8}$–$\frac{1}{4}$ in. long. Calyx campanulate, $\frac{1}{12}$ in. long, divided about $\frac{1}{3}$ the way down; teeth lanceolate or subdeltoid. Corolla $\frac{1}{8}$ in. long, divided about $\frac{1}{2}$ way down; lobes lanceolate, acute. Pods shortly stalked, 4–6 by $\frac{3}{4}$–1$\frac{1}{4}$ in., straight, strap-shaped, flat, thin, dry, obtuse at the apex, narrowed at the base, brown-tomentose when young, afterwards

glabrous, obscurely veined, dehiscent. Seeds 6–12. Fl. B. I. v. 2, p. 297; Grah. Cat. p. 59; Dalz. & Gibs. p. 88; Wight & Arn. Prodr. p. 278; Talb. Trees, Bomb. ed. 2, p. 154 (exclud. syn. *A. cæsia*); Woodr. in Journ. Bomb. Nat. v. 11 (1898) p. 429; Watt, Dict. Econ. Prod. v. 1, p. 50.—Flowers: Aug. VERN. *Chilhar.*

KONKAN: hilly tracts, *Graham.* DECCAN: Panchgani, *Cooke!*; Mahableshwar, *Cooke!*, *Woodrow!*; Fitzgerald Ghát, below Mahableshwar, *H. M. Birdwood.* GUJARAT: Ankleshwar, *Dalzell & Gibson*; Lalli, *Stocks*, 276!—DISTRIB. India (Tropical Himalayas, E. & W. Peninsulas); Ceylon.

15. **Acacia cæsia,** *Wight & Arn. Prodr.* (1834) p. 278. A scandent shrub armed with numerous hooked prickles; branches yellowish-brown. Leaves 2-pinnate, 4–6 in. long; main rhachis pubescent, occasionally armed with hooked prickles on the lower side, with a convex gland on the petiole below the leaflets and glands between the 2–4 uppermost pairs of pinnæ; pinnæ 8–15 pairs, 1–2 in. long, their rhachises densely pubescent. Leaflets 15–35 pairs, crowded, sometimes overlapping, $\frac{1}{8}$–$\frac{1}{6}$ by $\frac{1}{20}$–$\frac{1}{16}$ in., linear, very unequal-sided, the midrib near the upper edge, mucronate, pubescent on both surfaces, base truncate. Flowers in terminal panicles; heads globose, $\frac{3}{8}$ in. in diam.; peduncles in fascicles of 1–4; bracts linear-oblong, falcate, acute. Calyx campanulate, $\frac{1}{12}$ in. long; teeth ovate, subacute. Corolla $\frac{1}{8}$ in. long, divided $\frac{1}{2}$ way down; lobes lanceolate, acute. Pods strap-shaped, flat, thin, dry, subfalcate, 5–6$\frac{1}{2}$ by $\frac{7}{8}$ in., reticulately veined, shortly stalked, glabrous. Seeds 5–10. Dalz. & Gibs. p. 87. *A. Intsia* var. *cæsia*, Baker, in. Hook. f. Fl. B. I. v. 2, p. 297.

Not quite as common as the former species. DECCAN: Ganesh Khind near Poona, *Woodrow!* KANARA: Yellapur, *Talbot*, 467!

This plant is often confounded with *Acacia Intsia*, Willd., but to anyone who has seen both plants growing, their separation as distinct species presents no difficulty. See Prain, in Journ. As. Soc. Beng. v. 66 (1898) p. 510.

16. **Acacia pennata,** *Willd. Sp. Pl.* v. 4 (1805) p. 1090. A scandent shrub, armed with numerous stout slightly hooked or straight prickles (rarely unarmed); young branches pubescent. Leaves 2-pinnate, reaching 6 in. long; main rhachis densely pubescent, grooved, often prickly, with a large gland above the middle of the petiole and one between each of the 2–4 upper pairs of pinnæ; pinnæ 8–18 pairs, 1$\frac{1}{2}$–2$\frac{1}{2}$ in. long, subsessile, usually curved, their rhachises densely pubescent. Leaflets 40–50 pairs, slightly overlapping, $\frac{1}{6}$–$\frac{1}{3}$ by $\frac{1}{20}$ in., sessile, linear, obtuse, unequal-sided, glabrous, base oblique, rounded or truncate. Flowers white or pale-yellow, in large terminal panicles; heads globose, $\frac{3}{8}$–$\frac{1}{2}$ in. in diam.; peduncles pubescent, 2–4-nate; bracts linear. Calyx glabrous, $\frac{1}{10}$ in. long, divided $\frac{1}{3}$ of the way down; lobes linear-lanceolate, acute. Pods stalked, 4–8 by $\frac{3}{4}$–1$\frac{1}{4}$ in., straight, flat, thin, dry, strap-shaped, rounded or shortly apiculate, brown, glabrous. Seeds 8–14, ovoid-oblong, compressed, dark-brown. Fl. B. I. v. 2, p. 297; Grah. Cat. p. 59; Dalz. & Gibs. p. 87 (*pinnata*); Trim. Fl. Ceyl. v. 2, p. 127; Talb. Trees, Bomb. ed. 2, p. 154; Woodr. in Journ. Bomb. Nat. v. 11 (1898) p. 429; Watt, Dict. Econ. Prod. v. 1, p. 54.—Flowers: June–Aug. VERN. *Shembi*; *Shembáti.*

KONKAN: *Dalzell!*, *Law!*, *Woodrow*; Mumbra near Thana, *Kanitkar!* DECCAN: *Woodrow.* S. M. COUNTRY: Belgaum, *Ritchie*, 246! KANARA: *Talbot*; banks of Gatprabha river, *Law ex Graham.*—DISTRIB. India (Central and Eastern Himalayas, Behar, E. & W. Peninsulas, Birma); Ceylon, Malay Isles, Trop. Africa, Natal.

80. ALBIZZIA, Durazz.

Trees. Leaves 2-pinnate. Flowers (in the Indian species) in globose heads, sessile or pedicellate, hermaphrodite, usually 5-merous. Calyx campanulate or funnel-shaped, distinctly toothed. Corolla funnel-shaped, the petals connate below the middle. Stamens indefinite, monadelphous at the base; filaments much longer than the corolla; anthers minute, not gland-crested. Ovary sessile or shortly stalked; style filiform; stigma minute, capitate. Pod large, thin, flat, strap-shaped, straight, indehiscent or subindehiscent, continuous within, the sutures not thickened.—DISTRIB. Tropics of the Old World; species 25–30.

Pinnæ 2–4 (rarely 6) pairs; leaflets exceeding $\frac{1}{4}$ in. broad.
- Flowers pedicelled; calyx $\frac{1}{8}$ in. long .... 1. *A. Lebbek.*
- Flowers sessile; calyx less than $\frac{1}{8}$ in. long.
  - Calyx $\frac{1}{20}$ in. long, pubescent; teeth obsolete .... 2. *A. odoratissima.*
  - Calyx $\frac{1}{10}$ in. long, glabrous; teeth distinct .... 3. *A. procera.*

Pinnæ 6–20 pairs; leaflets less than $\frac{1}{4}$ in. broad.
- Stipules very large; heads of flowers panicled .... 4. *A. stipulata.*
- Stipules minute; heads of flowers not panicled .... 5. *A. amara.*

1. **Albizzia Lebbek,** *Benth. in Hook. Lond. Journ. Bot.* v. 3 (1844) p. 87. An unarmed deciduous tree 40–70 ft. high; bark pale; young shoots glabrous. Leaves abruptly 2-pinnate; main rhachis pubescent or glabrous, furnished with a large gland on the petiole above the base and one below the uppermost pair of pinnæ; petioles swollen and hairy at the base; pinnæ 2–3 (rarely 4) pairs, 4–5 in. long, their rhachises glabrous or pubescent, swollen and hairy at the base. Leaflets 5–9 pairs, 1–$1\frac{3}{4}$ by $\frac{3}{8}$–$\frac{3}{4}$ in., with glands between their bases, the lateral leaflets elliptic-oblong, the 2 terminal obovate-oblong, all pale green, unequal-sided, very obtuse, glabrous above, pubescent and reticulately veined beneath, base obliquely rounded or truncate; petiolules very short, hairy. Flowers white, fragrant, in globose umbellate heads $\frac{3}{4}$–$1\frac{1}{2}$ in. in diam. (not including the stamens); peduncles $1\frac{1}{2}$–3 in. long, more or less pubescent, solitary or 2–4 together from the axils of the upper leaves; pedicels $\frac{1}{10}$–$\frac{1}{8}$ in. long, pubescent. Calyx $\frac{1}{8}$ in. long, pubescent; teeth short, deltoid. Corolla $\frac{3}{8}$ in. long; tube glabrous; lobes $\frac{1}{10}$ in. long, triangular, acute, pubescent outside. Stamens much longer than the corolla; filaments connate at the base into a short tube. Pods 4–12 in. by $\frac{3}{4}$–$1\frac{3}{4}$ in., linear-oblong, bluntly pointed, thin, pale-yellow, reticulately veined above the seeds, smooth, shining. Seeds 4–12, ellipsoid-oblong, compressed, foveolate on the faces, pale-brown. Fl. B. I. v. 2, p. 298; Dalz. & Gibs. p. 88; Trim. Fl. Ceyl. v. 2, p. 128; Talb. Trees, Bomb. ed. 2, p. 154; Woodr. in Journ. Bomb. Nat. v. 11 (1898) p. 430; Watt, Dict. Econ. Prod. v. 1, p. 156. *Acacia speciosa,* Willd. Sp. Pl. v. 4 (1805) p. 1066; Grah. Cat. p. 58. *Mimosa speciosa,* Jacquin. Ic. t. 198.—Flowers: Mar.–May. VERN. *Siras*; *Chinchola.*

Throughout the Presidency, where it is often planted as a roadside tree.—DISTRIB. Throughout India, but usually planted; Tropical and Subtropical Asia and Africa, but usually planted.

2. **Albizzia odoratissima,** *Benth. in Hook. Lond. Journ. Bot.* v. 3 (1844) p. 88. A tall unarmed tree, often reaching 80 feet high; young shoots dark-colored, pubescent. Leaves abruptly 2-pinnate; main rhachis downy, 6–12 in. long, with a large sessile gland on the petiole a

little above its base and also at the bases of 1–2 of the upper pinnæ; pinnæ usually 4 pairs, rather distant, 3–6 in. long, their rhachises pubescent. Leaflets 8–15 pairs, sessile, $\frac{3}{4}$–$1\frac{1}{8}$ by $\frac{3}{8}$–$\frac{1}{2}$ in., obliquely oblong, rounded at the apex, reticulately veined, the midrib about $\frac{1}{3}$ the breadth of the blade from the upper edge, dark green and slightly pubescent above, glaucous and pubescent beneath, base very obliquely rounded. Flowers fragrant, sessile, in numerous small 10–12-flowered heads $\frac{3}{4}$–1 in. across; peduncles $\frac{1}{4}$ in. long, solitary or 2–4 together, arranged in terminal panicles. Calyx $\frac{1}{20}$ in. long, pubescent; teeth obsolete. Corolla white, $\frac{1}{8}$ in. long, grey-silky outside; teeth ovate-lanceolate, acute. Stamens twice as long as the corolla; filaments pale-yellow, connate at the base into a tube half as long as the corolla-tube. Pods shortly stalked, 4–8 by 1–$1\frac{1}{2}$ in., thin, flexible, glabrous, slightly reticulately veined, brown. Seeds 8–12, broadly ovate, $\frac{1}{3}$ by $\frac{1}{4}$ in., much flattened, yellow. Fl. B. I. v. 2, p. 299; Dalz. & Gibs. p. 88; Bedd. Flor. Sylvat. t. 54; Trim. Fl. Ceyl. v. 2, p. 129; Talb. Trees, Bomb. ed. 2, p. 155; Woodr. in Journ. Bomb. Nat. v. 11 (1898) p. 430; Watt, Dict. Econ. Prod. v. 1, p. 158. *Acacia odoratissima*, Willd. Sp. Pl. v. 4 (1805) p. 1063; Grah. Cat. p. 58.—Flowers: Apr.–June. VERN. *Kála-siras*; *Chichvá*.

KONKAN: *Graham*, *Dalzell & Gibson*, *Talbot*. DECCAN: Poona, *Woodrow*. KANARA: moist forests, *Talbot*; Sirsi (N. Kanara), *Woodrow*.—DISTRIB. Throughout India; Ceylon.

3. **Albizzia procera,** *Benth. in Hook. Lond. Journ. Bot.* v. 3 (1844) p. 89. An unarmed tree 60–80 ft. high; young shoots pale, lenticellate. Leaves abruptly 2-pinnate; main rhachis glabrous, 12–18 in. long, with a large gland on the petiole a little above its base; pinnæ 2–6 pairs, 5–6 in. long, their rhachises glabrous and with an oval gland below the uppermost pair of leaflets. Leaflets 6–12 pairs, 1–$1\frac{1}{2}$ by $\frac{5}{8}$–$\frac{7}{8}$ in., obtuse or subacute, dark green and glabrous above, more or less grey-pubescent beneath, base obliquely cuneate on the upper, rounded on the lower margin; petiolules $\frac{1}{20}$ in. long. Flowers sessile, in numerous small 12–20-flowered heads $\frac{3}{4}$ in. across; peduncles $\frac{1}{2}$ in. long, in fascicles of 3–5 (rarely solitary), arranged in terminal panicles. Calyx $\frac{1}{10}$ in. long, glabrous; teeth distinct, triangular. Corolla $\frac{1}{4}$ in. long, pubescent outside; teeth lanceolate, $\frac{1}{2}$ as long as the corolla-tube. Stamens $1\frac{1}{2}$ times as long as the corolla; filaments greenish-yellow, connate at the base into a tube as long as the corolla-tube. Pods scarcely stalked, at length dehiscent, 4–8 by $\frac{1}{2}$–$\frac{7}{8}$ in., thin, flexible, bright orange-brown, smooth and glossy, faintly reticulate above the seeds. Seeds 6–12, broadly ovate, $\frac{1}{4}$ by $\frac{1}{6}$ in., much flattened, pale-brown. Fl. B. I. v. 2, p. 299; Bedd. For. Man. p. xcvi; Talb. Trees, Bomb. ed. 2, p. 155; Woodr. in Journ. Bomb. Nat. v. 11 (1898) p. 430; Watt, Dict. Econ. Prod. v. 1, p. 159.—Flowers: May–June. VERN. *Kinhai*; *Belati*.

KONKAN: *Stocks*!, *Dalzell*!, *Talbot*. S. M. COUNTRY: Belgaum, *Ritchie*, 154! KANARA: *Talbot*.—DISTRIB. India (Central and E. Himalayas, Behar, W. Peninsula, Burma); China, Malay Archipelago, Philippines.

4. **Albizzia stipulata,** *Boivin, in Encyc. du xixᵉ Siècle*, v. 2, p. 33; *Benth. in Hook. Lond. Journ. Bot.* v. 3 (1844) p. 92. A tall unarmed evergreen tree; young shoots clothed with fine grey or golden-yellow pubescence. Leaves abruptly 2-pinnate; main rhachis 6–15 in. long, at first pubescent, afterwards glabrous, with a large sessile gland on the

petiole about 1 in. above its base and with smaller glands between each of the uppermost 2–9 pairs of pinnæ; stipules very large, soon deciduous, sometimes exceeding 1 in. long, unequally cordate, acuminate with a filiform tail, membranous, pubescent, orange-brown, the base much dilated on one side; pinnæ 7–20 pairs, shortly stalked, their rhachises tawny-pubescent, 2–5 in. long. Leaflets membranous, 30–45 pairs, $\frac{1}{4}$–$\frac{1}{3}$ by $\frac{1}{16}$–$\frac{1}{10}$ in. long, linear-oblong, falcate, pointed, pale-green and glabrous above, glaucous and pubescent beneath, the midrib close to the upper margin, base obliquely rounded at the lower side. Flowers in small panicled heads; peduncles $\frac{3}{4}$–$1\frac{1}{4}$ in. long, pubescent, solitary or in fascicles of 2–4; bracts ovate, acuminate, membranous, $\frac{1}{4}$–$\frac{1}{2}$ in. long, deciduous; pedicels $\frac{1}{20}$ in. long. Calyx $\frac{1}{10}$ in. long, funnel-shaped, pubescent; teeth short, acute. Corolla yellowish-white, densely pubescent outside, $\frac{1}{5}$–$\frac{1}{4}$ in. long; lobes half as long as the tube, lanceolate, acute. Stamens 4 times as long as the corolla, connate into a tube longer than the corolla-tube. Pods very shortly stalked, 5–7 by $\frac{3}{4}$–$1\frac{1}{8}$ in., thin, pale-brown, glabrous, faintly reticulately veined. Seeds 8–12, ovate, $\frac{1}{4}$ by $\frac{1}{6}$ in., much compressed, dark-brown, smooth. The large stipules are sufficiently characteristic to determine this species when growing. These, however, soon fall off and are often wanting in Herbarium specimens. Fl. B. I. v. 2, p. 300; Dalz. & Gibs. p. 88; Bedd. Flor. Sylvat. t. 55; Trim. Fl. Ceyl. v. 2, p. 129; Talb. Trees, Bomb. ed. 2, p. 155; Woodr. in Journ. Bomb. Nat. v. 11 (1898) p. 430; Watt, Dict. Econ. Prod. v. 1, p. 160. *Acacia stipulata*, DC. Prodr. v. 2, p. 469; Grah. Cat. p. 58.—Flowers: Apr.–June. VERN. *Udal*; *Phalára*.

KONKAN: *Law*!, *Stocks*; Matheran, *Cooke*!, *H. M. Birdwood*, *Dalzell*! DECCAN: Khandala, *Graham*; Fitzgerald Ghát below Mahableshwar, *Cooke*! S. M. COUNTRY: Ramghát, *Ritchie*, 248! KANARA: evergreen forests of N. Kanara Ghâts, *Talbot*; Sirsi (N. Kanara), *Talbot*!—DISTRIB. Throughout India; S.E. Asia.

5. **Albizzia amara,** *Boivin, in Encyc. du xix*[e] *Siècle*, v. 2, p. 34; *Benth. in Hook. Lond. Journ. Bot.* v. 3 (1844) p. 90. A small much-branched unarmed tree; young shoots clothed with yellowish-grey pubescence. Leaves abruptly 2-pinnate; main rhachis 2–4 in. long, densely pubescent, with a small gland about the middle of the petiole and another between the uppermost pair of pinnæ; stipules minute; pinnæ 6–15 pairs, 1–2 in. long, their rhachises pubescent. Leaflets 10–30 pairs, sessile, close, $\frac{1}{4}$–$\frac{1}{3}$ by $\frac{1}{20}$–$\frac{1}{12}$ in., linear-oblong, obtuse or subacute, the midrib nearly in the centre, green and glabrous above, glaucous and more or less pubescent beneath. Flowers subsessile, fragrant, in 12–20-flowered heads; peduncles solitary or in fascicles of 2–4 in the axils of the upper leaves, not forming a panicle, pubescent. Calyx $\frac{1}{15}$–$\frac{1}{10}$ in. long, funnel-shaped, pubescent, scarcely pedicelled; teeth short. Corolla yellow, nearly 3 times as long as the calyx, pubescent outside; lobes linear-lanceolate. Stamens $\frac{1}{2}$–$\frac{5}{8}$ in. long; filaments pinkish. Pods 4–7 by $\frac{3}{4}$–$1\frac{1}{8}$ in., stalked, thin, flat, abruptly pointed, slightly transversely veined. Seeds 6–8. Fl. B. I. v. 2, p. 301; Dalz. & Gibs. p. 88; Bedd. Flor. Sylvat. t. 61; Trim. Fl. Ceyl. v. 2, p. 130; Talb. Trees, Bomb. ed. 2, p. 155; Woodr. in Journ. Bomb. Nat. v. 11 (1898) p. 430; Watt, Dict. Econ. Prod. v. 1, p. 155. *Acacia amara*, Willd. Sp. Pl. v. 4 (1805) p. 1074; Grah. Cat. p. 58.—Flowers: Apr.–June. VERN. *Tugli*; *Lalai*.

Throughout the Presidency in dry forests. KONKAN: *Stocks*!, *Dalzell*!; Matheran hill, *Dalzell & Gibson*; Alexandra Point, Matheran, *H. M. Birdwood*; banks of the Kistna, *Graham*. DECCAN: Poona, *Woodrow*; Alandi, *Cooke*! S. M. COUNTRY: hills north of Belgaum, *Ritchie*, 1057!—DISTRIB. India (W. Peninsula); Ceylon, E. Tropical Africa.

Albizzia lucida, Benth. in Hook. Lond. Journ. Bot. v. 3 (1844) p. 86, an unarmed deciduous tree 50–60 ft. high, a native of the Eastern Himalaya and Indo-China, is frequently cultivated, but is not indigenous in the Bombay Presidency. The leaves are remarkable as having normally but 1 pair of pinnæ. The pod is 6–10 in. long, smooth and glossy, and of a bright orange-brown color. Fl. B. I. v. 2, p. 299; Woodr. in Journ. Bomb. Nat. v. 11 (1898) p. 430.

Woodrow in his list gives this as occurring at Matheran. I have ascertained from him, however, that the trees had been planted there and were not indigenous.

81. PITHECOLOBIUM, Mart.

Erect trees or shrubs, unarmed or with spinescent stipules or axillary spines. Leaves 2-pinnate; stipules various. Flowers usually in globose heads or cylindric spikes, 5- (rarely 6-) merous, usually hermaphrodite. Calyx campanulate or funnel-shaped, shortly toothed. Corolla funnel-shaped, the petals valvate, united below for $\frac{1}{2}$–$\frac{2}{3}$ of their length. Stamens monadelphous, much exserted; anthers not gland-crested. Ovary sessile or stalked; ovules many; style filiform; stigma minute, capitate. Pod strap-shaped, circinate or falcate (rarely straight), usually dehiscent throughout the lower suture and much twisted in a late stage, the sutures not or slightly thickened. Seeds often embedded in a scanty pulp, ovate or orbicular, compressed, the funicle filiform or variously expanded into a fleshy aril.—DISTRIB. Cosmopolitan in the Tropics; species about 100, chiefly American.

1. **Pithecolobium bigeminum**, *Mart. in Flora*, v. 20 (1837) ii, *Beibl.* p. 115 *in obs.*; *Benth. in Hook. Lond. Journ. Bot.* v. 3 (1844) p. 206. A middle-sized unarmed tree; young parts glabrous or slightly pubescent. Leaves 2-pinnate; main rhachis 4–6 in. long, glabrous, with a gland on the petiole and 1 below each pair of pinnæ; pinnæ stalked, 1–2 (rarely 3) pairs, the lowest pair the smallest, their rhachises with a gland beneath the insertion of each pair of leaflets except the lowest. Leaflets 1–2 (rarely 3) pairs, 3–6 by 1–1$\frac{1}{2}$ in., the terminal pair the largest, subcoriaceous, elliptic-lanceolate, or obovate-oblong, acuminate or acute, glabrous above, pubescent at first beneath, base acute; petiolules $\frac{1}{8}$ in. long. Flowers subsessile, in few-flowered heads in small peduncled clusters, arranged on the long branches of pubescent panicles usually shorter than the leaves. Calyx $\frac{1}{12}$–$\frac{1}{10}$ in. long, densely brown-silky; teeth short, triangular. Corolla pale-yellow or cream-colored, 2–3 times as long as the calyx, silky outside; lobes lanceolate, acute. Stamens $\frac{3}{8}$–$\frac{1}{2}$ in. long. Pods flat, once or twice spiral, bluntly pointed, roughish, but glabrous or nearly so, reddish-brown outside, bright red within, not indented between the seeds. Seeds 5–8. Fl. B. I. v. 2, p. 303; Dalz. & Gibs. p. 89; Bedd. For. Man. p. xcvi; Trim. Fl. Ceyl. v. 2, p. 132; Talb. Trees, Bomb. ed. 2, p. 156; Woodr. in Journ. Bomb. Nat. v. 11 (1898) p. 430; Watt, Dict. Econ. Prod.

v. 6, part 1, p. 281. *Inga bigemina*, Willd. Sp. Pl. v. 4, p. 1007; Grah. Cat. p. 57.—Flowers: Jan.–Feb. VERN. *Kachlor.*

KONKAN: *Stocks!*, *Dalzell & Gibson!*, *Talbot.* KANARA: evergreen forests, *Talbot*; Divimana (N. Kanara), *Woodrow*; Supa, *Ritchie*, 1728!—DISTRIB. India (E. Himalayas, W. Peninsula); Ceylon, Malay Islands, Philippines.

Pithecolobium dulce, Benth. in Hook. Lond. Journ. Bot. v. 3 (1844) p. 199. A moderately large tree, a native of Mexico, introduced into the Philippine Islands, and thence into India, is cultivated, often as a hedge plant, and may be met with in Bombay and Poona. The tree is armed with short straight stipular thorns, the pods are curiously twisted, and the seeds are embedded in a sweet whitish edible pulp. Fl. B. I. v. 2, p. 302; Talb. Trees, Bomb. ed. 2, p. 156; Woodr. in Journ. Bomb. Nat. v. 11 (1898) p. 430; Watt, Dict. Econ. Prod. v. 6, part 1, p. 281. *Inga dulcis*, Willd. Sp. Pl. v. 4, p. 1005; Wight, Icon. t. 198; Grah. Cat. p. 56; Dalz. & Gibs. Suppl. p. 25.—Flowers: Jan.–Mar. VERN. *Vilâyti-âmli*; *Vilâyti-chinch.*

Pithecolobium Saman, Benth. in Hook. Lond. Journ. Bot. v. 3 (1844) p. 216. A tree of rapid growth. A native of Central and Tropical S. America, whence it was introduced into Jamaica, and thence into India. It is called the *Rain Tree* and may be seen growing in Thana and Poona. It has also been introduced into N. Kanara. The pod is straight and indehiscent with a sweet pulp around the seeds. Talb. Trees, Bomb. ed. 2, p. 156; Woodr. in Journ. Bomb. Nat. v. 11 (1898) p. 430; Watt, Dict. Econ. Prod. v. 6, part 1, p. 283.

The following non-indigenous plants not belonging to any of the foregoing genera of the Suborder are occasionally cultivated in the Bombay Presidency:—

Parkia biglandulosa, Wight & Arn. Prodr. (1834) p. 279. A tall tree a native of Africa, with 2-pinnate leaves, 20–40 pairs of pinnæ and 60–100 pairs of leaflets, with flowers in dense subspherical heads 1½ in. in diam., on peduncles 5–8 in. long, is occasionally grown in gardens. The heads, when the flowers are in bud, are like balls of fawn-colored velvet and the pods reach 1 ft. or more in length. Fl. B. I. v. 2, p. 289; Dalz. & Gibs. Suppl. p. 25; Grah. Cat. p. 57; Woodr. in Journ. Bomb. Nat. v. 11 (1898) p. 428; Woodr. Gardening in India, ed. 5, p. 278.—Flowers: Dec. VERN. *Chenduphul.*

Desmanthus virgatus, Willd. Sp. Pl. v. 4 (1805) p. 1047. A glabrous, shrubby perennial, a native of Tropical America, has been extensively planted in gardens. It has flowers in solitary globose peduncled axillary heads and pods 2–3 in. long, each containing 20–30 seeds. Fl. B. I. v. 2, p. 290; Trim. Fl. Ceyl. v. 2, p. 122; Woodr. in Journ. Bomb. Nat. v. 11 (1898) p. 428.—Flowers: June–July.

Ceratonia Siliqua, Linn. Sp. Pl. (1753) p. 1026. The *Locust* or *Carob Tree*; *St. John's Bread*, a native of S. Europe, Syria, and Palestine, has been occasionally planted in gardens and thrives well if irrigated until well-established. The pods are large, dark-red and woody, with a sweet edible pulp. Dalz. & Gibs. Suppl. p. 28; Woodr. Gard. in Ind. ed. 5,

p. 275; Watt, Dict. Econ. Prod. v. 2, p. 254. *Tamarindus Siliqua*, Woodr. in Journ. Bomb. Nat. v. 11 (1898) p. 428.—VERN. *Meccani-amli.*

Hæmatoxylon Campechianum, Linn. Sp. Pl. (1753) p. 384. The *Logwood Tree*, a native of Tropical America, has been successfully grown in the Deccan, where it seems to thrive well. It has thick spikes of fragrant yellow flowers and small 1-seeded pods. Dalz. & Gibs. Suppl. p. 28; Woodr. in Journ. Bomb. Nat. v. 11 (1898) p. 427; Watt, Dict. Econ. Prod. v. 4, p. 108.—Flowers: Oct.

ORDER XLIX. ROSACEÆ.

Herbs, shrubs, or trees. Leaves simple or compound, alternate (rarely opposite), stipulate. Flowers usually regular and hermaphrodite. Calyx-tube free or rarely adnate to the ovary, the limb usually 5-lobed. Disk lining the calyx-tube or forming a ring at its base. Petals 5 (rarely 0), inserted under the margin of the disk, deciduous, usually imbricate. Stamens perigynous, usually indefinite, in one or many series; filaments subulate or filiform, usually incurved in bud; anthers small, didymous. Ovary of 1 or more free or connate carpels; ovules 1 or more in each carpel; styles as many as the carpels, free or connate, basal, lateral, or subterminal; stigmas simple, penicillate or capitate. Fruit variable, consisting of achenes, berries, or drupes, rarely capsular. Seeds erect or pendulous, exalbuminous; testa membranous or coriaceous, sometimes expanded into a wing; cotyledons large, plano-convex; radicle short.—DISTRIB. Throughout the world, chiefly in temperate regions; genera more than 70; species about 1200.

Unarmed trees .... 1. PYGEUM.
Prickly shrubs .... 2. RUBUS.
Herbs.
  Fruit of numerous small achenes .... 3. POTENTILLA.
  Fruit of 10 connate carpels .... 4. NEURADA.

1. PYGEUM, Gærtn.

Evergreen trees or shrubs. Leaves simple, alternate, persistent, usually quite entire, often with 2 glands at or near the base; stipules minute, fugacious. Flowers small, racemose or paniculate, sometimes unisexual by want of the ovary. Calyx deciduous; tube obconic, urceolate, or campanulate; limb 5–15-toothed, often unequally. Petals 5–6 in the 5–6-toothed calyx, 0 in the 8–15-toothed, villous or tomentose (rarely glabrous), often indistinguishable from the calyx-lobes. Stamens 10–50, in 1 or more series at the orifice of the calyx-tube; filaments filiform, incurved in bud; anthers small, didymous. Carpel 1, basal in the calyx-tube, ovoid or subglobose; ovules 2, collateral, pendulous; style terminal; stigma capitate. Fruit a transversely oblong 2-lobed indehiscent drupe; pericarp thin, dry or juicy; cotyledons very thick, hemispheric; radicle minute, superior.—DISTRIB. Tropical Asiatic with 1 African species; species about 30.

Petals 4–6; drupe less than 1 in. broad .... 1. *P. Wightianum.*
Petals 0; drupe 1 in. or more broad .... 2. *P. Gardneri.*

1. **Pygeum Wightianum,** *Blume, Mélanges Bot.* (1855) n. 2 (*ex Walp. Ann.* v. 4 (1857) p. 642). A moderate-sized tree; bark rough, pale-brown; young shoots slightly pubescent with appressed hairs. Leaves 2-5 by 1½–2½ in., coriaceous, dark-green above, paler beneath, elliptic-oblong, obtuse, entire, glabrous on both sides, with 2 large round or oval immersed glands on either side of the midrib, base rounded; nerves arched, spreading, prominent beneath; petioles ½–⅓ in. long, stout, rugose. Flowers ¼ in. in diam., in lax pubescent racemes 2–4 in. long; pedicels ⅛–⅓ in. long, pubescent with appressed hairs. Calyx ⅙ in. long, pubescent; tube obconic or turbinate; teeth usually 5, acute. Petals 4–6, elliptic-oblong, rounded at the apex, softly pubescent on the margins. Stamens 20 or more, much longer than the petals. Ovary glabrous; style stout. Drupe broader than long, ⅔ in. broad by ⅜ in. long, slightly bilobed, apiculate, glabrous; pericarp thin. Fl. B. I. v. 2, p. 319; Trim. Fl. Ceyl. v. 2, p. 134; Talb. Trees, Bomb. ed. 2, p. 157; Woodr. in Journ. Bomb. Nat. v. 11 (1898) p. 635. *P. ceylanicum*, Bedd. Flor. Sylvat. t. 59, exclud. syn. (*not* of Gærtn.).—Flowers: Nov.–Dec.

KANARA: S. Ghâts of N. Kanara in evergreen forests, *Talbot*; Divimana (N. Kanara), *Woodrow*.

These localities are given on the authority of Talbot and Woodrow. I have seen no specimens from Kanara, and there are none in Herb. Kew.—DISTRIB. India (W. Peninsula); Ceylon.

2. **Pygeum Gardneri,** *Hook. f. in Fl. B. I.* v. 2 (1878) p. 321. A middle-sized tree, glabrous except the inflorescence; bark of the branches dotted with white specks. Leaves coriaceous, 4–6 by 1¼–2¼ in., alternate, ovate or oblong-lanceolate, acute or acuminate, quite entire, glabrous, base acute or rounded, often unequal-sided, basal glands rarely present; petioles stout, ½–¾ in. long, rugose, glabrous. Flowers in axillary close racemes 1½–3 in. long; rhachis densely pubescent; pedicels ⅛–¼ in. long, stout, pubescent. Calyx ⅛–⅙ in. long, densely clothed outside with fulvous pubescence; tube urceolate; lobes 8–12, obtuse, densely pubescent. Petals 0. Stamens often more than 20, in 2 rows; filaments about as long as the calyx, much-exserted. Ovary glabrous, surrounded at the base by a ring of hairs. Fruit broader than long, 1–1¼ in. across, transversely oblong, bilobed, smooth, apiculate in the sinus at the top, the endocarp smelling strongly of prussic acid.

The ovary appears at first sight to be hirsute, especially in dried specimens, but it is really glabrous, being seated on a ring of hairs which surround it. I have examined numerous fresh specimens at Mahableshwar where the tree is common. Talb. Trees, Bomb. ed. 2, p. 157; Woodr. in Journ. Bomb. Nat. v. 11 (1898) p. 635; Watt, Dict. Econ. Prod. v. 6, part 1, p. 373. *Pygeum acuminatum*, Grah. Cat. p. 247 (*not* of Coleb.). *Pygeum zeylanicum*, Dalz. & Gibs. p. 89, exclud. syn. (*not* of Gærtn.).—Flowers: Nov. VERN. *Dáka*.

DECCAN: Mahableshwar, *Cooke*!, *Woodrow*; Khandala (rare), *Graham*. S. M. COUNTRY: Párva Ghát, *Dalzell & Gibson*; Ramghát, *Ritchie*, 1748! KONKAN: Gairsoppa Ghát, *Talbot*, 275!—DISTRIB. India (W. Peninsula).

2. RUBUS, Linn.

Suberect or sarmentose prickly shrubs. Leaves alternate, simple or compound; stipules free or adnate to the petiole. Flowers in terminal and axillary corymbose panicles (rarely solitary), white or red. Calyx peristent; tube broad; lobes 5. Petals 5. Stamens usually indefinite, inserted at the mouth of the calyx; filaments filiform. Disk lining the calyx-tube. Carpels many, on a convex receptacle; ovules 2, collateral, pendulous; style subterminal. Fruit of numerous small 1-seeded drupes crowded upon a dry spongy conical or cylindric receptacle. Seed pendulous.—DISTRIB. Abundant in the northern, rare in the southern hemisphere; species about 200.

Leaves simple .... 1. *R. moluccanus.*
Leaves 3-foliolate .... 2. *R. ellipticus.*
Leaves 5–9-foliolate .... 3. *R. lasiocarpus.*

1. **Rubus moluccanus,** *Linn. Sp. Pl.* (1753) p. 1197. An extensive subscandent shrub; young branches villous with yellowish hairs; prickles short, recurved, scattered over the branches, petioles and lower surfaces of the midribs of the leaves. Leaves about as broad or (not infrequently) broader than long, 3–6 in. in diam., palmately 5–7-lobed (the lobes obtuse or subacute), irregularly and finely serrate-dentate, bright-green rugulose and sparsely hispid above, clothed with soft yellowish tomentum, reticulately and prominently veined beneath, base deeply cordate; main nerves often prickly beneath; petioles 1–2½ in. long, densely fulvous-hairy; stipules usually large, toothed, pinnatifid or laciniate, densely silky-hairy. Flowers in terminal and axillary silky panicles usually shorter than the leaves; peduncles stout; pedicels short, fulvous-silky; bracts pectinate. Calyx densely silky; lobes more or less triangular, entire or pectinately toothed at the apex. Petals white, obovate, shorter than the calyx. Fruit globose, succulent, the individual carpels red, the receptacle hairy. Fl. B. I. v. 2, p. 330; Trim. Fl. Ceyl. v. 2, p. 136; Talb. Trees, Bomb. ed. 2, p. 157; Woodr. in Journ. Bomb. Nat. v. 11 (1898) p. 635; Watt, Dict. Econ. Prod. v. 6, part 1, p. 583. *Rubus rugosus*, Sm. in Rees, Cyclop. v. 30 (1819) *Rubus*, 34; Grah. Cat. p. 64; Dalz. & Gibs. p. 89; Wight, Icon. t. 225.—Flowers: May.

A rare plant. DECCAN: Mahableshwar, *Graham, Dalzell & Gibson, Cooke*! KANARA: on the Nilkund and Southern Ghâts of N. Kanara, *Talbot.*

I have found this at Mahableshwar in a ravine below the old temple, in which locality Graham also seems to have found it. I have not met with it elsewhere on the hill.—DISTRIB. India (Central, Eastern and Tropical Himalayas, Nipal, Sikkim, Birma, Assam, W. Peninsula); Ceylon, Malaya.

2. **Rubus ellipticus,** var. **hirta,** *Hook. f. in Fl. B. I.* v. 2 (1878) p. 336. A tall suberect bush; stems and branches somewhat sparsely armed with hooked scattered prickles, shaggy with long horizontal (often very dense) brown bristly hairs, covering a short greyish pubescence. Leaves pinnately 3-foliolate; leaf-rhachis (including the petiole) 1¼–2 in., shaggy; common petioles ¾–1 in. long, shaggy; stipules subulate. Leaflets broadly elliptic or obovate, acuminate, irregularly serrate-dentate, green on both sides, glabrous or nearly so, prominently reticulately veined beneath, the terminal leaflets 3½–5 by 2¾–3½ in. with petiolules ½–1 in. long, the lateral leaflets 1½–2½ by 1–1¾ in. with petiolules $\frac{1}{20}$ in. long. Flowers in axillary and terminal panicles; pedicels short. Calyx finely pubescent outside, sometimes with a few scattered bristly hairs; lobes ovate or elliptic, usually mucronate. Petals obovate, longer

than the calyx-lobes, white. Stamens 1-seriate. Fruit golden-yellow, globular, succulent, of numerous drupes on a cylindric hairy receptacle; stone rugose. *Rubus ellipticus*, Talb. Trees, Bomb. ed. 2, p. 157. *R. Wallichiania*, Wight & Arn. Prodr. p. 298. *R. Wallichianus*, Dalz. & Gibs. p. 89. *R. hirtus* (sp.), Roxb. Hort. Beng. p. 38.

KANARA: highest Ghâts to the southwards, *Dalzell & Gibson*; along the highest Ghâts southwards from Mahableshwar, *Talbot*.

Dalzell & Gibson (*l. c.*) state that the plant is found along with *R. lasiocarpus* which is abundant at Mahableshwar, but I have never found it there, nor does Woodrow include it in his list. There are no specimens from Bombay in Herb. Kew.—DISTRIB. India (Himalayas and Western Peninsula).

3. **Rubus lasiocarpus,** *Sm. in Rees, Cyclop.* v. 30 (1819) *Rubus*, 6. A rambling sarmentose prickly shrub; old branches reddish-brown, smooth; young shoots covered with a thin whitish tomentum; prickles compressed, hooked or rarely straight. Leaves 4-8 in. long. (including the petiole), imparipinnate; rhachis closely set with prickles of variable size and clothed with soft woolly pubescence; petioles $\frac{3}{4}$–$1\frac{1}{2}$ in. long: stipules linear, acute. Leaflets 5-9, ovate or elliptic, acute, the terminal leaflet sometimes lobed, longer than the sessile lateral ones, all dark-green, more or less pubescent and wrinkled on the upper side owing to the numerous prominent nerves below, hoary beneath with white woolly tomentum, the margins serrate, the serratures ending in a stout bristle, base cordate or rounded, rarely acute; petiolules of the terminal leaflets $\frac{3}{8}$-$\frac{5}{8}$ in. long. Flowers in terminal and axillary tomentose corymbs, the axillary corymbs sometimes reduced to a solitary flower; peduncles short, tomentose, rarely prickly; bracts linear-subulate. Calyx pubescent; tube small and broad; lobes ovate, with a long slender acumination. Petals pink, orbicular or broadly obovate, scarcely exceeding the calyx. Carpels numerous, tomentose; styles red. Fruit $\frac{1}{2}$–$\frac{3}{4}$ in. in diam.; globose; drupes numerous, dark-purple when ripe; stone pitted. Fl. B. I. v. 2, p. 339; Grah. Cat. p. 64; Dalz. & Gibs. p. 89; Wight, Icon. t. 232; Trim. Fl. Ceyl. v. 2, p. 138; Talb. Trees, Bomb. ed. 2, p. 158; Woodr. in Journ. Bomb. Nat. v. 11 (1898) p. 635; Watt, Dict. Econ. Prod. v. 6, part 1, p. 582.—Flowers: Nov. VERN. *Gauriphal.*

DECCAN: Panchgani, *Woodrow*; Mahableshwar, *H. M. Birdwood*, *Cooke*! KANARA: highest Ghâts to the southward, *Dalzell & Gibson*.

Very common at Mahableshwar, where it is found wild and where it is also cultivated, chiefly in the gardens below the lake, for its fruit which is largely eaten by the Europeans who frequent the hill and also made into jam. The fruit, which somewhat resembles a blackberry, is commonly known as the "*Mahableshwar Raspberry.*"—DISTRIB. India (Temperate Himalaya, Birma, W. Peninsula); Ceylon, Java.

Rubus rosæfolius, Sm. Ic. ined. t. 60, ex Hook. f. in Fl. B. I. v. 2, p. 341. A subscandent woody shrub, a native of the temperate Himalayas, the Khasia Hills, and Ava, is sometimes grown in gardens. The flowers are large, $\frac{3}{4}$–1 in. in diam., white, and the drupes are small. It flowers in August.

3. POTENTILLA, Linn.

Herbs usually perennial. Leaves compound; stipules adnate to the petiole. Flowers yellow or white (rarely red), solitary or in corymbose cymes. Calyx persistent, usually 5-bracteolate; lobes as many as the bracteoles, erect or spreading, valvate in bud. Petals as many as the calyx-lobes, obovate, orbicular, or linear-spathulate. Stamens usually numerous. Disk annular or lining the calyx-tube. Carpels many (rarely 1 or few), on a small dry receptacle; ovule solitary, pendulous; styles persistent or deciduous, ventral or terminal. Achenes many, on a dry receptacle.—DISTRIB. Chiefly in the colder regions of the northern, rare in the southern hemisphere; species about 120.

1. **Potentilla supina,** *Linn. Sp. Pl.* (1753) p. 497. An annual prostrate herb; stems very many from the root, 4–12 in. long, slender, spreading, leafy, dichotomously branched, hairy. Leaves pinnate, 1–2 in. long; rhachis densely hairy; petioles slender, hairy; stipules ovate, acute, entire, hairy. Leaflets 3–9, opposite and alternate, variable in size and form, usually obovate, sometimes oblong or cuneate, variously cut, hairy on both surfaces; petiolules very short or 0. Flowers axillary, solitary, $\frac{1}{4}$ in. in diam.; pedicels $\frac{1}{6}$–$\frac{1}{2}$ in. long, slender, hairy. Calyx hairy outside, $\frac{1}{8}$ in. long; lobes 5, ovate-oblong, subacute; bracteoles 5, oblong-elliptic, obtuse, about $\frac{1}{2}$ as broad as the calyx-lobes. Petals yellow, oblong, smaller than the calyx. Achenes numerous, small, smooth; receptacle globose. Fl. B. I. v. 2, p. 359; Boiss. Fl. Orient. v. 2, p. 725; Aitch. Pb. & Sind Pl. p. 57; Woodr. in Journ. Bomb. Nat. v. 11 (1898) p. 635; Watt, Dict. Econ. Prod. v. 6, part 1, p. 333.—Flowers: Oct.

GUJARAT: Karnáli, *Kanitkar*!, *Woodrow*. SIND: *Stocks*, 403!; banks of the Indus, *Stocks*!

It is VAR. 1 (Hook. f. Fl. B. I. l. c.) with smooth (not ribbed) achenes that is found in Gujarat and Sind.—DISTRIB. Throughout the warmer parts of the plains of India; Afghanistan and westward to the Atlantic, N. Asia, N. Africa.

4. NEURADA, Linn.

An annual woolly depressed branched herb. Leaves alternate, petiolate, ovate, lobed; stipules minute or obsolete. Flowers axillary, solitary, pedicelled. Calyx-tube flat, dilated, at length conic, spiny and forming with the ripe carpels an orbicular disk; lobes 5, triangular; bracteoles 5, subulate. Petals 5, small. Stamens 10, inserted in the contracted mouth of the calyx; filaments subulate. Carpels 10, whorled, united with one another and with the calyx; ovule solitary from the apex of the carpel; styles subulate, persistent. Fruit a depressed cone with spinous margins; carpels 10, horizontal, dehiscing above, terminated by the spinescent styles. Seeds curved, germinating within the carpels, exalbuminous.—DISTRIB. N. Africa, Arabia, Persia, Afghanistan, Sind, and the Panjáb; species 1.

1. **Neurada procumbens,** *Linn. Sp. Pl.* (1753) p. 441. A branched procumbent herb; branches 5–10 in. long, densely woolly. Leaves $\frac{1}{2}$–$\frac{3}{4}$ in. long, ovate-oblong, variously lobed, densely tomentose on both surfaces; petioles $\frac{1}{8}$–$\frac{1}{2}$ in. long, densely woolly. Flowers $\frac{1}{4}$ in.

in diam., axillary, solitary; pedicels short. Fruit $\frac{1}{4}$–$\frac{3}{4}$ in. in diam., orbicular, densely woolly, the lower surface quite flat. The seeds germinate within the carpels and the roots of the young plant carry the old fruit from which they have emerged as a persistent collar round them, the collar remaining even when the plant is fully grown. Fl. B. I. v. 2, p. 368; Boiss. Fl. Orient. v. 2, p. 735; Hook. Icon. Pl. t. 840; Aitch. Pb. & Sind Pl. p. 57; Focke, in Engl. & Prantl, Pflanzenf. v. 3, part 3, p. 50, fig. 23; Woodr. in Journ. Bomb. Nat. v. 11 (1898) p. 635.—Flowers: Nov.–Jan.

SIND: *Vicary*!, *Stocks*, 463!; in stony soil, *Dalzell*!; Karachi to Mugger Peer, *Perry*!; hills at the Hub river, near Karachi, *Bhola Puran*!—DISTRIB. India (Sind, Panjáb); N. Africa, Arabia, Persia, Afghanistan.

The following non-indigenous plants of the Order are grown more or less frequently in gardens throughout the Presidency:—

Prunus Amygdalus, Stokes, Bot. Mat. Med. v. 3, p. 101. "*The Almond*" is occasionally, though rarely, grown in gardens, but does not fruit well.—VERN. *Badám*.

Prunus Persica, Stokes, Bot. Mat. Med. v. 3, p. 100. "*The Peach*" is grown in some quantity at Panchgani. The fruit is, however, small and very unlike an English peach. It is used chiefly for stewing and making jam.—VERN. *A'lu*.

Fragaria vesca. "*The Strawberry*" is very extensively cultivated at Mahableshwar, especially along the banks of the river Yenna. It is one of the delicacies of the hill, and pounds of the fruit are daily consumed by the Europeans who visit the station in the hot season. It is in fruit from March to June.

Eriobotrya japonica, Lindl. in Trans. Linn. Soc. v. 13 (1822) p. 102. "*The Loquat*," a Chinese fruit, is occasionally grown in gardens, but does not fruit well, except perhaps about Belgaum.

Pyrus Malus, Linn. Sp. Pl. p. 479. "*The Apple*" has been planted at Ahmednagar, Poona, Panchgani, &c., but rarely bears fruit.

Pyrus communis, Linn. Sp. Pl. p. 479. "*The Pear*" has been planted at Mahableshwar below the forest officer's house at Lingmala, but the fruit is woody and of little value.

Roses are largely cultivated and succeed well with ordinary care. The soil and climate of the Deccan suit them. The varieties that have been introduced are numerous. An excellent description of the kinds introduced into Poona and their mode of culture may be found in *Gardening in India*, ed. 5, pp. 281–300, by Mr. G. M. Woodrow, who was, while in India, a most successful cultivator of roses.

Cotoneaster frigida, Wall., is mentioned by Mr. H. M. Birdwood [Cat. Flor. Matheran & Mahableshwar (1897) p. 15] as occurring above Rámbág Matheran. As this tree is an inhabitant of the Central and Eastern Himalayas and Nipal and grows at a high altitude, it is scarcely possible that it could be indigenous at Matheran. It has not been found anywhere else in the Bombay Presidency, and there is apparently but one tree on the Matheran hill.

ORDER L. SAXIFRAGACEÆ.

Trees, shrubs, or herbs of various habit. Leaves alternate and exstipulate or with stipules adnate to the base of the petiole, or opposite and exstipulate. Flowers usually hermaphrodite; sepals, petals, and stamens symmetrically regular. Calyx usually 5-merous, more or less adnate to the ovary; lobes imbricate or valvate. Petals 5 or 4 (rarely 0), usually perigynous, often small, imbricate or valvate. Stamens inserted with the petals, equalling or double their number, rarely indefinite. Ovary of 2 or 3–5 united carpels, usually 2- or 3–5-celled with axile placentas, occasionally 1-celled with parietal placentas; ovules numerous, anatropous, erect or pendulous; styles as many as the carpels, free or more or less connate; stigma capitate, or lateral and subcapitate. Fruit capsular or baccate. Seeds usually numerous, usually albuminous.—DISTRIB. Cold and temperate regions of the world and in the mountains of the Tropics; genera 72; species about 580.

1. VAHLIA, Thunb.

Annual or biennial herbs. Leaves opposite, entire; stipules 0. Flowers small, regular, axillary, usually in pairs, white or yellowish. Calyx-tube hemispheric, adnate to the ovary; lobes 5, ovate or lanceolate, valvate. Petals 5, usually shorter than the calyx-lobes. Stamens 5, epigynous; filaments subulate. Ovary inferior, 1-celled, with 2 pendulous placentas; ovules numerous; styles 2, distinct; stigma capitellate. Capsule dehiscing at the apex between the styles. Seeds numerous, minute, ellipsoid, smooth.—DISTRIB. Tropical and subtropical Asia, Tropical and S. Africa; species 3.

1. **Vahlia viscosa,** *Roxb. Fl. Ind.* v. 2 (1832) p. 89. A glandular-pubescent herb; stem 6–12 in. high, erect or diffuse, branched. Leaves $\frac{1}{2}$–1 by $\frac{3}{16}$–$\frac{1}{4}$ in., subsessile, oblong-lanceolate, acute or subobtuse, glabrous or nearly so; midrib prominent beneath. Flowers solitary or in pairs in most of the upper axils; pedicels very short. Calyx $\frac{1}{8}$–$\frac{1}{6}$ in. long, glandular-pubescent; tube hemispheric; lobes about as long as or a little shorter than the tube, triangular-ovate, acute. Petals white (Dalzell, following Roxburgh, says yellow), not exserted beyond the calyx-lobes, ovate-elliptic, acute. Stamens not exserted beyond the calyx-lobes. Capsules $\frac{1}{8}$ in. in diam., subglobose. Seeds minute, numerous. Fl. B. I. v. 2, p. 399; Wight, Icon. t. 563; Aitch. Pb. & Sind Pl. p. 58; Dalz. & Gibs. p. 90; Woodr. in Journ. Bomb. Nat. v. 11 (1898) p. 635.—Flowers: Jan.

KONKAN: Karanja (Bombay harbour), *Dalzell & Gibson*; Divale, 23 miles east of Ratnagiri, *Woodrow*; Murshi, foot of Ambeghát, between Kolapur and Ratnagiri, *Ranade*! GUJARAT: *Dalzell & Gibson*. SIND: *Stocks*!; near Karachi, *Cooke*!—DISTRIB. Throughout India in dry localities; Persia, Egypt, Tropical Africa.

ORDER LI. CRASSULACEÆ.

Herbs or undershrubs usually with fleshy or succulent stems and branches. Leaves alternate or opposite, simple or less commonly pinnately divided; stipules 0. Flowers usually cymose (paniculate in *Bryophyllum*), hermaphrodite or very rarely unisexual, regular. Calyx free, usually 4–5-fid or 4–5-partite. Petals as many as the sepals and alternate with them, free or more or less connate. Stamens adnate to the monopetalous corolla, or inserted alternately with the petals, sometimes double their number. Carpels usually as many as the petals and opposite to them, free or connate below, narrowed upwards into the styles, with a hypogynous gland or scale at the base of each; ovules numerous, 2-seriate along the ventral suture, horizontal or pendulous, anatropous. Follicles membranous or coriaceous, 1-celled, many or few-seeded, dehiscing down the ventral suture. Seeds albuminous, usually minute; embryo terete; cotyledons short.—DISTRIB. Spread over nearly the whole globe except Polynesia; genera 14; species about 400.

Stamens as many as the petals.
  Small herbs .... 1. TILLÆA.
Stamens twice as many as the petals.
  Tall erect herbs.
    Calyx shortly 4-fid .... 2. BRYOPHYLLUM.
    Calyx 4-partite.. 3. KALANCHOE.

1. TILLÆA, Linn.

Small subsucculent glabrous herbs. Leaves opposite, entire, flat in the Indian species. Flowers minute, axillary, often fasciculate, solitary or cymose, white or red. Calyx 4–5-lobed or 4–5-partite. Petals 4–5, free, or connate at the very base. Stamens 4–5; filaments filiform. Hypogynous scales 4–5 or 0. Carpels 4–5, free, attenuated into short subulate styles; ovules 2 to each carpel in the Indian species. Follicles 2-seeded.—DISTRIB. Cosmopolitan; species 20.

1. **Tillæa pentandra,** *Royle, Ill. Bot. Himal.* (1839) p. 222 (name only). Stems procumbent, branched; internodes shorter than the leaves. Leaves $\frac{1}{4}$–$\frac{3}{8}$ by $\frac{1}{10}$–$\frac{1}{8}$ in., linear-lanceolate, acute, connate at the base. Flowers minute, sessile, axillary, usually solitary in the upper, 2–3 together in the lower axils. Calyx-segments lanceolate, acuminate. Petals ovate, acuminate, white, not exceeding the sepals. Seeds minute. Fl. B. I. v. 2, p. 412; Oliver, Fl. Trop. Afr. v. 2, p. 386.

KONKAN: *Stocks!*

The plant is included on the authority of specimens marked as above in Herb. Kew. The ticket on the specimens is not, however, in the handwriting of Dr. Stocks, while the locality (Konkan) is printed (not written) on the ticket. No other botanist has found the plant in Bombay, and its occurrence in the moist Konkan would seem to be somewhat doubtful.—DISTRIB. India (Subtropical Himalaya, Mysore, Nilghiris); Tropical Africa, Abyssinia.

2. **BRYOPHYLLUM,** Salisb.

Tall erect perennial herbs, thickly fleshy. Leaves opposite, crenate. Flowers large, nodding, in spreading panicles with opposite branches. Calyx inflated, cylindric or 4-gonous, shortly 4-fid, valvate. Corolla urceolate or subcampanulate; limb shortly 4-fid, spreading. Stamens 8, in 2 series, inserted on the middle of the corolla-tube; filaments filiform. Carpels 4, free or connate at the base, attenuated into long styles; hypogynous scales 4, free or adnate to the carpels; ovules very numerous. Follicles 4, many seeded.—DISTRIB. Tropical Africa; species 4, of which 1 has been naturalized throughout the Tropics of the Old World.

1. **Bryophyllum calycinum,** *Salisb. in DC. Prod.* v. 3 (1828) p. 396. A succulent glabrous herb 1–4 ft. high; stems obtusely 4-angled, the older light-colored, the younger reddish speckled with white. Leaves variable, decussate, the lower usually simple or occasionally compound, the upper usually 3–5- or sometimes 7-foliolate, long-petioled, the petioles united by a ridge round the stem. Leaflets ovate or elliptic, crenate or serrate. Flowers pendent, in large spreading panicles with opposite stout branches; pedicels slender. Calyx 1–1½ in. long, striated red and green at the base, pale green above; teeth triangular. Corolla swollen and octagonal at the base, constricted in the middle, reddish-purple; lobes triangular. Filaments green at the base, pinkish below the anthers. Anthers hastate, black. Hypogynous scales subquadrate, free or slightly adherent to the carpels. Styles green. Fruit enclosed in the persistent papery calyx and corolla. Seeds small, oblong-ellipsoid, smooth, scarcely striate. The leaves often produce, on their crenatures at the extremities of the lateral nerves, buds furnished with root, stem, and leaves, which drop off and at once become new plants. (See Le Maout & Decaisne, Syst. Bot. p. 7.) Fl. B. I. v. 2, p. 413; Grah. Cat. p. 82; Trim. Fl. Ceyl. v. 2, p. 145; Woodr. in Journ. Bomb. Nat. v. 11 (1898) p. 636.—Flowers: Jan. VERN. *Pánphue*; *Ghaipát*.

KONKAN: *Stocks*!; Matheran, *H. M. Birdwood*; road to Gárbat Point, *Cooke*!; in gardens Bombay, *Graham*; Wari country, *Dalzell & Gibson*. DECCAN: Wai (Satara districts), *Woodrow*; Mahableshwar, *Cooke*!, *H. M. Birdwood*; Koina valley below Mahableshwar, abundant, *Cooke*! S. M. COUNTRY: near Belgaum, *Graham*, *Dalzell & Gibson*; Ramghát, *Law*.—DISTRIB. Supposed to be a native of Tropical Africa, but naturalized everywhere throughout the Tropics of the world.

3. **KALANCHOE,** Adans.

Erect stout perennial herbs. Leaves opposite, or the upper alternate, fleshy, sessile or petiolate, entire, crenate or pinnatifid. Flowers large, in many-flowered paniculate cymes, yellow, white, or purplish. Calyx 4-partite or 4-fid ½-way down, the segments shorter than the corolla-tube. Corolla with a flask-shaped tube and spreading 4-fid limb, persistent. Stamens 8, in 2 series, adnate to the corolla-tube. Hypogynous scales 4. Carpels 4, adnate to the base of the corolla-tube, attenuated into long subulate styles; ovules many. Follicles membranous. Seeds numerous, oblong-ellipsoid, with 8–15 longitudinal ribs.—DISTRIB. Tropical and S. Africa and Tropical Asia; one species in Brazil; species about 25.

Leaves simple.
  Flowers yellow.
    Calyx divided not more than ½-way .... 1. *K. glandulosa.*
    Calyx divided to the base or nearly so.
      Calyx ¼–⅜ in. long; segments ⅛ in. broad at the base... 2. *K. spathulata.*
      Calyx ⅜ in. long; segments 1/16 in. broad at the base ... 3. *K. floribunda.*
  Flowers white.
    Calyx glandular-hairy .... 4. *K. olivacea.*
    Calyx eglandular, glabrous .... 5. *K. Bhidei.*
Leaves pinnatifid .... 6. *K. laciniata.*

1. **Kalanchoe glandulosa,** *Hochst. in A. Rich. Flor. Abyss.* v. 1 (1847) p. 312. A stout perennial herb; stem thick at the base, 1–2 ft. high, clothed (especially towards the top) with glandular hairs. Leaves fleshy; radical ones ovate or obovate-lanceolate, 4–6 in. long, nearly entire, often glabrous, tapering to the base, scarcely petiolate; lower stem-leaves obovate, nearly entire, more or less pubescent, tapering to the base, amplexicaul; upper stem-leaves densely glandular-pubescent, lanceolate or oblanceolate, obtuse, amplexicaul. Flowers in dense paniculate glandular-pubescent cymes. Calyx ⅓ in. long, densely glandular-pubescent, divided about ½-way down into 4 segments; teeth triangular-ovate, acute or acuminate. Corolla ½–⅝ in. long, yellow; tube glandular-pubescent in the upper part; segments ovate-oblong, acuminate. Hypogynous scales narrow-linear, whitish, membranous. Carpels glabrous. Seeds longitudinally ribbed and transversely microscopically striate, oblong-ellipsoid, brown. Fl. B. I. v. 2, p. 414; Oliver, Fl. Trop. Afr. v. 2, p. 398; Woodr. in Journ. Bomb. Nat. v. 11 (1898) p. 636. *Kalanchoe Ritchieana,* Dalz. in Hook. Kew Journ. Bot. v. 4 (1852) p. 346; Dalz. & Gibs. p. 105.

DECCAN: Singhad (Poona districts), *Woodrow*; hills near Satara, *Woodrow*. S. M. COUNTRY: Kákti hill near Belgaum, *Ritchie*, 329!; Hubli, *Ritchie*!—DISTRIB. India (hills of the W. Peninsula); Tropical Africa.

2. **Kalanchoe spathulata,** *DC. Succ. Pl. & Grasses,* t. 65. Stem 1–4 ft. high, glabrous. Leaves spathulate-oblong, obtuse, crenate, cuneate at the base, glabrous; the lower petiolate, usually 3–5 by 1½–2 in. (sometimes reaching 10 by 4 in.); the upper distant, becoming very narrow, 3–4 by ½ in. (sometimes 3-foliolate), frequently sessile. Flowers in dense many-flowered cymose panicles; lower bracts leaf-like. Calyx ¼–⅜ in. long, glabrous, divided almost to the very base; segments oblong-lanceolate or triangular from a broad base, acute or acuminate, ⅛ in. broad at the base. Corolla clear yellow; tube glabrous, ½ in. long; lobes broadly lanceolate, acute or shortly acuminate. Hypogynous scales narrow-linear, ⅛ in. long, often bifid. Follicles glabrous. Fl. B. I. v. 2, p. 414; Woodr. in Journ. Bomb. Nat. v. 11 (1898) p. 636; Watt, Dict. Econ. Prod. v. 4, p. 564.—Flowers: Oct.–Nov.

DECCAN: Panchgani, *Woodrow*. S. M. COUNTRY: Badami, *Woodrow*.—DISTRIB. India (Tropical Himalaya, Birma); China, Java.

3. **Kalanchoe floribunda,** *Wight & Arn. Prod.* (1834) p. 359; var. **glabra,** *C. B. Clarke, in Hook. f. Fl. B. I.* v. 2, p. 415. A large perennial herb 2–3 ft. high, quite glabrous throughout; stem erect, not branched, hollow. Leaves fleshy, the lowest reaching 4 in. long, gradually becoming smaller upwards, the uppermost about 1½ in. long,

elliptic-spathulate, rounded or obtuse, gradually tapering to a long base, coarsely crenate-serrate, pale yellowish-green. Flowers numerous, in large flat-topped trichotomous corymbose cymes; bracts linear-lanceolate. Calyx $\frac{1}{8}$–$\frac{1}{4}$ in. long, divided nearly to the base, glabrous; segments narrowly lanceolate, $\frac{1}{16}$ in. broad at the base, very acuminate. Corolla $\frac{1}{2}$–$\frac{5}{8}$ in. long, yellow; tube inflated, glabrous; lobes broadly lanceolate, very acute. Hypogynous scales $\frac{1}{10}$ in. long, narrow-linear, usually acute. Follicles glabrous. Trim. Fl. Ceyl. v. 2, p. 144; Woodr. in Journ. Bomb. Nat. v. 11 (1898) p. 636.—Flowers: Nov.

DECCAN: hills near Satara, *Woodrow*.

4. **Kalanchoe olivacea,** *Dalz. in Dalz. & Gibs. Bomb. Fl.* (1861) p. 313. Whole plant of an olive-brown color; stem 1 ft. high, terete, glabrous. Leaves 3½–5 by 1–2 in., ovate, elliptic, or broadly lanceolate, irregularly crenate-serrate, fleshy, dotted with blood-red spots, glabrous, the upper leaves the smaller. Flowers in paniculate cymes; pedicels densely clothed with glandular viscid hairs. Calyx $\frac{3}{16}$–$\frac{1}{4}$ in. long, glandular-hairy; lobes lanceolate, acute or acuminate. Corolla white, sometimes slightly tinged with pink (especially when fading), $\frac{3}{4}$–$\frac{7}{8}$ in. long; tube clothed outside with glandular hairs; segments $\frac{1}{4}$–$\frac{3}{8}$ in. long, ovate, acute, apiculate, glandular-hairy outside. Hypogynous scales $\frac{1}{8}$ in. long, white, linear, slightly bifid at apex. Follicles glabrous.—Flowers: Oct.-Dec.

DECCAN: along the hill-side above the Ghát road from Wai to Panchgani abundant, *Cooke*!, *Bhide*!, *Dalzell & Gibson*, *H. M. Birdwood*; Pándughar hill fort near Wai, *Dalzell & Gibson*; Singhad, *Nairne*; N. Deccan hills, *Ritchie*. S. M. COUNTRY: hills near Belgaum, *Ritchie*, 330!

Note.—The description of this plant, owing no doubt to its having appeared in the *addenda and corrigenda* to the 'Bombay Flora' of Dalzell & Gibson (*l. c.*), has hitherto entirely escaped notice. No allusion to it is made in the 'Index Kewensis' nor apparently in any other botanical publication. I have, in my own Herbarium, several specimens obtained from the cliff at Panchgani, where Dalzell found it, and Mr. Gammie has recently sent me a large number of specimens from the same locality collected by Mr. Bhide, the Herbarium Keeper in the College of Science at Poona. There has been but one specimen of the plant in Herb. Kew. which was collected by *Ritchie* (n. 330, marked nov. sp.) on hills near Belgaum. Mr. C. B. Clarke in Hook. f. Fl. B. I. v. 2, p. 415, places Ritchie's plant under *K. brasiliensis*, Camb., a plant which in his original description (Fl. Bras. Merid. v. 2 (1829) p. 196) Cambessèdes describes as growing near the sea, and further describes the flowers as having a yellow tube and a rose-colored limb, characters which would seem to be sufficiently distinctive. Ritchie, in a note attached to his specimen in Herb. Kew., describes the flowers of his plant as white, and I can add my testimony to the correctness of Ritchie's statement, as I have seen the plant growing in abundance along the Panchgani Ghát, where its white flowers were a conspicuous object among the rocks.

5. **Kalanchoe Bhidei,** *T. Cooke.* Whole plant of a reddish color, glabrous; stem erect, 2–3 ft. high. Leaves 2½–3½ by 1½–2 in., elliptic, coarsely and irregularly crenate-serrate, tinged with red, running down into a flattened petiole which is enlarged at the base. Flowers numerous, in copious cymose panicles; pedicels slender, $\frac{1}{4}$–$\frac{3}{8}$ in. long; bracts linear-lanceolate, $\frac{1}{10}$–$\frac{1}{8}$ in. long. Calyx divided to the base; lobes $\frac{3}{16}$–$\frac{1}{4}$ in. long, $\frac{1}{10}$ in. broad at the base, triangular, acute, appressed to the corolla, glabrous, eglandular. Corolla $\frac{1}{2}$–$\frac{5}{8}$ in. long, pure white; segments $\frac{1}{8}$ in. long, $\frac{1}{16}$ in. broad, oblong or slightly obovate, acute, apiculate, glabrous. Hypogynous scales $\frac{1}{8}$ in. long, linear, acute. Follicles glabrous.—Flowers: Nov.

DECCAN: Shirgaon Ghát between Wathár and Wai, *Bhide*, 1243!

The above species was collected in November 1902 by Mr. Bhide, the Herbarium Keeper in the College of Science at Poona. I have named the plant after him.

6. **Kalanchoe laciniata,** *DC. Succ. Pl. & Grasses,* t. 100. A large succulent herb, glabrous or more or less pubescent, 3–4 ft. high; stems stout, slightly branched. Leaves numerous, large and very succulent, 3–4 in. long, very variable; the lowest deeply gashed, the segments usually narrow-oblong, acute, dentate, serrate or crenate; the middle-stem leaves more or less deeply pinnatifid; the uppermost entire or nearly so, all shining, pale glaucous-green; petioles 1–1½ in. long, flattened, fleshy, amplexicaul. Flowers in paniculate cymes; bracts linear. Calyx $\frac{1}{8}$–$\frac{1}{6}$ in. long, glabrous or glandular-pubescent, divided to the base; segments narrowly lanceolate, acute, somewhat spreading. Corolla yellow, $\frac{5}{8}$ in. long; tube $\frac{1}{2}$ in. long; lobes lanceolate, acute or acuminate, glabrous or pubescent. Hypogynous scales $\frac{1}{8}$–$\frac{1}{6}$ in. long, linear. Follicles $\frac{1}{3}$ in. long, glabrous. Fl. B. I. v. 2, p. 415; Grah. Cat. p. 81; Dalz. & Gibs. p. 105; Wight, Icon. t. 1158; Oliver, Fl. Trop. Afr. v. 2, p. 392; Trim. Fl. Ceyl. v. 2, p. 144; Watt, Dict. Econ. Prod. v. 2, p. 562.

The plants vary much in pubescence, the mode of division of the leaves and the shape of their ultimate segments. Mr. C. B. Clarke (Fl. B. I. l. c.) recognizes 2 varieties, in one of which the leaves are once-pinnatifid, the segments broad and the sepals glabrous, while in the other the leaves are 2–3-pinnatifid, the segments linear and the sepals pubescent.

DECCAN: Pándughar fort near Wai, *Gibson* ex *Graham*. S. M. COUNTRY: hills near Dharwar, *Lush* ex *Graham, Dalzell & Gibson*.

The localities named above have been given by Graham and by Dalzell & Gibson in their respective Floras. I have seen no Bombay specimens, nor has Mr. Woodrow included the plant in his list in Journ. Bomb. Nat. Hist. Soc. Graham is circumstantial enough in his description, but depends for localities on Dr. Lush and Dr. Gibson. Dalzell probably quotes Graham.—DISTRIB. India (Bengal, Birma, W. Peninsula); Ceylon, Malacca, Yunan, Java, Tropical Africa.

ORDER LII. DROSERACEÆ.

Perennial, glandular-hairy herbs. Leaves radical or alternate, usually circinate in vernation; stipules 0, represented by hairs edging the dilated base of the petiole, or scarious. Inflorescence various; flowers hermaphrodite, regular. Calyx 4–8-partite, or sepals free, imbricate, persistent. Petals 4–8, hypogynous or nearly so, imbricate in bud, marcescent. Stamens as many as the petals, hypogynous or nearly so. Ovary nearly free, globose or ovoid, 1–3-celled; ovules numerous, on 5–3 parietal placentas; styles 5–3, capitate, fimbriate or bifid. Capsule membranous, 5–3-valved. Seeds numerous, with fleshy albumen; embryo cylindric or minute.—DISTRIB. Throughout the world (except the Pacific Islands) in temperate and tropical regions; genera 6; species 110.

1. DROSERA, Linn.

Perennial herbs, scapigerous or with a leafy stem, grandular-hairy. Leaves alternate or rosulate, usually circinate in vernation; stipules 0 or scarious and adnate to the petiole. Flowers white or rosy, solitary, racemose, cymose or corymbose. Calyx free from the ovary, 4–8-partite, imbricate. Petals 4–8, hypogynous or scarcely perigynous, marcescent. Stamens as many as the petals and inserted with them. Ovary free, ovoid or globose, 1-celled; ovules numerous, parietal; styles 2–5. Capsule loculicidally 2–5-valved. Seeds numerous in the Indian species, obovoid-ellipsoid; testa black, smooth, reticulate, not lax.—DISTRIB. Throughout the world, except Polynesia; very numerous in Australia; species 100.

Leaves all radical, rosulate, spathulate-cuneate.................... 1. *D. Burmanni.*
Leaves cauline, linear .... 2. *D. indica.*

1. **Drosera Burmanni,** *Vahl, Symb.* v. 3 (1794) p. 50. Stem scarcely any. Leaves $\frac{1}{4}$–$\frac{5}{8}$ in. long, all radical, forming a close rosette on the ground, spathulate-cuneate, upper surface clothed with numerous gland-tipped tentacles longest at the margin; petioles flat; stipules nearly as long as the petioles, scarious, cut into long slender segments. Scapes 1–3, erect, glabrous, 2–8 in. long, from the axils of inner leaves. Flowers about 8–20, in secund racemes occupying the upper fourth of the scape only; pedicels $\frac{1}{8}$–$\frac{1}{4}$ in. long, slender, glabrous. Calyx $\frac{1}{8}$–$\frac{1}{6}$ in. long, papillose; segments linear-oblong, obtuse. Petals white, slightly longer than the calyx, spathulate. Styles 5, undivided. Capsules 5-valved. Seeds numerous, minute, black, reticulate. Fl. B. I. v. 2, p. 424; Grah. Cat. p. 11; Dalz. & Gibs. p. 12; Wight, Icon. t. 944; Trim. Fl. Ceyl. v. 2, p. 145; Woodr. in Journ. Bomb. Nat. v. 11 (1898) p. 636; Watt, Dict. Econ. Prod. v. 3, p. 195.—Flowers: Dec.–Feb.

KONKAN: Ratnagiri Collectorate, *Nairne*; Dapoli, *Nairne*; S. Konkan, *Dalzell & Gibson, Woodrow!* KANARA: Siddapur and Yacombi, *Woodrow.*—DISTRIB. Throughout India; Ceylon, China, Japan, Malaya, W. Africa, Australia.

2. **Drosera indica,** *Linn. Sp. Pl.* (1753) p. 282. Stem weak, suberect or decumbent, slightly branched, glandular-pubescent. Leaves cauline, alternate, 1–2$\frac{1}{2}$ in. long, narrow-linear, about $\frac{1}{30}$ in. broad, circinate in vernation, the upper portion copiously fringed with very fine gland-tipped tentacles, the lower half (petiole) glabrous. Flowers in leaf-opposed racemes, 3–8 in. long; pedicels $\frac{1}{4}$–$\frac{1}{2}$ in. long, glandular-hairy. Calyx $\frac{1}{6}$ in. long; segments oblong-lanceolate, subacute, more or less glandular-pubescent. Petals white, narrowly spathulate, slightly longer than the calyx. Capsules 3-valved; styles 3. Seeds minute, obovoid, strongly ridged and with raised reticulation. Fl. B. I. v. 2, p. 424; Grah. Cat. p. 11; Dalz. & Gibs. p. 12; Trim. Fl. Ceyl. v. 2, p. 146; Woodr. in Journ. Bomb. Nat. v. 11 (1898) p. 636.—Flowers: Oct.–Nov.

KONKAN: Salsette and the Konkans, *Nimmo ex Graham*; Vingorla, *Dalzell & Gibson*; N. & S. Konkan, *Law!*; Ratnagiri, *Nairne, Dr. E. H. R. Langley!*; Sávantwari, *Woodrow.* DECCAN: Mahableshwar, *Woodrow*; Lanoli, *Woodrow!* KANARA: *Law!*—DISTRIB. India (W. Peninsula, Birma); Ceylon, Malayan Archipelago, China, Tropical Australia, Africa.

ORDER LIII. HALORAGIDACEÆ.

Herbs often aquatic. Leaves alternate, opposite or whorled, often pectinately pinnatifid when submerged; stipules 0. Flowers hermaphrodite or unisexual, usually minute, often incomplete, axillary, solitary or fascicled, sessile or pedicelled, the nodes between the floral whorls sometimes developed. Calyx superior; tube adnate to the ovary; lobes of the limb 4 or 0. Petals 4, epigynous, or 0. Stamens 8, 4 or 1, epigynous in the bisexual flowers. Ovary 4-, 2-, or 1-celled: ovules 4 (1 in *Hippuris*), pendulous; styles equal in number to the cells; stigmas papillose or plumose. Fruit small, dry or drupaceous, with cells as in the ovary, indehiscent or separating into carpels. Seeds 4 or 1.—DISTRIB. Cosmopolitan; genera 9; species 80.

1. MYRIOPHYLLUM, Linn.

Glabrous aquatic herbs. Leaves entire, dentate, serrate, or pectinately pinnatifid, often whorled. Flowers monœcious or hermaphrodite, small, sessile or nearly so, in the axils of floral leaves or in nearly naked spikes. MALE FLOWERS: Calyx minute; tube short; limb 2–4-fid or 0. Petals 2–4. Stamens 2–8. FEMALE FLOWERS: Calyx-tube deeply 4-furrowed; limb 0 or of 4 minute lobes. Petals minute or 0. Ovary inferior, 4- or rarely 2-celled; ovule solitary in each cell, pendulous; styles 2 or 4, short; stigmas plumose. Fruit 4-furrowed or separating into 4 or 2 carpels.—DISTRIB. Cosmopolitan; species 15.

1. **Myriophyllum intermedium,** *DC. Prod.* v. 3 (1828) p. 69. An aquatic herb; stems long, the upper portion floating on the surface. Leaves $\frac{1}{2}$–$1\frac{1}{2}$ by $\frac{1}{20}$–$\frac{1}{10}$ in., alternate, solitary or in fascicles of 2–3, sometimes in whorls, linear, acute, entire or serrate; the submerged pectinately pinnatifid. Flowers subsessile, axillary. Fruit oblong, $\frac{1}{20}$ in. long, with rounded and minutely scabrous ridges and shallow furrows between them, ultimately separating into its component carpels. Fl. B. I. v. 2, p. 433; Woodr. in Journ. Bomb. Nat. v. 11 (1898) p. 636. *Myriophyllum tetrandrum* (?), Grah. Cat. p. 76; Dalz. & Gibs. p. 99 (*not* of Roxb.). *Haloragis oligantha*, W. & A. Prodr. p. 338; Wight, Icon. t. 1061 (*not* of Arn.).

DECCAN: Mahableshwar, side of the lake, *Cooke*!, *Woodrow*. S. M. COUNTRY: Belgaum, *Ritchie*, 1155! KANARA: Hulikal (N. Kanara), *Talbot*, 1353!—DISTRIB. India (W. Peninsula); Malaya, Australia, New Zealand, S. America.

ORDER LIV. RHIZOPHORACEÆ.

Trees or shrubs usually quite glabrous; branches terete, swollen at the nodes. Leaves opposite and stipulate (rarely alternate and exstipulate), usually coriaceous; stipules interpetiolar, very caducous. Flowers in axillary cymes, racemes, panicles or spikes, usually hermaphrodite, surrounded at the base by connate or cupuliform bracts, or ebracteate. Calyx-tube more or less adnate to the ovary, rarely free; calyx-lobes 4–14, valvate, persistent. Petals isomerous with the calyx-lobes, but usually shorter than them, entire, emarginate, 2-fid or lacerate. Stamens usually twice as many as the petals, often inserted in pairs opposite to and partly embraced by them, rarely indefinite (*Kandelia*); anthers 2-celled, rarely multiloculate (*Rhizophora*). Ovary more or less adnate to the calyx, 2-5- (rarely 3-6-) celled or 1-celled by the suppression of the septa; ovules usually 2 in each cell, pendulous; style usually simple; stigma simple or lobed. Fruit coriaceous or woody, crowned with or surrounded by the calyx-limb, usually indehiscent and 1-celled. Seed 1, pendulous, arillate or not; testa coriaceous or membranous, never lax; albumen fleshy or 0; embryo inverted, small in the albuminous seeds, elongate in the exalbuminous ones; radicle macropodous, in many of the genera perforating the apex of the pericarp and protruding while the fruit still adheres to the tree.—DISTRIB. Tropical plants; many sharing with an arboreal vegetation the muddy shores of the estuaries of rivers; genera 17; species about 70.

Seeds exalbuminous; radicle large, protruding while the fruit is still on the tree.
  Calyx 4-lobed; stamens 8-12; ovary 2-celled .... 1. RHIZOPHORA.
  Calyx 5-6-lobed.
    Stamens 10-12; ovary 3-celled........................... 2. CERIOPS.
    Stamens indefinite; ovary 1-celled .... 3. KANDELIA.
  Calyx 8-14-lobed; stamens 16-28; ovary 2-4 celled...... 4. BRUGUIERA.
Seeds albuminous; radicle not protruding while the fruit is still on the tree.. 5. CARALLIA.

Note.—Many of the species of this Order, which grow in muddy creeks and backwaters, are indiscriminately called "Mangroves," a term which is also applied to several bark-yielding plants of similar habit, even though belonging to other Natural Orders. Dr. Watt (Dict. Econ. Prod. v. 5, p. 157) enumerates the following as the chief species yielding what is known as mangrove-bark:—*Rhizophora mucronata* (the true mangrove), *Ceriops Candolleana* (the black mangrove), *Avicennia officinalis*, belonging to the Natural Order Verbenaceæ (the white mangrove), *Bruguiera gymnorhiza*, *Bruguiera parviflora*, *Ceriops Roxburghiana*, *Kandelia Rheedii*. Mr. Gamble (Indian Forester, v. 23 [1898] p. 413) adds to the above list the following plants not belonging to the Order RHIZOPHORACEÆ:—*Lumnitzera racemosa*, *Sonneratia acida*, *Sonneratia apetala*, *Ægiceras corniculata*, *Excæcaria Agallocha*.

1. RHIZOPHORA, Linn.

Trees; branches thick, terete, marked with leaf-scars. Leaves opposite, coriaceous, ovate or elliptic, mucronate, quite entire, glabrous; stipules large, in pairs, interpetiolar, caducous. Flowers rather large, in axillary 2-3-chotomously-divided and few-flowered cymes. Calyx 4-lobed, surrounded at the base by connate bracteoles; tube short, adnate to the ovary at the base. Petals 4, entire, inserted on a fleshy disk. Stamens 8-12; anthers subsessile, multiloculate. Ovary 2-celled, ½-inferior, produced beyond the calyx into a fleshy cone; ovules 2 in each cell; style conical at the base, subulate; stigma bifid. Fruit coriaceous, ovoid or obconic, girt at the base with the reflexed persistent calyx-teeth. Seed germinating while the fruit is still on the tree; radicle elongate, perforating the apex of the fruit and descending from the tree to the mud.—DISTRIB. Muddy shores of the Tropics; species about 5.

Many of the species of this genus which grow in muddy creeks and backwaters are indiscriminately called *mangroves*, a term which is also made to include several other plants of similar habit, even though belonging to different Natural Orders, as for example *Avicennia officinalis*, which is called the "white mangrove." *Rhizophora mucronata* is the "true mangrove," and *Ceriops Candolleana* is known as the "black mangrove."

Cymes usually 3-flowered; petals fleshy, villous on the inner faces and margins .... 1. *R. mucronata*.
Cymes 2-flowered; petals thin, glabrous .... 2. *R. conjugata*.

1. **Rhizophora mucronata,** *Lamk. Encyc. Méthod.* v. 6 (1804) p. 189. A large evergreen glabrous shrub or small tree; young branches thick, conspicuously marked with the scars of fallen leaves and stipules. Leaves 3–8 by 1¾–4 in., elliptic, acute, usually mucronate, glabrous, bright-green above, paler, minutely rugulose and dotted with black dots beneath, base tapering; petioles ¾–1½ in. long; stipules 2–3 in. long, glabrous, minutely rugulose, caducous. Flowers pedicelled, in axillary, usually 3- (rarely 2-) flowered cymes slightly longer than the petioles; peduncles stout, ¾–1½ in. long, from the axils of leaves of the same year; pedicels short, rugose. Calyx ½–⅝ in. long; lobes pale-yellow, coriaceous, triangular-oblong, subacute, glabrous, reticulato-rugose, keeled within, reflexed in fruit. Petals white, shorter than the calyx-lobes, oblong, obtuse, thick and fleshy, densely villous on the margins and less so on the inner faces. Stamens 8; anthers linear, acute. Fruit 1½ in. long, ovoid-conical, surrounded at the base by the persistent calyx-lobes; protruded radicle cylindric, sometimes reaching 2 ft. long before it falls from the tree. Fl. B. I. v. 2, p. 435; Dalz. & Gibs. p. 95; Wight, Icon. t. 238; Bedd. For. Man. in Flor. Sylvat. p. xcix, t. 13, fig. 4; Trim. Fl. Ceyl. v. 2, p. 151; Talb. Trees, Bomb. ed. 2, p. 158; Woodr. in Journ. Bomb. Nat. v. 11 (1898) p. 636; Watt, Dict. Econ. Prod. v. 6, part 1, p. 491. *Rhizophora candelaria*, Wight & Arn. Prodr. p. 310; Grah. Cat. p. 68.—Flowers: Aug.–Dec. VERN. *Kamo*; *Dumbi*; *Kándal*.

Salt-marshes and tidal creeks along the coast from Sind to Kanara.—DISTRIB. India, along muddy shores and tidal creeks; Ceylon, Tropics of the Old World and Australia.

This is the "*true mangrove*." Its bark supplies a useful tanning material. See Watt, Dict. Econ. Prod. l. c.

2. **Rhizophora conjugata,** *Linn. Sp. Pl.* (1753) p. 443. A glabrous shrub or small tree; young branches marked with the scars of fallen leaves. Leaves 4–6 by 1¾–2½ in., elliptic-lanceolate, acute, usually with a small mucro, dark-green above, paler, rugulose and minutely dotted beneath, base tapering; petioles ½–1 in. long; stipules 2–3 in. long. Flowers sessile, in axillary 2-flowered cymes usually shorter than the petioles; peduncles about ½ in. long or less, stout; pedicels 0. Calyx ⅜–½ in. long, externally rugose, glabrous; lobes ovate-oblong, acute. Petals white, slightly shorter than the calyx, linear, thin, flat, glabrous, caducous. Stamens 11–12; anthers linear, sessile or nearly so. Fruit 1 in. long, somewhat conical or obclavate, rugose, glabrous, surrounded at the base by the reflexed calyx-lobes; protruding radicle cylindric, sometimes reaching 1 ft. long before falling from the tree. Fl. B. I. v. 2, p. 436; Talb. Trees, Bomb. ed. 2, p. 159. *Rhizophora candelaria*, DC. Prodr. v. 3 (1828) p. 32 (*not* of Wight & Arn.); Trim. Fl. Ceyl. v. 2, p. 151.—Flowers: Aug.–Dec.

Found in the same localities as the preceding, which it much resembles but is not nearly so common.

2. CERIOPS, Arnott.

Shrubs or small trees with thick leafy branches. Leaves opposite, elliptic or obovate, entire; stipules interpetiolar, caducous. Flowers subcapitate; peduncles axillary. Calyx 5–6-merous, surrounded at the base by connate bracteoles; tube short, adnate to the ovary at the base; lobes coriaceous. Petals 5–6, inserted at the base of a 10–12-lobed fleshy disk, truncate or emarginate, appendiculate with clavate bristles. Stamens 10–12; filaments slender, inserted between the lobes of the disk; anthers oblong or linear, obtuse or acuminate. Ovary ½-inferior, 3-celled (at least above), produced beyond the calyx into a fleshy cone: ovules 2 in each cell, pendulous near its apex; style short; stigma simple. Fruit coriaceous, ovoid, girt above the base with the reflexed calyx-lobes, 1-celled. Seed 1, pendulous, germinating as in *Rhizophora*; cotyledons conferruminate; protruding radicle elongate, clavate.—DISTRIB. Muddy shores of Tropical Asia, Africa, Australia, and Polynesia; species 7.

1. **Ceriops Candolleana,** *Arn. in Ann. Nat. Hist.* v. 1 (1838) p. 364. A glabrous shrub or small tree 3–6 ft. high; branchlets marked with the scars of fallen leaves and stipules. Leaves 2–4 by 1¼–2 in., coriaceous, obovate-oblong, rounded at the apex, sometimes slightly emarginate, glabrous, much attenuated at the base; petioles ⅓–1 in. long, rugose, glabrous. Flowers in axillary, peduncled, branched cymes; pedicels short, stout. Calyx ¼ in. long; lobes 5, oblong, subobtuse. Petals 5, white, shorter than the calyx, oblong-obovate, truncate or emarginate, furnished at the apex with 3 short clavate appendages, glabrous, with a strong mid-nerve at the back of the petal. Stamens 10, about as long as the petals, alternately long and short. Fruit slightly conical, ½–⅝ in. long; protruded radicle sometimes reaching 1 ft. before falling, gradually thickening to near the apex and then becoming acute, deeply grooved and angled, reddish-brown. Fl. B. I. v. 2, p. 436; Wight, Icon. t. 240; Bedd. For. Man. in Flor. Sylvat. p. xcix, t. 13, fig. 5; Aitch. Pb. & Sind Pl. p. 59; Trim. Fl. Ceyl. v. 2, p. 152; Talb. Trees, Bomb. ed. 2, p. 159; Watt, Dict. Econ. Prod. v. 2, p. 261.—Flowers: July–Sept. VERN. *Kirrari*; *Chauri*.

Tidal swamps along the coast. KONKAN: *Law*!; Elephanta (Bombay), *Stocks*, 524! SIND: *Stocks*!, *Vicary*.—DISTRIB. India (muddy shores and tidal creeks); Ceylon, Tropics of the Old World.

The bark supplies an excellent tanning material, and a decoction of it is used to stop hæmorrhage and as an application to malignant ulcers. A decoction of the shoots is used as a substitute for quinine on the African coast. See Watt, Dict. Econ. Prod. l. c.

3. KANDELIA, Wight & Arn.

A small tree with terete leafy branches. Leaves opposite, oblong, obtuse, entire; stipules interpetiolar, caducous. Flowers large, few, on axillary dichotomously branched peduncles, white. Calyx 5–6-merous, surrounded at the base by connate bracteoles; tube short, adnate to the ovary; lobes linear. Petals 5–6, inserted at the base of a fleshy disk, bifid; lobes capillaceo-multifid. Stamens indefinite; filaments filiform; anthers small, oblong. Ovary ½-inferior, 1-celled, produced beyond the calyx into a fleshy cone; ovules 6, affixed in pairs to a central column; style filiform, conical at the base; stigma 3-fid. Fruit coriaceous, conical-ovoid, girt above the base by the reflexed calyx-lobes, 1-celled. Seed 1, germinating as in *Rhizophora*; cotyledons conferruminate; protruding radicle elongate, clavate, acuminate.—DISTRIB. Muddy shores of Tropical India and Ceylon; species 1.

1. **Kandelia Rheedei,** *Wight & Arn. Prodr.* (1834) p. 311. A small tree. Leaves 2½–5 by 1–2¼ in., elliptic-oblong, obtuse, dark green and polished above, reddish-brown beneath, glabrous, base narrowed; petioles ⅓–⅝ in. long; stipules ¾–1½ in. long. Flowers in axillary cymes; peduncles longer than the petioles, 4-9-flowered. Calyx ⅝–⅞ in. long, externally rugose; lobes narrow-linear, acute. Petals bifid; lobes divided into numerous capillary segments. Stamens indefinite, of unequal lengths. Fruit ½–1 in. long, obclavate, girt above the middle with the reflexed calyx-lobes; protruded radicle 6–15 in. long, cylindric, acuminate, usually not ridged nor grooved. Fl. B. I. v. 2, p. 437; Wight, Ill. t. 89; Bedd. For. Man. in Flor. Sylvat. p. c, t. 13, fig. 6; Talb. Trees, Bomb. ed. 2, p. 159; Woodr. in Journ. Bomb. Nat. v. 11 (1898) p. 636; Watt, Dict. Econ. Prod. v. 4, p. 565. *Rhizophora Candel*, Linn. Sp. Pl. (1753) p. 443; Grah. Cat. p. 68.—Flowers: Mar.

Tidal swamps along the coast. KANARA: Kumpta, *Woodrow*.—DISTRIB. Tidal shores of India and Ceylon, Malaya.

4. BRUGUIERA, Lamk.

Trees or shrubs. Leaves opposite, coriaceous, entire; stipules interpetiolar, caducous. Flowers large; peduncles axillary, 1-many-flowered. Calyx ebracteolate at the base; tube obconic or campanulate, adnate to the ovary at the base; lobes 8–14, subulate-lanceolate, valvate. Petals 8–14, inserted on the limb of the calyx, oblong, 2-fid, setigerous, convolute at the base, embracing the stamens. Stamens 16–28, in pairs opposite to the petals, at length springing from them elastically; filaments filiform, unequal in length; anthers linear, acute or apiculate. Ovary inferior, 2–4-celled; ovules 2 in each cell; style filiform; stigma minutely 2–4-fid. Fruit turbinate, thickly coriaceous, crowned at the apex by the lobes of the calyx, 1-celled. Seed 1, pendulous, germinating as in *Rhizophora*; protruding radicle elongate, clavate.—DISTRIB. Muddy shores of Tropical Asia, Africa, Australia, and Polynesia; species about 7.

Flowers solitary, 1–1½ in. long .... 1. *B. gymnorhiza.*
Flowers in axillary cymes, not exceeding ½ in. long.
  Lobes of calyx as long as the tube .... 2. *B. caryophylloides.*
  Lobes of calyx ½ as long as the tube .... 3. *B. parviflora.*

1. **Bruguiera gymnorhiza,** *Lamk. Tab. Encyc.* v. 2 (1793) p. 517, t. 397. A glabrous evergreen shrub or tree; young branches smooth, marked towards the apex with the scars of fallen leaves and stipules. Leaves 3–6 by 1¼–2½ in., elliptic or elliptic-oblong, acute or slightly acuminate (not mucronate), bright green above, paler and with a prominent midrib beneath, glabrous, cuneate at the base; petioles ½–1½ in. long; stipules 1½–2½ in. long, caducous. Flowers solitary, axillary; peduncles ¼–½ in. long, deflexed. Calyx 1–1½ in. long, orange-yellow, campanulate, ribbed,

divided about ½-way down into 10–14 (often 11) narrow acute erect segments keeled on the inner face. Petals shorter than the calyx-lobes and equal to them in number, 2-lobed at the apex, with 2–4 stout bristles at the point of each lobe and 1 in the notch, hairy at the base, glabrous above. Stamens 2 opposite to each petal and shorter than it; filaments of each pair alternately long and short. Fruit less than 1 in. long, obconic, crowned at first by the erect calyx-segments which afterwards drop off, scarlet; protruding radicle fusiform, more or less angled, often reaching 1 ft. in length before falling. Fl. B. I. v. 2, p. 437; Trim. Fl. Ceyl. v. 2, p. 153; Talb. Trees, Bomb. ed. 2, p. 160; Watt, Dict. Econ. Prod. v. 1, p. 541. *Bruguiera Rheedii*, Blume, Enum. Pl. Javæ, fasc. 1, p. 92; Dalz. & Gibs. p. 95; Wight, Icon. t. 239. *Rhizophora gymnorhiza*, Linn. Sp. Pl. (1753) p. 443; Grah. Cat. p. 68.—Flowers: Dec.–Feb.

Common along the sea-coast and in salt-marshes.—DISTRIB. Tropical Asia, Australia, Africa, and the Pacific.

2. **Bruguiera caryophylloides,** *Blume, Enum. Pl. Javæ*, fasc. 1 (1827) p. 93. A shrub or small tree, branched from the base; young branches with scars of fallen leaves and stipules towards the apex, slender. Leaves 2½–4 by 1–1¾ in., elliptic-lanceolate or slightly oblanceolate, subacute, pale, rather thin, shining above, dull beneath, glabrous, base cuneate; petioles ¾–1¼ in. long; stipules 1–2¼ in. long. Flowers in axillary 2–3- (usually 3-) flowered cymes; peduncles ⅜–⅝ in. long; pedicels very short. Calyx ⅜–½ in. long, not ribbed, divided about ½-way down; lobes usually 8, linear, subacute, erect or spreading at first, afterwards reflexed. Petals white, as many as the calyx-lobes and shorter than them, hairy outside and on the margins, 2-fid at the apex, the apical lobes obtuse, each furnished with 3–5 bristles at the end of each lobe and a longer one at the sinus. Stamens twice as many as the petals, 2 opposite to each petal and shorter than it; filaments of each pair unequal. Fruit ⅝ in. long, oblong-obovoid; protruding radicle slender, cylindric, reaching 6–8 in. long before falling. Fl. B. I. v. 2, p. 438; Trim. Fl. Ceyl. v. 2, p. 154; Talb. Trees, Bomb. ed. 2, p. 160.—Flowers: Aug.–Sept.

Not very common. In tidal mangrove-forests in the southern parts of the Presidency.

This species has been included on the authority of Mr. Talbot.—DISTRIB. India (muddy shores and tidal creeks of the W. Peninsula and Birma); Ceylon, Malaya.

3. **Bruguiera parviflora,** *Wight & Arn. Prodr.* (1834) p. 311 (*in adnot.*). A shrub; young branches with scars of fallen leaves and stipules, slender. Leaves 3–4 by 1–1½ in., oblong-lanceolate or elliptic-lanceolate, acute, shining above, dull beneath, glabrous, base cuneate; petioles ½–¾ in. long; stipules 1–2 in. long. Flowers in laxly 2–5-flowered erect cymes, longer than the petioles; pedicels slender. Calyx ⅜–½ in. long; tube cylindric or subfusiform, ribbed; lobes 8, about one-fourth the length of the tube, lanceolate, acute, erect. Petals as many as the calyx-lobes but shorter than them broadly oblong, 2-lobed, the lobes rounded and bearing short white hairs at the apex. Stamens twice as many as the petals, 2 opposite to each petal and embraced by it; filaments of each pair unequal. Ovary 3-celled. Fruit concealed by the enlarged calyx, ¾–1 in. long; protruding radicle cylindric, striate,

truncate, reaching 4-5 in. before falling. Fl. B. I. v. 2, p. 438; Bedd. For. Man. p. ci; Talb. Trees, Bomb. ed. 2, p. 160; Woodr. in Journ. Bomb. Nat. v. 11 (1898) p. 636. *Kanilia parviflora*, Blume, Mus. Bot. Lugd. Bat. v. 1 (1849) p. 140, t. 30; Dalz. & Gibs. p. 95. *Rhizophora parviflora*, Roxb. Fl. Ind. v. 2, p. 461; Grah. Cat. p. 68.—Flowers: Dec.

Salt-marshes, but not common. KONKAN: near Moul (Salsette), *Graham*. KANARA: Karwar, *Woodrow*.

5. CARALLIA, Roxb.

Trees or shrubs. Leaves opposite, petiolate, ovate or elliptic, glabrous, shining; stipules interpetiolar, caducous. Flowers small, sessile, often crowded in axillary trichotomously-branched cymes; peduncles short, stout. Calyx-tube cylindric or campanulate, minutely bracteolate at the base; limb 5-8-lobed, the lobes erect, valvate. Petals 5-8, inserted on the margin of a crenulate disk lining the calyx-tube, clawed, 2-fid or entire, subserrate or lacerate at the apex. Disk epigynous, 10-16-lobed. Stamens 10-16, inserted with the petals; filaments filiform; anthers small, oblong. Ovary ½-inferior; style subulate or filiform; stigma 3-5-lobed. Fruit small, globose, coriaceous, 1-celled. Seed 1, globose-reniform; testa fibrous; albumen fleshy; embryo curved.—DISTRIB. Tropical Asia and Australia, Madagascar; species about 12.

1. **Carallia integerrima,** *DC. Prodr.* v. 3 (1828) p. 33. A moderate-sized glabrous tree. Leaves 2-4 by 1-2½ in., very variable in shape, broadly elliptic, obovate-oblong or oblong-lanceolate, rounded or very shortly acuminate at the apex, entire, smooth and shining above, paler beneath, base acute or cuneate, rarely rounded; main nerves numerous, spreading and interarching freely; petioles stout, ⅛-$\frac{3}{16}$ in. long; stipules ⅜-⅝ in. long, caducous. Flowers sessile, in small heads, on stout branches of axillary trichotomous cymes shorter than the leaves; buds exuding a sticky resinous substance. Calyx $\frac{3}{16}$ in. long, campanulate, glabrous, divided about ½-way down; lobes 6-8 (commonly 7), triangular, acute. Petals white, as many as the calyx-lobes and shorter than them, broadly obovate or suborbicular, clawed, irregularly laciniate, with lanceolate segments. Stamens twice as many as the petals; one of each pair of filaments opposite to a petal and embraced by it, slightly longer than the other filament, which is opposite to a sepal. Stigma 4-5-lobed. Fruit filiform, about ¼ in. in diam. smooth, red. Seed 1; testa thick, bright-orange. Fl. B. I. v. 2, p. 439; Dalz. & Gibs. p. 96; Bedd. Fl. Sylvat. t. 193; Trim. Fl. Ceyl. v. 2, p. 155; Talb. Trees, Bomb. ed. 2, p. 160; Woodr. in Journ. Bomb. Nat. v. 11 (1898) p. 636; Watt, Dict. Econ. Prod. v. 2, p. 140. *Carallia ceylonica*, Wight, Illustr. t. 90. *Carallia integrifolia*, Grah. Cat. p. 68.—Flowers: Dec.-Mar. VERN. *Panschi*.

KONKAN: *Stocks*!, *Law*!; hills near Marmagoa, *Bhiva*!; Matheran, *Cooke*!, *Kanitkar*!; vale of the Savitri, between Poladpur and the Ghâts, *Graham*. DECCAN: hills about Pár, *Graham*; Khandala, *Graham*. S. M. COUNTRY, Ramghát, *Ritchie*, 279! KANARA: N. Kanara, *Talbot*, *Stocks*!, *Law*!—DISTRIB. Throughout India; Ceylon, Malaya, China, Australia.

The tree is very common and is quite distinct from *Carallia lucida*, Roxb. Hort. Beng. p. 92, & Cor. Pl. t. 211. Kurz (For. Fl. Brit. Burm. v. 1, p. 451) under the name *C. lucida* gives a correct description of *this* plant except for the statement that the petals do not embrace the stamens, an error into which Mr. Henslow (Fl. B. I. l. c.) has also fallen. Each petal embraces the longer stamen which is opposite to it, as figured in Wight, Ill. t. 90. The petals of *C. integerrima* are white, those of *C. lucida* in Roxburgh's figure yellow. The petals of *C. integerrima* are laciniate, as shown by both Wight and Beddome, whereas those of *C. lucida* are figured by Roxburgh as regularly crenate and the leaves of the latter plant are regularly and finely serrulate.

Order LV. COMBRETACEÆ.

Trees or shrubs, erect or climbing. Leaves alternate or opposite, coriaceous or membranous, simple, entire; petiole often glandular at the top; stipules 0. Flowers usually hermaphrodite, rarely unisexual or polygamous. Calyx bracteolate at the base; tube adnate to the ovary and prolonged above it; limb 4–5 (rarely 6–8) -fid or -partite, its lobes valvate in bud, deciduous or persistent. Corolla 0, or petals inserted on the calyx, alternate with its lobes, valvate in bud. Stamens inserted with the petals, sometimes alternate with them, sometimes double their number, of which the alternate 5 are inserted higher than and opposite to the petals; filaments free, filiform or subulate. Ovary inferior, 1-celled, usually crowned with a disk; ovules 1–7 (usually 2–4), pendulous from the apex of the cell; style terminal; stigma usually simple. Fruit usually indehiscent, coriaceous or drupaceous, ovoid, angular, frequently winged, crowned in *Calycopteris* by the greatly enlarged calyx. Seed 1, exalbuminous; cotyledons large, plaited or convolute.—Distrib. Tropics of the whole world; outside the Tropics in S. Africa; genera 15; species 320.

Anthers opening by slits.
  Petals 0.
    Flowers in spikes or racemes.
      Calyx-limb deciduous .... 1. Terminalia.
      Calyx-limb persistent, much enlarged in fruit ... 2. Calycopteris.
    Flowers in globose heads .... 3. Anogeissus.
  Petals 4 or 5.
    Leaves alternate; calyx-limb persistent .... 4. Lumnitzera.
    Leaves opposite; calyx-limb deciduous .... 5. Combretum.
Anthers opening by curved valves which open upwards .... 6. Gyrocarpus.

1. TERMINALIA, Linn.

Trees. Leaves alternate or subopposite, frequently crowded at the ends of the branches, often with glands on the petiole or at the base of the midrib beneath. Flowers green or white, rarely colored, small, spicate (the spikes sometimes panicled), hermaphrodite or often the upper flowers on the spikes male and the lower hermaphrodite. Calyx-tube ovoid or cylindric, constricted above the ovary; limb of 5 short valvate triangular lobes, soon deciduous. Petals 0. Stamens 10, inserted on the calyx-lobes (the epigynous disk within them densely hairy), biseriate, the 5 lower opposite the calyx-teeth, the 5 upper longer and alternate with the calyx-teeth; filaments subulate or filiform, exserted. Ovary inferior, 1-celled; ovules 2–3, pendulous from the apex of the cell; style subulate, often thickened and villous at the base; stigma simple. Fruit ovoid, various in size and texture, smooth or angular or 2–5-winged, indehiscent, coriaceous. Seed solitary, exalbuminous; cotyledons convolute.—Distrib. Tropics of both worlds; species 135.

Fruit not winged.
  Leaves alternate, clustered at the ends of the branches; flowers at top of spike male .... 1. *T. bellerica.*
  Leaves opposite, not clustered; flowers all hermaphrodite ... 2. *T. chebula.*
Fruit equally 5-winged.
  Veins of the wings curving upwards .... 3. *T. Arjuna.*
  Veins of the wings straight, horizontal .... 4. *T. tomentosa.*
Fruit unequally 3-winged .... 5. *T. paniculata.*

1. **Terminalia bellerica,** *Roxb. Cor. Pl.* v. 2 (1798) p. 54, t. 198. A large handsome tree 40–60 ft. high. Leaves collected about the extremities of the branches, alternate, coriaceous, 4–8 by 3–6 in., broadly elliptic or elliptic-obovate, rounded or rarely subacute or shortly acuminate at the apex, both surfaces puberulous when young, glabrous and reticulate when old, the margins entire, pellucid, base narrowed; main nerves 6–8 pairs, spreading, prominent, the midrib prominent on both sides; petioles $1\frac{3}{4}$–4 in. long, without glands at the apex. Flowers pale greenish-yellow, with an offensive odor, in axillary slender spikes longer than the petioles but shorter than the leaves, those in the upper part of the spike male, very shortly pedicelled, those in the lower part hermaphrodite, sessile. Calyx pubescent outside, densely villous within, the teeth broadly triangular, acute. Drupe $\frac{1}{2}$–1 in. in diam., suddenly narrowed into a very short stalk, clothed with minute pale tomentum, obscurely angled when dried.

Roxburgh (*l. c.*) describes and figures the plant with 2 glands at the apex of the petiole, but none of the specimens that I have seen possess these, while Wight & Arnott and Brandis have failed to find them in specimens of their collection. Fl. B. I. v. 2, p. 445; Grah. Cat. p. 69; Dalz. & Gibs. p. 91; Wight, Illustr. t. 91; Bedd. Flor. Sylvat. t. 19; Wight & Arn. Prodr. p. 313 (*exclud. syn.*); Trim. Fl. Ceyl. v. 2, p. 159; Talb. Trees, Bomb. ed. 2, p. 162; Woodr. in Journ. Bomb. Nat. v. 11 (1898) p. 636; Watt, Dict. Econ. Prod. v. 6, part 4, p. 18.—Flowers: Feb.–May. VERN. *Behada*; *Helá*.

In deciduous mixed forests throughout the Presidency. KONKAN: *Stocks*!, *Law*!; along the foot of the Ghâts, *Graham*; Malabar Hill (Bombay), *Graham*; Devale, *Woodrow*. DECCAN: *Cooke*! S. M. COUNTRY: Belgaum, *Ritchie*, 1064!—DISTRIB. Throughout India, except Sind and the desert region of the West; Ceylon, Malaya.

The fruit is one of those exported from India under the name of *Myrobalan* and is used for dyeing. The Myrobalans from the next species, *T. chebula*, are by far the most important of any exported from India. See Watt, Dict. Econ. Prod. l. c.

2. **Terminalia chebula,** *Retz. Obs.* fasc. 5 (1789) p. 31. A moderate-sized, much-branched tree. Leaves $2\frac{1}{2}$–6 by $1\frac{1}{2}$–3 in., not clustered, alternate or subopposite, elliptic-oblong, acute, penninerved, clothed when young with silky hairs, glabrous or nearly so when mature, rounded or cordate at the base; petioles $\frac{1}{2}$–1 in. long, pubescent, usually with 2 glands near their summit. Flowers all hermaphrodite, in terminal (often panicled) spikes; bracteoles exceeding the flowers, linear, acute, hairy, conspicuous among the buds but soon deciduous. Calyx campanulate, $\frac{1}{8}$ in. long, flat at the base, expanding a little towards the mouth, glabrous outside, hairy within; teeth 5, short, sometimes obscure. Drupe pendulous, $\frac{3}{4}$–$1\frac{1}{2}$ in. long, ellipsoid or obovoid from a broad base, glabrous, more or less 5-ribbed when dry, yellowish-green; stone oblong, bony, very thick, obscurely angled. Fl. B. I. v. 2, p. 446; Grah. Cat. p. 69; Dalz. & Gibs. p. 91; Bedd.

Flor. Sylvat. t. 27; Trim. Fl. Ceyl. v. 2, p. 159; Talb. Trees, Bomb. ed. 2, p. 162; Woodr. in Journ. Bomb. Nat. v. 11 (1898) p. 636; Watt, Dict. Econ. Prod. v. 6, part 4, p. 24.—Flowers: Apr.-May. VERN. *Hirdá*; *Hirad.*

Abundant along the line of the Ghâts. KONKAN: *Stocks*!, *Gibson*!, *Law*! DECCAN: table-land of Mahableshwar, *Graham*, *Cooke*!; Khandala, *Graham*. KANARA: abundant on the laterite of N. Kanara, *Talbot*.—DISTRIB. Throughout the greater part of India; Ceylon.

The dried fruit forms the Chebulic Myrobalan of commerce, one of the most valuable of Indian tanning materials and a very important source of revenue to the Bombay Forest Department. The gross revenue obtained in the southern circle of the Bombay Forest Department in 1893 from Chebulic Myrobalans considerably exceeded a lakh of rupees. See Watt, Dict. Econ. Prod. l. c.

3. **Terminalia Arjuna,** *Wight & Arn. Prodr.* (1834) p. 314, *in textu*. A large tree reaching 80 ft. high, with a very thick trunk and horizontally spreading branches; bark thick, smooth, greenish-white, flaking off in large flat pieces. Leaves usually subopposite, 4–6 by $1\frac{3}{4}$–$2\frac{3}{4}$ in., oblong or elliptic-oblong, obtuse or subacute, pale dull-green above, pale brown beneath, shallowly crenate-serrate in the upper part or sometimes throughout, base rounded or cordate, often unequal-sided; main nerves arcuate, 10–15 pairs, veins reticulate, pellucid; petioles $\frac{1}{4}$–$\frac{3}{8}$ in. long, with 1 or usually 2 prominent glands at the top immediately below the leaves. Flowers sessile, in short axillary spikes or in terminal panicles; bracteoles linear-lanceolate, shorter than the flowers, caducous. Calyx glabrous, $\frac{1}{6}$ in. long; mouth broadly campanulate; teeth triangular, $\frac{1}{16}$ in. long. Ovary quite glabrous. Disk clothed with yellowish or reddish hairs. Stamens much exserted. Drupe 1–2 in. long, ovoid- or obovoid-oblong, fibrous-woody, glabrous, dark-brown, with 5 hard projecting wings striated with numerous curved veins. Fl. B. I. v. 2, p. 447; Dalz. & Gibs. p. 91; Bedd. Flor. Sylvat. t. 28; Talb. Trees, Bomb. ed. 2, p. 162; Woodr. in Journ. Bomb. Nat. v. 11 (1898) p. 636; Watt, Dict. Econ. Prod. v. 6, part 4, p. 16. *Terminalia glabra*, Wight & Arn. Prodr. p. 314; Trim. Fl. Ceyl. v. 2, p. 160. *Pentaptera Arjuna*, Roxb. Hort. Beng. (1814) p. 34; Fl. Ind. v. 2, p. 438; Grah. Cat. p. 69.—Flowers: Apr.-May. VERN. *Kahu*; *Arjun*; *Arjuna-sádadá*.

KONKAN: *Stocks*!; Matheran, *Cooke*! DECCAN: rare, *Dalzell & Gibson*; Mul Zulla, Poona, *Dalzell & Gibson*; Koina valley, *Cooke*! GUJARAT: common in jungles south-east of Surat, *Law* ex *Graham*, *Dalzell & Gibson*. S. M. COUNTRY: Belgaum forests, *Dalzell & Gibson*.—DISTRIB. India (Sub-Himalayan tracts of the N.W. Provinces, W. Peninsula); Ceylon.

VAR. *angustifolia*, C. B. Clarke, in Hook. f. Fl. B. I. v. 2, p. 447. Branches drooping; leaves much narrower, oblong, attenuated into the petiole, sometimes very shortly acuminate at the apex. *Terminalia Berryi*, Wight & Arn. Prodr. p. 314; Dalz. & Gibs. p. 92. *Pentaptera angustifolia*, Roxb. Hort. Beng. (1814) p. 34; Fl. Ind. v. 2, p. 437 (not *Terminalia angustifolia* of Roxb. cited on the same page); Grah. Cat. p. 69.

KONKAN: *Stocks*! S. M. COUNTRY: banks of Kála naddi and Gatprabha rivers, *Law* ex *Graham*, *Dalzell & Gibson*.

4. **Terminalia tomentosa,** *Wight & Arn. Prodr.* (1834) p. 314 (*not* of Mart.). An erect-growing tree, reaching sometimes 80 ft. in

height; trunk straight; bark rough, deeply cracked; young parts more or less clothed with yellowish-brown pubescence. Leaves subopposite or the uppermost alternate, hard, coriaceous, 3–8 by 2–3 in., ovate-oblong or elliptic-oblong, rarely obovate, softly tomentose when young, becoming more or less glabrous when mature, with 1–2 glands (which are often turbinate or long-stalked) usually on the midrib but sometimes absent, base often cordate; main nerves arcuate, parallel, 10–20 pairs, prominent; petioles $\frac{3}{8}$ in. long, pubescent when young, glabrous or nearly so when old. Flowers hermaphrodite, dull-yellow, in axillary fulvous-pubescent spikes or terminal panicles. Calyx hairy or glabrous outside, $\frac{1}{8}$ in. long; mouth broadly campanulate; teeth $\frac{1}{16}$ in. long, triangular, slightly hairy within; bracteoles $\frac{1}{8}$ in. long, linear-lanceolate, hairy, caducous. Disk clothed with long fulvous hairs. Drupe $1\frac{1}{2}$–2 in. long, with 5 broad, coriaceous, brown, glabrous wings striated with numerous straight lines running horizontally from the axis to the edges. Fl. B. I. v. 2, p. 447; Wight, Icon. t. 195; Bedd. Flor. Sylvat. t. 17; Talb. Trees, Bomb. ed. 2, p. 162; Woodr. in Journ. Bomb. Nat. v. 11 (1898) p. 636; Watt, Dict. Econ. Prod. v. 6, part 4, p. 37. *Terminalia glabra*, var. *tomentosa*, Dalz. & Gibs. p. 91. *T. crenulata*, W. & A. Prodr. p. 314. *T. coriacea*, W. & A. Prodr. p. 315. *Pentaptera tomentosa*, Roxb. Hort. Beng. p. 34; Grah. Cat. p. 69.—Flowers: Apr.–June. VERN. *Ain*.

Common throughout the Presidency in mixed deciduous forests. KONKAN: *Stocks*!, *Law*!; common in the jungles at the foot of the Ghâts, *Dalzell & Gibson*. DECCAN: hills near Chattersinghi (Poona district), *Cooke*!; Gokak, *Ritchie*, 283!; Párghát, *Stocks*!—DISTRIB. Throughout the moister regions of India; Ceylon.

The well-known *Ain* tree, the timber of which is used for various purposes. Sleepers of the wood were at one time largely used on the Bombay Railways. The bark is useful as a tan, but the fruit is far inferior as a tanning material to Belleric and Chebulic Myrobalans. See Watt, Dict. Econ. Prod. l. c.

5. **Terminalia paniculata,** *Roth, Nov. Pl. Sp.* (1821) p. 383. A large tree; young parts rusty-tomentose. Leaves coriaceous, the upper alternate, the lower subopposite, 4–9 by $1\frac{3}{4}$–$3\frac{1}{2}$ in., oblong, acute or acuminate, nearly glabrous or with a few scattered hairs above (when adult), pale-brown, more or less pubescent and finely reticulately veined beneath, usually with 2 glands near the base of the midrib below, base cordate or rounded, often inequilateral; main nerves 10–15 pairs, arcuate, parallel; petioles $\frac{1}{2}$–$\frac{5}{8}$ in. long, pubescent. Flowers sessile, in slender spikes forming compound panicles; bracts at the forks $\frac{1}{8}$–$\frac{1}{5}$ in. long, ovate, acute, recurved; bracteoles $\frac{1}{12}$ in. long, acuminate from a triangular base, recurved. Calyx (free portion) $\frac{1}{12}$ in. long, reddish-brown, globose when in bud, afterwards cup-shaped; teeth broadly triangular, as long as the free portion of the calyx-tube, glabrous or nearly so outside, densely villous within. Disk densely clothed with long yellowish-white hairs. Ovary densely and softly pubescent. Fruit rusty-tomentose, $\frac{1}{4}$–$\frac{1}{2}$ in. long, sessile, closely set in dense spreading panicles, 3-winged, 2 of the wings much smaller than the other. Fl. B. I. v. 2, p. 448; Dalz. & Gibs. p. 92; Bedd. Flor. Sylvat. t. 20; Talb. Trees, Bomb. ed. 2, p. 163; Woodr. in Journ. Bomb. Nat. v. 11 (1898) p. 636; Watt, Dict. Econ. Prod. v. 6, part 4, p. 37. *Pentaptera paniculata*, Roxb. Hort. Beng. p. 34; Grah. Cat. p. 70.—Flowers: Aug.–Sept. VERN. *Kinjal*; *Honal*.

A common tree in the Bombay Presidency. KONKAN: common along the foot of the Ghâts in the S. Konkan, *Dalzell & Gibson*; common in the vales of Konkan rivers near their source, *Graham*; Poladpur, *Cooke*! GUJARAT: abundant in the jungles south-east of Surat, *Law* ex *Graham*. S. M. COUNTRY: hills north-east of Belgaum, *Ritchie*, 285! KANARA: one of the most common trees in N. Kanara, *Talbot*; near Sirsi, *Woodrow*.—DISTRIB. India from Bombay southwards to Cape Comorin.

Terminalia Catappa, Linn. Mantiss. (1771) p. 519. A small tree often with buttressed trunk, with branches in horizontal whorls, obovate leaves and an ellipsoid fruit keeled all round, a native of the Moluccas, is frequently cultivated. It is known as the *Bengal Almond*, but the kernel, though edible, is very insipid as compared with the almond. Fl. B. I. v. 2, p. 444; Grah. Cat. p. 69; Dalz. & Gibs. Suppl. p. 33; Talb. Trees, Bomb. ed. 2, p. 163; Woodr. in Journ. Bomb. Nat. v. 11 (1898) p. 636, & Gard. in India, ed. 5, p. 313; Watt, Dict. Econ. Prod. v. 6, part 4, p. 22.—VERN. *Deshi-badâm*; *Bengali-badâm*.

2. CALYCOPTERIS, Lamk.

A diffuse scandent shrub. Leaves opposite, petiolate, elliptic or ovate, acuminate, entire. Flowers in dense axillary racemes crowded towards the ends of the branches so as to form large panicles. Calyx-tube elongate-turbinate, 5-striate, produced above the ovary; limb broadly campanulate, 5-fid, accrescent, the lobes persistent, spreading. Petals 0. Stamens 10, biseriate, short; filaments subulate; anthers didymous. Ovary 1-celled, inferior; ovules 3, pendulous from the apex of the cell; style subulate; stigma simple. Fruit ovoid, 5-ribbed, villous, 1-seeded, surmounted by the enlarged calyx.—DISTRIB. India; species 1.

1. **Calycopteris floribunda,** *Lamk. Tab. Encyc.* v. 2 (1793) p. 485, t. 357. A scandent shrub; young branches slender, rusty-puberulous. Leaves opposite, 3–5 by $1\frac{1}{4}$–$2\frac{1}{4}$ in., ovate-lanceolate or elliptic-oblong, acute or acuminate, both surfaces more or less tomentose, the lower rusty and pitted, base usually rounded; main nerves 5–8 pairs, rather prominent beneath; petioles $\frac{1}{4}$–$\frac{3}{8}$ in. long. Flowers sessile, yellowish-green, in fulvous-pubescent terminal panicles; bracteoles short, lanceolate, pubescent. Calyx densely hairy within at the mouth of the tube; tube produced above the ovary; lobes accrescent, $\frac{3}{4}$–$\frac{7}{8}$ in. long in fruit, scarious, broadly linear-lanceolate, acute, strongly 3-nerved and reticulately veined, tomentose. Stamens unequal, much shorter than the calyx-lobes. Ovary densely villous outside; ovules 3, pendulous from the apex of the cell with long funicles. Fruit $\frac{1}{3}$ in. long, oblong or ellipsoid, 5-ribbed, pubescent or tomentose, crowned by the persistent calyx-lobes. Fl. B. I. v. 2, p. 449; Talb. Trees, Bomb. ed. 2, p. 163; Woodr. in Journ. Bomb. Nat. v. 11 (1898) p. 636; Watt, Dict. Econ. Prod. v. 2, p. 50. *Getonia floribunda*, Roxb. Cor. Pl. v. 1 (1795) p. 61, t. 87; Grah. Cat. p. 70; Dalz. & Gibs. p. 91.—Flowers: Mar.–May. VERN. *Ukshi*; *Bâguli*.

Common in the Konkan and on the Ghâts. KONKAN: Elephanta, *Graham*; Vingorla, *Ritchie*, 362!; Matheran, abundant, *Cooke*! DECCAN: hills, *Woodrow*!; Lanoli, *Woodrow*!—DISTRIB. India (Central and Southern Provinces, Assam); Malaya.

3. ANOGEISSUS, Wall.

Shrubs or small trees. Leaves alternate, petiolate, entire. Flowers small, yellow, in dense globose axillary heads; peduncles slender. Calyx-tube compressed, 2-winged, attenuated and produced above the ovary; limb campanulate or urceolate, 5-fid, deciduous. Petals 0. Stamens 10, biseriate, exserted; anthers small, cordate. Ovary inferior, 1-celled; ovules 2, pendulous from the top of the cell; style filiform, thickened at the base, villous; stigma simple. Fruit packed in dense heads, small, thickly coriaceous, broadly trapezoidal, 2-winged, terminated by the produced calyx-tube. Seed 1, ovoid; cotyledons convolute.—Distrib. India and Tropical Africa; species 5.

Beak of fruit as long as or longer than its nucleus.
  Fruit (including the wings) longer than broad; wings with entire margins; peduncles branched .... 1. *A. latifolia.*
  Fruit (including the wings) broader than long; wings with jagged margins; peduncles not branched .... 2. *A. sericea.*
Beak of fruit shorter than its nucleus .... 3. *A. pendula.*

1. **Anogeissus latifolia,** *Wall. Cat.* (1828) 4015. An erect tree sometimes reaching 60–70 ft.; bark smooth, light-colored; young parts glabrous or silky-pubescent. Leaves $2\frac{1}{2}$–4 by $1\frac{1}{4}$–2 in., alternate or subopposite, elliptic or oblong-elliptic, obtuse or very often shortly cuspidate, glabrous when fully grown, pale dull glaucous-green, base usually rounded, midrib prominent, pink; main nerves 6–10 pairs, arching, prominent on the lower side, the veins between them reticulate; petioles $\frac{1}{4}$–$\frac{1}{2}$ in. long. Flowers sessile, in small dense heads; peduncles 1 or more from the same axil, branched, not much longer than the petioles. Calyx-tube pubescent; teeth short, broadly triangular. Fruit small, several crowded in a globular head, the nucleus nearly plano-convex, $\frac{1}{8}$–$\frac{1}{6}$ in. long (excluding the beak), $\frac{1}{8}$–$\frac{1}{6}$ in. broad (including the wings), yellowish-brown, glabrous or more or less pubescent, winged down the two longest sides, beaked with the persistent calyx which is as long as or sometimes longer than the nucleus; wings with entire margins. Seed solitary. Fl. B. I. v. 2, p. 450. Bedd. Flor. Sylvat. t. 15; Trim. Fl. Ceyl. v. 2, p. 162; Talb. Trees, Bomb. ed. 2, p. 164; Woodr. in Journ. Bomb. Nat. v. 11 (1898) p. 636; Watt, Dict. Econ. Prod. v. 1, p. 256. *Conocarpus latifolia*, Roxb. Hort. Beng. p. 34; Grah. Cat. p. 70; Wight, Icon. t. 994; Dalz. & Gibs. p. 91.—Flowers: May–July. Vern. *Dhávda*; *Dhaura*; *Dábria.*

Throughout the Presidency usually in dry forests. Konkan: *Law*!; vales of Konkan rivers near their source, *Graham*; Kanheri jungles, *Graham*; Matheran Ghát, *H. M. Birdwood*; Mira hills, *Dalzell & Gibson*. Deccan: Kolapur, *Cooke*!; Ghát near Wai, *Woodrow*!; Ghát near Wathár, *Cooke*! S. M. Country: Belgaum hills, *Ritchie*, 922!—Distrib. Throughout the greater part of India; Ceylon.

The tree yields a useful gum and the wood is very strong and tough. See Watt, Dict. Econ. Prod. l. c.

2. **Anogeissus sericea,** *Brandis, in Indian Forester*, v. 25 (1900) p. 287. A middle-sized tree; branchlets clothed with silky pubescence. Leaves 1–$1\frac{1}{2}$ by $\frac{3}{4}$–1 in., elliptic, obtuse, apiculate or very shortly cuspidate, glabrous or nearly so above (when mature), clothed on the lower side and the nerves beneath with silky pubescence; main nerves 4–6 pairs; petioles $\frac{1}{8}$ in. long, pubescent. Flowers in globose heads,

$\frac{1}{2}$–$\frac{3}{4}$ in. in diam., on long axillary simple peduncles which often bear leafy bracts. Calyx densely pubescent. Fruit tomentose, broader than long, $\frac{1}{6}$ in. long by $\frac{1}{4}$ in. broad (including the wings), crowned by the pubescent calyx-tube, which is as long as the nucleus, and sometimes also by the subpersistent limb; wings pubescent in the upper part, jagged on the margins, each wing produced upwards beyond the top of the nucleus into a triangular lobe.

GUJARAT: Panch Maháls, *Dalzell!*

I have seen only one specimen from Bombay marked as above in Herb. Kew.—DISTRIB. India (Central Provinces, Gujarat).

3. **Anogeissus pendula,** *Edgew. in Journ. As. Soc. Beng.* v. 21 (1853) p. 171. A small tree; branches pendulous; young parts pubescent. Leaves $\frac{3}{4}$–$1\frac{1}{4}$ by $\frac{3}{8}$–$\frac{5}{8}$ in., alternate and subopposite, elliptic or obovate, obtuse or acute, usually mucronate, more or less clothed on both sides with appressed pubescence, or sometimes glabrous, attenuated at the base; main nerves 5–7 pairs, arcuate, with reticulate venation between; petioles $\frac{1}{12}$–$\frac{1}{8}$ in. long. Flowers in small globose heads $\frac{1}{4}$ in. across when in flower; peduncles usually solitary, not branched, pubescent. Fruit subquadrate, ultimately glabrous, the beak less than half the length of the nucleus. Fl. B. I. v. 2, p. 451. *Anogeissus myrtifolia*, Wall. Cat. 4017; Royle, Ill. p. 209.—Flowers: May–June. VERN. *Dhao*; *Dhankra*.

GUJARAT: Deesa, *Stocks!*

There is but one poor specimen in Herb. Kew. labelled as above. It is the only specimen I have seen from the Bombay Presidency.—DISTRIB. India (N.W. Provinces, Bandelkhand, Rajputana).

4. LUMNITZERA, Willd.

Large glabrous shrubs or small trees growing along tropical shores and in salt-marshes along with mangroves. Leaves clustered towards the ends of the branches, alternate, thickly coriaceous, subsessile, obovate-cuneate, entire or crenate. Flowers in short axillary or terminal spikes or racemes, scarlet or white. Calyx-tube elongate, oblong, attenuated at both ends, produced above the ovary, with 2 adnate bracteoles near the base; limb campanulate, 5-lobed, persistent. Petals 5, oblong, spreading. Stamens 5–10. Ovary 1-celled; ovules 2–5, pendulous from the apex of the cell; style filiform, glabrous; stigma simple. Fruit woody, ellipsoid-oblong or ovoid, crowned with the persistent calyx. Seed solitary; cotyledons convolute.—DISTRIB. Sea-shores of the Tropics of the Old World and Polynesia; species 2.

1. **Lumnitzera racemosa,** *Willd. in Ges. Naturf. Fr. Neue Schr.* v. 4 (1803) p. 187. A tall glabrous shrub or small tree. Leaves sessile, fleshy, crowded at the ends of the branches, 1–$2\frac{1}{2}$ by $\frac{1}{2}$–$\frac{7}{8}$ in., oblanceolate or obovate, glabrous, shallowly crenate or entire, rounded or emarginate at the apex, tapering much towards the base; main nerves 3–5 pairs, indistinct. Flowers sessile, in short lax axillary spikes. Calyx $\frac{3}{8}$–$\frac{1}{2}$ in. long; tube fusiform, glabrous; teeth obtuse, $\frac{1}{20}$ in. long, ciliolate; bracteoles 2, adnate to the calyx-tube, about $\frac{1}{12}$ in. long, ovate, acute, one of them higher up the tube than the other. Petals white, oblong, subacute. Stamens 10, almost equalling the petals; the alternate

filaments shorter. Fruit ½ in. long, ovoid, glabrous, longitudinally striate when dry, crowned by the persistent calyx-tube. Fl. B. I. v. 2, p. 452; Grah. Cat. p. 70; Dalz. & Gibs. p. 90; Bedd. For. Man. in Flor. Sylvat. p. ciii, t. 21, fig. 2; Trim. Fl. Ceyl. v. 2, p. 162; Talb. Trees, Bomb. ed. 2, p. 164; Woodr. in Journ. Bomb. Nat. v. 11 (1898) p. 636; Watt, Dict. Econ. Prod. v. 5, p. 97.—Flowers: Jan.–Apr.

KONKAN: S. Konkan along salt-water creeks and backwaters, *Talbot, Nimmo ex Graham*; Ratnagiri, *Woodrow*.

The tree grows with the mangrove along the muddy creeks and is, as are other shrubs which grow in similar localities, known also as a mangrove.

5. COMBRETUM, Linn.

Shrubs often scandent. Leaves usually opposite and simple, entire, petiolate. Flowers hermaphrodite or polygamo-diœcious, in spikes, racemes or panicles; bracteoles minute. Calyx-tube cylindric or 4–6-gonous, constricted above the ovary; limb campanulate, 4–5-fid, deciduous. Petals 4–5 (very rarely 0), inserted between the calyx-lobes. Stamens 8 or 10, biseriate; filaments filiform, elongate; anthers small, didymous. Ovary inferior, 1-celled; ovules 2–6, pendulous from the apex of the cell; style subulate; stigma simple. Fruit dry, usually indehiscent, 4–5-gonous or 4–5-winged, the wings often membranous. Seed 1; cotyledons plaited or flat, in a few species convolute.—DISTRIB. Tropics of America, Asia and Africa, also in S. Africa; species 160.

Calyx-limb cup-shaped .... 1. *C. ovalifolium.*
Calyx-limb funnel-shaped .... 2. *C. extensum.*

1. **Combretum ovalifolium,** *Roxb. Hort. Beng.* (1814) p. 28. A large scandent shrub; bark pale-brown, smooth; branches terete; young parts glabrous. Leaves 2–4 by 1¼–2½ in., opposite, elliptic or elliptic-lanceolate, obtusely acuminate, glabrous or nearly so, usually narrowed at the base into the petiole; main nerves 4–6 pairs; petioles $\frac{3}{8}$–$\frac{5}{8}$ in. long, channelled. Flowers sessile, $\frac{3}{16}$–¼ in. long, in short rather dense, often panicled axillary spikes, occasionally forming a large terminal panicle; main rhachis of the panicle densely pubescent, its branches slender, pubescent, often opposite or subopposite; buds globose, apiculate; bracteole at the base of the calyx minute. Calyx-tube glabrous outside, constricted into a short neck above the ovary, then suddenly expanded into a cup-shaped limb, densely hairy at the base within; lobes 4, ovate, acute, reflexed, $\frac{1}{16}$ in. long. Petals 4, oblong, obtuse, $\frac{1}{16}$ in. long by $\frac{1}{32}$ in. broad, white. Disk hairy. Stamens 8, in 2 series, those opposite to the petals inserted higher up than the others. Fruit pale-golden-brown, ¾–1 in. long and nearly as broad, with 4 papery finely transversely striate wings. Seed 4-sided. Fl. B. I. v. 2, p. 458; Grah. Cat. p. 70; Dalz. & Gibs. p. 90; Trim. Fl. Ceyl. v. 2, p. 163; Talb. Trees, Bomb. ed. 2, p. 165; Woodr. in Journ. Bomb. Nat. v. 11 (1898) p. 636; Watt, Dict. Econ. Prod. v. 2, p. 514. *Combretum Heyneanum*, Wall. Cat. 4001; Wight, in Hook. Miscell. v. 3 (1833) p. 86, Suppl. Tab. 22.—Flowers: Jan.–Mar. VERN. *Zellusi*; *Madbel*.

KONKAN: Jungles in the Konkan and Gháts, common, *Dalzell & Gibson*; Elephanta,

Graham; Konkan, *Stocks*! DECCAN: Karli, *Woodrow*. GUJARAT: *Graham*; Rajkot, *C. Macnaghten*! S. M. COUNTRY: Belgaum, *Ritchie*, 287!—DISTRIB. India (Gujarat to Cape Comorin); Ceylon.

2. **Combretum extensum,** *Roxb. Hort. Beng.* (1814) p. 28. A large scandent shrub, glabrous or nearly so. Leaves opposite, 2–6 by 1½–3 in. (sometimes, though rarely, reaching 8 by 4½ in.), usually broadly elliptic, shortly acuminate or cuspidate, glabrous on both sides, base usually rounded; main nerves 4–7 pairs; petioles ⅜–½ in. long. Flowers sessile, $\frac{1}{18}$ in. long, usually in solitary dense axillary spikes, rarely panicled or terminal; buds ovoid or subglobose, very acute at the apices. Calyx puberulous outside, contracted above the ovary and then at once expanding into a funnel-shaped limb; lobes 4, triangular, very acute or acuminate, reflexed, $\frac{1}{10}$ in. long. Petals yellowish-white, $\frac{1}{16}$ in. long and broad, oblong, truncate or very slightly emarginate at the apex. Disk hairy. Ovary 4-gonous. Fruit 1¼–1½ in. and (including the wings) almost as broad as long; wings scarious, horizontally striate, glabrous. Fl. B. I. v. 2, p. 458; Trim. Fl. Ceyl. p. 164; Talb. Trees, Bomb. ed. 2, p. 165; Woodr. in Journ. Bomb. Nat. v. 11 (1898) p. 636. *Combretum Wightianum*, Wall. Cat. 4007; Wight, Icon. t. 227; Grah. Cat. p. 70; Dalz. & Gibs. p. 90.—Flowers: Jan. VERN. *Piluki*.

KONKAN: hilly parts, *Dalzell & Gibson*; Vingorla, *Dalzell & Gibson*, *Ritchie*, 353! DECCAN: abundant at Khandala and Lanoli, *Graham*; Khandala, *Cooke*!, *Woodrow*! S. M. COUNTRY: Ramghât, *Ritchie*. KANARA: moist forests of N. Kanara, *Talbot*.—DISTRIB. India (W. Peninsula); Ceylon, Malaya.

Combretum coccineum, Lamk. Encyc. Méthod. v. 1 (1784) p. 734. A very beautiful plant, a native of Madagascar and the Mauritius. The foliage is dark-green, and the flowers, which are produced in dense elegant racemes, are of a brilliant scarlet color. It does not always flower freely in the Deccan. It is usually propagated by layers, but cuttings may be struck from young shoots in fine sand under a bell glass. Woodr. Gard. in Ind. ed. 5, p. 313. *Poivrea coccinea*, DC. Prodr. v. 3, p. 18; Dalz. & Gibs. Suppl. p. 34; Firminger, Man. Gard. ed. 3, p. 564.

6. GYROCARPUS, Jacquin.

A tall tree with thick branches. Leaves alternate, large, entire or lobed, membranous, crowded at the ends of the branches. Flowers small, unisexual and monœcious, or polygamous, in dense ebracteate cymes. MALE FLOWERS very numerous. Calyx 4–7-partite. Petals 0. Stamens 4–7, inserted at the bottom of the calyx, alternating with as many clavate fleshy staminodes; anthers 2-celled, dehiscing by valves. Ovary 0. FEMALE FLOWERS few. Calyx-tube adnate to the ovary, ovoid; limb 2-lobed, the lobes oblong, obtuse, persistent, much enlarged in fruit. Petals 0. Stamens 0. Ovary 1-celled; ovule 1, pendulous from the apex of the cell; style 0; stigma sessile. Fruit drupe-like, crowned with the long wing-like persistent calyx-segments; stone bony. Seed broadly oblong, terete; cotyledons large, convolute.—DISTRIB. Tropics generally; species 1.

1. **Gyrocarpus americanus,** *Jacquin, Select. Stirp. Amer.* (1763) p. 282, t. 178, fig. 80. A moderate-sized tree; bark smooth, shining, greenish-white; young branches stout, marked with leaf-scars, glabrous. Leaves 4–6 in. long and nearly as broad as long, ovate, acuminate, sometimes irregularly lobed, pubescent when young, afterwards glabrous or nearly so, base broad, truncate, cordate or sometimes shortly cuneate, 3-nerved from the base, the 2 lateral nerves soon forked, veins closely reticulate; petioles 1–5 in. long, slender. Flowers small, white, clustered in large branched cymes, the males very numerous, the females few; peduncles long, pubescent, several arising from the twigs above the new leaves. Calyx densely hairy on both sides. Stamens alternating with hairy clavate staminodes; anthers large, dehiscing by valves which open upwards (as the anthers of *Lauraceæ*). Fruit (without the wings) ½–¾ in. in diam., globose-ovoid, slightly pubescent, wrinkled in the lower part, furrowed in the upper, surmounted by 2 pubescent longitudinally striate oblanceolate or spathulate wings about ½ in. broad in the widest part and often 3 in. long. *Gyrocarpus Jacquini*, Gærtn. Fruct. v. 2 (1791) p. 92, t. 97, fig. 3; Roxb. Cor. Pl. v. 1 (1795) t. 1; Grah. Cat. p. 250; C. B. Clarke, in Hook. f. Fl. B. I. v. 2, p. 461; Bedd. Flor. Sylvat. t. 196; Trim. Fl. Ceyl. v. 2, p. 165; Talb. Trees, Bomb. ed. 2, p. 165; Watt, Dict. Econ. Prod. v. 4, p. 197.—Flowers: July–Aug. VERN. *Zaitun.*

DECCAN: banks of the Krishna river near Nalatwár, *Graham*. S. M. COUNTRY: Belgaum districts in dry forests, *Talbot*.—DISTRIB. India near the sea; Ceylon, Malaya.

Quisqualis indica, Linn. Sp. Pl. ed. ii, p. 556, a large subscandent shrub with elliptic acuminate leaves and handsome showy flowers, which are at first white, then orange, and finally red, a native of Java and the Malayan Peninsula, is very extensively cultivated in gardens as an ornamental plant. It rarely if ever produces fruit in the Bombay Presidency, where it is known as the *Rangoon Creeper*. Fl. B. I. v. 2, p. 459; Grah. Cat. p. 70; Dalz. & Gibs. Suppl. p. 33; Woodr. in Journ. Bomb. Nat. v. 11 (1898) p. 637, & Gardening in Ind. ed. 5, p. 312; Watt, Dict. Econ. Prod. v. 6, part 1, p. 388.—Flowers: Mar.–Aug. VERN. *Rangunachavel*; *Bármási*; *Ldlachameli.*

ORDER LVI. MYRTACEÆ.

Erect trees or shrubs, rarely herbs. Leaves usually opposite, petiolate, simple, entire, rarely denticulate or crenate, often with an intramarginal nerve and punctate with resinous or pellucid glands; stipules minute and deciduous or 0. Flowers usually regular, hermaphrodite or rarely polygamous, axillary, solitary, or in spikes, cymes, corymbs, or heads, naked or with an involucre, often with 2 bracts at the base. Calyx superior or ½-superior, the tube rarely produced beyond the ovary; limb usually 4–5-fid or -partite, persistent or deciduous, valvate or imbricate, often closed in bud. Disk lining the calyx-tube. Petals as many as the calyx-lobes and alternate with them (rarely 0), inserted on the margin of the disk, usually much imbricate in bud, sometimes more or less connate into a deciduous cap. Stamens usually numerous, inserted on the margin or within the margin of the disk, in one or several rows; filaments distinct or connate below, or in bundles opposite the petals; anthers 2-celled, usually dehiscing longitudinally. Ovary inferior or ½-inferior, 1-celled, with 1 or more ovules, or more commonly 2-many-celled with many ovules; style simple; stigma small, capitate or peltate. Fruit usually crowned with the calyx-limb, either 1-celled and 1-seeded by arrest, or 2-many-celled with loculicidal dehiscence, or baccate and indehiscent with the cells many-seeded or 1-seeded by arrest. Seeds angular, cylindric or compressed; testa hard or membranous, sometimes winged; albumen 0; embryo straight, curved or spirally twisted; cotyledons short and obtuse, sometimes combined into a mass with the radicle, very rarely leafy; radicle often thick.—Distrib. Tropical and subtropical regions of both hemispheres; genera 76; species upwards of 1800.

Leaves opposite, gland-dotted .... 1. Eugenia.
Leaves alternate, not gland-dotted.
  Fruit angular, fibrous, 1-seeded .... 2. Barringtonia.
  Fruit ovoid or globular, fleshy, many-seeded .... 3. Careya.

1. EUGENIA, Linn.

Evergreen trees or shrubs. Leaves opposite, penninerved, gland-dotted, exstipulate. Flowers in terminal or axillary paniculate cymes, or solitary in the axils of the leaves or of scales below the leaves, often on suppressed branchlets, appearing to be fasciculate or racemose; bracts usually small and deciduous. Calyx-tube globose, ovoid, turbinate, or elongate, not or more or less produced above the ovary; segments of the limb 4 (rarely 5), or the limb subtruncate. Petals 4 (rarely 5 or more or 0), free and spreading, or more or less connate into a calyptra which falls off on the expansion of the flower. Stamens ∞, in many rows, distinct or slightly combined into 4 bundles; filaments filiform; anthers small, versatile, dehiscing longitudinally. Ovary inferior, 2- (rarely 3-) celled; ovules many in each cell; style filiform; stigma small. Fruit usually a juicy berry (rarely dry), crowned with the remains of the calyx. Seeds few, globose or ellipsoid; albumen 0 or very scanty; embryo thick, fleshy; radicle short; cotyledons thick, more or less connate or distinct.—Distrib. Tropical Asia and America, a few in Tropical Africa and Australia; species about 650.

The name "Eugenia" was first given to this genus by P. Antonio Micheli (Nov. Pl. Gen. [1729] p. 226, t. 108) in honor of Prince Eugene of Savoy. The plant from which he established the genus was *E. Michelii*, Lamk., a native of S. America, and a very early introduction into India.

Flowers in cymes.
  Petals large, free; calyx with large staminal disk; fruit exceeding ¾ in. in diam.
    Calyx-tube hemispheric; stamens yellowish-white .... 1. *E. hemispherica.*
    Calyx-tube long-cylindric; stamens crimson.................. 2. *E. læta.*
  Petals small, usually calyptrate; staminal disk absent; fruit less than ¾ in. in diam. (except *E. lanceolata*).
    Petals usually 12 .... 3. *E. lanceolata.*

Petals 4–5.
  Cymes terminal or in the axils of present leaves (except sometimes in *E. Stocksii*).
    Calyx $\frac{1}{3}$–$\frac{1}{4}$ in. long.
      Calyx-tube slender, not thicker than the pedicels ... 4. *E. toddalioides.*
      Calyx-tube funnel-shaped; fruit globose, white ... 5. *E. spicata.*
    Calyx short, less than $\frac{1}{5}$ in. long.
      Branches 4-gonous.
        Lateral nerves very numerous, close .... 6. *E. rubicunda.*
        Lateral nerves few, distant .... 7. *E. Stocksii.*
      Branches cylindric or often compressed.
        A large shrub; leaves obovate......................... 8. *E. corymbosa.*
        Lofty trees; leaves elliptic.
          Fruit less than $\frac{3}{8}$ in. in diam., crowned with the calyx-segments .... 9. *E. utilis.*
          Fruit $\frac{3}{8}$–$\frac{1}{2}$ in. in diam., not crowned with the calyx-segments .... 10. *E. Gardneri.*
  Cymes in the axils of fallen leaves.
    A large forest tree; leaves exceeding 1 in. in breadth. 11. *E. Jambolana.*
    A large shrub growing in the beds of rivers and streams; leaves not exceeding 1 in. in breadth ... 12. *E. Heyneana.*
Flowers solitary or fascicled; petals free.
  Flowers sessile.
    Flowers lateral from the leafless axils; bracteoles linear . 13. *E. macrosepala.*
    Flowers axillary or terminal; bracteoles broadly ovate ... 14. *E. codyensis.*
  Flowers pedicelled .... 15. *E. Mooniana.*

1. **Eugenia hemispherica,** *Wight, Ill.* v. 2 (1850) p. 14. A moderate-sized tree; bark yellowish-grey; upper branches subtetragonous. Leaves 3–5 by $1\frac{1}{2}$–$2\frac{3}{4}$ in., ovate-lanceolate or sometimes oblanceolate, acuminate or sometimes rounded at the apex, minutely dotted, glabrous and shining, base tapering; nerves inconspicuous above, more prominent beneath, uniting, but not very regularly, within the margin, with sometimes a second but fainter nerve close to the edge; petioles $\frac{1}{4}$–$\frac{1}{2}$ in. long. Flowers fragrant, in axillary and terminal paniculate cymes which are sometimes in pairs in the axils. Calyx slightly rugose outside; tube hemispheric, $\frac{1}{4}$–$\frac{3}{8}$ in. long; lobes rounded, reflexed and with membranous margins. Disk thickened. Petals $\frac{3}{8}$ in. long, broadly ovate or suborbicular, concave, acute, gland-dotted, reflexed, cream-colored or with a pink tinge. Stamens yellowish-white. Berry globose, $\frac{7}{8}$–1 in. in diam., crowned with the calyx-segments. Fl. B. I. v. 2, p. 477; Wight, Icon. t. 525; Bedd. Flor. Sylvat. t. 203; Trim. Fl. Ceyl. v. 2, p. 170; Talb. Trees, Bomb. ed. 2, p. 167; Woodr. in Journ. Bomb. Nat. v. 11 (1898) p. 637; Watt, Dict. Econ. Prod. v. 3, p. 284. *Eugenia lanceolaria*, Roxb. Hort. Beng. (1814) p. 37; Wight, Icon. t. 613. *Jambosa lanceolaria*, Blume, Mus. Bot. Lugd. Bat. v. 1 (1850) p. 101; Dalz. & Gibs. p. 94.—Flowers: Mar.–Apr.

KONKAN: *Stocks*!, *Law*! S. M. COUNTRY: Ramghát, *Dalzell*! KANARA: Ghâts of N. Kanara, *Talbot*; Nilkund Ghât, *Dalzell & Gibson*, *Talbot*; Ainshi Ghât, *Talbot*, *Woodrow*.—DISTRIB. India (W. Peninsula); Ceylon.

2. **Eugenia læta,** *Buch.-Ham. in Trans. Wern. Soc.* v. 5 (1824) p. 338 (*excl. syn. Rumph.*). A small tree; branches slender, terete, smooth. Leaves 3–$4\frac{1}{2}$ by 1–$1\frac{3}{4}$ in., lanceolate or oblong-lanceolate, usually with a longish obtuse acumen, pellucid-dotted, glabrous, base tapering; main nerves 12–15 pairs, uniting into a somewhat indistinct intramarginal nerve; petioles $\frac{3}{16}$–$\frac{1}{4}$ in. long. Flowers $1\frac{1}{2}$–2 in. across when expanded, solitary or few, in terminal or less commonly axillary

cymes; pedicels jointed below the calyx. Calyx $\frac{7}{8}$ in. long; tube narrow, subcylindric or obconical, faintly striate, suddenly expanded at the mouth; lobes 4, about $\frac{1}{8}$ in. long, rounded, reflexed in flower. Petals white, $\frac{1}{2}$–$\frac{5}{8}$ in. long, orbicular, subacute, glandular and conspicuously veined; buds globose. Disk thickened, lining the calyx-tube. Stamens very numerous, bright crimson, much exceeding the petals. Style $1\frac{1}{2}$ in. long, persistent. Berry oblong-ellipsoid, 1 by $\frac{3}{4}$ in., glabrous, dark-brown, crowned conspicuously with the reflexed calyx-lobes. Fl. B. I. v. 2, p. 479; Talb. Trees, Bomb. ed. 2, p. 168; Woodr. in Journ. Bomb. Nat. v. 11 (1898) p. 637.—Flowers: Nov.–Jan.

KONKAN: *Stocks*!; W. Ghâts, *Woodrow*. DECCAN: Phunda Ghât, *Ritchie*, 1755! KANARA: *Gibson*; higher Ghâts of N. Kanara; common on the Gairsoppa Ghât, *Talbot*, *Woodrow*!; Yellapur, *Gibson*!—DISTRIB. India (W. Peninsula).

VAR. *pauciflora*, Duthie, in Hook. f. Fl. B. I. v. 2, p. 479. Pedicels solitary from the extreme axils, 1-flowered. Wight, Icon. t. 526 (sp.). *Eugenia Wightii*, Bedd. For. Man. in Flor. Sylvat. p. cix. *Jambosa pauciflora*, Wight, Ill. v. 2, p. 14.

DECCAN: *Dr. Gibson*!

3. **Eugenia lanceolata,** *Lamk. Encyc. Méthod.* v. 3 (1789) p. 200 (*not* of Berg). A small tree; bark grey; branchlets slender, terete, smooth. Leaves $2\frac{1}{2}$–$4\frac{1}{2}$ by $1\frac{1}{4}$–$1\frac{1}{2}$ in., elliptic-lanceolate, caudate-acuminate, acute, inconspicuously pellucid-dotted, base tapering; main nerves numerous, rather faint, parallel, uniting in an intramarginal nerve close to the edge; petioles $\frac{1}{8}$–$\frac{1}{4}$ in. long. Flowers nearly sessile, articulated, in short usually few-flowered cymes which are axillary or from the leafless branches. Calyx $\frac{1}{2}$–$\frac{5}{8}$ in. long, elongate, clavate or infundibuliform, glandular outside; lobes 4–5, very shallow, rounded, repand. Petals white, numerous, often as many as 12, usually calyptrate, broadly obovate or suborbicular. Fruit $\frac{3}{4}$–1 in. long, dark-brown, ellipsoid, tapering to a very slender base, crowned with the thickened calyx-lobes and persistent style. Wight, Ill. v. 2 (1850) p. 15; Icon. t. 530; Bedd. For. Man. in Flor. Sylvat. p. cix; Trim. Fl. Ceyl. v. 2, p. 172. *Eugenia Wightiana*, Wight, Ill. v. 2 (1850) p. 15; Icon. t. 529; Duthie, in Hook. f. Fl. B. I. v. 2, p. 485; Talb. Trees, Bomb. ed. 2, p. 168; Woodr. in Journ. Bomb. Nat. v. 11 (1898) p. 637.—Flowers: Feb.–Mar.

The specific name "*lanceolata*" given to the plant by Lamarck is 60 years prior to the name "*Wightiana*" given to it by Wight.

KONKAN: *Stocks*!, *Talbot*, *Woodrow*. KANARA: near rivers and along watercourses in N. Kanara, rare, *Talbot*.—DISTRIB. India (W. Peninsula); Ceylon.

4. **Eugenia toddalioides,** *Wight, Ill.* v. 2, p. 16. A small tree; young branchlets slender, subterete, smooth. Leaves $2\frac{1}{2}$–4 by 1–$1\frac{1}{4}$ in., lanceolate, with a long slender acumen, pellucid-dotted, glabrous, base tapering; main nerves numerous, close, parallel, uniting in an intramarginal nerve close to the edge; petioles $\frac{1}{4}$–$\frac{3}{8}$ in. long. Flowers less than $\frac{1}{2}$ in. across, in di- tri-chotomous axillary or extra-axillary cymes, each branch 1–3-flowered. Calyx $\frac{1}{6}$–$\frac{1}{4}$ in. long; tube very slender, scarcely thicker than the pedicels, suddenly dilated into a large cup-shaped limb; lobes 4, very short, rounded, sometimes almost obsolete.

Petals $\frac{1}{8}$ in. in diam., orbicular, tender, free. Fruit not seen. Fl. B. I. v. 2, p. 482; Wight, Icon. t. 542; Woodr. in Journ. Bomb. Nat. v. 11 (1898) p. 637.—Flowers: Jan.

S. M. Country: Castlerock, *Woodrow.*

This plant has been reported by Woodrow from Castlerock near the Railway Station on the Ghát at that place. It is no doubt a rare plant as it had not previously been collected in the Presidency.

5. **Eugenia spicata,** *Lamk. Encyc. Méthod.* v. 3 (1789) p. 201. A large shrub or small tree, very handsome when in full flower; bark pale-brown; branchlets slender, obsoletely 4-angled or terete, purplish-brown, shining. Leaves aromatically fragrant when bruised, coriaceous, variable, $1\frac{1}{2}$–4 by $\frac{3}{8}$–$1\frac{1}{2}$ in., ovate-elliptic to linear-lanceolate, usually caudate-acuminate, smooth and shining on both surfaces, paler and minutely glandular beneath, the margins slightly recurved, base acute; main nerves numerous, inconspicuous, uniting into an inconspicuous intramarginal nerve near the edge; petioles $\frac{1}{10}$–$\frac{1}{4}$ in. long. Flowers white, conspicuous, in axillary and terminal many-flowered paniculate cymes, in clusters of 3–5 at the ends of the ultimate cyme-branches. Calyx funnel-shaped, $\frac{1}{8}$ in. long, tubercled with glands on the outside, sessile or nearly so; lobes 4–5, broadly ovate or rotundate, concave, erect. Petals 4–5, orbicular, usually calyptrate but sometimes imperfectly so. Fruit pisiform, less than $\frac{1}{4}$ in. in diam., pure white, 1-seeded. Trim. Fl. Ceyl. v. 2, p. 171. *Eugenia zeylanica*, Wight, Ill. v. 2 (1850) p. 15; Bedd. Flor. Sylvat. t. 202; Duthie, in Hook. f. Fl. B. I. v. 2, p. 485; Talb. Trees, Bomb. ed. 2, p. 168; Woodr. in Journ. Bomb. Nat. v. 11 (1898) p. 637; Watt, Dict. Econ. Prod. v. 3, p. 290. *Syzygium zeylanicum*, DC. Prodr. v. 3, p. 260; Grah. Cat. p. 73; Wight, Icon. t. 73; Dalz. & Gibs. p. 94. *Myrtus zeylanica*, Linn. Sp. Pl. (1753) p. 472.—Flowers: Feb.–Apr. Vern. *Pitkuli.*

The specific name "*spicata*" was adopted by Lamarck in 1789, while Wight's name "*zeylanica*" (derived no doubt from *Myrtus zeylanica*, Linn.) was given in 1850. There can be no question as to the propriety of restoring the older nomenclature.

Konkan: *Law!*, *Stocks!*, *Dalzell!*; S. Konkan, *Nimmo* ex *Graham*. S. M. Country: Párva Ghát, *Ritchie*, 1752!; Ambgaon, *Ritchie*, 1752! Kanara: Sáwad, *Woodrow*; common in N. Kanara, *Talbot*; higher Ghâts south of Bombay, *Dalzell & Gibson*.—Distrib. India (W. Peninsula, Orissa, Silhet); Ceylon, Malaya, Sumatra, Borneo.

6. **Eugenia rubicunda,** *Wight, Ill.* v. 2 (1850) p. 15. A middling-sized tree; young branches quadrangular. Leaves variable, $1\frac{1}{2}$–$3\frac{1}{2}$ by $\frac{1}{2}$–$1\frac{1}{2}$ in., oblong-lanceolate, elliptic-lanceolate or sometimes oblanceolate, acuminate, glabrous on both surfaces, shining above, paler and minutely pellucid-dotted beneath, base tapering; mian nerves very numerous, fine, parallel, uniting in a distinct intramarginal nerve near the margin; petioles $\frac{1}{8}$–$\frac{1}{6}$ in. long. Flowers pinkish-white, sessile or nearly so, usually 3 together at the ends of the quadrangular branches of terminal and axillary cymes which are often longer than the leaves. Calyx $\frac{1}{8}$ in. long, shortly turbinate, rugose outside; lobes 4, very short, rounded or almost obsolete. Petals calyptrate. Berry round, size of a small pea, crowned with the persistent calyx-limb, black when ripe, glabrous. Fl. B. I. v. 2, p. 495; Wight, Icon. t. 538; Bedd. For. Man. in Flor. Sylvat. p. cviii; Talb. Trees, Bomb. ed. 2, p. 168; Woodr. in Journ.

Bomb. Nat. v. 11 (1898) p. 637. *Syzygium rubicundum*, Wight & Arn. Prodr. p. 330; Dalz. & Gibs. p. 94. *Syzygium salicifolium*, Wall. Cat. 3597 (*not* of Graham). *Eugenia lissophylla*, Duthie, in Hook. f. Fl. B. I. v. 2 (1878) p. 488; Bedd. For. Man. in Flor. Sylvat. p. cviii; Trim. Fl. Ceyl. v. 2, p. 173; Talb. Trees, Bomb. ed. 2, p. 168; Woodr. in Journ. Bomb. Nat. v. 11 (1898) p. 637. *Syzygium lissophyllum*, Thwaites, Enum. p. 117.—Flowers: Mar.-May. VERN. *Lendi-Jámbhal.*

Rare. Higher Gháts along streams, *Dalzell & Gibson*. KONKAN: *Stocks*! DECCAN: Singhad, near Poona, *Woodrow*.—DISTRIB. India (W. Peninsula); Ceylon.

7. **Eugenia Stocksii,** *Duthie, in Hook. f. Fl. B. I.* v. 2, p. 498. A lofty tree; branches 4-gonous. Leaves 4–6½ by 1¾–3 in., thin, lanceolate-oblong or obovate-oblong, rounded or shortly and obtusely acuminate, glabrous, finely dotted with opaque (not pellucid) dots, base tapering; main nerves 12–16 pairs, slender, curving upwards and becoming faint towards the margin, not uniting into an intramarginal nerve; petioles ½–⅝ in. long. Flowers about ⅛ in. across, numerous, in branched cymes which are axillary and from the leafless axils; peduncles 1–2 in. long. Calyx $\frac{1}{10}$–⅛ in. long, funnel-shaped, rugose outside; lobes 4, short, subacute or rounded. Petals calyptrate, gland-dotted. Fruit not seen. Talb. Trees, Bomb. ed. 2, p. 169; Woodr. in Journ. Bomb. Nat. v. 11 (1898) p. 637.

A rare plant. KONKAN: *Stocks*!, *Law*! KANARA: *Dalzell*!

8. **Eugenia corymbosa,** *Lamk. Encyc. Méthod.* v. 3 (1789) p. 199. A large shrub or small tree; branchlets terete or slightly compressed, brown. Leaves subcoriaceous, 2½–3½ by ⅞–1¾ in., obovate or rarely ovate-lanceolate, obtuse, or suddenly and shortly bluntly acuminate, bright-green and shining above, paler and inconspicuously dotted beneath, base tapering; main nerves numerous, fine, conspicuous beneath, uniting in a distinct intramarginal nerve; petioles ⅛–¼ in. long. Flowers numerous, small, sessile or nearly so, in terminal corymbose laxly trichotomous cymes with quadrangular branches; buds globose. Calyx ⅛ in. long, campanulate, externally rugose; lobes 4, shallow, subacute, often scarcely distinguishable. Petals white, calyptrate. Fruit depressed-globose, dark purple or nearly black, about the size of a pea, 1-seeded, shining, juicy, edible. Trim. Fl. Ceyl. v. 2, p. 174. *Eugenia caryophyllæa*, Wight, Ill. v. 2 (1850) p. 15; Icon. t. 540; Duthie, in Hook. f. Fl. B. I. v. 2, p. 490; Bedd. For. Man. in Flor. Sylvat. p. cviii; Talb. Trees, Bomb. ed. 2, p. 168; Woodr. in Journ. Bomb. Nat. v. 11 (1898) p. 637; Watt, Dict. Econ. Prod. v. 3, p. 283. *Syzygium caryophyllæum*, Gærtn. Fruct. v. 1 (1788) p. 166, t. 33; Grah. Cat. p. 73; Dalz. & Gibs. p. 93. *Syzygium rubicundum*, Grah. Cat. p. 73 (*not* of Wight & Arn.). *Myrtus caryophyllata*, Linn. Sp. Pl. (1753) p. 472.—Flowers: Mar.-May. VERN. *Nimbuli*; *Ránlavang.*

The specific name "*corymbosa*" is 60 years prior to that of "*caryophyllæa.*"

KONKAN: *Stocks*!; S. Konkan, *Nimmo* ex *Graham*; on the banks of streams, *Dalzell & Gibson*. DECCAN: Mahableshwar, bed of the Yenna river, *Graham*; on the banks of streams, *Cooke*!, *Woodrow*!; near the Fountain Hotel and Carnac Point, *H. M. Birdwood*. S. M. COUNTRY: Kála naddi, *Ritchie*, 1751! KANARA: moist forests, common near the sea, *Talbot*.—DISTRIB. India (W. Peninsula); Ceylon, Borneo.

9. **Eugenia utilis,** *Talbot, in Journ. Bomb. Nat. Hist. Soc.* v. 11 (1897) p. 235. A large quite glabrous tree; bark grey, scaly; branches terete. Leaves coriaceous, 2–3 by 1–1$\frac{1}{2}$ in., elliptic, abruptly and shortly acuminate, conspicuously gland-dotted, base acute; main nerves numerous, fine, close, uniting at the margin into an inconspicuous nerve; petioles $\frac{1}{4}$–$\frac{3}{8}$ in. long. Flowers small, in axillary and terminal corymbose panicled cymes which are shorter than the leaves, 2–3 flowers together on the ends of the slender angular branches of the cyme; buds globose or pear-shaped; bracteoles lanceolate. Calyx $\frac{1}{10}$ in. long, turbinate, rugulose externally, truncate or very indistinctly 4-lobed. Petals calyptrate. Fruit small, black, succulent, crowned with the persistent calyx-lobes. Talb. Trees, Bomb. ed. 2, p. 169.—Flowers: May–June.

Common in evergreen or on the borders of evergreen forests in the southern parts of N. Kanara, *Talbot.*

The wood is moderately heavy and tough, of a reddish-brown color and is greatly in demand in the Sirsi subdivision of N. Kanara for building purposes, *Talbot.*—Distrib. Apparently endemic.

10. **Eugenia Gardneri,** *Duthie, in Hook. f. Fl. B. I.* v. 2 (1878) p. 489. A large glabrous tree; bark smooth, pale-grey; branchlets terete, or sometimes somewhat compressed, white. Leaves 2$\frac{1}{4}$–3$\frac{1}{2}$ by $\frac{7}{8}$–1$\frac{1}{2}$ in., elliptic-oblong, usually caudate-acuminate, minutely pellucid-dotted, base acute; main nerves conspicuous, very numerous, parallel, close, uniting in an intramarginal nerve; petioles $\frac{3}{8}$–$\frac{3}{4}$ in. long. Flowers white, $\frac{1}{4}$–$\frac{1}{3}$ in. across, numerous, sessile or nearly so, usually in threes at the extremities of the branches of copious axillary and terminal cymes which are shorter than the leaves; buds globose. Calyx $\frac{1}{8}$–$\frac{1}{6}$ in. long, campanulate, rugulose outside, truncate, with obscure segments. Petals calyptrate. Fruit spherical, $\frac{3}{8}$–$\frac{1}{2}$ in. in diam., not crowned with the calyx-segments. Trim. Fl. Ceyl. v. 2, p. 174. *Syzygium Gardneri*, Thwaites, Enum. p. 117. *Eugenia kanarensis*, Talb. in Journ. Bomb. Nat. Hist. Soc. v. 11 (1897) p. 236, t. 4; Talb. Trees, Bomb. ed. 2, p. 169.

Kanara: Gnirsoppa Ghát above Mulamani (N. Kanara), 2000 ft., *Talbot*, 3552!—Distrib. India (Ghâts of the W. Peninsula); Ceylon.

11. **Eugenia Jambolana,** *Lamk. Encyc. Méthod.* v. 3 (1789) p. 198. A large tree; bark light-colored, thick, rough, exfoliating; branches terete, very pale when dry. Leaves coriaceous, variable, 2$\frac{1}{2}$–4$\frac{1}{2}$ by 1$\frac{1}{2}$–2$\frac{1}{4}$ in., lanceolate, elliptic-oblong or broadly ovate-elliptic, acute, subobtuse or shortly acuminate, smooth and shining, pellucid-dotted, slightly narrowed at the base; main nerves very many, slender, prominent on the lower surface, uniting into an intramarginal nerve, reticulations numerous between the main nerves; petioles $\frac{1}{2}$–1 in. long. Flowers dirty-white, fragrant, about $\frac{3}{16}$–$\frac{5}{16}$ in. across, sessile or shortly pedicelled, crowded in heads on the ends of laxly panicled cymes rising from the branches below the leaves (rarely axillary or terminal). Calyx $\frac{1}{6}$ in. long, rugulose externally, shortly turbinate; limb cup-shaped, yellow inside, truncate or with 4 very obscure segments. Petals calyptrate. Fruit the shape of an olive, or subglobose, varying in size from a pea to a pigeon's egg, dark-purple, smooth, juicy, crowned with the truncate calyx-limb, 1-seeded. Fl. B. I. v. 2, p. 499; Wight, Icon.

t. 535; Bedd. Flor. Sylvat. t. 197; Trim. Fl. Ceyl. v. 2, p. 179; Talb. Trees, Bomb. ed. 2, p. 169; Woodr. in Journ. Bomb. Nat. v. 11 (1898) p. 637; Watt, Dict. Econ. Prod. v. 3, p. 284. *Syzygium Jambolanum*, DC. Prodr. v. 3, p. 259; Grah. Cat. p. 73; Dalz. & Gibs. p. 93.—Flowers: Mar.–May. VERN. *Jámbhal.*

Throughout the Presidency (except Sind) both wild and cultivated. KONKAN: very common at Matheran, *Cooke*!, *Woodrow*! DECCAN: Mahableshwar, the commonest tree on the hill, *Cooke*! GUJARAT: Dangs, *Woodrow*. KANARA: common in the moist forests of N. Kanara, *Talbot*.—DISTRIB. Throughout India; Ceylon; Malaya, Australia.

The cultivated fruit is often as large as a pigeon's egg and is eaten largely by the natives. The flavor is subacid and rather astringent. For other uses of the products of the tree, see Watt, Dict. Econ. Prod. l. c.

12. **Eugenia Heyneana,** *Duthie, in Hook. f. Fl. B. I.* v. 2 (1878) p. 500. A shrub, scarcely a small tree, 12–15 ft. high, growing in the beds or on the banks of streams and rivers. Leaves 3–4 by ⅝–1 in., oblong-lanceolate, subobtuse, glabrous and shining, pellucid-dotted, base tapering; main nerves very numerous, fine, uniting in an intramarginal nerve; petiole ⅛–⅜ in. long. Flowers ¼ in. across, white, sessile or shortly pedicelled, in small heads at the ends of the branches of cymes which are lateral from the scars of fallen leaves, rarely axillary. Calyx ⅛–$\frac{3}{16}$ in. long, externally rugulose, funnel-shaped. Petals calyptrate. Fruit oblong-ellipsoid, ½ in. long, crowned with the cup-shaped calyx-limb. Talb. Trees, Bomb. ed. 2, p. 170; Woodr. in Journ. Bomb. Nat. v. 11 (1898) p. 637; Watt, Dict. Econ. Prod. v. 3, p. 284. *Eugenia salicifolia*, Wight, Ill. v. 2 (1850) p. 16; Icon. t. 539; Bedd. For. Man. in Flor. Sylvat. p. cix (not *E. salicifolia*, DC. Prodr. v. 3 (1828) p. 278, nor of Berg, in Mart. Fl. Bras. v. 14, part 1, p. 312). *Syzygium Heyneanum*, Wall. Cat. 3599. *Syzygium salicifolium*, Grah. Cat. (1839) p. 73; Dalz. & Gibs. p. 94 (*not* Wall. Cat. 3597).—Flowers: Mar.–May. VERN. *Pán-Jámbhal*; *Bedas.*

KONKAN: *Stocks*! DECCAN: Rotunda Ghát, Mahableshwar, also in the bed of the Koina river above Pár bridge, *Graham*; below Mahableshwar, *Woodrow*!; Koina valley, *H. M. Birdwood*. KANARA: common throughout N. Kanara in the beds of streams and rivers, *Talbot*, *Woodrow*; Chandvár, *Ritchie*, 1753!—DISTRIB. India (W. Peninsula, Berar, and Central Provinces).

VAR. *alternans*, Duthie, in Hook. f. Fl. B. I. v. 2, p. 500. Cymes from the axils of the upper leaves. *S. alternans* (sp.), Miq. in Herb. Hohenhacker.

KONKAN and KANARA: *Stocks*!, *Hohenhacker*.

13. **Eugenia macrosepala,** *Duthie, in Hook. f. Fl. B. I.* v. 2 (1878) p. 501. A spreading bushy shrub; bark brownish; upper branches stout. Leaves 2½–4½ by 1¼–1¾ in., elliptic-oblong or oblong-lanceolate, obtusely acuminate, base usually acute; main nerves slender, about 10–15 pairs, indistinct above, conspicuous beneath, uniting somewhat obscurely within the margin; petioles ¼ in. long. Flowers sessile, lateral from the leafless axils, solitary or in pairs; bracteoles 2 beneath the calyx, linear, pilose. Calyx ¼ in. long, clothed outside with long spreading white hairs; tube very short; lobes 4, lanceolate, acute, ciliate, usually exceeding the petals. Petals ovate-oblong, obtuse, ciliolate. Fruit not seen. There is no fruit on any of the specimens in

Herb. Kew. Talb. Trees, Bomb. ed. 2, p. 170; Woodr. in Journ. Bomb. Nat. v. 11 (1898) p. 637.—Flowers: Jan.–Feb.

DECCAN: Ahmednagar, *Woodrow*. KANARA: N. Kanara, *Stocks*!; border of Vaddi Ghát (N. Kanara), pretty common, *Talbot*.

14. **Eugenia codyensis,** *Munro, in Wight, Ill.* v. 2 (1850) p. 13. A small evergreen tree; bark smooth; branchlets slender, terete, pale. Leaves coriaceous, 1½–2¼ by ⅞–1½ in., elliptic, bluntly acuminate or subobtuse, finely pellucid-dotted, margins slightly recurved, base tapering; main nerves about 15–20 pairs, slender, uniting in an intramarginal nerve; petioles ¼–⅜ in. long. Flowers white, about ½ in. across, sessile or nearly so, axillary, solitary, or in fascicles of 2 or more, or in terminal heads at the ends of short abortive branches; bracteoles conspicuous, 1/16 in. long, broadly ovate, acute, pubescent. Calyx ¼ in. long, finely pubescent or tomentose outside; tube very short; lobes 4, broadly ovate, ciliate on the margins, gland-dotted. Petals 4, twice the length of the calyx, spreading. Fruit globose, ½ in. in diam., crowned with the persistent calyx-lobes; seeds 1–2. *Eugenia memecylifolia*, Talbot, in Journ. Bomb. Nat. Hist. Soc. v. 11 (1897) p. 236, t. 5, & Trees, Bomb. ed. 2, p. 170.—Flowers: Mar.–May.

I cannot separate Mr. Talbot's *E. memecylifolia* from *E. codyensis*, Munro. Mr. Talbot describes the fruit of the former as white, while Munro (*l. c.*) makes no mention of the color of the fruit of the latter.

KANARA: Kalpa on the Supa Ghâts of N. Kanara (3400 feet), *Talbot*, 3127! *Woodrow*.—DISTRIB. India (Nilghiri and Kurg mountains).

15. **Eugenia Mooniana,** *Wight, Ill.* v. 2 (1850) p. 13. (*Not* of Gardner, in Lond. Journ. Bot. v. 2 (1843) p. 352.) Shrubby, glabrous, or the young shoots puberulous. Leaves very variable in size and shape, 1½–2½ by ¾–1¼ in., ovate or elliptic or sometimes obovate, acuminate (the acumen either short and obtuse or prolonged to a more or less fine point), base usually tapering, but sometimes rounded; main nerves inconspicuous, slender, uniting in an intramarginal nerve; petioles 3/16–¼ in. long. Flowers white, about ¼ in. across, solitary or 2 together on filiform pedicels about ½ in. long which are axillary or from the old wood; bracteoles small, lanceolate-subulate. Calyx ⅛ in. long, pubescent outside; tube about equalling the lobes, funnel-shaped, not prolonged beyond the ovary; lobes 4, oblong, acute or obtuse, reflexed. Petals longer than the calyx-lobes, broadly ovate or elliptic, obtuse, glandular. Fruit globose, about the size of a cherry, scarlet or crimson (*Trimen*). Fl. B. I. v. 2, p. 505; Wight, Icon. t. 551; Trim. Fl. Ceyl. v. 2, p. 187. *Eugenia Wildenowii* (?), Dalz. & Gibs. p. 94 (*not* of DC.).

KONKAN: *Stocks*!

VAR. *gracilis*, Duthie, in Hook. f. Fl. B. I. v. 2 (1878) p. 505. Leaves longer; fruit oblong-ellipsoid (not globular). *E. gracilis* (sp.), Bedd. in Trans. Linn. Soc. v. 25 (1866) p. 217; Bedd. For. Man. in Flor. Sylvat. p. cx; Talb. Trees, Bomb. ed. 2, p. 170.—Flowers: Feb.–Mar.

Evergreen forests of the Konkan and N. Kanara, *Talbot*; Ainshi Ghát (N. Kanara), *Talbot*, *Woodrow*; common in the forests near Karwar on the coast, *Talbot*.—DISTRIB. India (W. Peninsula); Ceylon.

Eugenia malaccensis, Linn. Sp. Pl. (1753) p. 470. A small tree or large shrub with leaves 9–12 in. long and dense racemes of large bright-crimson flowers having 4 suborbicular glandular petals and numerous stamens about 1 in. long, a native of the Moluccas, is often grown in gardens in Bombay, where it thrives well. The fruit is of the size of a small apple and is eaten, although it is not very palatable. Fl. B. I. v. 2, p. 471; Talb. Trees, Bomb. ed. 2, p. 167; Woodr. in Journ. Bomb. Nat. v. 11 (1898) p. 637, & Gard. in Ind. ed. 5, p. 315; Watt, Dict. Econ. Prod. v. 3, p. 288. *Jambosa malaccensis*, DC. Prodr. v. 3, p. 286; Grah. Cat. p. 74; Dalz. & Gibs. Suppl. p. 35.—Flowers: Apr.–May. VERN. *Malake-jámb.*

Eugenia Jambos, Linn. Sp. Pl. (1753) p. 470. *The Rose-Apple.* A small tree, often cultivated in gardens. The flowers are large, greenish-white, and are followed by a subglobose berry 1–2 in. in diam., of rich pink and white coloration, but more pleasant to the sight than the taste. Some fine trees may be seen planted on the hill fort of Pertábghar near Mahableshwar. Fl. B. I. v. 2, p. 474; Talb. Trees, Bomb. ed. 2, p. 167; Woodr. in Journ. Bomb. Nat. v. 11 (1898) p. 637, & Gard. in Ind. ed. 5, p. 316; Watt, Dict. Econ. Prod. v. 3, p. 287. *Jambosa vulgaris*, DC. Prodr. v. 3, p. 286; Grah. Cat. p. 74; Dalz. & Gibs. Suppl. p. 35.—Flowers: Feb. VERN. *Guláb-jámb.*

Eugenia bracteata, Roxb. Hort. Beng. (1814) p. 37. A shrub or small tree, a native of Southern India and Ceylon, has been planted in Poona and N. Kanara. It has white flowers about as large as those of the common myrtle, borne on short axillary peduncles which are solitary or fascicled. Fl. B. I. v. 2, p. 502; Trim. Fl. Ceyl. v. 2, p. 182; Woodr. in Journ. Bomb. Nat. v. 11 (1898) p. 637.—Flowers: Apr.–July.

Eugenia Michelii, Lamk. Encyc. Méthod. v. 3 (1789) p. 203, a native of S. America (although a very ancient introduction into India), is occasionally met with in gardens, where it is known as the "*Brazil Cherry.*" It possesses considerable interest as being the plant from which, under the name *Eugenia indica*, the genus *Eugenia* was originally established by P. Antonio Micheli in 1729 (Nov. Pl. Gen. p. 226, t. 108) in honor of Prince Eugene of Savoy. Trimen (Journ. Linn. Soc. v. 24 [1888] p. 142) has shewn that the name *E. uniflora* subsequently given to the plant by Linnæus, which included both this and a form of *E. malaccensis*, must be abandoned in favor of *E. Michelii*, Lamk. *Eugenia uniflora*, Linn. Sp. Pl. (1753) p. 470; Fl. B. I. v. 2, p. 505; Woodr. in Journ. Bomb. Nat. v. 11 (1898) p. 637. *Eugenia zeylanica*, Willd. Sp. Pl. v. 2, p. 963 (*not* of Roxb. nor of Wight). *Eugenia Wildenowii*, DC. Prodr. v. 3, p. 265 (*not* of Wight). *Myrtus brasiliana*, Linn. Sp. Pl. (1753) p. 471.—Flowers: Aug.–Sept.

2. BARRINGTONIA, Forst.

Trees. Leaves alternate, crowded towards the ends of the branches, usually membranous, penninerved, not gland-dotted. Flowers in terminal and lateral racemes or interrupted spikes; bracts small, very caducous; bracteoles minute or 0. Calyx-tube ovoid or turbinate, not or scarcely produced above the ovary; lobes 2–4 (rarely 5). Petals 4 (rarely 5), imbricate, adnate at the base to the staminal-tube. Stamens numerous, in several rows, connate at the base into a ring or very short cup; filaments filiform, all antheriferous; anthers small. Disk annular, at the top of the ovary between the stamens. Ovary inferior, 2–4-celled; ovules 2–8 in each cell, pendulous or horizontal; style long, filiform; stigma small. Fruit fibrous or leathery, globose, ellipsoid, or quadrangular, crowned with the calyx-limb, usually 1-seeded. Seed ovoid or ellipsoid, exalbuminous; embryo thick, fleshy, consisting of two concentric homogeneous layers; cotyledons rudimentary, scale-like.—DISTRIB. Tropical Asia, Africa, Australia and Polynesia; species 25.

On the structure of seeds of *Barringtonia* and *Careya*, see Thomson, in Journ. Linn. Soc. v. 2 (1858) p. 47.

Leaves reaching 12 in. long; fruit ovoid .... 1. *B. racemosa.*
Leaves reaching 6 in. long; fruit quadrangular .... 2. *B. acutangula.*

1. **Barringtonia racemosa,** *Roxb. Hort. Beng.* (1814) p. 52; *Fl. Ind.* v. 2, p. 634. A glabrous tree often reaching 50 ft. high; bark grey. Leaves 4–12 by 2–5 in., membranous, obovate-oblong or oblanceolate, shortly acuminate, slightly crenate-denticulate, glabrous, base cuneate; main nerves 10–20 pairs, spreading or ascending, prominent beneath; petioles $\frac{1}{10}$–$\frac{1}{4}$ in. long. Flowers $1\frac{1}{2}$–2 in. across, distant, in pendulous many-flowered racemes 1–2 ft. long, terminal or from the axils of fallen leaves; buds globose; pedicels slender, $\frac{1}{4}$–$\frac{1}{3}$ in. long; bracteoles minute, caducous. Calyx turbinate; tube funnel-shaped in bud; lobes 2–3, ovate, acute, $\frac{3}{8}$–$\frac{1}{2}$ in. long. Petals 4, oblong-elliptic, acute, $\frac{3}{4}$–1 in. long. Stamens very numerous; filaments erect, spreading, about 1 in. long. Style $1\frac{1}{2}$–$1\frac{3}{4}$ in. long. Fruit 2–$2\frac{1}{2}$ by $1\frac{3}{4}$–2 in., ovoid, circular in horizontal cross-section or very bluntly 4-lobed, nearly smooth, crowned with the persistent calyx-lobes; pericarp leathery. Seed solitary, ovoid-ellipsoid, $1\frac{3}{4}$ in. long. Fl. B. I. v. 2, p. 507; Blume, in DC. Prodr. v. 3 (1828) p. 288; Grah. Cat. p. 74; Wight, Icon. t. 152; Bot. Mag. t. 3831; Dalz. & Gibs. p. 94; Trim. Fl. Ceyl. v. 2, p. 189; Talb. Trees, Bomb. ed. 2, p. 171; Watt, Dict. Econ. Prod. v. 1, p. 402.—Flowers: Apr.–May. VERN. *Nivdr*; *Samudra-phal.*

KONKAN: *Stocks*!, *Nimmo* ex *Graham*; Severndrug taluka, *Dalzell & Gibson*; near the coast, *Talbot*. KANARA: plentiful, *Dalzell & Gibson*; along rivers and nálas near the coast of N. Kanara, *Talbot*.—DISTRIB. India (eastern and western sea-coasts); Malaya, Polynesia.

2. **Barringtonia acutangula,** *Gærtn. Fruct.* v. 2 (1791) p. 97, t. 101. A glabrous tree 25–50 ft. high; young branches slender, pale-grey. Leaves $2\frac{1}{2}$–6 by $1\frac{1}{4}$–$3\frac{1}{4}$ in., obovate-oblong or elliptic-cuneate, the apex rounded or subacute, the margins minutely denticulate or crenulate, base much narrowed into the petiole; main nerves 10–13 pairs, spreading; petioles $\frac{1}{8}$–$\frac{1}{4}$ in. long. Flowers fragrant, dark-scarlet, $\frac{1}{3}$–$\frac{1}{2}$ in. across, in slender pendulous many-flowered racemes 6–15 in. long; pedicels $\frac{1}{16}$–$\frac{1}{8}$ in. long; bracteoles linear-lanceolate, acute, caducous. Calyx $\frac{1}{8}$ in. long; tube puberulous outside, about as long as the lobes; lobes 4, oblong, rounded, ciliolate. Petals $\frac{1}{6}$ in. long. Filaments $\frac{3}{4}$ in. long. Fruit $1\frac{1}{4}$–$1\frac{1}{2}$ by $\frac{1}{2}$–$\frac{3}{4}$ in., bluntly quadrangular, broadest in the middle, slightly narrowed towards and truncate at each end, crowned by the small persistent calyx. Fl. B. I. v. 2, p. 508; Grah. Cat. p. 74; Bedd. Flor.

Sylvat. t. 204; Dalz. & Gibs. p. 95; Trim. Fl. Ceyl. v. 2, p. 191; Talb. Trees, Bomb. ed. 2, p. 171; Woodr. in Journ. Bomb. Nat. v. 11 (1898) p. 637; Watt, Dict. Econ. Prod. v. 1, p. 401.—Flowers: Sept.-Oct. VERN. *Tivár*; *Ingli*.

KONKAN: banks of creeks in the S. Konkan, *Dalzell*!; Shrivardhan (S. Konkan), *Woodrow*; between Indapur and Dasgaon, *Dalzell & Gibson*; W. Ghâts widely, *Woodrow*. S. M. COUNTRY: near Belgaum, *Law* ex *Graham*. KANARA: banks of rivers and streams throughout N. Kanara, common near the coast, *Talbot*; island in the Kála naddi, *Ritchie*, 280!—DISTRIB. Throughout India; Ceylon, Malaya, N. Australia.

3. CAREYA, Roxb.

Trees or a small undershrub (*C. herbacea*). Leaves alternate, crowded at the ends of the branches, penninerved, not dotted. Flowers large and handsome, in racemes or interrupted spikes. Calyx-tube campanulate or ovoid, not produced above the ovary; limb deeply 4-lobed. Petals 4, imbricate. Stamens very numerous, epigynous, in several rows, slightly connate at the base; filaments very long, the innermost and outermost rows often without anthers, the intermediate perfect; anthers versatile, dehiscing longitudinally. Ovary inferior, 4- (rarely 5-) celled, crowned by an annular disk; ovules numerous, in 2 rows on axile placentas. Fruit large, globose, fleshy, indehiscent, crowned with the calyx-limb. Seeds numerous, nesting in fleshy pulp; albumen 0; embryo large; cotyledons obsolete.—DISTRIB. India, Ceylon, N. Australia, Queensland; species 4.

1. **Careya arborea,** *Roxb. Cor. Pl.* v. 3 (1819) p. 14, t. 218. A glabrous middle-sized or sometimes a large tree attaining 60 ft. with rounded head; bark thick, rough, dark-grey. Leaves 6–12 by 3–7 in., usually sessile, broadly obovate or oblong-obovate, rounded or shortly acuminate, crenate-denticulate, glabrous, tapering at the base; main nerves 10–12 pairs; petioles 0–¾ in. long, margined. Flowers yellowish-white, ill-smelling, sessile, 2½–3½ in. across, in thick swollen hard terminal spikes each with a central elliptic bract and 2 linear lateral ones. Calyx about 1 in. long; tube campanulate; segments rather shorter than the tube, oblong, obtuse, stiff, erect. Petals 1½–2 in. long, elliptic-oblong, obtuse or subacute. Filaments about equalling or slightly longer than the petals, red. Fruit 2½–3 in. in diam., globular, green, glabrous, somewhat like an apple in appearance. Fl. B. I. v. 2, p. 511; Grah. Cat. p. 74; Wight, Ill. tt. 99 & 100; Dalz. & Gibs. p. 95; Talb. Trees, Bomb. ed. 2, p. 172; Woodr. in Journ. Bomb. Nat. v. 11 (1898) p. 637; Watt, Dict. Econ. Prod. v. 2, p. 157.—Flowers: Mar.-Apr. VERN. *Kumbhá*; *Kubá*.

Throughout the Presidency in deciduous forests. KONKAN: common in S. Konkan, *Dalzell & Gibson*; W. Ghâts, widely, *Woodrow*; Matheran, abundant, *Cooke*!; Malabar and Parel hills (Bombay), *Graham*; jungles in Salsette, *Graham*; Indapur, *Dalzell & Gibson*. DECCAN: Khandesh, *Graham*. GUJARAT: where it attains a majestic size, *Gibson* ex *Graham*. S. M. COUNTRY: Belgaum jungles, *Ritchie*! KANARA: Kála naddi, *Ritchie*, 300!

The timber is useful, stands water well, and the heartwood takes a fine polish. From the inner bark fuses for matchlocks are made, and the bark is also used in native medicine. The dried calyces under the name "Vákumbha" are sold in the market and used as a demulcent in coughs and colds. See Watt, Dict. Econ. Prod. l. c. —DISTRIB. Throughout India; Ceylon.

Psidium Guyava, Linn. Sp. Pl. (1753) p. 470. The well-known *Guava Tree*, a native of Mexico and possibly other parts of Tropical America, is cultivated throughout and naturalized in India and in most tropical countries. It is valued for its fruit and is deserving of more attention than it generally receives. As the trees in cultivation are mostly seedlings, there is naturally an immense variety in the quality of the fruit, which could be much improved by a judicious system of grafting. Fl. B. I. v. 2, p. 468; Firminger, Man. Gard. ed. 3, p. 261; Woodr. in Journ. Bomb. Nat. v. 11 (1898) p. 637, & Gard. in Ind. ed. 5, p. 314; Watt, Dict. Econ. Prod. v. 6, part 1, p. 351. *Psidium pyriferum*, Linn. Sp. Pl. ed. 2 (1762) p. 672; Grah. Cat. p. 72; Dalz. & Gibs. Suppl. p. 34.—VERN. *Jámb*; *Peru.*

Myrtus communis, Linn. Sp. Pl. (1753) p. 471. *The Myrtle*, a well-known sweet-scented shrub, a native of S. Europe, is cultivated in every garden for its fragrant leaves. Dalz. & Gibs. Suppl. p. 34; Firminger, Man. Gard. ed. 3, p. 571; Woodr. in Journ. Bomb. Nat. v. 11 (1898) p. 637, & Gard. in Ind. ed. 5, p. 314; Watt, Dict. Econ. Prod. v. 5, p. 316.—VERN. *Vildyti-Mendhi.*

ORDER LVII. MELASTOMACEÆ.

Herbs or shrubs, rarely erect trees, sometimes climbers. Leaves opposite (rarely whorled), simple, equal or unequal, exstipulate, usually petiolate, often 3–11-nerved, the nerves converging from the base towards the apex (rarely penninerved). Flowers regular, hermaphrodite, in spikes, panicles or corymbs, rarely solitary or fascicled. Calyx-tube free or partly or entirely adherent to the ovary by longitudinal septa; limb truncate, 3–6-lobed, or calyptrate. Petals as many as the calyx-lobes, inserted on the mouth of the calyx-limb, sometimes oblique, very rarely cohering at the base, imbricate. Stamens as many or more commonly double as many as the petals and inserted with them (very rarely subindefinite), 1-seriate, the alternate stamens shorter or sometimes rudimentary, rarely all equal; filaments various, glabrous or glandular, inflexed in bud; anthers basifixed, opening at the apex by one or two pores, rarely by slits down the face, the connective sometimes appendaged. Ovary sometimes wholly free, usually variously adherent, 3–6-celled (1-celled in *Memecylon*); ovules numerous (except in *Memecylon*), on axile, parietal or free central placentas; style terminal, usually filiform. Fruit usually enclosed in the calyx-tube, capsular or baccate, breaking up irregularly or by slits through the top of its cells. Seeds many (usually 1 in *Memecylon*); albumen 0; cotyledons small (larger and much folded in *Memecylon*).—DISTRIB. Tropical with a few subtropical, very many in America, a smaller number in Asia, and a much less number in Africa and Polynesia; genera 138; species about 1800.

Seeds numerous.
  Petals 4 or 5.
    Stamens equal or subequal .... 1. OSBECKIA.
    Stamens very unequal .... 2. MELASTOMA.
  Petals 3 .... 3. SONERILA.
Seeds solitary (rarely 2) .... 4. MEMECYLON.

1. OSBECKIA, Linn.

Herbs or shrubs, usually erect and setose; branches commonly 4-gonous. Leaves subcoriaceous, sessile or petiolate, 3–7-nerved, usually quite entire. Flowers terminal, solitary, capitate or paniculate; bracts often forming an involucre. Calyx usually clothed with pectinate scales or stellate hairs; tube ovoid, urceolate or subglobose, sometimes much produced beyond the ovary; lobes 4–5, subulate or lanceolate, deciduous, generally with bristle-pointed teeth alternating with them. Petals 5 (rarely 4), obovate, often ciliate. Stamens twice as many as the petals, equal or subequal; anthers large, obtuse, or attenuated, or peaked, the connective rarely inconspicuously produced below the base, but usually dilated and with 2 tubercles there. Ovary ovoid, $\frac{1}{2}$-inferior, setose at the free vertex, 4-5-celled; ovules numerous in each cell. Capsule included in the calyx-tube and partially adnate to it below, 4–5-valved at the apex. Seeds minute, numerous, cochleate.—DISTRIB. Tropical Asia, Australia, Madagascar, and Tropical Africa; species 51.

Calyx-teeth $\frac{1}{12}$ in.; petals $\frac{1}{8}$–$\frac{1}{6}$ in. long; fruit 8-ribbed .... 1. *O. truncata.*
Calyx-teeth $\frac{1}{8}$–$\frac{1}{6}$ in.; petals $\frac{1}{3}$–$\frac{1}{2}$ in. long; fruit sometimes obscurely many-ribbed .... 2. *O. cupularis.*

1. **Osbeckia truncata,** *Don, in Wight & Arn. Prodr.* (1834) p. 322. Annual, herbaceous, 4–16 in. high; stem simple or more or less branched, 4-gonous, and as well as the branches clothed with long stiff spreading hairs. Leaves $\frac{1}{2}$–$1\frac{1}{4}$ by $\frac{1}{4}$–$\frac{5}{8}$ in., drying yellow, elliptic, subacute, densely clothed on both sides with rather long hairs, 3-nerved, entire or sometimes very slightly serrulate, base subacute; petioles $\frac{1}{12}$–$\frac{1}{8}$ in. long, bristly. Flowers capitate, often with 2 or 4 leaves close under the head; pedicels $\frac{1}{10}$–$\frac{1}{8}$ in. long; bracts ovate, $\frac{1}{12}$ in. long, bristle-ciliate, glabrous on their backs. Calyx $\frac{1}{4}$ in. long, clothed externally with long stellate, intermixed with simple bristly hairs; tube campanulate; teeth erect, $\frac{1}{12}$ in. long, broadly triangular, bristle-ciliate and with a tuft of long spreading bristles springing from an enlarged glandular apex; intermediate teeth scarcely $\frac{1}{30}$ in. long, stout, terete with a tuft of bristles from an enlarged glandular apex. Petals $\frac{1}{8}$–$\frac{1}{6}$ in. long, purple. Ovary with 16–20 bristles at the apex. Fruit ovoid-oblong, 8-ribbed. Fl. B. I. v. 2, p. 514; Wight, Icon. t. 375; Cogniaux, in DC. Monogr. Phan. v. 7, p. 327; Woodr. in Journ. Bomb. Nat. v. 11 (1898) p. 637. *Osbeckia zeylonica*?, Grah. Cat. p. 71 (*not* of Linn.). *Osbeckia Leschenaultiana*, Dalz. & Gibs. p. 92 (*not* of DC.).—Flowers: Oct.–Dec.

KONKAN: *Stocks*!, *Law*!, *Nimmo* ex *Graham*. S. M. COUNTRY: Londa, *Cooke*!, *Woodrow*!; Badami, *Woodrow*!; Rainghát, *Law* ex *Graham*. KANARA: Supa (N. Kanara), *Ritchie*, 1169!; Kála naddi, *Ritchie*; *Dalzell*!—DISTRIB. India (W. Peninsula, Chota Nagpur, East Bengal, Behar).

2. **Osbeckia cupularis,** *Don, in Wight & Arn. Prodr.* (1834) p. 323. Herbaceous, biennial or (not improbably) perennial, 8–20 in. high, branched; root thick, nodose. Stems many, 4-gonous, rather slender, densely clothed with simple appressed long bristly hairs. Leaves drying yellow, 1–$2\frac{1}{4}$ by $\frac{1}{2}$–$1\frac{1}{4}$ in., elliptic or elliptic-oblong, usually entire, 3- (or sometimes 5-) nerved, hairy on both surfaces, base acute or subobtuse; petioles $\frac{3}{16}$–$\frac{1}{4}$ in. long. Flowers 4–5-merous,

subcapitate (sometimes rather laxly arranged), often with 2 or 4 leaves under the head; bracts $\frac{1}{10}$ in. long, ovate, acute, ciliate on the margins and with a long bristle-point at the apex, glabrous on the back. Calyx $\frac{1}{4}$–$\frac{1}{3}$ in. long, densely clothed with stalked stellate long hairs; tube campanulate; teeth $\frac{1}{6}$–$\frac{1}{5}$ in. long, triangular, ciliate and with a tuft of long bristles from the enlarged glandular apex; intermediate teeth $\frac{1}{15}$ in. long, with a tuft of bristles from the enlarged glandular apex. Petals $\frac{1}{4}$–$\frac{1}{2}$ in. long, purple or sometimes white. Fruit ovoid-oblong, sometimes obscurely many-ribbed. Fl. B. I. v. 2, p. 514; Cogniaux, in DC. Monogr. Phan. v. 7, p. 328. *Osbeckia virgata*?, Grah. Cat. p. 71 (*not* of Wight & Arn.). *Osbeckia Leschenaultiana*, Wight, Icon. t. 996 (*not* of D.C.).

KONKAN: *Stocks* ex *Cogniaux* (l. c.).

The occurrence of this plant within the limits of the Bombay Presidency is somewhat doubtful. Cogniaux cites *Stocks* as an authority for its occurrence in the Konkan, but there is no specimen from *Stocks* in Herb. Kew. *Graham* includes in his Catalogue a plant which he calls *O. virgata*, W. & A., the habitat of which is given as S. Konkan on the authority of Nimmo, which may possibly be this plant.—DISTRIB. India (W. Peninsula).

2. **MELASTOMA,** Linn.

Shrubs, usually erect and strigose-hairy. Leaves petiolate, oblong or lanceolate, usually coriaceous and quite entire, 3–7-nerved. Flowers terminal, solitary, fasciculate or panicled, showy, purple, usually 5-merous. Calyx-tube strigose, setose or paleaceous, ovoid or campanulate; lobes deciduous, ovate or lanceolate, usually about as long as the tube and alternating with subulate teeth. Petals equal in number to the calyx-lobes, sometimes pilose on the back. Stamens twice as many as the petals, unequal; those opposite the calyx-lobes longer and with purple anthers, the connective produced below the cells and ending in 2 blunt lobes; those opposite the petals with yellow anthers, the connective not or scarcely produced and ending in 2 blunt tubercles. Ovary ovoid, more or less adnate to the calyx-tube, usually 5-celled, bristly on the apex; ovules numerous; style filiform; stigma obtuse. Berry coriaceous or fleshy, irregularly dehiscent, enclosed in the persistent calyx-tube. Seeds minute, numerous, cochleate.—DISTRIB. Tropical and East Asia, N. Australia, and Polynesia; species about 40.

1. **Melastoma malabathricum,** *Linn. Sp. Pl.* (1753) p. 390. A much-branched shrub sometimes reaching 8 ft. high. Young branches, petioles, and nerves of the leaves beneath densely clothed with appressed flat lanceolate acuminate paleaceous hairs. Leaves somewhat rigid, 2-4$\frac{1}{2}$ by $\frac{5}{8}$–1$\frac{3}{4}$ in., ovate-oblong or lanceolate-oblong, acute, strigose above with appressed thick hairs, softly hairy between the nerves beneath, 5-nerved, the outer nerves fine and close to the margin, base usually rounded; petioles $\frac{3}{8}$–$\frac{1}{2}$ in. long. Flowers in terminal corymbose 1–5-flowered panicles; pedicels about as long as the calyx-tube; bracts $\frac{1}{4}$–$\frac{5}{8}$ in. long, oblong-lanceolate, shortly stalked, clothed on the back with scaly hairs. Calyx clothed all over with silvery lanceolate scaly hairs; tube broadly campanulate; lobes $\frac{3}{8}$ in. long, lanceolate, acute, deciduous; intermediate teeth $\frac{1}{6}$ in. long, subulate, bristle-pointed. Petals $\frac{3}{4}$–1 in. long, obovate, rounded or truncate at the apex, narrowed at the base. Filaments yellow. Anthers alternately yellow and red. Ovary crowned at top with numerous silvery lanceolate hairs about

$\frac{1}{10}$ in. long; style nearly 1 in. long, exceeding the stamens. Fruit $\frac{1}{2}$ in. long, broadly ovoid, truncate, bursting irregularly usually in a circle, and exposing the 5 large purplish-black pulpy placentas covered with numerous minute seeds. Fl. B. I. v. 2, p. 523; Grah. Cat. p. 71; Wight, Ill. t. 95; Dalz. & Gibs. p. 92; Cogniaux, in DC. Monogr. Phan. v. 7, p. 349; Trim. Fl. Ceyl. v. 2, p. 199; Krasser, in Engler & Prantl, Pflanzenf. v. 3, part 7, p. 154, fig. 70, A, B; Talb. Trees, Bomb. ed. 2, p. 172. Woodr. in Journ. Bomb. Nat. v. 11 (1898) p. 637; Watt, Dict. Econ. Prod. v. 5, p. 210.—Flowers: Oct.-Mar. VERN. *Palore.*

KONKAN: *Stocks*!, *Dalzell*!, *Law*!; near Vingorla, *Cooke*!, *Woodrow*! S. M. COUNTRY: Asanwári, *Dr. Lush* ex *Graham*; Ramghát, *Ritchie*, 293! KANARA: N. Kanara in moist forests, often along the banks of nálas near evergreen forests, *Talbot*; Kumpta, *Woodrow*; Siddapur, *Woodrow*.—DISTRIB. Throughout India (except the desert); Ceylon.

The pulp of the fruit is edible, tasting something like a blackberry; it stains the mouth black.

3. SONERILA, Roxb.

Herbs often woody at the base, usually small, sometimes stemless. Leaves usually membranous, equal or dimorphous, entire or serrulate, 3-5-nerved. Flowers in racemes or scorpioid spikes, usually reddish. Calyx glabrous or setose; tube campanulate or funnel-shaped; teeth 3, short, usually deciduous. Petals 3, acute, acuminate, or obtuse. Stamens 3 (very rarely 6); anthers blunt, pointed or rostrate, the cells more or less divergent at the base, not produced below. Ovary adnate to the calyx-tube, 3-celled (the cells alternate with the petals), glabrous at the apex; ovules many; style filiform; stigma truncate or capitate. Capsule included in the calyx-tube, 3-gonous, dehiscing at the apex by 3 valves. Seeds numerous, usually muriculate with minute tubercles.—DISTRIB. India and Malaya with 1 species in S. China; species about 60.

Stem 0; leaves small; seeds small .... 1. *S. scapigera.*
Stem distinct; leaves large; seeds tuberculate .... 2. *S. Rheedei.*

1. **Sonerila scapigera,** *Hook. Lond. Journ. Bot.* v. 7 (1848) p. 672, t. 23. A small glabrous stemless herb 3–4 in. high. Leaves radical, $\frac{7}{8}$–$1\frac{1}{2}$ by $\frac{1}{2}$–1 in., ovate or ovate-oblong, sometimes tinged with purple, obtuse or subacute, minutely crenate-serrate, glabrous on both sides or sometimes minutely glandular-puberulous, base cordate; petioles $1\frac{1}{2}$–$2\frac{1}{2}$ in. long. Flowers 4–10, crowded, subumbellate; flowering scapes 1–3 in. long; pedicels slender, $\frac{1}{8}$–$\frac{1}{3}$ in. long. Calyx $\frac{1}{8}$–$\frac{1}{6}$ in. long, funnel-shaped, obscurely 3-sulcate; teeth short, triangular, acute, deciduous. Petals mauve-colored, $\frac{1}{3}$–$\frac{2}{5}$ in. long, obovate, obliquely acute. Stamens equalling the style; anthers $\frac{1}{8}$–$\frac{1}{6}$ in. long, bright-yellow. Capsule $\frac{1}{6}$–$\frac{1}{8}$ in. long. Seeds without raised points. Fl. B. I. v. 2, p. 538; Dalz. & Gibs. p. 93; Cogniaux, in DC. Monogr. Phan. v. 7, p. 513; Woodr. in Journ. Bomb. Nat. v. 11 (1898) p. 637.—Flowers: July–Aug. The plant was originally described by Hooker (Lond. Journ. Bot. l. c.) and not by Dalzell, as erroneously stated in Fl. B. I. (*l. c.*), a mistake which is followed by Cogniaux and by the 'Index Kewensis.'

KONKAN: *Dalzell*!; North and South Konkan, *Law*!; Ghâts near Bombay, *Dalzell*! DECCAN: Khandala, *Woodrow*!, *Cooke*!—DISTRIB. India (W. Peninsula).

2. **Sonerila Rheedei,** *Wight & Arn. Prodr.* (1834) p. 321 (*not* Wall. Cat. 4096). A small herb 4–6 in. high; stem distinct, quadrangular, sparsely clothed with weak hairs. Leaves 1¼–3 by ⅝–1½ in., ovate, remotely bristle-serrate, often tinged with purple, the upper surface sparsely clothed with short thick bristles, the lower surface paler and usually with minute scaly points, base subcordate or rounded; petioles ½–1½ in. long, usually with a few scattered weak hairs. Flowers 4–8, crowded, subumbellate on terminal or axillary peduncles which are sometimes 2½ in. long; pedicels ⅛–⅙ in. long, hairy. Calyx $\frac{3}{16}$–¼ in. long, hairy; lobes triangular, deciduous. Petals violet, ⅓ in. long, oblong-obovate, acute. Anthers $\frac{3}{16}$ in. long, bright-yellow, subulate, sagittate at the base. Capsule ⅛–⅙ in. long. Seeds with raised points. Grah. Cat. p. 71. *Sonerila Wallichii*, Woodr. in Journ. Bomb. Nat. v. 11 (1898) p. 637.—Flowers: July–Aug.

Triana (Trans. Linn. Soc. v. 28 [1873] p. 77) and, following him, Mr. C. B. Clarke (Hook. f. Fl. B. I. v. 2, p. 538) reduce this plant to *S. Wallichii* (Benn. Pl. Jav. Rar. p. 215) and cite *S. Rheedii*, Wall., 4096, as equivalent to *S. Rheedei*, Wight & Arn. Cogniaux (DC. Monogr. Phan. v. 7, p. 512) follows Mr. Clarke with a query, while the 'Index Kewensis' retains *S. Rheedii* as a separate species, citing both Wall. and Wight & Arn.

The two plants, *S. Rheedei*, Wight & Arn., and *S. Rheedii*, Wall., are, however, quite distinct and belong to different sections, the first having a stem and the latter (*S. Rheedii*, Wall.), which is conspecific with *S. Wallichii*, Benn., and with *S. acaulis*, Bedd. (Trans. Linn. Soc. v. 25 [1866] p. 216), being entirely stemless. *S. Rheedei*, Wight & Arn., should properly take its place in Fl. B. I. after no. 32, *S. maculata*, Roxb., to which it is nearly allied.

KONKAN: S. Konkan, *Nimmo ex Graham*. KANARA: Karwar, *Talbot*, 10!—DISTRIB. India (W. Peninsula).

4. MEMECYLON, Linn.

Trees and shrubs, quite glabrous; branches usually terete. Leaves sessile or shortly petiolate, coriaceous, ovate or oblong, quite entire, usually penninerved. Flowers usually axillary or from below the leaves (rarely terminal), in fascicles, panicles or short umbels, blue or white. Calyx quite glabrous; tube broadly campanulate or hemispheric; limb dilated, truncate or shortly 4-lobed. Petals 4, broadly ovate or orbicular, obtuse or apiculate. Stamens 8, equal; filaments filiform; anthers short, the cells opening by slits, the connective not elongate at the base, thickened at the back, ending in an obtuse spur or horn behind. Ovary inferior, 1-celled, glabrous, the apex convex or depressed; ovules 6–12, whorled about a free central placenta; style filiform; stigma punctiform. Berry globose, umbilicate at the apex, normally 1-seeded. Seed large; embryo involute; cotyledons acute.—DISTRIB. Asia, Australia, Pacific Islands, Tropical Africa; species about 130.

Trees.
  Berries blackish when ripe.
    Branchlets quadrangular, winged .... 1. *M. Wightii*.
    Branchlets terete, not winged.
      Leaves usually cordate at the base, sessile or nearly so. 2. *M. malabaricum*.
      Leaves not cordate, usually attenuate at the base, petiolate .... 3. *M. umbellatum*.
  Berries bright-yellow when ripe .... 4. *M. Talbotianum*.
A small shrub 2–3 ft. high .... 5. *M. terminale*.

1. **Memecylon Wightii,** *Thw. Enum.* (1859) p. 113. A small tree; branchlets slender, quadrangular, winged, the wings broader between each node. Leaves $2\frac{1}{2}$–$4\frac{1}{2}$ by $1\frac{1}{4}$–2 in., sessile or very nearly so, ovate-oblong or lanceolate-oblong, acute or somewhat acuminate, glabrous, thick, shining above, penninerved, base cordate. Flowers crowded, fascicled on tubercles usually on the old wood; peduncles 0; pedicels $\frac{1}{8}$–$\frac{1}{10}$ in. long, slender. Calyx $\frac{1}{16}$ in. long; tube campanulate; limb slightly 4-lobed or almost truncate. Petals blue, obtuse. Berry spherical, $\frac{1}{4}$–$\frac{1}{3}$ in. in diam., conspicuously crowned with the calyx-limb. Fl. B. I. v. 2, p. 554; Cogniaux, in DC. Monogr. Phan. v. 7, p. 1145; Talb. Trees, Bomb. ed. 2, p. 173; Woodr. in Journ. Bomb. Nat. v. 11 (1898) p. 638.—Flowers: Mar. and Sept.

KANARA: N. Kanara in evergreen forests, common in the forests near the Dodmune Ghát, *Talbot*; Mendele, *Ritchie*, 1740!

2. **Memecylon malabaricum,** *Cogniaux, in DC. Monogr. Phan.* v. 7 (1891) p. 1148 (*not* of Kostel). A small tree; branches robust, terete. Leaves 3–5 by 1–$2\frac{1}{2}$ in., oblong or ovate-oblong, acute or subobtuse, coriaceous, glabrous, shining above, amplexicaul or shortly petiolate, cordate or rounded at the base; nerves obscure. Flowers in umbels of 8–12 from the old wood; peduncles short, thickened at the apex and furnished there with numerous bracts below the pedicels; pedicels filiform, $\frac{1}{10}$–$\frac{1}{6}$ in. long. Calyx $\frac{1}{10}$ in. long and about as broad across the mouth when fully expanded; tube campanulate or subhemispheric, about $\frac{1}{20}$ in. long; limb saucer-shaped, subtruncate. Petals $\frac{1}{10}$ in. long, suborbicular, blue? Berry spherical, $\frac{1}{4}$–$\frac{1}{3}$ in. in diam., conspicuously crowned by the calyx-limb, blackish. Brandis, in Talb. Trees, Bomb. ed. 2 (Appendix). *Memecylon amplexicaule*, var. *malabarica*, C. B. Clarke, in Hook. f. Fl. B. I. v. 2, p. 560; Talb. Trees, Bomb. ed. 2, p. 173.—Flowers: May. VERN. *Limba*; *Limtoli*.

KANARA: Supa Ghâts of N. Kanara, *Talbot*!; Sampkhand, *Talbot*, 3689!; Yellapur Ghâts, *Talbot*.—DISTRIB. India (W. Peninsula).

3. **Memecylon umbellatum,** *Burm. Fl. Ind.* (1768) p. 87. A small tree; young branches terete, pale when dry. Leaves $1\frac{1}{2}$–3 by $\frac{5}{8}$–$1\frac{1}{2}$ in., elliptic or ovate, subacute or shortly and bluntly acuminate, glabrous, dark green and polished above, paler beneath, usually attenuated but sometimes rounded at the base, margins slightly revolute; midrib prominent; lateral nerves obscure; petioles $\frac{1}{10}$–$\frac{1}{8}$ in. long. Flowers numerous, in umbellate cymes from the axils of the fallen leaves on the old wood; peduncles several together, $\frac{1}{8}$–$\frac{3}{8}$ in. long, elongating in fruit; ultimate pedicels $\frac{1}{10}$–$\frac{1}{8}$ in. long, very slender; buds pyriform. Calyx $\frac{1}{10}$ in. long, campanulate before expansion (saucer-shaped when expanded), $\frac{1}{8}$ in. across the mouth when flowering; limb truncate or 4-toothed; teeth, when present, small, triangular. Disk without or with very faint rays. Berry globose, $\frac{1}{4}$ in. in diam., purplish-black, crowned, though rather inconspicuously, with the calyx-limb, 1- (less commonly 2-) seeded. Trim. Fl. Ceyl. v. 2, p. 216; Brandis, in Talb. Trees, Bomb. ed. 2 (Appendix). *Memecylon edule*, Roxb. Cor. Pl. v. 1 (1795) p. 59, t. 82; C. B. Clarke, in Hook. f. Fl. B. I. v. 2, p. 563; Dalz. & Gibs. p. 93; Cogniaux, in DC. Monogr. Phan. v. 7, p. 1155; Talb. Trees, Bomb. ed. 2, p. 174; Woodr. in Journ. Bomb. Nat. v. 11 (1898) p. 638; Watt, Dict. Econ. Prod. v. 5, p. 226. *M. tinctorium*,

Kœn. ex W. & A. Prodr. p. 319; Wight, Ill. t. 93; Grah. Cat. p. 71.—Flowers: Jan.–Mar. VERN. *Anjan.*

Roxburgh (*l. c.*) and Dalzell & Gibson (*l. c.*) notice the occurrence of 2 seeds. I can fully endorse this, as I have examined a large number of berries in the fresh state at Mahableshwar and frequently found them 2-seeded.

Burmann named the plant *M. umbellatum* in 1768, merely describing the leaves as ovate and the flowers as umbellate, but quoting the description of the elder Burmann (Thes. Zeyl. p. 76, t. 31). Roxburgh's name *M. edule* dates from 1795, and as the names are admittedly synonymous, the older name should have the preference.

Very common at Mahableshwar and Matheran, where it is called the *Ironwood Tree.* KONKAN: *Stocks*!; Matheran, *Cooke*! DECCAN: Mahableshwar, *Cooke*!; Khandala, *Nene*!; Lanoli, *Woodrow*! S. M. COUNTRY: Ramghát, *Ritchie*, 292! KANARA: *Law*!, *Mrs. Ward*, 118!; moist evergreen forests of N. Kanara, *Talbot.*—DISTRIB. India (E. & W. Peninsulas); Ceylon, Malaya.

VAR. *capitellata*, C. B. Clarke, in Hook. f. Fl. B. I. v. 2, p. 564 (exclud. syn.); peduncles more elongated, sometimes 1 in. long.

KONKAN: *Stocks*!

4. **Memecylon Talbotianum,** *Brandis, in Talb. Trees, Bomb.* ed. 2 (1902) (*Appendix*). A large shrub or small tree; branchlets terete, slightly quadrangular just below the nodes. Leaves 2–4 by 1–2 in., thickly coriaceous, elliptic, shortly and obtusely acuminate, margins slightly revolute, base acute; main nerves obscure; petioles $\frac{1}{4}$ in. long. Flowers small, sessile, few, in compact clusters, on bracteate, nearly sessile tubercles in the axils of present and former leaves; buds pyriform. Calyx $\frac{1}{10}$ in. long; tube campanulate; limb 4-lobed; teeth triangular. Petals $\frac{1}{16}$ in. long, orbicular, blue. Berry globose, $\frac{1}{4}$ in. in diam., yellow. —Flowers: Mar.–Apr.

The colour of the berry serves to distinguish this plant readily from *M. umbellatum.*

KONKAN: *Stocks*! DECCAN: hills near Mahableshwar, *Cooke, Brandis.* KANARA: Tinai (N. Kanara), *Ritchie*, 1738!; Bunwasi (N. Kanara), *Talbot*, 3658!, 3568!

5. **Memecylon terminale,** *Dalz. in Kew Journ. Bot.* v. 3 (1851) p. 121. A shrub 2–3 ft. high; branches dichotomous, very slender, terete or somewhat 4-gonous, smooth. Leaves subsessile, $1\frac{1}{2}$–3 by $\frac{1}{2}$–$1\frac{1}{2}$ in., ovate, ovate-oblong or ovate-lanceolate, very acute or acuminate, glabrous, obscurely penninerved, base cordate. Flowers in axillary and terminal umbels; peduncles $\frac{1}{2}$–$1\frac{1}{8}$ in. long, 1–3 together from the same point, very slender; pedicels $\frac{1}{4}$–$\frac{3}{8}$ in. long, filiform. Calyx $\frac{1}{8}$ in. across the mouth when fully expanded; tube very short, campanulate; limb saucer-shaped, truncate. Petals blue, $\frac{1}{10}$ in. long, ovate, obtuse. Berry globose, $\frac{1}{3}$ in. in diam., the areole at the apex about $\frac{1}{8}$ in. in diam. Fl. B. I. v. 2, p. 558; Dalz. & Gibs. p. 93; Cogniaux, in DC. Monogr. Phan. v. 7, p. 1163; Talb. Trees, Bomb. ed. 2, p. 173; Woodr. in Journ. Bomb. Nat. v. 11 (1898) p. 638. *M. amabile*, Bedd. Icon. Pl. Ind. Or. t. 163.—Flowers: Dec.–Feb.

I think that *M. amabile*, Bedd., from S. Kanara, should be included under the above. There is only one specimen of that plant in Herb. Kew.

KANARA: evergreen forests of N. Kanara from Ainshi southwards, *Talbot*; W. Ghâts southwards, *Woodrow*; Southern Ghâts, *Dalzell*!, *Gibson*!

ORDER LVIII. LYTHRACEÆ.

Trees, shrubs, or herbs; branches often 4-gonous. Leaves entire, usually opposite, sometimes alternate or whorled; stipules 0. Flowers hermaphrodite, usually regular, cymose or paniculate. Calyx usually free, persistent; primary teeth or lobes 3-6, with sometimes as many accessory teeth added, valvate. Petals as many as the primary teeth of the calyx, rarely fewer or 0. Stamens definite or indefinite, inserted at various heights on the calyx-tube. Ovary superior (rarely inferior), 1-6-celled; ovules many, placentas axile, rarely parietal; style usually filiform; stigma capitate, rarely 2-lobed. Fruit capsular or baccate, membranous or coriaceous, girt round the base by the calyx or entirely included in it (or rarely surmounted by it), 2-6-celled or, by the imperfection of the partitions, 1-celled, variously dehiscent (rarely indehiscent). Seeds numerous, sometimes winged; albumen 0; embryo usually straight; cotyledons usually oblong or orbicular, flat, 2-auricled at the base and with a short radicle.—DISTRIB. Chiefly tropical; genera 30; species about 275.

Herbs .... 1. AMMANNIA.
Shrubs or trees.
  Stamens 12............ 2. WOODFORDIA.
  Stamens 8 .... 3. LAWSONIA.
  Stamens indefinite.
    Fruit a 3-6-celled, 3-6-valved capsule .... 4. LAGERSTRŒMIA.
    Fruit a many-celled indehiscent berry .... 5. SONNERATIA.

1. AMMANNIA, Linn.

Annual usually glabrous herbs; stem usually 4-gonous. Leaves entire, opposite (rarely alternate) or whorled; stipules 0. Flowers small, axillary, solitary and subsessile, or in small trichotomous cymes; bracteoles usually 2. Calyx more or less deeply campanulate; teeth 3-7, often with intermediate teeth or folds. Petals 3-7 or 0, inserted between the calyx-teeth. Stamens 2-8, inserted in the middle of the calyx-tube; filaments filiform. Ovary superior, 1-5-celled, the septa often becoming absorbed; ovules very numerous, placentas axile; style filiform, exserted; stigma capitate. Capsule membranous, enclosed in (though free from) the persistent calyx, globose or ellipsoid, 1-5-celled, dehiscing by valves or irregularly breaking up or circumsciss. Seeds minute, very numerous.—DISTRIB. Marshy and moist places in the Tropics and warmer regions of the world; species 30.

Capsule 2-valved.
  Flowers axillary, solitary............ 1. *A. peploides.*
  Flowers in terminal spicate racemes.
    Leaves opposite .... 2. *A. tenuis.*
    Leaves alternate .... 3. *A. floribunda.*
Capsule 3-valved.
  Leaves in whorls of 3-6 .... 4. *A. Rotala.*
  Leaves in opposite pairs .... 5. *A. pentandra.*
Capsule 4-valved.
  Flowers axillary, solitary; leaves elliptic .... 6. *A. Ritchiei.*
  Flowers in terminal spicate racemes; leaves orbicular ...... 7. *A. rotundifolia.*
Capsule circumsciss or bursting irregularly.
  Capsule wholly covered by the calyx.
    Calyx distinctly 4-winged .... 8. *A. octandra.*

Capsule not wholly covered by the calyx.
  Calyx striate with 8 vertical lines .... 9. *A. multiflora.*
  Calyx not striate with vertical lines.
    Leaves narrowed at the base .... 10. *A. baccifera.*
    Leaves rounded or cordate at the base .... 11. *A. salicifolia.*

1. **Ammannia peploides,** *Spreng. Syst. Veg.* v. 1 (1825) p. 444. Stems 3-12 in., usually decumbent at the base and rooting at the lower nodes; branches ascending, 4-gonous. Leaves opposite; those on the main stem $\frac{1}{2}$-$\frac{3}{4}$ by $\frac{1}{4}$-$\frac{3}{8}$ in., sessile or nearly so, elliptic-spathulate, rounded at the apex, narrowed at the base, the midrib and lateral nerves prominent beneath; the leaves on the floriferous branches much smaller, linear-oblong, bract-like. Flowers very small, solitary in the axils of reduced leaves which are more or less approximated so that the branchlets appear like spikes; bracteoles 2, linear, acute, scarious, $\frac{1}{20}$ in. long. Calyx campanulate, $\frac{1}{10}$ in. long; teeth 4, acutely triangular; accessory teeth minute or 0. Petals 4, very small or 0. Stamens 4. Capsule ellipsoid, longer than broad, opening by 2 valves from the apex. Seeds very minute, narrowly ellipsoid, red. Fl. B. I. v. 2, p. 566; Trim. Fl. Ceyl. v. 2, p. 223; Woodr. in Journ. Bomb. Nat. v. 11 (1898) p. 638. *Ameletia indica*, DC. in Mém. Soc. Hist. Nat. Genèv. v. 3 (1825) part 2, p. 82; Dalz. & Gibs. p. 96.—Flowers: Nov.–Jan.

A common weed in wet places. KONKAN: Malwán, in rice-fields, *Woodrow.* GUJARAT: Surat, *Kanitkar,* 48!; Chikli near Surat, *Bhiva*!—DISTRIB. Throughout India in rice-fields and damp places; Ceylon, Malaya, Philippines, China, Afghanistan, Persia.

2. **Ammannia tenuis,** *C. B. Clarke, in Hook. f. Fl. B. I.* v. 2 (1879) p. 567. Stems often numerous, cæspitose, somewhat procumbent at the base, afterwards erect, simple, 3–4 in. long, or sometimes very compound, reaching 8–10 in. long, very slender (almost filiform), terete, shining, red. Leaves opposite, subsessile, broadly ovate or elliptic (the lower sometimes orbicular), obtuse or acute; lateral nerves inconspicuous. Flowers in dense terminal slender racemes (almost spikes) $\frac{1}{2}$–1 in. long on filiform peduncles; pedicels very short; bracts 1 to each flower, $\frac{1}{10}$–$\frac{1}{8}$ in. long, oblong-lanceolate, acute; bracteoles $\frac{1}{10}$ in. long, linear-lanceolate, acute, herbaceous. Calyx $\frac{1}{10}$–$\frac{1}{8}$ in. long, urceolate-campanulate, constricted at the top of the tube below the teeth; teeth $\frac{1}{30}$ in. long, triangular, acute; accessory teeth 0. Petals obovate, as long as the calyx-teeth, pink. Capsule narrowly ellipsoid, much longer than broad. Seeds narrowly ellipsoid, pink or yellow. Woodr. in Journ. Bomb. Nat. v. 11 (1898) p. 638. *Ameletia tenuis*, Wight, Icon. t. 257; Dalz. & Gibs. p. 96.—Flowers: Oct.–Dec.

KONKAN: in beds of rivers, *Law*!, *Woodrow*!; Sayu, *Gangaram*!; banks of Pen river, not common, *Dalzell & Gibson.* DECCAN: Kolapur, *Ritchie,* 1068! GUJARAT: Dangs, on rocks, *Woodrow,* 19! S. M. COUNTRY: Belgaum hills, *Ritchie,* 1068!—DISTRIB. India (Behar, Central India, E. Bengal, W. Peninsula).

3. **Ammannia floribunda,** *C. B. Clarke, in Hook. f. Fl. B. I.* v. 2 (1879) p. 567. Erect or shortly creeping at the base, 6–15 in. high; stems reddish, often much branched, the lower portion more or less angular, the upper terete and very slender. Leaves alternate, sessile, 1-nerved; the lower 1–2 by $\frac{1}{12}$–$\frac{1}{6}$ in., oblong, obtuse or acute; the upper $\frac{1}{4}$-$\frac{1}{2}$ in. long, often only $\frac{1}{25}$ in. broad, narrow-linear, acute. Flowers

dimorphic, in dense terminal racemes (almost spikes), $\frac{1}{3}$–$\frac{1}{2}$ in. long, on long filiform peduncles; pedicels very short; bracts 1 to each flower, $\frac{1}{8}$–$\frac{1}{5}$ in. long, linear-lanceolate, acute, 1-nerved; bracteoles $\frac{1}{12}$ in. long, linear, acute, herbaceous, 1-nerved. Calyx $\frac{1}{10}$–$\frac{1}{8}$ in. long; tube elongate-campanulate; teeth 4, triangular, acute, $\frac{1}{20}$ in. long; accessory teeth 0. Petals $\frac{1}{12}$ in. long, oblong-obovate, bright rose-colored. Stamens and style of 2 kinds, the flowers having either long exserted stamens and a short included style, or a long exserted style and stamens not exserted beyond the calyx; stamens 4. Stigma 2-lobed, the lobes $\frac{1}{80}$ in. long, papillose. Capsule ellipsoid, 2-valved, much longer than broad. Seeds ellipsoid, brown-yellow. Woodr. in Journ. Bomb. Nat. v. 11 (1898) p. 638. *Ameletia floribunda*, Wight, Ill. p. 206; Dalz. & Gibs. p. 96. *Nimmoia floribunda*, Wight, in Madr. Journ. Lit. & Science, v. 5 (1837) p. 312, t. 20. *Nimmonia floribunda*, Grah. Cat. p. 83.—Flowers: Dec.–Jan.

Bare rocky ground on the highest Ghâts, *Dalzell & Gibson*. DECCAN: Mahableshwar, *H. M. Birdwood, Cooke*!, *Woodrow*!, *Dalzell*!, *Law*!—DISTRIB. Apparently endemic on the hills of the Bombay Presidency.

The plant is very common in Mahableshwar, where it is known as the "Mahableshwar heather."—It grows in large dense patches on the bare damp rocks.

4. **Ammannia Rotala,** *F. Mueller, Fragm.* v. 3 (1862–63) p. 108. Stems 3–6 in., often procumbent and rooting at the very base, then erect, slightly branched, more or less striate. Leaves sessile, $\frac{1}{4}$–$\frac{3}{8}$ by $\frac{1}{30}$–$\frac{1}{16}$ in., in whorls of 4–8, linear, truncate or bifid at the apex, 1-nerved. Flowers 3–4-merous, sessile, in axillary whorls, 1 flower in the axil of each leaf, the lower whorls distant, the upper approximated. Calyx tubular, very thin, slightly constricted at the mouth; teeth 3–4, small, erect, triangular, acute. Petals usually 3 (rarely 4), small, fugacious or 0, when present rose-colored. Stamens 3. Ovary 3-celled. Capsule ellipsoid, nearly as broad as long, 3-valved. Seeds $\frac{1}{2}$-obovoid, yellowish-brown, the plane face often excavated. Fl. B. I. v. 2, p. 567; Trim. Fl. Ceyl. v. 2, p. 224. *Rotala verticillaris*, Linn. Mantiss. v. 2 (1771) p. 175; Wight, Icon. t. 260, A; Grah. Cat. p. 67; Dalz. & Gibs. p. 96.—Flowers: Dec.

KONKAN: *Law*! KANARA: Halihal, *Talbot* ex *Woodrow*.—DISTRIB. India (W. Peninsula); Ceylon, Australia, Tropical Africa.

5. **Ammannia pentandra,** *Roxb. Fl. Ind.* v. 1 (1832) p. 427. Stem stout, 4-gonous, rooting at the base, 3–12 in. long, with numerous 4-gonous opposite slender branches covered with flowers. Leaves opposite; those on the stem $\frac{1}{2}$–$\frac{3}{4}$ by $\frac{1}{4}$–$\frac{3}{16}$ in., sessile, oblong, obtuse or subacute, sometimes rounded at the base; those on the branches smaller and bract-like. Flowers sessile, solitary in the axils of nearly horizontal floral leaves (bracts), 1 flower to each bract, the lower whorls of flowers distant, the upper approximate, almost spicate; bracteoles subulate, as long as or longer than the calyx. Calyx shortly campanulate, $\frac{1}{8}$–$\frac{1}{10}$ in. long, very slightly longer than broad, semiglobose in fruit; teeth usually 5, small, triangular, very acute; accessory teeth longer than the primary, subulate. Petals 5, small, fugacious. Stamens 5. Capsule subglobose, 3-valved. Seeds hemispheric or broadly $\frac{1}{2}$-ellipsoid. Fl. B. I. v. 2, p. 568; Trim. Fl. Ceyl. v. 2, p. 224; Woodr. in Journ. Bomb. Nat. v. 11 (1898) p. 638.—Flowers: Aug.

KONKAN: Malwán, *Woodrow*; road Poladpur to Wada, *Kanitkar*!, *Woodrow*! DECCAN: Panchgani, *Cooke*! S. M. COUNTRY: Belgaum, *Ritchie*, 1750!; Londa, *Woodrow*. KANARA: on the Kála naddi, *Ritchie*, 1185!—DISTRIB. Throughout Tropical India in moist places, common; Ceylon, China, Malaya, Australia, Tropical Africa.

6. **Ammannia Ritchiei,** *C. B. Clarke, in Hook. f. Fl. B. I.* v. 2 (1879) p. 566. Stem 6–12 in. long, 4-gonous, creeping and rooting. Leaves opposite, the cauline $\frac{3}{8}$–$\frac{1}{2}$ by $\frac{3}{16}$–$\frac{1}{4}$ in., sessile, elliptic-oblong, rounded at the apex, not conspicuously nerved. Flowers solitary in each axil; pedicels $\frac{1}{20}$ in. long or less. Calyx $\frac{1}{10}$ in. long, tubular-campanulate; teeth 4, minute, the accessory teeth rather larger than the primary ones. Petals 4, ovate or obovate, longer than the calyx-teeth, pale rose-colored. Stamens 4, included. Style short. Capsule ellipsoid, included in the calyx, 4-valved. Seeds $\frac{1}{2}$-ellipsoid, brown. Woodr. in Journ. Bomb. Nat. v. 11 (1898) p. 638.—Flowers: Oct.

Belgaum in rice-fields, *Ritchie*, 1184! A very rare plant.

7. **Ammannia rotundifolia,** *Buch.-Ham. in D. Don, Prodr. Fl. Nep.* (1825) p. 220. Stems 4-gonous, creeping and rooting at the base, then ascending, leafy, 4–6 in. long. Leaves $\frac{1}{2}$–$\frac{5}{8}$ in. in diam., opposite, sessile or nearly so, orbicular or broadly obovate, strongly nerved beneath. Inflorescence in peduncled cylindric racemes (almost spikes), 1–8 (very commonly 3) together, forming a kind of terminal thyrsus; pedicels very short, scarcely more than $\frac{1}{30}$ in. long; flowers crowded towards the apex of the raceme, often lax towards its base; bracts cordate, orbicular, acute, sessile, about $\frac{1}{10}$ in. in diam., adnate to the pedicel by a short claw; bracteoles minute, linear-lanceolate, acute, scarious. Calyx $\frac{1}{12}$ in. long; lobes more or less unequal, triangular, acute, almost equalling the tube; accessory teeth 0. Petals $\frac{1}{18}$ in. long, obovate-spathulate, bright rose-colored. Capsule 4-valved, ellipsoid, slightly longer than broad. Seeds brownish-yellow, ellipsoid. Fl. B. I. v. 2, p. 566; Woodr. in Journ. Bomb. Nat. v. 11 (1898) p. 638. *Ameletia rotundifolia*, Wight, Icon. t. 258; Dalz. & Gibs. p. 96.—Flowers: Nov.

KONKAN: Sáwantwári in rice-fields, *Kanitkar*!, *Woodrow*!; Malwán, *Woodrow*. S. M. COUNTRY: Belgaum, *Ritchie*, 1069!—DISTRIB. Throughout the plains of India in damp localities; China, Formosa.

8. **Ammannia octandra,** *Linn. f. Suppl.* (1781) p. 127. Stem 6–36 in. high, erect, stiff, the upper part 4-gonous, the lower part subterete and often woody; branches numerous, sharply quadrangular. Leaves sessile, linear-lanceolate, tapering to an acute apex, subauriculate at the base, those of the stem $1\frac{1}{2}$–$2\frac{1}{2}$ by $\frac{1}{16}$–$\frac{3}{16}$ in., those of the branches smaller. Flowers in short-peduncled usually 3-flowered cymes; peduncles scabrous; pedicels short. Calyx $\frac{1}{8}$–$\frac{1}{4}$ in. long, campanulate, quadrangular, the angles winged and minutely serrulate, the faces between the wings furnished with a distinct rib in the middle of each face; mouth nearly truncate or with 4 very short teeth; accessory teeth short, horn-like, spreading. Petals 4, broadly obovate, $\frac{1}{8}$–$\frac{1}{6}$ in. long, irregularly crenulate, rose-colored, veined. Stamens 8, exserted; filaments dark-red. Capsule enclosed in the calyx and about equalling it, globose-ellipsoid. Seeds $\frac{1}{2}$-ovoid. Fl. B. I. v. 2, p. 571; Dalz. & Gibs. p. 97; Roxb. Cor. Pl. v. 2, p. 18, t. 133; Trim. Fl. Ceyl. v. 2, p. 225.

This plant is given as occurring in Bombay on the authority of *Dalzell & Gibson* (*l. c.*). I have seen no Bombay specimens, nor are there any in Herb. Kew.

9. **Ammannia multiflora,** *Roxb. Hort. Beng.* (1814) p. 11. Stem erect, 6–24 in. high, 4-gonous or sometimes almost 4-winged, more or less terete at the very base; branches numerous, slender, acutely quadrangular. Leaves opposite, sessile, linear-oblong or (rarely) elliptic-oblong, dilated and subauriculate at the base, the leaves on the stem $\frac{7}{8}$–$1\frac{1}{4}$ by $\frac{1}{8}$–$\frac{1}{4}$ in., those on the branches smaller. Flowers axillary, solitary, or in peduncled 3–many-flowered simple or compound cymes; peduncles and pedicels very slender, somewhat variable in length; bracts beneath the branches of the cyme linear, acute, $\frac{1}{30}$–$\frac{1}{20}$ in. long. Calyx $\frac{1}{20}$–$\frac{1}{16}$ in. long, campanulate or often hemispheric, marked with 8 faint vertical lines (scarcely ribs); teeth 4, shortly triangular, much shorter than the calyx-tube. Petals 4, obovate, about $\frac{1}{40}$ in. long, violet, very caducous, often wanting. Capsules globose, not wholly covered by the calyx, usually red. Seeds broadly $\frac{1}{2}$-obovoid, almost pointed at one end, excavated on the plane face. Fl. B. I. v. 2, p. 570; Dalz. & Gibs. p. 97; Woodr. in Journ. Bomb. Nat. v. 11 (1898) p. 638.—Flowers: Nov.

KONKAN: *Stocks!* DECCAN: in water-holes, *Dalzell & Gibson*; Kelgaon near Poona, *Woodrow!* S. M. COUNTRY: Belgaum, *Ritchie*, 1063!—DISTRIB. Throughout the plains of India; Afghanistan, Persia, Australia.

10. **Ammannia baccifera,** *Linn. Sp. Pl.* (1753) p. 120. Glabrous, 6–24 in. high; stems erect, 4-gonous, often with numerous horizontal or ascending branches which gradually become shorter towards the summit. Leaves opposite (rarely alternate), $\frac{3}{4}$–$2\frac{1}{2}$ by $\frac{1}{8}$–$\frac{3}{8}$ in., sessile, linear-oblong or oblong-lanceolate, subacute or obtuse, much narrowed at the base. Flowers in dense axillary clusters or in loose but very short cymes, forming whorls in the axils; bracts filiform, shorter than the pedicels. Calyx $\frac{1}{20}$–$\frac{1}{16}$ in. long; tube hemispheric; teeth 4 (rarely 5), short, broadly triangular, acute; accessory teeth inconspicuous. Petals 0 or minute. Capsule depressed, globose, red, irregularly circumsciss above the middle, not wholly covered by the calyx. Seeds subhemispheric, excavated on the plane face. Fl. B. I. v. 2, p. 569; Dalz. & Gibs. p. 97; Trim. Fl. Ceyl. v. 2, p. 224; Woodr. in Journ. Bomb. Nat. v. 11 (1898) p. 638; Watt, Dict. Econ. Prod. v. 1, p. 218. *Ammannia vesicatoria*, Roxb. Hort. Beng. (1814) p. 11; Grah. Cat. p. 67. —Flowers: Nov.—VERN. *Bhár-Jámbhal.*

Tolerably common in moist places. KONKAN: *Law!*; Salsette, *Graham*. DECCAN: margin of Páshan tank near Poona, *Woodrow!* GUJARAT: Surat, *Kanitkar!*, *Woodrow!* KANARA: Kála naddi, *Ritchie*, 1067! SIND: Mulir, near Karachi, *Woodrow*.—DISTRIB. Throughout India in moist places; Ceylon, Afghanistan, Malaya, China, Australia, Tropical Africa.

The plant has a strong muriatic but not disagreeable odor. Its leaves are used by the natives to raise blisters, for which purpose they are very efficacious, but cause much more pain than cantharides. See Watt, Dict. Econ. Prod. l. c.

11. **Ammannia salicifolia,** *Monti, in Comm. Bonon.* v. 1 (1767) p. 112. Stem erect, sometimes reaching 3 ft. high, purple, smooth, 4-gonous in the upper part, almost terete in the lower. Leaves opposite, sessile, oblong-lanceolate, obtuse or subacute, rounded or often cordate at the base, those on the stem $1\frac{1}{8}$–$2\frac{1}{2}$ by $\frac{1}{8}$–$\frac{1}{2}$ in., those on the branches $\frac{1}{4}$–1 by $\frac{1}{10}$–$\frac{3}{16}$ in. Flowers numerous, densely clustered in the axils in almost sessile cymes; pedicels very short. Calyx $\frac{1}{20}$–$\frac{1}{16}$ in. long, sub-

hemispheric; teeth about as long as the tube, broadly triangular, very acute; accessory teeth inconspicuous. Petals 0 or minute. Capsule not wholly covered by the calyx, globose, red, irregularly circumsciss. Seeds ½-obovoid, excavated on the plane face, much smaller at one end than the other, yellowish-brown.—Flowers: Nov.

May be distinguished from *A. baccifera* by the leaves which are rounded or cordate at the base, those of *A. baccifera* being attenuated. Fl. B. I. v. 2, p. 569; Dalz. & Gibs. p. 97; Woodr. in Journ. Bomb. Nat. v. 11 (1898) p. 638. *A. verticillata*, Lamk. Encyc. Méthod. v. 1 (1783) p. 131, & Ill. t. 77, f. 3 (*not* of Wight).

KONKAN: *Dalzell*!, *Stocks*!; Malwán, *Dalzell & Gibson*. DECCAN: Kelgaon near Poona, *Bhiva*!, *Woodrow*! S. M. COUNTRY: Belgaum, *Ritchie*, 268! SIND: *Woodrow*! —DISTRIB. Generally throughout India; Tropical Africa.

2. WOODFORDIA, Salisb.

Shrubs, often arborescent; younger branches quadrangular, more or less tomentose, the older terete or compressed beneath the nodes, glabrate. Leaves decussate, more or less coriaceous, nigro-punctate beneath, penninerved and reticulately veined. Flowers in paniculate cymes, on axillary peduncles, rarely solitary; pedicels bracteate at or near the base. Calyx tubular, the limb sometimes dilated, more or less contracted above the fruit; teeth 6, short, with as many minute accessory teeth. Petals 6, minute, or 0. Stamens 12, inserted near the bottom of the calyx-tube, much exserted, the alternate ones longer; filaments filiform; anthers broadly ovate or subrotund. Ovary sessile, cylindric, 2-celled (sometimes incompletely so); ovules numerous, minute, inserted on thick placentas adnate to the axis of the ovary; style filiform, longer than the ovary, slightly longer than the stamens, sometimes narrowed at the apex; stigma punctiform. Capsule covered by the calyx, ellipsoid, often splitting the calyx, thinly membranous, often bursting irregularly. Seeds small, narrowly cuneate-obovoid.—DISTRIB. India, China, Tropical Africa, Madagascar; species 2.

1. **Woodfordia floribunda,** *Salisb. Parad. Lond.* (1806) t. 42. A straggling leafy shrub reaching 12 ft. high; branches long, spreading; bark smooth, cinnamon-brown, peeling off in fibres; young shoots terete, often clothed with fine white pubescence. Leaves 2–3½ by ½–1 in., opposite or subopposite, sometimes in whorls of 3 (*Brandis*), sessile, ovate-lanceolate, acute, softly velvety above, usually hoary and always nigro-punctate beneath, base rounded or cordate; main nerves 6–12 pairs, arcuate, prominent beneath, uniting in a distinct intramarginal nerve. Flowers numerous, in short 2–15- (rarely 1-) flowered cymes from the axils of former, less commonly of present leaves; pedicels short, glandular-pubescent. Calyx ⅝ in. long, striate, covered with glandular dots, with a small campanulate base and a long slightly curved bright-red tube which is slightly contracted above the included capsule; mouth oblique; teeth about $\frac{1}{10}$ in. long, triangular, acute. Petals slightly longer than the calyx-teeth, narrowly linear, produced at the apex to a long fine point. Capsule ⅜ in. long, usually splitting the calyx near the base, irregularly dehiscent. Seeds cuneate-obovoid, brown, smooth. Fl. B. I. v. 2, p. 572 (exclud. syn. *Grislea uniflora*, Rich., and *Grislea*

micropetala, Hochst. & Steud.); Trim. Fl. Ceyl. v. 2, p. 226; Talb. Trees, Bomb. ed. 2, p. 174; Watt, Dict. Econ. Prod. v. 6, part 4, p. 312. *Grislea tomentosa*, Roxb. Cor. Pl. v. 1 (1795) p. 29, t. 31; Grah. Cat. p. 67; Dalz. & Gibs. p. 97. *Woodfordia tomentosa*, Bedd. For. Man. in Flor. Sylvat. p. cxvii, t. 14, fig. 4.—Flowers: Dec.–May. VERN. *Dhauri*; *Dhdyati*. The plant is trimorphic like *Lythrum Salicaria*.

DECCAN: Deccan hills widely, *Woodrow*; Poona, *Kusha*!; Poona near the river *Cooke*!; Khandesh, abundant, *Graham*. KANARA: N. Kanara near the sea-coast *Talbot*.—DISTRIB. Throughout India; Ceylon, Beluchistan, Tropical Africa, Madagascar, China, Japan, Sumatra, Java.

The leaves supply an excellent and largely used tanning material. The flowers also contain much tannin and are used throughout India as a dye. See Watt, Dict. Econ. Prod. l. c.

Grislea uniflora, Rich. (in union with *Grislea multiflora*, Rich.), has been made a separate species, viz. *Woodfordia uniflora*, Kœhne (Monogr. Lythr. in Engl. Jahrb. v. 1 (1881) p. 334), with which, according to Kœhne (*l. c.*), *Grislea micropetala*, Hochst. & Steud., is synonymous.

3. LAWSONIA, Linn.

A glabrous shrub; younger branches sometimes 4-gonous, the older terete, often spinescent. Leaves opposite, shortly petiolate, ovate-lanceolate, entire. Flowers in terminal panicled cymes. Calyx-tube short; lobes 4, spreading, broadly ovate; accessory teeth 0. Petals 4, very shortly clawed, inserted at the top of the calyx-tube. Stamens 8 (rarely 4), inserted at the base of the calyx-tube in pairs opposite the calyx-lobes; anthers broadly oblong, the connective thick. Ovary subglobose, 2–4-celled; ovules many, placentas axile; style thick, slightly longer than the stamens; stigma capitate. Capsule globose, stalked in the base of the calyx-tube, coriaceous, irregularly breaking up, ultimately 1-celled. Seeds closely packed on a central placenta, angular, pyramidal. —DISTRIB. Asia (probably); cultivated in many tropical and subtropical countries; species 1.

1. **Lawsonia inermis,** *Linn. Sp. Pl.* (1753) p. 349 (*charac. ampl.*). A glabrous much-branched shrub; lateral branches 4-gonous, often ending in a spinous point. Leaves $\frac{1}{2}$–$1\frac{1}{4}$ by $\frac{1}{4}$–$\frac{5}{8}$ in., elliptic or broadly lanceolate, acute or obtuse, often mucronulate, base tapering; petioles very short or 0. Flowers numerous, less than $\frac{1}{2}$ in. across, fragrant, white or rose-colored, in large terminal pyramidal panicled cymes; pedicels short, slender. Calyx $\frac{1}{8}$–$\frac{1}{6}$ in. long, broadly campanulate; lobes $\frac{1}{10}$–$\frac{1}{8}$ in. long, ovate, acute. Petals $\frac{1}{8}$ in. long, as broad as long, suborbicular or subreniform, undulate. Stamens 8, inserted in pairs on the calyx-tube. Capsule $\frac{1}{4}$ in. in diam., globose, slightly veined outside, supported by the persistent calyx and tipped with the style. Seeds trigono-pyramidal, about $\frac{1}{10}$ in. long, externally subtuberculate. Kœhne, in Engl. Bot. Jahrb. v. 4 (1883) p. 36, & in Engl. & Prantl, Pflanzenf. v. 3, part 7, p. 15, fig. 6. *Lawsonia spinosa*, Linn. Sp. Pl. (1753) p. 349 (*partly*). *Lawsonia alba*, Lamk. Encyc. Méthod. v. 3 (1789) p. 106; Fl. B. I. v. 2, p. 573; Grah. Cat. p. 67; Dalz. & Gibs. p. 97; Trim. Fl. Ceyl. v. 2, p. 228; Talb. Trees, Bomb. ed. 2, p. 175; Woodr. in Journ. Bomb. Nat. v. 11 (1898) p. 638; Watt, Dict. Econ. Prod. v. 4, p. 597.—Flowers: Apr.–July. VERN. *Mendhi*.

Doubtfully wild in the Bombay Presidency, said by *Dalzell & Gibson* (*l. c.*) to be indigenous in Gujarat. *Woodrow* mentions (*l. c.*) that it is plentiful in sandy salt land near Bombay and that seedlings are abundant. Cultivated throughout the Presidency, and often used as a hedge-plant in the same manner as privet in England.

The plant is the Henna of Egypt, and is largely used in India by the natives for dyeing the nails, skin, and hair. It is also used medicinally. See Watt, Dict. Econ. Prod. l. c., where a very full account of its various uses may be found.

4. LAGERSTRŒMIA, Linn.

Trees or shrubs. Leaves opposite, distichous or the uppermost alternate, petiolate, oblong or ovate, entire, often glaucous beneath. Flowers often large and showy, in axillary and terminal panicles, the ultimate branchlets usually cymose; peduncles 2-bracteate at their apex; pedicels 2-bracteolate. Calyx-tube campanulate, coriaceous, smooth or ribbed, or winged; lobes 6 (sometimes 7–9), ovate or triangular, often caudate, valvate; accessory teeth 0 or (rarely) minute. Petals 6 (sometimes 7–9) or 0, inserted at the summit of the calyx-tube, clawed, more or less orbicular, wrinkled, the margin crisped, erose or fimbriate. Stamens ∞, inserted near the bottom of the calyx-tube; filaments much exserted. Ovary sessile at the bottom of the calyx, 3–6-celled; ovules numerous, ascending; placentas axile; style long, bent; stigma capitate. Capsule more or less adnate to the calyx, ellipsoid, coriaceous, smooth, 3–6-celled, loculicidally 3–6-valved. Seeds many (rarely few), compressed, ascending or horizontal; testa membranous, winged at the summit.—DISTRIB. South-east Asia, extending to Australia; species 18.

Calyx not ribbed; petals less than ½ in. long.
  Capsule ¾–1½ in. long; calyx-lobes appressed to the fruit ... 1. *L. parviflora.*
  Capsule ½–¾ in. long; calyx-lobes spreading or reflexed ...... 2. *L. lanceolata.*
Calyx ribbed; petals 1 in. long or more .... 3. *L. Flos-Reginæ.*

1. **Lagerstrœmia parviflora,** *Roxb. Cor. Pl.* v. 1 (1795) p. 47, t. 66. A large tree attaining 50–70 ft. high; youngest branches sometimes slightly pubescent. Leaves 2–4 by 1½–2½ in., elliptic-oblong, acute or acuminate, green and glabrous above, pale or sometimes hoary-tomentose beneath, conspicuously reticulately veined, narrowed or cuneate at the base; main nerves 6–10 pairs, arcuate, prominent beneath; petioles 0–¼ in. long. Flowers white, fragrant, in axillary and terminal many- or few-flowered panicles; pedicels slender, short. Calyx ⅛ in. long in flower, enlarged to ½ in. or more in fruit, glabrous or finely cano-pubescent, not ribbed; tube subhemispheric, or in fruit somewhat funnel-shaped below; teeth 6, variable in size, triangular, acute, closely appressed to the fruit. Petals 6, white, broadly obovate-oblong, ¼ in. long, with a long slender claw, undulate. Capsules variable in size, but usually about ¾–1¼ by ½–¾ in., ellipsoid. Seeds (including the wing) ½–⅔ in. long, the wing much longer than the seed, about ⅜ in. long, cultriform, thin on the inside edge, thick on the outer. Fl. B. I. v. 2, p. 575; Brandis, For. Fl. p. 239; Talb. Trees, Bomb. ed. 2, p. 175; Woodr. in Journ. Bomb. Nat. v. 11 (1898) p. 638; Watt, Dict. Econ. Prod. v. 4, p. 583. *Lagerstrœmia lanceolata*, Dalz. & Gibs. p. 98; Bedd. Flor. Sylvat. t. 32 (*not* of Wall.).—Flowers: June. VERN. *Bondárá.*

KONKAN: *Stocks*!, *Law*!, *Gibson*!; Matheran, *Cooke*! DECCAN: hills near Poona, *Woodrow*!; Koina valley, *Cooke*!; Chattersinghi hill near Poona, *Kanitkar*! S. M.

COUNTRY: Belgaum, *Ritchie*, 276! & 949!—DISTRIB. India (base of the W. Himalaya, W. Peninsula); Ava.

The wood is valued for its timber, which is tough, elastic, and durable. The leaves are used to feed *tasar* silkworms. See Watt, Dict. Econ. Prod. l. c.

2. **Lagerstrœmia lanceolata,** *Wall. Cat.* (1828) 2120. A large tree 30–50 ft. high; bark ash-colored, peeling off in large strips. Leaves 2½–4 by ¾–2 in., elliptic-lanceolate, acute, glabrous above, usually hoary-tomentose beneath; main nerves 8–12 pairs, prominent; petioles ⅛–½ in. long. Flowers in large usually compound panicles; pedicels short, pubescent. Calyx ⅓ in. long, usually hoary-tomentose; tube hemispheric; lobes about 1/12 in. long, triangular, acute, patent or often reflexed. Petals ⅙–¼ by 1/10 in., oblong-obovate, with a long slender claw. Capsules ½–¾ in. long, ellipsoid, not ribbed. Seeds (including the wing) about ⅓ in. long, the wing about ⅙ in. long and ⅛ in. broad at the base, cultriform. Fl. B. I. v. 2, p. 576; Woodr. in Journ. Bomb. Nat. v. 11 (1898) p. 638; Watt, Dict. Econ. Prod. v. 4, p. 583. *Lagerstrœmia parviflora*, Dalz. & Gibs. p. 98 (*not* of Roxb.). *L. microcarpa*, Wight, Icon. (1840) t. 109; Bedd. Flor. Sylvat. t. 30; Talb. Trees, Bomb. ed. 2, p. 176.—Flowers: Mar.–Apr. VERN. *Náná*.

Dalzell & Gibson (Bomb. Fl. l. c.) have transposed the names *L. lanceolata* and *L. parviflora*.

KONKAN: *Stocks*!, *Law*!, *Dalzell*!, *Gibson*!; Wari country, common, *Dalzell & Gibson*. S. M. COUNTRY: Ramghát and Belgaum, *Ritchie*, 277! KANARA: North Kanara, *Talbot*; Kumpta-Sirsi Road, *Woodrow*.—DISTRIB. India (from Bombay southwards).

3. **Lagerstrœmia Flos-Reginæ,** *Retz. Obs.* (1789) fasc. 5, p. 25. A large tree 30–60 ft. high; branches widely spreading; bark pale, smooth, flaking off in irregular pieces. Leaves 4–8 by 1½–3 in., oblong-lanceolate or elliptic, subacute, glabrous and finely reticulate on both surfaces, pale beneath, base acute or rounded; main nerves 10–13 pairs, prominent, curving upwards; petioles ¼–⅜ in. long, stout. Flowers 2–3 in. across, in large panicles sometimes reaching 1 ft. long; pedicels stout, pubescent, thickened upwards and articulated below the middle. Calyx turbinate, ⅝ in. long, covered with white or ferruginous tomentum, ribbed with 12–14 prominent stout ridges, those opposite the calyx-teeth broader; teeth 6–7, triangular, acute, spreading, ¼ in. long, thickened at the edges. Petals 6–7, purple, 1–1½ in. long, suborbicular or rotund-ovate, clawed, much undulate and crumpled, spreading. Stamens all equal, shorter than the style. Capsules ellipsoid or subglobose, ¾–1¼ by ⅝–1 in., minutely apiculate. Seeds (including the wing) ½–9/16 by ¼–3/16 in., glabrous, pale-brown. Fl. B. I. v. 2, p. 577; Trim. Fl. Ceyl. v. 2, p. 228; Talb. Trees, Bomb. ed. 2, p. 176; Woodr. in Journ. Bomb. Nat. v. 11 (1898) p. 638; Watt, Dict. Econ. Prod. v. 4, p. 582. *Lagerstrœmia Reginæ*, Roxb. Cor. Pl. v. 1 (1795) p. 46, t. 65; Grah. Cat. p. 67; Dalz. & Gibs. p. 98; Wight, Icon. t. 413; Bedd. Flor. Sylvat. t. 29. *L. speciosa*, Pers. Syn. v. 2 (1807) p. 72; Kœhne, in Engl. & Prantl, Pflanzenf. v. 3, part 7, p. 14, fig. 5, P–T.—Flowers: Apr.–June. VERN. *Táman*; *Mota-bondárá*.

KONKAN: S. Konkan, *Woodrow*; wild in the vale of the Nagotna river near its source, *Graham*; Vingorla, *Dalzell & Gibson*. KANARA: N. Kanara Ghâts on the banks of nálas and rivers, *Talbot*.—DISTRIB. India (W. Peninsula, Assam); Ceylon, Malaya, China, in many cases only cultivated.

Sir G. King in his "Materials for a Flora of the Malayan Peninsula" (Journ. As. Soc. Beng. v. 67 [1898] p. 9) gives most convincing reasons for adopting the name *L. Flos-Reginæ*, Retz. (1789), instead of *L. speciosa*, Persoon (1807).

Lagerstrœmia indica, Linn. Syst. ed. 10 (1759) p. 1076. A very handsome shrub introduced from China and cultivated largely in gardens. It has glabrous leaves 2 in. long and showy flowers of every shade from pale rose to dark crimson. It is propagated by cuttings or seeds. Fl. B. I. v. 2, p. 575; Grah. Cat. p. 67; Dalz. & Gibs. Suppl. p. 33; Woodr. in Journ. Bomb. Nat. v. 11 (1898) p. 638, & Gard. in Ind. ed. 5, p. 318; Watt, Dict. Econ. Prod. v. 4, p. 583.—Flowers: June–July. VERN. *Chinai-Mendhi*.

5. SONNERATIA, Linn. f.

Trees growing near the sea. Leaves opposite, petiolate, coriaceous, entire. Flowers 3 together at the apices of the branches, or axillary and solitary, ebracteolate. Calyx thickly coriaceous; tube campanulate; lobes 4–8, triangular-ovate or lanceolate. Petals 0, or as many as the calyx-lobes. Stamens ∞, inserted in the throat of the calyx-tube, many-seriate; filaments filiform, at length reflexed; anthers versatile, reniform. Ovary free or adnate at the base to the calyx-tube, many-celled, with thin septa; ovules numerous, ascending, placentas axile; style elongate, filiform; stigma subcapitate. Berry subglobose, thick, supported by the persistent calyx, 10–15-celled, many-seeded. Seeds nesting in pulp, curved, angular; cotyledons short, foliaceous, convolute; radicle elongate, terete.—DISTRIB. Tropical sea-shores of the Eastern hemisphere; species 5–6.

Calyx-lobes 4; petals 0 .... 1. *S. apetala.*
Calyx-lobes 6; petals 6 .... 2. *S. acida.*

1. **Sonneratia apetala,** *Buch.-Ham. in Syme, Emb. Ava*, v. 3 (1800) p. 313. An erect tree reaching 40 ft. high growing in mangrove swamps; branches slender, drooping. Leaves 2–4 by 1–1½ in., oblong-lanceolate, obtuse, thick, glabrous, much attenuated at the base into a short petiole; main nerves 10–12 pairs, not conspicuous. Flowers solitary or, more commonly, 3 together, large, articulated on pedicels ½–¾ in. long. Calyx ¾ in. long; tube cup-shaped; lobes 4, ovate-oblong, acute, ½ in. long. Petals 0. Stamens slightly exserted; style shorter than the stamens; stigma umbrella-shaped. Capsule about ¾ in. broad, depressed-globose, tipped with the style, smooth. Fl. B. I. v. 2, p. 579; Grah. Cat. p. 72; Trim. Fl. Ceyl. v. 2, p. 229; Talb. Trees, Bomb. ed. 2, p. 177; Woodr. in Journ. Bomb. Nat. v. 11 (1898) p. 638; Watt, Dict. Econ. Prod. v. 6, part 3, p. 276.—Flowers: Feb.

Rather rare. KONKAN: *Law*!; salt-marsh by the road leading from Bombay to Sewree, *Graham*; Mumbra (Thana districts), *Woodrow*; Dharamtar, *Woodrow*.—DISTRIB. India (in tidal creeks of Bengal, the Western Peninsula, Birma).

This plant and the next have been included in the list of so-called "mangroves" given on page 471.

2. **Sonneratia acida,** *Linn. f. Suppl. Pl.* (1781) p. 252. A small tree rarely reaching 15 ft. high. Leaves nearly sessile, subfleshy, 2–3¾ by ¾–2¼ in., elliptic-oblong or obovate, obtuse, much attenuated at the base. Flowers large, terminal, solitary, on very short thick pedicels;

buds ellipsoid. Calyx 1¼–1⅝ in. long; tube hemispheric; lobes 6, lanceolate-oblong, acute, ¾ in. long. Petals 6, linear-oblong, ¾ by ⅛–⅙ in., dark rose-colored. Style very long, often exceeding 2 in. Fruit 1–2 in. in diam., cushion-shaped, supported by the persistent calyx which forms a shallow cup, and tipped by the persistent tapering style-base which forms a point about 1 in. long in its centre. Fl. B. I. v. 2, p. 579; Grah. Cat. p. 72; Dalz. & Gibs. p. 98; Trim. Fl. Ceyl. v. 2, p. 230; Talb. Trees, Bomb. ed. 2, p. 176; Woodr. in Journ. Bomb. Nat. v. 11 (1898) p. 638; Watt, Dict. Econ. Prod. v. 6, part 3, p. 275.—Flowers: Feb.–July.

KONKAN: salt-marshes of the Konkan, *Talbot*; salt-marsh on the Salsette side of Sion Causeway near Bombay, *Graham*, *Dalzell*; Ratnagiri, Vingorla, *Dalzell*; Hareshvar, *Kanitkar*!; Dharamtar, *Woodrow*! KANARA: salt-water creeks of N. Kanara, *Talbot*.—DISTRIB. India (tidal creeks and mangrove swamps); Ceylon, Java, Siam.

The erect root-branches, which reach 18–24 in. in length by 3 in. in diam., have a soft firm texture like cork and have been used as a substitute for it in Ceylon. (*Trimen*, l. c.)

Punica Granatum, Linn. Sp. Pl. (1753) p. 472. *The Pomegranate.* A small tree or large shrub, wild in Persia, Cabul, and Beluchistan, is cultivated throughout India for its fruit and flowers and has become naturalized in many places. It is largely cultivated in the Bombay Presidency at Alandi near Poona. The fruit is infested by a curious caterpillar which, in order to enjoy the fruit in safety, fastens it to the stalk with a web of silky threads, so that the fruit may not fall off the tree and the depredator be injured. Fl. B. I. v. 2, p. 581; Grah. Cat. p. 72; Dalz. & Gibs. Suppl. p. 34; Woodr. in Journ. Bomb. Nat. v. 11 (1898) p. 638, & Gard. in Ind. ed. 5, p. 319; Watt, Dict. Econ. Prod. v. 6, part 1, p. 368.—VERN. *Andr*; *Dálimbi*.

ORDER LIX. ONAGRACEÆ.

Herbs, rarely undershrubs, sometimes aquatic. Leaves opposite or alternate, membranous, entire or toothed, undivided (in *Trapa* the submerged leaves pinnatipartite), exstipulate. Flowers hermaphrodite, regular (rarely irregular), axillary and solitary, or in spikes or racemes towards the ends of the branches. Calyx-tube wholly adnate to the ovary (½-adnate in *Trapa*); limb 2–5-lobed, the lobes valvate. Petals epigynous, alternate with the calyx-lobes, rarely 0. Stamens as many or twice as many as the calyx-lobes, inserted with the petals when these are present. Ovary inferior (½-inferior in *Trapa*), 1–6- (commonly 4-) celled; ovules 1 or many in each cell, pendulous or ½-ascending, placentas axile; style cylindric or subulate; stigma capitate, entire, 2-lobed or 4-fid. Fruit various, dehiscent or indehiscent, membranous, capsular or bony, 1–many-celled, 1–many-seeded. Seeds exalbuminous or nearly so.—DISTRIB. Throughout the temperate regions of the world, rarer in the Tropics; genera 22; species 300.

Seeds very many.
  Stamens twice as many as the calyx-lobes.......................... 1. JUSSIÆA.
  Stamens as many as the calyx-lobes .... 2. LUDWIGIA.
Seeds 1–2.
  Aquatic; stamens 4 .... 3. TRAPA.

1. JUSSIÆA, Linn.

Herbs or undershrubs usually growing in swamps. Leaves alternate, usually membranous and entire, rarely coriaceous and serrate. Flowers yellow or white, axillary, solitary; pedicels usually 2-bracteate at the apex. Calyx-tube narrow, not or slightly produced above the ovary; teeth 4–6, acute, persistent. Petals 4–6, inserted beneath the margin of an epigynous disk. Stamens twice as many as the petals and inserted with them. Ovary 4-5-celled; ovules numerous, axile, in several vertical rows at the inner angle of each cell, placentas often prominent; style simple, sometimes very short; stigma 4–6-lobed. Capsule terete or 4–12-angled or ribbed, 4–6-celled, septicidally 4–5-valved, crowned with the disk and calyx-lobes. Seeds numerous, without a coma; cotyledons obtuse; radicle short.—DISTRIB. Chiefly Tropical American; species 30.

Stems creeping or floating; petals 5 .... 1. *J. repens.*
Stems erect; petals 4 .... 2. *J. suffruticosa.*

1. **Jussiæa repens,** *Linn. Sp. Pl.* (1753) p. 388. Herbaceous; stem rooting at the nodes, elongate, prostrate or creeping, or floating on the water, sustained by means of white spongy bodies which spring in tufts from each side of the base of the petioles and may be modified stipules. Leaves 1–2 by $\frac{1}{2}$–$\frac{7}{8}$ in., oblanceolate or obovate-oblong, rounded at the apex, glabrous or slightly pubescent, much narrowed into the petiole; main nerves 6–10 pairs, slender, nearly straight or slightly curved upwards; petioles very short. Flowers pale-yellow or white, with yellowish veins; pedicels usually as long as the capsule, more or less hairy. Calyx-tube about $\frac{1}{2}$ in. long, cylindric, glabrous or rarely pubescent; lobes 5, lanceolate, $\frac{1}{4}$–$\frac{5}{16}$ in. long. Petals 5, shortly clawed, $\frac{1}{2}$–$\frac{5}{8}$ in. long, obovate, obtuse, sometimes retuse. Stamens 10. Capsules $\frac{1}{2}$–$1\frac{1}{2}$ in. long, cylindric, glabrous or sparsely clothed with scattered hairs. Fl. B. I. v. 2, p. 587; Grah. Cat. p. 75; Dalz. & Gibs. p. 98; Hook. Bot. Misc. v. 3 (1833) p. 300, t. 40; Trim. Fl. Ceyl. v. 2, p. 233; Woodr. in Journ. Bomb. Nat. v. 11 (1898) p. 638.—Flowers: Nov.–Dec.

Common on the margins of tanks and in rice-fields. KONKAN: *Law*! GUJARAT: *Woodrow*. S. M. COUNTRY: Belgaum, *Ritchie*, 1758!; Dharwar, *Ritchie*, 1758! KANARA: Hulikal, *Bhiva*!—DISTRIB. Throughout the plains of India; Ceylon; generally distributed throughout the warmer regions of the world.

2. **Jussiæa suffruticosa,** *Linn. Sp. Pl.* (1753) p. 388. A semi-shrubby erect perennial, 1–4 ft. high; stem woody below, much-branched; branches stiff, terete, striate. Leaves nearly sessile, 2–3 by $\frac{1}{4}$–$\frac{3}{4}$ in., varying from linear to broadly elliptic, but usually lanceolate, acute, tapering much towards the base, villous, pubescent or subglabrous; main nerves numerous; petioles very short or 0. Flowers yellow; pedicels shorter than the calyx, pubescent; bracts minute. Calyx hairy; tube subquadrangular; lobes 4, ovate-elliptic, acute or subacuminate, $\frac{3}{8}$ in. long, hairy, obscurely nerved. Petals 4, broadly obovate, $\frac{1}{4}$–$\frac{3}{8}$ in. long, pinnately veined. Capsules 1–$1\frac{1}{2}$ in. long, subquadrangular, truncate, tapering towards the base, 8-ribbed, villous or pubescent, membranous, breaking up between the ribs which persist for some time. Seeds minute, ovoid, didymous, brown, polished. Fl. B. I. v. 2, p. 587;

Trim. Fl. Ceyl. v. 2, p. 233; Woodr. in Journ. Bomb. Nat. v. 11 (1898) p. 638; Watt, Dict. Econ. Prod. v. 4, p. 556. *Jussiæa villosa*, Lamk. Encyc. Méthod. v. 3 (1789) p. 331; Grah. Cat. p. 75; Dalz. & Gibs. p. 98.—Flowers: Aug.-Oct. VERN. *Pánlavang*.

KONKAN: *Graham*, *Law*!, *Stocks*!; Vingorla, *Dalzell & Gibson*. DECCAN: Tulsi tank near Poona, *Woodrow*!; Bowdhan near Poona, *Bhiva*!; road to Kadakvásla, *Cooke*!; Khandala, *Graham*. S. M. COUNTRY: Belgaum, *Ritchie*, 304!; Londa, *Cooke*! KANARA: Yellapur, *Talbot*!—DISTRIB. Throughout India; Ceylon, warmer regions of the world.

2. LUDWIGIA, Linn.

Perennial or annual herbs. Leaves alternate or opposite, usually lanceolate, entire, membranous. Flowers usually axillary, solitary, sessile or nearly so; peduncles when present 2-bracteate at the apex. Calyx-tube not or scarcely produced above the ovary; lobes 3–5, acute, persistent or tardily deciduous. Petals 3-5 (or 0), inserted beneath the margin of an epigynous disk, spreading. Stamens 3–5, inserted with the petals; filaments short. Ovary 4–5-celled; ovules numerous, attached in 2 or more vertical rows to the inner angle of each cell. Capsule crowned with the epigynous disk and calyx-lobes, opening by terminal pores or breaking up irregularly along the sides. Seeds very many, minute.—DISTRIB. Chiefly North American; species 20.

1. **Ludwigia parviflora**, *Roxb. Hort. Beng.* (1814) p. 11. An erect herb 6–24 in. high; stem more or less angular, much-branched, glabrous. Leaves variable in size, 1–3 by $\frac{1}{4}$–$\frac{3}{4}$ in., lanceolate or linear-lanceolate, narrowed to each end, glabrous; petioles obscure. Flowers small, solitary, axillary; pedicels very short. Calyx-tube subcylindric, glabrous or slightly pubescent; lobes 4, ovate, acute, $\frac{1}{10}$ in. long. Petals 4, elliptic-oblong, as long as the calyx-lobes. Style short, stout. Capsule $\frac{1}{3}$–$\frac{1}{2}$ in. long, obsoletely 4-angled, smooth, crowned for a time by the subpersistent calyx-lobes, breaking away from the ribs. Seeds very numerous, in several rows in each cell, minute, ellipsoid, yellowish-brown, polished. Fl. B. I. v. 2, p. 588; Grah. Cat. p. 75; Dalz. & Gibs. p. 99; Wight, Ill. t. 101; Trim. Fl. Ceyl. v. 2, p. 234; Woodr. in Journ. Bomb. Nat. v. 11 (1898) p. 638.—Flowers: May–June.

KONKAN: common, *Dalzell & Gibson*, *Graham*; Neral, *Woodrow*!; hills near Matheran, *Kanitkar*! DECCAN: Poona districts, *Cooke*!—DISTRIB. Throughout India; Ceylon, Malaya, N. Australia, Persia, Abyssinia.

3. TRAPA, Linn.

Aquatic herbs. Leaves alternate, floating, petiolate, rhomboid, toothed, stipulate; petiole spongy, inflated. Flowers axillary, solitary. Calyx-tube short, adnate to the lower part of the ovary; calyx-limb 4-partite, 2 or all the segments persistent and becoming spinescent on the fruit. Petals 4, sessile, inserted at the base of an undulate epigynous disk. Stamens 4, inserted with the petals. Ovary 2-celled, $\frac{1}{2}$-inferior, conical above the calyx, attenuated into a persistent subulate style; ovule solitary in each cell, pendulous; stigma capitate. Fruit bony, 1-celled, obovoid, with 4 angles 2 or all of which carry spines, indehiscent, with a short cylindric beak at the top through which the radicle is protruded. Seed 1, inverse; cotyledons very unequal; radicle incurved.—

DISTRIB. Central and Southern Europe, Tropical Asia and Africa; species 2–3.

1. **Trapa bispinosa,** *Roxb. Hort. Beng.* (1814) p. 11. Stems flexuose, often several feet long, ascending in the water, the submerged parts furnished with numerous opposite pairs of green root-like spreading pectinate organs (? floating roots), arising immediately below the position of the stipules of fallen leaves and reaching sometimes 2½ in. long. Leaves alternate, crowded on the upper part of the stem, the blade as broad as, or more commonly broader than long, 1½–2 by 1½–2¼ in., rhomboid with a triangular apex, somewhat truncate and entire at the base, irregularly inciso-serrate in the upper part, dark-green mottled with brown, glabrous and shining above, reddish-purple and densely pubescent beneath; petioles terete, at first short, but ultimately reaching as much as 5 in. in length, the upper part hairy, the lower glabrous, dilated near the apex into a large fusiform spongy float; stipules linear-lanceolate, acute, membranous, caducous. Flowers few, axillary, solitary; pedicels short, stout, hairy, incurved during flowering, afterwards bending down beneath the water in which the fruit ripens. Calyx pubescent; lobes 4, lanceolate, acute, of which 2 are persistent, becoming spines on the fruit. Petals 4, obovate, about twice as long as the calyx-lobes, crenulate on the margins, pure white. Fruit obovoid, angular, ¾–1 in. long and broad, with a short conical beak in the centre at the apex and a spreading flattened very sharp spinous horn at either side; radicle beneath the central beak, from which it protrudes in germination. Fl. B. I. v. 2, p. 590; Grah. Cat. p. 75; Dalz. & Gibs. p. 99; Roxb. Cor. Pl. v. 3 (1819) p. 29, t. 234; Trim. Fl. Ceyl. v. 2, p. 235; Woodr. in Journ. Bomb. Nat. v. 11 (1898) p. 639; Watt, Dict. Econ. Prod. v. 6, part 4, p. 73.—Flowers: Feb.–Mar. VERN. *Shingddá*.

In tanks throughout the Presidency, often cultivated; very abundant in tanks in Gujarat. The fruit is eaten by the natives and is much esteemed. It is known to Anglo-Indians as the water-chestnut.—DISTRIB. Throughout India; Ceylon, Malaya, Tropical Africa.

Note.—Considerable diversity of opinion exists as to the exact function of the "pectinate organs." Roxburgh (*l. c.*) considered them to be a second pair of stipules below the true ones, and gives an excellent figure. In the 'Genera Plantarum' (Benth. & Hook.) and in Hook. f. 'Flora of British India' they are called submerged leaves. Barnéoud (Mém. du Trapa natans, Ann. Sci. Nat. sér. 3, v. 9 [1848] p. 222) terms them adventitious floating roots. There is a good figure of *Trapa natans* in Engl. & Prantl, Pflanzenf. v. 3, part 7, p. 224, fig. 97, which shews these organs in their natural position in the water. They do not reach the bottom, but remain suspended in the liquid.

Fuchsias of several kinds are grown on the hills and are common in every garden at Mahableshwar, where they thrive very well. They do not, however, stand the climate of the Deccan plains. I have taken down large established plants in pots from Mahableshwar to Poona which all died after the second year. At an altitude of 4000 ft. and upwards they grow and flower freely.

Œnothera rosea, [Soland in] Ait. Hort. Kew. ed. 1, v. 2 (1789) p. 3. A small plant, a native of Mexico, is grown in gardens, especially on the hills, and thrives well at Mahableshwar. It is about 1 ft. high and has pink flowers with obovate petals. Woodr. in Journ. Bomb. Nat. v. 11 (1898) p. 639, & Gard. in Ind. ed. 5, p. 322.

Order LX. SAMYDACEÆ.

Trees or shrubs. Leaves usually alternate and distichous, petiolate, simple, entire or serrate, the teeth sometimes terminated by a gland; stipules small or 0. Flowers regular, usually hermaphrodite, inconspicuous, fasciculate, racemose, or paniculate, pedicelled, the pedicels articulated at the base, bracteolate. Calyx coriaceous, persistent; tube short or long, rarely adnate to the ovary; lobes 3–7, imbricate or valvate. Petals as many as the calyx-lobes or 0, perigynous, imbricate. Stamens definite or indefinite, often alternating with staminodes, equidistant or collected into fascicles opposite to the petals; filaments filiform or capillary, free or connate at the base or throughout their entire length. Ovary free or rarely adnate to the calyx-tube, sessile, 1-celled; ovules very many or few, attached to 2-5 (usually 3) parietal placentas; style 1, capitate or 3-fid at the apex, or styles 2–5, simple or capitellate. Fruit capsular or rarely indehiscent, 1-celled, 1–many-seeded, 2–5-(usually 3-) valved at the apex or throughout its entire length, the valves alternating with the placentas. Seeds usually few (always fewer than the ovules), oblong or angular, albuminous, usually arilled; cotyledons oblong, orbicular or cordate, often foliaceous; radicle very short or elongate and terete.—Distrib. Throughout the Tropics of both hemispheres, rare in subtropical regions; genera 17; species 150.

Flowers in axillary fascicles. Petals 0 .... 1. Casearia.
Flowers in axillary and terminal racemes. Petals 4 or 5 .... 2. Homalium.

1. CASEARIA, Jacq.

Shrubs or small trees. Leaves alternate, distichous, entire or serrate, often marked with pellucid dots or lines; stipules small, lateral, caducous. Flowers small (clustered in the axils in the Indian species); pedicels articulated above the base. Calyx inferior, deeply 4–5-lobed; lobes imbricate, obtuse, persistent. Petals 0. Stamens 6–15 (rarely 20–40), inserted on the tube or at the base of the calyx, alternating with as many staminodes; filaments free or connate into a ring at the base with one another and the staminodes; connective sometimes penicillate at the apex. Ovary free, ovoid, 1-celled; ovules many, parietal; style short; stigma capitate, or stigmas 3. Capsule succulent, globose or ellipsoid (when dry sometimes 3-angular or 6-ribbed), 3- rarely 2-valved. Seeds many, angular or obovoid, with a fleshy usually colored aril; testa coriaceous or crustaceous; albumen fleshy; embryo straight; cotyledons oblong or orbicular, flat; radicle terete.—Distrib. Warmer parts of the globe, most abundant in America; species 80.

Small trees.
  Stipules long, lanceolate-subulate.
    Leaves glabrous; calyx pubescent; lobes oblong; style $\frac{1}{8}$ in. long .... 1. *C. graveolens.*
  Stipules minute, scale-like.
    Leaves and calyx glabrous; calyx-lobes suborbicular; style almost 0 .... 2. *C. esculenta.*
    Leaves and calyx pubescent; calyx-lobes elliptic; style $\frac{1}{10}$ in. long .... 3. *C. tomentosa.*
A shrub 4–6 ft. high .... 4. *C. rubescens.*

1. **Casearia graveolens,** *Dalz. in Kew Journ. Bot.* v. 4 (1852) p. 107. A shrub or small tree; young branches obtusely angular, glabrous; new leaves appearing at the end of April. Leaves 3½–8 by 1½–4 in., coriaceous and hard when old, broadly elliptic, obtuse or shortly acuminate, more or less crenate-serrate, finely reticulately veined, glabrous; main nerves 8–12 pairs, slender, prominent beneath; petioles ¼–½ in. long; stipules ⅓ in. long, lanceolate-subulate, very deciduous. Flowers with a disagreeable odor, green, numerous, in axillary clusters; pedicels articulated above the base, very short when in flower, elongating in fruit, pubescent below the articulation, glabrous or subglabrous above it. Calyx pubescent outside, ⅛–⅙ in. long, deeply 5-lobed; lobes oblong, obtuse, concave, green. Stamens 8, equalling the calyx, the alternating staminodes villous; filaments glabrous. Style as long as the stamens, about $\frac{1}{16}$ in. long; stigma large, discoid. Fruit deep-yellow, ¾–1 in. long, ellipsoid or subglobose, smooth, shining, 3-valved. Seeds about 12, ovoid, compressed, with a scarlet aril. Fl. B. I. v. 2, p. 592; Talb. Trees, Bomb. ed. 2, p. 178; Woodr. in Journ. Bomb. Nat. v. 11 (1898) p. 639; Watt, Dict. Econ. Prod. v. 2, p. 209. *Casearia* ——?, *Bocarah*, Grah. Cat. p. 40.—Flowers: Aug.–Jan. VERN. *Bokhāda.*

KONKAN: *Stocks*!, *Law*!; open hills of the S. Konkan, *Dalzell*!; Matheran, *Cooke*! DECCAN: Fitzgerald Ghát below Mahableshwar, *Cooke*!; Mawal (Poona districts), *Woodrow*; hills near Kadkala, *Kanitkar*!; Hâtlot, *Woodrow*.—DISTRIB. India (Gurwhal, Kumaon, Sikkim, W. Peninsula, Birma).

2. **Casearia esculenta,** *Roxb. Fl. Ind.* v. 2 (1832) p. 422. A small tree reaching 20–30 ft. high; bark yellowish-white, smooth; young branches slender, pale, glabrous. Leaves thinly coriaceous, 3–6 by 1¼–2¼ in., elliptic-oblong to elliptic-lanceolate, subacute, usually shortly acuminate, tapering to the base; main nerves 6–10 pairs; petioles ¼–⅝ in. long, glabrous; stipules minute, scale-like. Flowers in clusters in the axils of past and present leaves; pedicels longer than the calyx, articulated above the base, glabrous above the articulation, surrounded at the base by numerous small bracts. Calyx glabrous; lobes 4 or 5, suborbicular, $\frac{1}{10}$ in. long and broad, sometimes ciliolate, concave. Stamens 8; staminodes oblong, truncate and villous at the apex, shorter than the stamens; filaments pubescent. Style scarcely any. Fruit ¾ in. long, ellipsoid or subglobose, orange-yellow, glabrous, dehiscing by 2 or 3 (usually 3) thick valves. Seeds many, covered by a large fleshy lacerate scarlet aril. Fl. B. I. v. 2, p. 592; Grah. Cat. p. 40; Trim. Fl. Ceyl. v. 2, p. 237; Talb. Trees, Bomb. ed. 2, p. 178; Woodr. in Journ. Bomb. Nat. v. 11 (1898) p. 639; Watt, Dict. Econ. Prod. v. 2, p. 209. *Casearia varians*, Thw. Enum. p. 19; Bedd. Flor. Sylvat. t. 208. *C. lævigata*, Dalz. in Kew Journ. Bot. v. 4 (1852) p. 108; Dalz. & Gibs. p. 11.—Flowers: May–June. VERN. *Modi*; *Kulkulta.*

KONKAN: *Stocks*!; hilly parts of the Konkan, *Nimmo* ex *Graham*; Ghâts, *Dalzell*! S. M. COUNTRY: Ramghât, *Ritchie*, 677!; Talaveri, *Ritchie*, 919!; Ambgaon, *Ritchie*, $\frac{919}{3}$! KANARA: moist forests of N. Kanara, *Talbot*; Yellapur, *Woodrow*; Karwar, *Talbot*, *Woodrow*.—DISTRIB. India (W. Peninsula); Ceylon, Malay Peninsula.

3. **Casearia tomentosa,** *Roxb. Fl. Ind.* v. 2 (1832) p. 421. A small tree attaining 30 ft. high; bark thick, ash-colored; branchlets tomentose or pubescent, rarely glabrous. Leaves 2½–7 by 1½–2¾,

oblong, acute, more or less serrulate, or sometimes almost entire, slightly pubescent or glabrous above, pubescent or tomentose (densely so on the nerves) beneath, base usually rounded or subcordate (more or less obliquely); main nerves 8–10 pairs; petioles $\frac{3}{16}$–$\frac{3}{8}$ in. long, densely pubescent; stipules minute, densely pubescent, deciduous. Flowers greenish-white, crowded in axillary fascicles; pedicels less than $\frac{1}{4}$ in. long, densely pubescent, articulated near the base. Calyx pubescent; tube scarcely $\frac{1}{30}$ in. long; lobes $\frac{1}{8}$ in. long, broadly elliptic, obtuse. Stamens usually 8; filaments glabrous; staminodes clavate, much shorter than the stamens, villous at the apex. Style $\frac{1}{30}$ in. long; stigma subglobose. Fruit broadly ellipsoid, $\frac{3}{4}$ in. long, smooth and shining, 3-valved. Seeds embedded in a soft pulpy scarlet mass consisting of the agglomerate arils. Fl. B. I. v. 2, p. 593; Trim. Fl. Ceyl. v. 2, p. 238; Talb. Trees, Bomb. ed. 2, p. 178; Woodr. in Journ. Bomb. Nat. v. 11 (1898) p. 639; Watt, Dict. Econ. Prod. v. 2, p. 209. *Casearia elliptica*, Willd. Sp. Pl. v. 2, p. 628; Wight, Icon. t. 1849. *C. ovata*, Roxb. Fl. Ind. v. 2 (1832) p. 420 (*not* of Willd.); Grah. Cat. p. 40. *C. Anavinga*, Dalz. & Gibs. p. 11.—Flowers: Jan.–May. VERN. *Chillá*; *Chari*.

Throughout the Presidency in deciduous forests, tolerably common. KONKAN *Stocks*!, *Law*!; Vingorla, *Stocks*! DECCAN: near Poona, *Woodrow*; hills near Poona, *Bhiva*! S. M. COUNTRY: Belgaum (east hills), *Ritchie*, 1011!—DISTRIB. Throughout India; Ceylon, Malaya, N. Australia.

4. **Casearia rubescens,** *Dalz. in Kew Journ. Bot.* v. 4 (1852) p. 108. A shrub 4–6 ft. high, all glabrous; branches pale. Leaves 2–5 by 1–1½ in., sometimes reaching 10 in. long in N. Kanara (*Talbot*), elliptic-oblong, shortly acuminate, obtuse or acute, entire, quite glabrous, base subacute; main nerves 6–8 pairs, the midrib of the young leaves red; petioles $\frac{3}{8}$–$\frac{1}{2}$ in. long, glabrous, channelled, those of the young leaves red. Stipules minute, scale-like, glabrous. Flowers in axillary clusters; pedicels minutely pubescent, articulated near the base. Calyx $\frac{1}{6}$ in. long, thick and fleshy, glabrous; lobes $\frac{1}{10}$ in. long, broadly elliptic-oblong, obtuse. Stamens 8; staminodes oblong, truncate and villous at the apex, shorter than the stamens; filaments pubescent. Ovary conical; style almost 0. Fruit ellipsoid, glabrous, $\frac{3}{4}$ in. long. Fl. B. I. v. 2, p. 593; Dalz. & Gibs. p. 11; Talb. Trees, Bomb. ed. 2, p. 178; Woodr. in Journ. Bomb. Nat. v. 11 (1898) p. 639.—Flowers: Feb. (*Dalzell*).

I am quite unable to separate this from *C. graveolens*, except by assuming Dalzell's description to be correct, viz. that it is a shrub 4–6 ft. high. Dalzell was himself doubtful of its being a good species.

KONKAN: *Stocks*!, *Woodrow*. S. M. COUNTRY: Talaveri, *Dalzell*!; Ramghát, *Ritchie*, 943! KANARA: forests near the Nilkund Ghát (N. Kanara), *Talbot*.—DISTRIB. India (W. Peninsula).

2. HOMALIUM, Jacq.

Shrubs or trees. Leaves alternate, petiolate, crenate or serrate, rarely entire; stipules small, rarely 0. Flowers small, in axillary slender panicles. Calyx-tube turbinate, adnate to the base of the ovary; lobes 4–7, persistent. Petals 4–7, inserted in the throat of the calyx, persistent. Stamens opposite to the petals and equal in number to them, or more, in fascicles opposite the petals, alternating with staminodes; filaments filiform; anthers small, didymous. Ovary ½-superior; ovules many or few, attached to 2–5 parietal placentas; styles 2–5, filiform; stigmas capitellate. Capsule ½-superior, coriaceous, 2–5-valved, few-seeded. Seeds angled or oblong; testa crustaceous; albumen fleshy; cotyledons foliaceous.—DISTRIB. Asia, Africa, N. Australia, Fiji Islands, Tropical America; species 30.

1. **Homalium zeylanicum,** *Benth. in Journ. Linn. Soc.* v. 4 (1860) p. 35. A tree reaching 60 ft. high and 2½ ft. in diam.; bark smooth, grey, lenticellate, breaking off in irregular pieces. Leaves 3–4½ by 1⅝–2¼ in., elliptic, acuminate, crenate-serrate, glabrous and shining on both sides, base narrowed into the petiole; main nerves 8–10 pairs, prominent and purplish-red beneath; petioles ¼–⅜ in. long, puberulous. Flowers greenish-white, in long panicles, arranged in numerous clusters along a slender rhachis 6–9 in. long; pedicels $\frac{1}{15}$ to $\frac{1}{10}$ in. long, articulated beneath the calyx; buds pear-shaped. Calyx pubescent, $\frac{1}{12}$ in. long; lobes 4–5, slightly longer than the turbinate tube, oblong, subacute, ciliate, open. Petals 4–5, equalling or a little longer than the calyx-lobes, obovate, ciliate. Stamens as many as the petals and longer than them; staminodes rounded, pubescent. Styles 3–4. Fruit not seen. Fl. B. I. v. 2, p. 596; Dalz. & Gibs. p. 53; Bedd. Flor. Sylvat. t. 210; Trim. Fl. Ceyl. v. 2, p. 239; Talb. Trees, Bomb. ed. 2, p. 178; Woodr. in Journ. Bomb. Nat. v. 11 (1898) p. 639; Watt, Dict. Econ. Prod. v. 4, p. 262.—Flowers: Apr.–May.

KONKAN: *Stocks*!, *Law*! S. M. COUNTRY: Párva Ghát, *Ritchie*, 1854!; Ramghát, *Dalzell & Gibson*. KANARA: evergreen forests of the N. Ghâts of N. Kanara, *Talbot*!—DISTRIB. India (W. Peninsula); Ceylon.

ORDER LXI. PASSIFLORACEÆ.

Shrubs or herbs usually twining. Leaves alternate, petiolate, simple, lobed, or palmately 3–7-foliolate, frequently glandular beneath; petiole usually glandular; stipules 0 or twin, deciduous or persistent. Tendrils axillary or 0. Flowers hermaphrodite or unisexual, solitary, racemose or cymoso-paniculate, often showy; bracteoles 3 (rarely 0), minute and scattered or foliaceous and forming an epicalyx. Calyx-tube short or long, coriaceous or herbaceous, persistent; lobes 5, imbricate. Petals 0 or as many as the calyx-lobes, inserted in the tube of the calyx, free or connate into a campanulate corolla, membranous, coriaceous or fleshy, imbricate, often marcescent. Corona simple or double, springing from the throat or bottom of the calyx, tubular or split into erect or radiating filaments (rarely 0). Stamens 5, on a gynophore or free at the base, perigynous; filaments subulate or filiform, free or monadelphous; anthers didymous or oblong, basifixed or versatile, the cells dehiscing introrsely. Ovary superior, free, 1-celled, sessile or stalked; ovules numerous, attached to parietal placentas, the funicle often expanded into a cup-shaped aril; styles 1 or 3; stigmas capitate, clavate or dilated, sometimes many-fid. Fruit baccate or capsular. Seeds numerous, usually ovoid, compressed, often pitted, covered with a fleshy aril; albumen fleshy; embryo rather large; cotyledons leafy; radicle terete.—

DISTRIB. Chiefly Tropical; most numerous in S. America; genera about 20; species about 300.

1. MODECCA, Lamk.

Glabrous herbs or undershrubs, scandent or twining. Leaves alternate, entire, palmi-lobed or pinnatifid, with 2 glands at the apex of the petiole; stipules 0 or inconspicuous. Tendrils lateral, undivided, circinate or twisted. Flowers unisexual, usually small; peduncles axillary, often produced into tendrils. MALE FLOWERS: Calyx turbinate or tubular; lobes 4–5, short or elongate. Petals 4–5, inserted on the throat or bottom of the calyx-tube and included in it, small, sometimes fimbriate. Corona 0, or a ring of white cilia arising from near the base of the calyx-tube. Stamens 4–5, inserted at the bottom of the calyx-tube, opposite to as many scales or glands; filaments free or connate below; anthers basifixed, oblong or linear, the connective usually apiculate. Ovary rudimentary or 0. FEMALE FLOWERS: Calyx and petals as in the male. Staminodes 4–5. Ovary stalked or subsessile, ovoid, terete or 4-gonous; ovules numerous, attached to 3 parietal placentas; style 0 or 3-fid; stigmas 3. Fruit capsular, dehiscing loculicidally by 3 valves. Seeds numerous, enveloped in a fleshy aril, flattened; funicle long; albumen fleshy; cotyledons foliaceous.—DISTRIB. Asia, Africa, and Tropical Australia; species about 25.

1. **Modecca palmata,** *Lamk. Encyc. Méthod.* v. 4 (1796) p. 209. A large perennial herb becoming woody at the base; root large, fusiform; stems long, thickened at the nodes, terete, smooth and shining, mottled with purple, not much branched. Leaves membranous, broader than long, 4–5 by 6–7 in., cordate, with 2 flat glands at the apex of the petiole and 1 at the base of each sinus in the divided leaves, usually very deeply palmately 5-lobed (rarely 3-lobed or undivided), glabrous and shining; lobes oblong-lanceolate, acute, entire; nerves and veins conspicuous; petioles 2 in. long, grooved, glabrous. Flowers in 2 opposite cymes (usually of 3) on a long axillary peduncle which is produced into a long simple tendril. MALE FLOWERS: Calyx broadly campanulate, $\frac{1}{2}$–$\frac{5}{8}$ in. long, dilated at the base; lobes 5, ovate, acute. Petals linear-oblong, acute, ciliate, inserted at the base of the calyx-tube. Corona a ring of threads from the calyx-tube just above the dilated portion. Stamens distant; filaments subulate, connate at the base; anthers linear-oblong. Ovary rudimentary. FEMALE FLOWERS: Calyx $\frac{1}{4}$ in. long, campanulate; lobes ovate, acute. Petals as in the male. Staminodes 5, erect, flat, strap-shaped, connate at the base into a membranous cup. Ovary shortly stalked, globose, smooth, tapering into 3 long styles; stigmas much divided, feathery. Fruit reaching 2 in. in diam., shortly stalked, globose, apiculate, smooth, orange-colored, splitting into 3 fleshy valves. Seeds nearly $\frac{1}{2}$ in. in diam., discoid, compressed, muriculate and pitted, each with a pulpy aril. Fl. B. I. v. 2, p. 603; Dalz. & Gibs. p. 104; Wight, Icon. t. 201; Trim. Fl. Ceyl. v. 2, p. 241; Woodr. in Journ. Bomb. Nat. v. 11 (1898) p. 639; Watt, Dict. Econ. Prod. v. 5, p. 254. —Flowers: Apr.–May.

Rather rare. KONKAN: *Stocks*!; Malwán, *Dalzell & Gibson*. KANARA: Divimana, Samptkhand (N. Kanara), *Woodrow*!; Chandvár, *Ritchie*, 1763!—DISTRIB. India (W. Peninsula); Ceylon.

Carica Papaya, Linn. *The Papaw*, a rapidly growing soft-wooded tree, considered by DeCandolle to be a native of the W. Indies, the shores of the Gulf of Mexico and doubtfully of Brasil, is widely cultivated throughout India. It has large glabrous pinnatifid and palminerved leaves 1–2 ft. across, and fragrant (diœcious) flowers of which the males are in long drooping panicles and the females in short clusters. The fruit, which is of the size of a small melon, with a soft yellow sweet pulp, is eaten and is regarded as possessing properties similar to pepsin. It seems to be a well-established fact that meat wrapped in the leaves or treated with the juice of the fruit becomes tender. The milky juice of the unripe fruit has been extensively used in medicine (see Watt, Dict. Econ. Prod. v. 2, p. 158). Fl. B. I. v. 2, p. 599; Grah. Cat. p. 80; Dalz. & Gibs. Suppl. p. 37; Woodr. in Journ. Bomb. Nat. v. 11 (1898) p. 639, & Gard. in Ind. ed. 5, p. 324.—Vern. *Papáya*; *Popai.*

Passiflora fœtida, Linn., a native of Tropical America, is a very common plant in gardens and is frequently found as an escape. It has small flowers and a remarkable pectinate and moss-like involucre.—Vern. *Veli-ghâni.*

Several other species of *Passiflora* are grown in gardens throughout the Presidency, of which may be mentioned:—*Passiflora edulis* with bluish-purple fragrant flowers, not fruiting much below 4000 ft. altitude and then bearing a plum-like edible yellow fruit; *P. laurifolia* with large blue fragrant flowers; *P. racemosa* with deep-red or scarlet flowers; *P. holosericea* with mottled flowers about 2 in. across; and *P. Raddiana* (better known as *P. kermesina*) which bears in great abundance bright-red flowers with narrow petals. (See *Woodrow*, Gard. in Ind. ed. 5, pp. 322–324.)

Order LXII. CUCURBITACEÆ.

Herbs or undershrubs usually climbing. Leaves alternate, petiolate, frequently cordate, simple, or palmately or pedately divided. Tendrils when present lateral, solitary, simple or divided, spirally twisted. Flowers monœcious or diœcious, yellow or white, solitary, paniculate or racemose. Calyx-tube adnate to the ovary; limb rotate, campanulate or tubular, 5- (rarely 3–6-) lobed, imbricate. Petals as many as the calyx-lobes, inserted on the limb of the calyx, free or rarely gamopetalous, sometimes lobed or fimbriate, valvate or involute in bud. Stamens inserted at the mouth, or about the middle, or at the base of the calyx-tube, usually 3 (rarely 5); anthers free, cohering, or confluent into a capitulum, one usually 1-celled, the other two 2-celled, the cells flexuose or conduplicate, extrorsely dehiscent; the connective sometimes produced beyond the cells. Ovary inferior, or rarely free at the apex only, usually 3-carpellary; ovules usually many, horizontal, rarely few and pendulous; style 1 with 3 large stigmas (more rarely styles 2–3–4); placentas usually 3, the edges of the carpellary leaves being often turned in so far that the ovary (even before fertilization) is spuriously 3-celled. Fruit usually a fleshy berry, indehiscent or dehiscing by valves or by a circumscissile lid. Seeds numerous, often packed in pulp or fibre; albumen 0.—DISTRIB. Warmer parts of the globe, especially in the Tropics; genera 80; species about 600.

Ovules horizontal.
  Stamens 3 (rarely 2 or 5); female flowers usually solitary, less commonly fascicled.
    Anther-cells flexuose or conduplicate.
      Corolla 5-partite to the base or 5-petalous.
        Petals fimbriate .... 1. TRICHOSANTHES.
        Petals not fimbriate.
          Stamens free, inserted on the mouth of the calyx.
            Calyx with scales at the bottom .... 2. MOMORDICA.
          Stamens free, inserted on the tube of the calyx.
            Male flowers racemose.
              Fruit dry, fibrous, dehiscing operculately at the apex .... 3. LUFFA.
            Male flowers solitary or fascicled.
              Pollen muriculate; rudimentary ovary 0 .... 4. BRYONOPSIS.
              Pollen smooth; rudimentary ovary glanduliform.
                Connective of anthers produced beyond the cells; tendrils simple. 5. CUCUMIS.
                Connective of anthers not produced beyond the cells; tendrils usually 2–3-fid .... 6. CITRULLUS.
      Corolla campanulate, divided to the middle or a little below it .... 7. COCCINIA.
    Anther-cells straight or curved, not flexuose.
      Style inserted on a cup-shaped or annular disk .... 8. MELOTHRIA.
      Disk at base of style 0 or obscure.
        Petiole with a stipuliform bract at the base .... 9. BLASTANIA.
        Petiole ebracteate at the base.
          Fruit indehiscent........ 10. KEDROSTIS.
          Fruit operculately dehiscent above the base .... 11. CORALLOCARPUS.
Ovules erect or ascending.
  Stamens 3 .... 12. DICŒLOSPERMUM.
Ovules pendulous.
  Stamens 5; female flowers in racemes .... 13. ZANONIA.

1. TRICHOSANTHES, Linn.

Scandent herbs. Leaves entire or 3–9-lobed, denticulate; tendrils simple or 2–5-fid. Flowers diœcious (rarely monœcious), white. MALE FLOWERS usually racemose (rarely solitary), often bracteolate. Calyx-tube cylindric, dilated above, 5-lobed. Corolla 5-fid nearly to the base; lobes long, fimbriate. Stamens 3, inserted in the calyx-tube; filaments very short; anthers almost included, usually connate, one 1-celled, the others 2-celled, the cells conduplicate; connective narrow, not produced. Rudimentary ovaries 3, filiform. FEMALE FLOWERS solitary. Calyx and corolla as in the male. Staminodes 0. Ovary inferior, ovoid or fusiform, 1-celled, 3-placentiferous; ovules very many, horizontal or semi-pendulous; style slender; stigmas 3, entire or bifid. Fruit fleshy, globose, ovoid or fusiform, indehiscent, many-seeded, usually smooth and glabrous. Seeds packed in pulp, ellipsoid, sometimes angular, usually margined.—DISTRIB. Tropical Asia, N. Australia, Polynesia; species 40.

Leaves entire.
  Male racemes with small bracts .... 1. *T. nervifolia.*
Leaves lobed or angled.
  Male racemes with large bracts .... 2. *T. palmata.*
  Male racemes ebracteate .... 3. *T. cucumerina.*

1. **Trichosanthes nervifolia,** *Linn. Sp. Pl.* (1753) p. 1008. Perennial; stems somewhat woody below, much-branched; branches slender, striate, glabrous. Tendrils 2-fid, glabrous. Leaves 2–4 by 1–2¼ in., ovate-oblong (not lobed), acute, mucronate, the margins minutely and remotely denticulate, glabrous on both surfaces, dark-green above, paler beneath, base cordate; main nerves 3 from the base, the two lateral not quite reaching the apex, with strong secondary nerves on the outside, the lowest pair of secondary nerves conspicuously branching into the basal lobes of the leaf at either side of the sinus; petioles ½–1 in. long. MALE FLOWERS in axillary 4–10-flowered corymbose racemes; peduncles slender, sulcate, 1–2½ in. long; pedicels $\frac{1}{5}$–$\frac{1}{3}$ in. long; bracts minute, caducous. Calyx-tube puberulous, ⅔–1¼ in. long, very narrow, about ⅛ in. wide at the mouth and $\frac{1}{20}$ in. wide in the middle; teeth linear, acute, $\frac{1}{16}$–$\frac{1}{10}$ in. long. Petals ovate-oblong, acute, the fimbriæ at the apex much branched and much longer than the blade of the petal, doubled inwards in bud. FEMALE FLOWERS axillary, solitary, on short peduncles. Calyx-tube nearly 2 in. long, much produced above the ovary. Fruit 1½–3 in. long, ellipsoid, shortly beaked, tapering to both ends, green with white lines when immature, scarlet when ripe; pericarp thin. Seeds semi-ellipsoid, ⅜–½ in. long, compressed, thickened at the margin, each enclosed in an envelope of scarlet pulp. Fl. B. I. v. 2, p. 609; Grah. Cat. p. 78; Trim. Fl. Ceyl. v. 2, p. 244; Watt, Dict. Econ. Prod. v. 6, part 4, p. 84.

KONKAN: *Graham.*

This is included on the authority of Graham (*l. c.*). It has not apparently been found by any other collector. I have seen no specimens from the Bombay Presidency.—DISTRIB. S. India; Ceylon.

2. **Trichosanthes palmata,** *Roxb. Fl. Ind.* v. 3 (1832) p. 704. Climbing often to a height of 30 ft.; stems robust, woody below, branched, grooved, the older light-grey with scabrous spots, the younger smooth, green. Tendrils 2-, more commonly 3-cleft. Leaves 2½–5 in. long and about as broad as long, variable, usually palmately 3–5-lobed to about the middle (more or less), dark-green above, paler beneath, frequently with dark-colored circular glands scattered along the lower side, glabrous, often scabrous with small scales above and on the nerves beneath, base cordate; lobes usually ovate-oblong, acute, more or less dentate or serrate; petioles 1–3 in. long, striate, puberulous or at length glabrous. MALE FLOWERS in axillary 5–10-flowered racemes 6–9 in. long (rarely solitary); pedicels thick, erect, very short; bracts 1 in. long and more, broadly ovate, pale-green, many-nerved, fringed, dotted with dark-green glandular spots. Calyx-tube 1½ in. long, pubescent, longitudinally striate; teeth lanceolate, erect or spreading, laciniate. Petals 1 in. long, wedge-shaped, fringed, exceeding the calyx-teeth. Filaments slightly villous. FEMALE FLOWERS axillary,

solitary; peduncles less than 1 in. long. Fruit 1½–2 in. in diam., globose, red when ripe, streaked with 10 orange streaks; pericarp thick. Seeds numerous, ⅜–½ in. long, ellipsoid, smooth, slightly attenuated at the base, not margined. Fl. B. I. v. 2, p. 606; Grah. Cat. p. 79; Dalz. & Gibs. p. 103; Wight, Ill. tt. 104, 105; Trim. Fl. Ceyl. v. 2, p. 244; Woodr. in Journ. Bomb. Nat. v. 11 (1898) p. 639; Watt, Dict. Econ. Prod. v. 6, part 4, p. 84. *Trichosanthes bracteata*, Voigt, Hort. Sub. Calc. (1845) p. 58; Cogniaux, in DC. Monogr. Phan. v. 3, p. 375.—Flowers: Apr.–July. VERN. *Kaundal*; *Mukál.*

KONKAN: *Law!* DECCAN: Lanoli, *Kanitkar!*, *Woodrow*; Mahableshwar, *Cooke!* S. M. COUNTRY: Castlerock, *Cooke!*; Kákti (Sángli State), *Ritchie*, 1071!—DISTRIB. Throughout India; Ceylon, Malaya, China, Japan, N. Australia.

The plant has some repute as a remedy in certain diseases of cattle.

3. **Trichosanthes cucumerina,** *Linn. Sp. Pl.* (1753) p. 1008. Annual, monœcious; stems 12–15 ft. long, slender, furrowed, slightly hairy or subglabrous, leafy. Tendrils 2–3- (usually 3-) fid. Leaves 2–5 in. long, usually a little broader than long, orbicular-reniform or broadly ovate, distantly denticulate, more or less deeply 5- (rarely 3–7-) lobed, the lobes broad, acute, glabrous or nearly so above, more or less pubescent, or, when old, sometimes scabrid beneath, base deeply cordate, the sinus often subrectangular; petioles 1–3 in. long, striate, pubescent. MALE FLOWERS in axillary racemes, with sometimes a solitary male flower from the same axil as the raceme; peduncles of the racemes 2–6 in. long, slender, striate, bearing 8–15 flowers near the apex; pedicels puberulous, ⅓–¾ in. long; bracts 0. Calyx-tube dilated at the apex, ¾–1 in. long, about ⅛ in. wide at the mouth; teeth short, acutely triangular. Petals white, ⅜ in. long, lanceolate-oblong, laciniate at the apex. FEMALE FLOWERS axillary, solitary, or occasionally a female flower in the same axil as the male peduncle; peduncles of female flowers ⅛–⅝ in. long. Fruit 1–3 in. long, ovoid-fusiform, tapering at both ends and with a long sharp beak, green and striped with white when immature, scarlet when ripe; pericarp thin. Seeds semi-ellipsoid, compressed, rugulose, surrounded with red pulp. Fl. B. I. v. 2, p. 609; Grah. Cat. p. 79; Dalz. & Gibs. p. 102; Trim. Fl. Ceyl. v. 2, p. 245; Woodr. in Journ. Bomb. Nat. v. 11 (1898) p. 639; Watt, Dict. Econ. Prod. v. 6, part 4, p. 82.—Flowers: July–Oct. VERN. *Jangli-padvel.*

KONKAN: S. Konkan, *Dalzell & Gibson*. DECCAN: Poona, *Woodrow*; Vitalwadi, 6 miles west of Poona, *Krishna!*; Shrivardhan (Jinjira State), *Kanitkar!* GUJARAT: common in hedges, *Dalzell & Gibson*; Baroda, *Cooke!*; Godra, *Cooke!*; Udwada, *Cooke!* KANARA: Karwar, *Woodrow*.—DISTRIB. Throughout India; Ceylon, Malaya, N. Australia.

Trichosanthes Anguina, Linn. Sp. Pl. (1753) p. 1008. *The Snake Gourd* of Anglo-Indians. The fruit of this gourd often attains 3 ft. in length with a thickness of 3 in. The leaves and flowers are like those of *T. cucumerina*, but the fruit is entirely different. Mr. C. B. Clarke suggests that it may perhaps be a cultivated form of that plant. It is cultivated as a rainy season crop throughout the Bombay Presidency, but is not known in the wild state. Fl. B. I. v. 2, p. 610; Grah. Cat. p. 78; Dalz. & Gibs. Suppl. p. 37; Duthie, Field and Gard. Crops, t. 46; Woodr. in Journ. Bomb. Nat. v. 11 (1898) p. 639, & Gard. in Ind. ed. 5, p. 330; Watt, Dict. Econ. Prod. v. 6, part 4, p. 81.—VERN. *Padvel*; *Chikonda.*

2. MOMORDICA, Linn.

Climbing annual or perennial herbs. Leaves entire, lobed or pedately 3–7-foliolate. Tendrils simple or bifid. Flowers yellow or white, monœcious or diœcious. Male flowers corymbose or racemose. Calyx-tube short, campanulate, closed at the bottom with 2–3 incurved oblong scales; lobes 5. Corolla usually 5-partite to the base or nearly so, rotate or broadly campanulate; segments obovate, costate. Stamens 3 (2 in *M. Cymbalaria*), inserted on the mouth of the calyx-tube; filaments short, free; anthers at first cohering, at length free, one 1-celled, the others 2-celled, the cells flexuose (rarely short and straight or curved), connective not produced at the apex. Rudimentary ovary 0 or glanduliform. Female flowers solitary. Calyx and corolla as in the male. Rudimentary stamens 0, or 3 glands surrounding the base of the style. Ovary oblong or fusiform, 3-placentiferous; ovules ∞, horizontal; styles slender; stigmas 3. Fruit oblong, fusiform, or cylindric, baccate, indehiscent or 3-valvate, few or many-seeded. Seeds tumid or flattened, smooth or variously sculptured.—Distrib. Chiefly African, a few scattered through the tropics of both hemispheres; species 25.

Male peduncles 1-flowered.
 Flowers monœcious.
  Bracts of male flowers about the middle or below the middle of the peduncle .... 1. *M. Charantia.*
  Bracts of male flowers at the apex of the peduncle ... 2. *M. Balsamina.*
 Flowers diœcious.
  Petioles without glands.
   Calyx-lobes linear-lanceolate, acute .... 3. *M. dioica.*
   Calyx-lobes ovate-oblong, obtuse .... 4. *M. subangulata.*
  Petioles glandular .... 5. *M. cochinchinensis.*
Male flowers in racemes .... 6. *M. Cymbalaria.*

1. **Momordica Charantia,** *Linn. Sp. Pl.* (1753) p. 1009. Annual; stem 3–6 ft. long, much branched, angled and grooved, more or less pubescent or hairy; young parts hairy or villous. Tendrils simple, slender, elongate, pubescent. Leaves almost orbicular in outline, 2–5 in. in diam., pubescent or subglabrous on both sides, cordate at the base, deeply divided into 5–7 lobes, the lobes acute or subacute, apiculate, coarsely spinous-dentate, constricted at the base, the sinus between them narrow, rounded; petioles 1–2 in. long, channelled, pubescent. Flowers monœcious. Male flowers solitary; peduncles 2–4 in. long, glabrous or pubescent, furnished with a large reniform or orbicular bract at or below the middle. Calyx $\frac{1}{3}$–$\frac{3}{8}$ in. long, pubescent; lobes $\frac{1}{5}$–$\frac{1}{4}$ in. long, elliptic, subacute. Corolla somewhat irregular, lemon-yellow; segments obtuse or emarginate, $\frac{2}{3}$–$\frac{3}{4}$ in. long, veined. Female flowers: Peduncles 2–4 in. long, slender, bracteate usually at or near the base. Staminodes 3, glanduliform. Ovary fusiform, muricate; stigmas 3, bifid. Fruit bright orange-colored, 2–6 in. long, pendulous, fusiform, usually pointed or beaked, ribbed, and bearing numerous triangular tubercles giving it the appearance of a crocodile's back (*Graham*), 3-valved at the apex when mature. Seeds $\frac{1}{3}$–$\frac{1}{2}$ in. long, compressed, corrugate on the margin, sculptured on both faces. Fl. B. I. v. 2, p. 616; Grah. Cat. p. 78; Dalz. & Gibs. p. 102; Trim. Fl. Ceyl.

v. 2, p. 248; Woodr. in Journ. Bomb. Nat. v. 11 (1898) p. 640; Watt, Dict. Econ. Prod. v. 5, p. 256.—Flowers: May–Aug. VERN. *Kdrale.*

Widely cultivated. DECCAN: *Woodrow*!; Poona districts, *Kanitkar*! SIND: Larkbána, *Cooke*!; near Karachi, *Bhola Puran*!—DISTRIB. Throughout India; Ceylon, Malaya, China, Tropical Africa.

The fruit is eaten, but requires steeping in salt water before use. The root, as well as the fruit, is also used medicinally.

2. **Momordica Balsamina,** *Linn. Sp. Pl.* (1753) p. 1009. Monœcious; stem 2–5 ft. long, very slender, branched, grooved, subglabrous. Tendrils simple, filiform, glabrous. Leaves membranous, orbicular in outline, 1½–3 in. in diam., cordate at the base with a broad sinus, palmately 3–5-lobed to about the middle, the lobes rhomboid, deeply lobulate, acute and mucronulate at the apex, usually constricted at the base, the sinus between the lobes broad and rounded; petioles ½–1¼ in. long, striate, pubescent. MALE FLOWERS: Peduncles 1-flowered, slightly pubescent at the apex, otherwise glabrous or nearly so, slender, 1–3 in. long; bract towards the apex of the peduncle, ¼–⅜ in. wide, cordate, orbicular, denticulate, variegated green and white, reticulately veined. Calyx ⅜ in. long, pubescent; lobes ¼ in. long, 5–7-nerved, triangular, acute, with a long slender mucro. Corolla subregular, yellowish with a dark base, ½ in. long, obovate, subobtuse, reticulately veined, sometimes apiculate. Anther-cells flexuous, the connective broad. FEMALE FLOWERS: Peduncles ⅕–½ in. long, usually ebracteate, or bracteate at the base. Calyx-lobes linear-lanceolate. Ovary fusiform, beaked, verrucose. Fruit 1–3 in. long, ovoid, narrowed to both ends, rostrate, fleshy, smooth or muricate. Seeds ash-colored, ellipsoid, compressed, ⅜ by ¼ by $\frac{1}{10}$ in., rugulose on the flat faces, and with a grooved margin which is tuberculate on the edges. Fl. B. I. v. 2, p. 617; Aitch. Pb. & Sind Pl. p. 63; Hook. f. in Oliver, Fl. Trop. Afr. v. 2, p. 537; Woodr. in Journ. Bomb. Nat. v. 11 (1898) p. 640; Watt, Dict. Econ. Prod. v. 5, p. 256.—Flowers: Nov. VERN. (Sindi) *Kurelo-jangro.*

Common in Sind, also found in Gujarat, but rare in the Deccan. GUJARAT: Pahlanpur, *Woodrow*; Ahmedabad, *Raoji*! SIND: indigenous, *Stocks & Aitchison, Bhola Puran*! *Woodrow*; Mulir near Karachi, *Cooke*!—DISTRIB. India (Panjáb, N.W. Provinces); Malaya, Australia, W. Asia, Africa.

3. **Momordica dioica,** *Roxb. in Willd. Sp. Pl.* v. 4 (1805) p. 605. Diœcious, perennial, with tuberous roots; stem slender, branched, furrowed, glabrous and shining. Tendrils simple, elongate, striate, glabrous. Leaves membranous, broadly ovate in outline, variable, 1½–4 by 1¼–3¼ in., cordate at the base, glabrous, minutely punctate, entire or more or less deeply 3–5-lobed, the lobes triangular, ovate or oblong, distantly denticulate; petioles ½–1¾ in. long, channelled above, pubescent, eglandular. MALE FLOWERS: Peduncle solitary, 1-flowered, 1½–5 in. long, slender, angled, usually pubescent near the top, otherwise glabrous; bract cucullate, inserted a little below the flower and enclosing it, orbicular-reniform, ½–¾ in. broad, usually pubescent on both sides, strongly nerved, often ciliolate. Calyx-lobes distant, ⅕–⅓ in. long, linear-lanceolate. Petals ½–1 in. long, wholly yellow, oblong-lanceolate. FEMALE FLOWERS: Peduncles nearly as long as those of the male, usually with a small bract near the base. Ovary clothed with long soft papillæ. Fruit 1–2½ in. long, ellipsoid, shortly beaked, densely echinate

with soft spines. Seeds many, $\frac{3}{8}$ in. long, broadly ellipsoid, slightly compressed, slightly and irregularly corrugated, enclosed in a red pulp. Fl. B. I. v. 2, p. 617 (exclud. syn. *M. subangulata*, Blume); Grah. Cat. p. 78; Dalz. & Gibs. p. 102; Wight, Icon. tt. 505, 506; Trim. Fl. Ceyl. v. 2, p. 249; Woodr. in Journ. Bomb. Nat. v. 11 (1898) p. 640; Watt, Dict. Econ. Prod. v. 5, p. 258.—Flowers: June–Aug. VERN. *Kartoli*.

Widely cultivated in the Deccan. KONKAN: *Law*! DECCAN: Kadakvasla, *Cooke*!; Kothrud near Poona, *Kanitkar*! S. M. COUNTRY: Badami, *Cooke*!; Castlerock, *Cooke*! GUJARAT: Godra, *Cooke*! Sind: *Stocks*!—DISTRIB. Throughout India; Ceylon, Malaya.

4. **Momordica subangulata,** *Blume, Bijdr.* (1825) p. 928. Diœcious; stem slender, branched, furrowed, glabrous or slightly puberulous at the nodes. Tendrils simple, slender, furrowed, glabrous. Leaves membranous, deeply cordate, the upper surface glabrous, the lower more or less pubescent, broadly ovate, acute, entire, or sub-3–5-lobed, the margins remotely denticulate, 2–4 by $1\frac{1}{2}$–$3\frac{1}{2}$ in. long; petioles 1–2 in. long, slender, striate, subglabrous, eglandular. MALE FLOWERS: Peduncle solitary, 1-flowered, 1–3 in. long, furrowed, pubescent, especially at the apex; bract cucullate, close to the flower, $\frac{1}{2}$–$\frac{3}{4}$ in. broad, not as long as broad, pubescent on both sides and with ciliate margin. Calyx dark-purplish; lobes ovate-oblong, obtuse, glandular, $\frac{1}{8}$–$\frac{1}{6}$ in. long. Corolla yellow, partite to the base, the segments oblong. FEMALE FLOWERS not known. Fruit ellipsoid, 2–3 in. long, attenuated at the base and apex, densely and softly echinate, obscurely ribbed, the ribs broken into joints. Cogniaux, in DC. Monogr. Phan. v. 3, p. 443; King, in Journ. As. Soc. Beng. v. 67, part 2 (1898) p. 36.

S. M. COUNTRY: *Ritchie*, 311!; Belgaum, *Ritchie*, 311!

A rare plant, of which only 2 specimens from Bombay exist in Herb. Kew.—DISTRIB. India (W. Peninsula); Java, Malaya.

5. **Momordica cochinchinensis,** *Spreng. Syst.* v. 3 (1826) p. 14. A strong climber ascending trees, diœcious; root tuberous, perennial; stem robust, angular, glabrous. Tendrils simple, stout, angled, glabrous. Leaves suborbicular in outline, cordate at the base, 4–7 in. long and broad, glabrous on both surfaces, the margin near the base furnished with umbilicate glands, divided to the middle or almost to the base into 3 (rarely 5) lobes, the lobes ovate or oblong-lanceolate, acute or acuminate, diverging, the margins entire or faintly toothed; petioles 2–3 in. long, stout, sulcate, almost invariably glandular at the middle and at the apex, glabrous or nearly so. MALE FLOWERS: Peduncles 1-flowered, 2–6 in. long, angularly furrowed, more or less pubescent, especially near the apex; bract at the top of the peduncle embracing the flower, broader than long, $1\frac{1}{8}$–$1\frac{3}{8}$ by $1\frac{1}{2}$–2 in., cordate at the base, pubescent or scabrid. Calyx hirsute or scabrid; lobes $\frac{1}{2}$–$\frac{5}{8}$ in. long, oblong-lanceolate, acute. Corolla white, tinged with yellow, pubescent outside and more or less so inside; segments reaching $2\frac{1}{4}$ by 1 in., obovate-oblong or elliptic-oblong, obtuse or subacute. FEMALE FLOWERS: Peduncles 1–2 in. long, with a small bract about the middle. Fruit 4–6 in. long, ovoid, pointed, red, fleshy, terete, densely covered with raised points about $\frac{1}{8}$ in. long. Seeds numerous, $\frac{7}{8}$ by $\frac{5}{8}$ by $\frac{1}{4}$ in., ovoid, much compressed, sculptured on both faces. Fl. B. I. v. 2, p. 618; Woodr. in Journ. Bomb. Nat.

v. 11 (1898) p. 640; Watt, Dict. Econ. Prod. v. 5, p. 257.—Flowers: June-Aug.

Rare. KANARA: *Law*!; N. Kanara, *Woodrow*.—DISTRIB. Throughout India; Malaya, Philippines.

6. **Momordica Cymbalaria,** *Fenzl, ex Naudin, in Ann. Sci. Nat.* sér. 4, v. 12 (1859) p. 134. Monœcious; root woody, tuberous, perennial; stem very slender, scandent, branched, striate, pubescent or subglabrous. Tendrils filiform, slightly pubescent, simple. Leaves orbicular-reniform in outline, $\frac{3}{4}$–$1\frac{3}{4}$ by 1–2 in., glabrous or with a few scattered hairs, punctate (but not scabrid) on both surfaces, deeply cordate at the base, obtusely but not deeply 5–7-lobed, the lobes short, acute or obtuse; petioles $\frac{1}{2}$–$1\frac{1}{2}$ in. long, striate, pubescent. MALE FLOWERS in 2–5-flowered racemes; peduncles $\frac{1}{4}$–1 in. long, filiform, pubescent, ebracteate; pedicels $\frac{1}{8}$–$\frac{3}{8}$ in. long. Calyx hairy; tube short, broadly campanulate, narrowed at the base; lobes $\frac{1}{4}$ in. long, lanceolate, acute. Corolla pale yellow; segments obovate, obtuse, $\frac{3}{8}$–$\frac{1}{2}$ in. long. Stamens 2; filaments very short, thick, flattened; anthers $\frac{1}{12}$ in. long, one 2-partite, the others 3-partite, the cells conduplicate, the connective broad. FEMALE FLOWERS: Peduncles $\frac{3}{4}$–$1\frac{1}{2}$ in. long, slender, ebracteate. Ovary fusiform, beaked; style stout; stigmas 2, spreading, 2-partite. Fruit $\frac{3}{4}$–1 in. long, pyriform or broadly fusiform, narrowed into the curved peduncle, fleshy, dark-green, 8-ribbed, sparsely hairy. Seeds $\frac{1}{6}$–$\frac{1}{4}$ in. long, broadly ovoid, slightly compressed, strophiolate, not margined; testa polished and shining, dark-brown. Fl. B. I. v. 2, p. 618; Hook. f. in Oliv. Fl. Trop. Afr. v. 2, p. 540; Woodr. in Journ. Bomb. Nat. v. 11 (1898) p. 640; Watt, Dict. Econ. Prod. v. 5, p. 258. *Momordica tuberosa*, Cogniaux, in DC. Monogr. Phan. v. 3 (1881) p. 454. *Luffa tuberosa*, Roxb. Hort. Beng. p. 104.—Flowers: Nov. VERN. *Kadvanchi.*

DECCAN: Sholapur districts, Igatpuri, Sattara, *Nairne*. S. M. COUNTRY: Dharwar, *Woodrow*!—DISTRIB. India (W. Peninsula); Tropical Africa.

3. LUFFA, Cav.

Annual herbs. Tendrils 2-many-fid. Leaves 5–7-lobed (rarely subentire); petiole without glands at the apex. Flowers monœcious (rarely diœcious), rather large, yellow or white, males and females often from the same axil. MALE FLOWERS racemose. Calyx-tube campanulate or turbinate; lobes 5, triangular or lanceolate. Petals 5, free, spreading, obovate or obcordate. Stamens 3 (rarely 5), inserted on the calyx-tube; filaments free or connate; anthers exserted, free, one 1-celled, the others 2-celled, the cells sigmoid, often on the margin of a broad connective. Rudimentary ovary glanduliform or 0. FEMALE FLOWERS solitary. Calyx-tube produced beyond the ovary; lobes as in the male. Corolla as in the male. Staminodes usually 3, thick. Ovary elongate, sulcate, angled or cylindric, 3-placentiferous; ovules numerous, horizontal; style columnar; stigma 3-lobed. Fruit dry, oblong or cylindric (not spherical), acutely ribbed or terete, smooth or echinate, fibrous within, 3-celled, terminated by the persistent style, usually circumscissile near the apex. Seeds many, oblong, compressed.—DISTRIB. Warmer regions of the Old World, one species indigenous in America; species 6.

Stamens 5.
Seeds winged, usually smooth .... 1. *L. ægyptiaca.*
Stamens 3.
Fruit 10-ribbed (not echinate); seeds rugose, wingless .... 2. *L. acutangula.*
Fruit echinate; seeds slightly verrucose, wingless .... 3. *L. echinata.*

1. **Luffa ægyptiaca,** *Mill. Dict.* ed. 8 (1768). Monœcious, climbing to a considerable height; stems stout, 5-angled, twisted, glabrous or slightly pubescent, often scabrous at the angles. Tendrils usually 3-fid. Leaves orbicular-reniform in outline, 4–8 in. long, often broader than long, palmately 5- (rarely 7-) lobed, the lobes acute or acuminate, lobulate and distantly denticulate, both surfaces finely scabrous, punctate, glabrous except the pubescent nerves beneath, base deeply cordate; petioles 1–4 in. long, angular, slightly scabrous. Male flowers in axillary 4–20-flowered racemes, usually crowded near the top of the raceme; peduncles 4–6 in. long; pedicels $\frac{1}{4}$–$\frac{1}{2}$ in. long, pubescent, articulated near the apex, each bearing a small lanceolate glandular bract at or, more commonly, a little above its base; buds ovoid, pointed. Calyx pubescent, $\frac{3}{4}$ in. long; lobes lanceolate, acute, $\frac{1}{2}$ in. long. Petals spreading, 1 in. long, obovate-oblong, yellow with green veins. Stamens 5, distinct. Female flowers solitary, usually from the same axils as the males; peduncles stout, 1–3 in. long. Staminodes usually 5. Ovary cylindric-oblong, glabrous or pubescent. Fruit 5–12 in. long, cylindric or somewhat trigonous, blunt at the end, marked with longitudinal lines. Seeds black or grey, $\frac{3}{8}$ by $\frac{1}{4}$ in., much compressed, narrowly winged, smooth or slightly tuberculate. Fl. B. I. v. 2, p. 614; Trim. Fl. Ceyl. v. 2, p. 251; Woodr. in Journ. Bomb. Nat. v. 11 (1898) p. 640; Watt, Dict. Econ. Prod. v. 5, p. 96. *Luffa pentandra*, Roxb. Hort. Beng. p. 70; Grah. Cat. p. 77; Dalz. & Gibs. Suppl. p. 36; Wight, Icon. t. 499.—Flowers: June–Sept. Vern. *Ghosdle*; *Ghiyd-turai.*

Very common in native gardens and sometimes as an escape, but scarcely to be regarded as a wild plant. The young fruit is eaten as a vegetable, and, as Mr. C. B. Clarke points out (Fl. B. I. l. c.), being the only part attended to in cultivation is hence too variable to afford good diagnostic characters. The seeds are used medicinally and the fibrous network in the fruit employed as a flesh-brush.

2. **Luffa acutangula,** *Roxb. Hort. Beng.* (1814) p. 70. Monœcious, climbing to a considerable height; stems 5-angled, glabrous, with sharp angles which are often scabrid. Tendrils usually 3-fid. Leaves orbicular in outline, pale green, 6–8 in. long and broad, palmately 5–7-angled or sublobate, scabrid on both sides, base cordate; nerves and veins prominent beneath; petioles 2–5 in. long, angular, scabrid. Male flowers in axillary 12–20-flowered racemes 4–6 in. long. Calyx pubescent, $\frac{1}{2}$ in. long; lobes lanceolate, $\frac{3}{8}$ in. long. Petals $\frac{3}{4}$ in. long, spreading, obovate, yellow with green hairy veins. Stamens 3. Female flowers solitary, in the same axils as the males; peduncles 2–4 in. long. Ovary strongly ribbed. Fruit 6–12 in. long, clavate-oblong, tapering towards the base, very obtuse, smooth, longitudinally ribbed (almost winged) with 10 sharp angles. Seeds $\frac{1}{2}$ by $\frac{1}{4}$–$\frac{1}{3}$ in., ovoid-oblong, much compressed, slightly corrugated on the sides, not winged, black.

Very closely allied to *L. ægyptiaca*, from which it differs in the number of stamens, the strongly ribbed ovary, the fruit, and the seeds. Fl. B. I. v. 2, p. 615; Grah. Cat. p. 77; Dalz. & Gibs. Suppl. p. 36;

Trim. Fl. Ceyl. v. 2, p. 252; Woodr. in Journ. Bomb. Nat. v. 11 (1898) p. 640; Watt, Dict. Econ. Prod. v. 6, p. 94.—Flowers: June–Sept VERN. *Shiráld*; *Shirol*; *Dodka-turai.*

S. M. COUNTRY: Belgaum hill south, *Ritchie*, $\frac{307}{2}$! KANARA: Halyal, *Ritchie* $\frac{307}{4}$! As in the case of the preceding species, this cannot be regarded as truly wild. It is cultivated extensively, and when half grown is an excellent and palatable vegetable. The seeds possess emetic and purgative properties and are used in medicine. See Watt, Dict. Econ. Prod. l. c.

VAR. *amara*, C. B. Clarke, in Hook. f. Fl. B. I. v. 2, p. 615. Leaves smaller, at first whitish and softly villous, at length scabrid. Flowers smaller. Fruit obovoid, obtusely conical at both ends, 2–4 in. long by about 1–1½ in. thick, 10-ribbed, bitter. Seeds smaller. Trim. Fl. Ceyl. v. 2, p. 252; Cogniaux, in DC. Monogr. Phan. v. 3, p. 461; Watt, Dict. Econ. Prod. v. 5, p. 95. *Luffa amara* (sp.), Roxb. Hort. Beng. p. 70; Grah. Cat. p. 77; Dalz. & Gibs. p. 102; Woodr. in Journ. Bomb. Nat. v. 11 (1898) p. 640.—Flowers: Sept. VERN. *Rán-turai.*

Common in hedges in the rains. KONKAN: wild about Bombay and in the Konkans, *Graham*; W. Ghâts, *Woodrow*. S. M. COUNTRY: Belgaum, *Ritchie*. GUJARAT: Godra, *Cooke*!, *Woodrow*.—DISTRIB. Throughout India, especially the Western Peninsula; Ceylon.

The whole plant is exceedingly bitter and the seeds are cathartic and emetic. Their action is said to be safe and sure, and more satisfactory than that of the seeds of *L. acutangula*. See Watt, Dict. Econ. Prod. l. c.

3. **Luffa echinata,** *Roxb. Hort. Beng.* (1814) p. 104. Climbing but not extensively; stem slender, branched, furrowed, glabrous. Tendrils 2-fid. Leaves 1½–2½ in. long, usually a little broader than long, reniform-suborbicular in outline, broadly cordate at the base, obscurely 5-angled or more or less deeply 5-lobed, the lobes rounded or rarely subacute at the apex, the margins minutely denticulate; petioles 1–2 in. long, striate, puberulous or sometimes slightly scabrid. Flowers usually diœcious. MALE FLOWERS: Peduncles 3–6 in. long, usually in pairs, one 1-flowered, the other with a raceme of 5–12 flowers at the apex; pedicels ⅜–¾ in. long, bracteate near the base. Calyx hairy, ¼ in. long; tube very short; lobes ovate-lanceolate, acute. Petals white, spreading, obovate, twice as long as the calyx, veined. Stamens 3, two with 2-celled anthers. FEMALE FLOWERS: Peduncles ½–2 in. long. Fruit broadly ellipsoid, 1–1½ by ½–¾ in., not ribbed, clothed with ciliate bristles ⅙–¼ in. long; operculum conical, without bristles. Seeds numerous, ⅙–⅕ by ⅛ in., not winged, slightly verrucose. Fl. B. I. v. 2, p. 615; Dalz. & Gibs. p. 102; Aitch. Pb. & Sind Pl. p. 63; Woodr. in Journ. Bomb. Nat. v. 11 (1898) p. 640; Watt, Dict. Econ. Prod. v. 5, p. 97.—Flowers: Sept. VERN. *Kukad-vel.*

Rare, except in Gujarat and Sind. GUJARAT: *Dalzell*!; Gundár, *Dalzell & Gibson*; Godra, *Woodrow*; Deesa, *Stocks*! SIND: *Stocks*.—DISTRIB. India (Gujarat, Sind, Dacca); Tropical Africa.

The fruit is used in medicine.

4. BRYONOPSIS, Arn. in Hook. Journ. Bot. v. 3, p. 274.

Annual scaberulous scandent herbs. Tendrils 2-fid. Leaves deeply palmately 5-lobed. Flowers monœcious, the male and female fascicled, often in the same axils. MALE FLOWERS: Calyx-tube broadly campanulate; lobes 5, subulate. Corolla campanulate, 5-partite; segments ovate. Stamens 3, free, inserted on the calyx-tube; filaments short; anthers cohering, one 1-celled, the others 2-celled; cells flexuose round the broad connective, which is not produced at the apex. Pollen muriculate. Rudimentary ovary 0. FEMALE FLOWERS: Calyx and corolla as in the male. Staminodes 3, small. Ovary globose or ovoid, 3-placentiferous; ovules numerous, horizontal; style slender; stigmas 3, papillose, deeply 2-lobed. Fruit baccate, spherical or ovoid-conical, pulpy, many-seeded. Seeds subpyriform, very turgid, surrounded by a very thick grooved crenulate ring, on each side of which the tumid faces of the seed project.—DISTRIB. S. Asia, Indian and Pacific Islands, Australia; species 2.

1. **Bryonopsis laciniosa,** *Naud. in Ann. Sci. Nat.* sér. 4, v. 18 (1862) p. 194. Stems much branched, slender, grooved, glabrous. Tendrils slender, striate, glabrous, 2-fid. Leaves membranous, 4–6 in. long and about as broad, green and scabrid above, paler and smooth or nearly so beneath, deeply cordate at the base, 5-lobed, the lobes oblong-lanceolate (the middle sometimes reaching 4 in. long), the margins sinuate, distantly denticulate, sometimes subserrate; petioles 1–3 in. long, striate, slender. MALE FLOWERS in small fascicles of 3–6; peduncles $\frac{1}{5}$–$\frac{3}{4}$ in. long, filiform, glabrous. Calyx glabrous, $\frac{1}{10}$ in. long; teeth subulate, less than $\frac{1}{20}$ in. long. Corolla $\frac{1}{8}$–$\frac{1}{6}$ in. long; segments ovate-oblong, acute, pubescent. FEMALE FLOWERS solitary, or few, or many; peduncles shorter than in the male. Fruit subsessile, $\frac{1}{2}$–1 in. in diam., globose, smooth, bluish-green streaked with broad vertical lines. Seeds $\frac{1}{5}$–$\frac{1}{4}$ in. long, yellowish-brown. Hook. f. in Oliv. Fl. Trop. Afr. v. 2, p. 556; Cogniaux, in DC. Monogr. Phan. v. 3, p. 477. *Bryonia laciniosa*, Linn. Sp. Pl. (1753) p. 1013; C. B. Clarke, in Hook. f. Fl. B. I. v. 2, p. 622; Grah. Cat. p. 78; Dalz. & Gibs. p. 101; Trim. Fl. Ceyl. v. 2, p. 254; Wight, Icon. t. 500; Woodr. in Journ. Bomb. Nat. v. 11 (1898) p. 640; Watt, Dict. Econ. Prod. v. 1, p. 542.—Flowers: Aug.–Sept. VERN. *Sivalingi*; *Kávdodi*.

Common in hedges, *Graham*, *Dalzell & Gibson*. DECCAN: Poona, *Woodrow*! S. M. COUNTRY: Belgaum, *Ritchie*, 314!—DISTRIB. Throughout India; Ceylon, Malaya, Mauritius, Tropical Africa, Australia.

5. CUCUMIS, Linn.

Annual herbs with a perennial root, climbing or trailing, hispid or scabrous. Tendrils simple, sometimes straight and spinescent. Leaves entire or palmately 3–7-lobed or 5-angled. Flowers yellow, monœcious. MALE FLOWERS fascicled (rarely solitary). Calyx-tube turbinate or campanulate; lobes 5. Corolla subcampanulate, deeply 5-lobed or 5-partite. Stamens 3, free; filaments short; anthers free, oblong, one 1-celled, the others 2-celled, the cells linear, straight, curved or flexuose, the connective produced above into a papillose appendage. Pollen smooth. Rudimentary ovary glanduliform. FEMALE FLOWERS solitary. Calyx and corolla as in the male. Rudimentary stamens 0. Ovary ovoid or globose, 3–5-placentiferous; ovules ∞, horizontal; style short; stigmas 3, obtuse. Fruit fleshy or corky, globose or cylindric, terete or obtusely 4-angled, smooth or echinate, indehiscent, or 3-valved and tardily dehiscent. Seeds numerous, oblong, compressed, usually smooth.—DISTRIB. Tropical Asia and Africa, a few in Australia and America; species 26.

Fruit smooth, glabrous or pubescent.
Perennial; leaves deeply cut into 5–7 obtuse lobes, scabrid .... 1. *C. trigonus.*
Annual; leaves usually 5-angled, softly hairy .... 2. *C. Melo.*
Fruit echinate .... 3. *C. prophetarum.*

1. **Cucumis trigonus,** *Roxb. Hort. Beng.* (1814) p. 70. Perennial, scabrid, monœcious; stems 3–5 ft. long, slender, angled, rough with short rigid hairs. Tendrils simple. Leaves suborbicular in outline, 1–2 in. long and broad (sometimes larger), scabrid on both surfaces, hispid on the nerves beneath, cordate at the base, deeply palmately 5–7-lobed, the lobes ovate-oblong or obovate, often narrowed at the base, rounded at the apex, lobulate or dentate; petioles slender, striate, scabrid, often hispid, ½–2 in. long. MALE FLOWERS: Peduncles slender, ⅛–⅜ in. long, in small clusters (rarely solitary). Calyx narrowly campanulate, hairy; tube ⅛–⅙ in. long; teeth short, subulate. Corolla yellow, ⅙–¼ in. long, more or less pubescent; segments elliptic, acute. Appendage of the connective of the anthers a little shorter than the anther. FEMALE FLOWERS: Peduncles slender, ½–1 in. long in fruit. Ovary hairy. Fruit ellipsoid or subglobose, 1½ by 1¼ in., longitudinally variegated with 10 green stripes, pale yellow when ripe, with bitter pulp. Seeds white, ellipsoid, not margined. Fl. B. I. v. 2, p. 619; Dalz. & Gibs. p. 103; Wight, Icon. t. 497; Trim. Fl. Ceyl. v. 2, p. 250; Woodr. in Journ. Bomb. Nat. v. 11 (1898) p. 640; Watt, Dict. Econ. Prod. v. 2, p. 635.—Flowers: June. VERN. *Kárit.*

DECCAN: very common, *Dalzell & Gibson*; jungles about Poona, *Woodrow*!; Bowdhan near Poona, *Kanitkar*!; Rajwadi, *Kanitkar*! SIND: *Dalzell*, 37!; Landhi near Karachi, *Cooke*!; Bhubak, *Cooke*!; Hyderabad, *Cooke*!—DISTRIB. Throughout India; Ceylon, Malaya, N. Australia, Afghanistan, Persia.

2. **Cucumis Melo,** *Linn. Sp. Pl.* (1753) p. 1011, var. **agrestis,** *Naud. in Ann. Sci. Nat.* sér. 4, v. 11 (1859) p. 73, & v. 12, p. 110. Annual; stems creeping, branched, obtusely angular, with stiff (sometimes hooked) hairs on the ridges. Tendrils simple. Leaves 2–4 in. long and about as broad as long, acute at the apex, cordate at the base, more or less hairy on both sides, denticulate, usually 5-angled; petioles 1–1½ in. long, grooved and roughly hairy. MALE FLOWERS in axillary fascicles of about 2 or 3; peduncles ¼–½ in. long, very slender, densely hairy. Calyx densely hairy; tube narrowly campanulate, ⅙–⅛ in. long; teeth $\frac{1}{10}$ in. long, subulate, densely hairy. Corolla ¼–⅜ in. long, the segments hairy outside, often terminated by a hairy apiculation. FEMALE FLOWERS: Calyx-tube constricted above the ovary. Ovary ellipsoid, clothed with long bristly deciduous hairs. Fruit ellipsoid or turbinate, about 1½ in. long, smooth or with a few small bristles. Seeds numerous, narrowly ovoid, compressed, smooth. Cogniaux, in DC. Monogr. Phan. v. 3 (1881) p. 483. *Cucumis Melo*, var. *pubescens*, Kurz, in Journ. As. Soc. Beng. v. 46, part 2 (1877) p. 103. *Cucumis pubescens* (sp.), Willd. Sp. Pl. v. 4 (1805) p. 614; Wight, Icon. t. 496; Dalz. & Gibs. p. 103; Fl. B. I. v. 2, p. 619 (under *C. trigonus*); Trim. Fl. Ceyl. v. 2, p. 250. *Cucumis madraspatanus*, Roxb. in Wall. Cat. 6734 (*not*

of Linn.). *Cucumis cicatrisatus*, Stocks, in Kew Journ. Bot. v. 4 (1852) p. 148.—VERN. *Takmak*; *Shinde*.

DECCAN: common, *Dalzell & Gibson*; Khandala, *Bhiva*! S. M. COUNTRY: Castle-rock, *Cooke*!; Londa, *Cooke*! SIND: (cultivated) *Dalzell & Gibson*, *Stocks*.
The plant is cultivated in Sind and the fruit is eaten (*Stocks*).

Cucumis Melo. The Melon (VERN. *Kharbuj*). The origin of the plant is uncertain. M. DeCandolle considers it to be probably a native of N.W. India, Beluchistan, and perhaps Tropical Africa. It is largely cultivated throughout India, especially in the sandy beds of rivers. A good figure may be seen in Duthie & Fuller's 'Field and Garden Crops' (1882) t. 50. (See also Firminger, Man. Gard. ed. 3, p. 189, and Watt, Dict. Econ. Prod. v. 2, p. 627.)

There are several varieties differing much in properties and in the size and appearance of the fruit. Duthie & Fuller (*l. c.*) give figures of two of the varieties, viz. *Momordica*, t. 49, and *utilissimus*, tt. 53 & 54.

3. **Cucumis prophetarum,** *Linn. Cent. Amœn. Academ.* v. 4 (1759) p. 295. Monœcious. Stems slender, branched, angled and grooved, scabrid. Tendrils very short, striate, sometimes 0. Leaves polymorphous, rigid, $\frac{3}{4}$–2 in. long and broad, somewhat ash-colored, scabrid, coarsely hairy on the nerves beneath, cordate or truncate at the base, frequently 3-lobed, the lobes often lobulate with rounded apices, the terminal lobe often contracted at the base; nerves prominent beneath; petioles $\frac{1}{2}$–1 in. long. MALE FLOWERS solitary or fascicled; peduncles filiform, densely hairy, $\frac{1}{20}$–$\frac{1}{5}$ in. long. Calyx-tube subcylindric, $\frac{1}{6}$ in. long, densely hirsute; teeth linear, $\frac{1}{8}$ in. long. Corolla hairy, $\frac{1}{8}$–$\frac{1}{6}$ in. long; segments ovate-oblong, subacute. Filaments filiform, slightly hairy; anthers oblong, the appendage to the connective slightly dilated at the apex. FEMALE FLOWERS: Peduncle (in fruit) stout, $\frac{1}{2}$–1 in. long. Fruit subglobose, 1–1$\frac{1}{2}$ in. long and nearly as broad, longitudinally striped with green and white, echinate, the spines not or scarcely pungent, $\frac{1}{20}$–$\frac{1}{8}$ in. long. Seeds ellipsoid, not margined, $\frac{1}{8}$ in. long. Fl. B. I. v. 2, p. 619; Woodr. in Journ. Bomb. Nat. v. 11 (1898) p. 640.

In the Bombay Presidency confined to Sind. SIND: *Dalzell & Gibson*, p. 103 (under *Cucumis pubescens*), *Dalzell*, 36!, *Stocks*! The Hub, near Karachi, *Bhola Puran*!; Mulir, *Woodrow*!—DISTRIB. India (Sind); Beluchistan, Arabia, Tropical Africa.

Cucumis sativus, Linn. The Cucumber (VERN. *Kakri*; *Khira*). DeCandolle considers N. India to be the original home of this plant. It is cultivated widely throughout India. Duthie & Fuller, 'Field and Garden Crops' (1882), give good figures (tt. 51 & 52). See also Watt, Dict. Econ. Prod. v. 2, p. 632.

6. CITRULLUS, Schrader.

Perennial herbs usually trailing. Tendrils 2–3-fid, rarely undivided. Leaves deeply 3–7-lobed, the lobes usually lobulate. Flowers rather large, yellow, monœcious, all solitary. MALE FLOWERS: Calyx-tube broadly campanulate; lobes 5. Corolla 5-partite beyond the middle, subcampanulate; segments oblong-ovate, obtuse. Stamens 3; filaments short, free; anthers scarcely cohering, one 1-celled, the others 2-celled, the cells linear, flexuose, the connective not produced. Pollen smooth.

Rudimentary ovary glanduliform. FEMALE FLOWERS: Calyx and corolla as in the male. Rudimentary stamens 3, setose or ligulate. Ovary ovoid, 3-placentiferous; ovules ∞, horizontal; style short; stigmas 3, thick, reniform. Fruit globose or ellipsoid, smooth, fleshy, indehiscent. Seeds very many, much compressed, smooth.—DISTRIB. Eastern Mediterranean region, Tropical Africa, Western Asia; species 3.

1. **Citrullus Colocynthis,** *Schrader, in Linnæa*, v. 12 (1838) p. 414. Monœcious; root perennial; stems diffuse or creeping, slender, angled, branched, hirsute or scabrid. Tendrils simple or 2-fid, slender, hairy. Leaves very variable, 1½–2½ by 1–2 in. in the wild form (larger in the cultivated one), usually deltoid in outline, pale-green above, ashy beneath, scabrid on both surfaces, 5–7-lobed or very commonly 3-lobed, the middle lobe the largest, each lobe deeply pinnatifid or sinuate-lobulate, the segments obtuse; petioles ½–1 in. (longer in the cultivated form), densely hirsute. MALE FLOWERS: Peduncles ¼–½ in. long, villous. Calyx hairy, campanulate, ⅙ in. long; teeth lanceolate, $\frac{1}{12}$ in. long. Corolla ¼ in. long, pale yellow; segments obovate, apiculate. FEMALE FLOWERS: Ovary ellipsoid, densely hairy. Fruit globular, slightly depressed, 2–3 in. in diam., variegated green and white, glabrous when ripe, filled with a dry spongy very bitter pulp; epicarp thin. Seeds ⅛–¼ in. long, pale brown. Fl. B. I. v. 2, p. 620; Dalz. & Gibs. p. 101; Wight, Icon. t. 498; Aitch. Pb. & Sind Pl. p. 64; Trim. Fl. Ceyl. v. 2, p. 253; Woodr. in Journ. Bomb. Nat. v. 11 (1898) p. 640; Duthie & Fuller, Field and Gard. Crops, t. 57; Watt, Dict. Econ. Prod. v. 2, p. 328. *Cucumis Colocynthis*, Linn. Sp. Pl. (1753) p. 1011; Grah. Cat. p. 77.—Flowers: Nov.–Jan. VERN. *Kadu-vrindavan*; *Kadu-indrdyan.*

KONKAN: Salsette jungles, *Graham*. DECCAN: *Graham, Dalzell & Gibson, Cooke!, Woodrow!* GUJARAT: *Graham* (sea-shores), *Dalzell & Gibson, Stocks!, Woodrow!* SIND: *Stocks!*; Sehwan, *Cooke!*—DISTRIB. Throughout India, wild or sparingly cultivated; Ceylon, W. Asia, Arabia, Africa, Spain.

Citrullus vulgaris, Schrad. The Water Melon (VERN. *Tarbuj*; *Kalingad*). The plant is indigenous in Tropical Africa, but is extensively cultivated in most warm countries. Duthie & Fuller, 'Field and Garden Crops' (1882), give figures of the typical plant (tt. 55 & 56) and of the variety *C. fistulosus*, Stocks (t. 47). See also Watt, Dict. Econ. Prod. v. 2, p. 331, and Woodrow, Gard. in Ind. ed. 5, p. 331.

7. COCCINIA, Wight & Arn. Prodr. (1834) p. 347.

CEPHALANDRA, Schrad. in Eckl. & Zeyh. Enum. Pl. Afr. Austr. (1836) p. 280.

Slender scandent or prostrate herbs; root often tuberous. Tendrils slender, simple. Leaves petiolate, deltoid or subrotund, angled or lobed, sometimes glandular beneath. Flowers rather large, white or yellow, diœcious. MALE FLOWERS solitary, or subcymose at the apex of a peduncle. Calyx short, campanulate or turbinate; limb 5-lobed. Corolla campanulate, shortly 5-fid. Stamens 3; filaments connate into a column, rarely free; anthers connate into a capitulum or cohering, the cells conduplicate. Rudimentary ovary 0. FEMALE FLOWERS solitary. Calyx and corolla as in the male. Rudimentary stamens 3, short or long. Ovary ovoid or ellipsoid, 3-placentiferous; ovules ∞, horizontal; style slender; stigmas 3, bifid. Fruit baccate, ovoid or ellipsoid, indehiscent. Seeds many, ovoid, compressed, margined; testa smooth or scrobiculate.—DISTRIB. Tropical Asia, Tropical and South Africa; species 13.

The genus was established as *Coccinia* by Wight & Arnott in 1834, two years prior to the publication of the genus as *Cephalandra* by Schrader.

1. **Coccinia indica,** *Wight & Arn. Prodr.* (1834) p. 347. Perennial, scandent or prostate, much branched; root thick; stems grooved, slender, glabrous. Tendrils slender, striate, simple. Leaves 2–4 in. long and broad, bright-green above, paler beneath, studded and sometimes rough with papillæ, palmately 5-nerved from a cordate base, often with circular glands between the nerves, obtusely 5-angled or sometimes deeply 5-lobed, the lobes broad, obtuse or acute, apiculate, more or less sinuate-toothed; petioles $\frac{3}{4}$–$1\frac{1}{4}$ in. long. MALE FLOWERS: Peduncles 1-flowered, $\frac{3}{4}$–$1\frac{1}{2}$ in. long, subfiliform. Calyx-tube glabrous, broadly campanulate, $\frac{1}{6}$–$\frac{1}{5}$ in. long; teeth $\frac{1}{10}$ in. long, linear. Corolla 1 in. long, veined, pubescent inside, glabrous outside; segments $\frac{3}{16}$–$\frac{5}{16}$ in. long, triangular, acute. Staminal column glabrous; capitulum of anthers subglobose. FEMALE FLOWERS: Peduncles $\frac{1}{2}$–1 in. long. Staminodes 3, subulate, $\frac{1}{8}$ in. long. Ovary fusiform, glabrous, slightly ribbed. Fruit fusiform-ellipsoid, slightly beaked, 1–2 by $\frac{1}{2}$–1 in., marked when immature with white streaks, bright scarlet when fully ripe. Seeds somewhat obovoid, rounded at the apex, slightly papillose, much compressed, yellowish-grey. Grah. Cat. p. 78; Dalz. & Gibs. p. 103; Hook. Icon. Pl. v. 2 (1837) t. 138; Wight, Ill. t. 105* (bis). *Cephalandra indica*, Naud. in Ann. Sci. Nat. sér. 5, v. 5 (1866) p. 16; C. B. Clarke, in Hook. f. Fl. B. I. v. 2, p. 621; Trim. Fl. Ceyl. v. 2, p. 247; Woodr. in Journ. Bomb. Nat. v. 11 (1898) p. 640; Watt, Dict. Econ. Prod. v. 2, p. 252. *Bryonia cordifolia*, Linn. Sp. Pl. (1753) p. 1012. *Coccinia cordifolia*, Cogniaux, in DC. Monogr. Phan. v. 3 (1881) p. 529.—Flowers: Aug.-Sept. VERN. *Tondli.*

DECCAN: *Woodrow.* S. M. COUNTRY: Badami, *Cooke*!; Belgaum, *Ritchie*, 306! GUJARAT: Rajkot, *Woodrow.* SIND: Mulir, near Karachi, *Bhola Puran*!—DISTRIB. Throughout India; Ceylon, Malaya, Tropical Africa.

8. MELOTHRIA, Linn.

Slender scandent or prostrate herbs, annual or with a perennial root, monœcious or very rarely diœcious. Tendrils simple, rarely bifid. Leaves usually membranous, entire or more or less lobed. Flowers small, yellow or white. MALE FLOWERS racemose or corymbose, less commonly fascicled or solitary. Calyx campanulate, 5-toothed. Corolla deeply 5-partite; segments entire. Stamens 3, inserted on the tube (rarely at the base) of the calyx; filaments free; anthers free or rarely slightly cohering, one 1-celled, the others 2-celled or sometimes all 2-celled, the cells straight, rarely curved, the connective sometimes produced. Rudimentary ovary globose or annular, rarely 3-lobed. FEMALE FLOWERS solitary, fascicled, or corymbose. Calyx and corolla as in the male. Staminodes 3 or 0. Ovary ovoid, globose or fusiform, 3-placentiferous, constricted beneath the flower; ovules usually numerous, horizontal; style short, surrounded at the base by an annular disk; stigmas 3, linear, rarely 2, or stigma 3-lobed. Fruit small, baccate, globose, ovoid or fusiform, usually many-seeded. Seeds ovoid or ellipsoid, compressed, usually margined, smooth or rarely scrobiculate.—DISTRIB. Warmer regions of the globe; species 54.

The genus has been enlarged by Cogniaux (DC. Monogr. Phan. v. 3 [1881] p. 572) so as to include the genera *Mukia*, Arn., and *Zehneria*, Endl., a course which has been followed by Jackson in 'Index Kewensis.'

Flowers monœcious.
  Male flowers fascicled.
    Seeds smooth; leaves softly villous beneath .... 1. *M. leiosperma.*
    Seeds scrobiculate; leaves hirsute or scabrid beneath. 2. *M. maderaspatana.*
  Male flowers subumbellate at the apex of the peduncle . 3. *M. perpusilla.*
Flowers diœcious .... 4. *M. heterophylla.*

1. **Melothria leiosperma,** *Cogniaux, in DC. Monogr. Phan.* v. 3 (1881) p. 622. Monœcious; stems hispid, furrowed, slightly branched; young parts densely and softly villous-hairy. Tendrils simple. Leaves 2–3½ by 1¾–3 in., bright-green above, paler beneath, broadly ovate in outline, acute, cordate at the base, scabrid and coarsely hairy above, softly villous beneath, usually 5-angled or slightly 3–5-lobed, strongly dentate; petioles ½-2 in. long, densely hairy. Flowers axillary. MALE FLOWERS fascicled; peduncles very short. Calyx densely hairy; tube ⅛ in. long, campanulate; teeth linear-subulate, ⅛-⅙ in. long. Corolla pubescent outside; segments ovate-oblong, ⅙ in. long. Anthers subsessile, oblong, the connective short, apiculate. FEMALE FLOWERS: Peduncles usually solitary, ¾-2 in. long, thickened in fruit, densely clothed with long hairs. Ovary densely hairy. Fruit ½ in. in diam., globose, glabrous or slightly hairy. Seeds ellipsoid, ⅙ by ⅛ by $\frac{1}{12}$ in., turgid, conspicuously margined, smooth on the faces. Jackson, in Index Kew. v. 3, p. 203. *Mukia leiosperma*, Wight, in Ann. Mag. Nat. Hist. v. 8 (1842) p. 268; C. B. Clarke, in Hook. f. Fl. B. I. v. 2, p. 623; Trim. Fl. Ceyl. v. 2, p. 255.—Flowers: July–Aug.

Rare. KONKAN: Matheran, *H. M. Birdwood.* DECCAN: Kolhapur, *Cooke*!—DISTRIB. India (W. Peninsula); Ceylon.

2. **Melothria maderaspatana,** *Cogniaux, in DC. Monogr. Phan.* v. 3 (1881) p. 623. Annual, monœcious; stems scandent or prostrate, slender, much branched, angular, very hispid; young parts densely covered with white hair. Tendrils simple, striate, sparingly hirsute. Leaves variable in size, 1–5 by 1–4 in., deltoid-ovate, entire, 5-angled or 3-5-lobed, very scabrid above, scabrid or shortly hispid beneath, acute at the apex, cordate at the base with a wide sinus, the lobes often overlapping, the margins dentate or subserrate; petioles ¼-1 in. long, hairy. MALE FLOWERS in small fascicles on very short peduncles. Calyx hairy; tube $\frac{1}{12}$ in. long, narrowly campanulate; teeth about $\frac{1}{20}$ in. long, subulate. Corolla pubescent; segments ovate-oblong, rounded at the apex, $\frac{1}{12}$ in. long. FEMALE FLOWERS almost sessile. Fruit the size of a pea, smooth or slightly echinulate, at first green and variegated with yellow, finally wholly red. Seeds ellipsoid, compressed, not or scarcely margined, scrobiculate on both faces. Jackson, in Index Kew. v. 3, p. 203. *Mukia scabrella*, Arn. in Hook. Journ. Bot. v. 3 (1841) p. 276; C. B. Clarke, in Hook. f. Fl. B. I. v. 2, p. 623; Dalz. &

Gibs. p. 100; Aitch. Pb. & Sind Pl. p. 64; Trim. Fl. Ceyl. v. 2, p. 254; Woodr. in Journ. Bomb. Nat. v. 11 (1898) p. 640; Watt, Dict. Econ. Prod. v. 5, p. 287. *Bryonia scabrella*, Linn. f. Suppl. p. 424; Grah. Cat. p. 78; Wight, Icon. t. 501. *Cucumis maderaspatanus*, Linn. Sp. Pl. (1753) p. 1012.—Flowers: July. VERN. *Chirdti.*

Very common in hedges, *Dalzell & Gibson*. KONKAN: common about Bombay in the rains, *Graham*. DECCAN: common, *Cooke*!, *Woodrow*!; Kolapur, *Cooke*!; Hotgi, *Woodrow*; Hombal, *Woodrow*!; hills near Poona, *Woodrow*. S. M. COUNTRY: Belgaum, *Ritchie*, 316!; Badami, *Cooke*! GUJARAT: Dakor, *Woodrow*. SIND: *Stocks*.—DISTRIB. Throughout India; Ceylon, Africa, Malaya, Australia.

3. **Melothria perpusilla,** *Cogniaux, in DC. Monogr. Phan.* v. 3 (1881) p. 607. Monœcious, climbing; root an oblong flattened tuber; stems deeply striate, glabrous. Tendrils simple, striate, glabrous. Leaves broadly ovate in outline, $1\frac{3}{4}$–$3\frac{1}{2}$ in. long and as broad or sometimes broader than long, acute or shortly acuminate and mucronate at the apex, usually 5-angled, the angles at the base rounded, the margins distantly toothed, the upper side usually rough with scabrous spots, the lower side smooth and prominently veined, base subcordate or nearly truncate; petioles $\frac{3}{4}$–1 in. long. MALE FLOWERS 3–10 at the apex of a peduncle, $\frac{3}{4}$–$1\frac{3}{4}$ in. long, capitate or in subumbellate racemes; pedicels short, filiform. Calyx-tube $\frac{1}{20}$–$\frac{1}{16}$ in. long, campanulate, rounded at the base; teeth very short, recurved. Corolla pale-yellow; segments $\frac{3}{4}$ in. long, ovate-oblong, subacute, slightly hairy within the throat. Filaments hairy. FEMALE FLOWERS solitary or rarely subumbellate; peduncles $\frac{1}{4}$–$\frac{1}{3}$ in. long, in the same axils as the males. Ovary globose. Fruit smooth, globose, minutely pitted, red when ripe, $\frac{3}{8}$–$\frac{1}{2}$ in. in diam. Seeds many, much flattened, smooth. Jackson, in Index Kew. v. 3, p. 203. *Bryonia perpusilla*, Blume, Bijdr. p. 926. *Zehneria Hookeriana*, Arn. in Hook. Journ. Bot. v. 3 (1841) p. 275; C. B. Clarke, in Hook. f. Fl. B. I. v. 2, p. 624 (exclud. syn.); Trim. Fl. Ceyl. v. 2, p. 256. *Bryonia maysorensis*, Wight, Icon. t. 758 (*not* of Wall.); Dalz. & Gibs. p. 101. *Zehneria Baueriana*, Woodr. in Journ. Bomb. Nat. v. 11 (1898) p. 640.—Flowers: June–Nov. VERN. *Varáli.*

KONKAN: *Stocks*!, *Law*!; Wari country, *Dalzell & Gibson*; Ambeghát, *Woodrow*!; Mahableshwar, abundant, *Cooke*!, *Woodrow*!, *H. M. Birdwood*.—DISTRIB. India (N. Bengal, Sikkim, Assam, Khasia, W. Peninsula); Ceylon, Malaya, Africa.

4. **Melothria heterophylla,** *Cogniaux, in DC. Monogr. Phan.* v. 3 (1881) p. 618. Diœcious; root perennial, consisting of several tubers; stems slender, branched, furrowed, glabrous. Tendrils simple. Leaves 3–6 in. long, polymorphous, regularly ovate, or 3–5-angled or lobed, or hastate, acute or acuminate, usually cordate at the base, generally scabrid and pale-green above, paler or cinereous and reticulately veined beneath, margins remotely denticulate; petioles $\frac{1}{4}$–$\frac{3}{8}$ in. long, pubescent. MALE FLOWERS subumbellate, 15–20 on a peduncle $\frac{1}{4}$–$\frac{3}{4}$ in. long; pedicels filiform, $\frac{1}{8}$–$\frac{1}{3}$ in. long. Calyx glabrous; tube campanulate, rounded at the base, $\frac{1}{6}$–$\frac{1}{4}$ in. long; teeth minute, subulate. Corolla small, yellowish-white; segments triangular, acute, $\frac{1}{16}$ in. long. Filaments slender, subglabrous, $\frac{1}{8}$ in. long. FEMALE FLOWERS: Peduncles solitary, $\frac{1}{4}$–$\frac{1}{2}$ in. long. Ovary narrowly oblong, glabrous or more or less pubescent, 10-ribbed. Fruit $1\frac{1}{2}$–2 in. long, oblong-ovoid, cylindric, tapering towards the apex, ribbed, bright red when ripe.

Seeds obovoid or subglobose, scarcely compressed, smooth, white. Jackson, in Index Kew. v. 3, p. 203. *Bryonia umbellata*, Klein, in Willd. Sp. Pl. v. 4, p. 618; Grah. Cat. p. 78; Dalz. & Gibs. p. 101. *Zehneria hastata*, Miq. Fl. Ind. Bat. v. 1, part 1, p. 656; Trim. Fl. Ceyl. v. 2, p. 256. *Zehneria umbellata*, Thwaites, Enum. p. 125; C. B. Clarke, in Hook. f. Fl. B. I. v. 2, p. 625; Woodr. in Journ. Bomb. Nat. v. 11 (1898) p. 640; Watt, Dict. Econ. Prod. v. 6, part 4, p. 355.—Flowers: June. VERN. *Gometi.*

The leaves are of very variable shape. Cogniaux (*l. c.*) distinguishes no less than 12 different forms.

KONKAN: *Stocks*!, *Law*!; Neral, *Bhiva*!; Amboli Ghát, *Kanitkar*! (all of Cogniaux's form 1). DECCAN: Mahableshwar, *Cooke*!, *Woodrow*! (form 1); Karli, *Bhiva*! (form 2); Kadkala, *Woodrow*! (form 8). S. M. COUNTRY: *Ritchie*, 308! (form 1).—DISTRIB. Throughout India; Ceylon, China, Cochinchina, Java.

9. **BLASTANIA,** Kotschy & Peyr. Pl. Tinn. (1865–66) p. 15, t. 7.

CTENOLEPIS, Hook. f. in Benth. & Hook. Gen. Pl. v. 1 (1867) p. 832.

Prostrate or scandent annual herbs. Tendrils simple. Leaves digitately 5–7-lobed or -partite. Bracts stipuliform, in the axils of the leaves, toothed or pectinately ciliate. Flowers minute, monoecious. MALE FLOWERS racemose, on slender pedicels. Calyx-tube short, campanulate; lobes 5, subulate, very small. Corolla rotate, deeply 5-partite. Stamens 3, inserted on the calyx-tube, free; filaments remote, very short; anthers small, one 1-celled, the others 2-celled, the cells short, straight, the connective not produced. Rudimentary ovary 0. FEMALE FLOWERS solitary, in the same axils as the males; peduncle short. Calyx and corolla as in the male. Staminodes 0. Ovary ovoid, 2–3-placentiferous; ovules few, horizontal; style columnar, without a basal disk; stigmas 2 (rarely 3). Fruit fleshy, globose or obliquely subquadrate. Seeds few, ovoid, much compressed or boat-shaped, the margins obtuse or acute; testa smooth.—DISTRIB. Tropical and subtropical Asia, Tropical Africa; species 2.

Fruit globose .... 1. *B. fimbristipula.*
Fruit inversely reniform or hammer-shaped .... 2. *B. Garcini.*

1. **Blastania fimbristipula,** *Kotschy & Peyr. Pl. Tinn.* (1865–66) p. 15, t. 7. An extensive climber; stems subfiliform, elongate, much-branched, grooved and angled, glabrous, smooth or slightly scabrid. Tendrils slender, elongate, striate, simple. Leaves membranous, $1\frac{1}{2}$–4 in. long and broad, scabrid on both surfaces with white spots, usually 3-partite (rarely 5-lobed), the segments ovate-oblong or lanceolate, acute, narrowed at the base, denticulate or crenulate, the lateral segments more or less 2-lobed, the intermediate segment entire or 3-lobed, often with a long mucro; petioles $\frac{3}{4}$–$1\frac{1}{2}$ in. long, slender, grooved, hirsute, at length scabrid with white spots. Stipular bracts $\frac{1}{4}$–$\frac{1}{2}$ in. long, orbicular, reniform or dimidiate, scabrid with minute white spots, ciliate with hairs as long as the breadth of the bract. MALE FLOWERS 5–10 at the apex of a glabrous filiform peduncle $\frac{3}{4}$–$1\frac{1}{2}$ in. long; pedicels ebracteate, $\frac{1}{20}$–$\frac{1}{8}$ in. long. Calyx-teeth minute. Corolla minute; segments ovate-oblong, obtuse, spreading. FEMALE FLOWERS solitary; peduncles short. Fruit subsessile, globose, scarlet, glabrous, $\frac{1}{2}$ in. in diam. Seeds 2, ovoid, $\frac{1}{3}$ in. long, $\frac{3}{16}$–$\frac{1}{4}$ in. broad,

smooth, yellowish-grey, convex on one side, deeply concave on the other, edge sharp. Jackson, in Index Kew. v. 1, p. 311. *Ctenolepis cerasiformis*, Hook. f. in Oliv. Fl. Trop. Afr. v. 2, p. 558; C. B. Clarke, in Hook. f. Fl. B. I. v. 2, p. 630; Woodr. in Journ. Bomb. Nat. v. 11 (1898) p. 641. *Zehneria cerasiformis*, Stocks, in Kew Journ. Bot. v. 4 (1852) p. 149; Dalz. & Gibs. p. 100; Aitch. Pb. & Sind Pl. p. 65.

GUJARAT: *Dalzell*!; Verawul (Kathiawar), *Woodrow*! SIND: *Dalzell*!, *Stocks* ex *Aitchison*.—DISTRIB. Tropical and S. Africa, Arabia.

2. **Blastania Garcini,** *Cogniaux, in DC. Monogr. Phan.* v. 3 (1881) p. 629. Climbing; stems slender, elongate, striate, branched, glabrous. Tendrils capillary. Leaves membranous, 1–2 in. long and broad, at first hirsute, afterwards scabrid with white spots, deeply 3–5-lobed, the lobes usually obovate, obtuse or acute, constricted at the base, denticulate or crenulately toothed, the intermediate lobe scarcely longer then the others, mucronate; petioles $\frac{1}{2}$–$1\frac{1}{2}$ in. long, slender, striate, shortly hirsute, at length scabrid. Stipular bracts $\frac{1}{8}$–$\frac{5}{16}$ in. long, ovate or rotundate, shortly hairy, fringed on the margin with long filiform cilia. MALE FLOWERS yellowish-white, 3–4 at the apex of a slender peduncle less than $\frac{1}{2}$ in. long; pedicels $\frac{1}{24}$–$\frac{1}{12}$ in. long. FEMALE FLOWERS solitary on very short peduncles. Fruit broader than long, $\frac{1}{8}$–$\frac{1}{4}$ by $\frac{1}{3}$–$\frac{3}{8}$ in., bright-red, glabrous, inversely subreniform or hammer-shaped. Seeds $\frac{1}{4}$–$\frac{1}{3}$ by $\frac{1}{8}$ in., oblong, yellowish-grey, rounded at the apex, slightly attenuated at the base, with a deep pit on one face, convex on the other, the edge thick and obtuse. Jackson, in Index Kew. v. 1, p. 311. *Ctenolepis Garcini*, C. B. Clarke, in Hook. f. Fl. B. I. v. 2, p. 629; Trim. Fl. Ceyl. v. 2, p. 250; Woodr. in Journ. Bomb. Nat. v. 11 (1898) p. 641; Watt, Dict. Econ. Prod. v. 2, p. 626. *Zehneria Garcini*, Stocks, in Kew Journ. Bot. v. 4 (1852) p. 149; Dalz. & Gibs. p. 99; Aitch. Pb. & Sind Pl. p. 65.—Flowers: Oct.

DECCAN: Dhulia, *Woodrow*! GUJARAT: Surat, *Woodrow*; Ahmedabad, *Raoji*!; Domas near Surat, *Dalzell*!; Deesa, *Stocks* ex *Aitchison*; Kathiawar coast plentiful, *Dalzell & Gibson*. S. M. COUNTRY: Badami, *Bhiva*!

10. **KEDROSTIS,** Medikus, in Phil. Bot. v. 2 (1791) p. 69.

RHYNCHOCARPA, Schrad. in Linnæa, v. 12 (1838) p. 403.

Prostrate or scandent herbs; root perennial. Tendrils simple. Leaves entire or lobed. Flowers small, monœcious (rarely diœcious). MALE FLOWERS racemose or corymbose. Calyx-tube campanulate, usually glabrous within; lobes 5, short. Corolla rotate, 5-partite. Stamens 3 (rarely 5), inserted in the calyx-tube; filaments short, glabrous; anthers short, glabrous, one 1-celled, the others 2-celled (or when 5, all 1-celled), free or slightly cohering, the cells straight or slightly curved, the connective usually 2-fid or 2-partite, produced beyond the cells. Rudimentary ovary 0 or glanduliform. FEMALE FLOWERS subsessile, solitary or aggregated, shortly pedicelled. Calyx and corolla as in the male. Rudimentary stamens 0 or 3, very small. Ovary usually ovoid, beaked, 2–3-placentiferous; ovules few, horizontal; style sometimes obscurely surrounded by a disk at the base; stigmas 2 or 3. Fruit baccate, ovoid, usually rostrate. Seeds usually few, tumid, margined; testa usually crustaceous, smooth.—DISTRIB. Tropical and subtropical Asia and Africa; species 11.

1. **Kedrostis rostrata,** *Cogniaux, in DC. Monogr. Phan.* v. 3 (1881) p. 636. Scandent, monœcious; stems slender, branched, angled, sparsely hairy. Tendrils simple, filiform, glabrous. Leaves ¾–2 in. long and as broad as long, membranous, orbicular in outline, bright-green, hairy and more or less scabrid on both sides, margins entire or distantly toothed, cordate at the base, sometimes 5-angled or sublobate, the lobes subacute, apiculate; petioles ½–1½ in. long, hairy. MALE FLOWERS: Peduncles filiform, ¼–¾ in. long, 2–4-flowered at the apex; pedicels capillary, $\frac{1}{10}$–¼ in. long, usually bracteolate at the base. Calyx hairy; tube campanulate, rounded at the base; teeth minute. Corolla pale-yellow; segments oblong-lanceolate, acute, ⅛–⅕ in. long, pubescent. FEMALE FLOWERS: Peduncles $\frac{1}{20}$–⅓ in. long. Ovary oblong, beaked, pubescent. Fruit subsessile, deep-red, about 1 in. long, ovoid, tapering into a long narrow beak, pubescent. Seeds ⅕ in. long, ovoid, with a narrow sharp wing, brown. Jackson, in Index Kew. v. 3, p. 4. *Rhynchocarpa rostrata,* Naud. in Ann. Sci. Nat. sér. 4, v. 16, p. 177; Kurz, in Journ. As. Soc. Beng. (1877) part 2, p. 105; Trim. Fl. Ceyl. v. 2, p. 258. *Rhynchocarpa fœtida,* C. B. Clarke, in Hook. f. Fl. B. I. v. 2, p. 627 (partly); Woodr. in Journ. Bomb. Nat. v. 11 (1898) p. 640; Watt, Dict. Econ. Prod. v. 6, part 1, p. 502. *Æchmandra rostrata,* Arn. in Hook. Journ. Bot. v. 3 (1841) p. 274; Dalz. & Gibs. p. 100. *Bryonia pilosa,* Roxb. Hort. Beng. p. 104; Grah. Cat. p. 248.—Flowers: Sept.–Nov. VERN. *Nurakvel.*

KONKAN: S. Konkan, *Nimmo ex Graham*; Miradonger near Pen, *Kanitkar*! GUJARAT: common in hedges, *Dalzell & Gibson, Dalzell,* 38! S. M. COUNTRY: Padshapur (Belgaum districts), *Ritchie,* 1761!—DISTRIB. India (W. Peninsula, Ava); Ceylon.

11. **CORALLOCARPUS,** Welw.

Prostrate or climbing herbs. Tendrils simple. Leaves roundish or cordate, lobed or palmate. Flowers minute, monœcious. MALE FLOWERS crowded at the apex of a long peduncle. Calyx-tube broadly campanulate; lobes 5, short. Corolla 5-partite; segments ovate-oblong. Stamens 3, free, inserted on the calyx-tube; filaments very short; anthers glabrous, entire or 2-partite, one 1-celled, the others 2-celled, the cells straight, the connective produced or not, often bifid. Rudimentary ovary 0 or minute. FEMALE FLOWERS sessile or shortly pedicelled, solitary or fascicled, sometimes subspicate. Calyx and corolla as in the male. Rudimentary stamens 0 or minute. Ovary ovoid, beaked, 2–3-celled; ovules few, horizontal; style straight, without a basal disk; stigma 3- (rarely 2–4-) lobed. Berry fleshy, ovoid or ellipsoid, rostrate or obtuse, operculately dehiscent near the base. Seeds few, obovoid or subglobose, tumid.—DISTRIB. India and Tropical Africa; species 15.

Seeds obovoid or pyriform, slightly attenuated at the base; stems slender.
  Female flowers usually solitary; seeds margined .... 1. *C. epigæus.*
  Females flowers usually fascicled or subspicate; seeds not margined .... 2. *C. conocarpus.*
Seeds globose or subglobose, not attenuated at the base; stems stout .... 3. *C. velutinus.*

1. **Corallocarpus epigæus,** *C. B. Clarke, in Hook. f. Fl. B. I.* v. 2 (1879) p. 628. Prostrate or climbing, monœcious; root large,

turnip-shaped; stems slender, grooved, zigzag, glabrous. Tendrils simple, slender, glabrous. Leaves suborbicular in outline, $\frac{3}{4}$–3 in. long, usually a little broader than long, light-green above, paler beneath, shortly roughly hairy on both surfaces, deeply cordate at the base, angled or more or less deeply 3–5-lobed, the lobes usually lobulate and obtuse, sometimes apiculate, more or less irregularly dentate on the margins; petioles $\frac{3}{4}$–$1\frac{1}{2}$ in. long, glabrous. MALE FLOWERS small, 5–15 at the apex of a straight stiff glabrous peduncle $1\frac{1}{2}$–$2\frac{1}{2}$ in. long; pedicels filiform, $\frac{1}{24}$–$\frac{1}{12}$ in. long. Calyx slightly hairy; tube $\frac{1}{16}$ in. long, slightly rounded at the base; teeth minute, erect, distant, subulate. Corolla greenish-yellow; segments $\frac{1}{24}$ in. long. Anthers yellow; connective green, produced beyond the cells, bifid. FEMALE FLOWERS usually solitary; peduncles short, stout, glabrous. Fruit stalked, $\frac{1}{2}$–1 in. long (including the beak), ellipsoid or ovoid, suddenly contracted into a slender beak $\frac{1}{4}$ in. long, scarlet in the middle, the base and beak green, circumscissilely dehiscent at the junction of the green and red portions near the base. Seeds 6–9, in orange-colored pulp, pyriform, $\frac{1}{8}$–$\frac{1}{6}$ by $\frac{1}{12}$–$\frac{1}{10}$ in., turgid, brown, with a whitish corded margin. Trim. Fl. Ceyl. v. 2, p. 258; Woodr. in Journ. Bomb. Nat. v. 11 (1898) p. 641. *Bryonia epigæa*, Wight, Icon. t. 503. *Æchmandra epigæa*, Arn. in Hook. Journ. Bot. v. 3 (1841) p. 274; Dalz. & Gibs. p. 100.—Flowers: June–Aug. VERN. *Karvina*; *Karmugli.*

DECCAN: *Dalzell & Gibson*; Poona, *Woodrow*! GUJARAT: *Dalzell*, 40! S. M. COUNTRY: Badami, *Bhiva*!; Karlimatti, *Cooke*!; Kakti hills near Belgaum, *Ritchie*, 1076! SIND: *Dalzell*, 40!—DISTRIB. India (Panjáb, Sind, Gujarat, W. Peninsula); Ceylon.

2. **Corallocarpus conocarpus,** *C. B. Clarke, in Hook. f. Fl. B. I.* v. 2 (1879) p. 628. Climbing, monœcious; stems slender, striate, glabrous. Tendrils simple, slender, glabrous. Leaves 2–$2\frac{3}{4}$ by $1\frac{1}{2}$–$2\frac{1}{2}$ in., pale-green above, ash-colored beneath, both surfaces and especially the lower clothed with minute white hairs (scarcely scabrid), cordate at the base, deeply palmately 3–5-lobed, the lobes oblong-lanceolate, acute or acuminate, the terminal lobe the longest much contracted at the base; petioles $\frac{3}{4}$–$1\frac{1}{4}$ in. long, slender, rugulose. MALE FLOWERS 6–15 at the apex of a slender glabrous peduncle $\frac{1}{2}$–$1\frac{1}{4}$ in. long; pedicels filiform, $\frac{1}{24}$–$\frac{1}{12}$ in. long. FEMALE FLOWERS fascicled or subspicate. Fruit glabrous or slightly pubescent, sessile, fascicled or sometimes subspicate, conical-oblong, not suddenly coutracted into the beak, orange-red except the cup-shaped base which remains green. Seeds pyriform, turgid, $\frac{1}{8}$–$\frac{1}{6}$ by $\frac{1}{12}$–$\frac{1}{10}$ in., dark-brown (nearly black), not margined. Woodr. in Journ. Bomb. Nat. v. 11 (1898) p. 641. *Æchmandra conocarpa*, Dalz. & Gibs. Bomb. Fl. p. 100.—Flowers: June–Aug.

Rare. GUJARAT: *Dalzell* (in Herb. Kew.), 39!; Malpor and Gundar, *Dalzell & Gibson*. There is a single specimen from *Herb. Stocks* at Kew without locality.

3. **Corallocarpus velutinus,** *Benth. & Hook. f. Gen. Pl.* v. 1 (1862–67) p. 831. A stout climber; root fibrous; stems stout, angular, hairy, deeply grooved, not much branched. Tendrils very long, striate, simple. Leaves fleshy, suborbicular in outline, 2–3 in. long and as broad as long, pale-green and at first softly villous, finally scabrid above, tomentose and ashy-grey beneath, cordate or subtruncate at the base, deeply palmately 3–5-lobed, the lobes rounded or oblong, sometimes

lobulate (the terminal lobe the longest), irregularly denticulate; petioles stout, $1\frac{1}{2}$–2 in. long, densely hairy. MALE FLOWERS in 15–20-flowered racemes at the top of a hairy slender peduncle 2–4 in. long; pedicels filiform, $\frac{1}{10}$–$\frac{1}{8}$ in. long. Calyx shortly hairy; tube subhemispheric, $\frac{1}{16}$ in. long; teeth narrowly triangular, less than $\frac{1}{20}$ in. long. Corolla greenish-yellow; segments ovate-oblong, subacute, $\frac{1}{16}$ in. long. Anthers subsessile; connective scarcely produced, bifid. FEMALE FLOWERS fascicled, subsessile. Fruit $\frac{3}{4}$ in. long (including the beak), sessile, ellipsoid, suddenly narrowed into a beak about $\frac{1}{8}$ in. long, red when ripe, finely velvety. Seeds $\frac{1}{8}$ in. in diam., globose, margined. Fl. B. I. v. 2, p. 628; Woodr. in Journ. Bomb. Nat. v. 11 (1898) p. 641. *Æchmandra velutina*, Dalz. & Gibs. p. 100.

Rare, apparently confined to Sind. SIND: *Dalzell*, 41!; Karachi, *Cooke*!—DISTRIB. Tropical Africa.

12. DICŒLOSPERMUM, C. B. Clarke.

A scabrid scandent slender herb. Tendrils simple. Leaves petiolate, ovate-cordate or subhastate. Flowers white, minute, shortly pedicelled, monœcious, the males and females in the same axils. MALE FLOWERS solitary or fascicled. Calyx-tube short, campanulate; teeth 5, minute. Corolla deeply 5-partite; segments entire, triangular-ovate. Stamens 3, free, inserted on the calyx-tube; filaments very short; anthers oblong, one 1-celled, the others 2-celled, the cells straight, connective narrow, scarcely produced at the apex. Rudimentary ovary glanduliform. FEMALE FLOWERS unknown. Fruit dry, depressed-globose, 1-celled. Seeds 3, erect, inserted at the bottom of the cell.—DISTRIB. India (W. Peninsula), apparently endemic.

1. **Dicœlospermum Ritchiei,** *C. B. Clarke, in Hook. f. Fl. B. I.* v. 2, p. 630. Stems elongate, not much branched, grooved, scabrid. Tendrils slender, elongate, striate, sparingly hairy. Leaves $1\frac{3}{4}$–3 in. long and about as broad as long, deep-green and sparingly hirsute above, paler, hirsute and at length scabrid beneath, denticulate, usually ovate-subtriangular and slightly 3-lobed, the lateral lobes very short, acute, divergent, the terminal triangular, acute or acuminate; petioles $\frac{3}{4}$–$1\frac{1}{2}$ in. long, very scabrid (almost echinulate). MALE FLOWERS fascicled; peduncles filiform, $\frac{1}{10}$–$\frac{1}{5}$ in. long, hairy. Calyx-tube $\frac{1}{10}$ in. long; teeth erect, subulate, $\frac{1}{24}$ in. long. Corolla pubescent; segments subacute, $\frac{1}{16}$ in. long. FEMALE FLOWERS not seen. Fruit sessile, glabrous, smooth, umbilicate at the apex, about $\frac{1}{5}$ in. long and somewhat broader than long, red when ripe. Seeds whitish-brown, $\frac{1}{6}$ by $\frac{1}{8}$ by $\frac{1}{10}$ in., broadly ovoid, compressed, slightly beaked, longitudinally ridged and slightly rugulose in the middle, containing 3 cavities, the central one enclosing the embryo, the 2 lateral empty. Woodr. in Journ. Bomb. Nat. v. 11 (1898) p. 641. —Flowers: July-Sept. VERN. *Gogara*.

Rare. *Stocks* (without locality) in Herb. Kew.! KONKAN: W. Ghâts near Matheran, *Woodrow*. DECCAN: Amboyne, 12 miles from Lanoli, *Woodrow*! S. M. COUNTRY: Belgaum, *Ritchie*, 316!—DISTRIB. Apparently endemic.

None of the specimens have female flowers, all having been collected in the fruiting stage.

13. ZANONIA, Linn.

Scandent glabrous or pubescent shrubs. Tendrils simple or bifid. Leaves petiolate, ovate or oblong, entire. Flowers diœcious, all racemose or the males panicled. MALE FLOWERS: Sepals 3, broadly oblong or orbicular, membranous, concave. Corolla rotate, 5-partite, coriaceous or fleshy; the segments narrowed at the apex. Stamens 5, free, inserted on a fleshy disk; filaments very short and thick; anthers transversely oblong, adnate to the filaments, 1-celled. Rudimentary ovary 0. FEMALE FLOWERS: Calyx and corolla as in the male. Staminodes very short, alternate with the petals. Ovary elongate, at first 3-celled, at length 1-celled by the absorption of the septa; ovules 2–many in each cell, attached at both sides to parietal placentas, pendulous. Fruit cylindric, clavate or hemispheric, terete or sub-trigonous, truncate and broadly 3-valved at the apex. Seeds large, pendulous, oblong, compressed, imbricate, surrounded by a large membranous wing.—DISTRIB. Tropical Asia, Java; species 2.

1. **Zanonia indica,** *Linn. Sp. Pl.* ed. 2 (1763) p. 1457. Scandent, climbing to a height of 30–50 ft. Stems stout, cylindric, striate, woody, glabrous. Tendrils elongate, terete, glabrous. Leaves coriaceous, deciduous (leaving a prominent circular scar), 3–6 by 2–4 in., ovate-oblong, acute, entire, bright-green and glabrous above, paler and conspicuously reticulate beneath, 3-nerved from a rounded or slightly cordate base; petioles $\frac{5}{8}$–1$\frac{1}{4}$ in. long, stout, glabrous. MALE FLOWERS in racemes or panicles 6–12 in. long, on slender grooved glabrous peduncles; pedicels somewhat stout, articulated about the middle, $\frac{1}{12}$–$\frac{1}{6}$ in. long, bracteolate at the base. Sepals $\frac{1}{12}$ in. long, ovate, acute, concave, glabrous. Petals greenish-yellow, oblong, obtuse, $\frac{1}{8}$ in. long, $\frac{1}{12}$ in. broad at the base. FEMALE FLOWERS in 5–12-flowered racemes 4–12 in. long. Sepals broadly triangular, $\frac{1}{8}$ in. long. Petals ovate-oblong, $\frac{1}{4}$–$\frac{1}{3}$ in. long. Ovary cylindric, $\frac{1}{2}$ in. long. Capsule in shape like a candle-extinguisher, 2–4 in. long, cylindric-obconic, slightly tapering towards a rounded base, truncate at the apex, glabrous, pale yellowish-brown. Seeds much compressed, $\frac{3}{4}$ by $\frac{3}{8}$ in., pale-yellow, smooth; the wing 2–2$\frac{1}{2}$ in. long by $\frac{1}{2}$ in. broad, rounded at the base and apex. Fl. B. I. v. 2, p. 633; Dalz. & Gibs. p. 99; Wight, Ill. t. 103; Trim. Fl. Ceyl. v. 2, p. 261; Woodr. in Journ. Bomb. Nat. v. 11 (1898) p. 641; Watt, Dict. Econ. Prod. v. 6, part 4, p. 322.—The fruit is ripe in May. VERN. *Chirpoti.*

Rare. *Stocks*!, without locality (Herb. Kew.). KONKAN: Vingorla, *Dalzell*!, *Woodrow*.—DISTRIB. India (Assam, E. Bengal, W. Peninsula); Ceylon, Java, Borneo, New Guinea, Malaya.

The following plants which do not belong to any of the genera in the preceding pages are cultivated:—

Lagenaria vulgaris, Seringe, the Bottle-Gourd (VERN. *Dudhi*; *Dudhya*; *Dudh-bhopalá*), said by DeCandolle to be wild in India (Malabar and the moist forests of Dehra Doon), the Moluccas and Abyssinia, is cultivated throughout India and in tropical and warm regions throughout the world. There are several varieties distinguished chiefly by the fruit which assumes a diversity of shapes. One of these which is shaped like a flask is, when emptied and dried, largely used by the natives for toddy-vessels and is also commonly carried by beggars as a receptacle for alms, &c. The fruit is eaten when young; when fully ripe it often weighs as much as 20 lbs. An inedible variety known as *Kadva-dudhya* (bitter *dudhya*) is used for floats by fishermen. Duthie & Fuller (Field and Garden Crops) give a description and figure (t. 48). Fl. B. I. v. 2, p. 613; Dalz. & Gibs. Suppl. p. 36; Woodr. in Journ. Bomb. Nat. v. 11 (1898) p. 639, & Gard. in Ind. ed. 5, p. 331; Watt, Dict. Econ. Prod. v. 4, p. 580.

Cucurbita moschata, Duchesne, the Musk Melon (VERN. *Kála-bhopalá*), is largely cultivated in India and in most tropical and subtropical countries. Its native country is unknown. The fruit is of various shapes, ovoid, clavate, or subglobose and depressed at the apex and base and more or less ribbed, dark-green when young, covered with a delicate glaucous bloom when ripe (*Duthie*). Duthie & Fuller (Field and Garden Crops) give 4 plates (tt. 58–61). The fruiting peduncle is angular and furrowed. Fl. B. I. v. 2, p. 622; Woodr. in Journ. Bomb. Nat. v. 11 (1898) p. 640; Watt, Dict. Econ. Prod. v. 3, p. 640.

Cucurbita maxima, Duchesne, the Melon-Pumpkin, Squash-Gourd, Red Gourd (VERN. *Támbada-bhopalá*; *Kadu*), is cultivated throughout India and in most warm regions of the world. The fruit is the largest of any produced by the Cucurbitaceæ, sometimes weighing 2 cwt. and measuring 6 to 8 feet in circumference. Woodrow (Gard. in Ind. ed. 5, p. 328) describes the mode by which very large fruit may be grown. The fruiting peduncle is round and smooth. Fl. B. I. v. 2, p. 622; Woodr. in Journ. Bomb. Nat. v. 11 (1898) p. 640; Watt, Dict. Econ. Prod. v. 2, p. 638.

Cucurbita Pepo, DC., the Pumpkin, Vegetable Marrow (VERN. *Káshi-bhopalá*; *Kaula*), is cultivated, but not extensively, in the Bombay Presidency, where the commonly grown *Lagenaria vulgaris* (dudhya) is used in preference. The fruiting peduncle is woody and strongly grooved. Fl. B. I. v. 2, p. 622; Woodr. in Journ. Bomb. Nat. v. 11 (1898) p. 640, & Gard. in Ind. ed. 5, p. 334; Watt, Dict. Econ. Prod. v. 2, p. 641.

The three plants *Cucurbita moschata*, *C. maxima*, and *C. Pepo* are somewhat difficult to distinguish from one another. Duthie & Fuller (Field and Garden Crops, p. 58) give the following distinguishing characters:—

The hairiness of *C. moschata* is harsher than that of *C. maxima*, but much less so than that of *C. Pepo*, which is decidedly pungent. The leaves of *C. moschata* are usually marbled with whitish blotches; not so in *C. maxima*, rarely in *C. Pepo*. The calyx-segments of the female flower of *C. moschata* are leaf-like, those of the other two subulate, while the glaucous bloom on the fruit of *C. moschata* is characteristic.

Benicasa cerifera, Savi, the White Pumpkin or White Gourd-Melon (VERN. *Bhura-kolá*; *Kohalá*), probably, according to DeCandolle, a native of Japan and Java, is cultivated more or less throughout India and in many warm countries, but not largely in the Bombay Presidency. The fruit, which is without ribs, softly hairy and covered when ripe with a waxy bloom, is eaten as a vegetable and used in the manufacture of a native sweetmeat. Duthie & Fuller (Field and Garden Crops) give a figure (t. 45). Fl. B. I. v. 2, p. 616; Woodr. in Journ. Bomb. Nat. v. 11 (1898) p. 640; Watt, Dict. Econ. Prod. v. 1, p. 439. *Benicasa hispida*, Cogniaux, in DC. Monogr. Phan. v. 3 (1881) p. 513.

ORDER LXIII. BEGONIACEÆ.

Succulent herbs, sometimes shrubs; stem sometimes reduced to a rhizome or tuber. Leaves alternate, more or less inequilateral, entire, lobed or digitately partite, usually dentate; stipules 2, free, usually caducous. Flowers handsome, white or rosy (rarely yellow or red), unsymmetrical, monœcious; peduncles axillary, bracteate, divided into dichotomous 1- or 2-sexual cymes; bracts and bracteoles usually opposite. MALE FLOWERS: Perianth-segments (of the only Indian genus) 2 or 4 in pairs, the outer pair valvate, the inner (when present) smaller. Stamens numerous, inserted on a more or less convex torus; filaments free or connate; anthers linear-oblong or clavate. Rudimentary ovary 0. FEMALE FLOWERS: Perianth-segments 2–5, of which the 2 exterior are larger and sepaloid. Staminodes 0. Ovary inferior, usually 3- (rarely 2- or 4-) celled; ovules numerous, crowded on axile placentas; styles 2–4, free or connate at the base; stigmas branched or tortuous. Fruit capsular, loculicidally (rarely septicidally) dehiscent, less commonly a fleshy berry breaking up irregularly, usually 3-celled and 3-gonous, often winged, more rarely 2- or 4-celled. Seeds numerous, minute; albumen scanty or 0.—DISTRIB. Tropical America, Asia, and Tropical and South Africa, not in Australia; genera 2, of which one only (*Begonia*) occurs in India; species about 400, of which the genus *Begonia* contains 398.

1. BEGONIA, Linn.

Characters of the Order.

Fruit not winged.
  Fruit 4-celled, 4-angled .... 1. *B. Roxburghii.*
Fruit winged.
  Capsule 2-celled.
    Leaves crenate-dentate, scarcely oblique at the base, whitish beneath .... 2. *B. crenata.*
    Leaves nearly entire, ciliate, very oblique at the base, blood-red beneath .... 3. *B. integrifolia.*
  Capsule 3-celled.
    Flowers rosy; wings of capsule unequal .... 4. *B. concanensis.*
    Flowers white; wings of capsule subequal .... 5. *B. trichocarpa.*

1. **Begonia Roxburghii,** *A. DC. Prodr.* v. 15, part 1 (1864) p. 398. A stout succulent plant 1–3 ft. high; root fibrous; stems many, erect, often nearly as thick as the thumb, striate, pubescent when young, afterwards glabrous. Leaves very unequal at the base, 6–12 by 4–8 in., ovate, acuminate, irregularly dentate, glabrous or minutely pubescent on the nerves, very obliquely cordate at the base, strongly nerved; petioles 3–9 in. long; stipules oblong-lanceolate, glabrous, deciduous. Flowers fragrant, white or very pale pink, in short dichotomous few- or many-flowered cymes; bracts linear-lanceolate. MALE FLOWERS: Sepals 2, orbicular, glabrous. Petals 2, smaller than the sepals. Stamens about 50. FEMALE FLOWERS: Ovary 4-celled; placentas equally 2-partite; styles 4, bifid almost from the base; stigmas spirally twisted. Fruit subpyramidal with thick walls, 4-celled, 4-angled, the angles obtuse, each ending in a small horn upwards.

Seeds small, obovoid. Fl. B. I. v. 2, p. 635. *Begonia malabarica*, Roxb. Fl. Ind. v. 3, p. 648 (*not* of Lamk.); Grah. Cat. p. 172.

Rare. KONKAN: S. Konkan, *Nimmo ex Graham*. This plant has been included on the authority of Graham (*l. c.*), who states that it was found by Nimmo in the S. Konkan. I have seen no specimens from the Bombay Presidency; there are none in Herb. Kew.—DISTRIB. India (North and East Bengal, Assam, Birma).

2. **Begonia crenata,** *Dryand. in Trans. Linn. Soc.* v. 1 (1791) p. 162, t. 14. A small herbaceous 1–4-leaved plant, 4–10 in. high; root subtuberous; stems usually red, smooth, slender. Leaves 1–3 by ¾–2 in., ovate, acute, or rarely suborbicular, with crenate margins (the crenatures crowned with a small subulate tooth), with a few scattered stout hairs above, glabrous (except on the nerves) and ashy grey or almost silvery white beneath, base cordate, the lobes at each side of the sinus slightly unequal or often quite equal; petioles of the radical leaves 2–5 in. long, those of the cauline ½–1½ in. long, usually red, glabrous or with a few scattered hairs; stipules small, triangular, acute. Flowers not very many, pinkish or pinkish-white, beautifully marked with glistening dots when fresh; peduncles weak, with a few scattered hairs which are tipped with black glandular dots; bracts minute, acute, glabrous. MALE FLOWERS: Sepals 2. Petals 2, narrower than the sepals. Stamens many, monadelphous; anthers yellow. FEMALE FLOWERS: Perianth-segments 5, the outer elliptic, the inner oblong and apiculate, soon becoming larger than the male flowers. Styles usually 3, connate ½-way up or more; stigmas reniform. Capsules ¼ by ⅓ in., membranous, crowned by the accrescent perianth, 3-winged (one wing smaller than the other two, the margins of all 3 ciliate with hairs tipped with glandular black dots), 2-celled, with one side, at which dehiscence takes place, concave. Seeds minute, ellipsoid. Fl. B. I. v. 2, p. 651; Grah. Cat. p. 172; Dalz. & Gibs. p. 104; Woodr. in Journ. Bomb. Nat. v. 11 (1898) p. 641. *Begonia minima*, Bedd. Icon. Pl. Ind. Or. t. 110.—Flowers: Aug.–Sept.

KONKAN: *Stocks!*, *Law!*; Salsette, *Graham*. DECCAN: hills, *Woodrow!*; Mahableshwar, *Cooke!*; Khandala, *Bhiva!* KANARA: *Law!*—DISTRIB. India (W. Peninsula).

I have examined numerous fresh specimens and have invariably found 3 styles. Beddome, in his figure of *B. minima* (Icon. Pl. t. 110), gives a correct drawing of the styles.

3. **Begonia integrifolia,** *Dalz. in Kew Journ. Bot.* v. 3 (1851) p. 230. A succulent herbaceous plant 6–12 in. high; rootstock tuberous, the tubers of the size of a large pea: stem herbaceous, slender, striate, pubescent or glabrous. Leaves 3–7 by 1½–4 in., very inequilateral, obliquely ovate, subobtuse, sparingly clothed with stout short hairs above, pubescent, especially on the nerves, and dark-red beneath, margins entire or nearly so, finely ciliate, base very unequally cordate; petioles 1–2 in. long, pubescent; stipules ¼ in. long, ovate or elliptic, obtuse. Flowers white, ⅜ in. in diam., few, glabrous; peduncles longer than the petioles, glabrous or nearly so; bracts broadly ovate, acute, ciliate, caducous. MALE FLOWERS: Sepals 2, orbicular. Petals 2, oblong. Stamens numerous (about 50), monadelphous. FEMALE FLOWERS: Perianth-segments 5, the inner the smaller. Styles 2, connate below, branched and much twisted upwards. Capsules ⅜ by

$\frac{5}{8}$–$\frac{3}{4}$ in., 3-winged (one wing much larger than the others), dehiscing by an elliptic line round the narrow face. Seeds minute, ellipsoid. Fl. B. I. v. 2, p. 648; Dalz. & Gibs. p. 104; Woodr. in Journ. Bomb. Nat. v. 11 (1898) p. 641.—Flowers: Aug.–Sept.

Rare. KONKAN: *Stocks*!; on rocks on the Ghâts, *Dalzell*! KANARA: *Law*!—DISTRIB. India (W. Peninsula, Birma).

4. **Begonia concanensis,** *A. DC. Prodr.* v. 15, part 1 (1864) p. 314. Succulent, about 1 ft. high; root tuberous; stem simple, glabrous. Leaves 2–5 by $1\frac{1}{4}$–4 in., ovate (sometimes lobed), acute or subacute, palmately 7–9-nerved, with a few short thick hairs above, glabrous or nearly so (except on the nerves) beneath, the margins serrate or undulate-dentate and denticulate, base almost subequally cordate or slightly oblique; petioles of the radical leaves often 6 in. long or more, those of the cauline leaves 1–$2\frac{1}{2}$ in. long; stipules ovate-lanceolate, $\frac{1}{8}$ in. long, glabrous. Flowers rosy, few, on elongate dichotomous nearly glabrous peduncles; pedicels hairy; bracts $\frac{1}{4}$ in. long, lanceolate, acuminate, subciliate. MALE FLOWERS: Sepals 2, broadly elliptic, $\frac{1}{2}$ in. long. Petals 2, obovate-oblong, $\frac{1}{4}$ in. long. Stamens numerous, nearly free. FEMALE FLOWERS: Perianth-segments 5, the exterior broadly ovate or suborbicular, much larger than the inner, clothed with short stout hairs outside. Styles 3, nearly free, bifid at the apex. Capsules turbinate, $\frac{1}{2}$–$\frac{5}{8}$ by $\frac{5}{8}$–$\frac{3}{4}$ in. (including the wings), terminated by the styles, 3-celled, hispid or at length glabrous, 3-winged, one wing larger than the others, the larger wing obtusely triangular. Seeds ellipsoid. Fl. B. I. v. 2, p. 653; Dalz. & Gibs. p. 104; Woodr. in Journ. Bomb. Nat. v. 11 (1898) p. 641.—Flowers: Aug.–Oct.

Not common. KONKAN: *Stocks*!; above the Ghâts, *Law*! DECCAN: Lanoli, *Woodrow*!—DISTRIB. India (W. Peninsula).

5. **Begonia trichocarpa,** *Dalz. in Kew Journ. Bot.* v. 3 (1851) p. 230. Root tuberous; stem 1–$1\frac{1}{4}$ ft. long, glabrous or nearly so. Leaves 2–5 by $1\frac{1}{2}$–3 in., ovate, acute or subacute, sparingly clothed with short thick hairs above, more or less pubescent (especially on the nerves) beneath, irregularly sinuate-dentate, lacerate and denticulate on the margins, palmately 7–9-nerved; petioles of the radical leaves 4–8 in. long, those of the cauline 1–2 in. long; stipules $\frac{1}{2}$–$\frac{5}{8}$ in. long, ovate-lanceolate, hairy on the back. Flowers white, 2 in. in diam.; peduncles longer than the petioles, 4–6-flowered at the apex, glabrous or nearly so; pedicels slender, hairy; bracts $\frac{1}{4}$–$\frac{1}{3}$ in. long, ovate, acuminate, dentate, pubescent, caducous. MALE FLOWERS: Sepals 2, broadly elliptic, or suborbicular, $\frac{2}{3}$–$\frac{3}{4}$ in. long, denticulate or subentire, glabrous or slightly pubescent. Petals $\frac{1}{2}$–$\frac{2}{3}$ in. long, obovate-oblong. Stamens numerous, nearly free. FEMALE FLOWERS: Perianth-segments 5, the inner narrower, the outer often denticulate. Ovary hispid. Styles 3, nearly free, each divided into 2 branches. Capsules 3-celled, at first hispid, at length glabrous, $\frac{1}{2}$–$\frac{5}{8}$ by $\frac{7}{8}$ (including the wings), with 3 almost equal obtuse ciliate wings. Seeds ellipsoid. Fl. B. I. v. 2, p. 653; Dalz & Gibs. p. 104; Woodr. in Journ. Bomb. Nat. v. 11 (1898) p. 641.—Flowers: Aug.–Oct.

Rare. KONKAN: *Stocks*!; W. Ghâts, *Dalzell*! KANARA: *Law*!—DISTRIB. India (W. Peninsula).

ORDER LXIV. DATISCACEÆ.

Trees or herbs. Leaves alternate, simple or pinnate; stipules 0. Flowers small, regular, diœcious (in the Indian species), fascicled, racemose or panicled. MALE FLOWERS: Calyx-tube very short or hemispheric; lobes 3–9. Petals 0 in the Indian species. Stamens 4–25. Rudimentary ovary 0 or small. FEMALE FLOWERS: Calyx-tube adnate to the ovary; lobes 3–8, short. Petals 0. Ovary 1-celled, open or closed; placentas parietal, alternating with the calyx-lobes; ovules numerous, ascending or horizontal; styles as many as the placentas and alternate with them, simple or 2-partite. Capsule membranous or coriaceous, dehiscing within the styles. Seeds very many, minute, albuminous; embryo cylindric; radicle elongate, next the hilum.—DISTRIB. South-eastern Europe, Western and Central Asia, East Indies, Java, North-west America; genera 3; species 4.

1. TETRAMELES, R. Br.

A tall tree. Leaves deciduous, ovate, acuminate, pubescent or tomentose beneath. Flowers diœcious, appearing before the leaves, in elongate slender many-flowered racemes or panicles. MALE FLOWERS: Calyx-tube very short; lobes 4, equal or unequal, ovate or oblong, with sometimes an interposed small tooth. Petals 0. Stamens 4, opposite the calyx-lobes, inserted round a flat central disk. Ovary rudimentary or 4-gonous. FEMALE FLOWERS: Calyx-tube connate with the ovary, sub-4-gonous; teeth 4, short. Ovary inferior, 1-celled; ovules numerous, on 4 parietal placentas; styles 4, subulate, distinct, persistent; stigmas club-shaped. Capsule membranous, subglobose or urceolate, 4- or 8-ribbed, dehiscing at the apex between the styles. Seeds very many, minute, flattened, ellipsoid; testa very lax and extending much beyond the nucleus as a loose ragged reticulated membrane.—DISTRIB. India, Ceylon, Java; species 1.

1. **Tetrameles nudiflora,** *R. Br. in Benn. Pl. Java Rar.* (1838) p. 79. A very large deciduous tree reaching 100–150 ft.; trunk straight, not branched below, buttressed at the base; bark smooth, grey, lenticellate. Leaves appearing after the flowers, 4½–6 by 4–5½ in., broadly ovate, acuminate, irregularly serrate or dentate, bright-green and (when mature) glabrous above, paler and with softly hairy reticulate venation beneath, base cordate; petioles 4–6 in. long, terete, softly pubescent. Flowers numerous, small, yellow. MALE FLOWERS subsessile, in pubescent panicles 6–10 in long. Calyx-lobes linear-oblong, subacute, glabrous, exceeding the tube. Stamens much exserted: filaments very long; anthers small, subglobose. FEMALE FLOWERS sessile or nearly so, in pendulous spicate pubescent racemes. Calyx urceolate, pubescent outside; teeth 4, short, triangular, acute. Ovary faintly 8-ribbed, slightly pubescent; styles much exserted; stigmas club-shaped. Fruit ⅕–¼ in. long, urceolate, truncate, 8-ribbed, glandular. Seeds minute, ellipsoid. Fl. B. I. v. 2, p. 657; Bedd. Flor. Sylvat. t. 212; Trim. Fl. Ceyl. v. 2, p. 265; Talb. Trees, Bomb. ed. 2, p. 170; Woodr. in Journ. Bomb. Nat. v. 11 (1898) p. 641; Watt, Dict. Econ. Prod. v. 6, part 4, p. 41. *Tetrameles* (without specific name), Dalz. & Gibs. p. 311.

Tetrameles Grahamiana, Wight, Icon. t. 1956. *Anictoclea Grahamiana*, Nimmo, in Grah. Cat. p. 252.—Flowers: Feb.–Mar. Vern. *Ugad*; *Bondsa*.

Konkan: *Stocks*!, *Law*!; W. Gháts, *Woodrow*. Deccan: foot of Párghát, *Graham* (Cat. p. 88). Kanara: *Law*!, *Woodrow*; common in the evergreen forests of the Gháts of N. Kanara, *Talbot*.—Distrib. India (W. Peninsula, Birma, Andamans); Ceylon, Java.

Order LXV. CACTACEÆ.

A large Order comprising perhaps 1000 species, confined almost entirely to the New World. It is introduced here in consequence of the naturalization of certain species of the genus *Opuntia* (*Opuntia Dillenii*, Haw., and *O. nigricans*, Haw.). The latter, commonly called the Prickly Pear, has spread widely throughout the Deccan, where it is known by the vernacular name *Nigadung* and has become so common about native villages as to be a regular pest, forming a harbor for snakes and filth of all kinds.

Several species of the Order are grown in gardens, but none of them are indigenous.

Order LXVI. FICOIDEÆ.

Annual or perennial herbs. Leaves simple, often fleshy, opposite, alternate or falsely whorled; stipules 0 or scarious. Flowers regular, hermaphrodite (rarely polygamous), in cymes or clusters, rarely solitary, never racemose. Calyx 4–5-sepalous or 4–5-partite, free or rarely adnate to the ovary, the lobes usually green, herbaceous, imbricate, always persistent in fruit. Petals usually wanting; when present, small. Stamens perigynous or hypogynous, definite or indefinite, when equal to the number of sepals usually opposite to them, when more, equidistant or in bundles; filaments subulate or dilated, free or connate into a membranous cup. Disk 0 or annular, often produced into subulate staminodes alternating with the stamens. Ovary usually free, 2–5-celled; ovules solitary in each cell and basal, or many, inserted on placentas adnate to the interior angle of the cell, amphitropous; styles as many as the cells of the ovary, free, or connate into one split at the apex. Fruit usually capsular, splitting dorsally or circumscissilely, or less commonly separating into cocci, usually smaller than the persistent calyx and included in it. Seeds solitary or numerous, usually reniform, compressed; testa membranous or crustaceous; embryo curved round farinaceous or fleshy albumen.—Distrib. Scattered throughout the tropical and subtropical regions of the globe; genera 22; species 450.

Stamens inserted on the calyx-tube.
- Capsule loculicidally or septicidally dehiscent .... 1. Aizoon.
- Capsule circumscissilely dehiscent.
  - Ovary 3–5-celled .... 2. Sesuvium.
  - Ovary 1–2-celled .... 3. Trianthema.

Stamens hypogynous.
- Fruit capsular.
  - Petals many .... 4. Orygia.
  - Petals 0 .... 5. Mollugo.
- Fruit of 2–5 one-seeded cocci.
  - Carpels 3–5; petals 0 .... 6. Giseria.
  - Carpels 2; petals 3-5 .... 7. Limeum.

1. AIZOON, Linn.

Herbs or undershrubs. Leaves alternate (rarely opposite), sessile or petiolate; stipules 0. Flowers axillary, solitary, or in spikes or cymes. Calyx-tube short, turbinate or hemispheric; lobes 4–5, spreading, valvate or imbricate, often colored within. Petals 0. Stamens many (usually about 20), inserted in the throat of the calyx, united into tufts alternating with the calyx-lobes; filaments filiform; anthers oblong. Ovary free, nearly included within the calyx-tube, 4–5-gonous, 4–5-celled; ovules 2–∞ in each cell; styles 4–5, free, papillose. Capsule subwoody, surrounded by the persistent calyx, 4–5-celled, loculicidally (rarely septicidally) 5-valved at the apex, the valves gaping, the cells 2–∞-seeded. Seeds small, pendulous, subreniform; embryo curved, cylindric.—DISTRIB. Southern Europe, North and South Africa, Arabia, Canary Islands, India, Australia; species 8.

1. **Aizoon canariense,** *Linn. Sp. Pl.* (1753) p. 488. A woody much-branched procumbent densely hairy annual or subperennial, 3–12 in. Leaves $\frac{1}{2}$–$1\frac{1}{4}$ in. long, alternate, obovate-spathulate, cuneate at the base and running down into the petiole, papillose and densely hairy with often medifixed hairs; petioles $\frac{1}{4}$–$\frac{3}{8}$ in. long. Flowers solitary, sessile, in almost every axil. Calyx $\frac{1}{8}$–$\frac{1}{6}$ in. long, hairy; tube subhemispheric; lobes broadly triangular-ovate, $\frac{1}{12}$–$\frac{1}{10}$ in. long, yellowish within. Capsules sessile, woody, pentagonal when looked down upon, much depressed, $\frac{1}{8}$–$\frac{1}{3}$ in. long, the valves inflexed. Seeds smooth, black, shining, with a few ridges on the back. Fl. B. I. v. 2, p. 659; Oliver, Fl. Trop. Afr. v. 2, p. 584; Woodr. in Journ. Bomb. Nat. v. 11 (1898) p. 642.—Flowers: Sept.–Nov.

In the Bombay Presidency confined to Sind. SIND: *Vicary*!, *Stocks*, 472!; Jemadar ka Landa, near Karachi, *Stocks*!; banks of the Hub river near Karachi, *Cooke*!, *Woodrow*!—DISTRIB. Africa, Canary Islands, Arabia, Beluchistan, Afghanistan.

2. SESUVIUM, Linn.

Herbs or undershrubs, erect or prostrate, branched, succulent. Leaves opposite, subfleshy; stipules 0, but the petioles are sometimes connate by a stipuliform membrane. Flowers axillary, sessile or peduncled, solitary or clustered (rarely subcymose), often flesh-colored or purple, bracteate or not. Calyx-tube turbinate; lobes 5, oblong or triangular, colored within. Petals 0. Stamens many or 5, inserted round the top of the calyx-tube; filaments filiform, sometimes connate at the base; anthers didymous. Ovary free, 3–5-celled; ovules numerous; styles 3–5, longitudinally papillose on the inside. Capsule ellipsoid or ovoid, membranous, 3–5-celled, circumscissilely dehiscent. Seeds very many in each cell, reniform; embryo annular.—DISTRIB. Throughout the Tropics of the world near sea-shores; species 4.

1. **Sesuvium Portulacastrum,** *Linn. Syst.* ed. 10 (1759) p. 1058. Herbaceous; stems prostrate, creeping and rooting at the nodes, often buried in the sand, stout, succulent, much branched, red, glabrous. Leaves opposite, 1–$1\frac{3}{4}$ by $\frac{1}{8}$–$\frac{1}{2}$ in., linear or spathulate-oblong, sometimes subcylindric, fleshy, obtuse, glabrous, tapering much towards the base; petioles short, much dilated and amplexicaul at the base, with broad scarious margins. Flowers axillary, solitary; pedicels about equalling

the calyx, filiform, glabrous. Calyx deeply 5-lobed, purplish outside, rosy within, $\frac{1}{4}$-$\frac{5}{16}$ in. long; lobes lanceolate-oblong, obtuse, with a mucro just below the apex behind. Stamens numerous, free or nearly so; filaments red. Ovary usually 3-celled; styles usually 3. Capsules 3-celled, $\frac{1}{6}$ in. long, enclosed within the persistent calyx, pointed, circumscissile. Seeds black, smooth and polished. Fl. B. I. v. 2, p. 659; Grah. Cat. p. 248; Dalz. & Gibs. p. 15; Trim. Fl. Ceyl. v. 2, p. 268; Pax, in Engl. & Prantl, Pflanzenf. v. 3, part 1, B, p. 42, fig. 17; Woodr. in Journ. Bomb. Nat. v. 11 (1898) p. 642.—Flowers: Nov.-Dec.

A tolerably common weed on the sea-coast throughout the Presidency. KONKAN: sea-shore near Bassein, *Bhiva*!; sea-shore, Revdanda, *Woodrow*!; Salsette, *Graham*; Ooran, *Graham*.—DISTRIB. India (on sea-shores); Ceylon, shores of tropical and subtropical regions.

3. TRIANTHEMA, Linn.

Diffuse prostrate branched herbs, glabrous, pubescent or papillose. Leaves petiolate, opposite, unequal, linear, ovate or obovate, quite entire; stipules 0, but the petiole dilated, with membranous stipuliform margins. Flowers axillary, sessile or peduncled, solitary, cymose or panicled. Calyx-tube short or long; lobes 5, colored within, mucronate at the back. Petals 0. Stamens 5–10 or many, inserted near the top of the calyx-tube. Ovary free, sessile, 1–2-celled, often truncate at the apex; ovules 1–∞, basal; styles 1 or 2. Capsule membranous below, with a hard thick cap which is detached by a circumscissile dehiscence and carries away one or more seeds, 1–2-celled. Seeds 1–∞, subreniform; embryo annular.—DISTRIB. Widely spread in tropical and subtropical regions; species 10.

Stamens 10 or more.
  Style 1 .... 1. *T. monogyna.*
  Styles 2 .... 4. *T. decandra.*
Stamens less than 10.
  Lower half of capsule 8–12-seeded .... 5. *T. hydaspica.*
  Lower half of capsule 1–2-seeded.
    Leaves less than $\frac{1}{2}$ in. long; style 1 .... 2. *T. triquetra.*
    Leaves $\frac{1}{2}$–$1\frac{1}{2}$ in. long; styles 2 .... 3. *T. pentandra.*

1. **Trianthema monogyna,** *Linn. Mantiss.* (1767) p. 69. A prostrate somewhat succulent herb; stems more or less angular, glabrous or pubescent, much branched. Leaves subfleshy, obliquely opposite, unequal, the upper one of the pair the larger, $\frac{3}{4}$–$1\frac{1}{2}$ by $\frac{3}{4}$–$1\frac{1}{4}$ in., the lower $\frac{3}{8}$–$\frac{1}{2}$ by $\frac{1}{4}$–$\frac{3}{8}$ in., broadly obovate, rounded and often apiculate at the apex, cuneate at the base, glabrous; petioles $\frac{1}{4}$–$\frac{1}{2}$ in. long, much dilated and membranous at the base, especially those of the smaller leaves in which the membranous enlargement forms a triangular pouch. Flowers solitary, sessile, almost concealed by the pouch of the petiole. Calyx-lobes ovate, acute. Stamens 10–20. Ovary truncate; style 1. Capsules small, almost concealed in the petiolar pouch, lid truncate, slightly concave, with 2 spreading teeth, carrying away at least one seed, the lower part 3–5-seeded. Seeds reniform, muriculate, dull-black. Fl. B. I. v. 2, p. 660; Trim. Fl. Ceyl. v. 2, p. 269; Woodr. in Journ. Bomb. Nat. v. 11 (1898) p. 642; Watt, Dict. Econ. Prod. v. 6, part 4, p. 77. *Trianthema obcordata*, Roxb. Hort. Beng. p. 34; Dalz. & Gibs. p. 14; Wight, Icon. t. 288; Aitch. Pb. & Sind Pl. p. 65.—Flowers: June-Aug. VERN. *Bis-khápra*.

A common weed. DECCAN: Poona, *Woodrow!* SIND: Karachi, *Woodrow!*—DISTRIB. Throughout India; Ceylon and most tropical regions.

2. **Trianthema triquetra,** *Rottl. & Willd. in Ges. Naturf. Fr. Neue Schr.* v. 4 (1803) p. 181. A small diffuse much-branched herb 3–12 in. high, with a woody rootstock; stems and branches slender, usually red, covered with minute papillæ; branches numerous, prostrate, divaricate, the upper part more or less triquetrous. Leaves opposite or alternate, $\frac{1}{4}$–$\frac{5}{8}$ by $\frac{1}{16}$–$\frac{1}{12}$ in., linear or linear-lanceolate, subacute, fleshy, more or less covered with crystalline papillæ; petioles short, dilated and slightly sheathing at the base. Flowers sessile or nearly so, several in an axil, not enclosed in the sheath of the petiole. Calyx $\frac{1}{10}$–$\frac{1}{8}$ in. long; tube obconic, with many slender ribs; lobes broad, triangular, about equalling the tube. Stamens 5; anthers purple. Style simple. Fruit enclosed in the calyx-tube, 2-seeded, the cap flat, much depressed in the centre, carrying away with it 1 seed. Seeds 2, orbicular-reniform, compressed, concentrically striate on the faces, about $\frac{1}{20}$ in. in diam., black. Trim. Fl. Ceyl. v. 2, p. 269; Aitch. Pb. & Sind Pl. p. 65. *Trianthema crystallina*, Wight & Arn. Prodr. p. 355 (*not* of Vahl); Dalz. & Gibs. p. 14; C. B. Clarke, in Hook. f. Fl. B. I. v. 2, p. 660; Woodr. in Journ. Bomb. Nat. v. 11 (1898) p. 642; Watt, Dict. Econ. Prod. v. 6, part 4, p. 76.—Flowers: Sept.–Oct.

As Trimen (*l. c.*) has pointed out, this plant appears to be quite distinct from *T. crystallina*, Vahl, from Arabia and Nubia.

KONKAN: *Stocks!* DECCAN: Bijapur, *Woodrow!* S. M. COUNTRY: Badami, *Cooke!* GUJARAT: Dehgaon near Cambay, *Dalzell & Gibson*. SIND: *Stocks*, 512!—DISTRIB. India (Panjáb, Sind, W. Peninsula); Ceylon.

3. **Trianthema pentandra,** *Linn. Mantiss.* (1767) p. 70. Diffuse, much-branched, from a few inches to $1\frac{1}{2}$ ft. high; stems and branches more or less papillose (sometimes glabrous), angled and grooved. Leaves $\frac{1}{2}$–$1\frac{1}{4}$ by $\frac{1}{4}$–$\frac{5}{8}$ in., elliptic-oblong, sometimes slightly obovate, glabrous or more or less papillose, rounded (rarely subacute) at the apex, narrowed at the base; petioles distinct, $\frac{1}{4}$–$\frac{1}{2}$ in. long, dilated at the base, slightly sheathing. Flowers sessile or subsessile, in few- or many-flowered axillary fascicles; bracteoles thinly membranous. Calyx $\frac{1}{10}$–$\frac{1}{8}$ in. long, deeply 5-lobed; lobes ovate-oblong, colored within, with a short apiculation at the back below the apex. Stamens 5. Styles 2. Capsules $\frac{1}{8}$ in. long, exserted, the cap with broad deflexed horns, mitriform, dividing into two 1-seeded portions, the lower half of the capsule containing 2 seeds. Seeds $\frac{1}{16}$–$\frac{1}{14}$ in. in diam., orbicular-reniform, compressed, rugulose, dull-black. Fl. B. I. v. 2, p. 660; Aitch. Pb. & Sind Pl. p. 65; Woodr. in Journ. Bomb. Nat. v. 11 (1898) p. 642; Watt, Dict. Econ. Prod. v. 6, part 4, p. 77.—Flowers: Oct.–Nov.

A common weed in Sind. KONKAN: *Stocks!* DECCAN: Poona, *Woodrow*. S. M. COUNTRY: Badami, *Woodrow!* SIND: *Stocks*, 36!; Mulir, *Cooke!*; Karachi, *Woodrow!* DISTRIB. India (Panjáb, N.W. Provinces, Sind, W. Peninsula); Tropical Africa.

4. **Trianthema decandra,** *Linn. Mantiss.* (1767) p. 70. Stems elongate, prostrate, not much branched, angular and striate, glabrous. Leaves subfleshy, $\frac{3}{4}$–$1\frac{1}{2}$ by $\frac{1}{4}$–$\frac{5}{8}$ in., the opposite pairs somewhat unequal, elliptic-oblong, rounded and usually apiculate at the apex; petioles $\frac{1}{4}$–$\frac{1}{2}$ in. long, puberulous, much dilated and amplexicaul at the base, but

not enclosing the flowers. Flowers in dense axillary subumbellate clusters; peduncles and pedicels very short; bracteoles thinly membranous. Calyx $\frac{1}{8}$ in. long; tube very short; lobes much longer than the tube, oblong, obtuse, with scarious margins and with a distinct long apiculation at the back below the apex. Stamens 10. Styles 2. Capsules not enclosed in the tube of the calyx, 4-seeded, the cap very truncate, $\frac{1}{8}$ in. long, solid, subcylindric with a narrow acute rim round its base, carrying away 2 seeds. Seeds orbicular-reniform, striate, black. Fl. B. I. v. 2, p. 661; Grah. Cat. p. 81; Dalz. & Gibs. p. 15; Wight, Icon. t. 296; Trim. Fl. Ceyl. v. 2, p. 270; Woodr. in Journ. Bomb. Nat. v. 11 (1898) p. 642; Watt, Dict. Econ. Prod. v. 6, part 4, p. 77.—Flowers: Dec.

S. M. Country: Adur village 10 miles west of Haveri (Dharwar Collectorate), *Woodrow*!; Badami, *Cooke*!—Distrib. India (W. Peninsula); Ceylon, Timor.

5. **Trianthema hydaspica,** *Edgew. in Journ. Linn. Soc.* v. 6 (1862) p. 203. A prostrate succulent papillose herb; branches dichotomous. Leaves $\frac{3}{8}$–$\frac{1}{2}$ by $\frac{1}{8}$–$\frac{1}{4}$ in., fleshy, elliptic-oblong, obtuse (the younger revolute), narrowed into the petiole; petioles $\frac{1}{8}$–$\frac{3}{16}$ in. long, dilated and membranous at the base. Flowers sessile, axillary, solitary or clustered. Calyx-tube obconic, $\frac{3}{16}$ in. long, many-ribbed; lobes 5, rose-colored within, about equalling the tube, triangular, acuminate, with a tooth or horn at the base of each at the sinus giving the lobe a somewhat hastate appearance. Stamens 5–7; filaments filiform; anthers rosy. Ovary 2-celled; styles 2. Capsules $\frac{1}{4}$ in. long, the cap conical, thin, membranous, hollow, not completely enclosing a seed, the lower part of the capsule containing 8–12 seeds. Seeds cochleate, rugose, black. Fl. B. I. v. 2, p. 661; Woodr. in Journ. Bomb. Nat. v. 11 (1898) p. 642; Watt, Dict. Econ. Prod. v. 6, part 4, p. 77. *Diplochonium Hochstetteri*, Stocks, ex Aitch. Pb. & Sind Pl. p. 66.—Flowers: Dec.

In the Bombay Presidency confined to Sind. Sind: Jemadar ka Landa near Karachi, *Stocks*, 476!; Karachi, *Woodrow*!, *Bhola Puran*!—Distrib. India (Multán); Tropical Africa.

4. ORYGIA, Forsk.

A somewhat rigid diffuse branched glabrous herb. Leaves opposite or alternate, rather fleshy, petiolate; stipules 0. Flowers rather large, pedicelled, in terminal or leaf-opposed lax few-flowered cymes. Sepals 5, ovate-cuspidate, with membranous margins. Petals 0. Staminodes many, narrow, connate at the base. Stamens numerous, inserted at the base of the calyx, subhypogynous; filaments filiform; anthers linear-oblong. Ovary subglobose, 5-celled; ovules many, attached to the interior angle of the cells; styles 5, filiform. Capsule subglobose, included in the calyx, 5-celled, loculicidally 5-valved, many-seeded. Seeds compressed, reniform, strophiolate.—Distrib. Warm parts of Africa, Arabia, and India; species 1.

1. **Orygia decumbens,** *Forsk. Fl. Ægypt.-Arab.* (1775) p. 103. A decumbent diffuse wiry herb, from a few inches to more than 1 ft. high; root woody at the crown; stems pale, obscurely angled. Leaves $\frac{3}{4}$–$1\frac{1}{4}$ by $\frac{1}{2}$–$\frac{7}{8}$ in., alternate, obovate, cuspidate, glabrous, glaucous; petioles $\frac{1}{8}$ in. long, with a small membranous wing. Flowers $\frac{1}{3}$ in. in diam., in racemose lax terminal or leaf-opposed cymes, sometimes (including the slender obscurely winged peduncle) reaching 3 in. long; pedicels $\frac{1}{8}$–$\frac{1}{6}$ in. long; bracts at the base of the peduncles $\frac{1}{8}$–$\frac{1}{6}$ in. long, membranous,

pinkish. Calyx glabrous, divided to the base; sepals $\frac{1}{6}$–$\frac{1}{4}$ in. long, ovate-elliptic, acute or acuminate, green, with pink membranous margins. Staminodes about 20, purple-red. Stamens 12 or more. Ovary 5-ribbed. Capsules $\frac{1}{6}$ in. long, pale-yellow, smooth and shining. Seeds reniform, minutely strophiolate, finely striate, black. Fl. B. I. v. 2, p. 661; Woodr. in Journ. Bomb. Nat. v. 11 (1898) p. 642.—Flowers: Dec.-Jan.

SIND: *Stocks*, 444!; Karachi district, *Woodrow*!, *Bhola Puran*!, *Cooke*!; Jemadar ka Landa near Karachi, *Stocks*!—DISTRIB. India (Panjab, Sind, Mysore); Western Asia, Africa.

5. MOLLUGO, Linn.

Erect or diffuse glabrous pubescent or stellately tomentose herbs, often dichotomously branched. Leaves often falsely whorled or alternate, or all radical, linear, obovate or spathulate; stipules membranous, fugacious. Flowers axillary, solitary, fascicled or in diffuse or umbelliform cymes, usually greenish. Sepals 5, subequal, persistent, with membranous margins. Petals 0. Stamens 3–5, subhypogynous, usually alternate with the sepals, sometimes intermixed with subulate staminodes. Ovary free, 3–5-celled; ovules ∞, attached to the interior angle of the cells; styles 3–5. Capsule membranous, included in the calyx, oblong, globose or subcylindric, 3–5-celled, loculicidally 3–5-valved. Seeds several (rarely 1) in each cell, reniform, appendaged at the hilum or not; embryo more or less curved.—DISTRIB. Tropical and subtropical regions of both hemispheres; species 12.

Flowers in axillary fascicles; seeds appendaged.
  Densely stellately hairy .... 1. *M. hirta.*
  Glabrous .... 2. *M. oppositifolia.*
Flowers in terminal cymes; seeds not appendaged.
  Seeds with raised tubercular points .... 3. *M. pentaphylla.*
  Seeds without raised tubercular points .... 4. *M. Cerviana.*

1. **Mollugo hirta,** *Thunb. Prodr. Pl. Cap.* (1794) p. 24. Annual, softly villous with (chiefly) stellate hairs; stems many, usually prostrate and spreading 6–18 in. from a centre, sometimes ascending, leafy. Leaves opposite or several at a node, $\frac{3}{8}$–$\frac{3}{4}$ by $\frac{5}{16}$–$\frac{1}{2}$ in., densely stellately villous on both sides, broadly obovate or suborbicular, very obtuse at the apex, cuneate at the base; petioles $\frac{1}{4}$–$\frac{5}{8}$ in. long, slender, stellately hairy. Flowers pinkish-white, in axillary fascicles, 1–6 together; pedicels unequal, $\frac{1}{12}$–$\frac{1}{6}$ in. long, divaricate. Calyx stellately hairy outside; sepals $\frac{1}{4}$–$\frac{1}{3}$ in. long, elliptic-lanceolate, acute. Stamens usually 10 or more, varying to 5. Ovary ovoid, quite glabrous, 5-lobed, 5-celled; ovules ∞; styles almost 0 or very short; stigmas usually 5, spreading. Capsules a little shorter than the sepals, ovoid. Seeds ∞, subreniform, with raised tubercular points, black, appendaged with a white scale at the hilum extended into a long filiform process which curves round the seed. Fl. B. I. v. 2, p. 662; Trim. Fl. Ceyl. v. 2, p. 270; Woodr. in Journ. Bomb. Nat. v. 11 (1898) p. 642; Watt, Dict. Econ. Prod. v. 5, p. 255. *Mollugo Glinus*, A. Rich. Tent. Fl. Abyss. v. 1 (1847) p. 48; Aitch. Pb. & Sind Pl. p. 66. *Glinus lotoides*, Lœfl. It. Hisp. (1758) p. 145; Linn. Sp. Pl. ed. 2 (1762) p. 663; Grah. Cat. p. 82; Dalz. & Gibs. pp. 16 & 311.—Flowers: Feb.-Apr. VERN. *Dasard-sdg*; *Kotrak.*

KONKAN: *Stocks*!; Bombay, common, *Graham*, *Dalzell & Gibson*. DECCAN: Khandala, *Woodrow*!; Mahableshwar, *Cooke*! S. M. COUNTRY: Belgaum, *Ritchie*, 51! SIND: *Dalzell*!; hills near Karachi, *Bhola Puran*!—DISTRIB. Throughout India, common; Ceylon, warmer regions of the world.

2. **Mollugo oppositifolia,** *Linn. Sp. Pl.* (1753) p. 89. Diffuse, prostrate or ascending; stems numerous, dichotomously branched, with long internodes, slender, glabrous or pubescent near the ends. Leaves $\frac{1}{2}$–$\frac{7}{8}$ by $\frac{1}{8}$–$\frac{1}{4}$ in., in whorls of 4–5, unequal, oblanceolate or linear-lanceolate or sometimes spathulate, rounded or acute and apiculate at the apex, much tapered into the petiole which is therefore obscure. Flowers white, in axillary fascicles of 2 or more; pedicels $\frac{1}{4}$–$\frac{1}{2}$ in. long, filiform. Calyx glabrous outside; sepals $\frac{1}{8}$ in. long, oblong, subacute, with membranous margins. Staminodes 0. Stamens usually 3. Ovary glabrous; styles 3, very short; stigmas spreading. Capsules ellipsoid, a little shorter than the sepals, 3-celled. Seeds very numerous, subreniform, with raised tubercular points, dark-brown, appendaged with a very small white scale at the hilum extended into a bristle which curves round the seed. Jackson, Index Kewen. v. 3, p. 254; Trim. Fl. Ceyl. v. 2, p. 271. *Mollugo Spergula*, Linn. Syst. ed. 10 (1759) p. 881; Grah. Cat. p. 12; C. B. Clarke, in Hook. f. Fl. B. I. v. 2, p. 662; Woodr. in Journ. Bomb. Nat. v. 11 (1898) p. 642.—Flowers: Sept.–Oct.

DECCAN: Bijapur, *Woodrow*! S. M. COUNTRY: Belgaum, *Woodrow*!; Badami, *Bhiva*! GUJARAT: Baroda, *Kanitkar*! KANARA: Kála naddi, *Ritchie*, 40!; Chandwár, *Ritchie*, 40!—DISTRIB. India (W. Peninsula, Birma); Ceylon, Tropical Africa, Australia.

3. **Mollugo pentaphylla,** *Linn. Sp. Pl.* (1753) p. 89. Annual, diffuse, glabrous, 6–12 in. high; stems numerous, with many more or less quadrangular leafy dichotomously arranged branches. Leaves $\frac{1}{2}$–$1\frac{1}{2}$ in. by $\frac{1}{8}$–$\frac{1}{4}$ in., in whorls of 2–9, linear-lanceolate to obovate, obtuse or acute, sometimes apiculate, much narrowed at the base; petioles obscure. Flowers white, numerous, in lax corymbose terminal cymes; peduncles and pedicels filiform; bracts lanceolate, scarious. Calyx glabrous; sepals $\frac{1}{16}$–$\frac{1}{10}$ in. long, broadly elliptic-oblong, obtuse, parallel-nerved. Stamens usually 3. Styles 3, short, linear. Capsules subglobose, as long as or slightly longer than the sepals, with thin walls. Seeds numerous, roundish-reniform, compressed, covered with raised tubercular points, dark-brown. Jackson, in Index Kewen. v. 3, p. 254; Grah. Cat. p. 12; Dalz. & Gibs. p. 16; Trim. Fl. Ceyl. v. 2, p. 271. *Mollugo stricta*, Linn. Sp. Pl. ed. 2 (1762) p. 131; Dalz. & Gibs. p. 16; C. B. Clarke, in Hook. f. Fl. B. I. v. 2, p. 663; Woodr. in Journ. Bomb. Nat. v. 11 (1898) p. 642; Watt, Dict. Econ. Prod. v. 5, p. 255. *Mollugo triphylla*, Lour. Fl. Cochinch. v. 1 (1790) p. 62 (*not* of Burm.); Grah. Cat. p. 12.—Flowers: Sept.–Nov. VERN. *Jharasi.*

A common weed, *Graham, Dalzell & Gibson.* DECCAN: Poona, *Woodrow*!; Panchgani, *Cooke*!, *Woodrow*! S. M. COUNTRY: Belgaum, *Woodrow*!; hills north of Belgaum, *Ritchie*, 950!; Dharwar districts, *Talbot*, 2536!; Badami, *Cooke*! —DISTRIB. Throughout India; Ceylon, Malacca, China, Japan, Fiji.

VAR. *rupestris*, A much smaller plant, $2\frac{1}{2}$–6 in. high. Leaves narrow-linear, $\frac{1}{2}$–1 by $\frac{1}{30}$ in., apiculate; in other respects as in *M. pentaphylla*.

I have found this very abundantly in October on the wet rocks of the hill called the Table rock just above the Travellers' Bungalow at Panchgani. I have also found it on wet rocks near Marmagoa, but it has not been reported from any other locality. The inflorescence and seeds are exactly as in *M. pentaphylla*, but the leaves are entirely different. It seems scarcely entitled to specific rank, but is quite distinct as a variety.

4. **Mollugo Cerviana,** *Seringe, in DC. Prodr.* v. 1 (1824) p. 392. An annular erect slender glabrous herb 3–8 in. high. Stems very many, almost filiform; branches umbellate, the nodes thickened. Radical leaves $\frac{1}{4}$–$\frac{1}{2}$ in. long, rosulate, spathulate or linear-spathulate. Cauline leaves $\frac{1}{4}$–$\frac{3}{4}$ by about $\frac{1}{30}$ in., narrow-linear, apiculate, 2–8 in a whorl; petioles obscure. Flowers numerous, on long filiform stiff pedicels sub-umbellately arranged, usually in threes on the top of long filiform axillary and terminal peduncles. Sepals $\frac{1}{10}$ in. long, elliptic-oblong, obtuse, with white membranous margins. Stamens 3–5. Styles 3, very short. Capsules subglobose, equalling the sepals. Seeds numerous, smooth, without tubercular points, yellowish-brown. Fl. B. I. v. 2, p. 663; Aitch. Pb. & Sind Pl. p. 66; Trim. Fl. Ceyl. v. 2, p. 272; Woodr. in Journ. Bomb. Nat. v. 11 (1898) p. 642; Watt, Dict. Econ. Prod. v. 5, p. 254.—Flowers: Sept.–Nov. VERN. *Padá.*

S. M. COUNTRY: Badami, *Woodrow*!, *Cooke*! GUJARAT: *Kanitkar*!; Deesa, *Raoji*! SIND: *Stocks* ex *Aitchison*.—DISTRIB. India (Panjáb, Sind, W. Peninsula); Ceylon, Tropical Africa, Australia.

6. GISEKIA, Linn.

Diffuse branched usually annual herbs. Leaves opposite or falsely whorled, subfleshy, linear or spathulate, abounding in raphides; stipules 0. Flowers small, in lax or dense axillary sessile fascicles or shortly peduncled umbellate cymes, hermaphrodite or polygamous. Sepals 5, equal, herbaceous or with membranous margins. Petals 0. Stamens 5–15, hypogynous; filaments dilated at the base; anthers oblong. Carpels usually 5, distinct, sessile on a small torus, 1-celled; ovules solitary, basal; styles as many as the carpels. Fruit of 5 free membranous compressed papillose indehiscent 1-seeded carpels. Seeds vertical, compressed, subreniform; embryo annular.—DISTRIB. Africa, Arabia, India; species 5.

1. **Gisekia pharnaceoides,** *Linn. Mantiss.* (1771) p. 562. A diffuse somewhat succulent glabrous herb; stems 6–18 in. long; branches prostrate or ascending. Leaves subfleshy, subopppposite, $\frac{3}{4}$–$1\frac{1}{2}$ by $\frac{1}{8}$–$\frac{1}{4}$ in., linear-oblong, elliptic-lanceolate or spathulate-oblong, obtuse or sub-acute, entire, tapering at the base, glabrous, glaucous; petioles 0–$\frac{1}{4}$ in. long. Flowers numerous, in almost sessile umbellate cymes; pedicels slender, $\frac{1}{10}$–$\frac{1}{6}$ in. long. Sepals $\frac{1}{12}$–$\frac{1}{10}$ in. long, elliptic-oblong, obtuse, with membranous margins. Stamens 5; filaments dilated at the base. Ripe carpels membranous, as long as the sepals and surrounded by them. Seed solitary, rounded on the back, black, with scattered white glandular prominences. Fl. B. I. v. 2, p. 664; Grah. Cat. p. 250; Wight, Icon. t. 1167; Aitch. Pb. & Sind Pl. p. 66; Trim. Fl. Ceyl. v. 2, p. 273; Woodr. in Journ. Bomb. Nat. v. 11 (1898) p. 642; Watt, Dict. Econ. Prod. v. 3, p. 502.—Flowers: Aug.–Sept.

KONKAN: *Nimmo* ex *Graham*. S. M. COUNTRY: Badami, *Woodrow*!, *Bhiva*! GUJARAT: *Stocks*! SIND: *Dalzell*!, *Stocks*, 6!—DISTRIB. India (Panjáb, W. Peninsula); Ceylon, Beluchistan, Afghanistan, Africa. VERN. *Váluchi-bháji.*

Strong anthelmintic properties have been claimed for this plant, which has been especially recommended as a specific for tape-worm. See Watt, Dict. Econ. Prod. l. c.

7. **LIMEUM,** Linn.

Annual or perennial low branched glabrous herbs, sometimes frutescent at the base; branches usually prostrate. Leaves alternate or subopposite, linear-lanceolate, elliptic or obovate, entire or obscurely ciliolate; stipules 0. Flowers small, bracteate, greenish, hermaphrodite or unisexual, in dense terminal and subaxillary cymes. Sepals 5, unequal, ovate, herbaceous or with membranous margins. Petals 3–5, oblong or spathulate, or minute, or 0. Stamens 5–10, sometimes imperfect, hypogynous; filaments dilated and connate at the base. Ovary free, globose, compressed, 2-celled; ovule solitary in each cell, ascending, with basal funicle; style very short, with 2 branches which are stigmatose within. Fruit separating into 2 orbicular or hemispheric cocci which at length dehisce ventrally. Seeds vertical; embryo annular; radicle inferior.—DISTRIB. Tropical and S. Africa, India; species 10.

1. **Limeum indicum,** *Stocks, ex T. Anders. in Journ. Linn. Soc.* v. 5, Suppl. 1 (1860) p. 30. A prostrate glandular herb; root perennial; stems diffuse, much-branched, glandular-pubescent. Leaves opposite or nearly so, $\frac{1}{4}$–$\frac{3}{8}$ by $\frac{3}{16}$–$\frac{1}{4}$ in., broadly elliptic or suborbicular, inequilateral, shortly apiculate, entire, glandular-pubescent; petioles distinct, $\frac{1}{8}$ in. long, slightly dilated at the base. Flowers crowded, in axillary subsessile cymes; pedicels short, glandular, bracteate at the base. Sepals $\frac{1}{10}$ in. long, glandular-pubescent, ovate, acute, with membranous margins. Petals much shorter than the sepals, clawed, truncate and 2-dentate at the apex. Stamens 7 (*Stocks*). Carpels in fruit as long as the sepals, hemispheric, dehiscing ventrally, the margins of the valves inflexed so as to retain the seed till moistened. Seeds broader than long, about $\frac{1}{12}$ in. broad, concavo-convex, quite smooth on the back, yellowish-white. Fl. B. I. v. 2, p. 664; Aitch. Pb. & Sind Pl. p. 67; Woodr. in Journ. Bomb. Nat. v. 11 (1898) p. 642.—Flowers: Oct.-Nov.

In the Bombay Presidency confined to Sind. SIND: *Woodrow, Dalzell*; Schwan, *Cooke*!; sandy bed of the Mulir river near Karachi, *Stocks*, 535!—DISTRIB. India (Panjáb, Multán); Beluchistan, Aden, Nubia.

Tetragonia expansa, Murr. in Comm. Gotting. v. 6 (1785) p. 13, t. 5. *New Zealand Spinach.* A creeping herb with succulent stems, small yellow flowers on short pedicels, triangular-ovate succulent leaves and a 4–5-horned fruit, a native of Australasia. It has been introduced recently into a few gardens in the Bombay Presidency. It grows exceedingly well and seeds abundantly in the Deccan, where it comes up self-sown when once introduced. Its leaves furnish an excellent spinach for the table. See Woodrow, Gard. in Ind. ed. 5, p. 339.

ORDER LXVII. **UMBELLIFERÆ.**

Herbs (rarely shrubs or trees). Leaves usually alternate, simple or compound, exstipulate (except *Hydrocotyle*); petiole generally sheathing at the base. Flowers usually bisexual, often slightly irregular, in simple or compound umbels, rarely in heads or whorls; umbels and umbellules each furnished with an involucre of bracts or one or both naked. Calyx-tube adnate to the ovary; teeth 5 or 0 (so that there seems to be no calyx). Petals 5, epigynous, distinct, sometimes unequal, often bifid, with an inflexed apex and an impressed midrib, imbricate in bud (sometimes valvate in *Hydrocotyle*). Stamens 5, epigynous, alternating with the petals. Ovary inferior, 2-celled, crowned by a large epigynous usually 2-lobed disk; ovule solitary in each cell, pendulous; styles 2, often dilated at the base into *stylopods* which crown the ovary; stigmas minute, capitellate. Fruit of 2 indehiscent dorsally or laterally compressed separable carpels (*mericarps*), separated by a commissure and attached to and often pendulous from a slender central axis (*carpophore*). The mericarps are usually marked by 5 longitudinal lines (*primary ridges*), 1 dorsal, 2 marginal and 2 intermediate, and often with 4 more (*secondary ridges*) alternating with the primary ones; pericarp often traversed by oil-canals (*vittæ*). Seed 1 in each carpel, pendulous from the point of attachment to the carpophore; testa thin; albumen cartilaginous; embryo minute, straight, near the apex of the seed; radicle superior.—DISTRIB. A large Order, abundant in temperate regions, especially in the Northern hemisphere, but more or less represented throughout the world; genera 152; species 1300.

Umbels simple .... 1. HYDROCOTYLE.
Umbels compound.
  Fruit laterally compressed, not winged; commissure narrow.
    Leaves quite entire, grass-like .... 2. BUPLEURUM.
    Leaves pinnate or decompound (sometimes simple and broadly ovate-cordate in *Pimpinella*).
      Ridges of fruit slender; furrows 1-vittate .... 3. CARUM.
      Ridges of fruit slender; furrows 2-3-vittate; root usually fusiform .... 4. PIMPINELLA.
  Fruit somewhat dorsally compressed, not winged; commissure broad; root tuberous .... 5. POLYZYGUS.
  Fruit much dorsally compressed; lateral ridges winged.
    Portion of the fruit between the margin and the seed hyaline .... 6. ZOSIMIA.
    Portion of the fruit between the margin and the seed not hyaline.
      Herbs, usually glabrous; petals not radiant; ovary glabrous; wings of fruit with thin margins .... 7. PEUCEDANUM.
      Herbs, usually hairy; petals often radiant; ovary usually pubescent; wings of fruit thickened at the margin .... 8. HERACLEUM.

1. HYDROCOTYLE, Linn.

Annual or perennial herbs growing in moist places, usually prostrate and creeping and rooting at the nodes. Leaves orbicular or reniform; stipules small, scarious, sometimes lacerate. Flowers (in the Indian species) in very small heads or simple umbels, white or purplish, sometimes unisexual. Involucre-bracts few or 0. Calyx-teeth minute or obsolete. Petals entire, valvate or imbricate. Fruit somewhat fleshy, laterally compressed; commissure narrow; mericarps with the primary and sometimes the secondary ridges visible; vittæ 0. Carpophore 0. Seed laterally compressed.—DISTRIB. Temperate and tropical regions of the world, abundant in Australasia, S. Africa and S. America; species about 70.

Petals valvate in bud; secondary ridges of fruit 0; pericarp not thickened .... 1. *H. javanica.*
Petals imbricate in bud; secondary ridges of fruit distinct; pericarp much thickened .... 2. *H. asiatica.*

1. **Hydrocotyle javanica,** *Thunb. Diss.* (1798); *edit. Pers.* v. 2 (1800) p. 415, t. 3. Stems long, succulent, pubescent beneath the nodes, sending up erect stout branching shoots more than 6 in. high. Leaves suborbicular, broader than long, 1¾–3 by 2–3½ in., subentire or palmately 7–9-lobed one-fourth of the way down, coarsely crenate, shining on both sides, with a few weak hairs on the nerves; petioles pubescent, those of the leaves of the prostrate stems sometimes reaching 10 in. long, those of the erect shoots much shorter; stipules entire, scarious. Flowers pale-green, very small, sessile or shortly pedicelled, 20 or more crowded in dense globular heads or umbels on the apex of peduncles ¼–2 in. long which are often in clusters of 2–6 from the nodes of the upright branches; pedicels 0–⅛ in. long; bracts small. Calyx-teeth 0. Petals lanceolate, acute, valvate in bud. Fruit $\frac{1}{16}$ in., orbicular or subquadrate; mericarps with acute primary but not secondary ridges. Fl. B. I. v. 2, p. 667; Wight, Icon. t. 1003; Trim. Fl. Ceyl. v. 2, p. 275; Woodr. in Journ. Bomb. Nat. v. 11 (1898) p. 642.—Flowers: Feb.

KANARA: Hulikal, *Woodrow.*
This plant has been included on Woodrow's authority, who gives the above-named locality as its habitat. I have seen no Bombay specimens, and there are none from that Presidency in Herb. Kew.

2. **Hydrocotyle asiatica,** *Linn. Sp. Pl.* (1753) p. 234. A slender herbaceous creeping plant; stems long, prostrate, coming off from the leaf-axils of a vertical rootstock, filiform, often reddish, and with long internodes, rooting at the nodes. Leaves ½–2½ in. in diam., several from the rootstock which often have much elongated petioles, and 1–3 from each node of the stems, orbicular-reniform, rather broader than long, more or less cupped, entire or shallowly crenate, glabrous on both sides, and with numerous slender nerves from a deeply cordate base; petioles very variable in length, 3–6 in. long or more, channelled, glabrous or nearly so; stipules short, adnate to the petioles, forming a sheathing base. Flowers in fascicled umbels, each umbel consisting of 3–4 pink, sessile (rarely pedicelled) flowers; peduncles pubescent or glabrous, short, pink; bracts ovate, acute, concave, 2 beneath each umbel. Calyx-teeth 0. Petals minute, pink, ovate, acute. Fruit ⅛ in. long, longer than broad, ovoid, hard, with thickened pericarp, reticulato-rugose, often crowned by the persistent petals, the primary and secondary ridges distinct. Fl. B. I. v. 2, p. 669; Grah. Cat. p. 84; Dalz. & Gibs. p. 105; Wight, Icon. t. 565; Trim. Fl. Ceyl. v. 2, p. 276; Woodr. in Journ. Bomb. Nat. v. 11 (1898) p. 642; Watt, Dict. Econ. Prod. v. 4, p. 311.—Flowers: May–Nov. VERN. *Brahmi.*

In moist situations throughout the Presidency. KONKAN: Matheran, *Cooke*! DECCAN: *Woodrow*!; banks of the Poona river, *Cooke*!; Mahableshwar, *Cooke*! S. M. COUNTRY: *Woodrow*; Belgaum, *Ritchie*, 1080!—DISTRIB. Throughout India; Ceylon, tropical and subtropical regions of the world.
The plant is extensively employed in medicine. It was employed by Dr. Bhau Daji as a remedy for leprosy and has considerable reputation as an alterative in skin-diseases. See Watt, Dict. Econ. Prod. l. c., where an exhaustive account of the medicinal uses of the plant may be found.

Hydrocotyle rotundifolia, Roxb. Hort. Beng. (1814) p. 21. A pretty little creeping plant occasionally grown in gardens, but not indigenous in the Bombay Presidency. It covers the surface of a flower-pot with a dense green mantle and is easy of culture if kept shaded from the noonday sun and well watered. It is propagated by division. The plant is commonly known by its synonym *H. nitidula*, Rich. See Woodrow, Gard. in Ind. ed. 5, p. 342.

2. BUPLEURUM, Linn.

Glabrous annual or perennial herbs or shrubs. Leaves quite entire, the lowest grass-like. Flowers in compound umbels, usually with involucres and involucels, small, yellow or lurid. Calyx-teeth 0. Petals broad, emarginate, inflexed. Disk broad, flat. Styles short. Fruit more or less laterally compressed, slightly constricted at a somewhat broad commissure; mericarps subpentagonal; primary ridges distinct, with 1–3 vittæ between them; secondary ridges 0 or obscure. Carpophore 2-fid or 2-partite. Seed subterete, sometimes grooved on the face.—DISTRIB. Europe, temperate Asia, N. Africa, Canary Islands and Azores, with one species in S. Africa and one in N.W. America; species about 60.

1. **Bupleurum virgatum,** *Wight & Arn. Prodr.* (1834) p. 370 (*not* of Wall.). Perennial; stem erect, 1–3 ft. high; branches numerous, ascending, cylindric, striate, glabrous. Leaves 2–5 by $\frac{1}{4}$–$\frac{1}{2}$ in., linear-oblong, grass-like, sessile, usually acute or acuminate (rarely subobtuse), mucronate, glabrous, glaucous, with numerous parallel prominent slender nerves, narrowed at the base, amplexicaul but not sheathing. Flowers in compound umbels, yellow. Primary umbels in lax elongated corymbose or subcorymbose panicles, 5–8-rayed; bracts 3–6, linear-lanceolate, acuminate. Partial umbels (*umbellules*) 6–8-flowered; pedicels short; bracteoles 4–5, linear-lanceolate, longer than the umbellules. Calyx-teeth 0. Petals distant, the apex much inflexed. Fruit $\frac{1}{8}$ in. long, longer than broad, ellipsoid, dark brown, shining; mericarps rounded on the back, the primary ribs prominent, rounded, with a broad vitta in each furrow, often with a smaller one on either side. Trim. Fl. Ceyl. v. 2, p. 277. *Bupleurum ramosissimum*, Wight & Arn. Prodr. p. 370; Wight, Icon. t. 1007. *B. falcatum*, Dalz. & Gibs. p. 108 (*not* of Linn.). *B. mucronatum*, Wight & Arn. Prodr. p. 370; C. B. Clarke, in Hook. f. Fl. B. I. v. 2, p. 676; Woodr. in Journ. Bomb. Nat. v. 11 (1898) p. 642.—Flowers: Dec.

The specific name *virgatum*, Wight & Arn. l. c., has precedence over that of *mucronatum*.

A rare plant in the Bombay Presidency. S. M. COUNTRY: Dharwar, *Dalzell & Gibson*.—DISTRIB. India (W. Peninsula); Ceylon.

3. CARUM, Linn.

Annual or perennial herbs. Leaves pinnate or decompound. Umbels compound. Bracts of the involucre few or 0; bracteoles of the involucel usually numerous, undivided. Flowers white (in the Indian species), hermaphrodite or polygamous, the petals of the sterile flowers often irregular. Calyx-teeth small or 0. Petals broad, obtuse, entire, emarginate or 2-lobed. Fruit ovoid or ellipsoid, more or less laterally compressed and more or less constricted at the commissure; mericarps subpentagonal, the primary ridges obtuse, the lateral marginal with a single vitta in the furrows. Carpophore 2-fid or 2-partite.—DISTRIB. Europe and most temperate and subtropical regions of the Old World; species about 50.

1. **Carum stictocarpum,** *C. B. Clarke, in Hook. f. Fl. B. I.* v. 2 (1879) p. 681. Annual, $\frac{1}{2}$–3 ft. high, erect, much branched; root fusiform; stem glabrous. Lower leaves 2-pinnate; leaflets deeply cut into linear-lanceolate apiculate glabrous or minutely pubescent segments, the segments of the upper leaves often linear; petioles with broad sheaths, their margins membranous, ciliolate. Flowers white. Primary umbels 5–10-rayed; bracts 3–6, linear, acute, $\frac{1}{4}$–$\frac{1}{3}$ in. long. Partial umbels 6–20-flowered; pedicels $\frac{1}{8}$–$\frac{1}{6}$ in. long; bracteoles 4–8, linear-lanceolate, $\frac{1}{8}$–$\frac{1}{4}$ in. long, with white scarious ciliate margins. Ovary minutely pubescent; styles long, recurved on the fruit; stigma capitate. Petals broadly obovate or suborbicular, rounded (not emarginate) at the apex, $\frac{1}{25}$ in. long. Fruit $\frac{1}{24}$–$\frac{1}{16}$ in. long, ovoid, glabrous or puberulous, brown; mericarps scarcely compressed, the ridges slender, faint. Trim. Fl. Ceyl. v. 2, p. 278; Woodr. in Journ. Bomb. Nat. v. 11 (1898) p. 642.—Flowers: Aug.–Oct. VERN. *Rán-onvá.*

KONKAN: *Law*!, *Stocks*! DECCAN: hills, *Woodrow*; Jejuri, *Ranade*!; Bowdhán 8 miles west of Poona, *Bhiva*!; Panchgani Ghát, *Cooke*!—DISTRIB. India (W. Peninsula); Ceylon.

VAR. *hebecarpa*, C. B. Clarke, in Hook. f. Fl. B. I. v. 2, p. 682. Fruit larger, $\frac{1}{18}$–$\frac{1}{12}$ in. long, hispidulous, sometimes densely so.

KONKAN: *Law*!, *Stocks*!

Carum Roxburghianum, Benth. & Hook. f. Gen. Pl. v. 1, p. 891, is cultivated in native gardens (extensively so in Gujarat) and is probably, as suggested by Mr. C. B. Clarke (Fl. B. I. v. 2, p. 682), a cultivated form of *C. stictocarpum*, from some forms of the variety *hebecarpa* of which it is hardly separable. It is not known wild (C. B. Clarke, l. c.). The seeds are used for flavoring curries and the leaves as a substitute for parsley. Woodr. in Journ. Bomb. Nat. v. 11 (1898) p. 642; Watt, Dict. Econ. Prod. v. 2, p. 201. *Pimpinella involucrata*, Wight & Arn. Prodr. p. 369; Dalz. & Gibs. p. 106. *Apium involucratum*, Roxb. Hort. Beng. p. 22; Dalz. & Gibs. Suppl. p. 41.—Flowers: Nov.–Dec. VERN. *Ajmod*; *Chanu*; *Randhuni.*

Carum copticum, Benth. & Hook. f. Gen. Pl. v. 1, p. 891. *The Bishop's Weed*; *Lovage.* A plant 1–3 ft. high, cultivated extensively for its seeds which are largely employed in medicine and also in England and Germany in the manufacture of *Thymol* which is used as an antiseptic. Fl. B. I. v. 2, p. 682; Woodr. in Journ. Bomb. Nat. v. 11 (1898) p. 642; Watt, Dict. Econ. Prod. v. 2, p. 198. *Ptychotis Ajowan*, Wight & Arn. Prodr. p. 368; Grah. Cat. p. 84; Dalz. & Gibs. Suppl. p. 41.—Flowers: Apr. VERN. *Ajván*; *Onvá.*

Carum Petroselinum, Benth. & Hook. f. Gen. Pl. v. 1, p. 891. *Parsley.* Cultivated occasionally in European gardens, but not much grown by the natives. *Apium Petroselinum*, Linn. Sp. Pl. (1753) p. 264; Grah. Cat. p. 84; Dalz. & Gibs. Suppl. p. 41. *Petroselinum sativum*, Hoffm. Gen. Umb. p. 177; Watt, Dict. Econ. Prod. v. 6, part 1, p. 181.

4. PIMPINELLA, Linn.

Annual or perennial herbs. Leaves simple or compound. Flowers in compound umbels, hermaphrodite or polygamo-monœcious. Bracts of the involucre 0 or few; bracteoles small or 0. Calyx-teeth obsolete or small. Petals usually with long inflexed points, more or less emarginate, retuse or entire. Fruit ovoid or broader than long, laterally compressed, often constricted at the commissure; mericarps subterete or subpentagonal, often dorsally compressed; ridges slender, obscure or prominent; vittæ 2–3 in each furrow. Carpophore entire, 2-fid or 2-partite. Seed subterete or dorsally subcompressed, the inner face flat or nearly so.—Distrib. Northern hemisphere of the world, S. Africa, a few in extratropical S. America; species about 70.

Fruit glabrous .... 1. *P. Heyneana.*
Fruit papillose, scabrid or pubescent.
  Lower cauline leaves simple .... 2. *P. Candolleana.*
  Lower cauline leaves pinnate.
    Flowers monœcious .... 3. *P. monoica.*
    Flowers hermaphrodite.
      Bracts 0 .... 4. *P. tomentosa.*
      Bracts 3–7.
        Leaves simply pinnate; flowers white .... 5. *P. adscendens.*
        Leaves ternate; leaflets 2-ternate; flowers pink ...... 6. *P. lateriflora.*

1. **Pimpinella Heyneana,** *Wall. Cat.* (1828) 566. Annual; root fusiform; stem erect, 1½–3 ft. high, with ascending glabrous branches. Leaves 3-foliolate, smaller upwards, the lateral leaflets usually ternate, the terminal leaflet sometimes ternate, but often simple, entire or lobed; ultimate segments of the lower cauline leaves usually stalked, ovate-lanceolate, ¾–2 by ⅜–¾ in., very acute, sharply serrate, glabrous or nearly so, base tapering; ultimate segments of the upper cauline leaves often much narrower; common petioles 1–1½ in. long, dilated and ciliate at the base. Primary umbels 6–20-rayed, the rays unequal, very slender, 1–2 in. long, glabrous; bracts 0. Partial umbels 4–12-flowered; pedicels filiform, very unequal, ⅛–⅜ in. long; bracteoles 1–2, linear, ⅛–¼ in. long, or 0. Styles short. Fruit subglobose, $\frac{1}{18}$ in. in diam., glabrous; primary ridges slender. Fl. B. I. v. 2, p. 684; Trim. Fl. Ceyl. v. 2, p. 279; Woodr. in Journ. Bomb. Nat. v. 11 (1898) p. 643. *Helosciadium Heyneanum*, DC. Prodr. v. 4, p. 106; Dalz. & Gibs. p. 106.—Flowers: Aug.–Oct.

Konkan: *Stocks*!. *Dalzell*!; near Marmagao, *Cooke*! Deccan: Bowdhán 8 miles west of Poona, *Cooke*! S. M. Country: *Woodrow*! Kanara: Kála naddi, *Ritchie*, 1767!—Distrib. India (Circars, Chittagong, W. Peninsula); Ceylon.

2. **Pimpinella Candolleana,** *Wight & Arn. Prodr.* (1834) p. 369. An erect herb 1–2½ ft. high; root fusiform, perennial; stems stout, striate, pubescent or villous. Leaves with cartilaginously crenate-serrate margins: lower cauline leaves simple (rarely pinnate), 1½–2½ by 1⅝–2¼ in., broadly ovate, usually acute, deeply cordate at the base, the lower surface pubescent, the upper more or less so; petioles long,

densely pubescent: middle cauline leaves 3-partite, the segments cut and sometimes lobed: upper leaves often irregularly 1–2-pinnatifid, the ultimate segments oblong, acute. Primary umbels with 10–16 pubescent equal rays, $\frac{1}{2}$–1 in. long; bracts 5–8, linear-subulate, $\frac{1}{8}$–$\frac{3}{8}$ in. long. Partial umbels 10–20-flowered; pedicels $\frac{1}{8}$ in. long; bracteoles $\frac{1}{8}$ in. long. Styles long, divaricate. Fruit $\frac{1}{10}$ in. long, ovoid, acutely pointed, covered with granular tubercles; mericarps rounded on the back, slightly concave on the inner face, the ridges prominent. Fl. B. I. v. 2, p. 687; Wight, Icon. t. 341; Woodr. in Journ. Bomb. Nat. v. 11 (1898) p. 643.—Flowers: Sept.-Oct.

Not very common in the Bombay Presidency. DECCAN: Poona districts, *Ranade*!; Panchgani, *Cooke*!, *Woodrow*.—DISTRIB. India (W. Peninsula).

3. **Pimpinella monoica,** *Dalz. in Kew Journ. Bot.* v. 3 (1851) p. 212. A tall plant reaching 6–8 ft. high; stem as thick as a goose-quill, terete, simple below, branched above, glabrous, smooth, striate; branches alternate and bifarious. Lower cauline leaves pinnately 3-foliolate; leaflets $1\frac{1}{2}$–4 by $\frac{3}{4}$–2 in., ovate or ovate-lanceolate, acute, more or less pubescent, sharply serrate, base cordate, truncate or sometimes tapering; common petioles 3–6 in. long, sheathing, ciliate; petiolules $\frac{1}{2}$–2 in. long: upper leaves often cut into numerous setaceous linear segments, or sometimes reduced to mere sheaths. Flowers in compound umbels, some of the umbels consisting wholly of male, the others of female flowers. Primary umbels with 6–12 slender rays, $\frac{3}{4}$–1 in. long; bracts 0, or 1 subulate. Partial umbels 8–20-flowered; bracteoles 1–4, linear-subulate, $\frac{1}{8}$–$\frac{1}{6}$ in. long, or often 0. Petals white, $\frac{1}{30}$ in. long, obovate or suborbicular, rounded at the apex. Fruit $\frac{1}{12}$ in. long, ovoid, crowned by the conspicuous disk, clothed when young with pellucid granules; mericarps rounded on the back. Fl. B. I. v. 2, p. 687; Dalz. & Gibs. p. 106; Woodr. in Journ. Bomb. Nat. v. 11 (1898) p. 643.—Flowers: Nov.

On the highest Ghâts, *Dalzell & Gibson*. KONKAN: *Stocks*!, *Law*! DECCAN: Mahableshwar, *Cooke*!; Panchgani, *Cooke*! S. M. COUNTRY: Belgaum south, *Ritchie*, 332!—DISTRIB. India (W. Peninsula).

4. **Pimpinella tomentosa,** *Dalz. ex C. B. Clarke, in Hook. f. Fl. B. I.* v. 2 (1879) p. 689. Erect, 2–3 ft. high; root narrowly fusiform; stems pubescent or tomentose; branches numerous. Lower cauline leaves 2–3-pinnatipartite; leaf-blade (excluding the petiole) 3–6 in. long; ultimate segments sharply inciso-serrate, the teeth pointed with a stout sharp bristle; common petioles sometimes 4 in. long, sheathing at the base, striate, pubescent or tomentose: upper leaves often reduced to sheaths. Flowers white. Primary umbels 4–8-rayed, the rays subequal, $\frac{3}{4}$ in. long, pubescent; bract 1, subulate, $\frac{1}{4}$ in. long, or 0. Partial umbels 3–12-flowered; pedicels short, pubescent; bracteoles 1–3, linear. Styles long, their bases enlarged into conical yellowish-brown stylopods persistent on the fruit. Fruit $\frac{1}{6}$ in. long, narrowly oblong, attenuate upwards, scabrid with numerous small whitish scales; ridges very obscure. Woodr. in Journ. Bomb. Nat. v. 11 (1898) p. 643. *Heracleum tomentosum*, Dalz. & Gibs. p. 108 & p. 313 (*not* of Smith).—Flowers: Nov.

KONKAN: *Stocks*!; S. Konkan, *Law*! DECCAN: Panchgani, *Cooke*!; Mahableshwar, *Cooke*!; Singhad near Poona, *Woodrow*.—DISTRIB. India (W. Peninsula).

5. **Pimpinella adscendens,** *Dalz. in Kew Journ. Bot.* v. 2 (1850) p. 261. Stems many, 6–18 in. long, terete, smooth, glabrous; branches few. Leaves mostly radical, simply pinnate, sometimes reaching 8 in. long (including the petiole); leaflets 4–8 pairs, rotund-ovate or obovate, cuneate at the base, acutely and irregularly serrate, the lateral leaflets $\frac{1}{2}$–$\frac{3}{4}$ in. long, the terminal leaflet usually longer than the lateral ones: cauline leaves few, the upper pinnatisect. Flowers in terminal compound umbels. Primary umbels 4–12-rayed, the rays subequal, $\frac{1}{4}$–$\frac{3}{4}$ in. long; bracts 4–8, linear-subulate, $\frac{1}{8}$–$\frac{1}{4}$ in. long. Partial umbels 8–16-flowered; pedicels $\frac{1}{10}$–$\frac{1}{6}$ in. long; bracteoles 3, linear-subulate, $\frac{1}{10}$–$\frac{1}{8}$ in. long. Petals white, broadly obovate, externally pubescent. Fruit $\frac{1}{18}$ in. long, brown, ovoid, subobtuse, laterally compressed, minutely pilose; disk not prominent; ridges obscure. Fl. B. I. v. 2, p. 689; Dalz. & Gibs. p. 106; Woodr. in Journ. Bomb. Nat. v. 11 (1898) p. 643.—Flowers: Jan.–Feb.

KONKAN: *Stocks*!; banks of rivers in the Konkan, *Dalzell*! DECCAN: *Stocks*!; Poona, *Woodrow*!; Singhad, *Woodrow*; between Nasik and Igatpuri, *Egdeworth*! S. M. COUNTRY: Belgaum, *Woodrow*!, *Ritchie*, 1081!—DISTRIB. India (W. Peninsula).

6. **Pimpinella lateriflora,** *Dalz. & Gibs. Bomb. Fl.* (1861) p. 106. Erect, 1–1$\frac{1}{2}$ ft. high; stems puberulous. Leaves ternate, the leaflets 2-ternate, the lobes of the lower leaves lanceolate, those of the upper linear, all acute, mucronate. Flowers pink; peduncles long, slender, leaf-opposed. Primary umbels 3–10-rayed; bracts 3–7, subulate. Partial umbels with 7 subulate bracteoles as long as the pedicels. Fruit densely covered with small granular tubercles. Fl. B. I. v. 2, p. 689; Woodr. in Journ. Bomb. Nat. v. 11 (1898) p. 643.

DECCAN: in ravines, common, *Dalzell & Gibson*.

This plant has been included on the authority of Dalzell & Gibson. It has not, as far as I am aware, been found by any other collectors, though Dalzell & Gibson state that it is common in ravines in the Deccan. I have never seen a specimen. There are none in Herb. Kew., and the description has been taken from Dalzell & Gibson, Bomb. Fl. l. c.

5. POLYZYGUS, Dalz.

A glabrous herb; root tuberous. Leaves ternately and pinnately decompound; segments rather broad, pinnatifid. Involucre-bracts very few, or 0; bracteoles of the involucels few, small, setaceous. Flowers white, in compound umbels. Calyx-teeth small, or the exterior larger. Petals oblong, inflexed at the apex, emarginate. Fruit small, ovoid, transversely subterete, with a broad commissure, glabrous; mericarps semiterete, primary ridges scarcely prominent, furrows broad, 1–3-vittate. Carpophore 2-partite. Seed flat on the inner face.—DISTRIB. India (W. Peninsula); species 1.

1. **Polyzygus tuberosus,** *Dalz. in Kew Journ. Bot.* v. 2 (1850) p. 260. A herb $\frac{3}{4}$–1$\frac{1}{2}$ ft. high, quite glabrous; root tuberous; stem erect, sparingly branched, terete below, angular and furrowed above. Radical leaves several, deltoid in outline, triternate; pinnæ distant; common petioles very long, 3–6 in. long or more; partial petioles of the lowest pinnæ 1–2 in. long, becoming shorter upwards; ultimate leaflets pinnatisect, the segments with irregular bristle-pointed serratures: cauline leaves few, smaller. Flowers white, in terminal and axillary compound umbels. Primary umbels 3–8-rayed, $\frac{3}{4}$–1$\frac{1}{4}$ in. long; bract 1,

subulate, $\frac{1}{8}$ in. long, or 0. Partial umbels 6–12-flowered, $\frac{1}{8}$–$\frac{1}{4}$ in. long, the outer flowers fertile with long divaricate purple styles, the inner sterile with scarcely any styles; bracteoles 3, unilateral. Fruit $\frac{1}{8}$ in. long, dorsally compressed, ovoid, glabrous, shining, many-ribbed. Fl. B. I. v. 2, p. 698; Dalz. & Gibs. p. 107.—Flowers: June–July.

A rare plant. KONKAN: *Stocks*!; Malwán, *Dalzell*!; Dapoli, *Nairne*. KANARA: *Law*!

6. **ZOSIMIA,** Hoffm.

A perennial pubescent or hirsute herb. Leaves pinnately decompound; segments small. Flowers white or greenish-yellow; umbels compound, many-rayed; bracts and bracteoles usually many, small. Calyx-teeth prominent. Petals equal or unequal, rarely radiant, with an inflexed acumen, emarginate or 2-lobed. Disk depressed, with undulate margin. Fruit orbicular or elliptic, dorsally much compressed, surrounded by a broad tumid margin before dehiscence; mericarps slightly convex in the middle of the back; dorsal and intermediate ridges slender, the lateral dilated into closely contiguous wings which form the margin of the fruit, the space between the margin and the seed-bearing cell hyaline; vittæ large, solitary in the furrows. Carpophore 2-partite. Seed flat or slightly convex on the back.—DISTRIB. W. Asia; species 1.

1. **Zosimia orientalis,** *Hoffm. Gen. Pl. Umbel.* ed. 1 (1814) p. 148, t. 1, B, fig. 7. A stout perennial pubescent or hirsute herb 1–3 ft. high; root large, fusiform; stems grooved, pubescent. Leaves reaching 8 in. long, decompound, oblong-lanceolate in outline, pubescent, much cut; ultimate segments narrow, linear, obtuse or subacute, $\frac{1}{30}$–$\frac{1}{20}$ in. broad. Flowers greenish-yellow; petals obovate-oblong, $\frac{1}{10}$–$\frac{1}{8}$ in. long with a very long inflexed acumen. Primary umbels 10–30-rayed, the rays unequal, 2–4 in. long, stout, pubescent; bracts about 10, linear-lanceolate, very acute, $\frac{3}{8}$ in. long, pubescent (often araneously so when young). Partial umbels 8–25-rayed; bracteoles 8–12, linear-lanceolate, $\frac{1}{4}$ in. long, pubescent; pedicels $\frac{1}{8}$–$\frac{3}{8}$ in. long. Disk very large. Ovary densely pubescent; style bases not dilated. Fruit pubescent until fully ripe, obovate or elliptic, $\frac{1}{2}$ by $\frac{3}{8}$ in. with a broad wing; dorsal and intermediate ridges prominent, very slender; vittæ thick, solitary in the furrows; commissural vittæ 2–4. Jackson, in Index Kewen. v. 4, p. 1254. *Zosimia absinthifolia*, DC. Prodr. v. 4 (1830) p. 195; C. B. Clarke, in Hook. f. Fl. B. I. v. 2, p. 717. *Heracleum absinthifolium*, Vent. Choix, t. 7.

A rare plant, confined in the Bombay Presidency to Sind. SIND: *Stocks*, 958!—DISTRIB. India (Panjáb); Afghanistan, Beluchistan.

7. **PEUCEDANUM,** Linn.

Perennial (rarely annual) usually glabrous herbs. Leaves pinnately or ternately decompound (rarely simply pinnate). Flowers white or yellow (rarely pink), often polygamous, those of the central umbels usually perfect. Umbels compound, usually with many rays; bracts various; bracteoles many, rarely minute or 0. Calyx-teeth obsolete or more or less prominent, small. Petals obovate, cuneate, or subovate, inflexed at the tip, emarginate or entire, not radiant. Disk undulate with flattened margin; stylopods usually small. Ovary glabrous. Fruit ellipsoid, oblong, or suborbicular, dorsally much compressed, more or less acutely winged on the margin; mericarps slightly convex on the back, the primary dorsal and intermediate ridges filiform or little elevated, the lateral dilated, winged; vittæ usually solitary in the furrows reaching the base of the fruit or rarely abbreviated, the commissural vittæ 2–6. Seed flat, slightly curved on the back, the face flat or rarely somewhat concave.—DISTRIB. Throughout the northern hemisphere of the world, Tropical and South Africa, Tropical America; species about 100.

Margins of leaflets entire; commissure 2-vittate .... 1. *P. Dhana.*
Margins of leaflets serrate; commissure 4-vittate .... 2. *P. grande.*

1. **Peucedanum Dhana,** *Ham. in Wall. Cat.* 7216, var. **Dalzellii,** *C. B. Clarke, in Hook. f. Fl. B. I.* v. 2 (1879) p. 709. Glaucous, glabrous; root large, fusiform; stem rigid, 6–8 in. high, scarcely branched. Leaves radical, lying on the ground, subcoriaceous, pinnately divided; leaflets 3–5, entire, or, more commonly, deeply 2–3-lobed, $\frac{3}{4}$–1 in. long, the lobes obovate-oblong, mucronate, entire; petioles 1–3 in. long. Flowers yellow. Calyx obscurely 5-toothed. Primary umbels 5–10-rayed, the rays $\frac{3}{4}$–$1\frac{1}{2}$ in. long; bracts 3–6, lanceolate, acute, $\frac{1}{8}$–$\frac{1}{6}$ in. long. Partial umbels 20-flowered; pedicels unequal, $\frac{1}{10}$–$\frac{1}{4}$ in. long; bracteoles 3–6, lanceolate, $\frac{1}{8}$–$\frac{1}{6}$ in. long. Styles long, recurved. Fruit $\frac{3}{8}$ by $\frac{1}{4}$ in., broadly elliptic; vittæ linear, solitary between the ridges and as long as them, the commissure 2-vittate, the vittæ marginal. Woodr. in Journ. Bomb. Nat. v. 11 (1898) p. 643. *Pastinaca glauca*, Dalz. in Kew Journ. Bot. v. 4 (1852) p. 293; Dalz. & Gibs. p. 107.—Flowers: July–Aug. VERN. *Koland.*

KONKAN: near Pen, *Woodrow.* S. M. COUNTRY: pastures near Belgaum, *Dalzell & Gibson*; Belgaum, *Dalzell*!, *Ritchie*, 1078!

The root is eaten and has the taste and odor of a carrot.—DISTRIB. India (W. Peninsula, Jabalpur, Chota Nagpur).

2. **Peucedanum grande,** *C. B. Clarke, in Hook. f. Fl. B. I.* v. 2, p. 710. Glabrous, 3 ft. high; root large, woody, perennial; stem erect, grooved, as thick as the little finger at the base. Leaves mostly radical, bipinnate, 8–12 in. long (including the common petiole which is 2–5 in. long), pinnæ usually 2 pairs and a terminal leaflet, the lowest pair ternately divided, with petioles $\frac{3}{4}$–1 in. long, the upper pair often simple, sessile or nearly so, the terminal leaflet 3-lobed nearly to the base, the ultimate leaflets 2–$2\frac{1}{4}$ by $1\frac{1}{4}$–$1\frac{1}{2}$ in., with deeply and irregularly gashed and serrate margins, the serratures ending in a stiff hard bristle: cauline leaves usually ternate, very variable in size and shape, usually deeply lobed (sometimes almost entire), with crenate-serrate margins and petioles much dilated at the base. Flowers yellow. Calyx-teeth 5, short, triangular. Petals $\frac{1}{12}$ in. long, ovate-oblong, with a long inflexed acumen. Primary umbels 10–20-rayed, the rays unequal, 1–$2\frac{1}{2}$ in. long; bracts 5, herbaceous, $\frac{1}{2}$ in. long, ovate-oblong, acuminate. Partial umbels 10–20-rayed; pedicels $\frac{1}{4}$–$\frac{1}{2}$ in. long; bracteoles 5, oblong, acute, $\frac{1}{6}$ in. long. Ovary glabrous. Fruit obovate, $\frac{3}{8}$–$\frac{1}{2}$ in. long, narrowly winged; dorsal and intermediate ridges prominent, the furrows 1-vittate, the vittæ nearly as long as the fruit; lateral usually 2-vittate, the vittæ abbreviated; commissural vittæ 4, abbreviated. Woodr. in Journ. Bomb. Nat. v. 11 (1898) p. 643; Watt, Dict. Econ. Prod. v. 6, part 1, p. 181.

Pastinaca grandis, Dalz. & Gibs. p. 107.—Flowers: July. VERN. *Báphali*.

Ghâts near Bombay, *Dalzell & Gibson*. KONKAN: Matheran, *H. M. Birdwood*; Pen, *Woodrow*! DECCAN: Mawal taluka, *Woodrow*!; Khandala, *Cooke*!; Karkala, *Cooke*!—DISTRIB. India (hills of the Western Peninsula), apparently endemic.

The plant has some repute in native medicine. The fruit collected from the Konkan hills is sold in the Bombay market. See Watt, Dict. Econ. Prod. l. c.

Peucedanum graveolens, Benth. & Hook. f. Gen. Pl. v. 1, p. 919. *The Dill* or *Sowa*. A glabrous herb 1-3 ft. high, with 2-3-pinnate leaves and yellow flowers, extensively cultivated for culinary and medicinal purposes. The seed is sold in every Indian market. Fl. B. I. v. 2, p. 709; Woodr. in Journ. Bomb. Nat. v. 11 (1898) p. 643; Watt, Dict. Econ. Prod. v. 6, part 1, p. 181. *Anethum Sowa*, Roxb. Hort. Beng. p. 22; Grah. Cat. p. 248; Dalz. & Gibs. Suppl. p. 41.—VERN. *Shepu* (the plant); *Balantshep* (the fruit).

Peucedanum sativum, Benth. & Hook. f. Gen. Pl. v. 1, p. 920. *The Parsnip*. Cultivated but very sparingly in the gardens of Europeans. It grows remarkably well in the Deccan, especially if irrigation be available. I have grown it most successfully in my own garden at Poona and it seems a pity that this valuable esculent is not more generally cultivated. *Pastinaca sativa*, Linn. Sp. Pl. (1753) p. 262; Grah. Cat. p. 84; Dalz. & Gibs. Suppl. p. 41.

8. HERACLEUM, Linn.

Perennial or biennial more or less hairy (rarely glabrous) herbs. Leaves lobed, pinnate or pinnately (rarely ternately) divided; segments broad, lobed and toothed, rarely small. Umbels compound, many-rayed, often large; bracts few, 0, or many, foliaceous; bracteoles usually many. Flowers often polygamous. Calyx-teeth obsolete or more or less conspicuous. Petals white (rarely yellow), usually unequal, often radiant, the lobes of the larger often widely spreading, emarginate or 2-lobed. Ovary usually pubescent, the fruit often at length glabrate. Fruit orbicular, obovate or elliptic, much dorsally compressed, winged, the wing with thickened margins (wing obsolete or nearly so in *H. concanense*); dorsal and intermediate ridges prominent or obscure, the lateral expanded into closely contiguous wings forming the wing of the fruit; vittæ usually solitary in the furrows, the commissural 2-4, all descending from a short thick stylopod to or beyond the middle of the fruit, often more or less dilated towards their extremities.—DISTRIB. Temperate regions of the northern hemisphere of the Old World, 1 widely spread through N. America, 1 in Abyssinia; species about 50.

Petals not radiant.
- Wing of fruit broad .... 1. *H. aquilegifolium*.
- Wing of fruit narrow .... 2. *H. Sprengelianum*.

Petals radiant.
- Bracts linear-lanceolate; bracteoles 5; commissure 6-vittate .... 3. *H. concanense*.
- Bracts broadly ovate; bracteoles 3; commissure 2-vittate. 4. *H. Pinda*.

1. Heracleum aquilegifolium, *C. B. Clarke, in Hook. f. Fl. B. I.* v. 2 (1879) p. 715. Glabrous, branched; root fusiform. Radical leaves usually 2-pinnate; petioles 4–8 in. long, dilated at the base; pinnæ usually 2 pairs and a terminal leaflet, the lowest pair of pinnæ usually ternate, with petioles 1–1½ in. long, the second pair sessile or nearly so, simple or lobed, the terminal leaflet undivided or more or less deeply 3-lobed, sometimes with a winged petiolule; ultimate leaflets 1½–3 in. long, all irregularly serrate-dentate and with many prominent slender nerves: cauline leaves usually ternate, the uppermost often reduced to sheaths. Umbels often in a nearly naked raceme. Primary umbels 6–10-rayed, the rays 1½–2 in. long; bracts 3–5, oblong-lanceolate, ¼–⅜ in. long. Partial umbels 6–10-rayed; bracteoles 3–5, linear-oblong, acute, ¼ in. long; pedicels unequal, ⅛–¼ in. long. Petals equal. Ovary glabrous. Stylopods small. Fruit ⅜ by ¼ in., ellipsoid, glabrous, the wing thickened at the margin; dorsal and intermediate ridges distinct, shortly excurrent, wing broad with a minute marginal vitta; vittæ on the back about 10–12, linear, produced nearly to the base of the fruit, not dilated at the lower end; commissural vittæ 4–6. Woodr. in Journ. Bomb. Nat. v. 11 (1898) p. 643.—Flowers: Sept.-Oct.

KONKAN: *Stocks*!, *Láw*!; Ooran, *Stocks*!

2. **Heracleum Sprengelianum,** *Wight & Arn. Prodr.* (1834) p. 372. A stout herb 2–4 ft. high; stem branched, much grooved. Lower leaves pinnate or 2-pinnate, 8–12 in. long, ovate in outline, clothed with minute scattered hairs above and slightly larger ones beneath; pinnæ 2–3 pairs and a terminal leaflet, the lower pair (or when 3 pairs are present, the 2 lower pairs) pinnate or undivided on petioles of variable lengths, the uppermost pair nearly sessile, not divided, the terminal leaflet large and usually deeply 3-lobed on a long petiolule; ultimate leaflets sometimes 4 in. long: upper leaves usually 3-foliolate, the uppermost often reduced to sheaths. Flowers small; petals equal. Primary umbels 8–20-rayed, the rays unequal, 1–3 in. long, pubescent; bracts 0 or 1–2, oblong-lanceolate. Partial umbels 8–16-rayed; bracteoles 3–5, lanceolate, caducous, ¼ in. long; pedicels ¼–½ in. long, pubescent. Ovary pubescent. Stylopods conical, large. Fruit ¼ by ⅛ in., ellipsoid, with a very narrow wing; dorsal and intermediate ridges often obscure; vittæ 4 on the back, about ¾ the length of the fruit, not dilated at the lower end; commissural vittæ 2–4. Fl. B. I. v. 2, p. 716; Dalz. & Gibs. p. 108; Woodr. in Journ. Bomb. Nat. v. 11 (1898) p. 643. *Pastinaca Sprengeliana*, Wight, Icon. t. 1008.—Flowers: Aug.

Rare. DECCAN: Khandala, *Woodrow*. S. M. COUNTRY: on the road between Belgaum and the Rámghát, *Dalzell & Gibson*.—DISTRIB. India (W. Peninsula).

3. **Heracleum concanense,** *Dalz. in Kew Journ. Bot.* v. 2 (1850) p. 260. Erect, 1½–2½ ft. high, more or less hairy; root pisiform; stem striate, dichotomously branched, usually with a few scattered hairs. Lower leaves 2-ternate; leaflets 3-lobed or ternately divided; segments 1–1½ in. long, pubescent, ovate, cuneate at the base, irregularly serrate, the serratures with a hard mucro: upper leaves often reduced to sheaths. Flowers white, the outer radiant. Calyx 5-toothed, the 2 exterior teeth ovate, subobtuse, subpersistent on the fruit beneath the stylopods, the 3 interior obsolete, but the margin of the calyx thickened there. Petals of the radiant flowers ⅓ by ¼ in., broadly obovate, cuneate, strongly veined, 2-lobed, with a shortly inflexed tooth

between the lobes; inner petals broadly elliptic, with a shortly inflexed acumen. Primary umbels 5–12-rayed, the rays unequal, $\frac{3}{4}$–$1\frac{3}{4}$ in. long, pubescent; bracts 1–3, linear-lanceolate, acute, unilateral, $\frac{1}{6}$ in. long. Partial umbels 5–10-rayed; bracteoles usually 5, lanceolate-acuminate, $\frac{1}{4}$ in. long, strongly nerved; pedicels $\frac{3}{8}$–$\frac{1}{4}$ in. long. Ovary pubescent when young. Stylopods large, conical. Fruit less flattened than in most of the other species of the genus, very hard, not or obsoletely winged, $\frac{1}{6}$–$\frac{1}{5}$ by $\frac{1}{8}$ in., glabrous; dorsal and intermediate ridges obtuse, equally prominent; vittæ on the back about 8–10, reaching nearly to the base of the fruit, solitary in the dorsal furrows, usually 2 in the lateral ones; commissural vittæ usually 6. Fl. B. I. v. 2, p. 716; Dalz. & Gibs. p. 107; Woodr. in Journ. Bomb. Nat. v. 11 (1898) p. 643. *Heracleum grandiflorum*, Dalz. & Gibs. p. 108.—Flowers: July–Aug.

KONKAN: *Stocks*!, *Dalzell*! DECCAN: Khandala, *Woodrow*!, *Cooke*!; Mahableshwar, *Cooke*!; Panchgani, *Woodrow*. S. M. COUNTRY: Rámghát, *Stocks*!—DISTRIB. India (W. Peninsula).

VAR. *Stocksii*, C. B. Clarke, in Hook. f. Fl. B. I. v. 2, p. 716. Dorsal and intermediate ridges (in the unripe fruit) slender; lateral ridges excurrent into a very thin wing.

KONKAN: *Stocks*!

4. **Heracleum Pinda,** *Dalz. & Gibs. Bomb. Fl.* (1861) p. 107. Perennial; root as thick as the finger; whole plant clothed with long weak white flat hairs; stem erect, branched. Leaves chiefly radical, 2-pinnate; segments cuneate at the base, coarsely toothed, the teeth mucronate; petioles long. Flowers white, in terminal umbels, radiant. Petals of the radiant flowers large, obcordate, deeply 2-lobed. Primary umbels 6–8-rayed, the rays unequal; bracts 1–3, foliaceous, broadly ovate, acute. Partial umbels with 3 bracteoles similar to the bracts. Fruit with 6 vittæ on the back, 2 on the commissure. Fl. B. I. v. 2, p. 717; Woodr. in Journ. Bomb. Nat. v. 11 (1898) p. 643.—Flowers: July–Aug. VERN. *Pandá*.

DECCAN: hill forts of Harishchandragad and Harsar, *Dalzell & Gibson*.
The above is included on the authority of Dalzell & Gibson, from whom the description has been taken (*l. c.*). I have never seen the plant, nor, as far as I know, has it been found by any collectors.—There are no specimens in Herb. Kew.

The following plants not belonging to any of the foregoing genera are cultivated more or less throughout the Presidency:—

Daucus Carota, Linn. Sp. Pl. (1753) p. 242. *The Carrot*. Extensively cultivated. Fl. B. I. v. 2, p. 718; Grah. Cat. p. 85; Dalz. & Gibs. Suppl. p. 41; Woodr. in Journ. Bomb. Nat. v. 11 (1898) p. 643; Watt, Dict. Econ. Prod. v. 3, p. 43.—VERN. *Gájar*.

Apium graveolens, Linn. Sp. Pl. (1753) p. 264. *Celery*. Cultivated occasionally in gardens. Fl. B. I. v. 2, p. 679; Grah. Cat. p. 84; Dalz. & Gibs. Suppl. p. 41; Watt, Dict. Econ. Prod. v. 1, p. 271.

Fœniculum vulgare, Gærtn. Fruct. v. 1, p. 105, fig. 5. *Fennel*. Cultivated throughout India, and, in the Bombay Presidency, largely in Khandesh and Gujarat. Fl. B. I. v. 2, p. 695; Grah. Cat. p. 84;

Dalz. & Gibs. Suppl. p. 41; Woodr. in Journ. Bomb. Nat. v. 11 (1898) p. 643; Watt, Dict. Econ. Prod. v. 3, p. 405.—VERN. *Badishep.*

Cuminum cyminum, Linn. Sp. Pl. (1753) p. 254. *The Cummin.* Widely cultivated in the Bombay Presidency. Fl. B. I. v. 2, p. 718; Grah. Cat. p. 84; Dalz. & Gibs. Suppl. p. 41; Woodr. in Journ. Bomb. Nat. v. 11 (1898) p. 643; Watt, Dict. Econ. Prod. v. 2, p. 642.—VERN. *Jire.*

Coriandrum sativum, Linn. Sp. Pl. (1753) p. 256. *Coriander.* Extensively cultivated throughout India, largely in the Deccan. Fl. B. I. v. 2, p. 717; Grah. Cat. p. 85; Dalz. & Gibs. Suppl. p. 41; Woodr. in Journ. Bomb. Nat. v. 11 (1898) p. 643; Watt, Dict. Econ. Prod. v. 2, p. 567.—VERN. *Kothmir* (the herb); *Dhand* (the fruit).

ORDER LXVIII. ARALIACEÆ.

Trees or shrubs sometimes climbing (very rarely herbs), glabrous or stellately pubescent or tomentose. Leaves alternate (rarely opposite), compound or decompound (rarely simple); petioles long; stipules within and partly adnate to the petiole (rarely free or 0). Flowers regular, hermaphrodite or polygamous, in umbels, racemes, or panicled heads (rarely solitary), with bracts and bracteoles; pedicels continuous with the base of the calyx, or there articulated. Calyx-tube adnate to the ovary; limb annular or shortly cup-shaped, truncate or more or less obscurely toothed or obsolete. Petals usually 5 (rarely 6 or 7), valvate or slightly imbricate, singly or calyptrately deciduous, rarely persistent. Stamens as many as the petals (rarely more), alternate with the petals and inserted with them within the margin of the calyx around an epigynous disk. Ovary inferior, 1–many-celled; ovules solitary in each cell, pendulous, anatropous; styles as many as the cells of the ovary, distinct or united, erect or recurved. Fruit usually drupaceous or dry, with as many cells and seeds as the ovary. Seed pendulous; albumen copious, uniform or ruminate; embryo next the hilum; radicle superior.—DISTRIB. Chiefly tropical and subtropical; genera 38; species about 340.

1. HEPTAPLEURUM, Gærtn.

Trees or shrubs often climbing. Leaves alternate, digitate, crowded near the ends of the branches; petioles long, dilated and clasping at the base; stipules usually connate within the petiole, prominent. Umbellules (rarely capitate) or racemes amply or shortly paniculate or rarely the umbellule subsolitary; bracts beneath the peduncles membranous, usually very caducous, those beneath the umbellules small or 0; pedicels usually not articulated. Calyx-teeth obsolete or the calyx-margin truncate. Petals 5–∞ (usually 5–6), valvate. Stamens as many as the petals; anthers ovate. Disk convex or conical; in male flowers concave. Ovary-cells as many as the petals; stigmas sessile in the middle of an umbonate or conical disk, which is more or less produced into a columnar style. Fruit subglobose, 5–6-angled. Seeds laterally compressed; albumen uniform.—DISTRIB. Asia, Tropical Africa, Pacific Islands, and Australia; species about 60.

1. **Heptapleurum venulosum,** *Seem. in Journ. Bot.* v. 3 (1865) p. 80. A climbing glabrous shrub, rarely a small tree. Leaves digitate; leaflets 3–7 (commonly 5), coriaceous, 3–4 by 1½–2 in., elliptic-oblong, acuminate, entire, glabrous, prominently reticulately veined, base rounded or acute; petioles stout, terete, 3–9 in. long; petiolules 1–2 in. long; stipules connate, ½ in. long. Flowers in terminal branched panicles, the branches numerous, sometimes reaching 10 in. long, with a number of stalked 8–12-flowered umbellules along a glabrous purple rhachis; ultimate pedicels ⅛–¼ in. long, filiform; bracts caducous. Calyx truncate. Petals 5, obovate-oblong, acute. Stamens 5. Styles almost 0. Fruit 5-angled, 5-celled. Fl. B. I. v. 2, p. 729; Talb. Trees, Bomb. ed. 2, p. 180; Woodr. in Journ. Bomb. Nat. v. 11 (1898) p. 643; Watt, Dict. Econ. Prod. v. 4, p. 222. *Paratropia venulosa*, Wight & Arn. Prodr. p. 377; Wight, Ill. t. 118; Grah. Cat. p. 85. *Hedera Wallichiana*, Dalz. & Gibs. p. 108.—Flowers: Mar.–June.

KONKAN: evergreen forests, *Talbot*; in gardens, Bombay, *Woodrow*. KANARA: evergreen forests of N. Kanara, *Talbot*.—DISTRIB. Throughout India; Malaya, Tropical Australia.

The following plants of the Order are grown in gardens:—

Panax fruticosum, Linn. Sp. Pl. ed. 2, p. 1513. A shrub 3–6 ft. high, a native of the Eastern Islands, with large supra-decompound leaves. It is commonly grown as a foliage plant in gardens and in pots about houses. Fl. B. I. v. 2, p. 725; Grah. Cat. p. 85; Dalz. & Gibs. Suppl. p. 42; Woodr. in Journ. Bomb. Nat. v. 11 (1898) p. 643.

Panax cochleatum, DC. Prodr. v. 4 (1830) p. 253. *The Shell-leaved Panax.* A shrub with long simple concave leaves, a native of the Eastern Islands, very common as a foliage plant in gardens. Grah. Cat. p. 85; Dalz. & Gibs. Suppl. p. 42; Woodr. in Journ. Bomb. Nat. v. 11 (1898) p. 643.

Fatsia papyrifera, Benth. & Hook. Gen. Pl. v. 1, p. 939. *The Chinese Rice-paper Plant.* A handsome shrub 8–12 ft. high, with large alternate 5–7-lobed leaves, a native of Formosa, sometimes grown in gardens. The Chinese rice-paper is made from thin slices of the pith. Woodr. in Journ. Bomb. Nat. v. 11 (1898) p. 643. *Aralia papyrifera*, Hook. in Kew Journ. Bot. v. 4 (1852) p. 50; Dalz. & Gibs. Suppl. p. 42.—Flowers: Dec.

Trevesia palmata, Vis. Mem. Accad. Torino, ser. 2, v. 4 (1842) p. 262. A small prickly tree with palmate or digitate leaves 1–2 ft. long, and straggling panicles 1½ ft. long, recently introduced into gardens at Poona. Fl. B. I. v. 2, p. 732; Woodr. in Journ. Bomb. Nat. v. 11 (1898) p. 643.

Hedera Helix, Linn. Sp. Pl. (1753) p. 202. *The Ivy.* The variety grown in the Bombay Presidency lacks the bright green of the ivy in Europe. It grows freely in the Deccan on the shady side of a house if regularly watered, but is not much cultivated. Fl. B. I. v. 2, p. 739; Woodr. in Journ. Bomb. Nat. v. 11 (1898) p. 643.

Order LXIX. CORNACEÆ.

Shrubs or trees. Leaves opposite or alternate, usually petiolate, generally quite entire, often unequal at the base; stipules 0. Flowers 1-sexual or hermaphrodite, regular, in terminal or axillary cymes, panicles or heads. Calyx-tube adnate to the ovary; limb 0, or truncate, or 4–10-toothed or lobed, persistent, valvate or open in æstivation. Petals 0 or 4–5 (rarely ∞), imbricate or valvate. Stamens inserted with the petals at the base of an epigynous disk, usually equal in number to the petals, rarely 2–4 times as many. Ovary inferior, 1–4-celled; ovules usually solitary (rarely 2), pendulous from the apex of the cell, anatropous. Fruit usually drupaceous; putamen 1–4-celled, less commonly with 2 bony or crustaceous pyrenes. Seed oblong, pendulous; embryo in the axis of copious usually fleshy albumen; cotyledons usually thinly foliaceous; radicle terete.—Distrib. Scattered throughout the world, but chiefly in the northern hemisphere; species 75.

Flowers fascicled; petals very long; stamens 15 or more .... 1. Alangium.
Flowers panicled; petals short; stamens 4–5 .... 2. Mastixia.

1. ALANGIUM, Lamk.

Shrubs or small trees, armed or not. Leaves alternate, petiolate, oblong, quite entire, 3-nerved from the base, persistent. Flowers white, subsilky, hermaphrodite, in axillary fascicles, ebracteate, shortly pedicelled, articulated with the pedicel. Calyx-tube turbinate, often sulcate; limb large, 5–10-toothed or truncate. Petals 5–10, linear-oblong, at length reflexed or revolute, valvate. Stamens usually 2–4 times as many as the petals; filaments filiform or flattened, more or less villous; anthers long. Disk cushion-shaped, depressed in the centre, lobed or crenulate. Ovary 1-celled; ovule solitary in each cell, pendulous; style narrowly clavate or filiform; stigma clavate or capitate, 4-many-fid or many-lobed, the lobes conduplicate. Berry crowned with the calyx-limb. Seed oblong; testa thin; albumen usually fleshy; cotyledons foliaceous; radicle elongate, cylindric, thick.—Distrib. Asia and Tropical Africa; species 8–10.

1. **Alangium Lamarckii,** *Thw. Enum.* (1859) p. 133. A small tree with more or less spinescent branches; bark light-colored; young parts pubescent. Leaves variable, 3–5 by 1–2¼ in., narrowly oblong or ovate-lanceolate, more or less acuminate, subobtuse, entire, glabrous above, pubescent on the nerves and prominently reticulately veined beneath, base rounded or acute; petioles ¼–½ in. long, densely pubescent. Flowers few, in axillary fascicles; pedicels ⅛–¼ in. long, densely pubescent, jointed at the top. Calyx turbinate, ⅛ in. long, densely silky-pubescent; teeth triangular, $\frac{1}{10}$ in. long. Petals 5–10 (usually 6), densely pubescent outside, ½–¾ in. long and about $\frac{3}{16}$ in. wide, narrowly linear, reflexed. Stamens numerous (usually more than 20), nearly as long as the petals; filaments hairy at the base. Style as long as the stamens; stigma very large. Fruit when young ovoid or ellipsoid, becoming nearly globular when ripe, ½–¾ in. in diam., crowned by the persistent calyx-limb, finely pubescent, not or obscurely ribbed, purplish-

red; endocarp bony; albumen fleshy outside, friable inside, not at all ruminate; cotyledons foliaceous, flat, not crumpled. Fl. B. I. v. 2, p. 741; Dalz. & Gibs. p. 109; Trim. Fl. Ceyl. v. 2, p. 285; Talb. Trees, Bomb. ed. 2, p. 181; Woodr. in Journ. Bomb. Nat. v. 11 (1898) p. 644; Watt, Dict. Econ. Prod. v. 1, p. 153. *Alangium decapetalum*, Lamk. Encyc. Méthod. v. 1, p. 174; Grah. Cat. p. 72; Wight, Icon. t. 194.—Flowers: Feb.–Apr. VERN. *A'nkul*; *Ansaroli.*

KONKAN: *Stocks*!, *Dalzell & Gibson*; Elephanta, *Graham*. DECCAN: *Dalzell & Gibson*; Poona, *Woodrow*! GUJARAT: Dangs, *Bhiva*!; Bodeli, *Woodrow*. S. M. COUNTRY: Belgaum, *Ritchie*, 1070! KANARA: Godhuli, *Talbot*, 521!—DISTRIB. Throughout India; Ceylon, S. China, Malaya, Philippines.

The fruit though astringent and acid is eaten. The wood is hard, tough, and close-grained, and is valuable as fuel.

2. MASTIXIA, Blume.

Trees with terete branches. Leaves alternate, subopposite, and opposite, oblong, quite entire, drying black. Flowers small, hermaphrodite, in terminal panicles, articulated with a 2-bracteolate pedicel. Calyx-tube campanulate; limb dilated, 4-5-toothed. Petals 4–5, ovate, leathery, valvate. Stamens 4–5; filaments short; anthers cordate. Disk fleshy. Ovary 1-celled; ovule 1, pendulous from one side of the cell near its summit. Drupe ovoid or ellipsoid, usually areolate at the apex; putamen woody, grooved down one face. Seed conform to the cell; testa membranous; albumen copious, fleshy; embryo small; cotyledons foliaceous, thin; radicle subelongate, cylindric.—DISTRIB. Indian Peninsula, Ceylon, Java; species about 8.

1. **Mastixia pentandra,** *Blume*, *Bijdr.* (1825) p. 654. A moderate-sized tree; bark smooth. Leaves 4–6 by $1\frac{3}{4}$–$2\frac{1}{2}$ in., elliptic-oblong, often obtusely acuminate, green and glabrous above, paler, reticulately veined, and, when young, puberulous beneath, base usually unequal-sided; main nerves 6–8 pairs; petioles $\frac{3}{4}$–1 in. long, glabrous. Flowers numerous, in terminal densely pubescent panicles; buds silky-pubescent; lower bracts foliaceous, sometimes nearly 1 in. long, the upper narrowly linear $\frac{1}{4}$ in. long; bracteoles $\frac{1}{12}$ in. long, acute, pubescent. Calyx $\frac{1}{8}$ in. long, pubescent outside; tube narrowly campanulate; teeth 5, ovate, subacute, $\frac{1}{12}$ in. long. Petals 5, ovate, very acute, leathery, a little longer than the calyx. Stamens 5. Style very short. Fruit $1\frac{1}{4}$ by $\frac{3}{4}$ in., ellipsoid. Fl. B. I. v. 2, p. 746; Talb. Trees, Bomb. ed. 2, p. 182; Woodr. in Journ. Bomb. Nat. v. 11 (1898) p. 644. *Bursinopetalum arboreum*, Dalz. & Gibs. p. 28 (*not* of Wight).—Flowers: Jan.–May.

KONKAN: *Stocks*!, *Dalzell*!, *Law*!; Western Ghâts from Bombay southwards, *Talbot*. S. M. COUNTRY: Dharwar, *Woodrow*; Párva Ghát, *Dalzell & Gibson*. KANARA: in evergreen forests and along nálas in N. Kanara, *Talbot*.—DISTRIB. India (W. Peninsula).

ORDER LXX. RUBIACEÆ.

Trees, shrubs or herbs, erect, prostrate, or scandent. Leaves opposite or whorled, simple, entire, stipulate (except in *Rubia*); stipules various, inter- or intra-petiolar, persistent or deciduous, sometimes free, sometimes united to the leaf or the neighbouring stipule, entire, toothed or setose. Flowers hermaphrodite (rarely 1-sexual), usually regular. Inflorescence various. Calyx-tube adnate to the ovary; limb various. Corolla regular, gamopetalous, infundibuliform, hypocrateriform or rotate; limb of 4–6 segments, usually equal, valvate or imbricate or contorted (to the left as seen from outside). Stamens as many as the segments of the corolla, inserted on its mouth or tube; filaments short or long; anthers 2-celled. Disk epigynous, usually annular or cushion-shaped. Ovary inferior, 2–10-celled; ovules 1 or more in each cell; style simple, 2-fid or multifid; stigmas various. Fruit berried, capsular, drupaceous or of dehiscent or indehiscent cocci, 2–10-celled. Seeds various; albumen fleshy or horny; embryo straight or curved; cotyledons flat or semi-terete; radicle superior or inferior.—DISTRIB. Chiefly tropical and subtropical; genera about 340; species about 4000.

Ovules more than 2, usually numerous in each cell [rarely solitary in some species of *Anotis* (12)].
- Flowers crowded in dense globose heads.
  - Calyx-tubes fused into a fleshy mass .... 1. SARCOCEPHALUS.
  - Calyx-tubes not fused into a fleshy mass.
    - Corolla-lobes imbricate.
      - Seeds not winged; stigma fusiform .... 2. ANTHOCEPHALUS.
      - Seeds winged; stigma globose........................ 3. NAUCLEA.
    - Corolla-lobes valvate.
      - Calyx cleft ½-way down; stigma clavate .... 4. ADINA.
      - Calyx truncate; teeth obscure; stigma mitriform, 5. MITRAGYNA.
- Flowers not in dense heads.
  - Fruit capsular.
    - Trees or shrubs.
      - Corolla-lobes valvate: seeds winged .... 6. HYMENODICTYON.
      - Corolla-lobes twisted; seeds not winged .... 7. WENDLANDIA.
    - Herbs (the Bombay species).
      - Corolla-lobes valvate.
        - Corolla-lobes with a tooth on each side ...... 8. DENTELLA.
        - Corolla-lobes entire.
          - Anthers connivent, dehiscing by apical pores; capsule bursting irregularly at the apex .... 9. ARGOSTEMMA.
          - Anthers not connivent, dehiscing laterally; capsule usually regularly dehiscing, rarely indehiscent.
            - Calyx-teeth 4.
              - Calyx-teeth contiguous on the capsule .... 10. HEDYOTIS.
              - Calyx-teeth distant on the capsule.
                - Seeds numerous, minute, angular .... 11. OLDENLANDIA.
                - Seeds few, plano-convex, or globose with a large ventral cavity............. .... 12. ANOTIS.
            - Calyx-teeth 5 .... 13. OPHIORRHIZA.
  - Fruit a fleshy berry.
    - Corolla-lobes valvate .... 14. MUSSÆNDA.
    - Corolla-lobes twisted.
      - Inflorescence terminal [sometimes axillary or leaf-opposed in *Randia* (16)].
        - Ovary 2-celled.
          - Seeds few .... 15. TARENNA.
          - Seeds numerous .... 16. RANDIA.
        - Ovary 1-celled .... 17. GARDENIA.
      - Inflorescence axillary [see also *Randia* (16)].
        - Flowers in clusters; ovary 2-3-celled .... 18. DIPLOSPORA.

Ovules solitary in each cell [see also *Anotis* (12)].
Leaves with stipules.
Radicle superior; corolla-lobes valvate.
Fruit of 2 cocci .... 19. KNOXIA.
Fruit a drupe with 2–many free or cohering pyrenes.
Ovary 2-celled .... 20. PLECTRONIA.
Ovary 5–3-celled .... 21. VANGUERIA.
Radicle inferior.
Corolla-lobes twisted.
Style shortly exserted, 2-branched .... 22. IXORA.
Style much exserted, entire .... 23. PAVETTA.
Corolla-lobes valvate.
Calyx-tubes confluent .... 24. MORINDA.
Calyx-tubes not confluent.
Ovules basilar, erect, anatropous.
Style-branches 2.
Trees or shrubs.
Stipules intrapetiolar.
Corolla-tube short, straight ... 25. PSYCHOTRIA.
Corolla-tube long, curved ...... 26. CHASALIA.
Stipules interpetiolar.
Corolla-tube funnel-shaped; berry blue; a fetid shrub ... 27. SAPROSMA.
Slender creeping herbs .... 28. GEOPHILA.
Style-branches 3–9.
Fruit drupaceous.............................. 29. LASIANTHUS.
Fruit capsular .... 30. HAMILTONIA.
Ovules attached to the septum, amphitropous.
Herbs.
Fruit of 2 indehiscent cocci .... 31. HYDROPHYLAX.
Fruit of 2 cocci, both or 1 only dehiscing ventrally .... 32. SPERMACOCE.
A small shrub; fruit of 2 connate cocci; calyx-limb greatly enlarged .... 33. GAILLONIA.
Leaves without stipules.
Herbs; leaves whorled .... 34. RUBIA.

1. SARCOCEPHALUS, Afzel.

Shrubs or trees. Leaves petiolate; stipules interpetiolar and caducous, or intrapetiolar and persistent. Flowers packed into globose heads, the calyx-tubes fused into a fleshy mass; peduncles simple, usually solitary, terminal, bracteate below the middle; bracts small. Calyx-lobes 4–5, persistent or caducous. Corolla-tube long, narrowly funnel-shaped, glabrous; lobes 4–5, imbricate, glabrous or pubescent. Stamens 4–5, inserted on the mouth or throat of the corolla. Ovary 2-celled; ovules numerous, imbricate, on pendulous placentas; style filiform, exserted; stigma fusiform. Fruits combined into a fleshy globose mass of 2-celled pyrenes with very thin septa. Seeds few in each cell, not winged; testa crustaceous; albumen fleshy.—DISTRIB. Tropical Asia, Africa and Australia; species 13.

1. **Sarcocephalus missionis,** *Haviland, Rev. Naucl. in Journ. Linn. Soc.* v. 33 (1897) p. 32. A small tree. Leaves 4–6 by $1\frac{1}{2}$–$2\frac{1}{4}$ in., elliptic-lanceolate, subobtuse, membranous, glabrous, shining above, running down wing-like into the petiole; main nerves 10–12 pairs, slender; petioles scarcely $\frac{1}{2}$ in. long; stipules intrapetiolar, persistent, $\frac{1}{4}$ in. long, triangular, acute, more or less connate, forming a sheath. Peduncles stout, solitary, usually inclined, $\frac{1}{2}$–1 in. long, with stipular sheathing bracts at the base and 4 small bracts $\frac{1}{6}$–$\frac{1}{4}$ in. long united

below into a cup attached on the peduncle below its middle. Heads of flowers 1–1¼ in. in diam. Calyx hairy, the calyx-tubes fused together, $\frac{1}{12}$ in. long; calyx-lobes $\frac{1}{8}$–$\frac{1}{6}$ in. long, oblong, subclavate at the apex, hairy inside and outside. Corolla yellow; tube $\frac{1}{4}$–$\frac{5}{16}$ in. long, glabrous; lobes oblong, obtuse, hairy on both sides, $\frac{1}{16}$ in. long. Anthers apiculate, reaching to about the middle of the corolla-lobes. Style exserted about $\frac{1}{8}$ in. beyond the corolla-lobes; stigma fusiform. Fruits connate into a fleshy globose mass. Seeds arillate, irregularly flattened, imbricate; testa black, crustaceous. *Nauclea missionis*, Wall. Cat. 6099; Fl. B. I. v. 3, p. 27; Talb. Trees, Bomb. ed. 2, p. 186; Woodr. in Journ. Bomb. Nat. v. 11 (1898) p. 644. *Nauclea elliptica*, Dalz. & Gibs. Bomb. Fl. p. 118 (*not* of Bedd.).—Flowers: Apr.–May. VERN. *Phuga*.

KANARA: along rivers and watercourses in N. Kanara, *Talbot*; N. Kanara, *Woodrow*!; common near Yellapur, *Talbot*; Sirsi, *Talbot*!; Karwar, *Woodrow*!—DISTRIB. India (southern districts of the Western Peninsula).

Note.—I have carefully examined the specimens of what Dalzell called *Nauclea elliptica*, which were sent by Dalzell himself to Kew in 1873, with a letter to Prof. Oliver (which is preserved in Herb. Kew.), and these specimens certainly do not belong to the genus *Nauclea*. Indeed Dalzell himself admits, in the letter referred to, that they do not belong to that genus. In his description of *N. elliptica* (Bomb. Flora, p. 118) Dalzell gives the length of the peduncle as 2¼ in., whereas it does not exceed 1 in., and he moreover describes the stigma as round-headed, whereas in his specimens it is distinctly fusiform. Dalzell's description would apply to *Nauclea purpurea*, but the plant he has himself sent is *Nauclea missionis*, Wall., *Sarcocephalus missionis*, Haviland.

2. ANTHOCEPHALUS, A. Rich.

Glabrous trees. Leaves petiolate, coriaceous; stipules interpetiolar, caducous. Flowers orange, crowded in terminal globose peduncled solitary heads, ebracteolate; peduncles with basal stipular bracts. Calyx-tubes closely pressed together but not fused; limb tubular, with 5 linear persistent or deciduous lobes. Corolla-tube long, funnel-shaped, the throat glabrous; segments 5, imbricate. Stamens inserted on the throat of the corolla; filaments short. Disk inconspicuous. Ovary 2-celled below, 4-celled above; ovules very many, horizontal, on 2 bifid placentas which ascend from the septum below its middle and send an arm into each of the upper cells; style filiform, exserted; stigma fusiform. Fruits packed into a fleshy globose mass of many few-seeded coriaceous pyrenes. Seeds minute; testa rather thin; embryo clavate, in fleshy albumen.—DISTRIB. Tropical Asia and the Indian Archipelago; species 2.

1. **Anthocephalus indicus,** *A. Rich. in Mém. Soc. Hist. Nat. Par.* (1834) v. 5, p. 238. A large tree with erect trunk and widely spreading horizontal branches; young parts pubescent. Leaves coriaceous, decussate, 5–8 by 2¾–4 in., elliptic-oblong, shortly acuminate, entire, glabrous and shining above, more or less pubescent beneath, base usually rounded, sometimes cordate; main nerves 8–12 pairs, parallel, prominent on both sides; petioles ¾–1¼ in. long; stipules lanceolate, acute, caducous. Flowers fragrant, in solitary terminal globular heads 1–1¾ in. in diam., on stout peduncles. Calyx $\frac{1}{6}$–¼ in. long; lobes 5, linear, obtuse, hairy at the top outside. Corolla orange, ⅜–½ in. long; tube infundibuliform, slender; segments about $\frac{1}{10}$ in. long, erect, linear-oblong, acute, imbricate, slightly pubescent outside. Styles and stigmas white. Fruit the size of a small orange, yellow when ripe. Seeds muriculate. *Anthocephalus morindæfolius*, Korth. Verh. Nat. Gesch. Bot. (1839–42) p. 154, & Obs.

Naucl. Ind. p. 20; Jackson, in Index Kewen. v. 1, p. 148. *Anthocephalus Cadamba*, Miq. Fl. Ind. Bat. v. 2 (1856) p. 135; Hook. f. in Fl. B. I. v. 3, p. 23; Trim. Fl. Ceyl. v. 2, p. 293; Talb. Trees, Bomb. ed. 2, p. 184; Woodr. in Journ. Bomb. Nat. v. 11 (1898) p. 644; Watt, Dict. Econ. Prod. v. 1, p. 266. *Nauclea Cadamba*, Roxb. Hort. Beng. p. 14; Grah. Cat. p. 87; Dalz. & Gibs. Suppl. p. 43.—Flowers: Nov.–Feb. VERN. *Niv*; *Kadam*.

A doubtful native, common near villages throughout the Konkan, but apparently not found unmistakably wild. KONKAN: Poladpur, *Graham*; Dasgaon (Ratnagiri districts), *Woodrow*!; Hátkhabe near Ratnagiri, *Bhiva*! KANARA: N. Kanara, rare, *Talbot*; Kála naddi, *Ritchie*, 987!—DISTRIB. Throughout India, often cultivated; Ceylon, Sumatra, Borneo.

There used to be a very large tree at the Wada Travellers' Bungalow below Mahableshwar.

3. NAUCLEA, Linn.

Trees or shrubs. Leaves opposite, sessile or petiolate; the secondary nerves usually few; stipules interpetiolar, flat, entire, deciduous. Flowers crowded in globose bracteate heads; peduncles terminal, simple, solitary or ternate; bracts often large, caducous; bracteoles 0 or glabrous, setiform, intermixed with the flowers. Calyx-tube prism-shaped; lobes 5, deciduous, linear-subulate, often tipped with valvate processes at the apex. Corolla-tube infundibuliform; lobes 5, imbricate. Stamens 5 on the throat of the corolla; anthers oblong or linear. Ovary 2-celled; ovules numerous in each cell on pendulous placentas; style long, thickened; stigma globose. Fruit of 2 cocci, the cocci often separating from a persistent axis. Seeds imbricate; testa winged, the upper wing 2-horned, the lower acuminate.—DISTRIB. Tropical Asia and Polynesia; species 30.

Linnæus is usually cited as the author of the genus *Nauclea*, but the plant (*Nauclea orientalis*) on which Linnæus founded the genus is now *Sarcocephalus cordata*; hence the real *Nauclea* of Linnæus does not now exist as *Nauclea*.

1. **Nauclea purpurea,** *Roxb. Cor. Pl.* v. 1 (1795) p. 41, t. 54. A small glabrous tree. Leaves 4–8 by 1½–4 in., membranous, elliptic or lanceolate, acute or acuminate, glabrous, base much tapering; main nerves 8–10 pairs; petioles ½–1 in. long, drying black. Peduncles 1–2¼ in. long, usually solitary, bracteate about the middle, terete, thickened above; bracts very caducous. Calyx ⅛ in. long; tube glabrous or nearly so; teeth triangular-subulate, $\frac{1}{16}$ in. long, silky. Corolla ⅜ in. long, externally glabrous or nearly so; lobes ⅛ in. long, oblong-obovate, obtuse, glabrous or slightly pubescent outside. Anthers included within the corolla-lobes, apiculate. Fruit of 2 dehiscent many-seeded cocci. Fl. B. I. v. 3, p. 26; Talb. Trees, Bomb. ed. 2, p. 185; Woodr. in Journ. Bomb. Nat. v. 11 (1898) p. 644. *Nauclea elliptica*, Bedd. Icon. Pl. Ind. Or. t. 19; For. Man. in Flor. Sylvat. p. cxxix, t. 29, fig. 3 (*not* of Dalzell & Gibson).—Flowers: Feb. VERN. *Dev-phanas*.

Not common in the Bombay Presidency. *Stocks* in Herb. Kew. (without locality)! KANARA: *Woodrow*; Tinai Ghát (N. Kanara), *Talbot*, 1601!—DISTRIB. India (W. Peninsula).

4. ADINA, Salisb.

Trees or shrubs with terete branches. Leaves petiolate, ovate, lanceolate or cordate; stipules interpetiolar, large, oblong, obtuse, caducous. Flowers small, crowded in solitary panicled globose heads surrounded by paleaceous bracteoles, the calyces not fused together. Calyx-tube angled; lobes 5. Corolla-tube elongate, funnel-shaped, the throat glabrous inside; segments 5, valvate. Stamens 5, inserted on the mouth of the corolla; filaments short. Disk cup-shaped. Ovary 2-celled; ovules numerous, inserted on a pendulous placenta, imbricate; style filiform; stigma clavate, rarely capitate. Capsule of 2 dehiscent cocci, many-seeded. Seeds oblong; testa winged; nucleus small; albumen copious, fleshy; radicle superior.—DISTRIB. Tropical and subtropical Asia and America; species 9.

1. **Adina cordifolia,** *Benth. & Hook. f. Gen. Pl.* v. 2 (1873) p. 30. A tree with erect trunk and horizontal branches; bark brownish-grey, thick, furrowed; young parts pubescent. Leaves 4–10 in. long and about as broad as long, orbicular, shortly acuminate, glabrous or slightly pubescent above, more or less densely so (especially when young) beneath; main nerves 5–7 pairs; petioles 2–4 in. long, softly pubescent; stipules oblong, obtuse, pubescent, $\frac{1}{2}$–$\frac{3}{4}$ in. long. Flowers numerous, in globose heads $\frac{3}{4}$–1 in. in diam.; peduncles 1–2 in. long, stout, axillary, 1–3 together, each bearing 1 (rarely 2) heads of yellow flowers. Calyx $\frac{1}{16}$ in. long, hairy; lobes club-shaped. Corolla $\frac{1}{4}$ in. long; tube slender, dilated above, pubescent; segments $\frac{1}{16}$ in. long, ovate-oblong, subacute, recurved. Style much exserted. Capsules $\frac{1}{8}$–$\frac{1}{6}$ in. long, cuneate, densely downy. Seeds about 6 in each cell. Fl. B. I. v. 3, p. 24; Trim. Fl. Ceyl. v. 2, p. 293; Talb. Trees, Bomb. ed. 2, p. 184; Woodr. in Journ. Bomb. Nat. v. 11 (1898) p. 644; Watt, Dict. Econ. Prod. v. 1, p. 114. *Nauclea cordifolia*, Roxb. Cor. Pl. v. 1 (1795) p. 40, t. 53; Grah. Cat. p. 87; Dalz. & Gibs. p. 118.—Flowers: June–Sept. VERN. *Hedu*; *Hedi*; *Hed*.

KONKAN: near Kalyan, *Woodrow*! DECCAN: Nasik, *Woodrow*; Chikli near Nasik, *Bhiva*!; Gokak, *Ritchie*, 1771!

5. MYTRAGYNA, Korth. Obs. Naucl. (1839) p. 19; Index Kewensis, v. 3, p. 249.

STEPHEGYNE, Korth. Verh. Nat. Gesch. Bot. (1840 ?) p. 160; Benth. & Hook. f. Gen. Pl. v. 2 (1873) p. 31.

Shrubs or trees. Leaves petiolate, usually with transverse parallel nerves; stipules interpetiolar, large, caducous. Flowers yellow, crowded in globose axillary and terminal solitary panicled or subumbellate usually 2-bracteate heads; bracteoles paleaceous. Calyx-tube short, ovoid or obconic; limb cupular or tubular, truncate or obscurely 5-toothed. Corolla funnel-shaped; tube long, the throat glabrous or pilose; lobes 5, short, valvate. Stamens 5, on the throat or below the apex of the corolla-tube; filaments short, filiform; anthers oblong, apiculate. Disk annular. Ovary 2-celled; ovules numerous, on pendulous placentas, imbricate upwards; style long, filiform; stigma much exserted, mitriform. Fruit of 2 dehiscent cocci. Seeds many; testa winged; albumen fleshy.—DISTRIB. Asia, Tropical Africa; species 8.

1. **Mitragyna parvifolia,** *Korth. Obs. Naucl. Ind.* (1839) p. 19. A large deciduous tree, glabrous or pubescent. Leaves variable in size and shape, 2–5 by 1$\frac{1}{2}$–3 in., elliptic, suborbicular, or obovate, rounded, acute or bluntly acuminate at the apex, glabrous on both sides, base

rounded or acute, sometimes cordate; main nerves 6–8 pairs, oblique; petioles $\frac{3}{8}$–$\frac{3}{4}$ in. long; stipules $\frac{1}{2}$ by $\frac{3}{16}$–$\frac{5}{16}$ in., oblong-spathulate, obtuse, parallel-nerved, pink. Flowers greenish-yellow, fragrant; peduncles solitary, terminal, short, each carrying a globose head of flowers $\frac{3}{4}$–1 in. in diam. Calyx $\frac{1}{12}$ in. long, funnel-shaped; limb truncate. Corolla $\frac{1}{4}$–$\frac{5}{16}$ in. long; tube narrowly infundibuliform, glabrous; lobes $\frac{1}{16}$ in. long, triangular-ovate, acute, recurved. Style white, much exserted; stigma mitriform. Head of fruits $\frac{1}{2}$–$\frac{5}{8}$ in. in diam.; capsules $\frac{1}{8}$ in. long, oblong, with blunt rounded tops and 10 blunt ribs. Jackson, in Index Kewen. v. 3, p. 249; Hav. Rev. Naucl. in Journ. Linn. Soc. v. 33 (1897) p. 69. *Stephegyne parvifolia*, Korth. Verh. Nat. Gesch. Bot. (1840?) p. 161; Hook. f. Fl. B. I. v. 3, p. 25; Trim. Fl. Ceyl. v. 2, p. 294; Talb. Trees, Bomb. ed. 2, p. 185; Woodr. in Journ. Bomb. Nat. v. 11 (1898) p. 644; Watt, Dict. Econ. Prod. v. 6, part 3, p. 360. *Nauclea parvifolia*, Roxb. Cor. Pl. v. 1 (1795) p. 40, t. 52; Grah. Cat. p. 87; Bedd. Flor. Sylvat. t. 34. *Nauclea parviflora* (an evident misprint for *N. parvifolia*), Dalz. & Gibs. p. 118.—Flowers: May–Aug. VERN. *Kadam*; *Kalam*.

In deciduous forests throughout the Presidency, *Talbot*. KONKAN: *Graham*. DECCAN: Máwal districts, *Graham*, *Dalzell*; Chinchwad (near Poona), *Ranade*! GUJARAT: *Cooke*!; Baroda, *Cooke*!; Dabhoi, *Woodrow*, *Kanitkar*! S. M. COUNTRY: Belgaum, *Ritchie*, 341! KANARA: Kála naddi, *Ritchie*, 341!—DISTRIB. Throughout the drier parts of India; Ceylon.

6. HYMENODICTYON, Wall.

Trees or shrubs with thick branches and bitter bark. Leaves opposite, petiolate, deciduous; stipules interpetiolar, glandular-serrate, deciduous. Flowers small, spicate, in axillary and terminal nodding panicles; bracts 1 or 2, foliaceous, reticulate, subpersistent; bracteoles small or 0. Calyx-tube short; lobes 5–6, ovate or subulate, deciduous. Corolla infundibuliform or narrowly campanulate, glabrous inside; lobes 5, short, erect, reduplicato-valvate. Stamens 5, inserted below the throat of the corolla; filaments short, dilated upwards; anthers linear. Ovary 2-celled; ovules numerous, on cylindric placentas adnate to the septum; style filiform, exserted; stigma fusiform. Capsule loculicidally 2-valved, many-seeded; placentas at length free. Seeds imbricating upwards; testa broadly winged; embryo small in fleshy albumen.—DISTRIB. Tropical Asia and Africa; species 4–5.

Flowers pedicelled; corolla $\frac{1}{4}$ in. long; capsules on decurved peduncles .... 1. *H. excelsum*.
Flowers sessile; corolla $\frac{1}{10}$ in. long; capsules erect .... 2. *H. obovatum*.

1. **Hymenodictyon excelsum,** *Wall. in Roxb. Fl. Ind. ed. Carey*, v. 2 (1824) p. 149. A tree 30–40 ft. high; bark usually smooth. Leaves membranous, 4–9 by 3–4$\frac{1}{4}$ in., ovate-elliptic, abruptly-acuminate, pubescent on both surfaces, base narrowed into the petiole; main nerves 7–10 pairs; petioles 1–3 in. long, pubescent; stipules broadly oblong, obtuse, recurved, deciduous. Flowers numerous, greenish-white, fragrant, pedicelled, in clusters along the rhachis of dense cylindrical pubescent spiciform racemes in erect terminal panicles; floral leaves shaped like the other leaves but smaller, colored, bullate, on petioles 1$\frac{1}{2}$–2$\frac{1}{2}$ in. long. Calyx $\frac{1}{12}$ in. long, narrowly campanulate, pubescent;

lobes $\frac{1}{30}$ in. long, acute. Corolla $\frac{1}{8}$ in. long, pubescent outside; tube slender; limb broadly campanulate with short acute lobes. Styles very long. Capsules $\frac{3}{4}$ in. long, ellipsoid, on stout decurved pedicels $\frac{1}{4}$–$\frac{1}{2}$ in. long. Fl. B. I. v. 3, p. 35; Grah. Cat. p. 87; Dalz. & Gibs. p. 117; Wight, Icon. t. 79; Talb. Trees, Bomb. ed. 2, p. 186; Woodr. in Journ. Bomb. Nat. v. 11 (1898) p. 644; Watt, Dict. Econ. Prod. v. 4, p. 317. —Flowers: June–Aug. VERN. *Kála-Kaddu*; *Bhorsal.*

Along the Ghâts, *Graham, Dalzell & Gibson.* KONKAN: *Law*!; Ghâts near Bombay, *Dalzell*!; Matheran (Porcupine Point), *H. M. Birdwood.* DECCAN: Kartriz Ghât, *Woodrow*! GUJARAT: Panch Máháls, *Talbot.* S. M. COUNTRY: hills near Belgaum, *Ritchie*, 289!—DISTRIB. India (base of the Himalayas, W. Peninsula, Birma); Java.

The inner coat of the bark is bitter and has been used as a febrifuge. The wood is fine and close-grained and is employed for making agricultural implements, scabbards, palanquins, toys, &c. See Watt, Dict. Econ. Prod. l. c.

2. **Hymenodictyon obovatum,** *Wall. in Roxb. Fl. Ind. ed. Carey*, v. 2 (1824) p. 153. A large tree reaching 50 ft. high. Leaves 4–6 by $1\frac{3}{4}$–3 in., elliptic or obovate, abruptly-acuminate, glabrous above, more or less pubescent beneath, narrowed into the petiole; main nerves 6–8 pairs; petioles 1–2 in. long; stipules obovate-oblong with glandular margins. Flowers small, inconspicuous, greenish, with a pungent odor, in sessile clusters along the rhachis of dense cylindric pubescent panicled spikes; floral leaves bullate, white or cream-colored, with petioles $1\frac{1}{4}$–2 in. long. Calyx broadly campanulate, $\frac{1}{12}$ in. long, pubescent outside; teeth triangular, acute, $\frac{1}{30}$ in. long. Corolla $\frac{1}{10}$ in. long, pubescent outside; tube very short; limb broadly campanulate, $\frac{1}{16}$ in. long, the lobes ovate-oblong, acute. Capsules $\frac{1}{2}$ in. long, ellipsoid, on very short erect pedicels. Fl. B. I. v. 3, p. 36; Grah. Cat. p. 88; Dalz. & Gibs. p. 117; Bedd. Flor. Sylvat. t. 219; Talb. Trees, Bomb. ed. 2, p. 186; Woodr. in Journ. Bomb. Nat. v. 11 (1898) p. 644; Watt, Dict. Econ. Prod. v. 4, p. 319.—Flowers: July–Sept. VERN. *Kadvá-sirid.*

KONKAN: moist forests, *Talbot*; Matheran, *Woodrow*; island of Karanja, *Dalzell & Gibson.* S. M. COUNTRY: Rámghát, *Law, Dalzell & Gibson, Ritchie*, 1048! KANARA: *Talbot.*—DISTRIB. India (W. Peninsula).

Mr. Talbot distinguishes 2 varieties of this tree, one with large obovate pubescent leaves and capsules 1 in. long, the other with small ovate nearly glabrous leaves and capsules $\frac{1}{2}$ in. long. The erect capsules serve to distinguish this species from *H. flaccidum*, which it otherwise much resembles.

7. **WENDLANDIA,** Bartl.

Shrubs or small trees. Leaves opposite or ternately whorled, subsessile or petiolate, ovate or oblong, subcoriaceous; stipules entire or 2-fid. Flowers rosy or white, in terminal dense thyrsoid or panicled cymes, 2–3-bracteate. Calyx-tube subglobose; lobes 4–5, subequal, persistent. Corolla tubular, salver-shaped or funnel-shaped, throat glabrous or hairy; lobes 4–5, imbricate in bud. Stamens 4–5, inserted between the corolla-lobes; filaments 0 or elongate; anthers versatile, exserted. Ovary 2 (rarely 3) -celled; ovules numerous, on small subglobose placentas adnate to the septum; style slender; stigma entire, 2-fid or 2-partite. Capsule small, globose, crustaceous, loculicidally (rarely septicidally) 2-valved, many-seeded. Seeds minute, horizontal, compressed; testa membranous, not winged; albumen fleshy; embryo short, cylindric.—DISTRIB. Tropical and subtropical Asia; species 16.

Leaves opposite; corolla-tube $\frac{1}{18}$ in. long, glabrous inside; filaments exserted .... 1. *W. exserta.*
Leaves usually ternately whorled; corolla-tube $\frac{1}{8}$–$\frac{1}{6}$ in. long, hairy inside; filaments not exserted .... 2. *W. Notoniana.*

1. **Wendlandia exserta,** *DC. Prod.* v. 4 (1830) p. 411. A small deciduous pubescent or tomentose crooked tree with brown rough bark; branches terete. Leaves coriaceous, opposite, 3–7 by $1\frac{1}{4}$–$3\frac{1}{4}$ in., lanceolate or ovate-lanceolate, entire, acute, more or less pubescent above, grey-tomentose or grey-pubescent beneath, base acute, often inequilateral; main nerves 10–18 pairs, arched; petioles $\frac{1}{2}$–1 in. long, downy; stipules interpetiolar, ovate, acute, softly downy, the upper part recurved. Flowers subsessile, fragrant, in sessile tomentose pyramidal panicles 6–10 in. long and as broad as long; bracteoles linear-lanceolate, hairy. Calyx hairy, $\frac{1}{10}$ in. long; tube subglobose; lobes 5, obtusely triangular, $\frac{1}{30}$ in. long. Corolla white; tube $\frac{1}{18}$ in. long, glabrous inside; lobes $\frac{1}{10}$ in. long, ovate-oblong, subacute, reflexed, veined with dark conspicuous veins. Filaments exserted, as long as the anthers. Style 2-fid nearly $\frac{1}{2}$-way down, the lobes oblong-spathulate, flattened on the inside. Capsules globose, $\frac{1}{12}$ in. in diam., pubescent. Seeds minute, black. Fl. B. I. v. 3, p. 37; Bedd. For. Man. in Flor. Sylvat. p. cxxx; Talb. Trees, Bomb. ed. 2, p. 187; Woodr. in Journ. Bomb. Nat. v. 11 (1898) p. 644; Watt, Dict. Econ. Prod. v. 6, part 4, p. 302.—Flowers: Mar.–Apr.

Rather rare. Konkan: *Law*!, *Gibson*! Deccan: N. Deccan, *Talbot.*—Distrib. India (Tropical Himalaya, Orissa, Central India, W. Peninsula).

2. **Wendlandia Notoniana,** *Wall. Cat.* (1828) 6273; *Wight & Arn. Prodr.* (1834) p. 403. A shrub or small tree; young branches pubescent, often reddish. Leaves usually ternately whorled (rarely opposite), 3–$4\frac{1}{2}$ by 1–2 in., elliptic-lanceolate, acuminate, glabrous or nearly so above, pubescent beneath, base much tapering; main nerves 8–10 pairs, prominent, pink on the young leaves; petioles $\frac{1}{8}$–$\frac{1}{4}$ in. long; stipules variable, about $\frac{1}{4}$ in. long, oblong and rounded at the apex, or linear-lanceolate, acute, sometimes 2-fid. Flowers fragrant, having somewhat the odor of newly mown hay, in dense pyramidal hirsute panicles 6–12 in. long. Calyx $\frac{1}{12}$ in. long; tube globose, pubescent; teeth as long as the tube, lanceolate, acute, more or less pubescent. Corolla white; tube cylindric, $\frac{1}{8}$–$\frac{1}{6}$ in. long, hairy inside; lobes $\frac{1}{18}$ in. long, oblong-orbicular, obtuse, not veined with dark veins. Filaments not exserted. Style 2-fid at the apex. Capsules globose, $\frac{1}{10}$ in. in diam., pubescent, crowned with the calyx-teeth. Fl. B. I. v. 3, p. 40; Grah. Cat. p. 89; Dalz. & Gibs. p. 117; Wight, Icon. t. 1033; Bedd. Flor. Sylvat. t. 224; Trim. Fl. Ceyl. v. 2, p. 297; Talb. Trees, Bomb. ed. 2, p. 187; Woodr. in Journ. Bomb. Nat. v. 11 (1898) p. 644; Watt, Dict. Econ. Prod. v. 6, part 4, p. 302.—Flowers: Feb.–Mar.

Konkan: Wari jungles, *Stocks*! Deccan: Koina river banks, *Dalzell & Gibson*; banks of the Yenna river below Lingmala, Mahableshwar, *Graham*, *Dalzell & Gibson*, *H. M. Birdwood*, *Cooke*! S. M. Country: Castlerock, *Woodrow*; Londa, *Cooke*!, *Woodrow*!; Rámghát, *Dalzell & Gibson*; Belgaum Gháts, *Ritchie*, 350! Kanara: Supa Gháts of N. Kanara, *Talbot.*—Distrib. India (hills of the W. Peninsula); Ceylon.

8. DENTELLA, Forst.

A small prostrate herb. Leaves small, opposite; stipules short, scarious, connate. Flowers minute, solitary, axillary and in the forks, sessile or shortly pedicelled, white. Calyx-tube subglobose; limb membranous, tubular, 5-fid, persistent. Corolla infundibuliform; tube hairy within; lobes 5, induplicato-valvate, 2–3-toothed. Stamens 5, inserted in the middle of the corolla-tube; filaments short; anthers linear. Ovary 2-celled; ovules numerous, on hemispheric placentas; style short; stigmas filiform. Fruit small, dry, globose, 2-celled, indehiscent, many-seeded. Seeds minute, angled; testa dotted; albumen fleshy.—DISTRIB. Asia, Tropical Australia and the Pacific Islands; species 1.

1. **Dentella repens,** *Forst. Char. Gen.* (1776) p. 26, t. 13. A slender prostrate herb; stems long, slender, rooting at the nodes. Leaves $\frac{3}{16}$–$\frac{5}{16}$ by $\frac{1}{16}$–$\frac{1}{8}$ in., lanceolate or subspathulate, glabrous or with a few bristly hairs on the margins; petioles obscure; stipules scarious. Flowers $\frac{1}{12}$ in., solitary, often in the forks of the stem, subsessile. Calyx-tube subglobose; limb persistent; teeth acute. Corolla-lobes ovate, acute, with a tooth on each side. Filaments very short. Stigmas 2, filiform. Capsules $\frac{1}{10}$–$\frac{1}{8}$ in. in diam., usually densely villous with coarse hair, crowned by the persistent calyx-limb. Fl. B. I. v. 3, p. 42; Grah. Cat. p. 90; Dalz. & Gibs. p. 115; Trim. Fl. Ceyl. v. 2, p. 298; K. Schum. in Engl. & Prantl, Pflanzenf. v. 4, part 4, p. 22, fig. 8, A; Woodr. in Journ. Bomb. Nat. v. 11 (1898) p. 644.—Flowers: Apr.–July.

Common in moist situations, *Dalzell & Gibson.* KONKAN: Bombay, *Law*!; Salsette, common, *Graham*; Dharamtar, *Woodrow*! DECCAN: border of Parvati tank, Poona, *Ranade*!; Bijapur, *Woodrow*! S. M. COUNTRY: Badami, *Cooke*! KANARA: Kála naddi, *Ritchie*, 421!—DISTRIB. Throughout India in moist places; Ceylon, Malay Islands, China, N. Australia, Polynesia.

9. ARGOSTEMMA, Wall.

Low fleshy or membranous delicate herbs. Leaves opposite, the pairs equal or very unequal, or falsely whorled; stipules interpetiolar, entire, persistent or obsolete. Flowers white, in peduncled cymes or umbels. Calyx-tube short; lobes 5, rarely 3–7. Corolla rotate, 4–5-partite, valvate. Stamens 4–5, inserted on the corolla-tube; filaments short; anthers conniving or cohering, dehiscing by terminal pores. Ovary 2-celled; ovules numerous, on swollen placentas attached to the middle of the septum; style filiform; stigma capitellate. Capsule coriaceous or membranous, 2-celled, many-seeded, dehiscing by a torn apex or by the top coming off operculately. Seeds minute, angled or compressed; testa granulate or reticulate; embryo very minute, in dense fleshy albumen.—DISTRIB. Mountains of India and the Indian Archipelago except one African species (which is also Indian); species about 40.

Flowers 4-merous .... 1. *A. courtallense.*
Flowers 5-merous .... 2. *A. verticillatum.*

1. **Argostemma courtallense,** *Arn. in Ann. Nat. Hist.* v. 3 (1839) p. 22. A small herb 3–6 in. high with a tuberous root. Leaves very variable in size and shape, in whorls of 4, thinly membranous, very un-

equal, 1 or 2 of the leaves of the whorl sometimes not being more than ½ in. long, while 1 or both of the other 2 may exceed 2½ in. long, subsessile or rarely shortly petioled, ovate or orbicular-ovate, obtuse or subobtuse (rarely acute), glabrous or sparsely puberulous on both sides; stipules obsolete. Flowers 4-merous, in terminal 3-many-flowered usually simple umbels; peduncles solitary, 1–1½ in. long; bracts foliaceous, conspicuous beneath the umbel. Calyx ⅛ in. long; teeth short, subacute. Corolla white, divided almost to the base; lobes ¼ in. long, ovate-oblong, subacute. Anthers 4, oblong-lanceolate, curved, opening by pores. Fl. B. I. v. 3, p. 42; Wight, Icon. t. 1160. *A. connatum*, Dalz. in Kew Journ. Bot. v. 3 (1851) p. 345. *A. cuneatum* (by error for *A. connatum*), Dalz. & Gibs. p. 118.—Flowers: Aug.

S. M. COUNTRY: on rocks at the Chorla Ghát, *Dalzell*! KANARA: *Law*!—DISTRIB. India (W. Peninsula).

2. **Argostemma verticillatum,** *Wall. in Roxb. Fl. Ind. ed. Carey*, v. 2 (1824) p. 325. Erect, 4–6 in. high. Leaves thinly membranous, 4 in a whorl, unequal, 1–4½ by ¾–1¼ in., sessile or nearly so, lanceolate or ovate-lanceolate, acuminate, glabrous, inequilateral at the base. Flowers white, 5-merous, in terminal peduncled few-flowered umbels shorter than the leaves, often 3 umbels together of which the central one is frequently compound, the lateral ones usually simple; bracts beneath the umbels conspicuous, oblong-lanceolate or linear-lanceolate. Calyx $\frac{1}{10}$ in. long; teeth $\frac{1}{18}$ in. long, subacutely triangular from a broad base. Corolla ¼ in. long, divided almost to the base; lobes narrowly triangular-oblong or ovate, very acute. Anthers linear-oblong, apiculate, opening by pores. Fl. B. I. v. 3, p. 43. *Argostemma glaberrimum*, Dalz. in Kew Journ. Bot. v. 3 (1851) p. 345; Dalz. & Gibs. p. 118.

KONKAN: on trees in the Wari country, *Dalzell*!

10. HEDYOTIS, Linn.

Herbs, undershrubs or shrubs (herbs in the Bombay species). Leaves opposite (rarely ternately whorled); stipules free, or connate with the petioles into a bristly sheath. Flowers usually white, in terminal or axillary dense or lax cymes. Calyx-tube ovoid, globose or turbinate; lobes 4, usually short, acute, persistent, without interposed teeth. Corolla infundibuliform or campanulate; lobes 4, ovate or linear, valvate in bud. Stamens 4, inserted in the tube or throat of the corolla. Ovary 2-celled; ovules numerous, on sessile or pedicelled placentas attached to the septum at or below the middle; style filiform; stigma 2-fid or 2-lobed. Fruit small, coriaceous or crustaceous (very rarely membranous), indehiscent or septicidally or loculicidally dehiscent, or separable into 2 indehiscent cocci, 2-many-seeded. Seeds plano-convex or angled; albumen horny.

Capsule indehiscent .... 1. *H. Auricularia.*
Capsule loculicidal on the crown only.
  Leaves linear-subulate, aristate .... 2. *H. cærulea.*
  Leaves elliptic or linear-lanceolate, acute .... 3. *H. nitida.*

1. **Hedyotis Auricularia,** *Linn. Sp. Pl.* (1753) p. 101. Annual; branches numerous, prostrate or suberect, spreading, not rooting at the nodes, glabrous or hairy especially at the nodes, often purple when young.

Leaves sessile, subsessile or shortly petioled, ovate or ovate-lanceolate or sometimes quite lanceolate, acuminate, glabrous or slightly pubescent on the nerves above, hairy on the nerves beneath, base acute or rounded; main lateral nerves impressed above, prominent beneath, curved; petioles very short or 0; stipules membranous, furnished with 3 or 5 unequal filiform bristles. Flowers white, sessile or very shortly pedicelled, in dense sessile or subsessile axillary cymes. Calyx-teeth small, triangular or lanceolate, acuminate. Corolla-tube very short; lobes oblong, obtuse, recurved, hairy at the base. Capsules globose, hard, hairy or nearly glabrous, indehiscent. Fl. B. I. v. 3, p. 58; Bedd. Icon. Pl. Ind. Or. t. 27; Trim. Fl. Ceyl. v. 2, p. 313; Watt, Dict. Econ. Prod. v. 4, p. 208. *Hedyotis vestita*, Woodr. in Journ. Bomb. Nat. v. 11 (1898) p. 644 (*not* of Br. in Wall. Cat.).—Flowers: Sept.–Nov.

KONKAN: *Kanitkar*!; Savantwari, *Woodrow*! S. M. COUNTRY: Londa, *Bhiva*!; Castlerock, *Cooke*!; north of Dharwar, *Ritchie*, 271! KANARA: Kumpta, *Woodrow*!; banks of the Kála naddi, *Ritchie*, 271!

2. **Hedyotis cærulea,** *Wight & Arn. Prodr.* (1834) p. 412. Annual, erect, 4–15 in. high, much-branched from a little above the base; branches terete, slender, rough to the touch. Leaves opposite or fascicled, usually $\frac{3}{8}$–$\frac{3}{4}$ by $\frac{1}{20}$–$\frac{1}{10}$ in., linear, sessile, bristle-pointed, minutely scaberulous above, 1-nerved, the margins reflexed; stipules pectinate with filiform bristles. Flowers blue (*Wight & Arn.*), sessile or nearly so, in axillary and terminal sessile capitate few-flowered cymes, or sometimes solitary in the forks. Calyx $\frac{1}{8}$–$\frac{1}{5}$ in. long; teeth lanceolate, rigid, tipped with a fine sharp bristle. Capsule globose, pubescent or glabrous, loculicidally dehiscent on the top only, crowned with the erect calyx-teeth which about equal the capsule. Fl. B. I. v. 3, p. 60; Bedd. Icon. Pl. Ind. Or. t. 30; Trim. Fl. Ceyl. v. 2, p. 312.

Rare. Herb. Stocks without locality! Kanara, Dharwar, and Bellary districts, *Law*! The plant is included on the authority of *Law*, who states that it has been found in the Dharwar districts. I have seen no specimens from the Bombay Presidency.

3. **Hedyotis nitida,** *Wight & Arn. Prodr.* (1834) p. 412. Annual; branches numerous, prostrate or ascending, 4-angled, slightly rough on the angles. Leaves subsessile, 1–$2\frac{1}{4}$ by $\frac{1}{4}$–$\frac{1}{2}$ in., lanceolate or ovate-lanceolate, acute, rigid, light-green, glabrous and shining above, scabrous towards the much-recurved margins, whitish and with the midrib often rough beneath, base usually acute; nerves (except the strong midrib) not visible; stipules with numerous long bristles. Flowers solitary or few, axillary, sessile. Calyx glabrous; teeth rigid, triangular, shortly spinoso-ciliate. Capsules $\frac{1}{4}$ in. long, dehiscent at the top only, ovoid, glabrous, veined, crowned by the erect calyx-teeth which about equal the capsule. Seeds numerous, pale-brown, angled. Fl. B. I. v. 3, p. 61; Trim. Fl. Ceyl. v. 2, p. 312. *Hedyotis glabella*, Br. in Wall. Cat. 886; Bedd. Icon. Pl. Ind. Or. t. 36; Watt, Dict. Econ. Prod. v. 4, p. 209.—Flowers: Sept.–Nov.

S. M. COUNTRY: north of Dharwar, *Ritchie*, 357!; Londa, *Woodrow*!, *Bhiva*! KANARA: Kála naddi, *Ritchie*, 357!—DISTRIB. India (W. Peninsula, Tenasserim); Ceylon.

11. OLDENLANDIA, Linn.

Slender erect or diffuse di- tri-chotomously-branched usually glabrous herbs. Leaves opposite, usually small, narrow; stipules acute or bristly. Flowers small, white or pink, in dichotomous axillary and terminal usually panicled cymes, rarely solitary. Calyx-tube turbinate, obovoid or subglobose; teeth 4 (rarely 5), usually erect and distant in fruit; sometimes with alternating teeth. Corolla rotate, infundibuliform or hypocrateriform; tube short or long; lobes 4 (rarely 5), obtuse, valvate. Stamens 4 (rarely 5), inserted in the throat of the corolla; filaments short: anthers usually exserted. Ovary 2-celled; ovules numerous, the placentas attached to the septum; style filiform; stigmas 2, linear. Capsule small, usually membranous, terete, didymous or angled, loculicidal at top, rarely indehiscent, many-seeded. Seeds angled, globose or ellipsoid; testa not winged, smooth or pitted; embryo clavate in fleshy albumen.—DISTRIB. Tropical and subtropical, chiefly Asiatic; species about 70.

Corolla-tube short.
  Peduncles 1–4-flowered from the lower or all the axils.
    Leaves linear, not exceeding $\frac{1}{8}$ in. broad; bases of calyx-teeth not touching in fruit.
      Top of capsule flat, not protruded.
        Flowers pedicelled, usually in pairs .... 1. *O. corymbosa.*
        Flowers sessile or nearly so, solitary .... 2. *O. diffusa.*
      Top of capsule rounded, protruded .... 3. *O. herbacea.*
    Leaves elliptic, exceeding $\frac{1}{8}$ in. broad; base of calyx-teeth touching in fruit .... 4. *O. crystallina.*
  Peduncles many-flowered, chiefly from the axils.
    Flowers in umbels; pedicels very short .... 5. *O. umbellata.*
    Flowers in axillary clusters, sessile or nearly so; capsule hairy .... 6. *O. trinervia.*
    Flowers on long capillary pedicels or in slender panicles; capsule minute, glabrous .... 7. *O. dichotoma.*
Corolla-tube long.
  Leaves whorled.
    Branches scabrid with whitish points; capsule scabrid ... 8. *O. aspera.*
    Branches retrorsely hispid; capsule glabrous .... 9. *O. retrorsa.*
  Leaves opposite, not whorled.
    Corolla-tube $\frac{1}{12}$ in. long; lobes obtuse; capsule obovoid... 10. *O. gracilis.*
    Corolla-tube $\frac{1}{4}$ in. long; lobes acuminate; capsule globose. 11. *O. senegalensis.*

1. **Oldenlandia corymbosa,** *Linn. Sp. Pl.* (1753) p. 119. Annual, varying from 3–15 in. high; stems terete, numerous, slender, erect, ascending or spreading, glabrous or pubescent. Leaves subsessile, $\frac{3}{4}$–1$\frac{3}{4}$ by $\frac{1}{16}$–$\frac{1}{8}$ in., linear or linear-lanceolate, acute, often with recurved and frequently scabrous margins; stipules short, membranous, truncate, with a few short bristles. Flowers on filiform pedicels longer than the calyx, usually 2–3 (rarely 1 or very rarely 4) on the top of a very slender axillary solitary peduncle; bract beneath the pedicels $\frac{1}{20}$–$\frac{1}{18}$ in. long, subulate. Calyx $\frac{1}{12}$ in. long, pubescent; teeth narrowly triangular, about equalling the calyx-tube when in flower. Corolla white, $\frac{1}{10}$ in. long; lobes acute, about $\frac{1}{20}$ in. long. Capsules globose or sometimes slightly pyriform, somewhat didymous, the top rather flat and not protruded beyond the calyx, glabrous. Seeds pale-brown, angular. Fl. B. I. v. 3, p. 64; Trim. Fl. Ceyl. v. 2, p. 314; K. Schum. in Engl. & Prantl, Pflanzenf. v. 4, part 4, p. 22, fig. 8, D–G; Woodr. in Journ. Bomb.

Nat. v. 11 (1898) p. 644; Watt, Dict. Econ. Prod. v. 5, p. 480. *Oldenlandia herbacea*, DC. Prodr. v. 4, p. 425 (*not* of Linn.). *Hedyotis Burmanniana*, Br. in Wall. Cat. 868 (in part); Grah. Cat. p. 90; Dalz. & Gibs. p. 116.—Flowers: Sept.–Nov. VERN. *Pitpápda*.

A common weed. KONKAN: *Stocks*!; Dharamtar, *Woodrow*!; Savantwari, *Kanitkar*!; Kalyan, *Woodrow*! DECCAN: Khandala, *Cooke*!; Poona, *Woodrow*!; Koina valley, *Cooke*! S. M. COUNTRY: Londa, *Cooke*!; Belgaum, *Ritchie*, $\frac{359}{3}$!—DISTRIB. Throughout India; Ceylon, Tropical E. Asia to Java and the Philippines, Tropical Africa, and America.

The plant has some repute in native medicine and is employed in the treatment of bilious fevers. See Watt, Dict. Econ. Prod. l. c.

2. **Oldenlandia diffusa,** *Roxb. Hort. Beng.* (1814) p. 11. Annual, diffuse, glabrous; stems numerous, prostrate, often rooting at the nodes. Leaves subsessile, $\frac{3}{4}$–$1\frac{1}{4}$ by $\frac{1}{20}$–$\frac{1}{8}$ in., linear or linear-lanceolate, acute, glabrous; stipules short, slightly pectinate. Flowers usually solitary (rarely 2 together), sessile or on very short pedicels. Calyx-teeth long, narrowly triangular, cuspidate, finely ciliate, very distant in fruit. Capsules larger than in *O. corymbosa*, broader than long, very truncate and flat on the top, not protruded beyond the calyx. Seeds angular. Fl. B. I. v. 3, p. 65; Trim. Fl. Ceyl. v. 2, p. 315; Woodr. in Journ. Bomb. Nat. v. 11 (1898) p. 644.—Flowers: Aug.–Oct.

Not common. S. M. COUNTRY: Belgaum, *Ritchie*, $\frac{359}{6}$! KANARA: N. Kanara, *Woodrow*; Sirsi, *Talbot* ex *Woodrow*.—DISTRIB. Throughout India; Ceylon, Borneo, Philippines, Japan.

3. **Oldenlandia herbacea,** *Roxb. Hort. Beng.* (1814) p. 11; *Fl. Ind.* v. 1, p. 424. An erect glabrous annual or biennial 3–18 in. high; branches numerous, dichotomous, slender, 4-gonous, divaricate. Leaves $\frac{3}{8}$–$1\frac{1}{4}$ by $\frac{1}{30}$–$\frac{1}{8}$, the lower leaves often broader than the upper ones, sessile, linear or linear-lanceolate, acute, glabrous, usually with recurved margins; stipules very short, inconspicuous or very shortly setose. Flowers usually on solitary or 2-nate axillary filiform peduncles, sometimes however (especially the upper flowers) forming a paniculate cyme. Calyx-teeth triangular-subulate, acute, distant on the fruit, very short. Corolla $\frac{1}{6}$ in. long; tube $\frac{1}{8}$ in. long, slender. Capsules $\frac{1}{10}$ in. in diam., ovoid or subglobose, somewhat didymous, the crown much protruded beyond the calyx, glabrous. Seeds somewhat ellipsoid in outline. Trim. Fl. Ceyl. v. 2, p. 315. *Oldenlandia Heynii*, G. Don, Gen. Syst. v. 3 (1834) p. 531; Hook. f. in Fl. B. I. v. 3, p. 65; Woodr. in Journ. Bomb. Nat. v. 11 (1898) p. 644. *Hedyotis herbacea*, Linn. Sp. Pl. (1753) p. 102. *Hedyotis Heynii*, Br. in Wall. Cat. 867; Grah. Cat. p. 90; Dalz. & Gibs. p. 116.—Flowers: Aug.–Oct. VERN. *Paripdth.*

KONKAN: *Stocks*!, *Ritchie*, $\frac{359}{2}$!; Malwán, *Woodrow*. DECCAN: Koina valley, *Cooke*! S. M. COUNTRY: Belgaum hills, *Ritchie*, 1162!; Belgaum, *Supekar*!, *Woodrow*. KANARA: *Thomson*!—DISTRIB. Throughout India in hilly districts; Malay Islands, Tropical Africa.

4. **Oldenlandia crystallina,** *Roxb. Hort. Beng.* (1814) p. 11. A prostrate glabrous herb, much-branched from the base; branches leafy, 2–6 in. long. Leaves $\frac{1}{2}$–$\frac{5}{8}$ by $\frac{1}{6}$–$\frac{1}{4}$ in., elliptic or elliptic-lanceolate, subacute, flat, sessile or nearly so, tapering to the base; stipules with a few short bristles. Flowers on solitary 1–2 (rarely 3) -flowered filiform peduncles about equalling the leaves. Calyx (in flower) $\frac{1}{12}$ in. long, the

teeth $\frac{1}{20}$ in. long; the teeth in fruit $\frac{1}{16}$ in. long, triangular, acute, their bases touching. Corolla white, short, but little exserted beyond the calyx; tube about $\frac{1}{16}$ in. long. Capsules $\frac{1}{6}$ in. long, obovoid or pyriform, glabrous, ribbed, crowned by the broad triangular calyx-teeth which touch at their bases, the crown of the capsule not protruded. Fl. B. I. v. 3, p. 65. *Oldenlandia pumila*, DC. Prodr. v. 4, p. 425.

Rare. S. M. COUNTRY: Belgaum, *Stocks*, 336! *Ritchie*, 1781!—DISTRIB. Sparingly throughout the plains of India; Java.

5. **Oldenlandia umbellata,** *Linn. Sp. Pl.* (1753) p. 119. Annual; stems semi-woody at the base, 6–10 in. high, much-branched from the base; branches more or less angular and rough. Leaves numerous, often fascicled, rather close, sessile, $\frac{1}{2}$–1 by $\frac{1}{8}$–$\frac{1}{6}$ in., linear, flat, very acute; stipules short, pectinate. Flowers 3–10, in small irregular axillary peduncled umbels; peduncles usually longer than the leaves, stout, erect, pubescent; pedicels very short, pubescent. Calyx (in flower) $\frac{1}{8}$ in. long; teeth $\frac{1}{12}$ in. long, triangular, cuspidate, ciliolate. Corolla $\frac{1}{8}$ in. long, glabrous on both sides; lobes triangular-oblong, equalling the tube. Capsules globose, $\frac{1}{10}$ in. in diam., glabrous, crowned with the not very distant calyx-teeth, the top of the capsule not protruded. Fl. B. I. v. 2, p. 66; Roxb. Cor. Pl. t. 3; Trim. Fl. Ceyl. v. 2, p. 316; Woodr. in Journ. Bomb. Nat. v. 11 (1898) p. 644; Watt, Dict. Econ. Prod. v. 5, p. 481.—Flowers: Aug.–Dec. VERN. *Chirval.*

DECCAN: Wadi on the G. I. P. Railway line, *Woodrow*! I have only had the plant from the locality above named.—DISTRIB. India (Orissa, Bengal, Birma, W. Peninsula); Ceylon.

The root of the plant known commercially as *Chay-root* or *Indian Madder* furnishes a permanent red dye which was much used in Madras where the plant has been extensively cultivated. See Watt, Dict. Econ. Prod. l. c.

6. **Oldenlandia trinervia,** *Retz. Obs. Bot.* fasc. 4 (1786) p. 23. A small procumbent leafy annual; stems weak, flaccid, slender, angular, glabrous or slightly hairy, often rooting near the base. Leaves numerous, $\frac{1}{4}$–$\frac{3}{8}$ in., broadly elliptic or suborbicular, tapering to the base or to an obscure petiole, glabrous or nearly so, very thin, distinctly 3-nerved from the base; stipules 2-partite, acuminate. Flowers 1–6 in the axils of the leaves, sessile or very shortly pedicelled. Calyx hairy; teeth short, narrowly lanceolate, acute. Corolla rotate, white (*Dalzell*). Fruit globose, very hairy, dehiscing by a wide circular opening at the top, the crown not protruded. Fl. B. I. v. 3, p. 66; Trim. Fl. Ceyl. v. 2, p. 316. *Hedyotis trinervia*, Rœm. & Schult. Syst. v. 3 (1818) p. 197; Dalz. & Gibs. p. 115; Bedd. Icon. Pl. Ind. Or. t. 29.—Flowers: July.

Ritchie (ex Herb. *Dalzell*), 1780! without locality. Herb. Stocks without locality in Herb. Kew.! KONKAN: Malwân, *Dalzell & Gibson*.

7. **Oldenlandia dichotoma,** *Hook. f. Fl. B. I.* v. 3 (1880) p. 67. A very slender annual 8–18 in. high; stem erect, terete, usually glabrous; branches filiform, the ultimate ones like fine hairs. Leaves linear-lanceolate, acute, flat, the lower leaves larger than the upper, 1–3 by $\frac{1}{8}$–$\frac{5}{16}$ in., some of the uppermost leaves sometimes not being more than $\frac{1}{2}$–$\frac{3}{4}$ by $\frac{1}{30}$–$\frac{1}{16}$ in.; stipules small, truncate, without bristles, or sometimes with 2–3 short bristles. Flowers white (*Ritchie*), on long capillary pedicels, rarely solitary, sometimes 2–3 from the apex of a

filiform elongated peduncle, or often arranged in terminal and axillary slender lax panicles. Calyx (in flower) $\frac{1}{16}$ in. long; teeth $\frac{1}{30}$ in. long, subulate, in fruit distant. Corolla $\frac{1}{8}$–$\frac{1}{6}$ in. long; tube $\frac{1}{16}$–$\frac{1}{12}$ in. long; lobes nearly as long as the tube. Capsules $\frac{1}{16}$–$\frac{1}{12}$ in. in diam., globose. Fl. B. I. v. 3, p. 67; Woodr. in Journ. Bomb. Nat. v. 11 (1898) p. 644. *Hedyotis Heynei*, Bedd. Icon. Pl. Ind. Or. t. 33 (*not* of Br.).—Flowers: July–Oct. VERN. *Kajuri.*

Rare. DECCAN: Poona districts, *Woodrow.* S. M. COUNTRY: Belgaum, *Ritchie*, 1162!—DISTRIB. India (Bandelkand, W. Peninsula).

8. **Oldenlandia aspera,** *DC. Prodr.* v. 4 (1830) p. 428. A stout annual herb 6–15 in. high; stems and branches scabrid with minute whitish points. Leaves whorled, 1–2 by $\frac{1}{8}$–$\frac{1}{4}$ in., linear, acute, subsessile, with slightly recurved margins; stipules membranous, with 1–3 bristles. Flowers pale blue (*Dalzell*), rose-colored (*Ritchie*), small, in terminal branched cymes, solitary or in pairs, sessile or shortly pedicelled along the branches of the cyme. Calyx (in flower) $\frac{1}{16}$ in. long; teeth $\frac{1}{25}$ in. long, triangular-subulate. Corolla infundibuliform, $\frac{1}{8}$–$\frac{1}{6}$ in. long; tube very slender, $\frac{1}{10}$ in. long. Capsules $\frac{1}{8}$–$\frac{1}{6}$ in. in diam., globose, somewhat didymous, scabrid with white points, crowned by the distant calyx-teeth. Fl. B. I. v. 3, p. 68; Woodr. in Journ. Bomb. Nat. v. 11 (1898) p. 644. *Hedyotis aspera*, Heyne, in Roth, Nov. Pl. Sp. p. 94; Dalz. & Gibs. p. 115.—Flowers: Aug.

DECCAN: Poona, *Cooke!*, *Woodrow!*, *Ranade!*, *Kanitkar!* GUJARAT: Surat, *Dalzell!* S. M. COUNTRY: Badami, *Woodrow!*; Pádshapur, *Ritchie*, 1782!—DISTRIB. India (W. Peninsula).

9. **Oldenlandia retrorsa,** *Boiss. Fl. Orient.* v. 3 (1875) p. 12. Rootstock woody; stems 12–18 in. long, numerous, terete, slender, retrorsely hispid with short stiff hairs. Leaves whorled, $\frac{1}{2}$–1 by $\frac{1}{8}$–$\frac{1}{4}$ in., subsessile, linear-oblong, subobtuse, flat, hispid on both sides with short stiff hairs; stipules membranous, with 1–3 bristles. Flowers sessile and pedicelled, scattered along the long branches of glabrous spreading terminal cymes. Calyx (in flower) slightly pubescent, $\frac{1}{10}$ in. long; lobes $\frac{1}{24}$ in. long, linear or subtriangular, acute. Corolla $\frac{1}{2}$–$\frac{5}{8}$ in. long; tube very slender (almost filiform), $\frac{3}{8}$–$\frac{1}{2}$ in. long, glabrous; lobes $\frac{1}{8}$ in. long, linear-oblong, obtuse. Capsules $\frac{1}{8}$–$\frac{1}{6}$ in. in diam., crowned by the distant calyx-teeth, subglobose, truncate, didymous, quite glabrous, the crown of the capsule about level with the top of the calyx or very slightly protruding. Fl. B. I. v. 3, p. 68; Woodr. in Journ. Bomb. Nat. v. 11 (1898) p. 644.—Flowers: Oct.–Nov.

Confined to Sind. SIND: *Stocks!*, *Bhola Puran!*; on sand-hills, *Dalzell!*; banks of Mulir river near Karachi, *Woodrow*; Jemadar ka Landa near Karachi, *Stocks*, 481!—DISTRIB. Arabia.

10. **Oldenlandia gracilis,** *Hook. f. in Fl. B. I.* v. 3 (1880) p. 68. A slender erect herb 6–12 in. high; branches few, erect, slender, glabrous. Leaves opposite (not whorled), 2–3 by $\frac{1}{10}$–$\frac{1}{4}$ in. (the uppermost leaves often much narrower, sometimes not more than $\frac{1}{30}$ in. wide), linear, acuminate, glabrous, flat; stipules truncate. Flowers in lax branched cymes, the branches slender, spreading in flower, erect in fruit; pedicels very slender. Calyx $\frac{1}{8}$ in. long, glabrous; teeth triangular-subulate, $\frac{1}{16}$ in. long, very acute. Corolla brown (*Hooker*);

tube $\frac{1}{16}$ in. long, very slender; lobes $\frac{1}{8}$ in. long, linear-oblong, obtuse. Capsules ellipsoid, $\frac{1}{8}$–$\frac{1}{4}$ in. long, glabrous, slightly protruded beyond the calyx. *Hedyotis aspera*, Bedd. Icon. Pl. Ind. Or. t. 32 (*not* of Heyne).—Flowers: Apr.

Rare in the Bombay Presidency. S. M. COUNTRY: Belgaum, *Ritchie*!—DISTRIB. Throughout India in hilly districts; Ava.

11. **Oldenlandia senegalensis,** *Hiern, in Oliver, Fl. Trop. Afr.* v. 3 (1877) p. 56. Annual, 8–16 in. high, sparingly branched; stem very erect, glabrous or minutely scaberulous, slender, wiry. Leaves $1\frac{1}{4}$–2 by $\frac{1}{20}$–$\frac{1}{8}$ in., not whorled, linear-lanceolate, acute or acuminate, apiculate, flat or with slightly recurved margins; stipules with lateral bristles. Flowers in very lax open terminal pyramidal panicled cymes; peduncles long, slender; pedicels capillary, 1–2 in. long. Calyx $\frac{1}{16}$ in. long; teeth subulate, slightly shorter than the obovoid calyx-tube. Corolla $\frac{1}{8}$–$\frac{1}{4}$ in. long; lobes $\frac{1}{12}$ in. long, linear, acute or acuminate. Capsules $\frac{1}{8}$ in. in diam., on long filiform pedicels, globose, crowned by the very distant calyx-teeth which are below the top of the capsule. Fl. B. I. v. 3, p. 68; Woodr. in Journ. Bomb. Nat. v. 11 (1898) p. 644.—Flowers: Sept.

DECCAN: Kirkee, *Woodrow*; Poona, *Woodrow*, 192!—DISTRIB. India (Chota Nagpore); W. Tropical Africa.

Sir J. Hooker (Fl. B. I. l. c.) referred this to the Senegal plant with hesitation. The flowers are smaller than those of the African plant, but as there are only 3 sheets in Herb. Kew., of which 2 (collected by one and the same collector) are from Chota Nagpore and the other from the Deccan, the material is still insufficient for accurate determination.

12. ANOTIS, DC.

Herbs prostrate or ascending, rarely erect, often with flaccid hairs. Leaves opposite; stipules interpetiolar, usually bristly. Flowers small, in heads or in axillary and terminal cymes. Calyx-tube compressed; lobes 4, erect or recurved, usually with broad sinuses. Corolla tubular or infundibuliform; lobes 4, ovate, usually shorter than the tube, valvate in bud. Stamens 4; filaments short or long; anthers included or exserted. Ovary 2 (rarely 3–4) -celled; ovules usually few (rarely 1) in each cell on placentas ascending from near the base of the septum; style filiform; stigmas 2–4, linear. Capsule didymous, laterally compressed, the crown produced, loculicidally 2-valved at top, rarely indehiscent; cells 1–few (rarely many) -seeded. Seeds peltate, boat-shaped or plano-convex; testa coarsely pitted; embryo clavate in horny albumen.—DISTRIB. Chiefly Tropical Asia; species about 25.

Cymes corymbose.
  Capsule subglobose; calyx-teeth suberect in fruit, a little below the top of the capsule .... 1. *A. Leschenaultiana.*
  Capsule broader than long, reaching $\frac{1}{4}$ in. broad; calyx-teeth large, deflexed in fruit, a little below the top of the capsule .... 2. *A. lancifolia.*
  Capsule globose, $\frac{1}{16}$ in. in diam.; calyx-teeth minute, $\frac{1}{2}$-way down or more from the top of the capsule in fruit ... 3. *A. Rheedei.*
Cymes clustered; capsules in clusters or heads.
  Leaves fleshy; calyx-teeth large .... 4. *A. carnosa.*
  Leaves membranous.
    Capsule usually 4-lobed and 4-celled; calyx-teeth minute........................ 5. *A. quadrilocularis.*

Capsule 2-lobed, 2-celled.
 Calyx-teeth nearer the pedicel than the top of the capsule, tipped with a fine bristle .... 6. *A. Montholoni.*
 Calyx-teeth not bristle-tipped.
  Leaves exceeding ⅓ in. long .... 7. *A. fœtida.*
  Leaves not exceeding ⅓ in. long .... 8. *A. Ritchiei.*

1. **Anotis Leschenaultiana,** *Benth. & Hook. f. Gen. Pl.* v. 2 (1873) p. 59, & *Hook. f. Fl. B. I.* v. 3 (1880) p. 72. A stout plant 1–2 ft. high with a perennial root; stems straggling, more or less hairy especially near the extremities and beneath the nodes, sometimes glabrous or nearly so. Leaves 1–2½ by ⅜–1⅛ in., sessile or petioled, ovate or ovate-lanceolate, acute or subobtuse, usually densely villous on both sides, base obtuse or acute, sometimes cordate; lateral nerves numerous, prominent beneath; petioles 0–½ in. long; stipules bristly. Flowers in corymbose usually hairy dense peduncled terminal cymes; pedicels slender, short, hairy. Calyx in flower $\frac{1}{16}$ in. long; teeth equalling the tube, narrowly triangular, acute. Corolla red-purple; tube $\frac{3}{16}$–¼ in. long; lobes $\frac{1}{12}$ in. long, oblong, obtuse. Anthers blue. Capsules subglobose, didymous, with the calyx-teeth near the top. Seeds 1–2, plano-convex, $\frac{1}{20}$–$\frac{1}{16}$ in. long, deeply pitted. The plant varies much in hairiness. *Hedyotis Leschenaultiana*, Wight & Arn. Prodr. p. 411; Wight, Ill. t. 125; Dalz. & Gibs. p. 115.

S. M. Country: Belgaum, *Dalzell & Gibson.*

I have seen no authentic specimens from the Bombay Presidency. Dalzell & Gibson (Bo. Fl. l. c.) give Belgaum as the locality in which the plant occurs, and there are in Herb. Kew. specimens of one of the varieties of the plant from Stocks' Herbarium and also one from Dalzell's Herbarium, but none of these have localities assigned to them. Woodrow does not include the plant in his list.

2. **Anotis lancifolia,** *Hook. f. in Fl. B. I.* v. 3 (1880) p. 73. Herbaceous, erect, diffusely branched, 2–3 ft. high; stems and branches glabrous. Leaves membranous, 1–3 by ⅜–1 in., ovate or ovate-lanceolate, acuminate, bright-green and pubescent above, paler and hairy on the nerves beneath, base acute or obtuse; petioles ¼–⅜ in. long; stipules pubescent, shortly bristly. Flowers purple, in terminal and subterminal many-flowered corymbose (usually glabrous) cymes which are sometimes 4–6 in. in diam.; peduncles 4-gonous, pubescent or glabrous. Calyx $\frac{1}{12}$ in. long, hairy; teeth $\frac{1}{16}$ in. long, triangular, acuminate. Corolla ¼ in. long; lobes triangular-oblong, acute, $\frac{1}{10}$ in. long, hairy outside. Capsules compressed, $\frac{3}{16}$–¼ in. broad, much broader than long, dehiscing across the top, 2-lobed at the apex, crowned by the large distant recurved calyx-teeth. Seeds 4–6, broadly ellipsoid or suborbicular, convex on the back, deeply excavated on the face, pitted, black. Woodr. in Journ. Bomb. Nat. v. 11 (1898) p. 645. *Hedyotis lancifolia*, Dalz. in Kew. Journ. Bot. v. 2 (1850) p. 135; Dalz. & Gibs. p. 116.—Flowers: Sept.–Oct.

Konkan: *Stocks*!, *Dalzell*! Deccan: Mahableshwar, *Cooke*!, *Woodrow*!; Purandhar, *Woodrow*; Phunda Ghát, *Dalzell & Gibson*. S. M. Country: Belgaum south, *Ritchie*, 1777!; Castlerock, *Cooke*!; Belgaum, *Ritchie*, 356!—Distrib. India (W. Peninsula).

3. **Anotis Rheedei,** *Benth. & Hook. f. Gen. Pl.* v. 2 (1873) p. 59, & *Hook. f. Fl. B. I.* v. 3 (1880) p. 73. Annual, slender; stem erect, glabrous, 4-gonous, almost 4-winged. Leaves 1½–3 by ¾–1 in., membranous, ovate, acute or acuminate, with a few scattered hairs on both surfaces, tapering at the base into the petiole; petioles slender, ⅛–½ in

long; stipules short, crenate. Flowers few, minute, in axillary and terminal very lax and open cymes; peduncles and pedicels long, capillary. Calyx-teeth very minute. Corolla pale rose-colored; tube short, cylindric. Capsules $\frac{1}{10}$ in. in diam., appearing after dehiscence as 4 connate cups, globose, puberulous, broadly didymous, much protruded, the calyx-teeth being about the middle of the capsule. Seeds 4–12, semiellipsoid, rounded on the back, deeply excavated on the face, microscopically reticulate, black. Woodr. in Journ. Bomb. Nat. v. 11 (1898) p. 645. *Hedyotis latifolia*, Dalz. in Kew Journ. Bot. v. 2 (1850) p. 133; Dalz. & Gibs. p. 116. *Hedyotis Rheedei*, Wight & Arn. Prodr. p. 409.—Rheede, Hort. Mal. v. 10, p. 49, t. 25.—Flowers: July.

KONKAN: *Stocks*!, *Dalzell*!; Malwán, *Dalzell & Gibson*; near Matheran, *Woodrow*; hills near Matheran, *Kanitkar*!; Gháts near Goa, *Woodrow*.—DISTRIB. India (W. Peninsula).

4. **Anotis carnosa,** *Benth. & Hook. f. Gen. Pl.* v. 2 (1873) p. 59, & *Hook. f. Fl. B. I.* v. 3 (1880) p. 74. Annual, 4–6 in. high, diffusely branched from the base. Leaves $\frac{3}{4}$–$1\frac{1}{4}$ by $\frac{1}{4}$–$\frac{3}{8}$ in., elliptic-lanceolate, subobtuse, thick and fleshy, scaberulous with papillæ above, pale beneath and with recurved margins, attenuated at the base into a short petiole or almost sessile; stipules truncate or almost obsolete. Flowers sessile, 3–6, in capitate cymes which are sessile and axillary, or peduncled and terminal, each head of flowers with 2 large floral leaves (bracts) at its base; peduncles $\frac{1}{4}$–1 in. long. Calyx $\frac{1}{6}$ in. long, externally papillose; teeth $\frac{1}{10}$ in. long, slightly longer than the tube, linear-oblong, acute, when in fruit about $\frac{1}{4}$ the way down from the top of the capsule. Corolla purple, $\frac{3}{16}$ in. long; lobes ovate, $\frac{1}{20}$ in. long. Capsules $\frac{1}{8}$–$\frac{1}{6}$ in., broader than long, sessile, 2-lobed, 2-celled, glabrous, crowned by the large papillose calyx-teeth; cells 3–6-seeded. Seeds elliptic or orbicular in horizontal section, compressed, convex on the back, excavated on the face, pitted, black. *Hedyotis carnosa*, Dalz. in Kew Journ. Bot. v. 2 (1850) p. 135; Dalz. & Gibs. p. 116.

KONKAN: on rocky sea-shore Malwán, *Dalzell*!; sandy margins of rivulets Ooran, *Dalzell*! KANARA: *Law*!—DISTRIB. India (W. Peninsula).

5. **Anotis quadrilocularis,** *Hook. f. Fl. B. I.* v. 3 (1880) p. 74. Annual, 6–18 in. high, with many flaccid spreading glabrous cylindric branches. Leaves $\frac{3}{4}$–$1\frac{1}{4}$ by $\frac{1}{2}$–$\frac{3}{4}$ in., thinly membranous, subacute, more or less hairy on both surfaces, pale beneath, shortly tapering at the base; petioles $\frac{1}{8}$–$\frac{1}{4}$ in. long; stipules short, truncate, the upper with short bristles. Flowers sessile or nearly so, solitary or 2–4 together in the axils (those on short branchlets with a single pair of leaves appearing terminal). Calyx-teeth $\frac{1}{20}$ in. long, broadly ovate, acute, apiculate, ciliate in fruit, about $\frac{1}{3}$ the way down from the top of the capsule. Corolla $\frac{1}{5}$ in. long; lobes $\frac{1}{16}$ in. long, ovate, subacute, pubescent on the back. Capsules sessile, broader than long, usually 4 (sometimes 2 or 3) -lobed, usually 4 (sometimes 2 or 3) -celled. Seeds 3 in each cell, hemispheric or semiellipsoid, deeply excavated on the face, pitted, black. Trim. Fl. Ceyl. v. 2, p. 318. *Hedyotis quadrilocularis*, Thw. Enum. p. 144.

Belgaum, *Ritchie*, 191!

I have seen only one specimen from the Bombay Presidency collected by *Ritchie* at Belgaum.—DISTRIB. India (W. Peninsula); Ceylon.

6. **Anotis Montholoni,** *Hook. f. in Fl. B. I.* v. 3 (1880) p. 73. Annual, erect, sparingly branched; stem and branches more or less hispid. Leaves 1$\frac{3}{8}$–2 by $\frac{5}{8}$–$\frac{3}{4}$ in., ovate or ovate-lanceolate, acute, more or less hairy on both surfaces; petioles $\frac{1}{10}$–$\frac{1}{4}$ in. long; stipules with short bristles. Flowers in terminal and axillary peduncled many-flowered (not capitate) cymes; peduncles hairy. Calyx $\frac{1}{16}$ in. long; teeth longer than the tube, in fruit below the middle of the capsule nearer to the pedicel than the crown, ovate, pointed with a fine capillary bristle. Corolla funnel-shaped, purple, $\frac{1}{4}$ in. long; lobes $\frac{1}{12}$ in. long, oblong, subacute, glabrous outside. Capsules clustered, subsessile, didymous, broader than long, with a large double convex crown giving the appearance of two hemispheric bosses, pubescent; cells 1–3-seeded. Seeds globose or somewhat beehive-shaped, deeply excavated on the face, pitted, black. The hair-points on the calyx-teeth are a good distinctive mark. Woodr. in Journ. Bomb. Nat. v. 11 (1898) p. 645.—Flowers: Aug.

DECCAN: Poona, *Ranade*!, *Woodrow*! S. M. COUNTRY: Belgaum, *Ritchie*, 1778!; banks of nálas near Belgaum, *Ritchie*! KANARA: *Law*!—DISTRIB. India (W. Peninsula).

7. **Anotis fœtida,** *Benth. & Hook. f. Gen. Pl.* v. 2 (1873) p. 59, & *Hook. f. Fl. B. I.* v. 3 (1880) p. 74. A slender annual 4–6 in. high; stem simple or sometimes excessively branched; branches erect, very slender, more or less 4-gonous, glabrous. Leaves sessile, $\frac{5}{8}$–1 by $\frac{1}{20}$–$\frac{3}{16}$ in., linear or narrowly linear-lanceolate, subacute, scaberulous with minute papillæ above, pale beneath and with recurved margins; stipules small, bristly. Flowers subsessile, in 2–3-flowered capitate cymes terminating simple or forked subterminal capillary erect peduncles. Calyx $\frac{1}{16}$ in. long; teeth $\frac{1}{32}$ in. long, narrowly triangular, acute, apiculate. Corolla $\frac{1}{4}$ in. long, funnel-shaped, purple; lobes ovate, acute, $\frac{1}{20}$ in. long, externally papillose. Capsules $\frac{1}{10}$–$\frac{1}{8}$ in., sessile, broader than long, didymous, the crown very prominent, with the calyx-teeth about $\frac{1}{2}$-way down from the top of the capsule; cells 1–6-seeded. Seeds elliptic or orbicular in horizontal section, compressed, convex on the back, excavated on the face, pitted, black. Woodr. in Journ. Bomb. Nat. v. 11 (1898) p. 645. *Hedyotis fœtida*, Dalz. in Kew Journ. Bot. v. 2 (1850) p. 134; Dalz. & Gibs. p. 116.—Flowers: July–Aug.

KONKAN: Malwân in stony ground during the rains, *Dalzell*!; Bombay, *Lambert*! DECCAN: Khandala, *Bhiva*! S. M. COUNTRY: Belgaum, *Ritchie*, 1163!; Londa, *Woodrow*. KANARA: *Woodrow*; Karwar, *Talbot*, 554!—DISTRIB. Apparently endemic.

8. **Anotis Ritchiei,** *Hook. f. Fl. B. I.* v. 3 (1880) p. 74. A small slender plant 4–7 in. high; stems cæspitose, more or less angled, glabrous or pubescent. Leaves $\frac{1}{4}$–$\frac{1}{2}$ by $\frac{1}{16}$–$\frac{1}{8}$ in., oblong-lanceolate, acute or obtuse, hairy on both surfaces, narrowed at the base into a very short petiole; stipules inconspicuous. Flowers in small terminal shortly peduncled cymes; branches of the cyme few, pubescent, each carrying a head of 2–3 sessile or subsessile flowers. Calyx $\frac{1}{10}$ in. long, hairy; teeth $\frac{1}{16}$ in. long, linear-lanceolate, acute. Corolla purple, $\frac{1}{8}$–$\frac{1}{6}$ in. long; tube very slender; lobes $\frac{1}{16}$ in. long, pubescent on both sides, with a darker purple spot at the base of each lobe (*Ritchie*). Stamens exserted; anthers linear, blue (*Ritchie*). Ovary 2-celled; cells 2–4-seeded. Fruit unknown.

There is but a single sheet of this species (without fruit) in Herb. Kew. The specimens on it were collected by Dr. Ritchie, but the locality whence they were obtained is not given. They may have been collected at or near Belgaum, where Dr. Ritchie collected largely, but there is absolutely no evidence that such was the case, or that they were found within the limits of the Presidency at all.

13. OPHIORRHIZA, Linn.

Erect, creeping or decumbent small herbs, rarely undershrubs. Leaves opposite; stipules interpetiolar, caducous. Flowers secund on the branches of axillary or terminal dichotomous cymes, with or without bracts. Calyx-tube short; lobes 5, small, persistent. Corolla tubular or funnel-shaped; lobes 5, valvate in bud, often winged or appendaged at the back, sometimes also with a fold in the sinus. Stamens 5, inserted below the throat of the corolla, usually included; anthers linear. Disk of 2 large prominent erect lobes which become much enlarged in fruit. Ovary 2-celled; ovules many in each cell, inserted on basal ascending placentas; style filiform; stigmas 2, broad or linear. Capsule coriaceous, compressed, obcordate, girt by the calyx-limb, the crown dehiscing by 2 broad gaping valves; placentas divaricating, many-seeded. Seeds minute, angled; testa thinly crustaceous; embryo clavate in fleshy albumen.—DISTRIB. Tropical Asian, with a few Australian and Polynesian; species about 50.

1. **Ophiorrhiza Harrisiana,** *Heyne, in Wall. Cat.* (1828) 6236. Herbaceous, woody at the base, 6–15 in. high; branches numerous, often rooting near the base, glabrous or more or less pubescent. Leaves 2–3½ by 1–1½ in., elliptic or elliptic-lanceolate, acute or acuminate, glabrous or with a few scattered hairs above, whitish on the lower surface and pubescent on the nerves beneath; petioles ⅛–⅜ in. long; stipules with 1 or more long rather stout bristles. Flowers in rather dense terminal cymes; peduncles and pedicels densely hairy; bracteoles at base of pedicels $\frac{1}{12}$ in. long, linear, acute, hairy. Calyx $\frac{1}{10}$ in. long, hairy; tube turbinate; teeth $\frac{1}{30}$ in. long, triangular, acute. Corolla ¼ in. long, externally pubescent; lobes $\frac{1}{12}$ in. long, triangular-oblong, acute, not keeled on the back, pubescent inside. Capsules somewhat canoe-shaped, pubescent, much compressed, ¼–⅓ in. broad, much broader than long, rounded at the ends, surmounted by the very distant short calyx-teeth. Fl. B. I. v. 3, p. 78; Trim. Fl. Ceyl. v. 2, p. 321. *Ophiorrhiza Harrisonii*, Wight, Icon. t. 1162; Dalz. & Gibs. p. 117.—Flowers: Aug.

KONKAN: *Stocks*!; Amba Ghát, *Woodrow*. S. M. COUNTRY: Rámghát, *Dalzell & Gibson*. KANARA: *Hohenhacker*, 792 *a*!; Divimana, *Woodrow*; near Gondabel, *Dalzell*; Bombardi, *Ritchie*, 1775!—DISTRIB. Throughout India in hilly districts; Ceylon.

14. MUSSÆNDA, Linn.

Shrubs or undershrubs (rarely herbs), erect or climbing. Leaves opposite or 3-nately whorled; stipules interpetiolar, solitary or twin, usually deciduous. Flowers yellow or scarlet (rarely white) in terminal cymes; bracts and bracteoles deciduous. Calyx-tube oblong or turbinate; lobes 5, usually deciduous, one frequently forming a large stalked white or colored leaf. Corolla infundibuliform; tube usually silky, throat villous; lobes 5, short, induplicato-valvate. Stamens 5, inserted in the throat of the corolla or lower down; filaments very short; anthers linear. Ovary 2-celled; ovules very numerous in each cell, on peltate fleshy placentas; style filiform; stigmas 2, linear. Fruit a fleshy berry, areolate at the apex, many-seeded. Seeds minute; testa pitted; embryo minute in dense fleshy albumen.—DISTRIB. Asia, Africa, and the Pacific Islands; species about 40.

1. **Mussænda frondosa,** *Linn. Sp. Pl.* (1753) p. 177. A rambling shrub, climbing by its long flexuose divaricate branches which are cylindric and appressedly hairy (rarely glabrous). Leaves 3–5 by 2–3½ in., broadly elliptic, shortly acuminate, more or less pubescent (rarely glabrous) above, pubescent on the nerves and on the numerous reticulate veins beneath, base rounded or often tapering into the petiole; main nerves 8–12 pairs conspicuous on both surfaces, curving upwards; petioles ¼–1 in. long, more or less appressedly hairy; stipules twin, ¼ in. long and about $\frac{1}{10}$ in. broad at the base, linear-lanceolate, very acute, hairy. Flowers in terminal somewhat open cymes; peduncles stout, coarsely hairy; pedicels short, hairy; buds densely hairy, clavate, 5-angled; bracteoles subulate. Calyx-teeth reaching ⅜ in. long, linear-subulate, hairy, the enlarged segments (only developed on the outer side of a few flowers) leaf-like, creamy-white, persistent, 2½–4½ by 1½–2½ in., broadly ovate or elliptic, acuminate, usually tapering at the base, more or less velvety when young, when older nearly glabrous or with a few scattered hairs, strongly 5–7-nerved from the base and reticulately veined between the nerves, the stalk about ½–1 in. long. Corolla 1⅛–1½ in. long, of a deep golden-yellow; tube slender, very hairy outside and with a dense lining of yellowish hairs completely blocking the mouth; lobes ¼ in. long, broadly ovate or elliptic, apiculate, pubescent on the back. Berries ⅜–½ in., subglobose or obovoid, glabrous. This is the var. *glabrata* of Hook. f. Fl. B. I. Fl. B. I. v. 3, p. 89; Grah. Cat. p. 88; Dalz. & Gibs. p. 121; Bedd. For. Man. in Flor. Sylvat. p. cxxxi, t. 16, fig. 3; Talb. Trees, Bomb. ed. 2, p. 187; Woodr. in Journ. Bomb. Nat. v. 11 (1898) p. 645.—Flowers: July–Oct. VERN. *Sarvad*; *Bhutkes.*

KONKAN: *Law*!; hills, *Dalzell & Gibson*; Matheran, *Cooke*!; near Simpson's Lake, *H. M. Birdwood*; Vingorla, *Kanitkar*! DECCAN: Khandala, *Woodrow*!; Koina valley, *Cooke*! KANARA: moist forests where there is a heavy rainfall, *Talbot*; N. Kanara, *Woodrow*.—DISTRIB. India (Tropical Himalaya, Assam, Andamans, W. Peninsula); Ceylon, Malay Islands.

15. TARENNA, Gærtn.

Shrubs or trees. Leaves opposite, petiolate; stipules usually deciduous. Flowers in terminal many-flowered corymbiform cymes. Calyx-tube obovoid or turbinate; limb small, shortly tubular, 5-fid or 5-partite (very rarely 4- or 6-fid or -partite), deciduous or subpersistent. Corolla infundibuliform or hypocrateriform; tube short or long, the throat glabrous or villous; lobes 5, spreading or reflexed, twisted in bud. Stamens 5, inserted on the mouth of the corolla; filaments short, or 0; anthers narrow, often acute. Ovary 2-celled; ovules few in each cell, immersed or ½-immersed in fleshy peltate placentas; style stout, usually pubescent; stigma fusiform, grooved, usually much exserted. Fruit a hard 2-celled berry. Seeds few.—DISTRIB. Tropical Asia and Africa.

The genus should properly be called *Chomelia*, Linn., which dates from 1737 (Gen. Pl. ed. 1, p. 55), but the name has been retained for another (American) genus of the

Order as *Chomelia*, Jacq. (1760). K. Schum. in Engl. & Prantl, Pflanzenf. v. 4, part 4, p. 74. adopts *Chomelia* as the name of the genus.

Note.—The genus was founded by Gærtner from the Ceylon plant *Tarenna zeylanica*. In his original description, Gærtner describes the calyx as 4-partite, a condition of rare occurrence, but, as has been pointed out by Wight & Arnott (Prodr. p. 401), the calyx is sometimes (though rarely), 4- or even 6-cleft, and from the fact that Gærtner does not describe the corolla, his specimens may have been few or imperfect. There can scarcely be any doubt as to the plant Gærtner, whose figures of the fruit are excellent, intended to describe; in fact *Tarenna zeylanica* appears to be generally recognized as a synonym for *Webera corymbosa*, Willd., and *Stylocoryna Webera*, A. Rich. It is significant too that the name *Tarenna* was derived from the Cinghalese name (Tarana) of *Tarenna zeylanica* (see Trim. Fl. Ceyl. v. 2, p. 328, and Wight & Arn. Prodr. l. c.). As the name *Tarenna* dates from 1788 it is clearly prior to *Webera*, Schreb. (1791), or *Stylocoryna*, Cav. (1797).

1. **Tarenna zeylanica,** *Gærtn. Fruct.* v. 1 (1788) p. 139, t. 28. A large shrub or small tree; bark smooth, pale-grey; twigs compressed, glabrous; young shoots often covered with a resinous exudation. Leaves coriaceous, 3–6 by $\frac{3}{4}$–$2\frac{1}{2}$ in., oblong-lanceolate, acute at both ends (sometimes acuminate at the apex), glabrous, polished above, pale beneath; main nerves 10–12 pairs, prominent on the lower side; petioles $\frac{1}{4}$–$\frac{1}{2}$ in. long, stout; stipules triangular from a broad base, acute, closely appressed to the stem and at first glued to it by a waxy secretion, $\frac{1}{4}$ in. long, subpersistent. Flowers faintly odorous, in terminal trichotomous corymbose cymes; peduncles stout; ultimate pedicels about $\frac{1}{10}$ in. long. Calyx $\frac{1}{8}$ in. long, slightly pubescent; teeth triangular, $\frac{1}{20}$ in. long, ciliolate. Corolla white, $\frac{1}{3}$ in. long; lobes $\frac{1}{6}$ in. long, oblong, subacute, hairy at the mouth. Berries the size of a pea, 2-celled, globose, glabrous, at first dark-green, becoming black when fully ripe, surmounted at first by the calyx-lobes, which however often drop off before maturity leaving a conspicuous scar. Seeds 6–10, semilunate, wedge-shaped, rounded on the back, in shape like a section of an orange, hard, rugose, black, shining. I have never found more than 10 seeds in a berry. Jackson, in Index Kewen. v. 4 (1895) p. 1038. *Webera corymbosa*, Willd. Sp. Pl. v. 1 (1797) p. 1224; Hook. f. in Fl. B. I. v. 3, p. 102; Trim. Fl. Ceyl. v. 2, p. 328; Talb. Trees, Bomb. ed. 2, p. 188; Woodr. in Journ. Bomb. Nat. v. 11 (1898) p. 645; Watt, Dict. Econ. Prod. v. 6, part 4, p. 300. *Stylocoryna Webera*, A. Rich. Mém. Fam. Rubiac. (1829) p. 168, & in Mém. Soc. Hist. Nat. Par. v. 5 (1834) p. 248. *Stylocoryne Webera*, Wight & Arn. Prodr. (1834) p. 401; Wight, Icon. tt. 309 & 584; Grah. Cat. p. 89; Dalz. & Gibs. p. 119.—Flowers: Apr.–June and again in Dec. Vern. *Kare.*

Konkan: S. Konkan, *Nimmo ex Graham, Dalzell & Gibson*; jungles near Goa, *Dr. Lush ex Graham*. Kanara: *Law*!, *Hohenhacker*, 1231; N. Kanara in moist forests on the Ghâts, common near the Ainshi Ghât, *Talbot*.—Distrib. India (southern parts of the Western Peninsula); Ceylon, Malay Islands.

16. RANDIA, Linn.

Trees and shrubs unarmed or spinous. Leaves opposite, or with one of the pair often arrested; stipules short, intrapetiolar, free or connate. Flowers rather large, solitary and terminal or in axillary or leaf-opposed cymes, white or yellowish. Calyx-tube ovoid or turbinate, ribbed or terete; limb often tubular, truncate, toothed or lobed, the lobes sometimes foliaceous. Corolla various; tube long or short, the throat glabrous or villous; lobes 5 (rarely more), short or long, twisted in bud. Stamens 5 (rarely more); anthers subsessile, narrowly linear. Disk annular or cushion-shaped. Ovary 2-celled; ovules numerous, sunk in fleshy placentas; style short or slender; stigma large, clavate or fusiform, entire or 2-fid. Berry globose, ovoid or ellipsoid, 2-celled, many-seeded. Seeds often immersed in pulp, angled; testa thin; albumen horny; cotyledons orbicular.—DISTRIB. Throughout the tropics of the world; species about 90.

Armed. Erect trees or shrubs.
Flowers 1-3, terminal; calyx-limb persistent.
Flowers exceeding $1\frac{1}{4}$ in. in diam.; fruit exceeding 2 in. in diam. .... 1. *R. uliginosa.*
Flowers and fruit both less than 1 in. in diam. .... 2. *R. dumetorum.*
Flowers in cymes; calyx-limb not persistent .... 3. *R. malabarica.*
Unarmed; a climbing shrub .... 4. *R. rugulosa.*

1. **Randia uliginosa,** *DC. Prodr.* v. 4 (1830) p. 386. A small tree rarely reaching 20 ft. high; bark reddish-brown, scaly; branches numerous, thick, horizontal (the younger 4-angled), many of them short and terminating in 1–2 pairs of strong sharp thorns $\frac{1}{2}$ in. long. Leaves fascicled on suppressed branchlets, thin, $2\frac{1}{2}$–5 by $1\frac{3}{8}$–2 in., obovate or obovate-oblong, obtuse, glabrous above, more or less pubescent and reticulately veined beneath, tapering to the base; main nerves 6–8 pairs; petioles very short; stipules acute from a broad base. Flowers solitary at the ends of suppressed branches, white, fragrant, $1\frac{1}{2}$–2 in. in diam.; pedicels short. Calyx $\frac{1}{2}$ in. long, fleshy, green; limb broadly tubular with 5–7 broad rounded ciliate shallow lobes scarcely $\frac{1}{8}$ in. long. Corolla glabrous outside; tube very short with a ring of white hairs at the mouth; lobes 5–7, orbicular, much overlapping. Stamens 5–7, sessile. Ovary 2-celled; ovules ∞; style ribbed; stigma large with subconvolute spiral laciniæ. Fruit 2–$2\frac{1}{2}$ in. long, ovoid, smooth, yellowish-brown, crowned with the persistent calyx-limb, 2-celled. Seeds numerous, compressed, smooth, closely packed in pulp. Fl. B. I. v. 3, p. 110; Grah. Cat. p. 89; Dalz. & Gibs. p. 119; Wight, Icon. t. 397; Trim. Fl. Ceyl. v. 2, p. 330; Talb. Trees, Bomb. ed. 2, p. 188; Woodr. in Journ. Bomb. Nat. v. 11 (1898) p. 645; Watt, Dict. Econ. Prod. v. 6, part 1, p. 391.—Flowers: May–June. VERN. *Pándhara*; *Pándri*.

Throughout the Presidency often in abandoned rice-fields, *Talbot*. KONKAN: banks of rivers in the Konkan, *Graham*; S. Konkan, *Dalzell & Gibson*; near Pen, *Woodrow*. GUJARAT: Porbander (Kathiawar), *Woodrow*. S. M. COUNTRY: *Graham*; S. of Belgaum, *Ritchie*, 343 (*a*)! KANARA: Kála naddi, *Ritchie*, 343! —DISTRIB. Throughout India; Ceylon.

The fruit is eaten when boiled or roasted. See Watt, Dict. Econ. Prod. l. c.

2. **Randia dumetorum,** *Lamk. Tab. Encyc.* v. 2 (1793) p. 227. A large shrub or small tree armed with strong straight nearly opposite decussate spines $\frac{1}{2}$–$1\frac{1}{2}$ in. long, coming off from above the branchlets; branches horizontal, rigid, many of the lateral ones suppressed and very short. Leaves usually fascicled on the suppressed branches, $1\frac{1}{4}$–$2\frac{1}{4}$ by $\frac{3}{4}$–$1\frac{1}{4}$ in., obovate, obtuse, wrinkled, shining above, more or less pubescent above and on the nerves beneath (especially when young), base cuneate; main nerves 6–10 pairs; petioles $\frac{1}{8}$–$\frac{3}{8}$ in. long, densely pubescent; stipules ovate, acuminate. Flowers at the ends of short leaf-bearing branchlets, fragrant, solitary or 2 (rarely 3) together; peduncles short. Calyx $\frac{1}{2}$ in. long, densely hairy; tube broadly campanulate; teeth 5,

foliaceous, $\frac{1}{5}$ in. long, ovate-oblong, subacute, often with small intermediate teeth between. Corolla $\frac{3}{4}$ in. long, at first white, afterwards becoming yellow; tube $\frac{1}{5}$–$\frac{1}{4}$ in. long, densely hairy outside; lobes $\frac{1}{2}$ in. long and nearly as broad as long, obovate-oblong, rounded at the apex, pubescent outside, spreading. Fruit like a small crab-apple, yellowish, globose or broadly ovoid, smooth or obscurely longitudinally ribbed, crowned with the large calyx-limb, 2-celled, glabrous; pericarp thick. Seeds many, flat, imbedded in pulp. Fl. B. I. v. 3, p. 110; Grah. Cat. p. 89; Dalz. & Gibs. p. 119; Wight, Icon. t. 580; Bedd. For. Man. in Flor. Sylvat. p. cxxxii, t. 16, f. 1; Trim. Fl. Ceyl. v. 2, p. 330; Talb. Trees, Bomb. ed. 2, p. 189; Woodr. in Journ. Bomb. Nat. v. 11 (1898) p. 645; Watt, Dict. Econ. Prodr. v. 6, part 1, p. 389. *Randia longispina*, DC. Prodr. v. 4, p. 386; Grah. Cat. p. 89; Dalz. & Gibs. p. 119.—Flowers: Mar.–June. VERN. *Geheld*; *Gel*.

Common throughout the Presidency in deciduous forests. KONKAN: Matheran *Woodrow*! DECCAN: Khandala, *Bhiva*!; Mahableshwar, *Cooke*!. *Woodrow*; Kadkalla near Lanoli, *Ranade*!; Karli, *Bhiva*!; Lanoli, *Bhiva*!; Khandesh, *Dalzell & Gibson*. S. M. COUNTRY: Sulebhavi near Belgaum, *Woodrow*. KANARA: Sampkhand, *Woodrow*.—DISTRIB. Throughout India; Ceylon, Java, Sumatra, South China, E. Tropical Africa.

The bark, rind, and fruit are used medicinally and the bruised root and unripe fruit are used to poison fish. See Watt, Dict. Econ. Prod. l. c.

3. **Randia malabarica,** *Lamk. Encyc. Méthod.* v. 3 (1789) p. 25. An erect much-branched glabrous shrub; branchlets sometimes reduced to short sharp spines which are, however, often absent. Leaves coriaceous, 1$\frac{1}{2}$–2$\frac{1}{2}$ by $\frac{3}{4}$–1$\frac{1}{4}$, elliptic-oblong or oblong-lanceolate, subacute, glabrous, tapering to the base; nerves not conspicuous; petioles $\frac{1}{8}$–$\frac{3}{8}$ in. long; stipules triangular, caducous. Flowers white, in leaf-opposed spreading glabrous cymes fascicled on the top of a very short peduncle; pedicels $\frac{1}{8}$–$\frac{1}{3}$ in. long, each with a pair of acute connate bracts forming a cup at its base. Calyx $\frac{1}{8}$ in. long, campanulate, glabrous; teeth triangular, acute, about $\frac{1}{20}$ in. long. Corolla lemon-yellow, hairy at the mouth; tube $\frac{1}{6}$ in. long, glabrous; lobes $\frac{1}{4}$ by $\frac{1}{10}$ in., ovate-oblong, acute, veined. Stigma fusiform. Anthers long, exserted. Fruit globose, $\frac{1}{4}$–$\frac{1}{3}$ in. in diam., red (*Graham*), marked at the apex with the scar of the calyx-limb. Seeds 6–8 in each cell, closely packed, angled, compressed. Fl. B. I. v. 3, p. 111; Trim. Fl. Ceyl. v. 2, p. 331. *Griffithia fragrans*, Wight & Arn. Prodr. p. 400; Wight, Icon. t. 310; Grah. Cat. p. 89; Dalz. & Gibs. p. 119.

S. KONKAN: *Dalzell & Gibson*, *Nimmo* ex *Graham*, l. c.

I have seen no specimens from Bombay and there are none from that Presidency in Herb. Kew. Nimmo ex Graham (Cat. p. 89) and Dalzell & Gibson (Bo. Fl. p. 119) give its habitat as S. Konkan. Neither Talbot nor Woodrow enumerates the species.—DISTRIB. India (W. Peninsula); Ceylon.

4. **Randia rugulosa,** *Hook. f. in Fl. B. I.* v. 3 (1880) p. 113. A large climbing unarmed shrub with many drooping branches; stem reaching 4 in. in diam. at the base. Leaves 2$\frac{1}{2}$–4$\frac{1}{2}$ by 1–2$\frac{1}{4}$ in., elliptic-oblong or elliptic-lanceolate, acuminate, glabrous; main nerves 5–6 pairs, prominent beneath; petioles $\frac{3}{8}$–$\frac{1}{2}$ in. long, glabrous; stipules ovate, cuspidate. Flowers in leaf-opposed paniculate cymes; peduncles very short; pedicels longer than the calyx; bracts numerous, connate, cuspidate. Calyx $\frac{1}{4}$ in. long, leathery, glabrous or puberulous; tube campanulate; limb

truncate, with minute distant triangular teeth not more than $\frac{1}{20}$ in. long. Corolla white; tube $\frac{1}{3}$ in. long; lobes $\frac{3}{8}$ by $\frac{1}{8}$ in., oblong, subacute, glabrous. Stigma very large, fusiform. Berry $\frac{3}{8}$ in. in diam., pisiform, the calyx-limb not persistent in fruit, but soon falling and leaving a conspicuous scar. Seeds rugose. Trim. Fl. Ceyl. v. 2, p. 331; Talb. Trees, Bomb. ed. 2, p. 189; Woodr. in Journ. Bomb. Nat. v. 11 (1898) p. 645. *Griffithia speciosa*, Bedd. Icon. Pl. Ind. Or. t. 37.—Flowers: Jan.-Mar.

KONKAN: Matheran, *Woodrow*; near Simpson's lake, *Cooke*!; Chowk plateau, *H. M. Birdwood*. S. M. COUNTRY: Castlerock, *Kanitkar*! KANARA: common in the forests near the Tinai and Gairsoppa Ghâts, *Talbot*; Divimana, *Woodrow*; Mendele (N. Kanara), *Ritchie*, 1772!—DISTRIB. India (W. Peninsula); Ceylon.

17. GARDENIA, Linn.

Shrubs rarely trees, armed or not. Leaves opposite, rarely 3-nately whorled; stipules intrapetiolar, often connate. Flowers often large, terminal or axillary, solitary, fascicled, or rarely cymose, sometimes dimorphic and polygamous. Calyx-tube ovoid or obconic; limb tubular or dilated, variously cleft or lobed. Corolla various; lobes 5–12, twisted in bud. Stamens as many as the corolla lobes, inserted in the throat of the corolla; anthers sessile or subsessile, linear, included. Ovary 1-celled; ovules numerous, 2-seriate, on 2–6 parietal placentas; style thick; stigma large, club-shaped or fusiform, usually 2-fid. Fruit often large, ovoid, ellipsoid or globose, coriaceous or fleshy and irregularly bursting, or with a hard bony endocarp which sometimes splits along the placental sutures. Seeds many, imbedded in the placentas, compressed; testa thin; embryo small, in horny albumen.—DISTRIB. Tropical and subtropical parts of the Old World; species 60.

Small trees.
  Armed; flowers dimorphic; placentas 5–6 .... 1. *G. turgida*, [var. *montana*.
  Unarmed; flowers not dimorphic.
    Leaves petioled; calyx-teeth long, subulate, erect; placentas 2 .... 2. *G. lucida*.
    Leaves sessile; calyx-teeth long, recurved; placentas 4–5 . 3. *G. latifolia*.
A shrub unarmed; leaves sessile; calyx-teeth minute; placentas 4–5 .... 4. *G. gummifera*.

1. **Gardenia turgida,** *Roxb. Hort. Beng.* (1814) p. 15, var. **montana,** *Hook. f. Fl. B. I.* v. 3 (1880) p. 118. A small deciduous tree reaching 25 ft. high; bark smooth, thick, soft, that on the young branches yellowish; branches numerous, thick and stout, usually armed with strong straight sometimes leaf-bearing thorns. Leaves 2–3½ by 1½–2¼ in., oblong or semiorbicular, obtuse, glabrous above, velvety-tomentose beneath, base much tapered into an obscure petiole; nerves inconspicuous; stipules triangular, cuspidate, caducous. Flowers from the young leafless shoots, dimorphic, the males in fascicles, the females solitary. MALE FLOWERS: Calyx $\frac{1}{6}$ in. long, turbinate, pubescent, the mouth wide, truncate; teeth minute. Corolla $\frac{3}{4}$–1 in. long, glabrous; lobes $\frac{1}{4}$–$\frac{1}{3}$ in. long, oblong, obtuse. FEMALE FLOWERS: Calyx $\frac{1}{3}$–$\frac{1}{2}$ in. long, flask-shaped, the mouth dilated; teeth foliaceous, $\frac{1}{8}$ in. long, narrowly linear, obtuse. Corolla as in the male. Fruit 1–3 in. in diam., ovoid or subglobose, often bluntly pointed but not beaked, smooth;

pericarp thick; endocarp woody, shining inside; placentas 5 or 6. Talb. Trees, Bomb. ed. 2, p. 190; Woodr. in Journ. Bomb. Nat. v. 11 (1898) p. 645; Watt, Dict. Econ. Prod. v. 3, p. 483. *Gardenia montana* (sp.), Roxb. Fl. Ind. v. 1, p. 709; Wight, Icon. t. 577; Grah. Cat. p. 88; Dalz. & Gibs. p. 120.—Flowers: Apr.–June.

Dalzell (without locality) in his Herbarium of Bombay Plants in Herb. Kew.! DECCAN: Poona districts, *Woodrow*! S. M. COUNTRY: Belgaum, *Ritchie*, 1087!; Dharwar, *Talbot*. KANARA: common in the N. Kanara jungles, *Talbot*.—DISTRIB. India (Himalayas, Behar, W. Peninsula).

2. **Gardenia lucida,** *Roxb. Hort. Beng.* (1814) p. 15. A large glabrous shrub or small tree reaching 20–25 ft. high; bark smooth, grey; young shoots greyish-green, smooth, resinous. Leaves 2½–8 by 1–3 in., elliptic-oblong, subacute or shortly acuminate, base narrowed into a short petiole; main nerves 20–25 pairs, slender, prominent beneath; petioles somewhat obscure, about ⅛ in. long; stipules large, broadly ovate, acute, membranous. Flowers fragrant, axillary, solitary, from the axils of the uppermost leaves near the ends of the branches; pedicels ¼–½ in. long. Calyx ⅝ in. long, pubescent or tomentose; teeth ⅜ in. long, erect, lanceolate, subulate. Corolla large, at first pure white, soon turning yellow; tube 1¼–2 in. long, slender, puberulous outside; lobes 5, obovate, obtuse, 1¼ by ¾ in., spreading, veined, glabrous. Fruit ellipsoid or globose, ¾–1 in. in diam., smooth, marked with longitudinal lines, crowned by the persistent calyx-limb; pericarp thick, woody; placentas 2. The flowers open in the evening, soon turn from white to yellow and die. Fl. B. I. v. 3, p. 115; Grah. Cat. p. 88; Dalz. & Gibs. p. 120; Wight, Icon. t. 575; Bedd. For. Man. in Flor. Sylvat. p. cxxxiv, t. 15, fig. 6; Talb. Trees, Bomb. ed. 2, p. 190; Woodr. in Journ. Bomb. Nat. v. 11 (1898) p. 645; Watt, Dict. Econ. Prod. v. 3, p. 482.—Flowers: Mar.–June. VERN. *Dikemáli*.

KONKAN: *Lambert*!, *Dalzell*!, *Law*!; Elephanta, *Graham*; Kanheri jungles, *Graham*. S. M. COUNTRY: *Graham*; Belgaum, *Talbot*. KANARA: N. Kanara, *Woodrow*.—DISTRIB. India (Birma, Chittagong, W. Peninsula).

This species is, as well as *G. gummifera*, one of the sources of the *Dikemáli* resin which is much used by the natives in medicine. The resin, which has a most offensive odor, is employed extensively to keep off flies from sores. See Watt, Dict. Econ. Prod. l. c.

3. **Gardenia latifolia,** *Ait. Hort. Kew.* v. 1 (1789) p. 294 (*not* of Roxb.). A small deciduous tree reaching 30 ft. high, with stiff divergent branches forming a rounded head; bark smooth, pale-grey, flaking off in small round pieces; young parts glabrous but coated with a resinous exudation. Leaves opposite or 3-nately whorled, crowded towards the ends of the branches, subsessile, 4–8 by 2½–6½ in., broadly elliptic or obovate, rounded or very shortly and obtusely acuminate at the apex, apple-green above, paler beneath, glabrous or more or less pubescent; main nerves 10–20 pairs; stipules adnate to the base of the petiole, connate, forming a thin truncate tube at first enclosing the young leaves, but, after the fall of the leaf, separating at the base and forming a loose ring round the stem. Flowers solitary or 2-nate, subsessile, white changing to yellow, fragrant. Calyx ¾–1 in. long, densely pubescent; limb broadly tubular, slightly dilated at the apex; teeth 5–9, lanceolate-subulate, unequal, recurved, and with ciliate margins. Corolla-tube 2 in. or more long, striate, densely pubescent outside; lobes 5–9,

obliquely obovate-oblong, obtuse, $1\frac{1}{2}$–$1\frac{3}{4}$ by $\frac{1}{2}$–$\frac{3}{4}$ in. Fruit nearly globose, $1\frac{1}{4}$–$1\frac{3}{4}$ in. in diam., without ribs, appressedly pubescent when young, pale-green and speckled, surmounted by the calyx-limb, which is $\frac{1}{2}$ in. or more long; epicarp dry, fleshy; endocarp bony, yellow, polished within, 3-valved. Seeds numerous, small, flattened, pale-brown, in purplish-grey pulp; placentas 4–5. Fl. B. I. v. 3, p. 116; Grah. Cat. p. 88; Dalz. & Gibs. p. 120; Wight, Icon. t. 759; Trim. Fl. Ceyl. v. 2, p. 332; Talb. Trees, Bomb. ed. 2, p. 190; Watt, Dict. Econ. Prod. v. 3, p. 482.—Flowers: Mar.–May.

S. M. COUNTRY: sandstone hills north of Belgaum, *Ritchie*, 1085! KANARA: *Law!*; near Duddi on the Gatprabа river, *Law* ex *Graham*, *Ritchie*, 1085!—DISTRIB. Dry hilly districts of Western, Central, and South-western India, Behar and W. Bengal; Ceylon.

The wood has been recommended as a substitute for boxwood for engravers' use. It is employed by the natives to make combs. See Watt, Dict. Econ. Prod. l. c.

4. **Gardenia gummifera,** *Linn. f. Suppl.* (1781) p. 164. A shrub about 6 ft. high, glabrous or nearly so, unarmed; buds resinous. Leaves sessile or nearly so, $1\frac{3}{4}$–$2\frac{3}{4}$ by $\frac{3}{4}$–1 in., elliptic-oblong or obovate-oblong, obtuse or subacute, glabrous, shining, base obtuse, acute, or sometimes cordate; main nerves 12–18 pairs; stipules connate, truncate or mucronate. Flowers not odorous (*Ritchie*), subsessile, 1–3 together. Calyx $\frac{3}{8}$ in. long, densely pubescent; teeth triangular, $\frac{1}{12}$–$\frac{1}{8}$ in. long. Corolla at first white, soon changing to yellow; tube pubescent outside, $1\frac{1}{4}$–$1\frac{1}{2}$ in. long; lobes oblong, obtuse, 1–$1\frac{1}{4}$ by $\frac{1}{2}$–$\frac{5}{8}$ in. Fruit 1–$1\frac{1}{2}$ in. long, oblong or ellipsoid, with numerous longitudinal elevated lines and with a stout beak, smooth; pericarp thin; placentas 4–5. Fl. B. I. v. 3, p. 116; Grah. Cat. p. 88; Dalz. & Gibs. p. 120; Wight, Icon. t. 576 (*figure not good*); Talb. Trees, Bomb. ed. 2, p. 190; Woodr. in Journ. Bomb. Nat. v. 11 (1898) p. 645; Watt, Dict. Econ. Prod. v. 3, p. 480.—Flowers: Feb.–June. VERN. *Dikemáli*; *Kamarri*.

S. M. COUNTRY: barren plains south of Dharwar, *Dalzell & Gibson*; Belgaum, *Ritchie*, 344! KANARA: *Dalzell & Gibson*; common on the laterite plains from Kumpta southwards, also near Siddapur, *Talbot*; Bhatkal (N. Kanara), *Woodrow!*, *Bhiva!*; Duddi on the Gatprabа river, *Law* ex *Graham*.—DISTRIB. India (W. Peninsula).

This shrub, as well as the small tree *G. lucida*, produces the resinous material known as *Dikemáli*, which is largely used by the natives in medicine and to keep flies off sores. See Watt, Dict. Econ. Prod. l. c.

Gardenia jasminoides, Ellis, in Phil. Trans. v. 51 (1761) part ii. p. 935, sometimes known as the *Cape Jasmine*, has been introduced from China and is much valued as an ornamental plant in gardens in districts where there is a tolerably heavy rainfall. The double-flowered variety is that most commonly cultivated. It has oblong-elliptic coriaceous leaves 2–4 in. long, large white very fragrant flowers, and oblong fruit about 1 in. long. *Gardenia florida*, Linn. Sp. Pl. ed. 2 (1762) p. 305; Bot. Mag. (1826) t. 2627 (the double-flowered variety); Grah. Cat. p. 88; Dalz. & Gibs. Suppl. p. 43; Woodr. in Journ. Bomb. Nat. v. 11 (1898) p. 645, & Gard. in Ind. ed. 5, p. 355; Watt, Dict. Econ. Prod. v. 3, p. 480.—Flowers in the rains. VERN. *Gandarájá*.

18. DIPLOSPORA, DC.

Evergreen shrubs or trees; branches terete. Leaves opposite, petiolate, coriaceous; stipules triangular, long-pointed or acuminate. Flowers small, inconspicuous, in axillary fascicles or short cymes, usually polygamo-diœcious; bracts connate, often involucellate. Calyx-tube short, obconic or hemispheric; limb truncate or 4–5-lobed or -toothed. Corolla-tube short, cylindric or campanulate; lobes 4–5, spreading, twisted in bud. Stamens 4–5, inserted at the mouth of the corolla; filaments short or long; anthers oblong or linear, often recurved, exserted. Ovary 2 (rarely 3)-celled; ovules 2–5 in each cell on placentas attached to the septum; style short or long, with oblong or linear branches. Berry ovoid or globose, 2-celled, few-seeded. Seeds rather large; testa various; embryo small.

Fruit umbonate with a conical beak within the calyx-limb...... 1. *D. apiocarpa.*
Fruit not umbonate, marked at the apex with the scar of the calyx-limb .... 2. *D. sphærocarpa.*

1. **Diplospora apiocarpa,** *Hook. f. Fl. B. I.* v. 3 (1880) p. 123. A moderate-sized tree; bark pale. Leaves 3½–6 by 1½–3 in., ovate or elliptic-lanceolate, obtusely acuminate, glabrous, base tapering; main nerves 6–8 pairs, sometimes with hairy glands (? galls) in their axils beneath; petioles ½–¾ in. long; stipules ⅜ in. long, triangular, acuminate. Flowers subsessile, in axillary fascicles; buds resinous; bracts connate into a cup or epicalyx. Calyx $\frac{1}{10}$ in. long, campanulate, covered with a resinous substance; limb truncate, entire or with several minute irregular teeth. Corolla ¼ in. long, glabrous; lobes ⅛ in. long, oblong, obtuse. Stamens in the male and 2-sexual flowers much exserted. Fruit ¾ in. long, sessile or subsessile, ellipsoid or pyriform, bluntly umbonate with a conical beak within the calyx-limb. Seeds flat, irregularly compressed, few. Bedd. Flor. Sylvat. t. 223 ?; Talb. Trees, Bomb. ed. 2, p. 191. *Discospermum apiocarpum*, Dalz. in Kew Journ. Bot. v. 2 (1850) p. 257; Dalz. & Gibs. p. 120; Watt, Dict. Econ. Prod. v. 3, p. 156.—Flowers: July–Oct.

KONKAN: *Stocks*; the Ghâts lat. 16°, *Dalzell & Gibson*; about the latitude of Vingorla, *Talbot*. KANARA: *Law*!—DISTRIB. Apparently endemic in the Western Peninsula of India.

I have cited Beddome's t. 223 in Flor. Sylvat. for this, with hesitation. The fruit, as figured by Beddome, does not agree at all with that of Dalzell's plant; in fact Beddome, in For. Man. p. cxxxiv–3, is himself doubtful of the correctness of the identification.

2. **Diplospora sphærocarpa,** *Hook. f. Fl. B. I.* v. 3 (1880) p. 123. A small glabrous tree. Leaves elliptic-lanceolate, obtuse, subacute or shortly acuminate, glabrous, base tapering; main nerves 4–6 pairs; petioles ¼–½ in. long; stipules ⅕–¼ in. long, triangular, acute. Flowers sessile, fascicled on a very short peduncle, without connate bracts. Calyx resinous outside, $\frac{1}{10}$ in. long; lobes 4, equalling the tube, orbicular-oblong, ciliolate. Corolla-tube very short, not as long as the lobes of the calyx, throat glabrous; lobes ⅛ in. long, oblong, obtuse. Fruit globose, ⅜ in. in diam., shortly pedicelled, marked at the apex with the scar of the calyx-limb, not umbonate. Seeds few, vertically imbricate, much compressed. Bedd. For. Man. in Flor. Sylvat. p. cxxxiv–3 (exclud. syn.); Talb. Trees, Bomb. ed. 2, p. 191. *Discospermum sphæro-*

carpum, Dalz. in Kew Journ. Bot. v. 2 (1850) p. 257; Dalz. & Gibs. p. 120.—Flowers: Oct.

Rare. KONKAN: Western Peninsula on the Ghâts from Bombay southwards, *Talbot*. Sahyádri mountains, lat. 16° N., *Dalzell & Gibson*.—DISTRIB. Endemic in the Western Peninsula of India.

19. KNOXIA, Linn.

Erect herbs or undershrubs; stems terete or obtusely angled. Leaves opposite; stipules connate with the petiole into an entire or bristly sheath. Flowers dimorphic, pink or lilac, subsessile on the elongating branches of terminal cymes (rarely spicate), ebracteolate. Calyx-tube ovoid or didymous; teeth 4, minute, and subequal or 1 or 2 elongate, persistent. Corolla-tube long, throat usually villous; lobes 4, valvate in bud, with inflexed tips. Stamens 4, inserted within the throat of the corolla; anthers linear, included or exserted. Ovary 2-celled; ovule 1, pendulous in each cell; style filiform; stigma 2-lobed. Fruit small, of 2 semi-terete or dorsally compressed indehiscent cocci. Seeds with a thickened funicle; testa membranous; albumen fleshy; embryo axile; cotyledons thin; radicle superior.—DISTRIB. India, Java, China, Philippines, Tropical Australia; species 6–8.

1. **Knoxia corymbosa,** *Willd. Sp. Pl.* v. 1 (1797) p. 582. An erect annual 1–4 ft. high; stem sparingly branched, somewhat stout, with long internodes, often obtusely 4-angled, softly and more or less densely hairy. Leaves 2–4 by $\frac{1}{2}$–1 in., lanceolate or linear-lanceolate, sessile or shortly petioled, acute, more or less hairy on both sides, tapering much at the base into a short petiole; main nerves 8–12 pairs, conspicuous on the lower side, very oblique; stipules with 3–5 filiform hairy bristles. Flowers small, numerous, on the sides of slender pubescent branches of large lax corymbose cymes; pedicels very short, almost 0. Calyx $\frac{1}{20}$ in. long; teeth minute, triangular, subequal. Corolla $\frac{1}{8}$ in. long, somewhat club-shaped; lobes short, $\frac{1}{30}$–$\frac{1}{20}$ in. long, triangular-oblong, subacute. Fruit $\frac{1}{18}$ in. long, sessile or shortly pedicelled, ellipsoid, 4-angled, secund, indehiscent, perforate at the base. The mericarps when ripe separate from the persistent columella with the least pressure. Fl. B. I. v. 3, p. 128; Dalz. & Gibs. p. 111; Wight, Ill. t. 128; Trim. Fl. Ceyl. v. 2, p. 340; Woodr. in Journ. Bomb. Nat. v. 11 (1898) p. 645.—Flowers: Aug.-Oct.

KONKAN: Wág Donger near Vingorla, *Dalzell & Gibson*. S. M. COUNTRY: Londa, *Cooke*!; Gamji Station (S. M. Railway), *Woodrow*!; Belgaum, *Ritchie*, 1089! KANARA: Kála naddi, *Ritchie*, 1089!—DISTRIB. Throughout Tropical India; Ceylon, Malay Archipelago, Tropical Australia.

20. PLECTRONIA, Linn.

Shrubs (sometimes small trees), armed or unarmed, sometimes scandent. Leaves opposite, shortly petiolate; stipules connate. Flowers axillary, fascicled, or in corymbose peduncled cymes, small, white or green. Calyx-tube short, obconic, turbinate or hemispheric; limb very short, truncate or 4–5-toothed. Corolla-tube infundibuliform, campanulate, globose or urceolate, usually with a ring of deflexed hairs within; lobes 4–5, at length reflexed, valvate in bud. Stamens 4–5, subsessile, on the throat or mouth of the corolla. Ovary 2-celled; ovules solitary in each cell, pendulous; style stout; stigma large. Drupe didymous or subglobose, or with one carpel suppressed, then reniform or oblong, with 1–2 pyrenes or a 2-celled putamen. Seeds oblong, pendulous; testa membranous; albumen fleshy; embryo elongate; cotyledons short; radicle superior.—DISTRIB. Tropical Asia, Africa and Australia, South Africa and Pacific Islands; species about 70.

Branches without spines.
  Flowers 5-merous .... 1. *P. Wightii.*
Branches with spines.
  Flowers 5-merous .... 2. *P. Rheedei.*
  Flowers 4-merous .... 3. *P. parviflora.*

1. **Plectronia Wightii,** *T. Cooke.* An unarmed handsome large erect shrub or small tree; young shoots 4-angled. Leaves 3½–4½ by 1½–2 in., elliptic-lanceolate, obtuse or shortly acuminate, coriaceous, entire, bright-green, polished and shining above, paler beneath, quite glabrous on both sides, base narrowed into a very short petiole; main nerves 4–6 pairs, oblique, often with hollow galls (the work of insects) in their axils; stipules rounded-ovate at base, with a long subulate acumination. Flowers 5-merous, in peduncled umbels in the opposite axils; peduncles stout, ¼ in. long, glabrous; pedicels very numerous, ¼–½ in. long, slender, glabrous. Calyx ⅛ in. long, glabrous; teeth triangular, $\frac{1}{32}$ in. long, slightly ciliolate. Corolla thick and subfleshy, ⅓ in. long, densely bearded with white hairs in the throat; lobes 5, oblong, acute, ⅙ by $\frac{1}{16}$ in. Fruit obovoid, didymous, ⅜–½ in. long, warted, black when ripe, polished. The wood is very hard; even the young branches test the penknife. *Canthium umbellatum*, Wight, Icon. t. 1034 (*not* of Korth.); Hook. f. Fl. B. I. v. 3, p. 132; Dalz. & Gibs. p. 113; Talb. Trees, Bomb. ed. 2, p. 192; Woodr. in Journ. Bomb. Nat. v. 11 (1898) p. 645; Watt, Dict. Econ. Prod. v. 2, p. 129. *Canthium didymum*, Grah. Cat. p. 91 (*not* of Gærtn.); Trim. Fl. Ceyl. v. 2, p. 343.—Flowers: Nov.–Jan. VERN. *Tupá*; *Arsul.*

KONKAN: evergreen forests, *Talbot*; hills in the Konkan, *Law*! DECCAN: Mahableshwar, common, *Cooke*!; Khandala, *Cooke*!, *Woodrow*! S. M. COUNTRY: Rámghát, *Ritchie*, 1787! KANARA: evergreen forests of N. Kanara, *Talbot*.—DISTRIB. India (W. Peninsula, Ava).

Trimen (*l. c.*) makes this synonymous with *Canthium didymum*, Gærtn., but the inflorescence is sufficiently distinctive to warrant its retention as a separate species. As the name *Plectronia umbellata* has been already adopted for a Madagascar plant with 4-merous flowers by Mr. Baker (Journ. Linn. Soc. v. 20 [1884] p. 168), Wight's specific name cannot be used for this plant. I have therefore named the plant *P. Wightii* after Dr. Wight, who first discovered, described, and figured it.

2. **Plectronia Rheedei,** *Bedd. For. Man. in Flor. Sylvat.* p. cxxxiv–5 (1874). A scandent armed shrub; stem slender, 1 in. in diam., spinous to near the base; bark smooth, shining; branches divaricate, slender, terete, more or less clothed with appressed pubescence, usually armed with straight or slightly curved sharp supra-axillary spines ¼–½ in. long. Leaves thin, 1–4 by ¾–2 in., ovate, acute or acuminate, glabrous on both sides or with a few scattered hairs on the nerves beneath, rounded or cordate at the base; main nerves 4–6 pairs, often with galls in their axils; petioles ⅛–¼ in. long; stipules ovate, cuspidate, hairy. Flowers greenish, axillary, solitary or in fascicles of 2–4 (rarely in very shortly peduncled cymes); pedicels very short; buds very acute. Calyx $\frac{1}{16}$–$\frac{1}{12}$ in. long, turbinate; limb truncate or with 5 very minute distant

teeth. Corolla $\frac{1}{3}$ in. long; tube short and wide; lobes 5, linear-lanceolate, acuminate, $\frac{3}{16}$-$\frac{1}{4}$ by $\frac{1}{16}$ in. Style hairy; stigma mitriform, bifid. Fruit slightly broader than long, about $\frac{1}{3}$ in. broad, didymous, compressed, 2-lobed at the apex, rugose. *Canthium Rheedei*, DC. Prodr. v. 4 (1830) p. 474; Hook. f. Fl. B. I. v. 3, p. 134; Grah. Cat. p. 91; Dalz. & Gibs. p. 113; Trim. Fl. Ceyl. v. 2, p. 344; Talb. Trees, Bomb. ed. 2, p. 192; Woodr. in Journ. Bomb. Nat. v. 11 (1898) p. 645. *Canthium angustifolium*, Roxb. Fl. Ind. v. 1 (1832) p. 533; Hook. f. Fl. B. I. v. 3, p. 135; Woodr. in Journ. Bomb. Nat. v. 11 (1898) p. 645. *Canthium Leschenaultii*, Wight & Arn. Prodr. p. 426; Dalz. & Gibs. p. 113.—Flowers: Feb.-May.

KONKAN: *Stocks*!; foot of the Ghâts, *Dalzell*!; evergreen forests, *Talbot*; near Sewree Fort (Bombay), *Graham*. S. M. COUNTRY: Râmghât, *Ritchie*, 1193!; Mulas, foot of Râmghât, *Dalzell & Gibson*; near Belgaum, *Cooke*!; Pârva Ghât, *Ritchie*, 1193! KANARA: evergreen forests of N. Kanara, *Talbot*; Yacombi, *Woodrow*!—DISTRIB. India (W. Peninsula); Ceylon.

The fruit has the taste of the blæberry, *Dalzell*.

3. **Plectronia parviflora,** *Bedd. For. Man. in Flor. Sylvat.* p. cxxxiv-5 (1874). A shrub usually rigid, but sometimes subscandent in hedges (*Talbot*); branches many, with opposite supra-axillary nearly horizontal sharp straight spines $\frac{3}{4}$-$1\frac{1}{2}$ in. long, the spines sometimes wanting when the branches are less rigid. Leaves $\frac{3}{4}$-$1\frac{1}{2}$ by $\frac{1}{2}$-1 in., often fascicled on the young shoots, ovate, obovate or suborbicular, obtuse, glabrous, green above, whitish beneath, base cuneate; main nerves 4-6 pairs; petioles $\frac{1}{10}$-$\frac{1}{4}$ in. long, slender; stipules shortly triangular at the base, with a long subulate point. Flowers 4-merous, small, yellowish, in many-flowered usually peduncled cymes which are sometimes fascicled; peduncles and pedicels slender, of variable length. Calyx $\frac{1}{20}$-$\frac{1}{16}$ in. long; lobes 4, triangular, acute, $\frac{1}{30}$ in. long. Corolla $\frac{1}{8}$ in. long; tube inflated; lobes as long as the tube, ovate, acute. Style glabrous; stigma large, globose. Drupe $\frac{3}{8}$-$\frac{7}{16}$ in. long, about $\frac{3}{16}$ in. broad, oblong-ellipsoid, compressed, didymous, areolate at the apex, yellow when ripe, edible. *Canthium parviflorum*, Lamk. Encyc. Méthod. v. 1 (1783) p. 602; Hook. f. Fl. B. I. v. 3, p. 136; Dalz. & Gibs. p. 113; Roxb. Cor. Pl. t. 51; Trim. Fl. Ceyl. v. 2, p. 346; Talb. Trees, Bomb. ed. 2, p. 192; Woodr. in Journ. Bomb. Nat. v. 11 (1898) p. 645; Watt, Dict. Econ. Prod. v. 2, p. 129.—Flowers: Apr.-May. VERN. *Kirni*.

DECCAN: Kothrud near Poona, *Woodrow*! S. M. COUNTRY: Ghâts between Belgaum and Nipani (rare), *Dalzell & Gibson*; Belgaum, *Ritchie*, 1007! KANARA: Mangod (N. Kanara), *Woodrow*!—DISTRIB. India (W. Peninsula); Ceylon.

The leaves are eaten in curries and the wood is hard and used for turning.

21. VANGUERIA, Juss.

A genus closely allied to *Plectronia*, from which it differs chiefly in the ovary which is 3-6 (usually 5) -celled, and in the fruit which is larger than that of *Plectronia*; pyrenes 5-3 or putamen 5-3-celled.

1. **Vangueria spinosa,** *Roxb. Hort. Beng.* (1814) p. 15. A large shrub or small tree with straight opposite (sometimes 3-nate) sharp spines $\frac{1}{2}$-$1\frac{1}{2}$ in. long; bark dark-colored, nearly smooth. Leaves 2-5 by $1\frac{1}{4}$-$2\frac{3}{4}$ in., membranous, elliptic-oblong, acuminate, glabrous, base shortly cuneate; main nerves 6-8 pairs; petioles $\frac{1}{4}$-1 in. long; stipules $\frac{1}{3}$ in. long, glabrous, broadly triangular at the base, with a slender subulate

acumination about $\frac{1}{8}$–$\frac{1}{6}$ in. long. Flowers greenish-white, in peduncled cymes from the old scars below the leaves; peduncles usually short; pedicels slender; buds acute, somewhat mitre-shaped. Calyx $\frac{1}{10}$ in. long, glabrous; tube cup-shaped, ribbed, rugose; teeth 5, somewhat scarious, $\frac{1}{30}$ in. long, distant, triangular, very acute. Corolla $\frac{1}{3}$ in. long; tube very broad, glabrous outside, the throat densely hairy within; lobes 5, ovate-lanceolate, acute, equalling the tube. Fruit about 1 in. in diam., on slender pedicels, globose, smooth, yellowish when ripe, edible; pyrenes 4–5, woody, smooth. Fl. B. I. v. 3, p. 136; Grah. Cat. p. 90; Talb. Trees, Bomb. ed. 2, p. 192; Woodr. in Journ. Bomb. Nat. v. 11 (1898) p. 645; Watt, Dict. Econ. Prod. v. 6, part 4, p. 221.—Flowers: Jan.–Apr. VERN. *A'lu.*

KONKAN: Thal Ghát, *Kanitkar*!; Matheran, *Cooke*!, *Kanitkar*! DECCAN: Lanoli, *Woodrow*! S. M. COUNTRY: near Belgaum; *Ritchie*, 1786/3; KANARA: common, *Ritchie*, 1786!—DISTRIB. India (N. Bengal, W. Peninsula, Birma, Pegu); Java.

22. IXORA, Linn.

Shrubs or small trees usually glabrous. Leaves opposite (rarely 3-nately verticelled); stipules interpetiolar. Flowers usually 4-merous, in terminal 3-chotomously branched often corymbose cymes, 2-bracteolate. Calyx-tube ovoid; limb short, 4 (rarely 5) -toothed, persistent. Corolla-tube long, very slender; lobes 4 (rarely 5), usually shorter than the tube, spreading, twisted in bud. Stamens 4 (rarely 5), on the mouth of the corolla; filaments short or 0; anthers slender, often with an apiculate tip. Ovary 2-celled; ovules solitary in each cell, peltately attached to the septum; style filiform; stigma slender, fusiform, 2-branched, the branches rarely persistently connate. Fruit globose or subdidymous, with 2 plano-convex or ventrally concave coriaceous pyrenes. Seeds peltate; testa membranous; albumen horny; cotyledons flat, thin; radicle inferior.—DISTRIB. Tropical Asia and Africa, America, Australia, and the Pacific Islands.

Calyx-teeth longer than the ovary.
- Calyx $\frac{1}{6}$ in. long; corolla-tube reaching $\frac{3}{4}$ in. .... 1. *I. lanceolaria.*
- Calyx $\frac{1}{6}$ in. long; corolla-tube reaching $1\frac{1}{4}$ in. .... 2. *I. polyantha.*

Calyx-teeth shorter than the ovary.
- Leaves and inflorescence turning black in drying .... 3. *I. nigricans.*
- Leaves and inflorescence not turning black in drying.
  - Peduncles 4–7 in. long .... 4. *I. elongata.*
  - Peduncles less than 3 in. long.
    - Flowers white.
      - Small trees.
        - Corolla-tube less than $\frac{1}{2}$ in. long; flower-buds globose. 5. *I. brachiata.*
        - Corolla-tube exceeding $\frac{1}{2}$ in. long; flower-buds ellipsoid .... 6. *I. parviflora.*
    - Flowers bright-scarlet.
      - A shrub; corolla-tube $1\frac{1}{2}$ in. long .... 7. *I. coccinea.*

1. **Ixora lanceolaria,** *Colebr. in Roxb. Fl. Ind. ed. Carey,* v. 1 (1820) p. 397. A small erect shrub; branches ash-colored. Leaves 4–$5\frac{1}{2}$ by 1–2 in., oblong-lanceolate, acute, glabrous, attenuate (rarely rounded) at the base; main nerves slender, 14–18 pairs; petioles $\frac{1}{8}$–$\frac{3}{8}$ in. long; stipules shortly triangular at the base, with a long slender point which is sometimes $\frac{1}{8}$ in. long. Flowers numerous, in brachiate cymes 2–3 in. in diam., supported by a pair of floral leaves; bracts beneath the branches of the cyme lanceolate-subulate, caducous; bracteoles 2,

appressed to the calyx, linear-lanceolate, acute, $\frac{1}{8}$ in. long. Calyx more or less pubescent, $\frac{1}{4}$ in. long; teeth 4, fleshy, linear-lanceolate, acute, $\frac{1}{8}$–$\frac{1}{6}$ in. long by $\frac{1}{20}$ in. broad. Corolla white; tube very slender, up to $\frac{3}{4}$ in. long, mouth naked; lobes linear-oblong, obtuse, $\frac{7}{18}$ by $\frac{1}{8}$ in. Filaments $\frac{1}{8}$–$\frac{1}{6}$ in. long, flattened, slender. Style exserted beyond the corolla-tube, but the exserted portion shorter than the corolla-lobes; branches of the stigma linear, $\frac{1}{20}$–$\frac{1}{16}$ in. long. Fruit globose or didymous, $\frac{1}{4}$ in. in diam., smooth, crowned with the 4 erect calyx-teeth. Fl. B. I. v. 3, p. 138; Wight, Icon. t. 827; Talb. Trees, Bomb. ed. 2, p. 193; Woodr. in Journ. Bomb. Nat. v. 11 (1898) p. 645.—Flowers: June–July.

Chiefly in the southern districts of the Presidency. KANARA: evergreen forests of N. Kanara particularly on the southern Ghâts, *Talbot*; Godhuli, *Woodrow*; Kanara, *Woodrow*; Elai jungles below Supa (N. Kanara), *Ritchie*, 1789.—DISTRIB. Southern districts of the Western Peninsula of India.

2. **Ixora polyantha,** *Wight, Icon.* t. 1066. A small shrub. Leaves 6–11 by 2½–5½ in., obovate, elliptic-oblong or oblong-lanceolate, acute or acuminate, coriaceous, glabrous on both sides, base usually acute; main nerves about 8–12 pairs; petioles $\frac{1}{8}$–$\frac{3}{8}$ in. long, rugose; stipules broadly ovate, cuspidate. Flowers in corymbiform cymes open or collected into a globose head; branches of the cyme usually densely clothed with white hairs; bracts ovate, acute, caducous; bracteoles reaching $\frac{1}{4}$ in. long, ovate, very acute. Calyx $\frac{3}{8}$–$\frac{1}{2}$ in. long; tube hairy, $\frac{1}{8}$–$\frac{1}{6}$ in. long; teeth $\frac{1}{4}$–$\frac{1}{3}$ by $\frac{1}{10}$–$\frac{1}{8}$ in., elliptic-lanceolate, acute, the upper part of each glabrous, the lower half with a few scattered hairs. Corolla-tube reaching 1½ in. long, slender, glabrous, without hairs in the mouth; lobes reaching $\frac{7}{16}$ by $\frac{1}{8}$ in., broadly elliptic, obtuse. Style exserted beyond the tube, the exserted portion much shorter than the corolla-lobes; branches of the stigma $\frac{1}{10}$–$\frac{1}{8}$ in. long, linear, recurved. Fruit $\frac{1}{2}$ in. long, ovoid, on hairy pedicels $\frac{1}{2}$ in. long, striate, sparsely hairy, crowned with the persistent calyx-teeth, red when ripe. Fl. B. I. v. 3, p. 140; Talb. Trees, Bomb. ed. 2, p. 193; Woodr. in Journ. Bomb. Nat. v. 11 (1898) p. 645.—Flowers: Mar.

KONKAN: N. & S. Konkan, *Law*! KANARA: Southern Ghâts of N. Kanara, *Talbot*; Gondabel Ghât, *Stocks*!; Nilkund, *Woodrow*!—DISTRIB. India (W. Peninsula).

3. **Ixora nigricans,** *Br. in Wall. Cat.* (1828) 6154. A large evergreen shrub or small tree; young branches, leaves, and inflorescence turning black in drying. Leaves 4–6 by 1½–2½ in., membranous, elliptic-oblong, elliptic-lanceolate, or (sometimes) elliptic-obovate, acute or shortly acuminate, glabrous, base acute or rounded; main nerves 12–15 pairs, slender, arched; petioles $\frac{1}{4}$–$\frac{3}{8}$ in. long; stipules shortly triangular at base, cuspidate with a long stiff bristle. Flowers white, odorous, in sessile or peduncled brachiate usually glabrous cymes which are broader than long; bracts at the base of the main peduncles foliaceous, $\frac{3}{8}$ in. long, lanceolate, cuspidate, those beneath the branches of the cyme subulate; bracteoles minute, subulate; buds very narrowly fusiform, not much broader than the corolla-tube. Calyx glabrous, $\frac{1}{10}$ in. long; teeth $\frac{1}{25}$ in. long, triangular, acute, subfleshy. Corolla-tube $\frac{3}{8}$ in. long, slender, glabrous, without hairs in the mouth; lobes $\frac{3}{16}$ by $\frac{1}{10}$ in., oblong, subacute, glabrous. Style glabrous. Stigma-branches recurved. Fruit globose or didymous, size of a pea. Seeds plano-convex, rugose on the back. Fl. B. I. v. 3, p. 148; Dalz. & Gibs. p. 113; Wight, Icon. t. 318;

Talb. Trees, Bomb. ed. 2, p. 195; Woodr. in Journ. Bomb. Nat. v. 11 (1898) p. 646.—Flowers more or less throughout the year. VERN. *Kát-kuda.*

Common in thick shaded jungles of the Gháts, *Dalzell & Gibson.* KONKAN: Miradonger near Pen, *Kanitkar*! DECCAN: Lanoli, *Woodrow*!; Khandala, *Woodrow*; Mahableshwar, *Cooke*!, *Woodrow.* KANARA: Kumpta, *Woodrow*; Kála naddi, *Ritchie*, 351!; common in the evergreen forests of N. Kanara, *Talbot.*—DISTRIB. India (E. & W. Peninsula, Birma); Malay Archipelago.

VAR. *arguta*, Hook. f. Fl. B. I. v. 3, p. 149. Leaves narrowly oblanceolate or elliptic-lanceolate, acuminate, 4–5 by 1–$1\frac{1}{4}$ in.

S. M. COUNTRY: Párva Ghát, *Ritchie*, $\frac{351}{2}$!

4. **Ixora elongata,** *Heyne, in Wall. Cat.* (1828) 6131. A small shrub, glabrous except the calyx, bracts and corolla-lobes. Leaves 4–7 by $1\frac{5}{8}$–$2\frac{1}{4}$ in., elliptic-lanceolate, obtuse, or subacute, glabrous, base narrowed into the petiole; main nerves 10–15 pairs; petioles $\frac{1}{4}$–$\frac{3}{8}$ in. long; stipules broadly ovate, with a long slender cuspidate point. Flowers pink, in peduncled brachiate cymes; main peduncles 4–7 in. long, with a pair of sessile leaves 1–4 in. long below the middle; branches of the cyme hairy, the lowest pair sometimes 3 in. long; bracteoles linear, $\frac{1}{20}$ in. long, very hairy. Calyx $\frac{1}{12}$ in. long, hairy; teeth 4, triangular, subobtuse, hairy, $\frac{1}{30}$ in. long. Corolla-tube $\frac{1}{3}$–$\frac{1}{2}$ in. long, without hairs at the mouth; lobes 4, ovate-oblong, acute, $\frac{1}{4}$ by $\frac{1}{10}$ in., usually hairy on the back. Filaments thick, short. Anthers sagittate at the base, apiculate at the apex. Branches of the stigma $\frac{1}{30}$ in. long, linear. Fruit glabrous, slightly 2-lobed (*Dalzell*), smooth, black when ripe. Fl. B. I. v. 3, p. 141; Talb. Trees, Bomb. ed. 2, p. 194; Woodr. in Journ. Bomb. Nat. v. 11 (1898) p. 645. *Ixora pedunculata*, Dalz. in Kew Journ. Bot. v. 3 (1851) p. 121; Dalz. & Gibs. p. 113.—Flowers: Feb.

KONKAN: *Stocks*! DECCAN: Bhimashankar, *Dalzell*!, *Woodrow.* S. M. COUNTRY: Párva Ghát, *Dalzell & Gibson.* KANARA: Gháts of N. Kanara, *Talbot.*—DISTRIB. India (W. Peninsula).

5. **Ixora brachiata,** *Roxb. Hort. Beng.* (1814) p. 10. A small tree 15–30 ft. high; bark smooth, grey. Leaves 3–$5\frac{1}{2}$ by $1\frac{1}{2}$–$2\frac{1}{4}$, pale when dry, elliptic-oblong or lanceolate, obtuse, reticulately veined, glabrous, usually attenuated at the base; main nerves numerous, faint, very slender; petioles $\frac{1}{4}$–$\frac{3}{4}$ in. long, stout, rugose; stipules short, broad, shortly cuspidate. Flowers white, odorous, in sessile or shortly peduncled cymes brachiate with 2–3 pairs of long puberulous or sometimes nearly glabrous branches; flower-buds globose; the lowest bracts like the stipules, the upper lanceolate-subulate united by a stipule-like membrane across the nodes; bracteoles minute, subulate. Calyx $\frac{1}{20}$ in. long, urceolate; teeth 4, minute, triangular, membranous. Corolla-tube $\frac{1}{8}$–$\frac{1}{6}$ in. long, without hairs in the mouth; lobes $\frac{1}{12}$ by $\frac{1}{16}$ in., broadly oblong, rounded at the apex, deflexed. Style clothed sparingly with long white hairs, not much exserted; branches of the stigma at first connate, usually separating later. Fruit globose or didymous, the size of a pea, smooth, purplish-black, edible. Seeds hemispheric, with a deep pit on the ventral side within which the funicle was attached, rugose. The flowers are the smallest of the genus and the only ones

with globose buds (*Hooker*). Fl. B. I. v. 3, p. 142; Wight, Icon. t. 710; Talb. Trees, Bomb. ed. 2, p. 194.—Flowers: Nov.–Feb. VERN. *Gorbále.*

KONKAN: *Law*!, *Stocks*!; S. Konkan, *Ritchie*, 354! DECCAN: Khandala, *Woodrow*! KANARA: *Mrs. Ward*!; Mendele, *Ritchie*, 354/2.—DISTRIB. India (W. Peninsula).

6. **Ixora parviflora**, *Vahl, Symb.* v. 3 (1724) p. 11, t. 52. A small much-branched evergreen tree; bark thick, reddish-brown; branchlets somewhat compressed, glabrous. Leaves 3–5 by $1\frac{1}{2}$–$2\frac{1}{4}$ in., very coriaceous and hard, reticulately veined, oblong or elliptic, obtuse, glabrous and shining, pale when dry, base usually rounded, sometimes cordate; main lateral nerves 8–10 pairs, slender, faint; petioles scarcely $\frac{1}{8}$ in. long, rugose; stipules $\frac{1}{8}$ in. long, broadly ovate, with a cuspidate point about $\frac{1}{8}$ in. long. Flowers white, odorous, small and very numerous, in subglobose clusters, in sessile cymes brachiate with 3–5 pairs of short branches; pedicels very short or 0; bracts and bracteoles as in *I. brachiata*; flower-buds ellipsoid. Calyx $\frac{1}{16}$ in. long, ovoid-oblong; teeth 4, minute, not more than $\frac{1}{50}$ in. long, triangular, subacute. Corolla-tube $\frac{1}{3}$–$\frac{7}{16}$ in. long, without hairs in the mouth; lobes 4, linear-oblong, obtuse, $\frac{3}{16}$–$\frac{1}{4}$ by $\frac{1}{20}$ in. Style densely clothed with white hairs; branches of the stigma elliptic-lanceolate. Fruit $\frac{1}{4}$ in. in diam., didymous. Fl. B. I. v. 3, p. 142; Grah. Cat. p. 92; Dalz. & Gibs. p. 113; Trim. Fl. Ceyl. v. 2, p. 348; Talb. Trees, Bomb. ed. 2, p. 194; Woodr. in Journ. Bomb. Nat. v. 11 (1898) p. 645; Watt, Dict. Econ. Prod. v. 4, p. 533.—Flowers: Jan.–Apr. VERN. *Rai-Kudá.*

Throughout the Presidency in deciduous forests, *Talbot*. KONKAN: Elephanta, *Graham*; Matheran, *Cooke*!, *Woodrow*! DECCAN: Nasik, *Kanitkar*!; Khandala, *Cooke*!; Gokak, *Bhiva*! S. M. COUNTRY: Kákti hills near Belgaum, *Ritchie*, 1788! KANARA: on the Kála naddi, *Ritchie*!—DISTRIB. Throughout a considerable part of India, chiefly in hilly districts; Ceylon.

The tree has been called the "*Torch Tree*" in consequence of its branches having been used by dák runners for torches. The wood is very hard and close-grained and takes a good polish.

7. **Ixora coccinea**, *Linn. Sp. Pl.* (1753) p. 110. A glabrous shrub 2–3 ft. high. Leaves 2–4 by $1\frac{1}{4}$–$2\frac{1}{2}$ in., coriaceous, pale when dry, sessile or nearly so, oblong, obtuse (rarely acute), apiculate, base rounded or subcordate; main nerves 8–12 pairs, slender; stipules with a long rigid cuspidate point. Flowers numerous, bright-scarlet, in dense sessile or very shortly peduncled corymbiform cymes; pedicels very short, glabrous or puberulous; bracts and bracteoles small, lanceolate-subulate, acute; buds fusiform, very acute. Calyx $\frac{1}{10}$ in. long, glabrous; teeth $\frac{1}{20}$ in. long, triangular, acute. Corolla-tube reaching $1\frac{1}{2}$ in. long, slender, without hairs in the mouth; lobes $\frac{1}{2}$ by $\frac{1}{6}$–$\frac{1}{5}$ in., elliptic-oblong, subacute. Fruit globose, size of a pea, smooth, fleshy, crowned with the calyx-teeth, purple when ripe. Seeds deeply ventrally concave. Fl. B. I. v. 3, p. 145; Grah. Cat. p. 91; Dalz. & Gibs. p. 112; Wight, Icon. t. 153; Trim. Fl. Ceyl. v. 2, p. 348; Talb. Trees, Bomb. ed. 2, p. 194; Woodr. in Journ. Bomb. Nat. v. 11 (1898) p. 646; Watt, Dict. Econ. Prod. v. 4, p. 533. *Ixora Bandhuca*, Roxb. Hort. Beng. (1814) p. 10; Grah. Cat. p. 92.—Flowers more or less throughout the year. VERN. *Bakorá.*

A handsome shrub known as the "*Flame of the Woods*," often grown in gardens, but indigenous in the Presidency. KONKAN: common, *Dalzell & Gibson*; S. Konkan, *Ritchie*, 348!; Vingorla, *Woodrow*!; Ooran (an island in Bombay harbour), *Cooke*!;

Salsette, *Graham*; Thana, *Woodrow*; Ratnagiri, *Kanitkar*! DECCAN: Kolhapur, *Cooke*! KANARA: common in the moist forests of N. Kanara near the sea-coast, *Talbot*; Kála naddi, *Ritchie*, 348!—DISTRIB. Cultivated throughout India as an ornamental shrub, indigenous in the W. Peninsula; Ceylon.

23. PAVETTA, Linn.

Shrubs or small trees. Leaves opposite, petiolate, usually membranous; stipules intrapetiolar, usually connate into a lax sheath, deciduous. Flowers in axillary or terminal 3-chotomously branched usually many-flowered corymbose cymes, white or greenish, bracteolate. Calyx-tube ovoid, turbinate or campanulate; lobes 4 (very rarely 5), short or long. Corolla hypocrateriform; tube slender, cylindric; throat naked or bearded; lobes 4 (very rarely 5), frequently longer than the tube, twisted. Stamens 4 (very rarely 5), inserted in the throat or mouth of the corolla; filaments short or long, or 0. Ovary 2-celled; ovules solitary in each cell, attached to the middle of the septum, amphitropous, the placenta fleshy, often tumid; style long, much exserted; stigma fusiform or somewhat clavate, undivided or 2-dentate. Berry pisiform, fleshy, with 2 pyrenes which are convex on the back and concave on the face. Seeds conform to the pyrenes; testa membranous; albumen horny; cotyledons foliaceous; radicle inferior.—DISTRIB. Tropics of the Old World and S. Africa; species about 60.

A genus very closely allied to *Ixora* from which it may be distinguished by the stipules, the very long style, and the tumid placentas.

Leaves pale when dry; corolla-tube $\frac{1}{2}$ in. long .... 1. *P. indica.*
Leaves black when dry; corolla-tube 1 in. long .... 2. *P. hispidula*, [var. *siphonantha*.

1. **Pavetta indica,** *Linn. Sp. Pl.* (1753) p. 110. A stout bushy shrub 2–4 ft. high; bark thin, smooth, yellowish; young branches terete, glabrous. Leaves 3–6 by 1–$2\frac{1}{2}$ in., membranous, variable in shape and size, elliptic-oblong or elliptic-lanceolate, sometimes obovate-oblong, obtuse, acute or acuminate, glabrous on both sides, base tapering; main nerves 8–10 pairs; petioles $\frac{1}{4}$–$\frac{1}{2}$ in. long; stipules connate, triangular, acute, thin, deciduous. Flowers white, odorous, in terminal sessile corymbose pubescent cymes; pedicels $\frac{1}{6}$–$\frac{1}{4}$ in. long, densely pubescent; bracts broad, membranous, the lower cupular; buds oblong-clavate. Calyx densely pubescent, $\frac{1}{8}$ in. long; tube narrowly campanulate; teeth $\frac{1}{10}$ in. long, triangular, acute, slightly reflexed at the tip. Corolla-tube $\frac{1}{2}$ in. long; lobes $\frac{1}{4}$–$\frac{5}{16}$ in. by $\frac{1}{10}$ in., linear-oblong, subacute. Style white, glabrous or nearly so; stigma green, narrowly clavate, puberulous. Fruit $\frac{1}{4}$–$\frac{3}{8}$ in. in diam., globose, black, smooth. In all the specimens I have examined from the Bombay hills I have found the pedicels and calyx to be densely pubescent even though the leaves were quite glabrous. Fl. B. I. v. 3, p. 150; Grah. Cat. p. 92; Dalz. & Gibs. p. 112; Wight, Icon. t. 148; Trim. Fl. Ceyl. v. 2, p. 349; Talb. Trees, Bomb. ed. 2, p. 195; Woodr. in Journ. Bomb. Nat. v. 11 (1898) p. 646; Watt, Dict. Econ. Prod. v. 6, part 1, p. 114.—Flowers: Mar.–May. VERN. *Pâpat*.

Very common on hills throughout the Presidency. KONKAN: Matheran, *H. M. Birdwood*, *Woodrow*; Karanja hill, *Dalzell & Gibson*. DECCAN: Mahableshwar, very common, *Cooke*!, *Graham*; Khandala, *Woodrow*!; Igatpuri, *Kanitkar*!—DISTRIB. Throughout India; Ceylon, Malay Archipelago, S. China, N. Australia.

VAR. *tomentosa*, Hook. f. in Fl. B. I. v. 3 (1880) p. 150. Leaves glabrous or slightly or harshly puberulous above, tomentose or softly villous beneath. Cymes pubescent, tomentose or softly villous. Talb. Trees, Bomb. ed. 2, p. 195. *Pavetta tomentosa* (sp.), Roxb. ex Sm. in Rees Cyclop. v. 26 (1819) n. 2; Wight & Arn. Prodr. p. 431. *P. Brunonis*, Wight, Icon. t. 1065; Dalz. & Gibs. p. 112.

2. **Pavetta hispidula,** *Wight & Arn. Prodr.* (1834) p. 431; var. **siphonantha,** *Hook. f. Fl. B. I.* v. 3, p. 151. A slender branched shrub 3–12 ft. high (*Ritchie*). Leaves 3–7 by 1–2½ in., elliptic-lanceolate, acuminate, black when dry, glabrous, attenuated into the petiole; petioles ½–1 in. long; stipules connate, triangular, acute, from a broad base, membranous, pilose within. Flowers white, in large terminal corymbose more or less pubescent peduncled cymes. Calyx pubescent, ⅛ in. long; teeth $\frac{1}{25}$ in. long, triangular, acute, slightly reflexed at the tip. Corolla-tube 1–1⅛ in. long, slender, glabrous; lobes ¼–⅓ by $\frac{1}{12}$–$\frac{1}{10}$ in., linear-oblong, subacute. Style very slender, exserted for 1½ in. or even more, gradually tapering; stigma hardly distinguishable from the style, scarcely if at all fusiform. Fruit size of a pea, globose, smooth, purple. Talb. Trees, Bomb. ed. 2, p. 195; Woodr. in Journ. Bomb. Nat. v. 11 (1898) p. 646. *Pavetta siphonantha* (sp.), Dalz. in Kew Journ. Bot. v. 2 (1850) p. 133; Dalz. & Gibs. p. 112; Bedd. For. Man. in Flor. Sylvat. p. cxxxiv–8.—Flowers: May.

KONKAN: *Stocks*!, *Dalzell*!; Matheran, *Woodrow*; Bhimashankar, *Woodrow*. S. M. COUNTRY: Parpoli Ghát (Belgaum districts), *Dalzell & Gibson*; Rámghát, *Ritchie*, 676! KANARA: Supa Ghâts of N. Kanara (rare), *Talbot*; Mendele, *Ritchie*, 676!—DISTRIB. India (W. Peninsula).

24. **MORINDA,** Linn.

Shrubs or trees; branches terete or obscurely 4-gonous. Leaves opposite, rarely 3-nately verticillate, usually membranous; stipules connate, sheathing. Flowers in axillary or terminal simple, panicled, or umbellate heads, white, more or less connate by the calyces. Calyx-tube urceolate or hemispheric; limb short, truncate or obscurely toothed, persistent. Corolla-tube short or long; lobes 4–7, coriaceous, valvate in bud. Stamens 4–7; filaments short; anthers linear or oblong. Ovary 2- or (sometimes imperfectly) 4-celled; ovules solitary, ascending from towards the base of the septum in each cell; style slender, with 2 short or long linear branches. Fruit a syncarpium formed by the succulent enlarged calyces enclosing many cartilaginous or bony 1-seeded pyrenes which sometimes cohere into a 2–4-celled putamen, rarely of nearly free drupes. Seeds obovoid or reniform; testa membranous; albumen fleshy or horny; embryo terete; radicle inferior.

Leaves 5–8 in. long, glabrous, shining .... 1. *M. citrifolia*.
Leaves 4–6 in. long, tomentose, dull, not shining .... 2. *M. tinctoria*, [var. *tomentosa*.

1. **Morinda citrifolia,** *Linn. Sp. Pl.* (1753) p. 176. A small glabrous tree; trunk straight; bark smooth, yellowish-white; branchlets obtusely 4-angled. Leaves 5–8 by 3–4 in., broadly elliptic, acute, acuminate or obtuse, bright-green, glabrous, shining, one of the pair next the peduncle often suppressed, base acute; main nerves 8–10 pairs, prominent; petioles ½ in. long; stipules connate, short, broad, obtuse,

membranous. Flowers white, in dense ovoid heads over 1 in. long; peduncles solitary (rarely 2–3 together), usually leaf-opposed, 1–2 in. long. Calyx-limb truncate. Corolla infundibuliform; tube ⅝ in. long, the mouth hairy; lobes 5, lanceolate, acute. Stamens 5; filaments hairy; anthers about ½-exserted. Fruit white when ripe, smooth and glossy, about the size of a small egg; pyrenes ovoid, compressed, concavo-convex, winged on the edge. Fl. B. I. v. 3, p. 155; Grah. Cat. p. 90; Dalz. & Gibs. p. 114; Gærtn. Fruct. v. 1, t. 29; Wall. Cat. 8418; Roxb. Fl. Ind. v. 1, p. 541; Talb. Trees, Bomb. ed. 2, p. 196; Woodr. in Journ. Bomb. Nat. v. 11 (1898) p. 646; Watt, Dict. Econ. Prod. v. 5, p. 261.—Flowers: May–June. Vern. *A'l*; *Bártondi.*

Cultivated widely in many places throughout India, found also as an escape, but not truly wild.—It has not been much cultivated in the Bombay Presidency except in Khandesh and less commonly at Pandarpur in the Deccan. The roots furnish a valuable red dye. A very full description of the mode of cultivation of the tree and of preparing and using the dye may be found in Watt's Dict. Econ. Prod. l. c.

Var. 1. *bracteata*, Hook. f. Fl. B. I. v. 3 (1880) p. 156. Anthers included within the hairy mouth of the corolla-tube. Calyx-limb often with a lanceolate or spathulate white foliaceous lobe sometimes nearly ½ in. long. Talb. Trees, Bomb. ed. 2, p. 196; Woodr. in Journ. Bomb. Nat. v. 11 (1898) p. 646. *Morinda bracteata*, Roxb. Hort. Beng. p. 15; Fl. Ind. v. 1, p. 544; Dalz. & Gibs. p. 114. *M. citrifolia*, Trim. Fl. Ceyl. v. 2, p. 354 (*not* of Linn.).

Konkan: Malwán, *Dalzell & Gibson*; Vingorla, *Dalzell & Gibson*; coast of the Konkan near the sea, *Talbot*; near Marmagao close to the sea, *Woodrow.*

This ought perhaps to take rank as a separate species. It is certainly indigenous along the coast, while *M. citrifolia* is an introduction.

Var. 2. *elliptica*, Hook. f. Fl. B. I. v. 3 (1880) p. 156. Leaves 6–8 in. long, elliptic, polished, acuminate; nerves strong on both surfaces.

I have seen no authentic specimens which can with certainty be referred to Bombay. There is one specimen in Herb. Kew. marked "Herb. Stocks," but, like many of the specimens in the Stocksian Herbarium, this has had no locality assigned to it. It is merely a supposition that this specimen was collected in the Konkan. Other specimens of the var. in Herb. Kew. have come from Tenasserim, the Andamans, Birma, the Malay Peninsula, Malacca.

2. **Morinda tinctoria,** *Roxb. Hort. Beng.* (1814) p. 15, var. **tomentosa,** *Hook. f. Fl. B. I.* v. 2, p. 156. A small tree; young branches 4-angled, tomentose. Leaves 4–6 by 2–3 in., elliptic, or oblong-lanceolate, acuminate, tomentose on both surfaces, one of the pair of leaves near the peduncle usually suppressed or its place sometimes taken by a small linear leaf from the axil of which the peduncle arises; petioles ¼–½ in. long, densely tomentose; stipules often bifid, the lobes triangular, acute. Flowers pure white, in globose heads; peduncles ¾–1 in. long, tomentose, solitary, leaf-opposed, or sometimes in the axil of a small linear leaf which has taken the place of the suppressed leaf. Calyx ⅛ in. long, truncate; the limb sometimes (though rarely) with a foliaceous oblong obtuse or subacute veined lobe reaching ⅝ in. long, hairy outside. Corolla-tube ⅞–1 in. long, very hairy outside, but not hairy at the mouth; lobes ⅜–$\frac{7}{16}$ by ⅛–⅙ in., oblong, obtuse or subacute, hairy on the back. Anthers included within the tube. Fruit globose

or ellipsoid, fleshy, ¾ in. in diam.—Flowers: Apr. Talb. Trees, Bomb. ed. 2, p. 196. *Morinda tomentosa* (sp.), Heyne, in Roth, Nov. Pl. Sp. (1821) p. 147; Dalz. & Gibs. p. 114.

DECCAN: Chattersingi hill near Poona, *Bhiva*!; Sholapur districts, *Woodrow*!; Gokák jungles, *Ritchie*, 1785!; Hotgi, *Cooke*! S. M. COUNTRY: Badami, *Woodrow*! KANARA: *Kanitkar*!

25. PSYCHOTRIA, Linn.

Shrubs or small trees, usually erect. Leaves opposite, rarely whorled; stipules intrapetiolar, often connate, solitary or in pairs, often with glandular hairs. Flowers in terminal (rarely axillary) cymes, heads or fascicles, bracteate or not. Calyx-tube short; limb often deciduous. Corolla-tube straight, short (in the Indian species), throat naked or hairy; lobes 5, rarely 4 or 6, valvate in bud. Stamens as many as the corolla-lobes, inserted on the throat or mouth of the corolla; filaments short or long; anthers included or exserted. Ovary 2-celled; ovules solitary in each cell, basal, erect, anatropous, usually cuneate; style long or short, with 2 branches. Fruit small, ovoid, globose or oblong (rarely didymous), with 2 plano-convex 1-seeded pyrenes, rarely separating into 2 cocci. Seeds usually plano-convex (the ventral base rarely concave), often longitudinally grooved; testa thin; albumen hard, sometimes ruminate; embryo small, basal; cotyledons broad, thin; radicle inferior.—DISTRIB. Tropics of the world; species about 500.

Albumen ruminate.
  Cyme-branches whorled.
    Flowers mixed with reddish-brown hairs .... 1. *P. Thwaitesii.*
    Flowers not mixed with reddish-brown hairs.
      Calyx truncate, teeth 0 or obscure; seeds without dorsal ridges .... 2. *P. truncata.*
      Calyx-teeth distinct, with membranous ciliate margins; seeds with 1 dorsal ridge .... 3. *P. Dalzellii.*
  Cyme-branches opposite, bright-yellow in fruit; seeds with 1 dorsal ridge .... 4. *P. flavida.*
Albumen uniform (not ruminate).
  Cyme-branches opposite or whorled; seeds with 1 dorsal ridge .... 5. *P. canarensis.*
  Cyme-branches opposite; seeds with 4 dorsal ridges .... 6. *P. octosulcata.*

1. **Psychotria Thwaitesii,** *Hook. f. Fl. B. I.* v. 3 (1880) p. 162. A stout glabrous shrub; branchlets smooth, compressed. Leaves 4–8 by 1½–2¾ in., subcoriaceous, elliptic-oblong, obovate-oblong or oblong-lanceolate, acuminate or acute, glabrous; base tapering into the petiole; main nerves 12–15 pairs, prominent; petioles ¼–¾ in. long; stipules variable, usually broadly ovate, acute, small. Flowers sessile or nearly sessile, with reddish-brown hairs at their bases, in small round heads on the usually whorled glabrous branches of pyramidal peduncled cymes. Calyx $\frac{1}{12}$ in. long; limb deciduous; segments broad. Corolla ⅛ in. long; tube short, straight, with a few white hairs at the mouth; lobes $\frac{1}{16}$ in. long, oblong, obtuse. Fruit ellipsoid or subglobose, ¼–⅜ in. in diam., marked with the scar of but not crowned by the calyx-limb; pyrenes without furrows, plano-convex. Seeds plano-convex; albumen very ruminate. Trim. Fl. Ceyl. v. 2, p. 358; Talb. Trees, Bomb. ed. 2, p. 197; Woodr. in Journ. Bomb. Nat. v. 11 (1898) p. 646.—Flowers: Mar.–Apr.

KANARA: Southern Ghâts of N. Kanara in evergreen forests; common on the Nilkund Ghât, *Talbot*; Falls of Gairsoppa, *Talbot*, 258!

VAR. *peninsularis*, Hook. f. Fl. B. I. l. c. Leaves smaller, more obovate; cymes always sessile, their branches moderate or short, or 0, or the inflorescence a peduncled globose head.

KONKAN: *Law*, 34!

2. **Psychotria truncata,** *Wall. in Roxb. Fl. Ind. ed. Carey*, v. 2 (1824) p. 162. A stout erect glabrous shrub. Leaves 4–7 by 2–3 in., green above, pale beneath, obovate, shortly and abruptly acuminate, margins slightly recurved, base cuneate; main nerves 14–16 pairs, arcuate, very prominent; petioles $\frac{1}{4}$–1 in. long, stout; stipules large, reaching sometimes 1 in. and even more in length, combined into a sheath, very caducous. Flowers sessile or shortly pedicelled, in dense terminal cymes; branches long or short, usually whorled. Calyx $\frac{1}{16}$ in. long, broadly campanulate, truncate; teeth 0 or very obscure. Corolla waxy-white; tube $\frac{1}{10}$ in. long, straight, broad, glabrous outside, with a ring of hairs at the mouth; lobes $\frac{1}{8}$ in. long, oblong, subacute. Fruit ellipsoid, $\frac{1}{3}$ in. long, smooth, crowned by the truncate calyx; pyrenes without furrows, plano-convex. Seeds plano-convex; albumen ruminate. Talb. Trees, Bomb. ed. 2, p. 197; Woodr. in Journ. Bomb. Nat. v. 11 (1898) p. 646. *Grumilea vaginans*, Dalz. in Dalz. & Gibs. Bo. Fl. (1861) p. 111. *Grumilea congesta*, Grah. Cat. p. 92 (*not* of Wight & Arn.).—Flowers: Apr.–May.

DECCAN: Mahableshwar, *Cooke*!, *Woodrow*; near Carnac Point, Mahableshwar, *H. M. Birdwood*. S. M. COUNTRY: Chorla Ghât, *Ritchie*, 1792! KANARA: *Law*!; Mendele, *Ritchie*, 1792!; Diggi, *Woodrow*; evergreen forests of N. Kanara Ghâts, *Talbot*.—DISTRIB. India (W. Peninsula).

3. **Psychotria Dalzellii,** *Hook. f. Fl. B. I.* v. 3 (1880) p. 163. A large shrub reaching 20 ft. high; stem 2 in. in diam. at the base, not much branched. Leaves coriaceous, $5\frac{1}{2}$–9 by 2–$3\frac{1}{4}$ in., obovate-oblong, rounded and apiculate at the apex, glabrous, cuneate at the base; main nerves 12–20 pairs, prominent; petioles $\frac{1}{4}$–$\frac{1}{2}$ in. long, stout; stipules $\frac{7}{8}$ in. long, broadly ovate, acuminate. Flowers in terminal peduncled brachiate cymes; branches whorled, the lower usually in whorls of 5, subtended by 4 large bracts, the upper in whorls of 3 subtended by 2 bracts; branches of the lower whorl often reaching 2 in. long; each branch carrying a head of 1–5 sessile or nearly sessile flowers surrounded by large oblong or suborbicular more or less cucullate bracteoles. Calyx broadly campanulate, glabrous, $\frac{1}{8}$ in. long; teeth a little shorter than the tube, oblong, rounded or truncate at the apex, emarginate, the margins membranous, ciliate. Corolla-tube very short, straight, densely bearded in the throat; lobes $\frac{1}{8}$ by $\frac{1}{20}$ in., ovate-oblong, acute. Fruit $\frac{3}{8}$ in. in diam., subglobose, smooth, succulent, black when ripe, edible, crowned by the calyx-limb; pyrenes with 1 conspicuous dorsal ridge. Seeds plano-convex, rugose, with a conspicuous dorsal ridge; albumen ruminate. Talb. Trees, Bomb. ed. 2, p. 197; Woodr. in Journ. Bomb. Nat. v. 11 (1898) p. 646. *Psychotria bracteata*, Wight & Arn. Prodr. (1834) p. 434 (not of DC.).—Flowers: June–July.

The name *P. bracteata* given to the plant by Wight & Arn. (1834) had been given by DC. in 1830 to a different plant, a native of Guiana.

KONKAN: *Stocks!*, *Dalzell!*; Banda (Wari Country), *Kanitkar!* KANARA: *Woodrow!*; common throughout the evergreen forests of N. Kanara, *Talbot*; Yellapur, *Talbot*, 235!—DISTRIB. India (W. Peninsula), apparently endemic.

4. **Psychotria flavida,** *Talbot, Trees & Shrubs, Bomb.* ed. 1 (1894) p. 113. A small shrub. Leaves coriaceous, 4–10 by 2–4 in., elliptic-oblong, acute or shortly acuminate, glabrous, tapering to the base; main nerves 10–12 pairs; petioles $\frac{1}{4}$–$\frac{3}{8}$ in. long; stipules ovate, acuminate, deciduous. Flowers numerous, small, in terminal peduncled cymes; peduncles 1–2 in. long; cyme-branches opposite, flattened, shorter than the peduncles; pedicels very short; bracts leafy, deciduous. Calyx $\frac{1}{16}$–$\frac{1}{12}$ in. long, truncate; teeth obscure or 0. Corolla $\frac{1}{8}$ in. long; tube $\frac{1}{10}$ in. long, densely hairy in the throat inside. Fruit $\frac{1}{4}$ in. in diam., ellipsoid, compressed, crowned with the calyx, black when ripe; pyrenes with 1 dorsal ridge. Seeds plano-convex, with a narrow dorsal ridge, rugose, black; albumen ruminate. Cyme-branches turning bright yellow in fruit. Talb. Trees, Bomb. ed. 2, p. 197. Closely allied to *P. nudiflora*, Wight & Arn., from which it differs by the short corolla-tube which is densely hairy within, that of *P. nudiflora* being longer and glabrous inside.—Flowers: May–July. VERN. *Shivan-Yallaki.*

KONKAN: *Hohenhacker*, 735 *a*!, *Law*! KANARA: abundant in the evergreen forests of Sirsi and Siddapur; Hulikal, *Talbot*, 3661!; Ghâts near Yellapur, *Talbot*, 236!—DISTRIB. Konkan and Kanara, apparently endemic.

5. **Psychotria canarensis,** *Talbot, Trees & Shrubs, Bomb.* ed. 1 (1894) p. 113. A small erect shrub with smooth branches. Leaves 2–5 by $\frac{1}{2}$–1$\frac{3}{4}$ in., ovate, obovate, or lanceolate, acute, thin, nearly glabrous, minutely punctate and pale beneath, attenuate at the base; main nerves 8 pairs, distinctly looping within the margin; petioles $\frac{1}{4}$ in. long; stipules short, acute, caducous. Flowers small, sessile, in few- or many-flowered mostly terminal cymes 1–3 in. long; branches opposite or whorled, slender, as long as or longer than the peduncles; bracts and bracteoles minute, linear, caducous. Calyx short, tubular, 4-toothed. Corolla white, tubular or slightly funnel-shaped, the mouth of the tube hairy inside; lobes 4, spreading or reflexed. Stamens at the mouth of the tube; filaments very short. Ovary 4-lobed; style as long as the corolla-tube. Fruit ovoid, slightly curved, black, shining, ridged, about $\frac{1}{2}$ in. long, crowned with the toothed calyx. Seeds with 1 ridge along the back, ventrally flat; albumen uniform. There is but 1 specimen in Herb. Kew. (in fruit). The description has been taken from Mr. Talbot (*l. c.*). Talb. in Journ. Bomb. Nat. v. 11 (1898) p. 691, t. 12; Trees, Bomb. ed. 2, p. 197.

KANARA: moist evergreen forests near the Falls of Gairsoppa in N. Kanara, *Talbot*!—DISTRIB. Apparently endemic.

6. **Psychotria octosulcata,** *Talbot, in Journ. Bomb. Nat. Hist. Soc.* v. 11 (1897) p. 237, t. 7. An erect shrub 10–20 ft. high; stem 1–2 in. in diam. at the base; bark smooth; branches green, glabrous. Leaves thin, 3–6 by 1–2 in., elliptic, obovate, or oblanceolate, shortly and abruptly acuminate, shining above, pale beneath, glabrous, base much tapered; main nerves 8–10 pairs, prominent, frequently with galls in their axils; petioles $\frac{1}{4}$–$\frac{1}{2}$ in. long; stipules connate at the base, acuminate, deciduous. Flowers white, in short terminal corymbose cymes 1–2 in. long; branches opposite. Calyx $\frac{1}{20}$ in. long; teeth 5, minute, triangular.

Corolla-tube very short, hairy at the mouth inside. Fruit obovoid or pyriform, $\frac{3}{8}$–$\frac{1}{2}$ in. long, straight or slightly curved, 8-ridged, black and succulent when ripe, soon drying and becoming regularly ridged with a flattened top. Seeds dorsally 4-ridged (*Talbot*); albumen uniform, horny. Talb. Trees, Bomb. ed. 2, p. 198. *Psychotria sarmentosa*, Woodr. in Journ. Bomb. Nat. v. 11 (1898) p. 646 (*not* of Blume).—Flowers: July–Aug.

KANARA: common in some of the evergreen forests of the Siddapur and Sirsi subdivisions of N. Kanara, *Talbot*; Yacombi, *Talbot*, 3556!, *Woodrow*!, *Bhiva*!—DISTRIB. Apparently endemic.

26. CHASALIA, Commers.

Shrubs or small trees; branchlets terete. Leaves opposite or 3-nately whorled, petiolate; stipules intrapetiolar, simple or 2-fid, free or connate. Flowers in terminal cymes. Calyx-tube ovoid or subglobose; limb truncate or 5-toothed, persistent. Corolla-tube elongate, terete, usually curved, the throat bearded or naked; lobes 5, much smaller than the tube, erect or spreading, valvate. Stamens 5, inserted in the corolla-tube; filaments 0 or short. Disk annular or tumid. Ovary 2-celled; ovules solitary in each cell, erect from the base. Fruit dry or slightly fleshy; pyrenes 2, very thin, very concave on the ventral face, cup-shaped (crescent-shaped in section). Seeds orbicular, compressed, convex on the back, concave on the ventral face; testa membranous; albumen horny, not ruminate; embryo small; cotyledons broad; radicle terete, inferior.—DISTRIB. Asia, Tropical Africa, Mascarene Islands; species 10.

1. **Chasalia curviflora,** *Thw. Enum.* (1859) p. 150. A small shrub 2–4½ ft. high; branchlets compressed, glabrous. Leaves 5–9 by 1½–2¾ in., elliptic, oblong-lanceolate, or sometimes obovate, acute, acuminate, or obtuse, glabrous, base tapering, sometimes much so; main nerves 8–10 pairs; petioles ¼–1¼ in. long, often obscure owing to the tapering of the leaf-blade; stipules short, ¼ in. long, usually 2-fid. Flowers dimorphic, one form with exserted anthers and included styles, the other the opposite, sessile or nearly so, in trichotomously branched terminal peduncled cymes 1½–2 in. long; peduncles 1–2 in. long; branches short, often purplish; bracts persistent, ovate-lanceolate or subulate. Calyx $\frac{1}{12}$ in. long, glabrous; limb slightly dilated above; teeth scarcely $\frac{1}{60}$ in. long, triangular, acute. Corolla waxy-white or pinkish, with a yellow throat, variable in length, sometimes reaching nearly ¾ in. long; tube slender, glabrous outside, hairy in the throat inside; lobes $\frac{1}{10}$ in. long, oblong, subobtuse. Berry size of a pea, depressed-globose or more or less didymous, dark-purple; pyrenes thin, dorsally compressed. Fl. B. I. v. 3, p. 176; Trim. Fl. Ceyl. v. 2, p. 362; Talb. Trees, Bomb. ed. 2, p. 198; Woodr. in Journ. Bomb. Nat. v. 11 (1898) p. 646. *Psychotria longifolia*, Dalz. in Kew Journ. Bot. v. 2 (1850) p. 133 (*not* of Beddome). *Psychotria ambigua*, Wight & Arn. Prodr. p. 433; Wight, Ill. t. 127; Dalz. & Gibs. p. 111.—Flowers: Apr.–July.

KONKAN: *Law*!; Malwán, *Ritchie*, 1793! S. M. COUNTRY: Párva Ghát, *Dalzell & Gibson*, *Ritchie*, 1795! KANARA: evergreen forests of N. Kanara, *Talbot*; Karwar, *Woodrow*; Divimana, *Woodrow*; Siddapur, *Woodrow*; Usheli, *Ritchie*, 1793!—DISTRIB. More or less throughout India; Ceylon, Malaya, Borneo.

27. SAPROSMA, Blume.

Shrubs usually glabrous, fetid when bruised, often with subulate bristles at the tips of the branches and bases of the peduncles. Leaves opposite or 3–4-whorled, membranous; stipules interpetiolar, broad, usually connate, 1–3-cuspidate, deciduous. Flowers small, white, sessile and congested, or on axillary or terminal peduncles, solitary or 3-nate; bracts and bracteoles minute, often connate. Calyx-tube obconic; limb dilated, 4–6-lobed or -toothed, persistent. Corolla campanulate or infundibuliform, throat villous; lobes 4–5, broad, obtuse, valvate, with inflexed flat or crisped margins. Stamens 4–5, in the corolla-throat; filaments short or 0. Ovary 2-celled; ovules solitary in each cell, erect from the base, anatropous. Drupe small; pyrenes 1–2, thin, crustaceous. Seeds erect, plano-convex, the ventral face not hollowed out; testa membranous; cotyledons foliaceous; radicle elongate, terete, truncate, inferior, next the hilum.—DISTRIB. Tropical Asia; species 8.

1. **Saprosma indicum,** *Dalz. in Kew Journ. Bot.* v. 3 (1851) p. 37. A shrub 3–4 ft. high; branches pale, terete, dichotomous, glabrous. Leaves opposite (one of the pair often smaller than the other), sessile or nearly so, $2\frac{1}{2}$–5 by $\frac{7}{8}$–$1\frac{3}{4}$ in., thin, elliptic-oblong or oblong-lanceolate, acute or acuminate, glabrous, base acute or rounded; main nerves 8–10 pairs; stipules usually 3-cuspidate, small. Flowers terminal, on short pedicels, 1–3 in a fascicle at the apices of twigs between the last pairs of leaves; pedicels $\frac{1}{20}$ in. long, with a cup-shaped whorl of rigid connate glabrous scaly bracts at the base. Calyx $\frac{1}{12}$ in. long, cup shaped, unequally 4–5 toothed; teeth triangular, acuminate, with broad sinuses between. Corolla $\frac{1}{4}$ in. long, white; lobes ovate, acute, as long as the tube. Style shortly 2-fid. Berry $\frac{1}{3}$–$\frac{1}{2}$ in. long, ellipsoid, smooth, crowned by the calyx, blue, very fetid, usually 1-seeded by suppression. Seeds broadly ellipsoid or globose. Fl. B. I. v. 3, p. 192; Dalz. & Gibs. p. 112; Trim. Fl. Ceyl. v. 2, p. 368; Talb. Trees, Bomb. ed. 2, p. 199; Woodr. in Journ. Bomb. Nat. v. 11 (1898) p. 646.

KONKAN: Western Ghâts, *Woodrow.* S. M. COUNTRY: Chorla Ghât, *Dalzell!* KANARA: common on the southern Ghâts of N. Kanara, *Talbot.*

28. GEOPHILA, D. Don.

Small slender perennial herbs, creeping and rooting. Leaves opposite, long-petiolate, orbicular-reniform or ovate-cordate; stipules interpetiolar, ovate, entire. Flowers small, solitary or umbelled, subsessile, or on axillary or terminal peduncles; bracts subulate, linear, or leafy. Calyx-tube obovoid; limb short, 5–7-toothed or -partite, persistent. Corolla elongate, infundibuliform, throat hairy; lobes 4–7, spreading or recurved, valvate. Stamens 4–7, inserted on the corolla-tube; filaments filiform; anthers linear. Ovary 2-celled; ovules solitary in each cell, erect from the base, anatropous; style slender, with 2 short or elongate branches. Drupe fleshy; pyrenes 2, plano-convex, not grooved on the ventral face; testa membranous; albumen horny; embryo basal, minute; radicle inferior.—DISTRIB. Tropical Asia, Africa, and America; species 8–10.

1. **Geophila reniformis,** *D. Don, Prodr. Fl. Nepal.* (1825) p. 136. A small creeping herb; stems prostrate, 1 ft. long or less, rooting at the nodes, filiform, puberulous. Leaves ½–1¼ in. in diam., orbicular, deeply cordate, pubescent or glabrous; petioles ½–2 in. long, pubescent; stipules broadly ovate, obtuse. Flowers terminal, solitary, or in peduncled 2–3-flowered umbels; peduncles ¼–1½ in. long; pedicels very short; bracts lanceolate-subulate. Calyx ⅛ in. long; teeth longer than the tube, lanceolate, acuminate, ciliate. Corolla glabrous or slightly pubescent outside; tube dilated upwards, hairy in the throat; lobes ovate-oblong, acute, shorter than the tube, recurved. Berry ¼–⅜ in. in diam., globose, crowned with the large calyx-limb, smooth, pulpy, red when ripe; pyrenes small, flat and smooth on the ventral, rough and bluntly keeled on the convex dorsal surface. Fl. B. I. v. 3, p. 178; Dalz. & Gibs. p. 111; Trim. Fl. Ceyl. v. 2, p. 363; Watt, Dict. Econ. Prod. v. 3, p. 488. *Psychotria herbacea*, Jacq. Enum. Pl. Carib. (1760) p. 16; Grah. Cat. p. 92.

Rare. KONKAN: S. Konkan, *Nimmo* ex *Graham*; Vingorla, *Dalzell & Gibson*.

The plant is said by Kurz to possess properties similar though inferior to those of *Cephælis Ipecacuanha*. See Watt, Dict. Econ. Prod. l. c.—DISTRIB. India (Silhet and Khasia hills, Tenasserim, the Andamans, W. Peninsula); Ceylon.

29. LASIANTHUS, Jack.

Shrubs often fetid; branches terete, compressed at the nodes. Leaves distichous, opposite, shortly petiolate, usually caudate-acuminate, with arching nerves and closely-set transverse veins which are simple or forked, or branched and reticulate; stipules interpetiolar, broad, rarely narrow. Flowers small, in axillary, rarely peduncled, often bracteate clusters, cymes or heads. Calyx-tube short, subglobose, ovoid or oblong; limb short or long, 3–7-toothed or -lobed, persistent. Corolla infundibuliform or hypocrateriform, throat villous; lobes 3-7, valvate. Stamens 4-6 on the corolla-throat; filaments short; anthers included, often apiculate. Ovary 4–9-celled; ovules solitary in each cell, erect from the base, anatropous. Drupes of 4–9 pyrenes; pyrenes cartilaginous or crustaceous, triquetrous, sometimes keeled or winged on the back, 1-seeded. Seeds narrowly oblong, slightly curved; testa membranous; albumen fleshy; embryo terete, elongate; cotyledons short, obtuse; radicle elongate, inferior.—DISTRIB. Chiefly Tropical Asian; species about 80.

Cymes sessile; corolla hairy outside; drupe black .... 1. *L. sessilis.*
Cymes peduncled; corolla glabrous outside; drupe black ...... 2. *L. venulosus.*

1. **Lasianthus sessilis,** *Talbot, Trees & Shrubs, Bomb.* ed. 1 (1894) p. 114. A stout gregarious shrub usually branched from the base; branchlets appressedly hairy. Leaves opposite, 2–5 by 1–2 in., elliptic, acuminate, glabrous above, hairy on the nerves beneath, base acute or rounded; main nerves 6 pairs, prominent beneath, curved upwards; petioles ¼ in. long, hairy; stipules broad, acuminate, hairy. Flowers small, white, sessile, in axillary fascicles; bracts triangular, hairy. Calyx-tube short; teeth triangular, hairy. Corolla tubular, slightly hairy outside, villous inside. Ovary 4-celled; style with 4 branches. Drupe fleshy, black; pyrenes 4, triangular, dorsally tubercled. The

leaves and fruit are fetid when bruised. Talb. Trees, Bomb. ed. 2, p. 199.—Flowers: Aug.-Sept.

The above description is taken from that of Mr. Talbot (*l. c.*). I have seen only 2 somewhat imperfect specimens which are in Herb. Kew.

KANARA: evergreen forests of N. Kanara from Yellapur southwards to Gairsoppa Falls, *Talbot*!

2. **Lasianthus venulosus,** *Wight, in Calc. Journ. Nat. Hist.* v. 6 (1846) p. 508. A large robust nearly glabrous leafy shrub. Leaves light-green, $1\frac{1}{2}$-$3\frac{3}{4}$ by $\frac{5}{8}$-$1\frac{1}{2}$ in., elliptic-oblong, acute, acuminate or cuspidate, glabrous above, more or less hairy on the midrib and nerves beneath, base rounded; main nerves 6–8 pairs, prominent on both sides, the veins between closely reticulated; petioles $\frac{1}{8}$ in. long; stipules small, triangular, hairy. Flowers yellowish-white, sessile, or shortly pedicelled and racemose, on short stout peduncles longer than the petioles; pedicels hairy; bracts hairy. Calyx hairy, $\frac{1}{5}$ in. long; teeth 4-5, linear-subulate, hairy, $\frac{1}{8}$ in. long. Corolla $\frac{1}{3}$ in. long; tube glabrous outside, throat hairy; lobes 4-5, shorter than the tube, villous inside. Stamens 4-5. Style 3-5-branched. Drupe globose, $\frac{1}{5}$ in. in diam., blue, crowned by the persistent calyx-teeth; pyrenes 3-5, with thick walls. Fl. B. I. v. 3, p. 190; Wight, Icon. t. 1032; Bedd. For. Man. in Flor. Sylvat. p. cxxxiv-11, t. 17, f. 5. *Santia venulosa*, Wight & Arn. Prodr. p. 422; Dalz. & Gibs. p. 114.

On the Ghâts but very rare, *Dalzell & Gibson*. Western Ghâts, *De Crespigny* ex *Woodrow*.

This is included on the authority of Dalzell & Gibson (Bo. Fl. p. 114). I am inclined to doubt its occurrence within the limits of the Bombay Presidency. Dalzell says that it is to be found on the Ghâts, and that it is very rare, but there are no specimens in Dalzell's Herbarium in Herb. Kew. The only specimen which reached the Poona Herbarium was furnished by Dr. DeCrespigny and ticketed "Western Ghâts." Neither Woodrow nor Talbot have found the plant, which seems to flourish at higher elevations than are obtainable in the Bombay Presidency.—DISTRIB. India (W. Peninsula).

30. HAMILTONIA, Roxb.

Trichotomously branched undershrubs; branches terete. Leaves opposite, petiolate, fetid when bruised, many nerved; stipules intrapetiolar, short, acute, persistent. Flowers small, in broad terminal trichotomously branched panicled or subumbellate cymes, white or blue, fragrant, bracteate and bracteolate. Calyx-tube ovoid; teeth 4-5, persistent. Corolla infundibuliform; tube long, straight; lobes 5, short, valvate. Stamens 5, inserted in the throat of the corolla; filaments short, subulate; anthers included, obovate-oblong, obtuse. Ovary 5-furrowed, 5-celled, the septa soon disappearing; ovules solitary in each cell, erect from the base, anatropous; style filiform, with 5 linear arms. Capsules 1-celled, from the absorption of the septa, 5-valved, 5- or fewer-seeded. Seeds surrounded by a loose clathrate envelope which splits into 3-4 segments from the base; cotyledons foliaceous, induplicate, cordate; radicle terete, inferior.—DISTRIB. Mountains of the East Indies, 1 species in Northern China; species 3-4.

1. **Hamiltonia suaveolens,** *Roxb. Hort. Beng.* (1814) p. 15. A small shrub with divaricate more or less herbaceous branches. Leaves

rather rigid, 5–8 by $1\frac{1}{2}$–$3\frac{1}{2}$ in., elliptic-lanceolate, acute, glabrous or pubescent above, more or less hairy especially on the nerves beneath, reticulately veined, base acute; main nerves 10–16 pairs, arcuate; petioles $\frac{1}{2}$–$\frac{3}{4}$ in. long; stipules triangular, hairy. Flowers numerous, sessile or nearly so, in subglobose heads in terminal trichotomous pubescent panicles, white or blue; bracteoles beneath the calyx minute, subulate. Calyx $\frac{1}{5}$–$\frac{1}{6}$ in. long, hairy; tube narrow; teeth 4–5, linear-lanceolate, acute, $\frac{1}{12}$ in. long, pubescent. Corolla up to $\frac{1}{2}$ in. long, pubescent outside; tube slender, slightly enlarged at the top, without hairs in the throat; lobes 4–5, ovate, acute, glabrous inside, $\frac{1}{5}$ by $\frac{1}{12}$ in. Capsules ellipsoid, $\frac{1}{5}$–$\frac{1}{6}$ in. long. Seeds 3-quetrous, with a loose arillate lace-like covering. Fl. B. I. v. 3, p. 197; Bedd. For. Man. in Flor. Sylvat. p. cxxxiv–12, t. 17, f. 3; Talb. Trees, Bomb. ed. 2, p. 200; Woodr. in Journ. Bomb. Nat. v. 11 (1898) p. 646; Watt, Dict. Econ. Prod. v. 4, p. 200. *Hamiltonia mysorensis*, Wight & Arn. Prodr. p. 423; Grah. Cat. p. 91; Dalz. & Gibs. p. 115.—Flowers: Oct.–Feb. VERN. *Gidesa*; *Gidas*; *Gidasdwa*.

Hills throughout the Presidency. KONKAN: island of Karanja, *Dalzell & Gibson*. DECCAN: Mahableshwar, *Woodrow*; Fitzgerald Ghát below Mahableshwar, *Cooke*!; Warra Ghát road and Falkland Point, Mahableshwar, *H. M. Birdwood*; Kartrix Ghát, *Woodrow*!; Kamatki Ghát, *Cooke*!; Sinhagad hill near Poona, *Bhiva*! KANARA: on the highest hills of the Supa taluka, N. Kanara, *Talbot*.—DISTRIB. India (tropical and subtropical Himalayas, Central India, W. Peninsula); China.

31. HYDROPHYLAX, Linn. f.

Subsucculent herbs, creeping, glabrous; branches terete. Leaves opposite, sessile, ovate or oblong; stipules combined into an entire or toothed cup-like sheath, persistent. Flowers solitary, axillary, sessile or shortly pedicelled, lilac. Calyx-tube 4-angled; limb 4-partite, the segments ovate-lanceolate, acute, persistent. Corolla subfleshy, between campanulate and infundibuliform; tube with a ring of hairs inside; lobes 4, ovate, valvate. Stamens 4, on the corolla-throat; filaments filiform; anthers linear. Ovary 2-celled; ovules solitary, peltately attached to the septum in each cell; style filiform, pubescent; stigma obscurely 2-lobed. Fruit large, corky, oblong-ovoid, compressed, slightly curved, acutely 3–4-keeled between the acute margins, 1–2-celled, 2-seeded. Seeds linear-oblong, convex on the back, longitudinally grooved on the face; testa minutely granulate; albumen cartilaginous; embryo straight; radicle elongate, terete, inferior.—DISTRIB. Species 3, of which 1 is in India, 1 in Madagascar, and 1 in Natal.

1. **Hydrophylax maritima,** *Linn. f. Suppl.* (1781) p. 126. A perennial herb; stems numerous, prostrate, rooting at the nodes, stout, glabrous, clothed with the cup-like persistent stipules of fallen leaves. Leaves $\frac{1}{2}$–$\frac{3}{4}$ by $\frac{1}{4}$–$\frac{3}{8}$ in., sessile, more or less recurved, ovate-oblong or obovate-oblong, acute, fleshy, much wrinkled when dry, smooth or papillose; stipules large, membranous, forming a cup round the stem, truncate or obscurely toothed, sometimes ciliate. Flowers sessile, solitary, axillary. Calyx $\frac{1}{2}$ in. long, glabrous; teeth lanceolate or narrowly triangular, acute, $\frac{1}{8}$ in. long. Corolla $\frac{1}{2}$ in. long; tube enlarged at the top and with a ring of hairs in the throat; lobes ovate, acute, much shorter than the tube. Fruit $\frac{1}{2}$–$\frac{2}{3}$ in. long, oblong, tapered at both ends,

with acute margins and with about 3 prominent acute ribs on each face, crowned with the large calyx-teeth, smooth, glabrous and shining. Seeds ¼ in. long, linear-oblong, ½-terete, rounded on the back and with a groove on the ventral face. Fl. B. I. v. 3, p. 199; Grah. Cat. p. 93; Trim. Fl. Ceyl. v. 2, p. 370; Woodr. in Journ. Bomb. Nat. v. 11 (1898) p. 646; Wight, Icon. t. 760.

KONKAN: *Dalzell*!; Ooran, *Nimmo ex Graham*. GUJARAT: Porbander (coast of Kathiawar), *Bhiva*!—DISTRIB. India (shores of W. Peninsula); Ceylon.

32. **SPERMACOCE,** Linn.

Annual or perennial herbs or low undershrubs; branches usually 4-gonous. Leaves opposite, sessile or petiolate; stipules connate with the petioles into a broad truncate tube with unequal bristles. Flowers small or minute, solitary, or in axillary or terminal fascicles, heads, or cymes. Calyx-tube various; limb 2–4 (rarely 5) -toothed, sometimes with interposed teeth or bristles. Corolla infundibuliform or hypocrateriform; throat naked or hairy; lobes 4, valvate. Stamens 4, on the throat or tube of the corolla; filaments short or long; anthers linear or oblong. Ovary 2-celled; ovules solitary in each cell, attached to the middle of the septum, amphitropous; style filiform, with 2 short arms or a capitate stigma. Fruit of 2 coriaceous or crustaceous mericarps which dehisce variously. Seeds oblong, ventrally grooved; testa thin, often granulate; cotyledons leafy; radicle terete, inferior.—DISTRIB. Scattered throughout tropical and subtropical regions, abundant in America; species about 150.

Stem erect; both mericarps ventrally dehiscent .... 1. *S. stricta*.
Stem procumbent; one mericarp only ventrally dehiscent .... 2. *S. hispida*.

1. **Spermacoce stricta,** *Linn. f. Suppl.* (1781) p. 120. Annual; stem erect, 6–14 in. long, slender, thickened at the nodes, quadrangular, the angles scabrid with recurved prickles; internodes long. Leaves subsessile, 1–2 by ⅛–½ in., linear-oblong or ovate-oblong, acute, mucronate, more or less scabrous on both sides, the margins often recurved, base much tapered; stipules hairy and with numerous long filiform bristles which are much longer than the sheath. Flowers in globose dense-flowered heads, surrounded by a whorl of 2–6 linear, acute, spreading or at length reflexed leaves; bracteoles filiform, hyaline, as long as or longer than the calyx. Calyx $\frac{1}{10}$–⅛ in. long; tube densely pubescent in the upper part, glabrous near the base; teeth about as long as the tube, linear-subulate, pubescent and with pointed hyaline tips. Corolla white, ⅛ in. long; tube almost filiform; lobes $\frac{1}{24}$ in. long, linear, acute. Stamens much exserted; filaments very long. Stigma subglobose or somewhat funnel-shaped. Capsules ⅛ in. long, membranous, narrowed, veined and glabrous at the base, densely pubescent towards the apex, crowned with the erect calyx-teeth, dehiscing from above, each mericarp ventrally dehiscent. Seeds $\frac{1}{10}$ in. long, ½-ellipsoid, rounded at both ends, smooth, polished, with a deep groove on the ventral face, brown. Fl. B. I. v. 3, p. 200; Trim. Fl. Ceyl. v. 2, p. 371; Woodr. in Journ. Bomb. Nat. v. 11 (1898) p. 646.—Flowers: Oct.–Nov.

KONKAN: *Stocks*!, *Lambert*!; Worlee (Bombay), *Stocks*! DECCAN: Poona, *Woodrow*!; Dongergaon near Ahmednagar, *Cooke*! S. M. COUNTRY: Badami, *Woodrow*; Belgaum, *Ritchie*, 1797!—DISTRIB. Throughout India; Ceylon, Tropical Asia and Africa.

2. **Spermacoce hispida,** *Linn. Sp. Pl.* (1753) p. 102. A procumbent herb; stems quadrangular, hirsute, hispid, or subglabrous, usually with long internodes. Leaves subsessile, $\frac{1}{2}$–2 by $\frac{1}{3}$–$\frac{3}{4}$ in., oblong or elliptic, acute, scabrid, pubescent, or nearly glabrous, with scabrid or ciliate margins; stipules membranous, hispid, with few bristles which are usually longer than the sheath. Flowers 4–6, in a whorl within the stipular cup; pedicels short; bracts lanceolate-subulate, hyaline. Calyx hispid, $\frac{1}{6}$ in. long; tube narrowly campanulate; teeth as long as the tube, linear-lanceolate, very acutely pointed, reflexed, hairy. Corolla pale-blue or white, $\frac{1}{8}$–$\frac{1}{5}$ in. long; lobes $\frac{1}{12}$ in. long, oblong, acute, bristly on the back near the tip. Stigmas 2, very short. Capsules $\frac{1}{5}$ in. long, hairy, ellipsoid, rounded at both ends, crowned with the calyx-teeth, one mericarp only ventrally dehiscent, the other closed by the septum which remains attached to it, finally separating as a membranous plate. Seeds $\frac{1}{8}$–$\frac{1}{6}$ in. long, $\frac{1}{2}$-ellipsoid, one end rounded, the other truncate, finely granulate, rounded on the back, with a deep groove on the flat face, brown. Fl. B. I. v. 3, p. 200; Grah. Cat. p. 93; Dalz. & Gibs. p. 111; Trim. Fl. Ceyl. v. 2, p. 371; Woodr. in Journ. Bomb. Nat. v. 11 (1898) p. 646; Watt, Dict. Econ. Prod. v. 6, part 3, p. 320.—Flowers: Sept.–Oct. VERN. *Madanghanti.*

KONKAN: *Law*!; Vingorla, *Kanitkar*! S. M. COUNTRY: Castlerock, *Cooke*!; Londa, *Bhiva*; Belgaum, *Ritchie*, 358!

33. GAILLONIA, A. Rich.

Low rigid branched shrubs. Leaves small, rigid, opposite, linear or subulate; stipules usually connate with the petioles into a 2-setose or 2-spinous sheath, rarely remote from the petiole or obsolete. Flowers small, solitary, or in simple spicate cymes, white. Calyx-tube ovoid; limb 2–7-toothed or -lobed, dilated after flowering into a scarious crenate wing or feathery bristles. Corolla infundibuliform; throat naked; lobes 4–5, valvate. Stamens 4–5, inserted on the throat or tube of the corolla; filaments short; anthers linear-oblong. Disk inconspicuous. Ovary 2-celled; ovules solitary in each cell, attached to the middle of the septum, amphitropous; style filiform, with 2 short linear branches. Fruit small, ovoid, of 2 terete indehiscent cocci, crowned with the enlarged calyx. Seeds oblong, ventrally grooved; albumen horny; cotyledons flat; radicle slender, inferior.—DISTRIB. W. Asia and N. Africa; species 10.

1. **Gaillonia hymenostephana,** *Jaub. & Spach, Ill. Pl. Or.* v. 1 (1842) p. 146, t. 79. A small shrub 6–12 in. high, fetid when fresh; stem as thick as a goose-quill, irregularly branched; branches numerous, terete, slender, hoary and scaberulous. Leaves $\frac{1}{4}$–$\frac{5}{8}$ by $\frac{1}{16}$–$\frac{1}{10}$ in., linear-oblong, sessile, subobtuse, attenuated at the base, scabrid, margins ciliate, sometimes recurved; stipules of the lower leaves usually obsolete, those of the upper small, membranous, connate. Flowers terminal, solitary, or in 2–3-flowered fascicles. Calyx-tube $\frac{1}{12}$ in. long, hairy; limb membranous, reticulately veined, subpellucid, pale-yellow, hairy, unequally 5–7-lobed, the lobes rounded or broadly ovate, apiculate or acuminate, small before flowering, afterwards enlarged to a diameter of about $\frac{1}{2}$ in. when spread out. Corolla white, $\frac{1}{8}$–$\frac{1}{6}$ in. long, infundibuliform; lobes 5, hairy outside, glabrous inside, much shorter than the tube, linear, subobtuse. Fruit small, of 2 terete

indehiscent cocci, crowned with the enlarged calyx. Fl. B. I. v. 3, p. 202; Boiss. Fl. Orient. v. 3, p. 15; Woodr. in Journ. Bomb. Nat. v. 11 (1898) p. 646.

A rare plant, confined (in the Bombay Presidency) to Sind. SIND: Thano-Bullo-Khan, *Woodrow*.

Woodrow reports this plant from Sind, but I have seen no specimens from there. The specimens in Herb. Kew. are from Waziristan, the Panjáb, Afghanistan, and Beluchistan.

34. RUBIA, Linn.

Scabrid hispid or prickly erect diffuse or climbing herbs; stems long, 4-gonous. Leaves 4–8 in a whorl, exstipulate. Flowers small or minute, in axillary and terminal cymes; pedicels articulate with the calyx. Calyx-tube ovoid or globose; limb 0. Corolla rotate or subcampanulate; lobes 4–5-valvate. Stamens 4–5, inserted on the corolla-tube; filaments short; anthers didymous, exserted. Ovary 2-celled; ovules solitary in each cell, attached to the septum, amphitropous; style 2-fid or styles 2; stigmas capitellate. Fruit small, fleshy, didymous or globose by the suppression of a carpel. Seeds subereet, adhering to the pericarp; testa membranous; cotyledons broad, thin; radicle slender, inferior.—DISTRIB. Chiefly in the temperate regions of the world; species about 30.

1. **Rubia cordifolia,** *Linn. Syst. Nat.* ed. 12, v. 3 (1768) p. 229.—Perennial, herbaceous, climbing; roots very long, cylindric, flexuose, with a thin red bark; stems often many yards long, rough, grooved, becoming slightly woody at the base; bark white; branches scandent by means of numerous divaricate or deflexed branchlets and petioles, quadrangular, sometimes prickly on the angles, glabrous, shining. Leaves $1\frac{1}{2}$–$3\frac{1}{2}$ by $\frac{5}{8}$–$1\frac{3}{8}$, in whorls of 4 (one pair of each whorl often larger and with longer petioles than the other), ovate, acute, the lower leaves larger than the upper, all scabrous above, on the nerves beneath, and on the margins with minute white prickles, base rounded or slightly cordate, the base of the upper leaves sometimes acute, all 5 (rarely 7)-nerved from the base; petioles triangular, with many sharp recurved prickles on the edges, often deflexed; stipules 0. Flowers in terminal panicled glabrous cymes; branches trichotomous, spreading; bracts ovate acute, leafy. Calyx $\frac{1}{30}$ in. long; tube globose, glabrous, limb 0. Corolla greenish, divided nearly to the base; tube scarcely any; lobes 5, ovate, acute, $\frac{1}{8}$ in long. Styles 2; stigmas globose. Fruit $\frac{1}{8}$–$\frac{1}{4}$ in. in diam., didymous or globose, smooth, shining, purplish-black when ripe. Fl. B. I. v. 3, p. 202; Grah. Cat. p. 93; Dalz. & Gibs. p. 121; Wight, Ill. t. 128, *bis*, fig. 1; Trim. Fl. Ceyl. v. 2, p. 372; Woodr. in Journ. Bomb. Nat. v. 11 (1898) p. 646; Watt, Dict. Econ. Prod. v. 6, part 1, p. 570.—Flowers: Oct.-Jan. VERN. *Manjishth*; *Itta*.

On the higher Gháts tolerably common. KONKAN: *Stocks*!; Amboli Ghát, *Kanitkar*! DECCAN: Phunda Ghát, *Ritchie*, 361!; hills at Bhor, *Kanitkar*!; hills at Pár, *Law*!; Mahableshwar, *Cooke*!; hills near Sinhagad (Poona districts), *Bhiva*! S. M. COUNTRY: Belgaum, *Ritchie*, 361!—DISTRIB. Throughout India in hilly districts; Ceylon, Malacca, Japan, Java, Tropical Africa.

The roots furnish a valuable dye which is used largely by the natives of India. The plant is known as *Indian Madder*. A very full description of the dyeing process will be found in Watt's Dict. Econ. Prod. l. c.

Rubia tinctorum, Linn. Sp. Pl. (1753) p. 109. The European Madder plant, not indigenous in India, but, according to De Candolle, a native of western temperate Asia and the south-east of Europe. It is cultivated in Sind and is a scandent herb with lanceolate acuminate obscurely penninerved leaves 4–6 in a whorl, leafy cymes, and didymous or globose fruit $\frac{1}{8}$–$\frac{1}{6}$ in. diam. Fl. B. I. v. 3, p. 203; Boiss. Fl. Orient. v. 3, p. 17; Watt, Dict. Econ. Prod. v. 6, part 1, p. 578.

Under genera not included in the foregoing pages the most important plants grown in the Bombay Presidency are the following:—

Coffea arabica, Linn. Sp. Pl. (1753) p. 172. The Coffee Plant, a native of Abyssinia, the Soudan, and the coasts of Guinea and Mozambique, has been cultivated on the hills between Panchgani and Mahableshwar at an altitude of about 4000 ft., but not to any great extent.—Flowers: Jan.–Apr.

Serissa fœtida, Lamk. Tab. Encyc. v. 2 (1793) p. 211. A small shrub about 2 ft. high, a native of China and Japan, is often grown in gardens. It has ovate-lanceolate dark-green shining myrtle-like leaves and axillary solitary small sessile white flowers, which, as well as the leaves, are fetid when bruised. Grah. Cat. p. 93; Dalz. & Gibs. Suppl. p. 44; Woodr. in Journ. Bomb. Nat. v. 11 (1898) p. 646; Firminger, Gard. ed. 3, p. 579.—Flowers: May.

Hamelia patens, Jacquin, Enum. Pl. Carib. (1760) p. 16. A shrub 4–6 ft. high with dense rich-green foliage, a native of Tropical America and the West Indies, is often cultivated in gardens. It has elliptic-lanceolate villous and strongly nerved petiolate leaves about 4 by 2 in. and scarlet and yellow flowers in terminal corymbose cymes; the corolla with a long tube and short lobes. Dalz. & Gibs. Suppl. p. 44; Woodr. in Journ. Bomb. Nat. v. 11 (1898) p. 645; Firminger, Gard. ed. 3, p. 586.

Pentas carnea, Benth. in Bot. Mag. v. 17 (1844) t. 4086. A plant about 1 ft. high, scarcely shrubby (the branches all herbaceous), is very commonly grown in gardens. It bears a constant succession of flowers of a delicate lavender-color in large corymbs. Dalz. & Gibs. Suppl. p. 44; Firminger, Gard. ed. 3, p. 586.

Rondeletia odorata, Jacq. Enum. Pl. Carib. (1760) p. 16. A hard-wooded shrub, a native of Cuba and Mexico, has been introduced into gardens in the Bombay Presidency. It has ovate, acute or acuminate leaves on very short petioles and scarlet or orange fragrant flowers. Dalz. & Gibs. Suppl. p. 45; Woodr. Gard. in Ind. ed. 5, p. 354.

INDEX OF GENERA, SPECIES AND SYNONYMS.

The Synonyms are printed in italics.

INDEX TO VERNACULAR NAMES.

END OF VOL. I.